PENGUIN REFERENCE

Roget's Thesaurus

George Davidson is a former senior editor with Chambers Harrap. In addition to writing dictionaries and thesauruses, he is the author of books on English grammar, usage, spelling and vocabulary. He lives in Edinburgh.

Roget's Thesaurus
of English words and phrases

New edition prepared by
GEORGE DAVIDSON

PENGUIN BOOKS

PENGUIN BOOKS

Published by the Penguin Group
Penguin Books Ltd, 80 Strand, London WC2R 0RL, England
Penguin Group (USA) Inc., 375 Hudson Street, New York, New York 10014, USA
Penguin Books Australia Ltd, 250 Camberwell Road, Camberwell, Victoria 3124, Australia
Penguin Books Canada Ltd, 10 Alcorn Avenue, Toronto, Ontario, Canada M4V 3B2
Penguin Books India (P) Ltd, 11 Community Centre, Panchsheel Park, New Delhi – 110 017, India
Penguin Group (NZ), cnr Airborne and Rosedale Roads, Albany, Auckland 1310, New Zealand
Penguin Books (South Africa) (Pty) Ltd, 24 Sturdee Avenue, Rosebank 2196, South Africa

Penguin Books Ltd, Registered Offices: 80 Strand, London WC2R 0RL, England

www.penguin.com

First published 1852
Abridged edition first published in Great Britain by Penguin Books 1988. Based on
Roget's Thesaurus, revised and edited by Betty Kirkpatrick, first published by Longman
Group UK Limited 1987
Revised edition published 2000
New edition, revised and edited by George Davidson, first published 2004
1

Set in ITC Stone Serif and ITC Stone Sans
Typesetting by Columns Design Ltd
Designed by Richard Marston
Printed in England by Clays Ltd, St Ives plc

Preface to the first edition, 1852

It is now nearly fifty years since I first projected a system of verbal classification similar to that on which the present Work is founded. Conceiving that such a compilation might help to supply my own deficiencies, I had, in the year 1805, completed a classed catalogue of words on a small scale, but on the same principle, and nearly in the same form, as the Thesaurus now published. I had often during that long interval found this little collection, scanty and imperfect as it was, of much use to me in literary composition, and often contemplated its extension and improvement; but a sense of the magnitude of the task, amidst a multitude of other avocations, deterred me from the attempt. Since my retirement from the duties of Secretary of the Royal Society, however, finding myself possessed of more leisure, and believing that a repertory of which I had myself experienced the advantage might, when amplified, prove useful to others, I resolved to embark in an undertaking which, for the last three or four years, has given me incessant occupation, and has, indeed, imposed upon me an amount of labour very much greater than I had anticipated. Notwithstanding all the pains I have bestowed on its execution, I am fully aware of its numerous deficiencies and imperfections, and of its falling far short of the degree of excellence that might be attained. But, in a work of this nature, where perfection is placed at so great a distance, I have thought it best to limit my ambition to that moderate share of merit which it may claim in its present form; trusting to the indulgence of those for whose benefit it is intended, and to the candour of critics who, while they find it easy to detect faults, can at the same time duly appreciate difficulties.

P. M. Roget
29 April 1852

Preface to the 2004 edition

Roget's Thesaurus is now more than one hundred and fifty years old.

The *Thesaurus* began life as a notebook of words and phrases that Peter Mark Roget created for his own use as a writer and lecturer. However, recognizing that other people might also find such a book useful, he eventually expanded the material in his notebook into the *Thesaurus of English Words and Phrases*, which was first published in 1852.

Reactions to the book were mixed. Not everyone recognized its purpose and value. One reviewer, however, did perceive that Roget would one day 'rank with Samuel Johnson as a literary instrument-maker of the first class', a prophecy that time has certainly confirmed. In the past century and a half, the *Thesaurus* has sold over 30 million copies, and has become one of the best-known and best-loved reference books in English.

The original purpose of the book was to 'facilitate the expression of ideas and assist in literary composition', and this is still its main purpose. Given an idea or concept that we wish to express, the *Thesaurus* helps us find the word or words with which to express it. Far more than a mere synonym dictionary, it is a creative reference work that allows users to both clarify and embody their thoughts, either by homing in quickly on the exact word or phrase they need or by browsing at leisure in search of ideas and expressions.

Helping people to write and speak with accuracy and elegance is, however, no longer the sole function of the *Thesaurus*: it is now not only the speaker's and writer's companion, it is also, as *The New York Times* magazine once described it, an 'efficacious poultice for [the] aching brow' of the crossword-puzzler, a valuable source of ideas and solutions for all those who enjoy word games.

Few changes have been made to the structure of the *Thesaurus* since it was first published. The classification system that Roget devised for the original book is still in use in this concise edition: it has stood the test of time and, in edition after edition, has fully demonstrated its capacity for absorbing not only new vocabulary but also concepts completely unknown to Roget, such as air and space travel and computing and the Internet. Some modernization of the original headings has been necessary, however, replacing words now rare or archaic by more common and up-to-date terms (for example, 'sciolism' by 'superficial knowledge' and 'imperspicuity' by 'lack of clarity').

The main change to the *Thesaurus* over the past hundred and fifty-two years has, of course, been the huge increase in its vocabulary coverage. The anniversary edition, published in 2002, is many times larger than the 1852 edition, and even this concise edition is far larger than the original *Thesaurus*. In all areas of life – science and medicine, health and beauty, computing and the Internet, telecommunication, music and entertainment, food and drink, sport and leisure, and social and environmental issues – new words are entering the language at a bewildering and, it seems, ever-increasing rate. This new concise edition of *Roget*, making its appearance only four years after the publication of the last edition, includes many of the new terms that have come into use or prominence in that time, such as *broadband, cannabis café, congestion charging, designer baby, domestic goddess, face transplant, family balancing, flash mob, foundation hospital, genetic timebomb, grooming, health tourism, metrosexual, panic room, regime change, sky marshal, watercooler TV* and *weapon of mass destruction*. And it is a sad reflection of the state of the world today that no fewer than 27 words and phrases denoting types of bomb have been added to the text.

There is one completely new feature in this edition of the *Concise Roget*: text boxes. These, covering particular areas of vocabulary such as phobias, chemical elements, oceans and seas, methods of divination and group nouns, have been introduced in order to allow greater, and more informative, coverage of these topics than has been provided up till now, without thereby interrupting the flow of the main text.

Born of an idea that Peter Mark Roget first had some two hundred years ago, *Roget's Thesaurus* has become a highly valued and much loved language resource in homes, offices and libraries throughout the English-speaking world. There may now be other thesauruses and word-finders on the market, but for the 21st century, as for the 19th and 20th centuries, 'the *Thesaurus*' is still *Roget*.

G.W.D.
July 2004

How to use this book

There are two ways into the text of the *Thesaurus*: via the classification system devised by Peter Mark Roget (see pages xv and xvi) and via the index that follows the main text (from page 427 onwards).

The Classification System

Classes

The *Thesaurus* is divided into six large groupings of vocabulary which Roget called **Classes**. The first three of these Classes cover the world around us: Class One, *Abstract Relations*, deals with concepts such as number, order and time; Class Two, *Space*, is concerned with movement, shapes and sizes; while Class Three, *Matter*, covers the physical world and our human perception of it by our five senses. Classes Four, Five and Six, on the other hand, deal with the internal world of human beings: the human mind (Class Four, *Intellect*), the human will (Class Five, *Volition*) and the human heart and soul (Class Six, *Emotion, Religion and Morality*).

For convenient reference, the name of the Class to which the entries on any given two-page spread belong is printed at the top of each **left-hand** page of the text.

Sections

The six Classes are subdivided into **Sections** (see again pages xv and xvi). For example, Class One, *Abstract Relations*, is subdivided into eight Sections, covering *Existence, Relation, Quantity, Order, Number, Time, Change* and *Causation*.

The name of the Section to which the entries on any two-page spread belong is printed at the top of each **right-hand** page of the text.

Heads

Sections are subdivided into **Heads**. For example, in Section Six of Class One (*Time*), there are 35 Heads, dealing with concepts such as 'Present Time', 'Past Time', 'Transience' and 'Age'. Each Head has a number, from 1 to 990, and a descriptive title, e.g. 45 *Union*, 46 *Separation*. The numbers of the Heads found on any given page are printed at the top of that page.

The Heads are the basic units of the *Thesaurus*, their numbers being used both in cross-references within the text and in the index to indicate where words and phrases can be searched for or found, as will be further explained below.

Paragraphs

Each Head is divided into *paragraphs* of related words and phrases. Paragraphs are grouped according to their part of speech, in the order Nouns (marked **N.**), Adjectives (**Adj.**), Verbs (**Vb.**), Adverbs (**Adv.**) and Interjections (**Int.**). Of course, not every Head has paragraphs belonging to all five parts of speech: for example, Head 489 (*Dissent*) has two paragraphs of nouns, one of adjectives, one of verbs, one of adverbs and one of interjections, whereas Head 490 (*Knowledge*) has four paragraphs of nouns, two of adjectives and two of verbs, but no adverbs or interjections at all.

The part-of-speech labels are not applied with any great strictness, words and phrases being allocated to the part of speech which most closely describes their general function rather than their true grammatical category. In particular, it should be noted that, following Roget's original scheme, the **Adv.** label is not limited solely to words and phrases that are grammatically adverbs but is a 'catch-all' category that also includes prepositions and conjunctions. Transitive and intransitive verbs are not listed separately.

Within the paragraphs, the words and phrases are grouped loosely according to their meaning, context of use (everyday language, technical jargon, poetic language, etc.) or level of formality (colloquial or formal language, etc.). Each such group ends with a semicolon. (Note that words having more than one meaning or context of use are not usually repeated within paragraphs, as this would take up too much space, so a word found in one group in a paragraph may well relate to other groups in that paragraph as well.)

Keywords

Each paragraph begins with a word or phrase in bold italics known as the *keyword*. The keyword is the 'key' to the contents of the paragraph it introduces, a clue to the broad area of meaning covered in that paragraph. For example, at Head 264 (*Closure*) there are three noun paragraphs, with the keywords *closure*, *stopper* and *doorkeeper*, indicating that within these three paragraphs will be found, respectively, words referring broadly to 'the action of closing', 'something that closes' and 'someone who closes'.

The keyword of a paragraph is usually one item of the vocabulary provided in that paragraph, but on occasion it may simply be a descriptive phrase, such as '*existence in many forms*' at the noun paragraph of Head 82.

Cross-references

At the end of many groups of words there are *cross-references* consisting of a Head number and a keyword. For example, at Head 52, the first noun paragraph begins '*whole*, wholeness, fullness 54 *completeness*; …'. This indicates that readers looking in Head 52 for words with the general sense of 'wholeness' or 'fullness' should also look at the noun paragraph in Head 54 beginning with the keyword *completeness*, where other possibilities may be found.

Cross-references of the form 'See also …' and 'see also … below/above' are used to refer the reader to another paragraph within the same Head.

Some Text Conventions

1) To avoid unnecessary repetition, words and phrases may be shortened and linked by '*or*', as in 'countryman *or* -woman', 'drop a brick *or* a clanger'.

2) 'etc.' is used to indicate open-ended lists. For example, '*be high*, be tall, etc. (see adj.)' at the Verb paragraph of Head 209 indicates that readers can form similar verb phrases for themselves by using other words in the Adjective list in that Head.

'etc.' is also used to indicate partial lists, with cross-references indicating where fuller lists are to be found. For example, 'bedding, duvet, etc. 226 *coverlet*' at 218 *bed* indicates that a fuller list of 'bedding' words is to be found at the *coverlet* paragraph in Head 226.

3) Bracketed information is occasionally used to clarify the context of a word, as in 'dissolve (a marriage)'.

4) 'Tdmk' indicates a registered trade mark. 'Vulg' indicates that word is rather vulgar (and often offensive).

5) An 'e' in brackets added to the end of a word means that it is of French origin and requires a final 'e' if applied to a woman; e.g. 'distrait(e)', 'blond(e)'.

6) A comma *within* a phrase is printed smaller than the comma used to separate words and phrases: e.g. 'day in, day out, morning, noon and night'.

7) A comma is replaced by a colon when the preceding term simply introduces or defines what follows, e.g. 'god or goddess of war: Mars, Ares, Bellona'.

Searching the Text by means of the Classification System

To find a word you are looking for, first consult the table on pages xv and xvi and decide what Class and Section of vocabulary the word is likely to be found in. (As you become familiar with the Classes and Sections, it will of course become less and less necessary to consult the table. You will know where to begin a search.)

Next, having identified and turned to the Section of the text you are looking for, scan through the Heads of that Section until you find the one (or ones) covering the broad area of vocabulary you are interested in. (Again, this will become a more rapid process with experience.) Using the part-of-speech labels and the keywords, identify the paragraph (or paragraphs) relating to the specific area of vocabulary you are interested in, and read through them. You will in this way find the exact word or phrase you are looking for or, by comparing the words and phrases offered, be able to select the most appropriate one to express your meaning. (Where the right word or phrase is not immediately apparent, but an unfamiliar one seems from the context as if it might be suitable, it is always advisable to check in a dictionary. It is never a good idea to use a word or phrase you have found in the *Thesaurus* if you are not absolutely sure of its meaning.)

You can widen your search in various ways:

1) By using the cross-references mentioned above, you will be led from one paragraph to another (or others) covering a similar or related area of vocabulary.

2) Since words related in meaning but belonging to different parts of speech are grouped together under one Head, it is always possible to find a different way of expressing an idea by considering a different part of speech.

Furthermore, the grouping together of words that are related in meaning but belong to different parts of speech allows you to start a search with, say, a noun even if you are looking for an adjective or a verb even if you are looking for a noun. For example, if you are looking for an adjective related to the noun 'funeral', you can go to the Head where the noun 'funeral' is found (Head 364), and then consult the Adjective paragraph where you will find the adjectives 'funereal' and 'funebrial' and many other adjectives relating to death and funerals.

3) Thirdly, it is often worth consulting the Heads before and after the one you

have looked up. Heads often come in pairs covering related ideas (e.g. 361 *Death*, 362 *Killing*). Sometimes there are several heads covering an idea: 'education', for example, is dealt with in 534 *Teaching*, 535 *Misteaching*, 536 *Learning*, 537 *Teacher*, 538 *Learner* and 539 *School*.

Adjacent pairs of Heads often express positive and negative aspects of the same idea (e.g. 852 *Hope*, 853 *Hopelessness*). This allows you to use the *Thesaurus* to quickly find words that are opposite in meaning.

The Index

Once familiar with Roget's *Plan of Classification*, many readers will be able to use it to find their way round the book easily and quickly. That is certainly the method of consulting the *Thesaurus* that Roget himself envisaged. However, if you are like most *Thesaurus* users, you will probably prefer to use the Index at the back of the book.

The Structure of the Index

The Index consists of an alphabetical list of words and phrases, each of which is followed by one or more references to the text, consisting of a keyword in italics, a Head number, and a part-of-speech label (n. for nouns, adj. for adjectives, vb. for verbs, adv. for adverbs and int. for interjections, as in the text). For example:

solely
singly 88 adv.

and

abstract
subtract 39 vb.
non-material 320 adj.
description 590 n.
abstract 592 vb.
compendium 592 n.

Points to note:

1) The Index is intended only as a guide to the text, not as a complete catalogue of its contents: it lists only words and phrases that are considered to be likely starting-points for searches, and it should not be assumed that a word or phrase is not included in the *Thesaurus* simply because it is missing from the Index.

2) Items are listed in the Index in alphabetical order, e.g. **hamburger, hamlet, hammer, hammer and tongs, hammer away at, hammer in, hammering, hammock.** 'The', 'a', and 'be' are disregarded for this purpose.

3) As in the text, variant forms are linked by *or*: '**principal boy** *or* **girl**', '**rooted to the ground** *or* **spot**'. In the case of idioms in which the first word is variable, e.g. 'go/sell like hot cakes', the phrase may be indexed under both variants or under the next word in the phrase, i.e. '**like hot cakes, go** *or* **sell**'.

4) Obvious derivatives of words, such as nouns ending in '-ness', adjectives in '-ing' or '-ed' and adverbs in '-ly', are not usually given an entry of their own in the Index unless they have a different meaning from the parent word.

In other cases, too, references to the same general concept are not always repeated under the different grammatical forms of the same word. For example, 'abundance' has references to Heads 32, 36, 171, 570 and 632, while 'abundant' has references to Heads 32, 104, 570, 635, 800 and 813. The *idea* of 'abundance', however, is present in all the Heads listed.

5) In addition to words and phrases, some general concepts such as 'animal that does not exist' and 'fat person' have been added to the Index as useful guides for the reader.

6) '(s)' after a word in the Index indicates that references may apply to either the singular or the plural form, e.g. **'appurtenance(s)'**, **'aspersion(s)'**.

Searching the Text via the Index

To find a word in the text by means of the Index, first think of some other word that is related in meaning to the word you are looking for or to the idea you are wanting to express and look it up in the Index. (It is usually best to look for simple or general terms, e.g. 'ship' rather than 'clipper', 'dog' rather than 'wolfhound', 'flag' rather than 'banneret'.) If there is only one reference (as for example in the entry for **solely**: *singly* 88 adv.), turn to the Head indicated by the number (in this case, 88), look for the section corresponding to the part of speech (in this case, adv.) and look at the paragraph that begins with the keyword (in this case, *singly*). There you will find a list of words and phrases related to the concepts of 'singly' and 'solely'.

Where there are several references given in one entry in the Index (as, for example, at the entry for **abstract**:

> *subtract* 39 vb.
> *non-material* 320 adj.
> *description* 590 n.
> *abstract* 592 vb.
> *compendium* 592 n.),

you should choose the most appropriate keyword or keywords, taking account of both the meanings of the keywords and their parts of speech.

A specific example will make this process clearer. Let us suppose that you are looking for a way of expressing the idea of 'being indignant', but while 'indignant' is the word you are looking for, all you can think of is the word 'cross'. Look up 'cross' in the index and you will find an entry with the following references:

hybrid 43 n.	*badge* 547 n.	*painfulness* 827 n.
mix 43 vb.	*heraldry* 547 n.	*discontented* 829 adj.
counteract 182 vb.	*indication* 547 n.	*angry* 891 adj.
cross 222 n.	*label* 547 n.	*irascible* 892 adj.
cross 222 vb.	*mark* 547 vb.	*sullen* 893 adj.
crossed 222 adj.	*bane* 659 n.	*means of execution* 964 n.
traverse 267 vb.	*encumbrance* 702 n.	*talisman* 983 n.
pass 305 vb.	*opposing* 704 adj.	*ritual object* 988 n.
funeral rites 364 n.	*decoration* 729 n.	*church interior* 990 n.
assent 488 n.	*adversity* 731 n.	

From this long list of references, it is immediately clear that the only ones that are likely to be of interest in this particular search are: *discontented* 829 adj., *angry* 891 adj., *irascible* 892 adj. and *sullen* 893 adj. A search in Heads 829, 891, 892 and 893 at the paragraphs indicated by the keywords will provide a large number of possible words for expressing the concept of indignation, including, of course, 'indignant' itself.

Once you have used the Index to find the appropriate Heads and paragraphs, the search process can be widened in exactly the same way as described above in **Searching the Text by means of the Classification System**. For example, Head 891 provides a further possible extension to the search in the paragraph beginning with the keyword *resentful*. And cross-references within the paragraphs allow you to widen the search even further, e.g. from 891 *angry* to 176 *furious*, from 891 *resentful* to 924 *disapproving*.

Finally, you should bear in mind that, as has already been pointed out, it really does not matter whether you start a search by looking up a noun, a verb or an adjective, because once you have found the right Head, you can move easily from one part of speech to another in search of the word or phrase you are looking for. Since references to a given concept are sometimes, though not always, repeated in the Index under different grammatical forms of a word (see above at Point 4 of **Points to Note**), it is often a good idea to check in the Index for related forms of the word you are looking up in order to obtain the fullest possible list of references to suitable Heads.

Plan of classification

Abstract relations

Existence

1 Existence
N. existence, being, entity; self-existence, aseity, uncreatedness; a being, an entity, ens, monad, quiddity; Platonic idea; subsistence 360 *life*; eternity 115 *perpetuity*; pre-existence 119 *previousness*; this life 121 *present time*; prevalence 189 *presence*; realization, evolution 147 *conversion*; creation 164 *production*; potentiality 469 *possibility*; metaphysics; realism, materialism, idealism, philosophy of existence, existentialism 449 *philosophy*.

reality, realness, actuality; material existence 319 *materiality*; historicity, factuality, factualness 494 *truth*; fact, fact of life, undeniable fact, positive fact, stubborn fact, brute fact, matter of fact, factoid; fait accompli 154 *event*; real thing, not a dream, no joke; basics, nitty-gritty, fundamentals, bedrock, nuts and bolts, brass tacks 638 *important matter*.

essence, nature, essential nature, very nature, individuality, quiddity, haecceity, inner being, sum and substance 5 *essential part*; soul, heart, heart of the matter, core, centre 224 *interiority*.

Adj. existing, existent; existential; essential 5 *inherent*; absolute, given; in existence, under the sun, living 360 *alive*; pre-existent 119 *prior*; coexistent 121 *present*; undying, immortal, eternal, enduring 115 *perpetual*; extant, surviving, indestructible 113 *lasting*; abroad, afoot, prevalent, rife 189 *present everywhere*; metaphysical, ontological.

real, essential, not imagined, actual, positive, factual, genuine, attested, documented, well-documented, historical, well-grounded 494 *true*; natural, physical, flesh and blood 319 *material*; concrete, solid, tangible 324 *dense*.

Vb. be, exist, have being; be the case 494 *be true*; consist in, reside in 5 *be inherent*; pre-exist; coexist, coincide, subsist 121 *be now*;

continue 146 *go on*; endure 113 *last*; pass the time, live out one's life, drag out one's life; be alive, breathe, live, have one's being, draw breath 360 *be alive*; be found, be met with, lie 186 *be situated*; be here 189 *be present*; prevail, be rife 189 *pervade*; take place, come about, occur 154 *happen*; hold good, stand 494 *be true*.

become, come to be, come into being, come into existence, first see the light of day 360 *be born*; spring up 68 *begin*; develop, grow, take shape 316 *evolve*; turn out, change into, metamorphose 147 *be turned to*.

Adv. actually, really, essentially, substantially; ipso facto; in essence, to all intents and purposes; in fact, in actual fact, in point of fact 494 *truly*.

2 Non-existence
N. non-existence, nothingness, nullity; blank, vacuum 190 *emptiness*; nothing, sweet nothing, nil, cipher, zilch, etc. 103 *zero*; a nothing, nonentity 4 *thing that lacks substance*; no such thing; no one, nobody, etc. 190 *nobody*; nonperson, unperson.

extinction, oblivion, nirvana; dying out, obsolescence 51 *decay*; annihilation, nihilism 165 *destruction*; cancellation, erasure, clean slate 550 *obliteration*.

Adj. non-existent, without being; missing, omitted 190 *absent*; negatived, nullified, null and void; cancelled, wiped out.

unreal, without reality, baseless, groundless, unfounded, without foundation; fictitious, fabulous, visionary 513 *imaginary*; intangible 4 *lacking substance*; only supposed.

unborn, uncreated, unmade; unbegotten, unconceived; undiscovered, uninvented, unimagined; as yet unborn, yet to come 124 *future*, 507 *expected*.

extinct, died out, vanished, lost and gone forever; no more, dead and gone, defunct 361 *dead*; obsolete, dead as the dodo; finished, over and done with 125 *past*.

Vb. not be, have no existence *or* life, be null

and void; fail to materialize, not come off, abort; be yet unborn.

pass away, cease to exist, become extinct *or* obsolete, die out; be no more 361 *die*; come to nothing, abort 728 *miscarry*; sink into oblivion 506 *be forgotten*; go, vanish, be lost to sight; dematerialize, melt into thin air, go up in a puff of smoke 446 *disappear*; evaporate 338 *vaporize*; melt, dissolve 337 *liquefy*.

reduce to nothing, nullify, annul, annihilate, extinguish; make null and void, suspend 752 *annul*; neutralize, negative 533 *negate*; cancel 550 *obliterate*; abolish, wipe out 165 *destroy*.

3 Having substance

N. *having substance*, substantiality, essentiality 1 *reality*; substantivity, objectivity; corporeality, visibility, tangibility, palpability, solidity, concreteness 319 *materiality*; weight 322 *gravity*; pithiness, meatiness; material 319 *matter*.

substance, core, nub, nitty-gritty 5 *essential part*; entity, thing, something, somebody 319 *object*; living matter 360 *life*; concretion 324 *solid body*; pith, marrow, meat 224 *interiority*.

Adj. *substantial*, real, actual, objective, natural, corporeal, phenomenal, physical 319 *material*; concrete, solid, tangible, palpable 324 *dense*; considerable 638 *important*; bulky 195 *large*; heavy 322 *weighty*; pithy, meaty, meaningful, full of substance.

Adv. *substantially*, really 1 *actually*; essentially 5 *intrinsically*; largely, in the main 32 *greatly*.

4 Lacking substance

N. *lacking substance*, insubstantiality, nothingness 2 *non-existence*; naught, nothing, nothing at all, zilch, not a whit *or* jot, not a scrap 103 *zero*; no one, not a soul 190 *nobody*; incorporeality 320 *non-materiality*; lack of substance, meagreness, sparseness 325 *lack of density*; superficiality 212 *shallowness*; intangibility, impalpability, invisibility; vacuity, vacancy, void, hollowness 190 *emptiness*; fatuity 497 *absurdity*; hallucination, self-delusion 542 *deception*; dream world, fantasy 513 *conception*; unreality.

thing that lacks substance, token, symbol 547 *indication*; soul 447 *spirit*; abstraction, shadow, ghost, phantom, spectre, vision, dream, mirage, optical illusion 440 *visual fallacy*; air, thin air, mist; bubble, gossamer, snowflake; bauble; vanity, inanity, fatuity, fool's paradise 499 *folly*; flight of fancy, figment, figment of the imagination, chimera, pipe dream, castle in the air 513 *fantasy*; all talk, moonshine, cock-and-bull story; hot air, idle talk, gossip, goss, speculation, rumour 515

empty talk; cry of 'wolf' 665 *false alarm*; mockery, pretence 875 *ostentation*; nine days' wonder, flash in the pan; cipher, figurehead, man of straw 639 *nonentity*; stuffed shirt 873 *vain person*; courtesy title; fictitious person; pseudonym, stage name 562 *no name*; air guitar.

Adj. *lacking substance*, insubstantial, inessential; non-physical, non-material 320 *non-material*; bodiless, incorporeal; ethereal 323 *light*; thin, gossamer 422 *transparent*; pale 426 *colourless*; misty 336 *gaseous*; fragile, delicate, ghostly, spectral 970 *spooky*; vague 419 *dim*, vacuous, vacant, void 190 *empty*; inane; honorary, nominal, fictitious; emblematic, symbolic, token; without substance, baseless, groundless, unfounded, without foundation; visionary, chimerical 513 *imaginary*; senseless 515 *meaningless*; blank, characterless, null; superficial, -light *or* -lite 212 *shallow*.

Vb. *not be*, not exist; die, pass away, etc. 2 *pass away*, 361 *die*; die away, fade away 37 *decrease*, 145 *cease*, 446 *disappear*; annul, nullify 752 *annul*.

5 Inherent state

N. *inherent state*, inherence *or* inherency, immanence; intrinsicality, essentialness; ego 80 *self*.

essential part, sine qua non; prime constituent 1 *essence*; principle, property, attribute 89 *concomitant*; virtue; quintessence, flower, distillation; stuff, quiddity 3 *substance*; incarnation, embodiment; life, lifeblood, heart's blood, sap; jugular vein, artery; heart, heart of the matter, soul, inner man 447 *spirit*; backbone, marrow, pith, fibre; core, kernel 225 *centre*; nub, nitty-gritty, nuts and bolts, business end, nucleus 638 *chief thing*.

character, nature, quality; make-up, personality, type, stamp, breed 77 *sort*; constitution, characteristics, traits, ethos; cast, colour, complexion, hue; aspects, features; assessment, diagnosis 480 *estimate*.

temperament, temper, frame of mind, humour, disposition, mood, spirit 817 *mental state*; strain, trait 179 *tendency*; idiosyncrasy, peculiarity 80 *speciality*.

heredity, DNA, chromosome, gene, inherited characteristic, genome, genetic map; original sin; ancestry 169 *genealogy*; genetics, Mendel's law; genetic counselling, genetic engineering, genetic modification, gene technology, biotechnology, biotech, clone, cloning, transgenics 358 *biology*.

Adj. *inherent*, immanent, deep down, deep-seated, deep-set, deep-rooted, ingrained; integral 58 *component*; inward, internal 224 *interior*; implicit, part and parcel of, built-in 78

included; indispensable, unalienable, inseparable 13 *identical*; characteristic; indigenous,
native; natural, instinctive, automatic; organic
156 *fundamental*; a priori, original, elemental,
cardinal; essential, constitutional.

characteristic, typical, representative 80 *spe-cial*; characterizing, qualitative; indicative,
unchanging 153 *established*.

hereditary, genetic, inherited, familial, ata-
vistic; native, inborn, innate, congenital,
inbred; genetically-modified, GM, transgenic.

Vb. *be inherent*, be immanent, etc. (see
adj.); inherit, take after, run in the family;
bear the mark of, involve, boil down to 523
imply.

6 Externality

N. *externality*, extrinsicality; transcendence
34 *superiority*; otherness, the other, outwardness, outer space 223 *exteriority*; externalization; projection, extrovert; objectification;
objectiveness, objectivity; accidence 7 *mode*;
accident, contingency 159 *chance*; accessory.

Adj. *external*, extrinsic, foreign 59 *extrane-ous*; transcendent 34 *superior*; outward, extramural 223 *exterior*; outward-looking,
extroverted; environmental, acquired,
implanted, inbred, instilled, inculcated; accessory, annexed, appended 38 *additional*; incidental, accidental, contingent, fortuitous 159
casual; non-essential, inessential; subsidiary,
subordinate 35 *inferior*.

Vb. *be external*, be extrinsic, etc. (see adj.);
lie outside *or* without, be outside *or* outwith;
transcend 34 *be superior*; come from outside *or*
without.

make external, externalize, objectify,
project, realize.

7 State: absolute condition

N. *state*, condition; lot, walk of life, station in
life, lifestyle; plight 8 *circumstance*; position,
place, echelon, category, status, footing, standing, rank; habit, disposition, attitude, frame of
mind, vein, temper, disposition, humour,
mood 817 *mental state*; state of mind, spirits,
morale; state of health; kilter, fettle.

mode, modality, manner, way, fashion,
trend, style; mould 243 *form*; shape, fabric 331
structure; aspect, character, guise 445
appearance.

8 Circumstance: relative condition

N. *circumstance*, situation, circumstances,
conditions, factors, the times; environment,
milieu 230 *surroundings*; context 9 *relation*; status quo, state of affairs, how things stand;
regime *or* régime, set-up 7 *state*; aspect,

appearances 445 *appearance*; lie of the land
186 *situation*; footing, standing, status, relative
position 73 *serial place*, awkward situation,
catch-22 situation, plight, pickle, pretty pass,
pretty kettle of fish, corner, fix, hole, jam,
quandary, dilemma 61 *complexity*, 700
predicament.

juncture, conjuncture, stage, point 154
event; contingency, eventuality; crossroads,
turning point, point of no return; moment,
hour, right time, opportunity 137 *occasion*;
critical moment, crucial moment, when the
chips are down.

Adj. *circumstantial*, situated; surrounding,
environmental, contextual; limiting; modifying 468 *qualifying*; temporary 114 *transient*;
variable 143 *changeable*, 152 *changing*; relative,
contingent, incidental; critical, crucial 137 *cru-cial*; suitable, seemly 24 *agreeing*; appropriate,
convenient 642 *advisable*.

Adv. *thus*, so; like this, in this way.

if, should it be that; in the event of, in the
case of, in case; provided that; given that, supposing, assuming, granting, allowing; if not,
unless, except, without.

SECTION TWO

Relation

9 Relation

N. *relation*, relatedness, connectedness, rapport, reference, respect, regard; bearing, direction; concern, interest, import 638 *importance*;
involvement, implication 5 *inherent state*; relationship, affinity; filiation, kinship 11 *kinship*;
homogeneity; classification; affiliation, alliance 706 *association*; relations, friendly terms,
intimacy 880 *friendship*; liaison, connection,
merger, take-over, link, tie-up 47 *bond*; something in common, common interest, common
denominator; context, milieu, environment 8
circumstance.

relativeness, relativity, interconnection,
mutual relation 12 *correlation*; correspondence
13 *identity*, 28 *equality*; analogy 18 *similarity*;
comparability 462 *comparison*; apposition,
approximation 89 *accompaniment*, 200 *near-ness*, 202 *contiguity*, 289 *approach*; collaterality
219 *parallelism*, 245 *symmetry*; perspective,
proportion, ratio; cause and effect 156 *cause*;
dependence 157 *effect*; relative position, status,
rank, echelon 27 *degree*; serial order 65
sequence.

relevance, logicality, logical argument 475
reasoning; thread; due proportion 24 *conform-ance*; suitability, application, appositeness, pertinence, propriety, comparability 24 *suitability*;

case in point, good example, classic example.

act of referring, reference, cross-reference; referral; application, allusion, mention; citation, quotation; frame of reference, referent.

Adj. *relative*, not absolute 8 *circumstantial*; relational, respective; referable; related, connected, associated, en rapport, linked, bearing upon, concerning; of import 638 *important*; belonging, appertaining, in common; mutual, reciprocal, corresponding, answering to 12 *correlative*; in the same category 62 *arranged*; consecutive 65 *sequential*; affiliated, filiated, cognate, kindred 11 *akin*; analogous, like 18 *similar*; comparative, comparable 462 *compared*; approximating, approaching 200 *near*; collateral; proportional, proportionate, varying as, in ratio, to scale; in due proportion, commensurate 245 *symmetrical*; in perspective; contextual.

relevant, apposite, pertinent, applicable; to the point, well-directed 475 *rational*; proper, appropriate, suitable, fitting 24 *apt*; alluding, allusive; quotable, worth mentioning.

Vb. *be related*, have a relationship; have reference to, refer to, have to do with; bear on *or* upon, have a bearing on, be a factor 178 *influence*; touch, concern, deal with, interest, affect; be a relation 11 *be akin*; belong, pertain, appertain; approximate to 289 *approach*; answer to, correspond, reciprocate 12 *correlate*; have a connection, tie in with; be proportionate, vary as; be relevant, serve as an example; come to the point, get down to brass tacks, get down to the nitty-gritty.

relate, put in perspective; connect with, gear to, apply, bring to bear upon; link, connect, bracket together, treat as one, tie up with 45 *tie*; put in its context, provide a background, sketch in the background; compare 18 *liken*; balance 28 *equalize*; establish a connection, draw a parallel; make a reference to, refer to, touch on, allude to, mention, mention in passing, refer to en passant.

Adv. *relatively*, not absolutely, in relation to; to some extent, comparatively; proportionally, in ratio, to scale, in perspective; depending on circumstance.

concerning, touching, regarding; as to, as regards, with regard *or* respect to; relative to, relating to, vis-à-vis, with reference to, about, re, on; in connection with; in relation to; speaking of, apropos, apropos of, by the way, by the bye, on the subject of; on the point of; in the matter of; whereas; forasmuch, inasmuch; concerning which; whereto, thereto, hereto; whereof, thereof, hereof.

10 Unrelatedness: absence of relation

N. *unrelatedness*, absoluteness; independence 744 *freedom*; arbitrariness; unilateralism; sepa-

rateness, isolation 46 *separation*; individuality 80 *speciality*; homelessness, no fixed abode; lack of connection; unclassifiability; randomness 61 *disorder*; inconsequence (see also *irrelevance* below); dissociation 46 *disunion*, 72 *discontinuity*; wrong association 495 *error*; disproportion, asymmetry 246 *distortion*; incommensurability, disparity 29 *inequality*; diversity, multifariousness 15 *difference*, 17 *nonuniformity*, 82 *existence in many forms*; incongruence 84 *nonconformity*; irreconcilability 14 *contrariety*; intrusiveness 138 *untimeliness*; no business of, nobody's business; square peg in a round hole, fish out of water 25 *misfit*; exotic, intruder, cuckoo in the nest 59 *extraneousness*.

irrelevance, irrelevancy; illogicality 477 *sophism*; inapplicability; inconsequence, non sequitur; parenthesis; diversion, red herring, dust in the eyes 282 *deviation*; incidental 154 *event*; non-essential 639 *unimportance*.

Adj. *unrelated*, absolute, independent; owing nothing to 21 *original*; irrespective, regardless, unilateral, arbitrary; unclassified, unidentified; homeless, of no fixed abode; wandering, astray; insular 88 *alone*; uninvolved 860 *indifferent*; floating, detached, unconnected, without context, unallied; parenthetic; episodic, incidental 72 *discontinuous*; separate, individual 80 *special*; without interest, nothing to do with; inessential 6 *external*; exotic, foreign, alien, strange, extraterrestrial 59 *extraneous*; intrusive; inappropriate, incompatible 25 *disagreeing*; not comparable, incommensurable, disparate 29 *unequal*; disproportionate, out of proportion, asymmetrical 246 *distorted*; discordant 84 *unconformable*; irreconcilable 14 *non-identical*; multifarious 82 *existing in many forms*.

irrelevant, illogical; inapposite, inapplicable; impertinent, inept 25 *unapt*; misapplied; misdirected 495 *erroneous*; off-target, off the beam, off-centre, peripheral; wandering 570 *diffuse*; beside the point, beside the mark, neither here nor there; trivial, inessential 639 *unimportant*; inconsequential, of no consequence, six (of one) and half a dozen (of the other); incidental 159 *casual*; remote, far-fetched, forced, strained, laboured; academic, immaterial.

Vb. *be unrelated*, have nothing to do with, have no bearing on; owe nothing to; have no right to be there; not be one's business, be nobody's business; not concern, not touch; be irrelevant, be beside the point, cloud the issue, draw a red herring, throw dust in one's eyes; force, strain, labour; drag in by the heels, drag in screaming *or* kicking and screaming; ramble, wander, lose the thread, stray from the point 570 *be diffuse*.

11 Consanguinity: relations of kindred

N. *kinship*, kindred, blood, consanguinity 169 *parentage*; affiliation, relationship, affinity, propinquity; blood relationship; ancestry, lineage, descent 169 *genealogy*; connection, alliance, family; ties of family, clanship, tribalism, nationality 371 *nation*; nepotism; atavism 5 *heredity*.

kinsman, kinswoman; kin, kindred, kith and kin, kinsfolk, relations; near relative, next of kin; distant relation, blood relation, kissing cousin; one of the family, relation by marriage, in-law, grandparent, father, mother 169 *parentage*; children, offspring, issue, one's flesh and blood 170 *posterity*; twin, identical twin, sibling, brother, sister, blood brother *or* sister, half-brother *or* -sister, stepbrother *or* -sister; cousin, first cousin, second cousin, cousin once removed; aunt, auntie, great-aunt, grand-aunt, great-great-aunt, maiden aunt; uncle, great-uncle, grand-uncle, great-great-uncle; nephew, niece, grand-nephew, grand-niece; clansman, tribesman, compatriot.

family, matriarchy, patriarchy; motherhood, fatherhood, brotherhood, sisterhood; fraternity, sorority; adopted son *or* daughter, foster child, fosterling, godchild, stepchild, adopted child; stepmother, stepfather, foster-mother, foster-father, adoptive mother *or* father, biological mother *or* father, natural mother, birth mother, surrogate mother, in-laws; one's people, one's folks; family circle, home circle 882 *fellowship*; the old folks at home, household, hearth and home 192 *home*; nuclear family, extended family; tribe, clan.

race, stock, breed, strain, line, house, tribe, clan, sept; ethnic group; nation, people.

Adj. *akin*, kindred, twin-born; matrilineal, patrilineal; maternal, paternal 169 *parental*; sibling, fraternal, brotherly, sisterly, cousinly; avuncular; related, family, allied; german; near, related 9 *relative*; once removed, twice removed; next-of-kin.

ethnic, racial, tribal, clannish 371 *national*; interbred, inbred 43 *mixed*; Australoid, Caucasoid, Mongoloid, Negroid.

Vb. *be akin*, share the blood of; claim relationship, etc. (see *n.*); own a connection 9 *be related*; marry into 894 *wed*; father, sire 167 *generate*; be brother *or* sister to; affiliate, adopt, foster.

Adv. *by*, out of.

12 Correlation: double or reciprocal relation

N. *correlation*, correlativity 9 *relation*; proportion 245 *symmetry*; design, pattern 62 *arrangement*; grid 222 *network*; correspondence 18 *similarity*; opposite number 13 *identity*; mutuality, interrelation, interconnection; interdependence, mutual dependence; interaction, interplay; alternation, turn and turn about, swings and roundabouts, seesaw 317 *oscillation*; reciprocity, reciprocation 151 *interchange*; each, each other, one another; give and take 770 *compromise*; exchange, change, payment in kind 791 *barter*; trade-off, tit for tat 714 *retaliation*.

Adj. *correlative*, reciprocal 9 *relative*; corresponding, opposite, answering to, analogous, parallel 18 *similar*; proportional, proportionate 245 *symmetrical*; complementary, interdependent; interconnecting; mutual, requited; reciprocating; alternating, alternate, seesaw; balancing 28 *equivalent*; interlocking, geared, interacting; patterned, woven; interchangeable, exchangeable; inter-, international; two-way.

Vb. *correlate*, interrelate, interconnect, interlock, interplay, interact; interdepend; vary as, be a function of; correspond, be analogous to, answer to, reflect 18 *resemble*; react 280 *recoil*; alternate 317 *oscillate*; reciprocate 714 *retaliate*; exchange, swap, barter, trade off 791 *trade*; balance 28 *equalize*; set off, act as a foil to 31 *compensate*.

Adv. *correlatively*, proportionately, as . . . , so . . . ; mutually, reciprocally, each to each, each other, one another; interchangeably, in mutual exchange; in kind; alternately, by turns, turn and turn about; vice versa 14 *contrarily*; between, shuttlewise 317 *to and fro*.

13 Identity

N. *identity*, identicalness, sameness; the same, the very same, the very one; genuineness 494 *authenticity*; the real thing, it 21 *no imitation*; the very words, ditto, tautology, redundancy 106 *repetition*; alter ego, genius, double; identification, coincidence, congruence 24 *agreement*; coalescence, absorption 299 *reception*; convertibility, interchangeability, equivalence 28 *equality*; no difference, indistinguishability; synonymity, synonymy 514 *meaning*; same kind, homogeneity 16 *uniformity*; no change, invariability, constant 153 *fixture*; duplicate 22 *copy*; look-alike, dead ringer, spitting image, speaking likeness; fellow, pair, match, twin 18 *analogue*; homonym, homograph, homophone, synonym 559 *word*.

Adj. *identical*, same, self, selfsame, of that ilk; one and the same, one and only 88 *one*; coalescent, merging, absorbed; identified with, indistinguishable, look-alike, identikit, one-size-fits-all, interchangeable, confusable, unisex, convertible, equivalent 28 *equal*;

synonymous, congruent 24 *agreeing*; always the same, invariable, constant, unchanging, unaltered 153 *unchangeable*; monotonous 838 *tedious*; homogeneous, monolithic 16 *uniform*; tautologous, redundant, repetitive, repetitional 106 *repeated*.

Vb. **be identical**, look the same, be as like as two peas in a pod, be look-alikes, be a dead ringer for, be the spitting image *or* speaking likeness of, ditto 106 *repeat*; coincide, coalesce, merge, be one with; be congruent, agree in all respects, be unanimous 24 *accord*; phase 123 *synchronize*.

treat as identical, treat as the same, identify, not distinguish; equate, tar with the same brush 28 *equalize*; make as one, unify; assimilate, match, pair 18 *liken*.

Adv. **identically**, interchangeably; ibidem, ditto; likewise, same here.

14 Contrariety

N. **contrariety**, difference, world of difference 15 *difference*; exclusiveness, irreconcilability 10 *unrelatedness*; antipathy, repugnance, hostility 888 *hatred*; adverseness, contrariness, antagonism 704 *opposition*; antidote 182 *counteraction*; conflict, confrontation, clash 279 *collision*; discord 25 *disagreement*; contradistinction, contrast, relief, light relief, variation, undertone, counterpoint 15 *differentiation*; contradiction 533 *negation*; contraindication 467 *counterevidence*; antonym 514 *meaning*; inconsistency 17 *non-uniformity*; paradox, ambivalence 518 *equivocalness*; oppositeness, antithesis, opposite, direct opposite, antipodes, poles apart; other extreme, quite the contrary, quite the reverse; other side, opposite side 240 *oppositeness*; reverse, wrong side 238 *rear*; inverse 221 *inversion*; converse, reverse image, mirror image, mirror 417 *reflection*; opposite direction, contraflow; headwind, undertow, countercurrent 182 *counteraction*.

polarity, contraries, opposites; positive and negative, north and south, hot and cold, black and white, etc. 704 *opposites*.

Adj. **non-identical**, not identical, contrary, as different as chalk and cheese, anything but 15 *different*; contrasting, contrasted, incompatible, clashing, conflicting, discordant 25 *disagreeing*; inconsistent, not uniform 17 *non-uniform*; ambivalent, bittersweet, love–hate, sweet and sour; contradictory, antithetic 533 *negative*; antithetical, antonymous; diametrically opposite, poles apart, antipodean 240 *opposite*; reverse, converse, inverse; antipathetic, hostile; adverse, antagonistic 704 *opposing*; antidotal; counter-, contra-, anti-.

Vb. **have nothing in common**, be contrary,

be poles apart 10 *be unrelated*, 15 *differ*; contrast 25 *disagree*; conflict with; run counter to 240 *be opposite*; speak with two voices 518 *be equivocal*; contravene 704 *oppose*, 738 *disobey*; contradict, contraindicate 533 *negate*; cancel out 182 *counteract*; turn the tables 221 *invert*.

Adv. **contrarily**, on the other hand, conversely, contrariwise; vice versa, topsy-turvy, upside down; inversely; on the contrary; otherwise, the other way round; in contrast, in opposition to.

15 Difference

N. **difference**, unlikeness 19 *dissimilarity*; disparity, odds 29 *inequality*; margin, differential, minus, plus 41 *remainder*; wide margin, clear blue water 199 *distance*; narrow margin 200 *nearness*; heterogeneity, variety, diverseness, diversity 17 *non-uniformity*; divergence, departure from 282 *deviation*; otherness, differentia, distinctness 10 *unrelatedness*, 21 *originality*; discrepancy, incongruity 25 *disagreement*; incompatibility, antipathy 861 *dislike*; disharmony, discord, variance 709 *dissension*; contrast 14 *contrariety*; opposite, antithesis 240 *oppositeness*; variation, modification, alteration 143 *change*, 147 *conversion*.

differentiation 463 *discrimination*; contradistinction, distinction, nice distinction, subtle distinction; nuance, nicety 514 *meaning*; conjugation, declension 564 *grammar*.

variant, different thing, another thing, something else, something else again; quite another matter, a different kettle of fish, a different ball game, a whole new ball game; another story, horse of another colour, another light on, the other side of the coin; freak, mutation; sport 84 *nonconformist*; variety 77 *sort*; version, new version, edition, new edition 589 *edition*; cut, director's cut.

Adj. **different**, differing, unlike, like chalk and cheese 19 *dissimilar*; original 126 *new*; various, diverse, diversified, heterogeneous 17 *non-uniform*; multifarious 82 *existing in many forms*; assorted, all manner of 43 *mixed*; distinct, distinguished, differentiated, discriminated 46 *separate*; departing from; odd 84 *unusual*; discordant, clashing, incongruent, incongruous 25 *disagreeing*; disparate 29 *unequal*; contrasting, contrasted, far from it, wide apart, poles apart 14 *non-identical*; other, not the same; in a different class 34 *superior*, 35 *inferior*; the same, yet not the same, altered, genetically modified 147 *converted*.

distinctive, diagnostic, indicative 5 *characteristic*; differentiating, distinguishing; comparative, superlative.

Vb. **differ**, be different, etc. (see adj.); vary

from, diverge from 282 *deviate*; contrast, conflict 25 *disagree*; be at variance 709 *quarrel*; change one's tune, modify, vary, make alterations; suffer *or* undergo a sea change 143 *change*.

differentiate, distinguish, single out 463 *discriminate*; refine, make a distinction; widen the gap 46 *set apart*. (See also 605 *choose*.)

16 Uniformity

N. *uniformity*, uniformness, consistency, constancy, steadiness 153 *stability*; persistence 71 *continuity*, 146 *continuance*; unfailing regularity, conveyor belt 141 *periodic recurrence*; order, regularity, method, centralization 60 *order*; homogeneity 18 *similarity*; monolithic quality; unity, unison, correspondence, accordance 24 *agreement*; evenness, levelness, flushness 258 *smoothness*; roundness 245 *symmetry*; sameness 13 *identity*; monotony; mixture as before, same old story; even pace, rhythm; daily round, routine, treadmill 610 *habit*; monotone; droning, sing-song, monologue; monolith; pattern, mould; type, stereotype 22 *copy*; stamp, set, assortment; suit; standard dress 228 *uniform*; standardization, mass production, automation, computerization 83 *conformity*; cliché 106 *repetition*; regimentation, totalitarianism, closed shop 740 *compulsion*.

uniformist, uniformitarian, egalitarian, equalitarian, leveller, regimenter.

Adj. *uniform*, all of a piece, one-piece; same all through, monolithic; of one kind, one-size-fits-all; homogeneous 18 *similar*; same, consistent, constant, steady 153 *fixed*; undeviating, unchanging, invariable 144 *permanent*; equable 823 *inexcitable*; rhythmic 258 *smooth*; undifferentiated, unrelieved 573 *plain*; without contrast, lacking variety, uniformed, characterless, featureless, blank; monotonous, droning, sing-song, monotone; monochrome; repetitive 106 *repeated*; normal 83 *typical*; patterned, standardized, stereotyped, mass-produced, conveyor belt, unisex; sorted, assorted, sized; drilled, aligned, in line; orderly, regular 245 *symmetrical*; straight, even, flush, level, dead level 216 *flat*.

Vb. *be uniform*, be homogeneous, etc. (see adj.); follow routine 610 *be in the habit of*; agree, sing in unison, chorus, harmonize 24 *accord*; typify 83 *conform*; toe the line, follow the crowd, fall in, wear uniform.

make uniform, homogenize; characterize, run through 547 *mark*; level, abolish differentials 28 *equalize*; assimilate, harmonize 18 *liken*; size, grade; drill, align; regiment, institutionalize; standardize, stereotype; mass-produce; put into uniform; regularize 83 *make conform*.

17 Non-uniformity

N. *non-uniformity*, variability, patchiness 72 *discontinuity*; unpredictability 152 *changeableness*; inconstancy, inconsistency, capriciousness, whimsy 604 *caprice*; irregularity, haphazardness 61 *disorder*; asymmetry 244 *formlessness*; unevenness 259 *roughness*; heterogeneity 15 *difference*; contrast 14 *contrariety*, 19 *dissimilarity*; divergence 282 *deviation*; diversity, variety 82 *existence in many forms*; all shapes and sizes, mixed bag, ragbag, lucky dip, hotchpotch, smorgasbord, odds and ends 43 *medley*; patchwork, motley, crazy paving, mosaic 437 *variegation*; abnormality, exception, special case, sport, mutation, freak 84 *nonconformity*; odd man out, rogue elephant 59 *extraneousness*; uniqueness.

Adj. *non-uniform*, variable, unpredictable 152 *changing*; sporadic 142 *fitful*; inconstant, inconsistent 604 *capricious*; temperamental 822 *excitable*; patchy 29 *unequal*; random, haphazard, unsystematic; asymmetrical 244 *formless*; untidy, out of order; uneven, bumpy 259 *rough*; erratic, out of step, out of time; contrasted 14 *non-identical*; heterogeneous, diverse 15 *different*, 19 *dissimilar*; multifarious, miscellaneous, of all sorts 82 *existing in many forms*; multicoloured, decorated 844 *ornamental*; divergent, diversified; dissenting 25 *disagreeing*; atypical 84 *unconformable*; unusual, unconventional 84 *abnormal*; unique, lone 80 *special*; individual, hand-made; out of uniform, in civvies, in mufti, in plain clothes.

18 Similarity

N. *similarity*, resemblance, likeness, similitude; seeming, look 445 *appearance*; fashion, trend, style 243 *form*; point of resemblance 9 *relation*; congruity 24 *agreement*; affinity, kinship 11 *kinship*; homogeneity, comparability, analogy, correspondence, parallelism 12 *correlation*; equivalence, parity 28 *equality*; no difference 13 *identity*; family likeness; close resemblance, perfect likeness, faithful likeness, photographic likeness 551 *representation*; lifelikeness 494 *accuracy*; approximation 200 *nearness*; faint resemblance; suggestion, hint.

assimilation, likening 462 *comparison*; identification 13 *identity*; simulation, camouflage 20 *imitation*; parable, allegory, metaphor; portrayal 590 *description*; portraiture 553 *picture*; alliteration, assonance, rhyme 593 *prosody*; pun, play on words 518 *equivocalness*.

analogue, the like, suchlike, the likes of; type, perfect example, classic example 83 *example*; correlative 12 *correlation*; simile, parallel, metaphor, allegory, parable; equivalent 150 *substitute*; twin; match, pair, fellow, mate, companion; complement, counterpart, other half, better half 89 *concomitant*; alter ego, genius, doppelgänger; double, dead ringer, lookalike; likeness, reflection, shadow, the picture of 551 *image*; dead spit of, spitting image, living image, speaking likeness, chip off the old block; two peas, couple, pair 90 *existence as two*; two of a kind, birds of a feather; clone 22 *duplicate*.

Adj. similar, resembling, like, alike, twin, matching, like as two peas (in a pod), out of the same mould; much of a muchness 13 *identical*; of a piece 16 *uniform*; analogous, homologous; parallel 28 *equivalent*; corresponding, bracketed with; homogeneous, close, approximate 200 *near*; representative; reproducing, reflecting; after, après, in the style of, à la; much the same, something like, such as, quasi.

lifelike, realistic, exact, faithful, typical; just one, true to life, true to type; graphic, vivid.

simulating 20 *imitative*; seeming, deceptive; mock, quasi, pseudo 542 *spurious*; synthetic, artificial, simulated, ersatz 150 *substituted*.

Vb. resemble, be similar to, pass for, bear a resemblance; mirror, reflect 20 *imitate*; seem like, sound like, look as if; look like, take after, favour, put one in mind of, have the look of; savour of, smack of; come near to 289 *approach*; match, answer to 24 *accord*; typify 551 *represent*.

liken, approximate 462 *compare*; reduce to 13 *treat as identical*; pair, twin, bracket with 28 *equalize*; allegorize; portray 20 *imitate*.

Adv. similarly, as, like, as if, quasi, so to speak, as it were; likewise, so, in the same category, by the same token.

19 Dissimilarity

N. dissimilarity, incomparability 10 *unrelatedness*; disparity 29 *inequality*; divergence 15 *difference*; variation, variety 17 *non-uniformity*, 82 *existence in many forms*; contrast 14 *contrariety*; little in common, nothing in common, no common ground, not a pair 25 *disagreement*; novelty, uniqueness 21 *originality*; dissemblance 527 *disguise*; poor likeness 552 *misrepresentation*; foreign body 59 *extraneousness*; odd man out 25 *misfit*.

Adj. dissimilar, unlike, diverse 15 *different*; various 82 *existing in many forms*; disparate 29 *unequal*; unalike, not comparable 10 *unrelated*; unpaired 17 *non-uniform*; unique, peerless, matchless, nonpareil, one and only, original 21 *inimitable*; incongruent 25 *disagreeing*; untypical, atypical, exotic 84 *unconformable*; novel 126 *new*; a far cry from 199 *distant*; not true to life, unrealistic.

Vb. be unlike, be dissimilar, etc. (see adj.); bear no resemblance, have nothing in common 15 *differ*.

make unlike, discriminate, distinguish 15 *differentiate*; modify 143 *change*, 147 *convert*, 246 *distort*; dissemble 542 *deceive*; disguise 525 *conceal*; fake 541 *fake*.

20 Imitation

N. imitation, copying, etc. (see vb.); sincerest form of flattery; rivalry, emulation 716 *contention*; doing as Rome does 83 *conformity*; lack of originality, slavish imitation; imitativeness, parrotry (see also *mimicry* below); affectedness 850 *affectation*; mimesis 551 *representation*; reflection, mirror, echo, shadow 18 *assimilation*; translation 520 *interpretation*; borrowing, copying, cribbing, hot-plating, piracy, plagiarism 541 *duplicity*, 785 *borrowing*, 788 *stealing*; forgery, falsification, counterfeit, fake 541 *falsehood*; copying, transcribing, tracing 22 *copy*; duplication 166 *reproduction*, 551 *photography*.

mimicry, mimesis 551 *representation*; onomatopoeia; mime, pantomime, sign language, gesticulation 547 *gesture*; ventriloquism 579 *speech*; portraiture 553 *painting*, 590 *description*; realism 494 *accuracy*; mockery, caricature, parody, spoof, burlesque 851 *satire*; travesty 246 *distortion*, 552 *misrepresentation*; mimicking, apishness, parrotry 106 *repetition*, 850 *affectation*; conjuring, illusionism; simulation, semblance, disguise, cosmetics, make-up, camouflage, mockery.

imitator, copycat, ape, sedulous ape; mockingbird, parrot, mynah, echo; sheep 83 *conformist*; poseur; follower of fashion, fashion victim, fashionista; mocker, parodist, caricaturist 839 *humorist*; mime, ventriloquist, mimic, impersonator, female impersonator, drag artist, illusionist, tribute band, cover band 594 *entertainer*, actor; portraitist 556 *artist*; copyist, tracer; translator, paraphraser 520 *interpreter*; simulator, hypocrite 545 *impostor*; borrower, plagiarist, pirate; counterfeiter, forger; duplicator, spirit duplicator, copier, photocopier, Xerox (tdmk), stencil.

Adj. imitative, mimetic; emulating; onomatopoeic, echoic; aping, parrot-like, following; echoing; posing 850 *affected*; disguised, camouflaged; mock, mimic, simulating; shamming 541 *hypocritical*; pseudo, quasi, sham, imitation, phony, counterfeit 541 *false*; artificial, ersatz, synthetic, man-made 150 *substituted*; run-of-the-mill, hackneyed 610 *usual*; unimaginative, derivative, second-hand, handed down 106 *repeated*; paraphrastic, modelled; copied, slavish; caricatured, parodied, travestied, burlesque.

Vb. *imitate*, emulate, ape, parrot, echo, mirror, reflect 18 *resemble*; pretend, masquerade, make believe, make as if, make like; act, mimic, mime, portray 551 *represent*; parody, take off, spoof, lampoon, caricature, burlesque, travesty 851 *ridicule*; sham, simulate, put on, feign 541 *dissemble*; camouflage 525 *conceal*.

copy, trace; catch; set up 587 *print*; reprint, duplicate, mimeograph, cyclostyle, photocopy, xerox, photostat; copy out, transcribe, type, paraphrase, translate 520 *interpret*; crib, plagiarize, pirate, lift, borrow 788 *steal*; counterfeit, forge 541 *fake*.

do likewise, do as the Romans do, mould oneself on; take a leaf out of another's book; follow suit, tread in the steps of, follow my leader, follow in the footsteps of 120 *ensue*, 284 *follow*; echo, ditto, chorus 106 *repeat*; follow precedent, follow another's example, jump on the bandwagon 83 *conform*; emulate.

21 Originality

N. *originality*, creativeness, creativity, inventiveness, thinking outside the box 513 *imagination*; all my own work, a poor thing but mine own 164 *production*; original thought, originality 10 *unrelatedness*, 119 *previousness*; uniqueness, the one and only 88 *unity*; new departure 68 *beginning*; something new, novelty, innovation, freshness 126 *newness*; eccentricity, idiosyncrasy, individuality 84 *nonconformity*.

no imitation, genuineness, sincerity 494 *authenticity*; the real thing, the real McCoy, the genuine article 80 *self*; autograph, holograph, manuscript, one's own hand.

Adj. *original*, creative, inventive 513 *imaginative*; underived; archetypal; primordial, primary; first, first-hand, first in the field, pioneering 119 *prior*; unprecedented, fresh, novel 126 *new*; individual; idiosyncratic 84 *unconformable*.

inimitable, incomparable, out of reach 34 *superior*; not imitated, not emulated, uncopied, atypical 15 *different*; unique, one and only 88 *one*; true 494 *genuine*.

22 Copy

N. *copy*, exact copy; clone 166 *reproduction*; replica, facsimile, tracing; fair copy, transcript, transcription; cast, death mask; ectype, stamp, seal, impression, imprint; stereotype, lithograph, print, offprint 555 *engraving*; photocopy, Xerox (tdmk), photograph 551 *photography*; Photostat (tdmk), microfilm, microfiche 548 *record*; an imitation, dummy, pastiche; fake 542 *sham*; plagiarism, piracy,

crib 20 *imitation*; a likeness, semblance 18 *similarity*; portrait, drawing 553 *picture*; icon, image 551 *representation*; model, effigy, statue 554 *sculpture*; reflex, echo, mirror 106 *repetition*, 417 *reflection*; poor likeness, apology for, mockery of 552 *misrepresentation*; caricature, cartoon, travesty, take-off, spoof, lampoon, parody 851 *ridicule*; shadow; outline, sketch, draft; metaphrase, paraphrase 520 *translation*.

duplicate, carbon copy; stencil, master copy; transfer, rubbing; photograph 551 *photography*; reprint, reissue 589 *edition*.

copier, photocopier, plagiarist, etc. 20 *imitator*; identikit 551 *representation*; pantograph, carbon paper, plaster of Paris.

23 Prototype

N. *prototype*, archetype; type, norm, everyman 30 *average*; protoplasm 358 *organism*; original, protoplast 68 *origin*; precedent 119 *previousness*; guide, rule, maxim 693 *precept*; standard, criterion, touchstone, standard of comparison, yardstick, bench mark, barometer, frame of reference 9 *act of referring*; ideal 646 *perfection*; keynote, tuning fork, metronome 465 *gauge*; module; specimen, sample 83 *example*; model, exemplar, pattern, template, paradigm; dummy, mock-up; copybook, copy, text, manuscript; blueprint, design, master plan, scheme 623 *plan*; rough plan, outline, draft, sketch.

living model, model, artist's model, poser, sitter, subject, nude model, glamour model; fashion model, mannequin 848 *fashion*; stroke, pacer, pacemaker; role model, exemplar, trendsetter; bandleader, conductor.

mould, matrix, mint; stencil, negative; frame 243 *form*; wax figure, lay figure, tailor's dummy; last; die, stamp, punch, seal, intaglio 555 *printing*.

Vb. *be an example*, set an example, serve as an example, act as a pattern; serve as a model, model, sit for, pose.

24 Agreement

N. *agreement*, consent 488 *assent*; accord, accordance, chorus, unison 16 *uniformity*; harmony 410 *melody*; consonance, concordance; concert, understanding, mutual understanding, rapport, entente; concordat, convention, pact 765 *pact*; unity, solidarity, unanimity 488 *consensus*; consortium 706 *cooperation*; union 50 *combination*; peace 710 *harmony*.

conformance 83 *conformity*; congruence, coincidence 13 *identity*; consistency, congruity 16 *uniformity*; coherence, consequence, logic, logical conclusion 475 *reasoning*; correspondence, parallelism 18 *similarity*.

suitability, propriety 642 *good policy*; fitness, aptness, qualification, capability 694 *aptitude*; the right man *or* woman in the right place, the right man *or* woman for the job, the very thing, dream team, horses for courses; relevancy, pertinence, admissibility, appositeness, case in point, good example 9 *relevance*; commensurability, proportion 9 *relation*; timeliness, right moment 137 *occasion*; mot juste.

adaptation, harmonization, synchronization, matching 18 *assimilation*; reconciliation 719 *pacification*; accommodation, negotiation 770 *compromise*; attunement, adjustment 62 *arrangement*; compatibility, fitting, suiting, good fit, perfect fit.

Adj. *agreeing*, right, in accord, in accordance with, in keeping with; corresponding, answering; proportional, proportionate, commensurate, according to 12 *correlative*; coinciding, congruent, congruous 28 *equal*; consistent with, conforming 83 *conformable*; in conformity, in step, in phase, in tune, synchronized 123 *synchronous*; of a piece with, consistent; harmonized 410 *harmonious*; combining, mixing; suiting, matching 18 *similar*; becoming 846 *tasteful*; sympathetic; reconcilable, compatible, coexisting, symbiotic; consentient, agreeable, acquiescent, cool 488 *assenting*; concurrent, agreed, at one, in unison, unanimous, united, concerted; in rapport with, likeminded; in treaty, negotiating 765 *contractual*.

apt, applicable, admissible, germane, appropriate, pertinent, to the point, well-aimed 9 *relevant*; to the purpose, bearing upon; pat, in place, apropos; right, happy, felicitous 575 *elegant*; at home, in one's element; opportune 137 *timely*.

fit, fitting, befitting, seemly, decorous; suited, well-adapted, capable, qualified, groomed for, cut out for 694 *skilful*; suitable, up one's street 642 *advisable*; proper 913 *right*.

adjusted, well-adjusted 60 *orderly*, 494 *accurate*; synchronized; focused, tuned, fine-tuned; strung, pitched, attuned 412 *musical*; trimmed, balanced 28 *equal*; well-cut, fitting, wellfitting; bespoke, made to measure, tailored, tailor-made.

Vb. *accord*, agree, concur 488 *assent*, 758 *consent*; respond, echo, chorus, chime in, ditto 106 *repeat*; coincide, mesh with, dovetail 45 *join*; fit, fit like a glove, fit like a second skin, fit to a T; tally, correspond, match 18 *resemble*; go with, tone in with, harmonize; come naturally to; take to like a duck to water; fit in, belong, feel at home, be in one's element; answer, do, meet, suit, suit down to the ground 642 *be expedient*; prove timely, fit the occasion; pull together 706 *cooperate*; be con-

sistent, hang together 475 *be reasonable*; negotiate 766 *make terms*; get on with, be of one mind, be on the same wavelength, sing from the same hymn sheet *or* song sheet, hit it off, fraternize 880 *befriend*.

adjust, make adjustments, alter, modify 143 *change, modify*; put right 654 *rectify*; readjust, repair 656 *restore*; fit, suit, adapt, accommodate, conform; attune, tune, pitch, string 410 *harmonize*; modulate; regulate 60 *order*; graduate, proportion 12 *correlate*; align 62 *arrange*; balance 28 *equalize*; cut, trim 31 *compensate*; tailor, make to measure; focus, synchronize.

25 Disagreement

N. *disagreement*, disaccord; non-agreement, agreement to disagree 489 *dissent*; conflict of opinion, controversy 475 *argument*; confrontation, wrangling, bickering 709 *quarrel*; disunity, faction 709 *dissension*; dissidence 978 *schism*; clash 279 *collision*; challenge, defiance, rupture, breach 718 *war*; variance, divergence, discrepancy 15 *difference*; ambiguity, ambivalence 518 *equivocalness*; inconsistency, credibility gap; variety, inconsistency 17 *nonuniformity*; contradiction, conflict 14 *contrariety*; dissonance, inharmoniousness 411 *discord*; incongruence, incongruity 10 *unrelatedness*; disparity 29 *inequality*; disproportion, asymmetry 246 *distortion*; incompatibility, irreconcilability, hostility 881 *enmity*.

inaptitude, unfitness, incompetence 695 *lack of skill*; unfittingness, unsuitability, impropriety 643 *inexpediency*, inapplicability, inadmissibility, irrelevancy 10 *irrelevance*; interruption 138 *untimeliness*; maladjustment, incompatibility 84 *nonconformity*.

misfit, maladjustment, bad fit; bad match, mésalliance, mismarriage 894 *marriage*; incongruity, false note, jar 411 *discord*; fish out of water, square peg in a round hole; outsider, alien, foreigner, foreign body 59 *outsider*; dissident 84 *nonconformist*; joker, odd man out, freak, mutation 84 *abnormality*; eccentric, oddity 851 *laughing-stock*.

Adj. *disagreeing*, dissenting, not unanimous 489 *dissenting*; in opposition, at odds, at cross purposes, at variance; at one another's throats, at loggerheads, at war 718 *warring*; bickering 709 *quarrelling*; hostile, antagonistic 881 *inimical*; antipathetic; conflicting, contradictory 14 *non-identical*; unnatural, against the grain, out of character; incompatible; odd, alien, foreign 59 *extraneous*; out of proportion, unsymmetrical 246 *distorted*; grating 411 *discordant*; mismatched, ill-matching, badly matched, illassorted, incongruous 497 *absurd*.

unapt, unsuited, incompetent 695 *unskilful*;

inept, maladjusted 695 *clumsy*; wrong, unfitting, unsuitable, unbecoming, not for one, improper, undue, inappropriate 643 *inexpedient*; impracticable 470 *impossible*; unfit for, ineligible; ill-timed 138 *inopportune*; inapplicable, inadmissible 10 *irrelevant*; out of character, out of keeping; out of one's element, like a fish out of water, like a square peg in a round hole; out of place, out of joint, out of tune, out of time, out of step, out of phase.

Vb. *disagree* 489 *dissent*; differ, dispute 475 *argue*; fall out 709 *quarrel*; clash, confront, collide, contradict 14 *have nothing in common*; be unapt, etc. (see adj.); diverge 15 *differ*; not play, not play ball 702 *be obstructive*; have nothing to do with 10 *be unrelated*; be incongruous, stick out like a sore thumb, jar.

SECTION THREE

Quantity

26 Quantity

N. *quantity*, amount, sum 38 *addition*; total 52 *whole*; extent 465 *measurement*; mass, substance, body, bulk 195 *size*; dimension, dimensions, longitude 203 *length*; width, thickness 205 *breadth*; altitude 209 *height*; deepness 211 *depth*; area, volume, extension 183 *space*; weight 322 *gravity*, 323 *lightness*; force, flow, potential, pressure, tension, stress, strain, torque 160 *energy*; numbers 104 *multitude*; quotient, fraction, multiple.

finite quantity, limited amount; lower limit, upper limit, ceiling 236 *limit*; quantum, quota, quorum; gross, quire; measure, dose 465 *measurement*; avoirdupois 322 *weighing*; ration, whack 783 *portion*; armful, handful, mouthful, bagful, boxful, sackful, capful, cupful, glassful, plateful, quiverful, spoonful, dessertspoonful, tablespoonful, teaspoonful, snootful, thimbleful; lot, batch; load, lorryload, containerful 193 *contents*; lock, stock and barrel 52 *whole*; large amount, masses, heaps, mountains 32 *great quantity*; small amount, bit 33 *small quantity*; greater amount, more, most, majority 36 *increase*; smaller amount, less, not so much 37 *decrease*.

Adj. *quantitative*, some, certain, any.

27 Degree: relative quantity

N. *degree*, relative quantity, proportion, ratio, scale 9 *relativeness*, 462 *comparison*; ration, stint 53 *part*, 783 *portion*; amplitude, extent, intensity, frequency, magnitude, size 26 *quantity*; level, pitch, altitude 209 *height*, 211 *depth*; key, register 410 *musical note*; reach, compass,

scope 183 *range*; rate, tenor, way, speed 265 *motion*; gradation, graduation, calibration 15 *differentiation*; differential, shade, nuance; grade, remove, stepping-stone; step, rung, tread, stair 308 *ascent*; point, stage, milestone, turning point, crisis 8 *juncture*; mark, peg, notch, score 547 *indicator*; bar, line, interval 410 *notation*; valuation, value 465 *measurement*; ranking, grading, league table 77 *classification*; class, kind 77 *sort*; standard, rank, grade 73 *serial place*; military rank, lieutenancy, captaincy, majority, colonelcy 741 *army officer*, naval officer, air officer; ecclesiastical rank 985 *church office*, 986 *church dignitary*; hierarchy 733 *authority*; sphere, station, status, social class, caste, standing, footing 8 *circumstance*; gradualism, gradualness 278 *slowness*.

comparative, relative, proportional, in scale 9 *relative*; within the bounds of; measured by.

Vb. *graduate*, rate, class, rank 73 *grade*; scale, calibrate; compare, measure.

Adv. *by degrees*, gradually, imperceptibly, slowly, steadily, little by little, step by step, drop by drop, bit by bit, inch by inch; by inches, slowly but surely, by slow degrees; to some extent, just a bit; however little, however much.

28 Equality: sameness of quantity or degree

N. *equality*, parity, equal opportunity, equal status, sexual equality, gender equality, level playing field, coincidence 24 *agreement*; symmetry, balance; evenness 216 *horizontality*; equability.

equivalence, likeness 18 *similarity*; sameness 13 *identity*, 219 *parallelism*; equation; interchangeability 151 *interchange*; isotropy; synonym; reciprocation, exchange, fair exchange, trade-off 791 *barter*; par, quits; equivalent, value 809 *price*; six of one and half a dozen of the other, nothing to choose between, nothing in it, level-pegging; even money.

equilibrium, equipoise, equiponderance, balance; even keel, steadiness; balance of nature, balance of power, balance of trade, balance of payments; deadlock, stalemate, logjam 145 *stop*; stable state, homoeostasis; sea legs, seat; fin, aileron, spoiler 153 *stabilizer*; balance.

equalization, equation; balancing 322 *weighing*; coordination, adjustment, levelling up *or* down 31 *compensation*, 656 *restoration*; positive discrimination, affirmative action, equal opportunities legislation; equal division, going halves 92 *division into two*; reciprocity 12 *correlation*; tit for tat 151 *interchange*, 714 *retaliation*; equalizer, counterpoise.

draw, drawn game, no result, drawn battle;

level-pegging; tie, dead heat; stalemate, deadlock; neck-and-neck race, photo finish; love all, deuce.

peer, compeer, equal, match, mate, twin; fellow, brother 18 *analogue*; equivalent, parallel, opposite number, pair, counterpart, shadow.

Adj. *equal*, same 13 *identical*; like 18 *similar*; coordinate, coincident, congruent, homologous, analogous 24 *agreeing*; equidistant; isotropic; balanced, in equilibrium; homoeostatic, steady, stable 153 *fixed*; even, level, round, square, flush 258 *smooth*; equilateral, regular 16 *uniform*, 245 *symmetrical*; equable, unvarying; well-matched, drawn, tied; parallel, level-pegging, running level, abreast, neck-and-neck, nip and tuck; bracketed; sharing; equally divided, half-and-half, fifty-fifty; impartial, equitable 913 *just*; on equal terms, on the same footing, on a par, on a level, even-stevens; par, quits, upsides with.

equivalent, comparable, parallel, interchangeable, synonymous, corresponding, reciprocal 12 *correlative*; worth; tantamount, virtually the same, more or less identical, indistinguishable 18 *similar*; much the same, all one, as broad as it is long; pot calling the kettle black.

Vb. *be equal*, equal, counterbalance, compensate; come to the same thing, coincide with, agree with 24 *accord*; be equal to, measure up to; cope with 160 *be able*; make the grade, measure up, come up to scratch, cut the mustard, pass muster 635 *suffice*; hold one's own, keep up with, keep pace with, be level; parallel; match, twin 18 *resemble*; tie, draw; break even; go halves.

equalize, equate; bracket, match; parallel 462 *compare*; balance, strike a balance, poise; trim, dress, square, round off, make flush, level 16 *make uniform*, 258 *smooth*; fit, accommodate, readjust 24 *adjust*; counterpoise, even up; redress the balance, handicap 31 *compensate*; set on an even keel, equilibrate, restore to equilibrium 153 *stabilize*; right oneself, keep one's balance.

Adv. *equally*, evenly, etc. (see adj.); at the same rate, on equal terms; to all intents and purposes; likewise.

29 Inequality: difference of quantity or degree

N. *inequality*, difference of degree 34 *superiority*, 35 *inferiority*; irregularity, patchiness 17 *non-uniformity*; unevenness 259 *roughness*; disproportion, asymmetry 25 *disagreement*, 246 *distortion*; oddness, lopsidedness 220 *obliqueness*; disparity 15 *difference*; asymmetric warfare; unlikeness 19 *dissimilarity*; imbalance; dizziness, the staggers; tilting of the scales, preponderance, top-hamper 322 *gravity*; short weight 323 *lightness*; inadequacy 636 *insufficiency*; odds 15 *difference*; counterpoise; partiality, discrimination 481 *bias*.

Adj. *unequal*, disparate, incongruent 15 *different*, 19 *dissimilar*; unique, unequalled 644 *excellent*; below par 35 *inferior*; disproportionate, asymmetrical 246 *distorted*; irregular, scalene, lopsided 17 *non-uniform*; awry; odd, uneven; variable, patchy 437 *variegated*; deficient, defective, falling short, inadequate 636 *insufficient*; underweight 323 *light*; overweight 322 *weighty*; unbalanced, swaying; untrimmed, unballasted, uncompensated; overloaded, topheavy, unwieldy 695 *clumsy*; listing, leaning, canting, heeling; off balance, dizzy, giddy, falling; inequitable, unequitable, partial 481 *biased*, 914 *unjust*.

Vb. *be unequal*, be mismatched 25 *disagree*; not balance, not equate 15 *differ*; fall short 35 *be inferior*; preponderate, have the advantage, give points to, outclass, outrank 34 *be superior*; outstrip 306 *outdo*; be deficient 636 *be insufficient*; overcompensate, overweight 322 *make heavy*; tip the scales 322 *weigh*; be underweight 323 *be light*; unbalance, throw off balance; overbalance, capsize; list, tilt, lean 220 *be oblique*; rock, sway 317 *fluctuate*; vary 143 *change*.

30 Mean

N. *average*, medium, mean, median; middle term 73 *serial place*; balance; happy medium, golden mean 177 *moderation*; standard product 79 *generality*; ruck, ordinary run 732 *averageness*; norm, par; the normal 610 *habit*.

middle point, midpoint, middle distance, half way 70 *middle*; middle years 131 *middle age*; middle class 869 *middle classes*; middle of the road, midway, middle course, middle ground 625 *middle way*; splitting the difference 770 *compromise*; neutrality 606 *no choice*; central position 225 *centre*.

common man 869 *commoner*, everyman *or* -woman, man *or* woman in the street; Joe Soap 79 *everyman*; average specimen 732 *averageness*.

Adj. *median*, mean, average 70 *middle*, 225 *central*; lukewarm; intermediate, grey; standard, par, ordinary, commonplace, run-of-the-mill, mediocre 732 *middling*; moderate, middle-of-the-road 625 *neutral*; middle class, middle brow.

Vb. *average out*, average, take the mean; split the difference, go halfway 770 *compromise*; strike a balance 28 *equalize*.

31 Compensation

N. compensation, weighting 28 *equalization*; rectification 654 *amendment*; reaction, neutralization, antidote, nullification 182 *counteraction*; commutation 150 *substitution*, 151 *interchange*; redemption, recoupment, recovery; retrieval 771 *acquisition*; indemnification, reparation, damages, redress 656 *restoration*, 787 *restitution*; amends, expiation 941 *atonement*; reimbursement, refund, one's money back; recompense, repayment 714 *retaliation*, 910 *revenge*, 962 *reward*; reciprocity, measure for measure 12 *correlation*.

Adj. compensatory, compensating, redeeming, countervailing, balancing 28 *equivalent*; self-correcting, self-cancelling; reimbursing, restitutory; amendatory, expiatory 941 *atoning*; weighed against 462 *compared*.

Vb. compensate, offer compensation, make amends, make compensation, etc. (see n.); do penance 941 *atone*; indemnify, restore, pay back 787 *make restitution*; make good, make up, make up for; add a make-weight, ballast; pay, repay 714 *retaliate*; bribe, square 962 *reward*; reimburse, pay overtime 804 *pay*; redeem, out-weigh; overcompensate, lean *or* bend over backwards.

recoup, recover 656 *retrieve*; make up leeway, take up the slack; indemnify oneself, take back, get back 786 *take*; make a comeback 656 *be restored*.

32 Largeness

N. largeness, greatness, bigness, girth 195 *size*; large scale, generous proportions, ample proportions, vastness, enormousness, gigantism; muchness, abundance 635 *plenty*; amplitude, ampleness, fullness, maximum 54 *completeness, fullness*; superabundance, superfluity, embarras de richesses, an arm and a leg, more than enough 637 *redundancy*; immoderation 815 *prodigality*; exorbitance, excessiveness, excess 546 *exaggeration*; enormity, immensity, boundlessness 107 *infinity*; numerousness, countlessness 104 *multitude*; dimensions, magnitude 26 *quantity*, 27 *degree*; extension, extent 203 *length*, 205 *breadth*, 209 *height*, 211 *depth*; expanse, area, volume, capacity 183 *space*; spaciousness 183 *room*; might, strength, intensity 160 *power*, 178 *influence*; intensification, magnification, multiplication 197 *expansion*; aggrandizement 36 *increase*; seriousness, significance 638 *importance*; eminence 34 *superiority*; grandeur, grandness 868 *nobility*, 871 *pride*; majesty 733 *authority*; fame, renown 866 *repute, prestige*; noise, din 400 *loudness*.

great quantity, galore 635 *plenty*; crop, profusion, abundance 171 *productiveness*; superfluity, superabundance, torrent 350 *stream*, 637 *redundancy*; expanse, lake, sea, ocean, world, universe, sight of, world of; much, lot, whole lot, fat lot, deal, good deal, great deal; not a little, not peanuts, not chickenfeed, not to be sneezed at; too much, more than one bargained for; stock, mint, mine 632 *store*; quantity, peck, bushel, pints, gallons; gross, quire; lump, heap, mass, stack, mountain 74 *accumulation*; load (of), shipload, lorryload, sackload, sackful, containerful 193 *contents*; quantities, lots, lashings, mountains, oodles, scads, shedloads, truckloads, gobs, tons, wads, pots, bags, heaps, loads, masses, stacks; pots of money, a bomb, a mint, a packet; telephone numbers; oceans, seas, floods, streams; volumes, reams, sheets, pages and pages, screeds; numbers, quite a flood, crowds, hordes, masses, hosts, swarms, multitudes 104 *multitude*; millions, billions, trillions, bazillions, gazillions, jillions, kazillions, squillions, zillions; all, entirety, corpus, caboodle 52 *whole*.

Adj. great, greater, main, most, major 34 *superior*; maximum, greatest 34 *supreme*; grand, big, muckle *or* mickle 195 *large*; fair-sized, largish, biggish; substantial, considerable, respectable; sizable, king-size, economy-size, full-size, man-size, life-size; industrial, industrial-size; bulky, massive, heavy 322 *weighty*; prolonged, lengthy 203 *long*; wide, thick 205 *broad*; swollen; ample, generous, voluminous, capacious 183 *spacious*; profound 211 *deep*; tall, lofty 209 *high*; mighty 160 *powerful*, 178 *influential*; intense, violent 174 *vigorous*; noisy 400 *loud*; soaring, climbing; culminating, at the peak, at its height, through the ceiling, at the limit *or* zenith, at the summit 213 *topmost*; plentiful, abundant, overflowing 635 *plentiful*; superabundant 637 *redundant*; many, swarming, teeming, hotching, alive with 104 *multitudinous*; antique, ancient, venerable, immemorial 127 *olden*, 131 *ageing*; imperial, august, of value 644 *valuable*, 868 *noble*; exalted 821 *impressive*; glorious, famed, famous 866 *renowned, worshipful*; grave, solemn, serious 638 *important*; excelling, excellent, cool, wicked, awesome 644 *best*.

extensive, wide-ranging, far-flung, far-reaching, widespread, prevalent, epidemic; worldwide, global, universal, cosmic; mass, wholesale, all-embracing, across-the-board, comprehensive 78 *inclusive*; full-scale, large-scale, farm-scale.

enormous, immense, vast, colossal, giant, gigantic, monumental 195 *huge*; towering, sky-high 209 *high*; full-scale, large-scale, industrial-scale.

prodigious, marvellous, astounding, amazing, astonishing 864 *wonderful*; fantastic, fabulous, incredible, unbelievable, passing belief

472 *improbable*, 470 *impossible*; arrant, — on stilts (see also *consummate* below); stupendous, tremendous, terrific; dreadful, frightful 854 *frightening*; seismic, breathtaking, overwhelming, out of this world 821 *impressive*.

remarkable, signal, noticeable 866 *noteworthy*; outstanding, extraordinary, exceptional, singular, uncommon 84 *unusual*; eminent, distinguished, marked, über- 638 *notable*.

flagrant, blatant, flaring, glaring, stark, staring, staring one in the face; shocking 867 *discreditable*.

unspeakable, unutterable, indescribable, beyond description, indefinable, ineffable; past speaking 517 *inexpressible*.

exorbitant, extortionate, harsh, stringent, severe, Draconian 735 *oppressive*; excessive, extreme, monstrous, outrageous, swingeing, unconscionable; unbearable 827 *intolerable*; inordinate, unwarranted, preposterous, extravagant, astronomical; beyond the pale, going too far.

consummate 54 *complete*; flawless 646 *perfect*; entire 52 *whole*; thorough, thoroughgoing; utter, total, out and out, dyed in the wool, arch, crass, gross, arrant, rank, regular, downright, desperate, unmitigated, — on stilts.

absolute, essential, positive, unequivocal; stark, pure, sheer, mere 44 *unmixed*; unlimited, unrestricted 107 *infinite*.

Vb. be great, be large, etc. (see adj.); loom, loom up; stretch 183 *extend*; rear, tower, soar, mount 308 *ascend*; scale, transcend 34 *be superior*; clear, overtop; exceed, know no bounds, run to extremes, go off the deep end 306 *overstep*; enlarge 36 *augment*, 197 *expand*.

Adv. greatly, much, well, very, right, so; very much, mighty, ever so; fully, quite, entirely, utterly, without reservation 54 *completely*; thoroughly, wholesale; widely, extensively, universally 79 *generally*; largely, mainly, mostly, to a large *or* great extent; something, considerably, fairly, pretty, pretty well; a sight, a deal, a great deal, ever so much, in spades; materially, substantially; increasingly, more than ever, doubly, trebly; specially, particularly; dearly, deeply; vitally; exceptionally; on a large scale, in a big way; vastly, hugely, enormously, gigantically, colossally; heavily, strongly, powerfully, mightily; actively, strenuously, vigorously, heartily, intensely; closely, narrowly, intensively, zealously, fanatically, hotly, bitterly, fiercely; acutely, sharply, shrewdly, exquisitely; enough, more than enough, abundantly, profusely, prodigiously; generously, richly, worthily, magnificently, splendidly, nobly; supremely, pre-eminently,

superlatively; rarely, unusually, wonderfully, incomparably, strangely; indefinitely, immeasurably, incalculably, infinitely, unspeakably, ineffably; seriously, big time, for Britain *or* England, etc; as all-get-out.

extremely, ultra, to extremes, to the highest degree, to the maximum, to the max, to the limit, to the nth degree 54 *completely*; no end of, no limit to; beyond measure, beyond all bounds; beyond comparison, beyond compare, incomparably, drop dead; overly, unduly, improperly, to a fault; out of all proportion; bitterly, harshly, drastically, rigorously, unconscionably, with a vengeance; immoderately, uncontrollably, desperately, madly, frantically, frenziedly, furiously, fanatically, bitterly; exceedingly, excessively, exorbitantly, inordinately, outrageously, prohibitively, preposterously; foully, abominably, grossly, monstrously, horribly; confoundedly, deucedly, devilishly, damnably, hellishly; tremendously, terribly, fearfully, dreadfully, awfully, frightfully, horribly.

remarkably, noticeably, markedly, pointedly; notably, strikingly, conspicuously, signally, emphatically, prominently, glaringly, flagrantly, blatantly, unashamedly, etc. 263 *openly*; publicly 400 *loudly*; pre-eminently 34 *eminently*; outstandingly, unco; singularly, peculiarly, curiously, oddly, queerly, strangely, strangely enough, uncommonly, unusually; surprisingly, astonishingly, amazingly, astoundingly, incredibly, magically.

33 Smallness

N. smallness, small size, diminutiveness, minuteness 196 *littleness*; brevity 204 *shortness*; leanness, meagreness 206 *thinness*; briefness, momentariness 114 *transience*; paucity 105 *fewness*; rareness, sparseness, sparsity 140 *infrequency*; scarceness, scarcity, inadequacy 307 *shortfall*, 636 *insufficiency*; exiguousness, scantiness; moderateness, moderation; pettiness, insignificance, meanness 35 *inferiority*, 639 *unimportance*; mediocrity 30 *average*, 732 *averageness*; tenuity 4 *lacking substance*; compression, abbreviation, abridgment 198 *contraction*; diminution 37 *decrease*; miniaturization.

small quantity, fraction, modicum, minimum 26 *finite quantity*; minutiae, trivia; peanuts, chickenfeed 639 *trifle*; detail, petty detail 80 *particulars*; nut-shell 592 *compendium*; drop in the bucket, drop in the ocean; tip of the iceberg; homoeopathic dose, trifling amount, infinitesimal amount; dribs and drabs; thimbleful, spoonful, mouthful, handful, cupful; trickle, dribble, sprinkling, sprinkle, dash, splash, squirt, squeeze; tinge, tincture, trace, smidgen, lick, smell, breath, whisper, suspicion, vestige, soupçon, thought, suggestion, hint, nuance, shade, touch; vein, strain, streak; glimmer, spark, gleam, flash, flicker, ray; pinch, snatch, handful; snack, sip, bite, scrap, morsel, sop; dole, pittance, iron ration; fragment 53 *piece*; whit, bit, mite; iota, jot, tittle, fig, toss; ounce, gram, pennyweight, scruple, minim 322 *weighing*; inch, micron, millimetre 200 *short distance*; second, moment, nanosecond 116 *instant*.

small thing 196 *miniature*; microcosm; particle, atom; dot, point, pinpoint; dab, spot, fleck, speck, mote; grain, granule, seed, mustard seed, crumb 332 *powder*; drop, droplet; thread, wisp, shred, rag, tatter, fragment 53 *piece*; smithereens, little pieces; flake, snip, snippet, gobbet, small slice, finger; confetti; splinter, chip, clipping, paring, shaving; shiver, sliver, slip; pinprick, prick, nick; hair 208 *filament*; groat, mite, widow's mite; dime, sou; gnat, flea; shrimp, minnow, sprat; manikin, midget, etc. 196 *dwarf*.

Adj. *small*, exiguous, not much, moderate, modest, homoeopathic, minimal, infinitesimal; microscopic, tiny, teeny, teeny-weeny, teensy, weeny, wee, minute, diminutive, miniature 196 *little*; smaller 35 *lesser*; least, minimum; small-sized, small-framed, small-built, small-boned, petite, undersized 196 *dwarfish*; slim, slender, slimline, lean, meagre, thin, anorexic 206 *narrow*; slight, feeble, puny, frail 163 *weak*; delicate, dainty, fragile 330 *brittle*; flimsy 323 *light*; fine, subtle, quiet, soft, low, faint, hushed 401 *muted*; squat 210 *low*; brief, minute, skimpy, abbreviated 204 *short*; shortened, abridged, cut, concise, compact, thumbnail; scanty, scant, scarce 307 *deficient*; dribbling, trickling 636 *insufficient*; reduced, limited, restricted 747 *restrained*; declining, ebbing, at low ebb, less 37 *decreasing*.

inconsiderable, minor, lightweight, trifling, trivial, petty, paltry, not to be taken seriously, insignificant 639 *unimportant*; not many 105 *few*; imperceptible; marginal, negligible, laughable, remote, slight; superficial, cursory 4 *lacking substance*; so-so 30 *median*; modest, humble, tolerable 732 *middling*; not much of a —, no great shakes, second-rate 35 *inferior*.

Vb. *be small*, fit into a nutshell, be put onto a thumbnail; be less 307 *fall short*; get less 37 *decrease*; shrink 198 *become small*.

Adv. *slightly*, exiguously, little; lightly, softly, faintly, feebly; superficially, cursorily, gradually, little by little, imperceptibly, insensibly, invisibly; on a small scale, in a small way, modestly; fairly, moderately, tolerably,

quite; comparatively, relatively, rather; indifferently, poorly, badly; hardly, scarcely, barely, only just, just and no more; narrowly, by the skin of one's teeth, by one's fingernails; hardly at all, no more than, at least, at the very least.

partially, to some degree, in some measure, to a certain extent, to some extent; somehow, after a fashion, sort of, in a kind of way, in a manner of speaking; some, somewhat, a little, a bit, just a bit, ever so little; not fully; in part, partly; not perfectly.

almost, all but, within an ace of, within an inch of, on the brink of, on the verge of, within sight of, in a fair way to 200 *near*; close upon, approximately 200 *nearly*; pretty near, just short of, not quite, virtually.

about, somewhere, somewhere about, thereabouts; more or less; near enough; at a guess, say.

in no way, no ways, no wise, by no means, not by any manner of means, in no respect, not at all, not in the least, not a bit, not the least bit, not in the slightest; not a whit, not a jot, not by a long chalk.

34 Superiority

N. *superiority*, higher position; loftiness 209 *height*; transcendance 32 *largeness*, 306 *overstepping*; top 213 *summit*; excellence 644 *goodness*; ne plus ultra 646 *perfection*; seniority 64 *precedence*, 119 *previousness*; eminence 866 *prestige*; higher rank, higher degree 27 *degree*, 868 *nobility*, *aristocracy*; paramountcy, supremacy, sovereignty, majesty 733 *authority*; ascendancy, domination, predominance 178 *influence*; leadership 689 *management*; prevalence 29 *inequality*; win, championship 727 *victory*; prominence 638 *importance*; one-upmanship 698 *cunning*, 727 *success*; excess 637 *superfluity*; climax, zenith, culmination 725 *completion*; maximum, top, ceiling, peak, pinnacle, crest, crest of the wave; record, high, new high 213 *summit*.

advantage, handicap, favour 615 *benefit*; head start, flying start, lead, commanding lead, winning position, pole position; odds, points, vantage, pull, edge; seeded position; command, upper hand, whip hand; one up, something in hand, reserves; trump card, card up one's sleeve, ace up one's sleeve; leverage, clout; vantage ground.

superior, superman or -woman, wonder-woman 864 *prodigy*; select few 644 *elite*; high-ups, one's betters, top people, best people 638 *bigwig*; aristocracy 868 *upper class*; overlord, sovereign 741 *master*; commander, chief, guide 690 *leader*; boss, foreman 690 *manager*; primate, president, prime minister, premier, first minister, primus inter pares 690 *director*; star, virtuoso 696 *proficient person*; mastermind 500 *sage*; world-beater, record-breaker; chart-topper; prizewinner, champion, record-holder 727 *victor*; prima donna, first lady, head boy *or* girl; big fish in a small pond.

Adj. *superior*, greater 32 *great*; upper, higher, senior, supernormal, above average, in a different class, in a class by himself *or* herself 15 *different*; better, a cut above, head and shoulders above 644 *excellent*; more than a match for; one up, ahead, always one step ahead, streets ahead 64 *preceding*; record, exceeding, overtopping, vaulting, outclassing; in the lead, on top, winning, victorious 727 *successful*; distinguished 866 *noteworthy*; rare 84 *unusual*; top-level, high-level, high-powered 638 *important*; commanding, in authority 733 *ruling*.

supreme, arch-, über-, greatest 32 *great*; highest, above all others, uppermost 213 *topmost*; first, chief, foremost 64 *preceding*; main, principal, leading, overruling, overriding, cardinal, capital 638 *important*; excellent, superlative, super, champion, tip-top, top-notch, first-rate, first-class, A1, 5-star, front-rank, world-beating 644 *best*; facile princeps, top of the class, second to none, none such, nonpareil; dominant, paramount, pre-eminent, sovereign; incomparable, unrivalled, matchless, peerless, unparalleled, unequalled 21 *inimitable*; unsurpassed, ultimate, the last word in; beyond compare 646 *perfect*; transcendental, out of this world.

Vb. *be superior*, transcend, rise above, surmount, overtop, tower over, overlook, command 209 *be high*; go beyond 306 *overstep*; exceed, out-Herod Herod, take the cake, take the biscuit; carry off the laurels, bear the palm, wear the crown; pass, surpass, beat the record, reach a new high; improve on, better, go one better, cap, trump; excel 644 *be good*; assert one's superiority, be too much for; steal the show, outshine, eclipse, overshadow, throw into the shade; put another's nose out of joint, have the laugh on 851 *ridicule*; best, outrival, outclass, outrank 306 *outdo*; outplay, outpoint, outmanoeuvre, outwit; overtake, leave behind, lap 277 *outstrip*; get the better of, worst, trounce, beat, beat hollow, knock into a cocked hat, beat all comers 727 *defeat*.

predominate, preponderate, tip the scale, turn the scale; change the balance 29 *be unequal*; override, sit on 178 *prevail*; have the advantage, have the whip hand, have the upper hand, have the edge on; hold all the cards, hold all the aces; lead, hold the lead, be up on, be one up.

culminate, come to a head; cap, cap it all, crown all 213 *crown*; rise to a peak; set a new record, reach new heights, reach a new high 725 *climax*.

Adv. *beyond*, more, over; over the mark, above the mark, above par, over the average; above the limit, upwards of, in advance of; over and above; at the top of the scale, on the crest, at its height, at the peak, at the zenith.

eminently, pre-eminently, outstandingly, surpassingly, prominently, superlatively, supremely; above all, of all things; to crown it all, to cap it all; par excellence; principally, especially, particularly, peculiarly, singularly; a fortiori; far and away, by far 32 *extremely*.

35 Inferiority

N. *inferiority*, minority, littleness 33 *smallness*; subordinacy, subordination, dependence 745 *subjection*; supporting role, second fiddle 639 *unimportance*; lowliness 872 *humility*; second rank, third class, back seat, obscurity; handicap 702 *hindrance*; defect 647 *imperfection*; inadequateness 307 *shortfall*, 636 *insufficiency*; failure 728 *defeat*; second best 645 *badness*, 812 *cheapness*; kitsch 847 *bad taste*; shabbiness 801 *poverty*; decline 655 *deterioration*; low, all-time low, minimum, lowest point, nadir, the bottom, rock bottom 214 *base*; depression, trough 210 *lowness*.

inferior, subordinate, subaltern, sub, underling, assistant, sidekick, subsidiary 707 *auxiliary*; agent 150 *substitute*, 755 *deputy*; tool, pawn 628 *instrument*; retainer 742 *dependant*; menial, hireling 742 *servant*; poor relation, small fry 639 *nonentity*; subject, underdog 742 *slave*; backbencher, private, other ranks, lower classes 869 *common people*; second, second best, second string, second fiddle, second-rater; also-ran; failure, reject, turkey 607 *rejection*; lesser creation, beast, brute, worm; minor, junior.

Adj. *lesser*, less, minor, small-time, one-horse, hick, small-beer 639 *unimportant*; small 33 *inconsiderable*; smaller, diminished 37 *decreasing*; reduced.

inferior, lower, junior; subordinate, subaltern 742 *serving*; dependent, parasitical 745 *subjected, subject*; secondary, tributary, ancillary, subsidiary, auxiliary 639 *unimportant*, 703 *helping*; second, second-best, second-class, second-rate, B-list, low-rent; third-rate 922 *contemptible*; lowly, below the salt; low-ranking; subnormal, substandard, not up to the mark, not up to scratch; underweight 307 *deficient*; spoilt; defective 647 *imperfect*; failing 636 *insufficient*; shoddy, jerry-built, crummy 645 *bad*, 812 *cheap*, 847 *vulgar*; low 869 *plebeian*; makeshift 670 *unprepared*; temporary, provisional 114 *ephemeral*; feeble 163 *weak*; in a lower class, outclassed, outshone, trounced, beaten 728 *defeated*; unworthy, not fit, not fit to hold a candle to, not in the same league as, not a patch on, a poor man's —.

Vb. *be inferior*, fall short, come short of, fall below 307 *fall short*; lag, fall behind; want, lack 636 *be insufficient*; not make the grade, not come up to scratch, not pass 728 *fail*; bow to 739 *obey*; concede the victory; yield, give in, cede, yield the palm, hand it to, knuckle under 721 *submit*; play second fiddle, play a supporting role 742 *serve*; take a back seat, retire into the shade; sink into obscurity; lose face 867 *lose repute*; get worse 655 *deteriorate*; sink, sink without trace, touch rock bottom, reach one's nadir 309 *descend*.

Adv. *less*, minus, short of; beneath 210 *under*; below average.

36 Increase

N. *increase*, increment, augmentation, waxing, crescendo; progress 285 *progression*; growth, growth area, development area, boom town; buildup, development 164 *production*; extension, protraction; widening; spread, escalation, amplification, inflation, dilation 197 *expansion*; proliferation, swarming 171 *productiveness, abundance*; multiplication; adding 38 *addition*; enlargement, aggrandizement 32 *largeness*; heightening, raising 310 *elevation*; concentration 324 *condensing*; intensification, stepping up, redoubling 91 *duplication*, acceleration, speeding 277 *spurt*; hotting up 381 *heating*; excitation 174 *stimulation*; exacerbation 832 *aggravation*; advancement, boost 654 *improvement*; rise, spiral, upward curve, upward trend, upswing, upturn 308 *ascent*; uprush, upsurge, flood, tide, surge 350 *wave*; progressiveness, cumulativeness, snowball 74 *accumulation*.

increment, augmentation, bulge; accretion, accrual, accession, contribution 38 *addition*; supplement, salary increase, pay rise 40 *extra*; padding, stuffing 303 *insertion*; percentage, commission, expenses, rake-off 771 *earnings*.

Adj. *increasing*, spreading, progressive, escalating; growing, waxing, filling, crescent, on the increase, on the up and up; supplementary 38 *additional*; ever-increasing, snowballing, cumulative 71 *continuous*; intensive; fruitful 171 *prolific*; increased, stretched, enlarged.

Vb. *grow*, increase, gain, develop, escalate; dilate, swell, bulge, wax, fill 197 *expand*; fill out, fatten, thicken; broad; become larger, put on weight 322 *weigh*; sprout, bud, burgeon, flower, blossom 167 *reproduce itself*; breed, spread, swarm, proliferate, mushroom, multi-

ply 104 *be many*, 171 *be fruitful*; grow up 669 *mature*; spring up, shoot up, grow taller, grow by leaps and bounds 209 *be high*; spiral, climb, mount, rise, go through the ceiling, rocket, skyrocket, take off 308 *ascend*; gain strength 162 *be strong*, 656 *be restored*; improve 654 *get better*; flourish, thrive, prosper; gain ground, advance, snowball, accumulate 285 *progress*; earn interest 771 *be profitable*; gain in value, appreciate, rise in price 811 *be dear*; boom, break all records, surge, exceed, overflow 32 *be great*, 637 *be overabundant*; rise to a maximum 34 *culminate*.

augment, increase, bump up, double; redouble; duplicate 106 *repeat*; multiply 166 *reproduce*; propagate, grow, raise, rear 369 *breed stock*; enlarge, magnify, distend, inflate, blow up 197 *expand*; amplify, develop, build up, fill out, fill in, pad out 54 *make complete*; supplement, enrich; contribute to; accrue 38 *add*; extend, prolong, stretch 203 *lengthen*; broaden, widen, thicken, deepen; heighten, enhance, send up 209 *make higher*; raise, exalt 310 *elevate*; advance, aggrandize 285 *promote*; speed up 277 *accelerate*; intensify, redouble, step up, stimulate, energize 174 *invigorate*; give a boost to, boost 162 *strengthen*, 656 *restore*, 685 *refresh*; glorify 482 *overrate*, 546 *exaggerate*; stoke, add fuel to the flame, exacerbate 832 *aggravate*; maximize.

37 Decrease: no increase

N. *decrease*, lessening, dwindling, falling off, de-escalation; waning, fading; dimming 419 *dimness*; wane 198 *contraction*; shrinking; ebb, reflux, retreat 286 *regression*; ebb tide, neap 210 *lowness*; descending order 71 *series*; subsidence, sinking, decline, declension, downward curve, downward spiral, downward trend, downturn, fall, drop, plunge 165 *ruin*, 309 *descent*; deflation, recession, slump 655 *deterioration*; retrenchment, cutback, cut, cutting back 814 *economy*; loss of value, depreciation 812 *cheapness*; weakening; shortage 636 *scarcity*; diminishing returns, exhaustion 190 *emptiness*; shrinkage, erosion, decay, crumbling 655 *dilapidation*.

diminution, making less; deduction 39 *subtraction*; abatement, reduction, de-escalation, restriction 747 *restraint*; deceleration 278 *slowness*; retrenchment, cut, economization 814 *economy*; cutting back, pruning, paring, shaving, clipping, docking, curtailment, abridgment, abbreviation 204 *shortening*; compression, squeeze 198 *contraction*; abrasion, erosion 333 *friction*; weeding out, elimination 62 *sorting*, 300 *ejection*; mitigation, minimization 177 *moderation*; belittlement, undervaluation 483 *underestimation*, 926 *detraction*; demotion, degradation 872 *humiliation*.

Adj. *decreasing*, dwindling; waning, fading; evaporating; de-escalating; declining, going down, sinking, ebbing; decaying.

Vb. *lessen*, abate, diminish, decrease, de-escalate, take away, detract from, deduct 39 *subtract*; except 57 *exclude*; reduce, scale down, whittle, pare, scrape 206 *make thin*; clip, trim 46 *cut*; shrink, abridge, abbreviate, boil down 204 *shorten*; squeeze, compress, contract 198 *make smaller*; limit, curtail 747 *restrain*; cut down, cut back, retrench 814 *economize*; decelerate 278 *retard*; depress 311 *lower*; minimize, mitigate, extenuate 177 *moderate*; allay, alleviate 831 *relieve*; deflate, puncture; disparage, decry, belittle, depreciate, undervalue 483 *underestimate*; dwarf, overshadow 34 *be superior*; steal one's thunder, put in the shade; degrade, demote 872 *humiliate*; exhaust 300 *empty*; let evaporate, boil away 338 *vaporize*; crumble 332 *grind*; rub away, abrade, file 333 *rub*; gnaw, nibble at, eat away 301 *eat*; erode, rust 655 *impair*; strip, peel, denude 229 *uncover*; unman 161 *disable*; dilute 163 *weaken*; thin out, weed out, depopulate 105 *cause to be few*; decimate 165 *destroy*; damp down, crack down on.

decrease, grow less, lessen, de-escalate; abate, slacken, ease, moderate, subside, die down; dwindle, shrink, contract 198 *become small*; wane, waste, decay, wear away, wither away, degenerate 655 *deteriorate*; fade, die away, grow dim 419 *be dim*; retreat, withdraw, ebb 286 *regress*, 290 *recede*; run low, run down, ebb away, drain away, fail 636 *be insufficient*; tail off, taper off, peter out 293 *converge*; subside, sink 313 *plunge*; come down, decline, fall, drop, slump, collapse 309 *descend*; level off, bottom out, lag 278 *slow down*; melt away 446 *disappear*; evaporate 338 *vaporize*; thin out 105 *be few*; become endangered, become extinct 2 *pass away*; reduce, lose weight, become anorexic 323 *be light*, 946 *starve*; lose one's voice, shut up 578 *be mute*; lose, shed; cast off.

38 Addition

N. *addition*, adding to, annexation, agglutination 45 *union*; superimposing 187 *location*; affixture 65 *sequence*; supplementation, contribution 703 *aid*; superaddition, imposition, load 702 *encumbrance*; accession, accretion, accrual, supervention; interposition, interjection 78 *inclusion*, 303 *insertion*; reinforcement 36 *increase*; increment, supplement, additive, E numbers; add-on; addendum, appendage, tailpiece, appendix 40 *adjunct*; extra time, over-

time 113 *protraction*; appurtenance 89 *accompaniment*; summation, adding up, counting up, totalling, total.

Adj. *additional*, additive; added, included, etc. (see vb.); adventitious; supplementary, conjunctive; subsidiary, auxiliary, contributory 703 *helping*; supernumerary; another, further, more; extra, spare 637 *superfluous*; interjected, interposed 303 *inserted*; prefixed 64 *preceding*; beyond the call of duty 597 *voluntary*.

Vb. *add*, add up, sum, total; carry over 272 *transfer*; add to, annex, append; attach, pin to, clip to, tag on, tack on; hitch to, yoke to, unite to 45 *join, tie*; stick on, glue on; add on; preface, prefix, affix, suffix, infix; introduce; interpose, interject; engraft, let in 303 *insert*; contribute to 36 *augment*; swell, extend, expand 197 *enlarge*; supplement; superadd, superimpose; ornament, embellish 844 *decorate*; mix in with 43 *mix*; annex 786 *take*.

accrue, be added 78 *be included*; supervene 295 *arrive*; join 708 *join a party*; combine with 50 *combine*; make one more; reinforce, swell the ranks.

Adv. *in addition*, additionally, more, plus, extra; -plus, -something; with interest, with a vengeance, with knobs on; and, too, also, item, furthermore, further; likewise, and also, to boot; else, besides; et cetera; and so on, and so forth, moreover, into the bargain, over and above, including, inclusive of, with, cum, as well as, apart from, not to mention, let alone, not forgetting; together with, along with, coupled with, in conjunction with.

39 Subtraction

N. *subtraction*, deduction, taking away; diminution 37 *decrease*; abstraction, removal, withdrawal; elimination 62 *sorting*; clearance 300 *ejection*; unpacking 188 *displacement*, 304 *extraction*; precipitation, sedimentation, ablation, abrasion, erosion, detrition 333 *friction*; retrenchment, cutting back, curtailment 204 *shortening*; severance, detruncation, amputation, excision 46 *splitting*; mutilation 655 *impairment*; expurgation; deletion 550 *obliteration*; minuend 85 *numerical element*; subtrahend.

Vb. *subtract*, take away, deduct, do subtraction; detract from, diminish, decrease 37 *lessen*; cut 810 *discount*; take off, knock off, allow; except, take out, leave out 57 *exclude*; expel 300 *eject*; abstract 786 *take*, 788 *steal*; withdraw, remove; unload 188 *displace*; shift 272 *transfer*; draw off 300 *empty*; abrade, scrape away, file down, erode 333 *rub*; eradicate, uproot, pull up, pull out 304 *extract*; pick, pick out, put on one side 605 *select*; cross out, blot out, delete, censor 550 *obliterate*; expurgate, mutilate 655 *impair*; sever, separate, amputate, excise; shear, shave off, clip 46 *cut*; retrench, cut back, cut down, whittle, lop, prune, pare, decapitate, behead, dock, curtail, abridge, abbreviate 204 *shorten*; geld, castrate, caponize, spay, emasculate 161 *unman*; peel, skin, fleece, strip, divest, denude 229 *uncover*.

40 Adjunct: thing added

N. *adjunct*, addition, additive, something added, add-on, contribution 38 *addition*; addendum, carry-over; supplement, annex; attachment, fixture; inflection, affix, suffix, prefix, adjective, adverb 564 *part of speech*; ticket, tag 547 *label*; appendage, tailpiece, train, following 67 *sequel*; wake 65 *sequence*; appendix, postscript, P.S., P.P.S., envoi, coda, ending 69 *extremity*; codicil, rider 468 *qualification*; marginalia, annotation, footnotes; corollary, complement 725 *completion*; appurtenance, accessory 89 *concomitant*; companion piece, fellow, pair 18 *analogue*; extension, continuation, second part; annexe, wing (of a house), outhouse 164 *building*; offshoot 53 *branch*; arm, extremity 53 *limb*; accretion 59 *extraneousness*; increment 36 *increase*; patch, reinforcement 656 *repair*; padding, stuffing 227 *lining*; interpolation 303 *insertion*; interlude, intermezzo 231 *betweenness*; insertion, gusset 228 *article of clothing*; flap, lappet, lapel; ingredient 58 *component*; fringe 234 *edge*; embroidery 844 *ornamentation*; garnish, seasoning; frills, trimmings, trappings, accoutrements 228 *dressing*.

extra, additive, addendum, increment, something over and above, by-product; percentage, interest 771 *gain*; bonus, tip, perk, perquisite, graft 962 *reward*; free gift, freebie, giveaway, gratuity, golden handshake, golden hello 781 *gift*; windfall; allowance; oddment, odds and ends; supernumerary; spare parts, spares 633 *provision*; reinforcement 707 *auxiliary*; surplus 637 *superfluity*; extra time, injury time, overtime.

41 Remainder: thing remaining

N. *remainder*, residue; result; balance; surplus; relic, rest, remains, remnant 105 *fewness*; rump, stump, stub, scrag end, fag end, butt end 69 *extremity*; torso, trunk 53 *piece*; fossil, skeleton, bones 363 *corpse*; husk, shell; wreck, wreckage, debris 165 *ruin*; ashes 332 *powder*; track, spoor, fingerprint 548 *record, trace*; afterglow 67 *sequel*; memorabilia 505 *remembrance*; survival 113 *durability*; vestige.

leavings, leftovers, doggy-bag; precipitate, deposit, sediment, residue, residuum; allu-

vium, silt 344 *soil*; drift, loess, moraine, detritus 272 *thing transferred*: grounds, lees, dregs; scum, dross, slag, sludge; bilge; scrapings, shavings, filings, sawdust, crumbs 332 *powder*; husks, chaff, stubble; peel, peelings; skin, slough, scurf; combings, trimmings, clippings, remnants, off-cuts; scraps, candle-ends, odds and ends, bin-ends, lumber 641 *rubbish*; rejects 779 *derelict*; sweepings, scourings, off-scourings; waste, sewage 302 *excrement*; refuse, litter 649 *dirt*.

Adj. *remaining*, surviving, left, vestigial, resultant; residual; deposited, sedimentary, precipitated; discarded 779 *not retained*; on the shelf 860 *unwanted*; left over, odd; net, surplus; unused; outstanding; spare; superfluous 637 *redundant*; orphaned, widowed.

Vb. *be left*, remain, result, survive.

leave over, leave out 57 *exclude*; leave, discard, abandon 607 *reject*.

42 Deduction: thing deducted

N. *deduction*, decrement, depreciation, cut 37 *diminution*; allowance; remission; clawback, rebate 810 *discount*; refund, shortage, slippage; defect 307 *shortfall*, 636 *insufficiency*; loss, sacrifice, forfeit 963 *penalty*; leak, leakage, escape 298 *outflow*; consumption 634 *waste*; subtrahend; rake-off 786 *taking*; toll 809 *tax*.

43 Mixture

N. *mixture*, mingling, mixing, stirring; blending, harmonization; admixture 38 *addition*; commixture 45 *union*; intermixture, interpolation 231 *betweenness*; interweaving, interlacing 222 *crossing*; amalgamation, integration 50 *combination*; merger 706 *association*; eclecticism; fusion, interfusion, infusion, suffusion, transfusion, instillation, impregnation; adulteration 655 *impairment*; contamination, infection 653 *unhealthiness*; infiltration, penetration 297 *entering*; crossbreeding, interbreeding, miscegenation, intermarriage 894 *marriage*; syngamy, allogamy 167 *propagation*; cross-fertilization, hybridism, hybridization, mongrelism; miscibility, solubility 337 *liquefaction*.

tincture, infusion, admixture; sprinkling; ingredient 58 *component*; strain, streak, element, vein; tinge, touch, drop, dash, soupçon 33 *small quantity*; smack, hint, suspicion, flavour 386 *taste*; seasoning; colour, dye 425 *hue*; stain 845 *blemish*.

a mixture, mélange; blend, harmony 710 *harmony*; composition 331 *structure*; amalgam, fusion, compound, confection, potpourri, concoction 50 *combination*; pastiche; alloy, bronze, brass, pewter, steel; paste; soup, stew, goulash, ragout, blanquette, olla podrida, salmagundi 301 *dish*; cocktail, punch, brew; solution, infusion.

medley, variety 17 *non-uniformity*, 82 *existence in many forms*; motley, mosaic 437 *variegation*; arrangement, array, assortment, choice, collection, diversity, gallimaufry, hotchpotch *or* hodgepodge, miscellany *or* miscellanea, mishmash, mixed bag, pick'n'mix, potpourri, raft, ragbag, range, selection, smorgasbord; jumble, job lot, lucky dip; conglomeration 74 *accumulation*; entanglement, imbroglio 61 *confusion*; phantasmagoria, kaleidoscope; clatter 411 *discord*; motley crew 74 *crowd*; circus 369 *zoo*; variety show 594 *stage show*; all sorts, odds and ends, paraphernalia.

hybrid, cross, cross-breed, mongrel; mule; half-breed, half-caste; mulatto.

Adj. *mixed*, mixed up, stirred; mixed up in, involved in; blended, harmonized, integrated, joined up; syncretic, eclectic; fused, alloyed 50 *combined*; tempered, qualified, adulterated, sophisticated, watered down 163 *weakened*; merged, amalgamated; composite, half-and-half, fifty-fifty; confused, jumbled; unclassified, out of order; heterogeneous 17 *non-uniform*; kaleidoscopic, phantasmagoric 82 *existing in many forms*; patchy, dappled, motley 437 *variegated*; shot; miscellaneous, random 464 *indiscriminate*; miscible, soluble; pervasive 653 *infectious*; hybrid, mongrel; cross-bred, crossed; half-caste; of mixed blood, multiracial.

Vb. *mix*, mix up, stir, shake; shuffle, scramble 63 *jumble*; knead, mash 332 *grind*; brew 56 *compose*; fuse, alloy, merge, amalgamate 45 *join*; blend, harmonize 50 *combine*; mingle, intermingle, intersperse 437 *variegate*; interleave 303 *insert*; intertwine, interweave 222 *weave*; tinge, dye 425 *colour*; imbue, instil, impregnate; sprinkle 341 *moisten*; water down, adulterate 163 *weaken*; temper, doctor, tamper with 143 *modify*; season, spice, fortify, lace, spike; hybridize, mongrelize, cross, cross-fertilize, cross-breed 167 *generate*.

Adv. *among*, amongst, amid, amidst, with; in the midst of; inter alia.

44 Simpleness: freedom from mixture

N. *simpleness*, homogeneity 16 *uniformity*; purity 648 *cleanness*; oneness 88 *unity*; absoluteness, sheerness; fundamentality 1 *essence*; indivisibility, insolubility; simplicity 516 *intelligibility*, 573 *plainness*, 699 *artlessness*.

Adj. *simple*, homogeneous, monolithic 16 *uniform*; sheer, mere, utter, nothing but; single, unified 88 *one*; elemental, indivisible, entire 52 *whole*; primary, fundamental, nuts

and bolts, basic, bog standard, no-frills, without bells and whistles 5 *inherent*; elementary, uncomplicated, simplified, user-friendly 516 *intelligible*; direct, unadulterated, unalloyed; unsophisticated 699 *artless*; sincere; naked.

unmixed, pure and simple, without alloy; clear, pure, undefiled, unpolluted, clarified, purified 648 *clean*; thoroughbred 868 *noble*; free from, excluding; unblemished, untarnished 646 *perfect*; unblended, unalloyed; uncompounded, uncombined; undiluted, unadulterated, neat 162 *strong*; unqualified, unmodified; unfortified; unseasoned.

Vb. *simplify*, make simple 16 *make uniform*; break down, factorize 51 *decompose*; disentangle, unscramble; unite.

45 Union

N. *union*, junction, joining, etc. (see vb.); coming together, meeting, concurrence, conjunction 293 *convergence*; clash 279 *collision*; contact 202 *contiguity*, 378 *touch*; congress, concourse, reunion 74 *assembly*; confluence, rendezvous, meeting-place 76 *focus*; coalescence, fusion, merger 43 *mixture*; unification, synthesis 50 *combination*; cohesion, agglutination 48 *cohesiveness*; concretion, consolidation, solidification, coagulation 324 *condensing*; coalition, alliance, symbiosis 706 *association*; connection, linkage, tie-up, hook-up, link-up, network 47 *bond*; fusion (of gametes): syngamy; wedlock 894 *marriage*; interconnection, interlocking 222 *crossing*; communication 305 *passage*; network, intercommunication; intercourse 882 *sociability*; trade, traffic, exchange 151 *interchange*, 791 *trade*; involvement 9 *relation*; meeting of minds, chemistry.

joint, joining, juncture; crease 261 *fold*; suture, seam, stitching 47 *bond*; bonding, English bond, Flemish bond; weld; splice; mitre, mitre joint, dovetail, dovetail and mortise joint, mortise and tenon joint, ball and socket joint; hasp, latch, sneck, catch 218 *pivot*; hinge-joint; finger, thumb, wrist, ankle, knuckle, knee, hip, elbow; node; junction, meeting-point, intersection, crossroads 222 *crossing*; decussation, figure X 222 *cross*.

sexual intercourse, sex, making love, consensual sex, rumpy-pumpy, bonk (vulg), fuck (vulg), ride (vulg), screw (vulg), shag (vulg); quickie; intimacy, coition, coitus, copulation, carnal knowledge; the beast with two backs; group sex, gang-bang, roasting; anal intercourse; pairing, mating, coupling; union 894 *marriage*; consummation; unprotected sex, bareback sex *or* barebacking; casual sex, espresso sex, sexual sorbet, dogging; safe sex 172 *contraception*; foreplay, fellatio, blowjob (vulg), cunnilingus; sexual assault 951 *rape*; prostitution, survival sex 951 *social evil*; sex addiction *or* sexual addiction; cybersex; generation 167 *propagation*.

sexual partner, lover 887 *lover*; husband, wife; mistress 887 *loved one*, 952 *kept woman*; prostitute, sex worker, hooker, tart, whore, male prostitute, rent-boy 952 *libertine*, *prostitute*; lay (vulg), ride (vulg), screw (vulg); dogger; Mile High Club; sex addict.

Adj. *connective*, conjunctive, adjunctive, copulative, adhesive 48 *cohesive*; coagulating, astringent; coincident; copulatory, coital, venereal, intimate.

firm, close, fast, secure, sound 153 *fixed*; solid, set, solidified 324 *dense*; glued, cemented, stuck 48 *cohesive*; put, pat; planted, rooted, deep-set; ingrown, impacted; close-set, crowded, tight, tight-fitting, wedged, jammed, stuck; inextricable, inseparable, immovable, unshakable; packed, jam-packed 54 *full*.

tied, bound, knotted, roped, lashed, secured, belayed, spliced; stitched, sewn, gathered; attached, fastened, adhering 48 *cohesive*; well-tied, tight, taut, tense, fast, secure; intricate, involved, tangled, inextricable, indissoluble.

Vb. *join*, conjoin, couple, yoke, hyphenate, harness together; pair, match 18 *liken*, 462 *compare*, 894 *marry*; bracket, bracket together 28 *equalize*; put together, throw together, piece together, unite 50 *combine*; gather 74 *bring together*; add to, amass, accumulate 38 *add*, 632 *store*; associate, ally, twin (town); merge 43 *mix*; incorporate, unify 16 *make uniform*; lump together, roll into one; include, embrace 78 *comprise*; grip, grapple 778 *retain*; hinge, articulate, dovetail, mortise, mitre, rabbet; fit, set, interlock, jam 303 *insert*; weld, solder, fuse, cement, glue; lace, knit, sew, seam, stitch; pin, buckle; do up, fasten, button up, zip up 264 *close*; lock, latch; darn, patch, mend, heal over 656 *repair*.

connect, attach, annex (see also *affix* below); staple, clip, pin together; string together, rope together, link together, contact 378 *touch*; make contact, plug in, earth; network, interconnect; link, bridge, span; communicate, intercommunicate; put through to, put in touch; hook up with, link up with, tie up with 9 *relate*.

affix, attach, fix, fasten; yoke, leash, harness, saddle, bridle; tie up, moor, anchor, tie to, tether, pin on, hang on, hook on, screw on, nail on; stick on, cement on, sellotape on, gum on; suffix, prefix 38 *add*; splice, engraft, implant 303 *insert*; impact, set, frame 235 *enclose*; drive in, knock in, hammer in 279

strike; wedge, jam; screw, nail, rivet, bolt, clamp, clinch.

tie, knot, hitch, lash, belay; knit, sew, seam, stitch, suture; tack, baste; braid, plait, crochet, twine, twist, intertwine, lace, interlace, interweave 222 *weave*; truss, string, rope, strap; do up, lace up, lash up; tether, picket, moor; pinion, manacle, handcuff; hobble, shackle 747 *fetter*; bind, splice, gird, girdle; bandage.

tighten, constrict, compress; fasten, screw up, make firm, make fast, secure; tauten, draw tight, pull tight.

unite with, join, meet 293 *converge*; hold tight, fit closely, adhere, hang together, stick together 48 *cohere*; mesh, interlock, engage, grip, grapple, clinch; embrace, entwine; link up with, hold hands; associate with, partner, mix with 882 *be sociable*; marry, get hitched 894 *wed*; live with, cohabit.

have sexual intercourse with, have intercourse, make love, have sex with, go to bed with, sleep with, sleep together, bed, bonk, do, fuck (vulg), give someone one, have, have it off *or* away with, get one's end away, knock off, lay, make, ride (vulg), roger (vulg), screw (vulg), shaft (vulg), shag (vulg), tumble; enjoy, know, lie with, possess; have carnal knowledge; consummate a marriage *or* a union; deflower, rape, ravish, violate, take by force 951 *debauch*; copulate, couple, mate, pair 167 *generate*; cover, mount, tup, serve; cross with, breed with.

46 Separation

N. *separation*, disjoining, severance, parting; uncoupling, breaking up, splitting up 896 *divorce*; untying, undoing, unfastening, unravelling; loosening, freeing 746 *liberation*; setting apart, discrimination, segregation, ghettoization, apartheid 883 *seclusion*; exemption 57 *exclusion*; boycott 620 *avoidance*; expulsion 300 *ejection*; selection 605 *choice*; putting aside 632 *storage*; taking away 39 *subtraction*; expropriation; detaching, withdrawal 188 *displacement*, 272 *transference*; stripping, peeling, plucking 229 *uncovering*; disjointing, dislocation; scattering 75 *dispersion*; dissolution, resolution, disintegration 51 *decomposition*; dissection, analysis, breakdown; disruption, fragmentation 165 *destruction*; splitting (see also *splitting* below), fission, nuclear fission 160 *nuclear physics*; breaking, cracking, rupture, fracture 330 *brittleness*; dividing line; caesura; wall, fence, hedge, ha-ha 231 *partition*; curtain 421 *screen*; boundary 236 *limit*; Styx, Rubicon.

disunion, disjunction, disconnection, disconnectedness, incoherence, break 72 *discontinuity*; diffusion, dispersal 75 *dispersion*; breakup, disintegration, dissolution, decay 51 *decomposition*, 655 *dilapidation*; absent-mindedness 456 *abstractedness*; dissociation, withdrawal, retirement 621 *relinquishment*, 753 *resignation*; moving apart, growing apart, widening 282 *deviation*, 294 *divergence*; split, schism (see also *separation* below); detachment, neutrality 860 *indifference*; isolation, quarantine, segregation 883 *seclusion*; insularity 620 *avoidance*; lack of unity 709 *dissension*; separateness, isolationism, separatism; no connection, no common ground 10 *unrelatedness*; distance apart; dichotomy 15 *difference*; interval, breathing space, space, opening, hole, breach, break, rent, rift, tear, split; fissure, crack, cleft, chasm; cleavage, slit, cut, gash, incision 201 *gap*.

splitting, scission, section, cleavage, cutting, tearing; division, dichotomy 92 *division into two*; subdivision, segmentation; partition 783 *allocation*; abscission; cutting off, decapitation, curtailment, retrenchment 37 *diminution*, 204 *shortening*; cutting away, resection, circumcision; cutting open, incision, opening 658 *surgery*; dissection; rending; clawing, laceration, tearing off, nipping, pinching, biting, etc. (see vb.).

Adj. *separate*, apart, asunder; adrift, lost; unjoined, unfixed, unfastened; unattached, unannexed, unassociated; distinct, discrete, differentiated, separable, distinguishable 15 *different*; exempt, excepted; hived off, abstracted; unassimilated 44 *unmixed*; alien, foreign 59 *extraneous*; external 6 *external*, 223 *exterior*; insular, lonely, isolated 88 *alone*; outside *or* not in the loop; shunned, dropped, avoided, boycotted, sent to Coventry; cast-off; set apart 605 *chosen*; abandoned, left 41 *remaining*; hostile, antipathetic 14 *nonidentical*, 240 *opposite*, 881 *hostile*; divorced; disjunctive, separative; dichotomous, dividing; selective, diagnostic 15 *distinctive*.

Vb. *separate*, stand apart 620 *avoid*; go away 296 *depart*; go apart, go different ways, radiate 294 *diverge*; go another way 282 *deviate*; part, part company, cut adrift, cut loose, divorce, split up; hive off; get free, get loose 667 *escape*; disengage, cast off, unmoor, leave, quit, fall away 621 *relinquish*; scatter, break up 75 *disperse*; spring apart 280 *recoil*; come apart, fall apart, break, come to bits, disintegrate 51 *decompose*; come undone, unravel; fall off 49 *come unstuck*; split, crack 263 *open*.

disunite, dissociate, divorce, decouple; split up, break up, part, separate, sunder, sever; uncouple, unhitch, disconnect, unplug; disengage; disjoint, displace, dislocate, wrench; detach, unseat; remove, detract, deduct 39 *subtract*, 272 *transfer*; skin, strip, flay, peel;

pluck 229 *uncover*; unfasten, undo, unbutton, unhook, unlace, unzip, unclasp, unlock, unlatch 263 *open*; untie, cut the knot, sever the tie, disentangle; unstitch, unpick; loosen, relax, slacken, unstring 177 *moderate*; unbind, unchain, unfetter, unloose, loose, free, set free, release 746 *liberate*; expel 300 *eject*; dispel, scatter, break up, disband, demobilize 75 *disperse*; disintegrate, break down 51 *decompose*, 165 *destroy*, 332 *grind*.

set apart, put aside, set aside, ring-fence 632 *store*; mark out, tick off, distinguish 15 *differentiate*, 463 *discriminate*; single out 605 *select*; exempt, leave out 57 *exclude*; boycott, send to Coventry 620 *avoid*; taboo, black, blacklist 757 *prohibit*; insulate, isolate, cut off 235 *enclose*; zone, compartmentalize, screen off, declare a no-go area 232 *encircle*; segregate, ghettoize, sequester, quarantine, maroon 883 *seclude*; keep apart, hold apart, drive apart; drive a wedge between, estrange, alienate, set against.

break, fracture, rupture, bust; split, burst; break in pieces, smash, smash to smithereens, shatter, splinter, shiver 165 *demolish*; fragment, crumble, grind 332 *grind*; disintegrate, cave in 51 *decompose*; break up, dismantle (see also *break up* below); chip, crack, damage 655 *impair*; bend, buckle, warp 246 *distort*; break in two, snap; cleave, force apart 263 *open*.

break up, break apart, sunder (see also *break* and *disunite* above); divide, fragment, fractionate, segment, sectionalize, fractionalize; reduce, factorize, analyse; dissect 51 *decompose*; dichotomize, halve 92 *divide*; divide up, split, partition, parcel out 783 *allocate*; dismember, quarter, carve (see also *cut* below); behead, decapitate, curtail, dock, amputate 204 *shorten*; take apart, take to pieces, cannibalize, dismantle, break up, dismount; force open 263 *open*; slit, split; cleave 263 *pierce*.

cut, hew, hack, slash, gash 655 *wound*; prick, stab, knife 263 *pierce*; cut through, cleave, saw, chop; cut open, slit 263 *open*; cut into, make an incision, incise 555 *engrave*; cut deep, cut to the bone, carve, slice; cut round, pare, whittle, chisel, chip, trim, bevel; clip; snip; cut short, shave 204 *shorten*; cut down, fell, scythe, mow; cut off, lop, prune, dock, curtail (see also *break up* above); cut up, chop up, quarter, dismember; dice, shred, mince, make mincemeat of, pound 332 *grind*; bite 301 *chew*; scratch, score, plough 262 *groove*; nick 260 *notch*.

rend, tear (see also *break up* above); scratch, claw, gnaw, fret, fray, make ragged; rip, slash, slit (see also *cut* above); lacerate, dismember; tear limb from limb, tear to pieces, tear to shreds 165 *destroy*; mince, grind, crunch, scrunch, pound 301 *chew*, 332 *grind*; blow to pieces, burst.

Adv. *separately*, severally, singly, one by one, bit by bit, piecemeal, in bits, in pieces, in halves, in twain, discontinuously, unconnectedly, disjointedly.

apart, open, asunder, adrift; to pieces, to bits, to smithereens, to shreds; limb from limb.

47 Bond: connecting medium

N. *bond*, vinculum, chain, shackle, fetter, handcuff, tie, band, hoop, yoke; sympathy, empathy, fellow feeling 905 *pity*; nexus, connection, link, liaison 9 *relation*; junction, hinge 45 *joint*; ramification, network 53 *branch*; hyphen, dash, bracket 547 *punctuation*; cement (see also *adhesive* below); bondstone, binder; tie-beam, stretcher, girder 218 *beam*; strut, stay 218 *prop*; channel, passage, corridor 624 *access*; stepping-stone, causeway 624 *bridge*; span, arch; isthmus, neck; col, ridge; stair, steps, stepladder, ladder 308 *ascent*; lifeline; umbilical cord.

cable, line, guy, hawser, painter, moorings; guest-rope, towline, towrope, ripcord, lanyard, communication cord; rope, cord, whipcord, string, tape, twine 208 *fibre*; chain, wire, earth.

ligature, ligament, tendon, muscle, abdominal muscle, abdominals, abs, six-pack, pectoral muscle, pectorals, pecs (inf), biceps, triceps; tendril, osier, raffia 208 *fibre*; lashing, binding; string, cord, thread, tape, sticky tape, Sellotape (tdmk), Scotch tape (tdmk), duct tape, Velcro (tdmk); band, fillet, ribbon, riband; bandage, tourniquet; drawstring, thong, lace, tag; braid, plait 222 *network*; tie, stock, cravat 228 *neckwear*; knot, hitch, clinch, bend; running knot, slip knot, granny knot, reef knot; clove hitch, half hitch, bowline, bowline on a bight, sheepshank, sheet bend; Gordian knot.

fastening, fastener, snap fastener, press-stud, pop-fastener, popper, zip fastener, zip; drawstring; stitch, basting; button, buttonhole, eyelet, loop, frog; hook and eye; Velcro (tdmk); stud, cufflink; garter, suspender, braces; tiepin, brooch 844 *jewellery*; clip, grip, slide, clasp, curlers; hairpin, hatpin; skewer, spit, pin, drawing pin, safety pin, toggle pin, cotter pin, linch pin, king pin; peg, dowel, treenail *or* trenail, nail, brad, tack, tintack 256 *sharp point*; Blu-tack (tdmk), Sellotape (tdmk), Scotch tape (tdmk); holdfast, staple, clamp, brace, batten, cramp 778 *pincers*; nut, wingnut, bolt, screw, rivet, buckle, clasp, morse; hasp, hinge 45 *joint*; catch, safety catch, spring catch; latch, bolt; lock, lock and key 264 *closure*; combination lock, yale lock, mortise lock;

padlock, handcuffs, bracelets 748 *fetter*; ring, cleat; hold, bar, post, pile, pale, stake, bollard.

adhesive, glue, fish glue, isinglass, lime, birdlime, gum, epoxy resin; fixative, hair lacquer, hair spray, brilliantine, grease; solder; paste, size, clay, cement, putty, mortar, stucco, plaster, grout 226 *facing*; wafer, sealing wax; sticker, stamp, adhesive tape, sticky tape, Sellotape (tdmk), Scotch tape (tdmk), Blu-tack (tdmk); flypaper 542 *trap*; sticking plaster, Elastoplast (tdmk), Band-Aid (tdmk) 48 *cohesiveness*.

48 Cohesiveness

N. *cohesiveness*, cohesion, tenacity 778 *retention*; coherence, connection, connectedness 71 *continuity*; chain 71 *series*; adherence, adhesion, adhesiveness; stickiness 354 *glutinousness*; cementation, cementing, sticking, soldering, agglutination 45 *union*; compaction, conglomeration, consolidation, set 324 *condensing*; inseparability, indivisibility, union 88 *unity*; phalanx, serried ranks, unbroken front, united front; birds of a feather; monolith, agglomerate, concrete 324 *solid body*.

Adj. *cohesive*, adhesive, adherent; clinging, tenacious; sticky, tacky, gummy, gluey, viscous 354 *glutinous*; well-knit, coagulated, concrete, frozen 324 *dense*; shoulder to shoulder, side by side, serried; monolithic 16 *uniform*; united, indivisible, inseparable, inextricable; close, tight, close-fitting, skintight, figure-hugging, clinging, moulding.

Vb. *cohere*, hang together, grow together 50 *combine*; stick close, hold fast; bunch, close the ranks, rally 74 *congregate*; take hold of 778 *retain*; hug, clasp, embrace, twine round; close with; fit, fit tight, mould the figure; adhere, cling, stick; stick to, cleave to, stick on to, freeze on to; stick like a limpet, cling like a shadow, cling like ivy; cake, coagulate, conglomerate, solidify.

49 Non-cohesiveness

N. *non-cohesiveness*, non-coherence, incoherence 72 *discontinuity*; uncombined state, non-combination, chaos 51 *decomposition*; scattering 75 *dispersion*; separability; looseness, bagginess; loosening, relaxation, freedom 46 *separation*; wateriness 335 *fluidity*; slipperiness 258 *smoothness*; frangibility, friability 330 *brittleness*; non-adhesion, aloofness.

Vb. *come unstuck*, peel off, melt, thaw, run 337 *liquefy*; totter, slip 309 *tumble*; dangle, flap 217 *hang*; rattle, shake, flap.

50 Combination

N. *combination*, composition; coalescence, symphysis 45 *union*; fusion, blending, conflation, synthesis, syncretism 43 *mixture*; amalgamation, merger, assimilation, digestion, absorption 299 *reception*; uniting, unification, integration, centralization 88 *unity*; incorporation, embodiment; synchronization 706 *cooperation*; marriage, union, league, alliance 706 *association*; cabal 623 *plot*; counterpoint 412 *music*; chorus 24 *agreement*; harmony, orchestration 710 *harmony*; assembly 74 *assemblage*; synopsis, conspectus, bird's-eye view 592 *compendium*.

compound, alloy, amalgam, blend, composite, chemical, chemical compound 43 *a mixture*.

Adj. combined, united, unified 88 *one*; coherent, integrated, joined up, systematized; centralized; embodied; inbred, ingrained, absorbed 5 *inherent*; fused 43 *mixed*; blended, adapted 24 *adjusted*; connected, linked, networked, conjoint; aggregated; synchronized 123 *synchronous*; in harmony, on the same wavelength, in partnership, in league; associated 706 *cooperative*; conspiratorial.

Vb. combine, put together; make up 56 *compose*; interweave 222 *weave*; harmonize, synchronize 24 *accord*; bind, tie 45 *join*; unite, unify, centralize; incorporate, embody, integrate, absorb, assimilate; merge, amalgamate; pool; blend, fuse 43 *mix*; impregnate, imbue, instil, inoculate; bracket together; lump together 38 *add*; group, rally 74 *bring together*; band together, associate, ally; go into partnership with, join hands, join forces with, team up with 706 *cooperate*; fraternize, make friends 880 *be friendly*; marry 894 *wed*; mate 90 *pair*; conspire 623 *plot*; coalesce, grow together.

51 Decomposition

N. decomposition 46 *disunion*; division, partition 46 *separation*; dissection, dismemberment; anatomization, analysis, breakdown; factorization; syllabification, parsing 564 *grammar*; resolution, electrolysis, hydrolysis, photolysis, catalysis; atomization; dissolving, dissolution 337 *liquefaction*; fission 160 *nuclear physics*; hiving off, decentralization, devolution, delegation; regionalism; collapse, breakup, disintegration, entropy 165 *destruction*; chaos 17 *non-uniformity*.

decay 655 *dilapidation*; erosion, wear and tear 37 *diminution*; disintegration 361 *death*; corruption, mouldering, rotting, putridness, putrefaction, adipocere, mortification, necrosis, gangrene, caries 649 *uncleanness*; rot, dry rot, wet rot, rust, mould 659 *blight*; carrion 363 *corpse*; composting.

Vb. decompose, resolve, reduce, factorize 44 *simplify*; separate, parse, dissect; break down, analyse, take to pieces 46 *break up*; electrolyse, catalyse; split, fission 46 *disunite*; atomize 165

demolish; disband, break up, hive off 75 *disperse*; decentralize 783 *allocate*; unsettle, disturb 63 *disarrange*; melt 337 *liquefy*; erode 37 *lessen*; rot, rust, moulder, decay, compost, consume, waste away, crumble, wear, perish 655 *deteriorate*; corrupt, putrefy, mortify, gangrene 649 *be unclean*; disintegrate, go to pieces 165 *be destroyed*.

52 Whole. Principal part

N. whole, wholeness, fullness 54 *completeness*; integration, indivisibility, integrity, oneness 88 *unity*; whole number, integer, entity 88 *unit*; entirety, ensemble, corpus, complex, totality, summation, sum 38 *addition*; holism, universalization, generalization 79 *generality*; comprehensiveness, inclusiveness 78 *inclusion*; collectivity, system, world, globe, cosmos 321 *universe*; microcosm; Lebensraum; bird's-eye view, panorama, overview, conspectus.

all, no exceptions, one and all, everybody, everyone 79 *everyman*; all the world 74 *crowd*; everything, aggregate, gross amount, sum, total, sum total; lot, whole lot, the whole caboodle, the whole bang shoot, the works, the whole nine yards, the full monty; ensemble, be-all and end-all, lock, stock and barrel, bag and baggage, hook, line and sinker; inventory 87 *list*.

chief part, best part, major part, nitty-gritty, nuts and bolts 638 *chief thing*; ninety-nine per cent, bulk, mass; heap 32 *great quantity*; tissue, staple, stuff; body, torso, trunk, bole, stem, stalk; hull, hulk, skeleton; lion's share, biggest slice of the cake; gist, sum and substance, the long and the short of it; almost all, nearly all, everything but the kitchen sink; all but a few, majority.

Adj. whole, total, universal; integral, pure 44 *unmixed*; sound 646 *perfect*; gross, full 54 *complete*; integrated 88 *one*; in one piece; fully restored.

intact, untouched, unaffected, unspoiled, virgin 126 *new*; undivided, undiminished, unclipped, uncut; undissolved; unbroken, unimpaired 646 *undamaged*; uncut, unabridged, unedited, uncensored, unexpurgated.

indivisible 324 *insoluble*; inseparable, monolithic 16 *uniform*.

comprehensive, omnibus, all-embracing, all-encompassing, across-the-board, full-length 78 *inclusive*; wholesale, all singing, all dancing, sweeping 32 *extensive*; widespread, epidemic 79 *general*; international, world, world-wide, global, cosmic 79 *universal*, 189 *present everywhere*.

Adv. on the whole, by and large, all in all, all things considered, in the long run; substantially, in essence; virtually, to all intents and purposes, in effect; as good as; mainly, in the main 32 *greatly*; almost, all but 200 *nearly*.

collectively, one and all, all together; comprehensively; in bulk; in the aggregate; en masse, en bloc.

53 Part

N. *part*, portion, tranche; proportion, fraction, half, quarter, tithe, percentage; factor, aliquot 85 *number*; surplus 41 *remainder*; quota, contingent; dividend, share 783 *portion*; item, particular, detail 80 *particulars*; clause, sentence, paragraph 563 *phrase*; ingredient, member, constituent, element 58 *component*; schism, faction 708 *party*; heat, leg, lap, round 110 *period*; side 239 *laterality*; group, species (see also *subdivision* below); detachment; attachment 40 *adjunct*; page, leaf, folio, sheet 589 *book*; excerpt, extract, passage, quotation, quote 605 *choice*; text; segment, sector, section 46 *splitting*; arc 248 *curve*; hemisphere 252 *sphere*; instalment, advance, down payment, deposit, earnest 804 *payment*; fragment (see also *piece* below).

subdivision, segment, sector, section 46 *splitting*; division, compartment; group, subgroup, species, subspecies, family 74 *group*; classification 62 *arrangement*; ward, community, parish, department, region 184 *district*; chapter, paragraph, clause, subordinate clause, phrase, verse; part, number, issue, instalment, volume 589 *edition*; canto 593 *poem*.

limb, member, organ, appendage; hind limb 267 *leg*; forelimb 271 *wing*; flipper, fin 269 *propeller*; arm, hand 378 *feeler*; artificial limb 150 *substitute*; shoulder, armpit, elbow, wrist, knee, ankle.

branch, ramification, offshoot 40 *adjunct*; bough, limb, spur, twig, tendril, leaf, switch, shoot, scion, sucker, slip, sprig, spray 366 *foliage*.

piece, torso, trunk, stump 41 *remainder*; limb, segment, section (see also *part* above); patch, insertion 40 *adjunct*; length, roll 222 *textile*; strip, swatch; fragment 55 *incompleteness*; bit, scrap, offcut, shred, wisp, rag 33 *small thing*; morsel, bite, crust, crumb 33 *small quantity*; splinter, skelf, sliver, chip, snippet; cut, wedge, finger, slice, rasher; collop, cutlet, chop, gigot chop, steak; hunk, chunk, wad, wodge, portion, slab, lump, mass 195 *bulk*; clod, turf, divot, sod 344 *soil*; shard, flake, scale; dose 783 *portion*; bits and pieces, odds and ends, oddments 43 *medley*; bin ends; clippings, parings, brash, rubble, scree, detritus, moraine, debris 41 *leavings*; parcel, plot, allotment.

Adj. *fragmentary*, broken, crumbly 330 *brit-*

tle; in bits, in pieces, in smithereens; not whole 647 *imperfect*; partial, bitty, scrappy 636 *insufficient*; fractional, aliquot; segmental, sectional, divided; shredded, sliced, minced, ground 33 *small*.

Vb. *part*, divide, partition, segment; compartmentalize 46 *break up*; share, share out 783 *allocate*; job-share; fragment 46 *disunite*.

54 Completeness

N. *completeness*, entireness, wholeness 52 *whole*; integration 88 *unity*; solidarity 706 *cooperation*; harmony 710 *harmony*; self-sufficiency 635 *sufficiency*; entirety, totality 52 *all*; comprehensiveness 79 *generality*; the ideal 646 *perfection*; ne plus ultra, the limit 236 *limit*; peak, culmination, zenith, crown 213 *summit*; finish 69 *end*; last touch, finishing touch 725 *completion*; fulfilment, consummation 69 *finality*; the whole hog, the full monty.

fullness, amplitude, plenitude, capacity, maximum, one's fill, saturation 635 *sufficiency*; saturation point 863 *satiation*; completion, filling; filling up, brimming, overrunning, swamping, drowning; full house, complement, full complement; requisite number, quorum; full measure, bumper; bellyful, skinful, repletion; full size, full length, full volume.

Adj. *complete*, plenary, full; total; integral 52 *whole*; entire 52 *intact*; full-blown, full-grown, fully-fledged 669 *matured*; full-on, no-holds-barred; unbroken, undivided 324 *dense*; self-contained, selfsufficient 635 *sufficient*; fully furnished; all-in, comprehensive 78 *inclusive*; exhaustive, detailed 570 *diffuse*; absolute, extreme; thorough, thoroughgoing, sweeping, wholesale, regular 32 *consummate*; unmitigated, downright, plumb, plain 44 *unmixed*; crowning, culminating, consummating, complementary.

full, replete 635 *filled*; topped up; well-filled, bulging; brimful, brimming; overwhelmed; overflowing, running over, slopping, swamped, drowned; saturated, oozing; bursting at the seams; gorged, fit to burst, full to bursting 863 *satiated*; chock-full, chock-a-block, crammed, stuffed, packed, jam-packed, packed like sardines; laden, heavy-laden, fully charged, all seats taken, standing room only; infested, overrun, crawling with, hotching with, alive with, seething with, jumping with, lousy with, stiff with; full of, rolling in; soaked in, dripping with.

Vb. *be complete*, be integrated; culminate, come to a head 725 *climax*; come to a close, be all over 69 *end*; be self-sufficient 635 *have enough*; want nothing, lack nothing 828 *be content*; become complete, fill out, reach maturity 669 *mature*; be filled.

make complete, complete, complement, integrate 45 *join*; make whole 656 *restore*; build up, construct, make up, piece together 56 *compose*; eke out, supplement; do thoroughly, leave nothing undone, carry out 725 *carry through*; put the finishing touch, put the icing on the cake, round off 69 *terminate*.

fill, fill up, brim, top; saturate 341 *drench*; overfill, swamp, drown, overwhelm; top up, replenish 633 *provide*; satisfy 635 *suffice*, 828 *content*, 863 *satiate*; fill to capacity, cram, pack, stuff, line, bulge out, pack in, pile in, squeeze in, ram in, jam in 303 *insert*; load, charge, ram down; freight; fill space, occupy 226 *cover*; reach to, extend to 183 *extend*; spread over, overrun 189 *pervade*; fit tight, be full to overflowing, be chock-a-block 45 *tighten*; fill in, enter 38 *add*.

Adv. *completely*, fully, wholly, totally, entirely, utterly, extremely, tout à fait 32 *greatly*; all told, in all, in toto; on all counts, in all respects, in every way; quite, altogether; outright, downright; thoroughly; to one's fill, to the top of one's bent, to the utmost, to the end, to the full, to the max; out and out, all out, heart and soul; head and shoulders, head over heels, neck and crop; to the brim, up to the hilt, up to the neck, up to the ears, up to the eyes; hook, line and sinker, root and branch; down to the ground; with a vengeance, with knobs on, with all the trimmings, and then some; to the last man, to the last breath; every whit, every inch; at full length, full out, in full; as far as possible; to capacity, not an inch to spare.

throughout, all the way, from first to last, from beginning to end, from end to end, from one end to the other, the length and breadth of, from coast to coast, from sea to sea, from Land's End to John o' Groats 183 *widely*; from north and south and east and west; fore and aft; high and low; from top to bottom; from top to toe, from head to foot, cap-à-pie; to the bitter end, to the end of the road, to the end of the chapter.

55 Incompleteness

N. *incompleteness*, defectiveness; unfinished state 647 *imperfection*; immaturity 670 *undevelopment*; sketch, outline 623 *plan*; skeleton, torso, trunk 53 *piece*; half measures, a lick and a promise 726 *non-completion*; perfunctoriness, superficiality 458 *negligence*; non-fulfilment, deficiency, slippage 307 *shortfall*, 636 *insufficiency*; dissatisfaction 829 *discontent*; impairment 655 *deterioration*; omission, break, gap, lacuna, missing link 72 *discontinuity*, 201 *interval*; part payment 53 *part*.

deficit, screw loose, missing link, omission 647 *defect*; shortfall, slippage 772 *loss*; default 930 *improbity*; want, lack, need 627 *requirement*.

Adj. *incomplete*, inadequate, defective 307 *deficient*; short, scant, unsatisfactory 636 *insufficient*; like Hamlet without the Prince 641 *useless*; omitting, wanting, lacking, needing, requiring; short of, shy of; halting, mutilated; without, -less, -free; garbled, impaired; cropped, abbreviated, shortened 204 *short*; flawed 647 *imperfect*; partial 53 *fragmentary*; half-finished, neglected 726 *uncompleted*; not ready 670 *unprepared*; undeveloped, underdeveloped, unripe 670 *immature*; raw, crude, rough-hewn 244 *formless*; sketchy, scrappy, bitty; thin, poor 4 *lacking substance*; perfunctory, half-hearted, half-done, undone 458 *neglected*; left in the air, left hanging; omitted, missing, lost 190 *absent*; interrupted 72 *discontinuous*.

unfinished, in progress, in hand; in embryo, begun 68 *beginning*; in preparation, on the stocks; on the back-burner.

Vb. *be incomplete*, miss, lack, need 307 *fall short*, 627 *require*; be wanting 190 *be absent*; default, leave undone 458 *neglect*; omit, miss out 57 *exclude*; break off, interrupt 72 *discontinue*; leave in the air, leave dangling, leave hanging 726 *not complete*.

56 Composition

N. *composition*, constitution, set-up, make-up; formation, construction, buildup, build 331 *structure*; organization 62 *arrangement*; nature, humour, character, condition 5 *temperament*; embodiment 78 *inclusion*; compound 43 *mixture*, 50 *combination*, 358 *organism*; syntax, sentence 563 *phrase*; artistic composition 412 *music*, 551 *art*, 553 *painting*, 554 *sculpture*; architecture 164 *building*; authorship 586 *writing*, 593 *poetry*; dramatic art 594 *drama*; composing, printing, typography 587 *print*; compilation 74 *assemblage*; construction 164 *production*; choreography 594 *ballet*; orchestration, instrumentation, score 412 *musical piece*; work of art, picture, portrait, sculpture, piece of sculpture, model; literary work 589 *book*, 593 *poem*, 591 *dissertation*, 592 *anthology*; play 594 *stage play*; dance 837 *dance*; pattern, design 12 *correlation*.

Vb. *constitute*, compose, form, make; make up; inhere, belong to, enter into.

contain, subsume, include, consist of 78 *comprise*; hold, have, take in, absorb 299 *admit*; comprehend, embrace, embody 235 *enclose*.

compose, compound 43 *mix*, 50 *combine*;

organize, set in order, put in order 62 *arrange*; synthesize, put together, make up 45 *join*; compile, assemble 74 *bring together*; compose, set up, computer-set 587 *print*; draft, draw up 586 *write*; orchestrate, score 413 *compose music*; draw 553 *paint*; sculpt, construct, build, make, fabricate 164 *produce*; knit 222 *weave*.

57 Exclusion

N. *exclusion*, pre-emption; forestalling 702 *hindrance*; exclusiveness, monopoly, closed shop, dog-in-the-manger policy; possessiveness 932 *selfishness*; exception, special case; exemption, dispensation 746 *liberation*; leaving out, including out, omission 607 *rejection*; blackball; no entry, no admission, no-go area, no-man's-land, exclusion order; closed door, lockout; picket line; embargo, ban, bar, taboo 757 *prohibition*; ostracism, boycott 620 *avoidance*; segregation, quarantine, caste system, colour bar, apartheid 883 *seclusion*; social exclusion; intolerance, repression, suppression, discrimination 481 *prejudice*; expulsion, eviction; disbarment, dismissal, suspension, excommunication; deportation, exile, expatriation; removal, elimination, eradication, carbon sink 188 *displacement*; dam, wall, barricade, screen, partition, pale, curtain, Iron Curtain, Bamboo Curtain, Berlin Wall, peace wall 235 *barrier*; great wall of China 713 *defence*; customs' barrier, economic zone, tariff wall 809 *tax*; ghetto.

Adj. *excluding*, exclusive, exemptive; restrictive, clannish, cliquish; preventive, prohibitive; pre-emptive.

Vb. *be excluded*, be outside the loop; not belong, stay outside, not gain admission; suffer exile, go into exile, go into voluntary exile 190 *be absent*, 296 *depart*.

exclude, preclude 470 *make impossible*; preempt, forestall 64 *come before*; keep out, warn off 747 *restrain*; blackball, vote against, deny entry, shut out, debar, shut the door on, spurn 607 *reject*; bar, ban, place an embargo on, taboo, black, disallow 757 *prohibit*; ostracize, cold-shoulder, boycott, send to Coventry 620 *avoid*, not include, leave out, include out; count out; exempt, dispense, excuse 746 *liberate*; except, make an exception, treat as a special case 19 *make unlike*; omit, miss out, pass over, disregard 458 *neglect*; lay aside, put aside, relegate 46 *set apart*; take out, strike out, cross out, cancel, elide 550 *obliterate*; disbar, strike off, remove, disqualify 188 *displace*, 963 *punish*; rule out, draw the line; wall off, fence off, screen off, curtain off, quarantine 232 *encircle*, 235 *enclose*; excommunicate, segregate, sequester 883 *seclude*; thrust out, dismiss, sack,

declare redundant, deport, extradite, exile, banish, outlaw, expatriate; weed, sift, sieve, sort out; eradicate, uproot 300 *eject*; expurgate, bowdlerize, censor 648 *purify*; deny 760 *refuse*; abandon 779 *not retain*.

Adv. *exclusive of*, excepting, barring, bar, not counting, including out, except, with the exception of, save; short of; let alone, apart from.

58 Component

N. *component*, component part, integral part, element, item; piece, bit, segment; link, stitch; word, morpheme, letter; constituent, part and parcel 53 *part*; factor, leaven 178 *influence*; additive, appurtenance, feature 40 *adjunct*; one of —, member, one of us; staff, workforce, crew, men, company, complement 686 *personnel*; ingredient 43 *tincture*, 193 *contents*; works, inner workings, insides, interior 224 *interiority*; nuts and bolts, machinery 630 *machine*; spare part 40 *extra*; components, set, outfit 88 *unit*.

Adj. *component*, constituent, ingredient; belonging, proper, native, inherent 5 *inherent*; built-in; admitted, one of —, on the staff.

59 Extraneousness

N. *extraneousness*, foreignness 6 *externality*, 223 *exteriority*; foreign parts; foreign body, foreign substance, accretion 38 *addition*; alien element 84 *nonconformity*; exotica.

foreigner, alien, stranger, emmet, outlander, Johnnie Foreigner; Southerner, Northerner, Easterner, Westerner; Martian, extraterrestrial, extraterrestrial being, ET, little green men; Celtic fringe; Sassenach, pommie (derog), limey (derog), rooineck (derog); Yank, Yankee, Aussie, Kiwi; wog (derog), wop (derog), dago (derog); gringo (derog), whitey (derog), honkie (derog), paleface; darkie (derog), nigger (derog), spade (derog); colonial, Creole 191 *settler*; resident alien, expatriate; migrant, economic migrant, migrant worker, guest worker, Gastarbeiter, emigrant, émigré, exile; immigrant, refugee, asylum-seeker; diaspora, ten lost tribes.

outsider, not one of us, stranger in our midst; muggle; intruder, interloper, alien, trespasser, cuckoo in the nest, squatter; uninvited guest, gatecrasher, stowaway; arrival, new arrival, nouveau arrivé, newcomer, new boy, newbie, tenderfoot 297 *incomer*; invader 712 *attacker*.

Adj. *extraneous*, ulterior, outside 6 *external*, 223 *exterior*; ultramundane, extragalactic 199 *distant*; not indigenous, imported; foreign, alien, unearthly; strange, outlandish, barbarian; overseas, transatlantic; continental, extraterrestrial; exotic, unacclimatized; gypsy,

nomad, wandering; unassimilated, uninte-
grated 46 *separate*; immigrant; intrusive, inter-
loping, trespassing, gate-crashing; infringing,
invading; exceptional 84 *unusual*; not of this
world, unnatural, paranormal, supernatural
983 *magical*; inadmissible.

SECTION FOUR

Order

60 Order

N. *order*, state of order, orderliness, tidiness,
neatness 258 *smoothness*, 648 *cleanness*; quiet
266 *quietness*; harmony 710 *harmony*; system,
method, methodology, prioritization; fixed
order, pattern, rule 81 *regularity*, 16 *uniformity*;
custom, routine 610 *habit*; rite 988 *ritual*; discipline 739 *obedience*; due order, hierarchy,
gradation, subordination, rank, position 73
serial place; unbroken order, even tenor, progression, series 71 *continuity*; logical order,
alphabetical order 12 *correlation*, 65 *sequence*;
organization, array 56 *composition*, 62 *arrangement*; a place for everything and everything in
its place.

Adj. *orderly*, harmonious 245 *symmetrical*;
well-behaved, decorous 848 *well-bred*; disciplined 739 *obedient*; well-regulated, according
to rule 81 *regular*; ordered, classified 62
arranged; methodical, systematic; strict 16 *uniform*; steady 610 *habitual*; correct, shipshape,
Bristol fashion, trim, neat, tidy, neat and tidy,
neat as a pin, out of a bandbox; spick and
span, spruce, dapper, well-groomed 648 *clean*;
in good trim, well-kept, in apple-pie order, in
perfect order, in its proper place 62 *arranged*;
direct 249 *straight*; lucid 516 *intelligible*.

Vb. *order*, dispose, prioritize 62 *arrange*;
schematize, systematize, organize 62 *regularize*;
regulate 24 *adjust*; normalize, standardize 16
make uniform; keep order, call to order, police,
govern 733 *rule*, 737 *command*.

be in order, be shipshape, harmonize 24
accord; range oneself, draw up, line up; fall
into place, find one's level; take one's place,
station oneself, take up one's position 187
place oneself; keep one's place; rally round 74
congregate; follow routine 610 *be in the habit
of*.

61 Disorder

N. *disorder*, random order, non-classification;
lack of coordination, incoordination, muddle,
no system; bedlam, chaotic state, chaos, may-
hem 734 *anarchy*; irregularity, anomalousness,
anomaly 17 *non-uniformity*; disunion, disac-

cord 25 *disagreement*; disharmony 411 *discord*;
disorderliness, unruliness, lack of discipline
738 *disobedience*; outbreak (see also *turmoil*
below); nihilism 738 *sedition*; untidiness, clutter, littering, slovenliness 649 *uncleanness*;
neglect 458 *negligence*; discomposure, disarray,
dishevelment 63 *disarrangement*; scattering 51
decomposition, 75 *dispersion*; upheaval 149 *revolution*; subversion 221 *overturning*; destruction;
welter, jumble, shambles, hugger-mugger, mix-
up, medley, embroilment, imbroglio 43 *mixture*; chaos, scramble 74 *crowd*; muddle, litter,
clutter, lumber 641 *rubbish*; farrago, mess,
mishmash, hash, hotchpotch, ragbag, Babel,
bedlam, madhouse (see also *turmoil* below).

complexity, complication, snarl-up 700 *difficulty*, 702 *hindrance*; implication, involvement,
imbroglio, embroilment; intricacy, kink 251
convolution; maze, labyrinth, warren; web 222
network; coil, tangle, twist, snarl, ravel; knot,
Gordian knot 47 *ligature*; puzzle 517 *unintelligibility*; awkward situation, how d'ye do, how-
do-you-do, pretty pass, pretty kettle of fish,
pickle 700 *predicament*.

turmoil, turbulence, tumult, frenzy, ferment,
storm, convulsion 176 *violence*; pandemonium, inferno; hullabaloo, hubbub, racket,
row, riot, uproar 400 *loudness*; affray, fracas,
dustup, stramash, brawl, mêlée 716 *fight*;
hurly-burly, to-do, rumpus, ruction, shemozzle, spot of bother, pother, trouble, disturbance 318 *commotion*; whirlwind, tornado,
hurricane 352 *gale*; beargarden, shambles,
madhouse, Bedlam; shindig, breach of the
peace; roughhouse, rough and tumble, free for
all, fisticuffs, all hell broken loose; bull in a
china shop; street fighting, gang warfare 709
quarrel; fat in the fire, devil to pay, hell to pay.

slut, sloven, slag, slattern, draggletail, lit-
terer, litter lout 649 *dirty person*; ragamuffin,
tatterdemalion 801 *poor person*.

anarchist, nihilist; lord of misrule, sons of
Belial 738 *rioter*.

Adj. *lacking order*, in disorder, in disarray,
disorganized, jumbled, disarranged; askew,
awry; unclassified, unorganized, unsorted;
irregular, random, unsystematic, unmethodical, confused, muddled, chaotic, shambolic, in
chaos, in a mess, all anyhow, haywire; untidy,
slovenly, sluttish, slatternly, messy 649 *dirty*;
sloppy, slipshod, slack, careless 456 *inattentive*;
bedraggled, dishevelled, tousled, tumbled,
unkempt, uncombed, windswept, windblown;
incoherent, rambling.

complex, intricate, involved, elaborate,
sophisticated, complicated; Heath Robinson;
overcomplicated, overinvolved 251 *coiled*,
problematic or problematical 517 *puzzling*;

winding, inextricable; entangled, enmeshed, balled up, snarled 702 *hindered;* knotted 45 *tied.*

disorderly, undisciplined, unruly; out of control, out of step, out of line, tumultuous, rumbustious; frantic 503 *frenzied;* orgiastic, Bacchic, Dionysiac, Saturnalian 949 *drunken;* rough, tempestuous, turbulent 176 *violent,* anarchical, nihilistic, lawless 954 *lawbreaking;* wild, harum-scarum, rantipole, tomboyish, boisterous, scatterbrained 456 *lacking concentration.*

Vb. *be disordered,* fall into disarray, scatter, break up 75 *disperse;* get in a mess, fall into confusion 49 *come unstuck;* get out of hand, riot 738 *disobey;* jump the queue 64 *come before;* disorder 63 *disarrange.*

rampage, go on the rampage, storm; rush, mob; riot 738 *revolt;* romp 837 *amuse oneself;* play the fool 497 *be absurd;* give a riotous welcome 876 *celebrate.*

62 Arrangement: reduction to order

N. *arrangement,* reduction to order; ordering, disposal, disposition, marshalling, arraying, placing 187 *location;* grouping 74 *assemblage;* division, distribution, allocation, allotment 783 *allocation;* method, systematization, organization, prioritization, reorganization; restructuring, perestroika; rationalization; streamlining 654 *improvement;* centralization 48 *cohesiveness;* decentralization, hiving off 49 *non-cohesiveness;* administration 689 *management;* planning 623 *contrivance,* 669 *preparation;* taxonomy, categorization, classification 561 *nomenclature;* analysis 51 *decomposition;* codification, consolidation; syntax, conjugation 564 *grammar;* grading, gradation, subordination, graduation, calibration 71 *series,* 465 *measurement;* synchronization 123 *simultaneousness;* construction 56 *composition;* array, system, form 60 *order;* cosmos 321 *universe;* orchestration, score 412 *music;* layout, pattern; choreography 837 *dance;* collection, assortment 74 *accumulation;* schematism; computer program; register, file 548 *record;* inventory, catalogue, table 87 *list;* code, digest; class, group, sub-group 77 *classification.*

sorting, grading, seeding, league table; cross-reference 12 *correlation;* file, computer file, folder, filing system, Filofax (tdmk), personal organizer, card index, pigeonhole, slot; sieve, strainer 263 *porousness.*

Adj. *arranged,* disposed, marshalled, arrayed, etc. (see vb.); ordered, schematic, tabulated, tabular; methodical, systematic, organizational; precise, definite, cut and dried; classified; straightened out; regulated 81 *regular;* sorted, seeded, graded, streamed, banded.

Vb. *arrange,* set, dispose, set up, set out, lay out; formulate, form, knock into shape, orchestrate, score 56 *compose;* range, rank, align, line up, form up; position 187 *place;* marshal, array; rally 74 *bring together;* put in order; grade, size, group, space; collocate, thread together 45 *connect;* settle, fix, determine, define; allot, allocate, assign, distribute, deal, parcel out 783 *allocate;* rearrange, neaten, tidy, tidy up, trim; clear, declutter 701 *disencumber;* feng-shui; arrange for, make arrangements 623 *plan,* 669 *prepare,* 689 *manage.*

regularize, reduce to order, straighten out, put to rights 24 *adjust,* 654 *rectify;* regulate; organize, systematize, prioritize, methodize, schematize; standardize, normalize, centralize 16 *make uniform.*

class, classify, subsume, group; specify 561 *name;* process; analyse, divide; dissect 51 *decompose;* rate, rank, grade, evaluate 480 *estimate;* sort, sift, sieve, seed; tag, label 547 *mark;* file, pigeonhole; index, cross-refer; tabulate, alphabetize; catalogue, register 548 *record;* program.

63 Disarrangement

N. *disarrangement,* derangement, shuffling 151 *interchange;* translocation, displacement 272 *transference;* obstruction 702 *hindrance;* disorganization, discomposure, dishevelment; dislocation 46 *separation;* disturbance, interruption 138 *untimeliness;* creasing, corrugation 261 *fold;* madness, derangement 503 *mental disorder;* upsetting 221 *inversion;* convulsion 176 *violence,* 318 *agitation;* state of disorder 61 *disorder.*

Vb. *disarrange,* derange, disorder; put out of gear, get out of order; disturb, touch 265 *move;* interfere 702 *hinder;* lose 188 *misplace;* disorganize, muddle, confuse, convulse, throw into confusion, make havoc; tamper, spoil, mar, damage, sabotage 655 *impair;* strain, bend, twist 176 *force;* unhinge, dislocate, sprain, rick 188 *displace;* unseat, dislodge, derail, throw off the rails; throw off balance, upset, overturn, capsize 149 *revolutionize,* 221 *invert;* declassify; shake, jiggle, toss 318 *agitate;* trouble, perturb, unsettle, discompose, disconcert, ruffle, rattle, flurry, fluster 456 *distract;* interrupt 138 *mistime;* misdirect, disorientate, throw one off one's bearings 495 *mislead,* 655 *pervert;* unhinge, dement, drive mad 503 *make mad,* 891 *enrage.*

jumble, shuffle, get out of order 151 *interchange,* 272 *transpose;* mix up 43 *mix;* toss, tumble 318 *agitate;* ruffle, dishevel, tousle; rumple, crumple, crease, wrinkle, crush 261 *fold*; untidy, mess, muck up; muddle, mess up; scatter, fling about 75 *disperse*.

throw into confusion, bedevil, make a mess or hash of; confound, complicate, perplex, involve, ravel, ball up, foul up, entangle, tangle, embroil; turn topsy-turvy, turn upside down 221 *invert*; send haywire.

64 Precedence

N. precedence, antecedence, going before, coming before, queue-jumping 283 *preceding*; front position, prosthesis 237 *front*; higher position, pride of place 34 *superiority*; preference 605 *choice*; pre-eminence, excellence 638 *importance*; captaincy, leadership, hegemony 733 *authority*; the lead, the pas; leading, guiding, pioneering; precedent 66 *precursor*; past history 125 *past time*.

Adj. preceding, foregoing, outgoing; former, ex-, previous 119 *prior*; before-mentioned, above-mentioned; aforesaid, said; forewarning, premonitory, prodromal; preliminary, prefatory, preparatory.

Vb. come before, be first to arrive 283 *precede*; go first, jump the queue; lead, guide, conduct, show the way, point the way 547 *indicate*; be the forerunner of, pioneer, clear the way, blaze the trail 484 *discover*; head, take the lead 237 *be in front*; have precedence, take precedence 34 *be superior*; lead the dance, set the fashion, be a trend-setter 178 *influence*; open, lead off, kick off, bully off 68 *begin*; preface; introduce, usher in, herald, ring in 68 *inaugurate*; get ahead; antedate 125 *be past*.

put in front, send a reconnaisance party, send ahead, station before 187 *place*; prefix 38 *add*; front, top 237 *be in front*; presuppose 512 *suppose*; preface.

Adv. before, in advance; preparatory to, as a prelude to, as a preliminary; earlier 119 *before*; ante, supra, above 237 *in front*.

65 Sequence

N. sequence, coming after, descent, line, lineage 120 *subsequence*; going after; inference 475 *reasoning*; suffixion 38 *addition*; succession, successorship, mantle, Elijah's mantle 780 *transfer*; rota, Buggin's turn; series 71 *continuity*; successiveness, alternation, serialization; continuation, prolongation 113 *protraction*, 146 *continuance*; pursuance 619 *pursuit*; overtaking 306 *overstepping*, 727 *success*; subordination, second place, proxime accessit 35 *inferiority*; last place 238 *rear*; consequence 67 *sequel*.

Adj. sequential, following, succeeding; ensuing; next 200 *near*; posterior, latter, later 120 *subsequent*; another, second 38 *additional*;

successive, consecutive 71 *continuous*; alternating 12 *correlative*; alternate, consequent, resulting 157 *caused*.

Vb. come after, ensue 284 *follow*; follow close, sit on one's tail, drive bumper to bumper, breathe down one's neck, tread on the heels; succeed, inherit, step into the shoes of, supplant 150 *substitute*; alternate, relieve, take over.

place after, add on, append, annex, subjoin, suffix, tack on.

Adv. after, following; afterwards 120 *subsequently*, 238 *rearward*; at the end, as follows, consequentially; in the end 69 *finally*; next, later; infra, below.

66 Precursor

N. precursor, predecessor, ancestor, forbear 169 *parentage*; Adam and Eve, early man, Lucy 371 *humankind*; the ancients 125 *antiquity*; eldest, firstborn; discoverer, inventor 461 *experimenter*; pioneer, pathfinder, explorer 268 *traveller*; guide, pilot, bell-wether 690 *leader*; scout, reconnaissance party; vanguard, avant-garde, innovator, trail-blazer; trend-setter; forerunner; herald, harbinger, announcer 529 *messenger*; anticipation, foretaste, preview, premonition 511 *omen*; trailer; prequel; precedent 83 *example*; antecedent, prefix, preposition 40 *adjunct*; eve, vigil, wake, day before 119 *previousness*.

prelude, preliminary, preamble, preface, front matter, prologue, foreword; opening, introduction 68 *beginning*; lead, heading, frontispiece 237 *front*; aperitif, appetizer, hors d'oeuvre, starter; overture 412 *musical piece*; presupposition 475 *premise*, 512 *supposition*.

Adj. precursory, preliminary, exploratory 669 *preparatory*; introductory, prefatory 68 *beginning*; inaugural; precedent 64 *preceding*.

67 Sequel

N. sequel, consequence, result, aftermath, by-product, spin-off 157 *effect*; conclusion 69 *end*; aftereffect; hangover, morning after 949 *hangover*; aftertaste, afterglow, fallout; afterbirth, placenta 167 *obstetrics*; inheritance, legacy 777 *dowry*; surprise 508 *lack of expectation*; afterthought, second thoughts; second try, second bite at the cherry; end matter, epilogue, postscript; envoi, last words; follow-up 725 *completion*; continuation, sequel 589 *book*; tailpiece, colophon, coda 238 *rear*; appendage, appendix, codicil, supplement 40 *adjunct*; suffix, affix, inflection 564 *grammar*; afters, pudding, dessert 301 *dish*; afterlife 124 *future state*; hereafter.

retinue, following, followers, camp followers, groupies 284 *follower*; queue 71 *series*;

train, cortege 71 *procession*; tailback, wake 89 *concomitant*; trailer 274 *vehicle*.

successor, descendant, future generations 170 *posterity*; heir 776 *beneficiary*; next man in; replacement, supplanter 150 *substitute*; newcomer, nouveau arrivé 297 *incomer*; satellite, hanger-on 742 *dependant*.

68 Beginning

N. *beginning*, birth, rise (see also *origin* below); infancy, babyhood 126 *newness*, 130 *youth*; primitiveness 127 *oldness*; commencement; onset 295 *arrival*; emergence 445 *appearance*; inception, institution, constitution, foundation 156 *causation*; starting point; origination, invention 484 *discovery*; creation 164 *production*; innovation 21 *originality*; initiative, introduction 66 *prelude*; alpha, first letter, initial; heading, headline; title page, front matter; van, front, forefront 237 *front*; dawn 128 *morning*; running in, teething troubles, growing pains; tip of the iceberg, thin end of the wedge; first sight, first impression, first lap, first round, first stage; early stages, early days, early doors; rudiments, elements, first principles, alphabet, ABC; leading up to 289 *approach*; onset 712 *attack*; starter 538 *beginner*; preliminaries 669 *preparation*.

debut, coming out, presentation, initiation, launching; inauguration, opening, unveiling; first night, premiere, first appearance, first offence; first step, first move; gambit; maiden voyage, maiden speech; baptism of fire.

start, outset; zero hour, D-day; send-off, embarkation, countdown 296 *departure*; rising of the curtain; kick-off; house-warming, honeymoon; flying start; start-up.

origin, derivation, conception, genesis, birth, nativity; provenance, ancestry 169 *parentage*; fount, fons et origo; rise 156 *source*; nest, womb; bud, germ, seed; egg, embryo, pre-embryo, protoplasm, endoderm, mesoderm, ectoderm 358 *organism*; first beginnings, cradle 192 *home*; Big Bang.

entrance 297 *way in*; inlet 345 *gulf*; mouth, opening 263 *aperture*; threshold 624 *access*; porch 194 *lobby*; gateway 263 *doorway*; border 236 *limit*; suburbs 230 *surroundings*; foothills, outlier; pass, corridor 289 *approach*, 305 *passage*.

Adj. *beginning*, introductory, prefatory 66 *precursory*; inaugural; rudimental 156 *fundamental*; primeval, primordial 127 *primal*; rudimentary, elementary; embryonic, nascent, budding, incipient, in preparation 726 *uncompleted*; early, infant 126 *new*.

first, initial, primary, maiden, starting, natal; pioneering 21 *original*; unprecedented

126 *new*; foremost, front 237 *frontal*; leading, principal, major, head, chief 34 *supreme*.

Vb. *begin*, commence; open, dawn, spring up; arise, emerge, appear; rise; spring from; sprout, germinate; come into existence, come into the world, see the light of day 360 *be born*; make one's debut, come out; start, enter upon, embark on 296 *start out*; fire away, kick off, strike up; start work, clock in, log on; roll up one's sleeves, limber up 669 *prepare*; run in; begin at the beginning, start from scratch; put one's hand to the plough, put one's shoulder to the wheel, set to, set to work, get cracking, get moving, get weaving; attack, tackle, address oneself; go to it 672 *undertake*.

initiate, found, launch; originate, invent 484 *discover*; usher in, herald, ring in, open the door to, introduce; start, start up, kickstart, switch on, ring up the curtain; set in motion, get under way; put to work 622 *employ*; handsel, run in; take the initiative, lead, lead off, lead the way, take the lead, pioneer, break new ground 64 *come before*; broach, open, raise the subject; break the ice, kick off, set the ball rolling; throw the first stone, open fire; take the first step, take the plunge; trigger off, spark off, set off.

inaugurate, auspicate, open; establish 156 *cause*; be a founder member, be in on the ground floor, be in with the bricks; baptize, christen, launch 561 *name*; initiate, blood; lay the foundations, cut the first turf 669 *prepare*.

Adv. *initially*, originally, in the beginning; at the very start, from its inception; from the beginning, from the word go; first, firstly, in the first place, primarily, first of all, first and foremost; as a start, for starters, for a kick-off, for a beginning; from scratch; back to basics.

69 End

N. *end*, close, conclusion, consummation 725 *completion*; payoff, result, end result 157 *effect*; end use; expiration, lapse; termination, closure, guillotine; finishing stroke, death blow, quietus, coup de grâce; knockout, clincher 279 *knock*; denouement; ending, finish, finale, curtain; term, period, stop, halt 145 *cessation*; final stage, latter end 129 *evening*; beginning of the end, last words, swan-song, envoi, coda 67 *sequel*; last stage, last round, last lap, home stretch; last over, last breath, last gasp 361 *decease*; terminal illness; final examination, finals 459 *exam*.

extremity, omega; extreme, pole, North Pole, South Pole, antipodes; extreme case, ne plus ultra; farthest point, world's end, ultima Thule, where the rainbow ends; fringe, verge, brink 234 *edge*; frontier, boundary 236 *limit*;

end of the road, end of the line, terminus, terminal 295 *goal*, 617 *objective*; dregs; foot, toe, bottom, nadir 214 *base*; bottom dollar, last cent, last penny 801 *poverty*; tip, cusp, point, finial 213 *apex*, 256 *sharp point*; vertex, peak, head, top, zenith 213 *summit*, *apex*; tail, tail end 67 *sequel*; arm, stump 53 *limb*; shirt-tail, coat-tail 217 *hanging object*; end, butt end, gable end, fag end 238 *rear*; tag, epilogue, postscript, end matter, appendix 40 *adjunct*; inflection, suffix 564 *grammar*.

finality, bitter end; time, time up, deadline; conclusion, ending 54 *completeness* (see also *end* above); end of the matter, closure; breakup, wind-up 145 *cessation*; dissolution 165 *destruction*; doom, destiny 596 *fate*; end of the world, Last Day, Judgment Day, Day of Judgment; last trump, crack of doom, Götterdämmerung, Armageddon; Big Crunch 124 *future state*.

Adj. *final*, ending, terminal, last, ultimate, supreme, closing; extreme, polar; definitive, conclusive, crowning, hindmost, rear 238 *back*; caudal.

Vb. *end*, come to an end, expire, run out, become invalid 111 *elapse*; close, finish, conclude, be all over; die out 2 *pass away*, 361 *die*; come to a close, draw to a close, have run its course; stop, clock out, go home 145 *cease*.

terminate, conclude, close, settle; apply the closure, bring to an end, put an end to, put a stop to, put paid to, pull the plug on; discontinue, drop; finish, consummate, see it out 725 *carry through*; ring down the curtain, put up the shutters, shut up shop, wind up, close down, call it a day; switch off, ring off, hang up, cut off, stop 145 *halt*.

Adv. *finally*, in conclusion; at last, at long last; once for all, for good and all; never again, nevermore; in the end, in the long run, in the final analysis, when all's said and done.

70 Middle

N. *middle*, midst, midpoint; mean 30 *average*; medium; thick, thick of things; heart, heart of the matter, kernel, nave, hub, navel 225 *centre*; nucleus 224 *interiority*; midweek, midwinter, half tide; midstream 625 *middle way*; bisection, midline, equator, the Line 28 *equalization*; midriff, diaphragm 231 *partition*; equidistance, halfway house; mezzo floor.

Adj. *middle*, medial, mean, mezzo, mid 30 *median*; middlemost 225 *central*; intermediate, betwixt and between 231 *lying between*; equidistant; mediterranean, equatorial.

71 Continuity: uninterrupted sequence

N. *continuity*, continuousness, uninterruptedness, monotony 16 *uniformity*; continuation;

successiveness, succession; line, lineage, descent, dynasty; one thing after another, serialization 65 *sequence*; continuum 115 *perpetuity*; assembly line, conveyor belt 146 *continuance*; endless band 315 *rotation*; recurrence, cycle 106 *repetition*, 139 *frequency*, 141 *periodic recurrence*; cumulativeness, snowball 36 *increase*; course, career, flow, steady flow, trend 179 *tendency*; progressiveness 285 *progression*; circuit, round 314 *circuitous motion*; daily round, routine, rut, practice, custom 610 *habit*; track, trail, wake 67 *sequel*; chain, food chain; chain reaction; round robin, chain letter; circle 250 *circularity*.

series, gradation 27 *degree*; succession, run; progression; ascending order 36 *increase*; descending order 37 *decrease*; family tree, lineage 169 *genealogy*; chain, line, string, thread; train, parade; unbroken line, line of battle; array 62 *arrangement*; row; range, ridge; colonnade, peristyle, portico; ladder, steps, stairs, staircase 308 *ascent*; range, tier, storey 207 *layer*; set, group, raft; suite, suit (of cards); assortment 77 *classification*; spectrum; gamut, scale 410 *musical note*; stepping stones 624 *bridge*; hierarchy, pyramid.

Adj. *continuous*, continued, run-on; consecutive, running, successive 65 *sequential*; serial, serialized, seriate, catenary; progressive; overlapping, unbroken, solid, smooth, uninterrupted, circular; continuing, ongoing; continual, incessant, ceaseless, unremitting, nonstop, constant 115 *perpetual*; cyclical, rhythmic 110 *periodic*; repetitive, recurrent, monotonous 16 *uniform*, 106 *repeated*; linear, lineal, rectilinear 249 *straight*.

Vb. *continue*, run on, prolong 203 *lengthen*; serialize, arrange in succession, catenate, string 45 *connect*; maintain continuity, keep the kettle boiling 600 *persevere*; keep the succession, provide an heir.

Adv. *continuously*, consecutively, etc. (see adj.); successively, in succession, in turn; one after another; at a stretch, together, running; at one go, without stopping, on the trot; around the clock, night and day, 24/7 115 *for ever*; progressively; in procession, in file, in single file, in Indian file, in a crocodile, nose to tail, bumper to bumper.

72 Discontinuity: interrupted sequence

N. *discontinuity*, intermittence; discontinuation 145 *cessation*; interval, hiatus, pause, time lag 145 *lull*; disconnectedness, randomness 61 *disorder*; unevenness 17 *non-uniformity*, 259 *roughness*; dotted line; broken ranks; ladder, run 46 *disunion*; disruption, interruption, intervention; parenthesis 231 *interjection*; caesura, division 46 *separation*, 547 *punctuation*;

break, fracture, flaw, fault, split, crack, cut 201 *gap*; lacuna; missing link; broken thread, anacoluthon, non sequitur; alternation 141 *periodic recurrence*; irregularity 142 *fitfulness*.

Adj. *discontinuous*, non-recurrent; discontinued; interrupted, broken; disconnected; discrete 46 *separate*; few and far between 140 *infrequent*; irregular, intermittent 142 *fitful*; alternate, alternating, stop-go, on-off 141 *periodical*; spasmodic 17 *non-uniform*; jerky, bumpy, uneven 259 *rough*; incoherent; parenthetic, episodic.

Vb. *be discontinuous*, halt, rest 145 *pause*; alternate.

discontinue, suspend, break off, refrain from; desist; interrupt, intervene, chip in, butt in, break, break in upon 231 *interfere*; interpose, interject, punctuate; disconnect, break the connection, break *or* interrupt one's train of thought, snap the thread 46 *disunite*.

73 Term: serial position

N. *serial position*, order, term, remove 27 *degree*; echelon, rank, ranking, grade, gradation; station, place, position, slot; status, standing, footing, social class, caste; point, mark, pitch, level, storey; step, tread, round, rung; stage, milestone, watershed.

Vb. *grade*, rank, rate, place, classify; class; stagger, space out 27 *graduate*, 201 *space*.

74 Assemblage

N. *assemblage*, collection 50 *combination*, 62 *arrangement*; collocation; compilation, corpus, anthology 56 *composition*; gathering, harvest 370 *agriculture*, 771 *acquisition*; consolidation, concentration; centring, focusing, zeroing in on; levy, call-up 718 *war measures*; roundup, line-up; herding, shepherding 369 *animal husbandry*; collectivization, collective 370 *farm*; conspiracy, caucus 708 *party*; collective noun 564 *grammar*.

assembly, getting together, ganging up; forgathering, congregation, concourse, conflux, concurrence 293 *convergence*; gathering, meeting, mass meeting, protest meeting, indignation meeting, sit-in, meet 762 *deprecation*; march, protest march, demonstration, rally 267 *marching*, 762 *deprecation*, 875 *pageant*; parade 875 *pageant*; flash mob; coven; conventicle; convention, convocation 985 *synod*; legislature, conclave 692 *council*; eisteddfod, mod, festival 876 *celebration*; reunion, get-together; jamboree, indaba, moot; -fest; gathering of the clans, ceilidh 882 *social gathering*; company, at-home, party 882 *fellowship*; circle, sewing-bee; encounter group 658 *therapy*; discussion group, symposium, focus group, quality circle

584 *conference*; bevy, galaxy, etc. 866 *person of repute*.

group, constellation, galaxy, cluster 321 *star*; troop, swarm, flight, flock, herd; drove, team, pack, kennel, stable, string, nest, eyrie, brood, hatch, litter, shoal, school;

Some Less Common Group Nouns

bask (crocodiles), bevy (quail, swans), building (rooks), cast (hawks), cete (badgers), charm *or* chirm (goldfinches), chattering (choughs), clamour (rooks), clowder (cats), company (wigeon), congregation (crocodiles, plovers), covert (coots), covey (grouse, partridges), crash (rhinoceroses), down (hares), drift (pigs), dule (doves), exaltation (larks), fall (woodcock), fesnyng (ferrets), fluther (jellyfish), gaggle (geese on the ground), gam (whales), gang (elk), grist (bees), herd (cranes, curlews, seals, swans), husk (hares), kindle (kittens), leap (leopards), murder (crows), murmuration (starlings), muster (peacocks), mute (hounds), nye *or* nide (pheasant), pace (asses), parliament (owls), pod (seals, whales), pride (lions), sedge *or* siege (bitterns, cranes, herons), skein (geese in flight), skulk (foxes), sleuth *or* sloth (bears), smack (jellyfish), sord (mallard), sounder (pigs), spring (teal), stand (plovers), team (ducks in flight), tok (capercailzies), unkindness (ravens), walk (snipe), watch (nightingales), wing (plovers).

---

unit, brigade 722 *formation*; batch, lot, clutch; brace, pair, span 90 *existence as two*; leash, four-in-hand 96 *existence as four*; set, class, genus, species, subspecies 77 *sort*; breed, tribe, clan, household 11 *family*; brotherhood, sisterhood, fellowship, guild, union 706 *association*; club 708 *society*; sphere, quarter, circle 524 *informant*; charmed circle, coterie 644 *elite*; social group, the caste system, the classes 868 *nobility*, 869 *common people*; in-group, us and them, they 80 *self*; age group, peer group, year group, stream, set 538 *class*; hand (at cards), set 71 *series*; rope (of onions, pearls), string (of pearls).

band, company, troupe; cast 594 *actor*; dance band, string band, jazz band, ragtime band, brass band, military band, marching band, pipe band, pipes and drums, fifes and drums; group, skiffle group, pop group, rock band *or* group, punk band *or* group, boy band, girl band, tribute band *or* group, cover band; steel band; bandsman, orchestra, etc. 413 *orchestra*; team, string, fifteen, eleven, eight; knot, bunch; set, coterie, clique, ring; dream team; gang, squad, party, work party; crew, complement, manpower, workforce, staff 686 *personnel*; following 67 *retinue*; squadron, troop, platoon, unit, regiment, corps 722 *formation*; squad, posse; force, body, host 722 *armed force*, 104 *multitude*; (Boy) Scouts, Girl Guides, etc. 708 *society*; band of brothers, sisters, merry men 880 *friendship*; committee, commission 754 *nominee*; panel 87 *list*.

crowd, throng 104 *multitude*; huddle, cluster,

swarm, colony; knot, bunch; the masses, the hoi polloi, mass, mob, ruck 869 *rabble*; sea of faces; full house 54 *completeness*; congestion, press, squash, squeeze, jam, scrum, rush, crush; rush hour 680 *haste*; flood, spate, deluge, stream, streams of 32 *great quantity*; volley, shower, hail, storm; infestation, invasion 297 *entering*.

bunch, assortment, lot, mixed lot 43 *medley*; clump, tuft, wisp, handful; hand (of bananas), pencil (of rays), fan; bag 194 *receptacle*; hand (of tobacco), bundle, packet, wad; batch, pack, package, parcel; portfolio, file, dossier 548 *record*; bale, roll, bolt; load, pack 193 *contents*; fascine, faggot; fascicle; tussock, shock, sheaf, stook, truss, heap; swathe, rick, stack 632 *storage*; thicket, copse 366 *wood*; bouquet, nosegay, posy, spray; skein, hank.

accumulation, agglomeration, conglomeration; massing, amassment; concentration, centralization; pile-up 279 *collision*; pile, heap; snowdrift; snowball 36 *increment*; debris, detritus 41 *leavings*; dustheap, midden, dump 641 *rubbish*; cumulus, storm cloud 355 *cloud*; store, storage 633 *provision*, 799 *treasury*; magazine, battery, armoury, quiver 723 *arsenal*; bus garage, car park, parking lot; set, lot 71 *series*; mixed lot, mixed bag 43 *medley*; kit, gear, stock; range, selection, assortment 795 *merchandise*; display 522 *exhibit*; museum 632 *collection*; menagerie, aquarium 369 *zoo*; literary collection 589 *library*; miscellanea, miscellany, compilation 56 *composition*; symposium, festschrift 591 *dissertation*.

Vb. congregate, meet, forgather, rendezvous; assemble; associate, come together, get together, join together, flock together, gather, gather round, collect, troop, rally, roll up, swell the ranks; resort to, centre on, focus on, zero in on, make for 293 *converge*; band together, gang up; mass, concentrate; conglomerate, huddle, cluster, bunch, crowd; throng, swarm, seethe, mill around; surge, stream, flood 36 *grow*; swarm in, infest, invade.

bring together, assemble, put together, draw together 45 *join*; draw 291 *attract*; gather, collect, rally, muster, call up, mobilize; concentrate, consolidate; collocate, lump together, group, brigade, unite; compile 56 *compose*; bring into focus, focus, zero in on, centre; convene, convoke, convocate, summon, hold a meeting; herd, shepherd, get in, whip in, call in, round up, corral 235 *enclose*; mass, aggregate, rake up, dredge up; accumulate, conglomerate, heap, pile, amass; catch, take, rake in, net 771 *acquire*; scrape together, garner 632 *store*; truss, bundle, parcel, package;

bunch, bind 45 *tie*; pack, cram, stuff 54 *fill*; build up, pile up, stack 310 *elevate*.

Adv. together, as one, in a oner; collectively, all together, en masse.

75 Non-assembly. Dispersion

N. dispersion, scattering, diffraction, breakup 46 *separation*; branching out, fanning out, spread, scatter, radiation 294 *divergence*; sprawl, suburbia; distribution 783 *allocation*; delegation, decentralization, regionalization; disintegration 51 *decomposition*; evaporation 337 *liquefaction*, 338 *vaporization*; dissipation 634 *waste*; circulation, diffusion; dissemination, broadcasting; spraying, sprinkling; dispersal; disbandment, demobilization.

Vb. be dispersed, disperse, scatter, spread, fan out, thin out 325 *rarefy*; spread like wildfire, be rampant, flood; radiate, branch, branch out 294 *diverge*; break up, break ranks, fall out 46 *separate*; break away 49 *come unstuck*; hive off, go each his *or* her own way 267 *wander*; drift away, drift apart; straggle, trail, fall behind 282 *stray*; spread over, sprawl over, cover, litter 226 *overlie*; explode, blow up, burst, fly apart; evaporate, melt 337 *liquefy*, 338 *vaporize*; disintegrate, dissolve, decay 51 *decompose*.

disperse, scatter, diffract; spread out, splay 294 *diverge*; separate 46 *break up*; thin out, string out; disseminate, diffuse, broadcast, sow, strew, spread; dissipate, dispel, disintegrate 51 *decompose*; scatter to the winds 634 *waste*; dispense, deal, deal out, dole out, allot 783 *allocate*; decentralize, regionalize; break up, disband, disembody, demobilize, dismiss, send home 46 *disunite*; draft, draft off, hive off, detach 272 *send*; sprinkle, splash, spray, spatter 341 *moisten*; circulate; rout 727 *defeat*.

76 Focus: place of meeting

N. focus, focal point, junction, town centre, city centre 225 *centre*, 293 *convergence*; crossroads; switchboard, exchange, nerve centre; hub, nub, core, heart, kernel 70 *middle*; civic centre, community centre, village hall, village green, town square; campus, quad; market place 796 *market*; stamping ground; club, pub, local 192 *tavern*; headquarters, HQ, depot; rallying point; venue, rendezvous, trysting place 192 *meeting place*; fireside, campfire; cynosure, centre of attraction, honeypot 291 *attraction*; place of pilgrimage: Mecca, Lourdes, Rome, Zion, promised land 295 *goal*, 617 *objective*.

Vb. focus, centre on 293 *converge*; centralize, concentrate, focus on, zero in on; point to.

77 Class

N. classification, categorization 62 *arrangement*; taxonomy; diagnosis, specification, designation; category, class, bracket; set, subset;

head, heading, subhead, section, subsection 53 *subdivision*; division, branch, department, faculty; pocket, pigeonhole, slot 194 *compartment*; tier, rank, caste, status, social class, standing 27 *degree*; province, domain, field, sphere, range; sex, gender; blood group, age group, stream 74 *group*; coterie, clique 74 *band*; persuasion, school of thought, denomination 978 *sect*.

sort, kind, species, type, order, version, variety 15 *variant*, 589 *edition*; manner, genre, style; nature, quality, grade, calibre 5 *character*; mark, brand 547 *label*; ilk, stripe, kidney, feather, colour; stamp, mould, shape, frame, make 243 *form*; assortment, kit, gear, set, suit, lot 71 *series*.

breed, strain, blood, family, kin, tribe, clan, sept, caste, line 11 *race*, 169 *genealogy*; kingdom, phylum, class, order, genus, species, subspecies; genotype, monotype.

78 Inclusion

N. *inclusion*, comprising; incorporation, embodiment, assimilation, encapsulation; comprehension, admission, integration, social inclusion 299 *reception*; admissibility, eligibility; membership 775 *participation*; inclusiveness, coverage, full coverage, blanket coverage 79 *generality*; all-roundness, versatility 694 *skill*; comprehensiveness; set, complete set, complement, package 52 *whole*; package deal 765 *pact*; constitution 56 *composition*; accommodation 183 *room*.

Adj. *inclusive*, including, comprising; counting, containing, having; holding, consisting of; incorporating; fully-furnished, all-inclusive, all-in; overall, all-embracing 52 *comprehensive*; wholesale, blanket, sweeping 32 *extensive*; total, across-the-board, global.

included, admitted, counted; admissible, eligible; integrated; constituent, making up; inherent 5 *intrinsic*, 58 *component*; belonging, pertinent 9 *relative*; classified with, in the same league 11 *akin*, 18 *similar*; entered, noted, recorded, on the list; merged 38 *additional*; in the loop, in the know, in the in-crowd.

Vb. *be included*, be contained, be comprised, make one of; enlist, enrol oneself, swell the ranks, join 708 *join a party*; come under, go under, fall under; merge in; appertain to, pertain, refer to 9 *be related*; come in, go in, enter into 297 *enter*; constitute 56 *compose*; overlap, inhere, belong 5 *be inherent*.

comprise, include, involve, mean, imply, consist of, hold, have, count, boast 56 *contain*; take, measure 28 *be equal*; receive, take in 299 *admit*; accommodate, find room for; compre-

hend, encapsulate, cover; embody, incorporate; encompass, embrace, encircle, envelop 235 *enclose*.

Adv. *including*, inclusively; A–Z; et cetera.

79 Generality

N. *generality*, universality; catholicity, catholicism; ecumenicity, ecumenicalism 976 *orthodoxy*; universalism; generalization, universal; macrocosm 321 *universe*; globalization, global view, world-view; panorama, synopsis, conspectus, bird's-eye view 52 *whole*; inclusiveness, dragnet 78 *inclusion*; prevalence, custom 610 *habit*, 848 *fashion*; pervasiveness, ubiquity 189 *presence*; pandemic, epidemic 651 *disease*; imprecision 464 *lack of discrimination*, 495 *inexactness*; commonness, ruck, run of the mill 30 *average*; ordinariness 732 *averageness*.

everyman, everywoman; man *or* woman in the street, Mr *or* Mrs Average, man on the Clapham omnibus, Joe Soap, Joe Bloggs, Joe Public, common type 30 *common man*; everybody, everyone, every one, each one, one and all, the long and the short and the tall, all and sundry, every mother's son, every man Jack, all hands 52 *all*; all the world and his wife, the world and his brother *or* his granny, Tom, Dick and Harry, Uncle Tom Cobley and all, the masses, the hoi polloi, the rabble 869 *common people*; all sorts, anyone, whosoever, N or M; anything, whatsoever, what have you, what you will 562 *no name*.

Adj. *general*, generic, typical, representative, standard; encyclopaedic, broad-based; collective, all-embracing, blanket, across-the-board 52 *comprehensive*; broad, sweeping, panoramic; prevalent 189 *present everywhere*; usual, normal, run-of-the-mill, customary 610 *habitual*; vague, loose, indefinite 495 *inexact*; unspecified, impersonal 10 *unrelated*; common, ordinary, average 30 *median*; commonplace 83 *typical*; popular, mass, vulgar 869 *plebeian*; multipurpose.

universal, catholic, ecumenical; national, international, cosmopolitan, global, worldwide, nationwide, widespread 32 *extensive*; pervasive, prevalent, epidemic, pandemic 189 *present everywhere*; every, each, any, all, all without exception 52 *whole*.

Vb. *generalize*, make general, etc. (see adj.); broaden, widen, universalize, globalize; spread, broadcast, diffuse 75 *disperse*.

Adv. *generally*, without exception, universally, etc. (see adj.); mainly; generally speaking, by and large; loosely, vaguely.

80 Speciality

N. *speciality*, personality, uniqueness; singularity 88 *unity*; originality, individuality, particularity; make-up 5 *character*; characteristic, one's middle name; idiosyncrasy, eccentricity, peculiarity, distinctive feature, trademark, mannerism, quirk, foible; signature dish, signature tune, signature song; trait, mark, feature, attribute; sine qua non 89 *accompaniment*; distinction, differentiae 15 *difference*; idiom; slang, jargon, brogue, patois 560 *dialect*; idiolect 557 *language*; version, lection 15 *variant*; exception, nonce word, special case 84 *nonconformity*; specialty, gift, special study, specialization 694 *skill*.

particulars, details, the nitty gritty, minutiae, items, special points, specification; circumstances; the ins and outs of.

self, ego, id, identity, selfhood, personality 320 *subjectivity*; psyche, soul 447 *spirit*; I, myself, number one, numero uno, me generation; we, ourselves; yourself, himself, herself, itself, themselves; us, in-group 74 *group*; being 371 *person*.

Adj. *special*, specific, particular; peculiar, singular, unique 88 *one*; individual, idiosyncratic, characteristic, idiomatic, original 21 *inimitable*; personal, private (see also *private* below); subjective 476 *intuitive*, 481 *biased*, *misjudging*; appropriate 24 *apt*; diagnostic 5 *characteristic*; distinctive, marked, out of the ordinary 84 *unusual*.

definite, definitive, defining; determinate, quantified, specified; distinct, concrete, explicit, clear-cut, cut and dried; certain, exact, precise 494 *accurate*; itemized, detailed.

private, intimate, esoteric, personal, personalized, exclusive, one-to-one, one-on-one; off the record, for one's private ear, confidential, secret 523 *latent*.

Vb. *specify*, enumerate, quantify 86 *number*; particularize, itemize, detail 87 *list*; cite, reel off, mention, name names 561 *name*; enter into detail, spell out 570 *be diffuse*; define, determine 236 *limit*, 463 *discriminate*; pinpoint, locate 187 *place*; come to the point, explain 520 *interpret*; point out 547 *indicate*; realize, translate into fact, substantiate 156 *cause*; individualize, personalize 15 *differentiate*; specialize.

Adv. *specially*, especially, in particular; personally, for one's own part; specifically, ad hoc, to order.

severally, each, apiece, one by one; respectively, in turn; in detail, bit by bit.

namely, that is to say, videlicet, viz., to wit, i.e.

81 Rule

N. *rule*, norm, formula, canon, code; maxim, principle 693 *precept*; law, law of nature, universal principle; firm principle, hard and fast rule; strict law, law of the Medes and Persians; law of the jungle, sod's *or* Sod's law, Murphy's law, Parkinson's law; unwritten rule *or* law, rule of thumb; statute, by-law 953 *law*; regulation, order, party line; guide, precedent, model, pattern 23 *prototype*; form, standard, keynote 83 *example*.

regularity, constancy 16 *uniformity*; order 60 *order*; normality, normal state; form, routine, drill, practice, custom 610 *habit*; fixed ways, rut, groove; treadmill; methodicalness, method, system 62 *arrangement*; convention 83 *conformity*.

Adj. *regular*, constant, steady 141 *periodical*; even 258 *smooth*; standardized 16 *uniform*; regulated, according to rule, according to the rule-book, methodical, systematic 60 *orderly*; normal, unexceptional 83 *typical*; customary 610 *usual*; conventional, right-on 83 *conformable*.

82 Multiformity: having many forms

N. *existence in many forms*, multiformity, multiplicity; heterogeneity, variety, diversity, biodiversity 17 *non-uniformity*; multifariousness, many-sidedness 101 *plurality*; schizophrenia, split personality 503 *personality disorder*; changeability 152 *changeableness*, 437 *variegation*; Proteus, Jekyll and Hyde; kaleidoscope.

Adj. *existing in many forms*, multiform, multifarious, polymorphous, polymorphic; multifid 100 *divided into many parts*; multiple, multiplex, multiplicate, manifold, many-headed, many-sided, many-faceted, hydra-headed, protean, versatile, all-round; variform, heterogeneous, diverse 17 *non-uniform*; motley, mosaic, kaleidoscopic 43 *mixed*; many-coloured 437 *variegated*; divers, sundry; of all sorts and kinds 15 *different*; changeable 152 *changing*; schizophrenic.

83 Conformity

N. *conformity*, conformation 24 *conformance*; faithfulness 768 *observance*; accommodation, adjustment, reconciliation, conciliation 24 *agreement*, *adaptation*; malleability 327 *softness*; acquiescence 721 *submission*; assimilation, acclimatization, naturalization 18 *similarity*, 147 *conversion*; conventionality 848 *etiquette*; political correctness, PC; traditionalism; orthodoxness 976 *orthodoxy*; formalism, strictness 735 *severity*; convention, form 610 *practice*, 848 *fashion*; emulation 20 *imitation*, 106 *repetition*, 925 *flattery*; ordinariness 79 *generality*.

example, exemplar, type, pattern, model 23 *prototype*; exemplification, stock example, classic example; case, case in point, instance; illustration, practical demonstration, object lesson;

sample, random sample, cross-section; representative, specimen, representative selection; trailer, teaser, foretaste 66 *precursor*; precedent.

conformist, conventionalist, traditionalist; follower of fashion, fashion victim, fashionista 848 *fashionable society*; company man; formalist, copycat, yes-man 20 *imitator*, 925 *flatterer*; follower, loyalist.

Adj. *conformable*, adaptable, adjustable; malleable, pliant 327 *flexible*; accommodating 24 *agreeing*; conforming, following, faithful, loyal, true-blue 768 *observant*; conventional, right-on; politically correct, PC; on-message; traditional 976 *orthodox*; slavish, servile 20 *imitative*.

typical, normal, natural, of daily occurrence, everyday, common, common or garden 79 *general*; average 30 *median*, 732 *middling*; true to type; commonplace, prosaic; conventional; habitual 610 *usual*; representative, standard; exemplary.

Vb. *conform*, correspond, conform to 24 *accord*; adapt oneself, accommodate oneself, adjust oneself, mould oneself; fit in; bend, yield, take the shape of 327 *soften*; fall into line, toe the line, fall in with 721 *submit*; comply with 768 *observe*; fit in with 24 *accord*; stick to the rules, obey regulations, follow precedent 739 *obey*; keep in step, follow the fashion, follow the trend, do as others do, do as the Romans do; join in the cry, jump on the bandwagon, keep up with the Joneses 848 *be in fashion*; follow suit 20 *imitate*, *copy*; drift with the tide, swim with the stream 601 *be irresolute*; keep to the beaten track, run on tramlines, run in a groove, stick in a rut 610 *be in the habit of*.

make conform, conform, assimilate, naturalize 18 *liken*; acclimatize 610 *accustom oneself*; systematize 62 *regularize*; normalize, conventionalize, standardize; drill 16 *make uniform*; train, lead 689 *direct*; bend, twist, force 740 *compel*; accommodate, fit, fit in, trim, cut down to size, knock *or* lick into shape 24 *adjust*.

exemplify, illustrate, cite, quote, reel off, instance.

84 Nonconformity

N. *nonconformity*, non-conformance, unconformity, inconsistency 17 *non-uniformity*, 25 *disagreement*; contrast 14 *contrariety*; exceptionality, strangeness 59 *extraneousness*; nonconformism, unorthodoxy 977 *heterodoxy*; disconformity, dissidence 489 *dissent*, 769 *nonobservance*; deviationism 744 *independence*; anomalousness, eccentricity, irregularity 282 *deviation*; unconventionality; freakishness,

oddity; rarity 140 *infrequency*; infringement, infraction 954 *illegality*; breach of practice; wonder, miracle 864 *prodigy*; anomaly, exception 57 *exclusion*; exemption, escape clause 919 *non-liability*; special case 80 *speciality*; homosexuality, lesbianism, Sapphism, bisexuality; individuality, trait, idiosyncrasy, quirk, kink, peculiarity, singularity, mannerism; uniqueness 21 *originality*.

abnormality, aberration 282 *deviation*; mutation 15 *variant*; abortion, teratogenesis, monstrosity, monster; sexual abnormality, fetishism, necrophilia, sadism, masochism, sadomasochism; transvestism, gender bending, gender identity disorder; hermaphroditism 161 *lack of power*.

nonconformist, dissident, deviationist, dissenter, maverick 489 *objector*, 977 *heretic*, 978 *sectarian*; blackleg, scab 938 *cad*; unconventionalist, Bohemian, hippie, beatnik, dropout, flower people; rebel, angry young man, punk, recalcitrant 738 *rebel*; contra; fanatic 504 *crank*; outlaw, criminal 904 *offender*; pariah 883 *outcast*; hermit, loner 883 *unsocial person*; gypsy, nomad, New Age traveller, tramp, bag lady 268 *wanderer*; odd man out, joker; square peg in a round hole, fish out of water 25 *misfit*; deviant, mutant, albino, freak, monster, oddity, original, character, card, caution, odd customer, queer customer, oddball, weirdo 504 *crank*; queer fish 851 *laughing stock*; curiosity, rarity, rara avis, one of a kind; neither fish, flesh, nor fowl *or* neither fish, flesh, nor good red herring; transsexual, hermaphrodite; homosexual, gay, lesbian; fairy, nancy, nancy boy, pansy, batty-boy, fruit, homo, poof, poofter, queen, queer, shirtlifter (all derog *or* offensive); dyke *or* dike, lez *or* les (usually considered derog or offensive); transvestite, trannie *or* tranny, cross-dresser, transsexual, gender-bender, ladyboy 143 *transformation*; drag artist, female impersonator; pervert, perv; sadist, masochist, sadomasochist; mongrel, cur 43 *hybrid*.

Adj. *unconformable*, unmalleable 326 *rigid*, 602 *obstinate*; recalcitrant 711 *defiant*; eccentric; a law unto oneself 744 *independent*; freakish, outlandish; unique 80 *special*; solitary 883 *unsociable*; blacklegging; nonconformist, dissident 489 *dissenting*, 978 *sectarian*; unorthodox, heretical; non-practising 769 *non-observant*; homosexual, lesbian, lez *or* les, gay, bent, queer, bisexual, AC/DC, LGBT, lesbian, gay, bisexual, transgender; unconventional, weird, offbeat, Bohemian, boho, hippie, beatnik, irregular, not done; infringing, lawless, criminal 954 *illegal*; aberrant, off the rails; misplaced, out of one's element, out of place, ectopic, out of order; incongruous, out of step, out of line, off-message, out of tune, out of keeping 25 *disagreeing*; alien, exotic 59 *extraneous*; wandering; ambiguous 518 *equivocal*.

unusual, uncustomary, unwonted 611 *unaccustomed*; unfamiliar 491 *unknown*; newfangled 126 *new*; exotic 59 *extraneous*; out of the ordinary, extraordinary, way-out; phenomenal; unparalleled; singular, unique 80 *special*, 140 *infrequent*; rare, choice, recherché 644 *excellent*; strange, bizarre, curious, odd, queer, rum, unco; funny, peculiar, fantastic, grotesque 849 *ridiculous*; noteworthy, remarkable, surprising, astonishing, miraculous 864 *wonderful*; mysterious, inexplicable, unaccountable 523 *occult*; unimaginable, incredible 470 *impossible*, 472 *improbable*; monstrous, teratoid, teratological; unnatural, preternatural, supernatural; outsize 32 *enormous*; outré.

abnormal, unnatural, supernatural, preternatural (see also *unusual* above); aberrant, teratological, teratoid, freakish; uncharacteristic, untypical, atypical, unrepresentative, exceptional; anomalous 17 *non-uniform*; kinky, deviant; epicene, androgynous, gynandrous; mongrel, hybrid 43 *mixed*; irregular; solecistic; non-standard, substandard, below par, subnormal; supernormal 32 *great*; asymmetrical, deformed, amorphous, shapeless 246 *distorted*.

Vb. be unconformable, be unconventional, etc. (see adj.); not fit in, be a fish out of water, be a square peg, be out of one's element; be the exception that proves the rule; infringe custom; break a law, commit a breach of etiquette, break a habit, break with custom; violate a law; drop out, freak out, do one's own thing 744 *be free*; make an exception; leave the beaten track.

S E C T I O N   F I V E

Number

85 Number

N. *number*, real number, imaginary number; natural number, cardinal number, ordinal number; round number, complex number; prime number, odd number, even number, whole number, integer; irrational number, transcendental number; numeral, cipher, digit, figure, character; Arabic numerals, Roman numerals; decimal system, binary system, duodecimal system; quantity, unknown quantity, unknown, X, symbol, constant; mapping; operator, sign; function, variable, argument; algorithm; vector, matrix, tensor, quaternion; surd; expression, equation, quadratics; formula, chemical formula, empirical formula,

molecular formula, structural formula; series, set.

numerical element, minuend, subtrahend; multiplicand, multiplier; coefficient, multiple, dividend, divisor, aliquant, aliquot; quotient, factor, submultiple, fraction, proper fraction, improper fraction, vulgar fraction; mixed number; numerator, denominator; decimal, recurring decimal, repetend; common factor, common denominator; reciprocal, complement; parameter; power, root, square root, cube root; exponent, index, logarithm, natural logarithm, mantissa, antilogarithm; modulus, differential, derivative, integral, integrand, determinant, fluxion.

ratio, proportion; progression, arithmetical progression, geometrical progression, harmonic progression; trigonometrical ratio, sine, tangent, secant; cosine, cotangent, cosecant; percentage, per cent, percentile.

numerical result, answer, product, equation; sum, total, aggregate 52 *whole*; difference, residual 41 *remainder*; bill, score, tally 38 *addition*.

Adj. *numerical*, numerary, numeral, digital; arithmetical; cardinal, ordinal; round, whole; even, odd; prime; figurate; positive, negative, surd, radical; divisible, aliquot; multiple; reciprocal, complementary; fractional, decimal; incommensurable; commensurable, proportional; exponential, logarithmic, differential, fluxional, integral; algebraic, transcendental; rational, irrational.

86 Numeration

N. *numbering*, numeration, enumeration, census, counting, ciphering, figuring, reckoning, calculating, computing; sum, tally, score; count, countdown; summation, calculation, computation, number-crunching 465 *measurement*; pagination; algorithm, decimal system; accountancy 808 *accounts*; poll, capitation; head-count.

mathematics, pure mathematics, applied mathematics, arithmetic, algebra; quadratic equations; set theory, modern maths; differential calculus, integral calculus, infinitesimal calculus, vector calculus; fluxions; calculus of variations; topology; geometry, trigonometry; graph, logarithm; algorithm, systems analysis (see also *computing* below); operational research, critical path analysis, linear programming 623 *policy*; axiomatics 475 *reasoning*.

statistics, figures, tables, averages; lies, damned lies, and statistics; mode, mean 30 *average*; significance, deviation, normal deviation, standard deviation, standard error; distribution curve, skew; regression; correlation, rank correlation test, chi-square test; statistical enquiry, market research, poll, Gallup poll (tdmk) 605 *vote*; census, capitation; roll call, muster, muster roll, account 87 *list*; demography, birth rate, death rate; vital statistics; price index, retail price index, cost of living, cost-of-living index 809 *price*; graph, bar graph, histogram, scatter diagram, chart, pie chart, flow chart 623 *plan*; cartogram 551 *map*.

person who counts, enumerator, numberer, census-taker; calculator, counter; mathematician, arithmetician, geometrician, algebraist; actuary, bookkeeper 808 *accountant*; statistician, statistics freak, quantoid; teller, pollster.

counting instrument, abacus; ready reckoner, multiplication table; tape measure, yardstick 465 *gauge*; sliding rule, slide rule; Cuisenaire rods, Napier's bones *or* rods; comptometer, adding machine, calculating machine, calculator, electronic calculator, pocket calculator; cash register, till, totalizator, tote.

computer, digital computer, analogue computer; mainframe; minicomputer, microcomputer, microprocessor, personal computer, PC, home computer, desktop computer, laptop computer, laptop, palmtop, notebook, handheld computer, personal digital assistant, PDA; workstation.

computing, computation, computer science, computer technology, computer literacy; artificial intelligence, AI, cybernetics, informatics, information science, information technology, IT, software engineering; data capture, data processing, electronic data processing, EDP; desk-top publishing; software, program, computer program, firmware, shareware; DOS, MS-DOS (tdmk), protocol, application, applet, interface; application service provider, ASP; input, output, throughput, feedback; storage, retrieval, information retrieval, database management system, data mining, text mining; batch processing, real-time processing, time-sharing, multiprogramming, downtime; machine code, machine language, computer language, programming language; hardware (see also *counting instrument* above), keyboard, keypad, mouse, mouse pad *or* mat; data, bit, byte, kilobyte, megabyte, gigabyte; megaflop, gigaflop; magnetic tape, floppy disk, digital video disk, digital versatile disk, DVD; disk drive; processor, word processor; central processing unit; database, data bank, memory, menu, visual display unit, VDU, visual display terminal, VDT 445 *appearance*; icon, earcon; hard copy, printout; spell-check, spelling check; viewdata, Prestel (tdmk), Ceefax (tdmk), Oracle (tdmk), teletext 524 *informa-*

tion; virus, computer virus, e-mail virus, micro virus, macro virus, computer bug, millennium bug, malicious code, malicious mobile code, Trojan horse, worm; antivirus software, virus detection, virus protection program, quarantine; firewall; computer programmer, computer buff, computernik, geek, hacker, techie; mouse potato, the digerati; computer game, video game, role-playing game; Internet, World Wide Web, etc. 531 *Internet*.

Adj. *statistical*, expressed in numbers, digital, ciphered, numbered; mathematical, arithmetical, algebraical; geometrical, trigonometrical; in ratio, in proportion, percentile, quartile.

computerized, automatic, cyber-, e-, robotic, electronic, on-line, off-line; programmable; real-time, random-access, on-screen, user-friendly; analogue, digital, binary, alphanumeric.

Vb. *number*, cast, count, reckon, calculate, compute, tell; score, keep the score, notch up; tick off, count down; paginate; enumerate, poll, count heads, count hands; take a poll, take a census; muster, take roll call; take stock, inventory 87 *list*; go over 106 *repeat*; check, audit, balance, keep accounts 808 *account*; aggregate, amount to, add up to, total, tot up to, come to.

computerize, automate; digitize, digitalize; program, process; debug; compute, log on, boot, reboot, key in, keyboard, dump, drag and drop, download, upload, log off; scroll, browse 173 *operate*; hack; benchmark; surf, surf the Net 531 *Internet*.

87 List

N. *list*, enumeration; inventory, stock list; chart, table, catalogue, listing; portfolio 767 *security*; statement, schedule, manifest, bill of lading; checklist; invoice; score; price list, tariff, bill, account 809 *price*; registry, Domesday Book; file, register 548 *record*; ticket, docket, tag, tally 547 *label*; ledger, books; table of contents, index, card index 547 *indication*; menu 86 *computing*; bill of fare, menu 301 *eating*; playbill, programme, prospectus, synopsis, syllabus 592 *compendium*; roll, electoral roll, voting list 605 *electorate*; constituency list, top-up list; payroll; Army List, Navy List, active list 686 *personnel*; census 86 *numbering*; book list, bibliography 589 *reading matter*; rota, roster, panel; waiting list, short list, short leet; dramatis personae; family tree, pedigree 169 *genealogy*; scroll, roll of honour, martyrology, beadroll, diptych; blacklist 924 *censure*, 928 *accused person*; sick list 651 *sick person*; book of days, calendar, Advent calendar; engagement book, diary 505 *reminder*; questionnaire; alphabetical list, A–Z, alphabet 60 *order*.

word list, vocabulary, glossary, lexicon, thesaurus 559 *dictionary*.

directory, gazetteer, atlas; almanac, calendar, timetable 117 *chronology*; Bradshaw, ABC 524 *guidebook*; Army List, Navy List, Crockford, Debrett, Burke's Peerage, Almanac *or* Almanach de Gotha, Who's Who 589 *reference book*; telephone directory, phone book, Yellow Pages.

Vb. *list*, enumerate; itemize, reel off, inventory, catalogue, index, tabulate; file, docket, schedule, enter, book 548 *register*; enlist, matriculate, enrol, empanel, inscribe.

88 Unity

N. *unity*, oneness, absoluteness 44 *simpleness*; integration, wholeness 52 *whole*; uniqueness, individuality 80 *speciality*; monotheism; monism; singleness 895 *celibacy*; isolation, solitude, loneliness 883 *seclusion*; union, undividedness, indivisibility, solidarity 48 *cohesiveness*, 706 *association*; unification 50 *combination*.

unit, integer, one, ace, item, article, piece; individual, atom, monad, entity 371 *person*; single piece, monolith; nonce word; isolated case, only exception; solo, monologue; single person, single, singleton, bachelor, bachelor girl 895 *celibate*; single parent 896 *divorce*; hermit, lone wolf, loner 883 *unsocial person*; set, kit, outfit, package 78 *inclusion*.

Adj. *one*, singular, sole, single, solitary; unique, only, lone, one and only; unrepeated, only-begotten; one-off, custom-built; a, an, a certain 562 *anonymous*; individual 80 *special*; absolute, universal 79 *general*; unitary, unific, univocal, unicameral, unilateral, unicellular; unisex; mono-; monolithic 16 *uniform*.

alone, lonely, homeless, orphaned, deserted, abandoned, forsaken; lonesome, solitary, lone 883 *unsociable*; isolated; insular 199 *distant*; single-handed, on one's own; by oneself, on one's tod; unaccompanied, unescorted, unchaperoned; celibate.

Adv. *singly*, one by one, one at a time; once, once only, once and for all, for the nonce, just this once, never again, only, solely, simply; alone, on one's own, by oneself, per se.

89 Accompaniment

N. *accompaniment*, concomitance 5 *inherent state*, 45 *union*, 71 *continuity*; inseparability; society 882 *sociability*; companionship, togetherness 880 *friendship*; partnership, marriage 706 *association*; coexistence 181 *concurrence*; coincidence, contemporaneity, simultaneity

123 *simultaneousness*; attendance, company; parallel course 219 *parallelism*.

concomitant, attribute, sine qua non 5 *essential part*; complement 54 *completeness*; accessory, appendage, appurtenance, fixture 40 *adjunct*; by-product, corollary; symptom, syndrome 547 *indication*; coincidence 159 *chance*; context, circumstance 7 *state*; background; accompaniment, obbligato; accompanist 413 *musician*; entourage, court 742 *retainer*; attendant, following, suite 67 *retinue*; groupie, camp follower; convoy, escort, guide 690 *leader*; chaperon, bodyguard 660 *protector*, 749 *keeper*; suitor, wooer 887 *lover*; tracker 619 *hunter*; inseparable, shadow, tail 284 *follower*; consort, cohabitee, lover 894 *spouse*; comrade, companion, boon companion, best friend 880 *friend*; stable companion, mate, co-worker, partner, associate 707 *colleague*; accomplice 707 *collaborator*; twin, pair, fellow 18 *analogue*; satellite, parasite, hanger-on 742 *dependant*.

Vb. *accompany*, coexist; cohabit, live with, keep company with, consort with, walk out with; string along with; bear one company, squire, chaperon, protect 660 *safeguard*; convoy, escort, guide, conduct, lead, usher 64 *come before*; track, dog, tail, shadow 619 *pursue*; associate with, partner 706 *cooperate*; gang up with, chum up with 880 *befriend*; carry with, bring in its train *or* wake 156 *cause*; be inseparable, go hand in hand with, follow as night follows day 157 *depend*; belong, go with, go together 9 *be related*.

Adv. *with*, together with, along with, cum, in company with; in the same boat; hand in hand, arm in arm, side by side; cheek by jowl.

90 Duality: existence as two

N. *existence as two*, duality, dualism; double-sidedness; double life, dual personality, split personality, Jekyll and Hyde; positive and negative, yin and yang, etc. 14 *polarity*, 704 *opposites*; dyad, two, deuce, duo, twain, partnership, couple, item, Darby and Joan, Jack and Jill, Romeo and Juliet; brace, pair, couple; binomial; doublets, twins, Castor and Pollux, Gemini, Siamese twins, conjoined twins, identical twins, Tweedledum and Tweedledee 18 *analogue*; two-wheeler, bicycle; bireme; yoke; couplet; twosome, duel; duet; Janus; double whammy.

Adj. *dual*, binary, binomial; bilateral, bicameral; twin, biparous; bisexual, double-sidedness, double-barrelled, duplex 91 *double*; paired, coupled, etc. (see vb.); two abreast, two by two; in twos, both; in pairs, tête-à-tête, à deux; double-sided, double-edged, bipartisan; amphibious; ambidextrous 91 *double*; bifocal;

biform, two-dimensional, two-faced.

Vb. *pair*, couple, match, bracket, yoke; mate, pair off.

Adv. *and*, cum, with 38 *in addition*, 89 *with*.

91 Duplication: multiplication by two

N. *duplication*, doubling, doubleness; reduplication, encore, repeat, iteration, echo, parrotry 106 *repetition*; renewal 656 *restoration*; copy, carbon copy, photocopy, Xerox (tdmk) 22 *duplicate*; living image, look-alike 18 *analogue*; doubling 261 *fold*.

Adj. *double*, doubled, twice; duplex; biform; twofold, two-sided, two-headed, two-edged; double-faced, two-faced; amphibious, ambidextrous; dual-purpose, dual-use, two-way; ambiguous 518 *equivocal*; ambivalent; bisexual, AC/DC, hermaphrodite; twin, duplicate; dualistic 90 *dual*.

Vb. *double*, redouble, square; encore, echo, second 106 *repeat*; renew 656 *restore*; duplicate, twin; reduplicate, stencil, xerox, photocopy 20 *copy*.

92 Bisection: division into two

N. *division into two*, bisection, bipartition, dichotomy; dividing by two, halving, etc. (see vb.); hendiadys; half, moiety, fifty per cent 53 *part*; hemistich; hemisphere 252 *sphere*.

forking, branching, bifurcation, furcation 294 *divergence*; swallowtail, fork, prong 222 *cross*.

dividing line, diameter, diagonal, equator, parting, seam; date line; party wall, garden fence 231 *partition*.

Adj. *divided*, bisected, halved, etc. (see vb.); bifid; bipartite; bicuspid; bifurcated, forked; dichotomous; split, cloven.

Vb. *divide*, split, cleave 46 *break up*; bisect, transect; cut in two, share, go halves, go fifty-fifty 783 *allocate*; halve, divide by two; job-share.

fork, bifurcate, separate; branch off, ramify 294 *diverge*.

93 Triality: existence as three

N. *existence as three*, triality, trinity; triplicity 94 *triplication*.

three, triad; Faith, Hope and Charity; threesome, triumvirate, troika; triplet, trio; trinomial; trimester, triennium; trefoil, shamrock, triangle, trident, tripod, trivet; three-wheeler; tricycle; trireme; three-headed monster, Cerberus; triphthong, triptych, trilogy; third power, cube; third person; Third World.

Adj. *three*, triform, trinomial; three in one, tripartite; tricolour; three-dimensional, three-sided, triangular, deltoid, trigonal, trilateral;

three-pointed; trifoliate, three-leaved *or* -leafed; three-pronged, three-cornered, three-legged; tricorn, tricuspid; three-monthly, trimestrial, quarterly.

94 Triplication: multiplication by three

N. *triplication*, trebling, tripling; triplicity, trebleness; hat trick; tercentenary.

Adj. *treble*, triple; trine, trinal, ternary; triplex, triplicate, threefold, three-ply; third, tertiary; trihedral; trilateral.

Vb. *treble*, triple, triplicate, cube.

95 Trisection: division into three

N. *division into three parts*, trisection, tripartition, trichotomy; third, third part; tierce.

Vb. *divide into three parts*, divide by three, trisect; split into three, trifurcate.

96 Quaternity: existence as four

N. *existence as four*, quaternity; four, tetrad, tetrarchy; square, tetragon, quadrilateral, quadrangle, quad; tetrahedron; quadrinomial; quadrature, quarter; fylfot, swastika 222 *cross*; tetrapod; tetrameter, quatrain; tetragram; quartet, foursome; four winds, four evangelists; four-in-hand, quadriga; quatrefoil; quadruplet, quad; quadruped, tetrapod; quadrennium; four corners of 52 *whole*.

Adj. *four*, quaternary, quadratic; quadrate, square, quadrilateral, tetrahedral, foursquare; four-leaved *or* -leafed; four-footed, four-legged, quadrupedal; quadrennial.

97 Quadruplication: multiplication by four

N. *multiplication by four*, quadruplication; quadruplicity; squaring; quatercentenary.

Adj. *fourfold*, quadruple, quadruplicate, quadruplex; squared.

Vb. *multiply by four*, quadruple, quadruplicate; square, quadrate.

98 Quadrisection: division into four

N. *division into four parts*, quartering, quadrisection; fourth, fourth part; quarterly; quart, quarter; farthing, quarto.

Vb. *divide into four parts*, divide by four, quarter, quadrisect.

99 Five and over

N. *five*, cinque, quintuplet, quin; quintet; pentagon, pentagram; pentameter; Pentateuch; pentathlon; cinquefoil; quinquereme; five senses, Five Towns, Cinque Ports; five-a-side; a bunch of fives.

over five, six, half-a-dozen, sextet, hexad, sixer; hexagon, hexagram; Hexateuch; hexameter; seven, heptad, week, sabbatical year; septennium; septenary, septet; pleiad;

Heptateuch; seven deadly sins, seven wonders of the world, seven seas; eight, octave, octet, octad, octagon, Octateuch; one over the eight, piece of eight, figure of eight; nine, three times three; nonary; novena; nine Muses, nine days' wonder; ten, tenner, decade; decagon, decahedron, Decalogue; Ten Commandments; eleven, hendecasyllable; twelve, dozen; dodecahedron; twelve apostles, the Twelve, twelve tribes; thirteen, baker's dozen, double figures, teens.

twenty and over, twenty, a score; icosahedron; four and twenty, two dozen; twenty-five, pony; forty, two score; fifty, half a hundred, jubilee; sixty, three score; sexagenarian; seventy, three score and ten, septuagenarian; eighty, four score, octogenarian; ninety, nonagenarian.

hundred, century, ton, centenary, centennial; hundredweight; centurion; centenarian; centipede; the hundred days; Old Hundredth; hundred per cent; treble figures.

over one hundred, a gross; hundreds and hundreds; thousand, grand; millennium; ten thousand, myriad; hundred thousand, lakh; million; ten million; thousand million, milliard; billion; million million, trillion, quadrillion, quintillion, sextillion, septillion, octillion, nonillion, decillion, centillion, multimillion; zillion, etc. 32 *great quantity*.

100 Multisection: division into many parts

N. *division into many parts*, fractionation, fractionalization, decimation, multisection.

Adj. *divided into many parts*, multifid, multifidous, multipartite; decimal, tenth, tithe; duodecimal, twelfth; sexagesimal, sexagenary; hundredth, centesimal; millesimal.

Vb. *divide into many parts*, fractionate, fractionalize, decimate, multisect.

101 Plurality

N. *plurality*, the plural; multiplicity 104 *multitude*; many-sidedness 82 *existence in many forms*; polygon, polyhedron; polytheism; a number; a few; majority.

Adj. *plural*, composite, multiple; polydactyl, polypod; multiparous; polymorphic, multiform; many-sided; multilateral, multipurpose; in the majority 104 *many*.

102 Fraction: less than one

N. *fraction*, decimal fraction, vulgar fraction, etc. 85 *numerical element*; fragment 53 *part*, 783 *portion*; shred 33 *small quantity*.

Adj. *fractional*, partial 33 *small*, 53 *fragmentary*.

103 Zero

N. *zero*, nil, nothing, simply nothing, damn all, bugger all, fuck all, sweet fuck all, SFA, sweet Fanny Adams, nada, zilch, zip, zippo; next to nothing, naught, nought, nix; no score, love, duck, blank; cipher; nothingness 2 *non-existence*, 4 *lacking substance*; none, nobody, not a soul 190 *absence*; nadir, rock bottom.

Adj. *not one*, not any, zero; infinitely little, null 2 *non-existent*, 4 *lacking substance*.

104 Multitude

N. *multitude*, numerousness, multiplicity; large number, million 99 *over one hundred*; lots, loads, heaps, masses, numbers, scores, shedloads, truckloads, myriads, millions, trillions, zillions, etc. 32 *great quantity*; a sea of, a mass of, a world of, a sight of; forest, thicket; host, array, fleet, battalions 722 *army*; throng, mob, all the world and his wife 74 *crowd*; tribe, horde.

Adj. *many*, myriad, several, sundry, divers, various, a thousand and one; quite a few, a good few; considerable, numerous, very many, a good many, ever so many, many more, no end of, umpteen, n, in telephone numbers; untold, unnumbered, innumerable, uncounted 107 *infinite*; multifarious, manifold 82 *existing in many forms*; ever-recurring 139 *frequent*, 106 *repeated*; much, ample, multiple; profuse, in profusion, abundant, superabundant, generous, lavish, overflowing, galore 635 *plentiful*, 32 *great*.

multitudinous, massed, crowded, thronged 54 *full*; populous, peopled, populated, high-density 324 *dense*; teeming, crawling, humming, lousy with, hotching with, alive with, bristling with 171 *prolific*; thick, thick on the ground, thick as flies; coming thick and fast 139 *frequent*; incalculable, innumerable, inexhaustible, countless, endless 107 *infinite*.

Vb. *be many*, be various, etc. (see adj.); swarm with, crawl with, hum with, bristle with, teem with, be hotching with, be lousy with, be alive with 54 *fill*; clutter, crowd, throng, swarm, mass, flock, troop 74 *congregate*; swarm like ants *or* locusts *or* like bees round a honey-pot; flood, overflow, snow under, swamp, overwhelm 637 *be overabundant*; infest, overrun; swell the ranks 36 *augment*; outnumber, make a majority 32 *be great*.

105 Fewness

N. *fewness*, paucity; exiguity, thinness, sparsity, sparseness, rarity 140 *infrequency*; scantiness 636 *scarcity*; a few, a handful; wisps, tuft; small number, trickle; soupçon, smidgen 33 *small quantity*; limited number, poor turnout, no quorum; minority, one or two, not enough to matter, a derisory amount.

Adj. *few*, precious few, scant, scanty, little 636 *scarce*; thin on the ground, sparse, rare, low-density, few and far between 140 *infrequent*; not many, hardly any; to be counted on the fingers of one hand; too few, in a minority, without a quorum.

Vb. *be few*, be few in number, be underpopulated; seldom occur.

cause to be few, reduce, diminish, pare 198 *make smaller*; scale down, slim down, cut back, decimate; eliminate, weed, thin, sort out 300 *eject*; understaff.

Adv. *here and there*, in dribs and drabs, in twos and threes, in a trickle; sparsely, rarely, infrequently.

106 Repetition

N. *repetition*, iteration, reiteration; doubling, ditto, reduplication 20 *imitation*, 91 *duplication*; recapitulation; renewal, resumption, reprise 68 *beginning*; saying again, repeating, anaphora 574 *ornament*; same old story; dripping tap; mantra; tautology, redundancy 570 *diffuseness*; stammering, stuttering 580 *speech defect*; repeat, repeat performance, encore; second helping, seconds; playback, replay, action replay; return match, revenge; chorus, refrain 412 *vocal music*; echo, repercussion, reverberation 404 *resonance*; quotation, plagiarism; hardy annual; old story, old news, ancient history, chestnut, Queen Anne's dead 838 *tedium*; reprint, reissue 589 *edition*; remake, rehash, recast, revival 656 *restoration*.

recurrence, repetitiveness, repetitive strain injury, RSI 139 *frequency*; cycle, round, return, rebirth, renaissance, reincarnation, Groundhog Day 141 *regular return*; succession, run, series, serial; serial killing, serial monogamy 71 *continuity*; recurring decimal, repetend, throwback, atavism 5 *heredity*; reappearance, comeback, curtain call; rhythm, biorhythm, drumming, hammering 141 *periodic recurrence*; alliteration, assonance, rhyme 18 *assimilation*, 593 *prosody*; monotony 838 *tedium*; same old round, mixture as before, rehash, routine 610 *habit*.

Adj. *repeated*, repetitional; recurrent, recurring, ever-recurring 141 *periodical*; haunting 505 *remembered*; tautological, redundant, repetitive, repetitious, harping, iterative; stale, cliché-ridden 572 *feeble*; echoing, rhyming, alliterative, assonant 18 *similar*; monotonous, singsong 16 *uniform*, 838 *tedious*; rhythmical, drumming, hammering; incessant, habitual 139 *frequent*; retold, said before, quoted, cited; above-mentioned, aforesaid 66 *precursory*; pla-

giarized 20 *imitative*; reheated, rehashed, recycled.

Vb. *repeat*, do again, iterate, cut and come again; duplicate, reduplicate, redouble 91 *double*; multiply 166 *reproduce*; reiterate, say again, recapitulate, go over, ring the changes on; retell, restate, reword, rephrase; trot out; recite, reel off, say over, say after; echo, ditto, parrot, plagiarize 20 *copy*, 925 *flatter*; quote, cite 505 *remember*; go over the same ground, retrace one's footsteps, practise, rehearse; play back, rerun, rewind; recycle, reprocess; begin again, restart, resume 68 *begin*; replay, give an encore; reprint, reissue, republish; rehash, remake, renew, revive 656 *restore*; reheat.

Adv. *again*, afresh, anew, over again, for the second time, once more; ditto; encore; de novo.

107 Infinity

N. *infinity*, infiniteness, boundlessness, limitlessness, illimitability; infinite space, outer space 183 *space*; eternity 115 *perpetuity*.

Adj. *infinite*, indefinite; immense, measureless; eternal 115 *perpetual*; countless, innumerable, immeasurable, illimitable, interminable; incalculable, unfathomable, incomprehensible, unapproachable, beyond comprehension; inexhaustible, without number, without limit, without end, no end of; without measure, limitless, endless, boundless; untold, unnumbered 104 *many*; unlimited.

Adv. *infinitely*, ad infinitum; indefinitely; immeasurably 32 *greatly*.

SECTION SIX

Time

108 Time

N. *time*, tide; tense 564 *grammar*; duration, extent 113 *long duration*; season, term, semester, tenancy, tenure; tour, shift, shot, spell, stint; span, space 110 *period*; a bit, a while; quality time; the whole time, the entire period, life, life-time; eternity 115 *perpetuity*; passage of time, lapse of time, lapse, course 111 *course of time*; years, days; Time, Father Time, Time's scythe, Time's hourglass, sands of time, ravages of time, time the enemy, time the healer; fourth dimension; time zone; indefinite time; past time, past tense 119 *previousness*, 125 *past time*; prospective time 124 *futurity*; contemporaneity 121 *present time*; recent time 126 *newness*; antiquity, distant time 127 *oldness*.

point in time 8 *juncture*; time of day 117

clock time; time of life, vintage, year 117 *chronology*; date, day, age, reign 110 *era*; birthday, saint's day 141 *anniversary*; day of the week; day of the month, calends, ides, nones; moment 116 *instant*; target date, zero hour, D-day; term, fixed day, quarter day, payday; equinox, solstice.

Adj. *continuing*, permanent 115 *perpetual*, in process of, pending; repetitive, recurrent 106 *repeated*; temporal 141 *periodical*.

Vb. *continue*, endure, drag on 113 *last*; roll on, pass 111 *elapse*; live through, sustain; stay, remain, abide, survive 113 *outlast*; wait 136 *be pending*.

pass time, vegetate, breathe, subsist, exist 360 *be alive*; age; spend time, consume time, use time, employ time 678 *be busy*; while away time, kill time; summer, winter, weekend; waste time, fritter away time 679 *be inactive*; mark time.

fix the time, date, put a date to, set the day, settle on a date for, pencil in 117 *time*.

Adv. *while*, whilst, during, pending; day by day 113 *all along*; in the course of, so long as; for the time being, for now, meantime, meanwhile; between whiles, in the meantime, in the interim; from day to day, from hour to hour; hourly 139 *often*; for a time, for a season; till, until, up to, yet; always, the whole time, all the time 115 *perpetually*; all along 54 *throughout*.

when, what time; one day, once upon a time, one fine morning; in the days of, in the time of, in the year of.

109 Neverness

N. *neverness*, Greek Calends; month of Sundays, blue moon, when pigs fly; jam tomorrow, mañana; dies non; eternity 115 *perpetuity*.

Adv. *never*, not ever, at no time, at no period, on no occasion; not in donkey's years; nevermore, never again; over one's dead body; never before, never in one's born days; without date, sine die.

110 Period

N. *period*, matter of time; season; time of day, morning, evening; time of year, spring, summer, autumn, fall, winter 128 *morning*, 129 *evening*; term; time up, full time 69 *finality*; spell, go, tour, stint, shot, shift, span, stretch, sentence; innings, turn; round, bout, lap; watch; length of time, second, minute, hour; particular term, rush hour; pause, interval; day, weekday, working day; week, working week, five-day week; fortnight, month, calendar month, lunar month, quarter, trimester; half year, semester; twelve month, year, solar year, sidereal year, light year, leap year; financial year, fiscal year; quinquennium; decade, Gay Nineties, Hungry Thirties, Swinging Sixties, Noughties; golden wedding, jubilee 141 *anniversary*; century, millennium.

era, time, period, generation, age, days; epoch; aeon; cycle, Ice Age; Stone Age, Bronze Age, Iron Age; Dark Ages, Middle Ages 125 *antiquity*; Renaissance, Age of Enlightenment, Age of Reason, belle époque, fin de siècle; modern times, Computer Age, Space Age; Golden Age, Age of Aquarius.

Adj. *periodic* 141 *seasonal*; hourly, daily, weekly, monthly, yearly; annual, biennial, quinquennial, centennial; period 127 *olden*.

111 Course: indefinite duration

N. *course of time*, matter of time, process of time, lapse of time, march of time, flight of time; duration 108 *time*, 146 *continuance*.

Vb. *elapse*, pass, lapse, flow, run, roll, proceed, advance, press on 285 *progress*; wear on, drag on, crawl 278 *move slowly*; flit, fly, fleet, slip, slide, glide 277 *move fast*; run its course; go by, pass by, slip by, fly past.

Adv. *in time*, in due time, in due season; in the course of time, in the process of time, in the fullness of time, with the years.

112 Contingent duration

Adv. *provisionally*, precariously, by favour; at the pleasure of; for the present; so long as it lasts; as or so long as.

113 Long duration

N. *long duration*, a long time, unconscionable time; a month of Sundays, years, donkey's years, years on end, yonks; a lifetime; generations, a century, an age, ages, aeons 115 *perpetuity*; longevity 131 *old age*; corridor of time, antiquity 125 *past time*.

durability, lasting quality, endurance; stamina, staying power 162 *strength*; survival 146 *continuance*; permanence 153 *stability*; long standing, good age, ripe old age 127 *oldness*; long run, long innings.

protraction, prolongation, extension; dragging out, spinning out, padding out, filibustering, stonewalling 702 *hindrance*, 715 *resistance*; interminability, long haul 136 *delay*, 278 *slowness*; extra time, injury time, overtime.

Adj. *lasting*, abiding; secular, agelong, lifelong, livelong; longtime, longstanding, inveterate, deep-seated, deep-rooted; of long duration, long-term, long-service, marathon 203 *long*; unconscionable; durable, enduring 162 *strong*; long-lived 127 *immemorial*; evergreen, unfading, fresh 126 *new*; eternal, perennial 115 *perpetual*; persistent, chronic 602 *obstinate*; indestructible 162 *unyielding*; constant, stable, permanent 153 *unchangeable*.

Vb. *last*, endure, stand, stay, remain, abide, continue 146 *go on*; defy time, stand the test of time, never end 115 *be eternal*; wear well 162 *be strong*.

outlast, outlive, outwear, outstay, survive; remain 41 *be left*; ride out the storm, live to fight another day; have nine lives.

Adv. *for a long time*, long, for long, for ages, for years, since time immemorial, many a long day; for good, for ever, for all time, for better, for worse; all one's life, from the cradle to the grave; till one is blue in the face; till the cows come home.

all along, all day, all day long, the livelong day, as the day is long; all the year round, round the clock; day in, day out, year in, year out; ever since.

long ago, long since, in the distant past, long long ago, when the world was young; in the past, in ancient days, in bygone times, once upon a time, etc. 125 *formerly*.

at last, at long last, in the end, in the long run, after many days, not before time.

114 Transience

N. *transience*, transientness, transitoriness 4 *lacking substance*; impermanence; evanescence 446 *disappearance*; volatility 338 *vaporization*; fugacity 277 *velocity*; fragility 330 *brittleness*; mortality, perishability 361 *death*; frailty, fragility 163 *weakness*; mutability 152 *changeableness*; capriciousness, fickleness 604 *caprice*; suddenness 116 *instantaneousness*; temporariness, interregnum.

brief span, short space of time, a minute or two, short while; briefness, momentariness, brevity 204 *shortness*; mortal span, a short life and a merry one; summer lightning, shooting star, meteor, flash in the pan, nine days' wonder; ephemera, bubble, mayfly, snow on a dyke, snows of yesteryear, smoke in the wind; April shower, summer cloud 4 *thing that lacks substance*; bird of passage, ship that passes in the night; brief encounter; short run 110 *period*, 277 *spurt*; spasm, moment 116 *instant*.

Adj. *transient*, temporal, impermanent, transitory, fading, passing 4 *lacking substance*; cursory, flying, fleeting, flitting, fugitive 277 *speedy*; volatile, written in water; evanescent; unsettled, restless; flickering, changeable 152 *changing*.

ephemeral, of a day, short-lived, fleeting, here today, gone tomorrow; disposable; mortal 361 *dying*; frail, fragile 163 *weak*, 330 *brittle*; impermanent, temporary.

brief, short-term, short-service 204 *short*;

summary, short and sweet, to the point 569 *concise*; quick, fleet, brisk 277 *speedy*; sudden, momentary, meteoric, like a flash 116 *instantaneous*; hurried 680 *hasty*.

Vb. *be transient*, be transitory, etc. (see adj.); not stay, not last; flit, fleet, fly, gallop 277 *move fast*; fade, flicker, vanish, evanesce, melt, evaporate 446 *disappear*; fade like a dream, flit like a shadow, pass like a summer cloud, burst like a bubble.

115 Perpetuity: endless duration

N. *perpetuity*, endless time 107 *infinity*; everlastingness; eternity, timelessness; neverendingness, interminability 113 *long duration*; endurance 71 *continuity*, 144 *permanence*; immortality 146 *continuance*; perpetuation, immortalization.

Adj. *perpetual*, perennial, longlasting, enduring, durable 113 *lasting*; agelong 127 *immemorial*; non-stop, constant, continual, ceaseless, incessant; flowing, ever-flowing, uninterrupted 71 *continuous*; dateless, ageless, unageing, unchanging, immutable 144 *permanent*; evergreen, unfading, everlasting; imperishable, undying, deathless, immortal; unending, never-ending, interminable; endless, without end, timeless, eternal.

Vb. *perpetuate*, make permanent, continue, establish; immortalize, eternalize.

be eternal, be perpetual, etc. (see adj.); last for ever, endure for ever, live for ever; go on for ever, have no end, never cease.

Adv. *for ever*, in perpetuity, on and on; ever and always, for always and always, for aye, evermore, for ever and ever, for ever and a day; time without end, world without end; for keeps, for good and all, for better, for worse; to the end of time, till doomsday, to the crack of doom; to infinity 107 *infinitely*. (See also 139 *perpetually*.)

116 Instantaneousness: point of time

N. *instantaneousness*, instantaneity, immediateness, immediacy; simultaneity 121 *present time*; suddenness, abruptness 508 *lack of expectation*; precise time 135 *punctuality*; momentariness 114 *transience*.

instant, moment, precise moment, point, point of time; second, split second, half a second, tick, trice, jiffy, half a jiffy, mo, half a mo; breath; burst; crack; stroke; coup; flash, lightning flash; twinkle, twinkling, the twinkling of an eye; two shakes, two shakes of a lamb's tail; the very moment, the very hour, the stroke of.

Adj. *instantaneous*, immediate, instant,

sudden, abrupt, snap; quick as lightning, with the speed of light, quick as a flash, like a flash 277 *speedy*.

117 Chronometry

N. *chronometry*, chronoscopy, horology; watch-making; calendar-making, timetabling; timing, dating; timekeeping 108 *time*.

clock time, right time, BBC time, astronomer's time, solar time, sidereal time, Greenwich Mean Time, GMT, British Standard Time, British Summer Time, BST, local time, Central European Time, continental time; time of day, time of night; bedtime; summer time, double summer time, daylight saving time. (See also 108 *time*.)

timekeeper, chronometer, timepiece; clock, dial, face; hand, pendulum 317 *oscillation*; electric clock, digital clock, quartz clock, long-case clock, grandfather clock, grandmother clock, calendar clock, carriage clock, cuckoo clock, alarm clock, travelling alarm, travel clock, clock radio; alarum; clock tower, Big Ben; water-clock; watch, ticker; fob-watch, hunter, repeater; wristwatch, digital watch, analogue watch; sundial; hour-glass, sandglass, egg timer; chronograph, chronoscope; time signal, pip, siren, hooter; gong, bell, five-minute bell, time-clock, timer, stopwatch; Tim, speaking clock; parking meter, traffic light 305 *traffic control*; time fuse, time switch, time bomb; metronome.

chronology, dating, radiocarbon dating, dendrochronology, vole clock, glottochronology; date, age, epoch, style 110 *era*; old style, O.S., new style, N.S.; almanac, calendar, perpetual calendar, fixed calendar, Gregorian calendar, Julian calendar; ephemeris, astronomical almanac; timeline; chronicle, annals, book of days, diary, journal, log-book 548 *record*; date list, time-chart 87 *list*; tide-table, timetable, schedule 87 *directory*.

chronologist, chronographer, chronologer, calendar-maker, calendarist; chronicler, annalist, diarist 549 *recorder*.

Vb. *time*, clock; timetable, schedule; match times 123 *synchronize*; phase 24 *adjust*; set the alarm 669 *make ready*; calendar, chronologize, chronicle 548 *record*; date, be dated; measure time, mark time, beat time, keep time; count the minutes, watch the clock; clock in 68 *begin*; clock out 145 *cease*.

Adv. *o'clock*, a.m., p.m.

118 Anachronism

N. *anachronism*, parachronism, wrong date, wrong day, chronological error; mistiming, previousness, prolepsis 135 *anticipation*; disregard of time, unpunctuality 136 *lateness*; neglect of time 506 *no memory*; wrong moment 138 *untimeliness*.

Adj. *anachronistic*, misdated; antedated, foredated, previous, before time, too early 135 *early*; parachronistic, postdated 136 *late*; too late, overdue, unpunctual, behind time; out of due time, out of season, out of date, old-fashioned, retro 127 *antiquated*.

119 Antecedence: coming before

N. *antecedence*, previousness, priority, pre-existence; primogeniture, birthright; eldest, firstborn, son and heir; flying start 64 *precedence*; leading 283 *preceding*; the past, yesteryear, yesterday 125 *past time*; eve, day before; precedent, antecedent; foretaste, trailer, teaser, preview, prerelease; herald 66 *precursor*; prequel.

Adj. *prior*, earliest, first, first in the field, precedent 64 *preceding*; previous, earlier, anterior, antecedent; antediluvian, prehistoric; pre-Christian, BC; pre-war, pre-existing, prenatal, antenatal; elder, eldest, firstborn; former, ci-devant, onetime, erstwhile, sometime, ex-, retired, emeritus; foregoing, aforementioned, above-mentioned; aforesaid, said; introductory, prefatory, preliminary 66 *precursory*; given, presupposed 512 *supposed*.

Vb. *do before*, presuppose 512 *suppose*; predecease, prefabricate, prearrange, pre-empt, prejudge, preview; be previous, anticipate, forestall, be beforehand with, jump the gun, jump the queue; steal a march on, have a start on 277 *outstrip*; lead 64 *come before*, 283 *precede*.

Adv. *before*, prior to, beforehand, by; just before, on the eve of; earlier, previously, formerly; ultimo, ult.; afore, ere; aforetime, ere now, before now; ere then, before then, already, yet; in anticipation; until now, up to now, hitherto, heretofore.

120 Subsequence: coming after

N. *subsequence*, posteriority; succession 65 *sequence*, days to come, time to come 124 *futurity*; line, lineage, descent, successor, descendant 170 *posterity*; cadet; aftermath 67 *sequel*.

Adj. *subsequent*, posterior, following, ensuing, next, to come, after, later; last in date, junior, cadet, younger, youngest 130 *young*; successive, consecutive, consequent; succeeding, designate, to be 124 *future*; postnatal; posthumous; postwar; after Christ, AD; postprandial 65 *sequential*.

Vb. *ensue*, supervene, follow after 65 *come after*; go after 157 *result*, 284 *follow*; succeed, follow in the footsteps of, step into the shoes of 771 *inherit*.

Adv. *subsequently*, later, in the process of time; after, afterwards; at a later date; next, next time; thereafter, thereupon; since, from that time, from that moment; from the start, from the word 'go'; after a while, after a time; soon after, close upon; next month, proximo.

121 Present time

N. *present time*, contemporaneity, contemporaneousness, topicality 126 *modernism*; time being, the present, present time, present day, present moment; this hour, this moment, this moment in time, this instant 116 *instantaneousness*; juncture, opportunity, crisis 137 *occasion*; the nonce; the times, modern times, these days, this day and age; today, twenty-first century, nowadays; one's age, present generation, one's contemporaries 123 *contemporary*.

Adj. *present*, actual, instant, current, extant 1 *existing*; of this date, of today's date; topical, contemporary, contemporaneous; present-day, latter-day, latest, up-to-the-minute, up-to-date, bang up-to-date, breaking, du jour, the new — 126 *modern*.

Adv. *at present*, now, right now, at this time, at this moment, at this moment in time; live; at the present time, contemporaneously, contemporarily; today, nowadays; at this time of day, at this stage, even now; already, but now, just now; this time, on the present occasion; for the time being, for now, for the nonce; on the spot; now or never; now as always.

until now, to this day, to the present day, up to now, to date; through; from the start, from the word go 113 *all along*.

122 Different time

N. *different time*, other times 124 *futurity*, 125 *past time*; another time, some other time, not now, not today, any time but this 109 *neverness*; parachronism 118 *anachronism*.

123 Same time

N. *simultaneousness*, simultaneity, same time 116 *instantaneousness*; synchrony, synchronism; coexistence, coincidence, concurrence, concomitance 89 *accompaniment*; contemporaneity, contemporaneousness, same date, same day 121 *present time*; coevality, same age, twin birth 28 *equality*; level-pegging, neck-and-neck, nip and tuck, dead heat 28 *draw*; synchronization, sync, phasing, isochronism.

contemporary, coeval, twin 28 *peer*; one's contemporaries, one's own generation; age group, peer group, class, year 74 *group*.

Adj. *synchronous*, synchronal; synchronic; contemporary, contemporaneous 121 *present*, 126 *modern*; simultaneous, coinstantaneous, coincident, coexistent, coeternal, conterminous, concomitant 24 *agreeing*; level, neck and neck 28 *equal*; matched in age, coeval, twin; of the same age, of the same year, of the same generation, of the same vintage; synchronized, timed, phased, isochronous, on the beat.

Vb. *synchronize*, sync, concur, coexist 89 *accompany*; encounter, coincide 295 *meet*; keep time 410 *harmonize*; say together, say in unison, chorus; tune, phase 24 *adjust*; be level-pegging, run neck and neck 28 *be equal*; pace, keep in step with; isochronize.

124 Futurity: prospective time

N. *futurity*, womb of time, time to come, days and years to come; morrow 120 *subsequence*; future, time ahead, prospect, outlook 507 *expectation*; coming events, fate 154 *event*, 155 *destiny*; near future, tomorrow, mañana, the day after tomorrow, next week, next year 121 *present time*, 200 *nearness*; advent 289 *approach*; long run, distant future 199 *distance*; future generations, descendants, heirs, heritage 170 *posterity*; successorship; future tense 564 *grammar*.

future state, what fate holds in store 155 *destiny*, 596 *fate*; latter days; doomsday, crack of doom 69 *finality*; afterlife, life after death, life to come, hereafter, kingdom come 971 *heaven*; damnation 972 *hell*; good time coming, mañana, jam tomorrow, millennium 730 *prosperity*; reincarnation 106 *repetition*.

Adj. *future*, to be, to come; coming 289 *approaching*; nigh, just round the corner, close at hand 200 *near*; on the horizon, in the wind; due, destined, fated, threatening, imminent, overhanging 155 *impending*; in the future, ahead, yet to come, waiting; in embryo, on the stocks 669 *preparatory*; prospective, designate, earmarked 605 *chosen*; promised, looked for, anticipated 471 *probable*, 507 *expected*; predicted, foreseeable; later, ulterior, posterior 120 *subsequent*.

Vb. *be to come*, lie ahead, lie in the future; have in store, be destined, threaten, overhang 155 *impend*; near, draw nigh 289 *approach*; be imminent, be just round the corner, cast its shadow before, stare one in the face.

Adv. *henceforth*, in future, from this time forth, from now on.

125 Past Time: retrospective time

N. *past time*, 119 *previousness*; retrospection, looking back 505 *remembrance*; the past, recent past, only yesterday 126 *newness*; distant past, history, antiquity; old story, matter of history

127 *oldness*; past times, days of yore, days of old, olden days, good old days, bygone days; auld lang syne, yesterday, yesteryear, former times; past tense, historic tense, preterite, perfect, pluperfect 564 *grammar*.

antiquity, rust of antiquity, eld; creation, when time began, when the world was young, time immemorial; prehistory, protohistory, ancient world, mediaeval times; Stone Age, etc., prehistoric age, Dark Ages, Middle Ages 110 *era*; the ancients, cavemen, Neanderthal man, Cro-Magnon, etc. 371 *humankind*; relics, neolith, microlith 41 *remainder*, 127 *archaism*; ruin, ancient monument, megalith, henge, Stonehenge 253 *earthwork*, 548 *monument*; excavation, dig, archaeology 484 *discovery*; museum 632 *collection*; ancient lineage 169 *genealogy*.

fossil, fossilized remains *or* relics, petrified forest, trilobite, ammonite; trace fossil 548 *record*; coal forest 385 *fuel*; sponge, coral 358 *organism*; Neanderthal man, etc. 371 *humankind*; mammoth, dinosaur 365 *animal*.

palaeology, palaeontology, palaeozoology, palaeography; palaeoanthropology 371 *humankind*; archaeology; antiquarianism.

antiquarian, palaeontologist, archaeologist; palaeologist, palaeographer; antiquary 492 *scholar*; historian, prehistorian; medievalist 549 *chronicler*; Egyptologist, classicist 557 *linguist*.

Adj. past, in the past, historical; ancient, prehistoric 127 *olden*; early, primitive 127 *primal*; gone, gone for good, bygone, lost, dead and buried 506 *forgotten*; passed away, no more, died out, dead as the dodo 2 *extinct*, 361 *dead*; passé, has-been, obsolete 127 *antiquated*, 674 *disused*; fossilized 326 *hard*; over, blown over, done, over and done with, behind one; elapsed, lapsed, expired, run out, ended, finished 69 *final*.

former, late, quondam, sometime, ex- 119 *prior*; retired, emeritus, outgoing.

foregoing, last, latter 64 *preceding*; recent.

retrospective, looking back, backward-looking, retro; reminiscing 505 *remembering*; historical; retroactive, going back; with hindsight, from experience.

Vb. be past, have elapsed, have expired; have run its course, have had its day, be burnt out; pass, die, elapse, blow over, be over, be at an end 69 *end*; be a dead letter.

Adv. formerly, aforetime, of old, of yore; time was, ago, in olden times; long ago, long since; a long while, a long time ago; once upon a time; years ago, ages ago; lately, some time ago, some time back; yesterday, the day before yesterday; yestreen, yesteryear; last year,

last season, last month, last week; in old money.

126 Newness

N. newness, recentness; recent date, recent occurrence, recent past 121 *present time*, 125 *past time*; innovation 21 *originality*, 560 *neologism*; novelty, freshness, dewiness 648 *cleanness*; greenness, immaturity, callowness, rawness 130 *youth*; renovation, restoration, renewal, resurrection 656 *revival*; clean slate, new leaf, new broom; new housing, new build.

modernism, modernity, modernness, modernization; up-to-dateness, topicality, contemporaneity 121 *present time*; the latest, the latest thing, the in-thing, latest fashion; the last word, dernier cri; new look, contemporary style, trendiness 848 *fashion*.

modernist, neologist, neoteric, futurist; advanced thinker, avant-garde; bright young thing, trendy, yuppy, baby-boomer; modern generation, younger generation.

Adj. new, newish, recent, of recent date, of recent occurrence; upstart, parvenu, nouveau arrivé, nouveau riche, mushroom; novel, inventive, innovative, unprecedented, unheard of 21 *original*; brand-new, spick and span, like new, in mint condition 648 *clean*; green, evergreen, dewy, juicy; fresh, fresh as a daisy, fresh as paint; maiden, virgin, virginal; newborn 130 *young*; raw, unfledged, callow 670 *immature*; just out, just published, hot from the press; new-made, new-laid; straight from the oven, factory-fresh; untouched by human hand; unused, first-hand; untried, untrodden, unbeaten, unexplored 491 *unknown*; untested 461 *experimental*; aspiring, budding, wannabe 68 *beginning*.

modern, late, latter-day; contemporary, topical 121 *present*; up-to-the-minute, up-to-date, bang up-to-date, with it; à la mode, in the latest fashion, trendy, latest, new 848 *fashionable*; cutting-edge, leading-edge, state-of-the-art, ultramodern, modernistic, advanced, avant-garde, futuristic, revolutionary; innovating, innovative, neoteric, newfangled, new-fashioned.

Vb. modernize, do up, renovate, refurbish; update, bring up to date, give a new lease of life; have the new look, go modern, go contemporary, get with it; move with the times 285 *progress*; innovate, try something new, push the envelope.

127 Oldness

N. oldness, primitiveness 68 *beginning*; olden times 110 *era*; age, eld; dust of ages, ruins 125 *antiquity*; maturity, mellowness 129 *autumn*; decline, rust 51 *decay*; senility 131 *old age*.

archaism, antiquities 125 *antiquity*; ancien régime; thing of the past, relic of the past; listed building, ancient monument; museum piece, antique, heirloom, bygone, Victoriana; dodo, dinosaur 125 *fossil*; golden oldie; old fogy, old fossil, fuddy-duddy, archaist, square, old-timer, has-been, back number; love of the past, antiquarianism, old-fashionedness, retromania.

tradition, lore, folklore, mythology; inveteracy, custom 610 *habit*; common law; word of mouth 579 *speech*.

Adj. *olden*, old, ancient, antique, antiquarian; veteran, vintage; venerable; archaic, ancient; time-worn; prehistoric, mythological; feudal, medieval; historical 125 *past*, 866 *renowned*.

primal, prime, primitive, primeval, primordial, aboriginal 68 *beginning*; fossil, palaeozoic; eolithic, palaeolithic, mesolithic, neolithic; early, antediluvian, before the Flood.

antiquated, of other times, of another age, archaic, in old money; old as the hills, old as Methuselah, old as time, age-old 113 *lasting*; old-world, old-time; olde worlde, ye olde —; prewar 119 *prior*; anachronistic 125 *retrospective*; fossilized, ossified; behind the times, out of date, out of fashion, dated, antediluvian, before the Flood, out of the ark, horse-and-buggy, silent-screen, black-and-white; conservative, Victorian, old-fashioned, old-school, square, not with it; outworn, outdated, outmoded; passé, démodé, vieux jeu, old hat, quaint, retro; gone by 125 *past*; perished 655 *dilapidated*; mouldering; obsolete, obsolescent; superannuated 674 *disused*; old 131 *ageing*.

Vb. *be old*, be antiquated, etc. (see adj.); belong to the past, have had its day, be burnt out 69 *end*; age; decline, fade, wither 655 *deteriorate*.

128 Morning. Spring. Summer

N. *morning*, morn, forenoon, a.m.; small hours, wee sma' hours 135 *earliness*; breakfast-time, drive-time; matins; dawn, dawning, cockcrow, dawn chorus 66 *precursor*; sunrise, sun-up, daybreak 417 *light*; peep of day, break of day, first blush of day; daylight, daytime; full day, full light of day, broad daylight; Aurora, rosy-fingered Dawn; daystar, orb of day 321 *sun*.

noon, high noon, meridian, midday, noonday, noontide; eight bells, twelve o'clock, twelve noon.

spring, springtime, springtide, Eastertide, vernal season, spring season, seed-time, blossom-time, maying; first cuckoo; vernal equinox, first point of Aries.

summer, summertime, summertide, Whitsuntide; midsummer, summer solstice, longest day, Midsummer's Day, high summer, dog days 379 *heat*; haymaking; aestivation; Indian summer.

129 Evening. Autumn. Winter

N. *evening*, eventide, even, eve, dewy eve; evensong, vespers, afternoon, p.m.; teatime, drive-time; matinée; afternoon tea, five o'clock; sundowner, soirée; dog-watches; sunset, sundown, setting sun, going down of the sun; evening star, Hesperus, Vesper; dusk, crepuscule, twilight, gloaming 419 *half-light*; candlelight, cockshut, dewfall; moonrise, moonset 321 *moon*; close of day, nightfall, dark, nighttime 418 *darkness*; bedtime 679 *sleep*; curfew, last post 136 *lateness*, 69 *finality*; nightbird, night-owl.

midnight, dead of night, witching hour, witching time; night-watch, small hours.

autumn, back-end, fall, harvest, harvesttime; harvest celebration, harvest home, harvest thanksgiving 876 *celebration*; harvest moon; Michaelmas; Indian summer; falling of leaves: abscission.

winter 380 *wintriness*; wintertime, wintertide; Advent, Christmas, Yule, Yuletide; midwinter; winter solstice, shortest day; hibernation; nuclear winter.

Adj. *wintry*, winter, brumal, brumous, snowbound 380 *cold*; stark, bleak.

130 Youth

N. *youth*, freshness 126 *newness*, 174 *vigorousness*; young blood, youthfulness, youngness, juvenility; babyhood, infancy, childhood, childish years, tender age 68 *beginning*; puppyhood; boyhood, girlhood; one's teens, adolescence, pubescence, age of puberty, boyishness, girlishness, awkward age, growing pains; younger generation, rising generation, yoof, middle youth 132 *young person*; growing boy *or* girl, minor, ward; Peter Pan.

tender age, nonage, immaturity, minority, infancy, pupillage, wardship; cradle, nursery, kindergarten.

salad days, school days, student days, college days, happiest days of one's life; heyday, heyday of the blood, springtime of youth; prime of life, bloom of youth, florescence.

Adj. *young*, youthful, childlike, boyish, girlish; virginal, maidenly, sweet-sixteen; adolescent, pubescent; teenage, preteen, juvenile; maturing, developing, growing; budding, burgeoning, blooming, flowering; unripe, green, callow, awkward, raw, unfledged, bumfluffed 670 *immature*; school-age, under-age, minor, infant, pre-school; younger, minor, junior, cadet; youngest; childish; juvenescent; young at heart, ageless.

131 Age

N. *age*, time of life, years, lifespan 113 *long duration*.

middle age, middle years, middle life, middle youth, adultescent, sandwich generation, years of discretion 134 *adultness*; maturity, prime of life; a certain age, climacteric, change of life, the change, menopause, male menopause, andropause, mid-life crisis; middle-aged spread.

old age, anno domini; pensionable age, retirement age; advanced years, three-score years and ten, allotted span, grey hairs, white hairs 133 *old person*; senescence, declining years, vale of years, evening of one's days, autumn *or* winter of life; infirmity, debility 163 *weakness*; second childhood, dotage, senility, Alzheimer's disease 655 *deterioration*; longevity, ripe old age.

seniority, old man's privilege 64 *precedence*; primogeniture 119 *previousness*; higher rank 34 *superiority*; doyen; gerontocracy, elders, presbytery, senate 692 *council*.

care of the aged, geriatrics, gerontology, nostology 658 *therapy*, old people's home, sheltered housing, eventide home.

Adj. *ageing*, aged, old, elderly, matronly; grey; middle-aged, adultescent, ripe, mature, mellow 669 *matured*; overblown, overripe, run *or* gone to seed; of a certain age, not so young as one was, no chicken; past one's prime, getting on, getting old, going grey, greying; white-haired, grey-haired, hoary, hoary-headed, long in the tooth; senescent, waning, declining, moribund 361 *dying*; wrinkled, lined, marked with crow's feet, rheumy-eyed, toothless, shrivelled, wizened, decrepit, rickety; drivelling, doddering, gaga 499 *foolish*; senile, failing; advanced in years, stricken in years, living on borrowed time, with one foot in the grave; longeval, old as the hills, old as Methuselah; well-preserved 650 *healthy*; venerable, patriarchal; too old, past it; retired 681 *leisurely*; superannuated, passé(e) 127 *antiquated*; gerontologic, geriatric.

older, major; elder, senior 34 *superior*; first-born, eldest, primogenital 119 *prior*; eldest, maximus.

132 Young person. Young animal. Young plant

N. *child*, baby, babe, bundle of joy; infant, nursling, suckling, weanling, fosterling; kid;

kiddie, kiddiewink, mite, moppet, nipper, toddler, tot, tiny tot; bairn, wean, smout *or* smowt; brat, ankle-biter, rug rat, sprog; bambino, papoose, piccaninny; little one, little chap, little darling, little angel, little monkey, little imp, tyke; cherub, young innocent; changeling; children, brood, issue, offspring, progeny, small fry; only child, twin, triplet, quad, quadruplet, quin, quintuplet, sextuplet, septuplet; Siamese twins, conjoined twins, identical twins; babes and sucklings 935 *innocent*.

young person, youngster, juvenile, minor, young adult, young hopeful, young 'un; young people 130 *youth*; boy, schoolboy, lad, laddie, sonny; young man, adolescent, youth, stripling, urchin, cub, young shaver, whippersnapper; Ted, Teddy boy, mod, rocker, punk, skinhead, yob 176 *violent person*; girl, schoolgirl, lass, lassie, missie; young woman, wench, maid, maiden, virgin; dolly bird, Sloane Ranger 848 *fashionable society*; chit, slip, chick, miss; teenager, tween, tweenager, tweeny, subteen, teenybopper, weenybopper, groupie; tomboy, hoyden, ladette; little minx, baggage, a right little madam; colleen, mademoiselle, damsel, nymph, nymphet.

young creature, young animal 365 *animal*, bird; puppy, pup, whelp; cub (badger, bear, fox, leopard, lion, otter, tiger); kitten (cat, beaver, rabbit); foal (horse, zebra), colt, filly; piglet, pigling; lamb, lambkin; calf, heifer, stirk, yearling; kid; fawn; calf (camel, elephant, elk, giraffe, hippopotamus, moose, reindeer, rhinoceros, seal, whale); pup (rat, seal, walrus); joey (kangaroo, possum, wallaby); kit (ferret, fox, weasel); leveret (hare); fledgling, nestling; chick, chicken, pullet; duckling, gosling, cygnet; eyas, squab; tadpole, polliwog, froglet, toadlet; elver (eel); alevin, fingerling, fry, grilse, parr, smolt (salmon); brood, clutch, farrow, fry, litter, spawn; larva, pupa, nymph; caterpillar, grub; chrysalis, cocoon; spiderling; embryo, pre-embryo, foetus 156 *source*.

young plant, seedling, set; plug plant; sucker, runner, spur, shoot, offshoot, sprout, slip; twig, sprig, scion, sapling, whip 366 *plant*.

133 Old person

N. *old person*, elderly person, retired person, pensioner, old-age pensioner, O.A.P., senior citizen; coffin-dodger, golden-ager; Chelsea pensioner.

old man, elderly gentleman, patriarch, elder statesman; grandfather, grandad 169 *paternity*; veteran, old soldier, old hand, old stager, old trouper, old-timer 696 *expert*; old 'un, old boy, gaffer; old geezer, old codger, old buffer, dotard; old fogy.

old woman, elderly lady, dowager; grandmother, grandma, gran, granny; old girl, old dear, old duck, old body, old bag, old trout; old dutch 894 *spouse*; no spring chicken, mutton dressed as lamb; gammer, crone, hag.

old couple, Darby and Joan.

134 Adultness

N. *adultness*, adulthood, grown-upness, development; years of discretion, matureness; age of consent, legal age, age of reason, majority; man's *or* woman's estate; manhood, womanhood, virility, nubility 372 *male*, 373 *female*; key of the door; maturity, prime of life 131 *middle age*.

adult, grown-up, big boy *or* girl; man, gentleman 372 *male*; woman, lady, matron 373 *female*.

Adj. *grown-up*, adult, of age, at the age of consent, old enough to know better; mature, fully-developed, full-grown 669 *matured*; nubile; virile, manly 372 *male*; womanly, matronly 373 *female*; full-blown, full-fledged; in one's prime, adult, X-rated, 18.

135 Earliness

N. *earliness*, early hour, unearthly hour, wee sma' hours; early stage, primitiveness 68 *beginning*; early riser, early bird; first arrival 66 *precursor*; original settler, earliest inhabitant 191 *native*.

punctuality, timeliness 137 *occasion*; promptness, promptitude 678 *activity*; immediacy 116 *instantaneousness*.

anticipation, a stitch in time 510 *foresight*, 669 *preparation*; prematurity, precocity; forestalling 64 *precedence*.

Adj. *early*, bright and early, good and early, in the small hours, in the wee sma' hours; timely, in time, on time, in good time, punctual, prompt; forward, in advance; precocious, ahead of its time 126 *new*; immediate 116 *instantaneous*, 508 *unexpected*; coming shortly, forthcoming, ready 669 *prepared*; imminent, at hand 200 *near*; premature 670 *immature*.

Vb. *be early*, be premature, etc. (see adj. and adv.); nip in the bud; forestall, pre-empt 64 *come before*; take the opportunity, take time by the forelock, steal a march on, catch napping 306 *outdo*; engage, book, reserve; secure; order; lose no time 680 *hasten*; jump the gun.

Adv. *early*, soon, betimes; before long; first thing, at the first opportunity; with time to spare; punctually, to the minute, in time, in good time.

beforehand, in advance; precipitately; pre-

cociously, prematurely, untimely, too soon.

suddenly, without notice 508 *unexpectedly*; forthwith, right away; at the drop of a hat.

136 Lateness

N. *lateness*, late hour, small hours, wee sma' hours 129 *midnight*; eleventh hour, last minute; backwardness, slow development 499 *unintelligence*, 670 *non-preparation*; tardiness, lagging, dragging one's feet 278 *slowness*; afterthought, delayed reaction; latecomer; late developer 538 *learner*; late riser 278 *slowcoach*; laggard 679 *idler*; Fabius Cunctator.

delay, cunctation, Fabian policy 858 *caution*; delaying tactics, gaining time, stonewalling, filibustering 113 *protraction*, 702 *hindrance*; deceleration 278 *slowness*; holdup 747 *restraint*; postponement, adjournment, cooling-off period; pause, time lag, jet lag 145 *lull*; deferment, moratorium, respite, days of grace; suspension, stay of execution; reprieve 752 *annulment*; putting off, procrastination, mañana 679 *sluggishness*; dilatoriness, bureaucracy, red tape 678 *overactivity*; shelving, putting on ice, putting on hold, putting on the back-burner, cold storage 679 *inactivity*.

Adj. *late*, late in the day, eleventh-hour, last-minute, deathbed; too late, time up; overdue, delayed, belated, benighted; held up, bogged down 702 *hindered*; behindhand, lagging, behind time, behind schedule; sluggish, tardy; backward 278 *slow*; Fabian 858 *cautious*; unpunctual; procrastinating, dilatory 679 *inactive*; delayed-action; deferred, etc. (see vb.); on ice, on hold, in cold storage, on the back-burner, posthumous 120 *subsequent*.

Vb. *be late*, sit up late, rise late, keep late hours, burn the midnight oil, burn the candle at both ends; lag behind 284 *follow*; drag one's feet, linger, loiter 278 *move slowly*; hang back 679 *be inactive*; miss a chance, miss the boat, oversleep 138 *lose a chance*; be behindhand, have leeway to make up, have a backlog; not move with the times; lose, stop (clock).

wait 507 *await*; bide one's time, hold one's horses, take one's time, wait and see 145 *pause*; sleep on it 677 *not act*; hang fire; hang on, hold on, hold the line; stand about, sit about, hang about; be kept waiting, wait impatiently, cool one's heels, play the waiting game; count to ten.

put off, defer, postpone, adjourn; hold over; file, pigeonhole; table; shelve, put in cold storage, keep on ice, put on the back-burner; hold in abeyance; procrastinate, protract, delay, retard, set back, hold up, gain time, stonewall, filibuster; temporize, tide over; stall, keep one waiting.

Adv. *late*, after time, behind time; late in the day, at sunset, at the eleventh hour, at the last minute, last thing; at length, at last, at long last, ultimately; till all hours; too late.

137 Occasion: timeliness

N. *occasion*, happy chance 154 *event*; juncture 181 *concurrence*; timeliness, opportuneness, ripeness; fittingness 24 *suitability*, right time; auspicious hour, right moment, nick of time.

opportunity, favourable opportunity, golden opportunity 469 *possibility*; one's chance, break, lucky moment, piece of luck, the main chance 159 *chance*; opening, look-in, field 744 *scope*; freedom of choice 744 *freedom*; convenience, clear field 159 *fair chance*; stepping-stone 624 *bridge*.

crisis, critical time, key moment; turning point, psychological moment, crucial moment, crux, emergency, extremity; eleventh hour, last minute 136 *lateness*; the chips are down.

Adj. *timely*, in time, within the time limit; on time, to the minute, on the dot, punctual 135 *early*; well-timed; just in time, not before time, in the nick of time, at the eleventh hour.

opportune, favourable, providential, heaven-sent, auspicious, propitious; fortunate, lucky, happy 730 *prosperous*; fitting 24 *apt*.

crucial, critical, key, momentous, climactic, pivotal, decisive 638 *important*.

Vb. *profit by*, seize or grab the chance, take the opportunity, create an opening; take time by the forelock, carpe diem, strike while the iron is hot, make hay while the sun shines; cash in on, capitalize, exploit, turn to good account 673 *use*.

incidentally, by the way, by the by; en passant, apropos; parenthetically, by way of parenthesis; while speaking of, while on this subject, talking of, that reminds me.

138 Untimeliness

N. *untimeliness*, wrong time, inopportuneness 643 *inexpediency*; mishap, contretemps; evil hour 731 *misfortune*; off day, time of the month; disturbance 72 *discontinuity*; mistiming 118 *anachronism*.

Adj. *ill-timed*, mistimed, ill-judged, ill-advised; out-of-turn, untimely, untoward; mal-apropos, inconvenient 25 *unapt*, 643 *inexpedient*; unseasonable, unpunctual, not in time 136 *late*; premature, too soon for 135 *early*.

inopportune, untoward, inauspicious, unpropitious, unfavourable, ill-omened, ill-starred, unlucky, unhappy, unfortunate 731 *adverse*.

Vb. *mistime*, time it or things badly 481 *misjudge*; disturb, find engaged.

be engaged, be busy, be occupied, not be at home; be otherwise engaged, have a previous engagement, have other fish to fry 678 *be busy*.

lose a chance, miss the bus, miss the boat 728 *fail*; bungle 695 *be unskilful*; lose one's chance, let the opportunity slip 136 *be late*; let slip through one's fingers 458 *neglect*; stand in one's own light, shut the stable door after the horse has bolted 695 *act foolishly*.

139 Frequency

N. *frequency*, rapid succession 71 *continuity*; oftenness, unfailing regularity 141 *periodic recurrence*; redoubling 106 *repetition*; frequenting, haunting, regular visits.

Adj. *frequent*, recurrent 106 *repeated*; common, of common occurrence 104 *many*; thick on the ground 104 *multitudinous*; continual, constant, steady; regular 141 *periodical*; haunting, frequenting, assiduous 610 *habitual*.

Vb. *recur*, reoccur; do nothing but; keep, keep on 146 *go on*, frequent, haunt 882 *visit*; pester 827 *trouble*.

Adv. *often*, oft, many a time, time after time, time and time again, times without number; a thousand times; frequently, commonly, generally; more often than not; not infrequently, again and again; in quick succession, in rapid succession; thick and fast; regularly, daily, hourly; ad libitum.

sometimes, occasionally, every so often, once in a while; at times, now and then, now and again, every now and again, from time to time. (See also 141 *periodically*.)

perpetually, continually, constantly, incessantly, steadily, without respite 71 *continuously*; at all times, night and day, day and night, day after day, day in, day out, morning, noon and night, 24/7.

140 Infrequency

N. *infrequency*, rarity 105 *fewness*; seldomness, uncommonness; intermittence 72 *discontinuity*.

Adj. *infrequent*, uncommon, sporadic, occasional; intermittent, few and far between 72 *discontinuous*; scarce, rare, scarce or rare as hen's teeth 105 *few*; like gold dust 811 *of value*; almost unheard of, unprecedented 84 *unusual*.

Adv. *seldom*, little, once in a while; rarely, scarcely, hardly, only occasionally; not often, infrequently; scarcely ever, hardly ever, once in a blue moon, once in a month of Sundays; few and far between.

141 Periodicity: regularity of recurrence

N. *periodic recurrence*, periodicity, regularity, rhythm, steadiness, evenness 16 *uniformity*; timing, phasing, serialization 71 *continuity*; alternation, turn and turn about, shot about; reciprocity 12 *correlation*; ebb and flow, alternating current, AC, wave movement 317 *fluctuation*; to-and-fro movement, pendulum movement, piston movement, shuttle movement; shuttle service; shuttle diplomacy; pulsation, pulse, tick, beat, throb, rhythm, swing 317 *oscillation*; chorus, refrain 106 *recurrence*; drumbeat, tattoo 403 *roll*; tide 350 *wave*; frequency, wave frequency; turn, go, round, circuit, lap; shift, relay 110 *period*; cycle.

regular return, rota, cycle, circuit, revolution, life cycle, wheel of life 314 *circuitous motion*, 315 *rotation*; Groundhog Day; biorhythm; menstrual cycle, menses; yearly cycle, seasons 128 *morning*, 129 *evening*; fixed interval 110 *period*; routine, daily round 60 *order*, 610 *habit*.

anniversary, birthday, saint's day, jubilee, silver jubilee, diamond jubilee, wedding anniversary, silver wedding, ruby wedding, golden wedding, diamond wedding; centenary, bicentenary; St George's Day, St Andrew's Day, St Patrick's Day, St David's Day, St Valentine's Day 988 *holy day*; Fourth of July, Independence Day, 14 Juillet, Bastille Day 876 *special day*.

Adj. *periodical*, periodic, cyclic, revolving; fluctuating; rhythmical, steady, even, regular, constant, punctual, clock-like, like clockwork 81 *regular*; breathing, pulsating, throbbing, beating; recurrent, intermittent, sporadic, spasmodic, on-again-off-again 106 *repeated*; reciprocal, alternate, alternating 12 *correlative*; serial, successive, serialized 65 *sequential*, 71 *continuous*.

seasonal, anniversary; hourly, daily, nightly, diurnal, quotidian, tertian, biweekly, weekly, hebdomadal, hebdomadary, fortnightly, monthly; menstrual; biannual; yearly, annual, biennial, triennial, quadrennial, quinquennial, sextennial, septennial, octennial, decennial; bissextile; centennial, sesquicentennial, bicentennial, tercentennial, quadricentennial, quincentennial, millennial; secular.

Adv. *periodically*, rhythmically, etc. (see adj.); at regular intervals; at fixed periods; punctually, etc. (see adj.); seasonally, hourly, daily, on a daily basis, weekly, monthly, yearly; per diem, per annum; at intervals, intermittently, sporadically, spasmodically, fitfully, every now and then, every so often, every once in a while, every now and again.

(See also 139 *sometimes*.)

142 Fitfulness: irregularity of recurrence

N. *fitfulness*, irregularity 61 *disorder*; fits and starts 17 *non-uniformity*, 318 *spasm*; remission 72 *discontinuity*, 114 *transience*; unsteadiness, variability 143 *change*, 152 *changeableness*; capriciousness, unpredictability 604 *caprice*; eccentricity; lurching 317 *oscillation*.

Adj. *fitful*, periodic, intermittent, on-off, on-again-off-again, stop-go 72 *discontinuous*; irregular 84 *unconformable*; uneven 29 *unequal*; occasional 140 *infrequent*; unsteady, unstable, fluttering 17 *non-uniform*; inconstant, variable 152 *changing*; spasmodic, jerky, restless; halting, wavering, flickering, unsystematic; erratic 604 *capricious*; moody.

SECTION SEVEN

Change

143 Change: difference at different times

N. *change*, alteration, variation 15 *difference*; mutation, permutation, modulation, inflexion, declension; mutability, variability 152 *changeableness*; modification, adjustment, process, treatment 468 *qualification*; remix; sea change, step change 147 *conversion*; sudden change 149 *revolution*; break, break with the past, innovation, new look, make-over 126 *newness*; winds of change; change for the better, reformation 654 *improvement*; change for the worse 655 *deterioration*; change of direction, U-turn, diversion, shift, turn 282 *deviation*, 286 *regression*; relocation, change of position, transition 305 *passage*; change of staff, turnover, staff turnover, churn; rate of change, churn rate; translation, transposition 151 *interchange*, 272 *transference*; alternation 141 *periodic recurrence*; overthrow 221 *inversion*; change of mind, change of heart 603 *change of mind*.

transformation, transfiguration; transmogrification; make-over, sea change, metamorphosis, metasomatism; metabolism, anabolism, catabolism; transmutation, transubstantiation 147 *conversion*; transmigration of souls; reincarnation, avatar; version, adaptation, transcription, translation 520 *interpretation*, 521 *misinterpretation*.

Adj. *changeable*, variable, mutable 152 *changing*; fickle 604 *capricious*; affected, changed, etc. (see vb.); newfangled 126 *new*; transitional, provisional, alternative, transmutative; chequered, kaleidoscopic 437 *variegated*.

Vb. *change*, be changed, alter 152 *vary*; wax and wane 36 *grow*, 37 *decrease*; change one's clothes; change colour, change countenance 426 *lose colour*; change one's tune 603 *change one's mind*; vacillate, blow hot and cold, chop and change, channel-hop, channel-graze 604 *be capricious*; turn, shift, veer, change course, do a U-turn 282 *deviate*; relocate, seek pastures new, make a transition, pass to 305 *pass*; turn the corner 656 *be restored*; turn over a new leaf, be converted 654 *get better*; submit to change 83 *conform*; move with the times 126 *modernize*.

modify, alter, vary, modulate, diversify 437 *variegate*; superimpose 38 *add*; introduce changes, innovate 126 *modernize*; computerize, automate; turn upside down, subvert 149 *revolutionize*, 221 *invert*; reverse, turn back 148 *revert*; make changes, rearrange, reorder; change the rules, move the goalposts; reset 62 *arrange*; adapt 24 *adjust*; conform 83 *make conform*; recast, remould, reshape 243 *form*; process, treat; revise, edit, correct 654 *rectify*; reform 654 *make better*; remix; revamp, patch, darn 656 *restore*; change for the worse 655 *pervert*; tamper with, meddle with, spoil 655 *impair*; warp, bend, deform 246 *distort*; dye, discolour 425 *colour*, adulterate, doctor, qualify 43 *mix*, 163 *weaken*; cover, mask, disguise 525 *conceal*; change round, ring the changes 151 *interchange*, 272 *transpose*; effect a change, leaven 156 *cause*; turn the scale 178 *influence*; transform, transfigure, metamorphose, transmute, transubstantiate 147 *convert*; metabolize, digest.

144 Permanence: absence of change

N. *permanence*, permanency, status quo; invariability, immutability 153 *stability*; persistence 600 *perseverance*; endurance, duration 113 *durability*, 115 *perpetuity*; fixity of purpose, immobility, intransigence 602 *obstinacy*; firmness, bedrock, foundation, solidity 324 *density*; conservation 146 *continuance*, 666 *preservation*; rule 81 *regularity*; fixed law, entrenched clause 153 *fixture*; standing, long standing, inveteracy 127 *oldness*; tradition, custom, practice 610 *habit*; fixed attitude, conservatism; routine, rut 60 *order*.

Adj. *permanent*, enduring, durable 113 *lasting*; persisting, continuing, maintained 115 *perpetual*; inveterate, rocklike, long-standing 127 *immemorial*; perpetuated, standing, well-established, entrenched, in with the bricks; fixed, unchangeable, immutable, written on tablets of stone 153 *established*; well-preserved 666 *preserved*; unchanging, conservative, reactionary, dyed in the wool, true blue, diehard

602 *obstinate*; stationary, static, immobile 266 *at rest*; always the same 13 *identical*.

Vb. *stay*, come to stay, be here for good, set in, take root; abide, endure, subsist, outlast 113 *last*; persist, hold, hold good; hold on, hold it, maintain, sustain, keep up, keep on 146 *go on*; rest, remain, tarry, live 192 *live*; stand fast, refuse to budge, dig one's toes in, dig one's heels in 600 *persevere*; stand one's ground, keep one's footing 599 *stand firm*; stand still, resist change 266 *be at rest*; grow moss 127 *be old*; remain the same, not change one's spots.

145 Cessation: change from action to rest

N. *cessation*, ceasing; desistance, discontinuance, discontinuation 72 *discontinuity*; arrest 747 *restraint*; withdrawal 621 *relinquishment*, 753 *resignation*.

stop, halt, dead stop; logjam, impasse, standstill, deadlock, gridlock, stalemate 28 *draw*; traffic jam 305 *traffic control*, 702 *obstacle*; checkmate 728 *defeat*; breakdown 728 *failure*; stoppage; shutdown, closing down, non-resumption 69 *end*; hitch, check 702 *hindrance*; blockage 264 *closure*; interruption 72 *discontinuity*; breaking-off, walkout 709 *dissension*; closure of debate, guillotine 399 *silence*.

strike, stopping work 679 *inactivity*, 715 *resistance*; industrial action, general strike, 'national holiday'; work to rule; stoppage, walkout, sit-in, work-in, sit-down strike, lightning strike; unofficial strike, wildcat strike, mutiny 738 *disobedience*; lockout 57 *exclusion*.

lull, interval, pause, remission, letup; break, screen break, breather, rest 685 *refreshment*; holiday, day off, time off, gap year, leisure time 681 *leisure*; interlude, cooling-off period, breathing space; abeyance, suspension; close season, respite, moratorium, truce, armistice, cease-fire, standstill 136 *delay*.

stopping place, port of call, port, harbour; stop, halt, pull-up, whistle-stop, station; bus stop, request stop; terminus, terminal, air terminal 271 *air travel*; dead end, blind alley, cul-de-sac; billet, destination, the grave 295 *goal*.

Vb. *cease*, stay, desist, refrain, hold, hold *or* stay one's hand; stop, halt, pull up, draw up; stand, rest, rest on one's oars, repose on one's laurels 683 *rest*; have done with, see the last of, end, finish 69 *terminate*; interrupt, leave off, knock off, break off, let up 72 *discontinue*; ring off, hang up 578 *be mute*; withhold one's labour, stop work, down tools, strike, come out, walk out, vote with one's feet 715 *resist*; lock out 57 *exclude*; pipe down 399 *be silent*; come to an end, dry up, peter out, run out, run down 636 *be insufficient*; slacken off, fade out, fade away 446 *disappear*; come off, end its run, be taken off; fold up, collapse 728 *fail*; die away, blow over, clear up 125 *be past*; stand down, withdraw, retire 753 *resign*; leave, leave off; give up, give over 621 *relinquish*; shut up, shut down, close; shut up shop, put up the shutters, go out of business, wind up; shut off steam, switch off; cease fire 719 *make peace*; sound the last post, ring down the curtain, call it a day 266 *be at rest*, 679 *sleep*.

halt, stop, put a stop to; arrest, check, stem 702 *obstruct*; hold up, call off; pull up, cut short, call a halt, interrupt 747 *restrain*; call out, stage a strike; bring to a standstill, cause a logjam, freeze; checkmate, stalemate, thwart 702 *hinder*; check oneself, stop short, stop in one's tracks, stop dead; grind to a halt, seize, seize up, stall, jam, stick, catch; brake, put on the brake 278 *retard*.

pause, halt for a moment, take a breather; hold back, hang fire 278 *move slowly*; stay one's hand, hold one's horses, hesitate 679 *be inactive*; wait awhile, suspend, adjourn, shelve, put on ice, mothball, put on the back-burner 136 *wait*; rest 683 *rest*.

146 Continuance in action

N. continuance, continuation 71 *continuity*, 144 *permanence*; flow 179 *tendency*; extension, prolongation 113 *protraction*; maintenance, perpetuation 115 *perpetuity*; sustained action, persistence 600 *perseverance*; progress 285 *progression*; uninterrupted course, break, run, rally 71 *series*; recurrence 106 *repetition*.

Vb. go on, keep going, march on, drive on, proceed, advance 285 *progress*; run on, never end 115 *be eternal*; — and — (e.g. rain and rain); roll on, pursue its course, take its course; endure, stick, hold, abide, rest, remain, linger 144 *stay*; haunt, frequent 139 *recur*; persist, carry on, peg away 600 *persevere*; stick it out to the bitter end, sit it out, wait, wait till the end, see the end of, hang on 725 *carry through*; be not out; survive; live out one's time 69 *end*.

sustain, maintain, uphold 218 *support*; follow through 71 *continue*; keep up 666 *preserve*; keep on, harp on 106 *repeat*; keep it up, prolong, protract 115 *perpetuate*; keep things moving, keep the pot boiling, keep the ball rolling.

147 Conversion: change to something different

N. conversion, converting, turning into, making into, etc. (see vb.); processing 164 *production*; reduction, crystallization; fermentation, leaven; chemistry, alchemy; mutation, trans-

figuration 143 *transformation*; enchantment 983 *sorcery*; course, lapse, flux 111 *course of time*; development 36 *increase*; evolution 358 *biology*; degeneration 655 *deterioration*; regeneration, reformation 654 *improvement*; rebirth 656 *restoration*; naturalization 78 *inclusion*; denaturalization 916 *loss of right*; brainwashing 178 *influence*; evangelization 534 *teaching*, 612 *inducement*; convertibility 469 *possibility*.

transition, transit 305 *passage*; movement, shift, relocation, translation, transfer 272 *transference*; alteration 143 *change*; life cycle.

Adj. converted, turned into, made into, etc. (see vb.); assimilated, naturalized; reborn, born again; brainwashed; becoming, transitional; evolving, embryonic, developing, growing into; changed, altered, modified, transformed, metamorphosed, transfigured; unrecognizable 15 *different*; bewitched; genetically modified, GM, transgenic.

Vb. be turned to, be converted into, become, get; come to, turn to, ferment, develop into, evolve into, ripen into 316 *evolve*; fall into, pass into, slide into, shift into 305 *pass*; melt into, merge into; settle into, sink into; mellow 669 *mature*; wax 36 *grow*; degenerate 655 *deteriorate*; take the shape of, assume the character of; be transformed; undergo a personality change, suffer a sea change, turn over a new leaf, reinvent oneself 143 *change*; metamorphose.

convert, reduce, process, ferment, leaven; make into, reduce to, resolve into, turn into; decimalize; conjure into, enchant 983 *bewitch*; metamorphose; transmute, alchemize; render, make, mould, shape, hew into shape, knock or lick into shape 243 *form*; brainwash 178 *influence*; proselytize, evangelize 534 *teach*; win over 485 *convince*; regenerate 656 *revive*; paganize 655 *pervert*.

transform, transfigure; landscape 844 *decorate*; camouflage, disguise, paper over the cracks 525 *conceal*; render 520 *translate*; traduce 521 *misinterpret*; reshape, deform 246 *distort*; change the face of, change out of recognition 149 *revolutionize*; metamorphose 143 *modify*; reform, make something of 654 *make better*; remodel, reorganize, restructure, rationalize.

148 Reversion

N. reversion, reverting, going back, return, regress, retrogression, retreat, withdrawal, ebb 286 *regression*; tracing back, derivation 156 *source*; return to the past, turning the clock back, harking back 127 *archaism*; atavism, throwback 5 *heredity*; looking back, retrospection 505 *remembrance*; retroaction; reaction 31 *compensation*, 182 *counteraction*; repercussion, boomerang effect, backlash, backfire, ricochet 280 *recoil*; revulsion, disenchantment 830 *regret*; counter-revolution, reversal 149 *revolution*; retraction, backdown 603 *change of mind*; volte face, about-turn, U-turn, right-about turn 240 *oppositeness*; backsliding, recidivism 657 *relapse*; retroversion 246 *distortion*; giving back, cession, replacement, reinstatement 787 *restitution*; getting back, recovery, retrieval 771 *acquisition*; taking back; reply, feedback 460 *answer*; retort 479 *confutation*; turn, turning point, watershed, crucial point, turn of the tide, calm before the storm 137 *crisis*; alternation, swing, swings and roundabouts, give-and-take, swing of the pendulum 106 *recurrence*, 141 *periodic recurrence*, 317 *oscillation*; recycling; to-and-fro movement, coming and going, shuttling, commuting; round trip, there and back; return journey, return ticket, day return; back where one started, status quo.

Vb. *revert*, go back, turn back, turn, return, retrace 286 *regress*; reverse, face about, turn about, do a U-turn 221 *invert*; ebb, retreat, withdraw 290 *recede*; kick back, rebound, backfire, ricochet, boomerang 280 *recoil*; slip back, slide back, backslide 657 *relapse*; back down, retract 603 *recant*; hark back, start again, turn the clock back, go back to the beginning, restore the status quo, revive 656 *restore*; disenchant, open one's eyes, remove the spell 613 *dissuade*.

149 Revolution: sudden or violent change

N. *revolution*, full circle, circuit 315 *rotation*; radical change, organic change; tabula rasa, clean slate, clean sweep 550 *obliteration*; sudden change, catastrophe, coup d'état 508 *lack of expectation*; landslide; violent change, bouleversement, upset, overthrow 221 *overturning*; convulsion, shake-up, upheaval, reorganization, restructuring, perestroika; eruption, explosion, cataclysm 176 *outbreak*; avalanche, crash, debacle 309 *descent*, rebellion, counter-revolution 148 *reversion*, 738 *revolt*; total change, sea change, metamorphosis, nullification 752 *annulment*, *deposing*.

revolutionary, revolutionist, abolitionist, radical, socialist, communist, Maoist, Marxist, Militant Tendancy, Trotskyist, Red 708 *political party*, 738 *rebel*; Red Guard 979 *zealot*; seditionist 738 *agitator*; anarchist 168 *destroyer*; idealist 654 *reformer*.

Adj. *revolutionary* 126 *new*; innovating, radical, thoroughgoing, out-and-out, root and branch 54 *complete*; cataclysmic, catastrophic,

seismic, earth-shaking, world-shaking 176 *violent*; seditious, subversive 738 *disobedient*; Marxist, etc. (see n.), red; anarchistic 165 *destructive*.

Vb. *revolutionize*, overturn 221 *invert*; switch over 603 *change one's mind*; uproot, eradicate, make a clean sweep 550 *obliterate*, 165 *demolish*; break with the past, remodel, restructure, reorganize, refashion 126 *modernize*; change the face of, metamorphose 147 *transform*.

150 Substitution: change of one thing for another

N. *substitution*, subrogation, surrogation; commutation, exchange, switch, shuffle 151 *interchange*; supplanting, replacement, transfer 272 *transference*.

substitute, sub, proxy, alternate, agent, representative 755 *deputy*; surrogate; twofer; understudy, stand-in, body double 594 *actor*; ghost, ghost-writer 589 *author*; locum tenens, locum 658 *doctor*; reserve, twelfth man 707 *auxiliary*; supply, replacement; relief 67 *successor*; double, ringer, look-alike, changeling 545 *impostor*; mother figure, father figure, foster parent; synonym, doublet 559 *word*; metaphor, symbol 551 *representation*; prosthesis, artificial limb, pacemaker; transplant, bone marrow transplant, heart transplant, facial *or* face transplant, xenotransplant; alternative, second best, ersatz 35 *inferiority*; whipping boy, scapegoat, sacrifice 981 *religious offering*; makeshift, temporary measure, stopgap; sticking plaster, Band-Aid (tdmk) 177 *moderator*; expedient, modus vivendi 770 *compromise*.

Adj. *substituted*, vicarious 931 *disinterested*; interchangeable 28 *equivalent*; dummy, imitation, plastic, mock, ersatz, counterfeit, false 542 *spurious*; makeshift, stopgap, provisional, acting, temporary 114 *ephemeral*.

Vb. *substitute*, change for; exchange, switch 151 *interchange*; take *or* offer in exchange, swap, compound 770 *compromise*; palm off with, fob off with 542 *deceive*; make do with, put up with, make shift with; put in the place of, replace with; count as, treat as, regard as; replace, step into the shoes of, succeed 65 *come after*; supersede, supplant, displace, oust 300 *eject*; replace, take the place of, be substitute for, do duty for, count for, stand in for, act for, understudy for 755 *deputize*; act the part of, ghost for; hold the fort; shoulder the blame for, accept responsibility for, take the rap for, cover up for; rob Peter to pay Paul.

Adv. *instead*, in place, in lieu; in favour of; in loco parentis; by proxy; alternatively, as an alternative; in default of, for want of better, faute de mieux.

151 Interchange: double or mutual change

N. interchange, interchangeability, reciprocality; swap, exchange, trade-off 791 *barter*; Book-Crossing (tdmk); commutation, permutation; transposition, metathesis, mutual transfer; all change; castling (chess), shuffle, shuffling 272 *transference*; reciprocity, mutuality; cross-fire, interplay, two-way traffic, reciprocation 12 *correlation*; quid pro quo; rally (tennis), give and take; retort, repartee 460 *rejoinder*; measure for measure, tit for tat, an eye for an eye and tooth for a tooth 714 *retaliation*.

Vb. interchange, exchange, counter-change; change money, convert; swap, barter, trade off 791 *trade*; permute, commute, shuttle; change places; switch, shuffle, castle (chess) 272 *transpose*; give and take 770 *compromise*; reciprocate 12 *correlate*; requite, give as good as one gets 714 *retaliate*; bandy words, answer back 475 *argue*; return the compliment, rejoin, retort 460 *answer*; take in each other's washing, scratch each other's back 706 *cooperate*.

152 Changeableness

N. changeableness, changeability, mutability 143 *change*; changefulness, variability, variety 17 *non-uniformity*, 437 *variegation*; inconsistency, inconstancy, irregularity; instability, imbalance 29 *inequality*; unsteadiness, rockiness; pliancy 327 *softness*; fluidness 335 *fluidity*; lubricity, slipperiness 258 *smoothness*; mobility, restlessness, fidgeting, disquiet 318 *agitation*; fluctuation, alternation 317 *oscillation*; turning, veering, chopping and changing 142 *fitfulness*; impermanence, flash 114 *transience*; vacillation, hesitation, wavering 601 *irresolution*; yea and nay 603 *change of mind*; fickleness, capriciousness 604 *caprice*; flightiness, light-mindedness 456 *inattention*; versatility 694 *aptitude*.

changeable thing, moon, Proteus, chameleon; kaleidoscope; shifting sands; man of straw; wax, clay; mercury, quicksilver 335 *fluid*; wind, weathercock, weathervane; eddy; April showers; wheel, whirligig; mobile 265 *motion*; fortune, wheel of Fortune; vicissitude, luck 159 *chance*; variable quantity 85 *numerical element*; mobile features 445 *appearance*; grasshopper mind 456 *inattention*; floating voter, don't know 603 *recanter*.

Adj. changing, changeful, mutable, alterable, phased 143 *changeable*; shifting, vicissitudinous; varying, variant, variable 17 *non-uniform*; kaleidoscopic; protean 82 *existing in*

many forms; quick-change, versatile 694 *skilful*; uncertain, unreliable, vacillating, wavering 601 *irresolute*; moody, unpredictable, unaccountable 508 *unexpected*; never the same, ever-changing, volatile, mercurial 15 *different*; rootless, of no fixed abode, vagrant, wandering; wayward, fickle, whimsical 604 *capricious*; vibratory, tidal 141 *periodical*; malleable, plastic 327 *soft*; giddy, dizzy, flighty, wanton, irresponsible, frivolous 456 *lacking concentration*; shifty, inconstant, unfaithful, disloyal, traitorous.

Vb. vary, be off with the old and on with the new, show variety 437 *variegate*; ring the changes, go through phases 143 *change*; chop and change, change and change about; dodge, double 620 *avoid*; shuffle, be shifty 518 *be equivocal*; writhe 251 *wriggle*; dart, flit, flitter 265 *be in motion*; leap, dance, flicker, gutter 417 *shine*; twinkle, flash; wave, flutter, flap 217 *hang*; shake, tremble 318 *be agitated*; wobble, stagger, teeter, totter, rock, reel, sway, swing, vibrate 317 *oscillate*; shuttle, alternate, ebb and flow, wax and wane 317 *fluctuate*; veer, tack, yaw 282 *deviate*, 269 *navigate*; puff 352 *blow*; vacillate, waver, shilly-shally, hesitate, float, drift, change one's mind 601 *be irresolute*; hover, blow hot and cold, play fast and loose 603 *change one's mind*; be inconstant 604 *be capricious*.

153 Stability

N. stability, immutability; irreversibility, constancy 16 *uniformity*; firmness 144 *permanence*; rest, immobility, immovability 266 *state of rest*; stableness, steadiness, steady state, homoeostasis, balance 28 *equality*; nerve, iron nerve, aplomb 599 *resolution*; stiffness, inflexibility 326 *hardness*, 602 *obstinacy*.

fixture, establishment, firm foundation; foundations, cornerstone, rock, bedrock, pillar, tower, pyramid; invariant, constant; fast colour, indelible ink; leopard's spots; law, law of the Medes and Persians, the Twelve Tables, the Ten Commandments, written constitution, droit du seigneur 953 *legality*.

stabilizer, fin, spoiler, keel; counterweight, ballast; buttress 218 *prop*.

Adj. unchangeable, inflexible 602 *obstinate*; unwavering, rocklike 599 *resolute*; predictable, reliable 473 *certain*; immutable, unalterable, written on tablets of stone, inconvertible; changeless, unchanging, inalterable, irreversible; unshrinkable, shrinkproof; stereotyped, unvarying, invariable, constant 16 *uniform*; steady, undeviating 81 *regular*; durable, as the hills 113 *lasting*, 144 *permanent*; undying, perennial, evergreen 115 *perpetual*; imperishable, indestructible, inextinguishable 660 *invulnerable*.

fixed, steadfast, firm, secure, immovable, irremovable; unassailable, unshakable, rock-like, steady as a rock; steady, stable, balanced, homoeostatic; fast, ingrained, indelible; engraved; ineradicable, rooted, deep-rooted; deep-seated, entrenched, in with the bricks, foursquare, well-founded, built on a rock; standing, pat; tethered, moored, anchored 45 *tied*; at rest, at anchor; run aground, stuck fast, stranded, grounded, high and dry; pinned down, transfixed; immobile, frozen, rooted to the ground *or* spot, like a statue, still as a stone 266 *still*.

Vb. stabilize, root, entrench, found, establish, build on a rock 115 *perpetuate*; erect, set up, set on its feet 218 *support*; float, set afloat; fix, set, stereotype; make valid, validate, confirm, ratify 488 *endorse*; retain, stet; bind, make sure, make fast 45 *tie*; keep steady, hold the road, retain equilibrium, balance 28 *equalize*.

154 Present events

N. event, phenomenon; fact, matter of fact, actual fact 1 *reality*; case, circumstance, situation, state of affairs 7 *state*; occurrence, eventuality, incidence, realization, happening, turn of events; incident, episode, adventure 137 *occasion*; milestone, watershed 8 *juncture*; fortune, accident, casualty, contingency 159 *chance*; misadventure, mishap 731 *misfortune*; emergency, pass 137 *crisis*; coincidence 181 *concurrence*; advent 289 *approach*; encounter, meeting; transaction, proceeding, affairs 676 *action*; result, product, consequence, issue, outcome, upshot, bottom line 157 *effect*; denouement, solution 316 *evolution*; catastrophe 69 *end*.

affairs, matters, doings, transactions 676 *deed*; agenda; involvement, concern, concerns, interests, business interests, irons in the fire, axes to grind 622 *business*; world, life, situation 8 *circumstance*; current affairs, affairs in general, state of affairs; course of events 111 *course of time*; chapter of accidents, ups and downs of life, vicissitudes 730 *prosperity*, 731 *adversity*.

Vb. happen, become, come into existence 360 *be born*; materialize, appear, be realized, come off 727 *succeed*; take place, occur, come about, come to pass, fulfil expectations; befall, betide 159 *chance*; turn up, pop up, crop up, start up, spring up, arise 295 *arrive*; present itself 189 *be present*; supervene 284 *follow*; issue, transpire, emanate 157 *result*; turn out, fall out, work out, pan out; be afoot, take its

course, advance 285 *progress*; continue 146 *go on*; go off, pass off 125 *be past*; fall to one's lot, be one's good fortune *or* misfortune; be the case, be so, prove, prove to be; bring about, occasion 156 *cause*.

meet with, incur, encounter 295 *meet*; realize, happen on, chance upon, stumble upon, find 484 *discover*; experience, pass through, go through; have been through 490 *know*, 818 *feel*; have adventures, endure, undergo 825 *suffer*.

Adv. eventually, ultimately; in due course, in the course *or* natural course *or* ordinary course of things; as times go; as the world goes.

155 Destiny: future events

N. destiny, what's to come, one's stars 596 *fate*; horoscope, forecast 511 *prediction*; prospect, outlook 507 *expectation*; coming events, future plans 124 *futurity*, 617 *intention*; trouble in store, danger 900 *threat*; proximity 200 *nearness*, 289 *approach*; future existence, hereafter 124 *future state*; next world, Hades, afterworld, world to come, life after death 971 *heaven*; predestination 473 *certainty*, 596 *necessity*.

Adj. impending, overhanging, louring, hovering, imminent; preparing, brewing, cooking 669 *preparatory*; destined, predestined, in the stars, in the lap of the gods 596 *fated*; predicted, forthcoming, forecast 511 *predicting*; inescapable, inevitable, going to be, bound to happen 473 *certain*; due, owing 596 *necessary*; in the wind, on the cards 471 *probable*; on the agenda, intended, decided on 608 *predetermined*; in prospect, in view, in the offing, on the horizon, looming on the horizon, in the distance 443 *visible*; in the future, to come, in the womb of time 124 *future*; at hand, close 200 *near*, 289 *approaching*; instant, immediate, about to be, on the point of 116 *instantaneous*; pregnant with, heavy with 511 *presageful*; in store, in reserve, ready, kept ready, on the stocks 669 *prepared*; in embryo, embryonic 68 *beginning*.

Vb. impend 124 *be to come*; hang over, lie over, hover, lour, loom, be on the horizon 900 *threaten*; come on, draw nigh 289 *approach*; front, face, stare one in the face 237 *be in front*; breathe down one's neck; ripen 669 *mature*.

SECTION EIGHT

Causation

156 Cause: constant antecedent

N. causation, causality, cause and effect, aetiology 158 *attribution*; authorship; origination, creation 21 *originality*; invention 484 *discovery*; inspiration 178 *influence*; evocation, provocation 164 *production*; stimulation, fomentation, encouragement, motivation 612 *motive*; planting, cultivation 370 *agriculture*; abetment 706 *cooperation*.

cause, material cause, prime mover, God 965 *the Deity*; creator, maker 164 *producer*; begetter, father 169 *parentage*; author, inventor, originator, founder; agent, leaven; stimulus 174 *stimulant*; contributor, factor, contributory factor, moment, determinant; inspirer, mainspring 612 *motivator*; fomenter, aider, abettor; power behind the throne, undercurrents 178 *influence*; planetary influence, astrological influence, stars 155 *destiny*; fate 596 *necessity*; force 740 *compulsion*.

source, fountain, fount 68 *origin*; spring, fountainhead, wellspring; mine, quarry 632 *store*; birthplace 192 *home*; breeding-place, hotbed; cradle, nursery; genesis, ancestry, lineage, descent 169 *parentage*; parent, ancestor, progenitor; loins 167 *genitals*; rudiment, element, principle, first principle; nucleus, germ, seed, sperm, spore; egg, foetus, embryo, pre-embryo; chrysalis, cocoon 132 *young creature*; bud, stem, stock, rootstock; root, bulb 366 *plant*; radix, radical, etymon, derivation, etymology; foundation, fundamentals, the nitty gritty, bedrock 214 *base*; groundwork, spadework, beginnings 68 *beginning*; nuts and bolts, raw material, ore 631 *materials*.

reason why, reason, cause, the why and wherefore; explanation, key 460 *answer*, 520 *interpretation*; excuse 614 *pretext*; ground, basis, rationale, motive, idea, occasion, raison d'être.

Adj. *fundamental*, primary, elemental, ultimate; foundational, radical, basic 5 *inherent*; crucial, central 638 *important*; original, aboriginal 68 *first*; primitive, primordial 127 *primal*.

Vb. *cause*, originate, bring into being, create, make 164 *produce*; beget, be the author of 167 *generate*; invent 484 *discover*; be the reason 158 *account for*; underlie, be *or* lie at the bottom of, be at the root of; sow the seeds of, be answerable, responsible, have a hand in, be to blame; institute, found, lay the foundations, inaugurate 68 *inaugurate*; set up, erect 310 *elevate*; launch, set afloat, set afoot, set going, trigger off, spark off, touch off 68 *begin*; open, open up, broach 68 *initiate*; seed, sow, plant, water 370 *cultivate*; contrive, effect, effectuate, bring about, bring off, bring to pass 727 *succeed*; procure, provide the means, put up the wherewithal; stage-manage, engineer 623 *plan*; bring on, induce, precipitate 680 *hasten*; bring out, draw out, evoke, elicit 291 *attract*; provoke, arouse, awaken 821 *excite*;

stimulate 174 *invigorate*; kindle, inspire, incite, tempt 612 *induce*; occasion 612 *motivate*; have an effect, be a factor, show its result, make or mar 178 *influence*; be the agent, do the deed 676 *do*; determine, decide, give the decision 480 *judge*; decide the result, turn the scale, come down on one side or the other, give the casting vote 178 *prevail*, 34 *predominate*.

157 Effect: constant sequel

N. *effect*, consequence, corollary 65 *sequence*; result; derivation, derivative, precipitate 41 *remainder*; upshot, outcome, issue, denouement 154 *event*; final result, end result, termination 725 *completion*; visible effect, mark, print, impress 548 *trace*; by-product, side-effect, spin-off; aftermath, legacy, backwash, wake, repercussion 67 *sequel*; resultant action, response 460 *answer*; performance 676 *deed*; reaction, backlash, boomerang effect 182 *counteraction*; offspring 170 *posterity*; handiwork 164 *product*; karma 596 *fate*; moral effect 178 *influence*.

growth, development, expansion, — creep 36 *increase*; carcinoma 651 *cancer*; bud, blossom, florescence, fruit; ear, spike; produce, crop, harvest; profit 771 *gain*; growth industry.

Adj. *caused*, owing to, due to, attributed to; consequential, resulting from, consequent upon 65 *sequential*; contingent, depending, dependent on 745 *subject*; resultant, derivative, descended; secondary 20 *imitative*; arising, emergent, emanating, developed from, evolved from; born of, out of, by; ending in, issuing in; effected, done.

Vb. *result*, be the result, come of; follow on, ensue, wait on, accrue 284 *follow*; owing to, be due to; owe everything to, borrow from 785 *borrow*; have a common origin 9 *be related*; take its source, have its roots in, derive from, descend from, originate from *or* in, come from *or* out of; issue, proceed, emanate 298 *emerge*; grow from, spring from, arise from, flow from; develop, unfold 316 *evolve*; bud, sprout, germinate 36 *grow*; show a trace, show an effect, receive an impression, bear the stamp 522 *be plain*; bear the consequences 154 *meet with*, 963 *be punished*; turn out, fall out, pan out, work out, eventuate 154 *happen*; result in 164 *produce*.

depend, hang upon, hinge on, pivot on, turn on, centre on 12 *correlate*, 745 *be subject*.

158 Attribution: assignment of cause

N. *attribution*, reference to, imputation, ascription; theory, hypothesis, assumption, conjecture 512 *supposition*; explanation 520 *interpretation*; aetiology 459 *enquiry*; rationale

156 *reason why*; affiliation 169 *parentage*; derivation, etymology 156 *source*; attribute 89 *concomitant*; credit, credit title, acknowledgment 915 *what is due.*

Vb. *attribute*, ascribe, impute; say of 532 *affirm*; accord, grant, allow 781 *give*; put down to, set down to; assign to, refer to, point to, trace to, connect with, derive from 9 *relate*; lay at the door of, affiliate, father upon; charge with, saddle with *or* on; found upon; make responsible, make a scapegoat, blame for 928 *accuse*; bring home to 478 *demonstrate*; credit, credit with, acknowledge.

account for, explain 520 *interpret*; theorize, hypothesize, assume 512 *suppose.*

Adv. *hence*, thence, therefore; whence, wherefore; for, since, on account of, because, owing to, thanks to, on that account, from this cause, from that cause, ergo, thus, so; that's why.

159 Chance: no assignable cause

N. *chance*, blind chance, fortuity, randomness; fortuitousness; unpredictability 474 *uncertainty*; inexplicability 517 *unintelligibility*; lot, fortune, wheel of fortune, lady luck 596 *fate*; potluck, luck of the draw, lottery, postcode lottery, postcode prescribing; good fortune, luck, good luck, run of good luck, purple patch 730 *prosperity*; bad luck, run of bad luck 731 *misfortune*; hazard, accident, misadventure, casualty, coincidence, chapter of accidents 154 *event*; lucky shot, lucky strike, fluke 618 *non-design*; chance in a million 140 *infrequency*; chance meeting, chance encounter 508 *lack of expectation*; serendipity 484 *discovery.*

equal chance, even chance, fifty-fifty 28 *equality*; toss-up, spin of the coin, heads or tails, throw of the dice, turn of the card, spin of the wheel; lucky dip, random sample; lottery, National Lottery, scratch card, raffle, tombola, sweepstake, premium bond 618 *gambling.*

fair chance, sporting chance, fighting chance 469 *possibility*; half a chance, small chance 472 *improbability*; good chance, main chance 137 *opportunity*; long odds, odds on, odds 34 *advantage*; safe bet, sure thing, the probabilities 471 *probability.*

Adj. *casual*, fortuitous, serendipitous, chance, haphazard, hit-or-miss, random, stray, out of a hat; adventitious, accidental, unexpected, incidental; coincidental 10 *unrelated*; chancy, fluky, dicey, incalculable.

Vb. *chance*, turn up, crop up, fall to one's lot, so happen 154 *happen*; chance upon, come upon, light upon, hit upon, stumble upon, bump into, run across 154 *meet with,*

484 *discover*; go out on a limb, risk it, try one's luck, chance it, leave it to chance 618 *gamble.*

Adv. *by chance*, by accident; accidentally, fortuitously, serendipitously; perchance, perhaps; according to chance, as it may be.

160 Power

N. *power*, potency, mightiness 32 *largeness*; prevalence, predominance 34 *superiority*; omnipotence, almightiness 733 *authority*; control, sway 733 *governing*; moral power, ascendancy 178 *influence*; spiritual power, charisma, mana; witchcraft 983 *sorcery*; staying power, endurance 153 *stability*; driving force 612 *motive*; physical power, might, muscle, brute force *or* strength 162 *strength*; might and main, effort, endeavour, blood, sweat and tears 682 *exertion*, labour; force 740 *compulsion*; stress, strain, shear; weight 322 *gravity*; weight of numbers; manpower 686 *personnel*; position of power, position of strength, vantage ground 34 *advantage.*

ability, ableness, capability, potentiality 469 *possibility*; competence, efficiency, efficacy, effectuality 694 *skill*; capacity, faculty, virtue, property 5 *inherent state*; qualification 24 *suitability*; attribute 89 *concomitant*; native wit, gift, flair, what it takes 694 *aptitude*; grasp 183 *range*; enablement.

energy, liveliness, vigour, drive, pep, zip, dynamism 174 *vigorousness*; work, kinetic energy, electrical energy, atomic energy, nuclear energy; mechanical energy, engine power, horsepower, HP, metric horsepower, Pferdestärke, PS; life-force, bio-energy, qi *or* ch'i; inertia; resistance 333 *friction*; force, field of force; force of gravity 322 *gravity*; pressure, head, charge, steam; steam up; tension, high tension; electromotive force; pulling power 288 *traction*; thrust, jet propulsion 287 *propulsion*; momentum, impetus 279 *impulse*; magnetic field 291 *attraction*, 292 *repulsion*; suction 299 *reception*; expulsion 300 *ejection*; unit of work, erg, joule; calorie.

sources of energy, coal, gas, oil, etc. 385 *fuel*; nuclear power; alternative energy; hydroelectricity, power house, power station, hydroelectrics; wave power; wind power, windmill, wind farm; solar energy, solar panel 383 *heater*; generator 630 *machine*; energy bar, energy snack, energy drink, sports nutrition, sports drink.

electricity, static energy; lightning; electrodynamics, electrostatics, electromagnetism; induction, inductance, capacitance; resistance, conduction; oscillation, pulsation, frequency; electric charge, pulse, shock; electric current, direct current, alternating current; circuit, short circuit, closed circuit; electrode, anode, cathode; positive, negative; voltage, volt, watt, kilowatt, megawatt; ohm; amperage, ampere, amp; conductor, semiconductor, non-conductor, insulator; lightning conductor, earth 662 *safeguard*; electrification, live wire 661 *danger*.

electronics, electronic engineering, optics; microelectronics; lasers 417 *radiation*; integrated circuit, microprocessor; computer electronics 86 *computing*; automation 630 *machine*; television, radio 531 *telecommunication*; electrical engineering, electricity supply; power line, lead, flex 47 *cable*; distributor; pylon, grid, national grid; generator, magneto, dynamo; oscillator, alternator; transformer, commutator, power pack; battery, accumulator; cell, photo cell, photoelectric cell; valve, tube, transistor.

nuclear physics, nucleonics; fission, fusion, thermonuclear reaction; cyclotron, synchrotron; atomic pile, nuclear reactor, fast breeder reactor; fuel rods, coolant; radioactivity, fall-out 417 *radiation*; radioactive waste 659 *poison*; nuclear warhead, nuclear missile, atomic bomb 723 *bomb*; nuclear winter.

Adj. *powerful*, potent 162 *strong*; mighty 32 *great*; prevalent, prevailing, predominant 178 *influential*; almighty, omnipotent, irresistible 34 *supreme*; empowered 733 *authoritative*; competent, capable, able, adequate, equal to, up to 635 *sufficient*; with resources 800 *rich*; more than a match for, efficacious, effectual, effective 727 *successful*; operative, workable, having teeth; in force, valid 153 *established*; cogent, compulsive 740 *compelling*.

dynamic, energetic, peppy 174 *vigorous*; supercharged, souped-up; magnetic; propelling; locomotive, kinetic 265 *moving*; powered, engined; mechanized, automated 630 *mechanical*; electric, electrical, electromagnetic, electronic; computerized, atomic, nuclear, thermonuclear; hydroelectric, wave-powered, solar-powered, wind-driven, water-driven, steam-operated.

Vb. *be able*, be powerful, etc. (see adj.); be forceful, be vigorous, kick ass; can, have it in one's power, have it in one; be capable of, have the talent for, have the virtue, have the property; manage 676 *do*; measure up to 635 *suffice*; have power, exercise power, control 733 *dominate*; force 740 *compel*.

161 Impotence

N. *lack of power*, impotence; invalidity 163 *weakness*; inability, incapacity; incapability, incompetence, inefficiency 695 *lack of skill*, 728 *failure*; ineptitude, unfitness 25 *inaptitude*;

decrepitude 131 *age*; frailness 114 *transience*; invalidation, disqualification 752 *annulment*; sterility, barrenness, impotence 172 *unproductiveness, contraception*; disarmament, demilitarization, decommissioning 719 *pacification*; demobilization 75 *dispersion*.

helplessness, defencelessness 661 *vulnerability*; harmlessness 935 *innocence*; powerlessness 745 *subjection*, 747 *restraint*; toothlessness, toothless tiger; stamping of feet, gnashing of teeth 891 *anger*; prostration, exhaustion 684 *fatigue*; collapse, breakdown 728 *failure*; unconsciousness, faint, swoon, coma, catatonia; numbness, narcosis 375 *insensitivity*; stroke, cerebrovascular accident, CVA, apoplexy, paralysis, hemiplegia, paraplegia 651 *disease*; atrophy 655 *deterioration*; senility, old age 131 *age*; incontinence; dementia, Alzheimer's disease 503 *mental disorder*; imbecility 499 *unintelligence*; pupillage, minority 130 *tender age*; babyhood, infancy 130 *youth*; invalid 651 *sick person*, 163 *weakling*.

Adj. *powerless*, toothless, impotent, unable; unauthorized; nominal, figurehead 4 *lacking substance*; invalid, null and void; without a leg to stand on 163 *weak*; inoperative, not working, unemployed, disemployed 677 *non-active*; suspended, in abeyance, cancelled, withdrawn; abolished, gone by the board; obsolete; mothballed, laid up, out of circulation, kaput; disqualified, deposed; inept 25 *unapt*; unworkable, dud, good for nothing 641 *useless*; inadequate 636 *insufficient*; ineffective, inefficacious, ineffectual, feeble 728 *unsuccessful*; incapable, incompetent, inefficient 695 *unskilful*; unpowered, unengined.

impotent, feeble 163 *weak*; emasculated, castrated, gelded, unsexed, unmanned, spayed, sterilized; sexless; sterile, barren, infertile 172 *unproductive*; worn out, exhausted, used up, effete; senile, gaga 131 *ageing*; paralytic, arthritic, stiff 326 *rigid*; unconscious, comatose, drugged, hypnotized, catatonic 375 *insensitive*; incapacitated, disabled, paralysed 163 *crippled*; incontinent; all in, dead-beat, clapped out 684 *fatigued*; prostrated 216 *flat on one's back*; shell-shocked 854 *nervous*; helpless, rudderless; laid on one's back; thwarted, gnashing one's teeth, stamping one's feet 702 *hindered*.

Vb. *disable*, incapacitate 641 *make useless*; disqualify 916 *disentitle*; deprive of power, invalidate 752 *annul*; disarm, demilitarize, decommission 163 *weaken*; neutralize 182 *counteract*; undermine, sap 255 *make concave*; exhaust, use up, consume, guzzle 634 *waste*; wind, prostrate, bowl over, knock out 279 *strike*; paralyse 679 *make inactive*; sprain, rick, wrench, twist, dislocate, break, fracture; cripple, lame, maim, hobble, nobble, hamstring

702 *hinder*, 655 *impair*; stifle, smother, throttle, suffocate, strangle 362 *kill*; muzzle, deaden 399 *silence*; spike the guns, draw the teeth, clip the wings, tie one's hands, cramp one's style; sabotage, put a spoke into one's wheel, throw a spanner in the works; deflate, take the wind out of one's sails; put out of action, put out of commission 674 *stop using*.

unman, unnerve, devitalize 163 *weaken*; emasculate, castrate, neuter, spay, geld, unsex.

162 Strength

N. strength, might, potency, horsepower, HP, metric horsepower, Pferdestärke, PS 160 *power*; energy 174 *vigorousness*; force 735 *brute force*; resilience; load-bearing capacity, tensile strength; steel 326 *hardness*; heart of oak 329 *toughness*; staying power, survivability, endurance, grit 600 *stamina*; life-force, bio-energy, qi or ch'i.

vitality, healthiness, fitness 650 *health*; vim, vigour, liveliness 360 *life*; virility 855 *manliness*; guts, nerve, spunk, pluck, backbone 599 *resolution*; aggressiveness 718 *aggressiveness*; physique, muscularity, muscle, biceps, sinews, thews and sinews; beefiness, burliness, brawn 195 *size*; grip, iron grip, vicelike grip 778 *retention*; Titanic strength, strength of Hercules.

athletics 716 *contest*, 837 *sport*; biathlon, triathlon, pentathlon, decathlon; athleticism, gymnastics, acrobatics, body-building, pumping iron, feats of strength, callisthenics, aerobics 682 *exercise*; stadium, gymnasium, astrodome 724 *arena*.

athlete, biathlete, triathlete, pentathlete, decathlete; gymnast, tumbler, acrobat, contortionist, trapeze artist, tightrope walker or ropewalker or wirewalker, aerialist, circus rider, bareback rider; stunt man, escapologist 594 *entertainer*; marathon runner; Blue, all-rounder 716 *contender*; wrestler 716 *wrestling*; heavyweight 722 *boxer*; weight-lifter, body-builder, strong man; champion 644 *exceller*; he-man, muscle man 372 *male*; Mr Universe, Tarzan, Hercules; Samson, Goliath, Atlas, Titan 195 *giant*; tower of strength 707 *auxiliary*.

Adj. strong, lusty, vigorous, youthful 130 *young*; mighty, armed 160 *powerful*; potent, double-strength, industrial-strength; high-powered, high-tension; all-powerful, omnipotent, overpowering, overwhelming 34 *superior*; incontestable, irresistible, more than a match for, victorious; sovereign, supreme 733 *ruling*; valid, in full force; like a giant refreshed; in high feather, in fine fettle, in tip-top condition, at one's peak, in top form, in good nick, fit as a fiddle, sound as a bell 650 *healthy*; heavy 322 *weighty*; forceful; urgent, compul-

sive 740 *compelling*; emphatic 532 *assertive*; hard as iron, steely, adamantine 326 *hard*; case-hardened, toughened 329 *tough*; solid, substantial, stable 153 *fixed*; well-built, stout; strong as a horse or as a lion or as an ox; heady, alcoholic 949 *intoxicating*; undiluted, neat; strengthened, fortified, double-strength; entrenched, unassailable 660 *invulnerable*; unyielding, staunch 599 *resolute*; stubborn, intransigent 602 *obstinate*; persistent; shatterproof, unbreakable, solid 324 *dense*; impregnable 660 *invulnerable*; indomitable, unconquerable, invincible, unbeatable; unquenchable, unallayed; unflagging, tireless, unexhausted 678 *industrious*; unwithered, indestructible; waterproof, showerproof, weatherproof, rustproof, damp-proof, impermeable, gasproof, leakproof, hermetic; fireproof, bulletproof, bombproof.

stalwart, stout, sturdy, hardy, rugged, robust, doughty 174 *vigorous*; of good physique, able-bodied, abled, muscular, brawny; sinewy, wiry 678 *active*; strapping, well-knit, well set-up, broadshouldered, barrel-chested, thickset, stocky, mesomorphic, burly, beefy, husky, hulking, hefty, butch 195 *large*; gigantic, colossal, titanic, Herculean, Atlantean 195 *huge*.

manly, masculine, macho 372 *male*; amazonian, butch; virile, red-blooded, manful 855 *courageous*; in the prime of manhood 134 *grown-up*.

Vb. be strong, be mighty, etc. (see adj.); pack a punch; come in force; overpower, be more than a match for 727 *overcome*; recover, convalesce, revive 656 *be restored*; blow hard, blow great guns 352 *blow*.

strengthen, confirm, give strength to, lend force to 36 *augment*; underline, stress 532 *emphasize*; reinforce, fortify; ruggedize; prop, sustain 218 *support*; brace, steel, screw up one's courage 855 *give courage*; stiffen, stiffen one's resolve, stiffen one's upper lip, toughen, temper, case-harden 326 *harden*; energize, act like a tonic, put body into, put beef into 174 *invigorate*; beef up, tone up, reinvigorate 685 *refresh*; set one on his legs 656 *cure*; set up, build up 310 *elevate*; power, engine.

163 Weakness

N. weakness, lack of strength, feebleness, puniness; vulnerability, helplessness 161 *lack of power*; slightness 323 *lightness*; flimsiness, fragility, frailness 330 *brittleness*; delicacy, tenderness 374 *sensitivity*; unsteadiness, shakiness, giddiness, vertigo, disequilibrium 29 *inequality*; feet of clay, instability 152 *changeableness*; ineffectiveness; moral weakness, frailty, infirmity of purpose 601 *irresolution*; debility, infirmity, decrepitude, senility 131 *old age*; delicate health 651 *ill health*; flaccidity, flabbiness 327 *softness*; fleshiness, corpulence 195 *bulk*; loss of strength, enervation, inactivity 679 *sluggishness*; exhaustion, prostration, collapse 684 *fatigue*; decline 655 *deterioration*; weakening, softening, mitigation 177 *moderation*; relaxation 734 *laxity*; loosening 46 *disunion*; adulteration, watering, watering down, dilution 43 *mixture*; debilitation 655 *impairment*; emasculation, evisceration; invalidation 752 *annulment*; crack, fault 201 *gap*; flaw 845 *blemish*; inadequacy 636 *insufficiency*; weak point, fatal flaw, Achilles' heel 647 *defect*.

weakling, pansy, patsy; lightweight, small fry 639 *nonentity*; softy, sissy, milksop, namby-pamby; old woman, invalid, hypochondriac 651 *sick person*; lame dog, lame duck, basket case, the weakest link 731 *unlucky person*; infant, babe-in-arms, kitten 132 *young creature*; baby, big baby, crybaby, chicken 856 *coward*; mummy's boy, mother's darling, teacher's pet 890 *favourite*; doormat, pushover, jellyfish, drip, weed, wimp, nerd, wet, big girl's blouse.

weak thing, broken reed, thread, rope of sand; sandcastle, house built on sand, house of cards, house of straw, cobweb 4 *thing that lacks substance*; matchstick, eggshell, paper, tissue paper; glass, china 330 *brittleness*; water, dishwater, milk and water.

Adj. weak, powerless 161 *impotent*; unconfirmed 161 *powerless*; unfortified, unstrengthened, vulnerable; harmless 935 *innocent*; namby-pamby, cissy *or* sissy, babyish; effeminate, limp-wristed, womanish 373 *female*; poor, feeble, frail, delicate, slight, puny 33 *small*; lightweight 323 *light*; slightly built, anorexic, skeletal, of poor physique 196 *little*; thin 206 *lean*; feeble-minded, weak *or* soft in the head, dim-witted, imbecile 499 *foolish*; weak-willed, half-hearted 601 *irresolute*; spineless, weak-kneed, lily-livered, chicken-hearted, yielding 721 *submitting*; pale 426 *colourless*; limp, flaccid, flabby, floppy 327 *soft*; drooping, sagging, giving 217 *hanging*; slack, loose, relaxed 734 *lax*; watery, wishy-washy, milk-and-water, insipid, wersh 387 *tasteless*; low, quiet, faint 401 *muted*; decrepit, old 131 *ageing*; past it, weak as a baby, weak as a kitten; wavering, unreliable 604 *capricious*.

weakened, debilitated, enervated, diminished, deflated 37 *decreasing*; depleted, impoverished, drained, dissipated; effete; sapped, undermined, disarmed, disabled, laid low; exhausted, wearied 684 *fatigued*; strained, overstrained 246 *distorted*; the worse for wear, not what it was, on its last legs, tottering; deactivated, neutralized 175 *inert*; diluted, adulterated, watered, watered down 43 *mixed*.

(See also *crippled* below.)

weakly, infirm, delicate, sickly 651 *unhealthy*; groggy, rocky; run down, seedy, under the weather, coming apart at the seams, below par, one degree under, poorly; underweight, anorexic, skinny 206 *lean*; listless; faint; sallow, wan, pallid, lacklustre 426 *colourless*.

crippled, disabled, impaired, incapacitated, handicapped 161 *impotent*; halt, lame, game, gammy, limping, hobbling; hamstrung, hobbled; knock-kneed 246 *deformed*; arthritic, rheumatic, gouty; limbless, legless, armless, handless, eyeless 647 *imperfect*.

flimsy, gossamer, wispy, tenuous 4 *lacking substance*; delicate, dainty 331 *textural*; frail, fragile 330 *brittle*; gimcrack, jerry-built, makeshift, shoddy 641 *useless*; rickety, ramshackle, tumbledown, on its last legs, shaky, tottery, teetering, wobbly, wonky, creaky, tumbledown 655 *dilapidated*.

Vb. be weak, grow weak, grow feeble, weaken; sicken, be in poor health 651 *be ill*; faint, fail, languish, flag 684 *be fatigued*; drop, fall 309 *tumble*; dwindle 37 *decrease*; decline 655 *deteriorate*; droop, wilt, fade; wear thin, crumble; yield, give way, sag 327 *soften*; split 263 *open*; dodder, totter, teeter, sway, stagger, reel 317 *oscillate*; tremble, shake 318 *be agitated*; halt, limp, go lame 278 *move slowly*; have one foot in the grave, not have long to go, be on the way out 127 *be old*.

weaken, debilitate, enervate; loosen 46 *disunite*; soften up 327 *soften*; strain, sprain 161 *disable*; hurt, injure 655 *wound*; cramp 702 *obstruct*; disarm, take the edge off, cushion 257 *blunt*; impoverish, starve; deprive, rob 786 *take away*; reduce, degrade, extenuate, thin, lessen 37 *lessen*; dilute, adulterate 43 *mix*; devitalize, eviscerate; deactivate, neutralize 182 *counteract*; decimate 105 *cause to be few*; muffle 401 *mute*; invalidate 752 *annul*; sap, deplete, undermine.

164 Production

N. production, producing, creation; origination, invention, innovation, original work 21 *originality*, 484 *discovery*; productivity 171 *productiveness*; endeavour 671 *attempt*, 672 *undertaking*; composition, authorship 551 *art*, 553 *painting*, 554 *sculpture*, 586 *writing*; musicianship; performance, output, turnout 676 *action*; execution, accomplishment, achievement; concoction, brewing 669 *preparation*; craftsmanship 243 *formation*; planning, design, blue-sky planning 623 *plan*; organization 62 *arrangement*, 331 *structure*; engineering, construction; building design, geomancy, feng shui, vaastu; establishment, erection 310 *elevation*; making, fabrication, manufacture, industry, sunrise industry 622 *business*; processing, process 147 *conversion*; production line 71 *continuity*, 630 *machine*; technology, computerization, new technology, high-tech, nanotechnology, robotics, third wave, increased output, kaizen, mass production; productivity deal, performance-related pay 706 *cooperation*, 771 *earnings*, 804 *pay*; development, growth 36 *increase*, 171 *abundance*; factory farming 370 *agriculture*; breeding 369 *animal husbandry*; procreation 167 *propagation*.

product, creature, creation, result 157 *effect*; output; printout; end-product, by-product; extract, essence; handiwork, artifact *or* artefact, manufacture, article, thing 319 *object*; goods, wares 795 *merchandise*; goods and services, gross national product, GNP; earthenware 381 *pottery*; stoneware, hardware, ironware; fabric, cloth 222 *textile*; production, work, opus, oeuvre, piece 56 *composition*; chef d'oeuvre, magnum opus, crowning achievement 694 *masterpiece*; fruit, flower, blossom, berry; produce, yield, harvest, crop, vintage 157 *growth*; interest, increase, return 771 *gain*; brainwave, brainchild, conception 451 *idea*; fiction 513 *conception*; offspring, young, egg, spawn, seed 132 *young creature*.

building, edifice, structure, erection, pile, dome, tower, high-rise building, block of flats, skyscraper 209 *high structure*; sick building; pyramid, ancient monument 548 *monument*; church 990 *temple*; mausoleum 364 *tomb*; habitation, mansion, hall 192 *house*; college 539 *school*; fortress 713 *fort*.

producer, creator, maker; Nature; the Creator 965 *the Deity*; originator, inventor, discoverer, mover, prime mover, instigator 612 *motivator*; founding father, founder, founder member, establisher 156 *cause*; begetter 169 *parentage*; creative worker, poet, writer 589 *author*; composer 413 *musician*; painter, sculptor 556 *artist*; deviser, designer, creative, imagineer 623 *planner*; developer, constructor, builder, architect, engineer; manufacturer, industrialist, technocrat 686 *agent*; executive 676 *doer*; labourer 686 *worker*; artificer, craftsman *or* -woman 686 *artisan*; grower, planter, cultivator, agriculturalist, gardener 370 *farmer*; stock farmer, stock breeder, sheep farmer, rancher 369 *breeder*; miner, extractor; play-producer 594 *stage manager*; film producer, film director 445 *cinema*.

Vb. produce, create, originate, make; invent 484 *discover*; think up, conceive 513 *imagine*; write, design 56 *compose*; operate 676 *do*; frame, fashion, shape, mould 243 *form*; knit,

spin 222 *weave*; sew, run up 45 *tie*; forge, chisel, carve, sculpture, cast; coin 797 *mint*; manufacture, fabricate, prefabricate, process, turn out, mill, machine; mass-produce, churn out, multiply 166 *reproduce*; construct, build, raise, rear, erect, set up, run up 310 *elevate*; put together, make up, assemble, compose, cobble together 45 *join*; synthesize, blend 50 *combine*; mine, quarry 304 *extract*; establish, found, constitute, institute 68 *initiate*; organize, get up 62 *arrange*; develop, exploit; industrialize, mechanize, automate, computerize; engineer, contrive 623 *plan*; perform, implement, execute, achieve, accomplish 725 *carry out*; bring about, yield results, effect 156 *cause*; unfold, develop 316 *evolve*; breed, hatch, rear 369 *breed stock*; sow, grow, farm 370 *cultivate*; bear young 167 *reproduce itself*; bring up, educate 534 *train*.

165 Destruction

N. destruction, undoing 148 *reversion*; blotting out 550 *obliteration*; blowing out, annihilation, nullification 2 *extinction*; abolition, suppression 752 *annulment*; suffocation, smothering, stifling, silencing 399 *silence*; subversion 149 *revolution*, 221 *overturning*; overthrow 311 *lowering*; felling, levelling, razing, flattening 216 *horizontality*; dissolution 51 *decomposition*; breaking up, tearing down, knocking down, demolition, demolishment 46 *disunion*, 655 *dilapidation*; disruption 46 *separation*; crushing, grinding, pulverization 332 *powderiness*; incineration 381 *burning*; liquidation, elimination, extermination; extirpation, eradication, rooting out, uprooting 300 *ejection*; wiping out, mopping up 725 *completion*; decimation, mass murder, massacre, genocide 362 *slaughter*; abortion 172 *contraception*; hatchet job; destructiveness, vandalism, iconoclasm 176 *violence*; sabotage 702 *hindrance*; fire-raising, arson 381 *incendiarism*.

ruin, downfall, ruination, perdition, one's undoing; crushing blow 731 *adversity*; catastrophe, disaster, act of God 731 *misfortune*; collapse, débâcle, landslide 149 *revolution*; breakdown, meltdown, break-up, crack-up 728 *failure*; crash, smash, smash-up 279 *collision*; wreck, shipwreck, wreckage, wrack, rack and ruin; sinking, loss; Waterloo 728 *defeat*; knockout blow, KO 279 *knock*; beginning of the end, slippery slope, road to ruin 655 *deterioration*; coup de grâce 725 *completion*; apocalypse, doom, crack of doom, knell, end 69 *finality*, 961 *condemnation*; ruins 127 *oldness*.

Adj. destructive, destroying, internecine, annihilating, etc. (see vb.); root and branch 54 *complete*; consuming, ruinous 634 *wasteful*;

sacrificial, costly 811 *dear;* exhausting, crushing; apocalyptic, cataclysmic, overwhelming 176 *violent;* raging 176 *furious;* merciless 906 *pitiless;* mortal, suicidal, cut-throat, life-threatening 362 *deadly;* subversive, subversionary 149 *revolutionary;* incendiary, mischievous, pernicious 645 *harmful;* poisonous 653 *toxic.*

Vb. destroy, undo, unmake, dismantle, take apart 148 *revert;* destruct, self-destruct; abolish, annihilate, liquidate, nuke, exterminate, axe, invalidate 2 *reduce to nothing;* devour, consume 634 *waste;* swallow up, engulf 299 *absorb;* swamp, overwhelm, drown 341 *drench;* incinerate, burn up, gut 381 *burn;* wreck, ship-wreck, sink (see also *suppress* below); end, exterminate, put an end to 69 *terminate;* do for, do in, put down, put away, do away with, make away with, get rid of 362 *kill;* poison 362 *murder;* decimate 105 *cause to be few;* exterminate, leave no survivor 362 *slaughter,* 906 *be pitiless;* remove, extirpate, eradicate, deracinate, uproot, root up 300 *eject;* wipe out, expunge, efface, erase, delete, rub out, blot out, strike out, cancel 550 *obliterate;* annul, revoke, tear up 752 *annul;* dispel, scatter, dissipate 75 *disperse;* dissolve 337 *liquefy;* evaporate 338 *vaporize;* mutilate, deface 244 *deform;* knock out, flatten out; put the kibosh on, nip in the bud, put the skids under, make short work of, seal the doom of, make mincemeat of, mop up; spifflicate, trounce 726 *defeat;* dish, cook one's goose, sabotage 702 *obstruct;* play hell with, play the deuce with 63 *throw into confusion,* 634 *waste;* ruin, bring to ruin, be the ruin of, be one's undoing:

demolish, unbuild, dismantle, break down, knock down, pull down, tear down 46 *disunite;* level, raze, raze to the ground, lay in the dust 216 *flatten;* throw down, steamroller, bulldoze 311 *fell;* blow down, blow away, carry away; cut down, mow down 362 *slaughter;* knock over, kick over; subvert, overthrow, overturn, topple, cause the downfall of, overset, upset 221 *invert;* explode, blast, blow up, blow sky-high; bombard, bomb, blitz, blow to bits 712 *fire at;* wreck, break up, smash up; smash, shatter, shiver, smash to smithereens 46 *break;* pulp, crush, grind 332 *grind;* crush to pieces, atomize, grind to bits, make mince-meat of; rend, tear up, rend to pieces, tear to bits, tear to shreds, tear to rags, pull to pieces 46 *break up;* shake to pieces 318 *agitate;* beat down, batter, ram 279 *strike;* gut, strip bare 229 *uncover.*

suppress, quench, blow out, put out, snuff out 382 *extinguish;* put the kibosh on, nip in the bud, cut short, cut off, abort 72 *discontinue;* quell, put down, stamp out, trample out, trample under foot, stamp on, sit on, clamp down on 735 *oppress;* squelch, squash 216 *flatten;* quash, revoke 752 *annul;* blanket, stifle, smother, suffocate, strangle 161 *disable;* keep down, repress 745 *subjugate;* cover 525 *conceal;* drown, submerge, sink, scuttle, scupper, torpedo, sink without trace 313 *plunge,* 311 *lower.*

consume, devour, eat up, lick up, gobble up; swallow up, engulf, envelop 299 *absorb;* squander 634 *waste.*

be destroyed, go west, go under, be lost 361 *perish;* sink, go down 313 *plunge;* have had it, be history, be all over with, be all up with 69 *end;* cop it, fall, bite the dust 309 *tumble;* founder, go on the rocks, break up, split, go to pieces, crumple up; fall into ruin, go to rack and ruin, crumble 655 *deteriorate;* go to the wall, succumb; go downhill, go to pot, go to the dogs, go to hell, go to blazes.

166 Reproduction

N. reproduction, procreation 167 *propagation;* remaking, re-fashioning, reshaping, remoulding, reconstruction 164 *production;* redoing 106 *repetition;* reduplication, mass production 171 *productiveness;* multiplication, duplication, printing 587 *print;* renovation, renewal 656 *restoration;* regeneration, resuscitation 656 *revival;* resurrection, resurgence; reappearance 106 *recurrence;* atavism 5 *heredity;* reincarnation 124 *future state;* copy 22 *duplicate;* phoenix.

Vb. reproduce, remake, refashion, remould, reconstruct; rebuild; duplicate, clone 20 *copy,* 106 *repeat;* inherit 18 *resemble,* 148 *revert;* renovate, renew 656 *restore;* regenerate, revivify, resuscitate, reanimate 656 *revive;* reappear, reoccur; resurrect, mass-produce, multiply; breed 104 *be many,* 167 *reproduce itself.*

167 Propagation

N. propagation 166 *reproduction;* fertility, fecundity 171 *productiveness;* proliferation, multiplication 36 *increase;* breeding, hatching, incubation 369 *animal husbandry;* eugenics 358 *biology;* sex, facts of life, the birds and the bees; copulation 45 *sexual intercourse;* procreation 156 *source;* parthenogenesis, virgin birth; spontaneous generation; fertilization, pollination, fecundation, impregnation, insemination, artificial insemination, AID, test-tube baby; fertility treatment, assisted reproduction, reproductive medicine, fertility drug, gamete intra-fallopian transfer, Gift, intra-cytoplasmic sperm injection, in-vitro fertilization, IVF, egg donation 171 *fertilizer;* designer baby; family balancing; conception, pregnancy, germination, gestation (see also *obstetrics* below); birth, nativity, happy event 68 *origin*; stillbirth, abortion 728 *failure*; birth rate; development 157 *growth*; fruition, flowering 669 *maturation*; puberty 134 *adultness*; parenthood, maternity; paternity 169 *parentage*; procreator, begettor; inseminator, donor; fertilizer, pollinator; propagator, cultivator 370 *gardener*.

obstetrics, midwifery; parturition, birth, childbirth, natural childbirth, active birth, water birth, childbed, confinement, lying-in; epidural, etc. 375 *anaesthetic*; labour, labour pains, contractions; delivery, breech delivery, forceps delivery, Caesarean *or* Caesarian section, Caesarean birth, Caesarean 304 *extraction*; amniotic fluid, waters, bag of waters; caul, umbilical cord, placenta, afterbirth; amniocentesis, alpha-fetoprotein test 658 *diagnosis*; birthing pool; gynaecologist, obstetrician, midwife, doula 658 *nurse*; stork, gooseberry bush.

genitals, genitalia, reproductive organs, sex organs, private parts, privates, pudenda; penis, male member, phallus, cock (vulg), dick (vulg), dong (vulg), prick (vulg), trouser snake (vulg), wang (vulg), willy; erection, boner (vulg), hard-on (vulg); testicles, scrotum, balls (vulg), goolies (vulg), nads (vulg); crown jewels, lunch box, the last turkey in the shop; prostate, prostate gland; vas deferens; vulva, clitoris, vagina, front bottom, cunt (vulg), fanny (vulg), pussy (vulg), uterus, cervix, ovary, Fallopian tubes; loins, womb 156 *source*; pubic hair; ovum, egg; semen, sperm, spermatozoa, seminal fluid, jism *or* jissom *or* gism (vulg), cum (vulg), spunk (vulg); seed, pollen.

Adj. *pregnant*, fertilized, impregnated, enceinte, gravid; in an interesting *or* delicate condition; heavy with, big with; expecting, expecting a happy event, expectant, carrying, with child, in the family way; in *or* with calf, in *or* with foal, in pup; up the spout, up the pole, in the club, having a bun in the oven, fallen, preggers; biparous, multiparous, oviparous, viviparous; parturient; obstetric; antenatal, perinatal, postnatal.

Vb. *reproduce itself*, yield, give increase 171 *be fruitful*; hatch, breed, spawn, multiply, teem 104 *be many*; germinate, sprout, burgeon 36 *grow*; bloom, flower, fruit, bear fruit, fructify 669 *mature*; seed; conceive, get pregnant, fall; carry, bear; be brought to bed of, bring forth, give birth, have a baby; have children, have young; lay (eggs), drop, farrow, lamb, foal, calve, cub, pup, whelp, kitten, litter; have one's birth 360 *be born*.

generate, evolve 164 *produce*; bring into being, bring into the world, give life to, bring into existence, beget, get, engender, spawn, father, sire; copulate 45 *unite with*; impregnate, inseminate, pollinate; procreate, propagate; breed, hatch, incubate, raise, bring up, rear 369 *breed stock*; raise from seed, take cuttings, bud, graft, layer 370 *cultivate*.

168 Destroyer

N. *destroyer*, demolisher, leveller; Luddite, iconoclast, annihilationist, nihilist, anarchist 149 *revolutionary*; wrecker, vandal, arsonist, pyromaniac 381 *incendiarism*; despoiler, ravager, pillager, raider 712 *attacker*, 789 *robber*; saboteur; defacer, eraser, extinguisher 550 *obliteration*; hatchet man, hitman, killer, assassin 362 *murderer*; executioner, hangman; barbarian, Vandal, Hun; time, hand of time, time's scythe 111 *course of time*; angel of death 361 *death*; destructive agency, locust 947 *glutton*; moth, woodworm, dry rot, wet rot, rust, erosion 51 *decay*; corrosive, acid, mildew, blight, poison 659 *bane*; earthquake, fire, flood; grim-visaged war 718 *war*; instrument of destruction, sword 723 *weapon*; gunpowder, dynamite, blasting powder 723 *explosive*; block-buster 723 *bomb*; nuclear warhead; juggernaut, bulldozer 216 *flattener*; Four Horsemen of the Apocalypse, Exterminating Angel.

169 Parentage

N. *parentage*, paternity, maternity; parenthood, fatherhood, motherhood; loins, womb 156 *source*; kinship 11 *family*; adoption, fostering, guardianship, surrogateship, surrogacy 660 *protection*; parent, first parents, Adam and Eve, Lucy 371 *humankind*; single parent 896 *divorce*, godparent, guardian, appropriate person 660 *protection*.

genealogy, family tree, lineage, kin 11 *kinship*; pedigree, heredity; line, blood, strain; blue blood 868 *nobility*; stock, stem, tribe, house, clan 11 *race*; descent, extraction, birth, ancestry 68 *origin*.

paternity, fatherhood; father, dad, daddy, pop, papa, pater, governor, the old man; head of the family, paterfamilias; procreator, begetter, author of one's existence; grandfather, grandsire, grandad, grandpa, great-grandfather 133 *old man*; ancestor, progenitor, forefather, forbear, patriarch, predecessor 66 *precursor*; father figure; adoptive father, foster-father, natural father, biological father, stepfather, father-in-law; fatherland.

maternity, motherhood; maternal instinct 887 *love*; expectant mother, mother-to-be 167 *propagation*; mother, unmarried mother; mamma, mummy, mum, mater; grandmother, grandma, granny, gran, nan; materfamilias, matron, matriarch; dam; ancestress, progenitrix; grandam 133 *old woman*; mother substitute; adoptive mother, foster-mother, stepmother, natural mother, biological mother, surrogate mother; mother-in-law; Mother Church, mother country, motherland.

Adj. *parental*, paternal, fatherly, fatherlike; maternal, matronly, motherly, stepmotherly; family, lineal, patrilineal, matrilineal; ancestral; hereditary 5 *hereditary*; patriarchal 127 *immemorial*; racial 11 *ethnic*.

170 Posterity

N. *posterity*, progeny, issue, offspring, young, little ones, etc. 132 *child*; breed 11 *race*; brood, seed, litter, farrow, spawn 132 *young creature*; children, grandchildren 11 *family*; succession, heirs, inheritance, heritage 120 *subsequence*; rising generation 130 *youth*.

descendant, son, daughter; chip off the old block, infant 132 *child*; scion, shoot, sprout 132 *young plant*; heir, heiress 776 *beneficiary*; son and heir, etc. 119 *previousness*; love child 954 *illegitimacy*; branch, ramification, colony; graft, offshoot, offset.

171 Productiveness

N. *productiveness*, productivity, mass production 164 *production*; boom, booming economy 730 *prosperity*; overproductivity, superabundance, glut, butter mountain, wine lake 637 *redundancy*; menarche, fecundity, fertility, luxuriance, lushness, exuberance, richness, embarras de richesses 635 *plenty*; baby boom, population explosion; procreation, multiplication 167 *propagation*; fructification 669 *ripening*; fertilization, pollination.

fertilizer, organic fertilizer, manure, farmyard manure, dung, guano, compost, bonemeal; artificial fertilizer, chemical fertilizer; phosphates, nitrates, potash, lime; topdressing, mulch 370 *agriculture*; semen, sperm, seed; fertility drug, gonadotrophin 167 *propagation*.

abundance, wealth, riot, profusion, harvest 32 *great quantity*; mother earth; hotbed, nursery, propagator 156 *source*; cornucopia, horn of plenty, land flowing with milk and honey; milch cow; aftermath 67 *sequel*; rabbit warren, ant heap 104 *multitude*.

Adj. *prolific*, fertile, productive, fecund; teeming, spawning; fruitful, fruitbearing, fructiferous; pregnant, heavy with, parturient; exuberant, rife, lush, leafy, verdant, luxuriant, rich, fat 635 *plentiful*; copious, streaming, pouring; paying 640 *profitable*; creative, scribacious.

Vb. *make fruitful*, make productive, etc. (see adj.); fertilize, irrigate, impregnate, inseminate; procreate, propagate 167 *generate*.

be fruitful, be prolific, etc. (see adj.); flour-ish; burgeon, bloom, blossom; germinate; conceive, bear, give birth, have children 167 *reproduce itself*; teem, proliferate, swarm, multiply, mushroom 104 *be many*; boom 36 *augment*; populate.

172 Unproductiveness

N. *unproductiveness*, unproductivity, dearth, famine 636 *scarcity*; sterility, barrenness, infertility, infecundity 161 *lack of power*; deforestation, erosion; defoliation; scorched earth policy, desertification, desertization; falling birthrate, zero population growth 37 *decrease*; virginity 895 *celibacy*; change of life, the change, menopause; unprofitableness 772 *loss*; unprofitability, fruitlessness 641 *uselessness*; aridity, aridness, fallowness, stagnation; slump, idleness 679 *inactivity*.

contraception, birth control, planned parenthood, family planning; contraceptive, barrier contraceptive; pill, minipill, morning after pill, abortion pill, abortifacient; abortion, partial-birth abortion; coil, loop, diaphragm, Dutch cap, French letter, condom, sheath, pessary; spermicide, C-film; rhythm method, Billing's method; chastity 747 *restraint*; sterilization, vasectomy, hysterectomy.

desert, dryness, aridity, aridness 342 *dryness*; desolation, waste, barren waste, wastelands, lunar landscape; heath, moor, bush, wild, wilderness; desert sands, sand dunes, Sahara; dustbowl 634 *waste*; desert island; salt flat 347 *marsh*; Arctic wastes 380 *ice*.

Adj. *unproductive*, dried up, exhausted, spent; sparse, scarce 636 *insufficient*; waste, desert, desolate; treeless, bleak, gaunt, bare 190 *empty*; poor, stony, shallow, eroded; barren, infertile, sour, sterile; withered, shrivelled, blasted; unprolific, unfruitful, arid, unirrigated 342 *dry*; fallow, stagnating 674 *disused*; unsown, untilled, uncultivated; impotent, sterilized, sterile, on the pill; childless, without issue; celibate; fruitless, unprofitable 641 *profitless*; inoperative, out of action, null and void, of no effect 161 *impotent*; ineffective 728 *unsuccessful*; addled, abortive 670 *unprepared*.

173 Agency

N. *agency*, operation, work, doing 676 *action*; job, position, office 622 *function*; exercise 673 *use*; force, strain, swing 160 *power*; interworking 178 *influence*; procurement 689 *management*; service 628 *instrumentality*; effectiveness, efficiency 156 *causation*; quickening power 174 *stimulation*; support 703 *aid*; co-agency 706 *cooperation*; execution; process.

Adj. *operative*, effectual, efficient, efficacious 727 *successful*; operational, functional, up and running; in force, in play, at work 673 *used*; afoot, up and doing 678 *active*.

Vb. operate, be in action, be operative, be in play, play; act, work, go, run 676 *do*; serve, execute, perform 622 *function*; do its job, do its stuff, do one's thing 727 *be successful*; take effect 156 *cause*; have effect 178 *influence*; take action, take industrial action, strike 678 *be active*; crew, man; activate, make operate, bring into play, bring into action, wind up, turn on, plug in, switch on, flick *or* flip the switch, press the button; actuate, power, drive 265 *move*.

174 Vigour: physical energy

N. vigorousness, lustiness, energy, vigour, life 678 *activity*; dynamism, pressure, force, impetus 160 *energy*; intensity 162 *strength*; dash, élan, pizzazz, impetuosity 680 *haste*; exertion, effort 682 *labour*; fervour, enthusiasm 571 *vigour*; gusto, relish, zest, zestfulness 824 *joy*; liveliness, spirit, vim, zing, zip, éclat; fire, mettle, pluck, smeddum, blood 855 *courage*; fizz, verve, snap, pep, drive, go, get up and go; enterprise, initiative 672 *undertaking*; vehemence 176 *violence*; aggressiveness, oomph, thrust, push, kick, punch 712 *attack*; grip, bite, teeth, backbone, spunk 599 *resolution*; guts, grit 600 *stamina*; virility 162 *vitality*.

stimulation, activation, turning on, galvanizing, whipping up; intensification, boost stepping up 36 *increase*; excitement 821, *excitation*; stir; bustle 678 *activity*; perturbation 318 *agitation*; ferment, fermentation.

stimulant, energizer, activator, booster; yeast, leaven, catalyst; stimulus, fillip, shot, shot in the arm; Viagra (tdmk); crack of the whip, spur, prick, prod, jolt, goad, lash 612 *incentive*; restorative, tonic, pep pill 658 *tonic*; pick-me-up, aperitif, appetizer 390 *savouriness*; seasoning, spice 389 *sauce*; liquor, alcohol 301 *alcoholic drink*; aphrodisiac, philtre; love potion; pep talk, rousing cheer, egging on 821 *stimulator*.

Adj. vigorous, energetic 678 *active*; forceful, robust, kick-ass, vehement 176 *violent*; vivid, vibrant 160 *dynamic*, intense, strenuous 678 *industrious*; enterprising, go-getting, go-ahead 285 *progressive*; aggressive, keen 597 *willing*; potent 160 *powerful*; hearty, virile, full-blooded 162 *strong*; full of beans, peppy, zippy, zingy, zestful, lusty, mettlesome 819 *lively*; blooming, bouncing 650 *healthy*; spry, brisk, nippy, snappy; fizzy, effervescent, heady, racy; tonic, bracing, rousing, invigorating, stimulating 821 *exciting*; thriving, lush 171 *prolific*.

keen, acute, sharp, trenchant 571 *forceful*; mordant, biting, pointed, sarcastic; virulent, corrosive, caustic 388 *pungent*; acrimonious, acrid, acid 393 *sour*.

Vb. be vigorous, thrive, be full of zip *or* zing, enjoy life 650 *be healthy*; burst with energy 162 *be strong*; show energy 678 *be active*; be always on the go, be up and doing 682 *exert oneself*; drive; cut right through 176 *force*; get up steam, put on a spurt, get psyched up, pull out all the stops 277 *accelerate*; be thorough, strike home 725 *carry through*; show one's power, make an impression 178 *influence*, 821 *impress*; throw one's weight about 678 *meddle*.

invigorate, energize, activate 173 *operate*; push one's buttons; galvanize, electrify, intensify, double, redouble; wind up, step up, bump up, hike up, pep up, ginger up, boost, soup up 162 *strengthen*; rouse, kindle, inflame, stimulate, psych up, enliven, quicken, hothouse 821 *excite*; act like a tonic, hearten, animate, egg on 833 *cheer*; go to one's head, intoxicate 949 *inebriate*; freshen, revive 685 *refresh*; give an edge to 256 *sharpen*.

Adv. vigorously, etc. (see adj.); hard; (work, etc.) one's socks off.

175 Inertness

N. inertness, inertia 677 *inaction*; lifelessness, languor, paralysis, torpor, torpidity 375 *insensitivity*; rest, vegetation, stagnation, passivity 266 *state of rest*; dormancy 523 *latency*; apathy, sloth 679 *sluggishness*; immobility, passive resistance 602 *obstinacy*; impassiveness, stolidity 823 *inexcitability*.

Adj. inert, passive, dead 677 *non-active*; lifeless, languid, torpid, numb 375 *insensitive*; heavy, lumpish, sluggish 278 *slow*, 679 *inactive*; hibernating 679 *sleepy*; quiet, vegetating, stagnant 266 *at rest*; fallow 172 *unproductive*; slack; limp, flaccid 163 *weak*; apathetic, neutral 860 *indifferent*, 820 *impassive*; deactivated, suspended, in abeyance; dormant 523 *latent*.

176 Violence

N. violence, vehemence, frenzy, fury, ferment, impetuosity 174 *vigorousness*; destructiveness, vandalism 165 *destruction*; boisterousness, turbulence, storminess 318 *commotion*; uproar, riot, row, roughhouse, rumpus, ruckus, brouhaha, stramash, furore 61 *turmoil*; roughness, rough handling 735 *severity*; fisticuffs; force, hammer blows, strong-arm tactics, terrorism 735 *brute force*; torture 898 *cruel act*; brutality, savagery, domestic violence 898 *inhumanity*; fierceness, ferocity 906 *pitilessness*; rage, air rage, etc. 891 *anger*; hysterics 822 *excitable state*; fit, throes, paroxysm 318 *spasm*; shock, clash 279 *collision*.

outbreak, outburst 318 *agitation*; flood, tidal wave 350 *wave*; cataclysm, convulsion, earthquake, quake, tremor 149 *revolution*; eruption, volcano 383 *furnace*; explosion, blow-up, flareup, burst, blast 165 *destruction*; bursting open 46 *disunion*; detonation 400 *loudness*; sortie 712 *attack*; gush, torrent 350 *stream*.

storm, turmoil, turbulence, war of the elements; weather, dirty weather, rough weather, inclement weather, inclemency; squall, tempest, typhoon, hurricane, tornado, cyclone 352 *gale*; thunder, thunder and lightning; rainstorm, downpour, cloudburst 350 *rain*; hailstorm, snowstorm, blizzard 380 *wintriness*; sandstorm, duststorm, sirocco 352 *gale*; magnetic storm.

violent creature, brute, beast, wild beast, savage beast; dragon, tiger, wolf, she wolf, mad dog; demon, devil, hellhound, Hound of the Baskervilles, hellcat 938 *monster*; savage, barbarian, vandal, iconoclast 168 *destroyer*; he-man, cave man, Neanderthal man 372 *male*; man of blood, assassin, executioner, Herod 362 *murderer*; homicidal maniac, psychopath 504 *madman*; rough, tough, rowdy, thug, mugger, hooligan, football hooligan, lout, lager lout, bovver boy, boot boy, mod, rocker, punk, skinhead, yob 132 *young person*, 904 *ruffian*; bully, bully boy, terror, holy terror 735 *tyrant*; firebrand, incendiary, pyromaniac 738 *agitator*; revolutionary, militant, nihilist, terrorist 149 *revolutionary*; rogue state; termagant, battleaxe, Amazon; spitfire, scold 892 *shrew*.

Adj. *violent*, vehement, forcible 162 *strong*; acute 256 *sharp*; unmitigated; excessive, outrageous, extravagant 32 *exorbitant*; rude; extreme, severe, tyrannical, heavy-handed 735 *oppressive*; barbarous, savage, brutal, bloody 898 *cruel*; hot-blooded 892 *irascible*; aggressive, bellicose 718 *warlike*; bad-ass, kick-ass; rampant, charging; struggling, kicking, thrashing about 61 *disorderly*; rough, wild, furious, raging, blustery, tempestuous, stormy 352 *windy*; drenching, torrential 350 *rainy*; uproarious, obstreperous 400 *loud*; rowdy, turbulent, tumultuous, boisterous; incendiary, nihilistic 149 *revolutionary*; intemperate, immoderate, unbridled, unrestrained; ungovernable, unruly, uncontrollable 738 *disobedient*; irrepressible, inextinguishable 174 *vigorous*; ebullient, hot, red-hot, inflamed 381 *heated*; inflammatory, scorching, flaming 379 *fiery*; eruptive, cataclysmic, overwhelming, volcanic, seismic 165 *destructive*; detonating, explosive, bursting; convulsive, spasmodic; full of violence, disturbed, troublous.

furious, fuming, boiling, towering; infuriated, mad, like a mad bull, mad with rage, maddened 891 *angry*; impetuous, rampant, gnashing; roaring, howling; headstrong 680 *hasty*; desperate 857 *rash*; savage, tameless, wild; blustering, threatening 899 *cursing*; vicious, fierce, ferocious 898 *cruel*; bloodthirsty, ravening, rabid, berserk, out of control 362 *murderous*; tigerish; frantic, frenetic, hysterical 503 *frenzied*.

Vb. *force*, use force, smash 46 *break*; tear, rend 46 *break up*, bruise, crush 332 *grind*; blow up 165 *demolish*; strain, wrench, pull, dislocate, fracture, sprain; twist, warp, deform 246 *distort*; force open, prise open, pry open, lever open, jimmy 263 *open*; blow open, burst open; shock, shake 318 *agitate*; do violence to, mug, beat up, abuse 675 *misuse*; violate, ravish, rape 951 *debauch*; torture 645 *ill-treat*.

Vb. *be violent*, be vehement, etc. (see vb.); run amok, run riot, run wild; tear, rush, rush headlong, dash, hurtle, hurl oneself, stampede, charge 277 *move fast*; break the peace, raise a storm, mob, riot, rampage, go on the rampage 61 *rampage*; resort to violence, take up arms 718 *go to war*, 738 *revolt*; go berserk, let fly, fulminate 891 *be angry*; break in, burst in; erupt, break out, burst out; struggle, strain 715 *resist*; beat up, mug, savage, maul, knock *or* beat six *or* seven *or* ten bells out of 655 *wound*; ride roughshod over, trample on, tyrannize 735 *oppress*.

Adv. *violently*, forcibly, by force *or* main force, by storm; with might and main; tooth and nail, hammer and tongs; at the point of a sword, at knife-point, at the end of a gun; bodily, neck and crop; with a vengeance, like mad; precipitately, headlong, slap bang; like a bull at a gate, like a battering ram.

177 Moderation

N. *moderation*, non-violence; mildness, gentleness 736 *leniency*; harmlessness, innocuousness 935 *innocence*; moderateness, reasonableness 502 *sanity*; golden mean 732 *averageness*; temperateness, restraint, self-control, anger management 942 *temperance*; soberness 874 *modesty*, 948 *sobriety*; impassivity 823 *inexcitability*; neutrality 625 *middle way*; correction, adjustment, modulation; mitigation 831 *relief*; relaxation, remission, letup 734 *laxity*; easing, alleviation; détente 719 *pacification*; tranquillization, sedation; quiet, calm, dead calm 266 *quietness*; control, check 747 *restraint*.

moderator, mollifier, peacemaker 720 *mediator*; palliative 658 *remedy*; alleviative 658 *balm*; soothing syrup, milk, oil on troubled waters; calmative, sedative, tranquillizer, Valium (tdmk), lullaby; nightcap, bromide, barbiturate, sleeping pill, Mogadon (tdmk); anodyne, opiate, opium, laudanum 375 *anaesthetic*; dummy, pacifier 264 *stopper*; wet blanket, damper, killjoy 613 *dissuasion*; cooler, cold water, cold shower 382 *extinguisher*; clamp, brake, rein 747 *restraint*; neutralizer; anaphrodisiac 658 *antidote*; cushion, shock absorber 327 *softness*.

Adj. *moderate*, not extreme, reasonable, unextreme, within reason 913 *just*; nonviolent; innocuous 163 *weak*, 935 *innocent*; measured, restricted, low-key, understated 747 *restrained*; self-controlled, tempered 942 *temperate*, 948 *sober*; cool, calm, composed 823 *inexcitable*; still, quiet, untroubled 266 *tranquil*; peaceable, pacific 717 *peaceful*; leftish, pink, non-extreme, non-reactionary, middle-American, middle-of-the-road 625 *neutral*, 860 *indifferent*.

Vb. *moderate*, mitigate, temper; correct 24 *adjust*; tame, check, curb, control, chasten, govern, limit, keep within limits 747 *restrain*; lessen, diminish, slacken 37 *lessen*; palliate, extenuate, qualify 163 *weaken*; take the edge off 257 *blunt*; break the fall, cushion 218 *support*; play down, soft-pedal, tone down, blue-pencil, euphemize 648 *purify*; sober, sober down, dampen, damp, cool, chill, throw cold water on 382 *refrigerate*, 613 *dissuade*; put a damper on, bank down the fires; blanket, muffle, smother, subdue, quell 382 *extinguish*.

assuage, ease, pour balm, mollify 327 *soften*; alleviate, lighten 831 *relieve*; deactivate, neutralize, act as an antidote, take the sting out 182 *counteract*; allay, dull, deaden 375 *make insensitive*; soothe, calm, tranquillize, comfort, still, quiet, hush, lull, rock, cradle, rock to sleep 266 *bring to rest*; disarm, appease, smooth over, bring round, pour oil on troubled waters 719 *pacify*; assuage one's thirst, quench one's thirst, slake 301 *drink*.

178 Influence

N. *influence*, capability, power, potency 160 *ability*; prevalence, predominance 34 *superiority*; mightiness 32 *largeness*, 638 *importance*; upper hand, whip hand, casting vote, final say; vantage ground, footing, hold, grip; leverage, play 744 *scope*; purchase 218 *pivot*; clout, weight, pressure; pull, drag, magnetism 291 *attraction*; counterattraction 182 *counteraction*, 292 *repulsion*; impact 279 *impulse*; climate 8 *circumstance*; occult influence, mana, magic, spell 983 *sorcery*; stars, astrology, horoscope, heavens, destiny 596 *fate*; hypnotism, mesmerism; curse, ruin 659 *bane*; persuasion, insinuation, inspiration 612 *motive*; personality, je ne sais quoi, charisma 866 *prestige*; ascendancy, domination, tyranny 733 *authority*; sway, control, dominance, control freakery, reign 733 *governing*; sphere of influence, orbit; factor, contributing factor, vital role, leading part 156 *cause*; power dressing; indirect influence, patronage, favour, pull, friend at court, wire-pulling 703 *aid*; strings, lever 630 *tool*; secret influence, wheels within wheels, hidden hand, hand that rocks the cradle, woman behind the great man, power behind the throne, kingmaker, power broker, Grey Eminence, éminence grise 523 *latency*; lobby, pressure group, vested interest 612 *inducement*; manipulator, mover, manoeuvrer 612 *motivator*; big noise, big shot, etc. 638 *bigwig*; superpower, hyperpower; Big Brother, the Establishment, the powers that be 733 *government*.

Adj. *influential*, dominant, predominant, prevalent, prevailing 34 *supreme*; ruling, reigning, commanding, in the driving seat, obeyed; recognized, with authority 733 *authoritative*; rising, ascendant 36 *increasing*; strong, potent, mighty, multinational 32 *great*, 160 *powerful*; leading, guiding; inspiring; active in, busy, meddling 678 *active*; contributing, effective; weighty, key, momentous, decisive, worldshattering, earth-shaking 638 *important*; telling, moving, attractive; fascinating, charismatic; irresistible, hypnotic, mesmeric 740 *compelling*; persuasive, suggestive, insinuating; addictive; instructive 534 *educational*; pervasive 189 *present everywhere*.

Vb. *influence*, have influence, carry weight, cut ice; be well-connected, know the right people, have friends at court, have friends in high places; have a hold on, have in one's power; have the ear of, be obeyed 737 *command*; dominate, tower over, bestride; lead by the nose, have under one's thumb, wind round one's little finger, wear the trousers 34 *be superior*; exert influence, make one's presence felt, assert oneself; put pressure on, lobby, pull strings 612 *motivate*; make one's voice heard 455 *attract notice*; have a voice, have a say in; affect, be a factor in, turn the scale; bear upon, tell upon 821 *impress*; work on 925 *flatter*; inspire, persuade, carry with one 612 *induce*; force 740 *compel*; brainwash, prejudice 481 *bias*; hypnotize, mesmerize 291 *attract*; put off 292 *repel*; militate against, counterbalance 182 *counteract*; actuate, work 173 *operate*; have a rôle, play a part, play a leading part, guide 689 *direct*; lead the dance, set the fashion, establish a trend, be the model for 23 *be an example*.

prevail, outweigh, override, turn the scale

34 *predominate*; overawe, overcome, subdue, subjugate; hold the whip hand, gain the upper hand, hold all the cards, master 727 *overcome*; control, rule, monopolize 733 *dominate*; hold 778 *retain*; take root, take hold, settle 144 *stay*; permeate, catch on, spread, rage, be rife, spread like wildfire.

179 Tendency

N. *tendency*, trend, tenor; tempo, rhythm, set, drift 281 *direction*; course, stream, main current, main stream, spirit of the times, spirit of the age, Zeitgeist; climate 178 *influence*; gravitation, affinity 291 *attraction*; polarity 240 *oppositeness*; aptness 24 *suitability*; gift, talent, instinct for 694 *aptitude*; proneness, proclivity, propensity, predisposition, readiness, inclination, penchant, predilection, liking, leaning, bias, prejudice; weakness 180 *liability*; cast, cast of mind, bent, turn, grain; a strain of 43 *tincture*; vein, humour, mood; tone, quality, nature, characteristic 5 *temperament*; special gift, genius, idiosyncrasy 80 *speciality*.

Vb. *tend*, verge, lean, incline; set towards, gravitate towards 289 *approach*; turn 178 *influence*; lead to 156 *conduce*; be calculated to 471 *be likely*.

180 Liability

N. *liability*, liableness, weakness 179 *tendency*; exposure 661 *vulnerability*; susceptibility 374 *sensitivity*; potentiality 469 *possibility*; likelihood 471 *probability*; obligation, responsibility, accountability, amenability 917 *duty*.

Adj. *liable*, apt to; subject to, given to 745 *subject*; open to, exposed to, in danger of 661 *vulnerable*; dependent on, contingent 157 *caused*; incident to, incidental; possible, within the realms of possibility, on the cards, within the range of 469 *possible*; susceptible 819 *impressible*; answerable, reportable, responsible, accountable 917 *obliged*.

Vb. *be liable*, be subject to, etc. (see adj.); be responsible, answer for, the buck stops here 917 *incur a duty*; incur, lay oneself open to, stand the chance of; run the risk of 661 *be in danger*.

181 Concurrence: combination of causes

N. *concurrence*, combined operation, joint effort, collaboration, synergy, synergism 706 *cooperation*; coincidence 24 *conformance*, 83 *conformity*; concord, harmony 24 *agreement*; compliance 758 *consent*; consensus 488 *assent*;

acquiescence, non-resistance 721 *submission*; concert, pooling of resources, two heads are better than one, two minds with but a single thought, joint planning, collusion, conspiracy 623 *plot*; league, alliance, partnership 706 *association*; conjunction, liaison 45 *union*; think tank.

Vb. *concur*, acquiesce 488 *assent*; collude, connive, conspire 623 *plot*; agree, harmonize 24 *accord*; hang together, stick together, pull together 706 *cooperate*; contribute, help, aid, abet, aid and abet, serve 703 *minister to*; promote, subserve 156 *conduce*; go with, go along with, go hand in hand with, keep pace with, keep abreast of, run parallel to 89 *accompany*; unite, stand together 48 *cohere*.

182 Counteraction

N. *counteraction*, polarity 240 *oppositeness*; antagonism, antipathy, clash, aggro, conflict, mutual conflict 14 *contrariety*, 279 *collision*; reaction, retroaction, repercussion, backfire, backlash, boomerang effect 280 *recoil*; recalcitrance, kicking back 704 *opposition*, 715 *resistance*; inertia, friction, drag, check 702 *hindrance*; interference, counterpressure, repression, suppression 747 *restraint*; intolerance, persecution 735 *severity*; neutralization, deactivation 177 *moderation*; nullification, cancellation 165 *destruction*; crosscurrent, headwind 702 *obstacle*; counterspell, counterirritant, neutralizer, antidote, antibiotic 658 *antidote*; counterbalance, counterweight; counterblast, countermove 688 *tactics*; defensive measures, deterrent 713 *defence*; prevention, preventive, preventative; contraception; inhibitor 757 *prohibition*.

Vb. *counteract*, counter, run counter, cross, traverse, work against, go against, militate against; not conduce to 702 *hinder*; react 280 *recoil*; persecute 881 *be inimical*; fight against, resist, withstand, defend oneself 704 *oppose*; antagonize, conflict with 14 *have nothing in common*; clash 279 *collide*; interfere 678 *meddle*; cancel out, counterpoise, counterbalance; repress 165 *suppress*; undo, cancel 752 *annul*; neutralize, act as an antidote, deactivate, demagnetize; cure 658 *remedy*; recover 656 *retrieve*; obviate, be a way round, prevent, inhibit 757 *prohibit*.

Adv. *although*, in spite of, despite, notwithstanding; against, contrary to 704 *in opposition*.

Space

Space in general

183 Space: indefinite space

N. *space*, expanse, expansion; extension, extent, surface, area; volume, cubic content; continuum, stretch 71 *continuity*; space-time 108 *time*; empty space 190 *emptiness*; abyss 211 *depth*; roominess; infinite space 107 *infinity*; sky, aerospace, air-space, outer space 321 *heavens*; world, length and breadth of the land; vastness, immensity; terrain, open space, open country; green belt, wide open spaces 348 *plain*; upland, moorland, veld, prairie, steppe 348 *grassland*; outback, hinterland 184 *region*; wild, wilderness, waste 172 *desert*.

measure, proportions, dimension 203 *length*, 205 *breadth*, 209 *height*, 211 *depth*; area, surface area; square measure, acreage; acres, rods, poles and perches; square inch, square yard, square metre, hectare, hide; volume, cubic content 195 *size*.

range, reach, carry, compass; stretch, grasp, span; radius, latitude, amplitude; sweep, spread, ramification; play, swing, margin 744 *scope*; sphere, field, arena 184 *region*; prospect 438 *view*; perspective, focal distance 199 *distance*; aim; magnifying power.

room, space, accommodation; capacity, stowage, storage space 632 *storage*; seating capacity, seating; standing room; margin, clearance, windage; elbowroom, legroom, room to swing a cat; headroom, headway; leeway, latitude; opening, way 263 *open space*; Lebensraum.

Adj. *spacious* 32 *extensive*; expansive, roomy, commodious; ample, vast, capacious, broad, deep, wide; voluminous, baggy, loose-fitting 195 *large*; broad-based 79 *general*; far-reaching, far-flung, widespread, wide-ranging, comprehensive, worldwide, global, world 52 *whole*; uncircumscribed, boundless 107 *infinite*; extending, branching.

Vb. *extend*, spread, outspread, spread out, range, cover, encompass; span, straddle, bestride; extend to, reach to 202 *be contiguous*; branch.

Adv. *widely*, extensively, everywhere, with no stone unturned; far and near, far and wide, all over, globally, universally, the whole world over; under the sun, on the face of the earth, in all quarters, from end to end, from pole to pole, from coast to coast, from Land's End to John o' Groats 54 *throughout*; from all the points of the compass, from the furthest *or* four corners of the earth; to the four winds, to the uttermost parts of the earth; here, there and everywhere, right and left, left, right and centre, high and low.

184 Region: definite space

N. *region*, locality, locale, parts 185 *place*; sphere, orb, hemisphere; zone, section, belt; latitude, parallel, meridian; time zone; clime, climate; tract, terrain, country, ground, soil 344 *land*; geographical unit, island, peninsula, continent, landmass; sea 343 *ocean*; Third World, FourthWorld 733 *political organization*; compass, circumference, circle, circuit 233 *outline*; boundaries, bounds, shore, confines, marches 236 *limit*; pale, precincts, close, enclave, salient 235 *enclosure*; corridor 624 *access*; area, field, theatre 724 *arena*; affected area, footprint; economic zone, exclusive area, charmed circle; red-light district, tolerance zone 951 *brothel*; financial district, City, Wall Street.

territory, sphere, zone; catchment area; beat, pitch, ground; plot, lot, holding, claim 235 *enclosure*; grounds, park 777 *estate*; national boundaries, domain, territorial waters, economic zone; continental shelf, airspace; possession, dependency, protectorate, dominion; colony, settlement; motherland, fatherland, homeland 192 *home*; commonwealth, republic, kingdom, realm, state, empire 733 *political organization*; no-man's-land, Tom Tiddler's ground 774 *non-ownership*; no-go area; turf war.

district, purlieus, neighbourhood, haunt 187 *locality*; subregion, quarter, division 53 *subdivision*; state, province, county, shire, bailiwick, riding, lathe, wapentake, hundred, soke, rape, tithing; diocese, bishopric, archbishopric; parish, ward, constituency; borough, community, township, municipality; county, district, metropolitan area; canton, department, arrondissement, commune; hamlet, village, town, market town, county town 192 *abode*; built-up area 192 *housing*; garden city, new town; suburb, suburbia, dormitory suburb, stockbroker belt; green belt 183 *space*; Home Counties, provinces, the back of beyond, the sticks; outback, backwoods, bush, brush, bundu; hinterland, heartland.

city, town, municipality (see also *district* above); metropolis, conurbation; capital; Greater London, the Big City, the Big Smoke; the Big Apple (New York), the Windy City (Chicago); Cinque Ports.

185 Place: limited space

N. *place*, emplacement, site, location, position 186 *situation*; station, substation; quarter, locality 184 *district*; pitch, beat, billet, socket, groove; centre, meeting place, rendezvous 76 *focus*; birthplace, dwelling place, fireside 192 *home*; address, habitat 187 *locality*, 192 *quarters*; premises, building, mansion 192 *house*; spot, plot; point, dot, pinpoint; niche, nook, corner, cranny, hole, pigeonhole, pocket, slot 194 *compartment*; confines, bounds, baseline, crease (cricket) 236 *limit*; confined place, prison, coffin, grave; precinct, paddock, compound, pen 235 *enclosure*; close, quadrangle, quad, square, town square; yard, area, backyard, courtyard, court 263 *open space*; farmyard, field 370 *farm*; every nook and cranny.

186 Situation

N. *situation*, position, setting; scene, locale; time and place, when and where; location, address, whereabouts; point, stage, milestone 27 *degree*; site, seat, emplacement, base 185 *place*; habitat, ecosphere, ecosystem, biotype, range 184 *region*; post, station; standpoint, standing, ground, footing 7 *state*; side, aspect, feng shui, vaastu; attitude, posture, asana; frontage, orientation 239 *laterality*, 240 *oppositeness*; geography, topography, chorography, cosmography, ecology 321 *earth sciences*; chart 551 *map*.

Vb. *be situated*, be located, be sited, be situate, centre on; be found at, have one's address at, be, lie, stand; be stationed, be posted; live, live at 192 *live*; touch.

187 Location

N. *location*, placing, siting, placement, emplacement, collocation, disposition; post-ing, stationing, relocation; locating, pinpointing; radiolocation, radar; centring, localization 200 *nearness*; settlement, resettlement, lodgment, establishment, fixation, installation; deposition; putting in 303 *insertion*.

locality, quarters, purlieus, environs, environment, surroundings, milieu, neighbourhood, parts, neck of the woods 184 *district*; vicinity; address, postal district, street, place of residence, habitat 192 *abode*; seat, site 185 *place*; meeting place, venue, haunt 76 *focus*.

station, seat, site, emplacement, position 186 *situation*; depot, base, military base, barracks, naval base, air base; colony, settlement; anchorage, roadstead, mooring 662 *shelter*; cantonment, lines, police lines; camp, encampment, laager, bivouac, campsite, caravan site, temporary abode; hostel 192 *abode*; halting place, lay-by, car park, parking bay, parking lot, parking place, park-and-ride 145 *stopping place*.

Vb. *place*, collocate, assign a place 62 *arrange*; situate, position, site, locate, relocate; base, centre, localize; narrow down, pinpoint, pin down; find the place, put one's finger on; place right, aim well, hit, hit the nail on the head, hit the mark 281 *aim*; put, lay, set, seat; station, post, park; install, ensconce, set up, establish, fix 153 *stabilize*; fix in, root, plant, implant, embed, graft, slot in 303 *insert*; bed, bed down, put to bed, tuck in, tuck up, cradle; accommodate, find a place for, find room for, put one up, lodge, house, quarter, billet; quarter upon, billet on; impose; moor, tether, picket, anchor 45 *tie*; dock, berth 266 *bring to rest*; deposit, lay down, put down, set down; stand, put up, erect 310 *elevate*; place with, transfer, bestow, invest 780 *assign*; array, deploy.

place oneself, stand, take one's place, take one's stand, anchor, drop anchor 266 *come to rest*; settle, strike root, take root, gain a footing, get a foothold, entrench oneself, dig in 144 *stay*; perch, alight, sit on, sit, squat, park; pitch on, pitch one's tent, encamp, camp, bivouac; stop at, lodge, put up; burrow; ensconce oneself, locate oneself, establish oneself, find a home, move in, put down roots; settle in, get one's feet under the table; settle, colonize, populate, people 192 *live*.

188 Displacement

N. *displacement*, dislocation, derailment 63 *disarrangement*; misplacement, wrong place, ectopia 84 *abnormality*; shift, move 265 *motion*; red shift, Doppler effect; parallax; aberration, perturbation (astronomy) 282 *deviation*; translocation, transposition, transhipment, transfer 272 *transference*; mutual transfer 151 *interchange*; relief, replacement 150 *substitution*; uprooting, removal, taking away 304 *extraction*; unloading, unpacking; expulsion 300 *ejection*; weeding, eradication 300 *clearing*; exile, banishment 883 *seclusion*; docker, stevedore, removal man.

displaced person, homeless person, the homeless, bag lady, bag people, rough sleeper, skell; refugee, asylum-seeker, economic migrant 268 *wanderer*; fish out of water, square peg in a round hole 25 *misfit*.

Vb. *displace*, disturb, disarrange, disorientate, derail, dislocate; dislodge, disestablish, unseat, unfix, unstick 46 *disunite*; dispel, scatter, send flying 75 *disperse*; shift, remove 265 *move*; cart away, transport 272 *transfer*; change round; transpose 151 *interchange*; dispatch, post 272 *send*; relegate, banish, exile, kick upstairs 300 *dismiss*; set aside, supersede 150 *substitute*, 752 *depose*; turn out, evict, unhouse 300 *eject*; wipe out, eradicate, uproot 165 *destroy*; discharge, unload, off-load, unship, tranship; clear away, rake, sweep, sweep up 648 *clean*; take away, take off, cart off; lift, raise, uplift 310 *elevate*; draw, draw out, pull out 304 *extract*.

misplace, mislay, lose; lose touch with, lose track of.

189 Presence

N. *presence*, being there, existence; whereabouts 186 *situation*; being somewhere, ubiety; being everywhere, ubiquity, ubiquitousness, omnipresence; permeation, pervasion, diffusion; availability, bird in the hand; attendance, presenteeism; residence, occupancy, occupation, sit-in 773 *possession*; visit, descent, stay; nowness, present moment 121 *present time*; man on the spot; spectator, attendee, bystander 441 *onlookers*.

Adj. *present everywhere*, ubiquitous, omnipresent, permeating, pervading, pervasive 79 *universal*.

Vb. *be present*, exist, be; take up space, occupy; colonize, inhabit 192 *live*; hold 773 *possess*; stand, lie 186 *be situated*; look on, stand by, observe, witness 441 *watch*; frequent, haunt; occur 154 *happen*; stay, sojourn, summer, winter, revisit 882 *visit*; attend, assist at, grace the occasion, honour with one's presence; take part; show up, turn up, present oneself, announce oneself 295 *arrive*; be in evidence, look in on, put in an appearance, show one's face, show support, fly or show the flag; face, confront 711 *defy*.

pervade, permeate, fill 54 *make complete*; be diffused through, be disseminated, imbue, impregnate, soak, saturate, run through; over-

run, swarm over, spread, filter through, meet one at every turn 297 *infiltrate*; make one's presence felt 178 *influence*.

190 Absence

N. *absence*, non-presence, disappearing trick 446 *disappearance*; lack 636 *scarcity*; deprivation 772 *loss*; being nowhere; non-existence 2 *non-existence*; being elsewhere, alibi; non-residence, living out; leave, leave of absence, sick leave, compassionate leave, maternity leave, paternity leave, parental leave, vacation, holiday, sabbatical, furlough 681 *leisure*; non-attendance, non-appearance, truancy, skiving, bunking off, absenteeism 620 *avoidance*; absentee, truant 620 *avoider*; absentee landlord; backwoodsman, non-voter.

emptiness, bareness, empty space, void, vacuity, inanity, vacancy; blank 201 *gap*; nothing inside, hollowness, shell; vacuum, air pocket; empties, dead men (empty bottles); blank cartridge, blank paper, clean sheet, tabula rasa; virgin territory, no-man's-land; waste, desolation, wilderness 172 *desert*; vacant lot, bomb site 183 *room*.

nobody, no one, nobody present, nobody on earth; not a soul, not a single person, not a living thing; empty seats.

Adj. *absent*, not present, not found, unrepresented; away, not resident; gone from home, on tour, on location; out, not at home; gone, flown, disappeared; lacking, wanting, missing, wanted; absent without leave, AWOL; truant, absentee; unavailable, unobtainable, off the menu, off 636 *unprovided*; lost, mislaid, missing, nowhere to be found; inexistent 2 *nonexistent*; exempt from, spared, exempted; on leave, on holiday, on vacation, on sabbatical, on furlough; omitted, left out.

empty, vacant, vacuous, inane, void, devoid, bare; blank, clean; characterless, featureless; hollow; vacant, unoccupied, unlived-in, uninhabited, untenanted, tenantless; unstaffed, crewless; depopulated; desert, deserted; unpeopled, unsettled, uncolonized; godforsaken, lonely; bleak, desolate 172 *unproductive*; uninhabitable.

Vb. *be absent*, have no place in, take no part in; absent oneself, not show up, stay away, keep away, keep out of the way, cut, skip, skive, play truant or hookey, bunk off, take French leave 620 *avoid*; be missed, leave a gap, be conspicuous by one's absence.

go away, withdraw, leave 296 *depart*; make oneself scarce, slip out, slip away, be off, naff off, retreat 296 *walk out*, 667 *escape*; vanish 446 *disappear*; vacate.

191 Inhabitant

N. *inhabitant*, dweller, habitant, denizen; sojourner, migrant, expatriate 59 *foreigner*;

mainlander, Continental; islander; boat-dweller, water gipsy; landsman *or* -woman, hill-dweller, dalesman, daleswoman, highlander, lowlander, plains-dweller, fenman, fenwoman, forest-dweller, bush-dweller; frontiersman *or* -woman, borderer; city-dweller, town-dweller, urbanite, suburbanite, commuter; metropolitan, provincial; country-dweller, countryman *or* -woman, ruralist, villager, parishioner; peasant 370 *farmer*; desert-dweller, tent-dweller, bedouin; cave-dweller, troglodyte; slum-dweller 801 *poor person*. (See also *native* below.)

resident, householder, ratepayer, housewife, hausfrau, chatelaine, housekeeper; cottager, crofter; addressee, owner-occupier, occupier, occupant, incumbent, residentiary 776 *possessor*; locum tenens 150 *substitute*; tenant, sitting tenant, protected tenant, renter, lessee, leaseholder; inmate, in-patient; house surgeon, house physician, house officer 658 *doctor*; garrison, crew 686 *personnel*; lodger, boarder, au pair, paying guest, p.g.; guest, visitor, commensal; cuckoo, squatter 59 *outsider*; parasite 659 *bane*.

native, aboriginal, abo (derog), aborigines, autochthones, indigenes, first-comers 66 *precursor*; people, tribe, clan 371 *nation*; local, local inhabitant; parishioner, villager; townsperson, townee, city person, urbanite, city slicker, cockney, suburbanite, weekender, holiday-homer; yokel, rustic 869 *country-dweller*; fellow countryman *or* -woman, fellow citizen; national, patrial, citizen, burgher, burgess, voter; John Bull, Uncle Sam; Briton, Britisher, Brit; Celt, Gael, Scot, Scotsman *or* -woman, North Briton, Caledonian, Welshman *or* -woman. Irishman *or* -woman, Hibernian; Jock, Jimmy, Taffy, Paddy; Englishman *or* -woman, Northerner, Southerner, Midlander, East Anglian, Westcountryman *or* -woman; Londoner, Brummie, Bristolian, Mancunian, Liverpudlian, Scouse, Geordie, Glaswegian, Aberdonian; New Yorker, Parisian, Muscovite 59 *foreigner*; earth-dweller, earthman *or* -woman, earthling, terrestrial, tellurian; space-dweller, extraterrestrial, ET, Martian, Venusian, little green men.

settler, pioneer, Pilgrim Fathers 66 *precursor*; immigrant, colonist, colonial; planter 370 *farmer*; economic migrant, resident alien 59 *foreigner*, 188 *displaced person*.

Adj. *native*, vernacular, popular, national, ethnic; indigenous, autochthonous, aboriginal; earthbound, terrestrial, tellurian; home, home-made; domestic, domiciliary, domesticated; settled, domiciled, naturalized; resident.

occupied, occupied by, inhabited, lived in,

tenanted, populated; garrisoned by, taken over by, manned, staffed.

192 Abode: place of habitation or resort

N. *abode*, habitat, haunt, station 186 *situation*; place of residence 187 *locality*; habitation, street, house, home, second home; address, house number, number; domicile, residence, residency; accommodation address; town, city, postal district 184 *district*; headquarters, base, seat 76 *focus*; temporary abode, hangout, camp, pad, pied-à-terre; weekend cottage, country seat, holiday home, timeshare flat *or* apartment, watering place, hill station 837 *pleasure ground*; cantonment, lines 187 *station*; bivouac, encampment; camp, refugee camp; campsite, caravan park; home from home.

quarters, living quarters, married quarters, barracks, accommodation, lodging, billet, berth, squat; lodgings, rooms, rooms, digs; residential hotel, guest house, boarding house, lodging house, pension; boarding school, hostel, youth hostel, hostel for the homeless, foyer; dormitory, dorm; hall of residence; convent 986 *monastery*; cardboard city.

dwelling, roof over one's head 226 *roof*; prehistoric dwelling, lake dwelling, pile dwelling, crannog; tower, keep, broch; cave, hut, kraal, igloo; wigwam, hogan, tepee, wickiup, tent, yurt, ger, sweat lodge 226 *canopy*; lair, den, hole, form, burrow, warren, earth, sett 662 *shelter*.

nest, nidus; drey; branch 366 *tree*; aerie *or* eyrie, perch, roost; covert, heronry, rookery, swannery, gannetry, hatchery, aviary, apiary, beehive, skep; wasp's nest: bike; antheap, anthill.

home, home-sweet-home, hearth and home, where one hangs one's hat, hearth, fireside, fireplace, chimney corner, inglenook, rooftree, roof, paternal roof, ancestral halls; homestead, household; bosom of one's family, family circle, cradle, birthplace, 'house where I was born' 68 *origin*; native land, la patrie, motherland, fatherland, homeland, one's country, God's own country, the Old Country, Blighty, Albion; native soil, native sod, native ground, native heath, home ground, home town, own backyard.

house, building 164 *building*; abode, home, residence, dwelling, dwelling house; country house, town house; villa, detached house, semidetached house, semi, terraced house; Queen Anne house, Georgian house, Regency house; council house, council flat, high-rise flat, prefab; ranch house, chalet, bungalow, chalet-bungalow; seat, place, mansion, hall, stately home; palace, dome, alcazar; chateau, castle, keep, tower, broch, crannog; manor house, dower house, manor, grange, lodge, priory, abbey; vicarage 986 *parsonage*; farm-house, farmstead, croft, hacienda 370 *farm*; official residence, Buckingham Palace, Holy-rood Palace, Chequers, Mansion House, White House, embassy, consulate.

small house, bijou residence; two-up two-down, back-to-back; chalet, lodge, cottage, thatched cottage, cot, but and ben; cabin, log cabin, hut, Nissen hut, shanty, bothy; hovel, dump, hole, slum dwelling; box, hunting-box *or* -lodge; shed, shack, lean-to, outhouse, out-building; shelter, tent 226 *canopy*; kiosk, booth, stall, shieling; houseboat 275 *boat*; mobile home, Dormobile (tdmk), caravan, trailer 274 *vehicle*. (See also *flat*.)

housing, high-density housing; bricks and mortar 631 *building material*; built-up area, urban sprawl; asphalt jungle, concrete jungle, urban blight; urbanization, conurbation; town, satellite town, new town, commuter town, dormitory town, burgh, suburb, garden city 184 *city*; housing estate, housing scheme, sink estate, residential area 184 *district*; villa-dom, suburbia; crescent, close, terrace, circus, square, avenue, street 624 *road*; block, court, row, mansions, villas, buildings; houses, tene-ments, high-rise flats; inner city, ghetto, slum; shanty town; hamlet, village, community; new housing, new build.

flat, flatlet, granny flat, tenement flat, high-rise flat, council flat, furnished flat, service flat, mews flat; garden flat 194 *cellar*; attic, penthouse 194 *attic*; apartment, suite, rooms; bedsitting-room, bed-sitter, bed-sit 194 *room*; maisonette, duplex; block of flats, apartment block, tower block; mews, tenements.

stable, byre, cowshed; kennel, dog-house; sty, pigpen, fold, sheepfold 235 *enclosure*; dovecote, pigeon loft; stall, cage, coop, hencoop, hutch, battery; stabling, mews, coach-house, garage, carport, hangar; boathouse; marina, dock, dry dock, graving dock, floating dock; basin, wharf, roads, roadstead, port 662 *shelter*; berth, quay, jetty, pier.

inn, hotel, boutique hotel, boarding house, guest-house, hostelry, roadhouse, motel, bed and breakfast (see also *quarters* above); hydro, spa; doss-house, bunk-house, kip, flophouse; youth hostel, auberge, trattoria.

tavern, alehouse, pothouse, boozer; public house, pub, local; free house, tied house; gin palace, saloon; speakeasy, dive, joint, honky-tonk; shebeen; wine cellar, wine bar, tapas bar, bodega; beer cellar, beer hall, beer garden; bar, public bar, spit-and-sawdust bar, lounge bar,

saloon bar, snug; tap-room; theme pub, theme bar; gastropub.

café, restaurant, self-service restaurant, caf-eteria; eating-house, eatery, steakhouse, diner, brasserie, bistro, pizzeria, kebab house, crep-erie, spaghetti house, trattoria, grill room, rotisserie; coffee bar, milk bar, juice bar, soup bar, sushi bar; ice-cream parlour, soda foun-tain; lunch counter, fast-food counter, snack bar, sandwich bar; teahouse, teashop, tearoom; buffet, canteen, Naafi; fish and chip shop, fish and chicken bar, chippie, baked potato shop, pancake house, take-away; coffee stall, pull-in, transport café, motorway services; cybercafé, Internet café; cannabis café.

meeting place, conventicle, meeting house 990 *church*; day centre, community centre, vil-lage hall; assembly rooms, pump room; club, clubhouse, night club, working men's club, holiday camp 837 *place of amusement*; football ground, racecourse, dog track 724 *arena*; thea-tre, concert hall, opera house, stadium, stand 441 *onlookers*; astrodome, sports centre, gym-nasium, drill hall, parade ground; piazza, quadrangle, quad, campus, village green, town square 76 *focus*; shopping centre, shopping mall 796 *market*.

park, park, grounds, pleasure grounds, pleas-ance, gardens, green; walk, mall, avenue, parade, promenade, boulevard; national park, theme park, adventure park, safari park; park-land, chase 837 *pleasure ground*.

pavilion, kiosk, stand, bandstand, rotunda, folly, bower, grotto 194 *arbour*; stoa, colon-nade, arcade, peristyle; tent, marquee 226 *canopy*.

retreat, sanctuary, sanctum sanctorum, ref-uge, asylum, haven, ark 662 *shelter*; priesthole, hidey-hole 527 *hiding-place*; cubbyhole, den, snuggery, snug, sanctum, study 194 *room*; cell, hermitage 883 *seclusion*; cloister 986 *monastery*; almshouse, grace and favour house; work-house, poorhouse; orphanage, home, old peo-ple's home, rest home, hostel, foyer, hospice, halfway house, sheltered housing.

Adj. provincial, parochial, parish-pump, local, domestic, vernacular; up-country, coun-trified, rural, rustic.

architectural, designer, architect-designer 243 *formed*; architectural style: classical, Byz-antine, Romanesque, Norman, Tudor, Renais-sance, Elizabethan, Jacobean, baroque, neo-classical, Palladian, Queen Anne, rococo, Georgian, Victorian, neo-gothic, Bauhaus; Gothic, Decorated, Perpendicular, etc. 990 *churchlike*; old-fashioned 127 *olden, antiquated*.

Vb. live, dwell; dwell in, inhabit, populate, people 189 *be present*; settle, colonize 786 *appropriate*; frequent, haunt 882 *visit*; take up one's abode, take up residence, hang up one's hat, move in; reside, remain, abide, sojourn 186 *be situated*; take rooms, put up at, stay, keep, lodge, lie, sleep at; live in, board out, be in digs; have an address, hang out at; tenant, occupy, squat 773 *possess*; nestle, perch, roost, nest, hive, burrow, stable; camp, encamp, bivouac, squat, doss down, pitch one's tent, make one's quarters 187 *place oneself*; tent, shelter 662 *seek refuge*; berth, dock, anchor 266 *come to rest*.

193 Contents: things contained

N. *contents*, ingredients, items, components, constituents, parts 58 *component*; inventory 87 *list*; furnishings, equipment 633 *provision*; load, payload, cargo, lading, freight, shipment, cartload, shipload, containerful 272 *thing transferred*; enclosure, inside 224 *insides*; stuffing, filling, stopping, wadding 227 *lining*; cupful, fistful, handful, spoonful, etc. 32 *great quantity*, 33 *small quantity*.

Vb. *load*, lade, freight, charge, burden; palletize, containerize; take in, take on board, ship; overload, overburden 322 *weigh*; pack, package, pack in, fit in, tuck in 303 *insert*; pack tight, squeeze in, cram, stuff 54 *fill*.

194 Receptacle

N. *receptacle*, container, holder; frame 218 *prop*; hutch, cage, fish tank 369 *stock farm*; folder, wrapper, envelope, cover, file 235 *enclosure*; net, safety net, fishing net 222 *network*; sheath, chrysalis, cocoon; scrotum; packaging 226 *wrapping*; capsule, ampoule; pod, calyx, boll; mould 243 *form*; socket, mortise 255 *cavity*; groove, slot 262 *furrow*; pigeon-hole, hole, cave, cavity 263 *opening*; bosom, lap 261 *fold*; pincushion; catch-all, trap; well, reservoir, hold, repository 632 *store*; drain, cesspit, sump 649 *sink*; crockery, chinaware, glassware 381 *pottery*.

stomach, maw, tummy, tum, abdomen, belly, corporation, pot belly, paunch 253 *swelling*; intestines, small intestine, duodenum, ileum, jejunum, large intestine, caecum, appendix, vermiform appendix, colon, rectum, back passage, arsehole (vulg); gizzard, gullet, crop, craw, jaws, mouth, oesophagus 263 *aperture*.

compartment, cell, cellule, loculus, follicle, ventricle; tray, cage; cubicle, carrel, booth, stall; sentry box; box 594 *theatre*; pew, choir-stall 990 *church interior*; niche, nook, cranny, recess, bay, oriel; pigeonhole, cubbyhole; drawer, locker; shelving, rack, wine rack 218 *shelf*; storey, floor, deck 207 *layer*.

cabinet, closet, commode, wardrobe, press, chest of drawers, chiffonier, tallboy; cupboard, corner cupboard, built-in cupboard, unit; whatnot, dresser, Welsh dresser, china cabinet; buffet, sideboard 218 *stand*; freezer, fridge-freezer 384 *refrigerator*; cocktail cabinet, dumbwaiter, lazy Susan, tea trolley; secretaire, escritoire, davenport, bureau, desk, writing desk; console; book-case.

basket, creel; hamper, picnic basket; pannier; trug, punnet, skep, rush basket; crib, cradle, bassinet; clothesbasket, laundry basket; workbasket, workbox; wastepaper basket; shopping basket.

box, chest, ark; coffer, locker; case, canteen; safe, till, moneybox 799 *treasury*; coffin, sarcophagus 364 *tomb*; packing case, tea chest; tuckbox; attaché case, briefcase, dispatch box; suitcase, expanding suitcase, overnight case, vanity case; trunk, valise, portmanteau; sea chest, ditty-box; bandbox, hat box; ammunition chest, canister, caisson 723 *ammunition*; boxes, luggage, baggage, impedimenta, paraphernalia, bits and pieces, gear; boot, trunk, luggage van.

small box, pill box, snuff box, cigar box, pencil box, matchbox; cardboard box, carton, packet; plastic box, lunch box, metal box, can, tin, caddy, tea-caddy, canister; juice box; casket, pyx 988 *ritual object*; cruet, salt cellar, pepper mill, coffee mill 332 *grinder*; castor; nest of boxes.

bag, sack, poke; handbag, vanity case, reticule, clutch bag, dorothy bag, shoulder bag, tote bag; bum bag; shopping bag, carrier bag, polythene bag, poly bag, plastic bag, paper bag; cornet, twist, sachet; Gladstone bag, carpet bag, travelling bag, overnight bag, flight bag, sponge bag; sleeping bag; bedding-roll; holdall, grip; haversack, knapsack, rucksack, backpack; kitbag, ditty bag, duffle bag; pouch, sling; pannier, saddlebag, nosebag; school bag, satchel, sports bag.

case, étui, housewife; wallet, pocket book, notecase, billfold; spectacle case, cigar case, cigarette case, compact, powder compact; attaché case, briefcase, portfolio; file, box file; scabbard, sheath; pistol case, holster; arrow case, quiver 632 *store*.

vat, butt, water butt, cask, barrel, tun, tub, keg; drum 252 *cylinder*; wine cask, pipe, hogshead, firkin, kilderkin 465 *weights and measures*; hopper, cistern, tank 632 *store*.

vessel, vase, urn, jar, amphora, ampulla, cruse, crock, pot, water pot; pipkin, pitcher, ewer, jug, toby jug; gourd, calabash 366 *plant*; carafe, decanter, bottle; empties, dead men (empty bottles); leather bottle, chagal *or* chagul, blackjack, wineskin; wine bottle, demijohn, magnum, jeroboam, rehoboam, methuselah, balthazar; flask, hip flask, flagon, vial, phial; honeypot, jamjar; Kilner (tdmk) jar; gallipot, carboy, crucible, retort, pipette, test tube, cupel 461 *testing agent*; room pot, bedpan, toilet bowl 649 *toilet*; pail, bucket, wooden bucket; churn, can, watering can; flowerpot, cachepot, planter, jardinière; bin, litter bin, rubbish bin, dustbin 649 *sink*; scuttle, coal scuttle, hod; skip, kibble; bath, tin bath, tub. (See also *bowl* below.)

pot 383 *heater*; boiler, copper, kettle, cauldron, cooking pot, skillet, pan, saucepan, stewpan, steamer, double-boiler; frying pan, wok, omelette pan, grill pan, girdle; casserole, Dutch oven, tandoor, bain-marie; mess tin, dixie, billycan; tea urn, teapot, samovar, coffeepot, cafetière, percolator; vacuum flask, Thermos (tdmk) flask; warming pan.

cup, teacup, coffee cup, breakfast cup; tea service, tea set; eggcup; chalice, goblet, beaker; drinking cup, loving cup, quaich; horn, drinking horn, tankard, stoup, can, cannikin, pannikin, mug, stein, toby, noggin, rummer, schooner, tassie; tumbler, glass, liqueur glass, wine-glass, brandy glass, brandy balloon, pony, fishbowl; Grail, Holy Grail.

bowl, basin, hand basin, wash basin; finger bowl, sugar bowl; pudding basin, mixing bowl, punch bowl, drinking bowl, jorum; porringer, ramekin; manger, trough; colander, strainer, vegetable dish, tureen, terrine, gravy boat; cereal bowl, fruit bowl, rice bowl, soup bowl (see also *plate* below); rose bowl, vase 844 *ornamentation*; toilet bowl. (See also *vessel* above.)

plate, dessert plate, dinner plate, pasta plate, salad plate, soup plate, side plate; salver, silver salver, tray, platter, ashet, trencher, charger, dish; palette; saucer; pan, scale 322 *scales*; pallet; mortarboard, hod.

ladle, skimmer, dipper, baler, scoop, cupped hands; spoon, tablespoon, dessertspoon, teaspoon, eggspoon, soupspoon, medicine spoon, apostle spoon; spade, trowel, shovel 370 *farm and garden tools*; spatula, slice, fish slice.

room, chamber, apartment 192 *flat*; cockpit, cubicle, cab; cabin, stateroom; audience chamber, throne room; cabinet, closet, study, den, snug, snuggery, sanctum 192 *retreat*; library, studio, atelier, workroom, office 687 *workshop*; playroom, rumpus room, nursery; reception room, drawing room, front room, sitting room, living room, lounge, parlour, salon, boudoir; bedroom, bed deck, dormitory; dressing room; bathroom, en-suite bathroom, en-suite, washroom, toilet, shower room, sauna; dining room, breakfast room, dinette; panic room; messroom, mess, hall, refectory, canteen 192 *café*; gunroom, wardroom; smoking room, billiard room; bar, snug 192 *tavern*; cookhouse, galley, kitchen, kitchenette; scullery, pantry, larder, stillroom; dairy, laundry, utility room, offices, outhouse; coachhouse, garage 192 *stable*; storeroom, box room, lumber room, glory hole 632 *storage*; cloakroom, smallest room, lavatory 649 *toilet*. (See also *compartment* above.)

lobby, vestibule, foyer, anteroom, antechamber, waiting room; corridor, passage, hall, entrance hall; gallery, verandah, stoop, patio, piazza, loggia, balcony, portico, porch 263 *doorway*; extension, lean-to.

cellar, cellarage, vault, crypt, basement, garden flat 214 *base*; coalhole, bunker 632 *storage*; hold, dungeon 748 *prison*.

attic, loft, hayloft; penthouse, garret 213 *summit*.

arbour, alcove, bower, grotto, grot, summerhouse, gazebo, folly, pergola 192 *pavilion*; sun lounge, solarium, conservatory, orangery, greenhouse, glasshouse, hothouse 370 *garden*.

SECTION TWO

Dimensions

195 Size
N. *size*, magnitude, order of magnitude; proportions, dimensions, measurements 183 *measure*; extent, expanse, area 183 *space*; extension 203 *length*, 209 *height*, 211 *depth*; width, amplitude 205 *breadth*; volume; girth, circumference 233 *outline*; bulk, mass, weight 322 *gravity*; capacity, intake, tonnage; measured size, calibre 465 *measurement*; real size, true dimensions 494 *accuracy*; greatest size, maximum 32 *largeness*; full size, life size 54 *fullness*; large size, king size, queen size, magnum; largest portion 52 *chief part*; excessive size, hypertrophy, giantism, gigantism.

bulk, mass, weight, heaviness, avoirdupois 322 *gravity*; lump, dod, block, clod, boulder 324 *solid body*; hunk, chunk 53 *piece*; mound, heap 32 *great quantity*; mountain, pyramid 209 *high structure*; massiveness, bulkiness; turgidity 197 *distension*; obesity, corpulence, fatness, stoutness, chubbiness, plumpness, embonpoint, chunkiness, fleshiness, meatiness, beefiness; flesh and blood, rotund figure, corporation, spare tyre, double chin, thunder thighs 253 *swelling*; muscle man 162 *athlete*; fat person, fatty, tub, dumpling, mound of flesh, tub of lard, hulk; Billy Bunter, Bessie Bunter, Falstaff, Teletubby Generation.

giant, giantess, colossus 209 *tall creature*; mountain of a man *or* woman, young giant;

ogre, monster, King Kong; leviathan, behemoth, Triton among the minnows; whale, hippopotamus, elephant, jumbo; mammoth, dinosaur; giantry, Titan, Titaness, Gargantua, Pantagruel, Brobdingnagian, Gog and Magog, Typhon, Atlas, Cyclops, Polyphemus, Goliath.

Adj. *large*, big 32 *great*; large-size, economy-size, king-size, queen-size, jumbo; fair-sized, considerable, sizable, good-sized; bulky, massive, massy 322 *weighty*; ample, capacious, voluminous, baggy; comprehensive 205 *broad*; vast, extensive 183 *spacious*; monumental, towering, mountainous 209 *tall*; fine, magnificent, spanking, thumping, thundering, whacking; man-size, life-size, large as life; well-grown, well-built, large-limbed, elephantine; macroscopic, large-scale, megalithic.

huge, immense, enormous, vast, mighty, stonking, mega, grandiose, stupendous, monstrous 32 *prodigious*; record size; colossal, mammoth, dinosaurian, gigantic, giant, giantlike, mountainous; Brobdingnagian, titanic, Herculean, gargantuan; Cyclopean, megalithic; outsize, oversize, overlarge, overweight 32 *exorbitant*; limitless 107 *infinite*.

fat, fleshy, stout, obese, overweight; well-covered, well-upholstered, Falstaffian; plump, ample, plumpish, sonsie, chubby, cuddly, fubsy, podgy, pudgy 205 *thick*; squat, squab, square, dumpy, chunky, stocky 205 *broad*; tubby, portly, corpulent, paunchy, pot-bellied 253 *convex*; puffy, bloated, bosomy, busty; round, rotund, roly-poly, full, full-faced, chubby-faced; double-chinned, dimpled, dimply, buxom, jolly, on the plump side; in condition, in good condition, well-fed, well-grown, strapping, hunky, lusty, burly, beefy, brawny 162 *stalwart*; plump as a partridge, fat as butter, fat as a pig.

unwieldy, cumbersome, hulking, lumbering, gangling, lolloping; hulky, lumpy, lumpish, lubberly; too big, elephantine, whale-like, overweight; awkward, muscle-bound 695 *clumsy*.

196 Littleness

N. *littleness*, daintiness, etc. (see adj.); small size 33 *smallness*; lack of height 204 *shortness*; diminutiveness, dwarfishness, stuntedness; scantiness, paucity, exiguity 105 *fewness*; meagreness 206 *thinness*.

minuteness, point; pinpoint, pinhead; crystal; atom, molecule, particle, electron, neutron, proton, quark; nucleus, cell; corpuscle; drop, droplet, dust, grain, grain of sand; seed, mustard seed 33 *small thing*; bubble, button, molehill 639 *trifle*.

miniature 553 *picture*; microphotograph,

microdot, microfilm, microfiche 551 *photography*; pocket edition, duodecimo 589 *edition*; thumbnail sketch, epitome 592 *compendium*; model, microcosm; mini version.

dwarf, midget, minikin, munchkin, pigmy, Lilliputian, halfling, hobbit; little people 970 *elf*; chit, slip, titch; teeny, mite, tot, tiddler 132 *child*; cocksparrow, bantam 33 *small quantity*; pipsqueak, squirt 639 *nonentity*; manikin, doll, puppet, Pinocchio; Tom Thumb, Thumbelina, Hop-o'-my-thumb, homunculus; shrimp, runt, weakling.

Adj. *little* 33 *small*; petite, dainty, dinky, dolly, elfin; diminutive, mini, pigmy, midget, Lilliputian; no bigger than; wee, titchy, tiny, teeny, teeny-weeny, itsy-witsy; toy, baby, pocket, pocket-size, pocket-handkerchief, pint-size, duodecimo, mini-; miniature, model; portable, handy, compact, bijou; snug, cosy; poky, cramped, no room to swing a cat, like the Black Hole of Calcutta 206 *narrow*; puny 163 *weak*; petty 33 *inconsiderable*; one-horse 639 *unimportant*.

dwarfish, dwarf, dwarfed, Lilliputian, pigmy, undersized, stunted, wizened, shrunk; squat, dumpy 204 *short*; knee-high, knee-high to a grasshopper.

Vb. *be little*, take up no room, lie in a nutshell, roll up into a ball, fit on the head of a pin.

197 Expansion

N. *expansion*, enlargement, augmentation, aggrandizement 36 *increase*; amplification, supplementation, reinforcement 38 *addition*; hypertrophy, giantism, gigantism; hyperbole 546 *exaggeration*; stretching, extension, spread, deployment, fanning out 75 *dispersion*; ribbon development, urban sprawl 192 *housing*; increment, accretion 40 *adjunct*; upgrowth, overgrowth, development 157 *growth*, 171 *productiveness*; overstaffing, Parkinson's law 637 *superfluity*.

distension, dilation, dilatation, diastole; inflation, reflation, puffing, puff 352 *blowing*; swelling up, turgescence, turgidity, tumescence, intumescence, tumefaction; puffiness, dropsy, tumour 253 *swelling*.

enlarger, magnifying glass, magnifier, microscope, binoculars, telescope. (See also 442 *spectacles, telescope, microscope*.)

Vb. *expand*, wax, grow larger, increase, snowball 36 *grow*; widen, broaden, flare, splay; spread, extend, sprawl; fan out, deploy 75 *be dispersed*; spread over, spread like wildfire, overrun, straddle 226 *cover*; rise, prove (e.g. dough); gather, swell, distend, dilate, fill out; mushroom, balloon, belly; get fat, gain flesh, put on weight, put on the flab; burst at the seams; grow up, spring up, bud, burgeon, shoot, sprout, open, put forth, burst forth, blossom, flower, blow, bloom, be out 171 *be fruitful*.

enlarge, aggrandize; make larger, expand; rarefy (by expansion); leaven 310 *elevate*; bore, ream; widen, broaden, let out; open, pull out; stretch, extend 203 *lengthen*; intensify, heighten, deepen, draw out; amplify, supplement, reinforce 38 *add*; double, redouble; develop, build up 36 *augment*; distend, inflate, reflate, pump up, blow up, puff, puff up, puff out 352 *blow*; bulk, thicken; stuff, pad 227 *line*; cram, fill to bursting 54 *fill*; feed up, fatten, plump up, bloat 301 *feed*; enlarge, blow up 551 *photograph*; magnify, overenlarge, overdevelop 546 *exaggerate*.

198 Contraction

N. *contraction*, reduction, abatement, lessening, deflation 37 *diminution*; decrease, shrinkage, diminuendo; curtailment, abbreviation, elision 204 *shortening*; consolidation 324 *condensing*; freezing 382 *refrigeration*; contracting, systole; contractions, labour pains 167 *obstetrics*; attenuation, emaciation, consumption, withering, atrophy; decline, retreat, recession, slump 655 *deterioration*; neck, isthmus, bottleneck, hourglass, wasp-waist 206 *narrowness*; epitome 592 *compendium*.

compression, pressure, compressure, compaction, squeeze, squeezing, stenosis, strangulation; constriction, constringency, astriction, astringency; contractility, contractibility, compressibility.

Vb. *become small*, grow less, lessen, dwindle; take a pay cut, downshift; wane, ebb, fall away 37 *decrease*; shrivel, wither, waste away 51 *decompose*; lose weight, lose flesh 323 *be light*; level off, bottom out; contract, shrink, narrow, taper, taper off, draw in; condense 324 *be dense*; evaporate 338 *vaporize*; pucker, purse.

make smaller, lessen, reduce, scale down, downsize 37 *lessen*; contract, shrink, abridge, take in, cut down to life size, dwarf, stunt 204 *shorten*; diet, slim, take off weight 323 *lighten*; taper, narrow, attenuate, thin, emaciate 206 *make thin*; puncture, deflate, rarefy; boil down; evaporate 338 *vaporize*; dehydrate 342 *dry*; cramp, constrict, pinch, nip, squeeze, bind, bandage, corset; draw in, draw tight, strain, tauten 45 *tighten*; draw together, clench 45 *join*, 264 *close*; hug, crush, strangle, strangulate; compress, compact, constipate, condense, nucleate 324 *be dense*; huddle, crowd together; squeeze in, pack tight, pack like sardines, cram, jam 54 *fill*; squash 216 *flatten*; cramp,

restrict 747 *restrain*; limit 232 *encircle*; chip away, whittle away, shave, shear, clip, trim, prune, pollard 46 *cut*; scrape, file, grind 332 *grind*; fold up, crumple 261 *fold*; roll, press, flatten 258 *smooth*.

199 Distance

N. *distance*, astronomical distance, light years 183 *space*; measured distance, footage, mileage, food miles 203 *length*; focal distance; elongation, aphelion, apogee; far distance, horizon, skyline; background 238 *rear*; periphery, circumference 233 *outline*; drift, dispersion 282 *deviation*; reach, grasp, compass, span, stride, giant's stride 183 *range*; far cry, long way, fair way, tidy step, day's march, long long trail, marathon.

Adj. *distant*, distal, peripheral, terminal; far, farther; ulterior; ultimate, farthest, furthest, furthermost; long-distance, long-range; yon, yonder; not local, away, far away; outlying, peripheral; offshore, on the horizon; remote, aloof, farflung, godforsaken; hyperborean, antipodean; out of range, telescopic; lost to sight, lost to view, out of sight 444 *invisible*; off-centre, wide, wide of the mark.

Vb. *be distant*, stretch to, reach to, extend to, spread to, go to, get to, stretch away to, carry to, carry on to 183 *extend*; carry, range; outdistance, outrange, outreach 306 *outdo*; keep one's distance, remain at a distance, stay at arm's length, keep off, hold off, stand off, lie off; keep clear of, stand aloof, stand clear of, keep a safe distance, give a wide berth 620 *avoid*.

Adv. *away*, far, far away, far afield, far off, afar; hence, thence; yonder, in the distance, at a distance, a great way off, a long way away, on the horizon, on the far horizon, beyond the blue horizon, as far as the eye can see; out of the way; to the ends of the earth, to the back of beyond, to the uttermost end; east of the sun and west of the moon; at arm's length.

beyond, further, farther; further on, ahead, in front; clear of, wide of, wide of the mark; below the horizon; up over, down under, over the border, over the hills and far away.

too far, at the back of beyond, out of reach, out of range, out of sight, out of hearing, out of earshot, out of the sphere of, out of bounds.

200 Nearness

N. *nearness*, proximity, propinquity, closeness, near distance, foreground 237 *front*; vicinage, vicinity, neighbourhood 230 *surroundings*; brink, verge 234 *edge*; adjacency

202 *contiguity*; collision course 293 *convergence*; approximation 289 *approach*.

short distance, no distance, shortest distance, bee-line, short cut; step, short step, no distance, walking distance; striking distance, close quarters, close grips; close range, earshot, stone's throw, spitting distance; short span, inch, millimetre, finger's breadth, hair's breadth 201 *gap*; close-up, close finish, photo finish, needle race, near thing 716 *contest*.

Adj. *near*, proximate, proximal; very near, approximate; approximating, close, getting warm, warm 289 *approaching*; about to meet 293 *convergent*; nearby, wayside, roadside 289 *accessible*; not far, hard by, inshore; near at hand, close at hand, at hand, handy, at one's fingertips, present; near the surface 212 *shallow*; home, local, vicinal, in the neighbourhood; close to, next to, next-door to, neighbouring, bordering on, verging on, adjacent, adjoining, jostling, rubbing shoulders; fronting, facing 237 *frontal*; close, intimate, inseparable; bumper-to-bumper; on one's tail, breathing down one's neck; at close quarters, at close grips; close-run, neck-and-neck, nip and tuck, with nothing between, level, level-pegging; near in blood, related 11 *akin*.

Adv. *near*, not far, locally, in the neighbourhood, in the vicinity; nigh, hard by, fast by, close to, close up to, close upon, in the way, at close range, at close quarters; close behind, right behind; within call, within hearing, within earshot, within a stone's throw, only a step, at no great distance, not far from; on one's doorstep, in one's own backyard; at one's door, at one's feet, at one's elbow, at one's side, under one's nose, at one's fingertips, within reach, close at hand; in the presence of, face to face, eyeball to eyeball; in juxtaposition, next door, side by side, cheek by jowl, tête-à-tête, arm in arm, beside, alongside; on the circumference, on the periphery, on *or* in the confines of, on the skirts of, on the outskirts, at the threshold; brinking on, verging on, on the brink of, on the verge of, on the tip of one's tongue.

nearly, practically, almost, all but; more or less, near enough, roughly, around, somewhere around; in the region of, in round figures, in round numbers; about, much about, hereabouts, thereabouts, nearabouts, there or thereabouts, circa; closely, approximately, hard on, close on; well-nigh, as good as, on the way to; within an ace of, just about to; pushing.

201 Interval

N. *interval*, distance between, space; narrow interval, half-space, hairspace 200 *short distance*; interspace, daylight, head, length; clearance, margin, freeboard 183 *room*; interval of time, timelag; pause, break, intermission, breather, time out, gap year, truce 145 *lull*; hiatus 72 *discontinuity*; interruption, incompleteness, jump, leap; musical interval, tone, semitone, third, fourth, fifth 410 *musical note*.

gap, interstice, mesh 222 *network*; lacuna, cavity, hole, opening, aperture 263 *aperture*; pass, defile, ghat, wind-gap 305 *passage*; firebreak 662 *safeguard*; ditch, dike, trench 351 *drain*; water jump, ha-ha, sunk fence 231 *partition*; ravine, gorge, gully, couloir, chimney, crevasse, canyon 255 *valley*; cleft, crevice, chink, crack, rift, cut, gash, tear, rent, slit 46 *splitting*; flaw, fault, breach, break, split, fracture, rupture, fissure, chap 46 *separation*; slot, groove 262 *furrow*; indentation 260 *notch*; seam, join 45 *joint*; leak 298 *outlet*; abyss, chasm 211 *depth*; yawning gulf, void 190 *emptiness*; inlet, creek, gulch 345 *gulf*.

Vb. *space*, interval, space out, place at intervals 46 *set apart*; crack, split, start, gape, dehisce 263 *open*; win by a head, win by a length; clear, show daylight between; lattice, mesh, reticulate.

202 Contiguity

N. *contiguity*, juxtaposition, apposition, proximity, close proximity 200 *nearness*; touching 378 *touch*; no interval 71 *continuity*; contact, tangency; abuttal, abutment; intercommunication, osculation; meeting, encounter, confrontation, interface 293 *convergence*; conjunction, syzygy (astronomy) 45 *union*; close contact, adhesion, cohesion 48 *cohesiveness*; coexistence, coincidence, concomitance 89 *accompaniment*; grazing contact, tangent; border, fringe 234 *edge*; borderland, frontier 236 *limit*; buffer state 231 *betweenness*.

Vb. *be contiguous*, overlap 378 *touch*; make contact, come in contact, brush, rub, skim, scrape, graze, kiss; join, meet 293 *converge*; stick, adhere 48 *cohere*; lie end to end, abut; abut on, adjoin, reach to, extend to 183 *extend*; sit next to, rub shoulders with, crowd, jostle, elbow; be bumper to bumper, be elbow to elbow, border with, march with, skirt 234 *hem*; coexist, coincide 89 *accompany*; osculate, intercommunicate 45 *connect*; get in touch, contact.

203 Length

N. *length*, longitude; extent, extension; reach, long arm; full length, overall length; stretch, span, mileage, footage 199 *distance*; perspective 211 *depth*.

line, bar, rule, tape, measuring tape, strip,

stripe, streak; spoke, radius; single file, line ahead, crocodile, queue 65 *sequence*; straight line, right line 249 *straightness*; bent line, fractal 248 *curvature*.

measurement of length, long measure, linear measure, micrometry 465 *measurement*; unit of length, finger, hand, hand's breadth, palm, span, cubit; arm's length, fathom; head, length; pace, step; inch, foot, yard; rod, pole, perch; chain, furlong; mile, statute mile, geographical mile, nautical mile, knot, league; millimetre, centimetre, metre, kilometre; degree of latitude, degree of longitude; microinch, micron, wavelength; astronomical unit, light year, parsec.

Adj. long, lengthy, extensive, a mile long; long-drawn out; lengthened, elongated, outstretched, extended, strung out; shoulder-length, ankle-length, down to —; wire-drawn, lank 206 *lean*; lanky, leggy, long-legged 209 *tall*; as long as my arm *or* as a wet week; interminable, no end to 838 *tedious*; polysyllabic, sesquipedalian 570 *diffuse*; uncut, full-length 54 *complete*.

longitudinal, oblong, linear; one-dimensional.

Vb. lengthen, stretch, elongate, draw out; wiredraw 206 *make thin*; pull out, stretch out, spreadeagle 197 *expand*; spread oneself out, sprawl 216 *be horizontal*; spread out, string out, deploy 75 *disperse*; extend, pay out, uncoil, unfurl, unroll, unfold 316 *evolve*; let down, drop the hem; produce, continue; prolong, protract; drawl 580 *stammer*.

Adv. lengthwise, longwise, longways; along, longitudinally, radially, in line ahead, in single file, in Indian file; one in front and one behind, in tandem; in a crocodile; in a line, in perspective; at full length, end to end, overall; fore and aft; head to foot, head to tail, stem to stern, top to toe, head to heels, from the crown of the head to the sole of the foot.

204 Shortness

N. shortness, squatness, etc. (see adj.); brevity, briefness; transience 114 *brief span*; inch, centimetre 200 *short distance*; low stature, dwarfishness, short legs, duck's disease 196 *littleness*; lack of inches, no height 210 *lowness*; shrinkage; scantiness, exiguity; scarceness 636 *insufficiency*; slippage; concision 569 *conciseness*; short hair, short back and sides, bob, crew cut; shorts, miniskirt.

shortening, abridgment, abbreviation; précis, summary 592 *compendium*; curtailment, cutback, cut, reduction 37 *diminution*; contraction 198 *compression*.

Adj. short, brief 114 *transient*; not big, not

tall, dwarfish, stunted, knee-high to a grasshopper, etc. 196 *little, dwarfish*; dumpy, squat, stocky, stubby, stumpy, thickset, etc. 195 *fat*, 205 *thick*; not high 210 *low*; pug-nosed, snubnosed; snub, retroussé, blunt; not long, inchlong; skimpy, scanty 636 *insufficient*; foreshortened 246 *distorted*; abbreviated, abridged; shortened, sawn-off; cut, curtailed, docked, beheaded, decapitated, truncated, topless, headless; shaven, shorn, mown; sparing of words, terse 569 *concise*; elliptical (of style); half-finished 55 *unfinished*; epitomized, potted, compact; compacted, compressed.

Vb. shorten, abridge, abbreviate, cut; pot, epitomize, boil down, précis, summarize 592 *abstract*; sum up, recapitulate 569 *be concise*; compress, contract, telescope 198 *make smaller*; reduce, diminish 37 *lessen*; foreshorten 246 *distort*; take up, put a tuck in, raise the hem, turn up, tuck up, kilt; behead, decapitate, guillotine, axe, chop up 46 *break up*; cut short, dock, curtail, truncate; cut back, cut down, slash, lop, prune; shear, shave, trim, crop, clip, bob, shingle 46 *cut*; mow, scythe; nip in the bud, stunt, check the growth of 278 *retard*; scrimp, skimp.

205 Breadth. Thickness

N. breadth, width, latitude; width across, span, fingerspan, wingspan, wingspread; diameter, radius, gauge, broad gauge, bore, calibre; broadness, expanse, superficial extent, amplitude 183 *range*; wideness, fullness, bagginess.

Adj. broad, wide, expansive, unspanned 183 *spacious*; wide-cut, full, flared, ample, baggy; fan-like, umbelliferous; outspread, outstretched, splayed out; bell-bottomed, broad-bottomed, broad-based; callipygian, steatopygous, wide-hipped; broad in the beam, beamy, wide-bodied; wide as a church door; broad-brimmed, wide-angle (lens); wide-mouthed 263 *open*; broad-shouldered, broad-chested 162 *stalwart*; wide-ranging, global 79 *general*.

thick, stout, dumpy, squat, etc. 204 *short*; thickset, tubby, beefy, stubby, etc. 195 *fat*; thick-lipped, full-lipped; thick-necked, bull-necked; thick-skinned, pachydermatous; thick-ribbed, barrel-chested, broad-shouldered 162 *strong*; thick as a rope; pyknic, endomorphic; solidly built 324 *dense*; semiliquid, ropy, lumpy, to be cut with a knife 354 *glutinous*.

Adv. breadthwise, breadthways, broadways, broadwise; widthways, widthwise; broadways on 239 *sideways*.

206 Narrowness. Thinness

N. narrowness, tightness, etc. (see adj.); narrow interval, closeness, tight squeeze, crack, chink, hair's breadth, finger's breadth 200 *short distance*; lack of breadth, length without breadth, line, strip, stripe, streak; vein, capillary 208 *filament*; knife-edge, razor's edge, tightrope, wire; narrow gauge; bottleneck, narrows, strait 345 *gulf*; ridge, col, saddle 209 *high land*; ravine, gully 255 *valley*; pass, defile 305 *passage*; neck, isthmus, land-bridge 624 *bridge*.

thinness, tenuity, fineness 325 *lack of density*; slenderness, gracility; skinniness, emaciation, anorexia (nervosa), consumption; scrag, skin and bone, skeleton; miserable specimen, scarecrow, rake, beanpole, broomstick, shadow, spindle-shanks, barebones; haggardness, lantern jaws, hatchet face, sunken cheeks; thread, paper, tissue 422 *transparency*; shaving, splinter 33 *small thing*; slip, wisp 208 *filament*.

Adj. *narrow*, not wide, single-track; strait, tight, close; compressed, pinched, unexpanded; not thick, fine, thin, wafer-thin 422 *transparent*; attenuated, spun, fine-spun, wiredrawn 203 *long*; thread-like, capillary; tapering 293 *convergent*; slight, slightly-built, wispy, delicate 163 *weak*; gracile, attenuate, slender, slim, slimline, svelte, slinky, sylph-like; willowy, rangy, skinny; long-legged, leggy, lanky, gangling; narrow-waisted, wasp-waisted; isthmian; bottlenecked.

lean, thin, ectomorphic, spare, rangy, wiry; meagre, skinny, bony; cadaverous, fleshless, skin-and-bone, skeletal, raw-boned, haggard, gaunt, drawn, lantern-jawed, sunken-eyed, hatchet-faced; twiggy, spindly, spindle-shanked, spidery; undersized, weedy, scrawny, scrubby, scraggy; consumptive, emaciated, anorexic, wasted, withered, wizened, pinched, peaky 651 *sick*; sere, shrivelled 131 *ageing*; starved, starveling 636 *underfed*; wraith-like, scarecrow-like, worn to a shadow, thin as a rake, thin as a lath, without an ounce of flesh to spare.

Vb. *make thin*, contract, compress, pinch, nip 198 *make smaller*; starve, diet, reduce, lose weight; slim; draw, wiredraw, spin, spin fine 203 *lengthen*; attenuate 325 *rarefy*.

207 Layer

N. *layer*, stratum, substratum, underlay, floor 214 *base*; outcrop 254 *projection*; bed, course, range, row; zone, vein, seam, lode; thickness, ply; storey, tier, floor, mezzanine floor, entresol, landing; stage, planking, platform 218 *frame*; deck, top deck, lower deck, upper deck, orlop deck, quarterdeck, bridge 275 *ship*; film 423 *opacity*; bloom, dross, scum; patina, coating, coat, undercoat, veneer, top layer, top-dressing, topcoat 226 *covering*; scale, scab,

membrane, peel, pellicle, sheathe, bark, integument 226 *skin*; level, water level, water table 216 *horizontality*; atmospheric layer 340 *atmosphere*.

208 Filament

N. *filament*, flagellum, cilium, lash, eyelash, beard, down, bumfluff 259 *hair*; barb, feather, harl 259 *plumage*; flock, lock, shred of wool, thread, lock of hair, strand, wisp, curl; fringe 234 *edging*; fibre, fibril, fibrilla, rootlet, stalk, tendril 366 *plant*; whisker, antenna, antennule 378 *feeler*; gossamer, cobweb, web 222 *network*; capillary, vein, jugular vein, venule, veinlet, artery 351 *water channel*; ramification, branch; wire, element, wick 420 *torch*.

fibre, natural fibre, animal fibre, hair, camel hair, rabbit hair; Angora, goat's hair, mohair, cashmere; llama hair, alpaca, vicuña; wool, Shetland wool, botany wool, merino, fingering; silk, real silk, wild silk, tussore, floss; vegetable fibre, cotton, cotton wool, silk cotton, kapok; linen, flax; manila, hemp; jute, sisal, coir; hards; tow, oakum; bast, raffia; worsted, yarn; spun yarn, continuous filament yarn; thread, twine, twist, strand, cord, string, line, rope 47 *cable*; artificial fibre, man-made fibre, acrylic fibre, microfibre; rayon, nylon 222 *textile*; staple, denier 331 *texture*.

strip, fascia, band, bandage; belt, cord, thong, braid, tape, strap, ribbon, riband; fillet; lath, slat, batten, stave; shaving, wafer; splinter, shiver, shred 53 *piece*; streak, stripe, strake 203 *line*.

209 Height

N. *height*, perpendicular length; altitude, elevation, ceiling, pitch 213 *summit*; loftiness, steepness, dizzy height; tallness, stature; eminence, sublimity; sky, stratosphere 340 *atmosphere*; zenith; altimeter.

high land, height, highlands, heights, steeps, uplands, moor, moorland, downs, rolling country; rising ground, rise, bank, ben, brae, slope, climb 220 *incline*; mount, mountain, Munro; fell, scar, tor, alp, mountain range, chain, sierra, cordillera, massif; ridge, col, saddle, spur, headland, foothill 254 *projection*; crest, peak, pike, hilltop 213 *summit*; steepness, precipice, cliff, white cliffs of Dover; crag, scar, bluff, steep, escarpment; gorge, canyon, ravine 255 *valley*; summit level, mesa; plateau, tableland 216 *horizontality*.

Mountains and Mountain Ranges
Mountains: Annapurna, Ben Nevis, K2, Kangchenjunga, Kilimanjaro, Matterhorn, Mont Blanc, Mount Everest, Mount Rushmore, Scafell, Snowdon.
Volcanoes: Cotopaxi, Mount Fuji, Krakatoa, Mount

Etna, Mount St Helens, Popocatepetl, Stromboli, Vesuvius.
Mountain ranges: Alps, Altai Mountains, Andes, Apennines, Atlas Mountains, Black Hills, Cambrian Mountains, Carpathian Mountains, Caucasus, Cordilleras, Grampians, Himalayas, Hindu Kush, Karakorams, Pennines, Pyrenees, Rocky Mountains *or* Rockies, Urals.

high structure, column, pillar, turret, tower, clock tower, Big Ben; pile, noble pile; skyscraper, high-rise flats, tower block 164 *building*; chimney stack, steeple, spire, flèche, belfry, campanile 990 *church exterior*; minaret; obelisk, Cleopatra's Needle 548 *monument*; dome, cupola 226 *roof*; colossus 554 *sculpture*; mausoleum, pyramid 364 *tomb*; pagoda 990 *temple*; ziggurat, Tower of Babel; Eiffel Tower 548 *monument*; mast, topmast; flagstaff, flagpole, pole, maypole; lamppost, standard; pylon, radio mast, telecommunication mast, telemast, mobile phone mast; masthead 213 *summit*; watchtower, lookout, crow's nest, eyrie 438 *view*; column of smoke, mushroom cloud.

tall creature, giraffe, elephant, mammoth, ostrich, moa; longlegs, beanpole, six-footer, grenadier, colossus 195 *giant*.

Adj. high, high-up, sky-high; eminent, uplifted, exalted, lofty, sublime, supernal; highest 213 *topmost*; perching, hanging (gardens); aerial, airborne, flying; soaring, aspiring; towering, skyscraping, steep, dizzy, giddy; knee-high, thigh-high, breast-high, shoulder-high.

tall, lanky, leggy, rangy 206 *narrow*; longlegged, ostrich-necked, giraffelike, beanpolelike; colossal.

Vb. be high, be tall, etc. (see adj.); tower, rear, soar; surmount, clear, overtop, overlook, dominate, command 34 *be superior*; overhang, overshadow 226 *cover*; beetle, impend 254 *jut*; hover, hang over 217 *hang*; culminate, peak, be at the zenith 725 *climax*; mount, bestride, bestraddle; grow taller, shoot up, add to one's inches; rise 308 *ascend*; stand on tiptoe, stand on another's shoulders 310 *lift oneself*.

make higher, heighten, build up, raise, hold aloft 310 *elevate*.

210 Lowness

N. lowness, debasement 311 *lowering*; prostration; sea level, flatness 216 *horizontality*; flats, levels 347 *marsh*; levelness, steppe 348 *plain*; low elevation, lowlands, pimple 196 *littleness*; gentle slope, nursery slope, slight gradient 220 *incline*; lower level, foothill 35 *inferiority*; bottom, hollow, depression 255 *valley*; sea-floor 343 *ocean*; depths, cellar, nether regions, basement, well, mine 211 *depth*; floor, foot 214 *base*; underside 240 *oppositeness*; nadir, lowest point, the pits; low water, low ebb, low tide 350 *current*.

Adj. low, not high, squat 204 *short*; crouched, crouching, stooping, slouching, bending; recumbent, laid low, prostrate 216 *flat on one's back*; low-lying, flat, at sea level 216 *flat*; low-level, single-storey; lower, under, nether 35 *inferior*; sunken, lowered 255 *concave*; flattened, rounded, blunt; subterranean, subterraneous, underground, below the surface, submarine 523 *latent*, 211 *deep*; underfoot 745 *subjected*.

Adv. under, beneath, underneath, neath; below, at the foot of; underfoot, underground, downstairs, below stairs; at a low ebb; below par.

211 Depth

N. depth, drop, fall; deepness, etc. (see adj.); perspective 203 *length*; vertical range, profundity, lowest point, nadir; deeps, deep water 343 *ocean*; unknown depths, unfathomable depths 663 *pitfall*; depression, bottom 255 *valley*; hollow, pit, shaft, mine, well 255 *cavity*; abyss, abysm, chasm 201 *gap*; vault, crypt, dungeon 194 *cellar*; cave, pothole, catacomb, bowels of the earth 210 *lowness*; pot-holing, diving, deep-sea diving 309 *descent*, 313 *diver*; caisson disease, the bends; underworld, bottomless pit 972 *hell*; diving bell, submarine.

Adj. deep, steep, plunging, profound; abysmal, yawning, cavernous; abyssal, deep-sea; deep-seated, deep-rooted 153 *fixed*; unplumbed, bottomless, fathomless; unsounded, unfathomed, subterranean, underground, underwater, undersea, submarine; buried, deep in, immersed, submerged; drowned; knee-deep, ankle-deep; infernal; benthic; depth-measuring, bathymetric.

Vb. be deep, be profound, etc. (see adj.); deepen, hollow, fathom, sound, take soundings, plumb, heave the lead; drop, lower 311 *let fall*; go deep, plumb the depths, touch bottom, reach rock bottom, be on one's knees, reach one's nadir; sink to the bottom, plunge 313 *go down*.

212 Shallowness

N. shallowness, no depth, superficiality 4 *lacking substance*; film 223 *exteriority*; veneer, thin coat 226 *skin*; superficial wound, scratch, pinprick, graze 639 *trifle*; shoals, shallows; pond, puddle 346 *lake*; light soil, stony ground 344 *soil*.

Adj. shallow, slight, superficial, -light *or*

-lite 4 *lacking substance*; surface, skin-deep; shoaly, light, thin 206 *narrow*.

213 Summit

N. *summit*, sky, heaven, seventh heaven, cloud nine; pole, North Pole, South Pole; top, peak, crest, apex, pinnacle, crown; maximum height, pitch; zenith, meridian, high noon, culmination, apogee; culminating point, crowning point; acme, ne plus ultra, peak of perfection 646 *perfection*; crest of the wave, top of the tree 730 *prosperity*; highwater mark 236 *limit*; climax, turning point 137 *crisis*; dividing line, watershed, Great Divide 231 *partition*; copingstone, keystone; lintel, pediment, entablature, architrave, epistyle; capital, cornice.

apex, vertex, crown, top, cap, brow, head; tip, cusp, spike, point, nib, end 69 *extremity*; spire, finial 990 *church exterior*; stairhead, landing 308 *ascent*; acropolis 713 *fort*; summit level, hilltop, mountaintop, plateau, tableland 209 *high land*; treetop, housetop, rooftop; gable, gable-end; leads, ceiling 226 *roof*; upper chamber, garret, loft 194 *attic*; top storey; topside, upper deck, bridge 275 *ship*; topmast, masthead, crow's nest 209 *high structure*.

head, headpiece, pate, poll, sconce; noddle, nob, nut, noggin, coco, conk, bonce, crumpet, bean, block, chump; upper storey, belfry; brow, dome, temple, forehead; loaf, brain, grey matter 498 *intelligence*; epicranium, pericranium; scalp, crown, double crown; skull, cranium, brainpan 255 *cavity*; fontanelle; craniology, craniometry, cranioscopy, craniotomy; phrenology; brain scanning, brain scan, neuroradiology, brain surgery, neurosurgery.

Adj. *topmost*, top, highest 209 *high*; uppermost, upmost 34 *supreme*; polar, apical, crowning; capital, head; culminating, meridian; tiptop, super 644 *best*.

Vb. *crown*, cap, head, top, pinnacle, tip, surmount, crest, overtop 209 *be high*; culminate, consummate 725 *climax*; go up top, take top place, go into the lead 34 *be superior*; top out, put the finishing touches to 54 *make complete*.

214 Base

N. *base*, foot, toe, skirt 210 *lowness*; bottom, fundus, root; lowest point, the depths, rock bottom, nadir, low water; footing, foundation 218 *basis*; the nitty gritty; fundamental 68 *origin*; groundwork, substructure, infrastructure, chassis 218 *frame*; baseboard, plinth, pedestal 218 *stand*; substratum, floor, underlayer, bed, bedrock; subsoil, pan, hardpan; ground, earth, foundations; footing, sill; damp course, dampproof course; basement, ground floor 194 *cellar*; flooring, pavement, paving-stone, flagstone; carpet 226 *floor-cover*; skirting board, wainscot, plinth, dado; keel, keelson; hold, bilge; sump, drain 649 *sink*.

foot, feet, tootsies, dogs, plates; beetle-crusher; forefoot, hindfoot; sole, heel, Achilles' tendon, instep, arch; toe, toe-nail, big toe, hallux; trotter, hoof, cloven hoof; paw, pad; claw, talon 778 *pincers*; ankle, ankle-bone, tarsus, metatarsus, fetlock, pastern.

215 Verticality

N. *verticality*, the vertical, erectness, uprightness, upright carriage; steepness, sheerness, precipitousness 209 *height*; perpendicularity, right angle, square; elevation, azimuth circle; vertical line, plumbline, plummet; vertical structure, upright, pole, stalagmite 218 *pillar*; precipice, cliff, bluff, scarp, steep 209 *high land*; perpendicular drop, vertical height, rise.

Adj. *vertical*, upright, erect, standing; perpendicular, rectangular, sheer, abrupt, steep, precipitous 209 *high*; straight, plumb; straight up, straight down; upstanding, standing up, on one's feet, on one's legs, on one's hindlegs; bolt upright, stiff as a ramrod, unbowed; rampant, rearing; on end.

Vb. *be vertical*, stick up, cock up, bristle, stand on end; stand erect, stand upright, hold oneself straight; sit up, stand up, straighten up; rise, stand, be upstanding, rise to one's feet, get to one's feet, ramp, rear; keep standing, have no seat, sit on one's thumb.

216 Horizontality

N. *horizontality*, horizontalness; horizontal angle, azimuth; horizontal line, rule; horizontal course, strike; flatness 258 *smoothness*; level, plane, level plane; sea level, water level, water table; stratum; slab, tablet, table 207 *layer*; level stretch, steppe 348 *plain*; flats 347 *marsh*; platform, ledge 254 *projection*; terrace, esplanade; plateau, tableland 209 *high land*; billiard table, bowling green, cricket ground, croquet lawn 724 *arena*; gridiron, platter 194 *plate*; spirit level, T square 465 *gauge*; skyline, horizon, false horizon, horizon line 236 *limit*.

flattener, iron, flatiron, steam iron, mangle, press, trouser press; rolling pin, roller, garden roller, steamroller 258 *smoother*; bulldozer, juggernaut 168 *destroyer*.

Adj. *flat*, horizontal, two-dimensional, level, plane, even, flush 258 *smooth*; trodden, flat as a pancake; unwrinkled, smooth, smooth as a baby's bottom, smooth as glass, calm, calm as a millpond.

flat on one's back, flat out, supine; face down, prone, prostrate; recumbent; lying down, couchant; abed, laid up, laid out; stretched out, sprawling, spread-eagled, lolling.

Vb. *be horizontal*, lie, lie down, lie flat, lie prostrate, lie on one's back; measure one's length, recline, couch, sprawl, spread-eagle, loll 311 *sit down*; straighten out, level out, bottom out.

flatten, lay out, roll out, lay down, spread; lay flat, beat flat, tread flat, stamp down, trample down, squash, squish; make flush, align, level, even, grade, plane 28 *equalize*; iron, iron out, roll out 258 *smooth*; pat down, smooth down, prostrate, knock down, floor, ground 311 *fell*.

217 Pendency: hanging

N. *suspension*, hanging, dangle, dangling, pendency; set, hang, drape; droop, drooping.

hanging object, hanging ornament, mobile, pendant, dangler, drop, eardrop, earring, dangling earring 844 *jewellery*; tassel, bobble, tag 844 *trimming*; hangings, draperies, drapes, curtains, arras, tapestry 226 *covering*; train, skirt, coat-tails; flap, lappet, tippet 228 *headgear*; pigtail, tail 67 *sequel*, 259 *hair*; dewlap, lobe, appendix 40 *adjunct*; pendulum, bob, swing, hammock 317 *oscillation*; chandelier 420 *lamp*; icicle, stalactite.

hanger, coat hanger, curtain rod, curtain ring, runner, rack; hook, coathook, peg, knob, nail, hatstand 218 *prop*; suspender, braces, suspender belt 228 *underwear*; clothes-line 47 *cable*; clothes-horse, airer 218 *frame*; crane; spar, mast 218 *pillar*; gallows, gibbet 964 *pillory*.

Adj. *hanging*, pendent, pendulous, pensile; hanging from, dependent, suspended, dangling, etc. (see vb.); hanging the head, nodding, drooping, lowering, overhanging; beetling 254 *projecting*.

Vb. *hang*, be pendent, drape, set; hang down, draggle, trail, flow; hang on to, swing from; swing, sway, dangle, bob; hang the head, nod, loll, droop, sag, swag; hang in the wind, hang over, hover, lour; suspend, hang up, append 45 *join*.

218 Support

N. *support*, support, mounting, bearing; carriage, undercarriage, carrier, underframe, chassis; buttress, flying buttress, abutment, bulwark, embankment, wall, retaining wall; underpinning, shore, jack; flagstaff, jackstaff, stanchion, rod, bar, transom, brace, strut; stay, mainstay, guy, shrouds, rigging; sprit, boom,

spar, mast, yard, yard-arm, crosstree 254 *projection*; trunk, stem, stalk, caudex, pedicle, pedicel, peduncle 366 *plant*; arch, ogive 248 *curve*; keystone, headstone, cornerstone, springer; cantilever; pier (see also *pillar* below); strapping, bandage, elastic bandage, jockstrap, truss, splint; stiffener, whalebone; corset 228 *underwear*; yoke 217 *hanger*; rest, headrest, backrest, footrest, stirrup; banisters, handrail (see also *handle* below); foothold 778 *retention*; wedge 702 *obstacle*; staff, baton, cane, alpenstock, crutch, crook, shepherd's crook, stick, walking stick, swordstick; leg support, splint, calliper, irons; bracket (see also *shelf* below); trivet, hob (see also *stand* below); life-support machine; collarbone; worldbearer; patron.

handle, holder, pen holder, cigarette holder 194 *receptacle*; hilt, pommel, haft; knob, doorhandle; lug, ear, loop; railing, handrail, rail, poop rail, taffrail, banisters, balustrade; shaft; handlebar, tiller; winder, crank, crankhandle; lever, trigger 630 *tool*.

basis, foundation, footings, deck; pallet, sleeper; substratum 207 *layer*; ground, groundwork, floor, bed, bedrock, rock bottom 214 *base*; sill *or* cill; flooring, pavement 226 *paving*; terra firma 344 *land*.

stand, tripod, trivet, hob; table mat, coaster; anvil, block, bench; trolley, tea trolley; table, console table, coffee table, gateleg table, dropleaf table, refectory table, board; card table, bridge table, snooker table, pool table; sideboard, dresser, Welsh dresser 194 *cabinet*; work table, desk, counter; sawhorse; pedestal, plinth, podium; reading desk, lectern; platform, launching pad, launchpad, gantry; emplacement; footplate; landing; landing stage, pier; dais, pulpit, stage; doorstep, threshold; step, stair, tread, rung.

seat, throne, woolsack; bank, bench, form, settle; front seat, back seat, booster seat; bucket seat, box seat, rumble seat, dicky; pew, choirstall, misericord 990 *church interior*; stall, fauteuil 594 *theatre*; chair, armchair, easy chair, wing chair, grandad chair, club chair, rocking chair, revolving chair, basket chair, Windsor chair, high chair, deck chair, lounger; chaise longue; sofa, settee, bed settee, futon, divan, couch, studio couch, ottoman, chesterfield, loveseat, windowseat; pouffe, stool, footstool, kitchen stool, campstool, prie-dieu, hassock; saddle, pillion, pad, howdah; ducking-stool 964 *pillory*; electric chair; lap; mat 226 *floor-cover*; chair cover, etc. 226 *covering*.

bed, cot, crib, cradle, bassinet; marriage bed, bridal bed, double bed, single bed, king-size bed, bunk bed, bunk, feather bed; bed settee, daybed, couch; tester, four-poster; charpoy, truckle bed, trundle bed, camp bed, pallet, airbed, futon, bedroll, shakedown; hammock 217 *hanging object*; sick bed, litter, hurdle, stretcher 658 *hospital*; bier 364 *funeral*; bedding, duvet, etc. 226 *coverlet*; sleeping bag; bedstead, divan; headboard.

   cushion, pillow; bolster; mattress, palliasse; squab, hassock, kneeler.

   beam, balk, joist, RSJ, girder, box girder, rafter, purlin, tie beam, truss 47 *bond*; summer, bressummer; wall-plate 226 *roof*; crossbeam, transom, crossbar, traverse; architrave, lintel.

   pillar, shaft, pier, pile, pole, stake, stud 331 *structure*; post, king post, queen post, crown post; jamb, door jamb, doorpost; stanchion, puncheon; newelpost, banister, baluster; mullion; pilaster, column, Doric column, Ionic column, Corinthian column, Tuscan column; caryatid, telamon, atlantes; spinal column, spine, backbone, vertebral column, vertebrae; neck, cervix; pole-vaulter; pole-dancer; stylite.

   pivot, fulcrum, lever, purchase; hinge 45 *joint*; pole, axis; gimbals; axle, swivel, spindle, arbor, pintle 315 *rotator*; bearing, gudgeon, trunnion; rowlock, tholepin; centreboard, keel.

   shelf, bookshelf, ledge 254 *projection*; corbel, bracket, console; retable, niche 194 *compartment*; sill, windowsill, mantelpiece, mantelshelf, rack, dresser 194 *cabinet*; desktop, counter, worktop, plank, board, table, leaf, slab.

   frame, skeleton, ribs; framework, infrastructure, staging, scaffolding 331 *structure*; trellis, espalier; chassis, fuselage, body (of a car), undercarriage; trestle; easel, clotheshorse; housing 235 *enclosure*; picture frame, window frame, sash 233 *outline*.

   Vb. *support*, sustain, bear, carry, hold, shoulder; uphold, hold up, bear up, buoy up; prop, shore up, underprop, underpin, jack up 310 *elevate*; buttress, bolster, bolster up, cushion; reinforce, underset 162 *strengthen*; bandage, brace, truss 45 *tighten*; steady, stay; cradle, pillow, cup, cup one's chin; maintain, give aliment, give alimony 633 *provide*; give one a hand, back up, give support, lend support, furnish support, afford support, supply support 703 *aid*; frame, set, mount 235 *enclose*; be the infrastructure, bottom, ground, found, base 153 *stabilize*; stand, endure, survive, stand up to, stand the strain, take the strain 635 *suffice*.

219 Parallelism

N. *parallelism*, non-convergence, non-divergence, equidistance, coextension, collimation, concentricity; parallel,

correspondence 28 *equality*; parallel lines, lines of latitude; tramlines, rails, railway lines; parallel bars; parallelogram, parallelepiped.

220 Obliqueness

N. *obliqueness*, obliquity, skewness; diagonal; rhomboid 247 *angular figure*; oblique angle, inclination 247 *angularity*; indirection, indirectness, squint; curvature, camber, bend, z-bend, chicane, humpback 248 *curve*; crookedness, zigzag, chevron; switchback 251 *meandering*; oblique motion, circumlocution, digression, swerve, lurch, stagger 282 *deviation*; splay, bias, twist, warp 246 *distortion*; leaning, list, tip, cant; slope, slant, tilt, pitch, angle, rakish angle; sloping face; sloping edge, bevel, bezel; inclined plane, ramp, chute, slide, slipway; Tower of Pisa, leaning tower; measurement of inclination 247 *angular measure*.

   incline, rise, ascent; ramp, acclivity, gradient; hill, rising ground, hillock; hillside 239 *laterality*; declivity, fall, dip, downhill 309 *descent*; gentle slope, nursery slope; escarpment, steepness, cliff, precipice 215 *verticality*; scarp 713 *fortification*; talus, bank, scree, landslip, landslide.

   Adj. *sloping*, uphill, rising; downhill, falling, declining, dipping; anticlinal, synclinal; declivitous, steep, abrupt, sheer, precipitous, vertiginous, breakneck 215 *vertical*.

   Vb. *be oblique*, be askew, be awry, be agley; incline, lean, tilt; pitch, slope, slant, shelve, dip, decline 309 *descend*; rise, climb 308 *ascend*; cut, cut across, transect 222 *cross*; lean, list, tip, lean over, bank, heel, careen, cant; bend, sag, give; bend over 311 *stoop*; walk sideways, edge, sidle, sidestep; look sideways, squint; zigzag; jink, dodge, duck, swerve; diverge, converge.

221 Inversion

N. *inversion*, turning back to front, palindrome; turning inside out, eversion; turning backwards, retroversion, reversal 148 *reversion*; turning inward, introversion; turning over, capsizal (see also *overturning* below); turn of the tide, return 286 *regression*; oppositeness 14 *contrariety*, 240 *oppositeness*; transposition, metathesis 151 *interchange*; inverted order, chiasmus 519 *figure of speech*; spoonerism.

   overturning, capsizal, upset, purler, spill; somersault, summerset, cartwheel, handspring; subversion, undermining, overthrowing 149 *revolution*.

   Vb. *be inverted*, turn round, go round, wheel round, swing round, turn about, face about, right about turn 286 *turn back*; turn over, heel over, keel over, capsize, turn head over heels, turn turtle, turn topsy-turvy, be arsy-versy; tilt over 220 *be oblique*; go over, topple over 309 *tumble*; do a handstand, stand on one's head; loop the loop; reverse, back, back away, go backwards 286 *regress*; be back to front, be inside out.

invert, transpose, put the cart before the horse 151 *interchange*; reverse, turn the tables; turn back; turn down 261 *fold*; introvert, turn inside out, upend, upturn, overturn, tip over, spill, upset, overset, capsize; turn topsy-turvy.

Adv. *inversely*, vice versa; contrariwise, quite the reverse, just the opposite, on the contrary, other way round; back to front, upside down; arsy-versy, topsy-turvy, head over heels; face down, face downwards, bottom side up.

222 Crossing: intertexture

N. *crossing*, crisscross, transection, intersection; decussation, X-shape; intertexture, interlacement, intertwinement, interweaving 844 *pattern*; braid, wreath, plait, pigtail 251 *convolution*; entanglement, intricacy, skein, cat's cradle 61 *complexity*; crossroads, intersection, roundabout, interchange, road junction 624 *road*; level crossing 624 *railway*; viaduct, flyover, overpass, underpass, subway 624 *bridge*, 305 *traffic control*.

cross, crux, rood, crucifix 988 *ritual object*; pectoral 989 *vestments*; ankh, ansate cross, tau cross, Latin cross, cross of Lorraine, Greek cross, Maltese cross, Celtic cross, St Anthony's Cross, St Andrew's Cross; saltire, crosslet 547 *heraldry*; gammadion, swastika, fylfot; crossbones, skull and crossbones 547 *flag*; crossbar, transom 218 *beam*.

network, reticulation, meshwork, netting, wire netting, chicken wire; webbing, matting, wickerwork, basketwork, trellis, wattle; honeycomb, lattice, grating, grid, grille, gridiron; craquelure; tracery, fretwork, filigree 844 *ornamental art*; lace, crochet, knitting, darning, tatting, macramé 844 *needlework*; web, cobweb; net, fishnet, seine, purse-seine, drag-net, trawl, beam trawl 235 *enclosure*; plexus, mesh, reticle; chain, group, interconnection.

textile, weave, web, loom; woven stuff; bolt, roll, length, piece, cloth, stuff, material; broadcloth, fabric, tissue, suiting; batik 844 *ornamental art*; jute, hessian, gunny, sacking, sackcloth, hopsack, canvas, sailcloth, duck; ticking, crash, huckaback, towelling, terry towelling, candlewick; chintz, cretonne, damask, brocade, brocatelle, grosgrain, rep, chenille, tapestry 226 *covering*; mohair, cashmere; alpaca, vicuña, angora 208 *fibre*; wool, worsted, grogram, shoddy, mungo; frieze, felt,

baize; homespun, khadar, duffel, kersey, tweed, serge, shalloon, bombazine, gabardine, doeskin; flannel, swanskin, swansdown; paisley, jacquard 844 *pattern*; stockinette, jersey, tricot, nainsook, flannelette, winceyette; velvet, velveteen, velour; corduroy, needlecord; cotton, chino, denim, drill, nankeen, twill, cavalry twill, khaki; fustian, moleskin, sharkskin; poplin, calico, dimity, gingham, madras, seersucker, piqué; batiste, organdie, organza; silesia, cheesecloth, muslin, tarlatan, mull, voile, percale; cambric, lawn, toile, holland, linen; silk, shot silk, surah, foulard, georgette, crêpe de chine, chiffon, mousseline; satin, sateen, taffeta, moiré; tussore *or* tussah, shantung, pongee; ninon; tulle, net, gauze; lace, guipure; rayon, nylon, Terylene (tdmk), Crimplene (tdmk), polyester, Courtelle (tdmk), Acrilan (tdmk), fibreglass 208 *fibre*.

weaving, texture; web, warp, weft, woof, selvedge; nap, pile 259 *hair*; frame, loom, shuttle; weaver, knitter; knitting machine, sewing machine; spinning wheel, distaff, whorl; spinner, spider, weaverbird; Arachne, Penelope.

Adj. *crossed*, crossing, cross, crisscross; quadrivial; diagonal, transverse, cross-eyed, squinting, squint-eyed; X-shaped, decussate, quincunxial; cross-legged, cruciform, crucial, cruciate, forked, furcate 247 *angular*; plexiform; knotted, matted, tangled, balled-up, ravelled 61 *complex*; pleached, plashed, plaited, braided, interlaced, interwoven; textile, loomed, woven, handwoven, tweedy; twill, herringbone; trellised, latticed, honeycombed, mullioned, barred; corded, ribbed, streaked, striped 437 *variegated*.

Vb. *cross*, cross over, cross under 305 *pass*; intersect, cut 220 *be oblique*; decussate, inosculate, interdigitate; splice, dovetail, link 45 *join*; reticulate, mesh, net, knot; fork, bifurcate.

weave, loom; pleach, plash, plait, braid; felt, twill, knit, crochet, darn; spin, slub.

223 Exteriority

N. *exteriority*, the external; outwardness, externality 230 *surroundings*; periphery, circumference, sidelines 233 *outline*; exterior, outward appearance 445 *appearance*; superficiality, surface, superstratum, crust, cortex, shell, integument 226 *skin*; outer side, face, facet, façade 237 *front*; other side 240 *oppositeness*; externalism; externalization, extroversion, extrovert 6 *externality*; outside, out of doors, open air; outer space 199 *distance*; extraterritoriality 57 *exclusion*; foreignness 59 *extraneousness*; eccentricity 84 *nonconformity*; outsider 84 *nonconformist*.

Adj. *exterior*, exoteric, outward; external 10

unrelated; peripheral; outer, outermost, outlying, extraterrestrial 199 *distant*; outside, outboard; outdoor, extramural; foreign 59 *extraneous*; extraterrestrial, extraterritorial 57 *excluding*; extrovert, outward-looking 6 *external*; centrifugal; exogenous; eccentric; surface, superficial, epidermal, cortical; skin-deep 212 *shallow*; facial 237 *frontal*.

Adv. *externally*, outwardly, outwards, superficially, on the surface; on the face of it, to the outsider; outside, out, out of doors, in the cold, in the sun, in the open, in the open air, al fresco.

224 Interiority

N. *interiority*, interior, inside, indoors; inner surface, undersurface; sapwood, heartwood 366 *wood*; inmost being, heart's blood, soul; heart, centre, breast, bosom 225 *centrality*; inland, Midlands, heartland, hinterland, up-country; the nitty gritty, pith, marrow 3 *substance*; substratum 214 *base*; pervasion 189 *presence*, 231 *betweenness*; deepness, cave, pit, pothole, recesses 211 *depth*; introversion 224 *introversion*; self-absorption, egocentrism, egocentricity, egomania 932 *selfishness*.

insides 193 *contents*; inner man *or* woman, viscera, vitals; heart, ventricle; lungs, lights; liver, kidneys, spleen; offal 301 *meat*; bowels, entrails, innards, guts, tripe; intestines, colon, rectum, back passage 194 *stomach*; abdomen, belly, paunch, underbelly; womb, uterus; stomach, tummy 194 *stomach*; chest, breast, bosom 253 *bosom*; solar plexus.

***introversion*,** inwardness, withdrawnness, autism; subjectiveness, subjectivity, subjectivism.

Adj. *interior*, internal, inward 5 *inherent*; inside, inner, innermost 225 *central*; inland; domestic, home; intimate, familiar 490 *known*; indoor, intramural, shut in, enclosed; built-in, inwrought; endemic; deep-seated, deep-rooted, in-grown 153 *fixed*; intestinal, visceral; intravenous, subcutaneous; interstitial 231 *lying between*; endogamous; endogenous.

***inward-looking*,** introspective, introverted, introvert, withdrawn, autistic, subjective, introversive, reflexive.

Adv. *inside*, within, in, deep down; inwardly, intimately; deeply, profoundly, at heart; within doors, indoors, at home, en famille, chez, at the sign of.

225 Centrality

N. *centrality*, centralness; concentricity; centralization, focalization, concentration 324 *condensing*; central position 231 *betweenness*; midriff, waistline, centreline.

***centre*,** dead centre; centroid, centre of gravity, centre of pressure, metacentre; nerve centre, ganglion; centre of activity, focal point 76 *focus*; epicentre; storm centre; ground zero; heart, core, kernel 5 *essential part*; nub; hub; nucleus, nucleolus; navel, umbilicus; spine, backbone, vertebrae, midrib; marrow, pith 224 *interiority*; pole, axis, fulcrum, centreboard 218 *pivot*; centre point, mid point 70 *middle*; fesspoint 547 *heraldry*; eye, pupil; bull's-eye, target 617 *objective*.

Adj. *central*, centric, centrical; nuclear, nucleolar; centremost, midmost 70 *middle*; axial, focal, pivotal; umbilical; concentric; geocentric; spinal, vertebral; centripetal; metropolitan, chief, head 34 *supreme*.

Vb. *centralize*, centre, focus; zero in on, centre upon; concentrate, nucleate, consolidate 324 *be dense*.

226 Covering

N. *covering*, capping, etc. (see vb.); superimposition, overlaying; overlap, overlapping; coating, stratification 207 *layer*; veneer, top layer, top dressing, mulch, topsoil 344 *soil*; topping, icing, frosting 844 *ornamentation*; cover, lid; ledger 364 *tomb*; hatch, trapdoor; flap, shutter; film 423 *opacity*; glass, watch glass, crystal 422 *transparency*; cap, top, plug, bung, cork 264 *stopper*; plaster, Elastoplast (tdmk), Band-Aid (tdmk) 658 *surgical dressing*; carapace, shell, tortoiseshell 326 *hardness*; mail, plate 713 *armour*; shield, cowl, bonnet, hood (of a car); scab; crust, fur 649 *dirt*; capsule, ferrule, sheath, involucre, envelope 194 *receptacle*; pillowcase, pillowslip, cushion cover; table cloth, tray cloth; chair cover, antimacassar; soft furnishings, loose covers; hangings, curtains, drapes 217 *hanging object*; wallpaper 227 *lining*.

***roof*,** cupola 253 *dome*; mansard roof, hipped roof, pitched roof, gable roof, flat roof, housetop, rooftop 213 *apex*; leads, slates, slating, tiles, tiling, pantile, shingle, thatch, thatching, corrugated iron 631 *building material*; eaves 234 *edge*; ceiling, deck; vaulting, vault; rafters 218 *beam*.

***canopy*,** tilt, awning, sunblind 421 *screen*; marquee, pavilion, big top; tent, bell tent, ridge tent, frame tent; tepee 192 *dwelling*; tent-cloth, canvas, tarpaulin, fly sheet; mosquito net 222 *network*.

***shade*,** hood, eyelid, eyelash; blind, venetian blind, roller blind, festoon blind, jalousie, shutters, slats; curtain, veil; umbrella, gamp, brolly; parasol, sunshade; sun hat, sun helmet, topee *or* topi 228 *headgear*; visor, eye shade 421 *screen*; peak (of a cap); dark glasses, sunglasses, shades 442 *spectacles*.

wrapping, wrapper, paper, tissue paper, cellophane, polythene; polystyrene 227 *lining;* packaging, blister pack, bubble pack, shrinkpack 194 *receptacle;* bandage, roller; plaster cast 658 *surgical dressing;* book cover, binding, boards, dust jacket *or* cover 589 *bookbinding;* tunic, coat 228 *jacket;* mantle 228 *cloak;* comforter, scarf 228 *neckwear;* life belt, life jacket 662 *safeguard;* lagging; cocoon, chrysalis; shroud, winding sheet 364 *grave clothes.*

skin, epithelium; outer skin, scarf skin, epidermis, cuticle; true skin, cutis, dermis, derma, corium; tegument 223 *exteriority;* integument, peel, bark, crust, rind, coat, cortex; pericarp, husk, hull, shell, pod, jacket; pellicle, membrane, film; scalp 213 *head;* scale; pelt, fleece, fell, fur; leather, hide, rawhide, imitation leather, leatheroid; shagreen, patent leather; crocodile, alligator; pigskin, morocco, calf, kid, chamois, suede, buff, buckskin, doeskin; rabbitskin, moleskin, sealskin; sheepskin, lamb, Persian lamb, astrakhan; mink, sable, ermine, miniver, cony; chinchilla 208 *fibre;* feathers, coverts 259 *plumage.*

paving, flooring, floor, parquet, quarry tiles; deck, floorboards, duckboards; pavement, sidewalk, pavé; flags, paving stone, crazy paving; sett, cobble, cobblestone; gravel, chippings, asphalt, tarmac 624 *road.*

coverlet, bedspread, counterpane, bedding, bedclothes, bed linen; sheet, quilt, eiderdown, duvet, continental quilt, Downie (tdmk); blanket, rug; caparison, housings, trappings; saddlecloth, horsecloth; pall.

floor-cover, carpeting, carpet, fitted carpet, wall-to-wall; broadloom, pile carpet, shagpile, Persian carpet; mat, doormat, bath mat, prayer mat; rug, hearth rug; linoleum, lino, vinyl, tiles; matting, coconut matting; red carpet 875 *formality.*

facing, cladding; veneer, coating, varnish, japan, lacquer, enamel, glaze; roughcast, pebbledash; ashlar, weather-boarding 631 *building material;* stucco, compo, plaster, pargeting, rendering, screed; wash, whitewash, distemper, emulsion, paint; stain, polish, smearing, anointment; coat of paint 425 *pigment.*

Vb. *cover,* superimpose; roof, cork, cap, tip; ice, frost, decorate (a cake); spread, lay (a table); overlay, smother; insulate, lag 227 *line;* lap, wrap up, enfold, envelope 235 *enclose;* blanket, shroud, mantle, muffle; hood, veil 525 *conceal;* case, bind, cover (books); box, pack, vacuum-pack; wrap, shrink-wrap; bandage, swathe, wrap round, dress 658 *practise medicine;* sheathe, encapsulate, encase 303 *insert;* wall in, wall up; cover up, keep under cover.

coat, face, front, revet; grout, roughcast, encrust, shingle; stucco, plaster, pebbledash, render, parget 844 *decorate;* thatch, tile; veneer, varnish, lacquer; japan, enamel, glaze, size; paint, whitewash, colourwash, distemper, emulsion, stain 425 *colour;* creosote; tar, pitch, pay; daub, bedaub, scumble, overpaint, grease, lard, lay it on thick; smear, butter, anoint, powder, sprinkle, gild, plate, silver; electroplate, silverplate; waterproof, fireproof, damp-proof 660 *safeguard.*

227 Lining

N. *lining,* liner, coating, inner coating; stuffing, wadding, padding, quilting; kapok, foam, polystyrene 631 *materials;* lagging, insulation, double-glazing, damp-proofing, soundproofing; backing; facing; doublure 589 *bookbinding;* upholstery; papering, wallpaper; wainscotting, panelling, wainscot, skirting board, dado, brattice; metal lining; brake lining; packing, dunnage; packaging 226 *wrapping;* filling, stopping (dentistry); washer.

Vb. *line,* encrust 226 *coat;* insulate 226 *cover;* interlard, inlay; back, face, paper, wallpaper, upholster, cushion; stuff, pad, wad; fill, pack.

228 Dressing

N. *dressing,* investment, investiture; clothing, covering, dressing up, toilet, toilette; overdressing, foppishness; underdressing, casualness 848 *fashion;* vesture, dress, garb, attire, rig, gear, clobber; panoply, array; garniture, trim, accoutrements, caparison, harness, housing, trappings; traps, paraphernalia, accessories; rig-out, turn-out; tailoring, dressmaking; millinery; haute couture; the rag trade, the fashion world; power dressing.

clothing, wear, apparel, raiment, linen; clothes, garments, vestments, habiliments; togs, gear, kit, clobber, get-up; outfit, wardrobe, trousseau; maternity wear; layette, baby clothes, swaddling clothes, Babygro (tdmk); old clothes, duds, reach-me-downs, cast-offs, rags, tatters; working clothes, hand-me-downs, second-hand clothes; livery, uniform (see also *uniform* below); sportswear, tracksuit, strip, team strip; leisure wear, casual clothes, dressdown Friday; best clothes, Sunday best, Sunday-go-to-meeting clothes, best bib and tucker; party dress, glad rags; ostrich feathers, frippery 844 *finery;* fancy dress, masquerade; motley; national costume.

article of clothing, garment, neck, collar, grandad collar (see also *neckwear, neckline* below); top, bodice, bosom; corsage, bib, stomacher; shirt-front, dickey; waistline (see also *belt* below); peplum, bustle, train; crutch, codpiece; arms (see also *sleeve* below); flaps, coat tails 217 *hanging object*; placket, fly 263 *opening*; cargo pocket, patch pocket; flap, gusset, gore, pleat, kick pleat; lapel, turn-up 261 *fold*; cuff, hemline 234 *edging*.

formal dress, correct dress, court dress, full dress 875 *formality*; grande toilette, evening dress, tails, white tie and tails; dinner jacket, black tie, tuxedo; morning dress; academic dress, academicals, cap and gown, subfusc; mourning, black, widow's weeds, black armband.

uniform, regimentals; dress uniform, undress, mess kit; battledress, fatigues, khaki; school uniform, academic dress; robes, vestments, clerical dress 989 *clerical dress*; livery.

informal dress, undress, mufti, civvies; casual clothes, leisure wear, slacks, jeans; dress-down Friday; déshabillé, dishabille, something more comfortable; dressing gown, loungewear, peignoir, bathrobe, robe, wrapper, housecoat; smoking jacket, slippers.

robe, gown, robes, sari; kimono, caftan; jubbah, djellaba, toga, cassock 989 *clerical dress*.

dress, frock, gown; creation, number, ballgown, cocktail dress, little black dress; sheath dress, tube dress, cheongsam, chemise, shift, shift dress, sack, sack dress; shirtwaister, coatdress, overdress, pinafore dress, jumper, gymslip; sundress; christening gown.

suit, outfit, ensemble; coordinates, separates; lounge suit, zoot suit, drape suit, pinstripe suit; costume, tweeds, trouser suit, pantsuit; jumpsuit, catsuit, leotard, unitard, biketard, body-suit, body stocking; overalls, dungarees, boiler suit, siren suit, tracksuit, sweats, leisure suit, skinsuit, wetsuit; G-suit, spacesuit.

jacket, coat, tail coat, dinner jacket, tuxedo; monkey jacket, mess jacket, Eton jacket; blazer, reefer, sports jacket, Norfolk jacket, hacking jacket, riding habit, hunting pink; donkey jacket, lumber jacket (see also *overcoat* below); parka, windcheater, anorak, cagoule *or* kagoul; bomber jacket, blouson, body-warmer, puffa jacket; jerkin, tunic, tabard, surcoat, waistcoat, vest, gilet, spencer; bolero, coatee, matinee jacket.

jersey, pullover, woolly, knit, homeknit, handknit, jumper, sweater, V-neck, polo neck, turtle neck, crew neck, sloppy joe, sweatshirt, guernsey, Fair Isle, cardigan, cardi, shrug, tank top, tank, twin set.

trousers, pants, trews, breeks; cords, flannels, pinstripes; hipsters, drainpipes, bellbottoms, flares; slacks, bags, Oxford bags, plus fours; breeches, britches, jodhpurs, knickerbockers, pedal-pushers, leggings, tights; chaps,

dungarees, denims, jeans, blue jeans, low-rise jeans, Levi's (tdmk), cargo pants *or* cargos, chinos, combat trousers *or* combats; cigarette pants, palazzo pants; shorts, Bermuda shorts, hot pants, culottes; lederhosen; bloomers, pantaloons, rompers.

skirt, maxi skirt, midi skirt, miniskirt; pleated skirt, flared skirt, A-line skirt, gored skirt, full skirt, dirndl, bubble skirt, kilt, kirtle, filibeg; sarong; straight skirt, slit skirt, hobble skirt; sports skirt, divided skirt, culottes; ballet skirt, tutu; crinoline, farthingale, hoop.

shirt, grandad shirt, tee shirt *or* T-shirt, polo neck, sweatshirt; blouse, camisole, top; smock, angel top.

underwear, underclothes, undies, linen; lingerie, smalls, unmentionables; underpants, shorts, pants, Y-fronts, boxer shorts; briefs, thongs, panties, scanties, French knickers, camiknickers, teddy knickers, bloomers, drawers; combinations, long johns, thermal underwear; singlet, vest, string vest, undershirt, semmit; camisole, chemise, slip, half-slip, underskirt, petticoat; foundation garment, body stocking, corset, stays, girdle, pantiegirdle, roll-on; brassiere, bra; suspender belt, braces; G-string, modesty pouch, posing pouch.

nightwear, nightclothes, sleeping suit; nightgown, nightdress, nightie, negligee; nightshirt, pyjamas; bedsocks, bed jacket, nightcap.

beachwear, sunsuit, sundress; bikini, bankini, monokini, trikini, tankini, bandeau; swimming costume, swimsuit, one-piece swimsuit, maillot, bathing suit, trunks, bathers; beach robe; aloha shirt.

overcoat, coat (see also *jacket* above); fur coat 226 *skin*; topcoat, greatcoat, frock coat; ulster, car coat, duffel coat, cagoule *or* kagoul; waterproof, oilskins; mac, mackintosh, raincoat, gabardine; Burberry (tdmk), trench coat; light coat, duster; fitted coat.

cloak, cape, cycling cape; poncho; shawl, pashmina, shatoosh.

neckwear, scarf, fichu; stole, boa, tippet; comforter, muffler; neckerchief, jabot, cravat, necktie, tie, bow tie; necklace 844 *jewellery*; ruff, collar, dog collar 989 *clerical dress*; Eton collar, mandarin collar, Peter Pan collar, Vandyke collar, Bertha, sailor collar, shawl collar; button-down collar, stand-up collar. (See also *neckline* below.)

headgear, millinery; hat, cap, lid, titfer, tile; headdress, mantilla; plumes, ribbons 844 *finery*; crown, coronet, tiara, diadem 743 *regalia*; fillet, snood; juliet cap, skull cap, coif; headscarf, kerchief, bandanna, headband, sweatband, Alice band; turban; hood, cowl, wimple;

veil, yashmak, hejab *or* hijab 421 *screen*; fez, tarboosh; kepi, busby, bearskin; helmet, tin hat 713 *armour*; crash helmet, safety helmet 662 *safeguard*; woolly hat, bobble hat, ski hat; rainhat, sou'wester; cap, cloth cap, beret, tam-o'-shanter, tammy; Balmoral, glengarry, deerstalker; Homburg, trilby, pork-pie hat, billycock, fedora, beaver, bowler, derby; slouch hat, stetson, ten-gallon hat, sombrero, shovel hat, picture hat, straw hat, boater, panama, coolie hat, bush hat, sunhat, pith helmet, topee *or* topi 226 *shade*; bonnet, Easter bonnet, poke bonnet, mob cap, toque, cloche, pillbox; top hat, topper, silk hat, stovepipe hat; cocked hat, mortarboard; biretta, mitre 989 *clerical dress*; witch's hat, wizard's hat, dunce's cap; ear muffs.

neckline, boat neck, crew neck, cowl neck, turtle neck, roll neck, polo neck, halter neck, V-neck, round neck, low neck 229 *bareness*.

belt, waistband; cummerbund, sash, obi; money belt, belt-bag, bum-bag; shoulder-belt, bandolier, baldric.

sleeve, arm, armhole; leg-of-mutton sleeve, raglan sleeve, dolman sleeve, batwing sleeve, magyar sleeve, puff sleeve, cap sleeve, short sleeve, long sleeve; wristband, cuff.

glove, gauntlet, driving gloves, long gloves, evening gloves; mitten, mitt, muff.

legwear, hosiery; stockings, nylons, tights, fleshings; trunks, hose; socks, knee-length socks, over-the-knee socks, ankle socks, bootees; leggings, gaiters, spats, puttees; garter, suspender 47 *fastening*.

footwear, footgear; slipper, carpet slipper, mule; patten, clog, sabot; flipflops, jelly sandals, jellies, sandals, Jesus sandals, Jesus boots, chappals; rope-soled shoes, espadrilles, rubber-soled shoes, crepe-soled shoes, creepers, brothel creepers, sneakers, plimsolls, gym shoes, trainers, high-tops, tennis shoes; pumps, ballet shoes, pointe shoes; tap shoes, taps; moccasins, slip-ons, casuals; winklepickers, beetlecrushers, clodhoppers; shoe, court shoe; high heels, stiletto heels, platform heels, Cuban heels, wedge heels, kitten heels, stilettos, platforms; peep-toed shoes, slingbacks, flat shoes, driving shoes, lace-ups, buckled shoes; Oxfords, brogues; boots, fashion boots, high boots, cowboy boots, thigh boots, waders, wellingtons, wellies, gumboots; Doc Martens (tdmk), Dr Martens (tdmk), DMs; skiboots 274 *sled*; running shoes, spikes; seven-league boots.

clothier, outfitter, costumier; tailor, couturier, couturière; fashion designer 848 *fashion*; dressmaker, seamstress, modiste; shoemaker, bootmaker; cobbler 686 *artisan*; hosier, hatter, milliner, draper, haberdasher; Savile Row,

Carnaby Street; boutique; valet, batman 742 *domestic*; dresser, mistress of the wardrobe.

Adj. *tailored*, tailor-made, bespoke, made-to-measure, custom-made; designer, ready-to-wear, off-the-peg; fully fashioned.

Vb. *dress*, clothe, array, garb, attire; robe, drape, sheet, mantle; invest, put in uniform, equip, rig out, fit out, harness 669 *make ready*; dress up, deck, prink 843 *primp*; envelop, wrap, lap, enfold, wrap up, fold up, muffle up, roll up in, swaddle, swathe, shroud, sheathe 226 *cover*.

wear, put on, don, slip on, slip into; clothe oneself, attire oneself, get dressed, get one's clothes on; have on, dress in, dress up 875 *be ostentatious*.

229 Uncovering

N. *uncovering*, divestment, undressing, etc. (see vb.); opening, openness, glasnost; exposure, indecent exposure 526 *disclosure*; nudism, naturism; striptease, stripping, dance of the seven veils, fan dance, burlesque show (US), balloon dancing 594 *stage show*; undress, dishabille, déshabillé 228 *informal dress*; moulting, ecdysis, shedding; decortication, exfoliation, abscission, excoriation, peeling, desquamation); depilation, shaving; denudation, devastation.

bareness, décolleté, décolletage, bare neck, plunging neckline; nudity, nakedness, birthday suit, the altogether, the buff, the raw, the full monty, starkers, not a stitch on; streaking, skinny-dipping; baldness, tonsure.

stripper, striptease artiste, exotic dancer, fan dancer, lap-dancer, table-dancer, ecdysiast; nude model, glamour model; flasher, dirty old man in a raincoat, streaker; nudist, naturist; paint stripper, hair-remover, depilatory, wax, electrolysis.

uncovered person, nude, nudist, naturist; bald-headed person: baldie, slaphead.

Adj. *uncovered*, bared; exposed, unveiled 522 *manifest*; divested; debagged; stripped; unclad, unclothed, undressed, unattired; décolleté(e), bare-necked, off-the-shoulder, topless; bare-backed, bare-armed, barelegged; barefoot, unshod, hatless, bareheaded; en déshabillé, in one's shirt-sleeves; miniskirted; bikini-clad, swimsuited; indecently dressed; bare, naked, nude, raw; mother naked, in a state of undress, in the buff, in one's birthday suit, with nothing on, without a stitch on; stark, stark naked, starkers; unsheathed.

hairless, bald, baldheaded, beardless, shaved, shaven, clean-shaven, tonsured; bald as a coot, bald as an egg, bald as a billiard ball; threadbare; thin on top.

Vb. *uncover*, unveil, unclothe; divest, debag; undress, strip *or* strip off, get naked, change *or* slip into something more comfortable; strip, skin, scalp, flay, tear off; pluck, peel, pare, bark, excoriate; hull, pod, shell, stone; bone, fillet 300 *empty*; denude, expose, bare, lay open 526 *disclose*; unsheathe, draw (a sword) 304 *extract*; unwrap, unpack; uncap, uncork 263 *open*; abrade 333 *rub*.

230 Surroundings

N. *surroundings* 223 *exteriority*; ambience, atmosphere, aura; ambient music, Muzak (tdmk); medium, matrix; encompassment, containment, surrounding 235 *enclosure*; compass, circuit, circumference, periphery, perimeter 233 *outline*; milieu, environment, entourage; background, setting, scene, scenario 186 *situation*; neighbourhood, vicinity; outskirts, environs, suburbs, precincts 192 *housing*; sticks, outpost, cordon.

Vb. *surround*, lie around, encompass, lap; encircle 314 *circle*; begird 235 *enclose*; twine around; embrace, cuddle, hug 889 *caress*; contain, keep in, cloister, shut in, close round, hem in 232 *encircle*; blockade 712 *besiege*.

Adv. *around*, about, on every side, round about, all round; on all sides; outside, in the outskirts.

231 Betweenness

N. *betweenness*, interjacency, intermediacy; intervention, penetration, permeation, infiltration 189 *presence*, dovetailing 45 *union*.

partition, curtain, Iron Curtain, Bamboo Curtain 421 *screen*; Great Wall of China 713 *defences*; Berlin Wall, peace wall 57 *exclusion*; wall, party wall, garden fence, hedge, dyke, dry-stone wall, dry-stane dyke 235 *fence*; divide, watershed, parting 46 *separation*; division, panel 53 *subdivision*; ditch 201 *gap*.

intermediary, medium, link 47 *bond*; negotiator, go-between, pander, broker 720 *mediator*; agent 755 *deputy*; middle-man, retailer 794 *merchant*; advocate 707 *patron*; buffer, bumper, fender, crumple zone, cushion, air bag 662 *safeguard*; air lock, buffer state, no-man's-land, no-go area, halfway house 70 *middle*.

interjection, interruption, intrusion, chipping in, butting in 72 *discontinuity*; interpolation 303 *insertion*; sandwiching; interference, meddling 702 *hindrance*; episode, parenthesis 40 *adjunct*; insert; embolism 264 *closure*.

interjector, interpolator; intruder, interloper 59 *outsider*.

Adj. *lying between*, interjacent, sandwiched; episodic, parenthetical, in brackets, in parentheses; intermediary, lying between, interven-

ing, etc. (see vb.); mediating; intrusive 59 *extraneous*; interplanetary; intermediate 303 *inserted*; median, medium, mean 70 *middle*; partitioning, dividing.

Vb. *lie between*, come between, stand between; intervene; mediate.

introduce, let in 299 *admit*; throw in, work in, edge in, force in, thrust in 303 *insert*; ingrain; splice, dovetail, mortise 45 *join*; smuggle in, worm in, insinuate 297 *infiltrate*.

interfere, come between, intercept 702 *hinder*; step in, intervene, intercede 720 *mediate*; interrupt, interject, interpolate 38 *add*; put in, chip in, get a word in; obtrude, thrust in, poke one's nose in, horn in, butt in 297 *intrude*; invade, trespass 306 *encroach*; put one's oar in; have a finger in the pie 678 *meddle*.

Adv. *between*, betwixt, 'twixt, betwixt and between; among, amongst, amid, amidst, mid, midst; in the middle of; in the thick of; parenthetically.

232 Encircling

N. *encircling*, circumscription, enclosing 235 *enclosure*; encompassing, circle, balloon; ringing round, hedging round, fencing round; surrounding, framing, girdling; siege, blockade 712 *attack*; envelopment, encirclement, containment, confinement, limitation 747 *restriction*; ring 235 *fence*.

Vb. *encircle*, describe a circle, ring round, circle, circumscribe, encompass; envelop, close in, cut off, cordon off, rope off, mark off, invest, beleaguer, blockade, picket 712 *besiege*; beset, hem in, pen in; enclose, rail in, hedge in, fence in; box, cage, wall in, immure, cloister 747 *imprison*; frame 230 *surround*; encase, enfold, enshrine, edge, border 236 *limit*; clasp 889 *caress*, embrace.

233 Outline

N. *outline*, circumference, perimeter, periphery; surround, frame, rim 234 *edge*; compass, circuit 250 *circle*; delineation, configuration, features 445 *feature*; profile, relief 239 *laterality*; silhouette, skyline, horizon 553 *picture*; sketch, rough sketch, draft 623 *plan*; figure, diagram, layout; trace, tracing; skeleton, framework 331 *structure*; contour, contour line, shape 243 *form*; coastline, bounds 236 *limit*.

Vb. *outline*, describe a circle 232 *encircle*; frame 230 *surround*; delineate, draw, silhouette, profile, trace 551 *represent*; etch 555 *engrave*; map, block out, rough out, sketch out, sketch; diagrammatize.

234 Edge

N. *edge*, verge, brim; tip, brink, skirt, fringe, margin 69 *extremity*; confines, bounds, boundary, frontier, border 236 *limit*; coast, beach, strand, seaside, seashore, water's edge, waterfront 344 *shore*; wharf, quay, dock 192 *stable*; sideline, side, brim, kerb *or* curb, wayside, roadside, bank 239 *laterality*; hedge 235 *fence*; lip, ledge, eave, cornice, rim, welt, flange 254 *projection*; horizon, skyline; knife edge, razor edge; sharpness, acrimony; advantage, upper hand.

threshold, sill, doorstep, door, portal, porch 263 *doorway*; mouth.

edging, frame 233 *outline*; selvedge; hem, border; binding, piping; fringe, frill, ruffle, flounce, furbelow, valance 844 *trimming*; scallop.

Adj. marginal, border, coastal; riverside, roadside, wayside; labial, edged, trimmed, bordered; borderline, peripheral.

Vb. hem, edge, lower edge, border, trim, piping, fringe; crenellate 260 *notch*; bound, confine 236 *limit*.

235 Enclosure

N. enclosure, envelope, case 194 *receptacle*; wrapper, packaging 226 *wrapping*; ring, perimeter, circumference, periphery 233 *outline*; surround, frame; cloister, courtyard 185 *place*; reserve 883 *seclusion*; lot, holding, claim 184 *territory*; fold, pen, sheepfold, sty 369 *cattle pen*; park 370 *garden*; compound, yard, pound, paddock, field; car park, parking lot 192 *stable*; corral, stockade, lines 713 *defences*; net, trawl 222 *network*; cell, cage 748 *prison*.

fence, ring fence, barbed-wire fence, razor-wire fence, electric fence 222 *network*; hurdle, wooden fence, picket fence, sunk fence, ha-ha, hedge, privet hedge, quickset hedge, hedgerow, espalier; rails, balustrade, banisters, paling, railing; pale, wall, boundary wall; moat, dike, ditch, fosse, trench 713 *defences*.

barrier, wall, cavity wall, brick wall, drystone wall 231 *partition*; fence, ring fence 46 *separation*; buffer zone, cordon sanitaire; soundproofing, double-glazing, damp-proofing 660 *protection*; barricade, cordon, pale; balustrade, parapet; turnstile 702 *obstacle*; palisade, stockade 713 *fort*; portcullis, gate, door, bolt, bar, padlock 264 *closure*.

Vb. enclose, fence in, cordon off, rope off, surround, wall; pen, hem, ring, corral, ring-fence 232 *encircle*; cloister, immure, wall up, confine, cage 747 *imprison*; wrap, enfold 261 *fold*; hug, embrace, cuddle 889 *caress*; frame.

236 Limit

N. limit, limitation, constraint 747 *restriction*, 468 *qualification*; delimitation, demarcation 783 *allocation*; parameter, upper limit, ceiling, high-water mark 213 *summit*; ceiling, glass ceiling 481 *prejudice*, 747 *restriction*; lower limit, threshold 214 *base*; legal limit, Plimsoll line; saturation point 54 *completeness*; utmost, uttermost, extreme, ne plus ultra, pole 69 *extremity*; ends of the earth; terminus, terminal 69 *end*; goal, target, winning post, touch, touch-line, home, base 617 *objective*; turning point, watershed 137 *crisis*; point of no return 599 *resolution*; line in the sand, Rubicon; threshold of pain, tolerance, capacity, end of one's tether; outside edge, perimeter, periphery, circumference 233 *outline*; tidemark, sea line 344 *shore*; landmark, boundary stone; milestone 27 *degree*; kerb *or* curb, kerbstone 624 *road*; boundary, verge; frontier, border, marches 234 *edge*; demarcation line, international date line, divide, parting 231 *partition*; skyline, horizon, equator, deadline, time limit, term 110 *period*; ultimatum 900 *threat*; speed limit 278 *slowness*; sound barrier.

Vb. limit, bound, border, edge 234 *hem*; top 213 *crown*; confine; restrict 747 *restrain*; encompass 232 *encircle*; delimit, demarcate; rope off, mark out 547 *mark*.

237 Front

N. front, fore, forefront 64 *precedence*; prefix, frontispiece, preface, foreword, front matter; forelock 259 *hair*; forecourt, anteroom, entrance, hall 263 *doorway*; foreground 200 *nearness*; front rank, front line; leading edge; forward line, centre forward; avant-garde, vanguard, advance guard; spearhead; outpost, scout, reconnaissance party; forerunner, pioneer 66 *precursor*; prequel.

face, frontage, façade, fascia; face of a coin, obverse, head; right side, outer side, recto; front view, front elevation; physiognomy, features, visage, countenance, phiz, phizog, mug, mush, dial, clock 445 *feature*.

Adj. frontal, fore, forward, front, obverse; full frontal, head-on, oncoming, facing 240 *opposite*; anterior, prefixed 64 *preceding*.

Vb. be in front, stand in front, etc. (see adv.); front, confront, face, eyeball, face up to 240 *be opposite*; breast; come to the fore, forge ahead, take the lead, head 283 *precede*.

Adv. in front, before, in advance, in the lead, in the van; ahead, ahead of one's time, further on 199 *beyond*; far ahead, before one's eyes; face to face, eyeball to eyeball, man to man, in the foreground, in the forefront, in the limelight.

238 Rear

N. rear, back end, rear end, tail end, stern 69 *extremity*; tailpiece, heel, colophon; coda 412 *musical piece*; tail, brush, scut 67 *sequel*; parson's nose; wake, train 67 *retinue*; booby prize, wooden spoon, back seat 35 *inferiority*; rear-guard 67 *successor*; background, backdrop 594 *stage set*; hinterland, far corner 199 *distance*; behind, backstage, back side; reverse side, wrong side, verso 240 *oppositeness*; reverse, other side, flip side, B-side; back door, back entrance, tradesmen's entrance, postern 263 *doorway*; back (of the body), dorsum; spine 218 *prop*; back of the neck, scruff of the neck, nape; back of the head.

buttocks, backside, behind, rear end, der-rière, posterior; bottom, btm, seat, sit-upon; bum, arse (vulg), ass, butt, booty, fanny; build-er's bum, butt crack; rear, stern, tail; hindquar-ters; hips, haunches, hams, hunkers; rump; lower back, coccyx; anus.

Adj. *back*, rear; posterior, after, hind, hinder, hindermost, rearmost, tail-end; back-swept 253 *convex*; reverse 240 *opposite*; placed last 35 *inferior*; spinal, vertebral, dorsal, lum-bar; anal; caudal, caudate.

Vb. *be behind*, back on, back; back up 703 *aid*; follow, bring up the rear 65 *come after*; lag, trail, drop behind 278 *move slowly*; trail, tail, shadow, dog 619 *pursue*; follow at heel 284 *follow*; bend backwards 220 *be oblique*.

Adv. *rearward*, behind; in the rear, at the end; at the back, in the background; behind one's back; behind the scenes, offstage; after; aft, abaft, astern, aback; to the rear, hindward, backward, above; overleaf; hard on the heels of, at the back of, close behind; one behind the other, back to back.

239 Laterality

N. *laterality*, sidedness, handedness 241 *right-handedness*, 242 *left-handedness*; side move-ment 317 *oscillation*; sidestep 282 *deviation*; sideline, side, bank 234 *edge*; coast 344 *shore*; siding, side entrance, side door; broadside; beam; quarter; flank, ribs; wing, fin, arm, hand; cheek, jowl; gills; side whiskers 259 *hair*; temples; profile, side elevation; lee side, lee-ward; windward 281 *direction*; off side, on side, near side.

Adj. *lateral*, side 234 *marginal*; sidelong; winglike; flanking, skirting; flanked, sided; manysided, multilateral, unilateral, bilateral, trilateral, quadrilateral; collateral; edging, sidling.

Vb. *flank*, side, edge, skirt, border 234 *hem*; coast, move sideways, sidle; side-step 282 *deviate*.

Adv. *sideways*, crabwise, laterally; askance, asquint; in profile, sideways on; sidelong; broadside on; aside; side by side, cheek by jowl 200 *near*.

240 Oppositeness

N. *oppositeness*, opposition, contraposition, antithesis, antipodes 14 *contrariety*; opposite side, other side, other side of the fence; reverse, back 238 *rear*; polarity, polarization; opposite poles, poles apart, North and South; crosscurrent, headwind 704 *opposition*; reversal, inverse 221 *inversion*.

Adj. *opposite*, contrapositive, reverse, inverse; contrary 14 *non-identical*; facing, face to face, vis-à-vis, eyeball to eyeball, man to man, confronting 237 *frontal*; diametrically opposed, antipodean, antithetical; polarized, polar.

Vb. *be opposite*, be facing, etc. (see adj.); stand opposite, lie opposite; subtend; face, confront 237 *be in front*; run counter 182 *coun-teract*; oppose, contrapose.

Adv. *against*, poles apart; facing, face to face, eyeball to eyeball, man to man, vis-à-vis; back to back; on the other side, on the other side of the fence, overleaf; contrariwise, vice versa.

241 Right-handedness

N. *right-handedness*, dextrality, right hand; ambidextrousness 694 *skill*; right, offside, star-board; right-hand page, recto; right wing, right-winger; dextral, ambidexter.

242 Left-handedness

N. *left-handedness*, cack-handedness, sinistral-ity, left hand; left, near side, on side; larboard, port; left-hand page, verso; left wing, left-winger; sinistral, southpaw.

SECTION THREE

Form

243 Form

N. *form*, idea; essence 3 *substance*; art form 551 *art*, 593 *verse form*; word form; shape, turn, lines, architecture; formation, conforma-tion, configuration, fashion, style, trend, design 331 *structure*; contour, silhouette, relief, profile, frame, outline; figure, cut, set, trim, build, cut of one's jib, lineament 445 *feature*; physiognomy 237 *face*; look, expression, appearance 445 *mien*; posture, attitude, stance, asana; get-up, turnout, rig, gear; type, kind, pattern, stamp, cast, mould, blank 23 *proto-type*; format; morphology.

formation, forming, shaping, creation 164 *production*; formulation 62 *arrangement*; design-ing 844 *ornamental art*; weaving, knitting 222 *network*; tailoring 844 *needlework*; throwing 381 *pottery*; moulding 554 *sculpture*; joinery 694 *skill*; word-formation.

Adj. *formed*, created, etc. (see vb.); sculp-tured, carved, moulded, thrown, turned;

shaped, fashioned, fully fashioned, styled; designer, tailor-made, custom-built; ready-made, off the peg; matured, ready 669 *prepared*; solid, concrete 324 *dense*.

Vb. *form*, create, make 164 *produce*; formalize, shape, fashion; throw (pots), blow (glass); turn; cut, tailor; cut out, silhouette 233 *outline*; sketch, draft, draw 551 *represent*; model, carve, whittle, chisel 554 *sculpt*; hew, rough-hew 46 *cut*; mould, cast; stamp, coin, mint; hammer out, block out, punch out; forge; knead, work, work up into; construct, build, frame 310 *elevate*; express, put into words, verbalize, formulate, put into shape, lick into shape, knock into shape.

244 Absence of form

N. *formlessness*, amorphism; chaos 61 *disorder*; amorphousness, shapelessness; vagueness, fuzziness; uncouthness 670 undevelopment; raw material 631 *materials*; rough diamond; disfigurement, defacement, deformity 246 *distortion*.

Adj. *formless*, amorphous, unformed, unstructured, structureless; liquid 335 *fluid*; shapeless, characterless; chaotic; undefined, ill-defined, indistinct, nondescript, nebulous, vague, fuzzy, blurred 419 *shadowy*; unformed; embryonic 68 *beginning*; raw, callow 670 *immature*; unhewn 55 *incomplete*; rude, uncouth, barbaric 699 *artless*; rugged 259 *rough*; unshapely 842 *unsightly*; malformed, misshapen 246 *deformed*.

Vb. *deform*, deprive of form 165 *destroy*; melt 337 *liquefy*; knock out of shape, batter 46 *break*; grind, pulp 332 *grind*; warp, twist 246 *distort*; deface, disfigure 842 *make ugly*; mutilate 655 *impair*; jumble 63 *disarrange*.

245 Symmetry: regularity of form

N. *symmetry*, proportion 12 *correlation*; balance 28 *equilibrium*; regularity, evenness 16 *uniformity*; branching, ramification 219 *parallelism*; shapeliness, regular features, classic features 841 *beauty*; harmony, congruity 24 *agreement*; rhythm 141 *periodic recurrence*; finish 646 *perfection*.

Adj. *symmetrical*, balanced, well-balanced 28 *equal*; proportioned, well-proportioned 12 *correlative*; rhythmical, harmonious, congruous 24 *agreeing*; congruent; corresponding; analogous 18 *similar*; smooth, even 16 *uniform*; squared, rounded; even-sided, isosceles, equilateral 81 *regular*; arborescent.

246 Distortion: irregularity of form

N. *distortion*, asymmetry, disproportion, disproportionateness 10 *unrelatedness*; fractal;

imbalance, disequilibrium 29 *in equality*; lopsidedness, crookedness, skewness 220 *obliqueness*; projection 551 *map*; contortion, twisting; thrust, stress, strain, shear; bias, warp; buckle, bend, screw, twist 251 *convolution*; grimace, moue, snarl 547 *gesture*.

deformity, malformation, disfigurement, monstrosity, mutation, abortion 84 *abnormality*; curvature of the spine 248 *curvature*; club-foot, knock knees, bow legs, rickets, hunchback 845 *blemish*; ugliness 842 *eyesore*; teratology.

Adj. *distorted*, contorted, etc. (see vb.); irregular, asymmetric, scalene, unsymmetrical, disproportionate 17 *non-uniform*; weighted, biased; not true, not straight; out of shape, warped, mutative 244 *formless*; mangled, buckled, twisted, gnarled 251 *convoluted*; wry, awry, askew, crazy, crooked, cock-eyed, on one side; grimacing.

deformed, ugly 842 *unsightly*; ill-proportioned; defective 647 *imperfect*; mutative, ill-made, malformed, misshapen; hunchbacked, bandy-legged, bowlegged, knock-kneed; pigeon-toed, splay-footed, club-footed, web-footed; round-shouldered, pigeon-chested; hare-lipped; stunted 204 *short*.

Vb. *distort*, weight, bias; contort, screw, twist, knot 251 *twine*; bend, warp 251 *crinkle*; buckle, crumple; strain, sprain, skew, wrest, rack 63 *disarrange*; misshape, botch 244 *deform*; mangle, batter, knock out of shape 655 *impair*; pervert, slant, spin, twist, sex up 552 *misrepresent*; misconstrue 521 *misinterpret*; grimace 547 *gesticulate*; frown.

247 Angularity

N. *angularity*, crotchet, bracket, crook, hook; bend, scythe, sickle, scimitar 248 *curvature*; chevron, zigzag 220 *obliqueness*; V-shape, elbow, knee; withers 253 *camber*; knuckle, ankle, groin 45 *joint*; crotch 222 *cross*; fork, branching 222 *crossing*; corner, cranny, nook, niche, recess 194 *compartment*; nose, Roman nose, hook nose 254 *protuberance*; flexure 261 *fold*; indentation 260 *notch*.

angle, right angle, acute angle, obtuse angle, salient angle, solid angle.

angular measure, trigonometry, altimetry; angular elevation, angular distance; zenith distance; second, degree, minute; radian; altimeter; clinometer, level, theodolite; transit circle; sextant, quadrant; protractor, set square.

angular figure, triangle, isosceles triangle, equilateral triangle, scalene triangle; parallelogram, rectangle, square, quadrangle; quadrilateral, diamond; rhomb; trapezium, tetragon, polygon, pentagon, hexagon, heptagon, octagon, nonagon, decagon, dodecahedron, icosahedron; cube, pyramid, wedge; prism.

Adj. *angular*, hooked, Roman-nosed, aquiline; angled, sharp-angled, cornered; staggered, crooked, zigzag; jagged, serrated, crinkled; bony, jointed; akimbo; knock-kneed; forked, bifurcate, V-shaped.

248 Curvature

N. *curvature*, curvation; inward curve 255 *concavity*; outward curve 253 *convexity*; flexure, inflexion, bending 261 *fold*; stooping 311 *bow*; bending down; turning away, swerve, detour 282 *deviation*; downward bend 309 *descent*; curliness, sinuosity 251 *convolution*; curvature of the spine 246 *deformity*.

***curve*,** elbow 247 *angularity*; corner, turn, bend, Z-bend, hairpin bend, U-turn; horseshoe; bay, bight 345 *gulf*; figure of eight 250 *loop*; S-shape; curl 251 *convolution*; bow, Cupid's bow, rainbow 250 *arc*; arch, ogee arch, arcade, vault 253 *dome*; sickle, scimitar, crescent, half-moon, lens; trajectory, parabola, hyperbola, conic section; cone biopsy; arch (of the foot), instep; swan neck; Peyronie's disease.

Adj. *curved*, cambered, etc. (see vb.); bent; bowed, stooping; bowlike, curvilinear; rounded, curvaceous, curvy, bosomy, busty, wavy, billowy 251 *undulatory*; aquiline, hook-nosed 247 *angular*; beaked, beaklike; bent back, retroussé, turned-up; circumflex, ogival, vaulted 253 *arched*; bow-legged, bandy-legged 246 *deformed*; hooked, semicircular 250 *round*; crescent, lunate, lunar; heart-shaped, bell-shaped, pear-shaped, hour-glass.

Vb. *be curved*, be bent, etc. (see adj.); curve, swerve, bend, loop, wind, arch, sweep, sag, give 217 *hang*; bend, crook; turn, round; bend in, bend back, bend over, bend down, bow, incline 311 *stoop*; turn over 261 *fold*; turn away 282 *deflect*; arch; coil 251 *twine*; loop, curl, kink, wave, perm 251 *crinkle*; loop the loop.

249 Straightness

N. *straightness*, directness; perpendicularity 215 *verticality*; inflexibility, intransigence, rigidity 326 *hardness*; chord, radius, tangent 203 *line*; straight line, beeline; Roman road; straight stretch; short cut 200 *short distance*.

Adj. *straight*, direct, even, right, true; in a line, linear; straight-lined, rectilinear, rectilineal; perpendicular 215 *vertical*; stiff, inflexible 326 *rigid*; straightened, dead straight, undeviating, unswerving, undeflected, on the beam, straight as an arrow; straight as a die 929 *honourable*; not bent, heterosexual 83 *typical*.

Vb. *straighten*, align; iron out 216 *flatten*; unbend (a bow); uncross (legs), unfold (arms);

uncurl 258 *smooth*; uncoil, unroll, unfurl, unfold 316 *evolve*.

250 Circularity: simple circularity

N. *circularity*, roundness 252 *roundness*.

***circle*,** full circle, circumference 233 *outline*; equator; horizon, azimuth circle; orb; areola; plate, saucer; round, disc, disk, discus; coin, button, sequin; washer, ferrule, hoop, ring, bracelet, quoit; eye, iris; eyelet, loophole, keyhole 263 *aperture*; circuit, circus, roundabout; zodiac; fairy ring; smoke ring; crop circle.

***loop*,** figure of eight 251 *convolution*; bow; ringlet, curl, kink 259 *hair*; bracelet, armlet, torque 844 *finery*; crown, coronet 743 *regalia*; halo; wreath, garland 228 *headgear*; collar, neckband, necklace, choker 228 *neckwear*; band, cordon, sash, girdle, cummerbund 228 *belt*; lasso.

***wheel*,** pulley, castor 315 *rotator*; hub; tyre; spare tyre, radial tyre, roller 252 *roundness*; cogwheel 260 *notch*.

***arc*,** semicircle; half-moon, crescent, rainbow 248 *curve*; sector, quadrant, sextant; ellipse, oval; horizon, azimuth.

***orbit*,** cycle; circuit; circulation 314 *circuitous motion*.

Adj. *round*, rounded, circular, cyclic, discoid; orbicular, ringlike, annular; semicircular, hemicyclic; oval; elliptic, ovoid, egg-shaped, crescent-shaped, pear-shaped 248 *curved*; cycloidal, spherical 252 *rotund*.

251 Convolution: complex circularity

N. *convolution*, involution, circumvolution; intricacy; sinuosity, sinuousness; tortuosity, tortuousness, reticulation 222 *network*; twist 208 *fibre*; ripple 350 *wave*; kink, wrinkle, corrugation 261 *fold*; indentation, scallop 260 *notch*; waviness, undulation, ogee 248 *curve*.

***coil*,** roll, twist; turban 228 *headgear*; spiral, helix; screw, worm, corkscrew; spring, coiled spring; intrauterine device 172 *contraception*; whorl, snailshell, whirlpool 315 *whirl*, 350 *eddy*; tendril 366 *plant*; scalloped edge 234 *edging*; kink, curl; ringlet, lovelock 259 *hair*; scroll, flourish, twirl, curlicue, squiggle 844 *ornamentation*.

***meandering*,** winding, twists and turns 282 *deviation*; labyrinth, maze 61 *complexity*; switchback, zigzag 220 *obliqueness*.

***serpent*,** snake, eel, worm 365 *reptile*; wriggler.

Adj. *convoluted*, twisted, contorted 246 *distorted*; cranky; winding, looping, twining, sinuous, tortuous, indented, ragged; crumpled, buckled.

snaky, serpentine, eel-like, wormlike, vermiform, undulating, curvy, sinuous, S-shaped; squirming, wriggling.

undulatory, undulating, rolling, heaving; up-and-down, switchback, wavy, curly, frizzy, kinky, crinkly; crimped, curled, permed; scalloped, wrinkled, corrugated, indented.

coiled, spiral, helical, cochlear; convolute, involute, turbinate, whorled, coiling, spiralling.

intricate, involved, complicated, knotted 61 *complex*.

Vb. *twine*, twist, twirl, roll, coil, spiral 315 *rotate*; entwine; be convoluted, be twisted, etc. (see adj.); turn and twist, bend 248 *be curved*.

meander, loop, snake, twist and turn, zigzag, corkscrew.

crinkle, crimp, frizz, perm, curl; wave, undulate, ripple, wrinkle, corrugate 261 *fold*; indent 260 *notch*; crumple 246 *distort*.

wriggle, writhe, squirm, shimmy, shake; worm.

252 Roundness

N. *roundness*, rotundity 250 *circularity*; sphericality, globularity, cylindricality.

sphere, globe, spheroid, ellipsoid, globoid, bladder; balloon 276 *airship*; soap bubble 355 *bubble*; ball, football, pelota, billiard ball, marble; crystal ball; cannonball, bullet, shot, pellet; bead, pearl, pill, pea, boll, globule; drop, droplet, dewdrop, blot; vesicle, bulb, onion, knob, pommel 253 *swelling*; boulder; round head.

cylinder, roll; roller, rolling pin; round, rung; round tower, martello tower, column; trunk, stalk, stem; pipe, drainpipe 263 *tube*; funnel, chimneypot; hat box, pillbox; drum, barrel, cask.

cone, conoid; penumbra; cornet, horn 194 *cup*; top, spinning top; pear shape.

Adj. *rotund* 250 *round*; spherical, globular, global; round-headed, bullet-headed, beadlike, hemispherical; spheroidal, ovoid, egg-shaped; pot-bellied 195 *fat*.

253 Convexity

N. *convexity*, convexness; arching 248 *curvature*; sphericality 252 *roundness*; bulginess, lumpiness, humpiness, bulge, bump, lump; projection, protrusion, protuberance 254 *prominence*; tumescence, swelling 197 *distension*; pot-belliedness 195 *bulk*; pimpliness, wartiness.

swelling, bump, lump, bulge, growth, excrescence, gall, knot, node, nodule; knuckle; oedema, emphysema; intumescence, tumescence, etc. 197 *distension*; tumour, sarcoma, neoplasm, carcinoma 651 *cancer*; goitre; Adam's

apple; bunion, corn, wart, verruca; cyst, sebaceous cyst, boil, carbuncle, stye, pimple, blister, vesicle; polyp, adenoids, haemorrhoids, piles; proud flesh, weal, welt; cauliflower ear; drop 252 *sphere*; air bubble 355 *bubble*; knob; bulb, button, bud; belly, potbelly, paunch 195 *bulk*; billow, swell 350 *wave*.

bosom, bust, breasts; boobs, bristols, knockers, tits; breast, areola, nipple, pap, dug, teat, mamma, mamilla, papilla, udder; thorax, chest; silicone implant, breast enlargement, breast reduction; breast-feeding; breast cancer, mammogram, mastectomy, lumpectomy; breastplate.

dome, cupola, vault 226 *roof*; beehive; brow, forehead 237 *face*; skull 213 *head*; hemisphere, mound; hillock, molehill, anthill, mushroom, umbrella.

earthwork, tumulus; barrow, hill fort 713 *defences*; embankment.

camber 248 *curve*; arch, bow, rainbow; hump, humpback 246 *deformity*.

Adj. *convex*, protruding 254 *projecting*; hemispheric, domelike 252 *rotund*; lentiform, lenticular; humpy, lumpy, bumpy; curvaceous, bosomy, busty, billowy 248 *curved*; bulging, bouffant; swelling, swollen; bloated, potbellied, barrel-chested 195 *fat*; turgid, tumid, tumescent, tumorous, tuberous; nubbly 259 *rough*; warty, pimply, spotty, acned; blistery, vesicular.

arched, cambered, bowed 248 *curved*; rounded.

254 Prominence

N. *prominence*, eminence 209 *high land*; conspicuousness 443 *visibility*.

projection, salient; outstretched arm, forefinger, index finger; bowsprit; tongue of land, point, mull, promontory, foreland, headland, ness 344 *land*; peninsula 349 *island*; spur, foothill; jetty, breakwater, pier 662 *shelter*; outwork 713 *fortification*; buttress 218 *prop*; shelf, sill, ledge, balcony; eaves 226 *roof*; overhang 220 *obliqueness*; lip 234 *edge*; nozzle, spout; tongue; tenon 45 *joint*; stump, outcrop; landmark 209 *high structure*.

protuberance, bump 253 *swelling*; nose, aquiline nose, Roman nose, snout, schnozz, schnozzle, conk, hooter; neb, pecker, bill, beak, rostrum; muzzle, proboscis, trunk; antenna 378 *feeler*; chin, double chin, jaw, forehead, brow, beetle brow 237 *face*; figurehead; horn, antler 256 *sharp point*.

Adj. *projecting*, jutting, prominent, salient, bold; protuberant, protruding, bulging, popping, etc. (see vb.); bug-eyed, goggle-eyed, pop-eyed, with eyes out on stalks; toothy;

beetle-browed; raised, embossed, in relief, ridged, nobbly 259 *rough*.

Vb. jut, jut out, project, protrude, pout, pop, pop out; stand out, stick out, stick out like a sore thumb, hang out 443 *be visible*; prick up, cock up 259 *roughen*; shoot up, swell up 197 *expand*; overhang 217 *hang*.

255 Concavity

N. concavity, concaveness 248 *curvature*; hollowness 190 *emptiness*; depression, dint, dimple, dent; impression, stamp, imprint, footprint 548 *trace*; intaglio 555 *engraving*; furrowing 262 *furrow*; indentation 260 *notch*; gap, lacuna 201 *interval*.

cavity, hollow, niche, nook, cranny 194 *compartment*; hole, den, burrow, warren; chasm, abyss 211 *depth*; cave, cavern; grotto, alcove 194 *arbour*; bowl, cup, saucer, basin, trough 194 *vessel*; saltcellar; sump 649 *sink*; cell, follicle, pore 263 *aperture*; dimple, pockmark, orange peel; armpit; honeycomb, sponge 263 *porousness*; funnel, tunnel 263 *tube*; groove, socket 262 *furrow*; sinus; bay, bight, cove, creek, inlet 345 *gulf*; channel, ditch, moat, canal 351 *water channel*; shaft, dip, depression, pothole, crater, pit; saltpan.

valley, vale, dell, dingle, corrie, strath; glen, dip, depression, ravine, gorge, canyon, gully 201 *gap*.

excavation, dugout, grave, gravepit 364 *tomb*; opencast mining; shaft, bore-hole, well, mine, diamond mine, salt-mine, coal mine, pit, coal pit, colliery, shale mine, quarry 632 *store*; trench, burrow, warren; underground railway, tube 263 *tunnel*; archaeological excavation, dig; cutting.

excavator, digger; JCB (tdmk); miner, mining engineer, etc. 686 *artisan*; navvy; archaeologist; spade, fork, etc. 370 *farm and garden tools*; pick, pickaxe, etc. 256 *sharp point*.

Adj. concave, hollow, cavernous; vaulted, arched 248 *curved*; hollowed out, dug out; caved in; depressed, sunk, sunken; spoonlike; cup-shaped; funnel-shaped; bell-shaped; cellular, dented, dimpled, pockmarked; full of holes, pincushion-like, honeycombed; spongy, porous.

Vb. make concave, depress, press in, stamp, impress, buckle, dent, dint, stave in; crush, push in, beat in; excavate, hollow, dig, canalize 262 *groove*; mine, undermine, burrow, tunnel, bore; perforate 263 *pierce*; scoop out, hollow out, dig out 300 *eject*; pockmark; indent 260 *notch*.

256 Sharpness

N. sharpness, acuity, acuteness, pointedness, sting; serration 260 *notch*; thorniness, prickliness; acridity 388 *pungency*.

sharp point, sting, thorn, prick, point, cusp 213 *apex*; nail, tack, drawing pin, staple 47 *fastening*; nib, tag, pin, needle, knitting-needle, stylus, bodkin, skewer, spit; awl, gimlet, drill, auger 263 *piercer*, 630 *tool*; arrow, shaft, bolt, arrowhead; barb, swordpoint, rapier, lance, pike 723 *spear*; gaff, harpoon; dagger, dirk, stiletto 723 *side arms*; spike, barbed wire, razor wire 713 *defences*; spur; goad 612 *incentive*; fork, prong, tine, pick, horn, antler; claw, talon, nails 778 *pincers*; spire, steeple; peak 213 *summit*.

prickle, thorn, brier, bramble, gorse, whin, thistle, nettle, cactus; bristle 259 *hair*; beard; spine, needle, quill; hedgehog, porcupine, echidna *or* spiny anteater; stickleback, sea urchin.

tooth, tusk, fang; milk tooth; canine tooth, eyetooth, incisor, grinder, molar, wisdom tooth; dentition, front tooth, back tooth, set of teeth, denture, false teeth, gold teeth, plate, bridge; dentist, dental nurse, etc. 658 *doctor*, *dentistry*, *nurse*; comb; saw, hacksaw, etc. 260 *notch*; cog, ratchet, sprocket.

sharp edge, cutting edge; jagged edge, broken glass, razor wire; cutlery, steel; razor, blade, razor blade; ploughshare, spade, mattock, trowel, shovel; scythe, sickle, hook, billhook 370 *farm and garden tools*; cutter, lawn mower; scissors, shears, clippers, secateurs, pruners, scalpel; chisel, cold chisel; plane, scraper 258 *smoother*; knife, bread-knife, kitchen-knife, cook's knife, carving knife, fish knife, fish slice, cake knife, cake slice, penknife, pocketknife, flick-knife, sheath knife, jack knife, hunting knife, bowie knife, Stanley (tdmk) knife; machete; chopper, cleaver, wedge; hatchet, axe, adze; battleaxe 723 *axe*; sword, broadsword, cutlass, scimitar 723 *side arms*.

Adj. sharp, stinging, keen, acute; edged, cutting; swordlike; pointed; sharp-pointed, barbed; spiky, spiny, spinose, thorny, thistly; needlelike, needle-sharp, acicular; prickly, bristly; spear-like, bayonet-like; craggy, jagged 259 *rough*; comblike, serrated; sharp-edged, knife-edged, razor-edged; sharp as a razor, sharp as a needle; sharpened, whetted, etc. (see vb.); razor-sharp.

toothed, toothy; tusky, fanged, dental, denticulate, dentiform; cogged, serrated, sawedged.

Vb. be sharp, be stinging, etc. (see adj.); have a point, prick, sting; bristle with; have an edge, bite, pierce 46 *cut*; taper, come to a point, end in a point 293 *converge*.

sharpen, edge, put an edge on, whet, hone, grind, file, strop; barb, point.

257 Bluntness

N. bluntness, obtuseness, flatness, bluffness; curves 258 *smoothness*; rustiness, dullness; toothlessness, toothless tiger, lack of bite; blunt instrument, foil; blunt edge, blade, flat.

Vb. blunt, make blunt; take off the point, bate (a foil); obtund, dull, rust; draw the teeth 161 *disable*; be blunt.

258 Smoothness

N. smoothness, evenness, etc. (see adj.); silkiness; silk, satin, velvet, velour; fleeciness, down, swansdown 327 *softness*; sleekness; baby's bottom; millpond; marble, glass, ice; dance floor, ice rink; flatness, levelness, lawn, bowling green, billiard table 216 *horizontality*; tarmac 226 *paving*; polish, wax, varnish, gloss, glaze, shine, finish; slipperiness, slipway, slide, chute; lubricity, oiliness, greasiness 334 *lubrication*; calm, dead calm 266 *state of rest*.

smoother, roller, garden roller, road roller, steamroller; bulldozer; rolling pin 216 *flattener*; iron, electric iron, smoothing-iron, flatiron; mangle, wringer; press, trouser press; plane 256 *sharp edge*; rake, harrow 370 *farm and garden tools*; card, comb, brush; sandpaper, glasspaper, emery paper, emery board; file, nail file; polish, French polish, varnish, enamel 226 *facing*; lubricator, grease, oil, grease gun, oilcan 334 *lubricant*.

Adj. smooth, streamlined; slippery; lubricious, oily, greasy, buttery, soapy; greased, oiled 334 *lubricated*; polished, shiny, gleaming, varnished, waxed, enamelled, lacquered, glazed; soft, suave, bland, soothing, silky, satiny, velvety; peachlike, downy, woolly; marble, glassy; bald 229 *hairless*; sleek, slick, brushed; combed, carded; rolled, even, level, flush 216 *flat*; glassy, calm, calm as a millpond 266 *still*; blunt; smooth-skinned; smooth-haired; smooth as glass *or* as a baby's bottom *or* as velvet, satin-smooth; slippery as an eel.

Vb. smooth, streamline; oil, grease 334 *lubricate*; smoothen, plane, even, level; rake, comb; file, rub down 333 *rub*; roll, calender, press, iron 216 *flatten*; mow, shave, cut 204 *shorten*; smooth over, slick down, plaster down; iron out; shine, burnish 417 *make bright*; buff, polish, glaze, wax, varnish 226 *coat*.

259 Roughness

N. roughness, asperity, harshness; broken ground; rough water, choppiness 350 *wave*; turbulence 352 *wind*; brokenness, jaggedness, broken glass, barbed wire, razor wire 256 *sharp*

edge; serration, saw edge, scalloped edge 260 *notch*; ruggedness, cragginess; sierra 209 *high land*; rough going, dirt road, dirt track; unevenness 17 *non-uniformity*; kink, corrugation, ripple, corrugated iron 261 *fold*; rut 262 *furrow*; coarseness, coarse grain 253 *convexity*; washboard, grater, file, sandpaper, glasspaper, emery paper, emery board; sackcloth, tweed, homespun 222 *textile*; gooseflesh, goose pimples; chap, hack, crack; shagginess; hairiness; stubble, five o'clock shadow, burr, bristle, scrubbing brush, nailbrush.

hair 208 *filament*; head of hair, shock of hair, matted hair, thatch, fuzz, wool; crop, mop, mane, fleece, shag; bristle, stubble, five o'clock shadow; locks, flowing locks; crowning glory, tresses, curls, ringlet; kiss curl; strand, plait, braid; pigtail, ponytail, bunches, rat's tails; topknot, forelock, lovelock, dread locks; fringe, bangs, cowlick, quiff, widow's peak; roll, French pleat, bun, chignon 843 *hairdressing*; false hair, hairpiece, hair extension, switch, wig, fright wig, toupee 228 *head-gear*; wisp; beard, full beard, beaver, goatee, imperial, Van Dyke, Abe Lincoln; whiskers, sideboards, sideburns, mutton-chops; moustache, moustachio, toothbrush, handlebars; facial hair, bumfluff; eyebrows, eyelashes; woolliness, fleeciness, downiness, fluffiness; down, pubic hair, wool, fur 226 *skin*; tuft, flock; mohair, cashmere, angora 208 *fibre*; fluff, fuzz; horsehair 227 *lining*.

plumage, feathering; quill, feathers; neck feathers, hackle, ruff, frill, plume, crest; peacock feathers, ostrich feathers 844 *finery*.

Adj. rough, irregular, uneven; rippling, choppy, storm-tossed; stony, rocky, rutted, pitted, potholed, bumpy; roughcast; lumpy, stony, nodular, studded, roughened, frosted; nubbly, slubbed, bouclé; crinkled 251 *undulatory*; knotted, gnarled, coarse-grained, coarse; cracked, hacked, chapped; lined, wrinkled, corrugated, ridged; rough-edged; craggy, jagged; scabby, pockmarked, acned, warty, scaly, blistered; ruffled, unkempt, unpolished; unsifted.

hairy, woolly, fleecy, furry; hirsute, shaggy, matted; bristly 256 *sharp*; wispy, straggly, fringed, bearded, moustached; unshaven, unshorn; curly, frizzy, fuzzy, permed, woolly.

Vb. be rough, be hairy, etc. (see adj.); bristle 254 *jut*; creep (of flesh); scratch; jolt, bump, jerk 278 *move slowly*.

roughen, roughcast, rough-hew; serrate, indent 260 *notch*; stud, boss; corrugate, wrinkle, ripple, kink 251 *crinkle*; disorder, ruffle, tousle, tangle 63 *disarrange*; rumple, crumple, crease 261 *fold*; rub up the wrong way, set on edge; chap, crack, hack.

260 Notch

N. *notch*, serration, ragged edge 256 *sharpness*; indentation, deckle edge; battlement, crenellation 713 *fortification*; nick, snip, cut, gash, crenation 201 *gap*; indent, dent, dint, dimple 255 *concavity*; scallop, dogtooth 844 *pattern*; comb; sprocket, cog, ratchet, cogwheel; saw, bow saw, fretsaw, hacksaw, jigsaw, tenon saw, band saw, chain saw, circular saw, cross-cut saw, pit saw.

Vb. *notch*, serrate, tooth, cog; nick, score, scratch, scarify, bite, slice 46 *cut*; crenellate, indent, scallop, jag, pink, slash; dent, knurl 259 *roughen*; pinch, snip, crimp 261 *fold*.

261 Fold

N. *fold*, flexure, doubling; facing, revers, hem; lapel, cuff, turn-up; plait, braid, ply, pleat, box pleat, accordion pleat, knife-edge pleat; tuck, gather, pucker, ruche, ruffle; flounce, frill; ruff, jabot; wrinkle, ruck; frown, lines, wrinkles, age zones, crow's feet 131 *age*; joint.

Vb. *fold*, double, turn over, bend over, roll; corrugate, furrow, wrinkle 262 *groove*; pucker; ruffle, gather, frill, ruck, shirr, smock; hem; cuff; turn up; enfold, wrap, swathe 235 *enclose*; fold up, furl.

262 Furrow

N. *furrow*, groove, slot, slit, rabbet, mortise; crack, split, chink, cranny 201 *gap*; trough, hollow 255 *cavity*; flute, fluting, goffering; chamfer, bezel, incision, gash, slash, scratch, score 46 *splitting*; streak, striation 437 *stripe*; rut 548 *trace*; gutter, ditch, dike, trench, dugout, moat, channel 351 *water channel*; ravine 255 *valley*; wrinkle, corrugation; corduroy, corrugated iron, washboard, ploughed field; ripple.

Vb. *groove*, slot, flute, chamfer; gash, scratch, score, incise 46 *cut*; claw, tear 655 *wound*; striate, streak 437 *variegate*; carve, bite in, etch 555 *engrave*; furrow, plough, channel, rut, wrinkle, line; corrugate, goffer 261 *fold*.

263 Opening

N. *opening*, throwing open, openness, glasnost; uncorking, uncapping 229 *uncovering*; yawn, yawning, splitting; gaping; hiatus, lacuna, space, interval 201 *gap*; aperture (see also *aperture* below); split, crack, leak 46 *disunion*; hole, potato; hollow 255 *cavity*; placket.

perforation, piercing, body-piercing, tattooing; puncture, acupuncture; pinhole, eyelet.

porousness, porosity, sponge; sieve, sifter, riddle, screen 62 *sorting*; strainer, tea strainer, colander; grater; honeycomb, pincushion; filter, filter paper 648 *cleaning utensil*.

aperture, orifice, slot; oral cavity, mouth, gob, trap, kisser, mush, moosh, jaws, muzzle; throat, gullet 194 *stomach*; sucker; vagina, anus; flue pipe 353 *air pipe*; nozzle, spout, vent, vent-hole 298 *outlet*; blowhole, air-hole; nostril; rivermouth, pore; hole, crater, pothole 255 *cavity*; manhole, armhole, keyhole, buttonhole, punch hole, pin hole; pigeonhole 194 *compartment*; eye, eye of a needle, eyelet; ring 250 *loop*.

window, fenestration; shop window, plate-glass window, glass front; embrasure 713 *fortification*; lattice, grille; casement window, leaded window, sash window, bay window, oriel window, dormer window, French window, picture window; stained-glass window, rose window, lancet window 990 *church interior*; light, fanlight, skylight, sunshine roof; companion, cabin window, port, porthole; peephole, keyhole; car window, windscreen, windshield (US); window frame, casement, sash, mullion, transom; window pane 422 *transparency*; throwing through a window: defenestration.

doorway, archway; doorstep, threshold 68 *entrance*; approach, drive, driveway, entry 297 *way in*; exit, way out; passage, corridor, gangway, drawbridge 624 *access*; gate, gateway; portal, porch; door, front door, Dutch door; swing doors, revolving doors, double doors; church door, lychgate; back door, tradesmen's door, tradesmen's entrance; postern 238 *rear*; small door, wicket; cat-flap; hatch, hatchway; trapdoor, companionway; stairwell; door jamb, gatepost, lintel; concierge 264 *doorkeeper*, entryphone.

open space 183 *space*; yard, court 185 *place*; opening, clearing, glade; panorama, vista 438 *view*; landscape, open country 348 *plain*.

tunnel, boring; subway, underpass, underground railway, underground, tube, metro; Channel Tunnel, chunnel; mine, shaft, pit, gallery, adit 255 *excavation*; cave 255 *cavity*; bolthole, rabbit hole, fox hole, mouse hole 192 *dwelling*; funnel 252 *cone*; sewer 351 *drain*; qanat.

tube, pipe, duct 351 *water channel*; tubule, pipette, cannula; catheter, tubing, piping, pipeline, hose; artery, vein, jugular vein, capillary; colon, gut 224 *insides*; funnel, fistula; cigarette holder.

opener, key, master key, skeleton key; doorknob, handle; corkscrew, tin opener, can opener, bottle opener; aperient, purgative; password, open sesame; passport.

piercer, perforator, borer, corer; gimlet, corkscrew; auger, drill, pneumatic drill, bit, brace and bit 630 *tool*; trepan; probe, lancet, lance, bodkin, needle, hypodermic needle; awl, brad-awl 256 *sharp point*; pin, nail 47 *fastening*; skewer, spit, broach, stiletto 723 *weapon*; punch, card punch, stapler; dibble or dibber 370 *farm and garden tools*; pickaxe, mattock, pick, ice pick.

Adj. open, exposed to view, on view 522 *manifest*; uncapped, uncorked, ajar, unbolted, unlocked, unbarred, unobstructed 289 *accessible*; open-plan; wide-open, gaping; yawning, open-mouthed, gaping; opening, aperient; in bloom, out.

porous, permeable, spongy, percolating, leachy, leaky, leaking.

Vb. open, declare open, give the open sesame, give a passport to, unfold, unwrap, unpack, unpackage, undo, unlock, unlatch, unbolt, open the door, fling wide the gates 299 *admit*; uncover, bare; unplug, unstop, uncap, uncork; lay open, throw open 522 *show*; force open 176 *force*; cut open, tear open, crack open; fly open, split, gape, yawn; burst, explode; open out, fan open, deploy 75 *be dispersed*; unclench, bloom, be out.

pierce, transfix, impale; gore, run through, stick, pink, lance, bayonet, spear 655 *wound*; spike, skewer, spit; prick, puncture, tattoo, body-pierce; probe, stab, poke; inject; perforate, hole, riddle, pepper, honeycomb; knock holes in, punch, punch full of holes; bore, drill, trepan; burrow, tunnel, mine 255 *make concave*; cut through, penetrate 297 *enter*.

Adv. openly, blatantly, brazenly, flagrantly, freely, publicly, unashamedly, unreservedly; in public, in full view; unguardedly, out in the open; bluntly, candidly, frankly, honestly, plainly, straight, straight from the shoulder.

264 Closure

N. closure, closing, closing down, shutting, etc. (see vb.); occlusion, stoppage; contraction, strangulation 198 *compression*; sealing off, blockade 232 *encircling*, 235 *enclosure*; embolism, obstruction, infarction, constipation, strangury; dead end, cul-de-sac, impasse, blank wall, roadblock, rolling roadblock 702 *obstacle*; caecum.

stopper, cork, plug, bung, peg; ear plugs; ramrod, piston; valve; wedge, tampon; wadding, padding, stuffing 227 *lining*; gag, muzzle 748 *fetter*; shutter 421 *screen*; tourniquet; damper, choke; tap, faucet, stopcock, top, lid, cap, cover, seal 226 *covering*; lock, Yale (tdmk) lock, mortise lock, key, bolt, latch, bar 47 *fastening*.

doorkeeper, doorman, gatekeeper, porter, janitor, commissionaire, concierge; sentry, sentinel, night watchman 660 *protector*; warden,

guard, guard dog, vigilante 749 *keeper*; jailer, prison warder, turnkey 749 *gaoler*; Cerberus.

Adj. closed, shut, etc. (see vb.); unopened; shuttered, bolted, barred, locked; stoppered, corked, unpierced, non-porous, impervious, impermeable 324 *dense*; impenetrable, impassable 470 *impracticable*; dead-end; airtight, hermetic; clogged up, stuffed up, bunged up; strangulated.

Vb. close, shut, occlude, seal, hermetically seal; clinch, fix, bind, make tight 45 *tighten*; put the lid on, cap 226 *cover*; batten down the hatches; slam, bang (a door); lock, fasten, plug, bung up, cork, stopper, button, zip up, do up 45 *join*; knit, furrow, clench (fist); block, dam, staunch, choke, throttle, strangle, smother, asphyxiate 702 *obstruct*; blockade 712 *besiege*; enclose, surround, shut in, seal off 232 *encircle*; trap, bolt, latch, bar, lock in 747 *imprison*; shut down, clamp down, batten down, ram down, tamp down, put up the shutters; close down, go out of business, flop, go bust, fail.

SECTION FOUR

Motion

265 Motion: successive change of place

N. motion, movement, move, march; speed, acceleration, pace, tempo; locomotion, motility, mobility, movableness; kinetic energy, motive power; psychokinesis; forward motion, advance, progress, headway 285 *progression*; backward motion 286 *regression*, 290 *movement away*; motion towards 289 *approach*, 293 *convergence*; motion away, shift 282 *deviation*, 294 *divergence*; motion into 297 *entering*; motion out of 298 *going out*; upward motion, rising 308 *ascent*; downward motion, sinking, plummeting 309 *descent*, 313 *plunge*; motion round, circumnavigation 314 *circuitous motion*; axial motion 315 *rotation*, 316 *evolution*; to and fro movement, fluctuation 317 *oscillation*; irregular motion 318 *agitation*; stir, bustle, unrest, restlessness 678 *activity*; rapid motion 277 *velocity*; slow motion, slo-mo 278 *slowness*; regular motion 16 *uniformity*, 71 *continuity*; recurring movement, cycle, rhythm 141 *periodic recurrence*; motion in front 283 *preceding*; motion after 284 *following*, 619 *pursuit*; conduction, conductivity 272 *transference*; current, flow, flux, drift 350 *stream*; course, career, run; traffic, flow of traffic; transit 305 *passage*; transportation 272 *transport*; running, jogging, walking, foot-slogging, marathoning 267 *walking*; riding 267 *horse riding*; travel 267 *land travel*, 269 *water travel*, 271 *air travel*; dancing, tangoing, gliding, sliding, skating, rolling, skipping; manoeuvre, manoeuvring, footwork; exercise, aerobics, gymnastics 162 *athletics*; gesticulation 547 *gesture*; motion picture, film 445 *cinema*; laws of motion, kinetics, dynamics.

gait, walk, carriage 688 *conduct*; pace, step, stride; run, lope, jog; hop, skip, jump 312 *leap*; skid, slide, slip; waddle, shuffle; undulate, swagger, stalk, strut, goosestep 875 *formality*; march; trot, amble, canter, gallop 267 *horse riding*.

Adj. *moving*, rolling, etc. (see vb.); in motion, under way; motive, motor; motile, movable, mobile; progressive, regressive; locomotive, automotive; transitional, shifting; mercurial 152 *changing*; restless 678 *active*; nomadic; drifting, erratic, meandering, runaway; kinetic; cinematographic.

Vb. *be in motion*, move, go, hie, gang, wend, trail; budge, stir; flutter, wave, flap 217 *hang*; march, tramp 267 *walk*; tread; trip, dance 312 *leap*; shuffle, waddle 278 *move slowly*; toddle, patter; run, jog 277 *move fast*; run on wheels, roll, taxi; stream, roll on, drift 350 *flow*; paddle 269 *row*; skitter, slide, slither, skate, ski, sledge, toboggan, glide; fly, frisk, flit, dart, hover; climb 308 *ascend*; sink, plunge, plummet 309 *descend*; coast, cruise, steam, chug, proceed 146 *go on*; make one's way, push one's way, elbow one's way, shoulder one's way 285 *progress*; pass through, wade through, pass by 305 *pass*; make a move, shift, dodge, duck, shift about, jink, jouk, tack, manoeuvre 282 *deviate*; twist 251 *wriggle*; creep, crawl, worm one's way, go on all fours; hover about, hang about 136 *wait*; move house, flit, relocate; change places 151 *interchange*; move over, make room 190 *go away*; travel, stray 267 *wander*.

move, put in motion; set going; put skates under; put a bomb under, galvanize, actuate, switch on, put into operation 173 *operate*; stir up, jerk 318 *agitate*; budge, shift, trundle, roll, wheel 188 *displace*; push, shove 279 *impel*; move on, drive, hustle 680 *hasten*; tug, pull 288 *draw*; fling, throw 287 *propel*; convey, transport 272 *transfer*; dispatch 272 *send*; mobilize 74 *bring together*; scatter 75 *disperse*; raise, uplift 310 *elevate*; throw down, drop 311 *let fall*; motion, gesture 547 *gesticulate*; transpose 151 *interchange*.

266 Quiescence: being at rest

N. *state of rest*, quiescence, motionlesness; subsidence 145 *cessation*; rest, stillness; deadness; stagnation 679 *inactivity*; pause, truce, standstill 145 *lull*; stoppage, halt; deadlock,

gridlock, full stop, dead stop 145 *stop*; embargo, freeze 757 *prohibition*; immobility, rigidity, stiffness 326 *hardness*; equilibrium 153 *stability*; trance.

quietness, quietude, quiet, stillness, hush 399 *silence*; tranquillity, peacefulness 717 *peace*; rest 683 *rest*; eternal rest 361 *death*; sleepiness, slumber 679 *sleep*; calm, millpond 258 *smoothness*; not a breath of air; dead quiet, not a mouse stirring; composure, cool 823 *inexcitability*; calm before the storm 148 *reversion*; passivity, quietism; tranquillizer, sedation 177 *moderator*.

Adj. *at rest*, resting, quiescent, quiet, still; asleep 679 *sleepy*; becalmed; at anchor, anchored, moored, docked; at a standstill, stopped, idle 679 *inactive*; unemployed, disemployed, out of commission, inoperative; dormant, stagnant, vegetating, static, stationary 175 *inert*; sedentary; on one's back 216 *flat on one's back*; disabled, housebound, confined to bed 747 *restrained*; settled; unmoved 860 *indifferent*.

tranquil, undisturbed, sequestered 883 *secluded*; peaceful, restful; unhurried, easy-going 681 *leisurely*; uneventful 16 *uniform*; calm, like a millpond, airless; glassy 258 *smooth*; sunny, halcyon 730 *halcyon*; at ease, comfortable, relaxed 683 *restful*; tranquillized, sedated, under sedation; cool, unruffled, serene 823 *inexcitable*.

still, unmoving, unstirring, not fizzy, flat 387 *tasteless*; immobile, motionless, expressionless, deadpan, poker-faced 820 *impassive*; steady, unblinking 153 *unchangeable*; rooted to the ground *or* spot 153 *fixed*; transfixed, spellbound; immovable, becalmed, stuck; stiff, frozen 326 *rigid*; paralysed 375 *insensitive*; quiet, so quiet you could hear a pin drop, hushed, soundless 399 *silent*; stock-still, still as a statue, still as death; quiet as a mouse.

Vb. *be at rest*, be still, etc. (see adj.); subside, die down 37 *decrease*; pipe down 399 *be silent*; stand still, lie still, keep quiet; stagnate, vegetate; stand, mark time 136 *wait*; stay put, sit tight, remain in situ, remain 144 *stay*; ride at anchor; tarry 145 *pause*; rest, sit down, take a breather, rest on one's laurels, rest on one's oars 683 *rest*; retire, go to bed, doss down, turn in 679 *sleep*; settle down 187 *place oneself*; stick fast; jam; stand firm; not move a muscle, not stir a step; be at a standstill 145 *cease*.

come to rest, stop, stop short, stop in one's tracks, stop dead in one's tracks, freeze 145 *halt*; pull up, draw up; anchor, alight 295 *land*; relax, cool it, rest, pause 683 *rest*.

bring to rest, quiet, quieten, quell, hush 399 *silence*; lull, soothe, calm down, tranquillize, sedate 177 *assuage*; lull to sleep, cradle, rock; let alone, let well alone, let sleeping dogs lie 620 *avoid*; bring to a standstill, bring to, heave to; brake, put the brake on 278 *retard*; stay, immobilize 679 *make inactive*.

Int. *stop!*, stay!, halt!, whoa!, hold hard!, hold on!, hold it!, don't move!, freeze!

267 Land travel

N. *land travel*, travel, travelling; globetrotting, tourism; medical *or* health *or* surgical *or* transplant tourism, cosmetic holiday, scalpel safari; sight-seeing 438 *inspection*; walking, hiking, riding, driving, motoring, cycling, biking; journey, voyage, odyssey; exodus, Hegira; course, passage; pilgrimage, hajj; place of pilgrimage: promised land, Mecca, etc. 76 *focus*; quest, expedition, safari, trek, field trip; reconnaissance, exploration, orienteering, youth hostelling, backpacking; visit, trip, business trip, tour, grand tour, coach tour, package tour; circuit, turn, round, patrol, commuting; round trip, day trip 314 *circuitous motion*; jaunt, hop, spin; ride, bike ride, joy ride, drive, lift; school run; excursion, outing, airing; ramble, constitutional, promenade.

walking, going on foot, footing it, pedestrianism, Shanks's pony; foot-slogging, striding, tramping, marching, backpacking; perambulation; walkabout 314 *circuitous motion*; walk, promenade, constitutional; stroll, saunter, amble, ramble; hike, tramp, march, walking tour; run, cross-country run, jog, trot, jog trot, lope 265 *gait*; foot race, racewalking, marathon 716 *racing*; sleepwalking, somnambulism.

marching, marching and countermarching; march, forced march, route march, quick march, slow march; march past, parade, cavalcade, procession, Orange Walk, protest march 74 *assembly*, 762 *deprecation*, 875 *pageant*.

horse riding, equitation, equestrianism, horsemanship *or* horsewomanship, manège, dressage 694 *skill*; riding, bareback riding 162 *athletics*; horse racing, steeplechasing, point-to-point racing, show jumping, eventing, gymkhana, speed jumping 716 *contest*.

conveyance, lift, elevator, escalator, paternoster, travelator 274 *conveyor*; feet, own two foot 214 *foot*; legs, Shanks's pony; horseback, mount 273 *horse*; microscooter, bicycle, moped, scooter, motor cycle, car, bus, train, coach, taxi, ambulance 274 *vehicle*; traffic.

leg, limb, foreleg, hindleg; shank, shin, calf; groin, thigh, ham, hamstrings; knee, kneecap 247 *angularity*; tibia, fibula, legs, pegs, pins 218 *prop*; stumps, stilts; stump, wooden leg, artificial leg, prosthesis 150 *substitute*; bow legs, bandy legs, knock-knees 845 *blemish*;

thick legs, piano legs, legs like tree stumps; long legs, spindle shanks.

itinerary, route 624 *way*; course 281 *direction*; route map, road map, plan, chart 551 *map*; guide, Baedeker, timetable, Bradshaw, A–Z 524 *guidebook*; milestone, fingerpost 547 *signpost*.

Vb. *travel*, journey, tour, see the world, go globetrotting, go on a world cruise, visit, explore 484 *discover*; get around, knock about, go places, sightsee, rubberneck; go on a pilgrimage; go on a trip, go on a journey; go on safari, trek, hump bluey; hike, backpack; be always on the move, live out of a suitcase; set out, take wing 296 *depart*; migrate, emigrate, immigrate, settle 187 *place oneself*; shuttle, commute; take oneself off, swan off, slope off; go to, hie to, repair to, resort to, betake oneself to 295 *arrive*, 882 *visit*; go 265 *be in motion*; wend one's way, stir one's stumps, bend one's steps, shape one's course, tread a path, follow the road; make one's way, pick one's way, thread one's way, elbow one's way, force a way, plough through; jog on, trudge on, shuffle on, pad on, plod on, tramp on, march on, chug on 146 *sustain*; course, race, post 277 *move fast*; proceed, advance 285 *progress*; coast, free-wheel, glide, slide, skate, ski, skim, roll along, bowl along, fly along.

traverse, cross, range, pass through, range through 305 *pass*; go round, beat the bounds 314 *circle*; go the rounds, make one's rounds, patrol; scout, reconnoitre 438 *scan*; scour, sweep, sweep through.

wander, migrate; rove, roam, bum around; ramble, amble, stroll, saunter, mosey along, potter, dawdle, walk about, trail around; gad, traipse, gallivant, gad about, hover, flit about, dart about 265 *be in motion*; prowl, skulk 523 *lurk*; straggle, trail 75 *be dispersed*; lose the way, get lost, wander away 282 *stray*.

walk, step, tread, pace, stride; stride out 277 *move fast*; strut, stalk, prance, mince 871 *be proud*; tread lightly, tiptoe, trip, skip, dance, curvet 312 *leap*; tread heavily, lumber, clump, stamp, tramp, goosestep; toddle, patter, pad; totter, stagger, lurch, reel, stumble 317 *oscillate*; limp, hobble, waddle, shuffle, shamble, dawdle 278 *move slowly*; paddle, wade; go on foot, go by Shanks's pony, foot it, hoof it, hike, footslog, wear out shoe leather; plod, stump, trudge, jog; go, go for a walk, perambulate, pace up and down; go for a run *or* a jog, take the air, take one's constitutional; march, troop; file, file past, defile, march in procession 65 *come after*; walk behind 284 *follow*; walk in front 283 *precede*.

ride, mount, hack, trot, amble, canter, gallop; prance, caper; cycle, bicycle, bike, motorcycle; freewheel, coast; drive, motor; go by bike, go by car, go by bus, bus it, go by coach, go by taxi, go by cab; go by road, go by tube, go by train; go by air 271 *fly*; take a lift, take a ride, cadge a lift, thumb a lift, hitchhike.

Int. *come along!*, move along there!, move it!, get along!, get going!, get out!, git!, go away!, be off!, buzz off!, piss off (vulg)!, hop it!, skedaddle!, scram!

268 Traveller

N. *traveller*, itinerant, wayfarer; explorer, adventurer, voyager 270 *mariner*; air traveller, spaceman *or* -woman, astronaut, astrotourist, space tourist 271 *aeronaut*; pioneer, pathfinder, explorer 66 *precursor*; alpinist, mountaineer, cragsman 308 *climber*; pilgrim; walker, hiker, rambler, trekker; backpacker, camper, caravanner, youth hosteller; globe-trotter, tourist, rubberneck, sightseer 441 *spectator*; tripper, daytripper, excursionist; sunseeker, holidaymaker, visitor; health *or* medical *or* surgical *or* transplant tourist; roundsman, hawker 794 *pedlar*; doorstepper, canvasser; travelling salesman, commercial traveller, rep 793 *seller*; messenger, errand boy 529 *courier*; daily traveller, commuter.

wanderer, migrant, bird of passage, visitant 365 *bird*; floating population; nomad, bedouin; gypsy, didicoi, Romany, Roma; tinker; New Age traveller; rover, ranger, rambler, promenader, stroller; strolling player, wandering minstrel, touring company 594 *entertainer*; rolling stone, drifter, vagrant, vagabond, tramp, knight of the road, bag lady; swagman, sundowner, hobo, bum; loafer, beachcomber 679 *idler*; emigrant, émigré, refugee, asylum-seeker, deportee, exile 59 *foreigner*; runaway, fugitive, escapee 620 *avoider*; waif, stray, the homeless, rough sleeper, skell 801 *poor person*.

pedestrian, foot passenger, walker, tramper; jogger, sprinter, runner 716 *contender*; toddler; wader, paddler; skater, skier; skateboarder, roller-skater; hiker, hitch-hiker, foot-slogger; marcher 722 *infantry*; somnambulist, sleepwalker; prowler, snooper, loiterer; footpad 789 *robber*.

rider, horse-rider, camel-rider, cameleer; elephant-rider, mahout; horseman, horsewoman, equestrian; postilion, postboy 529 *courier*; mounted police, Mounties; cavalier, knight, knight errant 722 *cavalry*; hunt, huntsman 619 *hunter*; jockey, steeplechaser, show jumper, eventer 716 *contender*; trainer, breaker 369 *breeder*; roughrider, bareback rider, broncobuster, cowboy, cowgirl, cowpuncher, gaucho, rodeo rider; circus rider, bareback rider, trick rider 162 *athlete*; cyclist, bicyclist, biker,

motorcyclist, moped rider, scooterist;

driver, coachman; carter, wagoner, drayman; car driver, chauffeur, motorist, white-van man, roadhog; joy rider; L-driver 538 *beginner*; taxi driver, cab driver, cabby; bus driver, coach driver; lorry driver, truck driver, van driver, trucker, routier, teamster; tractor driver; bad driver, white van man; motorman, train driver, engine driver; pilot 271 *aeronaut*.

269 Water travel

N. *water travel*, seafaring, life on the ocean wave; navigation, voyaging, sailing, cruising; coasting, longshore sailing; boating, yachting, rowing (see also *watersports* below); voyage, navigation, cruise, sail; maiden voyage; course, run, passage, crossing, ferry crossing; circumnavigation 314 *circuitous motion*; sea trip, river trip, canal trip, breath of sea air 685 *refreshment*; way, headway, steerage way, sternway, seaway 265 *motion*; leeway, driftway 282 *deviation*; wake, track, wash, backwash 350 *eddy*; sea-path, sea lane, approaches 624 *route*; boat, sailing ship 275 *ship*; sailor 270 *mariner*.

navigation, piloting, steering, pilotage 689 *directorship*; astronavigation; plane sailing, plain sailing, spherical sailing, great-circle sailing, parallel sailing; compass reading, dead reckoning 465 *measurement*; automatic pilot *or* autopilot; pilotship, seamanship 694 *skill*.

watersports, aquatic sports, aquatics 837 *sport*; boating, sailing, yachting, cruising; rowing, sculling, canoeing; yacht racing, speedboat racing, ocean racing 716 *racing*; waterskiing, surf-riding, surfing, body-surfing, windsurfing, skiboarding, boardsailing; jet-skiing; rafting, white-water rafting, hydrospeeding; natation, floating, swimming, snorkelling, etc. 837 *sport*; stroke, breast stroke, side stroke, back stroke, crawl, back crawl, front crawl, butterfly, dogpaddle; diving, plunging 313 *plunge*; wading, paddling; swimsuit 228 *beachwear*.

sailing aid, navigational instrument, sextant, quadrant 247 *angular measure*; chronometer, ship's chronometer 117 *timekeeper*; log, line; lead, plummet 211 *depth*; anchor, grapnel 662 *safeguard*; compass, astrocompass, magnetic compass, ship's compass; needle, magnetic needle; card, compass card *or* rose; binnacle; gyrocompass 689 *directorship*; radar 484 *detector*; helm, wheel, tiller, rudder, steering oar, sea mark, buoy, lighthouse, pharos, lightship 547 *signpost*; chart, Admiralty chart, portolano 551 *map*; nautical almanac, ephemeris 524 *guidebook*.

propeller, screw, twin screw, blade, rotor 287 *propellant*; paddle wheel, stern wheel, floatboard; oar, sweep, paddle, scull; pole, punt pole, barge pole; fin, flipper, fish's tail 53 *limb*; sails 275 *sail*.

Vb. *go to sea*, join the navy; become a sailor, get one's sea legs; sail before the mast; go sailing, boat, yacht, cruise.

voyage, sail, go by sea, go by ship, go by boat, take the ferry, take the sea route; work one's passage; embark, go on board, put to sea, set sail, up anchor 296 *start out*; disembark, land 295 *arrive*; cruise; steam, ply, run, tramp, ferry; coast, hug the shore; roll, pitch, toss.

navigate, man a ship, work a ship, crew; put to sea, set sail; launch, push off, boom off; unmoor, cast off, weigh anchor; get up steam; hoist sail, spread canvas; get under way, gather way, make way, carry sail 265 *be in motion*; drop the pilot; set a course, make for, head for 281 *steer for*; read the chart, go by the card 281 *orientate*; pilot, steer, hold the helm, captain 689 *direct*; stroke, cox, coxswain; trim the sails, square, square away; change course, veer, gybe, yaw 282 *deviate*; put about, wear ship 282 *turn round*; run before the wind, scud 277 *move fast*; put the helm up, fall to leeward, pay off; put the helm down, luff, bring into the wind; beat to windward, tack, weather; back and fill; round, double a point, circumnavigate 314 *circle*; be caught amidships 700 *be in difficulty*; careen, list, heel over 220 *be oblique*; turn turtle, capsize, overturn 221 *invert*; ride out the storm, weather the storm, keep afloat 667 *escape*; run for port 662 *seek refuge*; lie to, lay to, heave to 266 *bring to rest*; take soundings, heave the lead 465 *measure*; tide over 507 *await*; tow, haul, warp, kedge, clubhaul 288 *draw*; ground, run aground, wreck, be cast away 165 *destroy*; sight land, make a landfall, take on a pilot 289 *approach*; make port; cast anchor, drop anchor; moor, tie up, dock, disembark 295 *land*; cross one's bows, take the wind out of one's sails, outmanoeuvre, gain the weather gauge 702 *obstruct*; foul 279 *collide*; back, go astern 286 *regress*; surface, break water 298 *emerge*; flood the tank dive 313 *plunge*; shoot, shoot a bridge, shoot the rapids 305 *pass*.

row, ply the oar, get the sweeps out; pull, stroke, scull; feather; catch a crab; ship oars; punt; paddle, canoe; boat; shoot the rapids.

swim, go swimming, do the breast stroke, do the crawl (see also *watersports* above); aquaplane; strike out, breast the current, stem the stream; tread water; dive 313 *plunge*; bathe, dip, duck; wade, paddle; go skinny-dipping.

270 Mariner

N. *mariner*, sailor, seaman, seafaring man; salt, old salt, seadog, shellback; tar, Jack Tar, limey, matelot; bad sailor, fairweather sailor, landlubber 697 *bungler*; skipper, master mariner, master, ship master; mate, boatswain; bosun; coxswain; able seaman, A.B. 696 *expert*; deckhand, swabbie; ship's steward, cabin boy 742 *servant*; shipmates, hearties; crew, complement, ship's complement, men, watch 686 *personnel*; trawler, whaler, deep-sea fisherman; sea rover, privateer, buccaneer, sea king, Viking, pirate 789 *robber*; sea scout, sea cadet.

navigator, pilot, sailing master, helmsman, steersman, wheelman, man at the wheel, quartermaster; coxswain, cox 690 *leader*; leadsman, lookout man; foretop-man, reefer; boatswain, bosun's mate; circumnavigator; compass 269 *sailing aid*.

nautical personnel, marine, submariner, naval cadet, bluejacket, rating 722 *naval man*; petty officer, midshipman, middy, lieutenant, sub-lieutenant, commander, captain, commodore, admiral 741 *naval officer*; Admiralty, Sea Lord; Trinity House, lighthouse keeper, coastguard 660 *protector*; lifeboatman 703 *helper*; river police, naval patrol, harbour patrol, harbourmaster.

boatman, waterman, rowing man, wet bob; gigsman; galley slave; oar, oarsman, sculler, rower, punter; paddler, canoeist; yachtsman *or* -woman; gondolier, ferryman; ferryman in hell: Stygian Ferryman, Charon; wherryman, bargeman, bargee, lighterman; stevedore, docker, longshoreman; lock keeper.

271 Aeronautics

N. *aeronautics*, aeromechanics, aerodynamics, aerostatics; aerostation, ballooning; aerospace, astronautics; aeroballistics, rocketry 276 *rocket*; volitation, flight, vertical flight, horizontal flight; subsonic flight, supersonic flight 277 *velocity*; stratospheric flight, hypersonic flight, space flight; aviation, flying, night flying, blind flying, instrument flying; shoran, teleran; gliding, powered gliding, hang-gliding; parachuting, skydiving, free fall; flypast, formation flying, stunt flying, aerobatics 875 *ostentation*; skywriting, vapour trail; planing, volplaning; looping the loop; spin, roll, sideslip; volplane, nose dive, pull-out; crash dive, crash, prang 309 *descent*; pancake, landing, belly landing, crash landing, forced landing; talkdown, touchdown 295 *arrival*; takeoff, vertical takeoff 296 *departure*.

air travel, air transport, airlift 272 *transport*; air service, airline; shuttle service, scheduled flight, charter flight; air miles; airlane, airway, air route 624 *route*; flight path, glide path, line of flight 281 *direction*; airspace 184 *territory*; takeoff, touchdown, landing; airbase; airstrip, runway, tarmac, airfield, aerodrome, airport, heliport, helipad; terminal, air terminal, check-in desk, luggage carousel, baggage reclaim, airside, landside 295 *goal*; hangar 192 *stable*; fear of flying, aerophobia; jetlag; red-eye flight *or* red-eye.

space travel, space flight, manned space flight, spacefaring 276 *spaceship*; astrotourism, space tourism; lift-off, blast-off; orbit, flyby; docking, space walk; re-entry, splashdown, soft landing; cosmodrome, spaceport, space station, space platform, space shuttle; launching pad, silo; spacesuit.

aeronaut, balloonist; glider, hang-glider, sky diver, parachutist; paratrooper 722 *soldier*; aviator, aviatrix, airwoman, airman, birdman; astronaut, cosmonaut, taikonaut, spaceman, spacewoman, space traveller; air traveller, air passenger, jet set 268 *traveller*; air hostess, steward, stewardess, cabin personnel 742 *servant*; flier, pilot, test pilot, jet pilot, copilot; automatic pilot *or* autopilot; navigator, air crew; pilot officer, flying officer, etc. 741 *air officer*; aircraftman *or* -woman 722 *air force*; air personnel, ground crew 686 *personnel*.

wing, pinion, feathers, flight feathers, wing feather, wing spread 259 *plumage*; sweptback wing, deltawing, swingwing, variable wing; aerofoil, aileron, flaps.

Vb. *fly*, wing, be on the wing; wing one's way, be wafted; soar, rise 308 *ascend*; hover, hang over 217 *hang*; flutter, flit 265 *be in motion*; taxi, leave the ground, climb, circle 296 *depart*; be airborne, have lift-off; aviate, glide, plane; float, drift 323 *be light*; hit an air pocket, experience turbulence, stunt, spin, roll, side-slip, loop the loop, volplane; hedge-hop, skim the rooftops, buzz; stall, dive, power-dive, nose-dive, spiral 313 *plunge*; crash, prang, force-land, crash-land, pancake, ditch 309 *tumble*; pull out, flatten out; touch down 295 *land*; bale out, jump, parachute, eject; blast off, lift off, take off; orbit, go into orbit 314 *circle*.

272 Transference

N. *transference*, relocation, transplantation, transhipment, transfer, bussing, commuting, shuttling, teleporting; shifting, shift, drift, longshore drift, continental drift 282 *deviation*; posting 751 *mandate*; transposition, metathesis 151 *interchange*; removal, moving house, flitting, relegation, deportation, expulsion 300 *ejection*; unpacking, unloading, airdrop 188 *displacement*; exportation, export 791 *trade*; trade-off, mutual transfer 791 *barter*; importation, import 299 *reception*; distribution, logistics 633 *provision*; transmittal, forwarding,

sending, remittance, dispatch; recalling, recall, extradition 304 *extraction*; recovery, retrieval 771 *acquisition*; handing over, delivery; takeover 792 *purchase*; conveyance, transfer of property, donation 780 *transfer*; committal, trust 751 *commission*; gaol delivery, habeas corpus, release 746 *liberation*; transition, metastasis; passing over, ferry, ferriage 305 *passage*; transmigration 143 *transformation*; transmission, throughput; conduction, convection; transfusion; decantation; diffusion, dispersal 75 *dispersion*; communication, contact 378 *touch*; contagion, infection, contamination 178 *influence*; transcription, transumption, copying, transliteration 520 *translation*.

transport, transportation; conveyance, carriage, shipping, shipment; carrying, humping, portage, porterage, haulage, draught 288 *traction*; carting; freightage, air freight, airlift; rail, road 274 *vehicle*; sea, canal 275 *ship*; pipeline, conveyor belt 274 *conveyor*; flotsam, jetsam, trust 767 *security*; legacy, bequest 781 *gift*; lease 777 *property*; cargo, load, payload, freight; consignment, shipment 193 *contents*; goods, mails; luggage, baggage, impedimenta; container, container-load, lorryload, trainload, coachload, busload; person transferred: passenger, rider, commuter 268 *traveller*.

astral travel, astral projection, out-of-body travel, out-of-body experience, OBE, near-death experience, NDE.

Vb. *transfer*, hand over, deliver 780 *assign*; leave 780 *bequeath*; commit, entrust 751 *commission*; transmit, hand down, hand on, pass on; make over, turn over, hand to, pass to; transfer responsibility to, delegate, pass the buck; export, transport, convey, ship, airlift, fly, ferry 273 *carry*; infect, contaminate 178 *influence*; conduct, convect; carry over 38 *add*; transfer itself to, come off on, adhere, stick 48 *cohere*.

transpose, shift, move 188 *displace*; transfer, relocate, switch, shunt, shuffle, castle (chess) 151 *interchange*; detach, detail, draft; relegate, deport, expel, sack 300 *eject*; drag, pull 288 *draw*; push, shove 279 *impel*; containerize 193 *load*; channel, funnel, pour in *or* out, transfuse, decant, strain off, siphon off 300 *empty*; unload, remove 188 *displace*; download, upload; shovel, ladle, spoon out, bail out 255 *make concave*; transliterate 520 *translate*.

send, remit, transmit, dispatch; direct, consign, address; post, mail; redirect, readdress, post on, forward; send by hand, deliver in person, send by post; send for, order, mail-order, tele-order 627 *require*; send away, detach, detail 287 *propel*.

Adv. *in transit*, en route, on the way; in the post; in the pipeline.

273 Carrier
N. *carrier*, haulier, carter, wagoner; shipper, transporter, exporter, importer; ferryman 270 *boatman*; lorry driver, truck driver, van driver, bus driver, white van man 268 *driver*; delivery boy; delivery van, lorry, truck, juggernaut, cart, goods train 274 *vehicle*; barge, cargo vessel, freighter, tramp 275 *ship*; chassis, undercarriage 218 *prop*; pallet, container; carrier bag, plastic bag, poly bag 194 *bag*; conveyor belt, escalator 274 *conveyor*.

***beast of burden*,** packhorse, pack-mule; ass, she-ass, donkey, mule, moke, Neddy, cuddy, burro; ox, oxen, bullock, draught animals 365 *cattle*; sledge dog, husky; camel, dromedary, ship of the desert; elephant 365 *mammal*.

***horse*,** equine species, quadruped, horseflesh; dobbin, gee-gee; nag; Rosinante; mount, steed, trusty steed; stallion, gelding, mare, colt, filly, foal; stud horse, brood mare, stud, stable; cart-horse; circus horse, liberty horse; roan, strawberry roan, grey, dapple grey, bay, chestnut, sorrel, black, piebald, skewbald, pinto, dun, palomino; purebred, blood-horse, bloodstock; Arab, Barbary horse; pacer, stepper, high-stepper, trotter; courser, racehorse, racer, goer, stayer; sprinter; steeplechaser, hurdler, fencer, jumper, hunter, foxhunter; warhorse, charger, courser, steed 722 *cavalry*, winged horse, Pegasus; Houyhnhnm. (See also 267 *horse riding*, 268 *rider*.)

***draught horse*,** carthorse, dray horse; shaft-horse, trace-horse; carriage-horse, coach-horse; post-horse; plough-horse, shire-horse, Clydesdale, punch, Suffolk Punch, Percheron, pit pony.

***saddle horse*,** mount, hack, roadster; jade, screw, nag; pad, pad-nag, ambler; mustang, bronco; palfrey, jennet.

***pony*,** cob, galloway, garron, sheltie; Shetland pony, fell pony, Welsh pony, Dartmoor pony, Exmoor pony, New Forest pony.

Adj. *equine*, horsy, horse-faced; neighing; roan, grey, etc. (see n.); asinine; mulish.

Vb. *carry*, bear 218 *support*; hump, humf, lug, heave, tote; caddy; shoulder, bear on one's back, carry on one's shoulders; fetch, bring, reach; fetch and carry; transport, cart, truck, railroad; ship, waft, raft; lift, fly 272 *transfer*; carry over, carry across, traject, ferry; convey, conduct, convoy, escort 89 *accompany*; be saddled with, be lumbered with, be burdened with; be loaded with, be fraught 54 *be complete*.

274 Vehicle
N. *vehicle*, conveyance, public conveyance; public service vehicle, transport, public transport; vehicular traffic, motorized traffic, road traffic, wheeled traffic; pedal power, horse power; sedan chair, palanquin; litter, horse litter; brancard, stretcher, hurdle, crate; ambulance, bloodwagon; fire engine, Green Goddess; Black Maria, paddy wagon; tumbril, hearse; snowplough, snowmobile, weasel; breakdown van, recovery vehicle; tractor, caterpillar tractor, tracked vehicle, bulldozer, JCB (tdmk); amphibian, moon buggy, space vehicle; all-terrain vehicle, ATV; rollercoaster, switchback, dodgem car; time machine.

***sled*,** sledge, sleigh, dogsleigh; bobsleigh, bobsled, toboggan, sand yacht, surfboard, bodyboard, boogie board, sailboard; skate, ice skate, roller skate, in-line skate, Rollerblade (tdmk), skateboard; snowshoes, skis, snowboard.

***bicycle*,** cycle, pedal cycle, bike, push bike; wheel, gridiron, crate; velocipede, hobbyhorse, boneshaker, penny-farthing, sit-up-and-beg; folding bicycle, sports model, racer, tourist, roadster, mountain bicycle *or* bike; ladies' bicycle, man's bicycle; five-speed, ten-speed; BMX (tdmk), Chopper (tdmk); stabilized bicycle; small-wheeler; tandem, random; monocycle, unicycle, tricycle, fairy cycle, trike, quadricycle; motorized bicycle, moped; scooter, motor scooter, motorcycle, motorbike, trail bike, scrambler, quad bike; motorcycle combination, sidecar; invalid carriage; cycle-rickshaw, trishaw.

***pushcart*,** barrow, wheelbarrow, handcart, cart; pram, perambulator, baby buggy, buggy, pushchair, stroller; bath chair, wheelchair, invalid chair; rickshaw; go-kart *or* go-cart; trolley, truck, float.

***cart*,** ox-cart, bullock-cart, horse-and-cart; dray, milk float; farm cart, haywain, hay wagon; wain, wagon, covered wagon, prairie schooner; caravan, mobile home, trailer, horse-box, loose-box; dustcart, watercart; tumbril. (See also *lorry* below.)

***carriage*,** horse-drawn carriage, equipage, turnout, rig; chariot, coach, state coach, coach and four; barouche, landau, landaulet, berlin, victoria, brougham, phaeton, clarence; surrey, buckboard, buggy, wagonette; travelling carriage, chaise, shay, calèche, calash, britzka, droshky, troika; racing chariot, quadriga; four-in-hand, drag, brake, charabanc; two-wheeler; cabriolet, curricle, tilbury, whisky, jaunting car; trap, gig, ponycart, dogcart, governess cart; carriole, sulky; shandrydan, rattletrap.

***war chariot*,** scythed chariot; gun carriage, caisson, limber, ammunition wagon; tank, armoured car, armoured fighting vehicle 722 *cavalry*; jeep, staff car.

cab, hackney carriage, horsecab, four-wheeler, hansom, fly; fiacre, droshky; gharry, tonga; taxicab, taxi, minicab; rickshaw, jin-rickisha, pedicab, cycle-rickshaw.

bus, horsebus, motorbus; omnibus, double-decker, single-decker; autobus, trolleybus, motor coach, coach, postbus, minibus; airbus.

tram, horse tram, tramcar, trolley, streetcar, cablecar.

car, automobile, horseless carriage, motor car, motor, auto; limousine, limo, stretch limo; gas guzzler; saloon, two-door saloon, four-door saloon; tourer, roadster, runabout, buggy; hard-top, soft-top, convertible; coupé, sports car; racing car, stock car, dragster, hot-rod; go-kart *or* go-cart, kart; fastback, hatchback, estate car, people carrier; station wagon, shooting brake; Land Rover (tdmk), jeep, four-by-four, off-roader, sport utility vehicle, SUV; police car, patrol car, panda car; veteran car, Edwardian car, vintage car, model T; tin Lizzie, banger, bus, jalopy, old crock, rattletrap; bee-tle, bubble car, minicar; invalid car, three-wheeler; minibus, camper, Dormobile (tdmk); cannibalized car, Frankencar; automatic car, gear-shift car; zero-emission vehicle; concept car; car crime, car theft, autotheft, carjacking, twoc (taken without consent), joy-riding; hotting; drive-by crime, hit-and-run accident; car bomb; drink-driving, drug-driving.

lorry, truck, pickup truck, dump truck; refuse lorry, dustcart; container lorry, articu-lated lorry, roadliner, juggernaut; tanker; bowser; car transporter, low-loader; van, deliv-ery van, removal van, pantechnicon; break-down van; electric van, float; truck bomb.

train, railway train, passenger train, excur-sion train, boat train, motorail; express train, through train, intercity train, high-speed train, HST, advanced passenger train, APT, tilting train, bullet train, train à grande vitesse, TGV; slow train, stopping train; goods train, freight train, freightliner; milk train, mail train, night mail; rolling stock; coach, carriage, compart-ment, first-class class, second-class class, smoker, non-smoker; Pullman, wagon-lit, sleeping car, sleeper; restaurant car, dining car, buffet car, observation car; guard's van, lug-gage van, brake van, caboose; truck, wagon, tank wagon, hopper wagon, trolley; bogie; steam train, diesel train, electric train, tube train, model train; live rail, third rail, over-head wires, pantograph; cable railway, electric railway, underground railway 624 *railway*; Ori-ent Express, Eurostar, Le Shuttle.

locomotive, diesel engine, steam engine, ten-der; choo-choo, puff-puff, traction engine, steam roller.

conveyor; conveyor belt, escalator, moving staircase, moving pavement, moving walkway, travelator; shovel, hod 194 *ladle*; fork, trowel 370 *farm and garden tools*; crane.

275 Ship

N. *ship*, vessel, boat, craft; bark, barque, barquentine; great ship, tall ship; little ship, cockleshell; bottom, keel, sail; hooker, tub, hull; hulk, prison ship; Argo, Golden Hind, Noah's Ark; steamer, screw steamer, steamship, steamboat, motor vessel; paddle steamer, pad-dleboat, stern-wheeler, riverboat, showboat; passenger ship, liner, luxury liner, cruise ship; channel steamer, ferry; hovercraft, hydrofoil; rotor ship; mail-boat, packet, steam packet; dredger, hopper, icebreaker; transport, hospital ship; storeship, tender, escort vessel, pilot ves-sel; tug, launch; lightship, weather ship; underwater craft, submarine, U-boat 722 *war-ship*; aircraft carrier.

merchant ship, galleon, argosy, Indiaman; banana boat, tea clipper; slave ship; cargo boat, freighter, tramp; coaster; lugger, collier, tanker, oil tanker, supertanker; containership.

fishing boat, inshore fishing boat; fishing smack, drifter, trawler, purse-seiner; factory ship; whaler, whale-catcher.

sailing ship, sailing boat, sailboat, sailer; windjammer, clipper, tall ship; square-rigged ship, four-masted ship, three-masted ship, threemaster; barque, barquentine; two-masted ship, brig, hermaphrodite brig, brigantine, schooner, pinnace; frigate, corvette 722 *war-ship*; cutter, sloop, ketch, yawl; wherry; yacht, racing yacht; sailing dinghy, smack; multihull, catamaran; xebec, felucca, caïque, dhow, junk, sampan; ship-related crime: piracy, yachtjacking.

sail, sailcloth, canvas; square sail, lug-sail, lug, lateen sail, fore-and-aft sail, leg-of-mutton sail, spanker; course, mainsail, foresail, topsail, topgallant sail, royal, skysail; jib, staysail, spin-naker, balloon sail, studding sail; rigging; mast, foremast, mainmast, mizzenmast 218 *prop*.

boat, skiff, foldboat, cockboat; lifeboat; ship's boat, tender, dinghy, pram; longboat, jolly boat; whaleboat, dory; pinnace, cutter, gig; bumboat, surf boat; barge, lighter, pon-toon, wherry; ferry, ferryboat, canalboat, nar-rowboat; houseboat; towboat, tugboat, tug; sailing boat, sailboat, sailing dinghy, yacht, catamaran; powerboat, motorboat, motor launch; pleasure-boat, cabin cruiser; speed-boat.

rowing boat, galley; bireme, trireme, qin-quereme; eight, racing eight; sculler, shell, randan; skiff, dinghy, rubber dinghy, wherry; coracle, currach; punt, gondola; canoe, outrigger, dugout; pirogue, proa, kayak, umiak.

shipping, craft; argosy, fleet, armada, flotilla, squadron 722 *navy*; marine, mercantile marine, merchant navy, shipping line; flag of convenience 547 *flag*.

Adj. *marine*, maritime, naval, nautical, seagoing, ocean-going; sea-worthy, snug, shipshape, shipshape and Bristol fashion.

276 Aircraft

N. *aircraft* 271 *aeronautics*; flying machine; aeroplane, airplane, crate; plane, monoplane, biplane, triplane; amphibian; hydroplane, seaplane, flying boat, floatplane; airliner, airbus, transport, freighter; warplane, fighter, bomber 722 *air force*; stratocruiser, jet plane, jet, jumbo jet, jump jet, supersonic jet, Concorde, turbojet, turboprop, turbofan, propfan; VTOL, STOL, HOTOL; microlight; helicopter, autogyro, whirlybird, chopper, copter; ornithopter; hovercraft 275 *ship*; glider, sailplane; flying instruments, controls, flight recorder, black box, autopilot *or* automatic pilot, joystick, rudder; aerofoil, fin, tail; flaps, aileron 271 *wing*; prop 269 *propeller*; cockpit, flight deck; undercarriage, landing gear; safety belt, life jacket, parachute, ejection seat; test bed, wind tunnel; flight simulator; aerodrome, airport 271 *air travel*.

airship, aerostat, balloon, Montgolfier balloon, hot-air balloon; captive balloon, barrage balloon, observation balloon, weather balloon, blimp; dirigible, Zeppelin; kite, box-kite; parachute, chute; hang glider; magic carpet; balloon-basket, nacelle, car, gondola.

rocket, rocketry; step rocket, multistage rocket; booster; nose cone, warhead; guided missile, intercontinental ballistic missile, ICBM, Exocet (tdmk), nuclear missile, Cruise missile 723 *throwing weapons, projectiles and missiles*; V2; Star Wars, Strategic Defence Initiative, SDI, Son of Star Wars.

spaceship, spacecraft, space probe, space shot, space capsule, space shuttle, spaceplane, aerospaceplane; space lab; lunar module, command module; space tug, orbital manoeuvring vehicle; space platform, space station, sputnik 321 *satellite*; flying saucer, UFO, unidentified flying object.

squadron, flight, group, wing; airborne division.

277 Velocity

N. *velocity*, celerity, rapidity, speed, swiftness, fleetness, quickness, liveliness, alacrity, agility; speed of thought 116 *instantaneousness*; promptness, expedition, dispatch; speed, tempo, rate, pace, bat 265 *motion*; speed-rate, miles per hour, mph, knots; mach number; speed of light, speed of sound, supersonic speed; lightning speed; maximum speed, full speed, full steam; utmost speed, press of sail, full sail; precipitation, hurry, flurry 680 *haste*; fast lane, fast track; breakneck speed 857 *rashness*; streak of lightning, flash, lightning flash; flight, jet flight, supersonic flight; gale, hurricane, tempest, torrent; electricity, telegraph, lightning, greased lightning; speed measurement: tachometer, speedometer 465 *gauge*; wind gauge; log, logline; speed trap, radar trap 542 *trap*.

spurt, spirt, acceleration, speed-up, overtaking; burst of speed; thrust, drive, impetus 279 *impulse*; jump, spring, bound, pounce 312 *leap*; whizz, swoop, swoosh, vroom, zip, zing, zap, uprush, zoom; down rush, dive, power dive; flying start, rush, dash, scamper, run, sprint, gallop.

speedy thing, arrow; lightning; cheetah, greyhound, whippet; Concorde; high-speed train, bullet train, etc. 274 *train*; Gadarene swine.

Adj. *speedy*, swift, fast, quick, rapid, nimble, volant; darting, dashing, lively, brisk, smart, snappy, nifty, zippy 174 *vigorous*; expeditious, fast-track, hustling 680 *hasty*; double-quick, rapid-fire; prompt 135 *early*; immediate 116 *instantaneous*; fast-track, high-speed, streamlined, souped-up, go-go; speeding, racing, tonup; running, charging, runaway; flying, whizzing, hurtling, pelting; whirling, tempestuous; breakneck, headlong, precipitate 857 *rash*; fleet, fleet of foot, light-footed, nimble-footed; darting, starting, flashing; swift-moving, agile, nimble, mercurial, like quicksilver 152 *changing*; like a bird; arrowy, like an arrow; like a shot; like a flash *or* like greased lightning *or* like the wind, quick as lightning *or* as thought *or* as a flash *or* as the wind, like a bat out of hell; meteoric, jet-propelled.

Vb. *move fast*, move, shift, travel, speed; drive, pelt, streak, flash, shoot, scorch, burn up the miles, tear up the road; scud, careen; skim, nip, cut; bowl along; sweep along, tear along, rattle along, thunder along, storm along; tear, rip, vroom, zip, zing, zap, rush, dash; fly, wing, whizz, skirr; hurtle, zoom, dive; dash off, tear off, dart off, dash on, dash forward; plunge, lunge, swoop; run, trot, double, lope, spank, gallop; bolt, cut and run, hotfoot it, leg it, scoot, skedaddle, scamper, scurry, skelter, scuttle; show a clean pair of heels, be unable to be seen for dust 620 *run* *away*; hare, run like a hare, run like the wind *or* like mad *or* like the clappers; start, dart, dartle, flit; frisk, whisk; spring, bound, leap, jump, pounce; ride hard, put one's best foot forward, stir one's stumps, get cracking, get a move on, get one's finger out; hie, hurry, post, haste 680 *hasten*; chase, charge, stampede, career, go full tilt *or* full pelt *or* full lick *or* full steam, go all out; break the speed limit, break the sound barrier.

accelerate, speed up, raise the tempo; gather momentum, gather speed, spurt *or* spirt, sprint, put on speed, pick up speed, step on it, step on the gas, put one's foot down, open the throttle, open up, let it rip; crowd on sail; quicken one's speed, get a move on; put on one's running shoes, set off at a run, get off to a flying start; make up time, make up for lost time, make forced marches; quicken, step up, drive, spur, urge forward, urge on; lend wings to, put a bomb under, hustle, expedite 680 *hasten*.

outstrip, overtake, overhaul, catch up, catch up with; lap, outpace, outrun 306 *outdo*; gain on, outdistance, leave behind, leave standing, leave at the starting post; lose, shake off; make the running, romp home, win the race, take the chequered flag, outclass 34 *be superior*.

Adv. *swiftly*, rapidly, etc. (see adj.); trippingly, apace; posthaste, at full speed (at) full tilt; in full gallop, all out, flat out; helter-skelter, headlong, lickety-split, hell for leather; pronto, smartish, p.d.q., quick-smart; like greased lightning, like a shot, like the clappers, like snow off a dyke, in a flash, before you could say Jack Robinson; in full sail, under press of sail *or* canvas, full speed ahead; on eagle's wings, with giant strides; nineteen to the dozen, hand over fist; at a rate of knots, at the double, in double-quick time, as fast as one's legs would carry one; at full speed, for all one is worth; by leaps and bounds, like wildfire.

278 Slowness

N. *slowness*, slackness, languor 679 *sluggishness*; inertia 175 *inertness*; deliberation 823 *inexcitability*; tentativeness, Fabian tactics; hesitation 858 *caution*; reluctance 598 *unwillingness*; go-slow, working to rule 145 *strike*; slowing down, slow-down, deceleration, retardation 113 *protraction*; drag 333 *friction*; brake, curb 747 *restraint*; leisureliness, no hurry, time to spare, time on one's hands, all the time in the world, easy stages 681 *leisure*; slow motion, slo-mo; low gear; slow march, dead march; slow time, andante; slow pace, foot pace, snail's pace, crawl, creep, dawdle; drag-

ging one's feet; amble 265 *gait*; limping, hobbling; standing start, slow start; lag, time lag 136 *delay*.

slowcoach, snail, tortoise, tardigrade; stopping train, slow train; funeral procession; dawdler, loiterer, lingerer; slow learner, late developer; laggard, sluggard, sleepyhead, slouch; drone 679 *idler*.

Adj. *slow*, painfully slow; low-geared, slow-motion, time-lapse; snail-like, tortoise-like, creeping, crawling, dragging; tardigrade, slow-moving 695 *clumsy*; limping, halting; taking one's time, dragging one's feet, hanging fire, tardy, dilatory, lagging 136 *late*; unhurried 681 *leisurely*; sedate 875 *formal*; deliberate 823 *patient*; painstaking 457 *careful*; Fabian 858 *cautious*; groping, tentative 461 *experimental*; languid, slack, sluggish 679 *lazy*; apathetic, phlegmatic 375 *insensitive*; gradual, imperceptible.

Vb. *move slowly*, go slow, amble, traipse, wander; crawl, creep, inch; trickle, dribble 350 *flow*; drift 282 *deviate*; hover; slouch, shuffle; toddle, waddle, mince; plod, trudge, lumber, wobble, totter, teeter, stagger, lurch; struggle, toil, labour, chug, limp, hobble, schlep; drag one's steps, flag, falter 684 *be fatigued*; trail, lag, fall behind 284 *follow*; hang fire, drag one's feet, drag oneself 598 *be unwilling*; tarry, be long about it, take one's time 136 *be late*; laze, idle 679 *be inactive*; dawdle, linger, saunter, stroll, take it easy 267 *walk*; march in slow time, slow-march, tick over; grope, feel one's way 461 *be tentative*; soft-pedal, hesitate 858 *be cautious*; speak slowly, drawl; spin something out 580 *stammer*.

slow down, decelerate, slow up, ease up, let up, lose momentum; reduce speed, slacken speed, slacken one's pace, slacken off; relax, slacken, ease off 145 *pause*; lose ground, flag, falter, waver 684 *be fatigued*.

retard, check, curb, rein in, throttle down 177 *moderate*; reef, shorten sail, take in sail, strike sail 269 *navigate*; brake, put on the brake, put on the drag 747 *restrain*; backpedal, backwater, backpaddle, put the engines astern, reverse 286 *regress*; handicap, impair, clip the wings 702 *hinder*.

Adv. *slowly*, deliberately, etc. (see adj.); lazily, sluggishly; at low speed, in low gear, in bottom gear; at a snail's pace, at a funeral pace; with leaden step; in one's own good time; in slow time, adagio, largo; by degrees, by easy stages, little by little, step by step 27 *by degrees*.

279 Impulse

N. *impulse*, impulsion, pressure; impetus, momentum; boost 174 *stimulant*; encouragement 612 *incentive*; thrust, push, shove, heave;

stroke; throw, fling 287 *propulsion*; lunge, kick 712 *attack*; beating, tapping, drumming; beat, drumbeat 403 *roll*; thud; ramming, bulldozing, hammering; butting, butt (see also *collision* below); shaking, rattling; shock, impact; slam, bang; flick, clip, tap 378 *touch*; shake, jerk, wrench 318 *agitation*; pulsation, pulse 318 *spasm*; mechanics, dynamics.

knock, dint, dent 255 *concavity*; rap, tap, clap; dab, pat, fillip, flip, flick; nudge, dig 547 *gesture*; smack, slap; cuff, clip on *or* round the ear, clout, buffet, box on the ears; blow, fourpenny one; bunch of fives, knuckle sandwich; lash, stroke, hit, crack; cut, drive (cricket); thwack, thump, biff, bang, slug; punch, rabbit punch, left, right, straight left, upper-cut, jab, hook; body blow, swipe; knockout blow; stamp, kick; swat; spanking, licking, leathering, etc. 963 *corporal punishment*; trouncing, dusting, pasting, bashing, hammering, pummelling, rain of blows; assault, assault and battery 712 *attack*; exchange of blows, fisticuffs, cut and thrust, hammer and tongs 61 *turmoil*.

collision, encounter, meeting, confrontation; graze, scrape 333 *friction*; clash 14 *contrariety*; cannon; impact, bump, shock, crash, smash, smash-up, accident; brunt, charge, force 712 *attack*; collision course 293 *convergence*; head-on collision; bird strike; multiple collision, pile-up, motorway madness 74 *accumulation*; near miss, air miss, signal passed at danger, spad.

hammer, ballpeen hammer, claw hammer, sledge hammer, steam hammer, tilt hammer, trip hammer, drop hammer, drop forge; beetle, mallet, maul; hammerhead, peen; gavel, nutcracker; punch, puncher; flail; club, cosh, cudgel, etc. 723 *club*; pestle, anvil.

ram, battering ram, bulldozer; JCB (tdmk); piledriver, monkey; ramrod; rammer, tamper; cue, billiard cue, pusher 287 *propellant*.

Vb. impel, fling, heave, throw 287 *propel*; give an impetus, impart momentum; slam, bang 264 *close*; press, press in, press up, press down; push, thrust, shove; ram down, tamp; shove off, push off, pole, punt; hustle, prod, urge, spur, railroad, pressurize 277 *accelerate*; fillip, flip, flick; jerk, shake, rattle, shock, jog, jolt, jostle 318 *agitate*; shoulder, elbow, push out of the way, push around 282 *deflect*; throw out, run out, expel 300 *eject*; frogmarch; drive forward, flog on, whip on; goad 612 *incite*; drive, start, run, set going, set moving 173 *operate*; raise 310 *elevate*; plunge, dip, douse 311 *lower*.

collide, impinge 306 *encroach*; come into collision 293 *converge*; meet, encounter, con-

front, clash; cross swords, fence 712 *strike at*; ram, butt, batter, bash, dint, dent; bulldoze 165 *demolish*; cannon into, bump into, bump against; graze 333 *rub*; butt against; drive into, crash into, smash into, run into, run down, run over; clash with, collide with, fall foul of; run one's head against, run into a brick wall, run against, dash against; bark one's shins, stub one's toe; trip over 309 *tumble*; knock together, knock heads together, clash the cymbals, clap one's hands.

strike, smite, hit, land a blow, fetch one a blow; aim a blow, hit out at; lunge at; lash out at, lace into, let fly; hit wildly, swing, flail; strike hard, slam, bang, knock; knock for six, knock into the middle of next week, send flying; knock down, floor 311 *fell*; tap, rap; slap; smack; bop, clock, clout, bash, clobber, box the ears of, clip one's ear; box, spar, fisticuff 716 *fight*; buffet, punch, paste, thump, thwack, whack, wham, rain blows, pummel, trounce, beat up, sock it to, let one have it; give one a black eye *or* a bloody nose, make one see stars, knock *or* beat six *or* seven *or* ten bells out of; pound, batter, bludgeon 332 *grind*; biff, bash, dash, slosh, sock, slog, slug, cosh, cudgel, club, mug, spifflicate; blackjack, sandbag, hit over the head, crown; concuss, stun, knock out, leave senseless; spank, wallop, thrash, lash, lam, lambast, beat, whip, cane 963 *flog*; leather, strap, belt, tan one's hide, give a hiding 963 *punish*; thresh, flail; hammer, drum; swat 216 *flatten*; maul 655 *wound*; throw stones at, stone, pelt; head (a football); bat, swipe, lob, smash, volley 287 *propel*.

280 Recoil

N. recoil, revulsion, reaction, retroaction, reflux 148 *reversion*; repercussion, reverberation, echo 404 *resonance*; reflex 417 *reflection*; kick, kickback, backlash; ricochet, cannon; rebound, bounce, spring, springboard, trampoline 328 *elasticity*; ducks and drakes; swingback, swing of the pendulum 317 *oscillation*; volley, return (at tennis), boomerang; rebuff, repulse 292 *repulsion*; riposte, return fire.

Vb. recoil, react 182 *counteract*; shrink, wince, blench, quail, start, flinch, jib, shy, shy away, jump back, back off 620 *avoid*; kick back, hit back; ricochet, cannon, cannon off; uncoil, spring back, fly back, rebound; return, swing back 148 *revert*; have repercussions; reverberate, echo 404 *resound*; be reflected, reflect 417 *shine*; boomerang 714 *retaliate*.

281 Direction

N. direction, bearing, compass reading; lie of the land 186 *situation*; orientation, collimation, alignment; set, drift 350 *current*; tenor, trend, bending 179 *tendency*; aim, course, beam; beeline, straight shot, line of sight, optical axis 249 *straightness*; course, tack; line, line of march, track, way, path, road 624 *route*; steering, steerage 269 *navigation*; aim, target 617 *objective*; compass, pelorus 269 *sailing aid*; collimator, sights; fingerpost 547 *signpost*; direction finder, range finder 465 *gauge*; orienteering.

Adj. *directed*, orientated, directed towards, signposted; aimed, well-directed, well-placed 187 *located*; bound for; aligned with; axial, diagonal; sideways 239 *lateral*; facing 240 *opposite*; direct, undeviating 249 *straight*; unswerving, straightforward, one-way, directive, guiding.

Vb. *orientate*, orientate oneself, box the compass, take one's bearings, shoot the sun, plot one's course 269 *navigate*; find which way the wind blows, see how the land lies; ask the way, ask for directions; signpost, direct, show the way, put on the right track 547 *indicate*; pinpoint, locate 187 *place*.

steer for, shape a course for, be bound for, head for, make for, aim for; make towards, bend one's steps to, go to, go towards, go straight for, direct oneself towards, make a beeline for; go straight to the point, hold the line, keep on the beam, keep the nose down.

point to, point out, point, show, point towards, signpost 547 *indicate*; incline towards.

aim, level, point; take aim, aim at; train one's sights, draw a bead on, level at; have one covered; collimate, set one's sights; hit the mark, get a bull's-eye.

Adv. *towards*, versus, facing; on the way, on the road to, through, via, en route for, by way of; straight, direct, straight forwards; point blank, straight as an arrow; in a direct line, in a straight line, in a line with, in a line for; directly, full tilt at, as the crow flies; upstream, downstream; upwind, downwind; before the wind, close to the wind, near the wind; against the wind, in the wind's eye, seaward, landward, homeward; downtown; cross-country; up-country; in all directions 183 *widely*; from *or* to the four winds; hither, thither; clockwise, anticlockwise, counterclockwise, widdershins.

282 Deviation

N. *deviation*, disorientation, misdirection, wrong course, wrong turning; aberration, deflection, refraction; diversion, digression; shift, veer, slew, swing; departure, declension 220 *obliqueness*; flection, flexion, swerve, bend 248 *curvature*; branching off 294 *divergence*; deviousness, detour, long way round, scenic route, tourist route 626 *circuit*; vagrancy; fall, lapse 495 *error*; wandering mind 456 *abstractedness*; drift, leeway; sidestep, sideslip; break, leg break, off break, googly (cricket); knight's move (chess); yaw, tack; zigzag, slalom course.

Vb. *deviate*, digress, make a detour, go a roundabout way, go the long way round; branch out 294 *diverge*; turn, filter, turn a corner, turn aside, swerve, slew; go out of one's way, depart from one's course; step aside, make way for; alter course, change direction, yaw, tack; veer, back (wind); bend, curve 248 *be curved*; zigzag, twist 251 *meander*; swing 317 *oscillate*; steer clear of, give a wide berth, sheer off; sidle, skid, sideslip; break (cricket); fly off at a tangent 220 *be oblique*; sidestep 620 *avoid*.

turn round, turn about, about turn, wheel, wheel about, face about, face the other way, do a U-turn, change one's mind; reverse, reverse direction, return 148 *revert*; go back 286 *turn back*.

stray, err, ramble, maunder, straggle 267 *wander*; go astray, go adrift, lose one's way, get lost; miss one's footing, lose one's bearings, lose one's sense of direction, take the wrong turning 495 *blunder*; lose track of, lose the place, lose the thread 456 *be inattentive*.

deflect, bend, crook; warp, skew; put off the scent, lead astray, draw a red herring, throw dust in one's eyes, set off on a wild-goose chase, misdirect, misaddress 495 *mislead*; avert; divert, change the course of; sidetrack, draw aside, push aside, pull aside, elbow aside; bias, slice, pull, hook, glance, bowl a break, bowl wide (cricket); shift, switch, shunt 151 *interchange*.

283 Preceding: going before

N. *preceding* 64 *precedence*, 119 *previousness*; going before, going ahead of, leading, heading, flying start; pre-emption, queue-jumping; pride of place; head of the table, head of the river (bumping races); lead, leading role, star role 34 *superiority*; pioneer 66 *precursor*; van, vanguard, avant-garde 237 *front*; prequel, foreword, prelude.

Vb. *precede*, go before, go ahead of, be the forerunner of, herald, be the precursor of, be the prelude to; usher in, introduce; head, spearhead, lead, be in the vanguard, head the queue; go in front, go in advance, clear the way, light the way, lead the way; lead the dance, guide, conduct 689 *direct*; take the lead, have a head start; steal a march on, pre-empt, steal one's thunder; get in front, jump the queue; get ahead of, lap 277 *outstrip*; be beforehand 135 *be early*; take precedence over, take priority over, have right of way 64 *come before*.

284 Following: going after

N. *following* 65 *sequence*; run, suit 71 *series*; subsequence 120 *subsequence*; pursuit, pursuance 619 *chase*; succession, reversion 780 *transfer*; last place 238 *rear*.

follower, pursuer, tail, stalker, attendant, suitor, hanger-on, camp follower, groupie 742 *dependant*; train, tail, wake, cortege, suite, followers 67 *retinue*; following, party, adherent, supporter, fan, -ista 703 *helper*; satellite, moon, artificial satellite, space station 276 *spaceship*; trailer, caravan 274 *cart*; tender 275 *ship*.

Vb. *follow*, come behind, succeed, follow on, follow after, follow close upon, sit on one's tail, breathe down one's neck, be bumper to bumper, follow in the wake of, tread on the heels of, tread in the steps of, follow the footprints of, come to heel 65 *come after*; stick like a shadow, tag after, hang on the skirts of, beset; attend, wait on, dance attendance on 742 *serve*; tag along 89 *accompany*; dog, shadow, trail, tail, track, chase 619 *pursue*; trail, dawdle 278 *move slowly*; bring up the rear 238 *be behind*.

285 Progression: motion forwards

N. *progression*, going forward; procession, march, way, course, career; march of time 111 *course of time*; progress, steady progress, forward march 265 *motion*; giant strides, leap, quantum leap, jump, leaps and bounds 277 *spurt*; irresistible progress, relentless progress, majestic progress; flood, tide 350 *current*; gain, ground gained, advance, headway 654 *improvement*; getting ahead, overtaking 283 *preceding*; encroachment 306 *overstepping*; next step, development, evolution 71 *continuity*, 308 *ascent*; furtherance, promotion, step up the ladder, advancement, preferment, fast lane, fast track; rise, raise, lift, leg-up 310 *elevation*; progressiveness; enterprise, go-getting, go-go 672 *undertaking*; achievement 727 *success*; economic progress 730 *prosperity*.

Adj. *progressive*, enterprising, resourceful, go-ahead, go-go, go-getting, forward-looking, reformist; advancing, etc. (see vb.); flowing on 265 *moving*; advanced, state-of-the-art, cutting-edge, leading-edge 126 *modern*.

Vb. *progress*, proceed 265 *be in motion*; advance, go forward, take a step forward, come on, develop 316 *evolve*; show promise, promise well 654 *get better*; get on, get ahead, do well 730 *prosper*; march on, run on, flow on, pass on, jog on, wag on, rub on, hold on, keep on, slog on 146 *go on*; move with the times 126 *modernize*; never look back, hold one's lead; press on, push on, drive on, push forward, press forward, press onwards 680 *has-*

ten; make a good start, make good progress; gain, gain ground, make headway, make strides 277 *move fast*; get a move on, get ahead, forge ahead, advance by leaps and bounds; gain on, distance, outdistance, overtake, leave behind 277 *outstrip*; rise, climb the ladder 308 *climb*; reach out to, make up leeway, recover lost ground 31 *recoup*; gain time, make up time.

promote, further, contribute to, advance 703 *aid*; upgrade, move up, raise, lift 310 *elevate*; bring forward, develop 174 *invigorate*; speed up 277 *accelerate*; put ahead 64 *put in front*; favour, make for 156 *cause*.

Adv. *forward*, forwards, onward, forth, on, ahead, forrard; progressively, by leaps and bounds, with giant strides.

286 Regression: motion backwards

N. *regression*, regress; reverse direction, retroflexion, retrocession, retrogression, retrogradation, retroaction, backward step 148 *reversion*; retreat, withdrawal, retirement, disengagement 290 *movement away*; regurgitation 300 *clearing*; reversing, backing; falling away, decline, drop, fall, downward trend, slump 655 *deterioration*.

return, remigration, homeward journey; homecoming 295 *arrival*; reentrance, re-entry 297 *entering*; going back, turn of the tide, reflux, ebb, regurgitation 350 *current*; veering, backing; relapse, backsliding 603 *change of mind*; U-turn, volte-face, about turn 148 *reversion*; countermarch, countermovement, countermotion 182 *counteraction*; turn, turning point 137 *crisis*; resilience 328 *elasticity*; reflex 280 *recoil*.

Vb. *regress*, recede, retrogress, retreat, sound a retreat, beat a retreat; retire, withdraw, fall back, draw back; turn away, turn tail 620 *run away*; back out, back down 753 *resign*; backtrack, backpedal; give way, give ground; recede into the distance 446 *disappear*; fall behind 278 *move slowly*; reverse, back, go backwards; run back, regurgitate; slip back; ebb, slump, fall, drop, decline 309 *descend*; bounce back 280 *recoil*.

turn back, retrace one's steps; remigrate, go *or* come back, go *or* come home, return 148 *revert*; look back, look over one's shoulder, hark back 505 *retrospect*; turn one's back, turn on one's heel; veer round, wheel round, about face, execute a volte-face, do a U-turn 603 *change one's mind*; double back, countermarch.

287 Propulsion

N. *propulsion*, jet propulsion, drive; impulsion, push, forward thrust 279 *impulse*; projection, throwing, tossing, hurling, pelting, slinging, stone-throwing; precipitation; defenestration; cast, throw, chuck, toss, fling, sling, shy, cock-shy; pot shot, pot, shot, long shot; shooting, firing, discharge, volley 712 *bombardment*; bowling, pitching, throw-in, full toss, yorker, lob (cricket); kick, punt, dribble (football); stroke, drive, swipe 279 *knock*; pull, slice (golf); rally, volley, smash (tennis); ballistics, gunnery, musketry, sniping, pea-shooting; archery, toxophily; marksmanship 694 *skill*; gunshot, bowshot, stone's throw 199 *distance*.

missile, projectile, shell, rocket, cannonball, grapeshot, ball, bullet, shot, small shot; pellet, brickbat, stone, snowball; arrow, dart 723 *throwing weapons, projectiles and missiles*; ball, tennis ball, golf ball, lake ball, cricket ball, hockey ball; football, rugby ball; bowl, boule, wood, jack, puck, curling stone; quoit, discus; javelin; hammer, caber.

propellant, thrust, driving force, jet, steam 160 *energy*; spray, aerosol, CFC, chlorofluorocarbon, greenhouse gas; thruster, pusher, shover 279 *ram*; tail wind, following wind 352 *wind*; lever, treadle, pedal, bicycle pedal; oar, sweep, paddle; screw, blade, paddlewheel 269 *propeller*; coal, petrol, diesel oil 385 *fuel*; gunpowder, dynamite 723 *explosive*; shotgun, rifle 723 *firearm*; revolver 723 *pistol*; airgun, pop gun, water pistol; blowpipe, pea-shooter; catapult, sling, bow 723 *throwing weapons, projectiles and missiles*.

Vb. propel, launch, project, set on its way; throw, cast, deliver, heave, pitch, toss, cant, chuck, shy, bung; bowl, lob, york; hurl, fling, sling, catapult; dart, flick; pelt, stone, shower, snowball; precipitate, get moving, send flying, send headlong; expel, pitchfork 300 *eject*; blow up, explode, put dynamite under, put a bomb under; serve, return, volley, smash, kill (tennis); bat, slam, slog, wham; sky, loft; drive, cut, pull, hook, glance (cricket); slice 279 *strike*; kick, dribble, punt (football); putt, push, shove, shoulder, ease along 279 *impel*; wheel, pedal, roll, bowl, trundle 315 *rotate*; move on, drive, hustle 265 *move*; sweep, sweep before one, carry before one; put to flight 727 *defeat*.

shoot, fire, open fire; fire a volley; discharge, explode, let off, set off; let fly, draw a bead on, pull the trigger; bombard 712 *fire at*; snipe, pot, take a potshot at, pepper 263 *pierce*.

288 Traction

N. traction, drawing, etc. (see vb.); retraction; retractability; magnetism 291 *attraction*; haulage; pull, haul, tug, tow; towrope; rake, harrow; trawl, dragnet; hauler, haulier; retractor; lugsail, square sail 275 *sail*; windlass; tug 275 *ship*; tractor, traction engine 274 *locomotive*;

loadstone; rowing; tug of war 716 *contest*; trailer, caravan 274 *cart*.

Vb. draw, pull, haul, kedge 269 *navigate*; tug, tow, take in tow; lug, drag, trail, trawl; rake, harrow; winch, reel in, wind in, lift, heave, hitch 310 *elevate*; drag down 311 *lower*; suck in 299 *absorb*; pluck; pull out 304 *extract*; wrench, twist 246 *distort*; yank, jerk, twitch, tweak, pluck at 318 *agitate*, pull towards 291 *attract*; pull back, draw in, retract.

289 Approach: motion towards

N. approach, advance 285 *progression*; approximation 200 *nearness*; meeting, confluence 293 *convergence*; access, accession, advent, coming 189 *presence*, 295 *arrival*; overtaking, overlapping 619 *pursuit*; onset 712 *attack*; advances, pass, overture 759 *offer*; way in 624 *access*.

Adj. approaching, nearing, getting warm, etc. (see vb.); close 200 *near*; meeting 293 *convergent*; closing in, imminent 155 *impending*; advancing, oncoming.

accessible, approachable, get-at-able; within easy reach; attainable 469 *possible*; available, obtainable, on tap; nearby 200 *near*; welcoming, inviting 882 *sociable*; well-paved, made-up, metalled.

Vb. approach, draw near; approximate; come within range 295 *arrive*; come into view 443 *be visible*; come closer, meet 293 *converge*; near, draw near, go near, walk up to, run up to; roll up 74 *congregate*; come in 297 *enter*; accost 884 *greet*; make overtures, make passes 889 *court*; lean towards, incline 179 *tend*; move towards 265 *be in motion*; advance 285 *progress*; advance upon, bear down on 712 *attack*; close in, close in on 232 *encircle*; hover 155 *impend*; overtake 277 *outstrip*; narrow the gap, breathe down one's neck, tread on one's heels, sit on one's tail, drive bumper to bumper, run one close; be in sight of, be within shouting distance of.

290 Recession: motion from

N. movement away, stepping back, recession, retirement, retreat, withdrawal 286 *regression*; emigration, evacuation 296 *departure*; resignation 621 *relinquishment*; flight 667 *escape*; shrinking, shying, flinching 620 *avoidance*; revulsion 280 *recoil*.

Vb. recede, retire, withdraw, fall back, draw back, retreat, back off 286 *regress*; ebb, subside, shrink, decline 37 *decrease*; fade from view 446 *disappear*; go, go away, leave, clear out, evacuate, emigrate 296 *depart*; move from, move away, put space between, widen the gap 199 *be distant*; stand aside, make way, sheer off 282 *deviate*; drift away 282 *stray*; back away, flinch 620 *avoid*; flee 620 *run away*; get away 667 *escape*; go back 286 *turn back*; jump back 280 *recoil*; come unstuck 46 *separate*.

291 Attraction

N. attraction, pull, drag, draw, tug; suction; magnetism, magnetic field; force of gravity; itch for 859 *desire*; affinity, sympathy, empathy; attractiveness, seductiveness, allure, appeal, sex appeal, it; allurement, seduction, temptation, lure, bait, decoy, charm, siren song 612 *inducement*; charmer, temptress, siren, Circe 612 *motivator*; head-turner; centre of attraction, cynosure, honeypot 890 *favourite*.

Vb. attract, magnetize, pull, drag, tug 288 *draw*; adduct, exercise a pull, draw towards, pull towards, drag towards; appeal, charm, move, pluck at one's heartstrings 821 *impress*; lure, allure, bait, seduce 612 *tempt*; decoy 542 *ensnare*.

292 Repulsion

N. repulsion, repulsiveness 842 *ugliness*; reflection 280 *recoil*; driving off, beating off 713 *defence*; repulse, rebuff, snub, refusal, the cold shoulder, the bird 607 *rejection*; brush-off, dismissal 300 *ejection*.

Adj. repellent, repelling, etc. (see vb.); repulsive, off-putting, antipathetic.

Vb. repel, put off, make sick 861 *cause dislike*; push away, butt away 279 *impel*; drive away, repulse, beat off, stonewall, talk out; dispel 75 *disperse*; head off, turn away, reflect 282 *deflect*; be deaf to 760 *refuse*; rebuff, snub, brush off, reject one's advances 607 *reject*; give one the bird, cold-shoulder, keep at arm's length, make one keep his distance; show the door to, shut the door in one's face, send one off with a flea in his ear, send packing, send one about his business, give one his marching orders; boot out, give the boot, kick out, sack 300 *dismiss*.

293 Convergence

N. convergence, narrowing gap; confrontation, collision course 279 *collision*; concourse, confluence, conflux, meeting 45 *union*; congress, concurrence, concentration, resort, assembly 74 *assemblage*; closing in 232 *encircling*; centring, focalization, zeroing in 76 *focus*; narrowing, tapering, taper 206 *narrowness*; tangent; perspective, vanishing point 438 *view*.

Adj. convergent, converging, etc. (see vb.); focusing, zeroing in on, focused; centring; confluent, concurrent 45 *connective*; tangential; pointed, conical, pyramidal; knock-kneed.

Vb. converge, come closer, close in; narrow

the gap; come together 295 *meet*; unite, gather together, get together 74 *congregate*; enter in 297 *enter*; close with, intercept, close in upon 232 *encircle*; concentrate, focus, bring into focus; centre on, zero in on 225 *centralize*; taper, come to a point, narrow down.

294 Divergence

N. divergence, divergency, clear blue water 15 *difference*; contradiction 14 *contrariety*; moving apart, drifting apart, parting 46 *separation*; aberration, declination 282 *deviation*; spread, fanning out, deployment 75 *dispersion*; parting of the ways, fork, bifurcation, crossroads, watershed, points 222 *crossing*; radiation, ramification, branching out; Y-shape 247 *angularity*.

Adj. divergent, diverging, etc. (see vb.); separated; radiating, radiant, palmate, stellate; centrifugal, centrifuge; aberrant.

Vb. diverge 15 *differ*; radiate; ramify, branch off, branch out; split off, fork, bifurcate; part, part company, come to the parting of the ways 46 *separate*; file off, go one's own way; change direction, switch; glance off, fly off, fly off at a tangent 282 *deviate*; deploy, fan out, spread, scatter 75 *be dispersed*; straddle, spread-eagle; splay, splay apart.

295 Arrival

N. arrival, advent, accession, appearance, entrance 189 *presence*, 289 *approach*; onset 68 *beginning*; coming, reaching, making; landfall, landing, touchdown, docking, mooring 266 *state of rest*; debarkation, disembarkation 298 *going out*; rejoining, meeting, encounter 154 *event*; greeting, handshake, golden hello, formalities 884 *courteous act*; homecoming 286 *return*; prodigal's return, reception, welcome 876 *celebration*; guest, visitor, visitant, new arrival, nouveau arrivé, recent arrival, homing pigeon 297 *incomer*; finish, close finish, neck-and-neck finish, needle finish, photo finish 716 *contest*; last lap, home stretch.

goal 617 *objective*; journey's end, point of no return, terminus 69 *extremity*; stop, halt 145 *stopping place*; pier; harbour, haven, anchorage, roadstead 662 *shelter*; aerodrome, airport, airfield, heliport, terminal, air terminal 271 *air travel*; terminus, railway terminus, railway station, bus station, depot, rendezvous 192 *meeting place*.

Vb. arrive, come, reach, fetch up at, end up at, get there 189 *be present*; reach one's destination, make port; dock, moor, drop anchor 266 *come to rest* (see also *land* below); draw up, pull up, park; come home, return home 286 *regress*; hit, make, win to, gain, attain; finish the race, breast the tape; achieve one's aim, reach one's goal 725 *carry through*; be on the doorstep 297 *enter*; make an entrance; appear, show up, pop up, turn up, roll up, drop in, blow in 882 *visit*; put in, pull in, stop 145 *pause*; clock in 135 *be early*; arrive at, find 484 *discover*; arrive at the top 727 *be successful*, 730 *prosper*; be brought, come to hand.

land, beach, run aground; touch down, make a landing; step ashore, disembark, get off, get out, get down, alight, light on, perch 309 *descend*; dismount.

meet, join, see, see again; receive, greet, welcome, shake hands 882 *be sociable*; go to meet, come to meet; rendezvous; come upon, encounter, come in contact, run into, meet by chance; hit, bump into, knock into, collide with 279 *collide*; burst upon, light upon, gather, assemble 74 *congregate*.

Int. *greetings*, hi, how are you?, how do you do, hullo, welcome, pleased to meet you; aloha, namaste, salaam, shalom.

296 Departure

N. *departure*, leaving, parting, removal, going away; walkout, exit 298 *going out*; pulling out, emigration 290 *movement away*; migration, exodus, general exodus, Hegira; flight, moonlight flit, decampment, elopement, getaway 667 *escape*; embarkation 297 *entering*; saddling 267 *horse riding*; setting out, outset 68 *start*; takeoff, blast-off 308 *ascent*; zero hour, time of departure, moment of leave-taking; point of departure.

farewell, goodbye; leave-taking, congé, dismissal; goodbyes, goodnights, farewells, adieus; valediction, valedictory; funeral oration, epitaph, obituary 364 *funeral rites*; last handshake, waving goodbye, wave of the handkerchief 884 *courteous act*; send-off, farewell address; last post, last words, final goodbye, parting shot; stirrup cup, doch-an-dorris, one for the road, nightcap.

Vb. *depart*, quit, leave, abandon 621 *relinquish*; retire, withdraw, retreat 286 *turn back*; remove, move house, flit, leave the neighbourhood, leave the country, leave home, emigrate, absent oneself 190 *go away*; fly the nest, take one's leave, take one's departure, be going, be getting along; bid farewell, say goodbye, say good night, make one's adieus, tear oneself away, part, part company; receive one's congé, get one's marching orders; leave work, cease work 145 *cease*; clock out, go home 298 *emerge*; quit the scene, leave the stage, bow out, give one's swan song, exit, make one's exit 753 *resign*; depart this life 361 *die*.

walk out, march out, pack up, clear off; clear out, pull out, evacuate; make tracks; be off, beetle off, buzz off, slope off, swan off, push off, shove off, make oneself scarce; decamp, up sticks, strike tents, break camp, break up; take wing 271 *fly*; vamoose, skedaddle, beat it, hop it, scram, bolt, scuttle, skip, slip away, cut and run 277 *move fast*; flee, take flight, make a break for it 620 *run away*; flit, make a moonlight flit, make one's getaway 446 *disappear*; elope, abscond, give one the slip 667 *escape*.

start out, be off, get going, get on one's way, set out 68 *begin*; set forth, sally forth, take up one's bed and walk; issue forth, strike out, light out, march out 298 *emerge*; gird oneself, be ready to start, warm up 669 *make ready*; take ship, embark, go on board 297 *enter*; hoist the Blue Peter, unmoor, cast off, weigh anchor, push off, get under way, set sail, put out to sea 269 *navigate*; mount, bridle, harness, saddle 267 *ride*; hitch up, pile in, hop on; catch a train, catch a plane, catch a bus; pull out, drive off, take off, be on one's way, see off.

Int. *be seeing you*, bye-bye, bye for now, cheerio, farewell, goodbye, see you later, so long, ta-ta, adieu, adios, aloha, arrivederci, auf Wiedersehen, au revoir, ciao, hasta la vista, sayonara; have a good trip, God be with you, pleasant journey, bon voyage.

297 Ingress: motion into

N. *entering*, entry, entrance, incoming, ingress; re-entry 286 *return*; inflow, influx, flood 350 *stream*; inpouring, inrush; intrusion, trespass 306 *overstepping*; invasion, forced entry, inroad, raid, irruption, incursion 712 *attack*; immersion, diffusion, osmosis; penetration, infiltration, insinuation 231 *betweenness*, 303 *insertion*; immigration; intake 299 *reception*; import, importation 272 *transference*; right of entry, admission, admittance, access, entrée 756 *permission*; free trade 791 *trade*.

way in, way, path 624 *access*; entrance, entrance hall, entry, door 263 *doorway*; mouth, opening 263 *aperture*; inlet 345 *gulf*; channel 351 *water channel*; open door, free port 796 *market*.

incomer, newcomer, Johnny-come-lately; new arrival, nouveau arrivé, new member, new face, joiner, joinee; new boy, new girl 538 *beginner*; visitant, visitor, caller 882 *sociable person*; immigrant, migrant, asylum-seeker, economic migrant, colonist, settler 59 *foreigner*; stowaway, unwelcome guest 59 *outsider*; invader, raider 712 *attacker*; house-breaker, burglar 789 *thief*; entrant, competitor 716 *contender*.

Vb. enter, turn into, go in, come in, move in, drive in, run in, breeze in, venture in, sidle in, step in, walk in, file in; follow in 65 *come after*; set foot in, cross the threshold, darken the doors; let oneself in; unlock the door, turn the key 263 *open*; gain admittance, have entrée to, be invited; look in, drop in, pop in, blow in, call 882 *visit*; mount, board, get aboard; get in, hop in, jump in, pile in; squeeze into, creep in, slip in, edge in, slink in, sneak in, steal in; work one's way into, buy one's way into, insinuate oneself; worm into, bore into 263 *pierce*; bite into, eat into, cut into 260 *notch*; put one's foot in, tread in, fall into, drop into 309 *tumble*; sink into, plunge into, dive into 313 *plunge*; join, enlist in, enroll oneself; immigrate, settle in 187 *place oneself*; let in 299 *admit*; put in 303 *insert*; enter oneself, enter for 716 *contend*.

infiltrate, percolate, seep, soak through; leak into, sink in, penetrate, permeate, mix in, taint, infect 655 *impair*; filter in, worm one's way in.

intrude, trespass, gatecrash, outstay one's welcome, be de trop; horn in, barge in, push in, muscle in, break in on, burst in on, interrupt 63 *disarrange*; break in, burgle 788 *steal*.

298 Egress: motion out of

N. going out, egress, egression; exit; walkout, exodus, general exodus, evacuation 296 *departure*; emigration, expatriation, exile 883 *seclusion*; Hegira; emergence, emerging, debouchment; emersion, surfacing; emanation, efflux, issue; evaporation 388 *evaporation*; eruption, outburst 176 *outbreak*; sortie, breakout 667 *escape*; export, exportation 272 *transference*.

leaver, migrant, economic migrant, emigrant, émigré 59 *foreigner*; expatriate, colonist 191 *settler*; expellee, exile; deportee, refugee 883 *outcast*.

outflow, effluence, efflux, effusion; emission 300 *ejection*; issue, outpouring, gushing, streaming; exudation, oozing, dribbling, weeping; bleeding 302 *bleeding*; perspiration, sweating, sweat; percolation, filtration; leak, escape, leakage, seepage 634 *waste*; drain, running sore 772 *loss*; discharge, drainage, draining 300 *clearing*; overflow, spill, flood 350 *waterfall*; jet, fountain, spring 156 *source*; gush, squirt 350 *stream*; geyser; streaming eyes, runny nose, postnasal drip.

outlet, vent, chute; spout, nozzle, tap, faucet; pore, blowhole 263 *aperture*, 352 *breathing*; sluice, floodgate 351 *water channel*; exhaust pipe; drainpipe, overflow, gargoyle; exit, way out, path 624 *access*; escape, loop-hole 667 *means of escape*.

Vb. emerge, pop out, stick out, project 254 *jut*; peep out, peer out 443 *be visible*; surface 308 *ascend*; emanate, transpire 526 *be disclosed*; egress, issue, debouch, make a sortie; issue forth, sally forth, come forth, go forth; issue out of, go out, come out, creep out, sneak out, march out, flounce out, fling out 267 *walk*; jump out, bale out 312 *leap*; clear out, evacuate 296 *walk out*; emigrate 267 *travel*; exit, walk off 296 *depart*; erupt, break out 667 *escape*.

exude, perspire, sweat, steam 379 *be hot*; ooze, seep through, soak through, leak through; percolate, strain, strain out, filter, filtrate, distil; run, dribble, drip, drop, drivel, drool, slaver, slobber, salivate, water at the mouth 341 *be wet*; exhale 352 *breathe*.

299 Reception

N. reception, admission, admittance, entrance, entrée, access 297 *entering*; invitation 759 *offer*; receptivity, acceptance; open arms, welcome, liberty hall 876 *celebration*; enlistment, enrolment 78 *inclusion*; initiation, baptism, baptismal fire 68 *debut*; asylum, sanctuary, shelter, refuge 660 *protection*; introduction; importation, import 272 *transference*; radio receiver, telephone receiver 531 *telecommunication*; inhalation 352 *breathing*; sucking, suction; assimilation, digestion, absorption, resorption; engulfing, engulfment, swallowing, ingurgitation; ingestion (of food) 301 *eating*; imbibition, fluid intake 301 *drinking*; intake, consumption 634 *waste*; infusion 303 *insertion*; interjection 231 *betweenness*; admissibility.

Vb. admit, receive, accept, take in; grant asylum, afford sanctuary, shelter, give refuge 660 *safeguard*; welcome, invite, call in 759 *offer*; enlist, enrol, take on 622 *employ*; give entrance *or* admittance to, allow in, allow access, give a ticket to, grant a visa to; throw open, open the door 263 *open*; bring in, import, land 272 *transfer*; let in, show in, usher in, introduce 64 *come before*; send in 272 *send*; initiate, baptize 534 *teach*.

absorb, incorporate, engross, assimilate, digest; suck in; soak up, sponge, mop up, blot 342 *dry*; take in, ingest, imbibe; lap up, swallow, engulf, gulp, gobble, devour 301 *eat*, *drink*; keep down; breathe in, inhale 352 *breathe*; sniff 394 *smell*; get the taste of 386 *taste*.

300 Ejection

N. ejection, ejaculation, expulsion, defenestration; precipitation 287 *propulsion*; disbarment, striking off, disqualification, excommunication 57 *exclusion*; throwing out, chucking out, bum's rush; drumming out, marching orders; the heave-ho, dismissal, discharge, redundancy, golden handshake, decruitment, downsizing, outplacement, rightsizing, sack, boot, push, kick upstairs, garden leave *or* gardening leave 607 *rejection*; deportation, extradition; relegation, downgrading, exile, banishment 883 *seclusion*; eviction, dislodgment 188 *displacement*; dispossession, deprivation 786 *expropriation*; jettison, throwing overboard 779 *non-retention*; clean sweep, elimination 165 *destruction*; emission, effusion, shedding, spilling 298 *outflow*; libation 981 *religious offering*; secretion, salivation 302 *excretion*; radioactivity 417 *radiation*.

clearing, clearance, clearage, voidance, drainage, curettage, aspiration; emptying, etc. (see vb.); eruption, eruptiveness 176 *outbreak*; egestion, regurgitation, disgorgement; vomiting, throwing up, nausea, vomit, puke; gas, wind, burp, belch, fart; breaking wind, belching; elimination, evacuation 302 *excretion*.

Adj. *vomiting*, sick, sickened, nauseated, sick to one's stomach, throwing up, green, green around the gills; seasick, airsick, carsick; sick as a dog.

Vb. *eject*, expel, send down 963 *punish*; strike off, strike off the register, disbar, excommunicate 57 *exclude*; export, send away 272 *transfer*; deport, expatriate; exile, banish, transport 883 *seclude*; throw up, cast up, wash up; spit out, cough up, spew out; put out, push out, turf out, throw out, chuck out, fling out, bounce 287 *propel*; kick out, boot out, give the bum's rush, throw out on one's ear, give the heave-ho, bundle out, hustle out; drum out; precipitate 287 *propel*; pull out 304 *extract*; unearth, root out, weed out, uproot, eradicate 165 *destroy*; rub out, scratch out, eliminate 550 *obliterate*; exorcize, rid, get rid of, rid oneself, get shot of; shake off, brush off; dispossess, expropriate 786 *deprive*; out, oust, evict, dislodge, turn out, turn adrift, turn out of house and home 188 *displace*; smoke out 619 *hunt*; jettison, discard, throw away, throw overboard 779 *not retain*; blackball 607 *reject*.

dismiss, discharge, lay off, make redundant, drop 674 *stop using*; axe, sack, fire, give the sack, give the boot, give the push, give the heave-ho, give marching orders to 779 *not retain*; turn away, send one about his business, send one away with a flea in his ear, send packing 292 *repel*; see off, shoo away 854 *frighten*; show the door, show out; bowl out, run out, catch out; exorcize, order off, order away 757 *prohibit*.

empty, drain, void; evacuate, eliminate 302 *excrete*; discharge; pour out, decant 272 *trans-*

pose; drink up, drain to the dregs 301 *drink*; drain off, strain off, ladle out, bail out, pump out, suck out, run off, siphon off, open the sluices, open the floodgates, turn on the tap 263 *open*; draw off, tap, broach 263 *pierce*; milk, bleed, let blood, catheterize 304 *extract*; clear, sweep away, clear away, clean up, mop up, make a clean sweep of, clear the decks 648 *clean*; clean out, clear out; unload, unpack 188 *displace*; disembowel, eviscerate, gut, clean, bone, fillet 229 *uncover*; disinfect 648 *purify*; depopulate, desertize 105 *cause to be few*.

emit, let out, give vent to; send out 272 *send*; emit rays 417 *radiate*; emit a smell, give off, exhale, breathe out, perfume, scent 394 *smell*; vapour, fume, smoke, steam, puff 338 *vaporize*; spit, splutter; pour, spill, shed, sprinkle, spray; spurt *or* spirt, squirt, jet, gush, ejaculate 341 *moisten*; bleed, weep; drip, drop, ooze; dribble, drool, slobber 298 *exude*; sweat, perspire 379 *be hot*; secrete 632 *store*; egest, pass 302 *excrete*; drop (a foal), lay (an egg) 167 *generate*.

vomit, be sick, be sick to one's stomach, bring up, throw up, regurgitate, disgorge, retch, gag; not keep down; spew, puke, cat, honk, poop, barf, chunder, be seasick, feel nausea, heave, have a bilious attack.

belch, burp, eruct; break wind, blow off, fart; hiccup, cough, hawk, clear the throat, spit, expectorate, gob.

301 Food: eating and drinking

N. *eating*, munching, etc. (see vb.); ingestion; alimentation, nutrition; feeding, drip-feeding, force-feeding, gavage; consumption, devouring; swallowing, downing, getting down, bolting; biting, chewing, mastication; rumination, digestion; chewing the cud; cropping; table, diet, dining, lunching, breakfasting, supping, having tea, snacking, grazing; dining out 882 *sociability*; partaking; tasting, nibbling, pecking, licking, playing with one's food, toying with one's food; eating disorder; anorexia, anorexia nervosa; guzzling, gobbling; overeating, overindulgence, bingeing, binge-eating, bulimia nervosa, seesaw eating 944 *sensualism*, 947 *gluttony*; obesity 195 *bulk*; appetite, voracity, wolfishness 859 *hunger*; feeding frenzy; omnivorousness 464 *lack of discrimination*; eating habits, table manners 610 *practice*; carnivorousness, man-eating, cannibalism; herbivorousness, vegetarianism, veganism; edibility, digestibility, food chain.

feasting, eating and drinking, gormandizing, guzzling, swilling; banqueting, eating out, dining out, having a meal out; regalement; orgy, bacchanalia, feast; reception, wedding breakfast, annual dinner, do 876 *celebration*; harvest supper, beanfeast, bunfight, thrash; Christmas dinner, blowout, spread (see also *meal* below); loaded table, festive cheer, festive board, groaning board; fleshpots 635 *plenty*.

dieting, dietetics 658 *therapy*; slimming, losing weight, weight loss, weight-watching, reducing, yo-yo dieting, juice fasting 206 *thinness*, 946 *fasting*; diet, balanced diet, macrobiotic diet, diet plan, crash diet, Atkins diet, F-plan diet, Weightwatchers (tdmk); nouvelle cuisine, cuisine minceur, lean cuisine; regimen, regime *or* régime, course, diet sheet, calorie counter; malnutrition 651 *disease*; calories, vitamins (see also *food content* below); vitamin pill; additive, E number; dieter, etc. 942 *abstainer*.

gastronomy, epicureanism, epicurism 944 *sensualism*; gourmandism, foodism, good living, high living 947 *gluttony*; refined palate 463 *discrimination*.

cookery, cooking, baking, cuisine, haute cuisine, nouvelle cuisine, lean cuisine, fusion cuisine; food preparation, dressing; domestic science, home economics, catering 633 *provision*; food processing (see also *provisions* below); baker, cook, chef, sous chef, commis chef, cuisinier, cordon bleu 633 *caterer*; bakery, rotisserie, delicatessen, restaurant 192 *café*; kitchen, cookhouse, galley; microwave, oven 383 *furnace*; cooking medium, butter, margarine, ghee, corn oil, vegetable oil, sunflower oil, olive oil, extra virgin olive oil, rape seed oil 357 *oil*; dripping, lard 357 *fat*; yeast 323 *raising agent*; flour, cornflour 332 *powder*; vinegar, balsamic vinegar, malt vinegar, etc. 393 *sourness*; recipe, cookery book, cookbook.

eater, feeder, consumer, partaker, taster, etc. (see vb.); nibbler, picker, pecker; messmate; diner, banqueter, feaster, picnicker; diner-out, dining club 882 *sociability*; connoisseur, gourmet, epicure; gourmand, trencherman, trencherwoman, bon vivant, foodie 947 *glutton*; flesh-eater, meat-eater, carnivore; man-eater, cannibal; vegetarian, vegan, veggie, herbivore; omnivore, hearty eater; wolf, gannet, vulture, hyena, locust.

provisions, stores, commissariat; provender, foodstuff, groceries; tinned *or* canned food, frozen food, convenience food, junk food, fast food; keep, board, maintenance, aliment, sustenance 633 *provision*; self-sufficiency; commons, rations, iron rations; helping 783 *portion*.

animal food, feed, fodder, provender, pasture, pasturage, forage; corn, oats, barley, grain, hay, grass, clover, lucerne, silage; beechmast, acorns; foodstuffs, winter feed; chicken feed, pigswill, cattle cake; saltlick; meat and bonemeal, MBM.

food, meat, bread, staff of life; aliment, nutriment, liquid nutriment; alimentation, nutrition; nurture, sustenance, nourishment, food and drink, pabulum; manna; nectar and ambrosia, amrita; daily bread, staple food, wheat, maize, rice, pulses, beans, potatoes; foodstuffs, comestibles, eats, victuals, viands, provender, grub, tucker, nosh, scoff, chow, chuck, scran; biscuit, salt pork, pemmican; stodge 391 *unsavouriness*; processed food, carrion, offal; wholefood, health food, energy bar, energy snack, sports nutrition, functional food, organic foodstuff, high-fibre food, low-fat food; genetically-modified food, GM food, genetically-altered food, Frankenstein food, Frankenfood, irradiated food; good food, cakes and ale; titbits, snacks, delicacies, Gucci food, garnish, flavouring, herbs, sauce 389 *condiment*.

food content, vitamins; calories, roughage, bulk, fibre; minerals, salts; calcium, iron; protein, amino acid; fat, oil, cholesterol, saturated fats, unsaturated food, polyunsaturated food, polyunsaturate essential fatty acid, trans-fatty acid 357 *fat*; carbohydrates, carbs, starch; sugar, glucose, sucrose, lactose, fructose 392 *sweet thing*; additive, preservative, antioxidant; artificial flavouring; E numbers.

mouthful, bite, nibble, morsel 33 *small quantity*; sop, sip, swallow; titbit; sandwich, club sandwich, open sandwich, submarine sandwich *or* submarine, toasted sandwich *or* toastie; snack, savoury, burrito, fajita, nacho, tortilla, wrap; petit four, biscuit, chocolate, sweet, toffee, chewing gum (see also *sweets* below); popcorn, crisps, nuts, Bombay mix, pork scratchings.

meal, refreshment, fare; snack, bite to eat; piece, butty, sandwich (see also *mouthful* above); hamburger, hot dog, fish and chips, Buffalo wings; packed lunch, ploughman's lunch; square meal, three-course meal, sit-down meal, repast, collation, spread, feed, blowout, beanfeast (see also *feasting* above); beano, thrash, junket 837 *festivity*; picnic, barbecue; bread and cheese lunch, potluck; take away, food to go; breakfast, elevenses, luncheon, lunch, brunch, tiffin; tea, afternoon tea, high tea; dinner, supper, fork supper, buffet supper; table d'hôte, à la carte, cover, helping 783 *portion*; seconds.

dish, course; main dish; salad, side dish, entremets; dessert, pudding, savoury; speciality, pièce de résistance, plat du jour, dish of the day; meat and two veg (see also *meat* below); casserole, stew, Irish stew, hotpot, Lancashire hotpot, ragout, blanquette 43 *a mixture*; meat loaf, hamburger; goulash, curry;

moussaka; pilau, pilaff, paella, risotto, biryani; chop suey, chow mein, stir-fry; dhal, bhaji; pasta, ravioli, lasagne, macaroni, spaghetti, tagliatelle, fettuccine, vermicelli, tortellini, penne, cannelloni, noodles; pancake, pizza, taco, tortilla, burrito, chimichanga, fajita; pasty, pie, flan, quiche; fricassee, fritters, croquettes, spring roll; fry-up, mixed grill, fritto misto, kebabs; tandoori; fondue, soufflé, omelette, fu yung; Welsh rabbit *or* rarebit, buck rabbit, bread and cheese, bread and dripping; cauliflower cheese, ratatouille, bubble and squeak; pease pudding, baked beans, nut cutlet; leftovers.

hors-d'oeuvres, antipasto, smorgasbord; starter, appetiser, canapé; angels on horseback, devils on horseback; bruschetta, crostini; taramasalata, hummus, raita, mezze; vol-au-vent: blini, samosa, pakora; soup, cream soup, broth, brew, potage, clear soup, consommé; stock, bouillon, julienne, bisque, chowder, purée; cock-a-leekie, mulligatawny, minestrone, borscht, gazpacho, bouillabaisse; cold meats, cooked meats, cold cuts, salami, pâté, terrine, galantine; salad, side salad, green salad, mixed salad, potato salad, Russian salad, Waldorf salad, coleslaw, macedoine; mayonnaise, dressing, French dressing 389 *sauce*.

fish as food, fish 365 *marine life*; fish and chips, fish pie, fish cakes, gefilte fish, fish fingers, quenelles, kedgeree; white fish, oily fish, fresh fish, smoked fish; freshwater fish, eel, salmon, smoked salmon, lox, gravlax *or* gravadlax, trout, tilapia; seafish, cod, coley, rock salmon, dogfish, whiting, monkfish, plaice, sole, skate, hake, halibut, haddock, smoked haddock, finnan haddie, turbot, mullet, mackerel, herring, rollmops, brisling, whitebait, sprats; sardine, pilchard, anchovies, tuna, tunny; kippers, bloaters, Arbroath smoky; Bombay duck; seafood, shellfish, oyster, lobster, crayfish, crab, shrimp, prawn, scampi; squid, calamari; scallop, cockle, winkle, mussel, whelk; jellied eel; roe, soft roe, hard roe, caviar; sushi; Frankenfish.

meat, flesh; red meat, white meat; beef, mutton, lamb, veal, pork, venison, game, bushmeat; pheasant, grouse, partridge, chicken 365 *table bird, poultry*; soya flour, textured vegetable protein, TVP 150 *substitute*; roast meat, Sunday roast, Sunday joint, roast beef and Yorkshire pudding, tournedos; boiled beef and carrots; haggis, black pudding; shepherd's pie, cottage pie; minced meat, mince; meatballs, rissoles, hamburgers; mechanically recovered meat, MRM; sausage, banger, snorker, chipolata, frankfurter, knackwurst *or* knockwurst, smoked sausage, chorizo; toad in

the hole, Cornish pasty, steak and kidney pudding; cut, joint, leg; baron of beef, sirloin; shoulder, hand of pork, skirt, scrag end, breast, brisket; shin, loin, flank, ribs, topside, silverside; cutlet, chop, loin chop, chump chop, gigot chop, escalope; steak, fillet steak, rump steak, porterhouse steak, entrecôte steak, sirloin steak; pork pie, ham, bacon, bacon rasher, streaky bacon, back bacon, boiled bacon, gammon; luncheon meat, Spam (tdmk); tongue, knuckle, brawn, oxtail, cowheel, pig's trotters, sweetbreads, tripe, chitterlings; offal, kidney, liver, haslet 224 *insides*; human flesh, long pig.

dessert, pudding, sweet; milk pudding, rice pudding, semolina, tapioca, bread-and-butter pudding, steamed pudding, suet pudding, Christmas pudding, plum pudding, summer pudding, roly-poly, spotted dick, duff, plum duff; jam tart, mince pies (see also *bread, pastries and cakes* below); apple pie, tarte tatin; crumble, charlotte, strudel; sticky toffee pudding, baklava; stewed fruit, compôte, fool; fresh fruit, fruit salad; ice cream, sorbet, mousse, tiramisu, soufflé, sundae, trifle, blancmange, jelly, custard, syllabub, pannacotta, crème caramel 392 *sweet thing*; cheese board; yogurt.

sweets, boiled sweets, confectionery; candy, chocolate, caramel, toffee, fudge, Turkish delight, marshmallows, mints, liquorice; acid drops, pear drops, barley sugar, humbugs, butterscotch, nougat; gob-stopper, aniseed ball, chewing gum, bubble gum; lolly, lollipop 392 *sweet thing*; sweetmeat, comfit, bonbon; crystallized fruit; toffee apple, candy floss.

fruit and vegetables, soft fruit, berry, gooseberry, strawberry, raspberry, loganberry, blackberry, tayberry, bilberry, mulberry; currant, redcurrant, blackcurrant, whitecurrant; apricot, peach, nectarine, plum, greengage, damson, cherry; apple, crab apple, pippin, russet, pear; citrus fruit, orange, grapefruit, pomelo, lemon, lime, tangerine, clementine, mandarin; banana, pineapple, grape; rhubarb; date, fig; dried fruit, currant, raisin, sultana, prune; pomegranate, persimmon, Sharon fruit, passion fruit, guava, lichee, star fruit; mango, avocado; melon, cantaloupe, honeydew, water melon; pawpaw, papaya; breadfruit; nut, coconut, Brazil nut, cashew nut, pecan, peanut, groundnut, monkey nut, almond, walnut, chestnut, pine nut, hazel nut, cob nut, filbert, betel nut 366 *fruit*; bottled fruit, tinned fruit, preserves 392 *sweet thing*; vegetable, greens 366 *plant*; turnip, swede, parsnip, carrot, Jerusalem artichoke; potato, spud, baked potato, roast potato, boiled potato, mashed potato, duchesse potato, fried potato, sauté potato, French fries, chips; sweet potato, yam; green vegetable, cabbage, Chinese cabbage, red cabbage, green cabbage, white cabbage, savoy, cauliflower, broccoli, calabrese, kohlrabi, kale, curly kale, seakale; sprouts, Brussel sprout, spring greens; pulses, pea, chick pea, petits pois, mangetout, lentils, split peas, bean, French bean, broad bean, runner bean, haricot bean, butter bean, kidney bean, soya bean, adzuki bean; okra, lady's fingers, sorrel, spinach, chard, radicchio, spinach beet, seakale beet, asparagus, globe artichoke; leek, onion, shallots, garlic; marrow, courgette, zucchini, cucumber, pumpkin, squash, gourd, dudhi; gherkin, etc. 389 *sauce*; aubergine, eggplant, capsicum, pepper, red *or* green *or* yellow pepper, chilli; sweetcorn; salads, lettuce, cos lettuce, Chinese leaves, Chinese cabbage, pak choi; chicory, endive; spring onion, scallion, radish, celery, beetroot; tomato, beef tomato, cherry tomato, tomatoes on the vine, sundried tomatoes, love-apple; beansprouts, bamboo shoots; cress, watercress, mustard and cress; mushroom, boletus, cep, chanterelle, shiitake, truffle; laver, laverbread, samphire; tofu, bean curd, Quorn (tdmk).

herb, bouquet garni, fines herbes; marjoram, sweet marjoram, oregano, rosemary, sage, mint, parsley, chervil, chives, thyme, basil, balm, bergamot, savory, tarragon, bayleaf, dill, fennel, borage, hops, seasoning 389 *condiment*.

spice, spicery; coriander, cumin, cardamom, pepper, cayenne, paprika, chilli, curry powder, turmeric, allspice, mace, cinnamon, ginger, nutmeg, clove, caraway, juniper berries, capers, vanilla pod 389 *condiment*.

cereals, grains, wheat, buckwheat, oats, rye, maize, mealies, corn; rice, brown rice, unpolished rice, wild rice, long grain rice, patna rice, basmati rice, golden rice, short grain rice, pudding rice; millet, sorghum; breakfast cereal, cornflakes, muesli, oatmeal, porridge, gruel, skilly, brose; flour, plain flour, self-raising flour, meal, wholemeal, wheat germ, bran.

bread, *pastries and cakes*, dough, yeast; crust, crumb; white bread, sliced bread, soda bread, brown bread, wholemeal bread, malt bread, granary bread, black bread, rye bread, pumpernickel, corn bread, pitta bread, ciabatta; toast, rusk, croûton; loaf, pan loaf, cottage loaf, cob, tin, farmhouse, bloomer, baguette, French stick, bread stick; roll, breakfast roll, bridge roll, finger roll, bap, bagel, croissant, brioche, bun, currant bun; crumpet, muffin, scone, drop scone, pancake, crêpe; tea-cake, pikelet, oatcake, bannock; poppadom *or* pappadom, chapatti, nan, paratha, polenta, tortilla, taco, waffle, wafer, crispbread, cracker, cream cracker; confectionery; patty, pasty, turnover, dumpling; tart, flan, quiche, puff, pie, piecrust; pastry, shortcrust pastry, flaky pastry, puff pastry, rough puff pastry, choux pastry; patisserie, gateau, cake, lardy cake, fruit cake, Dundee cake, seed cake, sponge cake, Madeira cake, angel cake, battenburg cake, layer cake, galette, cheesecake; brownie, fairy cake, cup cake, meringue, éclair, macaroon, ratafia biscuit; Chelsea bun, Bath bun, Eccles cake, doughnut, flapjack, brandysnap, gingerbread, shortbread, cookie, biscuit, cracker, pretzel; digestive biscuit, tea biscuit, Abernethy biscuit, Nice biscuit, garibaldi biscuit, custard cream, gingernut.

dairy products and eggs (see also *dish* above and *milk* below); cream, clotted cream, curds, whey, junket, yogurt *or* yoghurt *or* yoghourt, fruit yogurt, low-fat yogurt; fromage frais; cheese, goat's cheese, cream cheese, cottage cheese, full-fat cheese, crowdie; ripe cheese, blue cheese; vegetarian cheese; grated cheese; mousetrap; egg, yolk, egg yolk, white, egg white, albumen; duck egg, quail's egg; scrambled eggs, poached egg, boiled egg, fried egg.

Cheeses

Bel Paese, Bleu d'Auvergne, Boursin, Brie, Caboc, Caerphilly, Cambozola, Camembert, Cashel Blue, Cheddar, Cheshire, Danish blue, Dolcelatte, Doolin, Dorset Blue Vinny, Double Gloucester, Dunlop, Edam, Emmental, Gouda, Gorgonzola, Gruyère, Halloumi, Havarti, Jarlsberg, Lancashire, Leerdammer, Leicestershire, Limburger, Lymeswold, mascarpone, mozzarrella, Munster, Parmesan, Pont-l'Éveque, Port Salut, Provolone, red Windsor, ricotta, Roquefort, sage Derby, Saint-Paulin, Stilton, Vacherin, Wensleydale.

---

drinking, imbibing, sipping, wine-tasting 463 *discrimination*; gulping; swilling, alcoholism, binge-drinking 949 *drunkenness*; libation 981 *religious offering*.

drink, draught, beverage, dram, bevvy; gulp, swallow, sip, sup; bottle, bowl, glass 194 *cup*; cuppa, pinta; glassful, bumper; snootful; swig, nip, noggin, jigger, tot, slug; peg, double peg, snorter, snifter, chaser; long drink; short; quick one, quickie, snort; sundowner, nightcap; loving cup; stirrup cup, doch-an-dorris, one for the road; hair of the dog; health, toast; mixed drink, concoction, cocktail, punch, spritzer 43 *mixture*; potion, decoction, infusion 658 *medicine*; the cup that cheers; nectar, amrita.

soft drink, non-alcoholic beverage; water, drinking water, spring water, fountain; soda water, soda, cream soda, soda fountain, siphon; table water, carbonated water, mineral water, Perrier (tdmk), tonic water, barley water, squash, low-calorie drink, mixer; energy drink, sports drink; iced drink, frappé; milk, milk shake; ginger beer, ginger ale, Coca Cola *or* Coke (tdmk), Pepsi (tdmk); fizz, pop, lemonade, orangeade, bitter lemon; cordial, juice, fruit juice, apple juice, tomato juice, vegetable juice, juice box; coconut milk; tea, char, cuppa, Indian tea, China tea, green tea, black tea, Russian tea, iced tea, lemon tea, pekoe, orange pekoe, oolong, lapsang souchong; herb tea *or* herbal tea, maté, bush tea *or* redbush tea *or* rooibos tea, tisane 658 *tonic*; coffee, decaffeinated coffee, decaf, white coffee, café au lait, black coffee, café noir, Irish coffee, Turkish coffee, mocha, espresso, latte, skinny, cappuccino, frappuccino, mochaccino; caffeine 658 *tonic*; cocoa (see also *milk* below); sherbet, syrup, julep, hydromel.

   alcoholic drink, strong drink, booze, bevvy, tipple, poison; brew, intoxicating liquor (see also *wine* below); alcohol; malt liquor, John Barleycorn, beer, small beer; draught beer, keg beer, bottled beer; strong beer; heavy, export; ale, real ale; barley wine; stout, lager, bitter, porter, mild, home brew; low-alcohol beer, no-alcohol beer, nab; shandy; cider, scrumpy; perry, mead, Athole brose; palm wine, rice wine, rice beer, toddy, sake, mescal, tequila; distilled liquor, spirituous liquor, spirits, ardent spirits, raw spirits, aqua vitae, firewater, hooch, moonshine, mountain dew, rotgut, hard stuff; brandy, cognac, eau-de-vie, armagnac, marc, applejack, Calvados, kirsch, slivovitz, jambava, cachaça; gin, mother's ruin, geneva, Hollands, schnapps, sloe gin; whisky, Scotch whisky, scotch, usquebaugh, water of life; rye, bourbon; Irish whiskey, poteen; vodka, aquavit, ouzo, raki, arrack; rum, white rum, Bacardi (tdmk), margarita; aperitif, absinthe, pastis, Pernod (tdmk); liqueur, cassis, Kir, Cointreau (tdmk), Drambuie (tdmk), curaçao, crème de menthe, ratafia; grog, hot toddy, punch, rum punch; spiced wine, mulled wine, negus, posset, claret cup; Pimms (tdmk), gin and tonic, pink gin, highball, brandy and soda, whisky and soda; mint julep; cocktail; alcopop. (See also *drink* above.)

Cocktails

Alaska, alexander, Algonquin, Americano, aviation, Bellini, between the sheets, black Russian, Black Watch, Bloody Mary, blue lagoon, Bronx, caipirinha, Clover Club, Collins, Combustible Edison, Cuba libre, daiquiri, death in the afternoon, Delilah, flaming Ferrari, Gibson, gimlet, gin rickey, godfather, golden dawn, grasshopper, Harvey Wallbanger, highball, hurricane, John Collins, maiden's prayer, mai tai, Manhattan, margarita, martini, mint julep, mojito, mimosa, negroni, old-fashioned, piña colada, pink gin, pink lady, planter's punch, presbyterian, Rob Roy, rusty nail, sazerac, screwdriver, sea breeze, sidecar, Singapore sling, slow comfortable screw, snowball, stinger, tequila sunrise, Tom Collins, whiskey sour, white lady, white Russian, yellow bird, Yokohama, zombie.

   wine, the grape; red wine, white wine, vin rosé, blush wine, vermouth; spumante, sparkling wine; sweet wine, dry wine, full-bodied wine, vintage wine; vin ordinaire, vin de table, vin du pays; vino, plonk; table wine, dessert wine; fortified wine, sack, sherry, manzanilla, port, vintage port, ruby port, white port, tawny port, champagne, champers, fizz, bubbly, buck's fizz; alcohol-free wine, low-alcohol wine; sangria; vintage wine, first great growth, premier cru; study of wine: oenology; study of vines: ampelology, ampelography.

Wines and Grapes

Auslese, Beerenauslese, Trockenbeerenauslese, Spätlese; Kabinett. Asti, Asti Spumante, Beaujolais, Beaujolais nouveau, Beaune, Bordeaux; burgundy, Cabernet Franc, Cabernet Sauvignon, Chablis, Chambertin, champagne, Chardonnay, Châteauneuf-du-Pape, Chianti, claret, Côtes-du-Rhône, Frascati, Gewürztraminer, Graves, hock, Lambrusco, Liebfraumilch, Macon, madeira, marsala, Mateus rosé, Médoc, Merlot, Moselle, Muscadet, muscat, muscatel, Niersteiner, Pinot Blanc, Pinot Noir, port, retsina, Riesling, Rioja, sack, Sauternes, Sauvignon, Sekt, Sémillon, Shiraz, Soave, Sylvaner, Tarragona, Tokay, Valpolicella, vinho verde.

   milk, top of the milk, cream; cow's milk, beestings; goat's milk, mare's milk, koumiss; mother's milk, breast milk; buttermilk, dried milk, skimmed milk, semi-skimmed milk, condensed milk, evaporated milk, pasteurized milk; milk drink, milk shake, malted milk, cocoa, chocolate, hot chocolate, Horlicks (tdmk); curdled milk, curds, junket. (See also *dairy products and eggs* above.)

   Adj. *feeding*, eating, grazing, etc. (see vb.); flesh-eating, meat-eating, cannibalistic; vegetarian, vegan.

Words Describing What is Eaten

carnivorous *or* creophagous (meat); frugivorous (fruit), graminivorous (grass or cereals), granivorous (seeds), herbivorous (plants), insectivorous (insects), mellivorous *or* meliphagous (honey), nucivorous (nuts), omnivorous (meat and plants), omophagous *or* omophagic (raw flesh), piscivorous (fish), vermivorous (worms).

   edible, eatable, digestible; palatable, succulent, moreish, delicious 386 *tasty*; kosher, halal; drinkable, potable.

   nourishing, sustaining, nutritious, nutritive, nutritional; protein-rich, body-building; non-fattening, wholesome 652 *healthy*.

   culinary, dressed, oven-ready, ready-to-cook, made-up, ready-to-serve; cooked, done to a turn, well-done; al dente; underdone, red, rare, raw; over-cooked, burnt, burnt to a cinder; roasted, etc. (see vb. *cook* below); au gratin, au naturel, mornay, au fromage, à la campagne, à la mode, à la maison, à la meunière; gastronomic, epicurean; prandial, post-prandial, after-dinner; meal-time.

Vb. *eat*, feed, mess; partake, partake of 386 *taste*; take a meal, have a feed, break one's fast, break bread; breakfast, have brunch, snack, graze, eat between meals, lunch, have tea, take tea, dine, sup; dine out, feast, banquet, carouse 837 *revel*; do justice to, be a good trencherman *or* woman, ask for more; water at the mouth, drool, raven 859 *be hungry*; fall to, set to, tuck in, lay into; stuff oneself, binge 863 *satiate*; guzzle, gormandize 947 *eat to excess*; eat up, leave a clean plate; lick the platter clean 165 *consume*; swallow, gulp down, devour, dispatch, bolt, wolf, make short work of; feed on, live on, fatten on, batten on, prey on; nibble, peck, lick, play *or* toy with one's food, be anorexic; nibble at, peck at, sniff at; be a seesaw eater; ingest, digest 299 *absorb*.

chew, masticate, champ, chomp, munch, crunch, scrunch; gnaw, grind 332 *grind*; chew up 46 *cut*.

graze, browse, crop, feed; ruminate, chew the cud; nibble.

drink, imbibe, suck 299 *absorb*; quaff, drink up, drink one's fill, drain, drink like a fish, slake one's thirst, lap, sip, gulp; wet one's lips, wet one's whistle; crack a bottle; lap up, soak up, wash down; booze, swill, swig, tipple, tope 949 *get drunk*; drain one's glass, knock it back; raise one's glass, pledge 876 *toast*; take one for the road, have one over the eight; refill one's glass 633 *replenish*.

feed, nourish, nurture, sustain, cater 633 *provide*; nurse, breast-feed, give suck; pasture, graze, put out to grass; fatten, fatten up 197 *enlarge*; dine, wine and dine, feast, fête, banquet 882 *be hospitable*.

cook, pressure-cook; microwave, bake, brown; roast, spit-roast, pot-roast, braise; broil, grill, charcoal-grill, barbecue, spatchcock, griddle, devil, curry; sauté, fry, deep-fry, shallow-fry, stir-fry; fry sunny side up, scramble; poach; boil, parboil; coddle, simmer, steam; casserole, stew; baste, lard, bard; whip, whisk, beat, blend, liquidize, stir; draw, gut, bone, fillet; stuff, dress, garnish; dice, shred, mince, grate; sauce, flavour, herb, spice 388 *season*.

Int. *cheers!*, here's health!, here's to you!, here's mud in your eye!, bottoms up!, down the hatch!, slàinte!, prosit!, skol! bon appétit!

302 Excretion

N. *excretion*, discharge, secretion 300 *ejection*; emanation 298 *going out*; exhalation, breathing out 352 *breathing*; exudation, perspiration, sweating 298 *outflow*; suppuration, maturation 651 *infection*; cold, common cold, coryza, catarrh, hay fever, allergic rhinitis; allergy, allergic reaction; salivation, expectoration, spitting; coughing, hawking, cough; urination, micturition, peeing, pissing (vulg); slashing; waterworks, plumbing; incontinence.

bleeding, haemorrhage, haemophilia 335 *blood*; period, time of the month, monthlies, menstruation, menses, menarche, menorrhoea, curse; dysmenorrhoea, menorrhagia; cessation of bleeding: clotting, coagulation, menopause, change of life.

defecation, evacuation, elimination, clearance 300 *clearing*; bowel movement, crap (vulg); number two, pooh, shit (vulg); motion; bodily functions; diarrhoea, the runs, the trots, Montezuma's revenge, Aztec two-step 651 *digestive disorder*; absence of defecation: constipation.

urination, micturition, leak, number one, pee, piddle, piss (vulg), slash (vulg), wee, wee-wee, widdle.

excrement, waste matter; faeces, stool, shit (vulg), crap (vulg), pooh; excreta, ordure; dung, cowpat, manure, muck; droppings, guano; urine, pee, piddle, piss (vulg), water, wee, wee-wee, widdle; sweat; spittle, spit, gob, sputum, saliva, slaver, slobber, rheum; phlegm; catarrh, mucus, snot; matter, pus; afterbirth, lochia; poop-scoop *or* pooper-scooper.

Vb. *excrete*, secrete; pass, move; move one's bowels, defecate, crap (vulg), shit (vulg); be taken short, have the trots; relieve oneself, answer the call of nature, go, go to the lavatory; urinate, micturate, piddle, pee, have a pee, piss (vulg), have a piss (vulg), have a slash (vulg), take a leak, make water, pay a visit, spend a penny, wee, widdle, wet oneself; sweat, perspire 379 *be hot*; salivate, slobber, snivel; cough, hawk, spit, gob 300 *belch*; weep 298 *exude*.

303 Insertion: forcible entry

N. *insertion*, interpolation, parenthesis 231 *interjection*; adding 38 *addition*; introduction, insinuation 297 *entering*; impaction; planting 370 *agriculture*; inoculation, injection, jab, shot; infusion, enema, barium enema; catheter; insert, inset; implant, silicone implant; stuffing 227 *lining*.

Vb. *insert*, introduce; weave into; put into, thrust into, intrude; poke into, jab into, stick into; transfix, run through 263 *pierce*; ram into, jam into, stuff into, pack into, push into, shove into, tuck into, press into, pop into 193 *load*; pocket; ease into place, slide in, fit in; knock into, hammer into, drive into 279 *impel*; put in, inlay, inset 227 *line*; subjoin 38 *add*; interpose 231 *put between*; drop in, put in the slot 311 *let fall*; pot, hole; bury 364 *inter.*

implant, plant, transplant, plant out, prick out, bed out, dibble; graft, engraft, bud; inoculate, vaccinate; embed, bury.

immerse, bathe, steep, souse, marinate, soak 341 *drench*; baptize, duck, dip 311 *lower*; submerge; immerse oneself 313 *plunge*.

304 Extraction: forcible exit

N. extraction, withdrawal, removal 188 *displacement*; elimination, eradication 300 *ejection*; abortion 172 *unproductiveness*; extermination 165 *destruction*; extrication, unravelment, disengagement, liberation 668 *rescue*; tearing out, ripping out; cutting out, excision; Caesarian birth, forceps delivery, etc. 167 *obstetrics*; expression, squeezing out; suction, sucking out, aspiration; vacuuming; pumping; drawing out, pull, tug, wrench 288 *traction*; digging out 255 *excavation*; mining, quarrying; fishery; distillation 338 *vaporization*; drawing off, tapping, milking; thing extracted, essence, extract.

Vb. extract, remove, pull 288 *draw*; draw out, elicit; unfold 316 *evolve*; pull out, take out, get out, pluck; withdraw, excise, cut out, rip out, tear out, whip out; excavate, mine, quarry, dig out, unearth; dredge, dredge up; expel, lever out, winkle out, smoke out 300 *eject*; extort, wring from; express, press out, squeeze out, gouge out; force out, wring out, wrench out, drag out; draw off, milk, tap; syphon off, aspirate, suck, void, pump; wring from, squeeze from, drag from; pull up, dig up, grub up, rake up; eliminate, weed out, root up, uproot, eradicate, extirpate 165 *destroy*; prune, thin out 105 *cause to be few*; distil 338 *vaporize*; extricate, unravel, free 746 *liberate*; unpack, unload 188 *displace*; eviscerate, gut 300 *empty*; unwrap 229 *uncover*; pick out 605 *select*.

305 Passage: motion through

N. passage, transmission 272 *transference*; transportation 272 *transport*; passing, passing through, traversing; traverse, crossing, journey, patrol 267 *land travel*; penetration, permeation, infiltration; osmosis 297 *entering*; intervention 231 *betweenness*; right of way 624 *access*; stepping-stone, flyover, underpass, subway 624 *bridge*; track, route, orbit 624 *path*; intersection, junction 222 *crossing*; waterway, channel 351 *water channel*.

traffic control, traffic engineering; traffic calming, traffic calming measures, speed bump, sleeping policeman, road hump, chicane; road pricing, road tolling, congestion charging; flow of traffic; traffic jam, tailback, gridlock; rush hour; highway code, Green Cross Code, green man 693 *precept*; traffic lane, motorway lane, bus lane, cycle lane, one-way street, carriageway, dual carriageway, clearway 624 *road*; diversion, alternative route 282 *deviation*; contraflow, lane closure; white lines, yellow lines, double yellow lines, red lines, red route; cat's-eyes (tdmk); sleeping policeman, chicane; street furniture, traffic lights, Belisha beacon, lamppost; roundabout, mini roundabout; crossing, pedestrian crossing, green man, zebra crossing, pelican crossing, puffin crossing, toucan crossing, subway (see also *passage* above); bollard, island, refuge; parking, zone parking, off-street parking; car park, parking lot, parking place, parking zone, park-and-ride; parking meter, parking ticket, waiting, loading, unloading; lay-by; point duty, road patrol, speed trap, radar trap, speed camera; traffic police, traffic cop; traffic warden, parking attendant, meter maid; lollipop man *or* lady; road user 268 *pedestrian, driver*.

Vb. pass, pass by, leave on one side, skirt, coast; flash by 114 *be transient*, 277 *move fast*; go past, not stop 146 *go on*, 265 *be in motion*; pass along, circulate, weave; pass through, transit, traverse; shoot through, shoot the rapids 269 *navigate*; pass out, come out the other side 298 *emerge*; go through, soak through, seep through, percolate, permeate 189 *pervade*; pass and repass, patrol, walk up and down, work over, beat, scour, go over the ground; pass into, penetrate, infiltrate 297 *enter*; bore, perforate 263 *pierce*; thread, thread through, string 45 *connect*; rake; force a passage; worm one's way, squeeze through, elbow through, clear the way 285 *progress*; cross, go across, cross over, make a crossing, reach the other side 295 *arrive*; wade across, ford; get through, get past, negotiate; pass beyond 306 *overstep*; pass in front, cut across 702 *obstruct*; step over, straddle; bridge 226 *cover*; carry over, carry across, transmit 272 *send*; pass to, hand, reach, pass from hand to hand, hand over 272 *transfer*.

306 Overstepping: motion beyond

N. overstepping, going beyond, overstepping the mark, stretching a point 305 *passage*; transcendence 34 *superiority*, digression 282 *deviation*; transgression 936 *guilty act*; encroachment 916 *unjustifed claim*; infringement, intrusion 916 *what is not due*; expansionism, greediness 859 *desire*; excessiveness

637 *redundancy*; overdoing it, going overboard 546 *exaggeration*; overindulgence 943 *intemperance*.

Vb. overstep, overstep the mark; go too far, throw out the baby with the bathwater; exceed, exceed the limit; overrun, overshoot the mark, aim too high; overlap; cross the Rubicon, pass the point of no return, burn one's boats; overfill, spill over 54 *fill*; overgrow 637 *be overabundant*; overdo 546 *exaggerate*; strain, stretch a point; overbid, have one's bluff called, overestimate 482 *overrate*; overindulge 943 *be intemperate*; outstay one's welcome, oversleep 136 *be late*.

encroach, invade, make inroads on 712 *attack*; infringe, transgress, trespass 954 *be illegal*; poach 788 *steal*; squat, usurp 786 *appropriate*; barge in, horn in, butt in 297 *intrude*; impinge; eat away, erode 655 *impair*; infest, overrun; overflow, flood 341 *drench*.

outdo, exceed, surpass, outclass; transcend, rise above, soar above, outrival 34 *be superior*; go one better, outbid; outwit; outmanoeuvre, outflank, steal a march on, steal one's thunder; outpace, outrun, outride; outdistance; overtake; leave standing, leave at the starting post 277 *outstrip*; leave behind, beat hollow 727 *defeat*.

307 Shortfall

N. shortfall, falling short, etc. (see vb.); negative equity, inadequacy 636 *insufficiency*; a minus, deficit, short measure, shortage, slippage, loss; leeway, drift 282 *deviation*; unfinished state 55 *incompleteness*; non-fulfilment 726 *non-completion*; half measures 641 *wasted effort*; shortcoming 647 *imperfection*; something missing, want, lack, need 627 *requirement*.

Adj. deficient, short, short of, minus, wanting, lacking, missing; underpowered, substandard; undermanned, short-staffed, half-done 55 *incomplete*; inadequate 636 *insufficient*; failing, running short 636 *scarce*; below par 647 *imperfect*.

Vb. fall short, run short 636 *be insufficient*; not reach to; lack, want, be without 627 *require*; underachieve, not make the grade, not come up to scratch; miss the mark; lag 136 *be late*; stop short, fall by the way, fall out, not stay the course; break down, get bogged down; fall behind, lose ground, slip back; slump, collapse 286 *regress*; fall through, come to nothing, fizzle out, fail 728 *miscarry*; labour in vain 641 *waste effort*; not come up to expectations 509 *disappoint*.

308 Ascent: motion upwards

N. ascent, ascension, lift, upward motion; levitation; taking off, takeoff, lift-off, blast-off

296 *departure*; soaring, spiral; zoom 271 *aeronautics*; culmination 213 *summit*; surfacing; going up, rising; rise, upturn, upward trend; uprush, upsurge, crescendo 36 *increase*; updraught, thermal; sunrise, sun-up, dawn 128 *morning*; mounting, climbing; hill-climbing, hill-walking, Munro-bagging, rock-climbing, mountaineering, alpinism, hill-running, mountain-running; ladder-scaling, escalade 712 *attack*; jump, vault, pole vault, pole jump 312 *leap*; bounce 280 *recoil*; rising ground, hill 209 *high land*; gradient, slope, ramp 220 *incline*; rising pitch 410 *musical note*; stairs, steps, stile, flight of stairs, staircase, spiral staircase, stairway, landing; ladder, step-ladder, accommodation ladder, Jacob's ladder, companionway; rope ladder, ratlines; stair, step, tread, rung; lift, ski ladder, chair ladder, elevator, escalator; fire escape 667 *means of escape*.

climber, mountaineer, rock-climber, alpinist, cragsman *or* -woman, fell walker, hill-walker, Munro-bagger; steeplejack.

Vb. ascend, rise, rise up, go up, leave the ground; defy gravity, levitate; take off, become airborne, have lift-off, fly up 271 *fly*; gain height, mount, soar, spiral, zoom, climb; reach the top, get to the top of the ladder, reach the zenith, culminate; float up, bob up, surface, break water; jump up, spring, vault 312 *leap*; bounce 280 *recoil*; push up, grow up, shoot up 36 *grow*; curl upwards; tower, aspire, spire 209 *be high*; gush, spurt *or* spirt, spout, jet, play; get up, start up, stand up, rear, rear up, ramp 215 *be vertical*; rise to one's feet, get up 310 *lift oneself*; slope upwards 220 *be oblique*.

climb, walk up, struggle up; mount, make one's way up, work one's way up; go climbing, go mountaineering, mountaineer; clamber, scramble, swarm up, shin up, go up hand over fist; surmount, top, breast, conquer, scale, scale the heights 209 *be high*; go over the top, escalade 712 *attack*; go upstairs, climb a ladder; mount (a horse).

Adv. up, uphill, upstairs; upwards 209 *aloft*.

309 Descent

N. descent, declension 282 *deviation*; falling, dropping; cadence; downward trend, decline, drop, slump 37 *decrease*; sunset, moonset; comedown, demotion 286 *regression*; downfall, collapse, setback 165 *ruin*; trip, stumble; lurch, capsize 221 *overturning*; tumble, crash, spill, fall; cropper, purler; downrush, swoop, stoop, pounce; dive, header, bellyflop 313 *plunge*; nosedive, power-dive 271 *aeronautics*; landing, crash landing, splashdown 295 *arrival*; sliding down, glissade; subsidence, landslide, avalanche; downdraught 352 *wind*; downpour, shower 350 *rain*; cascade 350 *waterfall*; downthrow (geology); declivity, slope, tilt, dip 220 *incline*; chute, slide, helter-skelter; precipice, sheer drop 215 *verticality*; submergence, sinkage, slippage 311 *lowering*; burrowing, mining, undermining 255 *excavation*; speleology, potholing, caving.

Vb. descend, come down, go down, dip down; decline, abate, ebb 37 *decrease*; slump, plummet, fall, drop, sink; sink like a lead balloon, sink without trace 322 *weigh*; soak in, seep down 297 *infiltrate*; reach the depths, touch bottom; bottom out, reach one's nadir 35 *be inferior*; sink to the bottom, gravitate, precipitate, settle, set; fall down, fall in, cave in, fall to the ground, collapse; sink in, subside, slip, give way; hang down, prolapse, droop, sag, swag 217 *hang*; go under water, draw; submerge, dive 313 *plunge*; drown 313 *go down*; go underground, dig down, burrow, mine, undermine 255 *make concave*; parachute; swoop, stoop, pounce; fly down, flutter down, float down; lose height, drop down, swing low; touch down, alight, light, perch 295 *land*; lower oneself, abseil; get down, climb down, step down, get off, fall off, dismount; coast down, slide down, glissade, toboggan; fall like rain, shower, cascade, drip 350 *rain*; bow down, dip, duck 311 *stoop*; flop, plop, splash down.

tumble, fall; topple, keel over, overbalance, capsize, tumble head over heels 221 *be inverted*; miss one's footing, trip, stumble; lose one's balance; take a header, dive 313 *plunge*; fall off, take a fall, be thrown, come a cropper, fall heavily, crash to the ground, fall flat on one's face, fall prostrate, bite the dust, measure one's length; plummet, plump down 311 *sit down*; slump, nosedive.

Adv. down, downwards; downhill, downstairs, downstream.

310 Elevation

N. elevation, raising, etc. (see vb.); erection, uplift, upheaval; picking up, lift; hoist, boost; leg-up 703 *aid*; levitation; exaltation, Assumption; uprising, uptrend, growth, upswing 308 *ascent*; eminence 209 *high land*, 254 *prominence*; height above sea level 209 *height*.

Vb. elevate, heighten 209 *make higher*; puff up, blow up, swell, leaven 197 *enlarge*; raise, erect, set up, put up, run up, rear up, build up, build; lift, lift up, raise up, heave up; uplift; jack up, lever up, hike up, prop 218 *support*; stand on end; hold up, bear up; buoy up; raise aloft, hold aloft, hold up, wave; hoist, haul up; pick up, take up; pull up, wind up; weigh; fish up, drag up, dredge up, pump

up 304 *extract*; chair, shoulder, carry shoulder-high; exalt, put on a pedestal 866 *honour*; mount 213 *crown*; jump up, bounce up 285 *promote*; give a lift, give a leg-up 703 *aid*; throw in the air, throw up, cast up, toss up; loft; send up, shoot up, lob 287 *propel*; perk up (one's head), prick up (one's ears); bristle, bristle up 215 *be vertical*.

lift oneself, arise, rise 308 *ascend*; stand up, get up, get to one's feet, pick oneself up, jump up, leap up, spring up, spring to one's feet; pull oneself up; hold oneself up, hold one's head up, draw oneself up to one's full height, stand on tiptoe 215 *be vertical*.

311 Lowering

N. lowering, depressing, hauling down, etc. (see vb.); pushing down 279 *impulse*; ducking, sousing 313 *plunge*; debasement, demotion, reduction 872 *humiliation*; subversion 149 *revolution*; overthrow, prostration; overturn, upset 221 *overturning*; precipitation, defenestration 287 *propulsion*; suppression; depression, dent, dip, dimple, hollow 255 *cavity*; low pressure 340 *weather*.

bow, kowtow, obeisance, namaskar, namaste, reverence, salaam 884 *courtesy*; curtsy, bob, duck, nod, salute 884 *courteous act*; kneeling, genuflexion 920 *respect*.

Vb. lower, depress, push down, thrust down 279 *impel*; shut down (a lid) 264 *close*; hold down, keep down, hold under 165 *suppress*; lower, let down, take down; lower a flag, dip; haul down, strike; deflate, puncture, flatten, squash, crush 198 *make smaller*; let drop (see also *let fall* below); sink, scuttle, drown 309 *descend*; duck, souse, douse, dip 313 *plunge*; weigh on, press on 322 *weigh*; tip, hollow 255 *make concave*.

let fall, drop, shed; let go 779 *not retain*; let slip or slide through one's fingers; pour, pour out, decant 300 *empty*; spill, slop 341 *moisten*; sprinkle, shower, scatter, dust, dredge; sow, broadcast 75 *disperse*; lay down, put down, set down, throw down, fling down (see also *fell* below); pitch or chuck overboard, jettison, drop over the side; precipitate, send headlong 287 *propel*.

fell, overthrow; prostrate; lay low, lay one on his back 216 *flatten*; knock down, bowl over; floor, raze to the ground, trample in the dust 165 *demolish*; hew down, cut down, axe 46 *cut*; bring down; shoot down 287 *shoot*.

abase, debase, lower one's sights; demote, reduce to the ranks, cashier 752 *depose*; humble, deflate, puncture, debunk, take down a peg, cut down to size, take the wind out of one's sails 872 *humiliate*; crush, squash, grind down 165 *suppress*.

sit down, sit, sit oneself down, be seated, squat, hunker; sink, lower oneself; take a seat, seat oneself, take a pew, park oneself; perch, alight 309 *descend*.

stoop, bend, bend down; bend over, bend forward, bend backward; lean forward, lean over backwards; cringe, crouch, cower 721 *knuckle under*; slouch, hunch one's back 248 *make curved*; bow, scrape, duck, bob, curtsy, bob a curtsy 884 *pay one's respects*; nod, incline one's head, bow down, make obeisance, kiss hands, salaam, prostrate oneself, kowtow 920 *show respect*; kneel, kneel to, genuflect, kiss the ground.

312 Leap

N. *leap*, leapfrogging; jump, hop, skip; spring, bound, vault, pole vault; high jump, long jump, running jump, triple jump, hop, skip and jump; bungee jump, base jumping 837 *sport*; caper, gambol, frolic; kick, cancan; jeté, entrechat; prance; dance step; dance, breakdance, reel, jig, Highland fling 837 *dancing*.

Vb. *leap*, jump, take a running jump; spring, bound, vault, pole-vault; hurdle, steeplechase, take one's fences; skip, hop, leapfrog, bob, bounce, rebound, buck, bob up and down 317 *oscillate*; stamp 837 *dance*; caper, cut capers, gambol, frisk, romp; prance; start, give a jump; jump on, pounce; jump up, leap up, spring up 308 *ascend*; jump over, clear.

313 Plunge

N. *plunge*, swoop, pounce, stoop, plummet 309 *descent*; nosedive, power dive 271 *aeronautics*; dive, header, bellyflop; swallow dive, duck dive; dip, ducking; immersion, submergence; crash dive.

diver, skin diver, scuba diver, free diver, deep-sea diver, frogman; underwater swimmer, aquanaut; diving, skin diving, etc.; the bends, caisson disease.

Vb. *plunge*, dip, duck 341 *be wet*; fall in, jump in, plump, plop, plummet; dive, take a header, go headfirst; souse, douse, immerse, submerse, drown; submerge, crash-dive 309 *descend*; sink, scuttle, send to Davy Jones's locker 311 *lower*.

go down, go to the bottom, go down like a stone, founder 309 *descend*; get out of one's depth, drown 211 *be deep*; plummet, sink, sink without trace, sink like lead, sink like a stone 322 *weigh*.

314 Circuitous motion: curvilinear motion

N. *circuitous motion*, circuition, circulation, circumnavigation, circling, wheeling, spiral

315 *rotation*; turning, cornering, turn, U-turn 286 *return*; orbit; lap; circuit, milk round, tour, round trip, full circle; figure of eight 250 *loop*; helix 251 *coil*; circuitousness, roundabout way, scenic route, tourist route 626 *circuit*.

Adj. *circuitous*, turning, etc. (see vb.); peripatetic; devious 626 *roundabout*.

Vb. *circle*, circulate, make *or* do the rounds, make the round of; circuit, make a circuit, lap; do the round trip; go round, skirt; circumnavigate, go round the world, go globetrotting; turn, round, weather a point; round a corner, turn a corner; revolve, orbit; wheel, spiral, come full circle, chase one's tail 315 *rotate*; do a U-turn, turn round, bend round; put about, wheel about, face about, turn on one's heel 286 *turn back*; draw a circle, describe a circle 232 *encircle*; curve, wind, twist, wind one's way 251 *meander*; make a detour 626 *circuit*.

315 Rotation: motion in a continued circle

N. *rotation*, revolving, orbiting; revolution, full circle; gyration, circling, wheeling, spiralling; circulation; circumrotation; rolling 285 *progression*; spiral, roll, spin, flat spin; turn, twirl, pirouette, waltz 837 *dance*; whirl; dizzy round, rat race, milk round 678 *overactivity*.

whirl, swirl, vortex; whirlwind, tornado, cyclone 352 *gale*; waterspout, whirlpool 350 *eddy*; whirlpool bath, Jacuzzi (tdmk); maelstrom, Charybdis; smoke ring 250 *loop*.

rotator, rotor, spinner; whirligig, top, spinning top, humming top; merry-go-round; churn, whisk; potter's wheel, lathe, circular saw; spinning wheel, spinning jenny; catherine wheel; flywheel, roulette wheel, wheel of Fortune 250 *wheel*; Hula-Hoop (tdmk); gyroscope, turntable; gramophone record, disc, magnetic tape, cassette, compact disc; wind pump, windmill, fan, sail; propeller, prop, screw; turbine; winder, capstan; swivel, hinge; spit, jack; spindle, axle, axis, shaft 218 *pivot*; spool, reel, roller 252 *cylinder*; rolling stone, planet, satellite 268 *wanderer*.

Adj. *with one's head spinning*, with one's head swimming, dizzy, giddy, light-headed, reeling, unsteady, wobbly, woozy.

Vb. *rotate*, revolve, orbit, go into orbit 314 *circle*; turn right round, chase one's own tail; spin, twirl, pirouette; turn 251 *twine*; gyrate, waltz, wheel; whirl, hum 404 *resound*; mill around, swirl, eddy 350 *flow*; bowl, trundle; roll, roll along; twirl, twiddle, twizzle; churn, whisk 43 *mix*; turn, crank, wind, reel, spool, spin; slew, slew round, swing round, swivel round; roll up, furl 261 *fold*; roll itself up, curl up.

316 Evolution: motion in a reverse circle

N. *evolution*, unrolling, unfolding, unfurling; development 157 *growth*; evolutionism, Darwinism, Neo-Darwinism 358 *biology*.

Vb. *evolve*, unfold, unfurl, unroll, unwind, uncoil, uncurl, untwist, untwine, disentangle; develop, grow into 1 *become*, 147 *be turned to*; roll back 263 *open*.

317 Oscillation: reciprocating motion

N. *oscillation*, harmonic motion, pendular motion, swing of the pendulum; vibration, tremor; vibrancy, resonance 141 *periodic recurrence*; pulsation, rhythm; throbbing, drumming, pulse, beat, throb; pitter-patter, flutter, palpitation 318 *agitation*; breathing 352 *breathing*; undulation, wave motion, frequency, frequency band, wavelength 417 *radiation*; sound wave, radio wave; tidal wave 350 *wave*; seismic disturbance, earthquake, tremor 176 *violence*; seismology, seismograph; oscillator, vibrator; metronome; pendulum, bob, yo-yo 217 *hanging object*.

fluctuation, wave motion (see also *oscillation* above); alternation, reciprocation 12 *correlation*; to and fro movement, coming and going, shuttling; ups and downs, rollercoaster, boom and bust, ebb and flow, flux and reflux; yo-yo dieting, yo-yo economy; night and day 14 *contrariety*; rolling, pitching; roll, pitch, lurch, shake, nod, wag; swing, seesaw; shuttle; wavering, vacillation 601 *irresolution*.

Vb. *oscillate*, emit waves 417 *radiate*; wave, undulate; vibrate, pulsate, pulse, beat, drum; tick, throb, palpitate; pant, heave 352 *breathe*; play, sway, nod; swing, dangle 217 *hang*; seesaw, rock; lurch, stagger, totter, teeter, waddle, wobble, wiggle, waggle, wag; bob, bounce, bob up and down, dance 312 *leap*; toss, roll, pitch; rattle, chatter, shake; flutter, quiver, shiver 318 *be agitated*; flicker 417 *shine*; echo 404 *resound*.

fluctuate, alternate, reciprocate 12 *correlate*; ebb and flow, come and go, pass and repass, shuttle; yo-yo.

brandish, wave, wag, waggle, shake, flourish; wave to and fro, shake up and down; flutter 318 *agitate*.

Adv. *to and fro*, backwards and forwards, back and forth; in and out, up and down, side to side; zigzag, seesaw, like a yo-yo; shuttlewise.

318 Agitation: irregular motion

N. *agitation*, jerkiness, fits and starts, unsteadiness, shakiness 152 *changeableness*; joltiness, bumpiness, choppiness, pitching, rolling 259 *roughness*; flicker, twinkle 417 *flash*; start, jump 508 *lack of expectation*; hop 312 *leap*; shake, toss 287 *propulsion*; shock, jar, jolt, jerk, judder, bounce, bump 279 *impulse*; nudge, dig, jog 547 *gesture*; vibration, thrill, throb, pulse, pit-a-pat, palpitation, flutter 317 *oscillation*; shuddering, shudder, shiver, frisson; quiver, quaver, tremor; tremulousness, trembling; restlessness, ants in one's pants, feverishness, fever; tossing, turning; jiving, rock 'n' roll, breakdancing 678 *activity*, 837 *dancing*; itchiness, itch 378 *formication*; twitchiness, twitch, grimacing, grimace; perturbation, disquiet 825 *worry*; trepidation, jumpiness, twitter, flap, butterflies, collywobbles 854 *nervousness*; delirium tremens, dt's, the shakes; Parkinson's disease, Parkinsonism; shivers, jumps, jitters, fidgets.

spasm, ague, shivering, chattering; twitch, tic, nervous tic; chorea, St Vitus's dance 318 *nervous disorder*; lockjaw, tetanus; cramp, the cramps; throe 377 *pang*; convulsion, paroxysm, orgasm 503 *frenzy*; fit, epilepsy 651 *nervous disorder*; pulse, throb 317 *oscillation*; attack, seizure, stroke.

commotion, turbulence, tumult 61 *turmoil*; hurly-burly, hubbub, brouhaha, hassle; fever, flurry, rush, bustle 680 *haste*; furore 503 *frenzy*; fuss, to-do, bother, kerfuffle, shemozzle 678 *restlessness*; racket, din 400 *loudness*; stir, ferment 821 *excitation*; boiling, fermentation, ebullition, effervescence 355 *bubble*; ground swell, heavy sea 350 *wave*; squall, tempest, thunderstorm, magnetic storm 176 *storm*; whirlpool 315 *whirl*; whirlwind 352 *gale*; disturbance, atmospherics.

agitated, shaken; shaking, etc. (see vb.); troubled; restless; jittery, jumpy, twitchy, wound up, wired up, flustered, in a flap 854 *nervous*.

Vb. *be agitated*, ripple, boil 355 *bubble*; stir, move, dash; shake, tremble, quiver, quaver, shiver; have a fever, throw a fit, be all of a doodah, be all of a dither; be in a flap; be like a cat on hot bricks; writhe, squirm, twitch 251 *wriggle*; toss, turn, toss about, thresh about; kick, plunge, rear; flounder, flop, wallow, roll, reel, pitch 317 *fluctuate*; sway 220 *be oblique*; pulse, beat, thrill, vibrate, judder, shudder; wag, waggle, wobble, stagger, lurch, dodder, totter, teeter, dither 317 *oscillate*; whirr, whirl 315 *rotate*; jig around, jig up and down, jump about, hop, bob, bounce, dance 312 *leap*; flicker, twinkle, gutter, sputter 417 *shine*; flap, flutter, twitter, start, jump; throb, pant, palpitate, miss a beat, go pit-a-pat 821 *be excited*; bustle, rush, mill around 61 *rampage*; ramp, roar 891 *be angry*.

agitate, disturb, rumple, ruffle, untidy 63

disarrange; discompose, perturb, worry, hassle, throw into a panic 827 *trouble*; ripple, muddy; stir, stir up 43 *mix*; whisk, whip, beat, churn 315 *rotate*; shake up, shake; wag, waggle, wave, flourish 317 *brandish*; flutter, fly (a flag); jog, joggle, jolt, jounce, nudge, dig; jerk, pluck, twitch.

effervesce, froth, spume, foam, foam at the mouth, bubble up 355 *bubble*; boil, boil over, seethe, simmer, sizzle, spit 379 *be hot*; ferment, work.

Matter

Matter in general

319 Materiality

N. *materiality*, materialness; corporeality, bodiliness; world of nature 3 *having substance*; physical condition 1 *existence*; plenum 321 *world*; concreteness, tangibility, palpability, solidity 324 *density*; weight 322 *gravity*; personality, individuality 80 *speciality*; embodiment, incarnation, reincarnation, realization, materialization; materialism; worldliness, sensuality 944 *sensualism*.

matter, stuff; prime matter; mass, material, fabric, body, frame 331 *structure*; substance, corpus; flesh, flesh and blood, plasma, protoplasm 358 *organism*.

object, bird in the hand; inanimate object; body, flesh and blood, real person 371 *person*; thing, gadget, gizmo, something, commodity, article, item.

element, principle, nitty-gritty 68 *origin*; the four elements, earth, air, fire, water; factor, ingredient, nuts and bolts 58 *component*; isotope, radioisotope;

Chemical Elements

actinium, aluminium, americium, antimony, argon, arsenic, astatine, barium, berkelium, beryllium, bismuth, bohrium, boron, bromine, cadmium, caesium, calcium, californium, carbon, cerium, chlorine, chromium, cobalt, copper, curium, dubnium, dysprosium, einsteinium, erbium, europium, fermium, fluorine, francium, gadolinium, gallium, germanium, gold, hafnium, hassium, helium, holmium, hydrogen, indium, iodine, iridium, iron, krypton, lanthanum, lawrencium, lead, lithium, lutetium, magnesium, manganese, meitnerium, mendelevium, mercury, molybdenum, neodymium, neon, neptunium, nickel, niobium, nitrogen, nobelium, osmium, oxygen, palladium, phosphorus, platinum, plutonium, polonium, potassium, praseodymium, promethium, protactinium, radium, radon, rhenium, rhodium, rubidium, ruthenium, rutherfordium, samarium, scandium, seaborgium, selenium, silicon, silver, sodium, strontium, sulphur, tantalum, technetium, tellurium, terbium, thalium, thorium, thulium, tin, titanium, tungsten, uranium, vanadium, xenon, ytterbium, yttrium, zinc, zirconium.

atom, molecule; nucleus, particle, free radical; quantum, quark 196 *minuteness*; ion.

Terms Used in Particle Physics

electron; positron; nucleon, neutron, proton; elementary particle, fundamental particle, subatomic particle, antiparticle; baryon, fermion, kaon, lepton, meson, muon, pi-meson, pion, neutrino, tau particle; boson, gluon, graviton, photon; tachyon; exciton; soliton; quark, antiquark; flavour, up, down, strange, charm, top or truth, bottom or beauty; colour; string theory, superstring; brane, brane theory, membrane theory; strong interaction, weak interaction; strangeness; quantum chromodynamics, quantum electrodynamics, quantum mechanics; grand unified theories; particle accelerator, cyclotron, synchrotron.

physics, physical science, natural science; natural history 358 *biology*; chemistry, organic chemistry, inorganic chemistry, physical chemistry, biochemistry; mechanics, theory of relativity; thermodynamics; electromagnetism, electrodynamics, electrostatics; atomic physics, nuclear physics 160 *nuclear physics*; applied physics, technology 694 *skill*; biophysics, biotechnology; natural philosophy 490 *science*.

Adj. *material*, real, natural; solid, concrete, palpable, tangible, weighty; physical, objective, impersonal, clinical, neuter; substantial; embodied, incarnate, personified, — on a stick; corporeal, bodily, fleshly, of flesh and blood, in the flesh, carnal; reincarnated, realized, materialized; materialistic, worldly, unspiritual 944 *sensual*.

Vb. *materialize*, substantiate, objectify 223 *externalize*; realize, body forth; embody, incarnate, personify.

320 Non-materiality

N. *non-materiality*, immateriality, unreality 4 *lacking substance*; incorporeality, disembodiment, intangibility, impalpability, ghostliness, shadowiness; immaterialism, idealism,

Platonism; spirituality, otherworldliness; animism; spiritualism 984 *occultism*.

subjectivity, personality, myself, me, yours truly 80 *self*; me generation; ego, id, super-ego; Conscious, Unconscious; psyche 447 *spirit*.

Adj. non-material, immaterial, incorporeal, aery, ethereal, ghostly, shadowy 4 *lacking substance*; intangible; bodiless, disembodied; unearthly; psychic, astral 984 *psychical*; spiritual, otherworldly 973 *religious*; abstract 447 *mental*.

321 Universe

N. *universe*, whole; cosmos, macrocosm, microcosm; multiverse; matter; world, globe, creation; outer space, intergalactic space; void; cosmology; big bang theory, steady state theory 68 *start*.

world, wide world; earth, mother earth, planet earth, four corners of the earth; space, globe, sphere; geosphere, biosphere, ecosphere; continental drift 344 *land*; waters of the earth 343 *ocean*; atlas 551 *map*; latitude 184 *region*; longitude; Old World, New World 184 *region*; Ptolemaic system; personal world 8 *circumstance*.

heavens, sky, ether, celestial sphere, hemisphere; firmament; music of the spheres; aurora borealis, northern lights, aurora australis.

star, heavenly body, celestial body 420 *light*; guiding star, lodestar; starlight 420 *light*; blue star, white star, yellow star, red star; double star, binary; multiple star; variable star, cepheid; giant, supergiant, red giant; subgiant, dwarf, red dwarf, white dwarf; X-ray star, radio star 417 *radiation*; quasi-stellar object, quasar, pulsar, neutron star, black hole, singularity, event horizon, Schwarzschild radius, white hole; nova, supernova; bright star, first-magnitude star; constellation; star cluster, globular cluster, galaxy, radio galaxy; the Galaxy, the Milky Way; island universe; nebula; Star of Bethlehem; Star of David.

Stars and Constellations

Stars: Aldebaran, Algol, Alpha Centauri, Altair, Arcturus, Betelgeuse, Canopus, Regulus, Rigel, Vega; Polaris, Pole Star, North Star, Pointers; Dog Star, Sirius.
Constellations: Great Bear, Ursa Major, Little Bear, Ursa Minor, Plough, Big Dipper, Charles' Wain; Cassiopeia, Cassiopeia's Chair; Orion, Orion's Belt; Pegasus; Perseus; Pleiades; Southern Cross.

---

zodiac, signs of the zodiac, ecliptic; house, mansion, lunar mansion; cusp; ascendant, rising sign.

Signs of the Zodiac

air sign, earth sign, fire sign, water sign.
Aries (the Ram), Taurus (the Bull), Gemini (the Twins), Cancer (the Crab), Leo (the Lion), Virgo (the Virgin), Libra (the Balance), Scorpio (the Scorpion), Sagittarius (the Archer), Capricornus (the Goat), Aquarius (the Watercarrier), Pisces (the Fishes).

---

planet, asteroid, planetoid; solar system; Venus, morning star, evening star, Lucifer, Vesper, Hesperus; Mars, red planet; Mercury, Earth, Jupiter, Saturn, Uranus, Neptune, Pluto; extrasolar planet, exoplanet; waterworld; comet, wandering star, Halley's comet; near earth object.

meteor, falling star, shooting star, fireball, bolide; meteorite, aerolite, siderite, chondrite; chondrule; meteoroid; micro-meteorite.

sun, day-star, eye of heaven, eye of day; midnight sun; sunlight, sunshine, sun spot, solar flare, corona; solar wind; inner space, solar system, Copernican system, Ptolemaic system; sun god: Phoebus, Apollo.

moon, satellite; new moon, waxing moon, waning moon, half-moon, crescent moon, horned moon, full moon, harvest moon, hunter's moon; mock moon; moonscape, crater, mare, rill; man in the moon; moonlight, moonshine; goddess of the moon: Diana, Phoebe; Queen of the night.

satellite, moon; earth satellite, artificial satellite, sputnik, weather satellite, communications satellite, comsat; space station, skylab; space lab; space shuttle 276 *spaceship*.

astronomy, stargazing; satellite tracking; radioastronomy; astrophysics, astrochemistry; uranography; search for extraterrestrial intelligence, SETI, astrobiology; astrology, horoscope 511 *divination*; observatory, planetarium; tracking station; telescope, refracting telescope, etc. 442 *telescope*; astronomical telescope, altazimuth, equatorial; transit instrument; radio telescope, parabolic reflector, dish; spectroscope 551 *photography*.

earth sciences, geography, orography, oceanography, physiography, geomorphology, speleology; geology, geodesy, geodetics; hydrology, hydrography.

Adj. cosmic, universal, cosmological; interplanetary; galactic, intragalactic; extragalactic.

celestial, heavenly, ethereal, empyreal; starry, sidereal, astral, stellar; solar, zodiacal; lunar, lunate; nebular, nebulous; heliocentric, geocentric; meteoric; equinoctial.

astronomic, astronomical, astrophysical, stargazing, star-watching; astrological, telescopic, spectroscopic.

geographic, geographical, oceanographic, orographical; geological, geomorphic, speleological; geodesic, geodetic; hydrographic, hydrological.

322 Gravity

N. *gravity*, gravitation, force of gravity, gravitational pull; gravity feed; weight, weightiness, heaviness, ponderousness 195 *bulk*; specific gravity; pressure, displacement, sinkage, draught; encumbrance, load, lading, freight; burden; ballast, makeweight, counterpoise; mass, lump 324 *solid body*; plummet 313 *diver*.

weighing, balancing, equipoise 28 *equalization*; weight, avoirdupois weight, troy weight, apothecaries' weight; grain, carat, scruple, pennyweight, drachm; ounce, pound, stone, quarter, quintal, hundredweight, ton; milligram, gram, kilogram, kilo; megaton, kiloton; axle load, laden weight. (See also 465 *weights and measures*.)

scales, weighing machine; steelyard, weigh-beam; balance, spring balance; bathroom scales, kitchen scales, pan, scale, weight; calibrator; platform scale, weighbridge.

Adj. *weighty*, heavy, heavyweight, ponderous; leaden; weighing, etc. (see vb.); cumbersome, cumbrous 195 *unwieldy*; massive 324 *dense*; heavy-handed, heavy-footed, pressing, incumbent, oppressive; weighing, with a weight of; weighted, loaded, laden, charged, burdened; overburdened, overloaded, top-heavy 29 *unequal*.

Vb. *weigh*, balance 28 *be equal*; counterpoise, counterweigh 31 *compensate*; outweigh 34 *predominate*; tip the scales, turn the scales, tip the balance; settle 309 *descend*, 313 *go down*; lie heavy; press, weigh on, weigh one down, oppress, hang like a millstone 311 *lower*; load, cumber 702 *hinder*; find the weight of, put on the scales, lay in the scale 465 *measure*; weigh oneself, stand on the scales.

make heavy, weight, hang weights on; charge, burden, overweight, overburden, overload 193 *load*.

323 Lightness

N. *lightness*, portability; thinness, air, ether 325 *lack of density*; buoyancy; volatility 338 *vaporization*; weightlessness; levitation 308 *ascent*; feather, thistledown, cobweb, gossamer; fluff, oose, dust, straw 4 *thing that lacks substance*; cork, buoy, lifebelt, life jacket; balloon, bubble; hot air, helium, hydrogen.

raising agent, leaven; ferment, enzyme, barm, yeast, baking-powder, self-raising flour.

Adj. *light*, underweight 307 *deficient*; lightweight, featherweight; portable, handy 196 *little*; light-footed; light on one's feet; having a light touch; weightless, lighter than air; ethereal, airy, gaseous, volatile 325 *rarefied*; doughy, barmy, yeasty, fermenting, zymotic, enzymic; aerated, frothy, bubbly, sparkling, pétillant, foamy, whipped; floating, buoyed up, buoyant, feathery, cobwebby, fluffy; light as a feather.

Vb. *be light*, be buoyant, etc. (see adj.); levitate, surface, float, swim; drift, waft, glide, be airborne 271 *fly*; soar, hover 308 *ascend*.

lighten, make light, make lighter, lose weight; ease 701 *disencumber*; jettison 300 *empty*; vaporize 340 *aerate*; leaven; raise, levitate 310 *elevate*.

Inorganic matter

324 Density

N. *density*, solidity, consistency; compactness, solidness, concreteness, thickness, concentration; incompressibility 326 *hardness*; impenetrability, impermeability; indissolubility, indivisibility; coalescence, cohesion, inseparability 48 *cohesiveness*; relative density, specific gravity.

condensing, making dense *or* denser, condensation, concentration; thickening, etc. (see vb.); coagulation, thrombosis; congealment, gelatinization; solidification, concretion, consolidation; constipation; glaciation; ossification, petrifaction, fossilization; crystallization; sedimentation, precipitation.

solid body, solid; block, mass, solid mass 319 *matter*; knot, nugget, lump, chunk, dod, burl; condensation, nucleus, hard core; aggregate, conglomerate, concretion; concrete, cement; stone, crystal, hard-pan 344 *rock*; precipitate, deposit, sediment, residue, residuum; silt, clay, cake, clod, clump; bone, ossicle; gristle, cartilage 329 *toughness*; coagulum, curd, clot, blood-clot.

Adj. *dense*, thick; close, heavy, stuffy (air); foggy, murky, smoky, to be cut with a knife; lumpy, clotted, coagulated, curdled; caked, matted, knotted, tangled 48 *cohesive*; consistent, monolithic; firm, close-textured, knotty, gnarled; substantial, massy, massive 322 *weighty*; concrete, solid, set, gelled *or* jelled, frozen, solidified, etc. (see vb.); crystalline, crystallized; condensed, nucleated; costive, constipated; compact, close-packed, firm-packed 54 *full*; thick, bushy, luxuriant 635 *plentiful*; serried, massed; impenetrable, impermeable, impervious; indivisible.

indissoluble, insoluble, infusible; precipitated, sedimentary.

Vb. *be dense*, be solid, etc. (see adj.); become solid, solidify, consolidate; conglomerate, cement 48 *cohere*; condense, nucleate, thicken; precipitate, deposit; freeze, glaciate 380 *be cold*; set, gel *or* jell; congeal, coagulate, clot, curdle; cake, crust; crystallize; fossilize, petrify, ossify 326 *harden*; compact, compress, firm down, contract, squeeze 198 *make smaller*; crowd 74 *bring together*.

325 Lack of density

N. *lack of density*, low pressure, rarity, vacuum, near vacuum 190 *emptiness*; compressibility, sponginess 327 *softness*; tenuity, fineness 206 *thinness*; lack of substance 4 *lacking substance*, 323 *lightness*; incorporeality, ethereality 320 *non-materiality*; airiness, ether, gas 336 *gaseousness*, 340 *air*; rarefaction, expansion, dilatation, attenuation.

Adj. *rarefied*, aerated 336 *gaseous*; rare, tenuous, thin, fine, subtle, flimsy, airy, airy-fairy, slight 4 *lacking substance*; low-pressure, uncompressed; spongy 328 *elastic*; void, hollow 190 *empty*; ethereal, aery 323 *light*; incorporeal 320 *non-material*; wispy, straggly 75 *unassembled*.

Vb. *rarefy*, reduce the pressure, expand, dilate; make a vacuum, hermetically seal, pump out, exhaust 300 *empty*; attenuate, refine, thin; dilute, adulterate 163 *weaken*; gasify 338 *vaporize*.

326 Hardness

N. *hardness*, intractability, intransigence, resistance 329 *toughness*; starchiness, stiffness, rigour, rigidity, inflexibility; inelasticity; firmness; callosity, callousness, lumpiness, nodosity, nodularity; grittiness, stoniness, rockiness, cragginess; grit, stone, pebble, boulder; flint, silica, quartz, granite, marble, diamond 344 *rock*; adamant, metal, duralumin; steel, iron, wrought iron, cast iron; nails, hardware, stoneware; cement, concrete, reinforced concrete, brick; block, board, heartwood, duramen; hardwood, teak, oak, heart of oak 366 *wood*; bone, gristle, cartilage; spine, backbone; lump, nodule, callosity, callus, corn, wart; horn, ivory; crust, shell, hard shell; hard core, hard centre, jawbreaker; brick wall; stiffener, starch, wax; whalebone, corset, splint 218 *prop*; ossification, sclerosis, hardening of the arteries.

Adj. *hard*, adamantine; indestructible, unbreakable 162 *strong*; shatterproof, fortified, armoured, armour-plated; steeled, proof; iron, cast-iron; steel, steely, hard as iron *or* as steel *or* as stone, rock-hard; sun-baked; stony, rocky, flinty; gritty, gravelly, pebbly; granitic, crystalline, vitreous, glassy; horny; calloused; bony; gristly 329 *tough*; hardened, tempered, case-hardened; vitrified, petrified, fossilized, ossified; icy, frozen.

rigid, stubborn, resistant, intractable, unmalleable, intransigent; firm, inflexible, unbending 162 *unyielding*; starchy, starched; boned,

reinforced; muscle-bound 695 *clumsy*; braced, tense, taut, tight, set, solid; crisp 330 *brittle*; stiff, stiff as a poker *or* as a board.

Vb. *harden*, make hard, etc. (see adj.); steel 162 *strengthen*; temper, vulcanize, toughen; crisp, bake 381 *heat*; petrify, fossilize, ossify; calcify, vitrify, crystallize 324 *be dense*; set, gel *or* jell, glaciate, freeze 382 *refrigerate*; stiffen, back, bone, starch, wax (a moustache), tauten 45 *tighten*.

327 Softness

N. *softness*, tenderness; pliableness, etc. (see adj.); compliance 739 *obedience*; pliancy, pliability, flexibility, plasticity, ductility, tractability; malleability, adaptability; suppleness, litheness; springiness, suspension 328 *elasticity*; impressibility, doughiness 356 *pulpiness*; sponginess, flaccidity, flabbiness, floppiness; laxity, looseness 354 *semiliquidity*; sogginess, squelchiness, marshiness, bogginess 347 *marsh*; downiness; velvetiness; butter, grease, oil, wax, putty, paste, Plasticine (tdmk), clay, dough, soap, plastic; padding, foam-filling, wadding, pad 227 *lining*; cushion, pillow, armchair, feather bed 376 *euphoria*; velvet, plush, down, thistledown, fluff, fleece 259 *hair*; feathers 259 *plumage*; snow, snowflake 323 *lightness*.

Adj. *soft*, tender 301 *edible*; melting 335 *fluid*; giving, yielding, compressible; springy, sprung 328 *elastic*; pneumatic, foam-filled, cushiony, padded, podgy; impressible, waxy, doughy, spongy, soggy, mushy, squelchy, boggy 347 *marshy*; juicy, overripe; fleecy; turfy, mossy, grassy; velvety, silky 258 *smooth*; unstiffened, unstarched, limp; flaccid, flabby, floppy; unstrung, relaxed, slack, loose; soft as butter *or* as wax *or* as soap *or* as down *or* as velvet *or* as silk; tender as a chicken; softening, emollient.

flexible, bendable; pliant, pliable, putty-like; ductile, tractile, malleable, tractable, mouldable, plastic; stretchable 328 *elastic*; lithe, willowy, supple, lissom, limber, loose-limbed, double-jointed; acrobatic.

Vb. *soften*, tenderize; mellow 669 *mature*; oil, grease 334 *lubricate*; knead, massage, mash, pulp, squash 332 *grind*; macerate, marinade, steep 341 *drench*; melt, thaw 337 *liquefy*; cushion, featherbed; relax, unstring 46 *disunite*; yield, give, give way, relax, loosen up, hang loose 328 *be elastic*.

328 Elasticity

N. *elasticity*, give, stretch; spring, springiness; suspension; stretchability, tensibility; resilience, bounce 280 *recoil*; buoyancy, rubber, india rubber, foam rubber; caoutchouc, gutta-percha, balata; elastic; elastic band, rubber band, rubber ball; bouncy castle; stretch jeans; gum, chewing gum, bubble gum.

Adj. *elastic*, stretchy, stretchable, tensile; rubbery, springy, bouncy, resilient; buoyant; flexible; sprung, well-sprung; ductile 327 *soft*.

329 Toughness
N. *toughness*, durability, survivability, infrangibility 162 *strength*; tenacity, cohesion 48 *cohesiveness*; viscidity 354 *semiliquidity*; leatheriness, inedibility, indigestibility; leather, gristle, cartilage 326 *hardness*.

Adj. *tough*, durable; strong-fibred 162 *strong*; tenacious, retentive, clinging, sticky 48 *cohesive*; viscid 354 *semiliquid*; infrangible, unbreakable, indestructible, shockproof, shatter-proof; vulcanized, toughened, strengthened, weather-beaten; hardboiled, overdone; stringy, sinewy, woody, fibrous; gristly, cartilaginous; rubbery, leathery, tough as old boots *or* as shoe leather; chewy, indigestible, inedible; stubborn 326 *rigid*.

330 Brittleness
N. *brittleness*, crispness, etc. (see adj.); frangibility; friableness, crumbliness 332 *powderiness*; fissility 46 *splitting*; laminability, flakiness; fragility, frailty, flimsiness 163 *weakness*; eggshell, matchwood, shale, slate; glass, porcelain 381 *pottery*; greenhouse, glasshouse.

Adj. *brittle*, breakable, frangible; inelastic 326 *rigid*; fragile, papery, parchment-like; splintery; friable, crumbly 332 *powdery*; crisp, flaky, laminable; fissile, splitting; frail, flimsy, eggshell 163 *weak*.

331 Structure. Texture
N. *structure*, organization, pattern, plan; complex, syndrome 52 *whole*; build 243 *form*; constitution, make-up, set-up, content, substance 56 *composition*; construction, make, works, workings, nuts and bolts; architecture; fabric, brickwork, stonework, woodwork, timberwork 631 *materials*; infrastructure, superstructure 164 *building*; scaffold, framework, chassis, shell 218 *frame*; infilling 303 *insertion*; lamination, cleavage; body, carcass, physique, anatomy 358 *organism*; skeleton, anatomy, physiology, histology 358 *biology*.

texture, tissue, fabric, stuff 222 *textile*; staple, denier 208 *fibre*; web, weave, warp and woof, warp and weft 222 *weaving*; nap, pile 259 *hair*; grain, grit; fineness of grain 258 *smoothness*; coarseness of grain 259 *roughness*; surface 223 *exteriority*; feel 378 *touch*.

Adj. *textural*, textile, woven 222 *crossed*;

fine-woven, close-woven; ribbed, twilled; grained, granular; fine-grained, silky, satiny 258 *smooth*; coarse-grained, gritty 259 *rough*; fine, cobwebby, filmy; coarse, rough, homespun, tweedy 259 *hairy*.

332 Powderiness
N. *powderiness*, friability, crumbliness 330 *brittleness*; dustiness 649 *dirt*; sandiness, grittiness; granulation; pulverization, attrition, attenuation, disintegration, erosion 51 *decomposition*; grinding, milling; abrasion, filing 333 *friction*; fragmentation 46 *disunion*; sprinkling, dusting, powdering, frosting.

powder, face powder, foot powder, talcum powder; talc, chalk; pollen, spore; dust, coaldust, soot, ash 649 *dirt*; icing sugar, flour, cornflour, farina, arrowroot, kuzu, starch; grist, meal, bran; sawdust, filings, swarf; efflorescence, flowers; scurf, dandruff; debris, detritus 41 *leavings*; sand, grit, gravel, hoggin *or* hogging, shingle; grain, seed, crumb 53 *piece*; granule, speck 33 *small thing*; flake, snowflake; smut, smoke; dust cloud; fog, smog 355 *cloud*; sandstorm, dust storm 176 *storm*.

grinder, pulverizer, miller; roller, crusher, masher, atomizer; mill, millstone, muller, quern, quernstone; pestle, pestle and mortar; hand mill, coffee mill, pepper mill; grater, grindstone, file; abrasive, sandpaper, emery paper, emery board; molar 256 *tooth*; chopper 256 *sharp edge*; sledgehammer 279 *hammer*; bulldozer 279 *ram*.

Adj. *powdery*, chalky, dusty, sooty, smoky 649 *dirty*; sandy 342 *dry*; farinaceous, floury; granulated, granular; gritty, gravelly; flaky, efflorescent; ground, sifted, sieved; crumbly, friable 330 *brittle*.

Vb. *grind*, pulverize, powder, reduce to powder; granulate; crush, mash, smash, shatter, fragment, disintegrate 46 *break*; mill, mince, beat, bruise, pound; crumble; crunch, scrunch 301 *chew*; abrade 333 *rub*; erode 51 *decompose*.

333 Friction
N. *friction*, frictional force, drag 278 *slowness*; rubbing, etc. (see vb.); attrition, rubbing against, rubbing together 279 *collision*; rubbing out, erasure 550 *obliteration*; abrasion, excoriation, scraping; filing 332 *powderiness*; wearing away, erosion 165 *destruction*; scrape, graze, scratch; brushing, rub; polish, elbow grease; massage, facial massage, cosmetic scrub, exfoliator, exfoliant, facial 843 *beauty treatment*; pumice stone; eraser, rubber, rosin; whetstone.

Vb. *rub*, rub against, strike (a match); gnash, grind; fret, fray, chafe; graze, scratch, bark, take the skin off 655 *wound*; rub off, abrade, excoriate; skin, flay; scuff, scrape, scrub, scour, burnish; brush, rub down, towel, curry, curry-comb 648 *clean*; polish, buff 258 *smooth*; rub out, erase 550 *obliterate*; erode, wear away 165 *consume*; rasp, file, grind 332 *grind*; shampoo, massage; rub in; anoint 334 *lubricate*; wax, rosin, chalk (one's cue); catch, stick; rub gently, stroke 889 *caress*; iron 258 *smooth*.

334 Lubrication

N. *lubrication*, greasing; anointment, unction, oiling, etc. (see vb.); lubricity 357 *greasiness*; non-friction 258 *smoothness*.

lubricant, graphite, plumbago, black lead; oil, glycerine, wax, grease, axle grease 357 *oil*; soap, lather 648 *cleanser*; saliva, spit, spittle; ointment, salve 658 *balm*; emollient, lenitive 357 *ointment*; lubricator, oil-can, grease-gun.

Vb. *lubricate*, oil, grease, wax, soap, lather; butter 357 *grease*; anoint.

335 Fluidity

N. *fluidity*, fluidness, liquidity, liquidness; wateriness, rheuminess 339 *water*; juiciness, sappiness 356 *pulpiness*; haemophilia; solubility, solubleness, liquescence 337 *liquefaction*; gaseous character 336 *gaseousness*; viscosity 354 *semiliquidity*; fluid mechanics.

fluid, liquid; water, running water 339 *water*; drink 301 *drink*; milk, whey; juice, sap, latex; humour, chyle, rheum, mucus, saliva 302 *excrement*; serum, lymph, plasma; pus, matter; gore (see also *blood* below); hydrocele, dropsy 651 *disease*.

blood, lifeblood 360 *life*; bloodstream, circulation; red blood 162 *vitality*; blue blood 868 *nobility*; blood of the gods; gore; clot, blood clot, coagulation 324 *solid body*; corpuscle, red corpuscle, white corpuscle, platelet; lymph, plasma, serum, blood serum; haemoglobin; factor VIII; haematosis; blood group, ABO system, Rhesus factor; blood count; haematology; blood transfusion; haemophilia, anaemia, leukaemia, AIDS.

Adj. *liquid*, in suspension; uncoagulated, unclotted, clarified; soluble, liquescent, melting; viscous 354 *glutinous*; fluent, running 350 *flowing*; runny, rheumy 339 *watery*; serous; suppurating 653 *toxic*.

bloody, sanguinary; gory, bleeding; haematic, sanguineous, haemic, haemal; serous, lymphatic, plasmatic; haemophilic, haemolytic.

336 Gaseousness

N. *gaseousness*, vaporousness, etc. (see adj.); windiness, flatulence 352 *wind*; aeration, gasi-

fication; volatility 338 *vaporization*; aerostatics, aerodynamics.

gas, vapour; ether 340 *air*; effluvium, exhalation, miasma 298 *going out*; flatus 352 *wind*; fumes, reek, smoke; steam, water vapour 355 *cloud*; hydrogen, oxygen, nitrogen, etc. 319 *element*; helium, hydrogen 323 *lightness*; laughing gas, gas and air, etc. 375 *anaesthetic*; coal gas, town gas, natural gas, North Sea gas, methane 385 *fuel*; damp, after-damp, black damp, choke damp, fire damp; gasworks, gas plant, gasification plant 687 *workshop*; gasometer 632 *storage*; gas-light, neon light 420 *lamp*; gas stove, gas cooker, gas fire 383 *furnace*; gas meter 465 *meter*; carbon monoxide, marsh gas, poison gas, CS gas, etc. 659 *poison*; greenhouse gas, CFC, chlorofluorocarbon; gasbag, balloon 276 *airship*.

Adj. *gaseous*, gasiform; vaporous, steamy, volatile 338 *vaporific*; aerial, airy, aeriform, ethereal 340 *airy*; carbonated, effervescent, pétillant 355 *bubbly*; gassy, windy, flatulent; effluvial, miasmic; pneumatic, aerostatic, aerodynamic.

Vb. *gasify*, steam, emit vapour 338 *vaporize*; let off *or* blow off steam 300 *emit*; oxygenate 340 *aerate*; carbonate; hydrogenate, hydrogenize.

337 Liquefaction

N. *liquefaction*, liquidization; fluidization; solubility, deliquescence 335 *fluidity*; fusion 43 *mixture*; dissolution; thaw, melting 381 *heating*; solvent, dissolvent, flux; liquefier, liquefacient; liquidizer; anticoagulant 658 *antidote*.

solution, decoction, infusion; aqua; suspension, colloid; flux, lye.

Vb. *liquefy*, liquidize, unclot, clarify, liquate, dissolve, deliquesce, run 350 *flow*; unfreeze, thaw, melt, smelt 381 *heat*; render, clarify; leach; fluidize.

338 Vaporization

N. *vaporization*, gasification; exhalation 355 *cloud*; evaporation, volatilization, distillation, sublimation; steaming, fumigation, vapourability, volatility; atomization.

vaporizer, evaporater; atomizer, spray, aerosol; retort, still, distillery, vaporimeter.

Adj. *vaporific*, volatilised, etc. (see vb.); reeking; vapouring, steaming, etc. (see vb.); vaporous, vapoury, vapourish; steamy, gassy, smoky; evaporable, volatile.

Vb. *vaporize*, evaporate 336 *gasify*; volatilize, distil, sublimate, exhale, transpire, emit vapour, blow off steam 300 *emit*; smoke, fume, reek, steam; fumigate, spray; atomize.

339 Water

N. *water*, H_2O, aqua; heavy water, D_2O; hard water, soft water; drinking water, tap water,

Adam's ale; mineral water, soda water 301 *soft drink*; water vapour, steam 355 *cloud*; rain water 350 *rain*; spring water, running water, fresh water 350 *stream*; holy water 988 *ritual object*; weeping, tears 836 *lamentation*; sweat, saliva 335 *fluid*; high water, high tide, spring tide, neap tide, low water 350 *wave*; standing water, still water, stagnant water 346 *lake*; sea water, salt water, brine, briny 343 *ocean*; water cure, taking the waters, hydrotherapy, hydropathy 658 *therapy*; bath water, bath, tub, whirlpool bath, Jacuzzi (tdmk), shower, douche, splash 648 *washing*; lotion, lavender water 843 *cosmetic*; diluent, adulteration, dilution 655 *impairment*; wateriness, damp, humidity, wet; watering; jug, ewer 194 *vessel*; tap, faucet, stand-pipe, hydrant 351 *water channel*; waterer, hose 341 *irrigator*; water supply, waterworks; hot spring, geyser; well, artesian well, borehole 632 *store*; hydrometry; water purification, desalination 648 *cleansing*.

Adj. *watery*, aqueous, aquatic, lymphatic 335 *fluid*; hydrated, hydrous; hydrological, hydrographic 321 *geographic*; adulterated, diluted 163 *weak*; wet, moist, drenching 341 *humid*; hydrotherapeutic; sudorific 658 *medical*.

340 Air

N. *air* 336 *gas*; thin air, ether 325 *lack of density*; air pocket 190 *emptiness*; wind, blast, etc. 352 *wind*; oxygen, nitrogen, argon, etc. 319 *element*; blue sky, blue, welkin, wide blue yonder; cloud 355 *cloud*; open air, open, out of doors, exposure 183 *space*; sea air, ozone; fresh air, country air, smokeless zone, non-smoking compartment 648 *cleanness*; airing 342 *drying*; aeration 338 *vaporization*; fanning 352 *ventilation*; air-conditioning, air-cooling 382 *refrigeration*; ventilator, blower, fan, air-conditioner 384 *refrigerator*; air-filter 648 *cleanser*; humidifier, vaporizer, atomizer, ionizer 341 *moisture*.

atmosphere, troposphere, tropopause, stratosphere, ionosphere; mesosphere, exosphere; aerosphere; aerospace; ozone layer, hole in the ozone layer, CFC, chlorofluorocarbons, greenhouse effect 381 *heating*.

weather, the elements; fine weather; balmy days, halcyon days; dry spell, heat wave, Indian summer 379 *heat*; doldrums; atmospheric pressure, anticyclone, high pressure; cyclone, depression, low pressure; rough weather 176 *storm*, 352 *gale*; bad weather, foul weather, wet weather 350 *rain*; cold weather 380 *wintriness*; changeable weather; meteorology; weather forecast 511 *prediction*; isobar; glass, mercury, barometer; vane, weathervane, weathercock; hygrometer; weather ship,

weather station, rain gauge, wind gauge; weatherman *or* -woman, meteorologist; climate, microclimate; climatology, climatography; climatologist.

Adj. *airy*, ethereal 4 *lacking substance*; aerial; pneumatic, aerated, oxygenated; inflated, blown up; flatulent 336 *gaseous*; breezy 352 *windy*; well-ventilated, fresh, air-conditioned 382 *cooled*; meteorological, weather-wise; atmospheric, barometric; cyclonic, anticyclonic; high-pressure 324 *dense*; low-pressure 325 *rarefied*; climatic, climatological.

Vb. *aerate*, oxygenate; air, expose 342 *dry*; ventilate, freshen 648 *clean*; fan, winnow, make a draught 352 *blow*; take the air 352 *breathe*.

Adv. *out of doors*, in the open air, in the open, alfresco, en plein air.

341 Moisture

N. *moisture*, humidity, sap, juice 335 *fluid*; dampness, wetness, moistness, dewiness; dew point; dankness, condensation, rising damp; sogginess, swampiness, marshiness, bogginess; saturation, saturation point 54 *fullness*; leakiness 298 *outflow*; raininess, showeriness; rainfall, high rainfall, wet weather 350 *rain*; damp, wet; spray, spindrift, froth, foam 355 *bubble*; mist, haar, fog, fog bank 355 *cloud*; Scotch mist, drizzle, smirr, drip, dew, morning dew; drop, droplet, raindrop, dewdrop, teardrop; tears 836 *lamentation*; saliva, salivation, slabber, slobber, spit, spittle 302 *excrement*; ooze, slime, mud, squelch, fen, bog 347 *marsh*; sop.

irrigator, sprinkler, waterer, water-cart; watering can; spray, rose; hose, garden hose, syringe, squirt; pump, fire engine; shadoof, Archimedes's screw; water butt, dam, reservoir 632 *store*; catheter; sluice, water pipe, qanat 351 *water channel*.

Adj. *humid*, moistened, wet 339 *watery*; pluvial; drizzling, drizzly; damp, moist, dripping; dank, muggy, foggy, misty 355 *cloudy*; steaming, reeking; undrained, oozy, muddy, slimy, sloppy, slushy, squashy, squelchy, splashy, plashy, fenny, boggy 347 *marshy*; dewy, fresh, bedewed; juicy, sappy 335 *fluid*; dribbling, seeping, percolating; wetted, steeped, soaked, sprinkled.

Vb. *be wet*, be moist, etc. (see adj.); be soaking wet, be wringing wet; be soaking, be sopping; squelch; slobber, salivate, sweat, perspire 298 *exude*; steam, reek 300 *emit*; percolate, seep 297 *infiltrate*; weep, bleed, stream; ooze, drip, leak; trickle, smirr *or* smurr, drizzle, rain, pour, rain cats and dogs 350 *rain*; get wet, get wet through, get drenched, dip, duck; bathe, wash, shower, douche; paddle.

moisten, humidify, wet, dampen; dilute, hydrate; lick, lap, wash; splash, splatter; spill, slop; flood, spray, shower, spatter, bespatter, sprinkle, besprinkle, syringe; bedew.

drench, saturate, imbue; soak, deluge, wet through; leach; wash, bathe, shower, douche; hose down, sluice, slosh, rinse 648 *clean*; baptize 988 *perform ritual*; plunge, dip, duck, submerge, drown 303 *immerse*; swamp, flood, inundate, flood out, waterlog; dunk, douse, souse, steep; macerate, marinate.

irrigate, water, hose, pump; flood, submerge; percolate 297 *infiltrate*; squirt, inject, douche.

342 Dryness

N. *dryness*, aridity, aridness; thirst, drouth 859 *hunger*; low rainfall, drought, drouth; sandiness, desertification, desertization 172 *desert*; dry climate, dry season; sun, sunniness 379 *heat*.

drying, desiccation, drying up; airing, evaporation 338 *vaporization*; draining, drainage, catheterization; dehydration, sunning 381 *heating*; withering, searing 426 *colourlessness*.

dryer, dehydrator, desiccator, evaporator; dehydrant, siccative, silica gel, sand, blotting paper; absorbent; mop, swab, sponge, towel, towelling; paper towel, kitchen tissue, tissue, toilet roll; hair drier, hand drier, spin drier, tumble drier; wringer, mangle; airer, clotheshorse 217 *hanger*; airing cupboard.

Adj. *dry*, thirsty 859 *hungry*; arid; sandy, dusty, desertized 332 *powdery*; bare, brown; desert, Saharan; dehydrated, desiccated; shrivelled, withered, seared, sere; dried up, parchment-like; sunned; aired; sun-dried, wind-dried; burnt, scorched, baked, parched 379 *hot*; sunny, fine, cloudless, fair; dried out, drained, evaporated; squeezed dry, wrung out, mangled; waterproofed, waterproof, rainproof, showerproof, dampproof; watertight; high and dry; dry as a bone.

Vb. *dry*, dehumidify, desiccate, freeze-dry; dehydrate; drain, catheterize, pump out, suck dry 300 *empty*; wring out, mangle; spin-dry, tumble-dry, drip-dry; hang out, peg out, air, evaporate 338 *vaporize*; sun, expose to sunlight, solarize, sun-dry; smoke, kipper, cure; parch, scorch, bake, burn 381 *heat*; sere, sear, shrivel, wither; mummify 666 *preserve*; dry up, stop the flow, apply a tourniquet 350 *staunch*; blot, blot up, mop, mop up, soak up, sponge 299 *absorb*; swab, wipe, wipe up, wipe dry.

343 Ocean

N. *ocean*, sea, blue, salt water, brine, briny; waters, billows, waves, tide 350 *wave*; Davy

Jones's locker; main, deep, deep sea; high seas, great waters; trackless deep, watery waste; herring pond, drink; sea lane, shipping lane; ocean floor, sea bed, sea bottom, ooze, benthos 365 *marine life*; the seven seas.

Oceans and Seas

Antarctic Ocean, Arctic Ocean, Atlantic Ocean, Indian Ocean, Pacific Ocean.
  Adriatic Sea, Aegean Sea, Andaman Sea, Arabian Sea, Baltic Sea, Barents Sea, Beaufort Sea, Bering Sea, Black Sea, Caribbean Sea, Coral Sea, East China Sea, Greenland Sea, Irish Sea, Mediterranean Sea, North Sea, Norwegian Sea, Red Sea, Sargasso Sea, Sea of Japan, Sea of Okhotsk, South China Sea, Tasman Sea, Tyrrhenian Sea.

Inland seas: Aral Sea, Caspian Sea, Dead Sea, Sea of Azov, Sea of Galilee.

sea god, Oceanus, Neptune, Poseidon, Triton; Nereus; merman 970 *mythical being*.

sea nymph, Oceanid, Nereid, siren; Amphitrite, Thetis, Tethys; Calypso; Undine; mermaid 970 *mythical being*; water sprite 970 *fairy*; bathing beauty 841 *a beauty*.

344 Land

N. *land*, dry land, terra firma; earth, ground, earth's crust 321 *world*; continent, mainland; heartland, hinterland; midland, inland, interior 224 *interiority*; peninsula, delta, promontory 254 *projection*; isthmus; terrain, heights, highlands 209 *high land*; lowlands 210 *lowness*; reclaimed land, polder; steppe, fields 348 *plain*; wilderness 172 *desert*; oasis; isle 349 *island*; zone, clime; country, district, tract 184 *region*; territory, possessions, acres, estate, real estate 777 *lands*; landscape.

shore, coastline 233 *outline*; coast 234 *edge*; strand, beach, sands, shingle; seaboard, seashore, seaside; sea cliff, sea wall; plage, lido, Riviera, Costa Blanca, Costa Brava, Costa del Sol; marina; bank, river bank, riverside; continental shelf.

soil, ground; farmland, arable land, cropland 370 *farm*; pasture 348 *grassland*; deposit, moraine, loess, silt, alluvium; topsoil, sand, dust, subsoil; mould, leaf mould, humus; loam, clay, bole, marl; fuller's earth, argil, potter's clay, china clay, kaolin 381 *pottery*; gravel, scree; stone, pebble, flint; turf, sod, clod 53 *piece*.

rock, cliff, scar, crag; stone, boulder; reef; stack, skerry; dyke, sill; igneous rock, plutonic rock, granite, basalt; volcanic rock, pumice, lava; sedimentary rock, sandstone, shale, limestone, chalk, schist, marble; pore 359 *mineralogy*; quartz, precious stone, semi-precious stone 844 *gem*.

345 Gulf: inlet

N. *gulf*, bay, bight, cove, creek, lagoon; slough; natural harbour, road, roadstead; inlet, outlet, fleet, bayou; fjord, sea loch; ria; mouth, estuary; firth, frith, kyle; sound, strait, channel; mud flat.

346 Lake

N. *lake*, lagoon; loch, lough, linn; freshwater lake, salt lake; inland sea, Aral Sea, etc. 343 *ocean*; oxbow lake, bayou lake; broads; sheet of water, standing water, stagnant water, backwater; wash 347 *marsh*; pool, tarn, mere, pond, dewpond; fishpond, stew; millpond; water feature, water garden; waterhole, puddle; artificial lake, dam, reservoir 632 *storage*; well 339 *water*; swimming pool, lido, swimming baths, Jacuzzi (tdmk) 648 *washing*; birthing pool.

347 Marsh

N. *marsh*, morass; marshland; flat, mud flat, salt marsh; fen, fenland, bog, peat bog, quagmire, quicksand; saltpan; mudhole, slough, mire, mud; swamp, swampland, mangrove swamp; Slough of Despond.

Adj. *marshy*, paludal; swampy, boggy, fenny; quaggy; squelchy, spongy 327 *soft*; slushy; muddy, miry 649 *dirty*; waterlogged.

348 Plain

N. *plain*, peneplain; dale, levels 216 *horizontality*; lowlands 255 *valley*; flats 347 *marsh*; delta, alluvial plain; sands, desert sands, waste 172 *desert*; tundra; ice field, ice floe 380 *ice*; grasslands, steppe, prairie, pampas, savanna, llanos, campos; heath, common, wold, downland, downs, moor, moorland, fell; upland, plateau, tableland 209 *high land*; bush, veld, range 183 *space*; fields, green belt, parkland, national park, safari park 263 *open space*; lowlands, low countries 210 *lowness*.

grassland, pasture, pasturage, grazing 369 *animal husbandry*; sheeprun, sheep track, sheep walk; field, meadow, mead, lea; chase, park, grounds; green, greensward, lawn, turf.

349 Island

N. *island*, isle, islet, skerry; eyot, inch, holm; atoll, reef, coral reef; cay, key; sandbank; iceberg, growler, ice floe; peninsula; archipelago; insularity.

350 Stream: water in motion

N. *stream*, running water, watercourse, river, subterranean river; waterway; tributary, branch, streamlet, rivulet, brook, bourne, burn, rill, beck, gill, runnel, runlet; freshet, torrent; wadi; spring, fountain, fountainhead, headwaters 156 *source*; jet, spout, gush; geyser, hot spring, well 632 *store*; water feature; Styx, Rubicon.

current, flow, flux 285 *progression*; effluence 298 *going out*; confluence 293 *convergence*; inflow 297 *entering*; outflow, reflux 286 *regression*; undercurrent, undertow, crosscurrent 182 *counteraction*; tide, spring tide, neap tide; tidal flow, tidal current, ebb and flow 317 *fluctuation*; bore, eagre; tidal race; millrace, millstream; bloodstream.

eddy, whirlpool, swirl, maelstrom 315 *whirl*; whirlpool bath, Jacuzzi (tdmk); wake 67 *sequel*.

waterfall, falls, cataract, Niagara, Victoria; linn, cascade, rapids, weir; water power 160 *sources of energy*.

wave, bow wave; wash, backwash; ripple, cat's-paw 262 *furrow*; swell, ground swell; billow, roller, comber; breaker, surf, spume, white horses; tidal wave; bore, eagre; choppiness 259 *roughness*; sea, choppy sea, waviness, undulation.

rain, rainfall 341 *moisture*; precipitation; drizzle, mizzle, Scotch mist, smirr or smurr; sleet, hail 380 *wintriness*; shower, downpour, deluge, cloudburst, thunderstorm 176 *storm*; flurry 352 *gale*; pouring rain, teeming rain, driving rain, torrential rain, sheets of rain; raininess, wet spell, foul weather; rainy season, the rains, monsoon; lovely weather for ducks; patter; dripping, etc. (see vb.); rainmaking, cloud-seeding; rain gauge; acid rain 659 *poison*.

Adj. *flowing*, falling, etc. (see vb.); runny 335 *fluid*; fluent, riverine, fluvial, tidal; running, coursing, racing; streaming; in flood, overflowing, in spate; flooding, inundatory, cataclysmic; pouring, lashing, driving, dripping, gushing.

Vb. *flow*, run, course, pour; ebb 286 *regress*; surge, gush, rush, spurt or spirt, spout, spew, play, squirt; well, well up, bubble up, issue 298 *emerge*; pour, stream, trickle, dribble 298 *exude*; drip, drop 309 *descend*; wash, slosh, splash 341 *moisten*; trill, murmur, babble, bubble, burble, gurgle; flow over, cascade, fall, flood, inundate, deluge 341 *drench*; flow into, drain into 297 *enter*; run off; leak, percolate, pass through 305 *pass*; ooze.

rain, shower, stream, pour, pelt; snow, sleet, hail; fall, come down, bucket, piss down, rain hard, pour with rain, rain cats and dogs; come down in torrents, come down in sheets, come down in stair-rods, rain pitchforks; patter, drizzle, mizzle, smirr, drip, spit, sprinkle; be wet, rain and rain.

staunch, stop a flow, apply a tourniquet; plug 264 *close*; stem, dam, dam up 702 *obstruct*.

351 Conduit. Channel

N. *water channel*, conduit, tideway, riverbed; arroyo, wadi; trough, basin, river basin; canyon, ravine, gorge, gully 255 *valley*; inland waterways, canal system; canal, channel, watercourse, qanat; ditch, dike; trench, moat; gutter, mill race; duct, aqueduct; water pipe, water main; pipe, hose, garden hose; standpipe, hydrant, siphon, tap, spout, funnel 263 *tube*; valve, flume, sluice, weir, lock, floodgate, watergate, spillway; chute 350 *waterfall*; oilpipe, pipeline; vein, artery.

drain, gully, gutter, gargoyle, water-spout; overflow, wastepipe, drainpipe 298 *outlet*; culvert; ditch, sewer 649 *sink*; alimentary canal; catheter 300 *clearing*.

352 Wind: air in motion
N. *wind* 340 *air*; draught, downdraught, updraught; blast, blow; air stream, jet stream; current, air current, crosswind, headwind 182 *counteraction*; tailwind, following wind 287 *propellant*; air flow, slip stream; air pocket; wind sock, wind gauge, anemometer; cold draught, icy blast; hot wind, sirocco, monsoon, Etesian winds; prevailing winds, trade winds, Roaring Forties; north wind, Boreas, mistral, tramontano; south wind, föhn, chinook; east wind, levanter; west wind, Zephyr; wind god: Aeolus.

breeze, zephyr; breath of air, waft, whiff, puff, gust, sough, light breeze, gentle breeze, fresh breeze, sea breeze, cooling breeze.

gale, high wind; blow, blast, gust, flurry; squall; nor'wester, sou'wester, hurricane, whirlwind, cyclone, tornado, twister, typhoon, simoom 315 *whirl*; thunderstorm, dust storm, sandstorm, dust devil, blizzard 176 *storm*; microburst; gale force.

blowing, inflation, insufflation 197 *distension*; blowing up, pumping up; pumping out 300 *clearing*; pump, air pump, stirrup pump, bicycle pump; bellows, windbag, bag-pipe; woodwind, brass 414 *musical instrument*; blowpipe; exhaust pipe, exhaust 298 *outlet*.

ventilation, airing 340 *air*; draught; fanning, cooling; ventilator 353 *air pipe*; blower, fan, extractor fan, electric fan, punkah, air-conditioner, air-conditioning 384 *refrigerator*.

breathing, respiration, inhalation, exhalation, expiration, inspiration; gills, lungs, bellows; respirator, iron lung, oxygen tent; windpipe 353 *air pipe*; sigh, sob, gulp, hiccup, catching of the breath, yawn; panting, gasping, huffing and puffing; breath, bad breath, halitosis.

Adj. *windy*, airy, exposed, draughty, breezy, blowy; ventilated, fresh; blowing, gusty, gusting, squally; blustery, stormy, tempestuous, boisterous 176 *violent*; windswept, windblown; storm-tossed, storm-bound; flatulent; fizzy, gassy 336 *gaseous*; aeolian, boreal, zephyrous;

cyclonic; gale-force, hurricane-force.

Vb. *blow*, puff, blast; insufflate, blow up, get up, blow hard, blow great guns, blow a hurricane, rage, storm; howl, roar 409 *howl*; screech, scream, whistle, pipe, sing in the shrouds 407 *shrill*; hum, moan, mutter, sough, sigh 401 *sound faint*; wave, flap, shake, flutter, flourish 318 *agitate*; draw, ventilate, fan 382 *refrigerate*; waft 287 *propel*; veer, back 282 *deviate*; die down, subside, drop, abate.

breathe, respire, breathe in, inhale; draw *or* take a deep breath, fill one's lungs; breathe out, exhale; aspirate, puff, huff, huff and puff, whiff; sniff, sniffle, snuffle, snort; breathe hard; gasp, pant, heave; wheeze, sneeze, cough 407 *rasp*; sigh, catch one's breath.

blow up, pump up, inflate, dilate 197 *enlarge*; pump out, exhaust 300 *empty*.

353 Air pipe
N. *air pipe*, airway, air shaft, air well; wind tunnel; blowpipe, peashooter 287 *propellant*; throat, gullet, oesophagus, windpipe, trachea, larynx, voice box, Adam's apple; bronchia, bronchus; nose, nostril, spiracle, blowhole, nozzle, vent, mouthpiece 263 *aperture*; flue pipe, mouth organ 414 *organ*; gas main, gas pipe; tobacco pipe, pipe, briar, hookah, etc. 388 *tobacco*; funnel, flue, chimney, stack, exhaust pipe.

354 Semiliquidity
N. *semiliquidity*, mucosity, viscidity; thickness, stodginess; semiliquid, colloid, emulsion, gore, albumen, mucus, phlegm, clot 324 *solid body*; pus, matter; juice, sap 335 *fluidity*; soup, slop, gruel, cream, curds 356 *pulpiness*; molten lava; oil slick; mud, glaur, slush, sludge, thaw, ooze, slime; silt 347 *marsh*.

thickening, coagulation, clotting 324 *condensing*; gelatinization; emulsification; thickener, starch, arrowroot, flour, cornflour, gelatine, isinglass, pectin.

glutinousness, stickiness, adhesiveness, viscidity, viscosity 48 *cohesiveness*; glue, gluten, gum 47 *adhesive*; emulsion, colloid; glair, size, paste, glaze; gel, jelly; treacle, jam, syrup, honey, goo; wax, mastic 357 *resin*; flypaper.

Adj. *glutinous*, gummy, gooey, viscid, viscous 48 *cohesive*; slimy, sticky, tacky; jammy, treacly, syrupy, gluey; glairy, glaireous; mucous.

Vb. *thicken*, inspissate, congeal 324 *be dense*; coagulate 48 *cohere*; emulsify; gelatinize, jelly, gel *or* jell; starch 326 *harden*; curdle, clot; churn, whip up, beat up, mash, pulp 332 *grind*.

355 Bubble. Cloud: air and water mixed
N. *bubble*, suds, soapsuds, lather, foam, froth; head; sea foam, spume, surf, spray, spindrift

341 *moisture*; mousse, soufflé, meringue, candyfloss; yeast, barm 323 *raising agent*; scum 649 *dirt*.

cloud, scud; cloudbank; rain cloud, storm cloud; woolpack, cumulus, altocumulus, cirrus, cirrocumulus, stratus, cirrostratus, nimbostratus; mackerel sky, mare's tail; vapour, steam 338 *vaporization*; brume, haze, mist, haar, fog, smog, pea-souper; cloudiness, film 419 *dimness*; nebulosity; nephology, nephoscope.

Adj. bubbly, bubbling, etc. (see vb.); effervescent, fizzy, sparkling, pétillant 336 *gaseous*; mousseux, foamy; spumy, spumous; frothy, soapy, lathery; yeasty, aerated 323 *light*; scummy 649 *dirty*.

cloudy, clouded, overcast, nebulous; cirrose, foggy, hazy, misty, filmy, brumous 419 *dim*; steamy 338 *vaporific*.

Vb. bubble, spume, foam, froth, cream, form a head; boil, simmer, seethe, fizzle, gurgle 318 *effervesce*; work, ferment, fizz, sparkle; aerate, carbonate; steam 338 *vaporize*.

cloud, cloud over, be cloudy, etc. (see adj.); befog, mist up 419 *be dim*.

356 Pulpiness

N. pulpiness, doughiness, sponginess; fleshiness, juiciness 327 *softness*; poultice, pulp, pith, paste, putty, porridge, pap, puree; mush, mash, squash; dough, batter, sponge; jam 354 *glutinousness*; puree, mousse 355 *bubble*; slush, papier mâché, wood pulp.

357 Greasiness

N. greasiness, oiliness, unctuousness. unctuosity, lubricity, soapiness 334 *lubrication*; fattiness; saponification; anointment, unction.

oil, volatile oil, essential oil; animal oil, whale oil, sperm oil, train oil, cod-liver oil; vegetable oil, corn oil, sunflower oil, olive oil, virgin olive oil, coconut oil, almond oil, linseed oil, cotton-seed oil, castor oil, rape oil, rape seed oil, groundnut oil, palm oil, jojoba oil; mineral oil, shale oil, rock oil, crude oil, petroleum; refined oil, coal oil; fuel oil, paraffin, kerosene, petrol, gasoline, gas 385 *fuel*; lubricating oil 334 *lubricant*; bath oil, suntan oil.

fat, animal fat, grease, adipocere, body fat, excess fat, cellulite; removal of fat: liposuction 843 *beauty treatment*; saturated fat, unsaturated fat, polyunsaturated fat, monounsaturated fat, essential fatty acid, trans-fatty acid, triglyceride; blubber, tallow, spermaceti; sebum, wax, beeswax; suet, lard, dripping, bacon fat 301 *cookery*; glycerine, stearin, olein; margarine, butter, ghee, spread; cream, Devonshire cream,

Cornish cream, top of the milk, buttermilk; soap, carbolic soap, soft soap, toilet soap, liquid soap, soap flakes, wash-cream 648 *cleanser*.

ointment, embrocation, lanolin, liniment, salve, unction, unguent; pomade, brilliantine, hair gel; cream, cold cream 843 *cosmetic*; lotion; suntan lotion, suntan oil, sunblock, suncream, sunscreen.

resin, rosin, gum, gum arabic, tragacanth, myrrh, frankincense, camphor; lac, amber, ambergris; pitch, tar, bitumen, asphalt; varnish, mastic, shellac, lacquer, japan; epoxy resin; polyurethane, plastics.

Adj. fatty, fat, adipose, blubbery, flabby 195 *fat*; sebaceous, waxy, waxen; lardaceous; saponaceous, soapy; buttery, creamy, milky, rich 390 *savoury*.

Vb. grease, oil, anoint 334 *lubricate*; baste, lard; butter; saponify; resin, rosin.

SECTION THREE

Organic matter

358 Organisms: living matter

N. organism, organic matter; living beings; animal and vegetable kingdom, flora and fauna, biota; ecosystem; ecotype, biotype 77 *breed*; living matter 360 *life*; microscopic life; cell, stem cell, protoplasm, cytoplasm, nucleus, nucleolus; nucleic acid, RNA, DNA; chromatin, chromosome, chromatid, gene 5 *heredity*; albumen, protein; rogue protein, prion; enzyme, globulin; antioxidants; organic remains 125 *fossil*.

biology, microbiology; natural history, nature study, biochemistry, biophysics, molecular biology, cell biology, cytology; histology; morphology, embryology; anatomy, physiology 331 *structure*; zoography 367 *zoology*; phytography 368 *botany*; ecology, biodiversity; biogeography; marine biology; genetics, eugenics, sociobiology; genetic engineering, genetic modification, gene technology; biotechnology, biotech, biomedicine; evolution, natural selection, survival of the fittest; Darwinism, Neo-Darwinism; biogenesis; biorhythm.

biologist, cytologist, etc. (see *biology* above).

Adj. biological, physiological, zoological, palaeontological; biogenetic; evolutionary, Darwinian.

359 Mineral: inorganic matter

N. mineral, inorganic matter, earth's crust 344 *rock*; ore, metal, precious metal, base metal;

alloy 43 *a mixture*; mineralogical deposit, coal measures 632 *store*.

   mineralogy, geology, lithology, petrography, petrology; metallurgy, metallography; speleology, glaciology 321 *earth sciences*.

   mineralogist, etc. (see *mineralogy* above).

360 Life

N. *life*, living, being 1 *existence*; the living, living being, being, soul, spirit; plant life 366 *plant life*; animal life 365 *animal life*; human life 371 *humankind*; gift of life, birth, nativity 68 *origin*; renaissance 656 *revival*; life to come, the hereafter 124 *future state*; immortal life 971 *heaven*; animation; vitality, vital force, élan vital, life force, bio-energy, qi or ch'i; biorhythm; soul 447 *spirit*; will to live, survival, cat's nine lives, longevity 113 *long duration*; liveliness, animation 819 *moral sensibility*; breathing 352 *breathing*; lifeblood, heart's blood 5 *essential part*; vital spark; heart, artery; staff of life 301 *food*; biological function, parenthood 167 *propagation*; sex, sexual activity 45 *sexual intercourse*; living matter, protoplasm, living tissue; cell, unicellular organism 358 *organism*; symbiosis 706 *association*; life-support system; lifetime, one's born days; life expectancy, allotted span, life cycle; survivability, viability, viableness 469 *possibility*.

   Adj. *alive*, living, quick, live, animate; breathing, alive and kicking; animated 819 *lively*; incarnate, in the flesh, personified; surviving, in the land of the living, above ground, with us, on this side of the grave; long-lived 113 *lasting*; survivable, viable; vital, enlivened.

   born, begotten, fathered, sired; mothered, dammed; foaled, dropped; out of, by 11 *akin*; spawned, littered; laid, new-laid, hatched.

   Vb. *be alive*, live, have life, have being; draw breath 352 *breathe*; exist 1 *be*; come to life, come to, liven up, quicken, revive 656 *be restored*; be spared, survive 41 *be left*; cheat death, have nine lives; live in 192 *live*.

   be born, come into the world, come into existence, first see the light 68 *begin*; have one's nativity; draw breath; be begotten, be conceived.

   vitalize, give birth to, beget, conceive, support life 167 *generate*; vivify, enliven, breathe life into, bring to life 174 *invigorate*; revitalize, give a new lease of life, put new life into, ginger, put zest into, reanimate 656 *revive*; maintain, provide for, keep body and soul together, make ends meet, keep the wolf from the door 301 *feed*.

361 Death

N. *death*, no life 2 *extinction*; dying (see also *decease* below); mortality, ephemerality 114 *transience*; sentence of death, doom, death knell, death penalty, extreme penalty, ultimate penalty 963 *capital punishment*; execution, martyrdom; ultimate price; curtains, death-blow, quietus 362 *killing*; necrosis, mortification 51 *decay*; the beyond, the great divide, crossing the Styx or Lethe; eternal rest, long sleep 266 *quietness*; Abraham's bosom 971 *heaven*; the grave 364 *tomb*; jaws of death, shadow of death; nether regions, Stygian darkness, Hades 972 *hell*; Death, the Grim Reaper, the Great Leveller; Angel of Death; post-mortem, autopsy, necroscopy 364 *inquest*; mortuary, charnel house, morgue 364 *cemetery*; near-death experience, NDE, out-of-body experience, OBE.

   decease, clinical death, brain death, cerebral death; cot death, sudden infant death syndrome, SIDS, sudden death syndrome, SDS, sudden adult death syndrome, SADS, sudden unidentified death syndrome, SUDS, sudden cardiac death, SCD; extinction, exit, demise, curtains 69 *end*; departure, passing, passing away, passing over, homecall; natural death, quiet end, euthanasia 376 *euphoria*; welcome end; loss of life, fatality; sudden death, violent death, untimely end; death by drowning, watery grave; death on the roads; accidental death, death by misadventure; karoshi 362 *suicide*; fatal disease, terminal illness or disease 651 *disease*; genetic timebomb; dying day, last hour; valley of the shadow of death; death-bed, deathbed repentance, death scene; last gasp, dying breath; swan song, death rattle, rigor mortis 69 *finality*; extreme unction; passing bell 364 *funeral rites*.

   the dead, forefathers 66 *precursor*; dear departed, souls 968 *saint*; the shades, ghosts, phantoms 970 *ghost*; dead body 363 *corpse*; next world 124 *future state*; world of spirits, netherworld, Styx; Hades, Stygian shore 972 *mythical hell*; Elysian fields, happy hunting grounds, Davy Jones's locker 971 *mythical heaven*.

   death roll, mortality, fatality, collateral damage, death toll, death rate; casualty list; death register 87 *list*; death certificate 548 *record*; martyrology; obituary, obit, deaths column, death notice; the dead, the fallen, the lost; casualties, the dead and dying.

   Adj. *dying*, expiring, etc. (see vb.); mortal, ephemeral, perishable 114 *transient*; moribund, with one foot in the grave, deathly; all over with, all up with, not long for this world, not long to go; done for, had it; going, slipping away, sinking fast; sick unto death 651 *sick*; on the danger list, in a critical condition, terminally ill, on one's deathbed, at death's door;

life hanging by a thread; at the last gasp; on one's last legs, at the point of death; under sentence of death, doomed.

dead, deceased; passed over, passed away, departed, gone, gone before; dead and gone, dead and buried, in the grave, six feet under; stillborn; lifeless; extinct, bereft of life; cold, stiff; dead as a doornail *or* as a dodo; kaput, done for, gone for a burton; out of one's misery; departed this life, called to one's eternal rest, gathered to one's fathers, in Abraham's bosom, on the other side, beyond the grave; gone to join one's forefathers, gone to the happy hunting-grounds; defunct, late, late-lamented, gone but not forgotten, of sainted memory; martyred, slaughtered, massacred, killed.

Vb. *die*, be dead, lie in the grave, be gone, be no more, cease to be, lose one's life 2 *pass away*; die young, not make old bones; die a natural death, die in one's sleep, die in bed; end one's life, decease; expire, give up the ghost, breathe one's last; close one's eyes, sleep one's last sleep; pass over, be taken; depart this life 296 *depart*; ring down the curtain, shuffle off this mortal coil, go the way of all flesh, go to one's last home, cross the Styx, join the angels, meet one's Maker, reach a better world, be called home; croak, peg out, snuff it; cop it, have bought it; cash in one's chips, conk out, pop off, go west, go for a burton, hop the twig, kick the bucket, bite the dust, turn up one's toes, push up the daisies, flatline.

perish, die out, become extinct 2 *pass away*; go to the wall 165 *be destroyed*; wither, come to dust 51 *decompose*; meet one's end, meet one's fate; die in harness, die with one's boots on; get killed, be killed, fall in action, lose one's life, be lost; lay down one's life; become a martyr, make the supreme sacrifice; die young, drop down dead; meet a sticky end, die a violent death, break one's neck; bleed to death; drown, go to Davy Jones's locker 313 *go down*; be put to death, walk the plank; commit suicide 362 *kill oneself*.

362 Killing: destruction of life

N. *killing*, slaying 165 *destruction*; taking life; blood sports, hunting, poaching, lamping, shooting 619 *chase*; poaching 788 *stealing*; blood-shedding, blood-letting; vivisection; cull; abortion, partial-birth abortion; mercy killing, euthanasia; murder, serial killing, assassination; bumping off (see also *homicide* below); poisoning, drowning, suffocation, strangulation, hanging; immolation; sacrifice; martyrdom; crucifixion, execution 963 *capital*

punishment; judicial murder, auto da fé, burning alive, the stake; deathblow, coup de grâce, quietus; death by misadventure, violent death, fatal accident, death on the roads, car crash, train crash, plane crash.

homicide, manslaughter; murder, premeditated murder, capital murder, first-degree murder, second-degree murder, third-degree murder, serial killing, contract killing, contract; corporate killing, corporate manslaughter; assassination; thuggery; crime passionel 911 *jealousy*; honour killing; genocide, ethnocide, ethnic cleansing; regicide 738 *revolt*.

Homicides and Victims

filicide (child), foeticide (foetus), fratricide (brother), giganticide (giant), homicide (human being), infanticide (child), matricide (mother), neonaticide (newborn baby), parricide (parent or relative), patricide (father), regicide (king), sororicide (sister), tyrannicide (tyrant), uxoricide (wife), vaticide (prophet).

---

slaughter, bloodshed, butchery, carnage; bloodbath, massacre, fusillade, holocaust; pogrom, purge, liquidation, decimation, extermination, annihilation 165 *destruction*; genocide, ethnocide, ethnic cleansing; war, battle 718 *warfare*; friendly fire, fratricide; Roman holiday, gladiatorial combat 716 *duel*; slaughter-house, abattoir, knacker's yard, shambles; bull-ring 724 *arena*; battlefield 724 *battleground*; killing-fields; gas chamber, gas oven, Auschwitz, Belsen.

killer, slayer; mercy killer 905 *pity*; abortionist; soldier, guerrilla, urban guerrilla 722 *combatant*; slaughterer, butcher; huntsman 619 *hunter*; trapper, mole-catcher, ratcatcher, pest exterminator; toreador, picador, matador 162 *athlete*; executioner, hangman; homicide (see also *murderer* below); lynch mob; homicidal maniac, psychopath; head-hunter, cannibal; predator, bird of prey, beast of prey, man-eater, insecticide.

murderer, homicide (see *Homicides* box above); killer, serial killer, mass murderer; Bluebeard, Cain, Doctor Crippen, Jack the Ripper, Sweeney Todd; assassin, terrorist; poisoner, strangler, garrotter, thug; hatchet man, hitman, gangster, contract killer, gunman; cutthroat 904 *ruffian*.

suicide, self-destruction, felo de se; suttee, hara-kiri, seppuku; assisted suicide, doctor-assisted *or* physician-assisted suicide; parasuicide, attempted suicide; suicide chatroom; mass suicide, Gadarene swine, lemmings.

Adj. *deadly*, killing, lethal; fell, mortal, fatal, deathly; life-threatening, capital; death-bringing, malignant, poisonous 653 *toxic*; asphyxiant, suffocating, stifling; miasmic 653 *unhealthy*; inoperable, incurable, terminal.

murderous, homicidal, genocidal; suicidal, self-destructive; internecine, death-dealing, trigger-happy; sanguinary, bloody, gory, blood-stained, red-handed; bloodthirsty 898 *cruel*; head-hunting, man-eating, cannibalistic.

Vb. *kill*, slay, take life, deprive of life; do in, do for, top 165 *destroy*; nip in the bud, shorten one's life; put down, put to sleep, euthanase; hasten one's end, drive to one's death, work to death, send to the scaffold, hang, behead, guillotine, electrocute, send to the electric chair 963 *execute*; stone to death; string up, lynch; make away with, do away with, dispatch, get rid of; deal a deathblow, give the coup de grâce, put one out of his misery, give one his quietus; shed blood, knife, put to the sword, lance, bayonet, stab, run through 263 *pierce*; shoot down, pick off, blow the brains out 287 *shoot*; strangle, garrotte, choke, suffocate, smother, stifle, drown; wall up, bury alive; brain, poleaxe, sandbag 279 *strike*; send to the stake 381 *burn*; immolate, sacrifice, offer up; martyr, condemn to death, sign the death warrant, ring the knell 961 *condemn*.

slaughter, butcher, poleaxe, cut the throat of; massacre, put to the sword; decimate, scupper, wipe out; cut to pieces, cut to ribbons, cut down, shoot down, mow down; give no quarter, spare none 906 *be pitiless*; annihilate, exterminate, liquidate, purge, send to the gas chamber, commit genocide 165 *destroy*.

murder, commit murder, commit homicide, commit manslaughter, assassinate, finish off, make away with, do in, do to death, do for, fix, settle, bump off, wipe out, liquidate, rub out, top; make to walk the plank; smother, suffocate, strangle, poison, gas.

kill oneself, do oneself in, do away with oneself, make away with oneself, commit suicide, suicide; commit hara-kiri, commit suttee; hang oneself, shoot oneself, top oneself, blow out one's brains, cut one's throat, slash one's wrists; fall on one's sword, die Roman fashion; put one's head in the oven, gas oneself; take poison, take an overdose; jump overboard, drown oneself.

363 Corpse

N. *corpse*, dead body, body; dead man *or* woman, deceased, victim; stiff; cadaver, carcass, skeleton, dry bones; death's-head, skull; mummy; mortal remains, relics, ashes; carrion, food for worms *or* for fishes; body-snatcher, resurrectionist; body bag, coffin.

364 Interment

N. *interment*, burial, entombment; inhumation, cremation, incineration; scattering of the ashes; embalming, mummification; embalmment, myrrh, spices, coffin, cist, shell, casket, urn; sarcophagus; pyre, funeral pile, crematorium; mortuary, morgue, charnel house; undertaker's, funeral parlour; sexton, gravedigger; undertaker, funeral director; mortician; embalmer.

funeral rites, burial service, obsequies; mourning, weeping and wailing, wake 836 *lamentation*; lying-in-state; last rites; cortege; knell; dead march, muffled drum, last post; memorial service, requiem, funeral hymn, funeral oration; elegy, dirge 836 *lament*; inscription, epitaph, obituary; tombstone, gravestone, headstone; cross, war memorial; cenotaph 548 *monument*; necrologist, obituary-writer.

funeral, hearse, bier, pall, coffin, body bag; mourner, weeper, keener; pallbearer; lychgate (see *funeral rites* above).

grave clothes, shroud, winding sheet.

cemetery, burial place, golgotha; churchyard, graveyard, God's Acre, potter's field; catacombs, cinerarium; necropolis, city of the dead; garden of remembrance, garden of rest.

tomb, vault, crypt; burial chamber; mausoleum, pyramid, sepulchre 548 *monument*; pantheon; grave, long home; cist; barrow 253 *earthwork*; cromlech, dolmen, menhir 548 *monument*; shrine, memorial, cenotaph 548 *monument*.

inquest 459 *enquiry*; autopsy, necropsy, post-mortem; exhumation, disinterment, disentombment.

Adj. *funereal*, funebral *or* funebrial; sombre, sad 428 *black*; mourning; elegiac, mortuary, cinerary, crematory, sepulchral; obsequial, obituary; epitaphic; necrological, dirgelike 836 *lamenting*.

Vb. *inter*, inhume, bury; lay out; embalm, coffin; urn, entomb; lay in the grave, consign to earth, lay to rest; cremate, incinerate 381 *burn*; pay one's last respects, go to a funeral, toll the knell, sound the last post; mourn, keen, hold a wake 836 *lament*.

exhume, disinter; disentomb; unearth, dig up.

365 Animal life

N. *animal life*, animality, wild life; animal kingdom, fauna; physique, flesh, flesh and blood; anthropomorphism; zoomorphism, Pan; animalism 944 *sensualism*; animal liberation movement, animal rights movement; antivivisectionist, animalist, animal liberationist, animal protectionist.

animal, living thing; viviparous animal, oviparous animal; carnivorous animal, herbivorous animal, omnivorous animal; birds, beasts and fishes; creature, brute, beast, dumb animal, creeping thing; protozoon, metazoon; zoophyte; mammal, amphibian, fish, bird, reptile; worm, mollusc, arthropod; crustacean, insect, arachnid; invertebrate, vertebrate; biped, quadruped; carnivore, herbivore, insectivore, ruminant, man-eater; wild animal, game, big game; prey, beast of prey; pack, flock, herd 74 *group*; farm animal, livestock, stock 365 *poultry, cattle, goat, sheep, pig*; farming 369 *animal husbandry, stock farm*; tame animal, domestic animal; pet, pet animal, household pet, animal companion, companion animal, cat, dog, gerbil, guinea pig, hamster, mouse, potbellied pig, rabbit, rat, terrapin, tortoise; catfish, goldfish, koi, shubunkin; cagebird (see *bird* below); cage, goldfish bowl, enclosure 369 *stock farm, cattle pen*; cyberpet, virtual pet, Pokémon (tdmk), Tamagotchi (tdmk); young animal 132 *young creature*; draught animal 273 *horse, beast of burden*; endangered species: African elephant, Indian elephant, black rhinoceros, Iberian lynx, snow leopard, tiger, red wolf, blue whale, right whale, giant panda, lesser panda, aye-aye, western gorilla, giant armadillo, oryx; extinct animal: aurochs, quagga; prehistoric animal: dinosaur, megathere, mammoth, mastodon, sabre-toothed tiger.

Dinosaurs and Related Animals

archosaur, dinosaur, pterosaur/-saurus, pteranodon, pterodactyl; ichthyosaur/-saurus, plesiosaur/-saurus, thecodont.

bird-hipped dinosaur, ornithischian; lizard-hipped dinosaur, saurischian.

allosaur *or* allosaurus, ankylosaur/-saurus, apatosaur/-saurus, argentinosaur/-saurus, brachiosaur/-saurus, brontosaur/-saurus, carnosaur, coelurosaur/-saurus, compsognathus, deinonychus, diplodocus, gigantosaur/-saurus, hadrosaur/-saurus, iguanodon, maiasaur/-saurus, megalosaur/-saurus, raptor, sauropod, stegosaur/-saurus, theropod, titanosaur/-saurus, triceratops, tyrannosaur/-saurus, tyrannosaurus rex, velociraptor.

mythical animal, fabulous beast, heraldic beast; unicorn, phoenix, griffin, roc; sphinx, hippogriff, chimera, centaur, Minotaur; dragon, wyvern, fire-drake, cockatrice, basilisk, salamander, hydra; sea serpent, leviathan, kraken, Loch Ness monster, Nessie; the Abominable Snowman, yeti, Bigfoot, Sasquatch, bunyip; Bandersnatch, Boojum, Jabberwocky, Snark. (See also 970 *mythical being*.)

mammal, man 371 *humankind*; primate, ape, anthropoid ape, gorilla, orang-utan *or* -utang *or* -outang, chimpanzee, bonobo, gibbon, siamang, baboon, drill, mandrill, monkey, marmoset, aye-aye, potto, agouti; lemur, tarsier, bush baby; sloth; marsupial, kangaroo,

wallaby, wombat, koala bear, opossum; platypus *or* duck-billed platypus, echidna *or* spiny anteater; rodent, rat, mouse, field mouse, dormouse, shrew, vole, lemming, porcupine, mongoose, chipmunk, squirrel, jerboa; aardvark, ant-eater, mole; bat, flying fox; raccoon, kinkajou, badger, hedgehog; stoat, weasel, ferret, mink, marten, polecat, skunk; civet *or* civet cat; fox, dog fox, vixen, Reynard; jackal, hyena; lion, etc. (see *cat* below); sheep, goat, etc. (see *sheep* etc. below); hare, mountain hare, rabbit, bunny; otter, beaver, water rat, water vole; walrus, seal, sea lion; cetacean, dolphin, grampus, porpoise, whale, blue whale, minke whale, right whale, sperm whale, narwhal, killer whale, orca; pachyderm, elephant, rhinoceros, hippopotamus; bear, polar bear, black bear, brown bear, grizzly bear; giant panda; ungulate, giraffe, zebra, zebu, yak (see *cattle* below); deer, stag, hart, buck, doe, fawn, pricket; red deer, fallow deer, roe deer, muntjac; reindeer, caribou, elk, moose; musk ox; llama, alpaca, guanaco, vicuña; gazelle, antelope, chamois, springbok, eland, hartebeest, wildebeest, gnu; horse, donkey, mule, camel 273 *beast of burden*. (See also 132 *young creature*, 372 *male animal*, 373 *female animal*.)

bird, winged thing, fowls of the air; fledgling, nestling, squab 132 *young creature*; avifauna, birdlife; cagebird, budgerigar, budgie, canary, cockatiel, cockatoo, lovebird, macaw, parakeet, parrot, polly, mynah; mockingbird; songbird, songster, warbler, nightingale, philomel, bulbul, lark, thrush, throstle, mavis, blackbird, linnet; curlew, plover, lapwing, peewit; dove, collared dove, turtle dove, pigeon, wood pigeon *or* ring dove; crow, jackdaw, jay, magpie, pie, rook, raven; finch, bunting, bullfinch, chaffinch, goldfinch, greenfinch, snow bunting, yellowhammer; tit, blue tit, great tit; wren, robin, sparrow, house sparrow, tree sparrow; hedge sparrow *or* dunnock; wagtail, woodpecker, humming bird, sunbird, weaver bird, bird of paradise, lyrebird, hoopoe, golden oriole; migrant, cuckoo, swallow, swift, martin; redwing, fieldfare; emu, ostrich, rhea, cassowary; kiwi, penguin, gentoo, rockhopper; nightbird, owl, tawny owl, barn owl, screech owl, nightjar; vulture, marabou, carrion crow; bird of prey, eagle, golden eagle, bald eagle, kite, kestrel, harrier, osprey, buzzard, hawk, sparrowhawk, falcon, peregrine falcon, merlin, shrike; pelican, kingfisher, gannet, cormorant, shag, skua, Arctic skua; gull, herring gull, kittiwake, tern; oyster-catcher, auk, puffin, guillemot; albatross, petrel, stormy petrel, Mother Carey's chickens; wader, stork, crane, heron, bittern; spoonbill, ibis, flamingo; water bird, waterfowl, swan, cob, pen, cygnet; duck, drake, duckling; goose, gander, gosling; merganser, pintail, teal, mallard, widgeon; moorhen, coot, lily-trotter, diver, dipper, grebe, dabchick; extinct bird: dodo, great auk, moa, passenger pigeon.

table bird, game bird, woodcock, wood pigeon, squab; peafowl, peacock, peahen; grouse, ptarmigan, capercaillie *or* capercailzie, pheasant, partridge, quail; goose, duck, snipe; turkey, guinea fowl, guinea hen.

poultry, fowl, hen; cock, cockerel, rooster; chicken, pullet; boiler, broiler, roaster, capon, poussin; bantam, Leghorn, Orpington, Rhode Island Red, Wyandotte; turkey; goose; duck, drake, duckling; Aylesbury, Indian Runner, Muscovy duck.

cattle, livestock, kine, neat; bull, cow, calf, heifer, stirk, yearling; bullock, steer; beef cattle, highland cattle, Aberdeen Angus, Belted Galloway, Charolais, Hereford, longhorn, Luing cattle; dairy cattle, milch cow, Ayrshire, Friesian, Guernsey, Jersey; dual-purpose cattle, Redpoll, shorthorn, Simmental; zebu, brahmin, zho *or* zo *or* dzo *or* dzho; ox, oxen; buffalo, beefalo, bison; yak, musk ox; cattle-farming 369 *animal husbandry, stock farm.*

goat, billy goat, nanny goat; mountain goat, ibex.

sheep, ram, tup, wether, bell wether, ewe, lamb; teg; blackface, Cheviot, Herdwick, Jacob sheep, Leicester, Lincoln, Merino, Southdown, Suffolk; mountain sheep, mouflon.

horse, pony, etc. 273 *horse, draught horse, saddle horse, pony.*

pig, swine, boar, warthog; hog, sow, piglet, pigling, sucking pig, porker; Berkshire, Large White, Tamworth, Wessex Saddleback, Vietnamese potbellied pig; Gadarene swine.

dog, canine, bow-wow, man's best friend; bitch, whelp, pup, puppy; cur, hound, tyke, pooch, mutt; mongrel, pariah dog, pye-dog; guide dog, hearing dog, house dog, watch dog, police dog, guard dog, sniffer dog, bloodhound, mastiff; sheepdog, Old English Sheepdog, collie, Border collie; Doberman pinscher, bull terrier; bulldog, boxer; wolfhound, borzoi, Afghan hound, Alsatian, Dalmatian; Great Dane; St Bernard; greyhound, courser, lurcher, whippet; foxhound, staghound, beagle; basset, dachshund; gun dog, retriever, golden retriever, Labrador retriever, Labrador, golden Labrador, Newfoundland, pointer, setter, Irish setter; terrier, smooth-haired terrier, wire-haired terrier, fox terrier, sealyham, Scottish terrier, Scottie, West Highland terrier, Yorkshire terrier; spaniel, cocker spaniel, springer spaniel, King Charles spaniel, cavalier King

Charles spaniel; show dog, fancy dog, toy dog, chihuahua, Pomeranian, chow; lapdog, Pekinese, peke, pug; Welsh corgi; poodle, French poodle, miniature poodle, toy poodle; schipperke, schnauzer; basenji, barkless dog; husky, sledge dog; wild dog, dingo; wolf, coyote; dangerous dog, fighting dog, bandog; Cerberus, Gelert, Greyfriars Bobby.

cat, feline; grimalkin, moggie, puss, pussy, kitten, pussycat; tom, tom cat, tabby; mouser; Persian cat, Siamese cat, Manx cat, calico cat, tortoiseshell cat, marmalade cat, tabby cat; Cheshire Cat.

big cat, lion, lioness, King of Beasts; tiger, tigress, tigon, leopard, leopardess, snow leopard, ounce, cheetah, panther, black panther, puma, jaguar, cougar, ocelot, bobcat, lynx, catamount *or* catamountain, wildcat.

amphibian, frog, bullfrog, tree frog, platanna frog; frogspawn, tadpole, polliwog; paddock, puddock, toad, natterjack; newt, eft; salamander, axolotl.

reptile, ophidian, saurian; serpent, sea serpent; snake, water snake, grass snake, venomous snake, viper, adder, asp; cobra, king cobra, hamadryad; puff adder, mamba, horned viper, rattlesnake; anaconda, boa constrictor, python; crocodile, alligator, cayman; lizard, slowworm, blindworm; chameleon, iguana, monitor, gecko; turtle, tortoise, terrapin.

marine life, denizens of the deep; marine organisms, nekton, plankton, benthos, krill; cetacean (see also *mammal* above); sea urchin, sea horse, sea anemone, coral, coral reef, jellyfish, Portuguese man of war, starfish, brittlestar; shellfish, mollusc, bivalve, clam, oyster, mussel, cockle; whelk, winkle, limpet; cephalopod, cuttlefish, squid, octopus; crustacean, crab, lobster, crayfish, shrimp; barnacle.

fish, flying fish, swordfish, angelfish, dogfish, shark; piranha, barracuda; stingray, electric ray; tuna *or* tunny *or* tunny fish, turbot, bass, conger eel 301 *fish as food*; coelacanth; blenny; pike, roach, perch, bream, carp; trout, grayling; salmon, grilse; eel, elver, lamprey; minnow, gudgeon, stickleback; fish-like animal: dolphin, porpoise, whale (see also *mammal* above).

insect, larva, pupa, imago; fly, house fly, horse fly, gadfly, cleg, bluebottle; mayfly, caddis fly; gnat, midge, tsetse fly, mosquito; greenfly, blackfly, aphid; thunder fly; ladybird, lacewing, hoverfly; firefly, glow-worm; dragonfly, crane fly, daddy longlegs; butterfly, cabbage white, Camberwell Beauty, fritillary, painted lady, peacock butterfly, red admiral, skipper, swallowtail, tortoiseshell; moth, hawk moth, clothes moth; bee, bumble bee, humble bee, honey bee, queen bee, worker bee, drone; wasp, hornet; beetle, stag beetle, dung beetle, cockroach; vermin, parasites, bug, bed bug, flea, louse, nit, mite, tick; jigger; woodworm, weevil, borer, cockchafer, deathwatch beetle, Colorado beetle, aphid, blackfly, greenfly, whitefly 659 *blight*; emmet, ant, soldier ant, worker ant, white ant, termite; stick insect, praying mantis; locust, grasshopper, cicada, cricket.

creepy-crawly, grub, maggot, gentle, caterpillar, looper, inchworm, silk worm; worm, earthworm, lugworm, wireworm, roundworm, flatworm, tapeworm, fluke; myriapod, centipede, millipede; slug, snail; earwig, woodlouse; spider, money spider; black widow spider, tarantula; scorpion.

Adj. *animal*, brutish, beastly, bestial; feral, domestic; human, manly, subhuman; therianthropic, theriomorphic, anthropomorphic, zoomorphic; zoological; vertebrate, invertebrate; mammalian; apelike, anthropoid, simian; horsey *or* horsy, equine, asinine, mulish; deerlike, cervine; bovine, taurine, ruminant; sheep-like, ovine, sheepish; goat-like, goatish; piggy, porcine; bearish, ursine; elephantine; doggy, canine; wolfish, lupine; catlike, feline, cattish, tigerish, leonine; foxy, vulpine; birdlike, avian; aquiline, vulturine; passerine; owlish; dovelike; gallinaceous, anserine; fishy, piscine, cold-blooded, molluscan, molluscoid; amphibian, amphibious, salientian; reptilian, saurian; snaky, ophidian, serpentine, viperish; wormy, vermicular, weevilly; verminous; lepidopterous, entomological.

366 Plant life

N. *plant life*, vegetable kingdom; flora, vegetation; biomass; plant community, biome; flowering, blooming, florescence; lushness, rankness, luxuriance 635 *plenty*, 171 *abundance*; wood nymph, etc. 967 *nymph*.

wood, timber, lumber, softwood, hardwood, heartwood, sapwood; forest, virgin forest, primeval forest; rain forest, cloud forest, jungle; coniferous forest, taiga; bush, heath, scrub, maquis, chaparral; woods, timberland, greenwood, woodland, bocage, copse, coppice, spinney; thicket, bosk, brake, covert; park, chase, game preserve; hurst, holt; plantation, arboretum, pinetum, pinery; orchard, orangery 370 *garden*; grove, clump; clearing, glade; brushwood, underwood, undergrowth; bushiness, bushes, shrubbery, wind-break, hedge, hedgerow.

forestry, dendrology, silviculture, treeplanting, afforestation; forester, woodcutter, dendrologist 370 *gardener*.

tree, shrub, bush, sapling, scion, stock; pollard; bonsai; shoot, sucker, trunk, bole; limb, branch, bough, twig; conifer, greenwood tree, evergreen tree, deciduous tree, softwood tree, hardwood tree; fruit tree, timber tree; mahogany, ebony, teak, iroko, sandalwood, walnut, oak, elm, ash, beech, sycamore, maple, plane, lime, linden; horse chestnut, copper beech, cedar of Lebanon, redwood, larch, fir, Douglas fir, spruce, pine, Scots pine, lodgepole pine, Christmas tree; poplar, Lombardy poplar, abele, aspen, alder, sallow, willow, weeping willow, pussy willow; birch, silver birch, rowan, mountain ash; crab apple, sweet chestnut; hazel, elder, spindle, hawthorn, may, blackthorn, sloe; privet, yew, holly, ivy, box, bay, laurel; rhododendron, camellia, azalea, fuchsia, hydrangea, magnolia, laburnum, lilac; wisteria, Virginia creeper; acacia, jacaranda; palm, date palm, coconut palm, oil palm; baobab, banyan, mangrove; gum tree, eucalyptus, rubber tree 370 *agriculture*; dating by tree rings: dendrochronology 117 *chronology*.

foliage, foliation, frondescence; greenery; verdure; leafiness, leafage; herbage; umbrage; limb, branch, bough, twig, shoot; spray, sprig; treetop; leaf, simple leaf, compound leaf; frond, flag, blade; leaflet, foliole; pine needle; seed-leaf, cotyledon; leaf-stalk, petiole, stipule, node, stalk, stem; tendril, prickle, thorn; falling of leaves: abscission.

plant, herb, wort, weed, superweed; root, tuber, rhizome, bulb, corm 156 *source*; stolon, rootstock, cutting 132 *young plant*; culinary herb 301 *herb*; medicinal herb 658 *remedy*; fodder 301 *fruit and vegetables, animal food*; national plant, rose, leek, daffodil, thistle, shamrock, fleur-de-lis; garden plant, pansy, primula, marigold, lupin, iris, dahlia, gladiolus, hyacinth, geranium, pelargonium, chrysanthemum, snapdragon, sweet william, pink, carnation, lily, sunflower, wallflower; lavender, honeysuckle 396 *fragrance*; wild plant, buttercup, daisy, dandelion, ox-eye, poppy, primrose, snowdrop, bluebell, harebell, foxglove, cowslip, forget-me-not, clover, heather; water lily, marsh marigold, flag; cactus, succulent; prickly plant, bramble, gorse, whin; insectivorous plant, Venus's *or* Venus flytrap, sundew, pitcher plant; deadly nightshade, etc. 659 *poisonous plant*; architectural plant; creeper, climber, twiner, vine, bine, convolvulus, bindweed, liane; parasite, mistletoe; horsetail, fern, bracken; moss, clubmoss, bog moss, sphagnum; liverwort; lichen, fungus, mushroom, toadstool, agaric, puffball; mould, penicillin; seaweed, wrack, bladderwrack, kelp, gulfweed; algae.

flower, floweret, floret, blossom, bloom, bud, burgeon; inflorescence, head, corymb, panicle, cyme, umbel, spike, catkin; petal, sepal; corolla, calyx; ovary, ovule, receptacle; pistil, style, stigma, stamen, anther, pollen; nectary; annual, biennial, perennial; house plant, pot plant; hothouse plant, exotic; garden flower, wild flower; flowerbed, seedbed, propagator, growbag; gardening, horticulture, floriculture 370 *garden*.

fruit, berry, nut, drupe; pip, spore, seed 156 *source*; seed vessel, pod, capsule, cone; acorn, beechmast, chestnut, elderberry, haw, hip *or* rosehip, key. (See also 301 *fruit and vegetables*.)

grass, hay; pasture, pasturage, herbage 348 *grassland*; verdure, turf, sod, lawn; meadow grass, rye grass, couch grass, bent grass, fescue; sedge, rush, bulrush, reed, papyrus; marram grass, esparto grass; Pampas grass, elephant grass, bamboo, sugar cane; grain plant, wheat, oats, barley, rye, millet, sorghum, rice 301 *cereals*; grain, husk, bran, chaff, stubble, straw.

Adj. *wooden*, wood, treen; woody, ligneous, ligniform.

Vb. *vegetate*, germinate, sprout, shoot 36 *grow*; plant, garden 370 *cultivate*; afforest.

367 Zoology: the science of animals

N. *zoology*, morphology 331 *structure*; embryology 358 *biology*; animal behaviour; anthropography 371 *anthropology*; ornithology, birdwatching, twitching; ichthyology, herpetology, ophiology, mammalogy, primatology, cetology, malacology, helminthology, nematology, entomology, lepidopterology, arachnology, conchology; palaeontology; cryptozoology, Nessiehunting.

zoologist, ornithologist, ichthyologist, entomologist, lepidopterist, etc. (see *zoology* above); bird-watcher, twitcher.

368 Botany: the science of plants

N. *botany*, taxonomy; plant ecology; dendrology 366 *forestry*; mycology, fungology, bryology, algology, phycology; palaeobotany; botanical garden 370 *garden*; herbarium.

botanist, taxonomist, etc. (see *botany* above), herbalist 658 *pharmacist*.

369 Animal husbandry

N. *animal husbandry*, farming, pharming (see also 370 *agriculture*); breeding, stock-breeding, horse-breeding, cattle-raising; dairy farming, beef farming 365 *cattle*; sheep farming, hill farming, pig-farming, bee-keeping, apiculture; poultry farming, aviculture, pisciculture, sericulture; selective breeding, stirpiculture; veterinary science; veterinary surgeon, vet,

veterinarian, animal doctor, horse doctor 658 *doctor*; groom 742 *servant*.

stock farm, stud farm, dairy farm, cattle farm, ranch, rancho, hacienda; fish farm, trout farm, hatchery; fish pond, fish tank; duck pond; pig farm, piggery; beehive, hive, apiary; pasture, grazing, sheep farm, hill farm, sheeprun, sheepwalk 348 *grassland*; poultry farm, chicken run, hen run, broiler house, battery, deep litter, enriched cage, free range; factory farm.

cattle pen, byre, cowshed 192 *stable*; sheepfold 235 *enclosure*; hutch, coop, hencoop, hen run, henhouse; cowshed, pigsty; swannery; cage, bird cage, aviary.

zoo, zoological gardens, menagerie, circus; Noah's Ark; aviary, aquarium, dolphinarium, terrarium, vivarium; reptile house, monkey house, monkey temple, bear pit; wildlife park, safari park; game park, game reserve, game preserve.

breeder, stockbreeder; apiarist; aviculturist, fancier, pigeon-fancier.

herdsman, herd; cowherd, stockman, cattleman, byreman, cowman, rancher; cowboy, cowgirl, cowpuncher; broncobuster, gaucho; shepherd, shepherdess; swineherd; goatherd; goosegirl; milkmaid, dairymaid; kennel maid.

Vb. *break in*, tame, domesticate, acclimatize 610 *accustom oneself*; train 534 *teach*; mount, whip, spur 267 *ride*; yoke, harness, hitch, bridle, saddle; round up, herd, corral, cage 235 *enclose*.

breed stock, breed, rear, raise, grow, hatch, culture, incubate, nurture, fatten; farm 370 *cultivate*.

groom, currycomb, rub down.

370 Agriculture and gardening

N. *agriculture*, agronomy, agronomics; Common Agricultural Policy, decerealization; butter mountain, grain mountain, wine lake; agribusiness, agro-industry, agrochemical industry 622 *business*; cultivation, ploughing, sowing, reaping; growth, harvest, produce, crop, vintage 632 *store*; cash crop, fodder crop; husbandry, farming, mixed farming, factory farming, macro-farming, cattle farming, dairy farming, horticulture 369 *animal husbandry*; cereal farming, arable farming; hydroponics, tank farming; biodynamic farming, biodynamics, permaculture; pharmaceutical farming, pharming; irrigation 341 *irrigator*; tillage, tilth; green fingers; floriculture, flower-growing; horticulture, gardening, market gardening; bonsai; vegetable growing, fruit growing, softfruit growing, mushroom growing; winegrowing, viticulture, viniculture; arboriculture, silviculture, afforestation 366 *forestry*; landscape gardening, landscape architecture.

farm, home farm, grange; arable farm, dairy farm, sheep farm, hill farm, cattle farm 369 *stock farm*; ranch, rancho, hacienda; model farm; farmstead, steading, farmhouse; farmyard, barnyard 235 *enclosure*; state farm, collective farm, kolkhoz, kibbutz; farmland, arable land, cropland, ploughed land, fallow 344 *soil*; field, corn field; crop circle; rice paddy, paddyfield; pasturage, pasture, corn field, crop circle, fields, meadows 348 *grassland*; demesne, manor farm, estate, holding, smallholding, croft 777 *lands*; allotment, kitchen garden; market garden, herb garden; nursery; vineyard, vinery, domaine; fruit farm, orchard; tea garden, tea estate, coffee estate, coffee plantation, cotton plantation, rubber plantation, sugar plantation.

garden, botanical garden, flower garden, rose garden, Dutch garden, herb garden, rock garden, alpine garden, cottage garden, indoor garden, container garden, winter garden; vegetable garden, cabbage patch, kitchen garden, potager, allotment; fruit garden, orchard; arboretum, pinetum, pinery 366 *wood*; patch, plot, lawn, park 235 *enclosure*; shrubbery, border, herbaceous border, bed, flowerbed, parterre 844 *ornamental art*; seedbed, frame, cold frame, propagator 167 *propagation*; cloche, conservatory, hothouse, greenhouse, glasshouse, orangery; grow bag *or* growing-bag; jardinière, planter, cachepot, flower-pot; water feature, patio.

farmer, husbandman, farm manager, grieve, factor, farm agent, bailiff; cultivator, planter, tea planter, coffee planter; agronomist, agriculturalist; peasant, paysan; serf; villein; tenant farmer; gentleman farmer, yeoman; hill farmer; smallholder, crofter, allotment-holder; fruit grower; wine-grower, vigneron; farm hand, farm labourer, orraman, agricultural worker; land girl; ploughman, tractor driver, sower, reaper, harvester, gleaner; thresher; potato picker, hop picker, fruit picker.

gardener, horticulturist, flower grower; topiarist, landscape gardener, garden designer; seedsman, nurseryman *or* -woman; market gardener; fruit-grower, vine-grower, vigneron; arborist, arboriculturalist, silviculturist 366 *forestry*.

farm and garden tools, tractor, plough, ploughshare, harrow, chain harrow, disc harrow, cultivator, rotary cultivator, drill, trimmer, binder, baler, combine harvester, thresher, pea viner, hayfork, pitchfork, farm fork, graip, flail, mattock, pick, pickaxe, hook, billhook; barrow, wheelbarrow 274 *pushcart*;

garden tool, spade, shovel, fork, hand fork, hoe, Dutch hoe, rake, lawn rake, cultivator, Rotovator *or* Rotavator (tdmk), trowel, dibble *or* dibber; digging stick, caschrom; scythe, sickle, shears, pruners, secateurs, pruning hook, pruning knife, pruning saw, edger 256 *sharp edge*; winepress, ciderpress; mowing machine, mower, Flymo (tdmk), rotary mower, cylinder mower; aerator; strimmer; watering can, hose, sprinkler, lawn sprinkler. (See also 630 *tool*.)

Vb. *cultivate*, bring under cultivation 171 *make fruitful*; farm, ranch, garden, grow; till, till the soil, dig, trench, dibble; sow, scatter the seed, set, plant, prick out, dibble in, transplant, plant out, bed out; plough, harrow, rake, hoe; weed, prune, thin out, deadhead 204 *shorten*; graft 303 *implant*; layer, take cuttings; force; fertilize, topdress, mulch, manure 174 *invigorate*; grass over, rotate the crop; leave fallow 674 *not use*; harvest 632 *store*; glean, reap, mow, cut, scythe, cut a swathe; bind, bale, stook, sheaf; flail, thresh, winnow, sift, bolt 46 *separate*; crop, pluck, pick, gather; tread out the grapes; ensile; ditch, drain, reclaim; water 341 *irrigate*.

371 Humankind

N. *humankind*, mankind, homo sapiens, womankind; humanity, human nature; flesh, mortality, human frailty; human race, human species; man; earthling; human being, Adam, Eve; civilized world, civilization; barbarians, savages; bushmen, aborigines; Stone-Age man, Cro-Magnon man, Neanderthal man, cavemen and -women, troglodytes; apemen and -women, Pithecanthropus, Australopithecus, Peking man, Java man; Piltdown man; ethnic type 11 *race*.

anthropology, anthropography; somatology; ethnology, ethnography; folklore; social anthropology, demography; social science, humanitarianism 901 *social care*; humanism; anthroposophy; anthropomorphism, pathetic fallacy; anthropologist, craniologist, ethnographer, demographer, folklorist, humanist.

person, individual, human being, everyman, everywoman; creature, mortal, body, bod; a being, soul, living soul; one, somebody, someone, so and so, such a one; party, customer, character, type, element; chap, fellow 372 *male*; girl, female, bird 373 *woman*; personage, figure, person of note, VIP 638 *bigwig*; celebrity, star 890 *favourite*; dramatis personae, all those concerned 686 *personnel*; unit, head, hand, nose; — monkey (derog).

social group, society, community, ethnic group, ghetto 74 *group*; kinship group 11 *family*; primitive society, tribalism; organized society; people, persons, folk; public, general public, man *or* woman in the street, Joe Bloggs, Joe Public, Joe Soap, the average punter, everyman, you and me, the 'me' generation 79 *generality*; population, populace, citizenry 191 *inhabitants*; the masses 869 *common people*; social classes 868 *upper class, aristocracy*, 869 *lower classes, middle classes*.

nation, nationality, statehood, nationalism; chauvinism, jingoism, gung-ho nationalism, expansionism, imperialism, colonialism; Lebensraum; body politic, people, demos; state; realm, commonwealth 733 *political organization*; democracy, republic 733.

Adj. *national*, state, civic, general, communal, tribal, social, societal; cosmopolitan, international.

372 Male

N. *male*, male sex, man, he, him; Adam; manliness, masculinity, manhood; virility, machismo; male chauvinism, male-dominated society, patriarchy, men's movement, mannishness, virilism; gentleman, sir, esquire, master; lord, my lord, his lordship; Mr, mister, monsieur, Herr, sahib, etc. 870 *title*; tovarich, comrade, citoyen; squire, guvnor, guv; buster, Mac, Jock, Jimmy; mate, buddy, butty, pal 880 *chum*; goodman, wight, swain; gaffer, buffer 133 *old man*; fellow, guy, scout, bloke, bugger, chap, chappie, johnny, gent; codger, card, cove, joker; blade, rake, gay dog 952 *libertine*; he-man, caveman, macho, Alpha Man; male chauvinist pig, MCP, New Lad, lad, laddism; New Man; sissy, mummy's boy 163 *weakling*; homosexual, homo, queer 84 *nonconformist*; eunuch, castrato; escort, beau, boy friend; bachelor, widower; bridegroom 894 *bridal party*; married man, husband, house husband, man, live-in 894 *spouse*; family man, paterfamilias, patriarch; father 169 *paternity*; uncle, brother, nephew; lad, stripling, boy 132 *young person*; blue-eyed boy, son; spear side; stag party, menfolk.

male animal, dog (coyote, dog, fox, otter, wolf), dog fox; tom cat; horse, stallion (horse, zebra), stud horse, colt; bull, bull-calf, bullock, ox, steer; boar, hog; ram, tup; he-goat, billy goat; buck (deer, reindeer), hart (red deer), roebuck, stag (caribou, deer, red deer); buck (antelope, goat, hare, kangaroo, rabbit); bull (buffalo, camel, elephant, elk, giraffe, hippopotamus, moose, rhinoceros, seal, walrus, whale); boar (badger, bear, beaver, hedgehog, raccoon); jack (donkey), jackass; hob, jack (ferret); cock, cockerel, rooster; drake, gander, cob (swan), tiercel *or* tercel (falcon); drone (bee); gelding, capon.

Adj. *male*, he-, masculine, manly, gentle-

manly, chivalrous; virile, macho; mannish, manlike, butch, unfeminine, unwomanly; effeminate, unmanly, womanish, pansy.

373 Female

N. *female*, feminine sex, woman, she, her, -ess; Eve, femininity, feminineness; womanhood 134 *adultness*; womanliness, girlishness; feminism, gynography, women's rights, Women's Lib *or* Liberation, Women's Movement; matriarchy, gynocracy, pornocracy, regiment of women; girl, little girl 132 *young person*; virgin, maiden; nun, unmarried woman, old maid 895 *spinster*; bachelor girl, career woman; feminist, sister, women's libber, bra burner; suffragette; bride, married woman, wife, 'trouble and strife', woman, live-in, squaw, widow, matron 894 *spouse*; dowager 133 *old woman*; mother, grandmother 169 *maternity*; unmarried mother, working wife *or* mother, housewife, superwoman, domestic goddess; aunt, auntie, niece, sister, daughter; wench, lass, lassie, nymph; colleen, damsel; petticoat, skirt, doll, chick, bird, totty; honey, hinny, baby; brunette, blonde, platinum blonde, peroxide blonde, bottle blonde, redhead; girl friend, sweetheart 887 *loved one*; moll, bint, crumpet, ho, bit of fluff; broad, courtesan 952 *loose woman*; lesbian, dyke *or* dike 84 *nonconformist*; minx, hussy, baggage, jade; shrew, virago, harridan, stramullion, termagant, ballbreaker; Amazon; lady, gentlewoman; dame; milady, her ladyship, donna; madam, ma'am, marm, mistress, Mrs, missus, Ms, miss, madame, mademoiselle, Frau, Fräulein, memsahib, etc. 870 *title*; goodwife; gynaecology; obstetrics 167 *propagation*.

womankind, second sex, female sex, fair sex, gentle sex, weaker sex; the distaff side, womenfolk, women; hen party; women's quarters, purdah, seraglio, harem.

female animal, bitch (dog, fox, otter, wolf); tabby cat; mare (horse, zebra), filly; cow, heifer; sow, gilt; ewe, ewe-lamb; nanny goat, she-goat; hind, doe; jenny (ass, donkey), jenny-ass; she-wolf, vixen; lioness, leopardess, tigress; she-bear, sow; cow (buffalo, camel, elephant, elk, giraffe, hippopotamus, moose, rhinoceros, seal, walrus, whale); doe (antelope, ferret, hare, kangaroo, rabbit, rat); sow (badger, guinea pig, hedgehog, mink, raccoon); gill *or* jill (ferret); hen, pullet; duck, goose, pen (swan); pea-hen (peafowl).

Adj. *female*, she-, feminine, petticoat, girlish, womanly, ladylike, maidenly, matronly; child-bearing; feminist, feministic; Amazonian; lesbian, lez *or* les (usually considered derog or offensive), dykey *or* dikey (usually considered derog or offensive); womanish, effeminate, unmanly, pansy; unfeminine, unwomanly, mannish, masculine, butch.

374 Physical sensitivity

N. *sensitivity*, sensitiveness, sensibility; soreness, tenderness, delicateness, threshold of pain; exposed nerve; perceptivity, awareness, consciousness 819 *moral sensibility*; susceptibility; allergy 302 *excretion*; funny bone; sensuousness, aestheticism, aesthetics; aesthete 846 *person of taste*; touchy person, sensitive plant, thin skin.

sense, sense organ, nervous system, sensorium; five senses, touch, hearing, taste, smell, sight; sensation, impression 818 *feeling*; effect, response, reaction, reflex, autosuggestion; sixth sense, feyness, second sight, extrasensory perception, ESP; telepathy, thought-transference 984 *psychics*.

Adj. *sentient*, perceptive, sensitive, sensitized; sensible, susceptible; sensory, perceptual; sensuous, aesthetic 818 *feeling*; percipient, aware, conscious 490 *knowing*; acute, sharp, keen 377 *painful*; ticklish, itchy; tender, raw, sore, exposed; impressionable, alive, alive to, warm, responsive; allergic, oversensitive, hypersensitive 819 *impressible*.

Vb. *have feeling*, sense, become aware; come to one's senses, awaken, wake up; perceive, realize 490 *know*; be sensible of 818 *feel*; react, tingle 819 *be sensitive*; have all one's senses, hear, see, touch, taste, smell; be alert, have one's wits about one, be on the ball, be on the qui vive.

cause feeling, stir the senses, stir the blood; arouse, awaken, excite, make *or* produce an impression 821 *impress*; cause a sensation 508 *surprise*; sensitize.

375 Physical insensitivity

N. *insensitivity*, insensitiveness, insensibility; imperceptiveness, obtuseness 499 *unintelligence*; impassivity 820 *moral insensibility*; anaesthesia; analgesia; hypnosis, hypnotism, hypnotherapy, autosuggestion; suspended animation; apoplexy, paralysis, palsy; numbness; catalepsy, stupor, coma, trance, freak-out; faint, swoon, blackout, unconsciousness, senselessness; narcolepsy, narcotism, sleeping sickness 651 *disease*; narcosis 679 *sleep*.

anaesthetic, dope 658 *drug*; local anaesthetic, general anaesthetic; ether, chloroform, morphine, cocaine; gas, nitrous oxide, laughing gas; gas and air, epidural, pethidene; narcotic, sleeping tablets, Mogadon (tdmk), draught; opium, laudanum; painkiller, analgesic 177 *moderator*.

Adj. *insensitive*, insensible, insentient; obtuse, imperceptive 499 *unintelligent*; unaware, oblivious; unhearing 416 *deaf*; unseeing 439 *blind*; senseless, unconscious; inert 679 *inactive*; out cold, out for the count, dead 266 *at rest*; numb, frozen; paralysed, paralytic, palsied; doped, dopy, drugged; freaked out, spaced out; stoned 949 *dead drunk*; anaesthetized, hypnotized; dazed, stupefied; semiconscious, in a trance; catatonic, cataleptic, comatose.

unfeeling, cold, callous, insensitive, inured, toughened, hardened; pachydermatous, thick-skinned; stony, shock-proof 820 *impassive*.

Vb. *make insensitive*, blunt, deaden; paralyse, benumb; freeze 382 *refrigerate*; put to sleep, send to sleep, hypnotize, mesmerize 679 *make inactive*; anaesthetize, put under, gas, chloroform; drug, dope; dull, stupefy; stun, concuss, brain, knock out, make unconscious 279 *strike*.

376 Physical pleasure

N. *pleasure*, thrill 821 *excitation*; enjoyment, gratification, sensuousness, sensuality; self-indulgence, luxuriousness, hedonism 944 *sensualism*; dissipation 943 *intemperance*; treat, diversion, entertainment, divertissement 837 *amusement*; feast, thrash 301 *feasting*; epicurism, epicureanism, relish 386 *taste*; gusto, zest, delight, happiness, ecstasy 824 *joy*.

sexual pleasure, sexual satisfaction; thrill 821 *excitation*; sexual intercourse, lovemaking, making love, sex, casual sex, foreplay, etc. 45 *sexual intercourse*; free love, wife-swapping, sharing, swinging, dogging, espresso sex, sexual sorbet 951 *illicit love*; masturbation, manual relief, autoeroticism *or* autoerotism, frigging (vulg), onanism, self-abuse, self-stimulation, wanking (vulg); dildo, vibrator; shrimping; frottage, tribadism, dry-humping; climax, orgasm; sex addiction *or* sexual addiction; oral sex, fellatio, blowjob (vulg), cunnilingus; G-spot *or* Gräfenberg spot; Viagra (tdmk); Mile High Club; cybersex.

euphoria, well-being, contentment 824 *happiness*, 828 *contentment*; quiet.

Adj. *pleasant*, pleasure-giving 826 *pleasurable*; pleasing, titillating, arousing; delightful; welcome, gratifying, satisfying 685 *refreshing*; genial, congenial, friendly, matey, cordial, heart-warming; nice, agreeable, enjoyable 837 *amusing*; palatable, delicious 386 *tasty*; tuneful 410 *melodious*; lovely 841 *beautiful*.

comfortable, affording comfort, comfy, homely, snug, cosy, warm, comforting, restful 683 *restful*; convenient, cushy; downy 327 *soft*; luxurious; in comfort, at one's ease; pampered, featherbedded, in clover, on a bed of roses, on velvet; happy, gratified 828 *content*; relieved.

sensuous, appealing to the senses; bodily, physical 319 *material*; voluptuous, pleasure-loving, luxuriating, enjoying, epicurean, hedonistic 944 *sensual*.

Vb. *enjoy*, relish, like, love, adore; feel pleasure, experience pleasure, take pleasure in 824 *be pleased*; thrill to 821 *be excited*; luxuriate in, revel in, bask in, roll in, wallow in; gloat over, get a kick out of; lick one's lips, smack one's lips 386 *taste*; live on the fat of the land, live comfortably, live in clover, rest on a bed of roses 730 *prosper*; give pleasure 826 *please*.

have or give sexual pleasure, have sex with, make love, sleep around, sleep together, sleep with 45 *have sexual intercourse with*; masturbate, frig (vulg), toss off (vulg), wank (vulg); climax, have an orgasm, orgasm, come (vulg); fellate, go down on (vulg); arouse, excite, turn on 821 *excite*; satisfy 826 *please*.

Adv. *in comfort*, at one's ease; in clover, on velvet, on a bed of roses.

377 Physical pain

N. *pain*, threshold of pain; no pain, no gain; discomfort, malaise; distress, hell 731 *adversity*; strain, stress 684 *fatigue*; hurt, bruise, sprain, break, fracture; cut, gash 655 *wound*; aching, smarting, throbbing; heartache, anguish, agony 825 *suffering*; torment, torture; crucifixion, martyrdom, vivisection; rack, wheel, thumbscrew 964 *instrument of punishment or torture*; painfulness, soreness, tenderness.

pang, throes; stab, labour pangs, hunger pangs, twinge, nip, pinch; pins and needles 378 *formication*; stitch, crick, cramp, convulsion 318 *spasm*; smart, sting, sharp pain; shooting pain; ache, headache, splitting head, migraine; toothache, earache; stomachache, bellyache, colic, collywobbles; neuritis, neuralgia, angina; arthritis, rheumatoid arthritis, rheumatism, fibrositis, repetitive strain injury, sciatica, lumbago, backache 651 *ill health*.

Adj. *painful*, aching, agonizing, excruciating, harrowing, racking, tormenting; burning, biting, searing, stabbing, shooting, tingling, smarting, throbbing; sore, raw, tender, exposed, grazed; bittersweet 393 *sour*; disagreeable.

Vb. *give pain*, hurt, pain, sting, graze; excruciate, lacerate, torment, twist the arm of 963 *torture*; flog, whip, crucify, martyr 963 *punish*; vivisect, tear, lacerate 46 *cut*; prick, stab 263 *pierce*; gripe, nip, pinch, tweak, twinge, shoot, throb; bite, gnaw; grate, jar, set on edge; fret, chafe, gall 333 *rub*; irritate 832

aggravate; put on the rack, break on the wheel; grate on the ear 411 *discord*; annoy, distress 827 *trouble*.

feel pain, feel the pangs 825 *suffer*; agonize, ache, smart, chafe; twitch, wince, flinch, writhe, squirm, creep, shiver, quiver 318 *be agitated*; tingle, get pins and needles; be a martyr, go through it 731 *have trouble*, groan 408 *cry*.

378 Touch: sensation of touch

N. *touch*, tactility, palpability; handling, feeling, palpation, manipulation; massage, kneading, squeeze, pressure 333 *friction*; graze, contact 202 *contiguity*; stroke, pat, caress; flick, flip, tap 279 *knock*; precision 494 *accuracy*; artistry 694 *skill*.

tingling, tingle, pins-and-needles, formication; creeps, gooseflesh, gooseskin, goose bumps, goose pimples; someone walking over one's grave; scratchiness, itchiness, itch; urticaria, nettlerash, hives, allergic reaction; rash, prickly heat 651 *skin disease*.

feeler, antenna, whisker, tentacle; proboscis, tongue; digit, forefinger, thumb (see also *finger* below); hand, paw, flipper.

finger, forefinger, index, middle finger, ring finger, little finger, pinkie; thumb, pollex; big toe 214 *foot*; five fingers, bunch of fives, knuckle sandwich, dukes, fingernail, talon, claw; cuticle.

Adj. *tactile*, tactual; prehensile; touching, licking, grazing, etc. (see vb.); touchable, tangible, palpable 319 *material*.

handed, right-handed 241 *right-handedness*; left-handed, cack-handed 242 *left-handedness*; manual.

Vb. *touch*, make contact, come into contact; graze, scrape, shave, brush, glance; kiss 202 *be contiguous*; impinge; hit, meet 279 *collide*; feel, palpate; finger, thumb, pinch, nip, massage 333 *rub*; palm, run the hand over; stroke 258 *smooth*; tap, tip, pat, dab, flick, flip, tickle, scratch; lick; nuzzle, rub noses; paw, fondle 889 *caress*; handle, twiddle, fiddle with, play with; manipulate, wield, ply, manhandle 173 *operate*; jab, poke, goose, bruise, crush 377 *give pain*; grope; put out a feeler 461 *be tentative*.

379 Heat

N. *heat*, radiant heat; convected heat; emission of heat, incandescence, flame, glow, flush, hot flush, blush; warmth, fervour, ardour; tepidity, lukewarmness; specific heat, blood heat, body heat; sweat, perspiration, swelter; pyrexia, fever, inflammation 651 *disease*; high temperature, white heat; ebullition, boiling point, flash point, melting point; tropical heat, sweltering heat, high summer, flaming June, Indian summer; dog days, heat haze 128 *summer*; heat wave, scorcher, sizzler; hot wind, simoom, sirocco; hot springs, thermal springs, geyser, hot water, steam; tropics, torrid zone; sun, midday sun, sunshine, solar heat 381 *heating*.

fire, flames; bonfire; beacon fire; St Elmo's fire 417 *glow*; hellfire; pyre 364 *funeral rites*; open fire, coal fire, log fire, gas fire, electric fire, wood-burning stove, chimenea 383 *furnace*; Greek fire, wild fire 723 *bomb*; conflagration, holocaust; forest fire, bush fire; fireball, blaze, flame, tongue of flame, sheet of flame, wall of flame; spark, scintillation, flicker, arc 417 *flash*; flare 420 *torch*; volcano, eruption, lava, pyroclastic flow; pyrotechnics; arson 381 *incendiarism*; fire worship 981 *worship*.

thermometry, thermometer, clinical thermometer, Fahrenheit thermometer, centigrade *or* Celsius thermometer, Réaumur thermometer; feverscan; thermostat; calorimeter; British Thermal Unit, BTU, therm, calorie; thermodynamics; thermography; temperature.

Adj. *hot*, heated, superheated; inflamed, fervent, fervid; flaming, glowing, fiery, red-hot, white-hot; piping hot, hot as hell; feverish, febrile, fevered; sweltering, sweating, perspiring; steaming, smoking; dripping with sweat; on the boil, boiling, seething, ebullient, scalding; tropical, torrid, scorching; grilling, broiling, searing, blistering, baking, toasting, roasting, etc. (see vb.); scorched, scalded 381 *heated*; thirsty, burning, parched 342 *dry*.

fiery, burning, blazing, flaming; smoking, smouldering; ablaze, afire, on fire, aflame; candescent, incandescent, glowing, aglow 431 *red*; pyrogenic, igneous; ignited, lit, alight, kindled, volcanic, erupting.

warm, tepid, lukewarm; temperate, mild, genial, balmy; fair, set fair, sunny, sunshiny 417 *undimmed*; summery; tropical, equatorial; torrid, sultry; stuffy, close, muggy; overheated, unventilated; oppressive, suffocating, stifling, like a hothouse 653 *unhealthy*; warm as toast; snug 376 *comfortable*; at room temperature, at blood heat.

Vb. *be hot*, be warm, get warm, etc. (see adj.); incandesce; burn, kindle, catch fire, draw; blaze, flare, flame, burst into flame, go up in flames; glow, flush; smoke, smoulder, reek, fume, steam 300 *emit*; boil, seethe 318 *effervesce*; toast, grill, broil, roast, sizzle, crackle, fry, bake 381 *burn*; get burnt, scorch, boil dry; bask, sun oneself, sunbathe; get sunburnt, tan; swelter, sweat, perspire, glow; thaw 337 *liquefy*; parch; suffocate, stifle, pant, gasp

for breath, fight for air; be in a fever, be feverish, have a fever, run a temperature; keep warm, wrap up, insulate, keep out the cold.

380 Cold

N. *coldness*, low temperature, drop in temperature; cool, coolness, freshness; cold, freezing cold, absolute zero; freezing point, frigidity; iciness, frostiness; chilliness, windchill factor, hypothermia, shivering, shivers, chattering of the teeth, chittering; gooseflesh, gooseskin, goose pimples, goose bumps, frostbite, chilblains, chap, hack; chill, cold, common cold, a cold in the head, coryza; cold climate, Siberia, North Pole, South Pole, Arctic, Antarctica; snowline, permafrost; Ice Age.

wintriness, winter, hard winter; nip in the air, cold snap; cold front; arctic conditions, degrees of frost; snowstorm, hailstorm, blizzard; frost, touch of frost, Jack Frost, rime, hoarfrost, hard frost; sleet, hail, hailstone, freeze.

snow, snowfall, snowflake; avalanche, snowdrift, snowfield; snowstorm; snow line, snowcap, snowball, snowman; snowplough, snowblower, snowshoe, snowmobile, snow tyre; winter sports 837 *sport*; snow blindness; snowbound.

ice, ice cube; icicle; black ice; ice cap, ice field, ice sheet, ice shelf, floe, ice floe, iceberg, tip of the iceberg, glacier, icefall; pack ice; icebreaker, ice yacht; ice house, icebox 384 *refrigerator*; glaciation 382 *refrigeration*.

Adj. *cold*, cool; shady, chilly, parky, nippy, perishing, Baltic; unheated; fresh, raw, keen, bitter, biting, piercing; freezing, ice-cold; frigid 129 *wintry*; winterbound, frosty, snowy, snow-covered; sleety, icy; glacial, ice-capped, glaciated; boreal, polar, arctic, Siberian.

chilly, shivering, chattering, chittering, shivery, blue with cold; perishing, starved with cold, chilled to the bone, hypothermic, frozen, frostbitten, like ice, stone-cold, cold as charity *or* as marble *or* as death.

Vb. *be cold*, be chilly, etc. (see adj.); grow cold, lose heat, drop in temperature; feel cold, chatter, chitter, shiver, tremble, shake, quake, quiver, shudder; freeze, starve, perish with cold, suffer from hypothermia; catch cold, get a chill; chill 382 *refrigerate*.

381 Heating

N. *heating*, superheating, warming, keeping warm; space heating, central heating 383 *heater*; solar heating, sunning 342 *drying*; greenhouse effect; melting, thawing 337 *liquefaction*; smelting, boiling, seething, simmering, ebullition; baking, cooking 301 *cookery*.

burning, combustion; inflammation, kindling, ignition; afterburning; conflagration 379 *fire*; incineration, roasting; cremation 364 *interment*; suttee, self-burning 362 *suicide*; holocaust 981 *religious offering*; cauterization, branding; scorching, singeing, charring, inflammability, flammability, combustibility; burner 383 *furnace*; vitriol; branding iron; match, touchpaper 385 *lighter*; burn, scorch mark, brand, sunburn, tan, sunstroke.

arson, fire-raising, pyromania, incendiarism; incendiary, arsonist, fire-raiser, fire-bug.

pottery, ceramics; earthenware, stoneware, lustre ware, glazed ware; majolica, faience, chinaware, porcelain; crockery, china, bone china, Wedgwood (tdmk) china, Spode china, Worcester china, Doulton china, Chelsea china, Staffordshire china, Derby china, Sèvres china, Dresden china; delft, willow pattern, terracotta; tile, brick, adobe; pot, urn 194 *vessel*; potter's wheel.

Adj. *heated*, superheated 379 *hot*; centrally-heated, winterized, insulated; fired; cooked; warmed up; overheated; steamy, smoky.

heating, warming, etc. (see vb.); calefactory, calorific, solid-fuel, coal-burning, oil-fired, gas-fired; incendiary, inflammatory; inflammable, flammable; anti-freeze.

Vb. *heat*, raise the temperature, warm; winterize, insulate; keep the cold out, take the chill off; hot up, warm up, stoke up; rub one's hands, stamp one's feet; thaw, thaw out; inflame, foment; overheat, stifle, suffocate; parch, shrivel, sear 342 *dry*; roast 301 *cook*; defrost 337 *liquefy*.

kindle, ignite, light, strike a light; set fire to, light the touchpaper, light the fuse, touch off; lay the fire, rub two sticks together; add fuel to the fire, poke the fire.

burn, burn up, burn out; consign to the flames; make a bonfire of, send to the stake; fire, set fire to, set on fire, set alight; cremate, incinerate; boil dry 342 *dry*; char, singe, sear, scorch; cauterize, brand; scald.

382 Refrigeration

N. *refrigeration*, cooling, reduction of temperature; icing, etc. (see vb.); freezing, freezing up, icing over, glaciation 380 *ice*; solidification 324 *condensing*; exposure; cold storage 384 *refrigerator*; cryonic suspension, cryonics 364 *interment*; cryogenics, cryosurgery.

extinguisher, fire extinguisher; foam, powder, water; hose, hydrant, fire hydrant, sprinkler, standpipe; fire blanket; fire engine, fire appliance, fire tender, fire truck, Green Goddess, fireboat, fire station; firefighter, fireman,

firewoman; fire brigade; firebreak, fire line; fire door, fire wall.

Adj. *cooled*, chilled, etc. (see vb.); ventilated, air-conditioned; iced up; frozen, deep-frozen, freeze-dried; frosted, iced, glacé, frappé; with ice, on the rocks 380 *cold*; cooling, etc. (see vb.); refrigeratory.

Vb. *refrigerate*, cool, air-cool, water-cool; reduce the temperature, turn off the heat; freeze, deep-freeze, freeze-dry; ice up, ice over; chill, benumb, starve, nip, pinch, bite, pierce, chill to the marrow, make one's teeth chatter; expose to the cold, frost-bite.

extinguish, quench, put out, blow out, snuff out; choke, suffocate, stifle, smother 165 *suppress*; damp, douse, damp down, bank down; stamp out; stub out; go out, burn out, die down.

383 Furnace

N. *furnace*, fiery furnace; the stake 964 *means of execution*; volcano (see 209 *high land*); touchhole, gun barrel; forge, blast furnace; kiln; oasthouse; incinerator; crematorium; brazier, stove, kitchen stove, wood-burning stove, gas stove, electric stove, primus stove, oil stove; oven, gas oven, electric oven, microwave oven; range, kitchen range; cooker, gas cooker, electric cooker, split-level cooker, turbo-fan cooker, ceramic hob; gas ring, burner, bunsen burner; blowlamp, oxyacetylene lamp; fire, coal fire, etc. 379 *fire*; brand 385 *lighter*; fireplace, grate, hearth, ingle; fire-irons, andirons, firedog; poker, tongs, shovel; hob, trivet; fireguard, fender; flue.

heater, space heater, paraffin heater, radiator, solar panel; hot-air duct, hot-water pipe, immersion heater, geyser, boiler, back boiler, central-heating boiler, combi-boiler, copper, kettle, electric kettle 194 *pot*; hotplate; warming pan, hot-water bottle; electric blanket; still, retort, crucible 461 *testing agent*; blowpipe, bellows, damper; hot baths, Turkish bath, sauna, Jacuzzi (tdmk) 648 *washing*; hotbed, hothouse, greenhouse, conservatory 370 *garden*; sun trap, solarium; kitchen, galley, cookhouse; grill, frying pan, saucepan; toaster, electric toaster; iron, flat iron, electric iron, steam iron, soldering iron, curling tongs; flame, sunlight 381 *heating*; gas, electricity, solar energy, greenhouse effect 160 *sources of energy*; steam, hot air; wood, coal, peat 385 *fuel*.

384 Refrigerator

N. *refrigerator*, cooler; frigidarium; refrigerating plant, fridge, chiller, wine cooler, ice bucket; coolant, snow, ice; icehouse, icebox, ice pack, ice cubes, rocks; cold storage, freezer, fridge-freezer, cooler cupboard, deep-freeze 382 *refrigeration*; refrigerant, chlorofluorocarbon, CFC, greenhouse gas.

385 Fuel

N. *fuel*, inflammable material, flammable material, combustible; wood, brushwood, firewood, faggot, log, Yule log, kindling; firewood, peat; coal (see also *coal* below); petroleum 357 *oil*; nuclear fuel 160 *nuclear physics*; petrol, high octane petrol, two-star, three-star, fourstar, unleaded petrol, lead-free petrol, lead replacement petrol, LRP, gasoline, gas, juice; diesel oil, derv; biodiesel, biofuel, alternative fuel; paraffin, kerosene, methylated spirit; gas, coal gas, natural gas, North Sea gas, town gas 336 *gas*; acetylene, propane, butane, methane.

coal, black diamond, brown coal, charcoal, lignite, anthracite, briquette; coal dust, slack; coal seam, coal deposit, coalfield 632 *store*; embers; coke; smokeless fuel.

lighter, fire-lighter, cigarette lighter, igniter, light, pilot light, illuminant, taper, spill, candle 420 *torch*; fire ship, incendiary bomb 723 *bomb*; touchpaper, match, safety match, lucifer, vesta, fusee; matchstick; percussion cap, detonator; flint, steel, tinder, touchwood.

386 Taste

N. *taste*, savour; flavour, flavouring; peppermint, spearmint, vanilla, coffee, chocolate, etc.; smack, tang, aftertaste; relish, gusto, zest, appetite 859 *liking*; palate, tastebuds.

Adj. *tasty*, palatable, mouth-watering, tempting, appetizing 390 *savoury*; wellseasoned, tangy 388 *pungent*; flavoured, spiced, spicy, herbed, herby, rich, strong, full-bodied, fruity, well-matured, mellow, vintage.

Vb. *taste*, lick one's lips, lick one's fingers 376 *enjoy*; savour, sample; sip, lick, sup, nibble 301 *eat*; have a taste, taste of, savour of, smack of 18 *resemble*; taste good, tickle the palate, tempt the appetite, stimulate the tastebuds 390 *make appetizing*.

387 Insipidness

N. *insipidness*, insipidity, vapidity, vapidness, tastelessness, etc. (see adj.); pap.

Adj. *tasteless*, wersh; vapid, insipid, watery; adulterated 163 *weakened*; wishy-washy; unappetizing 391 *unsavoury*; flavourless, unspiced, unseasoned.

388 Pungency

N. *pungency*, piquancy, poignancy, sting, kick, bite, edge; causticity; spiciness; acridity, sharpness, acerbity, acidity 393 *sourness*; roughness, harshness; strength, tang; bad taste 391 *unsa-*

vouriness; salt, brine, pepper, pickle, spice 389 *condiment*; sal volatile, smelling salts 656 *revival*.

tobacco, baccy, snout, the weed; nicotine 658 *tonic*; tobacco leaf, Virginia tobacco, Turkish tobacco, smoking mixture; snuff; plug, quid, twist; chewing tobacco, nicotine chew, tobacco sachet, tobacco teabag; pipe tobacco, shag; cigar, cigarillo, cheroot, panatella, Havana, corona; smoke, cigarette, cig, ciggie, fag, gasper, coffin-nail; reefer, joint 949 *drugtaking*; filter tip, cork tip, low-tar cigarette, menthol cigarette, roll-up; butt, stub, fag-end, dog-end; pipe, tobacco pipe, clay pipe, churchwarden, briar, corncob, meerschaum; water pipe, hubble-bubble, hookah, narghile; pipe of peace, calumet; bowl, stem; smoker's cough; snuff taker, smoker, pipe smoker, cigarette smoker, cigar smoker, chain smoker; smoking, passive smoker; tobacconist, cigarette machine; cigarette holder; snuff box, cigarette case, cigar case, cigarette box, cigar box; pipe rack; pipe cleaner, tobacco pouch, tobacco jar, smokeroom; smoker, non-smoker, smoking compartment, smoking zone; smokefree zone *or* area.

Adj. *pungent*, strong; stinging, biting 256 *sharp*; caustic, smoky; harsh 259 *rough*; bitter, acrid, tart, astringent 393 *sour*; strongflavoured, high, gamy, off; highly-seasoned, hot, gingery, peppery, fiery; zesty, tangy, piquant, aromatic 390 *savoury*.

salty, salt, brackish, briny, saline, pickled.

Vb. *season*, salt, marinade, souse, pickle; flavour; spice, herb, season, pepper, devil, curry; smoke, kipper 666 *preserve*.

smoke, smoke a pipe, pull, draw, suck, inhale; puff, blow smoke rings; chain-smoke, smoke like a chimney; chew a quid, suck tobacco sachets; take a pinch.

389 Condiment

N. *condiment*, seasoning, flavouring, dressing, relish, garnish; aspic; salt, garlic salt, celery salt; mustard, French mustard, Dijon mustard, German mustard, English mustard; pepper, black pepper, white pepper, peppercorn; vinegar, malt vinegar, balsamic vinegar, etc. 393 *sourness*; onion, garlic 301 *herb*; curry powder 301 *spice*; vanilla; cruet, salt cellar, etc. 194 *small box*.

sauce, roux; gravy, stock; brown sauce, white sauce, béchamel; parsley sauce, bread sauce, tartar sauce, mint sauce, horseradish sauce, sauce piquante; béarnaise sauce; apple sauce, cranberry sauce 392 *sweet thing*; tomato sauce, ketchup; chilli sauce, salsa, Tabasco (tdmk) sauce, soy sauce, Worcester *or*

Worcestershire sauce; chutney, sweet chutney, mango chutney, salad dressing, French dressing, Thousand Island dressing, mayonnaise, vinaigrette; relish, piccalilli, pickles, pickled onions, gherkins.

Vb. *spice* 388 *season.*

390 Savouriness
N. *savouriness,* tastiness, palatability; gaminess; body, bouquet; savoury, relish, appetizer; delicacy, dainty, titbit 301 *mouthful;* hors d'oeuvre.

Adj. *savoury,* seasoned, flavoured, spicy, herby 386 *tasty;* tempting, appetizing, aromatic, piquant 388 *pungent;* palatable, toothsome; delectable, delicious, choice, epicurean; ambrosial, fit for the gods, fit for a king; scrumptious, yummy, moreish; succulent; gamy, high; full-flavoured.

Vb. *make appetizing,* garnish, spice, pep up 388 *season;* tempt the appetite, tickle the palate, stimulate the tastebuds; smell good, taste good.

391 Unsavouriness
N. *unsavouriness,* unpalatability, sourness, rankness, rottenness, over-ripeness, unwholesomeness 653 *unhealthiness;* acerbity, acridity 393 *sourness;* austerity, prison fare, bread and water, nursery fare, iron rations; aloes, bitter aloes, rue; bitter pill, gall and wormwood *or* wormwood and gall.

Adj. *unsavoury,* tasteless; unpalatable, unappetizing, wersh; underdone, undressed 670 *uncooked;* overdone, burnt, burnt to a cinder, uneatable, inedible; stale, leathery 329 *tough;* soggy 327 *soft;* bitter, acrid, acid 393 *sour;* undrinkable, corked; overripe, rank, rancid, putrid, rotten, gone off, high, stinking 397 *fetid;* revolting, disgusting, loathsome 827 *unpleasant;* nauseating; poisonous 653 *toxic.*

Vb. *be unpalatable,* be unappetizing, etc. (see adj.); disgust, repel, sicken, nauseate, turn the stomach 861 *cause dislike;* poison; pall.

392 Sweetness
N. *sweetness,* sweetening, sugariness, sweet tooth.

sweet thing, sweetening, honey, honeycomb, honeypot; sucrose, glucose, dextrose, fructose, lactose, galactose; sugar, cane sugar, beet sugar, invert sugar; granulated sugar, caster sugar, icing sugar, demerara; molasses, syrup, maple syrup, treacle; sweetener, artificial sweetener, saccharin, aspartame, acesulfame K; custard, condensed milk; julep, nectar, hydromel, mead; conserve, preserve; candied peel, glacé cherries; jam, marmalade, jelly;

marzipan, icing, fondant, sugar coating; fudge, candy, sugar candy 301 *sweets;* jujube, cachou, lozenge, pastille; lollipop, ice cream, candyfloss, rock; confectionery, confection, cake 301 *bread, pastries and cakes, dessert.*

Adj. *sweet,* sweetened, honeyed, candied, crystallized; iced, glacé; sugared, sugary, saccharine, melliferous; ambrosial, luscious, delicious 376 *pleasant;* sweet as sugar *or* as a nut; cloying 390 *savoury.*

Vb. *sweeten,* sugar, add sugar, candy, crystallize, ice, glaze; sugar the pill; mull.

393 Sourness
N. *sourness,* acerbity; astringency; tartness, bitterness, vinegariness; sharpness 388 *pungency;* acidity, acidosis; acid, tartar; lemon, lime, vinegar, malt vinegar, white wine vinegar, red wine vinegar, cider vinegar, raspberry vinegar, sherry vinegar, tarragon vinegar, balsamic vinegar; sloe, crab apple; alum, bitter aloes, bitters; gall, wormwood, absinth.

Adj. *sour,* sourish, acid, acidy, acidulous, acidulated, acetic, tartaric; acerbic, crabbed, tart, bitter; sharp, astringent 388 *pungent;* vinegary 391 *unsavoury;* unripe, green 670 *immature;* sugarless; unsweetened, dry.

Vb. *be sour,* be acid, etc. (see adj.); sour, turn, turn sour; acetify, acidify, acidulate; ferment; set one's teeth on edge.

394 Odour
N. *odour,* smell, aroma, bouquet, nose; perfume, scent, essence 396 *fragrance;* pong, niff, stink, etc. 397 *stench;* smoke, fume, reek; whiff; odorousness, redolence; tang, scent 548 *trace;* olfaction, sense of smell; olfactories.

Adj. *odorous,* odoriferous, smelling; scented, perfumed 396 *fragrant;* smelly, redolent, reeking; malodorous, whiffy, niffy, ponging 397 *fetid.*

Vb. *smell,* have an odour, smell of, reek of, reek, pong of, pong; exhale; smell a mile off; smell out, scent, get wind of 484 *detect;* get a whiff of, get a niff of; sniff, inhale, nose 352 *breathe.*

395 Odourlessness
N. *odourlessness,* inodorousness, scentlessness; absence of smell, loss of smell; deodorant, deodorizer, incense, mouthwash; deodorization, fumigation, purification.

Adj. *odourless,* inodorous, scentless; unscented, unperfumed; deodorized; deodorizing.

396 Fragrance
N. *fragrance,* sweet smell, perfume; redolence, aroma, bouquet 394 *odour;* flower garden, rose

garden 370 *garden*; buttonhole, nosegay; fumigation; perfumery, perfumer.

scent, perfume, aromatic gum; balm, myrrh,
incense, frankincense, spikenard; spicery 389
condiment; cloves, cachou; musk, civet, ambergris, camphor; sandalwood, patchouli; essential oil, otto, attar; lavender, thyme,
spearmint, chypre, vanilla, citronella oil; fran-
gipani, bergamot, orris root, tonka bean;
honeysuckle, toilet water, eau-de-toilette, lavender water, rose water, attar of roses, eau-de-
cologne; scented soap 843 *cosmetic*; lavender
bag, pomander, potpourri, scent bottle, joss
stick, censer, thurible.

Adj. *fragrant*, redolent, odorous, odoriferous, aromatic, scented, perfumed 376 *pleasant*;
balmy; sweet-scented; musky, spicy, fruity.

397 Stench

N. *stench*, smell, bad smell, bad odour, stink,
pong, niff, reek; fetidity, fetidness, mephitis;
fumes, miasma 336 *gas*; rancidity, putrefaction
51 *decay*; foulness 649 *dirt*; mustiness, fusti-
ness, staleness, fug; fungus, stinkhorn, garlic,
asafoetida; body odour, BO, armpits; bad
breath, halitosis; breaking wind, fart; hydrogen sulphide, ammonia; skunk, polecat; stink
bomb, bad egg; dung 302 *excrement*; latrine,
sewer, septic tank 649 *sink*.

Adj. *stinking*, fetid, foul-smelling, ill-
smelling, reeking, malodorous, smelly, whiffy,
niffy, pongy, humming; rank; high, bad, gone
bad, rancid, putrid; stale, musty, fusty, fuggy,
smoky, stuffy, suffocating; foul, noisome, noxious, sulphurous, ammoniacal, miasmic 653
toxic; acrid 388 *pungent*.

Vb. *stink*, smell, reek, pong, niff, hum; fart,
blow off; have bad breath, have halitosis; have
a bad smell, smell bad 51 *decompose*; stink to
high heaven; smell like a bad egg, stink out.

398 Sound

N. *sound*, audibility, reception 415 *hearing*;
sounding, sonancy; audio, mono, monophonic sound, binaural sound, stereophonic
sound, stereo, quadraphonic sound, surround-
sound system; sound waves, vibrations 417
radiation; sound effect; sound track, voiceover; sonority, sonorousness 404 *resonance*;
noise, loud sound 400 *loudness*; softness 401
faintness; tone, pitch, level, cadence; accent,
intonation, twang, timbre 577 *voice*; tune,
strain 410 *melody*, 412 *music*; types of sound
402 *bang*, 403 *roll*, 404 *resonance*, 405 *non-
resonance*, 406 *hissing*, 407 *stridency*, 408 *cry*,
409 *howling*, 411 *discord*; transmission, telephone, cellular telephone, radio, etc. 531 *telecommunication*; recorded sound, high fidelity,

hi-fi; record-player 414 *music player*; ghetto
blaster, personal stereo; loudspeaker 415 *hearing aid*; decibel, phon, sone; sonic barrier,
sound barrier; noise pollution.

speech sound, phoneme, phone, allophone;
syllable, polysyllable; consonant, fricative, plo-
sive, sibilant; dental, alveolar, labial, nasal,
palatal, guttural, glottal stop; click; aspirate,
surd; semivowel; glide; vowel, diphthong 577
voice; ablaut; umlaut; vocable 559 *word*; International Phonetic Alphabet, IPA 586 *script*.

Adj. *making sound*, sounding, sonic; supersonic; audible, distinct; resounding, sonorous
404 *resonant*; stentorian 400 *loud*; auditory,
acoustic; monaural, monophonic, mono; binaural, stereophonic, stereo, high fidelity, hi-fi;
audio, audiovisual; phonic, phonetic; voiced;
unvoiced, voiceless.

399 Silence

N. *silence*, soundlessness, inaudibility, total
silence, not a sound, not a squeak; stillness,
hush, lull, rest, peace, quiet 266 *state of rest*;
taciturnity, muteness, speechlessness 578 *voicelessness*; solemn silence, dead silence, perfect
silence, uncanny silence, deathly hush;
enforced silence, gagging order.

Adj. *silent*, still, hushed; calm, peaceful,
quiet 266 *at rest*; soft, faint 401 *muted*; noise-
less, soundless, inaudible; soundproof; speechless, taciturn, mute 578 *voiceless*; unspoken;
silent as the grave.

Vb. *be silent*, not open one's mouth, not
say a word, hold one's tongue 582 *be uncommunicative*; not speak 578 *be mute*; make not a
sound, not utter a squeak; become silent,
relapse into silence, pipe down, be quiet, lose
one's voice, fall silent.

silence, still, lull, hush, quiet, quieten, make
silent; soft-pedal; stifle, muffle, gag, stop, stop
someone's mouth, muzzle; drown the noise.

Int. *hush!*, sh!, silence!, quiet!, peace!, soft!,
whist!, hold your tongue!, keep your mouth
shut!, shut up!, keep your trap shut!, dry up!,
pipe down!, cut the cackle!, stow it!, mum's
the word!

400 Loudness

N. *loudness*, audibility; noise; high volume;
broken silence, shattered silence, knock,
knocking; burst of sound, report; sonic boom,
slam, clap, thunderclap, burst, shell burst,
explosion 402 *bang*; siren, alarm, honk, toot
665 *danger signal*; reverberation, boom, rattle
403 *roll*; thunder 176 *storm*; war in heaven,
hissing 406 *hissing*; gunfire, drumfire, artillery,
blitz 712 *bombardment*; shrillness, blast, blare,
bray, fanfare, flourish 407 *stridency*; trumpet

blast, clarion call, view halloo 547 *call*; sonority, clang 404 *resonance*; bells, peal, chimes; crescendo, fortissimo, full blast; clamour, outcry, roaring, shouting, bawling, yelling, screaming, whoop, shout, howl, shriek, scream, roar 408 *cry*, 409 *howling*; cachinnation 835 *laughter*; stertorousness 352 *breathing*; noisiness, din, row; racket, crash, clash, clatter, hubbub, hullabaloo, ballyhoo, song and dance, slamming, banging, stamping, chanting, hooting, uproar, stramash, shemozzle, tumult, bedlam, pandemonium, all hell let loose 61 *turmoil*.

megaphone, amplifier, loud pedal; public address system, loudhailer, loudspeaker, speaker, microphone, mike; ear trumpet 415 *hearing aid*; loud instrument, whistle, siren, ghetto blaster; town crier.

Adj. *loud*, audible; at full volume, at full pitch, at the top of one's voice; noisy, uproarious, rowdy, rumbustious 61 *disorderly*; clamorous, shouting, yelling, whooping, screaming, bellowing; sonorous, booming, full-throated, stentorian, ringing, carrying; deafening, dinning; piercing, ear-splitting, thunderous, rattling, crashing, pealing, shrill 407 *strident*; blaring; crescendo; fortissimo, enough to waken the dead.

Vb. *be loud*, be noisy, etc. (see adj.); break the silence; raise the voice, caterwaul; skirl; scream, whistle 407 *shrill*; shout 408 *cry*; cachinnate 835 *laugh*; clap, stamp, raise the roof, raise the rafters; roar, bellow, howl 409 *howl*; din, sound, boom; rattle, thunder, fulminate, storm, clash; ring, peal, clang, crash; bray, blare; slam 402 *bang*; explode, detonate; knock, hammer, drill; deafen, stun; shatter the eardrums, ring in the ear; waken the dead; raise Cain, kick up a shindy 61 *rampage*.

Adv. *loudly*, distinctly, etc. (see adj.); noisily, aloud, at the top of one's voice; in full cry, full blast; fortissimo, crescendo.

401 Faintness

N. *faintness*, softness, indistinctness, inaudibility; low volume, sound-proofing, noise abatement; thud, thump, bump 405 *nonresonance*; whisper, bated breath; muffled tones 578 *voicelessness*; undertone; murmur, hum, drone 403 *roll*; sigh, sough, moan; scratch, squeak, creak, tick, click; tinkle, clink, chink; buzz, whirr, purr, swish; burble, gurgle; rustle, frou-frou; patter, pitter-patter, pit-a-pat; soft footfall, pad; quiet tone, hushed tones, conversation level.

Adj. *muted*, distant, faint, inaudible, barely audible, sotto voce; half-heard; weak, feeble, unemphatic, unstressed, unaccented; soft, low,

gentle; piano, subdued, hushed, stealthy, whispered; dull; muffled, suppressed, stifled, bated 407 *hoarse*.

Vb. *sound faint*, lower one's voice; whisper, breathe, murmur, mutter; hum; croon, purr; buzz, drone; babble, ripple, lap, gurgle 350 *flow*; tinkle, chime; moan, sigh, sough 352 *blow*; rustle, swish; tremble, melt; float on the air; fade away; squeak, creak; tick, click; clink, chink; thud, thump.

mute, soften, dull, deaden, dampen, softpedal; turn down the volume; hush, muffle, stifle 399 *silence*.

402 Bang: sudden and violent noise

N. *bang*, report, explosion, detonation, blast, blowout, backfire, sonic boom; peal, thunderclap, crash 400 *loudness*; crackle; smack, crack, snap; slap, clap, tap, rap, rat-tat-tat; thump, knock, slam; pop; burst, burst of fire, firing, volley, round, salvo; shot, pistol-shot; cracker, banger, squib.

Vb. *crackle*, sizzle, spit 318 *effervesce*; crack, split; click, rattle; snap, clap, rap, tap, slap, smack.

bang, slam, wham, clash, crash, boom; explode, blast, detonate; pop, go pop; backfire; burst.

403 Roll: repeated and protracted sounds

N. *roll*, rumbling, grumbling; mutter, witter, murmur, background murmur, rhubarb rhubarb, blah blah; din, rattle, racket, clack, clatter, chatter; booming, clang, ping, reverberation 404 *resonance*; chugging; knocking, drumming, tattoo; rub-a-dub, rat-a-tat, pit-a-pat, pitter-patter; peal, carillon; ding-dong, tick-tock, cuckoo 106 *repetition*; trill, tremolo, vibrato 410 *musical note*; quaver; hum, whirr, buzz, drone; ringing, singing; drumfire, barrage, cannonade.

Vb. *roll*, drum, tattoo, beat a tattoo; tap, thrum; chug, rev up, vroom; drum in the ear; boom, roar, din in the ear; grumble, rumble, drone, hum, whirr; trill, chime, peal, toll; tick, beat 317 *oscillate*; rattle, chatter, clatter, clack; reverberate, clang, ping, ring, sing, sing in the ear; quaver, shake, tremble, vibrate; patter 401 *sound faint*.

404 Resonance

N. *resonance*, sonorousness; vibration 317 *oscillation*; reverberation; echo 106 *recurrence*; twanging; ringing, ringing in the ear, tinnitus; singing, bell ringing, tintinnabulation; peal, carillon; sonority, boom; clang, peal, blare, bray; sounding brass, tinkling cymbal; tinkle, jingle; chink, clink; ping, ring, ting-a-ling, chime; low note 410 *musical note*; bass, baritone, basso profondo, bass contralto.

Adj. resonant, vibrant, reverberant, reverberative; carrying 400 *loud*; resounding, etc. (see vb.); booming, echoing, lingering; sonorous; ringing, tintinnabulary; deep-toned; booming, hollow, sepulchral.

Vb. resound, vibrate, reverberate, echo 403 *roll*; whirr, buzz; hum, ring in the ear, sing; ping, ring, ding; jingle, jangle, chink, clink, clank, clunk; ting, tinkle; twang, thrum; gong, chime, tintinnabulate; tootle, toot, trumpet, blare, bray 400 *be loud*.

405 Non-resonance

N. non-resonance, non-vibration, thud, thump, bump; plump, plop, plonk, plunk; cracked bell 411 *discord*; muffled sound, muffled drums 401 *faintness*; mute, damper.

406 Sibilation: hissing sound

N. hissing, sibilation, sibilance, hiss; sibilant; sputter, splutter; splash, rustle, frou-frou 407 *stridency*; squelch, squish; swish, swoosh.

Vb. hiss, sibilate; snort, wheeze, snuffle, whistle; buzz, fizz, fizzle, sizzle, sputter, splutter, spit; splash 318 *effervesce*; swish, swoosh, whizz; squelch, squish, suck; rustle 407 *rasp*.

407 Stridency: harsh sound

N. stridency, stridor, discordance, cacophony 411 *discord*; roughness, raucousness, hoarseness, huskiness, gruffness; guttural; squeakiness, rustiness 333 *friction*; scrape, scratch, jarring, creak, squeak; stridulation; shriek, screech, squawk, yawp, yelp; braying 409 *howling*; high pitch, shrillness, piping, whistling, wolf whistle; bleep; piercing note, sharp note 410 *musical note*; soprano, treble, falsetto, tenor, countertenor; nasality, twang, drone; skirl, brass, blare.

Adj. strident, grating, rusty, creaky, creaking, jarring (see also *hoarse* below); harsh, metallic; high-pitched, acute, shrill, bleeping; piercing, tinny, ear-splitting 400 *loud*; blaring, braying; reedy, squeaky, squawky, screechy, scratchy; cracked; cacophonous 411 *discordant*.

hoarse, husky, throaty, guttural, raucous, rough, gruff; rasping, jarring, scraping, creaking; grunting, growling; hollow, deep, sepulchral; snoring, stertorous.

Vb. rasp, grate, crunch, scrunch, grind, saw, scrape, scratch, squeak; snore, snort; cough, hawk, clear the throat, hem, choke, gasp, sob; bray, croak, caw, screech 409 *howl*; grunt, burr, break (of the voice); jar, grate on the ear, set

the teeth on edge, clash, jangle, twang, clank, clink 411 *discord*.

shrill, bleep; drone, skirl; trumpet, blare 400 *be loud*; whistle, catcall, caterwaul 408 *cry*; scream, squeal, yelp, yawl, screech, squawk; buzz, hum, whine 409 *howl*; go right through one; strain one's vocal chords.

408 Human cry

N. cry, exclamation, ejaculation 577 *voice*; utterances 579 *speech*; talk, chat, chitchat, conversation 584 *conversation*; raised voice, vociferousness, shouting, clamour, hullabaloo 400 *loudness*; yodel, song, chant, chorus 412 *vocal music*; shout, yell, whoop, bawl; howl, scream, shriek, screech 407 *stridency*, 377 *pain*; halloo, hail 547 *call*; view halloo, tallyho, hue and cry 619 *chase*; cheer, hurrah, hip-hip-hurrah, hooray 835 *rejoicing*; laugh, giggle, titter 835 *laughter*; hoot, boo, guffaw 924 *disapprobation*; sob, sigh 836 *lamentation*; caterwaul, yawl, squeal, wail, whine, boohoo; grunt, gasp 352 *breathing*; cheerleader; barker; town crier; animal cry 409 *howling*.

Vb. cry, cry out, exclaim, ejaculate, pipe up 579 *speak*; call, call out, hail 884 *greet*; whoop; hoot, boo, whistle 924 *disapprove*; cheer, hurrah (see also *shout* below); scream, screech, yawl, yowl, howl, groan 377 *feel pain*; snigger, titter, giggle 835 *laugh*; caterwaul, squall, boohoo, whine, whimper, wail, fret, mewl, pule 836 *weep*; yammer, moan, sob, sigh 836 *lament*; mutter, grumble 401 *sound faint*, 829 *be discontented*; gasp, grunt, snort, snore 352 *breathe*; squeak, squawk, yap, bark 409 *howl*.

shout, vociferate, clamour, bawl, yell, yawl, yowl, holler; chant, chorus 413 *sing*; cheer, give three cheers, hurrah, hooray, huzza, exult 835 *rejoice*; hiss, hoot, boo, shout down 924 *disapprove*; roar, bellow 409 *howl*; yell, cry out, sing out, thunder out; raise the voice, give voice, shout at the top of one's voice; strain one's voice, make oneself hoarse.

409 Howling, etc.: animal sounds

N. howling, wailing, yowling, yawling, ululation; barking, baying; buzzing, humming, drone; chattering, twittering, chirping, chirruping; warble, call, cry, note, woodnote, birdsong; squeak, cheep, twitter, tweet-tweet; buzz, hum; croak, caw, coo, hiss, quack, cluck, squawk, screech, yawp; baa, moo, neigh, whinny, heehaw; cock-a-doodle-doo, cuckoo, tu-whit tu-whoo; miaow, mew, bark, yelp, yap, snap, snarl, growl.

Vb. howl, cry, call, give tongue, squawk, screech, yawp, caterwaul, yowl, yawl, wail, ululate; roar, bellow, bell; hum, drone, buzz, spit 406 *hiss*; woof, bark, bay; yelp, yap; snap, snarl, growl, whine; trumpet, bell, troat; bray, neigh, whinny, whicker; bleat, baa; low, moo; miaow, mew, mewl, purr; quack, cackle, gaggle; gobble, gabble, cluck, clack; grunt, gruntle, snort, squeal; pipe, pule; chatter, sing, chirp, chirrup, cheep, peep, tweet, twitter, chuckle, churr, whirr, coo; caw, croak; hoot, honk, boom; grate, squeak 407 *rasp*; warble, carol, whistle 413 *sing*.

410 Melody: concord

N. *melody*, musicalness, melodiousness, tonality, euphony, euphoniousness; harmoniousness, chime, harmony, concord, concert 24 *agreement*; assonance; unison; resolution (of a discord), cadence, perfect cadence; harmonics, harmonization, counterpoint; part, second, chorus; orchestration, instrumentation; tone; phrasing; passage, theme, leitmotiv, coda; movement 412 *musical piece*.

musical note, note, keys, keyboard, manual; black notes, white notes, sharp, flat, double flat, double sharp, accidental, natural, tone, semitone; keynote, fundamental note; tonic, supertonic, mediant, subdominant, dominant, submediant, subtonic, leading note; interval, second, third, fourth, fifth, sixth, seventh, octave, ninth; diatesseron, diapason; gamut, scale (see also *key* below); chord, common chord, triad, tetrachord, arpeggio *or* broken chord; grace note, grace, ornament, crush note, appoggiatura, acciaccatura, mordent, turn, shake, trill, tremolo, vibrato, cadenza; tone, tonality, register, pitch, concert pitch, high pitch, low pitch; high note 407 *stridency*; low note 404 *resonance*; undertone, overtone, harmonic, upper partial; sustained note, monotone, drone.

notation, musical notation, tonic solfa; score; signature, key signature, clef, treble clef, bass clef, tenor clef, alto clef; bar, stave, staff; line, ledger line, space, brace; rest, pause, interval; breve, semibreve, minim, crotchet, quaver, semiquaver, demisemiquaver, hemi-demisemiquaver.

tempo, time, beat; rhythm 593 *prosody*; measure, timing; syncopation; upbeat, downbeat; suspension, long note, short note, suspended note, prolonged note; tempo rubato; rallentando, andante, adagio 412 *adagio*; metronome.

key, signature, clef, modulation, transposition, major key, minor key; scale, gamut, major scale, minor scale, diatonic scale, chromatic scale, harmonic scale, melodic scale, enharmonic scale, twelve-tone scale; series,

tone row; mode, Lydian mode, Phrygian mode, Dorian mode, mixolydian; Indian mode, raga.

Adj. *melodious*, melodic, musical, lyrical, lilting, tuneful, catchy, tripping; dulcet, mellifluous, sweet-sounding; chiming; silver-toned; golden-toned; euphonious, euphonic.

harmonious, harmonizing, consonant 24 *agreeing*; in pitch; in chorus; assonant, rhyming, matching 18 *similar*; symphonic, symphonious.

Vb. *harmonize*, blend 24 *accord*; chorus 413 *sing*; attune, tune, tune up, pitch, string 24 *adjust*; be in key, be in unison, be on the beat; compose, put to music, set to music, score, symphonize, orchestrate 413 *compose music*; modulate, transpose.

411 Discord

N. *discord*, discordance, dissonance, disharmony, jangle 25 *disagreement*; atonality, twelve-tone scale; imperfect cadence; preparation (of a discord); harshness, hoarseness, jarring, cacophony; Babel, cat's concert, caterwauling, yowling 400 *loudness*; row, din, noise, pandemonium, bedlam, tumult, racket 61 *turmoil*; atmospherics, wow.

Adj. *discordant*, dissonant, jangling, discording 25 *disagreeing*; conflicting 14 *non-identical*; jarring, grating, scraping, rasping, harsh, raucous, cacophonous 407 *strident*; inharmonious; unmelodious, unmusical; untuned, cracked; off pitch, off key, out of tune, sharp, flat; atonal, toneless, tuneless, droning, singsong.

Vb. *discord*, lack harmony 25 *disagree*; jangle, jar, grate, clash, crash; saw, scrape 407 *rasp*; be harsh, be out of tune, be off key; play sharp, play flat; thrum, drone, whine; prepare a discord.

412 Music

N. *music*, harmony 410 *melody*; musicianship 413 *musical skill*; minstrelsy, music-making, playing; strumming, thrumming; waltz-time; vamping, improvisation; jam session; orchestration, instrumentation, composing, composition; instrumental music, pipe music, military music; counterpoint, contrapuntal music; classical music, chamber music, organ music, choral music, operatic music, ballet music, sacred music; descriptive music, programme music; live music, recorded music, canned music, piped music, musical wallpaper, wall-to-wall music, Muzak (tdmk), ambient music; disco music, dance music; hot music, syncopation, jazz, progressive jazz, modern jazz, cool jazz, acid jazz, blue note, blues, mainstream jazz, traditional jazz, trad, Dixieland, ragtime, swing, swingbeat, doowop, bebop, bop, boogie-woogie; light music, popular music, pop music, pop, indie pop, Britpop, bhangra *or* bangra, house, acid house, gabba, garage, electronic music, techno, trance, salsa, skiffle, jive, rock 'n' roll, rock music, soft rock, glam rock, progressive rock *or* prog rock, hard rock, heavy metal, black metal, nu-metal, drum 'n' base, grunge, goth, jungle, jazz-funk, electro, hip-hop, new wave, mod, punk, rap, gangsta; ska, reggae; soul music, soul, northern soul; remixing, sampling, scratching; musique concrète; New Age music; rhythm and blues, country and western, blue grass, Western swing, folk, folk music, world music, roots music; pipe music, pibroch; sheet music, the music, score, full score; concert, orchestral concert, choral concert, promenade concert, prom; singsong; music festival, eisteddfod, feis, mod; conservatoire; Tin Pan Alley, Nashville.

tune, melody, strain; theme song, signature tune; descant; reprise, refrain; melodic line; air, popular air, aria, solo; peal, chime, carillon; phrase, passage, measure.

musical piece, piece, composition, opus, work; tape, cassette, recording 414 *music player*; orchestration, instrumentation; arrangement, adaptation, setting, transcription; accompaniment, obbligato; voluntary, prelude, overture, intermezzo, finale; incidental music, background music, wallpaper music, wall-to-wall music (see also *music* above); romance, rhapsody, extravaganza, impromptu, fantasia, caprice, divertissement, variations, raga; medley, potpourri; étude, study; suite, fugue, canon, toccata; sonata, sonatina, concerto, symphony, sinfonietta; symphonic poem, tone poem; pastorale, scherzo, rondo, gigue, jig, reel, strathspey; gavotte, minuet, tarantella, mazurka, passacaglia, polonaise, polka, waltz 837 *dance*; march, grand march, bridal march, wedding march, dead march, funeral march, dirge, pibroch; nocturne, serenade, berceuse, lullaby; introductory phrase, anacrusis; statement, exposition, development, recapitulation, variation; theme, motive, leitmotiv; movement; passage, phrase; chord, arpeggio, etc. 410 *musical note*; cadenza, coda.

vocal music, singing, vocalism, lyricism; vocalization; part; opera, operetta, light opera, comic opera, musical comedy, musical 594 *stage play*; choir-singing, oratorio, cantata, chorale; hymn-singing, psalmody, hymnology; descant, chant, plain chant, Gregorian chant, Ambrosian chant, plainsong; cantus, cantus firmus, recitative; bel canto, coloratura, bra-

vura; solfège, solfa; introit, anthem, canticle, psalm 981 *hymn*; song, theme song; lay, roundelay, carol, lyric, lilt, canzonet, cavatina, lied, lieder, ballad; folk song, popular *or* pop song, rap, gangsta, etc. (see also *music* above); top twenty, hit parade, the charts; karaoke; ditty, shanty, calypso; spiritual, blues; part song, glee, madrigal, round, catch, canon; chorus, refrain, burden; choral hymn, antiphony, dithyramb; boat song, barcarole; lullaby, cradle song, berceuse; serenade, aubade; bridal hymn, wedding hymn, epithalamium, prothalamium; love song, amorous ditty; song, birdsong, bird call, dawn chorus; requiem, dirge, threnody, coronach 836 *lament*; musical declamation, recitative; lyrics, libretto, explicit lyrics; songbook, hymnbook, psalter.

Adj. *musical* 410 *melodious*; philharmonic, symphonic; melodic; vocal, hummable; operatic, recitative; lyric; choral; hymnal, psalmodic; harmonized 410 *harmonious*; contrapuntal; orchestrated, scored; set to music, arranged; instrumental, orchestral, for strings; syncopated; doo-wop.

Adv. *adagio*, lento, largo, larghetto, andante, andantino, maestoso, moderato; allegro, allegretto; spiritoso, vivace, accelerando, presto, prestissimo; piano, mezzo-piano, pianissimo, forte, mezzo-forte, fortissimo, sforzando, con brio, capriccioso, scherzando; glissando, legato, sostenuto; staccato; crescendo, diminuendo, rallentando; affettuoso, cantabile, parlante; tremolo, pizzicato, vibrato; rubato; da capo.

413 Musician

N. *musician*, artiste, virtuoso, soloist; bravura player 696 *proficient person*; player, performer, concert artist; bard, minstrel, troubadour, trovatore, minnesinger; street musician, busker; composer, symphonist, contrapuntist; scorer, arranger, harmonist; syncopator, jazzman; librettist, lyricist, tunesmith, lieder-writer, hymnwriter, hymnographer, psalmist; musical director, music teacher, music master, kapellmeister, master of the music, bandmaster, conductor, orchestra player, bandsman (see also *orchestra* below); musicologist, musicotherapist, music critic, concertgoer, operagoer 504 *enthusiast*.

instrumentalist, pianist, accompanist; organist, cembalist, harpsichordist, accordionist, concertina player, harmonica player; violinist, fiddler; violist, cellist; harpist, lyre player, lute player, lutanist, sitarist, guitarist, bassist, mandolinist, banjoist; strummer, thrummer; piper, fifer, piccolo player, flautist *or* flutist, clarinettist, oboist, bassoonist; saxophonist, horn player, trumpeter, bugler; cornetist; bell ringer, carilloneur, campanologist;

drummer, drummer boy, drum major; percussionist, timpanist or tympanist; organgrinder, hurdy-gurdy man.

orchestra, symphony orchestra, chamber orchestra, sinfonietta, quartet, quintet; ensemble, wind ensemble; strings, brass, woodwind, percussion; wind, drums; band, brass band, etc. 74 *band*; conductor, maestro, bandmaster; bandleader, leader, first violin.

vocalist, singer, songster, caroller; chanteuse, songstress; troubadour, madrigal singer, minstrel, busker; ballad singer, folk singer, pop singer; crooner, jazz singer, blues singer; opera singer, prima donna, diva; castrato, treble, soprano, mezzo-soprano, contralto, alto, tenor, counter-tenor, baritone, bass baritone, bass, basso, basso profondo.

choir, chorus, waits, wassailers, carol singers, glee club, barbershop quartet; massed choirs, eisteddfod, mod; chorister, choirboy or -girl; precentor, cantor, choirmaster, choirleader.

Vb. *compose music*, compose; set to music, score, arrange, transpose, orchestrate, harmonize, improvise, extemporize.

play music, play, perform, execute, render, interpret; pick out a tune; conduct, wield the baton, beat time, syncopate; play the piano, accompany; pedal, vamp, strum; tickle the ivories; harp, pluck, pick, strike the lyre, pluck the guitar, bottleneck; thrum, twang; fiddle, bow, scrape, saw; play the concertina, squeeze the box, grind the organ; play the harmonica; wind, wind the horn, blow, bugle, blow the bugle, sound the horn, sound, trumpet, sound the trumpet, toot, tootle; pipe, flute, whistle; clash the cymbals; drum, tattoo, beat, tap, ruffle, beat the drum 403 *roll*; ring, peal the bells, ring a change; toll, knell; tune, string, set to concert pitch; practise, do scales, improvise, jam, extemporize, play a voluntary, prelude; strike up.

sing, chant, intone, descant; warble, carol, lilt, trill, croon, hum, whistle, yodel; belt out; harmonize; chorus; serenade; chirp, chirrup, twitter, pipe 409 *howl*; purr 401 *sound faint*.

414 Musical instruments

N. *musical instrument*, band, concert 413 *orchestra*; strings, brass, wind, woodwind, percussion; sounding board, diaphragm, sound box; synthesizer.

stringed instrument, harp, Aeolian harp, Celtic harp, clarsach; lyre, lute, sitar; theorbo; cithara, cithern, zither, gittern, autoharp, guitar, acoustic guitar, semi-acoustic guitar, electric guitar, bass guitar, rhythm guitar, lead guitar; mandolin, ukulele, banjo, balalaika, bouzouki; psaltery, vina; neck, bridge, fingerboard, fret, string, action, body, sounding board, plectrum, capo or capodastro or capotasto, tremolo; air guitar.

violin, Amati, Cremona, Stradivarius, viol, fiddle, kit, crowd or crwth, rebec; viola or tenor violin, viola d'amore, viola da gamba or bass viol, cello or violoncello, double bass or contrabasso; musical saw; bow, fiddlestick; string, catgut; bridge; resin.

piano, pianoforte, grand piano, concert grand, baby grand; upright piano, cottage piano; virginals, dulcimer, harpsichord, cembalo, spinet, clavichord, celesta; piano-organ, player piano, Pianola (tdmk); clavier, keyboard, manual, keys, ivories; loud pedal, soft pedal, celeste, damper.

organ, pipe organ, church organ, Hammond organ, electric or electronic organ, steam organ, calliope; reed organ, harmonium, American organ, melodeon; mouth organ, harmonica; kazoo, comb and paper; accordion, piano accordion, concertina; barrel organ, hurdy-gurdy; great organ, swell organ, choir organ; organ pipe, flue pipe, organ stop, flue stop; manual, keyboard.

flute, fife, piccolo, flageolet, cornetto, recorder, fipple flute; woodwind, reed instrument, clarinet, bass clarinet, basset horn; saxophone, sax, tenor sax; shawm, hautboy, oboe, tenor oboe, cor Anglais; bassoon, double bassoon, contrabassoon; ocarina; pipe, oaten pipe, reed, straw; pipes, bagpipes, small pipes, Northumbrian or Northumberland pipes, uillean or uilleann pipes or union pipes or Irish pipes, musette, chanter, drones; pan pipes, Pandean pipes, syrinx; nose flute; whistle, penny whistle, tin whistle; pitch-pipe; bazooka; mouthpiece, embouchure.

horn, brass; bugle horn, post horn, hunting horn; bugle, trumpet, clarion; alpenhorn, French horn, flugelhorn, saxhorn, althorn, helicon horn, bass horn, sousaphone; euphonium, ophicleide, serpent, bombardon; cornet, trombone, sackbut, tuba, saxtuba, bass tuba; conch, shell.

gong, bell, tintinnabulum; treble bell, tenor bell; church bell, Angelus bell, Bow Bells; Big Ben; alarm bell, tocsin 665 *danger signal*; tintinnabulation, peal, carillon, chimes, bells; bones, rattle, clappers, castanets, maracas, rain stick; cymbals; xylophone, marimba; vibraphone, vibes; musical glasses; tubular bell, glockenspiel; triangle; tuning fork; Jew's harp; sounding board; percussion instrument.

drum, big drum, bass drum, tenor drum, side drum, snare drum, kettle drum, timpani or tympani, timps, steel drum; war drum, tomtom, bongo; tabor, tabla; tambourine, bodhran; percussion instrument.

music player, record player, record deck, gramophone, phonograph, radiogram; tape recorder, cassette recorder, high-fidelity system, hi-fi, stereo set, stereo system, music centre, stack system, stereo tower, hi-fi tower; surround-sound system; personal stereo, personal hi-fi, personal headset, Walkman (tdmk), ghetto blaster, compact disc player, CD player, digital music player, MP3 player; recording, tape recording, tape, cassette, playback; gramophone record, disc, platter, long-playing record, LP, EP, 33, 45, 78; album, single, A-side, B-side, flip side, track, cut; compact disc, CD, laser disc, minidisc; jukebox; head, needle, stylus, pickup, cartridge; deck, turntable; amplifier, speaker, tweeter, woofer. (See also 549 *recording instrument*.)

415 Hearing

N. *hearing*, audition; sense of hearing, acute hearing; good ear, sharp ear, ear for music; audibility, good reception; earshot, range, reach.

listening, hearkening 455 *attention*; aural examination 459 *enquiry*; listening-in; lip-reading 520 *interpretation*; eavesdropping, wire-tapping, bugging 523 *latency*; sound recording 548 *record*; audition, voice testing 461 *experiment*; interview, audience, hearing 584 *conference*; legal hearing 959 *legal trial*.

listener, hearer, audience, bums on seats 441 *spectator*; auditorium, stalls, pit, gallery, the gods; radio listener, radio ham, CB user; hi-fi enthusiast, audiophile; disciple, lecture-goer 538 *learner*; monitor, auditor, examiner 459 *questioner*; eavesdropper, listener-in, little pitcher.

ear, lug, lobe, earhole, lughole; cauliflower ear; external ear, middle ear, internal ear; aural cavity, cochlea, eardrum, tympanum; auditory canal, labyrinth; aurist, audiologist, otologist, otolaryngologist, otorhinolaryngologist, ENT specialist, ear, nose and throat specialist; otology, etc.; Ménière's disease.

hearing aid, deaf-aid, ear trumpet; stethoscope, otoscope, auriscope; loudspeaker, loudhailer, Tannoy (tdmk), public address system 528 *publication*; microphone, mike, amplifier 400 *megaphone*; speaking tube; telephone, phone, blower, cellular telephone, car phone, mobile phone, etc. 531 *telecommunication*; receiver, handset, earpiece, extension, headphones, headset, earphones; entryphone; walkie-talkie 531 *telecommunication*; sound recorder, asdic, sonar, Dictaphone (tdmk), Dictograph (tdmk) 549 *recording instrument*; radiogram 414 *music player*, 531 *broadcasting*.

Adj. *auditory*, hearing, auricular, aural; audiovisual 398 *making sound*; otic, otological, stethoscopic; auditive, acoustic, audile, within earshot, within hearing distance, audible.

Vb. *hear*, catch; list, listen, lip-read 520 *interpret*; listen in, switch on, tune in, tune to; lift the receiver, answer the phone; overhear, eavesdrop, listen at keyholes, keep one's ears open; intercept, bug, tap; hearken, lend an ear, give audience, interview, grant an interview 459 *interrogate*; hear confession 526 *confess*; be all ears, hang on the lips of, lap up 455 *be attentive*; strain one's ears, prick up one's ears; hear it said, hear it on *or* through the grapevine, come to one's ears 524 *be informed*.

416 Deafness

N. *deafness*, defective hearing, imperfect hearing, hardness of hearing; deaf-mutism; deaf-and-dumb speech, sign language, dactylogy; deaf-and-dumb person, deaf-mute; inaudibility 399 *silence*; ringing in the ear, tinnitus.

Adj. *deaf*, hard of hearing, dull of hearing, hearing-impaired, profoundly deaf, stone-deaf, deaf as a post, deaf and dumb, deaf-mute; deafened, unable to hear, with ears bunged up; deaf to, not listening 456 *inattentive*; tone-deaf; inaudible, out of earshot, out of hearing 399 *silent*.

Vb. *be deaf*, hear nothing, fail to catch; not listen, shut *or* close one's ears, plug one's ears 458 *disregard*; turn a deaf ear to 760 *refuse*; have hearing difficulties, have impaired hearing, be hard of hearing, use a hearing aid; lip-read, use lip-reading 520 *translate*; talk with one's fingers, use sign language.

deafen, make deaf, split the eardrum, drown one's voice 400 *be loud*.

417 Light

N. *light*, daylight, light of day, noon, high noon, broad daylight 128 *morning*; sunbeam, sunlight, sun 420 *light*; starlight, moonlight, moonshine, half-light, twilight, gloaming 419 *dimness*; artificial light, electric light, gaslight, candlelight, firelight 420 *lighting*; floodlight, son et lumière; illumination, irradiation, splendour, resplendence, effulgence, refulgence, intensity, brightness, vividness, brilliance; luminousness, luminosity, luminance, candle power, magnitude; incandescence, radiance; sheen, shine, gloss, polish, lustre (see also *reflection* below); blaze, blaze of light; glare, dazzle; flare, flame 379 *fire*; halo, nimbus, aureole; spectrum, iridescence, rainbow 437 *variegation*.

flash, lightning, forked lightning, sheet lightning, etc. 420 *light*; beam, stream, shaft, ray; streak, meteor flash; scintillation, sparkle, spark; glint, glitter, glisten, play of light; blink, twinkle, twinkling, flicker, flickering, glimmer, gleam, shimmer, shimmering; spangle, tinsel; strobe light, searchlight, torchlight 420 *lamp*; firefly.

glow, flush, afterglow, dawn, rosy-fingered dawn, sunset; lambent light; aurora, aurora borealis, aurora australis; northern lights; zodiacal light 321 *heavens*; radiance, incandescence 379 *heat*; luminescence, fluorescence, phosphorescence, thermoluminescence; will-o'-the-wisp.

radiation, emission, absorption; radioactivity, irradiation 160 *nuclear physics*; radioisotope; Geiger counter; fallout, nuclear fallout, mushroom cloud 659 *poison*; radiation belt, Van Allen layer 340 *atmosphere*; radio wave, frequency wave; long wave, short wave, medium wave 317 *oscillation*; wavelength, waveband; high frequency, VHF, UHF; interference, static 160 *electricity*; electromagnetic radiation, microwave; infrared radiation, radiant heat *or* energy; ultraviolet radiation; X-ray, gamma ray, cosmic radiation; magnetic storm; photon; photoelectric cell; curie, millicurie, roentgen, rem, rad; half-life, radiology, industrial radiology, medical radiology, diagnostic radiology, radiotherapy; food irradiation.

reflection, refraction; diffraction, dispersion; scattering, interference, polarization; polish, gloss, sheen, shine, glisten, gleam, lustre; glare, dazzle, blink.

Adj. *luminous*, lucid; light, lit, well-lit, floodlit, bright, gay, shining, fulgent, resplendent, splendid, brilliant, flamboyant, vivid; colourful; radiant, effulgent, refulgent; dazzling, blinding, glaring, lurid, garish; incandescent, flaring, flaming, aflame, aglow, afire, ablaze 379 *fiery*; glowing, blushing, auroral 431 *red*; luminescent, fluorescent, phosphorescent; soft, lambent, beaming; glittery, flashing, glinting, etc. (see vb.); scintillating, sparkling; lustrous, chatoyant, shimmering, shiny, sheeny, glossy, polished; reflecting; refractive; optical, photosensitive.

undimmed, clear, bright, fair; cloudless, unclouded, sunny, sunshiny; moonlit, starlit, starry; burnished, polished, glassy, gleaming; lucid, pellucid.

Vb. *shine*, burn, blaze, flame, flare 379 *be hot*; glow, incandesce, luminesce, phosphoresce; glare, dazzle, bedazzle, blind; dance; flash, glisten, glister, blink; glimmer, flicker, twinkle; glitter, shimmer, glance; scintillate, sparkle, spark; come up, gleam, glint.

radiate, beam, shoot, send out *or* shoot out

rays 300 *emit*; reflect, refract; be radioactive, bombard; X-ray.

make bright, lighten, dawn, rise, wax (moon); clear, clear up, lift, brighten; light, ignite 381 *kindle*; light up; shed lustre, throw light on; shine upon, flood with light, irradiate, illuminate, illume; transilluminate; burnish, rub up 648 *clean*.

418 Darkness

N. *darkness*, dark; black 428 *blackness*; night, dark night, night-time, nightfall; dead of night, witching time 129 *midnight*; pitch darkness; Stygian gloom; murk, murkiness, gloom, dusk, gloaming, twilight, half-dark, semi-darkness; shadiness, shadows 419 *dimness*; shade, shadow; penumbra; silhouette, negative, radiograph; darkroom.

darkening, obfuscation 419 *dimness*; blackout; fadeout, eclipse, total eclipse 446 *disappearance*; lights out; sunset, sundown 129 *evening*; blackening, shading; chiaroscuro; dark lantern; dimmer, dip switch.

Adj. *dark*, sombre, dark-coloured, swarthy, dusky 428 *black*; poorly lit, obscure, pitch-dark, sooty, inky, jet-black, black as night *or* as ink *or* as hell *or* as pitch *or* as the ace of spades; murky; funereal, gloomy, sombre; louring; shady 419 *shadowy*; darkened; nocturnal; hidden, secret 523 *occult*.

unlit, unlighted, unilluminated; sunless, moonless, starless; eclipsed; overcast; hazy, cloudy 423 *opaque*; extinguished; dimmed, blacked out; obscured.

Vb. *be dark*, grow dark, get dark, lour; cloud over, look black.

darken, black out; lower the light, dim the light, put out the light, switch off the light, eclipse 226 *cover*; curtain, shutter, veil 421 *screen*; obscure, obfuscate; cloud, dim, tone down 419 *dim*; overcast, overshadow, spread gloom; cast a shadow; silhouette 551 *represent*; shade, underexpose 428 *blacken*.

419 Dimness

N. *dimness*, indistinctness, vagueness, fuzziness, blur, lack of definition, soft focus; loom; faintness, paleness 426 *colourlessness*; grey 429 *greyness*; dullness, lacklustre; matt finish; leaden skies; cloudiness, smokiness, poor visibility, impaired visibility, white-out 423 *opacity*; mistiness, fogginess; murk, gloom 418 *darkness*; fog, mist, haar 355 *cloud*; shadowiness, shadow, shade.

half-light, semidarkness, half-dark, bad light; waning light, gloaming 129 *evening*; twilight, dusk; daybreak, break of day, penumbra, half-shadow, partial eclipse.

Adj. *dim*, darkish, sombre, dusky, dusk, twilight, wan, dun, grey, pale 426 *colourless*; faint, faded, waning; imperceptible, indistinct, blurred, bleary; dull, lustreless, lacklustre, leaden; flat, matt; filmy, hazy, fuzzy, foggy, fogbound, misty, nebulous 355 *cloudy*; thick, smoky, sooty, muddy 423 *opaque*; dingy, grimy, rusty, rusted, mildewed, unpolished, unburnished 649 *dirty*.

shadowy, shady, shaded, overshadowed, overcast; vague, indistinct, undefined, ill-defined, obscure, confused, fuzzy, blurry; deceptive; half-glimpsed, half-hidden 444 *invisible*; half-lit 418 *unlit*; dreamlike, ghostly 4 *lacking substance*; coming and going.

Vb. *be dim*, be faint, etc. (see adj.); be indistinct; lose definition, fade, wane, grow pale 426 *lose colour*; lour; glimmer, flicker, gutter.

dim, dip; bedim; lower *or* turn down the lights, fade out; obscure, blur; smear, besmirch, sully; rust, mildew, muddy, dirty 649 *make unclean*; fog, mist; becloud; overcast; shade, shadow, veil 226 *cover*.

420 Source of light

N. *light*, naked light, flame, luminary 379 *fire*; flare; sun; moon; star, starlight 321 *star*; evening star, Hesperus, Vesper, Venus; morning star, Lucifer; shooting star, fireball 321 *meteor*; galaxy, Milky Way, northern lights 321 *heavens*; lightning, bolt of lightning, sheet lightning, forked lightning, ball lightning, summer lightning, lightning flash, levin; scintilla, spark, sparkle 417 *flash*.

torch, brand; torchlight, flambeau, match 385 *lighter*; candle, bougie, tallow candle, wax candle; flower candle, cake candle, Christmas candle; taper; wax taper; spill, wick, dip, rushlight, nightlight, naked light, flare, gas jet, burner, Bunsen burner.

lamp, lamplight; lantern; safety lamp, Davy lamp, acetylene lamp; oil lamp, hurricane lamp, paraffin lamp, spirit lamp; gas lamp, Calor gas (tdmk) lamp, gas mantle; electric lamp, flash gun, torch, pocket torch, penlight, flashlight, Aldis lamp, searchlight, arc light, floodlight; headlamp, headlight, side light; foglamp, foglight; tail light, brake light, reflector; bulb, electric bulb, light bulb, flashbulb, photoflood; strobe light, stroboscope, strobe; vapour light, neon light, strip light, fluorescent light; street light, mercury vapour lamp, sodium lamp; Chinese lantern, fairy lights, Christmas tree lights; magic lantern, projector; light fitting, chandelier, candelabra; standard lamp, table lamp, lava lamp, desk lamp, reading lamp, Anglepoise (tdmk) lamp; uplighter, downlighter; sun lamp, sunray lamp; lamppost; candle holder, candlestick, sconce; Aladdin's lamp.

lighting, illumination, irradiation 417 *light*; artificial lighting, street lighting; indirect lighting; gas lighting, electric lighting, neon lighting, fluorescent lighting; floodlighting, son et lumière; limelight, spotlight, footlights, houselights.

signal light, warning light 665 *danger signal*; traffic light, red light, green light, amber light; trafficator, indicator; Very light, Bengal light, rocket, star shell, flare, parachute flare; flare path, beacon, beacon fire, balefire 547 *signal*; lighthouse, lightship.

421 Screen

N. *screen*, shield 660 *protection*; shelter; bower 194 *arbour*; shady nook 418 *darkness*; sunshade, parasol; sun hat, solar topee 226 *shade*; awning 226 *canopy*; sunscreen, visor; lampshade; eyeshade, blinkers; eyelid, eyelashes 438 *eye*; dark glasses, tinted glasses, sun glasses, shades 442 *spectacles*; smoked glass, frosted glass, opaque glass, polarized glass 424 *semitransparency*; stained glass 437 *variegation*; double glazing, soundproofing, partition, wall, hedge 235 *fence*; filter 57 *exclusion*; mask 527 *disguise*; hood, veil, mantle 228 *cloak*; cloud; mist; smokescreen.

curtain 226 *shade*; window curtain, net curtain, bead curtain; drapes, shade, blind, sunblind; persienne, jalousie, venetian blind, roller blind, festoon blind; shutter.

Vb. *screen*, shield, shelter 660 *safeguard*; protect 713 *defend*; ward off, fend off, keep at bay; keep off, keep out, filter out 57 *exclude*; cover up, veil, hood 226 *cover*; mask, hide, shroud 525 *conceal*; intercept 702 *obstruct*; blinker, blindfold 439 *blind*; shade, shadow, darken; curtain, curtain off, canopy, draw the curtains, pull down the blind; put up the shutters, close the shutters 264 *close*; cloud, fog.

422 Transparency

N. *transparency*, transmission of light; transparence, translucence; thinness; lucidity, pellucidity, limpidity; clearness, clarity; glassiness; water, ice, crystal, Perspex (tdmk), cellophane, shrink-wrapping, bubble pack, blister pack, glass, plate glass; magnifying glass, lens, eyepiece 442 *spectacles*; pane, window pane; sheer silk, gossamer, gauze, lace, chiffon 4 *thing that lacks substance*.

Adj. *transparent*, diaphanous, revealing, sheer, see-through; thin, fine, filmy, gauzy, pellucid, translucent; lucent 424 *semitransparent*; liquid, limpid; crystal, crystalline, glassy; clear, lucid; crystal-clear.

423 Opacity

N. *opacity*, opaqueness; thickness, solidity 324 *density*; filminess, frost; turbidity, muddiness, dirtiness 649 *dirt*; fog, mist, haar, dense fog, smog, pea-souper 355 *cloud*; film, scale 421 *screen*; smoke-screen.

Adj. opaque, non-transparent, thick, impervious to light, blank, windowless; not clean, unclarified, cloudy, milky, filmy, turbid, muddy, muddied; foggy, hazy, misty, murky, smoky, sooty 419 *dim*; frosted, misted, clouded.

424 Semitransparency

N. semitransparency, milkiness; pearliness, opalescence; smoked glass, ground glass, frosted glass; tinted spectacles, dark glasses; gauze, muslin, net; pearl, opal 437 *variegation*.

Adj. semitransparent, gauzy, filmy; translucent, opalescent; milky, pearly; frosted; smoked 419 *dim*, 355 *cloudy*.

425 Colour

N. colour, primary colour, three primaries, secondary colour; chromatism, chromatic aberration; chromatic scale; prism, spectrum, rainbow 437 *variegation*; colour chart, colour circle; colour scheme, palette; coloration 553 *painting*; colour photography, Technicolor (tdmk); heraldic colour, tincture, chromatics; spectroscope, prism.

hue, chromaticity, tone; brilliance, intensity, warmth, loudness; softness, deadness, dullness; coloration, livery; pigmentation, colouring, complexion; flush, blush, glow; rosy cheek, ruddiness 431 *redness*; sickly hue, pallor 426 *colourlessness*; discoloration; tint, shade, nuance, cast, dye; tinge, patina; half-tone, half-light, mezzotint.

pigment, colouring matter, rouge, blusher, warpaint 843 *cosmetic*; dyestuff, dye, fast dye; natural dye, vegetable dye, madder, cochineal 431 *red pigment*; indigo 436 *purpleness*; woad 435 *blueness*; artificial dye, synthetic dye, aniline dye; stain, fixative, mordant; wash, colourwash, whitewash, distemper; paint, emulsion paint, gloss paint; matt *or* matte *or* mat, satin, eggshell; top coat, undercoat, primer; oil paints, acrylic paints, watercolours.

Adj. florid, colourful, high-coloured; overstated; ruddy 431 *red*; intense, deep, strong, emphatic; unfaded, vivid, brilliant 417 *luminous*; warm, glowing, rich, painted, gay; bright; gaudy, garish, showy, flashy; glaring, flaring, flaunting, spectacular; harsh, stark, raw, crude; lurid, loud, screaming, shrieking; clashing, discordant 25 *disagreeing*.

soft-hued, soft, quiet, under-stated, tender, delicate, refined, discreet; pearly, creamy 427 *whitish*; light, pale, pastel, muted; simple; faded; weathered, mellow; harmonious 24 *agreeing*.

Vb. colour, colorize, colour in, block in, crayon, daub 553 *paint*; rouge 431 *redden*, 843 *primp*; pigment, tattoo; dye, tie-dye, dip, imbue; tint, touch up; shade; tincture, tinge; wash, colourwash, distemper, lacquer 226 *coat*; stain, run, discolour; come off (e.g. on one's fingers); tan, weather, mellow; illuminate, emblazon; whitewash; enamel 437 *variegate*.

426 Absence of colour

N. colourlessness, achromatism, achromaticity; discoloration, etiolation, weathering, fading, bleaching 427 *whiteness*; overexposure 551 *photography*; pallor, pallidity, paleness; lightness, faintness, etc. (see adj.); absence of colour, anaemia, bloodlessness; pigment deficiency, albinism, albinoism; neutral tint; monochrome; black and white; albino; blond(e), ash-blond(e), artificial blond(e), platinum blond(e), peroxide blond(e), bottle blond(e).

bleacher, decolorant, peroxide, bleaching powder, bleach, lime.

Adj. colourless, neutral; uncoloured, achromatic; bleached, etiolated, overexposed; weathered, faint, faded, fading; unpigmented, albino, light-skinned, fair-skinned, fair, blond(e) 427 *whitish*, 433 *yellow*; lustreless, mousy; bloodless, anaemic; without colour, drained of colour, washed out, wishy-washy, peaky; pale, pallid 427 *white*; ashen, livid, whey-faced; pasty, doughy, sallow, sickly 651 *unhealthy*; dingy, dull 429 *grey*; lacklustre; wan 419 *dim*; deathly, deathly pale, white as a sheet, ghostlike.

Vb. lose colour 419 *be dim*; pale, fade, bleach, blanch, turn pale, change countenance, go as white as a sheet 427 *whiten*; run.

427 Whiteness

N. whiteness, etiolation; albinism *or* albinoism 426 *colourlessness*; whitishness, creaminess, off-whiteness, pearliness; hoariness; white light 417 *light*; white heat 379 *heat*; white, Caucasian, paleface; albino.

white thing, alabaster, marble; hoar frost, snow, new-fallen snow; chalk, paper, milk, flour, salt, ivory, lily, swan; albino; silver, pewter, platinum; pearl, teeth.

Adj. white, pure; light, bright 417 *luminous*; silvery, silver, alabaster, marble; chalky, snowy, snow-capped, snow-covered; hoary, frosty, frosted; foaming, spumy, foam-flecked; soapy, lathery; white hot 379 *hot*; white as a sheet *or* as the driven snow; pure white, lily-white, milk-white, snow-white; white-skinned, Caucasian; whitened, whitewashed, bleached 648 *clean*.

whitish, pearly, milky, creamy 424 *semitransparent*; ivory, waxen, sallow, pale 426 *colourless*; off-white, oyster-white, mushroom, magnolia; ecru, beige 430 *brown*; hoary, grizzled 429 *grey*; pepper-and-salt 437 *mottled*; blond(e), fair, Nordic; ash-blond(e), platinum blonde, etc. 426 *colourlessness*; fair-haired, golden-haired, flaxen-haired, tow-headed.

Vb. *whiten*, white, blanco, pipeclay, whitewash, wash 648 *clean*; blanch, bleach; pale, fade; frost, silver, grizzle.

428 Blackness

N. *blackness* 418 *darkness*; inkiness, lividity, black, sable; melanism, swarthiness, duskiness, pigmentation, dark colouring, colour; depth, deep tone; black and white, monochrome; blackening, darkening 418 *obscuration*; black, Negro, Negress; coloured; African-American, Afro-American, African Caribbean, Afro-Caribbean, West Indian; person of colour.

black thing, coal, charcoal, soot, pitch, tar; ebony, jet, ink, smut; blacklead; burnt cork; melanin; sable; bruise, black eye; blackberry, sloe; crow, raven, blackbird; black clothes, mourning, widow's weeds.

Adj. *black*, sable, ebony; inky, black as thunder 418 *dark*; sooty, smoky, smudgy, smutty 649 *dirty*; blackened, singed, charred; black-haired, raven-haired, dark-headed; black-eyed, sloe-eyed; dark, brunette; black-skinned, Negro, Negroid, of colour, African-American, Afro-American, African Caribbean, Afro-Caribbean, West Indian; pigmented, coloured; sombre, gloomy, mourning 364 *funereal*; coal-black, jet-black, pitch-black; blue-black; black as ink *or* as pitch *or* as the ace of spades *or* as hell *or* as night.

blackish, swarthy, dusky, dark, dark-skinned, tanned, sun-tanned; coloured, pigmented; livid, black and blue.

Vb. *blacken*, black, blacklead, japan, ink, ink in; dirty, blot; char 381 *burn*.

429 Greyness

N. *greyness*, neutral, greige, grisaille; pepper and salt, grey hairs, hoary head; pewter, silver; gun-metal, ashes, slate; monochrome; grey, dove grey, etc. (see adj.); oyster, taupe.

Adj. *grey*, neutral, dull, sombre, leaden, livid, greying, grizzled, grizzly, hoary, silvery, pearly, frosted 427 *whitish*; greige; light-grey, pale-grey, ash-grey, dove-grey, pearl-grey; mouse-coloured, mousy, dun, drab, donkey-grey; steely, charcoal-grey; slate-coloured; greyish, ashen, smoky; dapple-grey; cheerless, dreich 834 *cheerless*.

430 Brownness

N. *brownness*, brown, bronze, copper, amber; tobacco leaf, autumn colours; cinnamon, coffee, chocolate; butterscotch, caramel, toffee, burnt almond; walnut, mahogany; dark skin *or* complexion, suntan; brunette.

brown pigment, bistre, ochre, sepia, burnt sienna, burnt umber, Vandyke brown.

Adj. *brown*, bronze, mahogany, etc. (see n.); browned, toasted; bronzed, tanned, sunburnt; dark, brunette; nut-brown, hazel; light brown, ecru, oatmeal, beige, buff, fawn, biscuit, mushroom, café-au-lait; brownish, greyish-brown, dun, taupe, mud-coloured; yellowish-brown, snuff-coloured, khaki; tawny, tan; reddish-brown, bay, roan, sorrel, chestnut, auburn, copper-coloured; russet, rust-coloured; maroon; puce; dark brown, peat-brown, mocha, chocolate, coffee-coloured, etc. (see n.); brown as a berry *or* as a nut.

Vb. *brown*, bronze, tan, sunburn; singe, char, toast 381 *burn*.

431 Redness

N. *redness*, blush, flush, hectic flush; sunset, dawn, rosy-fingered dawn 417 *glow*; reddening, warmth; rosiness, ruddiness, bloom, red cheeks, rosy cheeks, cherry lips; high colour, floridness; red colour, crimson, scarlet, red, etc. (see adj.); carnation, rose, geranium, poppy; cherry, tomato; burgundy, port, claret; gore 335 *blood*; ruby, garnet, cornelian; flame 379 *fire*; red ink, rubric; red planet, Mars; redbreast, robin redbreast; redskin, Red Indian, Indian, Native American, Native Canadian, First Nation; redhead, carrot-top, gingernob.

red pigment, red dye, cochineal, carmine, kermes; cinnabar, vermilion; madder; crimson lake, Venetian red, red ochre, red lead, rouge, blusher, lipstick 843 *cosmetic*.

Adj. *red*, reddish, ruddy, sanguine, florid, blowzy; warm, hot, fiery, glowing, red-hot 379 *hot*; flushed, fevered, flushing, blushing; red-cheeked, rosy-cheeked; bright red, red as a lobster *or* as a beetroot; red-haired, ginger-haired; carroty, sandy, auburn, titian-red, flame-coloured; russet, rusty, rust-coloured; pink, roseate, rosy, rose-coloured, peach-coloured, flesh-coloured, salmon-pink, shocking-pink; coral, carnation, damask, crushed strawberry; crimson, cherry-red, cerise, carmine, cramoisy; fuchsia, magenta, maroon 436 *purple*; wine-coloured; oxblood, sanguine; scarlet, cardinal-red, vermilion, pillarbox red; reddened, rouged, painted.

Vb. *redden*, rouge, apply blusher, raddle 843 *primp*; dye red, flush, blush, glow; colour, colour up, crimson, go red, go pink.

432 Orange

N. *orange*, red and yellow, gold, old gold; amber; sunflower, marigold; apricot, tangerine;

marmalade; ochre, cadmium orange, henna.

Adj. *orange*, apricot. etc. (see n.); coppery, ginger; orangeish, orangey, orange-coloured, flame-coloured, copper-coloured, brass-coloured, brassy.

433 Yellowness

N. *yellowness*, yellow, sunshine yellow, etc. (see adj.); brass, gold, old gold, topaz, amber, old ivory; sulphur, brimstone; buttercup, daffodil, primrose, dandelion; lemon, honey; saffron, mustard; jaundice, yellow fever; sallow skin, fair hair, golden hair; blond(e), ash blond(e), platinum blond(e), strawberry blond(e); yellow rain, cadmium yellow, chrome yellow, lemon yellow, yellow ochre, xanthin.

Adj. *yellow*, gold, amber, etc. (see n.); tawny, sandy; fair-haired, golden-haired, yellow-haired 427 *whitish*; honey-coloured, straw-coloured; pale yellow, acid yellow, lemon yellow; primrose yellow, jasmine, chartreuse, champagne; canary yellow, sunshine yellow, bright yellow; sulphur yellow, mustard yellow; golden, gilded; deep yellow, yellowy, yellowish, flavescent, xanthic; sallow, jaundiced, bilious; yellow with age.

434 Greenness

N. *greenness*, green, etc. (see adj.); verdancy, greenery, greenwood; verdure; grass, moss, turf, green leaf 366 *foliage*; lime, greengage; jade, emerald, beryl, aquamarine, olivine; verdigris; Lincoln green.

Adj. *green*, verdant; grassy, leafy; bright green, deep green, dark green, pale green; grass-green, leaf-green, moss-green; emerald, sea-green, Nile green 435 *blue*; jade-green, bottle-green, sage-green, willow-green; pea-green, acid-green, apple-green, lime-green, chartreuse; eau-de-Nil, avocado, olive, olive-green; greenish.

435 Blueness

N. *blueness*, blue, azure; blue sky, blue sea; sapphire, aquamarine, turquoise; lapis lazuli; bluebell, cornflower, forget-me-not, gentian; sky blue, etc. (see adj.); bluishness, cyanosis; lividness.

blue pigment, blue dye, indigo, woad; cobalt blue; bluebag.

Adj. *blue*, cyanic, azure; sky-blue, duck-egg blue, eggshell blue, turquoise; light blue, pale blue, ice-blue, powder-blue, Cambridge-blue; air-force blue, Saxe-blue, slate-blue, steel-blue, electric-blue; sapphire, aquamarine, peacock-blue, kingfisher-blue, teal, Nile blue 434 *green*; bright blue, royal-blue, ultramarine, deep blue, dark blue, Oxford-blue, midnight-blue, navy-blue, navy, French navy; gentian-blue, indigo; blue-black, black and blue, livid; cold, steely, bluish.

436 Purpleness

N. *purpleness*, purple, blue and red; imperial purple; amethyst; lavender, violet, heliotrope, heather, foxglove; plum, damson, aubergine; gentian violet; amaranth, lilac, mauve.

Adj. *purple*, plum, etc. (see n.); purplish, violet, mauve, pale purple, lavender, lilac; bright purple, fuchsia, magenta, plum-coloured, damson-coloured, puce; heliotrope; deep purple, dark purple, mulberry; purple with rage.

437 Variegation

N. *variegation*, variety, diversification, diversity 15 *difference*; dancing light; play of colour, shot colours, iridescence, chatoyance; tiger's eye, opal, nacre, mother-of-pearl; shot silk, moire; peacock's tail, tortoiseshell, chameleon; Joseph's coat, motley, harlequin, patchwork, patchwork quilt; enamelwork; stained glass, kaleidoscope; rainbow, spectrum, prism; collage.

chequer, check, Prince of Wales check, hound's tooth, pepper-and-salt; plaid, tartan; chessboard, draughtboard; marquetry, inlay, inlaid work 844 *ornamental art*; mosaic, crazy paving 43 *medley*.

stripe, striation; line, streak, band, bar, bar code; agate; zebra, tiger; streakiness, mackerel sky; crack, craze; reticulation 222 *network*.

mottle, maculation; dappling, stippling, marbling; spottiness, patchiness 17 *non-uniformity*; patch, speck, speckle, macula, spots, pimples, pockmarks 845 *blemish*; freckle, fleck, dot, polka dot; blotch, splotch, splodge, splash; leopard, Dalmatian.

Adj. *variegated*, fretted, etc. (see vb.); diversified; patterned, embroidered, worked 844 *ornamental*; colourful 425 *florid*; multi-coloured, parti-coloured, motley, patched; tortoiseshell, chameleon, harlequin, kaleidoscopic 82 *existing in many forms*; plaid, tartan; rainbow-coloured, prismatic; mosaic, tessellated, parquet.

pied, parti-coloured, black-and-white, pepper-and-salt, grizzled, piebald, skewbald, roan, pinto, chequered, check, dappled, patchy.

mottled, marbled, veined, reticulated; studded, maculose, spotted, patchy; speckled, freckled; streaked, striated, lined, barred, banded, striped 222 *crossed*; brindled, tabby; pocked, pockmarked.

Vb. *variegate*, diversify, pattern; chequer; patch 656 *repair*; embroider, work 844 *decorate*; braid, quilt; inlay, tessellate; stud, pepper, dot with, mottle, speckle, freckle, spangle, spot; tattoo, stipple, dapple; streak, stripe, striate; craze, crack; marble, vein; discolour 649 *make unclean*; make iridescent.

438 Vision

N. *vision*, sight, power of sight; eyesight; seeing, visualization, mind's eye 513 *imagination*; perception, recognition; acuity (of vision), good eyesight; long sight, far sight; defective vision, short sight 440 *dim sight*; second sight 984 *occultism*; double vision, binocular vision; magnification; winking, blinking, tic, squint; eye-testing; oculist, optician, ophthalmologist, optometrist; optometer, ophthalmoscope; eye bath, eye drops, eye lotion, eyewash.

eye, eyeball, iris, pupil, white, cornea, retina, optic nerve; optics, orbs, sparklers, peepers; saucer eyes, goggle eyes; eyelashes, eyelid 421 *screen*; lashes; naked eye; sharp eyes, gimlet eyes, X-ray eyes; hawk, eagle, cat, lynx; weak eyes 440 *dim sight*; glass eye 439 *blindness*; evil eye, jettatura 983 *spell*; basilisk, cockatrice; eye-testing, eye drops, optician, etc. (see *vision* above); eye make-up 843 *cosmetic*.

glance, look, sideways look, squint; tail *or* corner of the eye; glint, blink, flash; gaze, steady gaze; observation, close observation, contemplation, watch; stare, fixed stare; come-hither look, glad eye, sheep's eyes, ogle, leer 889 *wooing*; wink 524 *hint*; grimace, dirty look, scowl, evil eye (see *eye* above); peep, peek, glimpse, rapid glimpse, brief glimpse.

inspection, examination, autopsy 459 *enquiry*; view, preview, sneak preview 522 *manifestation*; supervision 689 *management*; survey, overview, bird's-eye view; reconnaissance, reconnoitre, recce, surveillance; sightseeing, rubbernecking, gawping; look, butcher's, lookaround, look-see, dekko, once-over, shufti, skimread; second glance, double take; review, revision; viewing, home viewing 445 *cinema*, 531 *broadcasting*; discernment, espial, view, first sight; looking round, observation, prying, spying; espionage; peeping, voyeurism, peeping Tom; window shopping.

view, eyeful, vista, prospect, outlook, perspective; aspect 445 *appearance*; panorama, bird's-eye view; horizon, false horizon; line of vision; range of view; field of view; scene, setting, stage 594 *theatre*; angle of vision, point of view, viewpoint, standpoint; vantage point, lookout, crow's nest, watchtower 209 *high structure*; camera obscura; astrodome, conning tower; observatory; grandstand, ringside seat

441 *onlookers*; peephole 263 *window*.

Adj. *seeing*, glimpsing, etc. (see vb.); visual, perceptible 443 *visible*; panoramic, ocular, ophthalmic; optical, optometric; stereoscopic, binocular; orthoptic, perspicacious, sharp-eyed, gimlet-eyed, eagle-eyed, vigilant, with eyes in the back of one's head.

Vb. *see*, behold, visualize; perceive, discern, distinguish, make out, pick out, recognize; take in, see at a glance 498 *be wise*; descry, discover 484 *detect*; sight, espy, spy, spot, observe 455 *notice*; lay *or* set eyes on, catch sight of, sight; catch a glimpse of, glimpse; view, command a view of, have in sight; look on 441 *watch*.

gaze, quiz, gaze at, look, look at; look straight at, look in the eyes; look intently, eye, stare, peer; stare at, stare hard, goggle, gape, gawk, gawp; focus, rivet one's eyes, fix one's gaze; glare, glower, look daggers, give a black look, look black 891 *be angry*; glance, glance at; squint, look askance, look down one's nose; wink, blink 524 *hint*; make eyes at, give the glad eye, give a come-hither look, ogle, leer 889 *court*; feast one's eyes on, gloat over 824 *be pleased*; steal a glance, peep, peek, take a peep; direct one's gaze, turn one's eyes on; notice, take notice, look upon 455 *be attentive*; lift up one's eyes, look up; look down, look round, look behind, look in front; look ahead 858 *be cautious*; look away, avert one's gaze 439 *be blind*; exchange glances.

scan, scrutinize, inspect, examine, take stock of, look one up and down; contemplate, pore over, post-mortem 536 *study*; look over, look through, read through, riffle through, leaf through, skim through; have *or* take a look at, have a dekko, have a butcher's, take a shufti at, take a gander *or* a squint at, run one's eye over, give the once-over; see, go and see, take in, sight-see, rubberneck, gawp; go to see 882 *visit*; view, survey, sweep, reconnoitre; scout, spy out the land, take a recce; peep, peek 453 *be curious*; spy, pry, snoop; observe, keep under observation, keep under surveillance, watch 457 *keep watch*; hold in view, keep in sight; watch out for, look out for 507 *await*; keep watch, look out, keep a lookout for, keep an eye out for, keep a weather eye open for, keep cave, keep looking, keep one's eyes skinned *or* peeled; strain one's eyes, peer; squint at, squinny; crane, crane one's neck, stand on tiptoe.

439 Blindness

N. *blindness*, unawareness 491 *ignorance*; sightlessness; glaucoma, river blindness, cataract; night blindness, snow blindness, colour

blindness; dim-sightedness 440 *dim sight*;
blind spot 444 *invisibility*; tunnel vision; blind
eye 456 *inattention*; word blindness, dyslexia;
glass eye, artificial eye; blind man *or* woman,
the blind; Braille, Moon *or* Moon type, talking
book; white stick, guide dog.

Adj. *blind*, sightless, unsighted, visually
challenged, dark; unseeing, undiscerning,
unperceiving, unobserving 456 *inattentive*;
blinded, blindfold, blinkered; in the dark,
benighted 440 *dim-sighted*; stone-blind; blind
as a bat.

Vb. *be blind*, not use one's eyes; go blind,
lose one's sight, not see; grope in the dark,
feel one's way 461 *be tentative*; be blindfolded,
wear blinkers; be blind to 491 *not know*;
ignore, have a blind spot, not see for looking,
not see what is under one's nose; not see the
wood for the trees, close *or* shut one's eyes to,
turn a blind eye, avert one's gaze, look the
other way 458 *disregard*; blink, squint 440 *be
dim-sighted*.

blind, gouge one's eyes out; dazzle; obscure
419 *dim*; screen from sight; blinker, blindfold,
bandage 421 *screen*; throw dust in one's eyes
495 *mislead*.

440 Dim-sightedness: imperfect vision

N. *dim sight*, failing sight, defective eyesight,
dim-sightedness, purblindness 439 *blindness*;
defective vision, impaired vision; eyestrain;
short sight, short-sightedness, near sight, near-
sightedness, myopia; hypermetropia, presby-
opia, long sight, long-sightedness, far sight,
far-sightedness; double vision; astigmatism;
cataract; glaucoma; colour-blindness; snow-
blindness; night-blindness; ophthalmitis; conjunctivitis, pink eye; cast; strabismus, squint,
cross-eye, wall-eye; wink, blink, nictitation,
nervous tic; eyeshade, blinker 421 *screen*; tunnel vision, blind spot 444 *invisibility*.

visual fallacy, refraction 417 *reflection*; aberration of light 282 *deviation*; false light 552
misrepresentation; optical illusion, trick of the
light, mirage, Brocken spectre, ignis fatuus,
will-o'-the-wisp 542 *deception*; spectre, apparition 970 *ghost*; vision, dream 513 *fantasy*; dis-
torting mirror, hall of mirrors, magic lantern.

Adj. *dim-sighted*, purblind, half-blind, semi-
blind; visually impaired, bespectacled; myopic,
short-sighted, near-sighted; hypermetropic,
presbyopic, long-sighted, far-sighted, astig-
matic; colour-blind; wall-eyed, squinting; stra-
bismal, strabismic, cross-eyed, squint-eyed;
wall-eyed, boss-eyed, bug-eyed; nystagmic;
blinking, dazzled; blinded, temporarily
blinded 439 *blind*; cataractous, glaucomatous.

Vb. *be dim-sighted*, be myopic, etc. (see

adj.); not see well, need spectacles; have a
mist before the eyes; get something in one's
eye; peer, screw up the eyes, squint; blink,
wink, nictate *or* nictitate, have a nervous tic;
see double, be blinded by, dazzle; grow
blurred, dim, fail; see through a glass darkly.

blur, confuse; dim, mist, fog, smudge; be
indistinct, be hazy.

441 Spectator

N. *spectator*, beholder; viewer, observer,
watcher, invigilator; inspector, examiner, scru-
tinizer, overseer 690 *manager*; witness, eyewitness; bystander, onlooker; gazer, starer, gaper,
gawper, goggler; ogler, voyeur, Peeping Tom;
window shopper; sightseer, globetrotter, rubberneck, tourist, astrotourist, space tourist 268
traveller; stargazer, astronomer; bird watcher;
twitcher; train spotter; lookout 484 *detector*;
watchman, night-watchman, security officer,
security man, sentinel, sentry 664 *warner*;
patrolman, patrol; scout, spy, mole, spook,
snoop 459 *detective*; filmgoer, cinemagoer 445
cinema; theatregoer 594 *theatregoer*; televiewer,
viewer, TV addict, square-eyes; captive
audience.

onlookers, audience, auditorium, sea of
faces; box office, gate; house, gallery, gods,
circle, dress circle, pit, stalls; stadium, grandstand, terraces; crowd, supporters, followers,
aficionados, fans 504 *enthusiast*, 707 *patron*;
bums on seats.

Vb. *watch*, spectate, look on, look at, view
438 *see*; witness 189 *be present*; follow with the
eyes, observe 455 *be attentive*; attend, eye,
ogle, give the glad eye, quiz; gape, gawk, stare;
spy, spy out, scout, scout out, reconnoitre 438
scan.

442 Optical instrument

N. *spectacles*, eyeglass, specs, goggles, glasses,
reading glasses, pince-nez, sunglasses, shades,
dark glasses, Polaroid (tdmk) glasses, bifocals;
pebble glasses; contact lens, hard contact lens,
soft contact lens; lorgnette, monocle; magnifying glass.

telescope, terrestrial telescope, astronomical
telescope, refracting telescope, reflecting telescope, Newtonian telescope, Cassegrainian
telescope, Gregorian telescope 321 *astronomy*;
collimator; sight, finder, viewfinder, rangefinder; periscope; spyglass, night glass; binoculars, prism binoculars, field glasses, opera
glasses.

microscope, electron microscope, photo-
microscope, ultramicroscope.

mirror, reflector; concave mirror, speculum;
rear-view mirror, wing mirror; glass, looking

glass, cheval glass, full-length mirror, dressing-table mirror, hand mirror.

camera, camera lucida, camera obscura, spectrograph 321 *astronomy*; box camera, disc camera; instant camera, Polaroid (tdmk) camera, digital camera, digicam; cinecamera; television camera, videopack, camcorder; electric eye, closed-circuit television 484 *detector*; webcam; shutter, aperture, stop; flashgun 420 *lamp*; film 551 *photography*; lens, telephoto lens, zoom lens, wide-angle lens; light meter; slide projector, overhead projector, magic lantern 455 *cinema*.

443 Visibility

N. *visibility*, perceptibility 445 *appearance*; sight, exposure; distinctness, clearness, clarity, definition, conspicuousness, prominence; eyewitness, visible evidence, object lesson 522 *manifestation*; visual aid 534 *teaching*; scene, field of view, field of vision 438 *view*; seeing, impaired visibility, reduced visibility; horizon, skyline, visible distance 183 *range*; landmark 547 *signpost*; symptom.

Adj. *visible*, perceptible, perceivable, discernible, observable, detectable; noticeable, remarkable; recognizable, unmistakable, palpable, tangible; symptomatic; apparent 445 *appearing*; showing 522 *manifest*; exposed, open, naked; exposed to view, in full view; before one's eyes, under one's nose, for all to see; visible to the naked eye; telescopic, panoramic.

obvious, showing, for all to see 522 *shown*; plain, clear, clear-cut, crystal-clear, as clear as day; definite, well-defined, well-marked; distinct, unblurred; undisguised; conspicuous, pointed, prominent; eye-catching, striking, shining 417 *luminous*; glaring, staring; pronounced, highlighted, spotlit; vivid, eidetic; under one's nose, before one's very eyes, staring one in the face, plain to see, plain as plain, plain as a pikestaff *or* as the nose on your face.

Vb. *be visible*, be seen, be obvious, etc. (see adj.); show, shine through; attract attention, ask to be noticed 455 *attract notice*; strike, catch the eye, stand out, act as a landmark; come to light, dawn upon; heave in sight, come into view, show its face 445 *appear*; pop up, crop up, turn up, show up 295 *arrive*; spring up, start up, arise 68 *begin*; surface, break surface 308 *ascend*; come out, creep out 298 *emerge*; stick out, project 254 *jut*; show, materialize, develop; manifest itself, expose itself, betray itself 522 *be plain*; symptomize 547 *indicate*; make one's entry, make an entrance 297 *enter*; step forward, advance; daz-

zle; break through the clouds 417 *shine*; stay in sight; make visible, expose 522 *manifest*.

444 Invisibility

N. *invisibility*, imperceptibility, indistinctness, poor definition; poor visibility, reduced visibility, obscurity 419 *dimness*; distance 199 *farness*; smallness 196 *minuteness*; privacy 883 *seclusion*; submergence 523 *latency*; hiding 525 *concealment*; mystery 525 *secrecy*; smoke screen, mist, fog, haar, veil, curtain; blind spot, blind eye 439 *blindness*; blind corner 663 *pitfall*; hidden menace, tip of the iceberg 661 *danger*.

Adj. *invisible*, imperceptible, indiscernible; indistinguishable, unrecognizable; unseen; sightless; unnoticed 458 *neglected*; out of sight, not in sight, remote 199 *distant*; sequestered 883 *secluded*; lurking 523 *latent*; camouflaged 525 *concealed*; shadowy, mysterious; obscured, eclipsed.

indistinct, unclear, poorly-defined, indefinite, indistinct 419 *dim*; faint, microscopic; confused, vague, blurred, out of focus; fuzzy, misty, hazy 424 *semi-transparent*.

Vb. *be unseen*, hide, lie low, go to earth, go to ground, lie in ambush 523 *lurk*; escape notice, blush unseen 872 *be humble*; pale, fade, die 419 *be dim*; be lost to view, vanish 446 *disappear*; hide away, submerge 525 *conceal*; veil 421 *screen*; darken, eclipse 419 *dim*.

445 Appearance

N. *appearance*, first appearance 68 *beginning*; materialization, bodying forth, presence 1 *existence*; exhibition, display, view, demonstration 522 *manifestation*; revelation 484 *discovery*; outside 223 *exteriority*; appearances, look of things; visual impact, face value; first impressions, effect; image, front, public persona, corporate identity, façade, angle, slant, spin 541 *duplicity*; veneer, show, seeming, semblance; side, aspect, facet, guise 228 *dressing*; shape, dimension 243 *form*; look; emanation; vision 513 *fantasy*; mirage, hallucination, illusion 440 *visual fallacy*; spectre 970 *ghost*; reflection, image, likeness 551 *representation*.

spectacle, impression, effect, something to write home about; decoration 844 *ornamentation*; eyeful, vision, sight, sight for sore eyes; scene; scenery, landscape, seascape, townscape, estatescape; panorama, bird's-eye view 438 *view*; display, pageantry, pageant, parade, review 875 *ostentation*; revue, extravaganza, pantomime, floor show 594 *stage show*; television, video 531 *broadcasting*; illuminations, son et lumière; pyrotechnics; presentation, show, demonstration, exhibition, exposition

522 *exhibit*; art exhibition 553 *picture*; visual entertainment, in-flight entertainment, peep show, slide show, film show, picture show, home movies; kaleidoscope 437 *variegation*; panorama, staging, tableau; set, decor, scenario 594 *stage set*.

cinema, cinematography; big screen, silver screen, Hollywood, Bollywood, film industry; film studio, film production, film-making, shooting 551 *photography*; direction, continuity, editing, cutting, montage, projection; photoplay, screenplay, scenario, script, shooting script; credits, titles; special effects, animation, computer animation, synthespian, claymation, animatronics, anime, hentai; voiceover, sound effects, soundtrack; cinematograph, projector; multiplex cinema *or* multiplex; picture house, drive-in cinema, flea pit 594 *theatre*; film director, film star 594 *actor*; filmgoer 504 *enthusiast*.

film, picture, motion picture, movie; pictures, movies, flicks, films; Technicolor (tdmk), 3-D, Cinerama (tdmk), Cinemascope (tdmk); silent film, talkie; Uc, U, PG, 12, 12A, 15, 18, R18; big picture, supporting film, B movie, B picture, newsreel, trailer; cartoon, animated cartoon, toon, anime, hentai; travelogue, documentary, docudrama, docusoap, documentainment, drama documentary, dramadoc, feature film; art film, nouvelle vague; epic, blockbuster, musical; low-budget movie; costume drama, period drama; weepie, bodice-ripper, thriller, cliffhanger, war film; horror film, slasher movie, splatter movie, gore movie, snuff movie; revenge movie; road movie; buddy movie; blue movie, stag movie, skinflick; Western, spaghetti western; romantic comedy, romcom; chick flick; space odyssey; Britflick, Ealing comedy; oldie, remake; rush, preview, cut, rough cut, director's cut; general release.

expression, look, mien, face; countenance, looks; complexion, colour, cast; air, demeanour, carriage, bearing, deportment, poise, presence; gesture, posture, behaviour 688 *conduct*.

feature, trait, mark, lineament; lines, cut, shape, fashion, figure 243 *form*; outline, contour, relief, elevation, profile, silhouette; visage, physiognomy, cut of one's jib 237 *face*.

Adj. *appearing*, apparent; seeming, ostensible; deceptive; outward, external, superficial 223 *exterior*; on view 443 *visible*; visual, showing, exhibited, hung 522 *shown*; impressive, effective, spectacular 875 *showy*; revealed 522 *manifest*; dreamlike 513 *imaginary*.

Vb. *appear*, show 443 *be visible*; seem 18 *resemble*; have the look of, have an air of, take the shape of; figure in, cut a figure 875 *be ostentatious*; be on show; be showing; appear on television, star in; exhibit 522 *manifest*; arise; dawn, break 68 *begin*; materialize, pop up 295 *arrive*.

446 Disappearance

N. *disappearance*, loss, vanishing; disappearing trick, escapology 542 *sleight of hand*; flight 667 *escape*; exit 296 *departure*; evaporation 338 *vaporization*; dissipation, dissolution 51 *decomposition*; extinction 2 *non-existence*; occupation, eclipse 418 *obscuration*; fadeout; thin air 444 *invisibility*.

Vb. *disappear*, vanish, do the vanishing trick; dematerialize, melt into thin air; evaporate 338 *vaporize*; dissolve, melt away 337 *liquefy*; dwindle to vanishing point 37 *decrease*; fade away 114 *be transient*; suffer an eclipse 419 *be dim*; disperse, dissipate, diffuse, scatter 75 *be dispersed*; fail to appear, play truant, bunk off, take French leave, go AWOL, go walkabout 190 *be absent*, 738 *disobey*; go, be gone, depart 296 *walk out*; run away, get away 667 *escape*; hide, lie low, be in hiding 523 *lurk*; leave no trace 525 *conceal*; be lost to sight 444 *be unseen*; become extinct 2 *pass away*; erase, dispel 550 *obliterate*.

Intellect: the exercise of the mind

4.1
Formation of Ideas

SECTION ONE

General

447 Intellect
N. intellect, mind, psyche, mentality; understanding, conception; powers of thought; rationality, reasoning power; reason, association of ideas 475 *reasoning*; philosophy 449 *thought*; awareness, sense, consciousness, self-consciousness, stream of consciousness 455 *attention*; tabula rasa; cognition, perception, percipience, insight; extra-sensory perception, ESP, instinct, sixth sense 476 *intuition*; flair, judgment 463 *discrimination*; intellectualism; mental capacity, brains, wits, senses, sense, grey matter, IQ, intelligence quotient 498 *intelligence*; genius; brain.

spirit, soul, inner mind, inner child; inner sense, inner being; heart, breast, bosom, inner man 5 *essential part*; double, genius 80 *self*; psyche, id, ego, superego, animus, self, the unconscious, the subconscious; personality, dual personality, multiple personality, split personality 503 *personality disorder*; spiritualism, psychical research 984 *occultism*; spiritualist, occultist.

psychology, Freudian psychology, Jungian psychology, Adlerian psychology, Gestalt psychology, behaviourism; clinical psychology; psychiatry, psychoanalysis, psychopathology, psychotherapy, psychodrama, cognitive therapy, cognitive behaviour *or* behavioural therapy, Neuro-Linguistic Programming 658 *therapy*; self-analysis, enneagram; psychological profiling, profiling; psychological warfare; parapsychology 984 *psychics*; pop psychology, cod psychology; pseudopsychology 984 *occultism*; phrenology; psycholinguistics.

psychologist, psychiatrist, psychoanalyst, psychotherapist 658 *doctor*; analyst, head

shrinker, shrink, trick cyclist; profiler; sports psychologist.

Adj. mental, cerebral, intellectual, conceptual; theoretical; perceptual, perceptive; cognizant 490 *knowing*; thinking, reasoning 475 *rational*; inward-looking, introverted 224 *inward-looking*.

Vb. perceive, perceive 490 *know*; realize, sense, become aware of, become conscious of; note 438 *see*; mark 455 *notice*; reason; use one's head, understand 498 *be wise*; conceptualize, intellectualize 449 *think*; conceive, invent 484 *discover*; imagine.

448 Absence of intellect
N. absence of intellect, stocks and stones; brainlessness, mindlessness 450 *absence of thought*; brain damage, unsound mind, insanity 503 *mental disorder*.

Adj. mindless, unintelligent; inanimate; unreasoning; brainless, empty-headed, vacuous 499 *foolish*; moronic, wanting 503 *mentally disordered*.

449 Thought
N. thought, mental process, thinking, thought processes; intellectual exercise, mental exercise, cogitation, cerebration, thinking cap; brainwork; hard thought, concentration 455 *attention*; deep thought, profundity 498 *wisdom*; thoughts, ideas 451 *idea*; conception, inmost thoughts 513 *conception*; train of thought; association of ideas, reason 475 *reasoning*; unreason, believing six impossible things before breakfast, intellectual suicide; brown study, deep thought, reverie 456 *abstractedness*; thinking out; second thoughts, after-thought 67 *sequel*; retrospection, hindsight, wisdom after the event 505 *memory*; forethought, forward planning, telepathy 984 *psychics*.

meditation, thoughtfulness, speculation 459 *enquiry*; lateral thinking; reflection, deep thought, brooding, rumination, consideration, pondering; contemplation 438 *inspection*;

absorption, pensiveness; introspection, self-absorption, self-communing, navel-gazing; transcendental meditation, TM, yogic flying; retreat, mysticism 979 *piety*; deliberation, thinking out 480 *judgment*; application 536 *study*.

philosophy, metaphysics, ethics, ontology; speculation, abstract thought, scientific thought, natural philosophy; philosophical system, philosophical theory 512 *supposition*; school of philosophy 485 *opinion*; monism, dualism; idealism, conceptualism, transcendentalism; phenomenalism, phenomenology, realism, nominalism, positivism, logical positivism, analytic philosophy 475 *reasoning*; epistemology, intuitionism 490 *knowledge*; philosophy of existence, existentialism, voluntarism; determinism, mechanism; vitalism; holism, organicism, structuralism, functionalism, reductionism, reductivism; rationalism, humanism, hedonism; utilitarianism, materialism; empiricism, pragmatism; relativism, relativity; agnosticism, scepticism, irrationalism 486 *doubt*; eclecticism; atheism 974 *lack of religion*; nihilism, fatalism 596 *fate*; literary theory, deconstruction; Pythagoreanism, Platonism, Aristotelianism; Scepticism, Stoicism, Epicureanism, Cynicism; Neo-Platonism, gnosticism; scholasticism, Thomism, Neo-Thomism, Cartesianism, Kantianism, Neo-Kantianism, Hegelianism, Neo-Hegelianism, Spinozism; dialectical materialism, Marxism; anthroposophy, theosophy; Hinduism, Buddhism, Sufism, Yoga, Zen 973 *religion*.

Adj. *thoughtful*, speculative; cogitative, deliberative; pensive, meditative, ruminative, contemplative, reflective; introspective; wrapt *or* rapt *or* wrapped in thought; absorbed 455 *obsessed*; musing, daydreaming, dreamy 456 *abstracted*; concentrated 455 *attentive*; studying 536 *studious*; considerate 901 *philanthropic*; prudent 510 *foreseeing*.

Vb. *think*, ween 512 *suppose*; form ideas, fancy 513 *imagine*; ponder, cogitate (see also *meditate* below); put on one's thinking cap, use one's grey matter; concentrate, collect one's thoughts 455 *be attentive*; apply the mind, trouble one's head about, cerebrate, mull over, puzzle over 536 *study*; think hard, rack one's brains; think through, reason out 475 *reason*; think up, invent 484 *discover*; devise 623 *plan*; take it into one's head, harbour a notion, have a sudden fancy, have an idea, toy with an idea, kick an idea around; cherish an idea 485 *believe*; become obsessed, get a bee in one's bonnet, have a hang-up about 481 *be biased*; bear in mind, take account of, think on 505 *remember*.

meditate, ruminate; wonder about, enquire into 459 *enquire*; reflect, contemplate, study; speculate, philosophize, theorize; think about, consider, take into account, take into consideration; take stock of, ponder, weigh 480 *estimate*; think over, run over in the mind 505 *memorize*; reconsider, have second thoughts; think better of; take counsel, sleep on it 691 *consult*; brood, brood upon, muse, fall into a brown study.

dawn upon, occur to, cross the mind; come into one's head, come to one in a blinding flash, strike one.

cause thought, provoke thought, make one think, make one stop and think 821 *impress*; sink in, become a hang-up, obsess 481 *bias*.

absorb, engross, absorb, preoccupy, monopolize; be never out of one's thoughts, go round and round in one's head, occupy the mind, be uppermost in one's mind; prey on one's mind, obsess 481 *bias*; fascinate 983 *bewitch*.

450 Absence of thought

N. *absence of thought*, blank mind, abstraction 456 *abstractedness*; inanity, vacuity, blankness, fatuity, empty head 499 *unintelligence*; thoughtlessness 456 *inattention*; conditioned reflex; knee-jerk response, gut reaction; instinct 476 *intuition*; intellectual suicide, unreason.

451 Idea

N. *idea*, notion, a thought; abstract idea, concept; theory 512 *supposition*; mental image; Platonic idea; conception, perception, apprehension 447 *intellect*; observation 449 *thought*; impression, fancy 513 *imagination*; figment of imagination; associated ideas, complex; stream of consciousness, free association of ideas; invention, brainchild; brain wave, happy thought 484 *discovery*; wheeze, device 623 *contrivance*; point of view, slant, way of thinking, attitude, mindset, culture 485 *opinion*; principle, main idea; obsession, hang-up 481 *prejudgment*.

452 Topic

N. *topic*, food for thought; gossip, rumour 529 *news*; subject matter, subject; contents, chapter, section 53 *subdivision*; what it is about, argument, plot, theme, message; text, commonplace, burden, motif; musical topic, statement, leitmotiv 412 *musical piece*; concern, interest, human interest; matter, affair; shop 622 *business*; topic for discussion, business on hand, agenda, any other business, AOB, order paper 623 *policy*; item on the agenda, motion

761 *request*; resolution 480 *judgment*; problem, problematics, gist, drift; theorem, proposition 512 *supposition*; thesis, case, point 475 *argument*; issue, moot point, debatable point, point at issue; field of enquiry, field of study 536 *study*.

Adj. topical, thematic; thought about, uppermost in the mind, fit for consideration, worthy of discussion.

Adv. in question, in one's thoughts; afoot, on the agenda, on the table; before the house, before the committee, under consideration, under discussion.

S E C T I O N   T W O

Precursory conditions and operations

453 Curiosity: desire for knowledge

N. curiosity, intellectual curiosity, speculativeness, enquiring mind, thirst *or* itch for knowledge 536 *study*; interest, inquisitiveness, curiousness; zeal, meddlesomeness, officiousness, nosiness 678 *overactivity*; quizzing 459 *question*; sightseeing, rubbernecking 267 *land travel*; morbid curiosity, ghoulishness; voyeurism 951 *impurity*.

Adj. inquisitive, curious, interested; speculating, searching, seeking, avid for knowledge, hungry for information 536 *studious*; morbidly curious, ghoulish, prurient; newsmongering, agog, all ears 455 *attentive*; burning with *or* consumed with *or* eaten up with curiosity; itching, hungry for; overcurious, nosy, snoopy, prying, spying, peeping, peeking; questioning, inquisitorial 459 *enquiring*; meddlesome, interfering, officious.

Vb. be curious, want to know; look for 459 *search*; research 461 *experiment*; be interested, take an interest; show interest, show curiosity, prick up one's ears, be all agog 455 *be attentive*; mosey around, dip into; dig up, nose out; peep, peek, spy 438 *scan*; snoop, pry, nose into 459 *enquire*; eavesdrop, tap the line, intercept, bug, listen, listen in, eavesdrop 415 *hear*; poke *or* stick one's nose in, be nosy, interfere, act the busybody 678 *meddle*; quiz, question, bombard with questions 459 *interrogate*; stand and stare, gape, gawk 438 *gaze*.

454 Lack of curiosity

N. lack of curiosity, incuriosity; uninterest, unconcern 860 *indifference*; mental inertia; apathy, phlegmatism 820 *moral insensibility*.

Adj. incurious, uninquisitive; uninterested; aloof, distant, blasé; unconcerned, uninvolved 860 *indifferent*; inert, apathetic 820 *impassive*.

Vb. be incurious, be indifferent, etc. (see adj.); have no curiosity, take no interest 456 *be inattentive*; feel no concern, couldn't care less, not trouble oneself, not bother with 860 *be indifferent*; mind one's own business, go one's own way 820 *be insensitive*; look the other way 458 *disregard*.

455 Attention

N. attention, notice, regard 438 *glance*; consideration 449 *thought*; heed, alertness, readiness, attentiveness, solicitude, observance 457 *carefulness*; observation, watchfulness, vigilance, watch, guard, invigilation 457 *surveillance*; wariness, circumspection 858 *caution*; contemplation, introspection 449 *meditation*; intentness, earnestness, seriousness 599 *resolution*; undivided attention, quality time; concentration, application, studiousness, close study 536 *study*; examination, scrutiny, checkup, review 438 *inspection*; close attention; meticulousness, attention to detail, minuteness, pernicketiness; diligence, trouble 678 *assiduousness*; rapt attention; single-mindedness; absorption, preoccupation 456 *inattention*; interest 453 *curiosity*; one-track mind, fixation, obsession, hang-up, hobbyhorse, thing.

Adj. attentive, intent, diligent, assiduous 678 *industrious*; considerate, caring, thoughtful 884 *courteous*; heedful, mindful; alert, ready, on one's toes, on the qui vive, on the ball, with it; wakeful, awake, wide-awake; awake to, alive to, sensing 819 *sensitive*; aware, conscious, thinking 449 *thoughtful*; observant, sharp-eyed, watching, watchful 457 *vigilant*; attending, rapt, missing nothing; all eyes, all agog 438 *seeing*; all ears; concentrating; serious, earnest; eager to learn 536 *studious*; meticulous, punctilious 494 *accurate*; on the lookout 507 *expectant*.

obsessed, single-minded, engrossed, preoccupied, wrapped up in, taken up with, into, hooked on, addicted to, hung up; haunted by 854 *afraid*; monomaniacal 503 *crazy*.

Vb. be attentive, attend, pay attention; heed, pay heed, take notice of, mind 457 *be careful*; care, take trouble, take pains, put oneself out for, bother 682 *exert oneself*; listen, prick up one's ears, sit up and take notice; take seriously; devote *or* give one's attention to, bend the mind to; direct one's thoughts to 449 *think*; think of nothing else, be obsessed with, be preoccupied with 481 *be biased*; keep one's eye on the ball, concentrate, miss nothing; watch, be all eyes, be all agog 438 *gaze*; be all ears, drink in, hang on the lips of 415 *hear*; focus one's mind on, rivet one's attention to, concentrate on, fix on; scrutinize; study closely.

pay some attention, dip into, look into, browse through, flick through, flip through, leaf through, glance at, skim, skim-read, flick over the pages, turn the pages.

be mindful, keep in mind, bear in mind, have in mind, be thinking of 505 *remember*; not forget, think of, spare a thought for, regard, look on 438 *see*; care about, be concerned for, have a heart for, pray for; lend an ear to 415 *hear*; take care of, see to 457 *look after*; have regard to, have an eye to.

notice, note, take note, register; mark, recognize, spot; take cognizance of, take into consideration, take into account, review, reconsider 449 *meditate*; take account of, consider, weigh 480 *judge*; comment upon, remark on, talk about 584 *converse*; mention, just mention, mention in passing, refer to en passant, touch on 524 *hint*; think worthy of attention, have time for, spare time for; acknowledge.

attract notice, draw the attention, hold the attention, engage the attention, focus the attention, rivet the attention, be the cynosure of all eyes, draw the crowds, cut a figure 875 *be ostentatious*; stick out like a sore thumb, arouse notice, interest 821 *impress*; excite attention, demand attention; catch the eye 443 *be visible*; bring to one's notice or attention 522 *show*; call attention to, advertise, publicize 528 *publish*; point out, point to, show 547 *indicate*; stress, underline 532 *emphasize*; fascinate; warn 665 *raise the alarm*; call to attention 737 *command*.

456 Inattention

N. *inattention*, inadvertence, forgetfulness 506 *no memory*; oversight; lapse 495 *error*; lack of interest 454 *lack of curiosity*; unconcern, apathy 860 *indifference*; disregard 458 *negligence*; thoughtlessness, heedlessness 857 *rashness*; carelessness, inconsiderateness 481 *misjudgment*, 932 *selfishness*; deaf ears 416 *deafness*; unseeing eyes, blind spot, tunnel vision 439 *blindness*; diversion, distraction, dust in the eyes, wild-goose chase, red herring 612 *inducement*; attention deficit disorder, attention-deficit hyperactive disorder, ADHD; absent-mindedness 450 *absence of thought*; stargazer, daydreamer, woolgatherer, head in the clouds, Johnny-head-in-air, Walter Mitty; scatterbrain, grasshopper mind, butterfly.

abstractedness, abstraction, absent-mindedness, wandering attention; woolgathering, daydreaming, stargazing, doodling; reverie; distraction, divided attention.

Adj. *inattentive*, careless 458 *negligent*; off one's guard, with one's trousers or pants down

508 *inexpectant*; unobservant, unnoticing 454 *incurious*; unseeing 439 *blind*; unhearing 416 *deaf*; undiscerning 464 *undiscriminating*; unmindful, unheeding, inadvertent, not thinking, unreflecting; half asleep; uninterested 860 *indifferent*; apathetic, unaware 820 *impassive*; oblivious 506 *forgetful*; inconsiderate, thoughtless, tactless, heedless; regardless 857 *rash*; cavalier, offhand, cursory, superficial 212 *shallow*.

abstracted, distrait(e), absent-minded, not with it, miles away; lost in thought; rapt, with one's head in the clouds, stargazing; bemused, sunk in a brown study, deep in reverie, pensive, dreamy, daydreaming, mooning, woolgathering; half-awake 679 *sleepy*.

distracted, preoccupied, engrossed; diverted; put off, put off one's stroke; unnerved 854 *nervous*.

lacking concentration, light-minded, desultory, trifling, frivolous, flippant, light-headed; mercurial, bird-witted, flighty, giddy; grasshopper-minded, scatty, scatterbrained, harebrained, featherbrained; harum-scarum, inconstant 604 *capricious*.

Vb. *be inattentive*, pay no attention, pay no heed; turn a blind eye 439 *be blind*; stop one's ears 416 *be deaf*; not register, not use one's eyes; not get the message, not click; overlook 495 *blunder*; be off one's guard, be caught with one's trousers or pants down, let the cat out of the bag, let slip, be caught out; lose track of, lose sight of; not remember 506 *forget*; dream, nod 679 *sleep*; trifle, play at, toy with; be abstracted, let one's thoughts wander; go woolgathering, build castles in Spain, build castles in the air 513 *imagine*; fall into a brown study, muse, be lost in thought, moon, stargaze, have one's head in the clouds; idle, doodle 679 *be inactive*; be distracted, digress, lose the thread, lose the train of thought, fluff one's lines 282 *stray*; be disconcerted, be rattled 854 *be nervous*; be put off, be put off one's stroke 702 *hinder*; disregard, ignore 458 *neglect*.

distract, divert, divert one's attention; put out of one's head, drive out of one's mind; entice, throw a sop to Cerberus 612 *tempt*; muddle 63 *disarrange*; disturb, interrupt 72 *discontinue*; disconcert, upset, perplex, hassle, fluster, bother, flurry, rattle, throw 318 *agitate*; put one off his stroke 702 *obstruct*; bewilder, flummox, throw off the scent, draw a red herring 474 *puzzle*; fuddle.

457 Carefulness

N. *carefulness*, attentiveness, diligence, pains 678 *assiduousness*; heed, care, utmost care 455 *attention*; anxiety, solicitude 825 *worry*; loving care 897 *benevolence*; orderliness, neatness 60 *order*; attention to detail, thoroughness, meticulousness; exactitude 494 *accuracy*; perfectionism 862 *fastidiousness*; scruples 929 *probity*; vigilance, watchfulness, alertness, readiness; wariness 858 *caution*; forethought 510 *foresight*.

surveillance, watching, guarding, neighbourhood watch, home watch 660 *protection*; houseminding, homesitting, caretaking, vigilance, invigilation, inspection; baby-sitting, childminding, chaperonage; lookout, weather eye, electronic surveillance, hoolivan; vigil, watch, deathwatch; doomwatch

carer, nurse, care assistant, home help, granny-sitter, buddy; baby-sitter, child-minder, minder; house-sitter, home-sitter; cat-sitter, dog-sitter, pet-sitter.

guard, sentinel, sentry 660 *protector*, 749 *keeper*.

Adj. careful, thoughtful, considerate, heedful 455 *attentive*; painstaking; solicitous, anxious; cautious; conscientious, scrupulous; diligent, assiduous 678 *industrious*; meticulous; nice, exact 494 *accurate*; pedantic, perfectionist 862 *fastidious*; neat 60 *orderly*; miserly 816 *parsimonious*.

vigilant, alert, ready 669 *prepared*; on the alert, on guard, on the qui vive, on one's toes; keeping cave, watchful, wide-awake; observant, sharp-eyed; eagle-eyed 438 *seeing*; prudent, far-sighted 510 *foreseeing*; circumspect, guarded, wary 858 *cautious*.

Vb. be careful, heed, beware 455 *be attentive*; take precautions, think twice; be on the qui vive, be on the alert, have one's eyes open, have one's wits about one, keep a lookout, keep cave, watch one's step, mind how one goes; look before one leaps; feel one's way 461 *be tentative*; be on one's guard, mind one's p's and q's; dot one's i's and cross one's t's; walk *or* tread on eggs *or* eggshells.

look after, look to, see to, take care of, caretake, homesit 689 *manage*; take charge of; care for, mind, tend, keep 660 *safeguard*; baby-sit, childmind; nurse, foster, take into care, cherish 889 *pet*; keep a sharp eye on, keep tabs on, monitor; escort, chaperon.

keep watch, invigilate, keep vigil, watch; stand sentinel; keep a sharp lookout, watch out for; keep one's wits about one, keep one's eyes peeled, keep one's weather-eye open, sleep with one eye open, keep one's ear to the ground; mount guard, post sentries.

458 Negligence

N. negligence, carelessness 456 *inattention*; forgetfulness 506 *no memory*; neglect, oversight, omission; default 918 *undutifulness*; unwariness, unguarded hour *or* minute, unpreparedness 670 *non-preparation*; disregard; unconcern, don't-care attitude, couldn't-care-less attitude 860 *indifference*; recklessness 857 *rashness*; procrastination 136 *delay*; laziness 679 *inactivity*; slovenliness, sluttishness, untidiness 61 *disorder*; sloppiness, inexactitude 495 *inexactness*; offhandedness, casualness, laxness 734 *laxity*; perfunctoriness, superficiality 212 *shallowness*; trifling, scamping, skipping, dodging, botching 695 *bungling*; scamped work, skimped work, botched job, loose ends 728 *failure*.

Adj. negligent, neglectful, careless 456 *inattentive*; remiss 918 *undutiful*; thoughtless; oblivious 506 *forgetful*; uncaring; reckless 857 *rash*; heedless 769 *non-observant*; casual, offhand 734 *lax*; sloppy, slipshod, slapdash, couldn't care less, perfunctory, superficial, with a lick and a promise; hit-and-miss, hurried 680 *hasty*; inaccurate 495 *inexact*; slack 679 *lazy*; procrastinating 136 *late*; sluttish, untidy, slovenly 649 *dirty*; unwary, unguarded, off guard 508 *inexpectant*; improvident 670 *unprepared*; disregarding, ignoring; lapsed 974 *irreligious*.

neglected, uncared for, untended; unkempt 649 *dirty*; unprotected, unguarded, unchaperoned; deserted; unattended, left alone, home alone; unheeded 860 *unwanted*; disregarded, ignored, out in the cold; overlooked, omitted; unnoticed, unmarked 444 *invisible*; shelved, pigeonholed, put aside, mothballed, on the back-burner 136 *late*; unread, unexplored; skimped, perfunctory 726 *uncompleted*; hid under a bushel.

Vb. neglect, omit; pass over; lose sight of, overlook 456 *be inattentive*; leave undone, leave half-done, leave loose ends, do by halves 726 *not complete*, botch, bungle 695 *be clumsy*; skimp, scamp 204 *shorten*; skip; skate over, gloss over 525 *conceal*.

disregard, ignore, pass over, give the go-by, dodge, shirk 620 *avoid*; let pass connive at, take no notice 734 *be lax*; pay no attention to, turn a blind eye to, dismiss 439 *be blind*; excuse, overlook 909 *forgive*; discount 483 *underestimate*; pass by 282 *deviate*; turn one's back on, slight, cold-shoulder, cut, cut dead, send to Coventry 885 *be rude*; turn a deaf ear to 416 *be deaf*; take lightly, not take seriously, not trouble one's head about 860 *be indifferent*; have no time for, laugh off, pooh-pooh 922 *hold cheap*; leave out in the cold 57 *exclude*; leave to their own devices, leave in the lurch, desert, abandon 621 *relinquish*.

be neglectful, doze, nod 679 *sleep*; be off one's guard; be caught napping, oversleep; be caught with one's pants *or* trousers down 508 *not expect*; procrastinate, put off until tomorrow, let slide, let slip, let the grass grow under one's feet 677 *not act*; take it easy, coast 679 *be inactive*; shelve, pigeonhole, lay aside, mothball, put on the back-burner, put aside.

459 Enquiry

N. enquiry, asking, questioning (see also *interrogation* below); challenge (see also *question* below); asking about 524 *information*; close enquiry, witch-hunt (see also *search* below); inquisition, examination, investigation; checkup, medical; inquest, post mortem, autopsy, audit, trial 959 *legal trial*; public enquiry; commission of enquiry, working party (see also *enquirer* below); census, canvass, survey, market, research; poll, public opinion poll, Gallup poll (tdmk), straw poll *or* vote 605 *vote*; probe, test, means test, check, spot check, trial run 461 *experiment*; review, scrutiny 438 *inspection*; IQ test; introspection, self-examination, navel-gazing; personality testing, Rorschach *or* inkblot test; research 536 *study*; analysis, dissection; exploration, reconnaissance, recce, reconnoitre, survey 484 *discovery*; discussion, canvassing, consultation 584 *conference*; scientific enquiry 449 *philosophy*.

interrogation, questioning; forensic examination, leading question, cross-examination; quiz, brains trust; catechism; inquisition, third degree, grilling; dialogue; question time, Prime Minister's question time.

question, question mark, interrogation mark 547 *punctuation*; query; questions, questionnaire 87 *list*; question paper, examination paper; Parliamentary question; challenge; trick question, catch, loaded question; indirect question, feeler, leading question; rhetorical question; moot point; point at issue 452 *topic*; crucial question, burning question, sixty-four-thousand-dollar question; vexed question, controversy, bone of contention 475 *argument*; problem, knotty problem, brain-teaser, poser, mind-boggler, unsolved mystery 530 *enigma*.

exam, examination, oral examination, viva voce examination, viva; interview, audition 415 *hearing*; practical examination, written examination, multiple choice examination; test, series of tests, battery; continuous assessment; intelligence test, IQ test; 11-plus, qualifying examination, entrance examination, common entrance, matriculation; Certificate of Secondary Education, CSE, 16-plus, General Certificate of Education, GCE, General Certificate of Secondary Education, GCSE; O level, A level, S level, A/S level; O grade, Standard grade, Higher, Advanced Higher, CSYS, bacca-

laureate; prelims, pre-Meds, Responsions; tripos, Moderations, Mods, Greats, finals, degree exams; doctorate examination, bar examination; degree level, pass level, honours level.

search, probe, investigation, enquiry; quest, hunt, witch-hunt 619 *pursuit*; treasure hunt, geocaching; metal detecting, mudlarking; house-to-house search; close search, fingertip search; frisking, skin-search, strip-search; rummaging, turning over; exploration, excavation, dig; speleology, potholing; searchparty; search warrant.

police enquiry, investigation, criminal investigation, detection 484 *discovery*; detective work, shadowing, tailing, house-watching; profiling, psychological profiling, geographical profiling; grilling, third degree; Criminal Investigation Department, CID, Federal Bureau of Investigation, FBI, Interpol; secret police, Gestapo.

secret service, espionage, counter-espionage, spying, intelligence, counter-intelligence, MI5, Security Service, MI6, Secret Intelligence Service, SIS, CIA, KGB; informer, spy, intelligence officer, operative, mole, sleeper, spook, 007, undercover agent, secret agent, cloak-and-dagger man; double agent, inside agent; counterspy; spy ring.

detective, investigator, criminologist; plain-clothes man; enquiry agent, private detective, private investigator, private eye; hotel detective, store detective; amateur detective, Sherlock Holmes, Miss Marple, Hercule Poirot; Federal agent, FBI agent, G-man, CID man; tec, sleuth, bloodhound, gumshoe, dick, snooper, nose, spy 524 *informer*; graphologist, handwriting expert; forensic expert, forensic scientist, forensic pathologist, forensic psychologist, profiler.

enquirer, investigator; journalist 529 *news reporter*; student, seeker for truth; search party; water diviner 484 *detector*; prospector, gold-digger, treasure-hunter, metal detectorist; talent scout; scout, spy, surveyor, reconnoitrer; inspector; checker screener, scrutineer, censor, ombudsperson 480 *estimator*; scanner, examiner, board of examiners; tester, test pilot, researcher, research worker, analyst, dissector 461 *experimenter*; market researcher, sampler, pollster, canvasser; explorer 268 *traveller*.

questioner, cross-questioner, cross-examiner, interrogator, inquisitor, Grand Inquisitor; interviewer; challenger, heckler; question master *or* quiz master.

Adj. enquiring, curious, prying, nosy 453 *inquisitive*; quizzing, quizzical; interrogatory, interrogative; examining, inquisitional; probing, poking, digging, investigative; testing, searching, fact-finding, exploratory, empirical, tentative 461 *experimental*; analytic, diagnostic.

Vb. *enquire*, ask 491 *not know*; demand 761 *request*; canvass, query, bring in question 475 *argue*; ask for, look for, enquire for, seek (see also *search* below); hunt for 619 *pursue*; check on, vet; enquire into, make enquiries, probe, delve into, dig into, sound, look into, investigate, throw open to enquiry, hold *or* conduct an enquiry, call in Scotland Yard; try, hear 959 *try a case*; review, overhaul, audit, scrutinize, monitor, screen; analyse, dissect, sift; research 536 *study*; examine 449 *meditate*; check, check on; take the temperature, put a toe in the water, take soundings; follow up an enquiry, pursue an enquiry, get to the bottom of, fathom, X-ray 438 *scan*; ferret out, nose out; peer, peep, peek, snoop, spy, pry, nose around 453 *be curious*; survey, reconnoitre, case, suss out; explore, feel one's way 461 *be tentative*; test, road-test, trial, try, sample, taste 461 *experiment*; post-mortem, hold a post-mortem.

interrogate, ask questions; question; cross-question, cross-examine, badger, challenge, heckle; interview, hold a viva; examine, subject to questioning, sound out, probe, quiz, catechize, grill, give the third degree; put to the question 963 *torture*; pump, pick one's brains; move the question, put the question, pop the question; pose, moot, propose *or* raise a question, frame a question, postulate a question.

search, seek, look for; conduct a search, rummage, ransack, comb; scrabble, forage, fossick, root about; scour, clean out, turn over, rake over, pick over, turn out, turn inside out, rake through, rifle through, go through, search through, look into every nook and corner *or* cranny; look high and low; sift through, winnow, go over with a fine-tooth comb; pry into, peer into, peep into, overhaul, frisk, strip-search, skin-search, go over, search one's pockets, search for, feel for, grope for, hunt for, drag for, fish, fish for, dig for; leave no stone unturned, explore every avenue 682 *exert oneself*; cast about, seek a clue, follow the trail 619 *pursue*; probe, explore, go in quest of 461 *be tentative*; dig, excavate, prospect, embark on a treasure-hunt.

460 Answer

N. *answer*, reply, response; reaction; answer by return of post, acknowledgment, return 588 *correspondence*; official reply; returns, results 548 *record*; feedback 524 *information*; echo 106 *repetition*; password 547 *identification*; keyword, open sesame; answering back, back-chat, repartee; retort, counterblast, riposte 714 *retaliation*; give and take, question and answer, dialogue, discussion 584 *conversation*; last word, final answer; Parthian shot; clue, key, right answer, explanation 520 *interpretation*; solution 658 *remedy*; oracle 530 *enigma*.

rejoinder, counterstatement, reply, counterblast, rebuttal; defence, reply; refutation, contradiction 467 *counterevidence*, 533 *negation*; countercharge, counterclaim.

respondent, defendant; answerer, responder, replier, correspondent; examinee; candidate, applicant, entrant, sitter, examinee 716 *contender*.

Vb. *answer*, reply, reply by return of post, reply to an invitation, RSVP, write back, acknowledge, respond, echo; answer back, retort, riposte 714 *retaliate*; say in reply, rejoin, rebut, counter 479 *confute*; field; parry 620 *avoid*; contradict 533 *negate*; defend; get the right answer, solve the riddle 520 *interpret*; settle, decide 480 *judge*; suit the requirements, suit one down to the ground 642 *be expedient*; answer to, correspond to 12 *correlate*.

461 Experiment

N. *experiment*, practical experiment, scientific experiment, controlled experiment; experimentalism, experimentation, experimental method, verification, verification by experiment; exploration, probe; analysis, examination 459 *enquiry*; object lesson, proof 478 *demonstration*; assay 480 *estimate*; testability; check, test, crucial test, acid test, test case; probation; double-blind test; practical test, beta test, trial, trials, try-out, trial run, practice run, dry run, test flight 671 *attempt*; audition, voice test; pilot scheme.

empiricism, speculation, guesswork, guesstimation 512 *conjecture*; tentativeness; experience, practice, rule of thumb, trial, trial and error, hit and miss; random shot, shot in the dark, leap in the dark, gamble 618 *gambling*; instinct 476 *intuition*; sampling, random sample, straw vote; feeler 459 *question*; straw to show which way the wind is blowing, kite-flying, toe in the water, trial balloon.

experimenter, experimentalist, empiricist, researcher, research worker, analyst, vivisector; assayer, chemist; tester; test driver, test pilot; speculator, prospector; prober, explorer.

testing agent, criterion, touchstone; standard, yardstick, benchmark 465 *gauge*; breathalyser, sniffer torch; control; indicator, reagent, litmus paper, retort, test tube; proving ground, wind tunnel; simulator, flight simulator, test track; laboratory.

Adj. *experimental*, analytical, probationary; provisional, tentative 618 *speculative*; trial, exploratory 459 *enquiring*; empirical; in the experimental stage 474 *uncertain*.

Vb. experiment, experimentalize; put to the proof; assay, analyse; research; experiment upon, vivisect, make a guinea pig of, practise on; test, put to the test, run a test on, put through a battery of tests, beta-test, target-test 459 *enquire*; give something a try; try out, give a trial to, trial 671 *attempt*.

be tentative, feel one's way, proceed by trial and error; feel 378 *touch*; grope, fumble; get the feel of 536 *learn*; put out a feeler, dip a toe in, put a toe in the water, fly a kite, feel the pulse, consult the barometer, take the temperature, see how the land lies, see how the wind blows; fish for, angle for, cast one's net; wait and see, see what happens; try it on, see how far one can go; try one's fortune, try one's luck, speculate 618 *gamble*; venture, explore, prospect 672 *undertake*; probe, sound 459 *enquire*.

462 Comparison

N. comparison, comparing, likening; juxtaposition 202 *contiguity*; comparability, points of comparison, analogy, parallel, likeness, similitude 18 *similarity*; identification 13 *identity*; antithesis 14 *contrariety*; contrast 15 *differentiation*; simile, allegory 519 *metaphor*; criterion, pattern, model, check list, control 23 *prototype*.

Adj. compared, compared with, in comparison with, likened, measured against, contrasted; comparative, comparable, analogical; relative, correlative; allegorical, metaphorical 519 *figurative*.

Vb. compare, collate, confront; set side by side, bring together; draw a comparison 13 *treat as identical*, 18 *liken*; parallel; contrast 15 *differentiate*; compare and contrast 463 *discriminate*; match, pair, balance 28 *equalize*; view together, check with 12 *correlate*; draw a parallel; compare to, compare with; compare notes.

463 Discrimination

N. discrimination, distinction 15 *differentiation*; discernment, discretion, connoisseurship 480 *judgment*; insight, perception, acumen, flair 498 *intelligence*; appreciation, critique 480 *estimate*; sensitivity 494 *accuracy*; sensibility 819 *moral sensibility*; tact, delicacy, kid gloves, refinement 846 *good taste*; timing, sense of timing; nicety, particularity 862 *fastidiousness*; sublety, hair-splitting 475 *reasoning*; sorting out 62 *sorting*; selection 605 *choice*; nuance 15 *difference*.

Adj. discriminating, discriminative, selective, judicious, discerning, discreet; sensitive

494 *accurate*; fine, delicate, nice, particular 862 *fastidious*; thoughtful, tactful 513 *imaginative*; tasting, appraising, critical 480 *judicial*; distinguishing 15 *distinctive*.

Vb. discriminate, distinguish 15 *differentiate*; compare and contrast 462 *compare*; sort out, sieve, sift; separate, separate the sheep from the goats, winnow, sort the wheat from the chaff 46 *set apart*; pick out 605 *select*; exercise discretion, make a distinction, make an exception, draw the line 468 *qualify*; make a value judgment 480 *judge*; be a good judge of, have a feel for, have an eye *or* an ear for; know what's what, know how many beans make five, know one's way about, know one's stuff, know a hawk from a handsaw 490 *know*.

464 Lack of discrimination

N. lack of discrimination, indiscrimination, promiscuity 79 *generality*; lack of judgment, simplicity, naiveté; obtuseness 499 *unintelligence*; indiscretion 857 *rashness*; imperceptivity 439 *blindness*; insensitiveness, insensibility; lack of refinement, coarseness, vulgarity 847 *bad taste*.

Adj. indiscriminate, random, unaimed, undirected; confused, undefined, unmeasured 474 *uncertain*; promiscuous, haphazard, wholesale, blanket, global 79 *general*; unsorted; undifferentiated, undistinguished, same for everybody 16 *uniform*.

undiscriminating, indiscriminating, unselective, undiscerning, uncritical 499 *unintelligent*; imperceptive, obtuse; tactless, insensitive, unimaginative 820 *impassive*; unrefined, tasteless, coarse 847 *vulgar*; indiscreet, ill-judged 857 *rash*; tone-deaf 416 *deaf*; colour-blind 439 *blind*; inaccurate 495 *inexact*.

465 Measurement

N. measurement, quantification; mensuration, surveying; geodetics, geodesy; dose, dosage 26 *finite quantity*; rating, valuation, evaluation; appraisal, assessment, appreciation, estimation 480 *estimate*; calculation, computation, number-crunching, reckoning 86 *numbering*; gauging; checking, check; biological monitoring *or* biomonitoring; reading; trigonometry; second, degree, minute, quadrant 247 *angular measure*.

geometry, plane geometry, planimetry; solid geometry, stereometry; altimetry, hypsometry; Euclidean geometry, non-Euclidean geometry; geometer.

weights and measures, avoirdupois, metric system, unit of measurement; weights 322 *weighing*; science of weights and measure: metrology, dimensions, length, breadth, height, depth, thickness 195 *size*; axle load; linear measure 203 *measurement of length*; measure of capacity, volume, cubic contents 183 *measure*; liquid measure, gill, pint, imperial pint, quart, gallon, imperial gallon; barrel, pipe, hogshead 194 *vessel*; litre; apothecaries' fluid measure, minim, dram; dry measure, peck, bushel, quarter; unit of energy, ohm, watt, amp, volt 160 *electricity*; horse power 160 *energy*; candle-power 417 *light*; decibel, sone. (See also 322 *weighing*.)

gauge, measure, scale, graduated scale; time scale 117 *chronometry*; balance 322 *scales*; vernier, micrometer; footrule; yardstick, metre bar; yard measure, tape measure, measuring tape, metal rule; chain, link, pole, perch, rod; lead, log, log-line; echo sounder; ruler, slide rule; straightedge, T-square, try square, set square; dividers, callipers, compass, protractor; sextant, quadrant 269 *sailing aid*; theodolite, astrolabe 321 *astronomy*; index, Plimsoll line, Plimsoll mark, bench mark 547 *indication*; high-water mark, tidemark, floodmark, water line 236 *limit*; axis, coordinate; rule of thumb, standard, criterion, norm 23 *prototype*; milestone 547 *signpost*.

meter, measuring instrument; gas, etc. meter; tachograph, spy-in-the-cab; metronome, time switch, parking meter 117 *timekeeper*; Geiger counter; seismograph; wind gauge.

Meters and What They Measure
accelerometer (acceleration), altimeter (altitude), ammeter (electric current), anemometer (wind speed), barometer (atmospheric pressure), bathometer (depth), chronometer (time), cyclometer (revolutions of a wheel; distance travelled by a wheeled vehicle), dynamometer (force or power), fluviometer (height or flow of river), hydrometer (density of solutions), hygrometer (atmospheric humidity), micrometer (precise measurements), mileometer *or* milometer (distance travelled in miles), odometer (distance travelled), pedometer (distance travelled by a person on foot), pluviometer (rainfall), speedometer (speed), sphygmometer (blood pressure), swingometer (swing of votes in an election), tacheometer *or* tachymeter (distance, bearings and elevation in surveying), tachometer (speed of rotation of an engine, etc.), thermometer (temperature).

Adj. *metrical*, mensural; imperial, metric; metrological; dimensional, three-dimensional, 3-D; cubic, volumetric, linear, micrometric; cadastral, topographical; geodetic.

Vb. *measure*, mensurate, survey, triangulate; compute, calculate, count, reckon 86 *number*; quantify, take the measurements, measure the length and breadth, measure up; size up, estimate the average 30 *average out*; beat the bounds, pace out; tape, span; calliper, use the dividers; probe, sound, fathom, plumb 313

plunge; take soundings, heave the lead; pace, check the speed 117 *time*; balance 322 *weigh*.

gauge, meter, take a reading, read, read off; standardize 16 *make uniform*; grade, mark off, mark out, calibrate 27 *graduate*; reduce to scale, draw to scale, map 551 *represent*.

appraise, gauge, value, cost, fix the price of 809 *price*; evaluate, estimate, make an estimate, form an estimate; appreciate, assess, assay 480 *estimate*; form an opinion 480 *judge*; tape, have taped, have the measure of, size up.

mete out, mete, measure out, weigh, weigh out, dole out, allocate, divide, share, share out, portion out 775 *participate*, 783 *allocate*.

SECTION THREE

Materials for reasoning

466 Evidence

N. *evidence*, facts, data, biodata, curriculum vitae, case history; grounds 475 *reasons*; premises 475 *premise*; hearsay 524 *report*; circumstantial evidence 8 *circumstance*; constructive evidence 512 *supposition*; prima facie evidence; proof, conclusive evidence, incriminating evidence, substantive evidence, smoking gun 478 *demonstration*; corroboration; verification, confirmation 473 *certainty*, 467 *counterevidence*; fact, relevant fact; document, exhibit, fingerprints, DNA fingerprinting, genetic fingerprinting 548 *record*; clue 524 *hint*; symptom, syndrome, sign, sure sign 547 *indication*; mention, reference, quotation, citation, chapter and verse; one's authorities, documentation.

testimony, witness; statement 524 *information*; admission, confession 526 *disclosure*; one's case, plea 614 *pretext*; word, assertion, allegation 532 *affirmation*; evidence on oath; legal evidence; deposition, affidavit, attestation 532 *oath*; State's evidence, King's *or* Queen's evidence; word of mouth, verbal; documentary evidence; character reference, compurgation 927 *vindication*; case record, dossier 548 *record*; written contract, contract of employment 765 *pact*; deed, testament 767 *security*.

credential, testimonial, chit, character, recommendation, references; seal, signature, countersignature, endorsement, docket, counterfoil; voucher, warranty, warrant, certificate, diploma 767 *security*; ticket, one-way ticket, single, return ticket, day return, cheap day return, season ticket, railcard, bus pass; passport, visitor's passport, visa, pet passport, animal passport 756 *permit*; authority, scripture.

witness, eye witness 441 *spectator*; indicator,

informant, telltale, grass, supergrass 524 *informer*; deponent, testifier, swearer, attestor 765 *signatory*; witness to character, referee; expert witness, forensic expert 459 *detective*; sponsor 707 *patron*.

Adj. evidential, show, evince, furnish evidence; significant 514 *meaningful*; indicative, symptomatic, identifying, diagnostic, deducible, verifiable 471 *probable*; corroborative, confirmatory; damning; presumptive, reliable 473 *certain*; proving, demonstrative, conclusive; factual, documented, well-documented 473 *positive*; well-grounded, well-founded 494 *true*; authoritative 178 *influential*; testified, attested, witnessed; in evidence, on the record.

Vb. evidence, show, evince, furnish evidence; show signs of, betray symptoms of, have the makings of; betoken 551 *represent*; breathe of, declare witness to 522 *manifest*; lend colour to 471 *make likely*; tell its own tale, speak for itself, speak volumes; carry weight 178 *influence*; suggest 547 *indicate*; argue, involve 523 *imply*.

testify, witness; take one's oath, swear, be sworn, speak on oath 532 *affirm*; bear witness, take the stand, give testimony, give evidence, witness for *or* against, swear to, vouch for, give one's word; authenticate, validate, give credence, certify 473 *make certain*; attest, subscribe, countersign, endorse, sign; plead, state one's case 475 *argue*; admit, avow, acknowledge 526 *confess*; give a character reference, act as referee.

corroborate, support, buttress 162 *strengthen*; sustain, uphold in evidence, substantiate 927 *vindicate*; bear out, verify; validate, confirm, ratify, establish, make a case for 473 *make certain*; lead evidence; produce one's witnesses; produce the evidence; document, give credence; collect evidence; cite the evidence; refer to a precedent, quote one's authorities; give chapter and verse.

467 Counterevidence

N. counterevidence, contraindication 14 *contrariety*; evidence against, defence, rebuttal, rejoinder 460 *answer*; refutation 479 *confutation*; denial 533 *negation*; justification 927 *vindication*; one word against another; counteroath, counterclaim; conflicting evidence, contradictory evidence; mitigating evidence 468 *qualification*; hostile witness.

Vb. tell against, weigh against, countervail; contravene, run counter, contradict, contraindicate; rebut 479 *confute*; oppose, point the other way 14 *have nothing in common*; cancel out 182 *counteract*; cut both ways 518 *be equivocal*; lead for the other side; fail to confirm, alter the case;

weaken, damage, spoil; undermine, subvert 165 *destroy*; demolish the case, turn the tables, contradict oneself, turn hostile.

Adv. conversely, on the other hand; in rebuttal.

468 Qualification

N. qualification, specification 80 *speciality*; prerequisite 627 *requirement*; assumption 512 *supposition*; leaven, colouring, tinge; modification 143 *change*; mitigation 177 *moderation*; stipulation, condition, sine qua non 766 *conditions*; limitation 747 *restriction*; proviso, reservation, exception, salvo, escape clause, let-out clause, get-out clause, exemption 919 *nonliability*; penalty clause; demur, objection, but 704 *opposition*; consideration, concession, allowance; extenuating circumstances; redeeming feature, saving grace.

Adj. qualifying, restricting, limiting; modifying; mitigatory; extenuating, palliative, excusing, weakening, colouring, leavening; contingent, provisional 766 *conditional*; discounting, allowing for, taking into account; saving, excepting, exempting; qualified, not absolute; exceptional, exempted, exempt.

Vb. qualify, condition, limit, restrict 747 *restrain*; colour, shade; leaven, alter 143 *modify*; temper, season, palliate, mitigate 177 *moderate*; adulterate 163 *weaken*; excuse 927 *extenuate*; grant, concede, make allowance for, take into account, take cognizance of; lessen 37 *lessen*; make exceptions 919 *exempt*; alter the case; insert a qualifying clause; insist on 627 *require*; relax 734 *be lax*; take exception, object, demur, raise an objection 762 *deprecate*.

Adv. provided, provided always, with the proviso that, according as, subject to, conditionally, with the understanding that, so *or* as long as; granting, admitting, supposing; allowing for; with a pinch of salt; not absolutely, not invariably; if, if not, unless 8 *if*; though, although, even if.

nevertheless, even so, all the same, for all that, after all; despite, in spite of; but, yet, still, at all events; whether, whether or no.

469 Possibility

N. possibility, potentiality; capacity, viability, viableness, workability 160 *ability*; what might be; best one can do, all in one's power, contingency, eventuality, a possibility, chance, off-chance 159 *fair chance*; good chance 137 *opportunity*; bare possibility, ghost of a chance, outside chance; likelihood 471 *probability*; conceivability; practicability; practicableness, feasibility; availability, accessibility; risk of. (See also 471 *probability*.)

Adj. *possible*, potential, hypothetical; able, capable, viable; arguable, reasonable; feasible, practicable, negotiable 701 *easy*; workable, achievable; doable, operable; attainable, approachable, accessible, obtainable, realizable; surmountable; within the bounds *or* realms of possibility; available, still open, not excluded, not too late; conceivable, imaginable; practical; allowable; contingent 124 *future*; on the cards 471 *probable*; liable, tending.

Vb. *be possible*, be feasible, etc. (see adj.); may, might; be a possibility, depend, be contingent, lie within the bounds *or* realms of possibility; stand a chance 471 *be likely*.

make possible, enable; allow 756 *permit*; give the green light, clear the path, smoothe the way, remove the obstacles.

Adv. *possibly*, conceivably; perhaps, perchance, for all one knows; within reach, within one's grasp; may be, could be; if possible, if humanly possible; wind and weather permitting, God willing, Deo volente, D.V.

470 Impossibility

N. *impossibility*, inconceivability, etc. (see adj.); unthinkableness, no chance, no way, not a chance of, not a cat's *or* cat in hell's chance, not a snowball's chance in hell *or* in an oven, not a hope 853 *hopelessness*; irrevocability; impasse, deadlock, logjam 702 *obstacle*; impracticability 643 *inexpediency*; unavailability, inaccessibility, sour grapes; impossible task, no go 700 *hard task*. (See also 472 *improbability*.)

Adj. *impossible*, not possible; ruled out, excluded; not to be thought of, out of the question, hopeless; unreasonable; incompatible with the facts 495 *erroneous*; inconceivable, unthinkable, unimaginable, unheard of; miraculous 864 *wonderful*; unrealistic 513 *imaginary*.

impracticable, not feasible, unworkable; out of the question, unattainable, insoluble, inextricable, beyond one 700 *difficult*; insuperable, insurmountable, impenetrable, unnavigable, inaccessible, unobtainable, not within one's grasp; elusive.

Vb. *be impossible*, be impracticable, etc. (see adj.), have no chance whatever.

make impossible, rule out, exclude; put out of reach, set an impossible task; eat one's hat if … 533 *negate*.

attempt the impossible, labour in vain 641 *waste effort*; have nothing to go upon, grasp at shadows, clutch at straws; be in two places at once, square the circle, discover the philosopher's stone, find the elixir of life, find a nee-

dle in a haystack; weave a rope of sand, gather grapes from thorns *or* figs from thistles, get blood from a stone, fetch water in a sieve; make bricks without straw, make a silk purse out of a sow's ear, change a leopard's spots; have one's cake and eat it; walk on water, set the Thames on fire.

Adv. *impossibly*, nohow, no way.

471 Probability

N. *probability*, likelihood 159 *chance*; good chance, fair chance, sporting chance, odds-on chance 469 *possibility*; excellent prospect 511 *prediction*; fair expectation 507 *expectation*; well-grounded hope 852 *hope*; safe bet, sure thing 473 *certainty*; credibility; likely belief 485 *belief*; plausibility, good reason 475 *reasons*; verisimilitude, semblance 445 *appearance*; theory of probability. (See also 469 *possibility*.)

Adj. *probable*, likely 180 *liable*; on the cards, in a fair way; to be expected, foreseeable, foreseen; presumptive; promising 507 *expected*; on the horizon, in the wind 155 *impending*; highly possible 469 *possible*.

plausible, specious; to all intents and purposes, to all appearances 445 *appearing*; reasonable 475 *rational*; convincing, persuasive 485 *credible*; well-grounded, well-founded 494 *true*.

Vb. *be likely*, be probable, etc. (see adj.); have a chance, be on the cards, stand a chance, be in with a chance, run a good chance 469 *be possible*; bid fair to, be in danger of 179 *tend*; show signs, have the makings of, promise.

make likely, make probable, increase the chances; involve 523 *imply*; entail; put in the way to, promote 703 *aid*; point to 466 *evidence*.

assume, presume, take for granted; conjecture, guess, dare say 512 *suppose*; think likely; count upon 473 *be certain*; gather, deduce, infer 475 *reason*.

Adv. *probably*, presumably; in all probability, in all likelihood, doubtless, as is to be expected, all things considered; very likely, most likely, ten to one, by all odds, a pound to a penny; seemingly, apparently, on the face of it, to all intents and purposes, to all appearances; like enough, as likely as not.

472 Improbability

N. *improbability*, doubt, real doubt 474 *uncertainty*; little chance, little or no chance, chance in a million, off-chance, small chance, poor chance, slim chance, outside chance, long shot; not a ghost of a chance, no chance, not a hope 470 *impossibility*; long odds, barest of possibilities; pious hopes, forlorn hope, poor prospect 508 *lack of expectation*; rare occurrence, rarity 140 *infrequency*; implausibility, traveller's tale, fisherman's yarn 541 *falsehood*. (See also 470 *impossibility*.)

Adj. improbable, unlikely, more than doubtful, dubious 474 *uncertain*; hard to believe, fishy, unconvincing, implausible; rare 140 *infrequent*; inconceivable 470 *impossible*; incredible, too good to be true.

Vb. be unlikely, be improbable, look impossible, etc. (see adj.); have the barest of chances, show little hope, be implausible, not wash, be hard to believe, strain one's credulity 486 *cause doubt*; think unlikely, whistle for 508 *not expect*.

Int. not likely!, no fear!, no way!, not on your life!, not on your nelly!, not a hope!, some hopes!

473 Certainty

N. certainty, certain knowledge 490 *knowledge*; certainness, assuredness, sureness; inevitability, inexorability, irrevocability, necessity 596 *fate*; infallibility; reliability, unimpeachability 494 *truth*; unambiguity, unequivocalness; incontrovertibility, irrefutability, indisputability, proof 478 *demonstration*; authentication, ratification, validation; certification, verification, confirmation; attestation 466 *testimony*; check 459 *enquiry*; ascertainment 484 *discovery*; dead certainty, cert, dead cert, sure thing, safe bet, cinch, open-and-shut case, foregone conclusion; fact; matter of fact, fait accompli 154 *event*; settled decision 480 *judgment*.

positiveness, moral certainty; assurance, confidence, conviction, persuasion 485 *belief*; unshakable opinion 485 *opinion*; idée fixe, obsession 481 *bias*; dogmatism; infallibility, self-confidence; pontification, laying down the law; confidence-building, assertiveness training.

dogmatist, self-opinionated person; bigot, fanatic, zealot 979 *zealot*; oracle, knowall, smarty-pants 500 *wiseacre*.

Adj. certain, sure, solid, unshakable, well-founded, well-grounded 3 *substantial*; cast-iron, reliable 929 *trustworthy*; authoritative, official 494 *genuine*; factual, historical 494 *true*; authenticated, ascertained, certified, attested, guaranteed, warranted; tested, tried, foolproof 660 *safe*; infallible, unerring 540 *truthful*; axiomatic, dogmatic, taken for granted; self-evident, evident, apparent; unequivocal, unambiguous; unmistakable, clear, clear as day 443 *obvious*; inevitable, irrevocable, inexorable 596 *fated*; bound, bound to be, in the bag; sure as fate, sure as death; inviolable, safe as houses, safe as the Bank of England 660 *invulnerable*; verifiable, demonstrable.

positive, confident, assured, self-assured, self-confident, certain in one's mind, undoubting, convinced, persuaded, certified, sure; opinionated, self-opinionated; pontificating, oracular 532 *assertive*; dogmatic, doctrinaire 976 *orthodox*; obsessed, bigoted, fanatical 481 *biased*; unshaken, set in one's ways, fixed in one's opinions 153 *unchangeable*; clear-cut; definite, decisive, defined, unambiguous, unambivalent, unequivocal; convincing 485 *credible*; affirmative, categorical, absolute, unqualified, unreserved; conclusive.

undisputed, beyond doubt, beyond all reasonable doubt, without a shadow of doubt, axiomatic, uncontroversial; unquestioned, undoubted, uncontested, unarguable, undebatable, indubitable, unquestionable, incontrovertible, incontestable, unimpeachable, undeniable, irrefutable.

Vb. be certain, be sure, etc. (see adj.); leave no doubt, be clear as day, be plain as the nose on your face, stand to reason, be axiomatic; be positive, be assured, satisfy oneself, convince oneself, feel sure, be clear in one's mind, have no doubts; know for certain 490 *know*; stick to one's guns, have made up one's mind, dismiss all doubt; depend on it, rely on, bank on, trust in, swear by; put one's shirt on, lay one's bottom dollar.

dogmatize, pontificate, lay down the law 532 *affirm*; know all the answers.

make certain, certify, authenticate, ratify, seal, sign 488 *endorse*; guarantee, warrant, assure; finalize, settle, decide 480 *judge*; remove doubt, persuade 485 *convince*; make sure, ascertain, check, run a check, double-check, verify, confirm, confirm in writing, clinch 466 *corroborate*; reassure oneself, take a second look, do a double take; insure against 660 *safeguard*; reinsure 858 *be cautious*; ensure, make inevitable 596 *necessitate*.

Adv. certainly, definitely, for sure, to be sure, no doubt, doubtless, indubitably, as sure as anything, as sure as eggs is eggs, as sure as God made little green apples, as night follows day, of course, as a matter of course, no question; no two ways about it, no ifs or buts; without fail, sink or swim, rain or shine, come hell or high water, come what may, whatever happens.

474 Uncertainty

N. uncertainty, doubtfulness, dubiousness; ambiguity, ambivalence 518 *equivocalness*; vagueness, haziness, obscurity 418 *darkness*; mist, haze, fog 423 *opacity*; grey area; yes and no, don't know, floating voter, vacillation, indeterminacy, borderline case; indefiniteness, roving commission; query, question mark 459 *question*; open question, anybody's guess, a matter of tossing a coin; guess, guesswork, guesstimate, nothing to go on, estimate 480 *estimate*, 512 *conjecture*; contingency 159 *chance*; gamble, toss-up, wager 618 *gambling*; leap *or* shot in the dark, bow at a venture, pig in a poke, blind date; something or other, this or that.

dubiety, a matter of doubt 486 *doubt*; open verdict, a verdict of not proven; suspense, waiting 507 *expectation*; doubt, indecision, hesitancy, shilly-shallying, vacillation 317 *fluctuation*; seesaw, floating vote 601 *irresolution*; bafflement, quandary; dilemma, cleft stick, Morton's fork.

unreliability, fallibility 495 *error*; precariousness, unstable condition, touch and go 661 *danger*; untrustworthiness, treacherousness; variability, changeability 152 *changeableness*; unpredictability, unexpectedness 508 *lack of expectation*; fickleness, capriciousness; slipperiness; lack of security, no guarantee, no collateral, gentleman's agreement, handshake deal.

Adj. *uncertain*, unsure, doubtful, dubious; chancy, risky 661 *unsafe*; treacherous (see also *unreliable* below); subject to chance, at the mercy of events; sporadic 140 *infrequent*; fluid; contingent, depending on 766 *conditional*; unpredictable, unforeseeable 508 *unexpected*; indeterminate, undefined; random; indecisive, undecided, vacillating, in suspense; in question, under enquiry; open to question, questionable, not decided, undecided, the jury is out; arguable, debatable, disputable, controvertible, controversial; suspicious 472 *improbable*; problematic *or* problematical, hypothetical, speculative; undefinable, borderline, grey-area, marginal; ambiguous 518 *equivocal*; paradoxical 477 *illogical*; oracular, enigmatic, cryptic, obscure 517 *puzzling*; vague, hazy, misty, cloudy 419 *shadowy*; mysterious, veiled 523 *occult*; unresolved, unexplained 517 *unintelligible*; perplexing, bewildering.

unreliable, undependable, untrustworthy; treacherous 930 *dishonest*; unsteady, unstable, variable, vacillating, changeable 152 *changing*; unpredictable, unforeseeable; fickle 604 *capricious*; fallible, open to error 495 *erroneous*; precarious, touch and go.

doubting, in doubt, doubtful, dubious, full of doubt, riddled with doubt, plagued by uncertainty; agnostic, sceptical; sitting on the fence, hedging one's bets, in two minds; in suspense, open-minded; distrustful, mistrustful

858 *cautious*; uncertain, diffident; hesitant, undecided, wavering, vacillating, unsure which way to jump 601 *irresolute*; unable to say; baffled 517 *puzzled*; in a cleft stick, on the horns of a dilemma; disorientated; clueless 491 *ignorant*.

Vb. *be uncertain*, be contingent, lie in the lap of the gods; hinge on, be dependent on 157 *depend*; be touch and go, hang by a thread, tremble in the balance, go to the wire; be open to question, be ambiguous 518 *be equivocal*; have one's doubts 486 *doubt*; wait and see 507 *await*; have a suspicion, suspect, wonder, wonder whether; dither, be in two minds, hover, float, be a don't know, sit on the fence, sway, seesaw, waver, teeter, vacillate, shilly-shally, falter, pause, hesitate 601 *be irresolute*; demur; flounder; be in the dark, have nothing to go on, grope 461 *be tentative*; cast about, lose the thread, miss one's way, get lost 282 *stray*; lose the scent, lose track of; not know which way to turn, be at one's wits' end, be at a loss, not know what to make of, be in a dilemma, be in a quandary; wouldn't swear, could be wrong; hem and ha 580 *stammer*.

puzzle, perplex, confuse, daze, bewilder, baffle, boggle the mind, nonplus, flummox, stump, floor 727 *defeat*; mystify, keep one guessing; bamboozle; fox, throw off the scent 495 *mislead*; plague or riddle with doubt 486 *cause doubt*; make one think.

Adv. *in suspense*, in a state of uncertainty, on the horns of a dilemma, in a maze, in a daze.

Reasoning processes

475 Reasoning

N. *reasoning*, force of argument; reason, discursive reason; lateral thinking 476 *intuition*; sweet reason, reasonableness, rationality; dialectics, logic; logical process, logical sequence, inference, generalization; distinction 463 *discrimination*; deductive reasoning, deduction; inductive reasoning, empirical reasoning; rationalism, dialectic 449 *philosophy*; modern maths 86 *mathematics*; simple arithmetic.

premise, postulate, basis of reasoning; principle, general principle, first principle; lemma, starting point; assumption, stipulation 512 *supposition*; axiom, self-evident truth 496 *maxim*; datum, data; hypothesis.

argument, discussion, symposium, dialogue;

exchange of views, cut and thrust; disputation, controversy, debate 489 *dissent*; set *or* formal argument, plea, pleading; thesis, case; reasons, submission; defence; polemics; war of words, paper war 709 *quarrel*; propaganda, agitprop, spin, pamphleteering 534 *teaching*; controversialism, argumentativeness, hairsplitting, logic-chopping, contentiousness, wrangling, jangling 709 *dissension*; sophism 477 *sophistry*; legal argument, pleadings 959 *litigation*.

reasons, grounds; where one is coming from; arguments, pros and cons; case, good case, case to answer; sound argument, conclusive argument 478 *demonstration*; point, valid point, point well taken.

Adj. rational, clear-headed, reasoning, reasonable; rationalistic, logical; cogent, acceptable, admissible, to the point, pointed, well-grounded, well-argued 9 *relevant*; sensible, fair 913 *just*; analytic; consistent, systematic, methodological; dialectic, discursive, deductive, inductive, axiomatic 473 *certain*; tenable 469 *possible*; a posteriori, a priori, a fortiori.

Vb. be reasonable 471 *be likely*; stand to reason, follow, hang together, hold water; appeal to reason; listen to reason, be guided by reason; yield to argument; admit, concede; have a case, have a case to be answered, have logic on one's side.

reason, philosophize 449 *think*; syllogize, rationalize; apply reason, bring reason to bear, use one's grey matter, put two and two together; infer, deduce, induct; explain 520 *interpret*.

argue, argufy, argy-bargy, bandy words, bandy arguments, cut and thrust; hold a symposium; exchange opinions, have an exchange of views, discuss; debate, dispute; quibble, split hairs, chop logic; argue the case, argue the point; stick to one's guns; work an argument to death 532 *emphasize*; put one's case, plead; pamphleteer 534 *teach*; take up the case, defend; attack; cross swords, take up a point with, join issue, demur, cavil 489 *dissent*; analyse, pull to pieces; out-argue; have words, have a confrontation, wrangle; answer back, make a rejoinder 460 *answer*; start an argument, move a motion, open a discussion *or* debate.

postulate, posit, stipulate, lay down, assume 512 *suppose*; take for granted, refer to first principles.

476 Intuition: absence of reason

N. intuition, instinct, association, Pavlovian response, automatic reaction, gut reaction, knee-jerk reaction 450 *absence of thought*; sixth sense, extrasensory perception, ESP; telepathy; insight, second sight, clairvoyance 984 *psychics*; id, subconscious; intuitiveness; divination; inspiration, presentiment, impulse 818 *feeling*; feminine logic; rule of thumb; hunch.

Adj. intuitive, instinctive, impulsive; devoid of logic 477 *illogical*; impressionistic, subjective; involuntary 609 *spontaneous*; subconscious 447 *psychic*; beyond reason; inspirational, inspired, clairvoyant, ESP, telepathic.

Vb. know intuitively, know by instinct, intuit, have a sixth sense; sense, feel in one's bones, have a funny feeling, have a hunch; have a gut reaction, react instinctively; play it by ear, go by impressions, rely on intuition, dispense with reason, use feminine logic; use guesswork, work on a hunch.

477 Sophistry: false reasoning

N. sophistry, illogicalness, illogicality, illogic; feminine logic 476 *intuition*; sophistical reasoning; false reasoning, rationalization; double think, self-deception; mental reservation 525 *concealment*; equivocation, blinding with science, casuistry; subtlety, over-subtlety; hairsplitting, logic-chopping; claptrap, mere words 515 *empty talk*; quibbling; chicanery, subterfuge; evasion 614 *pretext*.

sophism, a sophistry, specious argument; illogicality, fallacy; loose thinking, sloppy thinking; solecism, flaw in the argument; begging the question, circular reasoning; non sequitur, irrelevancy, contradiction in terms, Irishism; weak case.

Adj. illogical, contrary to reason, irrational, unreasonable; unreasoned, arbitrary; fallacious, fallible; contradictory, self-contradictory, inconsistent, incongruous; unwarranted, invalid, untenable, unsound; unfounded, ungrounded, groundless; irrelevant, inconsequent, inconsequential; incorrect, unscientific, false 495 *erroneous*.

poorly reasoned, unrigorous, inconclusive; unproved; weak, feeble; flimsy; loose, woolly, muddled, confused.

Vb. reason badly, argue in a circle, beg the question, fail to get to the point, not see the wood for the trees, strain at a gnat and swallow a camel; not have a leg to stand on; talk at random.

use sophistry, sophisticate, mislead 535 *misteach*; mystify, quibble, cavil, split hairs 475 *argue*; equivocate 518 *be equivocal*; dodge, shuffle, fence; not come to the point, beat about the bush 570 *be diffuse*; evade 667 *elude*; draw a veil over, varnish, gloss over, whitewash; colour 552 *misrepresent*; pervert, misapply 675 *misuse*; pervert reason, twist the argument, torture logic; prove that white is black.

478 Demonstration

N. *demonstration*, documentation, authentication 466 *evidence*; proven fact 494 *truth*; proof; conclusive proof; conclusiveness 473 *certainty*; verification, ascertainment 461 *experiment*; deduction, inference, argument, triumph of argument 475 *reasoning*; exposition, clarification 522 *manifestation*; burden of proof, onus.

Vb. *demonstrate*, prove; show, evince 522 *manifest*; justify 927 *vindicate*; bear out 466 *corroborate*; produce the evidence, document, provide documentation, substantiate, establish, verify 466 *evidence*; infer, deduce, draw, draw a conclusion 475 *reason*; settle the question, satisfy 473 *make certain*; make out a case, prove one's point, clinch an argument, have the best of an argument, win an argument 485 *convince*.

be proved, prove to be true, stand to reason 475 *be reasonable*; stand up to investigation, hold water, hold good 494 *be true*.

Adv. *of course*, undeniably, without doubt; as already proved, quod erat demonstrandum, QED.

479 Confutation

N. *confutation*, refutation, disproof, invalidation; conviction 961 *condemnation*; rebuttal, rejoinder, clincher, knock-down argument; last word, retort, repartee 839 *witticism*; contradiction, denial, denunciation 533 *negation*; exploded argument.

Vb. *confute*, refute, invalidate; rebut, rejoin, retort, have an answer, explain away; deny, contradict 533 *negate*; give the lie to, force to withdraw; prove the contrary, show the fallacy of; cut the ground from under, leave someone without a leg to stand on; confound, rout, silence, reduce to silence, stop the mouth, shut up, floor, gravel, nonplus; condemn one out of his own mouth; show up, expose; convict 961 *condemn*; defeat one's logic; blow sky-high, shoot full of holes, puncture, riddle, destroy, explode, demolish one's arguments, drive a coach and horses through, knock the bottom out of 165 *demolish*; have, have in one's hand, have one on the hip; overthrow, squash, crush, overwhelm 727 *defeat*; riddle the defence, outargue, have the better of the argument, get the better of, score off, parry, avoid the trap; stand, stand up to argument; dismiss, override, sweep aside, brush aside; brook no denial, affirm the contrary 532 *affirm*.

480 Judgment: conclusion

N. *judgment*, judging (see also *estimate* below); good judgment, discretion 463 *discrimination*; bad judgment, lack of discretion 464 *lack of discrimination*; arbitration, umpirage; verdict, finding; sentence, tariff 963 *punishment*; summing-up, pronouncement; act of judgment, decision, adjudication, award; order, court order, ruling, fatwa, decree, order of the court, county court judgment, CCJ 737 *decree*; decree nisi, decree absolute; judgment in appeal, irrevocable decision; settled decision; final judgment, conclusion, result, upshot; moral 496 *maxim*; value judgment 476 *intuition*; reasoned judgment, deduction, inference, corollary 475 *reasoning*; wise judgment, judgment of Solomon 498 *wisdom*; fair judgment, unclouded eye 913 *justice*; vox populi, voting, referendum, plebiscite, poll 605 *vote*.

estimate, estimation, view 485 *opinion*; assessment, valuation, evaluation, calculation 465 *measurement*; diagnosis; guess, guesstimate 474 *uncertainty*; consideration, comparing, contrasting 462 *comparison*; appreciation, appraisal, appraisement 520 *interpretation*; criticism, constructive criticism 703 *aid*; destructive criticism 702 *hindrance*; critique, crit, review, notice, press notice, comment, comments, observations, remarks, profile 591 *article*; summing-up; survey 438 *inspection*; favourable report 923 *approbation*; unfavourable report, censure 924 *disapprobation*.

estimator, judge, adjudicator; arbitrator, umpire, referee, assistant referee, linesman *or* -woman, fourth official; surveyor, valuer, valuator; inspector, inspecting officer, reporter, examiner, ombudsman, ACAS (=Advisory, Conciliation and Arbitration Service) 459 *enquirer*; counsellor 691 *adviser*; censor, critic, reviewer 591 *dissertator*; commentator, observer 520 *interpreter*; juror, assessor 957 *jury*; voter, elector 605 *electorate*.

Adj. *judicial*, judicious 463 *discriminating*; shrewd 498 *wise*; unbiased, dispassionate 913 *just*; arbitral, judicatory, conclusive; sententious.

Vb. *judge*, sit in judgment, hold the scales; arbitrate, referee, umpire; hear, try, hear the case, try the cause; uphold an objection, disallow an objection; rule, pronounce; find, find for, find against; decree, award, adjudicate; decide, settle, conclude; confirm, make absolute; pass judgment, deliver judgment; sentence, pass sentence, doom 961 *condemn*; agree on a verdict, return *or* bring in a verdict; sum up.

estimate, form *or* make an estimate, measure, calculate, make 465 *gauge*; value, evaluate, appraise; rate, rank; sum up, size up; conjecture, guess 512 *suppose*; take stock 808 *account*; diagnose; consider, weigh, ponder, weigh the pros and cons, take everything into consideration 449 *meditate*; criticize, review 591 *dissertate*.

Adv. *sub judice*, under investigation, under trial, under sentence.

481 Misjudgment. Prejudice

N. *misjudgment*, miscalculation, misreckoning, misconception, wrong impression 495 *error*; loose thinking, sloppy thinking 495 *inexactness*; bad judgment, poor judgment 464 *lack of discrimination*; lack of vision, blindness, short-sightedness, short-termism; fallibility, gullibility 499 *unintelligence*; misconstruction 521 *misinterpretation*; wrong verdict, miscarriage of justice 914 *injustice*; overvaluation 482 *overestimation*; undervaluation 483 *underestimation*; autosuggestion, self-deception, self-delusion, wishful thinking 542 *deception*; fool's paradise 513 *fantasy*; false dawn 509 *disappointment*.

prejudgment, foregone conclusion 608 *predetermination*; preconception, mind made up; preconceived idea; idée fixe, obsession, hang-up, hobbyhorse, thing, fixation, bee in the bonnet, monomania, emotional baggage, — on the brain 503 *personality disorder*.

prejudice, predilection; partiality, favouritism 914 *injustice*; penchant, bias, biased judgment, warped judgment, jaundiced eye; blind spot, blind side, tunnel vision, mote in the eye, beam in the eye 439 *blindness*; onesidedness, party spirit 708 *party*; partisanship, clannishness, cliquishness, esprit de corps; -ism; parochialism, provincialism, insularity 978 *sectarianism*; nationalism, chauvinism, gung-ho attitude, xenophobia, my country right or wrong; snobbishness, class war, class prejudice, classism, postcode discrimination; ageism, granny-bashing; sexism, sex prejudice, sex discrimination, gender discrimination, gender apartheid, gendering, male chauvinism, glass ceiling; ableism, fattism, heightism, sizeism; phobia 854 *phobia*; heterosexism, homophobia; xenophobia, race prejudice, racialism, racism, institutional racism, race hate; colour prejudice, colour bar, apartheid, segregation, discrimination 57 *exclusion*; intolerance, persecution, anti-Semitism 888 *hatred*.

narrow mind, narrow-mindedness, smallmindedness; insularity, parochialism, provincialism; closed mind, one-track mind, tunnel vision; one-sidedness; legalism, pedantry 735

severity; intolerance, dogmatism 473 *positiveness*; bigotry, fanaticism 602 *opinionatedness*; pedant, stickler 862 *perfectionist*; faddist 504 *crank*; zealot, bigot, fanatic 473 *dogmatist*; racialist, racist, white supremacist; chauvinist, sexist.

bias, unbalance, disequilibrium 29 *inequality*; warp, bent, slant, liability, penchant 179 *tendency*; angle, point of view 485 *opinion*; mind made up, obsession (see also *prejudgment* above); Afrocentrism, Anglocentrism, Eurocentrism.

Adj. *misjudging*, misconceiving, misinterpreting, etc. (see vb.); miscalculating, in error, out 495 *mistaken*; fallible, gullible 499 *foolish*; wrong, wrong-headed; unseeing 439 *blind*; myopic, purblind, short-sighted 440 *dim-sighted*; misguided, superstitious 487 *credulous*; subjective, unrealistic, visionary, impractical; crankish, faddy, faddish, whimsical 503 *crazy*; besotted, infatuated 887 *in love*; haunted, obsessed, hung up, eaten up with.

narrow-minded, petty-minded, narrow, hidebound; short-sighted, tunnel-visioned; parochial, provincial, insular; pedantic, donnish 735 *severe*; legalistic, literal, literal-minded, unimaginative, matter-of-fact; hypercritical, over-scrupulous, picky, fussy 862 *fastidious*; stiff, unbending 602 *obstinate*; dictatorial, dogmatic 473 *positive*; opinionated, opinionative; self-opinioned, self-conceited 871 *proud*.

biased, warped, twisted, swayed; jaundiced, prejudiced; snobbish, cliquish, clannish; partisan, one-sided, party-minded 978 *sectarian*; nationalistic, chauvinistic, gung-hoish, jingoistic, xenophobic; Afrocentric, Anglocentric, Eurocentric; racist, racialist; sexist, ageist, classist; class-prejudiced, colour-prejudiced; predisposed, preconceived; prejudging 608 *predetermined*; subjective, personal 80 *private*, *special*; discriminatory 914 *unjust*; intolerant 735 *oppressive*; bigoted, fanatic 602 *obstinate*; blinded 439 *blind*.

Vb. *misjudge*, miscalculate, miscount 495 *blunder*; not take into account, reckon without; undervalue, minimize 483 *underestimate*; overestimate, overvalue 482 *overrate*; guess wrong, come to the wrong conclusion, misconceive 521 *misinterpret*; overreach oneself, overplay one's hand; get the wrong end of the stick 695 *act foolishly*; not see the wood for the trees; not see beyond one's nose 499 *be foolish*; fly in the face of facts 477 *reason badly*.

prejudge, judge beforehand, make up one's mind in advance 608 *predetermine*; prejudice the issue, precondemn; preconceive, presuppose, presume 475 *postulate*; jump to conclusions 857 *be rash*.

bias, warp, twist, bend; jaundice, prejudice; predispose 178 *influence*.

be biased, be prejudiced, etc. (see adj.); be one-sided, see one side only, show favouritism, favour one side 914 *do wrong*; lean, favour, take sides, have a down on, have it in for, hold it against one, be unfair, discriminate against 735 *oppress*; lose one's sense of proportion; suffer from tunnel vision, blind oneself to, have a blind side, have a blind spot 439 *be blind*.

482 Overestimation

N. *overestimation*, overestimate, overenthusiasm, overvaluation 481 *misjudgment*; overstatement 546 *exaggeration*; boasting 877 *boast*; ballyhoo, hype, buildup, overkill 528 *publicity*; overpraise, panegyric, gush, hot air 515 *empty talk*; storm in a teacup, much ado about nothing; megalomania, vanity 871 *pride*; overconfidence 857 *rashness*; egotism 932 *selfishness*; overoptimism; defeatism 853 *hopelessness*; optimist 852 *hope*; pessimist, prophet of doom, doom-watcher, doomster, Jonah, defeatist; exaggerator, puffer, barker, advertiser, promoter 528 *publicizer*.

Adj. *optimistic*, can-do, upbeat, sanguine, overconfident; overpitched; overenthusiastic, raving.

Vb. *overestimate*, overrate, count all one's geese swans; overvalue, overprice, set too high a value on 811 *overcharge*; rave, idealize, overpraise, think too much of; make too much of 546 *exaggerate*; overemphasize, overstress, overdo, play up, overpitch, inflate, magnify 197 *enlarge*; boost, puff, panegyrize, hype 923 *praise*; attach too much importance to, make mountains out of molehills; maximize, make the most of; whitewash, paper over the cracks.

483 Underestimation

N. *underestimation*, underestimate, undervaluation, minimization; conservative estimate, modest calculation 177 *moderation*; depreciation 926 *detraction*; understatement, litotes, meiosis; euphemism 950 *prudery*; self-depreciation, self-effacement, overmodesty 872 *humility*; false modesty, mock modesty, irony 850 *affectation*; pessimism 853 *hopelessness*; pessimist, minimizer, cynic 926 *detractor*.

Vb. *underestimate*, underrate, undervalue, underprice; mark down, discount 812 *cheapen*; depreciate, underpraise, run down, cry down, disparage 926 *detract*; slight, pooh-pooh 922 *hold cheap*; not do justice to, do less than justice 481 *misjudge*; understate; play down, soft-pedal; shrug off 458 *disregard*; make little of, minimize; make light of, set no store by, think

too little of 922 *despise*.

484 Discovery

N. *discovery*, finding; invention; exploration, archaeology, speleology, potholing; excavation 459 *search*; detection 438 *inspection*; radio-location 187 *location*; water divining; exposure, revelation 522 *manifestation*; illumination, realization, lightbulb moment, eureka moment, when the penny drops; hitting upon, serendipity; strike, find, lucky find, treasure trove; eye-opener 508 *lack of expectation*; open sesame 263 *opener*; disenchantment.

detector, probe; space probe, spy satellite 276 *spaceship*; asdic, sonar; early warning system; radar, radar trap, speed trap; breathalyser, breath test, sniffer torch; finder 442 *telescope*; lie detector, polygraph; Geiger counter 465 *meter*; metal detector; divining rod; water diviner; talent scout; discoverer, inventor; explorer 268 *traveller*; archaeologist, speleologist, potholer 459 *enquirer*; prospector 461 *experimenter*; gastroscope, auriscope, ophthalmoscope, colposcope 658 *diagnosis*.

Vb. *discover*, invent, explore; find out; strike, hit, hit upon; come upon, happen on, stumble on; meet, encounter 154 *meet with*; tumble to, awake to, see the truth, see the light, see in its true colours 516 *understand*; find, locate 187 *place*; recognize, identify 490 *know*; unearth, uncover, bring to light 522 *manifest*; elicit, worm out, ferret out, nose out, sniff out, smell out 459 *search*; get wind of 524 *be informed*.

detect, find a clue, be on the track, be getting warm, see daylight; put one's finger on the spot, hit the nail on the head; discern, perceive, notice, spot, catch sight of 438 *see*; sense, trace; smell a rat; nose, scent out; follow, tail, trail, trace, track down 619 *hunt*.

Int. *eureka!*, got it!

485 Belief

N. *belief*, suspension of disbelief; credence, credit; assurance, conviction, persuasion; dependence on, trust, faith; religious belief 973 *religious faith*; implicit belief, firm belief, unshakable belief 473 *certainty*; obsession, self-conviction; expectation 852 *hope*; popular belief, public opinion; one's word of honour 929 *probity*.

creed, credo, what one believes; dogma 976 *orthodoxy*; precepts, principles, tenets, articles; catechism, articles of faith; rubric, canon, rule 496 *maxim*; declaration of faith, confession of faith, shahada 526 *disclosure*; doctrine, system, school.

opinion, sentiment, mind, view; point of

view, viewpoint, stand, position, attitude, angle 438 *view*; received wisdom 488 *consensus*; impression 818 *feeling*; conception, thought 451 *idea*; thinking, way of thinking, school of thought, outlook on life 449 *philosophy*; assumption, presumption, principle 475 *premise*; theory, hypothesis 512 *supposition*; surmise, guess 512 *conjecture*; conclusion 480 *judgment*.

Adj. credible, plausible, believable, tenable, reasonable 469 *possible*; likely, to be expected 471 *probable*; reliable, trustworthy, trusty; persuasive, convincing 178 *influential*; trusted, believed; held, maintained; accepted, credited, accredited.

credal, taught, doctrinal, dogmatic, confessional; canonical, orthodox, authoritative, accredited, ex cathedra; of faith, accepted on trust; sacrosanct, unquestioned, God-given; undeniable, absolute, unshakable 473 *undisputed*.

Vb. believe, be a believer; credit, put faith in; hold, hold to be true; maintain, declare 532 *affirm*; believe religiously, perceive as true, take for gospel; take on trust, take on credit; buy, swallow, swallow whole 487 *be credulous*; have no doubt, know for certain, be convinced, be sold on; rest assured, be easy in one's mind about, be secure in the belief, believe implicitly; have confidence in, trust, rely on, depend on, take one at his *or* her word; give one credit for, pin one's faith on, pin one's hopes on; have faith in, believe in, swear by, reckon on, count on, bank on; come to believe, be converted; realize 484 *discover*; take as proven.

be of the opinion that, opine, think, conceive, fancy; have a hunch, surmise, guess 512 *suppose*; suspect, be under *or* have the impression 818 *feel*; deem, assume, presume, take it, hold; get hold of an idea, get it into one's head; have views, have a point of view, view as, take as, regard as, consider as, look upon as, set down as; cherish an opinion; express an opinion; hazard an opinion 532 *affirm*; shove *or* put *or* stick one's oar in 678 *meddle*; change one's mind 603 *recant*.

convince, make believe, assure, persuade, satisfy; bring home to 478 *demonstrate*; make confident, restore one's faith; convert, win over, bring over, bring round, wean from; evangelize, spread the gospel; propagandize, indoctrinate, din into 534 *teach*; cram down one's throat; sell an idea to, put over, put across; gain one's confidence, sway one's belief 178 *influence*, mesmerize, hypnotize.

be believed, be widely believed, be received, gain wide acceptance; go down well, be swallowed; find willing ears; carry conviction; find credence, pass for truth.

486 Unbelief. Doubt

N. unbelief, disbelief, incredulity, discredit; disagreement 489 *dissent*; agnosticism; denial 533 *negation*; lack of faith; misbelief 977 *heresy*; atheism 974 *lack of religion*; derision, scorn, mockery 851 *ridicule*; loss of faith, lapse of faith, crisis of conscience, retraction 603 *recantation*; incredibility 472 *improbability*.

doubt 474 *dubiety*; hesitation, wavering, vacillation, shilly-shallying, uncertainty; misgiving, distrust, mistrust; suspiciousness, scepticism, agnosticism; reserve, reservation, second thoughts 468 *qualification*; demur, objection 704 *opposition*; scruple, qualm, suspicion 854 *nervousness*.

unbeliever, disbeliever; heathen, infidel 977 *heretic*; atheist; sceptic, agnostic; doubter, doubting Thomas; dissenter 489 *objector*; retractor, recanter 603 *recanter*; denier, Holocaust denier 533 *negation*; cynic, pessimist; scoffer, mocker, scorner 926 *detractor*.

Vb. disbelieve, be incredulous, find hard to believe, explain away, discredit, greet with scepticism, withhold assent, disagree 489 *dissent*; not fall for, not buy; mock, scoff at 851 *ridicule*; deny, deny outright 533 *negate*; refuse to admit, ignore; retract, lapse 603 *recant*.

doubt, half-believe 474 *be uncertain*; demur, object, cavil, question, scruple, boggle, have reservations 468 *qualify*; pause; hesitate, waver 601 *be irresolute*; distrust, mistrust, suspect, have fears 854 *be nervous*; shy at; be sceptical, doubt the truth of, take leave to doubt; not trust, set no store by; have one's doubts, take with a pinch of salt, harbour doubts, cherish scruples; entertain suspicions, smell a rat; hold back, not go all the way with one 598 *be unwilling*.

cause doubt, cast doubt, raise questions; cast a shadow over, make suspect; call in question, discredit 926 *defame*; shake, shake one's faith, undermine one's belief; pass belief 472 *be unlikely*; keep one guessing 517 *be unintelligible*.

Int. you're kidding!, you're joking!, you can't be serious!, please!

487 Credulity

N. credulity, credulousness; simplicity, gullibility, naiveté; blind faith 612 *persuadability*; self-delusion, self-deception, wishful thinking 481 *misjudgment*; superstition, superstitiousness; sucker, mug 544 *dupe*.

Adj. credulous, believing, persuadable, amenable; easily taken in, easily deceived, easily duped; unworldly; naive, simple, unsophisticated, green; overcredulous; infatuated; confiding, trustful, unsuspecting.

Vb. *be credulous*, be easily persuaded; kid oneself, fool oneself; suspend one's judgment 477 *reason badly*; follow implicitly, believe every word, fall for, buy it, take on trust, take for granted, take for gospel 485 *believe*; accept 299 *absorb*; rise to the bait, swallow, swallow hook, line and sinker 544 *be duped*; run away with an idea *or* a notion, rush *or* jump to a conclusion; be superstitious, touch wood, keep one's fingers crossed; think the moon is made of green cheese, not hear a word against.

488 Assent

N. *assent*, hearty assent; welcome; agreement, concurrence 758 *consent*; acceptance, agreement in principle 597 *willingness*; acquiescence 721 *submission*; acknowledgment, admission, clean breast, plea of guilty, plea bargain, plea-bargaining 939 *penitence*; confession; declaration of faith, profession 532 *affirmation*; sanction, nod, OK, imprimatur, thumbs up, go-ahead, green light 756 *permission*; approval, vote of confidence 923 *approbation*; corroboration 466 *evidence*; confirmation, verification 478 *demonstration*; ratification; authentication; certification, endorsement, seal, signature, mark, cross; visa, passport, pass 756 *permit*; stamp, rubber stamp 547 *label*; support 703 *aid*.

consensus, same mind 24 *agreement*; concordance, harmony, unison 710 *harmony*; unanimity, common consent, universal agreement; popular belief, public opinion, received wisdom; single voice; likemindedness, same wavelength, two minds with but a single thought 18 *similarity*; mutual understanding, bargain 765 *pact*.

assenter, follower 83 *conformist*; fellow traveller, ally 707 *collaborator*; yes-man 925 *flatterer*; the ayes; upholder, supporter, active supporter, abettor 703 *helper*; seconder 707 *patron*; subscriber, endorser 765 *signatory*; consenting party, covenanter.

Adj. *assenting*, concurring, party to 24 *agreeing*; aiding and abetting, supporting, collaborating 706 *cooperative*; likeminded, sympathetic, on the same wavelength, welcoming 880 *friendly*; unanimous, with one voice, in chorus; acquiescent 597 *willing*; granting 756 *permitting*; sanctioning, ratificatory; not opposed, conceding.

Vb. *assent*, concur, agree with 24 *accord*; welcome, acclaim 923 *applaud*; have no reservations 473 *be certain*; accept, agree in principle, like the idea, buy it; not deny, concede,

own, acknowledge, grant, allow 475 *be reasonable*; plead guilty, avow 526 *confess*; signify assent, nod, say aye, say yes, raise one's hand in assent, agree to, give one's assent, go along with 758 *consent*; sanction 756 *permit*; ratify (see also *endorse* below); agree with, see eye to eye, be on the same wavelength; echo, say amen, say hear hear; back up; be a yes-man, rubber-stamp 925 *flatter*; side with 708 *join a party*; collaborate 706 *cooperate*; tolerate (see also *acquiesce* below); agree upon, come to an understanding, have a mutual agreement 765 *contract*.

acquiesce, accept, abide by 739 *obey*; tolerate, put up with, suffer, bear, endure, wear it, bite the bullet; sign on the dotted line, toe the line 721 *submit*; yield, defer to, withdraw one's objections; let the ayes have it, allow 756 *permit*; let it happen, look on 441 *watch*; go with the stream *or* crowd, float with the current, join in the chorus, follow the fashion *or* trend, run with the pack, jump on the bandwagon 83 *conform*.

endorse, second, support, back up, vote for, give one's vote to 703 *patronize*; subscribe to, attest 547 *sign*; rubber-stamp, ratify, sanction, authorize 758 *consent*; authenticate 473 *make certain*; countersign.

Int. *yes*, okay, OK, uh-huh, aye, amen, yea; hear, hear!, absolutely!, aye, aye!, well said!, you can say that again!, how right you are!, I couldn't agree more!, yes indeed!

489 Dissent

N. *dissent*, agreement to disagree *or* differ; dissidence, difference 704 *opposition*; difference of opinion, a vote against, disagreement, controversy 709 *dissension*; faction 708 *party*; disaffection 829 *discontent*; dissatisfaction, disapproval 924 *disapprobation*; repudiation 607 *rejection*; protestantism, nonconformism, schism 978 *sectarianism*; alternative life style, alternative medicine, alternative birth 84 *nonconformity*; withdrawal, secession 621 *relinquishment*; walkout 145 *strike*; reluctance 598 *unwillingness*; recusancy 738 *disobedience*; noncompliance 769 *non-observance*; denial 760 *refusal*; contradiction 533 *negation*; recantation, retraction 603 *change of mind*; doubtfulness 486 *doubt*; demur, objection, reservation 468 *qualification*; protest; challenge 711 *defiance*; passive resistance 738 *sedition*.

objector, critic, dissentient 926 *detractor*; interrupter, heckler, obstructor; dissident, dissenter, protester; sectary 978 *sectarian*; separatist, seceder, withdrawalist 978 *schismatic*; rebel 738 *rebel*; dropout 84 *nonconformist*; grouser 829 *malcontent*; odd man out, minority; splinter group, breakaway party, cave, faction 708 *party*; the noes, the opposition 704 *opposition*; conscientious objector, peace women, CND, green party, ecowarrior 705 *opponent*; agitator, revolutionary, contra 149 *revolutionary*.

Adj. dissenting, differing, dissident 709 *quarrelling*; agnostic, sceptical; separatist, schismatic 978 *sectarian*; nonconformist 84 *unconformable*; malcontent, dissatisfied 829 *discontented*; recanting; not consenting; noncompliant 769 *non-observant*; loath, reluctant 598 *unwilling*; obstructive; challenging 711 *defiant*; resistant 704 *opposing*.

Vb. dissent, differ, agree to differ 25 *disagree*; beg to differ, pick a bone with, take one up on 479 *confute*; demur, object, raise objections, have reservations, cavil, boggle; protest, raise one's voice against, demonstrate against 762 *deprecate*; resist 704 *oppose*; challenge 711 *defy*; show reluctance 598 *be unwilling*; withhold assent, say no, shake one's head, not wear it 760 *refuse*; shrug one's shoulders, wash one's hands of it 860 *be indifferent*; disallow 757 *prohibit*; negative, contradict 533 *negate*; repudiate, hold no brief for; look askance at, not hold with 924 *disapprove*; secede, form a breakaway party, form a splinter group, withdraw 621 *relinquish*; recant, retract 603 *apostatize*; argue, wrangle, bicker 709 *quarrel*.

Adv. no, on the contrary, no way; in the negative.

Int. God forbid!, not on your life!, not on your nelly!, over my dead body!, tell that to the marines!, not likely!

490 Knowledge

N. knowledge, ken; knowing, cognition, cognizance, recognition, realization, apprehension, comprehension, perception, understanding, grasp, mastery 447 *intellect*; conscience, consciousness, awareness; insight 476 *intuition*; precognition 510 *foresight*; illumination 975 *revelation*; enlightenment 498 *wisdom*; learning, lore (see also *erudition* below); folklore; occult lore 983 *sorcery*; education, background; experience, practical experience, hands-on experience, acquaintance, nodding acquaintance, acquaintanceship, familiarity, intimacy; private knowledge, being in the know, sharing the secret 524 *information*; public knowledge, common knowledge, open secret 528 *publicity*; omniscience; intimation, glimpse, glimmering, inkling, suggestion 524 *hint*; suspicion, scent; self-knowledge, introspection, navel-gazing; detection, clue 484 *discovery*; expert knowledge, specialization savoir-faire, savvy, know-how, expertise 694 *skill*; smattering 491 *superficial knowledge*; science of knowledge, epistemics; theory of knowledge, epistemology; cognitive science.

erudition, lore, wisdom, scholarship, letters, literature 536 *learning*; acquired knowledge, general knowledge, practical knowledge, professional knowledge, encylopaedic knowledge, universal knowledge; profound learning; smattering, dilettantism 491 *superficial knowledge*; reading, wide reading; learning by rote, book-learning, bookishness, bibliomania; pedantry, donnishness; information; mine of information, store of knowledge, encyclopaedia 589 *library*.

culture, letters 557 *literature*; the humanities, the arts, the visual arts; education, instruction 534 *teaching*; literacy, numeracy; liberal education, scientific education; self-education, self-instruction, personal development; civilization; attainments, accomplishments, proficiency, mastery.

science, natural science, the life sciences; natural philosophy; scientific knowledge; applied science, technology, computer science; ologies and isms; pseudoscience.

Adj. knowing, all-knowledge, encyclopaedic, comprehensive, omniscient 498 *wise*; cognizant, cognitive 447 *mental*; conscious, aware, mindful of 455 *attentive*; alive to, sensible of 819 *impressible*; experienced, competent, no stranger to, at home with, acquainted, familiar with, au fait with 610 *accustomed to*; intimate, privy to, wise to, on to, in the know, in on 524 *informed*; fly, canny, shrewd 498 *intelligent*; conversant, practised, versed in, proficient 694 *expert*; having hands-on experience.

known, perceived, seen, heard; ascertained, verified 473 *certain*; discovered, explored; noted, celebrated, famous 866 *renowned*; no secret, open secret; familiar, intimate, dear; hackneyed, stale, trite; proverbial, household, commonplace 610 *usual*; prevalent 79 *general*; memorized, learnt off 505 *remembered*.

Vb. know, savvy; ken; have a nodding acquaintance with, be acquainted; apprehend, conceive, catch, grasp, twig, click, have, take in, get 516 *understand*; comprehend, master; come to know, latch on, get the hang of, get into one's head, realize; get to know, acquaint oneself, familiarize oneself, become au fait with; know again, recognize; be conscious of, be aware, be cognizant 447 *perceive*; discern 463 *discriminate*; perceive 438 *see*; know well, know full well, be thoroughly acquainted with, see through, read one like a book, have one's measure, have one taped, have one sized up, know inside out; know down to the ground, know from A to Z, know like the back of one's hand; know for a fact 473 *be certain*; know of, have knowledge of, know something; be in the know, be in the secret, have the lowdown 524 *be informed*; know by heart, know by rote 505 *memorize*; know backwards, have it pat, have at one's finger tips, be master of, know one's stuff 694 *be expert*; have a little knowledge of 491 *not know*; know by experience; get the picture, see the light; know all the answers, be omniscient; know what's what, see one's way, know one's way about 498 *be wise*.

be known, become known, come to one's knowledge, be brought to one's notice, come to one's ears; be a well-known fact, be public knowledge, be an open secret, be no secret 528 *be published*.

491 Ignorance

N. *ignorance*, no news, no word of; unawareness, unconsciousness 375 *insensitivity*; incognizance, non-recognition, non-realization; incomprehension, incapacity, backwardness 499 *unintelligence*; inappreciation, Philistinism 439 *blindness*; obstacle to knowledge, superstition 495 *error*; crass ignorance; lack of knowledge; lack of education, no schooling; blank mind, tabula rasa; unfamiliarity, inexperience, greenness, rawness; gaucherie, awkwardness, Asperger's syndrome; inexpertness, amateurishness 695 *lack of skill*; innocence, simplicity, naivety 699 *artlessness*; nothing to go on, no lead, lack of information, general ignorance, anybody's guess, bewilderment 474 *uncertainty*; moral ignorance, unwisdom 499 *folly*; darkness, benightedness, unenlightenment; savagery, heathenism, paganism 982 *idolatry*; Age of Ignorance, Dark Ages; imperfect knowledge, semi-ignorance (see also *superficial knowledge* below); ignorant person, illiterate 493 *ignoramus*; layman, autodidact, amateur, no expert 697 *bungler*; obscurantist; Philistine.

unknown thing, obstacle to knowledge; unknown quantity, matter of ignorance; prehistory 125 *antiquity*; sealed book, closed book, Greek, all Greek to me; Dark Continent, terra incognita, unknown country, unexplored ground, virgin soil, lion country; frontiers of knowledge; dark horse, wild card, enigma, mystery 530 *secret*; unidentified flying object, UFO; unidentified body; unknown person, mystery person, Mr *or* Miss X, anonymity 562 *no name*; unsung hero.

superficial knowledge, smattering, smatter, a little learning; glimmering, glimpse, half-glimpse 524 *hint*; vagueness, half-knowledge 495 *inexactness*; unreal knowledge 495 *error*; superficiality 212 *shallowness*; dilettantism, dabbling; pretension to knowledge, sciolism; affectation of knowledge, pedantry, quackery, charlatanism, bluff 850 *affectation*, smatterer 493 *dabbler*.

Adj. *ignorant*, unknowing; uncomprehending; unwitting; unaware, unconscious, oblivious 375 *insensitive*; unfamiliar with, not au fait with, unacquainted, a stranger to, not at home with; in the dark (see also *uninstructed* below); mystified 474 *uncertain*; clueless, with nothing to go on; blindfolded 439 *blind*; groping 461 experimental; amateurish, inexpert, ham 695 *unskilful*; unversed, inexperienced, uninitiated, green, raw, wet behind the ears; innocent of, guiltless 935 *innocent*; naive, simple, unworldly 699 *artless*; unenlightened, benighted; savage, uncivilized; pagan, heathenish; backward, dull, dense, dumb 499 *unintelligent*; empty-headed, foolish 499 *unwise*; half-baked; out of touch, not in the loop; behind the times 125 *retrospective*; wilfully ignorant, indifferent 454 *incurious*.

uninstructed, uninformed, kept in the dark; ill-informed, vague about 474 *uncertain*; untaught, untutored, untrained; illiterate, innumerate, uneducated; uncultivated, uncultured, lowbrow; unscholarly, unread, Philistine; dense, dumb (see also *ignorant* above).

unknown, unbeknown, untold, unheard; unspoken, unsaid, unvoiced, unuttered; unseen 444 *invisible*; hidden, veiled 525 *concealed*; unrecognized 525 *disguised*; unperceived; unexplained 517 *unintelligible*; dark, enigmatic, mysterious 523 *occult*; strange, new, newfangled, unfamiliar, unprecedented; unnamed 562 *anonymous*; unidentified, unclassified, uninvestigated 458 *neglected*; undiscovered, unexplored, uncharted, untravelled, unplumbed, unfathomed; untried, untested; virgin, novel 126 *new*; unforeseeable, unpredictable 124 *future*; unheard of, obscure 639 *unimportant*; unsung.

dabbling, unqualified; shallow, superficial, dilettante.

Vb. *not know*, be ignorant, be in the dark, have nothing to go on, have no lead; be unacquainted, not know — from Adam; be green, be wet behind the ears, know no better; cannot say; not know the half of, have no conception, have no notion, have no clue, not have a Scooby, have no idea, have not the remotest idea, not have the foggiest, not have an inkling, be reduced to guessing 512 *suppose*; know nothing of, not hear 416 *be deaf*; not see, suffer from tunnel vision 439 *be blind*; be at a loss, be stumped, not know what to make of 474 *be uncertain*; not know the first thing about, have to start at the bottom 695 *be unskilful*; not know chalk from cheese, not know one's arse from one's elbow; misunderstand 517 *not understand*; misconstrue 481 *misjudge*; half know, know a little, have a smattering, dabble in; suspect 486 *doubt*; ignore 458 *disregard*; profess ignorance, shrug one's shoulders, not want to know 860 *be indifferent*; grope, fumble 461 *be tentative*.

492 Scholar

N. *scholar*, savant(e), learned person, erudite person, educated person, man *or* woman of learning, man *or* woman of letters, bookman, bookwoman, bibliophile; don, reader, professor, pedagogue 537 *teacher*; pedant, bookworm, bluestocking; encyclopaedist; mine of information, walking encyclopaedia, talking dictionary; student, serious student 538 *learner*; degree-holder, graduate, diplomaholder; academic circles, academia, groves of academe; professoriate.

intellectual, academic, scholastic; genius, gifted child, prodigy 500 *sage*; know-all, brainbox; highbrow, egghead, bluestocking, intelligentsia, literati, illuminati, intellectual snob; academician.

collector, connoisseur, dilettante 846 *person of taste*; completist; book-collector, coincollector, egg-collector, stamp-collector 504 *enthusiast*; librarian, curator 749 *keeper*; antiquary 125 *antiquarian*; lexicographer, philologist 557 *linguist*.

Collectors and Collecting

Collectors: arctophile (teddy bears), bibliophile *or* bibliophilist *or* bibliomaniac *or* bibliomane (books), cartophilist (cigarette cards), deltiologist (postcards), discophile *or* discophil (gramophone records), lepidopterist (butterflies and moths), medallist (medals), notaphilist (banknotes and cheques), numismatist (coins and medals), philatelist (stamps), phillumenist (match-boxes), scripophilist (bonds and share certificates), tegestologist *or* tegetologist (beer mats).

Collecting: arctophily (teddy bears), bibliophily *or* bibliomania (books), cartophily (cigarette cards), deltiology (postcards), notaphily (banknotes and cheques), numismatics (coins and medals), philately (stamps), phillumeny (match-boxes), scripophily (bonds and share certificates), tegestology *or* tegetology (beer mats).

---

493 Ignoramus

N. *ignoramus*, illiterate, lowbrow; philistine; duffer, thickhead, numskull, bimbo, airhead, empty suit 501 *dunce*; bonehead, blockhead, goof, goose, bungler 501 *fool*; greenhorn, novice, raw recruit 538 *beginner*; simpleton 544 *dupe*.

dabbler, dilettante; quack, charlatan 545 *impostor*.

494 Truth

N. *truth*, verity, rightness; basic truth; truism, platitude 496 *axiom*; accordance with fact;

truth of the matter, honest truth, plain truth, simple truth; gospel, Holy Writ, Bible 975 *revelation*; facts, lowdown, skinny, the heart of the matter; actuality; factualness, fact, matter of fact, factoid 3 *having substance*; home truth, candour, frankness 929 *probity*; naked truth, unvarnished truth; the truth, the whole truth, and nothing but the truth; truthfulness 540 *truthfulness*; appearance of truth, verisimilitude 471 *probability*.

authenticity, validity, realness, genuineness; the real McCoy, the real thing, the genuine article, it 13 *identity*; no illusion, not a fake 21 *no imitation*.

accuracy, attention to fact; verisimilitude, local colour, realism, 'warts and all'; fidelity, high fidelity, exactitude, exactness, preciseness, precision, mathematical precision, clockwork precision; micrometry 465 *measurement*; mot juste, hitting the nail on the head, aptness 24 *adaptation*; meticulousness, punctiliousness 455 *attention*; letter of the law, acting according to the book 735 *severity*; literalness 514 *meaning*; true report, the very words, a verbatim account 540 *truthfulness*; chapter and verse, facts, statistics 466 *evidence*.

Adj. *true*, correct, right, so; real, tangible 3 *substantial*; actual, factual, historical; wellgrounded, well-founded, well-thought-out; well-argued, well-taken; literal, truthful 540 *truthful*; true to the facts, true to scale, true to the letter, according to the book (see also *accurate* below); unquestionable 473 *undisputed*; reasonable 475 *rational*; true to life, true to nature, faithful, verbatim; realistic; unromantic, down to earth; candid, honest, warts and all.

genuine, authentic, bona fide, valid, guaranteed, authenticated, official; sound, solid, reliable, honest 929 *trustworthy*; natural, pure, sterling, hallmarked; fair dinkum; true-born; rightful, legitimate; unadulterated, unvarnished, uncoloured, straight from the shoulder, undisguised, undistorted, unexaggerated.

accurate, exact, precise, definite, defined; well-adjusted, well-pitched, high-fidelity, dead-on 24 *adjusted*; well-aimed, direct, straight, dead-centre 281 *directed*; unerring, undeviating, constant, regular 16 *uniform*; punctual, right, correct, true, bang on, bang to rights, spot on, on the button, on the mark; infallible; close, faithful; fine, nice, delicate, sensitive; micrometric; mathematically exact, scientifically exact; scrupulous, punctilious, meticulous, strict, severe 455 *attentive*; word for word, verbatim, literal; literal-minded, just so 862 *fastidious*.

Vb. *be true*, be so, be just so, be the case,

happen, exist 1 *be*; hold, hold true, hold good, hold water, wash, stand, stand the test, ring true; conform to fact, prove true, hold together; speak the truth, omit nothing 540 *be truthful*; seem real, copy nature 551 *represent*; square, set, trim 24 *adjust*; substantiate 466 *corroborate*; prove 478 *demonstrate*; be right, be correct, have the right answer; get at the truth, hit the nail on the head, hit the mark, be spot on 484 *detect*.

Adv. *truly*, undeniably, indubitably, certainly, undoubtedly, really, genuinely, indeed; as a matter of fact 1 *actually*; to tell the truth 540 *truthfully*; frankly, candidly, etc. 263 *openly*; strictly speaking; sic, literally, to the letter, word for word, verbatim; exactly, accurately, precisely, right, to an inch, to a nicety, to a turn, to a T, just right, spot on; in every detail, in all respects, tout à fait.

495 Error

N. *error*, erroneousness, wrongness, unsoundness; silliness 497 *absurdity*; untruth, falsity; straying from the truth, inexactitude 282 *deviation*; inaccuracy, fallacy, self-contradiction 477 *sophism*; unorthodoxy 977 *heterodoxy*; old wives' tales, superstition, popular misconception 491 *ignorance*; pathetic fallacy; fallibility 481 *misjudgment*; mistaken belief, wishful thinking, doublethink, self-deception; misunderstanding, misconception, misconstruction, cross-purposes 521 *misinterpretation*; falseness, untruthfulness 541 *falsehood*; illusion, hallucination, mirage 440 *visual fallacy*; lapse of memory, false memory syndrome 506 *no memory*; false pregnancy, pseudocyesis; false light, false dawn 509 *disappointment*; delusion 503 *mental disorder*; dream 513 *fantasy*; false impression; prejudice 481 *bias*.

inexactness, inexactitude, inaccuracy, imprecision, non-adjustment; faultiness; looseness, laxity, generalization 79 *generality*; loose thinking, sloppy thinking 477 *sophistry*; carelessness 458 *negligence*; mistiming 118 *anachronism*; misinformation 552 *misrepresentation*; misquotation (see also *mistake* below); malapropism 565 *bad grammar*.

mistake, miscalculation 481 *misjudgment*; blunder, botch-up 695 *bungling*; mistaken identity, own goal, friendly fire; wrong address; glaring error, bloomer, clanger, howler, gaffe, bull, Irish bull 497 *absurdity*; oversight 456 *inattention*; bungle, foul-up, louse-up, screw-up, balls-up, cock-up, boo-boo, slip-up, boob, goof, blooper; fluff, muff; leak, slip, slip of the pen, lapsus calami, slip of the tongue, lapsus linguae, spoonerism, Bushism 565 *bad grammar*; typist's error; typographical

error, printer's error, misprint, typo, literal, erratum, corrigendum; human error, computer error; inadvertency; bad tactics, faux pas; solecism 847 *bad taste*; blot, flaw 845 *blemish*.

Adj. *erroneous*, erring, wrong; in error (see also *mistaken* below); unfactual, unhistorical, mythical 2 *unreal*; aberrant; wide of the mark, wide of the truth, devoid of truth 543 *untrue*; unsound, unscientific, unreasoned, cock-eyed, ill-reasoned, self-contradictory 477 *illogical*; implausible 472 *improbable*; unsubstantiated, uncorroborated, unfounded, ungrounded, groundless, disproved; exploded, discredited 924 *disapproved*; fallacious, misleading; unauthentic, apocryphal; perverted, unorthodox, heretical; untruthful, lying 541 *false*; flawed, fake, simulated, bogus 542 *spurious*; hallucinatory, illusive, illusory, delusive, deceptive; unrealistic, fantastical 513 *imaginary*; wild, crackpot 497 *absurd*; fallible, perverse, prejudiced 481 *biased*; superstitious 491 *ignorant*.

mistaken, misunderstood, misconceived; misrepresented, perverted; misinterpreted, misconstrued, misread, misprinted; miscalculated, misjudged; in error, misled, misguided; misinformed, ill-informed, deluded 491 *uninstructed*; slipping, blundering 695 *clumsy*; straying, wandering; wide, misdirected, off-target, off-beam, out to lunch 25 *unapt*; at fault, cold, off the scent, off the track, off the beam, wide of the mark, on the wrong tack, on the wrong scent, off the rails, at sea 474 *uncertain*.

inexact, inaccurate; loose; broad, generalized 79 *general*; incorrect, misreported, garbled; imprecise, erratic, wild, hit-or-miss; wildly out, maladjusted; untuned, out of tune, out of gear; out of synch, unsynchronized, slow, losing, fast, gaining; uncorrected, unrevised; faulty, full of holes, flawed, botched, mangled 695 *bungled*; misprinted, misread, mistranslated.

Vb. *err*, commit an error, go wrong, stray from the straight and narrow, mistake, make a mistake; labour under a misapprehension, bark up the wrong tree, be on the wrong scent; be in the wrong, be mistaken; delude oneself, suffer hallucinations 481 *misjudge*; be misled, be misguided; receive a wrong impression, get hold of the wrong end of the stick, be at cross-purposes, misunderstand, misconceive, misapprehend, get it wrong 517 *not understand*; miscount, misreckon 482 *overrate*, 483 *underestimate*; go astray 282 *stray*; gain, be fast 135 *be early*; lose, be slow, stop 136 *be late*.

blunder, trip, stumble, miss, fault 695 *be clumsy*; slip, slip up, drop a brick, drop a clanger, boob, goof, foul up, screw up, mess up, make a hash of; commit a faux pas, put one's foot in it; betray oneself, give oneself away 526 *disclose*; blot one's copybook, blot, flaw; fluff, muff, botch, bungle; blow it 728 *fail*; play into one's hands 695 *act foolishly*; miscount, miscalculate 481 *misjudge*; misread, misquote, misprint, misapprehend, mistranslate 521 *misinterpret*.

mislead, misdirect 282 *deflect*; misinform, lead astray, pervert; beguile, lead one a dance, lead one up the garden path 542 *deceive*; give *or* create a false impression, falsify, garble, sex up 541 *dissemble*; gloss over, whitewash, cover up 525 *conceal*.

496 Maxim

N. *maxim*, adage, saw, proverb, byword, aphorism; dictum, tag, saying, stock saying, common saying, truth; epigram, mot 839 *witticism*; wise maxim; truism, cliché, commonplace, platitude, banality, hackneyed saying, trite remark, statement of the obvious, bromide; motto, watchword, slogan, catchword; formula, mantra; text, canon, sutra, rule, golden rule 693 *precept*; gloss, comment, note, remark, observation 520 *commentary*; moral, edifying story, fable, cautionary tale 590 *narrative*.

axiom, self-evident truth, truism; principle, postulate, theorem, formula; sod's *or* Sod's law, Murphy's law.

Adj. *proverbial*, aphoristic, moralizing, holier than thou 498 *wise*; epigrammatic, pithy 839 *witty*; snappy 569 *concise*; enigmatic 517 *puzzling*; common, banal, trite, corny, hackneyed, platitudinous, clichéd, commonplace, stock 610 *usual*; axiomatic.

Adv. *proverbially*, as the saying goes, as they say, as the old adage has it, to coin a phrase; in a nutshell; epigrammatically, by way of moral.

497 Absurdity

N. *absurdity*, height of absurdity, height of nonsense, absurdness 849 *ridiculousness*; inconsequence 10 *irrelevance*; false logic 477 *sophistry*; foolishness, silliness, silly season 499 *folly*; senselessness, futility, fatuity 641 *wasted effort*; nonsense verse, doggerel; talking through one's hat; rot, rubbish, nonsense, stuff and nonsense, gibberish, jargon, twaddle 515 *silly talk*; Irishism, Irish bull, malapropism, howler 495 *mistake*; limerick 839 *witticism*; pun, play upon words 518 *equivocalness*; riddle, riddle-me-ree 530 *enigma*; anticlimax, bathos, descent from the sublime to the ridiculous.

foolery, tomfoolery, fooling about, antics, capers, horsing around, silliness, shenanigans,

high jinks, skylarking 837 *revel*; vagary, whimsy, whimsicality 604 *whim*; extravagance, extravaganza; escapade, scrape 700 *predicament*; practical joke, monkey trick, piece of nonsense; drollery 849 *ridiculousness*; clowning, buffoonery, burlesque, parody, caricature 851 *ridicule*; farce, mummery, pretence 850 *affectation*; showing off 875 *ostentation*.

Adj. *absurd*, ludicrous, laughable, risible, farcical, comical, grotesque, Pythonesque 849 *ridiculous*; rash, silly, asinine, idiotic, cockeyed, moronic, tomfool 499 *foolish*; nonsensical, senseless 515 *meaningless*; preposterous, without rhyme or reason 477 *illogical*; wild; pretentious 850 *affected*; frantic 503 *frenzied*; mad, crazy, crackpot, harebrained 495 *erroneous*; fanciful, fantastic 513 *imaginative*; futile, fatuous 641 *useless*; punning 518 *equivocal*.

Vb. *be absurd*, play the fool, play the clown, act like a fool, behave like an idiot 499 *be foolish*; fool, fool about, lark about, muck about, horse about, monkey around, play practical jokes 837 *amuse oneself*; be a laughing stock 849 *be ridiculous*; clown, clown about, parody, caricature, mimic, guy, make a fool of 851 *ridicule*; talk rot, talk nonsense, talk through one's hat, talk gibberish 515 *mean nothing*; rave 503 *be insane*.

498 Intelligence. Wisdom

N. *intelligence*, powers of thought, intellectualism 447 *intellect*; brains, brain, grey matter, head, loaf, upper storey, upstairs, noddle; nous, wit, common sense; understanding, sense, good sense, horse sense, savvy, gumption, knowhow; wits, sharp wits, ready wits, quick thinking; ability, capacity, mental capacity, mental grasp; calibre, mental calibre, intelligence quotient, IQ; high IQ, Mensa, brightness, forwardness; braininess, cleverness 694 *aptitude*; mental gifts, giftedness, brilliance, talent, genius; ideas, inspiration, sheer inspiration 476 *intuition*; brainwave, bright idea 451 *idea*.

sound judgment, judgment, discretion, discernment, sagacity 463 *discrimination*; perception, perspicacity, clear thinking, clearheadedness; acumen, sharpness, acuteness, acuity, penetration; shrewdness; levelheadedness, balance 502 *sanity*; prudence, forethought, farsightedness 510 *foresight*; craftiness 698 *cunning*; worldly wisdom; vigilance, alertness, awareness 457 *carefulness*; tact, statesmanship, strategy 688 *tactics*.

wisdom, sapience; profundity of thought 449 *thought*; breadth of mind; experience, lifelong experience; soundness; mental balance, enlightenment; Age of Enlightenment 110 *era*.

Adj. intelligent, brainy, clever, forward, bright, bright as a button; brilliant, scintillating, talented 694 *gifted*; capable, able 694 *skilful*; apt, ready, quick, quick on the uptake, receptive; acute, sharp, sharp as a needle, sharp-witted, quick-witted, nimble-witted; aware, on one's toes, streetwise, with it 455 *attentive*; astute, shrewd, fly, smart, canny, not born yesterday, all there, on the ball; knowing, sophisticated, worldly-wise; too smart for one's own good, too clever by half; sagacious, prudent, watchful 457 *careful*; far-seeing, farsighted 510 *foreseeing*; discerning 463 *discriminating*; penetrating, perspicacious, clearheaded; politic, statesmanlike.

wise, sage, sagacious, sapient; thinking, reflecting 449 *thoughtful*; reasoning 475 *rational*; knowledgeable; highbrow, intellectual, profound, deep; down to earth, sound, sensible, well-balanced 502 *sane*; not born yesterday, experienced; level-headed, grounded; judicious 913 *just*; enlightened, prudent, tactful, politic 698 *cunning*; wise as a serpent *or* as an owl *or* as Solomon, like a Daniel come to judgment; well-advised, well-considered, well-judged.

Vb. be wise, be intelligent, etc. (see adj.); use one's head *or* one's brains *or* one's intelligence, use one's loaf *or* one's noddle; have a fund of wisdom 490 *know*; have brains, have plenty of grey matter, have a head on one's shoulders, have one's wits about one, know how many beans make five, see with half an eye, see at a glance; have one's head screwed on the right way, know a thing or two, know what's what, know the score; be up on, be in the know, be au courant; show foresight 510 *foresee*; know which side one's bread is buttered on, be prudent, take care 858 *be cautious*; have sense, listen to reason 475 *be reasonable*; be politic 623 *plan*; have tact 698 *be cunning*; learn from one's mistakes, come to one's senses.

499 Unintelligence. Folly

N. unintelligence, lack of intelligence, lack of intellect 448 *absence of intellect*; feeblemindedness, low IQ, low mental age, brain damage, dementia, mental deficiency; mental handicap, arrested development, retardation, backwardness; cretinism, imbecility, idiocy; stupidity, slowness, dullness, obtuseness, thickheadedness, denseness; oafishness; no head for; incapacity, incompetence 695 *lack of skill*; gullibility 481 *misjudgment*; inanity, vacuity, vacuousness, superficiality 212 *shallowness*.

folly, foolishness, eccentricity 849 *ridiculousness*; tomfool idea, tomfoolery, act of folly 497

foolery; giddiness 456 *inattention*; irrationality, illogicality 477 *sophistry*; indiscretion, tactlessness; fatuity, fatuousness, pointlessness; wildgoose chase 641 *wasted effort*; silliness; idiocy, lunacy, utter folly; recklessness, wildness 857 *rashness*; infatuation 481 *misjudgment*; puerility, childishness 130 *tender age*; second childhood, senility, dotage, senile dementia 131 *old age*; drivelling, babbling, maundering, wandering.

Adj. unintelligent, unintellectual, low-brow; talentless, no genius; incompetent 695 *clumsy*; dull; subnormal, ESN, mentally handicapped, having a learning disability, mentally disadvantaged, mentally deficient; backward; retarded, feeble-minded, moronic, cretinous, imbecile 503 *mentally disordered*; deficient, wanting, not all there, vacant, not quite the full pound note, not right in the head; limited, weak, weak in the upper storey; slow, slow on the uptake, slow to learn; stupid, obtuse, dense, thick, gormless, bovine, blockish, oafish, doltish; dumb, dopey, dim, dim-witted, dull-witted, slow-witted, half-witted; pig thick *or* ignorant, dead from the neck up, thick as two short planks; thick-skulled, bone-headed, muddle-headed; cracked, barmy 503 *crazy*; unteachable; muddled, addled.

foolish, silly, idiotic, imbecile, asinine; non-sensical, senseless, fatuous, futile, inane 497 *absurd*; ludicrous, laughable, risible 849 *ridiculous*; like a fool, like an idiot 544 *gullible*; inexperienced 491 *ignorant*; tactless, impolitic; soft, wet, soppy, sappy, gormless; goofy, dopey; puerile, infantile; gaga, senile, away with the fairies; besotted, doting; spoony 887 *in love*; dazed, fuddled, maudlin 949 *drunk*; babbling, burbling, drivelling, maundering, wandering; mindless (see also *unintelligent* above); bird-witted, feather-brained, crack-brained, scatter-brained, hare-brained 456 *lacking concentration*; eccentric, unstable, wild, madcap, scatty, nutty, dotty, daft 503 *crazy*.

unwise, unenlightened; unintellectual; irrational 477 *illogical*; indiscreet 464 *undiscriminating*; injudicious; short-sighted 439 *blind*; unteachable; thoughtless; impatient 680 *hasty*; foolhardy, reckless 857 *rash*; unbalanced; unreasonable; unseemly, improper 643 *inexpedient*; ill-considered, ill-advised, ill-judged 495 *mistaken*.

Vb. be foolish, maunder, dote, drivel, babble, burble, wander, talk through one's hat 515 *mean nothing*; go haywire, lose one's wits, take leave of one's senses, go off one's head, go off one's rocker 503 *be insane*; have no sense, not have the sense one was born with; not see farther than one's nose, not see the wood for the trees; never learn; invite ridicule, look like a fool, look foolish 849 *be ridiculous*; make a fool of oneself, play *or* act the fool, act the giddy goat 497 *be absurd*; burn one's fingers 695 *act foolishly*; go on a fool's errand 641 *waste effort*; miscalculate 481 *misjudge*.

500 Sage

N. sage, nobody's fool; learned person 492 *scholar*; wise man, wise woman, statesman *or* -woman; elder statesman *or* -woman, consultant, authority 691 *adviser*; expert 696 *proficient person*; genius, master mind; master, mentor, guide, guru, pundit 537 *teacher*; Buddha 973 *religious teacher*; seer, prophet 511 *oracle*; yogi 945 *ascetic*; leading light, shining light, luminary; mahatma; doctor, thinker; egghead, boffin, highbrow, blue stocking 492 *intellectual*; wizard, witch doctor 983 *sorcerer*; magus, Magi, wise men from the East; Solomon, Daniel, Daniel come to judgment, learned judge; Grand Old Man.

wiseacre, wise guy, know-all, smarty-pants, smart ass 873 *vain person*; smart alec, clever dick.

501 Fool

N. fool, silly fool, tomfool 504 *madman*; buffoon, clown, comic, jester, zany 594 *entertainer*; perfect fool, complete idiot, big girl's blouse, geek, ninny, nincompoop, ass, jackass, donkey, goose, cuckoo; zombie, idiot, born fool; cretin, moron, imbecile; half-wit, dimwit, silly, silly-billy, twerp; stooge, butt, turkey 851 *laughing stock*; fathead, pinhead, muddle-head, incompetent, nit, nitwit, twit, clot, wally, plonker, nerd, clown, dipstick, numskull 697 *bungler*; birdbrain, featherbrain, airhead, bimbo, dingbat; flibbertigibbet; crackpot, eccentric, anorak, geek 504 *crank*; babbler, burbler, driveller; dotard 133 *old man*.

ninny, simpleton, Simple Simon; charley; nincompoop, juggins, muggins, booby, sap, big stiff, dope, jerk, gowk, galoot, goof; greenhorn 538 *beginner*; wet, weed, drip, milksop, wimp 163 *weakling*; sucker, mug 544 *dupe*.

dunce, dullard; blockhead, wooden-head, numskull, duffer, dummkopf, dolt, dumb cluck, bimbo, himbo 493 *ignoramus*; fat-head, bonehead, pinhead, blockhead, dunderhead, nitwit, dimwit; chump, clot, clod.

502 Sanity

N. sanity, saneness, soundness of mind; rationality, reason; balance of the mind, mental equilibrium; common sense, mother wit; coherence 516 *intelligibility*; lucidity, lucid moment; proper mind, right mind, senses; sound mind.

Adj. sane, of sound mind, all there; compos mentis, in one's right mind, in possession of one's faculties, with all one's wits about one; showing good sense, commonsensical, grounded, sober, sober-minded, with both feet on the ground; rational, reasonable 498 *intelligent*; coherent 516 *intelligible*, lucid, clear-headed.

503 Insanity: mental disorder

N. mental disorder, insanity, lunacy, madness, certifiability; mental illness; mental instability; mental derangement, unsound mind, delirium, brain damage; CJD, Creutzfeldt-Jakob disease, new variant Creutzfeldt-Jakob disease, Kuru, persistent vegetative state, PVS, Alzheimer's disease, softening of the brain 131 *age*; dementia, senile dementia, psychiatry, clinical psychology 447 *psychology*; psychotherapy 658 *therapy*; psychoanalyst, analyst, psychiatrist, shrink 658 *doctor*.

psychosis, paranoia, delusions, hallucinations; catatonia, schizophrenia; confusion; melancholia 834 *melancholy*; clinical depression, manic depression, mania, persecution mania, religious mania, spy mania.

Manias

ablutomania (an obsession with washing and cleanliness), Anglomania (obsession with all things English), arithmomania (a compulsion to count people and things), bibliomania (a mania for collecting books), demonomania (belief that one is possessed by the Devil), dipsomania (a craving for alcoholic drinks), egomania (extreme egotism), eleutheromania (obsessive desire for freedom), erotomania (excessive sexual desire), Gallomania (obsession with all things French), graphomania (obsession with writing), hydromania (craving for water), hypomania (a mild form of mania), idolomania (idol-worship), kleptomania (obsessive impulse to steal), megalomania (delusions of power or importance), metromania (mania for writing verse), monomania (obsession with a single idea), mythomania (a tendency to lie or exaggerate), nostomania (a great desire to return to familiar places), nymphomania (excessive sexual desire in a woman), pyromania (obsessive desire to set fire to things), sitomania (an abnormal craving for food), theomania (belief that one is a god).

---

learning disability, special needs, learning difficulty, mental handicap, mental deficiency, idiocy, imbecility, cretinism, feeblemindedness; Down's syndrome, mongolism; Asperger's syndrome, autism 84 *abnormality*.

personality disorder, psychopathology, psychopathy, maladjustment; split personality, dual personality, multiple personality, multiple personality disorder; persecution mania; kleptomania; nymphomania, satyriasis; inferiority complex.

neurosis, psychoneurosis, anxiety neurosis;

nervous disorder, nerves, social phobia, performance anxiety; hysteria; nervous breakdown, brainstorm; shell-shock, combat fatigue, post-traumatic stress disorder; obsession, compulsion, phobia, claustrophobia, agorophobia, etc. 854 *phobia*; hypochondria; depressed state, depression, manic depression, cyclothymia, blues.

frenzy, furore; ecstasy, raving, hysteria; distraction 456 *abstractedness*; incoherence 517 *unintelligibility*; delirium tremens, DTs; epilepsy, fit, epileptic fit, epileptic frenzy, paroxysm 318 *spasm*.

eccentricity, craziness, crankiness; queerness, oddness, weirdness; oddity, twist, quirk, kink, craze, fad 84 *abnormality*; a screw loose, bats in the belfry; fixation, hang-up, obsession, infatuation, bee in one's bonnet, etc. 604 *whim*.

mental hospital, psychiatric hospital, psychiatric unit, mental institution; mental home, madhouse, lunatic asylum, Bedlam; loony-bin, nuthouse, bughouse, funny farm; locked ward, padded cell 658 *hospital*.

person with a learning disability, mentally-handicapped person, idiot, congenital idiot, natural, cretin, moron 501 *fool*.

Adj. *mentally disordered*, insane, mad, barking mad, lunatic, of unsound mind, non compos mentis, not in one's right mind, out of one's mind, deranged, demented; certifiable, mental; psychologically abnormal, mentally disturbed, mentally ill, of diseased or disordered or distempered mind; unbalanced; brain-damaged; raving mad, stark staring mad, mad as a hatter, mad as a March hare, off one's rocker (see also *frenzied* below); gaga, loony, certified; locked up, put away.

having a learning disability, imbecile, moronic, cretinous, defective, feebleminded, subnormal; autistic.

psychotic, paranoiac, paranoid, schizophrenic, schizoid; manic, maniacal; catatonic, depressive, clinically depressed, cyclothymic 834 *melancholic*; hyperactive.

neurotic, hypochondriac; kleptomaniac; nymphomaniac, claustrophobic, agoraphobic.

maladjusted, psychopathic, psycho-pathological.

crazy, bewildered, wandering, bemused, pixilated, moidered 456 *abstracted*; not all there, not right in the head; off one's head or one's nut, off one's trolley, round the bend or the twist, up the pole; crazed, demented, driven mad, maddened (see also *frenzied* below); unhinged, unbalanced, off one's rocker; deluded; infatuated, possessed; besotted 887 *in love*; drivelling, gaga, in one's sec-

ond childhood, away with the fairies; touched, wanting; idiotic, scatterbrained, crack-brained 499 *foolish*; crackers, cracked, scatty, screwy, nutty, nutty as a fruit cake, nuts, bananas, batty, bats, cuckoo, barmy, bonkers, meshuga; daft, dippy, loony, loopy, goofy, potty, dotty; cranky, wacky, out to lunch, flaky, eccentric, erratic, funny, queer, odd, peculiar 84 *abnormal*; crotchety, whimsical 604 *capricious*; dizzy, giddy 456 *lacking concentration*.

frenzied, rabid, maddened; furious, foaming at the mouth 891 *angry*; wild, distraught 825 *suffering*; possessed; frantic, frenetic, demented, like one possessed, out of one's mind, beside oneself, uncontrollable; berserk, seeing red, running amok, running wild 176 *violent*; having fits; hysterical, delirious, hallucinating, raving, rambling, wandering, incoherent, fevered.

Vb. *be insane*, be mad, be crazy, etc. (see adj.); have bats in the belfry, have a screw loose; drivel 499 *be foolish*; ramble, wander; babble, rave; foam at the mouth; be delirious, see things.

go mad, go off one's head, go off one's rocker *or* nut, go crackers, lose one's marbles, go out of one's mind, crack up; go berserk, run amok, see red, foam at the mouth, lose one's head 891 *get angry*.

make mad, drive mad, drive insane, madden; derange; send one off his head *or* out of his mind; send round the bend *or* the twist, drive up the wall; turn one's brain; blow one's mind 821 *excite*; unhinge, unbalance, send off one's rocker; infuriate, make one see red 891 *enrage*; possess; go to one's head, turn one's head.

504 Madman

N. *madman*, madwoman, lunatic; raving lunatic, maniac; screwball, nut, nutcase, fruitcake, loon, loony, kook, bunny-boiler, meshuggenah (see also *the maladjusted* below).

psychotic, paranoiac, schizoid, schizophrenic, manic depressive, megalomaniac; catatonic.

neurotic, hysteric; neuropath; hypochondriac; obsessive; phobic, claustrophobic, agoraphobic; depressive, melancholic; kleptomaniac, pyromaniac; control freak.

the maladjusted, psychopath, psycho, psychopathic personality, sociopath, unstable personality, aggressive personality, antisocial personality; dipsomaniac 949 *drunkard*; drug addict, dope addict, dope fiend, junkie 949 *drug-taker*; crank, crackpot, nut, nutter, crackbrain; eccentric, oddball 851 *laughing stock* (see also *madman* above); freak 84 *nonconformist*; fanatic, extremist, lunatic fringe.

enthusiast, zealot; devotee, aficionado, addict, freak, buff, anorak, geek, wonk, trainspotter, big fan, supporter, -ista 707 *patron*; Europhile; connoisseur, fancier 846 *person of taste*; computer buff, fitness freak, radio ham, balletomane, opera buff, film buff; completist; bibliophile, etc. 492 *collector*; bird-lover, cat-lover, etc.

SECTION SIX

Extension of thought

505 Memory

N. *memory*, good memory, retentiveness; photographic memory, eidetic memory; tribal memory, atavism.

remembrance, recollection, recall, total recall; commemoration, evocation, mind's eye; recapitulation 106 *repetition*; memorization, remembering, learning by heart, committing to memory, learning by rote 536 *learning*; reminiscence, retrospection, review, retrospect, hindsight; flashback, recurrence, voice from the past; déjà vu 984 *psychics*; afterthought 67 *sequel*; nostalgia, regrets 830 *regret*; memorabilia, memoirs, reminiscences, recollections; place in history 866 *fame*; memoranda.

reminder, memorial, testimonial, commemoration, garden of remembrance; souvenir, keepsake, relic, memento, autograph; trophy, bust, statue 548 *monument*; prompter; testifier 466 *witness*; memorandum, memo, chit, note, notebook, memo pad, aidemémoire, diary, engagement diary, Filofax (tdmk), personal organizer; telephone book; album, autograph album, photograph album, scrapbook, commonplace book, promptbook; leading question, prompt, prompting, suggestion, cue 524 *hint*; memory aid, mnemonic, knotted handkerchief.

Adj. *remembered*, recollected, etc. (see vb.); retained, not forgotten, green, fresh, fresh in one's memory, of recent memory, as clear as if it were yesterday; uppermost in one's thoughts; of blessed memory, missed, regretted; memorable, unforgettable; haunting, persistent, undying; deep-rooted, indelible, inscribed upon the mind, stamped on one's memory; got by heart, memorized 490 *known*.

remembering, mindful, keeping in mind; evocative, commemorative 876 *celebratory*; reminiscent, recollecting; living in the past, dwelling upon the past, nostalgic; haunted; recalling, reminding, mnemonic, prompting, suggesting.

Vb. *remember*, bring to mind, call to mind; recognize, know again 490 *know*; recollect; not forget, bottle up 778 *retain*; hold in mind; enshrine in one's memory, store in one's mind, cherish the memory; never forget, be unable to forget; recall, call to mind, return to thoughts of, think of; reflect, review, think back, muse upon, keep in mind 455 *be mindful*; recapture, hark back, cast one's mind back; conjure up, rake up the past, reminisce; live in the past; reopen old wounds, recapture old times; remind oneself, make a note of, tie a knot in one's handkerchief; rack one's brains, tax one's memory.

remind, jog one's memory, refresh one's memory, renew one's memory; put one in mind of, take one back; drop a hint, cue, prompt, suggest 524 *hint*; not allow one to forget, haunt; not let sleeping dogs lie, fan the embers, keep the wounds open 821 *excite*; turn another's mind back, make one think of, awake memories of; commemorate, keep the memory green, toast 876 *celebrate*; recount, recapitulate 106 *repeat*.

memorize, commit to memory; get by heart, learn by rote 536 *learn*; fix in one's memory, implant in one's memory, impress on one's memory, engrave on one's memory, hammer into one's head, din into one's head; cram the mind with.

be remembered, linger in the memory, stick in the mind, make a lasting impression; recur, reoccur; flash across one's mind, ring a bell; run in one's mind, haunt, haunt one's thoughts or mind, be at the back of one's mind, lurk in one's mind, make history; live on 115 *be eternal*.

Adv. *in memory*, in memory of, to the memory of, as a memorial to, in memoriam, lest we forget; by heart, by rote, from memory.

506 Oblivion: no memory

N. *no memory*, no recollection, blankness, oblivion; obliviousness, forgetfulness, absent-mindedness, senior moment 456 *abstractedness*; loss of memory, amnesia, blackout, total blank, mental block; insensibility of the past; dim memory, hazy recollection; short memory, poor memory, defective memory, failing memory, faulty memory, false memory syndrome; lapse of memory, memory like a sieve; effacement 550 *obliteration*; Lethe, waters of oblivion; good riddance.

amnesty, letting bygones be bygones, burial of grievances, burial of the hatchet, shaking of hands; pardon, free pardon, absolution 909 *forgiveness*.

Adj. *forgotten*, clean forgotten, beyond recall; not missed, unremembered; out of sight, out of mind; in limbo 458 *neglected*; misremembered, etc. (see vb.); on the tip of one's tongue; in the recesses of one's mind, gone out of one's head; buried, suppressed; out of mind, over and done with, dead and buried, sunk in oblivion, amnestied.

forgetful, forgetting, oblivious; sunk in oblivion; unconscious of the past; unable to remember, suffering from amnesia, amnesic; unmindful, heedless, mindless 458 *negligent*; absent-minded 456 *abstracted*; conveniently forgetting 918 *undutiful*.

Vb. *forget*, clean forget, not remember, have no recollection of; not give another thought to, think no more of; suppress the memory, consign to oblivion, be oblivious; amnesty, let bygones be bygones, bury the hatchet 909 *forgive*; break with the past; suffer from amnesia, lose one's memory, remember nothing; misremember; be forgetful, have a poor memory, need reminding; lose sight of, leave behind, overlook; be absent-minded, fluff one's notes 456 *be inattentive*; forget one's lines, dry; have a memory like a sieve, go in one ear and out of the other, forget one's own name; have on the tip of one's tongue, not quite recall, draw a blank.

be forgotten, slip one's memory; sink into oblivion, be consigned to oblivion; become passé, be overlooked.

507 Expectation

N. *expectation*, state of expectation, expectancy 455 *attention*; contemplation 617 *intention*; confidence, trust 473 *certainty*; presumption 475 *premise*; foretaste 135 *anticipation*; eager expectation 859 *desire*; breathless expectation 852 *hope*; waiting, suspense, cliffhanger 474 *uncertainty*; dread, feelings of doom, doom-watching, apprehension, apprehensiveness 854 *fear*; anxiety 825 *worry*; expectance, one's expectations 471 *probability*; prospect, lookout, outlook, forecast 511 *prediction*; contingency 469 *possibility*; destiny 596 *fate*; unfulfilled expectation 509 *disappointment*; what is expected, the usual thing 610 *practice*.

Adj. *expectant*, expecting, in expectation, in hourly expectation; in suspense, on the waiting list, on the short list, on the short leet; sure, confident 473 *certain*; anticipatory, anticipating, banking on, putting all one's money on; presuming, taking for granted; predicting 510 *foreseeing*; forewarned, forearmed, ready 669 *prepared*; waiting, waiting for, awaiting; on the lookout, keeping cave, on the

watch for, standing by, on call 457 *vigilant*; keyed up 821 *excited*; on tenterhooks, on the rack, in agonies of expectation, agog; hopeful, sanguine 852 *hoping*; dreading, anxious 854 *nervous*; doom-watching 853 *hopeless*; expecting a baby, expecting a happy event, parturient 167 *fertilized*.

expected, long expected; up to expectation, as one expected; anticipated, presumed, predicted, on the cards, foreseen 471 *probable*; prospective, future, on the horizon 155 *impending*; promised, intended, in prospect; longed for 859 *desired*; dreaded, feared 854 *frightening*.

Vb. *expect*, look for, face the prospect; have in mind; calculate 480 *estimate*; forecast 510 *foresee*; see it coming 865 *not wonder*; think likely, presume 471 *assume*; bank on, count on, put one's money on 473 *be certain*; count one's chickens before they are hatched 509 *be disappointed*; anticipate 669 *prepare oneself*; look out for, watch out for, be waiting for, be ready for 457 *be careful*; stand by, be on call; hang around (see also *await* below); dread, doomwatch 854 *fear*; look forward to, hope for 852 *hope*, 859 *desire*.

await, be on the waiting list; stand and wait, watch and pray 136 *wait*; queue up, line up, mark time, bide one's time; stand by, hold oneself ready, be on call; keep one waiting; have in store for, be in store for.

Adv. *expectantly*, in suspense, with bated breath, on edge, on the edge of one's chair.

508 Lack of expectation

N. *lack of expectation*, false expectation 509 *disappointment*; resignation, no hope 853 *hopelessness*; apathy 454 *lack of curiosity*; unpreparedness 670 *non-preparation*; unexpectedness, unforeseen contingency; miscalculation 495 *error*; surprise; the unexpected, the unforeseen, surprise packet; windfall, gift from the gods, something to one's advantage 615 *benefit*; shock, nasty shock, jolt, blow, sudden blow, bolt from the blue, thunderbolt, thunderclap, bombshell; revelation, eye-opener; culture shock; reversal; amazement 864 *wonder*.

Adj. *unexpected*, unanticipated, unlooked for; unpredicted, unforeseen; unheralded, unannounced; without warning; astounding, mind-boggling, eye-opening, staggering, amazing 864 *wonderful*; shocking, startling 854 *frightening*; sudden 116 *instantaneous*; like a bombshell, like a thunderbolt, like a bolt from the blue, dropped from the clouds; unbargained for, uncatered for 670 *unprepared*; contrary to expectation; beyond one's wildest dreams, unprecedented 84 *unusual*; freakish 84 *abnormal*; unaccountable 517 *puzzling*.

not expecting, unexpecting, unexpectant, unsuspecting, off guard 456 *inattentive*; uninformed 491 *ignorant*; not forewarned; surprised, disconcerted, taken by surprise, taken aback, caught napping, caught with one's pants *or* trousers down, caught on the hop, on the wrong foot 670 *unprepared*; astonished, amazed, thunderstruck, dumbfounded, gobsmacked, dazed, stunned 864 *wondering*; startled, jolted, shocked; without expectations.

Vb. not expect, not look for, think unlikely, not foresee 472 *be unlikely*; not hope for 853 *despair*; be caught out, fall into the trap; be taken aback, be taken by surprise, be caught with one's pants *or* trousers down, not bargain for 670 *be unprepared*; get a shock, start, jump out of one's skin; have one's eyes opened; look surprised, goggle, stare, gawp.

surprise, take by surprise, spring something on one, catch, trap, ambush 542 *ensnare*; catch unawares, catch napping, catch off one's guard, catch with one's pants *or* trousers down; startle, make one jump, give one a turn, make one jump out of one's skin; take aback, leave speechless, stagger, stun; take one's breath away, knock one down with a feather, bowl one over, strike one all of a heap; be one in the eye for 509 *disappoint*; give one a surprise, pull out of the hat; astonish, amaze, astound, dumbfound, etc. 864 *be wonderful*; astound, shock, electrify, sock it to, etc. 821 *impress*; flutter the dovecotes, set the cat among the pigeons, let all hell loose 63 *disarrange*; drop from the clouds, come out of the blue; fall upon, spring upon, pounce on; steal upon, creep up on; come up from behind, appear from nowhere.

509 Disappointment

N. disappointment, sad disappointment, bitter disappointment, cruel disappointment; regrets 830 *regret*; frustration, bafflement; blighted hopes 853 *hopelessness* false expectation, unfulfilled expectation 482 *overestimation*; bad news 529 *news*; not what one expected, disenchantment, disillusionment 829 *discontent*; miscalculation 481 *misjudgment*; mirage, trick of the light, false dawn, fool's paradise; shock, blow, setback, double whammy, balk 702 *hitch*; non-fulfilment 726 *non-completion*; bad luck, slip 'twixt the cup and the lip, sod's *or* Sod's law, Murphy's law 731 *misfortune*; one in the eye for, letdown 872 *humiliation*; damp squib 728 *failure*.

Adj. disappointed, expecting otherwise 508 *inexpectant*; frustrated, thwarted, balked 702 *hindered*; baffled, foiled 728 *defeated*; crest-

fallen, chagrined, humiliated; disgruntled, dischuffed, soured 829 *discontented*; sick with disappointment 853 *hopeless*; let down; refused, turned away.

disappointing, unsatisfying, unsatisfactory 636 *insufficient*; not up to expectation 829 *discontenting*; abortive 728 *unsuccessful*.

Vb. be disappointed, be unsuccessful, etc. (see adj.); try in vain 728 *fail*; have hoped for something better, not realize one's expectations 307 *fall short*; expect otherwise, be let down, be left in the lurch, be jilted, laugh on the wrong side of one's face, be crestfallen, look blue; be sick with disappointment.

disappoint, not come up to expectations 307 *fall short*; dash one's hopes; burst the bubble, disillusion; let one down, leave one in the lurch, not come up to scratch; balk, foil, thwart, frustrate 702 *hinder*; amaze, dumbfound, boggle one's mind 508 *surprise*; betray, play one false 930 *be dishonest*; jilt; dash the cup from one's lips, leave unsatisfied, spoil one's pleasure, dissatisfy, turn away 607 *reject*.

510 Foresight

N. foresight, anticipation, foretaste; foreknowledge, second sight, clairvoyancy; premonition, presentiment, foreboding, forewarning 511 *omen*; prognosis, prognostication 511 *prediction*; foregone conclusion 473 *certainty*; programme, prospectus 623 *plan*; forward planning, forethought, vision, far-sightedness 498 *sound judgment*; premeditation 608 *predetermination*; prudence, providence 858 *caution*; provision 669 *preparation*.

Adj. foreseeing, prospective, prognostic, predictive 511 *predicting*; clairvoyant, second-sighted, prophetic; far-sighted, sagacious 498 *wise*; provident, prudent 858 *cautious*; anticipatory 507 *expectant*.

Vb. foresee, divine, prophesy, forecast 511 *predict*; forewarn 664 *warn*; see *or* peep *or* pry into the future, look into one's crystal ball, read one's palm, have second sight; be forewarned, know in advance 524 *be informed*; look ahead, see it coming, scent, feel in one's bones; look for 507 *expect*; be prepared, anticipate, forestall 135 *be early*; make provision 669 *prepare*; surmise, make a good guess 512 *suppose*; forejudge 608 *predetermine*; plan ahead 623 *plan*; look to the future, have an eye to the future, see how the cat jumps *or* how the wind blows 124 *look ahead*; have an eye on the main chance 498 *be wise*; feel one's way, keep a sharp lookout 455 *be attentive*; lay up for a rainy day 633 *provide*; take precautions, provide against 858 *be cautious*.

511 Prediction

N. prediction, foretelling, forewarning, prophecy; apocalypse 975 *revelation*; forecast, weather forecast; prognostication, prognosis; presentiment, foreboding 510 *foresight*; 1984 (book title); programme, prospectus, forward planning 623 *plan*; announcement, advance notice 528 *publication*; warning, preliminary warning, warning shot 665 *danger signal*; prospect 507 *expectation*; shape of things to come, horoscope, fortune.

divination, clairvoyancy; augury; soothsaying; astrology, horoscopy, casting nativities; fortune-telling, sortilege, palm-reading, palmistry; crystal gazing, scrying; reading teacups *or* tea leaves, runes, tarot cards; I Ching; casting lots; dowsing 484 *discovery*; futurology, scenario planning.

Some Other Methods of Divination

aeromancy (by atmospheric phenomena), ailuromancy (from the behaviour of cats), alectryomancy (from a cockerel eating grain placed on the letters of the alphabet, so spelling out something), alomancy (from random patterns of salt), anthropomancy (from human entrails), arithmancy *or* arithmomancy (by numbers), astromancy (= astrology), axinomancy (by means of an axe), belomancy (by means of arrows), bibliomancy (by opening a book, such as the Bible, at random; 'rhapsodomancy' if it is a book of poetry), botanomancy (by means of plants, especially by burning leaves or branches), capnomancy (by means of smoke), cartomancy (by means of playing cards), ceromancy (by dropping melted wax into water), cheiromancy *or* chiromancy (= palmistry), cleromancy (by casting lots), coscinomancy (by means of a sieve, and sometimes shears), crithomancy (by scattering meal over sacrificial animals), crystallomancy (by looking into transparent bodies such as crystals or water), dactyliomancy (by means of a ring), geomancy (from the shapes formed when earth is thrown down onto a surface, or by shapes formed by joining dots on paper or points on the ground), gyromancy (by walking round and round in a circle until you fall down from giddiness), hieromancy (by observing objects offered in sacrifice), hydromancy (by means of water), lampadomancy (by means of a flame), lithomancy (by means of stones), molybdomancy (from the shape of molten lead dropped into water), myomancy (from the movements of mice), necromancy (by consulting spirits of the dead), oenomancy (from the appearance of wine poured out in libations), omphalomancy (from the form of a baby's umbilical cord), oneiromancy (from dreams), onychomancy (by means of fingernails), ornithomancy (from the flight of birds), pyromancy (by means of fire), rhabdomancy (by means of a rod, e.g. in water-divining), scapulimancy (from the cracks that form in a burning shoulder-blade), spodomancy (by means of ashes), tasseomancy (by the patterns formed by tea leaves in a cup), tephromancy (by means of the ashes from sacrificial pyres), theomancy (by means of divinely inspired oracles), theriomancy *and* zoomancy (from the appearance or behaviour of animals).

omen, portent, writing on the wall; symptom, syndrome, sign 547 *indication*; forewarning, caution 664 *warning*; harbinger, herald 529 *messenger*; ominousness, portentousness, gathering clouds, signs of the times 661 *danger*; luck-bringer, black cat, horseshoe 983 *tal-*

isman; portent of bad luck, broken mirror, spilt salt, shooting star, walking under a ladder; bird of ill omen, owl, raven.

oracle, consultant 500 *sage*; meteorologist, weatherman *or* -woman; doom merchant, doomster, doomwatcher, Cassandra 664 *warner*; prophet, prophetess, seer, futurologist, forecaster; soothsayer 983 *sorcerer*; clairvoyant, medium 984 *occultist*; Delphic oracle; Sibyl; Nostradamus; cards, tarot cards, dice; crystal ball, tea leaves, palm.

diviner, water diviner, dowser; tipster 618 *gambler*; astrologer, stargazer; fortune-teller, palmist, crystal-gazer.

Adj. *predicting*, predictive, foretelling; clairvoyant 510 *foreseeing*; fortune-telling; weather-forecasting; prophetic, apocalyptic; oracular; foreboding; heralding 66 *precursory*; ominous, portentous; auspicious, promising, favourable 730 *prosperous*; inauspicious, sinister 731 *adverse*.

Vb. *predict*, forecast, make a prediction, make a prognosis; foretell, prophesy, forebode, bode, augur, spell; foretoken, presage, portend; foreshow, foreshadow, prefigure, shadow forth, forerun, herald, be harbinger, usher in 64 *come before*; point to, betoken, typify, signify 547 *indicate*; announce, give notice, notify 528 *advertise*; forewarn, give warning 664 *warn*; look black, look ominous, lour, menace 900 *threaten*; promise, augur well, bid fair to, give hopes of, hold out hopes, build up hopes, raise expectations, excite expectations.

divine, auspicate, haruspicate; read the entrails, take the auspices, take the omens; soothsay, vaticinate; cast a horoscope, cast a nativity; cast lots 618 *gamble*; tell fortunes; read the future, read the signs, read the stars; read the cards, read one's hand, read one's palm.

SECTION SEVEN

Creative thought

512 Supposition

N. *supposition*, notion 451 *idea*; fancy; pretence, pretending 850 *affectation*; presumption, assumption, presupposition, postulation, postulate 475 *premise*; condition, stipulation, sine qua non 766 *conditions*; proposal, proposition 759 *offer*; submission 475 *argument*; hypothesis, working hypothesis, theory; thesis; basis of supposition, datum 466 *evidence*; association of ideas 449 *thought*; supposability, conjecturability 469 *possibility*.

conjecture, guess, surmise, suspicion; bare supposition, vague suspicion, rough guess, crude estimate, guesstimate; shrewd idea 476 *intuition*; guesswork, guessing, speculation; gamble, shot, shot in the dark 618 *gambling*.

Adj. supposed, conjectured, etc. (see vb.); assumed, presumed, taken as read, postulated; proposed, mooted 452 *topical*; given, granted, granted for the sake of argument; putative, presumptive; so-called, quasi; not real 2 *unreal*; alleged.

Vb. suppose, just suppose, fancy; think, conceive, take into one's head, get into one's head 485 *opine*; surmise, conjecture, guess, hazard a guess, make a guess; suppose so, dare say; presume, assume, presuppose; posit; take for granted, take it, postulate 475 *reason*; speculate, have a theory, theorize 449 *meditate*; rely on supposition 618 *gamble*.

propound, propose 759 *offer*; put on the agenda, moot, move, propose a motion, postulate 761 *request*; put a case, submit, make one's submission 475 *argue*; put forth, make a suggestion, venture to say, put forward a notion, throw out an idea, throw something into the melting-pot 691 *advise*; suggest.

513 Imagination

N. imagination, vivid imagination, fertile imagination, wild imagination; imaginativeness, creativeness, inventiveness, creativity, imagineering 21 *originality*; ingenuity, resourcefulness 694 *skill*; thinking outside the box; fancifulness, fantasy, stretch of the imagination; understanding, insight, empathy, sympathy 819 *moral sensibility*; poetic imagination, ecstasy, inspiration, fancy, the mind's eye, recollection, recollection in tranquillity, visualization, image-building, imagery, word-painting; artistry, creative work.

conception, conceptualization, ideality 449 *thought*; idealization; mental image, projection 445 *appearance*; concept, image, conceit, fancy, notion 451 *idea*; whim, whimsy 497 *absurdity*; vagary 604 *caprice*; figment, figment of the imagination, fiction 541 *falsehood*; work of fiction, story 590 *novel*; science fiction, space odyssey, cyberpunk, steam punk; fairy tale; flight of fancy, uncontrolled imagination, romance, fantasy, extravaganza, rhapsody 546 *exaggeration*; imaginary being 970 *mythical being*; imaginary animal 365 *mythical animal*; poetic licence 593 *poetry*; skiamachy.

fantasy, wildest dreams; vision, dream, nightmare, night terror; Jabberwocky 970 *mythical being*; bogey, phantom 970 *ghost*; shadow, vapour 419 *dimness*; mirage 440 *visual fallacy*; delusion, hallucination, chimera 495 *error*; reverie, day dream, brown study 456 *abstractedness*; trance, somnambulism 375

insensitivity; delirium 503 *frenzy*; autosuggestion; wishful thinking 477 *sophistry*; make-believe, vapourware, golden dream, pipe dream 859 *desire*; romance, stardust; romanticism, escapism, idealism, Utopianism; Utopia, Erewhon; promised land, El Dorado, the end of the rainbow; Happy Valley, Fortunate Isles, Isles of the Blest; land of Cockaigne, Ruritania, Shangri-la, Atlantis, Lyonesse, Middle Earth, Narnia, San Serif; fairyland, wonderland; cloud-cuckoo-land, dream land, dream world; castles in Spain, castles in the air; pie in the sky, good time coming, millennium 124 *future state*; idle fancy, myth 543 *fable*; fantasy fiction; fantasy game, fantasy football.

visionary, seer 511 *diviner*, dreamer, day-dreamer; fantasist; idealist, Utopian 901 *philanthropist*; escapist; romantic, romancer, romanticist, rhapsodist, myth-maker; creative worker 556 *artist*.

Adj. imaginative, creative, lively, original, inventive, fertile, ingenious; resourceful 694 *skilful*; nifty 640 *useful*; romancing, romantic; high-flown, rhapsodical, carried away; poetic, fictional; Utopian, idealistic; rhapsodic, enthusiastic; dreaming, daydreaming, in a trance; extravagant, grotesque, bizarre, surreal, surrealistic, fantastical, unreal, whimsical, airy-fairy, preposterous, impractical, Heath Robinson 497 *absurd*; visionary.

imaginary, unreal, unsubstantial 4 *lacking substance*; notional, chimerical, illusory 495 *erroneous*; dreamy, visionary, not of this world, of another world, ideal; vaporous 419 *shadowy*; fictitious, fabulous, fabled, legendary, mythological 543 *untrue*; fanciful, fancied, imagined, fabricated; thought-up, dreamed-up; hypothetical; pretended, make-believe.

Vb. imagine, fancy, dream; think of, think up, conjure up, dream up; make up, devise, invent, originate, create, have an inspiration 609 *improvise*; coin, hatch, concoct, fabricate 164 *produce*; visualize, envisage, see in the mind's eye 438 *see*; conceive, form an image of; picture to oneself; paint, write a pen portrait of, conjure up a vision, capture, recapture 551 *represent*; use one's imagination, give a free rein *or* the reins to one's imagination, run riot in imagination 546 *exaggerate*; pretend, make believe, daydream 456 *be inattentive*; build castles in the air *or* castles in Spain; see visions, dream dreams; fantasize, idealize, romanticize, fictionalize, rhapsodize 546 *exaggerate*; enter into, empathize, sympathize 516 *understand*.

4.2
Communication of Ideas

SECTION ONE

Nature of ideas communicated

514 Meaning
N. meaning, substance, essence, spirit, sum and substance, gist, pith, nitty-gritty; contents, text, matter, subject matter 452 *topic*; semantic content, sense, drift, tenor, purport, import, implication; relevance, bearing; meaningfulness, context; semantics.

connotation, denotation, signification, significance, reference, application; construction 520 *interpretation*; context; derivation, etymology 156 *source*; semantic field, comprehension; extended meaning, core meaning, leading sense; specialized meaning, idiom 80 *speciality*; usage, accepted meaning 610 *practice*; single meaning 516 *intelligibility*; double meaning, ambiguity 518 *equivocalness*; many meanings, polysemy; same meaning; synonym, synonymousness, synonymity, equivalence 13 *identity*; opposite meaning, antonym, antonymy 14 *contrariety*; contradictory meaning, countersense; changed meaning, semantic shift; level of meaning, literal meaning, literality 573 *plainness*; metaphorical meaning 519 *metaphor*; hidden meaning, esoteric sense 523 *latency*; constructive sense, implied sense; no sense 497 *absurdity*.

Adj. meaningful, significant, of moment 638 *important*; substantial, pithy, meaty, full of meaning, packed with meaning, pregnant; meaning, etc. (see vb.); importing, purporting indicative; telling 516 *expressive*; pointed, epigrammatic 839 *witty*; suggestive.

semantic, semiological, philological, etymological 557 *linguistic*; connotational, connotative; denotational, denotative; literal, verbal 573 *plain*; metaphorical 519 *figurative*; univocal, unambiguous 516 *intelligible*; polysemous, ambiguous 518 *equivocal*; synonymous, homonymous 13 *identical*; tantamount, equivalent 18 *similar*; tautologous 106 *repeated*; antonymous 14 *non-identical*; idiomatic 80 *special*; paraphrastic 520 *interpretive*; obscure 568 *unclear*; clear; implied, constructive 523 *tacit*; nonsensical 497 *absurd*; without meaning 515 *meaningless*.

Vb. mean, mean something; convey a meaning, get across 524 *communicate*; symbolize 547 *indicate*; signify, denote, connote; purport; point to, add up to, boil down to, spell; involve 523 *imply*; convey, express, declare, assert 532 *affirm*; bespeak, tell of, speak of,

breathe of, savour of, speak volumes 466 *evidence*; be getting at, be driving at, have in mind; be synonymous, have the same meaning; say it in other words, put it another way; mean the same thing, be the same thing in the end.

515 Lack of meaning
N. lack of meaning, meaninglessness, nonsignificance 639 *unimportance*; inanity, emptiness, triteness; truism, platitude, cliché 496 *maxim*; mere words, empty words; illogicality 477 *sophistry*; invalidity, dead letter; illegibility, scribble, scribbling, scrawl 586 *script*; daub 552 *misrepresentation*; empty sound, strumming; sounding brass, tinkling cymbal 400 *loudness*; jargon, rigmarole, gobbledygook, galimatias, psychobabble, bafflegab; abracadabra, hocuspocus, mumbo jumbo; gibberish, gabble, double Dutch, Greek, Babel 517 *unintelligibility*; incoherence, raving, delirium 503 *frenzy*; double-talk.

silly talk, nonsense 497 *absurdity*; stuff and nonsense, balderdash, rubbish, load of rubbish, rot, tommyrot, pants; drivel, twaddle, fiddle-faddle, bosh, tosh, tripe, piffle, bilge, bull, bollocks (vulg), crap (vulg), shite (vulg).

empty talk, sweet nothings; wind, gas, hot air, verbiage 570 *diffuseness*; rant, bombast 877 *boasting*; blether, blather, blah-blah, flimflam; guff, pi-jaw, eyewash, claptrap, poppycock 543 *fable*; humbug 541 *falsehood*; moonshine, malarkey, hokum, bunkum, boloney, hooey; flannel, flummery, blarney 925 *flattery*; sales talk, patter, sales patter, spiel; talk, chatter, prattle, prating, yammering, wittering, babble, gabble, jabber, jabber jabber, jaw, yackety yack, yak yak, rhubarb rhubarb 581 *chatter*.

Adj. meaningless, nonsensical 497 *absurd*; senseless; unexpressive; insignificant, inane, empty, trivial, trite 639 *unimportant*; fatuous, piffling; waffling; incoherent, raving, gibbering 503 *frenzied*.

Vb. mean nothing, make no sense, be irrelevant; scribble, daub, talk bunkum 497 *be absurd*; babble, prattle, prate, gabble, gibber, jabber, witter, yak 581 *be talkative*; talk double dutch, talk gibberish; rant 546 *exaggerate*; rave, drivel, blether, waffle, talk hot air; not mean what one says; be Greek to, pass over one's head 474 *puzzle*.

516 Intelligibility
N. intelligibility, cognizability; explicability; comprehensibility; readability; legibility; clearness, clarity, coherence, limpidity, lucidity 567 *clarity*; precision, unambiguity 473 *certainty*; simplicity, straightforwardness, plain speaking,

plain speech, plain words, plain English, no gobbledygook; simplification 701 *easiness*.

Adj. intelligible, understandable, comprehensible; coherent 502 *sane*; audible, recognizable, distinguishable, unmistakable; cognizable 490 *known*; unambiguous, unequivocal 514 *meaningful*; explicit; distinct, clear-cut, precise 80 *definite*; articulate, eloquent; plain-spoken, downright, forthright 573 *plain*; straightforward, simple 701 *easy*; obvious, self-explanatory; explained, simplified, user-friendly; clear, limpid 422 *transparent*; lucid; readable, legible, decipherable, crystal clear, plain as a pikestaff 443 *visible*.

expressive, telling, meaningful, informative, striking, vivid, graphic, emphatic; illustrative, explicatory 520 *interpretive*.

Vb. be intelligible, be clear, be easy, etc. (see adj.); be readable, be an easy read, read easily; make sense, add up 475 *be reasonable*; tell its own tale, speak for itself, be self-explanatory 466 *evidence*; have no secrets 443 *be visible*; be understood, come over, get across, sink in, dawn on; clarify, clear up, open one's eyes, elucidate 520 *interpret*; simplify.

understand, comprehend, apprehend 490 *know*; master 536 *learn*; have, hold, retain 505 *remember*; have understanding 498 *be wise*; see through, penetrate, fathom, get to the bottom of 484 *detect*; spot, descry, discern, distinguish, make out, see at a glance, see with half an eye 438 *see*; recognize, make no mistake 473 *be certain*; grasp, get hold of, be on to it, cotton on to, dig; get the hang of, take in, register; be with one, follow, savvy; collect, get, catch on, latch on to, twig; catch one's drift, get the idea, get the picture; realize, get wise to, tumble to, rumble; have one's eyes opened, see the light, see through, see it all; get to know, get the hang of.

517 Unintelligibility

N. unintelligibility, incomprehensibility, unaccountability, inconceivability; inexplicability; difficulty 474 *uncertainty*; obscurity 568 *obscurity*; ambiguity 518 *equivocalness*; mystification 515 *lack of meaning*; incoherence 503 *mental disorder*; double Dutch, gibberish; jargon, psychobabble, bafflegab; foreign tongue, idiolect 560 *dialect, slang*; stammering 580 *speech defect*; undecipherability, illegibility; scribble, scrawl 586 *lettering*; inaudibility 401 *faintness*; Greek, sealed book 530 *secret*; paradox, knotty point, riddle, koan 530 *enigma*; mysterious behaviour, sphinx-like attitude.

Adj. unintelligible, incomprehensible, inconceivable, inexplicable, unaccountable; unrecognizable, all Greek to me, like double

Dutch 491 *unknown*; unfathomable, inscrutable, impenetrable; blank, poker-faced, expressionless 820 *impassive*; inaudible 401 *muted*; illegible, scrawly, scribbled, undecipherable; undiscernible 444 *invisible*; arcane 523 *occult*; cryptic; esoteric 80 *private*; Sphinx-like, enigmatic.

puzzling, complex 700 *difficult*; hard, beyond one, over one's head, recondite, abstruse, elusive; sphinxian, enigmatic, mysterious 523 *occult*; nebulous, obscure 419 *shadowy*; clear as mud *or* as ditch water 568 *unclear*; ambiguous 518 *equivocal*; paradoxical 508 *unexpected*; fishy, strange, odd 84 *abnormal*; unexplained, insoluble, unsolvable.

inexpressible, unspeakable, untranslatable; unpronounceable, unutterable, ineffable; incommunicable, indefinable.

puzzled, mystified, out of one's depth, flummoxed, stumped, baffled, perplexed, nonplussed 474 *uncertain*.

Vb. be unintelligible, be puzzling, be inexpressible, etc. (see adj.); be hard, be difficult, make one's head ache *or* swim 474 *puzzle*; talk in riddles 518 *be equivocal*; talk double dutch, talk gibberish 515 *mean nothing*; speak badly 580 *stammer*; write badly, scribble, scrawl; keep one guessing 486 *cause doubt*; perplex; require explanation, have no answer, need an interpreter; go over one's head; elude one's grasp, escape one; pass comprehension, baffle understanding.

not understand, not get it, not grasp it; find unintelligible, not make out, not know what to make of, make nothing of, make neither head nor tail of, be unable to account for; puzzle over, rack one's brains over, be floored by, be stumped by, give up; be out of one's depth 491 *not know*; be at sea 474 *be uncertain*; have no grasp of 695 *be unskilful*; have a blind spot 439 *be blind*; be on different wavelengths, be at cross-purposes 495 *blunder*; get one wrong 481 *misjudge*.

518 Equivocalness

N. equivocalness, ambiguity, ambivalence 517 *unintelligibility*; vagueness 474 *uncertainty*; newspeak, doubletalk, weasel word 515 *lack of meaning*; conundrum, riddle 530 *enigma*; prevarication; equivocation, white lie 543 *untruth*; quibble, quibbling 477 *sophistry*; word-play, play upon words; pun, double entendre 839 *witticism*; faux ami, confusible; anagram, acrostic; synonymy, homonymy, homonym, homograph, homophone 18 *analogue*.

Adj. equivocal, ambiguous, ambivalent; two-edged; left-handed, back-handed; equivocating, prevaricating; evasive; anagrammatic.

Vb. *be equivocal*, cut both ways; play upon words, pun; have two meanings; speak with two voices 14 *have nothing in common*; fudge, waffle, stall, not give a straight answer, beat about the bush, sit on the fence 620 *avoid*; equivocate, prevaricate.

519 Metaphor: figure of speech

N. *metaphor*, mixed metaphor; transference; pathetic fallacy; allusion; extended metaphor, allegory; fable, parable 534 *teaching*; symbol; symbolism, figurativeness, imagery 513 *imagination*; simile, likeness 462 *comparison*; personification.

figure of speech, turn of speech, trope, flourish; manner of speech; irony, sarcasm 851 *satire*; rhetorical figure 574 *ornament*; metonymy, antonomasia, synecdoche, transferred epithet; zeugma, anaphora; litotes 483 *underestimation*; hyperbole; stress, emphasis; circumlocution, euphuism, euphemism, dysphemism 850 *affectation*; anacoluthon, colloquialism 573 *plainness*; contrast, antithesis 462 *comparison*; metathesis 221 *inversion*; paradox, epigram, paronomasia, wordplay 518 *equivocalness*; aposiopesis; apostrophe.

Adj. *figurative*, metaphorical, allusive, symbolical, allegorical; parabolical; euphemistic 850 *affected*; hyperbolic 546 *exaggerated*; flowery.

520 Interpretation

N. *interpretation*, explanation, explication, exposition; elucidation, clarification, illumination; illustration, exemplification 83 *example*; solution, key, clue 460 *answer*; decipherment, decoding, decryption, cracking 484 *discovery*; construction, reading; allegorization 519 *metaphor*; accepted reading, vulgate; alternative reading, variant reading; criticism, textual criticism, literary criticism, practical criticism, appreciation 557 *literature*; critique, review, notice 480 *estimate*; insight.

commentary, comment, editorial comment, gloss, footnote; caption, legend 563 *phrase*; motto; annotation, notes, marginalia; exposition 591 *dissertation*; critical edition, variorum; glossary, lexicon 559 *dictionary*.

translation, version, rendering, free translation; literal translation; key, crib; paraphrase; précis, abridgment; adaptation; decoding, decryption, etc. (see also *interpretation* above); encoding, encryption.

interpreter, explainer, exponent, expounder 537 *teacher*, 973 *religious teacher*; demythologizer; editor, copy editor, proofreader 528 *publicizer*; textual critic; emender, emendator; commentator, annotator; glossarist, critic,

reviewer; medium 984 *spiritualism*; translator, paraphraser; cryptographer, encoder, codetalker; code-breaker; decoder; cryptanalyst, cryptologist; lip-reader; spokesman, mouthpiece; public relations officer, PR consultant, press officer, spin-doctor 524 *informant*; executant, performer 413 *musician*; player 594 *actor*.

guide, precedent 83 *example*; light, guiding light, star, guiding star; courier 690 *director*; demonstrator 522 *exhibitor*.

Adj. *interpretative*, interpretive, constructive; explanatory, explicatory, elucidatory; expository 557 *literary*; defining; illuminating, illustrative, exemplary; glossarial, annotative, editorial; lip-reading; mediumistic; literal; faithful; free 495 *inexact*.

Vb. *interpret*, define, clarify; explain, expound, elucidate 516 *be intelligible*; illustrate 83 *exemplify*; demonstrate 522 *show*; act as guide; comment on, edit, write notes for, add footnotes to, annotate, gloss; read, spell out; construe, put a construction on, understand by, make sense of; illuminate, throw light on; enlighten 524 *inform*; deduce, infer 475 *reason*; act as interpreter, be spokesman *or* -woman *or* -person 755 *deputize*; put a spin on, spin-doctor.

translate, render, do into, turn into; re-word, paraphrase; abridge, précis, adapt; transliterate, transcribe; encode, encrypt; lip-read.

decipher, crack, decode, decrypt; read, spell out, puzzle out, make out, work out; piece together, find the sense of; solve, resolve, unravel, disentangle, read between the lines.

Adv. *in plain words*, in plain English; by way of explanation; that is, i.e.; in other words, to put it another way, to wit, namely, viz.; to explain.

521 Misinterpretation

N. *misinterpretation*, misunderstanding, misconstruction, misapprehension, wrong end of the stick; cross-purposes, different wavelengths, crossed lines 495 *mistake*; mistranslation, misconstrue; wrong interpretation, false construction; false reading; dark glasses, rose-coloured spectacles; falsification 552 *misrepresentation*; travesty 851 *ridicule*; misapplication 565 *bad grammar*.

Vb. *misinterpret*, misunderstand; get wrong, get one wrong, get hold of the wrong end of the stick, bark up the wrong tree 495 *blunder*; misread, misspell 495 *err*; mistranslate, misconstrue, put a false sense *or* construction on; give a twist *or* turn, strain the sense; twist, twist the words 246 *distort*; equivocate, play upon words 518 *be equivocal*; read into, write into 38 *add*; misquote; garble 552 *misrepresent*; parody, caricature; misrepresent 926 *defame*.

SECTION TWO

Modes of communication

522 Manifestation

N. manifestation, revelation, unfolding, discovery, daylight, exposure 526 *disclosure*; expression; proof 466 *evidence*; presentation; sign, token 547 *signal*; symptom, syndrome 511 *omen*; press conference, prerelease, preview 438 *view*; demonstration, exhibition; display, showing off 875 *ostentation*; proclamation 528 *publication*; candour; conspicuousness 443 *visibility*; apparition, vision, materialization 445 *appearance*; séance 984 *occultism*; incarnation.

exhibit, specimen, sample 83 *example*; piece of evidence, quotation, citation 466 *evidence*; model, mock-up 551 *image*; show piece, museum piece, collector's item, antique, curio; display, show, dress show, mannequin parade 445 *spectacle*; scene 438 *view*; exhibition hall, exhibition centre, showplace, showroom, showcase, placard, hoarding, bill 528 *advertisement*; sign 547 *label*; shop window, museum, gallery 632 *collection*; exhibition, exposition; fair 796 *market*.

exhibitor, advertiser, publicist, promotion manager 528 *publicizer*; displayer, demonstrator; showman; impresario 594 *stage manager*; exhibitionist; model, male model, mannequin; flaunter.

Adj. manifest, apparent, ostensible 445 *appearing*; plain, clear, defined 80 *definite*; explained, plain as a pikestaff *or* as the nose on one's face, clear as daylight 516 *intelligible*; unconcealed, showing 443 *visible*; conspicuous, noticeable, notable, prominent, pronounced, signal, marked, striking, in relief, in the foreground, in the limelight 443 *obvious*; open, evident; gross, crass, palpable; self-evident, written all over one, for all to see, unmistakable, recognizable, identifiable, incontestable, staring one in the face 473 *certain*; public, famous, notorious, infamous; catching the eye, eye-catching, gaudy 875 *showy*; arrant, glaring, stark staring, flagrant, loud, on the rooftops, shouting from the rooftops, — on stilts.

shown, manifested, etc. (see vb.); declared, divulged, made public; unconcealed, overt, explicit, full-on, in the open, public; showing, featured, on show, on display, on view, on 443 *visible*; exhibited, shown off; brought forth, produced; mentioned, brought to one's notice; adduced, cited, quoted; confronted, brought face to face; worn, sported; paraded; unfurled, flaunted, waved, brandished; naked and unashamed; advertised, publicized, promoted 528 *published*; expressible, producible, showable.

Vb. manifest, reveal, divulge, give away, betray 526 *disclose*; evince, betoken, show signs of 466 *evidence*; bring to light, unearth 484 *discover*; explain, make plain, make obvious 520 *interpret*; expose, lay bare, unroll, unfurl, unsheathe 229 *uncover*; open up, throw open, lay open 263 *open*; elicit, draw forth, drag out 304 *extract*; invent, bring forth 164 *produce*; bring out, shadow forth, body forth; incorporate, incarnate, personify; typify, symbolize, exemplify 547 *indicate*; point up, accentuate, enhance, develop 36 *augment*; throw light on; highlight, spotlight, throw into relief 532 *emphasize*; express, formulate 532 *affirm*; bring, bring up, make reference to, mention, cite, quote; bring to the fore, place in the foreground; bring to notice, produce, trot out, come out with, proclaim, publicize, promote 528 *publish*; show for what it is (see also *show* below).

show, exhibit, display; set out, put on display, put on show, put on view, expose to view, offer to one's view, set before one's eyes; flourish 317 *brandish*; sport 228 *wear*; flaunt, parade 875 *be ostentatious*; make a show of, affect 850 *be affected*; present, feature, enact 551 *represent*; put on, stage, release 594 *dramatize*; televise, screen, film; stage an exhibition, put on a show *or* display, hang (a picture); show off, set off, model (garments); put one through his paces; demonstrate 534 *teach*; show round, show over, give a guided tour, point out, draw attention to, bring to notice 547 *indicate*; confront, force a confrontation, bring face to face, bring eyeball to eyeball; reflect, image, mirror, hold up the mirror to 20 *imitate*; tear off the mask, show up, expose 526 *disclose*.

be plain, be explicit, etc. (see adj.); show one's face, unveil, unmask; show one's true colours, have no secrets, make no mystery, not try to hide, wear one's heart on one's sleeve; have no shame, wash one's dirty linen in public; speak one's mind, speak out, tell to one's face, make no secret of, give straight from the shoulder, make no bones about 573 *speak plainly*; speak for itself, tell its own story, require no explanation 516 *be intelligible*; be obvious, stand to reason, go without saying 478 *be proved*; be conspicuous, be as plain as the nose on one's face, stand out, stand out a mile 443 *be visible*; fly *or* show the flag, be seen, show up, show up well, hold the stage, be in the limelight, have the spotlight on one, stand in full view 455 *attract notice*; loom large, stare one in the face; appear on the horizon, rear its head, show its face, transpire, emanate, come to light 445 *appear*.

523 Latency

N. *latency*, insidiousness; dormancy, potentiality 469 *possibility*; esotericism; occultness, mysticism; hidden meaning; symbolism, allegory 519 *metaphor*; implication, mystery 530 *secret*; inmost recesses 224 *interiority*; dark 418 *darkness*; shadowiness 419 *dimness*; imperceptibility 444 *invisibility*; more than meets the eye; deceptive appearance, hidden fires, hidden depths; iron hand in a velvet glove; slumbering volcano, sleeping dog, sleeping giant 661 *danger*; dark horse, mystery man; red under the bed, nigger in the woodpile, snake in the grass, mole 663 *pitfall*; manipulator, puppeteer, hidden hand, wirepuller, strings, friends in high places, friend at court, power behind the throne, éminence grise 178 *influence*; old-boy network, networking; subconscious; subliminal influence, subliminal advertising; something rotten; innuendo, insinuation, suggestion 524 *hint*; sealed lips 582 *uncommunicativeness*; undercurrent, undertone, aside 401 *faintness*; clandestineness, secret society, cabal, intrigue 623 *plot*; code, cryptography.

Adj. *latent*, lurking, skulking 525 *concealed*; dormant, sleeping 679 *inactive*; passive 266 *at rest*; in abeyance 175 *inert*; undeveloped 469 *possible*; unsuspected; subconscious, subliminal, underlying; in the background, behind the scenes, backroom, undercover; unmanifested, unseen, undetected, unexposed 444 *invisible*; arcane, impenetrable 517 *unintelligible*; sequestered 883 *secluded*; undiscovered, unexplored.

tacit, unsaid, unspoken, unpronounced, unexpressed, unvoiced, unmentioned, unarticulated, untold of, unsung; undivulged, unproclaimed, unprofessed, undeclared; unwritten, unpublished; understood, implied, inferred, implicit, between the lines; allusive.

occult, mysterious, mystic; symbolic, allegorical 519 *figurative*; cryptic, esoteric; veiled, masked, covert; clandestine, secret; insidious 930 *perfidious*; underhand 525 *stealthy*; undiscovered, hush-hush, top-secret; off the record 80 *private*; cryptographic 525 *disguised*.

Vb. *lurk*, hide, be latent, lie dormant, be a stowaway; burrow, stay underground; lie hidden; lie low, lie doggo; evade detection, escape recognition; act behind the scenes; creep, slink; pull the strings, stage-manage, underlie, be at the bottom of 156 *cause*; smoulder; be subliminal.

imply, insinuate, whisper, murmur, suggest 524 *hint*; understand, infer, allude; connote, carry a suggestion, involve, spell 514 *mean*.

524 Information

N. *information*, informatics; computerized information, information technology, IT, database, Internet, the Net, World Wide Web, website, information highway *or* superhighway, etc. 86 *computing*, 531 *Internet*; customer service; mailing list, distribution list 588 *correspondence*; hearsay, word of mouth; enlightenment, instruction, briefing 534 *teaching*; thought-transference; communication; mass media 528 *the press*, 531 *broadcasting*; notification, announcement, intimation, warning, advice, notice, mention, tip, tip-off (see also *hint* below); newspaper announcement, hatches, matches and dispatches, obit, small ad, advertisement, circular 528 *publicity*; common knowledge, gen, info; background, facts, the goods; credit-rating, black information, white information; documentary 494 *truth*; material, literature 589 *reading matter*; instructions, directions for use, care label, user's manual; stage directions; inside information, king's *or* queen's evidence, dope, lowdown, skinny, undisclosed source, confidence 530 *secret*; scoop; the know 490 *knowledge*; file, dossier 548 *record*; word, report, intelligence, item of news 529 *news*; wire, telegram, telemessage, telex, cable, cablegram 529 *message*; communicativeness; leak, disinformation 526 *disclosure*.

report, review, annual report; paper, Green Paper, White Paper, Black Paper; account, eyewitness account 590 *narrative*; statement, return, annual return, tax return 86 *statistics*; specification, estimates 480 *estimate*; progress report, confidential report; dispatch, bulletin, communiqué, handout, press release 529 *news*; presentation, case; petition 761 *entreaty*; round robin 762 *deprecation*; letters, letters to the editor, dispatches 588 *correspondence*.

hint, gentle hint, whisper, aside 401 *faintness*; intimation; broad hint, signal, nod, a nod is as good as a wink to a blind horse, wink, look, nudge, kick, kick under the table, gesticulation 547 *gesture*; prompt, cue 505 *reminder*; suggestion; caution 664 *warning*; tip, tip-off (see also *information* above); word in the ear, word to the wise; insinuation, innuendo; clue, symptom 520 *interpretation*; sidelight, glimpse, inkling; suspicion, inference.

informant, teller; spokesman *or* -woman *or* -person 579 *speaker*; mouthpiece, representative 754 *delegate*; announcer, radio announcer, television announcer, weather-forecaster, weatherman *or* -woman *or* -girl 531 *broadcaster*, notifier, advertiser, promoter 528 *publicizer*; harbinger, herald 529 *messenger*; testifier 466 *witness*; one in the know, authority, source, informed circles; quarter, channel, circle, grapevine; pander, go-between, contact 231 *intermediary*; information centre, information bureau, information desk, help desk, call centre; news agency, wire service, Reuter, TASS 528 *the press*; communicator, correspondent, special correspondent, reporter, newshound, chequebook journalist, commentator, columnist, gossip writer 529 *news reporter*; tipster 691 *adviser*; guide; source, little bird; chattering classes.

informer, spy, spook, snoop, sleuth 459 *detective*; undercover agent, inside agent, mole; stool pigeon, nark, copper's nark, snitch, sneak, nose, squealer, whistle-blower, grass, supergrass; eavesdropper, telltale, talebearer, clype, tattler, tattletale, gossip 581 *chatterer*.

guidebook, Baedeker, Rough Guide (tdmk); travelogue; handbook, book of words, manual, vade mecum, ABC, A–Z, bible; timetable, Bradshaw; roadbook, itinerary, route map, chart, plan 551 *map*; gazetteer 589 *reference book*; nautical almanac; telephone directory, phone book, Yellow Pages; index, catalogue 87 *directory*; courier 520 *guide*.

Adj. informative, communicative, newsy; instructive, documentary 534 *educational*; oral, verbal, spoken; explicit; indiscreet 581 *talkative*.

informed, well-informed, kept informed, au fait, au courant; posted, primed, briefed, instructed 490 *knowing*; au courant, genned-up, clued-up, wised-up; in the know, in on, in the picture, sussed, up to speed; brought up to date.

Vb. inform, certify, advise, beg to advise; intimate, impart, convey (see also *communicate* below); apprise, acquaint, have one know, give to understand; give one the facts, brief, instruct 534 *teach*; let one know, put one in the picture, fill one in on; enlighten 534 *educate*; point out, direct one's attention 547 *indicate*; insinuate (see also *hint* below); confide, mention privately; put one wise, put right, correct, disabuse, disillusion; be specific, state, name, signify 80 *specify*; mention, mention en passant, refer to, touch on, speak of 579 *speak*; gossip, spread rumours; be indiscreet, open one's mouth, let the cat out of the bag, blurt out, talk 581 *be talkative*; leak information, give disinformation, break the news, reveal 526 *disclose*; tell, clype, blab, split, grass, snitch, squeal, blow the gaff 526 *confess*; rat,

turn Queen's *or* King's evidence, turn State's evidence; betray one, blow the whistle on, sell one down the river; tell tales, tell on, clype on; inform against, shop, denounce 928 *accuse*.

communicate, transmit, pass on, pass on information; dispatch news 588 *correspond*; report, cover, make a report, submit a report; report progress, keep posted; get through, get across, put it over; contact, get in touch; convey, bring word, send word, leave word, write 588 *correspond*; beam; post; send a message, speak, semaphore 547 *signal*; wire, telegraph, telex, radio; send a telemessage; send a singing telegram, kissogram, etc.; telephone, phone, call, dial, ring, ring up, give one a ring *or* a tinkle *or* a buzz; text, send a text-message; disseminate, broadcast, telecast, televise; announce, notify, give notice, serve notice 528 *advertise*; give out, put out, carry a report, issue a press notice *or* release, publicize 528 *publish*; retail, recount, narrate 590 *describe*; commune 584 *converse*; swap news, exchange information, pool one's knowledge.

hint, drop a hint, suggest, throw out a suggestion; put an idea in one's head; prompt, give the cue 505 *remind*; caution 664 *warn*; tip off 691 *advise*; wink, tip the wink; nudge 547 *gesticulate*; insinuate, breathe, whisper, say in one's ear, touch upon, just mention, mention in passing *or* en passant, say by the way, let fall, imply, allude, leave one to gather, intimate.

be informed, be in possession of the facts 490 *know*; have it on good authority; keep one's ear to the ground, hear it on the grapevine, be a fly on the wall, overhear 415 *hear*; be told by a little bird, get wind of; have a line on, have the dope *or* gen *or* info.

525 Concealment

N. concealment, confinement, purdah 883 *seclusion*; hiding 523 *latency*; covering up; cache 527 *hiding-place*; disguise, camouflage 542 *deception*; masquerade, anonymity, incognito 562 *no name*; smoke screen 421 *screen*; reticence, reserve; mental reservation, ulterior motive, hidden agenda; evasion, evasiveness 518 *equivocalness*; misinformation, disinformation; white lie; subterfuge 542 *trickery*; suppression, D notice, Official Secrets Act; cover-up 543 *untruth*; deceitfulness, dissimulation 541 *duplicity*.

secrecy, secretness, mystery 530 *secret*; seal of secrecy, hearing in camera; secret society, clandestineness, secretiveness, furtiveness, stealthiness; underhand dealing 930 *improbity*; conspiracy 623 *plot*; cipher, code, encoding, encryption 517 *unintelligibility*.

Adj. concealed, crypto-, hidden, closet; hiding, in ambush; confined; mysterious, recondite, arcane 517 *unintelligible*; cryptic 523 *occult*; private 883 *secluded*; confidential, off the record; secret, top secret, restricted, hush-hush; unrevealed, ex-directory; undisclosed; unsigned, unnamed 562 *anonymous*; covert, behind the scenes; covered; hooded, masked, veiled, eclipsed; smothered, stifled, suppressed, clandestine, undercover, underground, subterranean 211 *deep*.

disguised, camouflaged; incognito 562 *anonymous*; unrecognizable 491 *unknown*; masked 421 *screened*; codified, cryptographic 517 *unintelligible*.

stealthy, silent, furtive, catlike, on tiptoe; prowling, skulking, loitering, lurking; clandestine, hugger-mugger, conspiratorial, cloak-and-dagger; hole-and-corner, backdoor, underhand, surreptitious 930 *dishonest*.

reticent, reserved, shy, self-contained, withdrawn; non-committal, uncommunicative, uninformative, cagey, evasive; vague, studiously vague; keeping one's own counsel, discreet, silent 582 *uncommunicative*; tight-lipped, poker-faced; close, secretive, buttoned-up, close as an oyster, clamlike; in one's shell 883 *unsociable*.

Vb. conceal, hide, hide away, squirrel away, plank, secrete, ensconce, confine, keep in purdah 883 *seclude*; stow away, lock up, seal up, bottle up 632 *store*; hide underground, bury 364 *inter*; put out of sight, sweep under the carpet, cover up, paper over, whitewash 226 *cover*; gloss over; blot out 550 *obliterate*; slur over, not mention 458 *disregard*; smother, stifle 165 *suppress*; veil, muffle, mask, disguise, camouflage; shroud, draw a veil over 421 *screen*; obscure, eclipse 418 *darken*; obfuscate 419 *dim*; go incognito, masquerade 541 *dissemble*; encode, encrypt.

keep secret, keep it dark, keep under wraps, keep close, keep under one's hat; look blank, look poker-faced, give nothing away, keep a straight face, keep mum, keep one's mouth shut, hold one's tongue, not breathe a word, not utter a syllable, not talk, keep one's counsel, make no sign 582 *be uncommunicative*; be discreet, neither confirm nor deny, make no comment; keep back, reserve, withhold, keep it to oneself, let it go no further; hush up, cover up, suppress; keep a low profile, keep in the background, stay in the shadows; let not one's right hand know what one's left hand does; blindfold, bamboozle, keep in the dark 542 *deceive*.

be stealthy, be furtive, be evasive, etc. (see

adj.); hugger-mugger, conspire 623 *plot*; snoop, sneak, slink, creep; glide, steal, steal along, steal by, steal past; tiptoe, go on tiptoe, pussyfoot; prowl, skulk, loiter; lie doggo 523 *lurk*; dodge 620 *avoid*.

Adv. secretly, in secret; hugger-mugger, confidentially, sotto voce, with bated breath; entre nous, between ourselves, between you and me and the gatepost *or* bedpost; aside, to oneself; not for publication, privately, in private, in camera, behind closed doors; behind one's back; anonymously, incognito; in pectore; under wraps.

stealthily, furtively, like a thief in the night; under cloak of darkness; underhand, by the back door, in a hole-and-corner way, under-the-counter; on the sly, on the quiet, on the QT.

526 Disclosure

N. disclosure, revelation, apocalypse; daylight, cold light of day; discovery, uncovering; unwelcome discovery, disillusionment 509 *disappointment*; denouement; lid off, exposé, divulgence 528 *publication*; exposure, showing up 522 *manifestation*; telling all, explanations, showdown; communication, leak, indiscretion 524 *hint*; betrayal, giveaway; tell-tale sign; State's evidence, Queen's *or* King's evidence 603 *change of mind*; acknowledgment, admission, avowal, confession, coming clean; confessional 939 *penitence*; clean breast, whole truth, cards on the table 494 *truth*.

Vb. disclose, reveal, expose, take the wraps off, disinter 522 *manifest*; bare, lay bare, strip bare, denude; unfold, unroll, unfurl, unpack, unwrap 229 *uncover*; unveil, lift the veil, raise the curtain, let some light in; break the seal, unclose 263 *open*; lay open, open up 484 *discover*; catch out 484 *detect*; not hide; make known, give away, betray, blow one's cover; unmask, tear off the mask; expose oneself, betray oneself, give oneself away 495 *blunder*; declare oneself, drop the mask; show oneself in one's true colours, show for what it is, debunk; disabuse, set right, undeceive, disillusion, open the eyes 524 *inform*; take the lid off, unleash, let the cat out of the bag.

divulge, declare, bring into the open, express, vent, give vent to 579 *speak*; ventilate, air, canvass, publicize 528 *publish*; tell all, let on, blurt out, blow the gaff, talk out of turn, spill the beans, let the cat out of the bag, give the show *or* the game away; speak of, talk; utter, breathe; let out, leak 524 *communicate*; let drop, let fall 524 *hint*; come out with, spit it out 573 *speak plainly*; get it off one's chest, unburden oneself; confide, let one into the secret, open one's mind *or* heart to; declare one's intentions, show one's hand, put one's cards on the table; report, tell, tell tales out of school, tell on, kiss and tell, clype, name names 928 *accuse*; split, squeal, blab, grass 524 *inform*; rat.

confess, admit, avow, acknowledge; concede, grant, allow, own 488 *assent*; own up, cough up, fess up; plead guilty, admit one's guilt, hold one's hands up, put one's hand up to; talk, sing, sing like a canary; come out with, come across with, come clean, tell all, speak the truth 540 *be truthful*; make a clean breast of it, go to confession; turn Queen's evidence 603 *change one's mind*.

be disclosed, come out, break 445 *appear*; come to light 478 *be proved*; show the cloven hoof, show its face, show its true colours, stand revealed 522 *be plain*; transpire, become known, become public knowledge 490 *be known*; leak out 298 *emerge*; show 443 *be visible*; show through; come as a revelation, break through the clouds, come with a blinding flash, flash on the mind 449 *dawn upon*; give oneself away, there speaks —.

527 Hiding. Disguise

N. *hiding-place*, hide, hideout, hideaway, hidey-hole, priesthole, safe house 662 *refuge*; lair, den 192 *retreat*; cache, secret place, oubliette; crypt, vault 194 *cellar*; closet, secret drawer, hidden panel, safe place, safe, safe deposit 632 *storage*; recess, corner, nook, cranny, niche, holes and corners, secret passage, underground passage; cover, underground 662 *shelter*; inmost recesses 224 *interiority*.

ambush, spider's web 542 *trap*; catch 663 *pitfall*; stalking horse, Trojan horse, decoy, stool pigeon 545 *impostor*; agent provocateur 663 *troublemaker*.

disguise, blind, masquerade 542 *deception*; camouflage 20 *mimicry*; veneer 226 *covering*; mask, visor, veil, domino 228 *cloak*; fancy dress; smoke screen, cover 421 *screen*.

Vb. *ambush*, set an ambush, lie in wait 523 *lurk*; set a trap for 542 *ensnare*; waylay.

528 Publication

N. *publication*, dissemination 526 *disclosure*; proclamation; edict; beat of drum, flourish of trumpets 400 *loudness*; press conference, press release, advance publicity (see also *advertisement* below); notification, public notice, official bulletin; announcement, press announcement, pronouncement, manifesto, programme, platform; the media, meeja, mass media; publishing, book trade, book-selling

589 *book*; broadcasting, narrowcasting, televising 531 *telecommunication*; broadcast, telecast, newscast, webcast 529 *news*; kite-flying; circulation, circular, bull, encyclical.

publicity, limelight, spotlight, public eye; common knowledge 490 *knowledge*; open discussion, seminar, ventilation; canvassing; blatancy 522 *manifestation*; open secret; notoriety, fame 866 *fame*; currency, wide currency; circulation, wide circulation; readership, audience, viewership; viewing *or* listening figures, ratings; public relations, PR, promotion, sales promotion, propaganda, spin, party political broadcast, PPB, soundbite, gesture politics; photocall, photo-opportunity, display, showmanship, salesmanship, window dressing 875 *ostentation*; sensationalism, ballyhoo, hype 546 *exaggeration*; publicization, advertising, shockvertising; medium of publicity: television, radio 531 *broadcasting* (see also *the press* below); skywriting; public address system, loudspeaker, loud hailer 415 *hearing aid*; public comment, journalism, reporting, the media, the meeja, rapportage, coverage, report, notice, write-up (see also *the press* below); investigative journalism, chequebook journalism 459 *enquiry*; newsreel, newsletter, news round-up 529 *news*; sounding board, correspondence column, open letter, letters to the editor; editorial 591 *article*; pulpit, platform, hustings, soapbox; printing press 587 *print*; blaze of publicity, letters a foot high; name in lights.

advertisement, notice, insertion, advert, ad, small ad, classified ad, advertorial; personal column; headline, banner headline, streamer; puff, blurb, buildup, hype, ballyhoo; spam; promotional literature, unsolicited mail, handout, handbill; bill, poster, flyer 522 *exhibit*; billboard, hoarding, placard, sandwich board, display board, notice board, bulletin board; Yellow Pages; advertising copy, slogan, jingle; plug, teaser, trailer, commercial, infomercial 531 *broadcasting*; hard sell, soft sell, subliminal advertising; cold-calling.

the press, the fourth estate, Fleet Street, the papers; newspaper, newssheet, freesheet, paper, rag, tabloid, red-top; comic; underground press, gutter press, yellow press, tabloid press; organ, journal, daily paper, daily, quality daily, broadsheet, heavy; morning paper, evening paper, Sunday paper, local paper; issue, edition, stop-press edition, sports edition, extra; magazine section, supplement, colour supplement; insert, leaflet, hand-bill, pamphlet, brochure, newsletter; editorial, column, agony column, classified advert (see also *advertisement* above); scoop, feeding frenzy; press officer.

journal, review, magazine, glossy magazine, glossy, specialist magazine, women's magazine, male-interest magazine, listings magazine, pulp magazine, fanzine, zine, e-magazine, e-mag, e-zine; part-work, periodical, serial, daily, weekly, monthly, quarterly, annual; gazette, trade journal, house magazine, trade publication 589 *reading matter*.

publicizer, notifier, announcer; herald, trumpet 529 *messenger*; proclaimer, crier, town crier; barker, tout; bill sticker, bill poster, sandwichman; demonstrator, promoter, publicist, publicity agent, press agent, advertising agent; adman, advertiser, hidden persuader; copywriter, blurb writer, commercial artist, public relations officer, PRO, image-maker, propagandist, pamphleteer 537 *preacher*; printer, publisher 589 *book-person*; reporter, journalist, investigative journalist, chequebook journalist 529 *news reporter*.

Adj. *published*, in print 587 *printed*; in the news, public 490 *known*; broadcast, on the air; on television; multi-media.

Vb. *publish*, make public; report, cover, write up; bring into the open, reveal 526 *divulge*; highlight, spotlight 532 *emphasize*; radio, broadcast, narrowcast, tape, telecast, televise, relay, diffuse 524 *inform*; spread, circulate, distribute, disseminate, circularize; canvass, ventilate, discuss 475 *argue*; pamphleteer, propagate, propagandize 534 *teach*; use the press 587 *print*; syndicate, serialize, edit, subedit, sub; issue, release, get out, put out, give out, send forth, lay before the public; bring to public notice, let it be known; spread a rumour, fly a kite; spread abroad; talk about, pass round, put about, bandy about; voice, broach, talk of, speak of, utter, emit 579 *speak*.

proclaim, announce, herald, notify; pronounce, declare, go on record 532 *affirm*; make one's views public, make a proclamation, issue a public statement; publish a manifesto; noise, trumpet, blaze abroad, declaim, shout from the rooftops; beat the big drum; announce with a flourish of trumpets.

advertise, publicize; place an ad, bill, post, put up a poster; tell the world, put on the map, headline; make a cynosure of, put in lights, spotlight, build up, promote, big up; make much of, feature; sell, boost, puff, hype up, write up, extol, rave about 482 *overrate*; plug 106 *repeat*.

be published, become public, come out; hit the headlines, make the front page; become the talk of the town, circulate, pass from mouth to mouth, go the rounds, get about, be bruited abroad, spread, spread like wildfire, find a publisher, see oneself in print, get printed, get into the papers; sell well, go like a best-seller, become a blockbuster 793 *be sold*.

529 News

N. *news*, good news, no news is good news; bad news 509 *disappointment*; tidings, glad tidings; gospel, evangel 973 *religion*; dispatches, diplomatic bag; intelligence, report, dispatch, word, intimation, advice; titbit 524 *information*; bulletin, communiqué, handout, press release; newspaper report, press notice; news item, news flash, soundbite 531 *broadcast*; latest news, breaking news, stop-press news; sensation, scoop, exclusive; old news, stale news, ancient history, Queen Anne's dead; copy, filler; yarn, story, tall story; newscast, newsreel 528 *publicity*; news value, newsworthiness.

rumour, unconfirmed report; hearsay, gossip, talk, talk of the town, tittle-tattle 584 *chat*; scandal 926 *calumny*; whisper, buzz, noise; false report, hoax; grapevine, bush telegraph.

message, word of mouth, word, tip 524 *information*; communication 547 *signal*; wireless message, cable, telegram, telemessage, wire, fax, electronic mail, e-mail, attachment, text-message, post 531 *Internet, telecommunication*; postcard, pc, note, letters, dispatches 531 *postal communications*, 588 *correspondence*; ring, phone call, buzz, tinkle; radiopaging; errand 751 *commission*.

news reporter, newspaperman *or* -woman, reporter, cub reporter, journalist, correspondent, legman, stringer 589 *author*; gentleman *or* lady of the press, pressman *or* -woman, press representative 524 *informant*; newsreader, newscaster 531 *broadcaster*; chequebook journalist, muckraker, scandalmonger.

messenger, forerunner 66 *precursor*; harbinger 511 *omen*, announcer, town crier 528 *publicizer*; ambassador, spokesman *or* -woman *or* -person 754 *envoy*, apostle, emissary; herald; go-between, pander, contact, contact man *or* woman 231 *intermediary*.

courier, runner, Queen's Messenger, express messenger, dispatch rider, delivery-man *or* -woman; postman *or* -woman 531 *postal communications*; telegraph boy *or* girl, messenger boy *or* girl, errand boy *or* girl, office boy *or* girl; call-boy, bellhop, page, buttons, commissionaire; carrier pigeon 273 *carrier*; messenger of the gods: Mercury.

530 Secret

N. *secret*, esotericism; mystery 984 *occultism*; confidential information, sealed orders, top-secret file, state secret, affairs of state; confidential communication; sphinx, man *or* woman of mystery, enigmatic personality,

Gioconda smile, inscrutable smile; Mr *or* Miss X 562 *no name*; dark horse, unknown quantity; unknown warrior; skeleton in the cupboard; nigger in the woodpile; sealed book; unknown country, terra incognita 491 *unknown thing*.

enigma, mystery, puzzle, Chinese puzzle, Rubik's cube (tdmk), Rubik's snake (tdmk), Rubik's magic (tdmk); problem, poser, brainteaser; hard nut to crack, vexed question; cipher, code, cryptogram, hieroglyphics 517 *unintelligibility*; word-puzzle, anagram, acrostic, crossword; riddle, riddle-me-ree, conundrum; charade; intricacy, labyrinth, maze 61 *complexity*.

531 Communications

N. *telecommunication*; teleinformatics; long-distance communication, telephony, cellular telephony, telegraphy, radio *or* wireless telegraphy; signalling, semaphore, morse 547 *signal*; cable, cablegram, telegram, telemessage, wire, fax, electronic mail, e-mail, spam, voicemail, text-message 529 *message*; bush telegraph, grapevine; radar 484 *discovery*; telex, teleprinter, tape machine, ticker; teleconferencing; videoconferencing; intercom, walkie-talkie, bleeper, bleep, pager; microphone 400 *megaphone*; headset 415 *hearing aid*; telephone, phone, blower, radio telephone, cellular telephone, cellphone, car telephone, car phone, cordless telephone, mobile phone, mobile, mobe *or* mobie, hands-free mobile phone, hands-free set; camera phone, videophone; texting *or* text-messaging, multimedia messaging, photo-messaging, picture messaging; m-commerce, m-business; ringtone; Short Message System, SMS; Wireless Application Protocol, WAP; line, party line, hot line; extension; telephone exchange, switchboard; call centre, customer service; telesales; telephonist, telephone receptionist, wireless operator, radio ham, telegrapher; tone dialling, pulse dialling; broadband.

postal communications, postal services, Royal Mail, GPO; post, first-class post, second-class post, mail, snail mail, letters 588 *correspondence*; letter, air letter, aerogramme, postcard, letter-card; surface mail, sea mail, air mail; parcel post, registered post, recorded delivery, express delivery, red star delivery; postcode, zip code *or* ZIP code (US); stamp, postage stamp, first-class stamp, second-class stamp, definitive stamp, commemorative stamp; address, accommodation address; mailing list, mailshot, mail merge; mail order; pillarbox, postbox, letterbox; post office, sorting office, mailbag; postmaster *or* -mistress, post-

man *or* -woman 529 *messenger*; pigeon post; diplomatic bag, dispatch box; hate mail, poison-pen letter, letter bomb, parcel bomb.

broadcasting, the media, meeja 528 *publicity*; broadcasting authority, BBC, Beeb, Auntie; IBA, ITA; independent television *or* radio; commercial television *or* radio, local television *or* radio, cable television *or* radio, satellite television, pirate radio, Citizens' Band *or* CB radio; transmitter, booster, communications satellite; aerial, antenna; radio waves, wavelengths, modulation, AM, FM 417 *radiation*; radio station, television channel, network; wireless, radio, cellular radio, mobile radio, steam radio, clock radio, cat's whisker, crystal set; radiopaging; portable, transistor, tranny *or* trannie, ghetto blaster, personal stereo; television, cable television, digital television, telly, TV, the box, gogglebox, the small screen, talking head; colour television, black-and-white television, monochrome television; cable TV, digital TV, satellite TV, terrestrial TV, pay TV, free-to-air broadcasting, free-to-view programmes; actuality TV, reality TV; watercooler television, car-crash TV, tabloid TV; net-top box, set-top box; screen, plasma screen; closed-circuit television 442 *camera*; videorecorder, videocassette, videocassette recorder, VCR, video, videotape, video nasty, video game 549 *recording instrument*; Teleprompter (tdmk), autocue; teletext, Ceefax (tdmk), Oracle (tdmk), Prestel (tdmk) 524 *information*; Open University; radio listener 415 *listener*; viewer, televiewer, TV addict 441 *spectator*; listings magazine.

broadcast, outside broadcast, telecast, transmission, relay, live relay 528 *publication*; recording, repeat, transcription 548 *record*; programme, request programme, phone-in, telethon, quiz, chat show, music 837 *amusement*; news, newsflash, soundbite, news roundup 529 *news*; time signal, pips; talk, feature, documentary, infotainment 524 *report*; actuality TV, reality TV; series, soap opera, situation comedy, sitcom, saga, docudrama, faction 594 *drama*; cartoon, film 445 *cinema*; commercial, commercial break, infomercial 528 *advertisement*.

broadcaster, announcer, commentator, talking head, newsreader, newscaster 524 *informant*; presenter, frontman *or* -woman, anchorman *or* -woman, linkman *or* -woman, compere, question master; disc jockey, DJ, deejay, shock jock; media personality 866 *person of repute*.

Internet, the Net, World Wide Web, the Web, information highway, information superhighway, router, portal, Usenet; computer, zombie computer; website, web page, home page, weblog, blog; webcast, webcam, livecam; FAQ, Frequently Asked Questions; hypertext markup language, HTML; e-mail, e-address, domain, domain name, URL, cybersquatter; Internet service provider, ISP, music service provider, MSP; net-top box; hypertext link, bookmark, search engine, browser, net-surfing, surfing, chatroom; emoticon *or* smiley; netiquette, flame, flaming, flame war, spam, spamming, smurfing; cyberspace, virtual reality; P2P, peer-to-peer; local area network, LAN, intranet; wi-fi; geek, hacker, web architect, internaut, netizen, silver surfer, telecommuter, e-lancer; cybercafé, Internet café; dotcom, dotcom company, cyberpreneur; e-business, e-commerce, e-sales, e-tailing, electronic shopping, cybershopping, e-shopping, virtual shopping, virtual storefront, virtual mall, clicks and mortar, shopping engine; e-cash, e-money; mousetrapping, page-jacking; computer crime, computer fraud, cybercrime, cybercriminal, e-stalking, cyberterrorism, cyberterrorist, cyberwar, cyberwarfare, electronic civil disobedience, hacktivism, hacktivist, information warfare, logic bomb; cyber cop, cyber court, cyberlaw, cyber lawyer; electronic virtual assistant, EVA; e-health, cyberchondriac; e-learning; cyberflirtation, cybersex; e-voting; electronic book, e-book; MP3, ripper 414 *music player*; Wireless Application Protocol, WAP; intelligent wear, I-wear; digital divide; electronic publishing, e-magazine, e-mag, e-zine. (See also 86 *computer, computing*.)

532 Affirmation

N. *affirmation*, saying, dictum 496 *maxim*; statement; submission, thesis 512 *supposition*; expressed opinion, conclusion 480 *judgment*; voice, suffrage, ballot 605 *vote*; expression, formulation; written statement, mission statement, prepared text; one's position, one's stand *or* stance; declaration, profession; allegation 928 *accusation*; assertion, ipse dixit, say-so; averment; admission, confession, avowal 526 *disclosure*; corroboration, confirmation, assurance, one's word, warrant 466 *testimony*; insistence, vehemence, peremptoriness 571 *vigour*; stress, accent, emphasis, protesting too much; observation 579 *speech*; comment, criticism 480 *estimate*; assertiveness, self-assertion, pontification 473 *positiveness*; assertiveness training.

oath, swearing, swearing on the Bible, statement on oath, deposition, affidavit 466 *testimony*; promissory oath, word of a gentleman, word of honour, pledge, promise, warrant, guarantee 764 *promise*.

Adj. *affirmative*, affirming, professing, etc. (see vb.); not negative 473 *positive*; declaratory; pronouncing; unretractable 473 *undisputed*; committed, promised; earnest; solemn, sworn, formal.

assertive, telling; assured, dogmatic, pontificating, confident, self-assured 473 *positive*; pushing, trenchant, incisive, pointed, decisive; peremptory, categorical, absolute, brooking no denial, emphatic, insistent; vehement; making no bones, blunt, outspoken, strongly-worded, straight from the shoulder 573 *plain*.

Vb. *affirm*, state, express, formulate, set down; declare, pronounce, deliver, enunciate 528 *proclaim*, 579 *orate*; give expression to, voice 579 *speak*; remark, comment, observe, say; state with conviction, be bound, dare swear 485 *opine*; mean what one says, vow, protest; make a statement, make a verbal, assert; maintain, hold, contend 475 *argue*; make one's point 478 *demonstrate*; urge 512 *propound*; put one's case, put forward, submit; appeal, claim 761 *request*; allege, aver; bear witness 466 *testify*; certify, confirm, warrant, guarantee 466 *corroborate*; commit oneself, go as far as; pledge; hold out 759 *offer*; profess, avow; admit 526 *confess*; abide by, stick to one's guns 599 *stand firm*; speak up, speak out, put it bluntly, make no bones about 573 *speak plainly*; brook no denial, shout, shout down; lay down the law, pontificate 473 *dogmatize*; get on one's soapbox, hold the floor, have one's say, have the last word.

swear, take one's oath; attest, confirm by oath 466 *corroborate*; cross one's heart; kiss the book, swear on the Bible.

emphasize, stress, lay stress on, accent, accentuate; underline, italicize, dot the i's and cross the t's, put in bold letters; raise one's voice, speak up, shout, thunder, roar, bellow, fulminate 400 *be loud*; bang one's fist down, thump the table; urge; insist 737 *command*; drive home, impress on, din in, rub in; plug, dwell on, labour 106 *repeat*; highlight, enhance, point up.

533 Negation

N. *negation*, negative, nay, no; denial 760 *refusal*; disbelief 486 *unbelief*; disagreement 489 *dissent*; rebuttal, appeal 460 *rejoinder*; refutation 479 *confutation*; emphatic denial, contradiction, gainsaying; challenge 711 *defiance*; demurrer 468 *qualification*; protest 762 *deprecation*; repudiation, disclaimer, dissociation 607 *rejection*; abnegation, renunciation 621 *relinquishment*; abjuration 603 *recantation*; negative attitude, negativism, negativity; noncorroboration; contravention 738 *disobedience*;

cancellation, invalidation, nullification, revocation.

Adj. *negative*, denying, negating, contradictory 14 *non-identical*; contravening 738 *disobedient*; protesting; abnegating, renunciatory; denied, disowned, dissociated.

Vb. *negate*, negative; contravene 738 *disobey*; deny, gainsay, give the lie to, belie, contradict; eat one's hat if … 470 *make impossible*; repudiate, disclaim, disown 607 *reject*; refuse to corroborate; hold no brief for 860 *be indifferent*; demur, object 468 *qualify*; disagree 489 *dissent*; dissociate oneself 704 *oppose*; impugn, question, call in question, express doubts, refute, rebut, disprove 479 *confute*; protest, appeal against 762 *deprecate*; challenge 711 *defy*; thwart 702 *obstruct*; say no, decline, shake one's head, disallow 760 *refuse*; not allow 757 *prohibit*; revoke, invalidate, nullify 752 *annul*; abnegate, renounce 621 *relinquish*; abjure, forswear, swear off 603 *recant*; go back on one's word, do a U-turn 603 *change one's mind*.

534 Teaching

N. *teaching*, pedagogy, pedagogics, tutoring; education, schooling; tutelage; direction, guidance, instruction, edification; dictation; chalk and talk, the chalk face; programmed instruction, direct method, immersion method, induction 475 *reasoning*; computer-aided *or* -assisted instruction, CAI; tuition, preparation, coaching, cramming; seminar, teach-in, workshop, tutorial; initiation, introduction; training, basic training, cascade training 536 *learning*; discipline, drill 682 *exercise*; inculcation, indoctrination, preaching; propagandism; pamphleteering, propaganda, agitprop 528 *publicity*; conversion; conditioning; brainwashing; assertiveness training; animal training: obedience class, manège.

education, liberal education 490 *culture*; classical education, scientific education, technical education; moral training; technical training, technological training, vocational training; coeducation, progressive education, Froebel system, Froebelism, kindergarten method, Montessori system; elementary education, grounding; nursery education, preschool education, primary education, secondary education, further education, higher education, tertiary education, university education, adult education, adult learning, lifelong learning, community education; distance learning, e-learning; day release, block release; sandwich course, refresher course; advanced studies, postgraduate studies; remedial education; physical education, PE.

curriculum, National Curriculum, course of study 536 *learning*; core curriculum, common core; ABC, the three R's 68 *beginning*; foundation course, access course; set books, prescribed text; module, project, exercise, homework, prep; Open University course, correspondence course, in-service course.

lecture, talk, illustrated talk; documentary 531 *broadcasting*; reading, discourse; sermon, homily 579 *oration*; lesson, parable.

Adj. *educational*, pedagogic, tutorial; scholastic, scholarly, academic; instructional, informational; audiovisual, instructive 524 *informative*; educative, didactic, doctrinal, edifying, moralizing; primary, secondary, etc. (see n.); single-sex, coeducational, comprehensive, all-ability, all-in; set, streamed, creamed, mixed-ability; extramural, intramural, extracurricular; university, redbrick, Oxbridge, Ivy League; cultural.

Vb. *educate*, edify (see also *teach* below); rear, nurture, bring up, develop, form, mould, shape, lick into shape; send to school, tutor, teach, school; ground, coach, cram, prime 669 *prepare*; guide 689 *direct*; instruct 524 *inform*; enlighten; sharpen the wits, open the eyes; stuff with knowledge, cram with facts; impress on the memory, din in, inculcate, indoctrinate, imbue, impregnate, infuse, instil, infix, implant, engraft, sow the seeds of.

teach, give lessons, take a class, lecture, deliver lectures; tutor, give tutorials, hold seminars; dictate, read out; preach, harangue, sermonize, pontificate; discourse, hold forth; moralize; expound 520 *interpret*; indoctrinate; pamphleteer, disseminate propaganda, condition, brainwash 178 *influence*.

train, coach 669 *prepare*; take on, take in hand, initiate, tame 369 *break in*; foster, cultivate; inure, keep one's nose to the grindstone; drill, exercise, practise, familiarize, accustom, groom one for 610 *accustom oneself*; show one the ropes; make fit, qualify; house-train, teach manners, teach etiquette.

535 Misteaching

N. *misteaching*, misdirection; the blind leading the blind; misinformation, disinformation 552 *misrepresentation*; propaganda, spin, brainwashing 534 *teaching*, 541 *falsehood*; perversion 246 *distortion*; false logic.

536 Learning

N. *learning*, lore, scholarship, attainments 490 *erudition*; tutelage, apprenticeship, initiation 669 *preparation*; computer-aided *or* -assisted learning, CAL, computer-assisted language learning, CALL; basic training, basics, first steps, teething troubles 68 *beginning*; teachability 694 *aptitude*; self-improvement, personal development, self-cultivation; culture, cultivation. (See also 534 *teaching*.)

study, studying; application, studiousness; cramming, swotting, grind, mugging up, burning the midnight oil; studies, course of studies, lessons, class, classwork, deskwork; homework, prep, preparation; revision, refresher course, further reading, further study; crash course; perusal, reading 455 *attention*; research, research work, field work, investigation 459 *enquiry*; learning curve.

Subjects of Study: -ics, -ologies and others

acoustics (sound), aesthetics (beauty and fine arts), aetiology (causation), agrostology (grasses), algology (algae), ampelology *or* ampelography (vines), anatomy (structure of the body), anthropology (human beings), arachnology (spiders), archaeology (human antiquities), astrology (stars and planets as supposed indicators of character and events), astronomy (stars and planets), bacteriology (bacteria), ballistics (projectiles), biochemistry (chemistry of living organisms), biology (living things), botany (plants and flowers), bryology (mosses), cereology (crop circles), cetology (whales), chemistry (structure and properties of substances), chiroptology (bats), chronology (measuring time), climatology (climate), conchology (molluscs and shells), cosmography *and* cosmology (the universe), craniology (skulls), criminology (crime and criminals), cryptozoology (undiscovered animals), cybernetics (control systems in the brain and computers, etc), cytology (cells), demography (population), dendrology (trees), deontology (duty), dermatology (skin), dialectology (dialects), ecology (the relationship between plants and animals and the environment), economics (the production and use of goods and services), electronics (conduction of electricity and its uses), embryology (embryos), entomology (insects), epidemiology (epidemics), epistemology (knowledge), eschatology (death, heaven and hell), ethics (morality and duty), ethnology (human culture), ethology (animal behaviour), etymology (word origins), genetics (biological heredity), geography (the earth), geology (rocks and minerals), geometry (the measurement and relationships of points, lines, angles, etc), geriatrics *and* gerontology (ageing and old people), glaciology (ice), graphology (handwriting), gynaecology (diseases of women), hagiology (saints), helminthology (worms), herpetology (reptiles and amphibians), horology (measurement of time; clock-making), ichthyology (fish), immunology (immunity against disease), informatics (processing of informationm, especially by computer), lepidopterology (butterflies and moths), lexicology (words), linguistics (language), malacology (molluscs), mammalogy (mammals), mathematics (numbers and quantities), mechanics (the effect of energy and forces on bodies), metallurgy (metals and ores), metaphysics (the nature of things), meteorology (atmospheric phenomena, the weather), microbiology (bacteria and viruses), mineralogy (minerals), morphology (structure, e.g. of words or of bodies), mycology (fungi), myrmecology (ants), nematology (parasitic worms), nosology (classification of diseases), obstetrics (childbirth), oenology (wine), onomastics *or* onomasiology (proper names), ontology (being), ophiology (snakes), ophthalmology (eye), optics (light),

orismology (definition of technical terms), ornithology (birds), otology (ear), otorhinolaryngology (ear nose and throat), paediatrics (diseases of children), palaeography (ancient writing), palaeontology (fossils), parapsychology (psychic phenomena), parasitology (parasites), pathology (diseases), penology (punishment of crime), phaleristics (medals and decorations), pharmacology (drugs and their effects), philology (ancient texts, or the development of language), philosophy (the nature of existence, knowledge, morality, etc), phonetics *and* phonology (speech sounds), phrenology (the skull as a supposed indicator of character and aptitudes), phycology (algae), physics (matter and energy), physiology (functions of cells, organs, etc), posology (administration of drugs), primatology (primates), psephology (elections), psychology (the mind), radiology (use of radioactivity in diagnosing and treating disease), robotics (robots), seismology (earthquakes), semantics (meaning), semiotics *or* semiology (signs amd symbols), taxonomy (classification), theology (God or gods), thermodynamics (heat and energy), toponymy (place names), toxicology (poisons), trichology (hair), trigonometry (triangles), virology (viruses), zoology (animals).

---

learning difficulty, learning disability 503 *learning disability*; dyslexia, dysgraphia, dyscalculia, attention deficit disorder, attention-deficit hyperactive disorder, ADHD; dyspraxia, mental retardation; person with learning difficulties, person with learning disabilities.

Adj. *studious*, academic, bookish, well-read, scholarly, erudite, learned, scholastic 490 *knowing*; diligent 678 *industrious*; receptive, teachable, self-taught, immersed in one's books 455 *attentive*.

Vb. *learn*, pursue one's education, go to school, attend college, take lessons, sit at the feet of, take a course; acquire knowledge, glean information, drink in, cram oneself with facts, know one's facts 490 *know*; apprentice oneself, learn one's trade, serve an apprenticeship, article oneself 669 *prepare oneself*; train, practise, exercise 610 *be in the habit of*; learn the basics, get the feel of, get the hang of, master; get by heart, learn by rote 505 *memorize*; finish one's education, graduate.

study, apply oneself, burn the midnight oil; do, take up; research into 459 *enquire*; specialize, major in; swot, cram, mug, get up; revise, go over, run over, brush up, take a refresher course; read, peruse, pore over, wade through; thumb, browse, skip, skim, skim-read, flip through, turn the leaves, dip into; be studious, be bookish, always have one's nose in a book; bury oneself in one's books, become a polymath.

Adv. *studiously*, at one's books; under training, in articles.

537 Teacher

N. *teacher*, mentor 520 *guide*; minister 986 *pastor*; guru 500 *sage*; instructor, educator;

tutor, crammer, coach; governor, governess, nursemaid 749 *keeper*; educationist, educationalist, pedagogue; pedant 500 *wiseacre*; dominie, beak, schoolmarm; master *or* mistress, school teacher, supply teacher, class teacher, form teacher; house master *or* mistress; assistant teacher, teaching assistant, classroom assistant; deputy head, head teacher, head, headmaster *or* -mistress, principal, rector; pupil teacher, trainee teacher, proctor; dean, don, fellow; lecturer, demonstrator, exponent 520 *interpreter*; reader, professor, Regius professor, professor emeritus; consultant 691 *adviser*; teaching staff, faculty, professoriate.

trainer, personal trainer, instructor, coach, team coach; sensei; sports psychologist; life coach; choirmaster; dancing-master *or* -mistress; animal trainer, dog trainer; horse trainer, breaker-in, broncobuster, horsebreaker, horse-tamer, horse whisperer; liontamer, puppy-walker; falconer.

preacher, lay preacher 986 *pastor*; pulpiteer, hot gospeller, evangelist; apostle, missionary; prophet.

538 Learner

N. *learner*, disciple, follower; proselyte, convert, initiate; mature student; self-taught person; do-it-yourself fan; swot, mugger, bookworm 492 *scholar*; pupil, scholar, schoolboy *or* -girl, student; day pupil, boarder; sixthformer; schoolfellow, schoolmate, classmate, fellow student; gifted child, high flier; slow learner, late developer, under-achiever, remedial pupil; school-leaver; old boy, old girl, former pupil.

beginner, novice, debutant; new boy *or* girl, tyro, greenhorn, tenderfoot, neophyte; rabbit, amateur 987 *lay person*; raw recruit, rookie; colt, cadet, trainee, apprentice, articled clerk, cub reporter; probationer, L-driver, examinee.

student, university student, college student; undergraduate, undergrad, freshman, fresher, sophomore; former student, alumnus, alumna; foundationer, exhibitioner; scholarship-holder, bursary-holder, Rhodes Scholar; honours student; graduand, graduate, postgraduate, fellow; mature student, research worker.

class, form, grade, remove; set, band, stream; age group; house; lower form, upper form; workshop; seminar.

539 School

N. *school*, nursery school, crèche, playgroup, kindergarten; infant school; private school, independent school, public school, state-aided school, state school; preparatory school, prep

school, crammer; primary school, middle school, secondary school, high school, secondary modern school, grammar school, senior secondary school; comprehensive school, sixth form college, FE college; Beacon school, city academy, specialist school, arts college, city technology college, languages college, sports college, technology college; faith school; boarding school, day school; night school, evening classes; Sunday school; special school; approved school, List D school, reform school, Borstal; remand home, detention centre; catchment area, parents' charter.

academy, institute, educational institute; college, lycée, gymnasium, senior secondary school; conservatoire, ballet school, art school, academy of dramatic art; finishing school; correspondence college; university, campus; Open University; redbrick university, Oxbridge, varsity; sixth-form college, FE college, college of further *or* higher education; polytechnic, poly; alma mater, old school, groves of academe.

540 Truthfulness

N. *truthfulness*, veracity; the truth, the whole truth, and nothing but the truth, fidelity, verisimilitude, realism, exactitude 494 *accuracy*; candour; honour bright, scout's (etc.) honour, no kidding; honesty, sincerity 929 *probity*; ingenuousness 699 *artlessness*; plain speaking, speaking straight from the shoulder 573 *plainness*; plain words, words of one syllable, home truth, honest truth 494 *truth*; clean breast 526 *disclosure*.

Adj. *truthful*, veracious 494 *true*; as good as one's word, reliable 929 *trustworthy*; factual, ungarbled, unembroidered, exact, just 494 *accurate*; full 570 *diffuse*; ingenuous 699 *artless*; bona fide; unaffected, unpretentious, open, above-board; frank, candid; blunt, forthright, outspoken, straightforward, straight from the shoulder, honest to God 573 *plain*; honest, sincere, on the level 929 *honourable*.

Vb. *be truthful*, tell the truth, tell the truth and shame the devil, tell the truth, the whole truth, and nothing but the truth, stick to the facts, play it according to the letter 494 *be true*; mean it; weigh one's words 834 *be serious*; speak one's mind, keep nothing back 522 *show*; come clean, make a clean breast of it; appear in one's true colours 526 *disclose*; be prophetic 511 *predict*.

541 Falsehood

N. *falsehood*, falseness, spuriousness, falsity; treachery, bad faith 930 *perfidiousness*; untruthfulness, mendacity, deceitfulness; lie, terminological inexactitude; lying, pathological lying, perjury 543 *untruth*; fabrication, fiction; faking, forgery, falsification 542 *deception*;

invention 513 *imagination*; prevarication, equivocation, ambivalence, evasion, double-talk 518 *equivocalness*; economy of truth, whitewashing, cover-up; overstatement 546 *exaggeration*; perversion 246 *distortion*; misrepresentation, spin; humbug, bunkum, boloney, hooey, rubbish, bull, flimflam 515 *empty talk*; cant, eyewash, hogwash; blarney.

duplicity, double life, double-dealing 930 *improbity*; guile 542 *trickery*; front, facade, mask, show, window-dressing, fanfaronade 875 *ostentation*; pretence, hollow pretence, bluff, act, fake, counterfeit, imposture 542 *sham*; hypocrisy; playacting, dissimulation, dissembling, insincerity, tongue in cheek, cant; lip service, cupboard love; false piety; outward show, crocodile tears; Judas kiss; fraud, sting, diplomatic illness; cheating, sharp practice; copying, cribbing, hot-plating; collusion, a nod and a wink; put-up job, frame-up; quackery, charlatanism 850 *pretension*.

Adj. *false*, not true; imagined, made-up; untruthful, lying, mendacious 543 *untrue*; perfidious, treacherous, perjured; disingenuous, dishonest; falsified, garbled; touched up; overdone; imitation, simulated, counterfeit, fake, faux, phoney, sham, pseudo, quack, bogus 542 *spurious*; cheating, deceptive, deceitful, fraudulent 542 *deceiving*; fiddled, fixed, engineered, rigged, packed; trumped up.

hypocritical, insincere, diplomatic, put on, imitated, pretended, simulated, economical with the truth, feigned; make-believe, play-acting; two-faced, shifty, sly, treacherous, double-dealing, designing, Machiavellian 930 *perfidious*; sanctimonious; plausible, smooth, smooth-tongued, oily; creepy, goody-goody; mealy-mouthed, euphemistic 850 *affected*.

Vb. *be false*, be perjured, be forsworn, etc. (see adj.); perjure oneself, bear false witness, swear that black is white; lie, tell lies, lie in one's teeth *or* one's throat, fib, tell a fib, tell a whopper; stretch the truth, tell a tall story 546 *exaggerate*; tell a white lie; invent, make believe, make up, romance 513 *imagine*; swing the lead, malinger; put a false construction on 521 *misinterpret*; garble, doctor, tamper with, falsify, spin 246 *distort*; misquote, misinform, cry wolf 535 *misteach*; play false; run with the hare and hunt with the hounds, have a foot in both camps; break faith, betray 603 *change one's mind*.

dissemble, dissimulate, disguise 525 *conceal*; simulate, counterfeit 20 *imitate*; put on, assume, affect, dress up, play-act, play a part, go through the motions, make a show of 594 *act*; feign, pass off for, sham, pretend, be under false pretences, sail under false colours;

malinger 542 *deceive*; be less than honest, say one thing and mean another; keep something back, fail to declare; fudge the issue, prevaricate, beat about the bush, dodge.

fake, fudge, fabricate, forge, plagiarize, counterfeit 20 *imitate*; get up, trump up, frame; manipulate, fiddle, fix, wangle, rig, pack (a jury); spin, weave, cook, cook up, concoct, hatch, invent 623 *plot*; touch-up, embroider; gloss over.

542 Deception

N. *deception*, kidding, kidology, tongue in cheek; self-deception, wishful thinking 487 *credulity*; fallacy 477 *sophistry*; illusion, delusion, hallucination; deceptiveness; false appearance, mockery, mirage, will-o'-the-wisp 440 *visual fallacy*; false show, meretriciousness, paint (see also *sham* below); feet of clay; bubble 4 *lacking substance*; falseness, deceit, quackery, imposture, lie, terminological inexactitude, pious fraud 541 *falsehood*; deceitfulness, guile, craft, artfulness 698 *cunning*; hypocrisy, insincerity 541 *duplicity*; treachery, betrayal 930 *perfidiousness*; machination, hanky-panky, jiggery-pokery, monkey business, wheeler-dealing, collusion 623 *plot*; fraudulence, cozenage, cheating, cheat, diddling; cheat 545 *deceiver*.

trickery, dupery, swindling, skulduggery, shenanigan; sharp practice, wheeler-dealing, chicanery, pettifoggery; swindle, ramp, racket, wangle, fix, fiddle, diddle, swizzle, swiz, sell, fraud, cheat; cardsharping; trick, dirty trick, bag of tricks, tricks of the trade, confidence trick, con trick, fast one, wiles, ruse, shift, dodge, artful dodge, blind, feint, funny business 698 *stratagem*; wrinkle 623 *contrivance*; bait, gimmick, shtick; diversion, red herring, smoke screen, hoax, bluff, spoof, leg-pull; game, sport, joke, practical joke, rag 839 *witticism*; April fooling; Piltdown man.

sleight of hand, sleight, legerdemain, conjuring, hocus-pocus, illusion, ventriloquism; juggling, three-card trick; magic 983 *sorcery*.

trap, deathtrap 527 *ambush*; catch 530 *enigma*; plant, frame-up; snare, gin, man trap; net, meshes, web; blind, decoy, decoy duck, bait, lure, sprat to catch a mackerel; baited trap, mousetrap, rat-trap, fishtrap, flypaper, birdlime; booby trap, mine, tripwire, pit 663 *pitfall*; car bomb, letter bomb, parcel bomb; trapdoor, sliding panel, false bottom 530 *secret*; poisoned apple, poisoned chalice, Trojan horse, Greek gift; honey trap.

sham, false front, veneer 541 *duplicity*; lip service, tokenism; make-believe, pretence 850 *affectation*; whitewash, gloss; whited sepulchre, man of straw, paper tiger; wolf in sheep's clothing 545 *impostor*; dummy, scarecrow, tattie bogle; imitation, simulacrum, facsimile 22 *copy*; mockery; counterfeit, forgery, fake; masquerade, mummery, mask, veil, cloak, disguise, borrowed plumes, false colours 525 *concealment*; imitation ware, tinsel, paste.

Adj. *deceiving*, deceitful, lying, economical with the truth 543 *untrue*; deceptive 523 *latent*; hallucinatory, illusive, illusory; specious 445 *appearing*; glib, oily, slick, slippery 258 *smooth*; fraudulent, humbugging, cheating; lulling, soothing 925 *flattering*; beguiling, treacherous, insidious 930 *perfidious*; trumped-up, framed 541 *false* (see also *spurious* below); feigned, simulated, pretended 541 *hypocritical*; tricky, crafty, wily, guileful, artful, on the fiddle 698 *cunning*.

spurious, false, faked, fake; sham, counterfeit 541 *false*; trumped-up, pretended; make-believe, mock, ersatz, bogus, phoney; pseudo-, so-called; cosmetic; artificial, simulated, man-made, plastic, paste, cultured, imitation; shoddy, rubbishy 641 *useless*; tinsel, meretricious, flash, gaudy, pasteboard 330 *brittle*; whitewashed, varnished.

Vb. *deceive*, delude; beguile, sugar the pill, gild the pill, give a false impression, belie; let down 509 *disappoint*; pull the wool over one's eyes, blindfold 439 *blind*; kid, bluff, bamboozle, hoodwink, hoax; throw dust in the eyes, create a smoke screen, lead up the garden path 495 *mislead*; spoof, mystify 535 *misteach*; play false, leave in the lurch, betray, two-time, double-cross 930 *be dishonest*; steal a march on 135 *be early*; pull a fast one, take one for a ride, outsmart 698 *be cunning*; trick, dupe; cheat, cozen, con, swindle, sell, rook, do 788 *defraud*; diddle, do out of, bilk, fleece, rip off, shaft, shortchange, obtain money by false pretences 788 *defraud*; juggle, conjure, palm off, foist off; fob, fob off with; live on one's wits, try it on; tinker with, fiddle, wangle, fix; load the dice, mark the cards; counterfeit 541 *fake*.

fool, make a fool of, make an ass of make a wally of, make one look silly; mock, make fun of 851 *ridicule*; play tricks on, play practical jokes on, pull one's leg, have one on, make an April fool of, play a joke on 497 *be absurd* throw over, jilt; take in, have, have on, put on, dupe, bull, victimize, gull, outwit, outsmart; trick, trap, catch out, take advantage of, manipulate, twist round one's little finger; kid, spoof, bamboozle, string along, lead one on (see also *deceive* above); cajole, wheedle, get round; play fast and loose with, leave in the lurch, leave one holding the baby 509 *disappoint*; be unfaithful to, cuckold 951 *be impure*;

send on a fool's errand, send on a wild-goose chase 495 *mislead*; make one an applepie bed.

ensnare, snare, trap, set a trap for, lay a trap for; entangle, net; trip, trip up, catch, catch out, hook; bait, bait the trap, bait the hook, lure, decoy, lead astray, entice, inveigle 612 *tempt*; lie in wait, waylay 527 *ambush*; nab, nick, kidnap, shanghai, hijack, take hostage 788 *steal*.

543 Untruth

N. *untruth*, more than the truth, lie, downright lie, barefaced lie, fib, porky, porky pie; white lie, diplomatic excuse, whopper; false statement, terminological inexactitude; breach of promise 930 *perfidiousness*; perjury; pack of lies, tissue of lies, trumped-up story, frame-up 466 *evidence*; fabrication, invention 513 *conception* (see also *fable* below); false excuse; misinformation, disinformation; misrepresentation, perversion 246 *distortion*; gloss, varnish, falsification 521 *misinterpretation*; disingenuousness, economy of truth; lie detector, polygraph, truth drug, truth serum, thiopentone sodium, Pentothal (tdmk). (See also 541 *falsehood*.)

fable, invention, fiction; story, tale 590 *narrative*; tall story, shaggy dog story, fisherman's yarn, traveller's tale 546 *exaggeration*; fairy tale, nursery tale, romance, tale, yarn, story, cock-and-bull story, all my eye and Betty Martin 497 *absurdity*; claptrap, gossip, guff, bull; myth; old wives' tale, urban myth, urban legend, friend-of-a-friend tale, foaf tale; moonshine, farce, mare's nest, sell, swiz, hoax, humbug, flummery 515 *empty talk*.

Adj. *untrue*, lying, mendacious 541 *false*, 542 *deceiving*; trumped-up, framed, cooked, fixed, hatched, concocted; mythological, fabulous; unfounded, ungrounded, empty; fictitious, imagined, hallucinatory, make-believe; artificial, synthetic, simulated; phoney, bogus, so-called 542 *spurious*; perjured, forsworn 930 *perfidious*.

Vb. *be untrue*, not hold water, not stand up in court, be wide of the mark; not ring true 472 *be unlikely*; lie, be a liar 541 *be false*; spin a yarn, tell a tall story, draw the long bow 546 *exaggerate*; make believe 20 *imitate*, 513 *imagine*; be phoney, pretend, sham, counterfeit, forge, falsify 541 *dissemble*.

544 Dupe

N. *dupe*, fool, April fool 851 *laughing stock*; Simple Simon; easy prey, sitting duck, soft touch, soft mark, pushover, cinch; fair game, victim, schlemiel, fall guy, patsy, stooge, mug, sap, sucker, schmuck, schnook, dude, greenhorn, innocent 538 *beginner*; puppet, cat's-paw, pawn 628 *instrument*; admass.

Vb. *be duped*, be had, be done, be taken in; be sold a pup, be sold a pig in a poke, be diddled; fall for walk into the trap, rise, nibble, swallow the bait, swallow hook, line and sinker; get taken for a ride; carry the can; catch a Tartar 508 *not expect.*

545 Deceiver

N. *deceiver*, leg-puller; practical joker; dissembler; whited sepulchre, false friend, fair-weather friend; rat, two-timer, double-crosser, double agent; traitor, Judas 938 *knave*; seducer 952 *libertine*; serpent, snake in the grass, joker in the pack 663 *troublemaker*; plotter, Guy Fawkes, intriguer, conspirator 623 *planner*; counterfeiter, forger; propagandist, spin-doctor; Holocaust denier.

liar, pathological liar; fibber, storyteller; romancer; yarn-spinner; fabricator.

impostor, shammer, malingerer, lead-swinger; adventurer, carpetbagger; usurper; cuckoo in the nest 59 *outsider*; wolf in sheep's clothing; pretender, charlatan, quack, mountebank; fake, fraud, con man, humbug; pseud, pseudo, phoney; masquerader.

trickster, hoaxer, spoofer, hood-winker, bamboozler; cheat, cozener; sharper, card-sharp; shyster; fraudster, swindler, bilker, diddler, hustler, shark 789 *defrauder*; twister, rogue 938 *knave*; confidence trickster, con man; decoy, decoy duck, agent provocateur; fiddler, manipulator, rigger, fixer.

546 Exaggeration

N. *exaggeration*, overemphasis, inflation, magnification, enlargement 197 *expansion*; straining; extravagance, exaggerated lengths, gilding the lily, extremes, immoderation, extremism; overkill; excess, excessiveness, feeding frenzy; violence 943 *intemperance*; inordinacy, exorbitance, overdoing it, piling it on; overacting, histrionics 875 *ostentation*; sensationalism, ballyhoo, hype 528 *publicity*; overstatement, hyperbole 519 *figure of speech*; embroidery 38 *addition*; disproportion 246 *distortion*; caricature, burlesque 851 *satire*; exacerbation 832 *aggravation*; big talk 877 *boasting*; grandiloquence 574 *grandiloquence*; overpraise, chauvinism 481 *prejudice*; tall story 543 *fable*; flight of fancy, stretch of the imagination 513 *imagination*; fuss, storm in a teacup, much ado about nothing 318 *commotion.*

Vb. *exaggerate*, maximize, magnify, expand, inflate, blow up, blow up out of all proportion 197 *enlarge*; overamplify, overelaborate; add to, pile up, pile it on 38 *add*; touch up, enhance, heighten, add a flourish, touch up, embroider, varnish 844 *decorate*; lay it on thick *or* with a trowel, depict in glowing terms, overvalue; overdo, overcolour; overemphasize; overpraise, puff, hype up, oversell; make too much of 925 *flatter*; stretch, strain, labour 246 *distort*; caricature 851 *satirize*; go to all lengths, gild the lily, not know when to stop, protest too much; overact, dramatize, out-Herod Herod; talk big, bull 877 *boast*; run riot, go to extremes; draw the long bow, overshoot *or* overstep the mark, go too far 306 *overstep*; spin a yarn, tell a tall tale; make mountains out of molehills, make a storm in a tea cup; awfulize; exacerbate 832 *aggravate*; overcompensate, lean over backwards.

SECTION THREE

Means of communicating ideas

547 Indication

N. *indication*, signification, meaning 514 *connotation*; notification 524 *information*; symbolization, symbolism 551 *representation*; symbol; rune, hieroglyph 530 *enigma*; cross; pentacle 983 *talisman*; image, type, figure; token, emblem, figurehead (see also *badge* below); symptom, syndrome, sign 466 *evidence*; tell-tale sign, blush 526 *disclosure*; nudge, wink, kick 524 *hint* (see also *gesture* below); kite-flying, straw in the wind, sign of the times 511 *omen*; clue, scent, whiff, trace 484 *discovery*; noise, footfall 398 *sound*; semiology, semiotics; pointer, finger, forefinger, index finger (see also *indicator* below); guide, index, thumb index 87 *directory*; key 520 *interpretation*; marker, mark; blaze; nick, scratch 260 *notch*; stamp, print, impression; stigma, stigmata; tattoo mark; scar 845 *blemish*; wrinkle, line, score, stroke; note, catchword (see also *punctuation* below); legend, caption 590 *description*; inscription, epitaph; motto, cipher, monogram.

identification, naming 77 *classification*, 561 *nomenclature*; brand, earmark, trademark, imprint (see also *label* below); name and address; autograph, signature, hand 586 *script*; fingerprint, footprint, spoor, track, trail, scent 548 *trace*; dental record; genetic fingerprinting, DNA fingerprinting, iris recognition (see also *label* below); password, open sesame, watchword, shibboleth; markings, colouring, characteristic, trait, lineament, outline, form, shape 445 *feature*; personal characteristic, mannerism, idiolect; mole, scar, birthmark, strawberry mark 845 *blemish*.

gesture, gesticulation, sign language; deaf-and-dumb language; sign 524 *hint*; pantomime, dumb show, charade, mime, air guitar, air quotes; body language, kinesics; demean-our, tone of one's voice 445 *mien*; motion, move; tic, twitch 318 *spasm*; shrug, shrug of the shoulders; raising of the eyebrows, nod, beck, wink, flicker of the eyelash, batting of the eyelids *or* eyelashes, twinkle, glance, ogle, leer, grimace 438 *glance*; smile, laugh 835 *laughter*; touch, kick, kick under the table, nudge, jog, dig in the ribs 279 *knock*; hug; squeeze of the hand, handshake, grip; push, shove 279 *impulse*; pointing, signal, waving, wave, hand-signal, wave of the hand, Mexican wave; raising one's hand; drumming one's fin-gers, tapping one's foot, stamp of the foot 822 *excitable state*; clenching *or* gritting one's teeth 599 *resolution*; gnashing *or* grinding one's teeth; wringing one's hands, tearing one's hair 836 *lamentation*; clenched fist 711 *defiance*; V-sign, flag-waving 876 *celebration*; clapping, cheer 923 *applause*; hissing, hooting, booing, catcall, Bronx cheer, raspberry 924 *disapproba-tion*; V-sign, two-finger gesture, two-finger salute, Harvey Smith salute; stuck-out tongue 878 *sauciness*; frown, scowl 893 *sullenness*; pout, moue, pursing of the lips 829 *discontent*.

signal 529 *message*; sign, symptom, syn-drome 522 *manifestation*; flash, rocket; railway signal, smoke signal, heliograph, semaphore, tick-tack; telegraph, morse 531 *telecommunica-tion*; flashlamp, signal lamp 420 *lamp*; warning light, beacon 379 *fire*; red flag, warning light, red light, Belisha beacon, green light, all clear 420 *signal light*; alarum, alarm, fire alarm, bur-glar alarm, warning signal, distress signal, SOS 665 *danger signal*; whistle, police whistle; siren, hooter; bleeper, bleep, pager, radiopager; buzzer, knocker, doorknocker 414 *gong*; bell, doorbell, alarm bell, ringtone; church bells, angelus, carillon; time signal, pip, dinner gong, dinner bell 117 *chronometry*; passing bell, knell, muffled drum 364 *funeral rites*.

indicator, index, pointer, arrow, needle; arm, finger, index finger; hand, hour hand, minute hand, second hand 117 *timekeeper*; Plimsoll line 465 *gauge*; traffic indicator, traffi-cator; direction finder, radar; cursor, white line, cat's-eyes (tdmk) 305 *traffic control*; weathercock, wind sock, vane, weathervane 340 *weather*; biological indicator *or* bioindica-tor, indicator species.

signpost, fingerpost; milestone, waymark; lighthouse, buoy 662 *safeguard*; compass 269 *sailing aid*; lodestar, guiding star, Pole Star, Southern Cross 321 *star*; landmark; cairn 253 *earthwork*; benchmark.

call, hue-and-cry 528 *publication*; shout, hail; call to prayer, church bell 981 *worship*; summons 737 *command*; call for help, cry of help, distress call, Mayday; bugle, trumpet; reveille, rally; last post; peal, flourish; drum, drumbeat, drum-roll, tattoo 403 *roll*; call to arms, fiery cross; battle cry, war cry, rallying cry.

badge, token, emblem, symbol, sign, totem (see also *indication* above); insignia (see also *heraldry* below); markings; throne, sceptre, orb, crown 743 *regalia*; badge of office, robes of office, Black Rod, mace 743 *badge of office*; pips, stripes, epaulette 743 *badge of rank*; medal, gong, cross, Victoria Cross, George Cross, Iron Cross, Croix de Guerre; order, star, garter, sash, ribbon 729 *decoration*; badge of merit, laurels, wreath 729 *trophy*; colours, blue, half-blue, cap; favour, rosette; black armband, widow's weeds 228 *clothing*.

heraldry, armory, blazonry; heraldic register, Roll of Arms; armorial bearings, coat of arms, blazon; achievement, funereal achievement, hatchment; shield, escutcheon; crest, torse, wreath, helmet, crown, coronet, mantling, lambrequin; supporters, motto; field, quarter, dexter, sinister, chief, base; charge, device, bearing; ordinary, fess, bar, label, pale, bend, bend sinister, chevron, pile, saltire, cross; can-ton; inescutcheon, bordure, lozenge, fusil, gyron, flanches; marshalling, quartering, impaling, dimidiation; differencing; fess point, honour point, nombril point; animal charge, lion, lion rampant, lion couchant, unicorn, griffin, cockatrice, eagle, falcon, martlet; floral charge, Tudor rose, cinquefoil, trefoil, planta genista; badge, rebus, antelope, bear and rag-ged staff, portcullis; national emblem, rose, thistle, leek, daffodil, shamrock, lilies, fleur-de-lis; device, national device, lion and unicorn, spread eagle, bear, hammer and sickle, triskelion; swastika, fylfot; skull and cross-bones; heraldic tincture, colour, gules, azure, vert, sable, purpure, tenné, murrey; metal, or, argent; fur, ermine, ermines, erminois, pean, vair, potent; heraldic personnel, College of Arms, Earl Marshal, King of Arms, Lord Lyon King of Arms; herald, herald extraordinary, pursuivant, Bluemantle, Rouge Croix, Rouge Dragon, Portcullis.

flag, ensign, white ensign, blue ensign, red ensign, Red Duster; jack, pilot jack, merchant jack; flag of convenience; colours, ship's col-ours, regimental colours, King's Colour, Queen's Colour; guidon, standard, vexillum, labarum, banner, gonfalon; bannerette, banne-rol, banderole, oriflamme; pennon, streamer, pennant, swallowtail, triple tail; pendant, broad pendant, burgee; bunting; Blue Peter, yellow flag; white flag 721 *submission*; eagle, Roman eagle; tricolour; Union Jack; Stars and

Stripes, Old Glory, star-spangled banner; Red Flag, Black Flag; pirate flag, black flag, Jolly Roger, skull and crossbones; parts of a flag: hoist, fly, canton; flagpole, flagstaff.

label, tattoo, caste mark (see also *identification* above); ticket, bus ticket, raffle ticket, cloakroom ticket, bill, docket, chit, counterfoil, stub, duplicate; counter, chip; mark, countermark; luggage label, sticky label, sticker; tie-on label, tab, tag; name badge, name tape, nameplate, signboard; numberplate, cherished number-plate; sign, inn sign, barber's pole, three balls 522 *exhibit*; brass plate, trademark, logotype, logo, hallmark; earmark, brand; electronic tag; dunce's cap; seal, signet, stamp, impression; letterhead, masthead, caption, heading, title, headline, superscription, rubric; imprint, colophon, watermark; bookplate, name, name and address, personal details; card, visiting card; birth certificate, marriage certificate, death certificate, identification papers, identity card, ID card, biometric ID card, entitlement card, tag, identification tag, electronic tag (see also *identification* above); passport, pass, visa, pet passport, animal passport 756 *permit*; endorsement 466 *credential*; bar code; swipe card, PIN, pin number, signature, autograph, cipher, mark, cross, initials, monogram, tag; fingerprint, thumbprint, footprint 548 *trace*; genetic fingerprint; International Mobile Equipment Identity, IMEI, International Mobile Subscriber Identity, IMSI.

punctuation, punctuation mark, point, stop, full stop, period; comma, colon, semi-colon; inverted commas, quotation marks, quotes, air quotes, apostrophe; exclamation mark, interrogation mark, question mark, query; parentheses, brackets, square brackets, crotchet, crook, brace; hyphenation, hyphen, en rule, em rule, dash, swung dash; dot, caret, omission mark, ellipsis, blank; slash, forward slash, back slash, solidus; asterisk, dagger; accent, grave accent, acute accent, circumflex accent; diaeresis, cedilla, tilde; macron, breve, umlaut; paragraph; plus sign, minus sign, multiplication sign, division sign, equals sign, decimal point; italics 587 *print-type*.

Adj. *heraldic*, emblematic; crested, armorial, blazoned, emblazoned, etc. (see vb.); paly, barry; dexter, sinister; gules, azure, vert, purpure, sable, tenné, murrey, or, argent, ermine; fleury, semé, pommé; rampant, gardant, regardant, couchant, statant, sejant, passant.

Vb. *indicate*, point 281 *point to*; point out, exhibit 522 *show*; blazon; delineate, demarcate, mark out, blaze, signpost; register 548 *record*; name, give a name to, identify, classify 80 *specify*; index, supply references, refer; point the way, show the way, guide 689 *direct*; signify, denote, connote, suggest, imply, involve, spell, bespeak, argue 514 *mean*; symbolize, typify, betoken, stand for, be the sign of 551 *represent*; declare 532 *affirm*; highlight 532 *emphasize*; show signs of, bear the stamp of, give evidence of, witness to 466 *evidence*; smack of, smell of, hint at 524 *hint*; reveal 526 *disclose*; herald, prefigure, forebode, presage 511 *predict*.

mark, mark off, mark out, demarcate, delineate, delimit 236 *limit*; label, ticket, docket, tag, tab, microchip; earmark, designate; annotate, score, underline; number, letter, page, paginate, index; tick, tick off; nick, scribe 260 *notch*; chalk, chalk up; scratch, scribble, cover 586 *write*; blot, stain, blacken 649 *make unclean*; scar, disfigure 842 *make ugly*; punctuate, dot, dash, cross, cross out, asterisk; put one's mark on, leave fingerprints *or* footprints; blaze, brand, earmark, burn in; tag, tag electronically, chip, microchip; tattoo 263 *pierce*; stamp, seal, punch, impress, emboss; imprint, overprint 587 *print*; etch 555 *engrave*; emblazon, blazon.

sign, autograph, write one's signature, inscribe; subscribe, undersign; initial; put one's cross.

gesticulate, mime, mimic, suit the action to the word 20 *imitate*; wave one's hands, talk with one's hands; wave 318 *agitate*; wave to, hold out one's hand 884 *greet*; stamp 923 *applaud*; wave one's arms, gesture, motion, sign; point, beckon, raise one's hand, bat one's eye-lashes 455 *attract notice*; nod, wink, shrug; jog, nudge, kick, poke, prod, dig in the ribs, clap on the back; look, look volumes, look daggers, glance, leer, ogle 438 *gaze*; twinkle, smile 835 *laugh*; raise one's eyebrows, wag one's finger, shake one's head, purse one's lips 924 *disapprove*; wring one's hands, tear one's hair 836 *lament*; grit *or* clench one's teeth 599 *be resolute*; gnash one's teeth 891 *be angry*; snap, bite; grimace, pout, scowl, frown 829 *be discontented*; shrug one's shoulders, curl one's lip 922 *despise*; shuffle, pat, stroke 889 *caress*.

signal, send a signal, send smoke signal, speak 524 *communicate*; tap out a message, semaphore, heliograph; flag down, thumb; wave on; unfurl the flag, fly the flag, dip the flag, salute; alert, sound the alarm, cry help, send an SOS, dial 999 665 *raise the alarm*; beat the drum, sound the trumpets; fire a warning shot 664 *warn*.

548 Record

N. *record*, recording, documentation; historical record, memoir, chronicle, annals, history, official report 590 *narrative*; case history, case notes, curriculum vitae 590 *biography*; photograph, portrait, sketch 551 *representation*; file, dossier, rogues' gallery; public record, gazette, official journal, Hansard, official report, official publication, blue book, White Paper; minutes, transactions; notes, annotations, marginalia, jottings, cuttings, press cuttings; memorabilia, memorandum, memo 505 *reminder*; reports, annual report, returns, tax returns, statements 524 *report*; tally, scoresheet, scoreboard; document; voucher, certificate, diploma, charter 466 *credential*; birth certificate, death certificate, marriage certificate, marriage lines 767 *title deed*; copy, spare copy, carbon copy, Xerox (tdmk) 22 *duplicate*; records, files, archives, papers, correspondence; record, book, roll, register, registry; notebook, memo pad, logbook, log, diary, journal, commonplace book, scrap-book, album; ledger, cashbook, chequebook; catalogue, index, waiting list 87 *list*; card, index card, microfilm, microfiche 196 *miniature*; tape, computer tape 86 *computing*; magnetic tape, pressing 414 *music player*; inscription, legend, caption, heading 547 *indication*; graffiti 586 *script*.

monument, memorial, war memorial, cenotaph 505 *reminder*; mausoleum, Taj Mahal 364 *tomb*; statue, bust 551 *image*; brass, tablet, inscription 364 *funeral rites*; memorial arch, Marble Arch, Arc de Triomphe; monolith, obelisk, pillar, Cleopatra's Needle 209 *high structure*; Eros, Statue of Liberty; national monument, ancient monument, cromlech, dolmen, menhir, megalith 125 *antiquity*; cairn, barrow 253 *earthwork*.

trace, vestige, relic, remains 41 *leavings*; archaeological remains, archaeology; track, tracks, footstep, footprint, footmark, hoof-mark, clawmark, tread; spoor; scent, smell; wake, wash, trail, vapour trail; furrow, swathe, path; scuffmark, skidmark, tyremark, finger-mark 547 *indication*; fingerprint, dabs 466 *evidence*; mark, tidemark, stain, scar, scratch, weal 845 *blemish*.

Vb. *record*, tape-record, telerecord, tape, videotape, video; store in a database, input, burn; film 551 *photograph*; paint 551 *represent*; document, put *or* place on record; docket, file, index, catalogue; inscribe, carve; take down, note down, set down in black and white, commit to writing 586 *write*; capture on film, preserve for posterity; log, write down, jot down; note, make a note of; take minutes of, minute; chronicle 590 *describe*.

register, mark up, chalk up, cross off, notch up, score; tabulate, enrol 87 *list*; enter 808

account; reserve, put on the waiting list; inscribe, log.

549 Recorder

N. *recorder*, registrar, record-keeper, archivist; Master of the Rolls; amanuensis, stenographer, scribe; secretary; writer, clerk, filing clerk, book-keeper 808 *accountant*; photographer, cameraman 551 *photography*; Record Office; Recording Angel.

chronicler, annalist, diarist, historian, historiographer, biographer, autobiographer; archaeologist 125 *antiquarian*; reporter, journalist.

recording instrument, recorder, tape recorder, videotape recorder, VTR, videocassette recorder, VCR, videorecorder, video disc, digital video disc, digital versatile disc, DVD; record, disc, compact disc, laser disc, etc. 414 *music player*; dictaphone, teleprinter, tape machine 531 *telecommunication*; cash register, till, checkout; turnstile; speedometer, tachograph 465 *gauge*; flight recorder, black box; time-recorder, stopwatch 117 *timekeeper*; hygrometer; anemometer; camera, speed camera, etc. 442 *camera*; photocopier, Xerox (tdmk); pen, pencil, etc. 586 *stationery*.

550 Obliteration

N. *obliteration*, wiping out, etc. (see vb.); erasure, effacement; defacement; deletion; crossing out, cancellation; annulment 752 *annulment*; oblivion 506 *amnesty*; blot 649 *dirt*; clean sweep 149 *revolution*; rubber, eraser.

Vb. *obliterate*, remove the traces, cover, cover up 525 *conceal*; deface; efface, eliminate, erase, scratch out, rub out; expunge, wipe out; blot out; wipe off, wash off, brush off; cancel, delete; cross out, score out, censor, blue-pencil; raze 165 *demolish*; cover 364 *inter*; submerge 311 *lower*; drown 399 *silence*.

551 Representation

N. *representation*, personification, incarnation, embodiment, bodying forth; typifying, typification, symbolization 547 *indication*; diagram, hieroglyphics, runes 586 *writing*; presentation; impersonation, identity theft, identity fraud; enactment, performance; role-playing, psychodrama 658 *therapy*; mimicry, charade, mime, dumb show 20 *imitation*; depiction, characterization 590 *description*; delineation, drawing, illustration, artwork, graphics 553 *painting*; creation, work of art 164 *product*; impression, likeness, identikit, Photofit (tdmk), E-fit, electronically generated picture 18 *similarity*; exact likeness, double, spitting image, look-alike, facsimile 22 *duplicate*; tracing 233 *outline*; reflection (see also *image*

below); portrayal; striking likeness, realism
553 *picture*; bad likeness 552 *misrepresentation*;
reproduction, copy, Xerox (tdmk), lithograph;
etching 555 *engraving*; design, blueprint, draft,
cartoon, sketch, outline 623 *plan*.

image, spitting image 22 *duplicate*; mental
image, after-image 451 *idea*; reflected image,
hologram, silhouette 417 *reflection*; pixel;
magic eye, autostereogram; visual aid 445 *spectacle*; idol, graven image 982 *idolatry*; icon;
cherub; statue, colossus; statuette, bust, torso,
head 554 *sculpture*; effigy, figure, figurine, figurehead; gargoyle; wax figure, waxwork;
dummy, tailor's dummy, manikin; model, lay
figure; doll, china doll, rag doll, Cabbage
Patch (tdmk) doll, Cindy (tdmk) doll, Barbie
(tdmk) doll, golliwog, teddy bear; marionette,
puppet, finger puppet, glove puppet, string
puppet; snowman, gingerbread man; scarecrow, tattie bogle, guy, Guy Fawkes; robot,
automaton, bot, cyborg, Dalek; type, symbol.

art, architecture 243 *formation*; fine arts;
graphic art 553 *painting*; plastic art 554 *sculpture*; classical art, Byzantine art, Renaissance
art, Baroque, Rococo; art nouveau, art deco,
modern art, abstract art, conceptual art; Surrealism, Expressionism 553 *school of painting*; op
art, pop art; kitsch, camp, high camp 847 *bad
taste*; Turner Prize; aestheticism, functionalism,
De Stijl, Bauhaus; functional art, commercial
art; useful arts; decorative art 844 *ornamental
art*; the minor arts, illumination, calligraphy,
weaving, tapestry, collage, embroidery, pottery.

photography, radiography, scanning; timelapse photography, aerial photography, telephotography, microphotography, macrophotography; cinematography 445 *cinema*;
photograph, photo, picture, snapshot, snap;
plate, film; exposure, negative, print, sepia
print, colour print, slide, transparency; thumbnail; frame, still; reel, spool, cassette; filmstrip,
microfilm, microfiche, movie, home movie 445
film; hologram; radiograph, X-ray, scan 417
radiation; photocopy, Xerox (tdmk) 22 *copy*;
shot, close-up, mug shot, pan, zoom, fade; lens
442 *camera*; cameraman, photographer, lensman, paparazzo; radiographer.

map, chart, plan, town plan, outline 86 *statistics*; sketch map, relief map, survey map,
Ordnance Survey map, road map, star map;
Admiralty chart; ground plan, elevation; projection, Mercator's projection, Peters projection; atlas; globe; map-making, cartography,
computerized cartography.

Vb. *represent*, stand for, denote, symbolize
514 *mean*; typify, embody, body forth, personify; act the part of, assume the role of,
role-play; impersonate, pose as 542 *deceive*;

pose, model, sit for 23 *be an example*; enact
594 *dramatize*; suggest; reflect, hold the mirror
up to nature; mimic, mime, copy 20 *imitate*;
depict, characterize 590 *describe*; delineate,
draw, picture, portray; illustrate 553 *paint*;
catch a likeness, capture; carve, cast 554 *sculpt*;
cut 555 *engrave*; mould, shape 243 *form*; fashion upon; design, draft, sketch out, rough out,
block out 623 *plan*; make a diagram, construct
a figure, describe a circle 233 *outline*; sketch;
map, chart, survey, plot.

photograph, photo, take a photo *or* a picture; snap; take, shoot, film; X-ray, scan;
expose, develop, process, print, enlarge, blow
up, reduce.

552 Misrepresentation

N. *misrepresentation*, not a true picture 19
dissimilarity; false light 541 *falsehood*; bad likeness, poor likeness 914 *injustice*; travesty,
parody 546 *exaggeration*; caricature; flattering
portrait 925 *flattery*; non-representational art
551 *art*; daub, botch; distorted image 246 *distortion*; misinformation, disinformation.

Vb. *misrepresent*, give a twist *or* turn, tone
down 925 *flatter*; overdramatize 546 *exaggerate*;
gild the lily, overembellish, caricature; parody,
daub, botch; lie, spin, sex up 541 *be false*.

553 Painting

N. *painting*, graphic art, colouring, illumination; daubing, finger painting; washing, colourwashing, tinting, touching up; depicting,
drawing, sketching 551 *representation*; artistry,
composition, design, technique, draughtsmanship, brushwork; line, perspective, golden section; treatment, tone, values, atmosphere,
ambience; highlight, local colour, shading,
contrast; monotone, monochrome, polychrome 425 *colour*; black and white,
chiaroscuro, grisaille.

art style, style of painting, grand style,
grand manner 243 *form*; intimate style, genre
painting (see also *art subject* below); pasticcio,
pastiche; trompe l'oeil; iconography, portrait-painting, portraiture; scenography, scene
painting, sign painting, poster painting, miniature painting; oil painting, watercolour, tempera, gouache; fresco painting, mural painting,
encaustic painting, impasto, secco.

school of painting, the Primitives, Byzantine
school, Renaissance school, Sienese school,
Florentine school, Venetian school, Dutch
school, Flemish school, French school, Spanish school; Mannerism, Baroque, Rococo, Pre-Raphaelitism, Neo-Classicism, Realism,
Romanticism, Impressionism, Post-Impressionism, Neo-Impressionism, Pointillism, Symbolism, Fauvism, Dada, Cubism,

Expressionism, Die Brücke, Der Blaue Reiter, Vorticism, Futurism, Surrealism, Abstract Expressionism, Tachism, action painting; minimal art, Minimalism, Conceptualism;

art subject, modernism 551 *art*; landscape, seascape, skyscape, cloudscape; scene, prospect, diorama, panorama 438 *view*; interior, conversation piece, still life, pastoral, nocturne, nude.

picture, pictorial equivalent 551 *representation*; tableau, mosaic, tapestry; collage, montage, photomontage; frottage, brass rubbing; painting, pastiche; icon, triptych, diptych, panel; tondo; fresco, mural, wall painting; poster; canvas, daub; drawing, line drawing; sketch, outline, cartoon; oil painting, oleograph, gouache, watercolour, aquarelle, pastel, wash drawing, pen-and-ink drawing, pencil drawing, charcoal drawing; design, pattern, doodle; cartoon, toon, manga, hentai, chad, caricature, silhouette; miniature, vignette, thumbnail sketch, illuminated initial; old master, masterpiece; study, portrait, full-length portrait, half-length portrait, kit-cat, head, profile, full-face portrait; studio portrait, snap, Polaroid (tdmk), pin-up 551 *photography*; rotogravure, photogravure, chromolithograph, reproduction, photographic reproduction, halftone; aquatint, woodcut 555 *engraving*; print, plate; illustration, fashion plate, picture postcard, cigarette card, tea card, stamp, transfer, scrap, sticker; picture book, illustrated book, scrapbook, photograph album, illustrated work 589 *book*.

Adj. *painted*, graphic, pictorial, scenic, picturesque, decorative 844 *ornamental*; pastel, in paint, in oils, in watercolours, in tempera; linear, black-and-white, chiaroscuro, shaded, stippled, sfumato; grisaille 429 *grey*; painterly, paintable.

Vb. *paint*, wash 425 *colour*; tint, touch up; lay on the colour 226 *coat*; slap on paint; paint a picture, do a portrait, portray, draw, sketch, limn, cartoon 551 *represent*; illuminate; do in oils *or* watercolours *or* tempera, do in black-and-white; ink, chalk, crayon, pencil, stencil, shade, stipple; block in.

554 Sculpture

N. *sculpture*, plastic art 551 *representation*; modelling 243 *formation*; carving, stone cutting, wood carving; moulding; paper modelling, origami; rock carving; toreutics 844 *ornamental art*; constructivism, etc. 553 *school of painting*; kinetic art; statuary; statue; statuette, figurine, bust, torso, head; model, cast, plaster cast, death mask, waxwork 551 *image*; anatomy art, plastination; ceramics 381 *pot-*

tery; medallion, cameo, intaglio; relief, bas-relief, tondo; stone, marble; bronze, clay, modelling clay, wax, Plasticine (tdmk), papier-mâché, plaster of Paris; claymation.

Vb. *sculpt*, sculpture, rough-hew 243 *form*; cut, carve, whittle, chisel, chip; chase, engrave, emboss; model, mould, cast.

555 Engraving. Printing

N. *engraving*, etching, line engraving, plate engraving, steel engraving, copper engraving; photogravure, photoengraving; zincography, cerography, glyptography, gem cutting, gem engraving; glass engraving; mezzotint, aquatint; wood engraving, xylography, lignography, woodcut; linoprinting, linocut; scraperboard; silverpoint; dry-point; steel plate, copper plate; stone, block, wood-block; chisel, graver, burin, burr, needle, dry-point, etching-point, style.

printing, type-printing, typography 587 *print*; laser printing; plate printing, copperplate printing, intaglio printing; lithography, photolithography, photogravure, chromolithography, colour printing; fabric printing, batik; silk-screen printing, stereotype; impression.

Vb. *engrave*, grave, cut; etch, stipple, scrape; bite, bite in, eat in; sandblast; impress, stamp; lithograph 587 *print*.

556 Artist

N. *artist*, craftsman *or* -woman 686 *artisan*; architect 164 *producer*; art master *or* mistress, designer, graphic designer, draughtsman *or* -woman; dress-designer, couturier; drawer, sketcher, delineator; caricaturist, cartoonist; illustrator, commercial artist; painter, colourist; pavement artist, graffiti artist; scene-painter, sign-painter; oil-painter, watercolourist, pastellist; miniaturist; portrait painter, landscape painter, marine painter, genre painter, still-life painter; Academician, RA; old master, primitive; Pre-Raphaelite, Impressionist, Fauve, Dadaist, Cubist, Vorticist, Surrealist, action painter, Minimalist 553 *school of painting*; art historian.

557 Language

N. *language*, tongue, speech, idiom, parlance, talk, dialect, patois 560 *dialect*; spoken language, living language; patter, lingo 560 *dialect*; idiolect; mother tongue, native tongue; vernacular, common speech, vulgar tongue; colloquial speech, English as she is spoken 579 *speech*; Received Pronunciation, Standard English, BBC English, Queen's English, correct speech, idiomatic speech; slang, jargon, argot, vulgarism; Estuary English; lingua franca, pidgin, creole, pidgin English; sign language 547 *gesture*; Basic English, Esperanto; official language, Mandarin, Hindi, etc.; officialese 560 *neologism*; machine language 86 *computing*; dead language, Latin, Greek, Sanskrit; metalanguage; Babel, babble 61 *confusion*; speaking in tongues, glossolalia, xenoglossia; language study, linguistics, linguistic science, descriptive linguistics, general linguistics, synchronic linguistics, theoretical linguistics; dialectology, philology, comparative philology; palaeography; comparative linguistics, comparative grammar; morphology, syntax 564 *grammar*; phonetics, phonology 577 *pronunciation*; historical linguistics, diachronic linguistics, applied linguistics; clinical linguistics, neurolinguistics, psycholinguistics; lexicography, lexicology, etymology; semantics 514 *meaning*; onomasiology, onomastics; sociolinguistics; computational linguistics, mathematical linguistics; bilingualism, multilingualism.

literature, creative writing, belles lettres; letters, classics, humanities; literary genre, fiction, metafiction, faction, non-fiction 590 *narrative*, *description*; lyricism, poetry 593 *poem*; plays 594 *drama*; criticism 480 *estimate*; literary criticism 520 *interpretation*; literary movement, Classicism, Neo-classicism, Sturm und Drang, Romanticism, Symbolism, Idealism, Expressionism, Surrealism, Realism, Naturalism; literary theory, structuralism, poststructuralism; deconstruction; literary history; Golden Age, Silver Age, Augustan Age, Classical Age 110 *era*.

linguist, philologist, etymologist, lexicographer, lexicologist; semanticist; grammarian, morphologist, syntactician 564 *grammar*; phonetician, phonologist; dialectologist; clinical linguist, psycholinguist, neurolinguist.

Adj. *linguistic*, philological, etymological, grammatical, morphological; lexicographical, lexicological, semantic; monosyllabic; inflected; written, literary, standard; spoken, living, idiomatic; vulgar, colloquial, vernacular, slangy, jargonistic 560 *dialectal*; current, common, demotic; bilingual, multilingual.

literary, written, polished; humanistic; classical, romantic, naturalistic, surrealistic, futuristic, decadent; learned; formal; critical 520 *interpretive*.

558 Letter

N. *letter*, sign, symbol, character 586 *writing*; alphabet, ABC; International Phonetic Alphabet, IPA; Chinese character, pictogram, cuneiform, hieroglyph 586 *lettering*; ogham alphabet, runic alphabet, futhorc; Greek alphabet, Roman alphabet, Cyrillic alphabet, Hebrew alphabet, Arabic alphabet; Devanagari; runic letter, rune, wen; Pinyin; lettering, Gothic, italic; ampersand; capital letter, cap, upper case; small letter, lower case, minuscule; block letter, uncial; cursive; printed letter, letterpress, type, bold type, ascender, etc. 587 *print-type*.

spelling, misspelling; orthography; spelling check, spell-check; phonography; spelling game, spelling bee; transliteration 520 *translation*.

Vb. *spell*, spell out, read, syllabify; alphabetize; transliterate; form letters 586 *write*; initial 547 *sign*.

559 Word

N. *word*, term 561 *name*; phoneme, syllable 398 *speech sound*; synonym 13 *identity*; homonym, homograph, homophone; palindrome, pun, weasel word 518 *equivocalness*; antonym 14 *contrariety*; etymon, root, back-formation, folk etymology; derivation, derivative, doublet; morpheme, etc. 564 *grammar*; stem, root, inflection *or* inflexion, affix, prefix, infix, suffix; part of speech 564 *grammar*; diminutive, intensive; contraction, abbreviation, acronym, portmanteau word 569 *conciseness*; cliché, catchword, vogue word, buzz word, nonce word, neologism, loan word 560 *neologism*; rhyming word; swearword, four-letter word, oath 899 *curse*; hard word, long word, polysyllable; short word, monosyllable, word of one syllable; verbiage, wordiness, verbal diarrhoea, loquacity, verbosity, bafflegab 570 *pleonasm*.

dictionary, rhyming dictionary, reverse word dictionary, reverse dictionary, monolingual dictionary, learners' dictionary, school dictionary, illustrated dictionary, bilingual dictionary, multilingual dictionary; lexicon, wordbook, word list, glossary, vocabulary; thesaurus 632 *store*; concordance.

Adj. *verbal*, literal; etymological, lexical; philological, lexicographical; derivative, conjugate, cognate; synonymous; verbose.

Adv. *verbally*, verbatim, word for word.

560 Neologism

N. *neologism*, neology 126 *newness*; coinage, new word, nonce word, vogue word, buzz word, catch phrase, cliché; borrowing, loan word; newfangled expression, slang expression; technical language, jargon, technical term, psychobabble, technospeak; barbarism, hybrid; corruption, dog Latin; novelese, journalese, legalese, officialese, telegraphese; baby talk; gobbledygook, newspeak, doubletalk, bafflegab; archaism; malapropism 565 *bad grammar*; word-play, spoonerism 839 *witticism*.

dialect, idiom, lingo, patois, vernacular 557 *language*; idiolect, burr, brogue, accent 577 *pronunciation*; cockney, mockney, rockney, Geordie, Scots, broad Scots, Doric, Lallans; broken English, pidgin English, pidgin; lingua franca, hybrid language; Briticism, Strine, Franglais; anglicism, Americanism, Hibernicism, Irishism, Scotticism.

slang, vulgarism, colloquialism; jargon, psychobabble, technospeak, argot, cant, patter, Polari *or* Parlyaree; Romany; thieves' Latin, rhyming slang; Billingsgate 899 *scurrility*; gobbledygook 515 *empty talk*.

Adj. *dialectal*, vernacular; Doric, cockney, broad; local; colloquial; non-standard, slangy, cant; jargonistic, journalistic.

561 Nomenclature

N. *nomenclature*, naming, etc. (see vb.); eponymy; terminology; description, designation, appellation, denomination; addressing, roll-call 583 *address*; christening, baptism 988 *Christian rite*; study of place names, toponymy.

name, first name, forename, Christian name; middle name, surname, family name, patronymic, matronymic; maiden name, married name; appellation, moniker; nickname, pet name, diminutive; sobriquet, epithet, description; handle, style 870 *title*; heading, caption 547 *indication*; designation; name and address, signature 547 *label*; domain name; term, technical term, trade name 560 *neologism*; namesake, synonym, eponym; pen name, pseudonym, stage name 562 *misnomer*; noun, proper noun 564 *part of speech*.

Adj. *named*, called, etc. (see vb.); entitled, christened; known as, alias, under the name of; so-called, soi-disant, self-styled; named after, eponymous.

Vb. *name*, call, christen, baptize 988 *perform ritual*; give one's name to; nickname, dub; address, sir; entitle, style, term 80 *specify*; call by name, call the roll, call out the names, announce.

562 Misnomer

N. *misnomer*, malapropism 565 *bad grammar*; false name, alias, assumed title; nom de guerre, nom de plume, pen name; stage name, pseudonym; nickname, pet name 561 *name*.

no name, anon, certain person, so-and-so, what's his name, what's his face; N or M, Miss X, A. N. Other; what d'you call it, thingummy, thingummyjig, thingamabob, whatsit, oojakapivvy; this or that; and co., etc.; some, any, what-have-you.

Adj. *anonymous*, unknown, faceless, nameless; incognito, unnamed, unsigned; a certain, certain, such; some, any, this or that.

Vb. *misname*, misterm, mistitle; nickname; assume an alias, go under a false name; be anonymous; write under an assumed name, pass oneself off as 541 *dissemble*.

563 Phrase

N. *phrase*, form of words; collocation; expression; idiom, mannerism 80 *speciality*; fixed expression; set phrase; euphemism, metaphor; catch phrase, slogan; hackneyed expression, cliché, commonplace 610 *habit*; saying, proverb, motto, moral, epigram, adage 496 *maxim*; epitaph 364 *funeral rites*; inscription, legend, caption 548 *record*; empty phrases, words, empty words, compliments 515 *empty talk*; terminology 561 *nomenclature*; phraseology, phrasing, diction, wording, turn of phrase; well-turned phrase; circumlocution 570 *diffuseness*; paraphrase 520 *translation*; epigrammatist.

Vb. *phrase*, word, verbalize, voice, articulate, syllable; reword, rephrase 520 *translate*; express, formulate, put in words, clothe in words, find words for, state 532 *affirm*; sloganize, talk in clichés; put words together, turn a sentence, round a period 566.

564 Grammar

N. *grammar*, analysis, parsing, construing; accidence, inflection *or* inflexion, declension, case, nominative, vocative, accusative, genitive, dative, ablative, locative, instrumental, ergative; conjugation, mood, indicative, imperative, infinitive, optative, subjunctive, voice, active, passive, middle, tense, present, future, past, perfect, imperfect, past perfect, pluperfect; number, singular, plural, dual, gender, masculine, feminine, neuter, agreement, concord; morphology, morpheme, morph, allomorph; affix, etc. (see also *part of speech* below); syntax, word order, parataxis, asyndeton, ellipsis, apposition; comparative grammar, philology; punctuation, pointing 547 *punctuation*; bad grammar 565 *bad grammar*; good grammar, grammaticalness, Standard English, Queen's English, BBC English, good English.

part of speech, substantive, noun, common noun, proper noun, collective noun, abstract noun, concrete noun, count noun, mass noun; pronoun, demonstrative pronoun, indefinite pronoun, interrogative pronoun, personal pronoun, reflexive pronoun, relative pronoun; adjective; verb, intransitive verb, transitive verb, reflexive verb, deponent verb, auxiliary verb, modal verb; adverb, sentence adverb, preposition, conjunction, interjection;

subject, object, direct object, indirect object; predicate, copula, complement; article, definite article, indefinite article, determiner; particle, affix, suffix, infix, prefix; inflection *or* inflexion, case-ending, conjugation, verb-ending; formative, morpheme, sememe, semanteme; diminutive, intensive, augmentative.

Adj. *grammatical*, correct; syntactic, inflectional; irregular, anomalous; masculine, feminine, neuter; singular, dual, plural; substantival, adjectival, attributive, predicative; verbal, adverbial; participial; prepositional; conjunctive; positive, comparative, superlative.

565 Bad grammar
N. *bad grammar*, bad English, faulty syntax; incorrectness, solecism, misusage; barbarism 560 *neologism*; malapropism, slip of the pen, slip of the tongue; mispronunciation, dropping one's aitches 580 *speech defect*; misspelling.

566 Style
N. *style*, fashion, mode, tone, manner, vein, strain, idiom; idiosyncrasy, mannerism 80 *speciality*; mode of expression, diction, phrasing, phraseology 563 *phrase*; idiolect, vocabulary; literary style, command of language *or* idiom, raciness, power 571 *vigour*; feeling for words; literary charm, grace 575 *elegance*; word power; vernacular speech 573 *plainness*; elaborate style 574 *ornament*; clipped speech 569 *conciseness*.

Adj. *stylistic*, mannered, literary; elegant, ornate, rhetorical; expressive, eloquent, fluent; racy, idiomatic; plain, perspicuous, forceful.

567 Clarity
N. *clarity*, clearness, lucidity, perspicuity, perspicuousness; limpidity 422 *transparency*; lucid prose 516 *intelligibility*; directness 573 *plainness*; definition, definiteness, exactness 494 *accuracy*.

568 Lack of clarity
N. *obscurity*, imperspicuity, obfuscation 517 *unintelligibility*; fogginess 423 *opacity*; abstraction, abstruseness; complexity, involved style 574 *ornament*; purple prose *or* passage *or* patch 574 *ornament*; hard words, Johnsonese 700 *difficulty*; imprecision, impreciseness, vagueness 474 *uncertainty*; inaccuracy 495 *inexactness*; ambiguity 518 *equivocalness*; mysteriousness 530 *enigma*; profundity 211 *depth*; ellipsis 569 *conciseness*; verbiage 570 *diffuseness*.

Adj. *unclear*, not transparent, muddied,

cloudy 423 *opaque*; obscure 418 *dark*; mysterious, enigmatic, clear as mud *or* as ditch water 517 *unintelligible*; abstruse, profound 211 *deep*; allusive, indirect 523 *latent*; vague, imprecise, indefinite 474 *uncertain*; ambiguous 518 *equivocal*; muddled, confused, tortuous, convoluted, involved 61 *complex*; hard, Johnsonian 700 *difficult*.

569 Conciseness
N. *conciseness*, succinctness, brevity; pithiness 496 *maxim*; aphorism, epigram, clerihew 839 *witticism*; economy of words, terseness, words of one syllable, laconicism; compression, telegraphese; overconciseness; ellipsis, abbreviation, contraction 204 *shortening*; epitome, précis, outline, brief sketch 592 *compendium*; compactness, portmanteau word; clipped speech, monosyllabism 582 *uncommunicativeness*; nutshell.

Adj. *concise*, brief, not long in telling, short and sweet 204 *short*; laconic, monosyllabic, sparing of words 582 *uncommunicative*; succinct; crisp, brisk, to the point; trenchant, mordant, incisive; terse, curt, brusque; condensed, tight-knit, compact; pithy, neat, exact, epigrammatic; elliptic, telegraphic, contracted, compressed; summary, cut short, abbreviated, truncated.

Vb. *be concise*, be brief, etc. (see adj.); need few words, not beat about the bush, pull no punches, come straight to the point, cut the cackle, cut a long story short, get down to brass tacks, talk turkey; telescope, compress, condense, contract, abridge, abbreviate, truncate 204 *shorten*; summarize; be short with, be curt with, cut short, cut off; waste no words.

Adv. *concisely*, in brief, in short, in a word, in a nutshell; to put it succinctly, to cut a long story short; to sum up.

570 Diffuseness
N. *diffuseness*, profuseness, copiousness, etc. (see adj.); amplification 197 *expansion*; abundance, superabundance, exuberance, redundancy 637 *redundancy*; expatiation, minuteness, blow-by-blow account; productivity 171 *productiveness*; inspiration, vein, flow, outpouring; richness; verboseness, verbosity, wordiness, verbiage; fluency, verbal diarrhoea 581 *talkativeness*; long-windedness, prolixity, epic length; repetitiveness, reiteration 106 *repetition*; twice-told tale 838 *tedium*; gush, rigmarole, waffle, blah 515 *empty talk*; effusion, tirade, harangue, sermon, speeches 579 *oration*; superfluity, redundancy 637 *redundancy*; tautology; circumlocution, periphrasis; beating about the bush 518 *equivocalness*; padding,

filler 40 *extra*; digression 10 *irrelevance*.

Adj. *diffuse*, profuse, copious, ample, rich; fertile, abundant, superabundant, voluminous, scribacious 171 *prolific*; verbose, non-stop, in love with one's own voice 581 *talkative*; fluent; exuberant, overflowing 637 *redundant*; expatiating, detailed, minute; gushing, effusive; windy, turgid, bombastic, orotund; polysyllabic, redundant, excessive, repetitious, repetitive; tautological; padded out.

long-winded, prolix, wordy, prosy; spun out, long-drawn-out; boring 838 *tedious*; lengthy, epic, never-ending, going on and on 203 *long*; discursive, digressing, episodic; rambling, wandering; loose-knit, incoherent; desultory, waffling, pointless 10 *irrelevant*; indirect, circumlocutory, periphrastic, round-about.

Vb. *be diffuse*, be profuse, be long-winded, etc. (see adj.); expatiate, amplify, particularize, detail, go into detail, expand, enlarge upon; descant, discourse at length; repeat; pad out, draw out, spin out, protract 203 *lengthen*; gush, be effusive 350 *flow*; let oneself go, rant, rant and rave, harangue 579 *orate*; have swallowed the dictionary; launch out on, spin a long yarn 838 *be tedious*; blether on, rabbit on, go on and on 581 *be talkative*; wander, waffle, digress 282 *deviate*; ramble, drivel, beat about the bush, not come to the point 518 *be equivocal*.

Adv. *diffusely*, verbosely, long-windedly; on and on, ad nauseam.

571 Vigour

N. *vigour* 174 *vigorousness*; power, strength, vitality, drive, force, forcefulness, oomph, go, get-up-and-go 160 *energy*; vim, punch, pep, guts, smeddum; verve, élan, panache, vivacity, liveliness, gusto, pizzazz, raciness; spirit, fire, ardour, glow, warmth, fervour, vehemence, enthusiasm, passion 818 *feeling*; stress, underlining, emphasis 532 *affirmation*; gravity, weight; impressiveness; declamation 574 *grandiloquence*; rhetoric 579 *eloquence*.

Adj. *forceful*, powerful, strenuous 162 *strong*; energetic, peppy, zingy, punchy 174 *vigorous*; racy; bold, dashing, spirited, vivacious 819 *lively*; fiery, ardent, enthusiastic, impassioned 818 *fervent*; kick-ass; vehement, emphatic, insistent, positive 532 *affirmative*; grave, sententious, strongly-worded, pulling no punches 834 *serious*; heavy, meaty, solid; weighty, forcible, cogent 740 *compelling*; vivid, graphic, effective; inspired 579 *eloquent*.

Vb. *be forceful*, be powerful, etc. (see vb.); kick ass.

572 Feebleness

N. *feebleness* 163 *weakness*; ineffectiveness, flatness, staleness, vapidity 387 *insipidness*; jejuneness, poverty, thinness; enervation, flaccidity; anticlimax.

Adj. *feeble*, weak, thin, flat, vapid, insipid 387 *tasteless*; wishy-washy, watery, wersh; sloppy, sentimental, schmaltzy, cutesy, novelettish; meagre, jejune, exhausted, spent; wan, colourless, bald 573 *plain*; languid, flaccid, nerveless, emasculated; uninspired, unimpassioned; ineffective, prosaic, uninspiring, a poor man's —; monotonous, pedestrian, dull, dry, boring 838 *tedious*; hackneyed, platitudinous, stale, starkness; matter-of-factness, childish; limping, lame, unconvincing 477 *poorly reasoned*; limp, loose, lax, inexact; poor, trashy 847 *vulgar*.

573 Plainness

N. *plainness*, naturalness, simplicity 699 *artlessness*; austerity, severity, baldness, spareness, bareness, starkness; matter-of-factness, plain English 516 *intelligibility*; home truths 540 *truthfulness*; homespun, vernacular, common speech, vulgar parlance; unaffectedness 874 *modesty*; bluntness, frankness, speaking straight from the shoulder, mincing no words, coarseness, four-letter word.

Adj. *plain*, simple 699 *artless*; austere severe; bald, spare, stark, bare, unfussy, bog standard, minimalist, no-frills, vanilla, without bells and whistles; neat 648 *clean*; pure, unadulterated 44 *unmixed*; unadorned, unvarnished, unembellished 540 *truthful*; played down, understated; unassuming, unpretentious 874 *modest*; chaste, restrained; unaffected, honest, natural, straightforward; homely, homey, homespun; prosaic, sober 834 *serious*; workaday, everyday, commonplace 610 *usual*; uninspired.

Vb. *speak plainly*, call a spade a spade, use plain English 516 *be intelligible*; moderate one's language; say outright, tell it like it is, spell it out, tell one straight, tell one to his *or* her face; not mince words, speak straight from the shoulder, not beat about the bush, come to the point, come down to brass tacks, talk turkey.

574 Ornament

N. *ornament*, embellishment, colour, decoration, embroidery, frills, flourish 844 *ornamentation*; floridness, floweriness, flowers of speech, arabesques 563 *phrase*; euphuism; preciousness, euphemism; rhetoric, purple patch *or* passage, purple prose; figure of speech 519 *figure of speech*; alliteration, assonance; paralipsis, aposiopesis; inversion, chiasmus; zeugma; metaphor, simile, antithesis.

grandiloquence, high tone 579 *eloquence*;

declamation, rhetoric 571 *vigour*; overstatement, extravagance, hyperbole 546 *exaggeration*; turgidity; pretentiousness, affectation, pomposity 875 *ostentation*; talking big 877 *boasting*; highfalutin, bombast, rant 515 *empty talk*; Johnsonese, long words.

Adj. *ornate*, beautified; rich, luxuriant, florid, flowery; precious, euphuistic, euphemistic; pretentious 850 *affected*; meretricious, flashy, flamboyant, frothy 875 *showy*; alliterative 519 *figurative*; stiff, stilted; pedantic, longworded, Latinate, Johnsonian.

Vb. *ornament*, beautify, grace, adorn, enrich, gild 844 *decorate*; charge, overlay; elaborate, smell of the lamp, overelaborate, overembellish, gild the lily.

575 Elegance

N. *elegance*, style, grace, gracefulness 841 *beauty*; refinement, taste 846 *good taste*; propriety; classicism; harmony, euphony, balance, proportion 245 *symmetry*; rhythm, ease, fluency, felicity, the right word in the right place, the mot juste; neatness, polish, finish; wellturned phrase; flourish.

Adj. *elegant*, majestic, stately 841 *beautiful*; graceful; stylish 846 *tasteful*; dignified; expressive; unaffected 573 *plain*; unlaboured, fluid, fluent, rhythmic, mellifluous, euphonious; harmonious, balanced, well-proportioned 245 *symmetrical*; neat, felicitous, happy, right, neatly put, well-turned; artistic; polished, finished, soigné; flawless 646 *perfect*; classic, classical, Attic, Ciceronian, Augustan.

576 Inelegance

N. *inelegance*, awkwardness, roughness, uncouthness 699 *artlessness*; coarseness 647 *imperfection*; harshness, stiltedness 326 *hardness*; unwieldiness; impropriety, barbarism; vulgarity 847 *bad taste*; artificiality 850 *affectation*; lack of style; anti-chic; turgidity, pomposity 574 *grandiloquence*.

Adj. *inelegant*, ungraceful, graceless 842 *ugly*; unpolished, unrefined 647 *imperfect*; coarse, crude, barbarous 699 *artless*; tasteless 847 *vulgar*; meretricious; turgid; forced, laboured, artificial; jarring, grating; insensitive; harsh; halting, unfluent; clumsy, awkward, gauche; wooden, stiff, stilted 875 *formal*.

577 Voice

N. *voice*, vocal sound; speaking voice 579 *speech*; singing voice; tongue, vocal organs, vocal cords; lungs, bellows; larynx, voice box; phoneme, vowel, diphthong; open vowel, close vowel, voiced consonant, syllable 398 *speech sound*; articulation; utterance, enuncia-

tion, delivery, articulation; exclamation, ejaculation, gasp; mutter, whisper, stage whisper, aside 401 *faintness*; tone of voice, accents, timbre, pitch, tone, intonation, modulation.

pronunciation, articulation, elocution, enunciation, inflection, accentuation, stress, emphasis; accent, broad accent, posh accent, foreign accent; burr, brogue, drawl, twang 560 *dialect*; trill; aspiration, glottal stop; nasality; lisping, stammer 580 *speech defect*; mispronunciation 565 *bad grammar*.

Vb. *voice*, pronounce, verbalize, put into words 579 *speak*; mouth, give tongue, give voice, express, utter, enunciate, articulate; vocalize; inflect, modulate; breathe, aspirate, sound one's aitches; trill, roll, burr, roll one's r's; accent, stress 532 *emphasize*; raise the voice, lower the voice, whisper, stage-whisper, make an aside, speak sotto voce; exclaim, ejaculate, rap out 408 *cry*; drone, intone, chant, warble, carol, hum 413 *sing*; bellow, shout, roar, vociferate, use one's voice 400 *be loud*; mispronounce, lisp, drawl, swallow one's consonants, speak thickly 580 *stammer*.

578 Voicelessness

N. *voicelessness*, no voice, loss of voice; difficulty in speaking, dysphonia, inarticulation; thick speech, hoarseness, huskiness, raucousness; muteness 399 *silence*; dumbness, mutism, deaf-mutism; childish treble, falsetto; breaking voice; sob, sobbing; undertone, aside, low voice, muffled tones, whisper, bated breath 401 *faintness*; surd, unvoiced consonant; sign language, deaf and dumb language 547 *gesture*; meaningful look; body language, kinesics.

Adj. *voiceless*, aphonic, dysphonic; unvoiced, surd; breathed, whispered, muffled, low-voiced, inaudible 401 *muted*; mute, dumb, deaf and dumb, deaf-mute; speechless, at a loss for words; inarticulate, tongue-tied; silent, mum, shtum 582 *uncommunicative*; silenced; gagged; croaking, hoarse as a raven 407 *hoarse*; breathless.

Vb. *be mute*, keep mum 582 *be uncommunicative*; be silent, keep quiet, hold one's tongue 525 *keep secret*; bridle one's tongue, dry up, shut up, ring off, hang up; lose one's voice, be struck dumb, lose the power of speech; make sign language, exchange meaningful glances 547 *gesticulate*; have difficulty in speaking 580 *stammer*.

make mute, strike dumb, dumbfound, take one's breath away, rob one of words; stick in one's throat, choke on; muffle, hush, deaden 401 *mute*; shout down, make one inaudible, drown one's voice; muzzle, gag, stifle 165 *suppress*; stop one's mouth, reduce one to silence, shut one up, cut one short, hang up on; still, hush, put to silence 399 *silence*.

579 Speech

N. *speech*, faculty of speech, gift of speech, tongue, lips 577 *voice*; parlance 557 *language*; word of mouth, personal account 524 *report*; spoken word, accents, tones 559 *word*; discourse, colloquy, conversation, talk, chat, rap, palaver, prattle, chinwag 584 *conversation*; address; fluency, talkativeness, volubility 581 *talkativeness*; prolixity; elocution, voice production; articulation, utterance, delivery, enunciation 577 *pronunciation*; ventriloquism; sign language, eye language, meaningful glance *or* look 547 *gesture*; body language; speech, dictum, utterance, remark, observation, comment, interjection 532 *affirmation*; fine words 515 *empty talk*; spiel, patter 542 *trickery*.

oration, speech; one's say, a word in edgeways; public speech, formal speech, discourse, disquisition, address, talk; maiden speech; welcoming address 876 *celebration*; panegyric, eulogy; valedictory, funeral oration 364 *funeral rites*; after-dinner speech, toast, vote of thanks; broadcast, commentary 534 *lecture*; recitation, recital, reading; set speech, declamation; sermon, homily, exhortation; harangue, ranting, tub-thumping, tirade, diatribe, invective; monologue 585 *soliloquy*; written speech, dictation, paper, screed 591 *dissertation*; preamble, prologue, foreword, narration, account, digression, peroration.

oratory, art of speaking, rhetoric, public speaking, stump oratory, tub-thumping; speech-making, speechifying; declamation, rhetoric, elocution, ranting, rant; vituperation, invective; soapbox; Hyde Park Corner.

eloquence, gift of the gab, fluency, articulacy; blarney; way with words, word power 566 *style*; power of speech; grandiloquence; elocution, good delivery; peroration, purple passage.

speaker, utterer; talker, prattler, gossiper 581 *chatterer*; conversationalist; speechifier, speech-maker, speech-writer, rhetorician, elocutionist; orator, Cicero; public speaker, after-dinner speaker, toastmaster *or* -mistress; raconteur 839 *humorist*; improviser, adlibber; declaimer, ranter, soap-box orator, tub-thumper, haranguer 738 *agitator*; lecturer; pulpiteer 537 *preacher*; presenter, announcer 531 *broadcaster*; narrator, chorus 594 *actor*; mouthpiece, spokesman *or* -woman, spokesperson 754 *delegate*; advocate, pleader, mediator 231 *intermediary*; salesman *or* -woman, salesperson, rep 793 *seller*.

Adj. *speaking*, talking; with a tongue in one's head, vocal; bilingual, polyglot; articulate, fluent, talkative 581 *talkative*; oral; well-spoken, soft-spoken; audible, spoken, verbal; elocutionary.

eloquent, spellbinding, silver-tongued; smooth-tongued 925 *flattering*; elocutionary, oratorical; grandiloquent, declamatory 571 *forceful*; tub-thumping, fire-and-brimstone, ranting, rousing 821 *exciting*.

Vb. *speak*, mention, say, be like; utter, articulate 577 *voice*; pronounce, declare 532 *affirm*; let out, blurt out, come clean, tell all 526 *divulge*; whisper, breathe 524 *hint*; talk 584 *converse*; give utterance, deliver oneself of; break silence, open one's mouth *or* lips, find one's tongue; pipe up, speak up, raise one's voice; give tongue, rattle on, gossip, prattle, chatter, rap 581 *be talkative*; patter, give a spiel, jabber, gabble; sound off, speak one's mind, tell a thing or two, have one's say, expatiate 570 be *diffuse*; trot out, reel off, recite; read, read aloud, read out, dictate; have a tongue in one's head, speak for oneself; use sign language 547 *gesticulate*.

orate, speechify; declaim, deliver a speech; hold forth, spout, be on one's hind legs; take the floor *or* the stand, rise to speak; preach, harangue; lecture, address 534 *teach*; perorate, mouth, rant, rail, sound off, tub-thump; spellbind, hold enthralled, be eloquent, have the gift of the gab, have kissed the Blarney Stone 925 *flatter*; talk to oneself 585 *soliloquize*; speak off the top of one's head, ad-lib 609 *improvise*.

580 Speech defect

N. *speech defect*, loss of speech, dysphasia, aphasia, aphonia; paraphasia, paralalia; idiolalia; stammering, stammer, stutter, lallation, lisp; sigmatism 406 *hissing*; speech impediment, dysphonia, dysarthria, dyspraxia, hesitation, drawl, slur; indistinctness, inarticulateness, thick speech, cleft palate; burr, brogue 560 *dialect*; accent, twang, nasal twang 577 *pronunciation*; treatment for speech defect: speech therapy, speech pathology and therapeutics 658 *therapy*; clinic; speech therapist, clinician.

affected accent, affectation, plum in one's mouth, marble in one's mouth, Oxford accent, haw-haw 246 *distortion*.

Vb. *stammer*, stutter, trip over one's tongue; drawl, hesitate, falter, quaver, hem and ha, hum and haw; um and ah, mumble, mutter; lisp; splutter; speak through the nose, drone; clip one's words, swallow one's words, gabble, slur; mispronounce.

581 Talkativeness

N. *talkativeness*, loquacity, loquaciousness, garrulity, communicativeness, yak, yackety-yack; volubility, runaway tongue, flow of words, fluency 570 *diffuseness*; verbosity, wordiness, prolixity; running on, spate of words, logorrhoea, verbal diarrhoea, inexhaustible vocabulary; patter, spiel, bafflegab, gab, gift of the gab 579 *eloquence*.

chatter, chattering, gossiping, gabble, jabber, rap, palaver, jaw-jaw, yackety-yack; clack, cackle, babble, prattle; small talk, gossip, idle gossip, tittle-tattle; waffle, blether, gush, guff, gas, hot air 515 *empty talk*.

chatterer, chatterbox; gossip, tittle-tattler 529 *news reporter*; haverer, ranter; preacher, sermonizer; windbag, gasbag, conversationalist; the chattering classes.

Adj. *talkative*, loquacious, garrulous, gossiping, tattling, tittle-tattling, yakking; communicative, rapping, chatty, gossipy, newsy 524 *informative*; gabbing, babbling, gabbling, gabby, gassy, windy, verbose, long-winded 570 *long-winded*; non-stop, voluble, going on and on, fluent, glib; conversational.

Vb. *be talkative*, be loquacious, etc. (see adj.); have a long tongue, chatter, rattle, go on and on, run on, bang on, reel off, talk nineteen to the dozen; gossip, tattle 584 *converse*; clack, gabble, jabber 515 *mean nothing*; talk, jaw, yak, go yackety-yack, gab, prate, gas, waffle, haver, blether, twitter, ramble on, rabbit on; rap; drone, drivel; launch into speech, start talking, give tongue, shoot; have one's say, talk at length; expatiate, spout 570 *be diffuse*; talk down; filibuster, stonewall; talk one's head off, talk the hind leg off a donkey; talk shop, bore 838 *be tedious*; engage in conversation, buttonhole; monopolize the conversation, hold the floor, not let one get a word in edgeways, never stop talking.

582 Uncommunicativeness

N. *uncommunicativeness*, incommunicativeness, taciturnity, reserve, reticence 525 *secrecy*; few words, brusqueness, curtness, gruffness 885 *rudeness*; muteness 578 *voicelessness*; economy of words; no orator; person of few words; clam; Trappist.

Adj. *uncommunicative*, incommunicative, not talking, saying little, taciturn, mute, mum 399 *silent*; sparing of words, monosyllabic, short, curt, laconic, brusque, gruff 569 *concise*; withdrawn, reserved, keeping oneself to oneself, guarded, with sealed lips 525 *reticent*; close, tight-lipped, shtum; not to be drawn, keeping one's counsel, discreet 858 *cautious*; inarticulate, tongue-tied 578 *voiceless*.

Vb. *be uncommunicative*, be laconic, etc. (see adj.); spare one's words 569 *be concise*; not talk, say nothing, have little to say; observe silence, make no answer; not be drawn, refuse comment, neither confirm nor deny; keep one's counsel 525 *keep secret*; hold one's tongue, put a bridle on one's tongue, keep one's mouth *or* one's trap shut; fall silent, relapse into silence, pipe down, dry up 145 *cease*; be speechless, lose one's tongue 578 *be mute*; waste no words on, save one's breath to cool one's porridge; not mention, leave out, pass over, omit 458 *disregard*.

Int. *hush!*, sh!, shut up!, mum's the word!, no comment!, a word to the wise!

583 Address

N. *address*, lecture, talk, speech, pep talk, sermon 579 *oration*; allocution, apostrophe; greeting, salutation; invocation, appeal, interjection, buttonholing, word in the ear, aside.

Vb. *speak to*, address, talk to, lecture to; turn to, direct one's words at, appeal to, pray to; sir; approach, accost; hail, call to, salute, say good morning 884 *greet*; pass the time of day, parley with 584 *converse*; take aside, buttonhole.

584 Conversation

N. *conversation*, interlocution, parley, colloquy, converse, talk, chat, rap, cybertalk; dialogue, question and answer; exchange, repartee, banter, badinage; slanging match 709 *quarrel*; confab, social intercourse 882 *fellowship*; commerce, communion, communication, intercommunication 524 *information*; tête-à-tête.

chat, chinwag, natter; chit-chat, talk, small talk, rap; gossip; tattle, tittle-tattle, tongue-wagging 581 *chatter*; fireside chat, cosy chat, tête-à-tête, heart-to-heart.

conference, colloquy, talks, parley, pow-wow; discussion, debate, forum, focus group, quality circle, symposium, seminar, teach-in, talk-in, controversy; exchange of views, high-level talks, summit meeting, summit conference, summit; negotiations, proximity talks, bargaining 765 *treaty*; conclave, convention, meeting, gathering 74 *assembly*; working lunch; reception 882 *social gathering*; audience, interview; consultation, huddle, council, war council, family council, round-table conference 691 *advice*.

Vb. *converse*, parley, talk together (see also *confer* below); pass the time of day, exchange pleasantries; draw one out; buttonhole, engage in conversation, carry on a conversation, join in a conversation, butt in, put in a word, bandy words, exchange words; chat, have a chat *or* a natter *or* a good talk; be drawn out 579 *speak*; natter, chinwag, chew the fat *or* rag, rap, gossip, tattle 581 *be talkative*; commune with; be closeted with; whisper together, talk tête-à-tête, go into a huddle, indulge in pillow talk.

confer, talk it over, sit in council *or* in conclave, sit in committee, hold a council of war, pow-wow; discuss, debate 475 *argue*; parley, negotiate, hold talks, hold a summit, get round the table; consult with 691 *consult*.

585 Soliloquy

N. *soliloquy*, monologue; stream of consciousness; apostrophe; aside; one-man *or* one-woman show.

Vb. *soliloquize*, say to oneself, make an aside, think aloud; apostrophize; talk to the wall, address an empty house, have an audience of one.

586 Writing

N. *writing*, creative writing, literary composition, authorship, journalism 590 *description*; literary output 557 *literature*, 593 *poem, prose*; script, copy, works, books 589 *reading matter*; pen-pushing, hackwork, Grub Street; paperwork 548 *record*; copying, transcribing, transcription, rewriting, editing; holography; handwriting, longhand, shorthand, stenography, speedwriting, typewriting, typing 587 *print*; braille; cipher, code, mirror writing, invisible ink 530 *secret*; automatic writing, spirit writing, psychography 984 *spiritualism*; hieroglyphics; sign-writing, skywriting 528 *advertisement*; graffiti; inscribing, carving; graphology.

lettering, stroke of the pen, up-stroke, down-stroke; line, dot, point; flourish, scroll; handwriting, joined-up writing; calligraphy, penmanship; fair hand; script, italic, copperplate; printing, block letters; scribble, scrawl; letters, characters, alphabet 558 *letter*; runes, pictogram, hieroglyph, cuneiform; palaeography.

script, written matter, illuminated address; calligraph; writing, screed, scrawl, scribble; manuscript, MS; original, one's own hand, autograph, holograph; signature; copy, transcript, transcription, fair copy 22 *duplicate*; typescript, stencil; newsprint; printed matter; letter, epistle, written reply 588 *correspondence*; inscription, graffito 548 *record*; superscription, caption, heading; illuminated letters.

stationery, writing materials, pen and paper, pen and ink; pen, quill-pen, fountain pen, cartridge pen, felt-tip pen, ballpoint pen, Biro (tdmk); nib; stylo; pencil, propelling pencil, lead pencil, coloured pencil; crayon, chalk; papyrus, parchment, vellum; foolscap 631 *paper*; writing paper, notepaper, lined paper, blank paper, notebook, pad, jotter; slate, blackboard; inkstand, inkwell; pencil sharpener, penknife; blotting paper, blotter; typewriter, ribbon, daisy wheel; stencil.

shorthand writer, stenographer, typist, shorthand typist, stenotypist, audiotypist, secretary, personal secretary, personal assistant, PA, Girl Friday.

Adj. *written*, inscribed, in black and white; in writing, in longhand, in shorthand; handwritten, manuscript, signed; penned, pencilled, scrawled, scribbled, etc. (see vb.); copybook, copperplate; italic, calligraphic; hieroglyphic, lettered, alphabetic; runic, roman, italic 558 *literal*; upright, sloping, bold, spidery.

Vb. *write*, form characters, inscribe; letter, block, print; write well; write badly, scribble, scrawl; put in writing, confirm in writing, set down in black and white, commit to paper, write down, jot down, note 548 *record*; transcribe, copy out, make a fair copy, rewrite, write out; take down, take dictation, take down in shorthand, type, key; take down longhand, write in full; draft; compose; pen, pencil, dash off; write letters 588 *correspond*; write one's name 547 *sign*; take pen in hand, put pen to paper; be an author.

587 Print

N. *print*, printing, laser printing, typing, typewriting 586 *writing*; typography, lithography, litho, photolithography, photolitho 555 *printing*; photocopying 551 *photography*; photocomposition, phototypesetting, computer typesetting, cold type; composition, typesetting, make-up; monotype, linotype, stereotype, electrotype; impression, printout; proof, galley proof, bromide, page proof, revise; proofcopy.

print-type, type, stereotype, plate; flong; matrix; broken type, pie; upper case, lower case, capitals, small capitals, caps; fount, face, typeface, boldface, bold, clarendon, lightface, old face, bastard type; roman, italic, Gothic, black letter 558 *letter*; body, bevel, shoulder, shank, beard, ascender, descender, serif, sanserif; lead, rule, en, em; space, hairspace, quad; type bar, slug, logotype.

press, printing press, printing works, printers; composing room; machining room; handpress, flatbed, platen press, rotary press, Linotype (tdmk), Monotype (tdmk), offset press.

Adj. *printed*, in print 528 *published*; cold-type, hot-metal; set, composed, machined, etc. (see vb.); in type, in italic, in bold, in roman; typographic; leaded, spaced, justified; solid, tight, crowded.

Vb. *print*, stamp; typeset, key, compose, photocompose; align, register, justify; set up in type, make ready, impose, machine, run off, pull off, print off; collate, foliate; paginate, lithograph, litho, offset, stereotype; put to bed; proofread; bring out 528 *publish*.

588 Correspondence

N. *correspondence*, exchange of letters, barrage of correspondence, backlog of correspondence; communication 524 *information*; mailshot, mailing list, distribution list; letters, mail, post, postbag 531 *postal communications*; letter, epistle, missive, dispatch, bulletin; postcard, pc, picture postcard, card, letter card, notelet; air letter, aerogramme, air mail, sea mail; business letter, bill, account, enclosure; open letter 528 *publicity*; love letter, billet doux, greetings card, Christmas card, Easter card, birthday card, Valentine 889 *endearment*; hate mail, poison-pen letter, letter bomb; unsolicited mail, junk mail, circular, round robin, chain letter, begging letter; note, line, chit; answer, acknowledgment, RSVP; envelope, cover, seal, stamp, postmark 531 *postal communications*; postcode, zip code *or* ZIP code (US).

correspondent, letter writer, penfriend, penpal, poison pen; foreign correspondent, contributor 529 *news reporter*.

Vb. *correspond*, correspond with, exchange letters, maintain *or* keep up a correspondence, keep in touch with 524 *communicate*; write to, send a letter to, drop a line; report 524 *inform*; deal with one's correspondence, catch up on one's correspondence, acknowledge, reply, write back, reply by return 460 *answer*; circularize 528 *publish*.

589 Book

N. *book*, title, volume, tome, roll, scroll, document; codex, manuscript, MS; script, typescript; published work, publication, best-seller, blockbuster, page-turner; potboiler; sleeper, remainder; standard work, classic, definitive work, collected works; major work, monumental work, magnum opus; slim volume; booklet; illustrated work, picture book, coffee-table book 553 *picture*; chapter book; magazine, periodical, rag 528 *journal*; brochure, pamphlet, leaflet 528 *the press*; bound book, cased book, hardback, softback, limpback, paperback (see also *edition* below); electronic book,

e-book; BookCrossing (tdmk).

reading matter, printed word, written word 586 *writing*; forms, papers, bumf, literature 548 *record*; circular, junk mail; script, copy; text, the words, libretto, lyrics, scenario, screenplay, book of words; proof, revise, pull; writings, prose literature 593 *prose*; poetical literature 593 *poetry*; classical literature, serious literature, light literature, chick lit, lad lit, bloke lit, mummy lit 557 *literature*, 590 *novel*; books for children, children's book, picture book, chapter book, juvenile; history, biography, travel 590 *description*; work of fiction 590 *novel*; biographical work, memoirs, memorabilia 590 *biography*; addresses, speeches 579 *oration*; essay, tract, treatise 591 *dissertation*; piece, occasional pieces 591 *article*; miscellanea, marginalia, jottings, thoughts, pensées; poetical works 593 *poem*; selections, flowers 592 *anthology*; dedicatory volume, festschrift; early works, juvenilia; posthumous works, literary remains; complete works, oeuvre, corpus; newspaper, magazine 528 *journal*; issue, number, back number; fascicle, part, instalment, serial, sequel, prequel.

reference book, encyclopaedia, cyclopaedia 490 *erudition*; lexicon, thesaurus 559 *dictionary*; biographical dictionary, dictionary of quotations, rhyming dictionary, reverse dictionary, dictionary of reverse words, technical dictionary, gazetteer, year-book, annual 87 *directory*; calendar 117 *chronology*; guide 524 *guidebook*; notebook, diary, album 548 *record*; bibliography, reading list.

edition, impression, issue, run; series, set, collection, library; bound edition, library edition, de luxe edition, school edition, trade edition, standard edition, definitive edition, omnibus edition, complete edition, collected edition, complete works; first edition, new edition, revised edition; reissue, reprint; illustrated edition, special edition, limited edition, expurgated edition; critical edition, annotated edition, variorum edition; adaptation, abridgment 592 *compendium*; quarto, folio; layout, format; house style; front matter, prelims, preface, prefatory note; dedication, acknowledgments; title, half-title; flyleaf, title page, endpaper, colophon 547 *label*; contents, errata, corrigenda, addenda; back matter, appendix, supplement, index, thumb index, bibliography; caption, heading, headline, running headline, footnote; guide word, catchword; margin; gutter; folio, page, leaf, recto, verso; sheet, forme, signature; chapter, section; inset; plate, print, illustration, halftone, line drawing 553 *picture*.

bookbinding, binding, spiral binding, perfect

binding, stitching, casing; case, slip case, cover, jacket, dust jacket 226 *wrapping*; boards 631 *paper*; cloth, limp cloth, linen, scrim, buckram, leather, pigskin, calf, morocco, vellum, parchment; spine, headband; tooling, gilding, marbling.

library, national library, public library, local library, reference library, mobile library, lending library, circulating library.

book person, man *or* woman of letters, bluestocking; reader, bookworm 492 *scholar*; bibliophile, book lover, book collector, bibliographer; librarian; stationer, bookseller, antiquarian bookseller, secondhand bookseller, publisher; editor, book reviewer, critic, reviewer 480 *estimator*.

author, authoress, writer, creative writer, wordsmith; man *or* woman of letters; fiction-writer, novelist, crime writer, historian, biographer, essayist 591 *dissertator*; prose writer; verse writer 593 *poet*; playwright, librettist, script writer 594 *dramatist*; freelance; copywriter 528 *publicizer*; pressman *or* -woman, journalist 529 *news reporter*; editor, subeditor, copy editor, contributor, correspondent, special correspondent, war correspondent, sports correspondent, columnist, gossip writer, diarist; agony aunt; scribbler, penpusher, hack, Grub Street hack; ghost writer.

590 Description

N. *description*, account, detailed account; statement, exposé, summary 524 *report*; brief, abstract, inscription, caption, subtitle, legend 592 *compendium*; narration, relation, recital, version (see also *narrative* below); documentary account; specification, characterization, details, particulars 87 *list*; portrayal, delineation, depiction; portrait, word portrait, sketch, character sketch, profile; case history 548 *record*; documentary, drama documentary, dramadoc, documentary drama, docudrama, faction, actuality TV, reality TV; picture, true picture, realism; travelogue 524 *guidebook*; vignette, cameo, thumbnail sketch, outline; idyll, parody 851 *satire*; epitaph 364 *funeral rites*.

narrative, storyline, plot, subplot, scenario 594 *stage play*; episode 154 *event*; dénouement 725 *completion*; dramatic irony, comic relief; catharsis; stream of consciousness; fantasia 513 *fantasy*; fiction, faction, story, tale, romance, fairytale, folk tale; tradition, legend, myth, saga, river saga, soap opera, serial, epic; ballad 593 *poem*; allegory, parable, cautionary tale; yarn 543 *fable*; bedtime story; anecdote, reminiscence 505 *remembrance*; annals, chronicle, history, historiography 548 *record*.

biography, real-life story, human interest; life, curriculum vitae, CV, biodata, life story *or* history, background, back story; experiences, adventures, fortunes; hagiology, hagiography, martyrology; obituary, obit; autobiography, confessions, memoirs 505 *remembrance*; diary, journals 548 *record*; letters 588 *correspondence*.

novel, fiction, literary fiction; roman fleuve; anti-novel, metafiction; genre fiction; historical novel, novelization; short story, novelette, novella; light reading, bedside reading 589 *reading matter*; adventure story, Western; fairy story, fantasy, science fiction, sci-fi, cyberpunk, steam punk, urban fantasy, magic *or* magical realism, sword and sorcery, gothic novel, ghost story, picaresque novel; crime story, detective story, spy story, whodunit, whydunit; cliffhanger, thriller, horror story, shocker, penny dreadful, horror comic; romance, love story, doctor–nurse story, bodice-ripper, bonkbuster, sex-and-shopping novel, Aga saga, family saga, clogs-and-shawls saga; paperback, pulp literature, pulp fiction, airport fiction; chick lit, mummy lit, lad lit, bloke lit; potboiler, trash; popular novel, blockbuster, best-seller, page-turner 589 *book*, *reading matter*; fanfic.

Adj. *descriptive*, graphic, colourful, vivid; well-drawn, sharp; true-to-life, realistic, real-life, photographic, impressionistic, evocative, emotive, full, detailed 570 *diffuse*; documentary.

Vb. *describe*, delineate, draw, picture, depict, paint 551 *represent*; evoke, bring to life, capture; characterize, detail; sketch 233 *outline*; relate, recount, recite, report, give an account 524 *communicate*; write, write about 548 *record*; narrate, tell, spin a yarn, unfold a tale; make a story out of; recapitulate 106 *repeat*; reminisce, relive the past 505 *retrospect*.

591 Dissertation

N. *dissertation*, treatise, tract, exposition, summary 592 *compendium*; theme, thesis 475 *argument*; disquisition, essay, examination, survey 459 *enquiry*; discourse, discussion; paper, monograph, study; homily, sermon 534 *lecture*, commentary.

article, news article, column; leader, editorial; essay; literary composition; comment, review, rave review, notice, critique, criticism, write-up 480 *estimate*.

dissertator, essayist; pamphleteer, publicist 528 *publicizer*; editor, leader writer, writer, contributor 589 *author*; reviewer, critic, commentator, pundit 520 *interpreter*.

Vb. *dissertate*, treat, handle, write about, deal with; discourse upon 475 *argue*; develop a thesis; go into, go into in depth, conduct an in-depth-enquiry, survey; set out, discuss, ventilate, air one's views; criticize, comment upon; write an essay, write a treatise, do a paper, write an article, do a piece; annotate, commentate 520 *interpret*.

592 Compendium

N. *compendium*, epitome, résumé, summary, brief; contents, heads, analysis; abstract, sum and substance, gist, drift; consolidation, digest, pandect; multum in parvo, précis; aperçu, conspectus, synopsis, bird's-eye view, survey; review, recapitulation, recap; rundown, runthrough; draft, minute, note 548 *record*; sketch, thumbnail sketch, outline, brief outline, skeleton; blueprint 623 *plan*; syllabus, prospectus, brochure 87 *list*; abridgment, abbreviation, concise version 204 *shortening*; contraction, compression 569 *conciseness*.

anthology, treasury, flowers, gems; selections, extracts 589 *textbook*; collection, compilation, miscellany; ephemera; gleanings; cuttings, album, scrapbook, sketchbook, commonplace book.

Vb. *abstract*, sum up, resume, summarize, run over; epitomize, make a synopsis of, reduce, abbreviate, abridge 204 *shorten*; capsulize, encapsulate; docket 548 *record*; condense, pot, give an out-line 569 *be concise*; compile 87 *list*; collect 74 *bring together*; conflate 50 *combine*; excerpt, select; sketch out 233 *outline*.

593 Poetry. Prose

N. *poetry*, poesy, balladry; versification (see also *prosody* below); poetic art, poetics; verse, rhyme; poetic licence; poetic inspiration, muse, Muses.

poem, versification, piece of verse, lines, verses, stanzas, strains; verse, stanza, canto; narrative verse, heroic poem, epic, dramatic poem, dramatic monologue, verse drama; light verse, lyric verse; comic verse, nonsense verse, limerick; acrostic; ode; dirge, elegy; idyll, eclogue, aubade; occasional poem; song, shanty, lay, ballad 412 *vocal music*; war-song, marching song; love song, drinking song; collected poems 592 *anthology*; cycle, sequence.

doggerel, jingle, ditty, nursery rhyme, Mother Goose rhyme; nonsense verse, comic verse; clerihew, limerick; burlesque.

verse form, sonnet, sestet, Petrarchan or Italian sonnet, Shakespearean or English sonnet; ballade, rondeau, virelay, triolet, villanelle, bouts rimés; burden, refrain, envoi; couplet, distich, sloka; haiku, tanka; triplet, tercet, terza rima, quatrain, ghazal; sestina, rhyme royal, ottava rima, Spenserian stanza; accentual verse, syllabic verse, metrical verse, blank verse; concrete poetry; Sapphics, Alcaics; limping iambics, scazon; free verse, vers libre; verse, versicle, stanza, stave, laisse, strophe, antistrophe; stichomythia; broken line, half line, hemistich.

prosody, versification, metre; scansion; rhyme, masculine rhyme, feminine rhyme, internal rhyme, eye rhyme; rhyme scheme; assonance, alliteration; cadence, rhythm; metrical unit, foot; iamb, trochee, spondee, pyrrhic; dactyl, anapaest; tetrameter, pentameter, hexameter, heptameter, octameter; iambic pentameters, blank verse; alexandrine, heroic couplet; beat, stress, accent; elision; caesura.

poet, poet laureate; Lake poet, Georgian poet, Metaphysical poet, beat poet, modern poet; versemonger, poetaster; versifier, rhymer, bard, minstrel, balladeer, troubadour, Meistersinger, epic poet, lyric poet, dramatic poet, elegiac poet; sonneteer, ballad-monger; songwriter, librettist.

prose, prose poem; piece of prose, prose composition, prosaicness, prose-writing, everyday language 573 *plainness*; purple prose or passage or patch 574 *ornament*; prose writer 589 *author*.

Adj. *poetic*, poetical; Parnassian, satiric; elegiac, lyrical, lyric, rhyming, jingling, etc. (see vb.); doggerel, prosodic, metrical, measured, rhythmic, scanning; iambic.

prosaic, pedestrian, uninspired, unpoetical, in prose, matter-of-fact 573 *plain*.

Vb. *write poetry*, poetize, rhyme, versify, put into verse; compose an epic, write a lyric, write a sonnet; make up a limerick; celebrate in verse; lampoon 851 *satirize*; scan.

594 Drama. Ballet

N. *drama*, the theatre, the stage, the boards, the footlights; theatreland, Broadway, West End; silver screen, Hollywood 445 *cinema*; show business, show biz, dramatic entertainment, straight drama, legitimate theatre, live theatre; intimate theatre, theatre in the round, total theatre, alternative theatre, street theatre, the Fringe, off-off-Broadway; repertory, rep; theatricals, amateur dramatics, am-dram, dressing-up; masque, charade, dumb show, puppetry, tableau, tableau vivant 551 *representation*; tragic mask, comic mask, sock, buskin; Melpomene, Thespis; psychodrama.

dramatic theory, dramaturgy, dramatic form 590 *narrative*; dramatic unities; dramatization, theatricals, dramatics; melodramatics, histrionics; theatricality, staginess; good or bad theatre or cinema or television, etc.; play writing, script writing, libretto writing; stagecraft; action, plot, subplot 590 *narrative*; characterization 551 *representation*; production, new production; revival; auditions, casting; walkthrough, rehearsal, dress rehearsal; direction, stage management; continuity; staging, stage directions; choreography; dialogue, soliloquy, stage whisper, aside, cue; entrance, exit (see also *acting* below); rising of the curtain, prologue, chorus; act, scene, opening scene, coup de théâtre, deus ex machina, alarums and excursions; curtain, drop of the curtain, blackout; finale, final curtain, epilogue; curtain call, encore; interval, intermission, break; enactment, performance, command performance, benefit performance; première, preview, first night, gala night; matinée, first house, second house; one-night stand, road show; sell-out, hit, smash hit, box-office hit, long run; flop.

stage play, play, drama, work; show, libretto, scenario, script, text, prompt book; part, lines 579 *speech*; dramatic representation 551 *representation*; five-act play, one-act play, playlet; sketch, skit; double bill; curtain-raiser, monologue, duologue, two-hander; masque; mystery play, miracle play, morality play, passion play, Oberammergau; commedia dell'arte; No, Kabuki; Greek drama, trilogy, tetralogy, cycle; poetic drama, verse drama; melodrama, gothic drama, blood and thunder; tragedy; tragicomedy, comedy, comedy of manners, Restoration comedy; situation comedy, sit-com; kitchen-sink drama, theatre of the absurd, theatre of cruelty; black comedy, farce, slapstick, burlesque 849 *ridiculousness*; pantomime, panto, musical comedy, musical, light opera, comic opera, grand opera 412 *vocal music*; television play 531 *broadcast*; screenplay 445 *cinema*; mime, puppet show, Punch and Judy show.

stage show 445 *spectacle*; live show; ice show, circus 837 *amusement*; variety, music hall, vaudeville; review, revue, intimate revue, late-night revue; Follies, leg show, strip show; floor show, cabaret; song and dance, act, turn; star turn; tableau.

ballet, dance, ballet dancing 837 *dancing*; choreography; classical ballet, modern dance; toe dance 837 *dance*; solo, pas seul, pas de deux; chassé, glissade; arabesque; fouetté, plié, pirouette 315 *rotation*; pas de chat, entrechat, jeté 312 *leap*; ballet enthusiast, balletomane 504 *enthusiast*.

stage set, set, setting, décor, scenery, scene 445 *spectacle*; drop curtain, backdrop, backcloth; screen, wings; background, foreground, front stage, upstage, down stage, stage, boards; apron, proscenium, proscenium arch, apron

stage, picture-frame stage; stage in the round, curtain; prompt box (see also *theatre* below); properties, props, costume; make-up, greasepaint.

theatre, amphitheatre, stadium 724 *arena*; circus, hippodrome; fleapit, picture house, movie theatre 445 *cinema*; theatre in the round, open-air theatre; pavilion; big top; playhouse, opera house, music hall, vaudeville theatre, variety theatre; night club, cabaret; stage, boards, proscenium, wings, flies; dressing room, green room; footlights, spotlight, limelight, houselights; auditorium, orchestra; seating, stalls, front stalls, back stalls, orchestra stalls, front rows; pit, box, circle, dress circle, upper circle, gallery, balcony, gods; front of house, foyer, box office, stage door.

acting, impersonation; interpretation; improvisation, improv, pantomime, miming, taking off 20 *mimicry*; histrionics, play-acting, the Method; hamming, barn-storming; overacting, camping it up, staginess, theatricality; repertoire; character, personage, role; leading role; part, fat part; vignette, cameo; supporting part, bit part, speaking part; walk-on part; stock part, stereotype, ingenue, heavy father, injured husband, merry widow, stage villain. stage Irishman; principal boy *or* girl; Harlequin, Columbine, Pierrot, pantomime dame; hero, heroine, antihero; stage fever; stage fright, first-night nerves, performance anxiety.

actor, actress, Thespian, luvvy, mimic, mime 20 *imitator*; mummer, play-actor, player, strolling player, trouper, ham; rep player, character actor; actor-manager, star, star of stage and screen, film star, starlet, tragedian, tragedienne; comedian, comedienne, funnyman, comedy actor *or* actress; opera singer, prima donna, diva; protagonist, lead, leading man, leading lady, juvenile lead, understudy, stand-in, body double, stunt man *or* woman, stunt double; extra, bit player; chorus, gentlemen *or* ladies of the chorus; troupe, company, repertory company; characters, cast, dramatis personae performance artist, flash mob.

entertainer, performer, artiste, artist, drag artist, striptease artist, exotic dancer, fan dancer; impressionist, impersonator, female impersonator; troubadour, minstrel; busker; crooner, pop singer 413 *vocalist*; comic, comedian, comedienne, stand-up comedian 839 *humorist*; ventriloquist, fire-eater, juggler; circus artiste, tightrope-walker, acrobat, bareback rider, etc. 162 *athlete*; clown, pierrot, Punch; dancer, dancing girl, hoofer, show girl, chorus girl, cancan dancer, belly dancer, gogo dancer, flashdancer, pole dancer, table dancer, lap dancer; ballet dancer, ballerina, prima ballerina, corps de ballet.

stage manager, producer, director, actor manager, business manager, press agent *or* officer; impresario, showman; backer, sponsor, angel.

dramatist, playwright, dramaturge, scenario writer, script writer, librettist; choreographer.

theatregoer, playgoer, operagoer, filmgoer, cinemagoer; film fan, opera buff, balletomane 504 *enthusiast*; first-nighter; stage-door Johnny; audience, house, packed house, full house, sell-out; stalls, pit, gods, gallery; dramatic critic, play *or* film reviewer.

Adj. *dramatic*, theatrical, stagy; operatic, balletic, Terpsichorean, choreographic; live, legitimate; Thespian; histrionic, camp; tragic, comic, tragicomic; farcical, burlesque, knockabout, slapstick 849 *funny*; melodramatic, sensational, horrific, blood and thunder 821 *exciting*; avant-garde; released, showing, running 522 *shown*; dramatized; camped up; barnstorming; on the stage; stagestruck, filmstruck.

Vb. *dramatize*, write plays, write for the stage; make a play of, adapt for the stage *or* for radio; stage, mount, produce, direct, stage-manage; cast; star, feature; present, put on, release 522 *show*; open, raise *or* ring up the curtain.

act, go on the stage, tread the boards; face the cameras; perform, enact, play, playact, do a play; impersonate; take the part; mime, take off 20 *imitate*; create a role, play a part, play the lead; play opposite, support; star, co-star, get one's name in lights, steal the show, upstage, take all the limelight; play to the gallery, ham, camp it up, send up, barnstorm, overact 546 *exaggerate*; underact, throw away; walk on; understudy, stand in 150 *substitute*; rehearse, say one's lines, cue in; fluff, forget one's lines, dry; ad-lib, gag; take a curtain call, do an encore, receive a standing ovation.

Volition: the exercise of the will

5.1
Individual Volition

SECTION ONE

Volition in general

595 Will

N. *will*, volition; disposition, inclination, mind, cast of mind, fancy, preference 597 *willingness*; act of will; strength of will, willpower, determination, firmness of purpose 599 *resolution*; self-control 942 *temperance*; purpose 617 *intention*; decision 608 *predetermination*; one's own sweet will 932 *selfishness*; iron will, wilfulness 602 *obstinacy*; whimsicality 604 *caprice*; free will, self-determination 744 *independence*; free choice, option, discretion 605 *choice*; voluntariness, spontaneousness, spontaneity 597 *voluntary work*.

Adj. *volitional*, willing; unprompted, unasked, unbidden, freewill, spontaneous, original 597 *voluntary*; discretionary, optional; self-willed, iron-willed, wayward, wilful 602 *obstinate*; arbitrary, autocratic, dictatorial 735 *authoritarian*; independent; determined, hell-bent 599 *resolute*; intentional, willed, intended 608 *predetermined*.

Vb. *will*, exercise the will; impose one's will, have one's way, have it all one's own way 737 *command*; do what one chooses, do as one likes 744 *be free*; be so minded, have a mind to, see fit, think fit, think best 605 *choose*; determine 617 *intend*; wish 859 *desire*; have a mind of one's own, be independent, go one's own way, do as one chooses, be one's own man *or* woman; exercise one's discretion, judge for oneself 480 *judge*; take the responsibility, take it upon oneself; be hell-bent on, take the law into one's own hands, take the bit between one's teeth 602 *be obstinate*; know one's own mind 599 *be resolute*; volunteer, offer, do of one's own accord, do without prompting 597 *be willing*.

596 Necessity

N. *necessity*, stern necessity, no alternative, no escape, no option, zero option, Hobson's choice, the only show *or* game in town 606 *no choice*; last shift, last resort 700 *predicament*; inevitability, the inevitable, inescapability, sure thing, what must be 155 *destiny*; determinism, fatalism 608 *predetermination*; pressure of events, pressure of work, force of circumstances, circumstances beyond one's control, act of God, fatality 154 *event*; no freedom 745 *subjection*; law of nature; superior force 740 *compulsion*; logical necessity, necessary conclusion, proof 478 *demonstration*; force of law 953 *law*; obligation, conscience 917 *duty*; indispensability, acid test, sine qua non, a necessity, a must, matter of life and death, must-do, must-have, must-see 627 *requirement*; want, lack 801 *poverty*; involuntariness, reflex action; instinct, impulse, blind impulse 476 *intuition*.

fate, inexorable fate, lot, portion; weird, karma, kismet; doom, die, predestination, destiny; book of fate, God's will, will of Allah; fortune, wheel of fortune 159 *chance*; stars, planets, astral influence; Dame Fortune, the Fates; Destinies; Weird Sisters, Lachesis, Clotho, Atropos.

Adj. *necessary*, indispensable, essential, vital, important, requisite, must-do, must-have, must-see 627 *required*; imperative; overriding, irresistible; compulsory, mandatory, binding 917 *obligatory*; necessitated, inevitable, unavoidable, inescapable, inexorable, life-and-death 473 *certain*; sure thing, leaving no choice, deterministic.

involuntary, instinctive 476 *intuitive*; unpremeditated, unintended 618 *unintentional*; unconscious, subliminal, unthinking, gut, unwitting, blind, impulsive 609 *spontaneous*; under a spell 983 *bewitched*; conditioned, reflex, automatic, mechanical.

fated, karmic, fatal; predestined, preordained 608 *predetermined*; doomed, precondemned 961 *condemned*.

Vb. *be forced*, compelled, etc. (see adj.);

incur the necessity; submit to the necessity 721 *submit*; be fated, bow to fate, dree one's weird; be cornered, be driven into a corner, be pushed to the wall 700 *be in difficulty*; be faced with a sine qua non, have no choice, have no option, have zero option, needs must; make a virtue of necessity; be unable to help it.

necessitate, dictate, impose, oblige 740 *compel*; bind by fate, destine, doom, foredoom, predetermine 155 *predestine*; brook no denial, not take no for an answer; leave no choice, face with a sine qua non, impose the necessity, drive into a corner, bulldoze; demand 627 *require*.

Adv. *necessarily*, as a matter of course, by force of circumstances, of necessity, perforce, when *or* if push comes to shove, willy-nilly; nothing for it, no help for it, needs must.

597 Willingness

N. *willingness*, voluntariness, volunteering; spontaneousness 609 *spontaneity*; free choice, option 605 *choice*; disposition; inclination, fancy, leaning, bent, bias, penchant, propensity 179 *tendency*; facility 694 *aptitude*; predisposition, readiness, right mood, receptive frame of mind; acquiescence 488 *assent*; compliance 758 *consent*; cheerful consent, alacrity, gameness, eagerness, enthusiasm; initiative, impatience, over-eagerness; dedication, sacrifice 931 *disinterestedness*; helpfulness 706 *cooperation*; loyalty 739 *obedience*; pliancy, putty in one's hands, docility, tractability 612 *persuadability*; submissiveness 721 *submission*; obsequiousness 879 *servility*.

voluntary work, voluntary service, VSO 901 *philanthropy*; honorary employment, unpaid labour, labour of love, self-appointed task.

volunteer, unpaid worker, willing horse; no slouch; do-gooder 901 *philanthropist*.

Adj. *willing*, ungrudging, acquiescent 488 *assenting*; compliant, game for, up for it; in the mood, feeling like, receptive, inclined, disposed, well-disposed, predisposed, amenable; cordial; happy, pleased, glad, delighted; ready 669 *prepared*; ready and willing, prompt, quick 678 *active*; forward; eager, enthusiastic, dedicated, overeager, impatient, raring to go; doing one's best; helpful 706 *cooperative*; docile, biddable, easy-going 24 *agreeing*; submissive 721 *submitting*; obsequious 879 *servile*; desirous, dying to.

voluntary, unprompted, unsought, unasked, unbidden 609 *spontaneous*; unsolicited, uncalled for, self-imposed; beyond the call of duty; discretionary, optional 605 *chosen*; volunteering, on one's own initiative, off one's own bat, of one's own free will; gratuitous,

honorary, unpaid 812 *free of charge*.

Vb. *be willing*, be ready, etc. (see adj.); have half a mind to; feel like, have a fancy to, have a good mind to 595 *will*; agree, acquiesce 488 *assent*; show willing, be ready and waiting, comply 758 *consent*; be found willing 739 *obey*; try, do one's best 671 *attempt*; go out of one's way to, lean over backwards; collaborate 706 *cooperate*; meet halfway; jump at, leap at; can't wait, be burning to, be thrilled at the idea; not hesitate; volunteer, sacrifice oneself 759 *offer oneself*.

Adv. *willingly*, with a will, with relish, cordially; voluntarily, spontaneously, without being asked; like a shot, at the drop of a hat; with open arms, with all one's heart, heart and soul, with a good grace, without demur, nothing loath; gladly, with pleasure.

598 Unwillingness

N. *unwillingness*, disinclination, reluctance; disagreement 489 *dissent*; demur, objection 468 *qualification*; protest 762 *deprecation*; recalcitrance 704 *opposition*; rejection 760 *refusal*; unhelpfuless, non-cooperation 702 *hindrance*; dissociation; faintheartedness, lack of zeal 860 *indifference*; backwardness 278 *slowness*; hesitation 858 *caution*; scruple, repugnance 861 *dislike*; recoil, aversion; bashfulness 874 *modesty*; negative attitude, negativeness, negativity, negativism; non-compliance 738 *disobedience*; refractoriness; grudging service; unreliability 474 *uncertainty*; shelving, postponement, procrastination, laziness 679 *sluggishness*; neglect, remissness 458 *negligence*.

Adj. *unwilling*, indisposed, loath, reluctant, averse; not prepared, not so minded, not in the mood, not feeling like; unconsenting, opposed; demurring; regretful, with regret 830 *regretting*; hesitant 858 *cautious*; shy, bashful 874 *modest*; unenthusiastic, half-hearted, lukewarm; backward; uncooperative; recalcitrant; perfunctory, remiss 458 *negligent*; grudging; unspontaneous, forced, begrudged, with bad grace.

Vb. *be unwilling*, be reluctant, etc. (see adj.); not have the heart to, not stomach 861 *dislike*; disagree, boggle, scruple 489 *dissent*; object, demur, protest 762 *deprecate*; resist 704 *oppose*; reject, give the thumbs down, give the red light 760 *refuse*; recoil, blench, fight shy, duck, shirk 620 *avoid*; drag one's feet, hold back, hesitate, tread warily, hang fire, go slow 278 *move slowly*; not play ball, abstain 702 *obstruct*; grudge, begrudge, turn up one's nose; force oneself; have regrets 830 *regret*; tear oneself away 296 *depart*.

599 Resolution

N. *resolution*, sticking point, resoluteness, determination, grim determination; zeal, ardour, earnestness, seriousness; resolve, mind made up, decision 608 *predetermination*; drive, vigour 174 *vigorousness*; energy; concentration, iron will, willpower 595 *will*; strength of character, self-control, self-restraint, self-possession; tenacity 600 *perseverance*; aplomb, mettle, daring, dash, élan 712 *attack*; guts, pluck, spunk, grit, backbone, spirit; fortitude, stiff upper lip, gritted teeth, moral fibre 855 *courage*; single-mindedness, commitment, total commitment, devotedness, devotion, dedication; reliability, staunchness, steadiness, constancy, firmness 153 *stability*; insistence, pressure 740 *compulsion*; sternness, relentlessness, ruthlessness, inexorability, implacability 906 *pitilessness*; inflexibility, steeliness 326 *hardness*; iron, steel, rock; clenched teeth, hearts of oak, bulldog breed 600 *stamina*.

Adj. *resolute*, resolved, made up, determined 597 *willing*; desperate, stopping at nothing, all out; serious, earnest, concentrated; intent upon, set upon, bent upon; insistent, pressing, urgent, driving, forceful, energetic, heroic 174 *vigorous*; firm, staunch, reliable, constant 153 *unchangeable*; iron-willed, strong-willed, strong-minded, decisive, unbending, immovable, unyielding, inflexible, uncompromising, intransigent 602 *obstinate*; stern, grim, inexorable, implacable, relentless, ruthless, merciless 906 *pitiless*; iron, steely; undaunted, nothing daunted; steadfast, unwavering, unshaken, unshakable, unflinching, game, tenacious 600 *persevering*; indomitable; steeled, armoured, proof; self-controlled, self-restrained 942 *temperate*; self-possessed, self-reliant, self-confident; purposeful, single-minded, whole-hearted, committed, devoted, dedicated, card-carrying.

Vb. *be resolute*, be determined, etc. (see adj.); steel oneself, brace oneself; clench *or* grit one's teeth (see also *stand firm* below); make up one's mind, take a resolution, will, resolve, determine, purpose 617 *intend*; decide, fix, seal, conclude, finish with 69 *terminate*; take on oneself, accept responsibility 595 *will*; know one's own mind, insist, press, urge, not take no for an answer 532 *emphasize*; cut through, override, put one's foot down, stand no nonsense; mean business, stick at nothing, not stop at trifles, go to all lengths, go to any length, push to extremes; go the whole hog, see it through 725 *carry through*; face, face the odds, take on all comers 661 *face danger*; bell the cat, outface, dare 711 *defy*; endure, go through fire and water 825 *suffer*; face the issue, bring to a head, take the bull by the horns; take the plunge, cross the Rubicon, burn one's boats, burn one's bridges, throw

down the gauntlet, nail one's colours to the mast; be single-minded, set one's heart on, take up, go in for, take up in earnest, devote *or* dedicate oneself, commit oneself, give oneself to, give up everything for; set to, buckle to, go to it, put one's shoulder to the wheel, put one's heart into, grapple, strain 682 *exert oneself*.

stand firm, not be moved, dig one's toes *or* heels in, stand one's ground, stay put; not budge, not yield, not compromise, not give an inch; never despair, stand fast, hold out 600 *persevere*; be hell-bent on, bear the brunt, have what it takes, fight on, soldier on, stick it out, grin and bear it, endure 825 *suffer*; fight to the death, die with one's boots on; go down with colours flying.

600 Perseverance

N. *perseverance*, persistence, tenacity, pertinacity, stickability, stubbornness 602 *obstinacy*; staunchness, constancy, steadfastness 599 *resolution*; single-mindedness, commitment, singleness of purpose, concentration 455 *attention*; sedulousness, application, tirelessness, indefatigability, assiduousness, industriousness 678 *assiduousness*; doggedness, plodding, hard work 682 *exertion*; endurance, patience, fortitude 825 *suffering*; maintenance 146 *continuance*; ceaselessness 144 *permanence*; repeated efforts, unflagging efforts 106 *repetition*.

stamina, endurance, staying power, indefatigability, fortitude 162 *strength*; grit, true grit, backbone, gameness, guts, gutsiness, pluck; bulldog courage 855 *courage*.

Adj. *persevering*, persistent, tenacious, stubborn 602 *obstinate*; game, gutsy, plucky; patient, plodding, dogged, trying hard 678 *industrious*; strenuous 682 *labouring*; steady, unfaltering, unwavering, enduring, unflagging, unwearied, untiring, indefatigable; unfailing, unremitting, constant, unceasing; indomitable, unconquerable; undaunted, nothing daunted, undiscouraged, game to the last, going down fighting, true to the end 599 *resolute*.

Vb. *persevere*, persist, keep at it, not take no for an answer, hold out for; not despair, never despair, never say die, never give up hope, hope on 852 *hope*; endure, have what it takes, come up for more 825 *suffer*; try, keep on trying, try and try again, renew one's efforts 671 *attempt*; maintain, keep up, follow up 146 *sustain*; plod, slog away, peg away, plug away, hammer away at, work at 682 *work*, 689 *deal with*; continue, go on, keep on, keep the pot boiling, keep the ball rolling, rally, keep going;

not let go, cling, hold fast, maintain one's grip, hang on like grim death 778 *retain*; hang on, stick it out, sweat it out, stay the course, stick with it, see it through, stay till the end; be in at the death, survive 41 *be left*; maintain one's ground, not budge, dig in one's heels, grit one's teeth 602 *be obstinate*; stick to one's guns, hold out, hold out to the last, die at one's post 599 *stand firm*; work till one drops, die with one's boots on, die in harness; spare no pains, move heaven and earth 682 *exert oneself*; bring to conclusion, see the end of, complete 725 *carry through*.

601 Irresolution

N. *irresolution*, irresoluteness, faintheartedness, squeamishness, loss of nerve, spinelessness, no backbone, no grit 856 *cowardice*; non-perseverance, broken promise 603 *change of mind*; indecision, uncertainty, doubt, floating vote 474 *dubiety*; hesitation, inconstancy, fluctuation, vacillation, variability, blowing hot and cold 152 *changeableness*; levity, fickleness, whimsicality, irresponsibility 604 *caprice*; passivity 679 *inactivity*; compromise 734 *laxity*; lukewarmness, apathy 860 *indifference*; weak will 163 *weakness*; suggestibility 612 *persuadability*; pliancy, putty in one's hands, obsequiousness 879 *servility*; submissiveness.

Adj. *irresolute*, undecided, indecisive, in or of two minds, wavering, vacillating; unable to make up one's mind, stalling, undetermined, unresolved, uncertain 474 *doubting*; hesitating 598 *unwilling*; faint-hearted; lukewarm 860 *indifferent*; infirm of purpose 474 *unreliable*; characterless; compromising, weak-willed, weak-kneed, spineless 163 *weak*; flexible, pliant, putty-like 327 *soft*; inconstant, variable; whimsical, mercurial, not to be pinned down, grasshopper-like 604 *capricious*; restless, unsteady; uncommitted, giddy; superficial 456 *inattentive*.

Vb. *be irresolute*, be undecided, etc. (see adj.); back away, shy, shirk 620 *avoid*; shilly-shally 518 *be equivocal*; fluctuate, vacillate, seesaw, waver, sway, hover, teeter, stall, dither 317 *oscillate*; not know one's own mind, blow hot and cold, back and fill, be in two minds, go round in circles, not know what to do, be at one's wits' end 474 *be uncertain*; hum and haw, etc. 280 *stammer*; leave in suspense, delay, put off a decision, put off until tomorrow 136 *put off*; dilly-dally 136 *wait*; debate, balance, weigh up the pros and cons, seesaw 475 *argue*; have second thoughts, hesitate 858 *be cautious*; falter, not persevere, give up 621 *relinquish*; make a compromise, take half meas-

ures 770 *compromise*; yield, give way 721 *submit*; change sides.

602 Obstinacy

N. *obstinacy*, mind of one's own; determination, will, single-mindedness 599 *resolution*; doggedness, tenacity, bulldog tenacity, pertinacity 600 *perseverance*; stubbornness, obduracy, obdurateness; pigheadedness; inflexibility, immovability, toughness 326 *hardness*; intransigence, hard line, hard core, no compromise; constancy, irreversibility, fixity 153 *stability*; stiff neck; incorrigibility 940 *impenitence*; intractability, mulishness, dourness, sulkiness 893 *sullenness*; perversity, wrongheadedness, cussedness, bloody-mindedness.

opinionatedness, dogmatism, bigotry, zealotry; intolerance, fanaticism 735 *severity*; ruling passion, obsession, idée fixe, monomania 481 *bias*; old school.

Adj. *obstinate*, stubborn, obdurate; pigheaded, mulish; pertinacious, unyielding, firm, determined 599 *resolute*; dogged, bulldog-like, tenacious; adamant, inflexible, unbending; obdurate, hard-nosed, hardened, case-hardened; uncompromising, hard-core, intransigent; unrelenting, immovable 153 *unchangeable*; inexorable, implacable; set in one's ways, hidebound; impervious; opinionated, dogmatic, pedantic 473 *positive*; obsessed, bigoted, fanatical 481 *biased*; contumacious, rebellious 738 *disobedient*; dour, grim 893 *sullen*; stiff-necked; perverse, incorrigible, bloody-minded, plain cussed; persistent, incurable, chronic 113 *lasting*.

wilful, self-willed, pig-headed, bull-headed, mulish, wayward; headstrong, perverse; unruly, refractory; unmanageable, intractable, uncontrollable 738 *disobedient*; incorrigible.

Vb. *be obstinate*, be stubborn, etc. (see adj.); persist 600 *persevere*; brazen it out 940 *be impenitent*; stick to one's guns, dig in one's heels, stand out, not budge, stay put 599 *stand firm*; insist, brook no denial, not take no for an answer; must have one's way; not change one's mind 473 *dogmatize*; stay in a rut, cling to custom 610 *be in the habit of*; not listen, stop up one's ears, take no advice, take the bit between one's teeth, damn the consequences 857 *be rash*; not yield to treatment, become chronic 113 *last*.

603 Change of mind

N. *change of mind*, tergiversation, better thoughts; afterthought, second thoughts 67 *sequel*; change of allegiance, conversion; change of purpose, alteration of plan, mission creep; new resolve; break with the past, repentance 939 *penitence*; revulsion 280 *recoil*; backsliding; shifting ground, change of direction 282 *deviation*; reversal, back-pedalling, veering round, about-face, about-turn, U-turn, volte-face, looking back 286 *return*; apostasy, turning renegade *or* traitor, defection, desertion 918 *undutifulness*; ratting, going over, treachery 930 *perfidiousness*; secession; abandonment 621 *relinquishment*; change of mood, mood swing.

    recantation, eating one's words, retraction, withdrawal, apology; renunciation, forswearing; disclaimer, denial 533 *negation*; revocation.

    recanter, tergiversator, turncoat, rat; back-pedaller; opportunist, timeserver, Vicar of Bray 518 *equivocalness*; double-dealer, two-faced person 545 *deceiver*; jilt; apostate, renegade; traitor, Judas, betrayer 938 *knave*; quisling, fifth columnist, collaborationist 707 *collaborator*; deserter, defector, quitter, ratter; grass 524 *informer*; strike-breaker, blackleg, scab; seceder 978 *schismatic*; runaway; backslider 904 *offender*; convert.

    Vb. *change one's mind*, tergiversate, think again, think better of it 601 *be irresolute*; change one's tune, shift one's ground 152 *vary*; get cold feet, back out, scratch, withdraw 753 *resign*; back down, crawl 872 *be humbled*; apologize (see also *recant* below); change round, swerve, tack, veer round, do a U-turn, backpedal, wheel about 282 *turn round*; turn one's back on 286 *turn back*; turn over a new leaf, repent 939 *be penitent*; reform, mend one's ways 654 *get better*; backslide 657 *relapse*; ditch, jilt, throw over, desert, walk out on 918 *fail in duty*; turn against.

    apostatize, turn one's coat, be a turncoat, change sides, change one's allegiance, turn renegade *or* traitor; switch over, join the opposition, cross over, cross the floor, go over, desert, defect; blackleg, rat; betray, collaborate 930 *be dishonest*; be off with the old love, follow the rising star.

    recant, unsay, eat one's words, eat one's hat; eat humble pie, apologize; take back, go back on, backpedal, backtrack, do a U-turn; withdraw 769 *not observe*; retract, disclaim, repudiate, deny 533 *negate*; renounce, abjure, forswear, recall, revoke, rescind 752 *annul*.

604 Caprice

N. *caprice*, capriciousness, arbitrariness; whimsicality, freakishness; faddishness, faddism, fad-surfing; inconsistency 25 *disagreement*; fitfulness, changeability, variability, fickleness, unreliability, levity, giddiness, irresponsibility 152 *changeableness*; inconstancy, coquettishness, flirtatiousness; channel-hopping.

    whim, whimsy, caprice, fancy; passing fancy, impulse 609 *spontaneity*; vagary, humour, mood, fit, bee in the bonnet, quirk, kink, fad, craze, freak, idiosyncrasy 503 *eccentricity*; escapade, prank; coquetry, flirtation.

    Adj. *capricious*, whimsical, fanciful, fantastic; eccentric, temperamental, crotchety, freakish, fitful; mad 503 *crazy*; mischievous; wayward, perverse; faddy; arbitrary, unreasonable; fretful, moody, contrary 892 *irascible*; refractory 602 *wilful*; erratic, uncertain, unpredictable 508 *unexpected*; volatile, mercurial, skittish, giddy, frivolous 456 *lacking concentration*; inconsistent, inconstant, variable; irresponsible, unreliable, fickle, feckless; coquettish.

    Vb. *be capricious*, be whimsical, etc. (see adj.); take it into one's head, have a sudden fancy for; chop and change, blow hot and cold 152 *vary*; be fickle; vacillate 601 *be irresolute*; flirt.

605 Choice

N. *choice*, election 463 *discrimination*; picking and choosing, finickiness 862 *fastidiousness*; picking out, selection; triage; co-option, adoption; nomination, appointment 751 *commission*; option; freedom of choice, discretion, pick; decision 480 *judgment*; third way; preference, predilection, partiality, inclination, leaning, bias 179 *tendency*; taste 859 *liking*; availability 759 *offer*; range of choice, assortment, list, raft, range, selection, embarras de choix 43 *medley*; possible choice, alternative, short list, short leet; difficult choice, difficult decision, tough call; dilemma 474 *dubiety*; limited choice, no real alternative; no choice, no alternative, nothing for it but 606 *no choice*; preferability, desirability; favour, fancy; first choice, top seed; selection, excerpts; the best of; literary selection 592 *anthology*; deselection.

    vote, voice 485 *opinion*; representation, proportional representation; cumulative vote, transferable vote, single transferable vote; majority vote, first past the post; one man one vote, OMOV; alternative voting, additional member system; casting vote; ballot, secret ballot, postal vote; vote of confidence; vote of no confidence, blackballing; vote-counting, show of hands, division, poll, straw poll, plebiscite, referendum; suffrage, universal suffrage; franchise, votes for women, women's suffrage, suffragettism; electoral system, ballot box, vox populi; polling, counting heads; straw vote, Gallup poll (tdmk), Mori poll (tdmk), opinion poll; election, general election; by-election; local election, local-government election; primary; polls, voting, e-voting; election campaign, electioneering, whistle-stop tour, battle bus, canvassing; door-stepping, polling, hustings, candidature; gerry-mandering; election fatigue; chad; return; psephology, psephologist; suffragette.

electorate, voters, elector, electoral college; quorum; electoral roll; constituent, constituency, marginal constituency; borough, pocket borough, rotten borough; polling booth, ballot box, voting paper; ticket, manifesto.

Adj. *chosen*, well-chosen; select, choice, hand-picked 644 *excellent*; seeded 62 *arranged*; elect, designate; elected; adopted, selected; deselected; on approval, on appro; favourite, pet; God's own; by appointment.

Vb. *choose*, make one's choice, make one's bed; shop around, be choosy, be picky; exercise one's discretion, accept, opt for, take up an option; elect, co-opt, adopt; favour, fancy; incline, lean, have a bias 179 *tend*; prefer, have a preference; think it best to, make up one's mind 480 *judge*; settle on, fix on, plump fur; take sides, back, support, embrace, espouse, throw in one's lot with 703 *patronize*.

select, pick, single out; pass 923 *approve*; nominate, appoint 751 *commission*; designate, detail, mark out; preselect, earmark, reserve 46 *set apart*; recommend, put up, propose, second 703 *patronize*; cull; glean, winnow, sift 463 *discriminate*; separate; skim off, cream, pick the best; take one's pick, cherry-pick, pick and choose 862 *be fastidious*.

vote, have a vote, have a voice, have a say; be enfranchised, be on the electoral roll; poll, go to the polls; cast a vote, register one's vote, raise one's hand; vote for, elect, return; deselect, vote with one's feet 607 *reject*; electioneer, canvass; stand 759 *offer oneself*; put to the vote, hold a referendum; count heads, count noses, count straws; hold an election, go to the country, appeal to the electorate, ask for a vote of confidence.

606 Absence of choice

N. *no choice*, Hobson's choice, no alternative, no option, zero option, the only game or show in town 596 *necessity*; any, the first that comes 464 *lack of discrimination*; neutrality; no difference, six of one and half a dozen of the other, a plague on both your houses 28 *equality*.

Vb. *be neutral*, take no sides, not vote, be a don't know, abstain; sit on the fence 601 *be irresolute*; not know.

have no choice, have no alternative, have Hobson's choice; have no or zero option; take it or leave it, make a virtue of necessity, make the best of a bad job 596 *be forced*; have no say.

Adv. *neither*, neither . . . nor . . .

607 Rejection

N. *rejection*, non-acceptance; repudiation, denial 533 *negation*; rebuff, frozen mitt, cold shoulder 760 *refusal*; spurning, kick, more kicks than ha'pence, more bricks than bouquets; electoral defeat; elimination 300 *ejection*; exemption 57 *exclusion*; discarding, deselection, disemployment 674 *non-use*; reject, wallflower; no-hoper, lost cause.

Vb. *reject*, decline, say no to, draw the line at, rebuff, repulse, spurn, dismiss out of hand, opt out 760 *refuse*; send back; pass over, ignore 458 *disregard*; vote against; scrap, discard, deselect, ditch, junk, throw away, throw aside, lay aside, give up 674 *stop using*; disallow, revoke 752 *annul*; set aside; expel, cast out, throw out, chuck out, sling out, kick out, fling out 300 *eject*; kick upstairs; sort out 44 *eliminate*; exempt 57 *exclude*; blackball, cold-shoulder, hand the frozen mitt to, turn one's back on, give the brush-off 885 *be rude*; disclaim, deny 533 *negate*; abnegate, repudiate; disdain, deride 851 *ridicule*; turn up one's nose at, sniff at, look a gift horse in the mouth 922 *hold cheap*; opt out.

Int. *thanks but no thanks.*

608 Predetermination

N. *predetermination*, predestination, preordination, foreordination 155 *destiny*, 596 *fate*; decree 595 *will*; premeditation; prearrangement 669 *preparation*; order of the day, order paper, agenda 622 *business*; frame-up, put-up job, packed jury 623 *plot*; closed mind 481 *prejudice*; foregone conclusion.

Adj. *predetermined*, decreed, premeditated, etc. (see vb.); predestined, preordained, foreordained; deliberate, aforethought; with a motive, studied, calculated, measured; weighed, considered, advised; devised, controlled, contrived 623 *planned*; put-up, framed, stacked, packed, prearranged 669 *prepared*.

Vb. *predetermine*, predestine, preordain; premeditate, preconceive; agree beforehand; fix; contrive, arrange, prearrange 623 *plan*; frame, put up, pack a jury, stack the cards 541 *fake*.

609 Spontaneity

N. *spontaneity*, ad-hoc measures, improvisation; extemporization, ad-libbing, impromptu, thinking on one's feet 670 *non-preparation*; involuntariness, reflex, automatic reflex; automatic pilot; impulsiveness, impulse, blind impulse, instinct 476 *intuition*; spur of the moment; snap decision; burst of confidence

526 *disclosure*; inspiration, sudden thought, hunch, flash 451 *idea*.

Adj. spontaneous, off-the-cuff, ad hoc, improvised, ad-lib, extemporaneous, extemporary, sudden, snap; ad-libbing; makeshift; impromptu, unpremeditated, unrehearsed 618 *unintentional*; unprompted, unmotivated, unprovoked; instinctive, involuntary, automatic, knee-jerk; impulsive.

Vb. improvise, extemporize, think on one's feet, vamp, ad-lib, busk it 670 *be unprepared*; obey an impulse, act on the spur of the moment 604 *be capricious*; blurt, come out with, say whatever comes into one's head, have a sudden brainwave; rise to the occasion.

Adv. extempore, impromptu, ad hoc, on the spur of the moment, off the cuff, off the top of one's head, ad lib.

610 Habit

N. habit, disposition; force of habit; second nature; occupation; addiction, confirmed habit, constitutional; trait, idiosyncrasy; knack, trick, mannerism; instinct, leaning 179 *tendency*; bad habit; usage, custom, old custom, mores; use, wont 146 *continuance*; inveteracy; tradition, law, precedent; way, ways, the old ways; lifestyle, way of life; beaten track, tramlines, groove, rut; fixed ways, daily round, daily grind, regularity 141 *periodic recurrence*; routine, drill, system 60 *order*; red tape, bureaucracy, conventionalism, traditionalism, conservatism, old school 83 *conformity*; usual suspects.

practice, common practice, matter of course; conventionality 83 *conformity*; mores, behaviour patterns; institution, ritual, observance 988 *rite*; religious observance; mode, vogue, craze, in-thing; order of the day 848 *fashion*; convention, protocol, unwritten law, done thing, the usual thing; recognized procedure, drill, fire drill, fire practice; form, good form, netiquette 848 *etiquette*; manners, table manners, eating habits; rules and regulations, house rules, standing order, routine 688 *conduct*.

habituation, training, indoctrination 534 *teaching*; inurement, hardening; naturalization, acclimatization; conditioning, reflex, conditioned reflex, drill, routine.

creature of habit, habitué, addict; traditionalist, conventionalist 83 *conformist*; regular, client 792 *purchaser*; frequenter, devotee, fan, groupie, camp follower 504 *enthusiast*.

Adj. habitual, customary; routine; conventional, traditional 976 *orthodox*; inveterate, time-honoured; habit-forming; ingrained, dyed-in-the-wool, bred in the bone 5 *inherent*;

rooted, deep-rooted, deep-seated; imbued, soaked, permeated.

usual, accustomed, normal, traditional, wonted; in character, natural; household, familiar, well-known 490 *known*; unoriginal, hackneyed; banal, commonplace, common, ordinary 79 *general*; set, stock, stereotyped 83 *typical*; widespread 79 *universal*; monthly, daily, everyday 139 *frequent*; practised, done; acknowledged, received, accepted, understood; established, official, hallowed by custom; de rigueur 740 *compelling*; invariable 153 *unchangeable*; in, in vogue 848 *fashionable*.

accustomed to, habituated, in the habit of, given to, addicted to; devoted to, wedded to; used to, familiar with, conversant with, au fait with, at home in 490 *knowing*; inveterate, confirmed; practised, inured, seasoned, incorrigible, hardened 669 *prepared*; broken in, trained, tame 369 *tamed*; naturalized, acclimatized.

Vb. be in the habit of, be wont, be used to, be a creature of habit; haunt, frequent; make a habit of, take up, embrace, go in for; be set in one's ways, be in a rut, stick in a groove, become a habit, catch on, grow on one, take hold of one, stick; take root; be the rule, obtain, hold good 178 *prevail*; acquire the force of custom.

accustom oneself, habituate, habituate oneself, get used to, get into the way of, get the knack of, get the feel of, get the hang of, warm up, get into one's stride; take to, acquire the habit; get into a habit, catch oneself doing; keep one's hand in, practise 106 *repeat*; accustom, inure, season, train; domesticate, tame 369 *break in*; naturalize, acclimatize; imbue 534 *teach*; condition, brainwash 178 *influence*.

611 Disuse

N. disuse, desuetude, discontinuance 674 *nonuse*; rust, decay 655 *deterioration*; rustiness, lack of practice 695 *lack of skill*; discarded custom 550 *obliteration*; weaning 134 *adultness*; not the thing, not etiquette, unconventionality 84 *nonconformity*; inexperience, unfamiliarity 491 *ignorance*.

Adj. not customary, unwonted, not done; not de rigueur; unfashionable, bad form, non-U 847 *vulgar*; out of fashion, old hat, defunct 125 *past*; discarded 674 *disused*; unconventional 84 *unconformable*; untraditional, unprecedented,

unaccustomed, unhabituated, not in the habit of 769 *non-observant*; untrained, undomesticated; unfamiliar, inexperienced, new, raw, fresh, callow, green, bumfluffed 491 *uninstructed*; weaned; out of the habit, rusty 695 *unskilful*.

Vb. *disaccustom*, wean from, cure of 656 *cure*; break a habit, kick the habit; dry out; wean oneself from, outgrow; give up, throw off, slough off, shed.

612 Motive

N. *motive*, cause of action, what is behind it; rationale, reasons, grounds 156 *reason why*; motivation, driving force, impetus, mainspring, what makes one tick, what turns one on 156 *causation*; intention 617 *objective*; ideal, principle, guiding principle; aspiration 852 *hope*; ambition 859 *desire*; calling, call 622 *vocation*; conscience, dictate of conscience, personal reasons, ulterior motive, hidden agenda 932 *selfishness*; impulse.

inducement, pressure, urgency, insistence, pester power, toddler tourism; lobbying 178 *influence*; indirect influence; provocation, urging, incitement, encouragement, incitation, instigation, prompting; support, abetment 703 *aid*; solicitation, invitation 761 *request*; temptation, enticement, carrot, allurement, seduction, seductiveness, fascination, charm, charm offensive, sex appeal, it, attractiveness, magnetism 291 *attraction*; blandishment 925 *flattery*; coaxing, wheedling 889 *endearment*; persuasion, persuasiveness, salesmanship, sales talk, spiel, patter 579 *eloquence*; pep talk, rallying cry 547 *call*; exhortation 534 *lecture*; pleading, advocacy 691 *advice*; propaganda, spin, agitprop; advertising, sales promotion, soft sell, hard sell 528 *advertisement*; promises, election promises; bribery, bribery and corruption, graft, palm-greasing, back-scratching 962 *reward*; honeyed words, winning ways.

persuadability, persuasibility, docility, tractability, willingness; pliancy, pliability, putty in one's hands 327 *softness*; susceptibility, impressibility; credulousness 487 *credulity*.

incentive, inducement; stimulus, fillip, tickle, prod, spur, goad, lash, whip; rod, big stick, crack of the whip 900 *threat*; energizer, tonic, carrot, carrot and stick, jam tomorrow, sop, sop to Cerberus 174 *stimulant*; charm 983 *spell*; attraction, magnet; lure, decoy, decoy duck, bait 542 *trap*; come-on, loss leader, special offer; profit 771 *gain*; cash, gold 797 *money*; pay, salary, perks, pay increase, increment, rise, raise, bonus 804 *payment*; donation, handout, freebie 781 *gift*; gratuity, tip, bribe, hush money, slush fund 962 *reward*; forbidden fruit; tempting offer, offer one cannot refuse 759 *offer*.

motivator, prime motivator 156 *cause*; manipulator, wire-puller 178 *influence*; manoeuvrer, tactician, strategist 623 *planner*; instigator, prompter; inspirer; aider and abet-

tor 703 *helper*; agent provocateur 545 *deceiver*; tempter, seducer, seductress, temptress, vamp, femme fatale, siren, Circe, Lorelei; hypnotizer, hypnotist; orator, rhetorician 579 *speaker*; advocate; wheedler 925 *flatterer*; advertiser, promotion manager, propagandist 528 *publicizer*; ringleader 690 *leader*; firebrand, rabblerouser 738 *agitator*; lobbyist, lobby, pressure group, ginger group.

Vb. *motivate*, move, actuate, manipulate 173 *operate*; work upon, play upon, act upon, operate upon 178 *influence*; weigh, count, be a consideration, sway 178 *prevail*; call the tune, override 34 *predominate*; work on the feelings, appeal, challenge, shame into; infect, inject with, infuse into 534 *educate*; interest, intrigue 821 *impress*; charm, fascinate, captivate, hypnotize, spellbind 983 *bewitch*; turnon; pull 291 *attract*; push 279 *impel*; force, enforce 740 *compel*; bend, incline, dispose; predispose, prejudice 481 *bias*; predestine 608 *predetermine*; lead, direct 689 *manage*; lead astray 495 *mislead*; give a lead, set the fashion, be a trendsetter, set an example, set the pace 283 *precede*.

incite, energize, galvanize, stimulate 174 *invigorate*; encourage, cheer on, act as cheerleader, root for 855 *give courage*; inspire, animate, provoke, rouse, rally 821 *excite*; evoke, call forth, challenge; exhort, invite, urge, exert pressure, bring pressure to bear on, lobby; nag, needle, goad, prod, jog, jolt; spur, prick; whip, lash, flog; spur on, egg on; drive, hurry up 680 *hasten*; instigate, prompt, put up to; abet, aid and abet 703 *aid*; start, kindle 68 *initiate*.

induce, instigate, bring about 156 *cause*; persuade, carry with one 485 *convince*; prevail upon, talk into, push into, drive into, nag into, bully into, browbeat (see also *motivate* above); twist one's arm 740 *compel*; wear down, soften up; get round, bring round, talk round 147 *convert*; bring over, win over, procure, enlist, engage; talk over, sweet-talk into, coax into, cajole 925 *flatter*; entice, seduce.

tempt, lead into temptation; entice, hold out a carrot to, dangle before one's eyes, make one's mouth water; tantalize, tease; allure, lure, inveigle 542 *ensnare*; coax, wheedle.

bribe, offer an inducement, hold out a carrot 759 *offer*; suborn, seduce, corrupt; square, buy off; oil, grease the palm, give a sop to Cerberus; tip 962 *reward*.

Int. *encore!*, hear hear!, more!, right on!, way to go! 488 *yes*, 923 *bravo*.

613 Dissuasion

N. *dissuasion*, caution 664 *warning*; discouragement, setback 702 *hindrance*; deterrence

854 *intimidation*; objection, expostulation, remonstrance, reproof, admonition 762 *deprecation*; rebuff 715 *resistance*; disincentive; health warning; deterrent, red light 665 *danger signal*; contraindication; cold water, damper, wet blanket; killjoy, spoilsport.

Vb. dissuade persuade against, convince to the contrary, talk out of 479 *confute*; caution 664 *warn*; remonstrate; expostulate, protest against 762 *deprecate*; make one stop in one's tracks, give one pause 486 *cause doubt*; head off, steer one away from, turn one aside 282 *deflect*; keep back; disenchant, disillusion, disincline; set against, turn against, put off, repel; dishearten, discourage; throw cold water on, dampen, quench, cool, damp the ardour, be a wet blanket; take the edge off 257 *blunt*.

614 Pretext

N. pretext, ostensible motive, alleged motive, reason given; statement, allegation, profession, claim 532 *affirmation*; plea, excuse, defence, apology, rationale, justification 927 *vindication*; alibi 667 *means of escape*; peg to hang something on 218 *prop*; shallow pretext, lame excuse, quibble 477 *sophism*; proviso 468 *qualification*; subterfuge 698 *stratagem*; pretence, previous engagement, Bunbury, diplomatic illness 543 *untruth*; blind, red herring, dust thrown in the eyes; stalking horse, smoke screen, cloak, cover 421 *screen*; apology for, pale imitation of; colour, guise 445 *appearance*; bluff.

Adj. ostensible, alleged, pretended; seeming.

Vb. plead, allege, claim, give as one's reason *or* rationale, profess 532 *affirm*; make one's pretext, make a plea of 475 *argue*; make excuses, offer an excuse, excuse oneself, defend oneself 927 *justify*; gloss over; shelter behind, use as a stalking horse; make capital out of, cash in on 137 *profit by*; find a loophole, wriggle out of 667 *escape*; bluff; varnish, colour; blind, throw dust in the eyes, draw a red herring across.

615 Good

N. good, one's (own) good, what is good for one; advantage, benefit; the best; common good; lesser evil, utilitarianism 642 *good policy*; well-being, welfare 730 *prosperity*; riches 800 *wealth*; luck, good luck, fortune, good fortune; happy days, happy ending 824 *happiness*; blessing, world of good; well-wishing.

benefit, something to one's advantage, advantage, interest; convenience; crop, harvest, return 771 *acquisition*; profit, increment, gain; edification, betterment 654 *improvement*; boon 781 *gift*; good turn; favour, blessing,

blessing in disguise; turn-up for the book, godsend, windfall, legacy, piece of luck, treasure trove, find, prize; good thing.

Adj. good, goodly, fine; blessed, happy; advantageous, heaven-sent 644 *beneficial*; worthwhile 644 *valuable*; helpful 706 *cooperative*; praiseworthy, commendable, recommended 923 *approved*; edifying, moral 933 *virtuous*; pleasure-giving 826 *pleasurable*.

Vb. benefit, do good, help, avail, be of service; edify, advantage, profit; repay 771 *be profitable*; do one a power of good 654 *make better*; turn out well, be all for the best, come right in the end.

flourish, thrive, do well, be on top of the world, be on the crest of a wave; rise, rise in the world 730 *prosper*; arrive 727 *succeed*; benefit by, gain by, be the better for, improve 654 *get better*; turn to good account, cash in on 137 *profit by*; make a profit 771 *gain*; make money 800 *get rich*.

Adv. well, satisfactorily, favourably, profitably, happily, healthily, not amiss, all to the good; to one's advantage, to one's benefit, for the best, in one's best interests; in fine style, on the up and up; like hot cakes, like a bomb, like gangbusters.

616 Evil

N. evil, wickedness, iniquity, mischievousness, injuriousness, disservice, injury, putting the boot in, dirty trick; wrong, injury, outrage 914 *injustice*; crying shame, shame, abuse; curse, scourge, poison, pest, plague, sore, running sore 659 *bane*; ill, ills that flesh is heir to, Pandora's box; sad world, vale of tears; trouble, troubles 731 *adversity*; affliction, misery, distress 825 *suffering*; grief, woe 825 *sorrow*; unease, malaise, angst, discomfort 825 *worry*; nuisance 827 *annoyance*; hurt, bodily harm, wound, bruise, cut, gash 377 *pain*; blow, mortal blow, death blow, buffet, stroke 279 *knock*; body blow; outrageous fortune, slings and arrows, calamity, bad luck, sod's *or* Sod's law, Murphy's law 731 *misfortune*; casualty, accident 154 *event*; fatality 361 *death*; catastrophe 165 *ruin*; tragedy, sad ending 655 *deterioration*; mischief, devilry, harm, damage 772 *loss*; ill effect, bad result; disadvantage 35 *inferiority*; drawback, fly in the ointment 647 *defect*; setback 702 *hitch*; indigence 801 *poverty*; sense of injury, grievance 829 *discontent*; vindictiveness 910 *vengefulness*.

Adj. evil, wicked, iniquitous, sinful 934 *villainous*; black, foul, shameful 914 *wrong*; bad, too bad 645 *damnable*; unlucky, inauspicious, sinister 731 *adverse*; insidious, injurious, prejudicial, disadvantageous 645 *harmful*; troublemaking; troublous 827 *distressing*; fatal, fell, mortal, deathly 362 *deadly*; ruinous, disastrous 165 *destructive*; catastrophic, calamitous, tragic 731 *unfortunate*; all wrong, awry, out of joint, out of kilter.

Adv. *amiss*, wrong, awry, sour.

SECTION TWO

Prospective volition

617 Intention

N. *intention*, intent, meaning; deliberateness; calculation, calculated risk 480 *estimate*; purpose, determination, predetermination, resolve 599 *resolution*; mind 447 *intellect*; criminal intent 936 *guilt*; good intentions 897 *benevolence*; view, prospect; proposal; design 623 *plan*; enterprise 672 *undertaking*; ambition 859 *desire*; decision 480 *judgment*; ultimatum 766 *conditions*; bid, bid for 671 *attempt*; destination, end use 69 *end*.

objective, destination, object, end, end in view, aim, mission statement; axe to grind; target, butt, tape, winning post, goal, wicket, stumps, touch, touchline; bull's-eye 225 *centre*; Mecca 76 *focus*; quarry, game, prey 619 *chase*; prize, crown, wreath, laurels 729 *trophy*; dream, aspiration, vision 513 *conception*; heart's desire, Promised Land, El Dorado, land flowing with milk and honey, pot *or* crock of gold at the end of the rainbow, Holy Grail 859 *desired object*.

Vb. *intend*, propose; have in mind, have in view, have an eye to, contemplate, think of; study, meditate; reckon on, calculate, look for 507 *expect*; foresee the necessity of 510 *foresee*; have a mind to, mean to, have every intention 599 *be resolute*; resolve, determine, premeditate 608 *predetermine*; project, design, plan for 623 *plan*; intend for, destine for 155 *predestine*; earmark 547 *mark*; put aside for, reserve for; intend for oneself (see also *aim at* below); declare one's intention, set out one's stall.

aim at, make one's target; go after, go all out for, work towards, strive after 619 *pursue*; try for 671 *attempt*; be after, have an eye on, have designs on, promise oneself, aspire to; take aim, zero in on, focus on, point at, level at, train one's sights on, aim high, hitch one's wagon to a star 281 *aim*.

Adv. *purposely*, on purpose, in cold blood, deliberately, intentionally; knowingly, wittingly; with forethought, with malice aforethought; in order to; with the intention of, with a view to, with the object of, by design, as planned, according to plan, as arranged.

618 Non-design. Gamble

N. *non-design*, indeterminacy; involuntariness, instinct 609 *spontaneity*; coincidence; accident, fluke, luck; good luck, windfall, stroke of luck; bad luck, hard luck 616 *evil*; lottery, luck of the draw, postcode lottery; potluck; wheel of Fortune 596 *fate*.

gambling, risk-taking; flier, risk, hazard, Russian roulette 661 *danger*; calculated risk 617 *intention*; gamble, potluck 159 *chance*; venture, speculation, flutter 461 *experiment*; shot, shot in the dark, leap in the dark, pig in a poke, blind bargain 474 *uncertainty*; bid, throw; toss of a coin, turn of a card; wager, bet, stake, ante; dice, die; element of risk, game of chance; bingo; fruit machine, gaming machine, slot machine, one-armed bandit; roulette, rouge et noir 837 *gambling game*; roulette wheel; betting, spread betting, turf, horse-racing, dog-racing 716 *racing*; football pool, treble chance, pools; tote; draw, lottery, National Lottery, Scratch card, raffle, tombola, sweepstake; raffle ticket; premium bond.

gambling den, gaming-house; betting shop, bookie's, bookmaker's, turf accountant's; casino, pool room, bingo hall, amusement arcade; racecourse, turf.

stock exchange, exchange, share shop, bucket shop.

gambler, gamester, player, better, backer, punter; turf accountant, bookmaker, bookie, tout, tipster; risk-taker; venture capitalist, adventurer, entrepreneur 672 *undertaking*; speculator; bear, bull, stag; arbitrageur.

Adj. *unintentional*, inadvertent, unintended, unmeant 596 *involuntary*; unpremeditated; accidental, coincidental 159 *casual*.

aimless, desultory, motiveless, planless, purposeless 641 *useless*; happy-go-lucky, devil-may-care 833 *cheerful*; random, haphazard 158 *casual*, 464 *indiscriminate*.

speculative, experimental 474 *uncertain*; hazardous, risky, chancy, dicey; risk-taking, adventurous, enterprising.

Vb. *gamble*, do the pools; bet, stake, wager; call one's hand; play for high stakes; take bets, offer odds, make a book; back, punt; cover a bet; play the market, speculate, arbitrage, have a flutter 461 *experiment*; run a risk, take risks, push one's luck, tempt Providence; buy a pig in a poke, buy something sight unseen 857 *be rash*; venture, chance it, chance one's arm, tempt fortune, tempt fate, try one's luck, trust to chance; raffle, draw lots, cut straws, cut for aces, spin a coin, toss up.

619 Pursuit

N. *pursuit*, pursuance, follow-up 65 *sequence*; seeking, looking for, quest 459 *search*; hunting, tracking, spooring, trailing, tailing, dogging, poaching, lamping, hounding, persecution, witch-hunt; affairs 622 *business*.

chase, run; steeplechase, paperchase 716 *racing*; hunt, hunting, hounding, hue and cry, tally-ho; beat, drive; shooting, gunning, hunting, shooting and fishing 837 *sport*; blood sport, fox hunt, stag hunt; big-game hunt, lion hunt, tiger hunt, elephant hunt, boar hunt; pigsticking; stalking, deer stalking; poaching; hawking, fowling, falconry; fishing, angling, fly fishing, coarse fishing, sea fishing; inshore fishing, deep-sea fishing, whaling; beagling, coursing, ratting, trapping, ferreting, rabbiting, mole-catching; fishing tackle, rod and line, bait, fly, fly-tying; fowling-piece 723 *firearm*; mousetrap, etc. 542 *trap*; manhunt, dragnet; game, quarry, prey, victim 617 *objective*; catch 771 *acquisition*.

hunter, quester, seeker, searcher 459 *enquirer*; search party; pursuer, tracker, trailer, sleuth, tail, shadow; huntsman, huntress; Diana the Huntress, Herne the Hunter, the Wild Huntsman; beater; sportsman, sportswoman, sportsperson 837 *player*; gun, shot, marksman *or* -woman; head-hunter 362 *killer*; big-game hunter, fox hunter, deer stalker; poacher, guddler, trout-tickler; trapper, rat-catcher, rodent officer, mole-catcher; bird-catcher, fowler, falconer, hawker; fisherman; angler; shrimper; trawler, trawlerman, whaler; pack, hounds; hound, foxhound, otterhound, bloodhound 365 *dog*; hawk 365 *bird*; beast of prey, man-eater 365 *mammal*; mouser 365 *cat*.

Vb. *pursue*, seek, look for, cast about for; be gunning for, hunt for, fish for, dig for 459 *search*; send out a search party; stalk; shadow, dog, track, trail, sleuth, tail, dog one's footsteps, follow the scent 284 *follow*; scent out 484 *discover*; witch-hunt, harry, persecute 735 *oppress*; chase, give chase, hunt; raise the hunt, raise the hue and cry; mark as one's prey, make one's quarry 617 *aim at*; run after, set one's cap at, throw oneself at, woo 889 *court*; be after; pursue one's own interests 622 *busy oneself*; follow up.

hunt, go hunting, go big-game hunting, go shooting, ride to hounds; go fishing, fish, angle, fly-fish; trawl; whale; shrimp; net, catch 542 *ensnare*; mouse; stalk, deer-stalk, fowl, hawk; course; flush, beat; set snares, poach, guddle.

620 Avoidance

N. *avoidance*, prevention 702 *hindrance*; abstinence, abstention 942 *temperance*; forbearance, refraining 177 *moderation*; non-intervention, non-involvement; evasiveness 518 *equivocalness*; evasive action, dodge, duck, sidestep; delaying action; evasion, flight 667 *escape*;

shrinking 854 *fear*; shunning, wide berth, safe distance 199 *distance*; shirking 458 *negligence*; non-attendance 190 *absence*; escapism.

avoider, abstainer; dodger, evader, tax evader, moonlighter, bilker, welsher 545 *trickster*; shrinker, quitter 856 *coward*; shirker, skiver, slacker, sloucher, leadswinger 679 *idler*; skulker; draft-dodger, truant, deserter 918 *undutifulness*; runaway, fugitive, escapee 667 *escaper*; refugee, displaced person, asylum-seeker; escapist, dreamer 513 *visionary*; head in the sand, ostrich.

Vb. *avoid*, not go near, keep off, keep away; bypass, circumvent 282 *deviate*; turn aside, look the other way, turn a blind eye, cold-shoulder; stand apart, have no hand in, play no part in, not soil one's fingers, keep one's hands clean, wash one's hands of, shun, eschew, leave, let alone, have nothing to do with, not touch with a bargepole; give a miss, give the go-by; fight shy, break away, draw back, back off 290 *recede*; hold off, stand aloof, keep one's distance, keep a respectful distance, keep at arm's length, give a wide berth; keep out of the way, keep clear, stand clear, get out of the way; forbear; refrain, abstain, forswear; hold back, hang back, balk at 598 *be unwilling*; pass the buck, get out of; cop out, funk, shirk 458 *neglect*; shrink, flinch, jib, refuse, shy; take evasive action, shy away, lead one a dance, draw a red herring, throw dust in one's eyes, throw one off the scent, play hide-and-seek; sidestep, dodge, duck; deflect, ward off; not talk about, not go there; duck the issue, fudge the issue, get round, obviate, skirt round, fence, hedge, pussyfoot 518 *be equivocal*; evade, escape, give one the slip 667 *elude*; hide 523 *lurk*; bury one's head in the sand, be ostrich-like; deny 533 *negate*.

run away, desert, play truant, jump bail, take French leave, go AWOL 918 *fail in duty*; abscond, welsh, flit, elope 667 *escape*; absent oneself 190 *be absent*; withdraw, retire, retreat, beat a retreat, turn tail, turn one's back 282 *turn round*; flee, flit, fly, take to flight, run for one's life; make off, slope off, bolt, run, run for it, cut and run, show a clean pair of heels, take to one's heels, beat it, make oneself scarce, scarper, scoot, scram, skedaddle 277 *move fast*; slip the cable, break away 296 *walk out*; shake the dust from one's feet, steal away, sneak off, slink off, scuttle, do a bunk.

621 Relinquishment

N. *relinquishment*, abandonment; leaving, evacuation 296 *departure*; desertion, truancy, defection 918 *undutifulness*; withdrawal, secession 978 *schism*; walk-out 145 *strike*; cop-out

620 *avoidance*; yielding, giving up; abnegation, renunciation 779 *non-retention*; abdication, retirement 753 *resignation*; disuse 674 *non-use*; discontinuance 611 *disuse*; cancellation, annulment 752 *annulment*.

Vb. relinquish, drop, let go, leave hold of; surrender, resign, give up, yield; waive, forgo; cede, hand over, transfer 780 *assign*; forfeit 772 *lose*; renounce, abnegate, recant, change one's mind 603 *change one's mind*; not proceed with, drop the idea, forget it 506 *forget*; wean oneself 611 *disaccustom*; forswear, abstain 620 *avoid*; shed, slough, cast off, divest; drop, discard, get rid of, jettison, write off 674 *stop using*; lose interest, have other fish to fry 860 *be indifferent*; abdicate, back down, scratch, stand down, withdraw, retire, drop out 753 *resign*; jack it in, give in, throw in the sponge *or* the towel, throw in one's hand 721 *submit*; leave, quit, move out, vacate, evacuate 296 *depart*; forsake, abandon, run out on, leave stranded, quit one's post, desert 918 *fail in duty*; play truant 190 *be absent*; down tools, strike, come out 145 *cease*; walk out, secede; throw over, ditch, jilt, break it off, go back on one's word 542 *deceive*; pass on to the next, shelve, postpone 136 *put off*; annul, cancel 752 *annul*; unsubscribe.

622 Business

N. business, affairs, business interests, irons in the fire; occupation, concern; business on hand, case, agenda 154 *affairs*; enterprise, venture, undertaking, pursuit 678 *activity*; new business, new enterprise, start-up, spin-off company, spin-out company, venture capital; office routine, daily round 610 *practice*; daily work; commerce, business circles, business world, City, world of commerce; technology, industry, light industry, heavy industry, sunrise industry; big business multinational, business company 708 *corporation*; retailing; dotcom, e-commerce, e-business, e-tailing, dot commerce 531 *Internet*; m-commerce, m-business 531 *telecommunication*; cottage industry; industrialism, industrialization, industrial arts, manufacture 164 *production*; trade, craft, handicraft; guild, union, chamber of commerce, business association 706 *association*; employment, work, black economy, grey economy.

vocation, calling, life work, mission; life, lifestyle, walk of life, career, chosen career; labour of love; living, livelihood, daily bread, one's bread and butter; profession, métier, craft, trade, line, line of country 694 *skill* (see also *function* below); ministry; cloth, veil, habit 985 *the church*; military profession, arms

718 *war*; naval profession, sea; legal profession 953 *law*; teaching profession, education 534 *teaching*; medical profession, medicine, practice; industry, commerce 791 *trade*; diplomatic service, civil service, administration 689 *management*; public service, public life; social service 901 *social care*.

job, chores, odd jobs, work, task, exercise 682 *labour*; duty, charge, commission, mission, errand; employ, service, employment, self-employment; hours of work, working day, working week, man-hour; occupation, situation, position, appointment, post, office; full-time job, permanency; temporary job, part-time job, freelance work, casual work; hiring, appointment, employment, recruitment, milk round; casualization, contractorization, outsourcing, subcontracting; dead-end job, McJob; situation wanted; situation vacant, opening, vacancy; labour exchange, employment agency, Job Centre, Department of Employment;

function, capacity, office, duty; area of interest, realm, province, domain, orbit, sphere; scope, field, terms of reference 183 *range*; department, line, line of country; role, part; business, job; responsibility, brief, concern, care, look-out, baby, pigeon.

Vb. employ, busy, occupy, take up one's time, fill one's time; give employment, engage, recruit, hire, enlist, appoint, post 751 *commission*; take on, take on the payroll 804 *pay*; offer a job to, fill a vacancy, staff.

busy oneself, work, work for 742 *serve*; have a career, be employed, be self-employed, be free-lance, work from home, do a job, hold down a job, earn, earn one's living; earn an honest crust, turn an honest penny, keep the wolf from the door 771 *acquire*; take on a job, apply for a job; be up and doing, bustle 678 *be busy*; concern oneself with, make it one's business, take a hand in 678 *meddle*; work at, ply; engage in, turn one's hand to, take up, engage in, go in for; have one's hands full, take on oneself, bear the burden, assume responsibility, bear the brunt, take on one's shoulders 917 *incur a duty*; work with one's hands, work with one's brains; pursue one's hobby 837 *amuse oneself*.

function, work, go 173 *operate*; fill a role, play one's part, carry on; officiate, act, discharge one's duties, serve as, do duty for, perform the duties, do the work of; substitute, stand in for 755 *deputize*; hold office, hold down a job, have a brief.

do business, transact, negotiate 766 *make terms*; ply a trade, follow a career; have a business, engage in, carry on a trade, keep shop;

do business with, deal with, enter into trade relations 791 *trade*; transact business, go about one's business; pursue one's vocation, earn one's living (see also *busy oneself* above); be self-employed, work from home, run a cottage industry, freelance, set up in business, go into business.

623 Plan

N. plan, scheme, design; planning, geomancy, feng shui, vaastu; organization, systematization, rationalization, centralization 60 *order*; programme, project, proposal 617 *intention*; proposition, suggestion, motion, resolution; master plan, five-year plan, road map; ground plan, drawing, scale drawing, blueprint 551 *map*; diagram, flow chart 86 *statistics*; sketch, outline, draft, first draft, schedule; skeleton; model, pattern, pilot scheme 23 *prototype*; drawing board, planning office.

policy, forethought 510 *foresight*; statesmanship 498 *wisdom*; course of action, procedure, strategy 688 *tactics*; approach, attack 624 *way*; steps, measures 676 *action*; proposed line of action, programme, prospectus, platform, outline, ticket, slate; party line; formula 81 *rule*; schedule, agenda, order of the day, any other business, AOB 622 *business*.

contrivance, expedient, resource, recourse, resort, last resort, card, trump card, card up one's sleeve, nuclear option 629 *means*; recipe; loophole, escape clause, way out, alternative, artifice, device, gimmick, dodge, ploy, shtick 698 *stratagem*; wangle, fiddle; trick 694 *skill*; flag of convenience; stunt; inspiration, brainwave, brainstorm, happy thought, bright idea; notion, invention; tool, weapon, contraption, gadget, gizmo 628 *instrument*; improvisation 609 *spontaneity*; feat, tour de force; bold move, masterstroke 676 *deed*.

plot, intrigue; web of intrigue; cabal, conspiracy, inside job, insider trading *or* dealing; scheme, racket, game 698 *stratagem*; frame-up, put-up job, fit-up, machination; manipulation, wire-pulling 612 *motive*.

planner, inventor, originator, deviser; proposer; founder, author, architect, designer; town-planner; backroom boy, boffin 696 *expert*; brains, mastermind; organizer, systems analyst; strategist, tactician; statesman *or* -woman, politician; wheeler-dealer, axe-grinder; plotter, intriguer; conspirator 545 *deceiver*; control freak.

Adj. planned, under consideration, at the planning stage, on the stocks, strategic, tactical.

Vb. plan, form a plan; make a plan, draw up, design, draft, blueprint; frame, shape 243 *form*; project, plan out, sketch out, map out, lay out, design a prototype; draw up a programme, lay the foundation; shape a course, mark out a course; organize, systematize, rationalize; schedule, draw up a schedule, phase; invent, think up 484 *discover*; conceive a plan 513 *imagine*; devise, engineer; hatch, concoct; prearrange 608 *predetermine*; calculate, think ahead, look ahead 498 *be wise*; follow a plan, work to a schedule; have an axe to grind.

plot, scheme, have designs, be up to something, wheel and deal; manipulate, pull strings 178 *influence*; conspire, intrigue, machinate; cook up; hatch a plot 698 *be cunning*; undermine; work against; frame 541 *fake*.

624 Way

N. way, route 267 *itinerary*; manner, guise; fashion, style 243 *form*; method, mode, line, approach, address, attack; procedure, process, way of, way of doing things, modus operandi 688 *tactics*; operation, treatment; routine 610 *practice*; technique, know-how 694 *skill*; gait 265 *motion*; progress 285 *progression*; primrose path; way of life, lifestyle.

access, right of way, communications; way to 289 *approach*; entrance, door 263 *doorway*; side-entrance, back-entrance, tradesman's entrance; drive, driveway, gangway; porch, hall, hallway, corridor, vestibule 194 *lobby*; way through, pass, passageway 305 *passage*; intersection, junction, crossing; zebra crossing, pedestrian crossing, pelican crossing 305 *traffic control*; strait, sound 345 *gulf*; channel, fairway, canal 351 *water channel*; lock, stile, turnstile, tollgate; stairs, flight of stairs, stairway, ladder 308 *ascent*.

bridge, brig; footbridge, flyover, road bridge, aqueduct; suspension bridge, swing bridge, Bailey bridge, humpback bridge; viaduct, span; railway bridge; pontoon bridge, floating bridge, transporter bridge; drawbridge; causeway, stepping-stone, gangway, gangplank, catwalk, duckboards; ford, ferry 305 *passage*; way under, subway, underpass 263 *tunnel*; isthmus.

route, direction, way to *or* from, course, march, tack, track; trajectory, orbit; carriageway, lane, bus lane 305 *traffic control*; air lane, sea lane, seaway, fairway, waterway 351 *water channel*; short cut, bypass; detour; line of communication.

path, pathway, footpath, pavement, sidewalk; towpath, bridlepath; lane, track, sheep track, trail, heritage trail; right of way, public footpath; walk, promenade, esplanade, front, avenue, drive, boulevard, mall; pedestrian precinct, arcade, colonnade, aisle, cloister, ambulatory; racetrack, running track, speed track 724 *arena*; fairway, runway.

road, high road, highway, Queen's highway, highways and byways; main road, A road, minor road, B road, dirt road, cinder track; side road; toll road, turnpike, route nationale; thoroughfare, trunk road, artery, bypass, ring road; motorway, M-way, autoroute, autobahn, autostrada, E road; turnpike, interstate; expressway, throughway, clearway; slip road, fast lane; crossroads, junction, T-junction, turn-off; intersection, roundabout, mini roundabout, cloverleaf, gyratory system *or* gyratory; crossing, pedestrian crossing, zebra crossing, pelican crossing, puffin crossing, toucan crossing 305 *traffic control*; roadway, carriageway, dual carriageway; central reservation, crash barrier; cycle track, cycleway; street, high street, one-way street, side street, back street; alleyway, wynd, alley, blind alley, cul de sac; close, avenue 192 *housing*; pavement, sidewalk, kerb; paving, cobbles, setts, paving stone, flagstones; hard shoulder, verge; macadam, tarmac, asphalt, road metal; surface; bend, corner 248 *curve*; road-user 268 *traveller*, *driver*, *pedestrian*.

railway, railroad, line; permanent way, track, lines, railway lines, electrified lines, main line, branch line; tramlines, tramway; monorail; funicular; overhead railway, elevated railway, underground railway, electric railway, subway, tube, metro 274 *train*; light railway, narrow gauge, standard gauge; junction, crossover, level crossing, tunnel, cutting, embankment; siding, marshalling yard, goods yard, shunting yard; station, railway station, halt; platform 145 *stopping place*; signal; rails, points, sleepers; track spread *or* track gauge spread; rail crash, signal passed at danger, spad.

Adv. via, by way of, in transit.

625 Middle way

N. middle way, middle course, middle of the road; balance, golden mean, happy medium 30 *average*; halfway, halfway house, midstream 30 *middle point*; half tide; neutrality 177 *moderation*; half measures 601 *irresolution*; mutual concession 770 *compromise*.

moderate, non-extremist, wet, Girondist, Menshevik; neutral, don't know; Laodicean.

Adj. neutral, impartial 913 *just*; uncommitted, unattached, free-floating, don't know; detached 860 *indifferent*; moderate, wet, non-extreme, middle-of-the-road 225 *central*; sitting on the fence, lukewarm, half-and-half, shilly-shallying 601 *irresolute*; neither one thing nor the other, grey.

626 Circuit

N. circuit, roundabout way, circuitous route, scenic route, bypass, detour, ring road, loop,

diversion; orbit, round, lap 314 *circuitous motion*; circumference 250 *circle*.

Adj. roundabout, circuitous, indirect, meandering; circumlocutory 570 *diffuse*; skirting.

Vb. circuit, lap, beat the bounds, go round, make a circuit, loop the loop 314 *circle*; make a detour, go a roundabout way, go out of one's way 282 *deviate*; short-circuit 620 *avoid*; encircle, encompass 230 *surround*; skirt.

Adv. round about, round the world, in a roundabout way, circuitously, indirectly, from pillar to post.

627 Requirement

N. requirement, essential, sine qua non, a must, acid test 596 *necessity*; needs, necessities; indent, order, requisition, shopping list; stipulation, prerequisite; need 636 *insufficiency*; gap, lacuna 190 *absence*; demand, call for, run on, seller's market, bearish market, bullish market 792 *purchase*; consumption, input, intake; shortage 307 *shortfall*; slippage; balance due, what is owing 803 *debt*; claim 761 *request*; ultimatum, injunction 737 *command*.

needfulness, necessity for, indispensability, desirability; necessitousness, want, breadline, poverty level 801 *poverty*; exigency, urgency, emergency 137 *crisis*; matter of life and death 638 *important matter*; bare minimum.

Adj. required, requisite, prerequisite, needful, needed; necessary, essential, vital, indispensable; called for, in demand 859 *desired*.

necessitous, in want, in need, feeling the pinch, on the breadline, in the poverty trap; lacking, deprived of; destitute 801 *poor*; starving 636 *underfed*; disadvantaged.

Vb. require, need, have need of, want, lack 636 *be unsatisfied*; be without, feel the need for, have occasion for; have a vacancy for; miss; crave 859 *desire*; cry out for; claim, put in a claim for, apply for 761 *request*; find necessary, be unable to do without, must have; create a need, necessitate; make demands 737 *demand*; order, tele-order, indent, requisition; reserve, book.

628 Instrumentality

N. instrumentality, operation 173 *agency*; use, employment; medium 629 *means*; occasion 156 *cause*; pressure 178 *influence*; result 157 *effect*; efficacy 160 *power*; services 703 *aid*; intervention, interference 678 *activity*; instrumentation, mechanization, automation, computerization 630 *machine*.

instrument, tool 630 *tool*; organ, hand, sense organ; amanuensis, scribe, lackey, slave 742 *servant*; agent, midwife, medium, help, assistant 703 *helper*; go-between, pander 720 *mediator*; catalyst; vehicle; pawn; robot 630 *machine*; cat's paw, stooge, puppet, creature 707 *auxiliary*; weapon, implement, appliance, lever 630 *tool*; magic ring, Aladdin's lamp 983 *spell*; key, skeleton key, master key, passkey 263 *opener*; open sesame, watchword, password, slogan, shibboleth, passport 756 *permit*; stepping-stone 624 *bridge*; highway 624 *road*; controls; device, gadget, gizmo 623 *contrivance*.

Adj. *instrumental*, working 173 *operative*; manual; automatic, computerized, electronic, push-button 630 *mechanical*; effective 160 *powerful*; conducive; applied; serviceable, promoting, assisting, helpful 703 *helping*; functional.

Vb. *be instrumental*, work, act 173 *operate*; perform 676 *do*; serve, work for, lend oneself *or* itself to; help, assist 703 *aid*; advance, promote 703 *patronize*; have a hand in 775 *participate*; be to blame for 156 *cause*; be the creature of, be a cat's paw, pull another's chestnuts out of the fire; use one's influence, pull strings 178 *influence*.

Adv. *through*, per, by the hand of, by means of, with the help of, thanks to.

629 Means

N. *means*, ways and means, wherewithal; power, capacity 160 *ability*; conveniences, facilities; appliances, tools, tools of the trade, bag of tricks 630 *tool*; technology, new technology, high technology, high tech, third wave 490 *knowledge*; technique, know-how 694 *skill*; equipment, supplies, ammunition 633 *provision*; resources, raw material 631 *materials*; nuts and bolts 630 *machine*; workforce, manpower 686 *personnel*; cash flow 797 *money*; capital, working capital 628 *instrument*; assets, stock-in-trade 777 *property*; stocks and shares, investments, investment fund, investment portfolio, tracker fund, zombie fund, PEP, ISA, Tessa-only ISA, TOISA; revenue, income; borrowing capacity; reserves, something in reserve, shot in one's locker, card up one's sleeve, two strings to one's bow 662 *safeguard*; method, measures, steps 624 *way*; expedient, device, resort, recourse 623 *contrivance*; last resort.

Adv. *by means of*, with, by, using, through; with the aid of; by dint of.

630 Tool

N. *tool*, precision tool, machine tool, hand tool, implement 628 *instrument*; apparatus, appliance, utensil (see also *utensil* below); weapon, arm 723 *arms*; device, contraption, gadget, gizmo, doodah, thingummy, whatsit 623 *contrivance*; screwdriver; hammer, mallet,

etc. 279 *hammer*; drill, electric drill, etc. 263 *piercer*; awl, bradawl, gimlet, pickaxe, etc. 256 *sharp point*; spanner, wrench, monkey wrench, pipe wrench, mole wrench, Stillson (tdmk) wrench; pliers, pincers, tweezers, etc. 778 *pincers*; axe, chisel, wedge, knife, adze, etc. 256 *sharp edge*, saw, etc. 260 *notch*; file, plane, etc. 258 *smoother*; fire-irons 383 *furnace*; glue gun; peg, nail 217 *hanger*, 218 *support*; screw, nail, tack, bolt, nut, etc. 47 *fastening*, 256 *sharp point*; rope 47 *cable*; leverage, lever, jemmy, crowbar, jack 218 *pivot*; grip, haft, shaft, tiller, helm, rudder 218 *handle*; pulley, sheave 250 *wheel*; switch, stopcock; trigger; pedal, pole, punt-pole 287 *propulsion*; ram 279 *hammer*; lathe; laser; prehistoric tool, flint; tools of the trade, tool-kit, do-it-yourself kit, bag of tricks. (See also 370 *farm and garden tools*.)

utensil, kitchen utensil; knife, cake knife, fish knife, etc. 256 *sharp edge*; fork, cake fork; ladle, spoon, teaspoon, etc. 194 *ladle*.

machine, machinery, mechanism, works; clockwork, wheels within wheels; nuts and bolts 58 *component*; spring, mainspring, hairspring; gears, gearing, bevel gears, syncromesh, automatic gear change; motor, engine, internal combustion engine, lean-burn engine, diesel engine, steam engine; turbine, dynamo 160 *sources of energy*; servomechanism, servomotor; robot, automaton, cyborg; computer 86 *computing*.

equipment, gear, tackle; outfit, kit; furnishing; trappings, accoutrement 228 *dress*; utensils, impedimenta, paraphernalia, chattels 777 *property*; wares, stock-in-trade 795 *merchandise*; plant 687 *workshop*.

machinist, operator, operative; driver; engineer, technician, mechanic, fitter; craftsman, skilled worker 686 *artisan*.

Adj. *mechanical*, mechanized, motorized, powered, power-driven; labour-saving, automatic 628 *instrumental*; automated, computerized, electronic.

631 Materials

N. *materials*, resources 629 *means*; material, stuff; raw material; meat, fodder 301 *food*; ore, mineral, metal; iron, pig iron, ingot, cast iron, wrought iron; aluminium, copper, lead, tin, zinc, brass, bronze; clay, adobe, china clay, potter's clay, gypsum 344 *soil*; glass 422 *transparency*; plastic, polythene, polyethylene, polypropylene, polystyrene, polyvinyl chloride, PVC, polytetrafluoroethylene, latex, celluloid, fibreglass; rope, yarn, wool 208 *fibre*; leather, hide 226 *skin*; timber 366 *wood*; rafter, board 218 *beam*; plank, plywood, lath; stuffing 227 *lining*; cloth, fabric 222 *textile*.

building material, building block, breeze block, brick 381 *pottery*; bricks and mortar, lath and plaster, wattle and daub; thatch, slate, tile 226 *roof*; stone, marble, granite, flint, ashlar, masonry; rendering 226 *facing*; cement, concrete, reinforced concrete, flag, cobble 226 *paving*; gravel, tarmac, asphalt 624 *road*.

paper, pulp, newsprint; card, art paper, cartridge paper, carbon paper, tissue paper, crepe paper, tracing paper, cellophane; papier mâché, cardboard, pasteboard; sheet, foolscap, quarto, imperial, A1, A2, A3, A4, A5; quire, ream; notepaper 586 *stationery*.

632 Store

N. *store*, mass, heap, load, stack, stockpile, mountain, butter mountain, lake, wine lake, buildup 74 *accumulation*; packet, bundle, bagful, bucketful 26 *quantity*; harvest, crop, vintage, mow 771 *acquisition*; haystack, haycock, hayrick; stock, stock-in-trade 795 *merchandise*; assets, capital, holding, investment 777 *property*; fund, reserves, something in reserve, backlog; savings, savings account, nest egg, baby bond; deposit, hoard, treasure, pot *or* crock of gold at the end of the rainbow; buried treasure, cache 527 *hiding-place*; bottom drawer, hope chest, trousseau 633 *provision*; pool, kitty; appeal fund; quarry, mine, goldmine; natural resources, mineral deposit, coal deposit; coalfield, gasfield, oilfield; coal mine, colliery, working, shaft; coalface, seam, lode; vein; well, oil well, gusher; fountain, fount 156 *source*; supply, stream; tap, pipeline, artesian well 341 *irrigator*; milch cow, the goose that lays the golden eggs, cornucopia, abundance 635 *plenty*.

storage, stowage, gathering, garnering 74 *accumulation*; conservation, bottling 666 *preservation*; safe deposit 660 *protection*; stabling, warehousing; mountain, butter mountain, lake, wine lake; storage space, shelf-room, space, accommodation 183 *room*; boxroom, loft; hold, bunker 194 *cellar*; storehouse, storeroom, stockroom; warehouse, goods shed; depot, dock, wharf 192 *stable*; magazine, arsenal, armoury, gunroom; treasure house 799 *treasury*; exchequer, strongroom, vault, coffer, moneybox, moneybag, till, safe, night safe, bank; blood bank, sperm bank; data bank 86 *computing*; store of memories 505 *memory*; hive, honeycomb; granary, garner, barn, silo; water tower, reservoir, cistern, tank, gas-holder, gasometer; battery, garage, petrol station, gas station, filling station, petrol pump; dump, sump, drain, cesspool, sewage farm 649 *sink*; pantry, larder, buttery, stillroom 194 *room*; cupboard, shelf 194 *cabi-

net*; refrigerator, fridge, deep freeze, freezer, fridge-freezer; portmanteau, holdall, packing case 194 *box*; container, holder, quiver 194 *receptacle*.

collection, set, complete set; archives, file 548 *record*; portfolio 74 *accumulation*; museum 125 *antiquity*; gallery, art gallery, art museum; library; thesaurus 559 *dictionary*; menagerie, aquarium 369 *zoo*; waxworks, Madame Tussaud's; exhibition 522 *exhibit*; repertory, repertoire, bag of tricks.

Vb. *store*, stow, pack, bundle 193 *load*; roll up, fold up; lay up, stow away, mothball; dump, garage, stable, warehouse; gather, harvest, reap, mow, pick, glean 370 *cultivate*; stack, heap, pile, amass, accumulate 74 *bring together*; stock up, stock up one's cupboards *or* larder, lay in, bulk-buy, panic buy, stock-pile, pile up, build up; take on, take in, fuel; fill, fill up, top up, refill, refuel 633 *replenish*; put by, save, keep, hold, file, hang on to 778 *retain*; bottle, pickle, conserve 666 *preserve*; leave, set aside, put aside, lay by, put by, reserve; bank, deposit, invest; hoard, treasure; bury, stash away, secrete 525 *conceal*; husband, save up, salt away, make a nest egg, prepare for a rainy day 814 *economize*; equip oneself, put in the bottom drawer 669 *prepare oneself*; pool, put in the kitty.

633 Provision

N. *provision*, furnishing, equipment; catering; service, delivery, distribution; self-service; procuring; feeding, entertainment, bed and breakfast, board and lodging, maintenance; assistance, lending 703 *subvention*; supply, food supply, water supply, feed; pipeline 272 *transference*; commissariat, provisioning, supplies, stores, rations, iron rations, reserves 632 *store*; refill, filling-up 54 *fullness*; food, provender 301 *provisions*, helping, portion 301 *meal*; grist to the mill, fuel to the flame; produce 164 *product*; budgeting.

provider, donor 781 *giver*; supplier, one-stop shop; retailer, shopkeeper, storekeeper 794 *tradespeople*; grocer, greengrocer, baker, poulterer, fishmonger, butcher, vintner, wine merchant, ship's chandler, drysalter, victualler, sutler; creditor, moneylender 784 *lender*; commissary, quartermaster; middleman; Internet service provider, ISP, music service provider, MSP 531 *Internet*: application service provider, ASP 86 *computing*; procurer, pander, pimp 952 *pimp*.

caterer, purveyor, hotelier, hotelkeeper, hotel manager, restaurateur, head waiter, maître d'hôtel; innkeeper, landlord, landlady, licensee, mine host, publican; housekeeper, housewife; cook, chef; pastrycook, confectioner.

Vb. *provide*, afford, offer, lend 781 *give*; equip, furnish, arm, man, fit out, kit out 669 *make ready*; supply; yield 164 *produce*; cater, purvey; procure, pander, pimp; service, service an order, meet an order 793 *sell*; distribute, deliver, deliver the goods; hand out, hand round, serve, serve up, dish up; feed, do for, board, put up, maintain, keep, clothe; stock; budget, make provision, make due provision; provide for oneself, do for oneself; stock up, lay in a stock 632 *store*; fuel; forage, water.

replenish, reinforce, top up, refill 54 *fill*; restock, refuel.

634 Waste

N. *waste*, wastage; leakage; depletion, exhaustion, drainage 300 *clearing*; dissipation 75 *dispersion*; evaporation 338 *vaporization*; melting 337 *liquefaction*; damage 772 *loss*; wear and tear, built-in obsolescence 655 *deterioration*; wastefulness, improvidence, lavishness, extravagance, overspending, squandering; overproduction 637 *superfluity*; misapplication, frittering away; vandalism, sabotage 165 *destruction*; waste product, litter, refuse 641 *rubbish*.

Adj. *wasteful*, extravagant, uneconomic 815 *prodigal*; time-consuming; damaging 165 *destructive*.

Vb. *waste*, deplete, drain 300 *empty*; dissipate, scatter; abuse, overwork, overfish, overgraze; wear out, erode, damage 655 *impair*; misapply, fritter away, cast pearls before swine; make no use of 674 *not use*; labour in vain 641 *waste effort*; be extravagant, overspend, squander, throw away, pour down the drain, throw out the baby with the bath water 815 *be prodigal*; be careless, spill; be destructive, destroy, sabotage, vandalize; be wasted, decay 37 *decrease*; leak; melt, melt away 337 *liquefy*; evaporate 338 *vaporize*; run to seed 655 *deteriorate*; go down the drain.

635 Sufficiency

N. *sufficiency*, elegant sufficiency, right amount; right number, quorum; adequacy, enough; assets, competence, living wage; subsistence farming; self-sufficiency; exact requirement, no surplus; breadline; minimum, bare minimum, least one can do; full measure; fulfilment 725 *completion*; one's fill.

plenty, horn of plenty, cornucopia 171 *abundance*; showers of, flood, spate, oceans, streams 350 *stream*; lots, lashings, oodles, galore 32 *great quantity*; copiousness 54 *fullness*; affluence, riches 800 *wealth*; fat of the land, luxury, groaning board, feast, banquet 301 *feasting*; orgy, profusion 815 *prodigality*; richness, fat; fertility, productivity, luxuriance, lushness 171 *productiveness*; harvest, rich harvest, vintage harvest, bumper crop; bonanza; endless supply; more than enough, too much, superabundance, embarras de choix, embarras de richesses 637 *redundancy*.

Adj. *sufficient*, sufficing; self-sufficient 54 *complete*; enough, adequate, competent; enough to go round; satisfactory; up to the mark; just right, not too much not too little; only just enough.

plentiful, plenteous, ample, enough and to spare, more than enough 637 *superfluous*; lavish 813 *liberal*; without stint, unsparing, inexhaustible 32 *great*; luxuriant, riotous, lush, fertile, fat 171 *prolific*; profuse, abundant, copious, overflowing 637 *redundant*; rich, opulent, affluent 800 *moneyed*.

filled, full up, chock-full, chock-a-block, replete, satiated, had it up to here, ready to burst 863 *satiated*; satisfied; teeming, overflowing with.

Vb. *suffice*, be enough, do, just do, do and no more, serve; qualify, make the grade 727 *be successful*; pass, pass muster, cut the mustard, measure up to, meet requirements, fill the bill, 'it does exactly or just what it says on the tin or box or packet'; rise to the occasion; stand up to, take the strain 218 *support*; do what is required 725 *carry out*; satisfy 828 *content*; more than satisfy, satiate; make adequate provision 633 *provide*.

abound, proliferate, teem, swarm, bristle with, crawl with 104 *be many*; riot, luxuriate 171 *be fruitful*; flow, shower, snow, pour, stream, sheet 350 *rain*; brim, overflow, flow with milk and honey 637 *be overabundant*.

have enough, be satisfied 828 *be content*; eat one's fill 301 *eat*; drink one's fill 301 *drink*; be sated, be chock-full, have had enough, have had it up to here, have had one's bellyful, be fed up 829 *be discontented*; have the means 800 *afford*; survive, scratch a living 801 *be poor*.

Adv. *enough*, sufficiently, amply, to the full, to one's heart's content; on tap, on demand; abundantly.

636 Insufficiency

N. *insufficiency*, not enough, drop in the bucket; non-satisfaction 829 *discontent*; inadequacy, incompetence; mingines, nothing to spare, too few; deficiency, imperfection 647 *defect*; deficit 55 *incompleteness*; non-fulfilment 726 *non-completion*; half measures, failure, weakness, slippage 307 *shortfall*; bankruptcy

805 *insolvency*; subsistence level, breadline, poverty level, pittance, dole, mite; stinginess, meanness 816 *parsimony*; short commons, iron rations, starvation rations, half rations; austerity, Spartan fare, starvation diet, bread and water 945 *asceticism*; malnutrition, vitamin deficiency 651 *disease*.

scarcity, scarceness, paucity 105 *fewness*; dearth, seven lean years; drought, famine, starvation; shortage 307 *shortfall*; slippage; power cut 37 *decrease*; short supply, seller's market, bearish market; scantiness, meagreness; deprivation 801 *poverty*; lack, want, need 627 *needfulness*.

Adj. insufficient, disappointing 829 *discontenting*; inadequate, not enough, too little; scant, scanty, skimpy, slender; deficient, light on, low on, lacking, 55 *incomplete*; wanting, poor, a poor man's — 35 *inferior*; incompetent, unequal to, not up to it 695 *unskilful*; weak, thin, watery, wersh, jejune, unnourishing 4 *lacking substance*; niggardly, miserly; stingy 816 *parsimonious*.

unprovided, unfurnished, ill-equipped; bare; unfilled, unsated 829 *discontented*; unprovided for, unaccommodated; lacking in, hard up 801 *poor*; undercapitalized, underfinanced, understaffed, undermanned, shorthanded, unavailable, off the menu, off 190 *absent*.

underfed, undernourished; half-starved, on short commons; famished, starved, starving ravening, ravenous 946 *fasting*; skin and bone, anorexic, emaciated.

scarce, rare 140 *infrequent*; sparse 105 *few*; in short supply, at a premium, hard to get, hard to come by, not to be had for love or money, not to be had at any price, unavailable, unobtainable, out of season, out of stock.

Vb. be insufficient, be inadequate, etc. (see adj.), not suffice; not meet requirements 647 *be imperfect*; want, lack; fail 509 *disappoint*; fall below 35 *be inferior*; come short, default 307 *fall short*; run out, dry up; paper over the cracks 726 *not complete*.

be unsatisfied, ask for more, come again, take a second helping; feel dissatisfied; spurn an offer, reject; miss, feel the lack, stand in need of; be a glutton for, be unable to have enough of 947 *eat to excess*.

637 Redundancy

N. redundancy, redundance, overspill, overflow; overabundance, superabundance; embarras de richesses, avalanche, spate 32 *great quantity*; too many, mob 74 *crowd*; saturation, saturation point 54 *fullness*; excess 634 *waste*; excessiveness, exorbitance, extremes, too much 546 *exaggeration*; overdoing it, over-stretching oneself, overextension, too many irons in the fire 678 *overactivity*; officiousness, red tape; overpraise, overoptimism 482 *overestimation*; overweight; overload, last straw 322 *gravity*; lion's share; overindulgence 943 *intemperance*; plethora, congestion 863 *satiation*; more than enough; glut; obesity 651 *disease*.

superfluity, more than is needed, luxury; frills, luxuries, non-essentials; overkill, duplication; something over, bonus, spare cash, money to burn 40 *extra*; margin, overlap, excess, surplus, balance 41 *remainder*; superfluousness, accessory, fifth wheel, parasite 641 *uselessness*; padding; tautology 570 *diffuseness*; redundancy; overmanning 678 *activity*; too much of a good thing, embarras de richesses, glut, drug on the market; surfeit, overdose 863 *satiation*.

Adj. redundant, one too many, one over the eight 104 *many*; overmuch, overabundant, excessive, immoderate 32 *exorbitant*; overdone, overflowing, overfull, running over, brimming over 54 *full*; flooding; snowed under, overwhelmed; cloying; replete, stuffed, overfed; overstretched; overloaded; congested.

superfluous, more than is needed, redundant, supernumerary; needless, unnecessary, uncalled for, otiose 641 *useless*; excessive; luxurious; surplus, extra, over and above 41 *remaining*; spare 38 *additional*; de trop, on one's hands, left over, going begging 860 *unwanted*; dispensable, expendable.

Vb. be overabundant, superabound, luxuriate 635 *abound*; run riot 171 *be fruitful*; bristle with, swarm with, teem with, hotch with, crawl with; overflow, brim over, burst at the seams 54 *be complete*; flood, inundate, burst its banks, deluge, overwhelm 350 *flow*; engulf 299 *absorb*; know no bounds, spread far and wide 306 *overstep*; overlap 183 *extend*; saturate 341 *drench*; stuff, gorge, cram 54 *fill*; congest, choke, suffocate; overdose, glut, cloy, satiate, sate; pamper oneself, overindulge oneself, overeat, overdrink, binge-eat, binge-drink 943 *be intemperate*; oversubscribe, do more than enough; oversell, flood the market; overstock; overdo, go over the top, overstep the mark, pile it on, lay it on thick, lay it on with a trowel 546 *exaggerate*; overload, overburden; overcharge; lavish upon 813 *be liberal*; be lavish, make a splash 815 *be prodigal*; roll in, stink of 800 *be rich*.

be superfluous, be redundant, etc. (see adj.); go begging, remain on one's hands 41 *be left*; have time on one's hands 679 *be inactive*; do twice over, duplicate; carry coals to Newcastle, gild the lily, teach one's grandmother to suck eggs; labour the obvious, take a sledgehammer to crack a nut, break a butterfly on a wheel, hold a candle to the sun; exceed requirements.

638 Importance

N. *importance*, priority, urgency 64 *precedence*; paramountcy, supremacy 34 *superiority*; essentialness; import, consequence, significance, weight, weightiness, gravity, seriousness; substance, moment 3 *having substance*; interest, consideration, concern 622 *business*; notability, memorability, mark, prominence, distinction, eminence 866 *repute*; influence 866 *prestige*; size, magnitude 32 *largeness*; rank; value, merit 644 *goodness*; stress, emphasis.

***important matter*,** vital concern, hot-button issue, bottom line, crucial moment, turning point 137 *crisis*; be-all and end-all; no joke, no laughing matter, matter of life and death; big news 529 *news*; exploit 676 *deed*; landmark, milestone; red-letter day, great day 876 *special day*.

***chief thing*,** what matters, the thing, great thing, main thing; supreme issue, crux 452 *topic*; fundamentals, bedrock, nitty-gritty; nuts and bolts, sine qua non 627 *requirement*; priority 605 *choice*; substance 5 *essential part*; highlight; cream, crème de la crème, pick 644 *elite*; key-note, cornerstone, mainstay, linchpin, kingpin; head, spearhead; sum and substance, heart of the matter, heart, core, kernel, nucleus, nub 225 *centre*; hub 218 *pivot*; chief hope, trump card, main chance; numero uno.

***bigwig*,** personage, notable, personality, heavyweight, somebody 866 *person of repute*; local worthy, pillar of the community; great man *or* woman, VIP, brass hat; his *or* her nibs, big gun, big shot, big noise, big wheel, big white chief, Mr Big, the main man; leading light; top dog, queen bee; kingpin, key player; numero uno; star, top of the bill, headline act, headliner; prima donna, lion, catch 890 *favourite*; head, chief, godfather, Big Brother 34 *superior*; the greatest 644 *exceller*; grandee 868 *aristocrat*; magnate, mogul, mandarin; baron, tycoon 741 *autocrat*; captains of industry, big battalions; movers and shakers; top brass, top people, establishment 733 *authority*; the great and the good; superpower, hyperpower 178 *influence*.

Adj. *important*, weighty, grave, serious, pregnant; of consequence, of importance, of concern; considerable; world-shattering, earth-shaking, momentous, critical, fateful 137 *timely*; chief, capital, cardinal, major, main, paramount, staple 34 *supreme*; crucial, essential; pivotal, hot-button 225 *central*; basic, fundamental, bedrock, radical, grass-roots;

primary, prime, foremost, leading; worthwhile, not to be sneezed at 644 *valuable*; necessary, vital, indispensable, key 627 *required*; significant, telling; imperative, urgent, high-priority; high-level; hush-hush 523 *latent*; high, grand, noble 32 *great*.

***notable*,** memorable, signal, unforgettable 505 *remembered*; first-rate, A1, outstanding, superior; top, top-rank, top-flight, A-list, über- 644 *excellent*; conspicuous, prominent, eminent, distinguished, exalted, august 866 *noteworthy*; imposing 821 *impressive*; formidable, powerful 178 *influential*; newsworthy, front-page; eventful, world-shattering, earth-shaking, epoch-making.

639 Unimportance

N. *unimportance*, inconsequence, insignificance 35 *inferiority*; immateriality, lack of substance 4 *lacking substance*; nothingness; pettiness 33 *smallness*; triviality; worthlessness 812 *cheapness*; uselessness 641 *uselessness*; irrelevance, red herring 10 *unrelatedness*.

***trifle*,** inessential, triviality; nothing, mere nothing, no great matter, secondary matter, nothing of note, matter of indifference, not the end of the world; no great shakes, nothing to speak of, nothing to write home about, nothing to worry about, storm in a teacup 482 *overestimation*; bagatelle, tinker's cuss, fig, damn, toss, straw, chaff, pin, button, feather, dust; tuppence, small change, small beer; paltry sum, peanuts, chickenfeed, flea-bite; pinprick, scratch; nothing to it, child's play 701 *easy thing*; peccadillo; trifles, trivia, minutiae, petty detail 80 *particulars*; whit, jot, the least bit, drop in the ocean 33 *small quantity*; cent, brass farthing 33 *small quantity*; nonsense.

***bauble*,** toy 837 *plaything*; geegaw *or* gewgaw, doodad, knick-knack, bric-a-brac, novelty, trinket; tinsel, trumpery, frippery, trash, gimcrack.

***nonentity*,** nobody, non-person; man of straw 4 *thing that lacks substance*; figurehead, cipher, sleeping partner; lightweight, small beer; small fry, small game; pipsqueak, squirt; other ranks, lower orders 869 *common people*; second fiddle 35 *inferior*; underling; pawn in the game, cat's paw, stooge, puppet 628 *instrument*; poor relation 801 *poor person*.

Adj. *unimportant*, immaterial 4 *lacking substance*; inconsequential, of no consequence, of no great weight; insignificant 515 *meaningless*; inessential, non-essential, fringe; unnecessary, expendable; small, petty, trifling, paltry 33 *inconsiderable*; negligible, inappreciable, not worth considering; weak; measly; obscure; beneath contempt 922 *contemptible*; jumped-up, no-account, tinpot; low-level, secondary, minor, subsidiary, peripheral 35 *inferior*.

trivial, trifling, piffling, piddling; pettifogging, nit-picking; footling, frivolous, puerile, childish 499 *foolish*; airy 4 *lacking substance*; superficial 212 *shallow*; slight 33 *small*; lightweight 323 *light*; parish-pump, small-time, B-list; twopenny-halfpenny, one-horse, second-rate, third-rate; grotty, rubbishy, trashy, tawdry, shoddy, gimcrack 645 *bad*; two-a-penny 812 *cheap*; worthless, valueless 641 *useless*; not worth a second thought 922 *contemptible*; token, nominal, symbolic; mediocre, nondescript, eminently forgettable; commonplace, ordinary, uneventful 610 *usual*.

640 Utility

N. *utility*, use, usefulness; employability, serviceability, handiness 628 *instrumentality*; efficacy, efficiency 160 *ability*; adequacy 635 *sufficiency*; applicability, suitability 642 *good policy*; availability 189 *presence*; service, avail, help; value, worth, merit 644 *goodness*; virtue, function, capacity, potency, clout 160 *power*; advantage, commodity; profitability, bottom line, earning capacity, productivity 171 *productiveness*; profit, mileage 771 *gain*; convenience, benefit, common weal, public good 615 *good*; utilitarianism, functionalism; employment, utilization 673 *use*.

Adj. *useful*, of use, helpful, of service, user-friendly, -friendly 703 *helping*; sensible, practical, applied, functional; versatile, multipurpose, all-purpose, of all work; practicable, convenient, expedient 642 *advisable*; handy, nifty; at hand, available, on tap; serviceable, fit for, good for, applicable; ready for use, operative, on stream, usable, employable; valid, current; able, competent, efficacious, effective, effectual, efficient 160 *powerful*; conducive; adequate 635 *sufficient*; pragmatic, utilitarian.

profitable, paying, remunerative 771 *gainful*; beneficial, advantageous, to one's advantage, edifying, worthwhile 615 *good*; worth one's salt, worth one's keep, worth one's weight in gold, invaluable, priceless 644 *valuable*.

find useful, find a use for, make use of, utilize 673 *use*; turn to good account, make capital out of 137 *profit by*; reap the benefit of 771 *gain*; be the better for 654 *get better*.

641 Uselessness

N. *uselessness*; inutility, superfluousness 637 *superfluity*; futility, inanity; worthlessness; inadequacy 636 *insufficiency*; inefficacy, ineffectualness, inability 161 *lack of power*; inefficiency, incompetence, ineptitude 695 *lack of skill*; unserviceableness, unfitness 643 *inexpedi-*

ency; inapplicability, no benefit 172 *unproductiveness*; unhelpfulness.

wasted effort, lost labour 728 *failure*; game not worth the candle; waste of breath, waste of time, dead loss, no-win situation; labours in vain, wild-goose chase, fool's errand; labour of Sisyphus, rearranging the deckchairs on the Titanic.

rubbish, load of old rubbish, trash, dreck; waste, refuse, lumber, junk, scrap, litter; wastage, bilge, wastepaper; scourings, sweepings, shavings 41 *leavings*; chaff, husks, bran; scraps, crumbs; offal, carrion; dust, muck, debris, slag, clinker, dross, scum 649 *dirt*; crap (vulg); peel, orange peel, peelings, banana skin, dead wood, stubble, weeds; rags and bones, old clothes, cast-offs; reject; midden, rubbish heap, tip, slag heap, dump.

Adj. *useless*, functionless, purposeless, pointless; naff; futile 497 *absurd*; unpractical, impracticable, unworkable, no go; nonfunctional 844 *ornamental*; redundant; expendable, dispensable, unfit, inapplicable 643 *inexpedient*; fit for nothing, unusable, unemployable; inefficient, incompetent 695 *unskilful*; unable, ineffective, feckless, ineffectual 161 *impotent*; non-functioning, inoperative, dud, kaput; invalid; out of order; broken down, worn out, hors de combat, past it, obsolete; hopeless, vain.

profitless, loss-making, unprofitable, wasteful, ill-spent; vain, abortive, Sisyphean 728 *unsuccessful*; nothing to show for; unrewarding, thankless; fruitless, valueless, not worth the effort, not worth the paper it is written on 645 *bad*; unsaleable, dear at any price 811 *dear*.

Vb. *make useless*, disqualify, unfit, disarm, decommission, make harmless, take the sting out of 161 *disable*; castrate, emasculate 161 *unman*; cripple, lame, clip the wings 655 *impair*; put out of commission, lay up 679 *make inactive*; sabotage, throw a spanner in the works, put a spoke in one's wheel, cramp one's style 702 *obstruct*; take to pieces, break up 46 *disunite*; deface.

waste effort, labour the obvious; waste one's breath, waste one's time, talk to a brick wall; beat one's head against a brick wall; preach to the converted 637 *be superfluous*; be on a hiding to nothing, get nowhere, labour in vain; go round in circles; flog a dead horse, beat the air, tilt at windmills; cry for the moon 470 *attempt the impossible*.

642 Good policy

N. *good policy*, expediency, expedience; right answer, advisability, desirability, worthwhileness, suitability 640 *utility*; fitness, propriety

915 *what is due*; proper time, opportunity 137 *occasion*; convenience, pragmatism, utilitarianism, opportunism; profit, advantage 615 *benefit*; facilities.

Adj. advisable, commendable; as well to, better to, desirable; fitting, seemly, proper 913 *right*; well-timed, opportune 137 *timely*; prudent, politic, judicious 498 *wise*; expedient, advantageous; practical, pragmatic; applicable.

Vb. be expedient, not come amiss, come in useful, suit the occasion; be to the purpose, help 703 *aid*; forward, advance, promote; have the desired effect, produce results; work, do, serve, be better than nothing, deliver the goods, fill *or* fit the bill 635 *suffice*; achieve one's aim 727 *succeed*; fit, be just the thing 24 *accord*; profit, advantage, benefit 644 *do good*.

643 Inexpediency

N. inexpediency, inexpedience; not the answer, lack of planning; inadvisability, undesirability; unsuitability, unfitness 25 *inaptitude*; impropriety, unfittingness, unseemliness 916 *what is not due*; wrongness 914 *wrong*; inopportuneness 138 *untimeliness*; inconvenience, disadvantage; mixed blessing, two-edged weapon, last resort 596 *necessity*.

Adj. inexpedient, better not, as well not to, inadvisable, undesirable, not recommended; ill-advised, impolitic, imprudent, injudicious, off-message 499 *unwise*; inappropriate, unfitting, out of place, unseemly; improper; unfit, inadmissible, unsuitable, unhappy, inept 25 *unapt*; unseasonable, inopportune, untimely 138 *ill-timed*; unsatisfactory 636 *insufficient*; inconvenient; detrimental, disadvantageous; unhealthy, unwholesome 653 *unhealthy*; unprofitable 641 *useless*; unhelpful; untoward 731 *useless*; awkward 695 *clumsy*; cumbersome.

644 Goodness

N. goodness, soundness 650 *health*; virtuosity 694 *skill*; quality, vintage; good points, redeeming feature; merit, desert, claim to fame; excellence, eminence; virtue, worth, value 809 *price*; pricelessness; flawlessness 646 *perfection*; quintessence 1 *essence*.

elite, chosen few; pick, prime, flower; cream, crème de la crème, salt of the earth, pick of the bunch, meritocracy; crack troops; top people, the great and the good 638 *bigwig*; charmed circle, top drawer, upper crust, aristocracy, Sloane Rangers 868 *upper class*; titbit, prime cut, pièce de résistance; plum, prize 729 *trophy*.

exceller, nonpareil; prodigy, gifted child, genius; superman, wonderwoman, wonder, wonder of the world 864 *prodigy*; Admirable

Crichton 646 *paragon*; one in a thousand, one in a million, treasure; jewel, pearl, ruby, diamond 844 *gem*; gem of the first water, pure gold, chef-d'oeuvre, pièce de résistance, collector's item, museum piece 694 *masterpiece*; record-breaker, best-seller, chart-topper, best ever, last word in, ne plus ultra, best thing since sliced bread; bee's knees, cat's whiskers, cat's pyjamas; the goods, winner, corker, humdinger, wow, knockout, hit, smash hit; smasher, charmer 841 *a beauty*; star, idol 890 *favourite*; best of its kind, Rolls-Royce, the tops, the greatest, top of the pops, top twenty, hit parade, chart-topper; top-notcher, top seed, first-rater; cock of the walk, toast of the town, Queen of the May; champion, titleholder, world-beater, prizewinner 727 *victor*.

Adj. excellent, fine, braw; exemplary; good, good as gold 933 *virtuous*; above par, preferable, better 34 *superior*; very good, first-rate, ace, A1, alpha plus; prime, quality, fine, superfine, killer, to die for; God's own, superlative, in a class by itself, beyond one's wildest dreams; all-star, of the first water, rare, vintage, classic 646 *perfect*; choice, select, handpicked, exquisite, recherché 605 *chosen*; exclusive, pure 44 *unmixed*; worthy, meritorious; admired, admirable, estimable, praiseworthy, creditable; famous, great; lovely 841 *beautiful*; glorious, dazzling, splendid, splendiferous, magnificent, marvellous, wonderful, terrific, sensational, superb, cool, wicked, def, awesome, phat.

super, superduper, fantastic, way-out, fabulous, fab, groovy, brill, magic, wizard, wizzo; spot-on, bang-on; top-notch, top-flight, über- (see also *best* below); lovely, glorious, gorgeous, heavenly, out of this world 32 *prodigious*; smashing, stunning, spiffing, ripping, topping, swell, great, grand, famous, capital, dandy, bully, hunky-dory; scrumptious, delicious, juicy, plummy, jammy 826 *pleasurable*.

best, optimum, A1, champion, tiptop, top-notch, ace; first-rate, crack; second to none 34 *supreme*; unequalled, unparalleled, unmatched, peerless, unbeatable, unsurpassable 646 *perfect*; best-ever, record, record-breaking, best-selling, chart-topping.

valuable, invaluable, inestimable, priceless, costly, rich 811 *of value*; rare, precious, worth its weight in gold, worth a king's ransom; sterling, gilt-edged, blue-chip.

beneficial, wholesome, healthy, salutary; edifying, worthwhile, advantageous, profitable 640 *useful*; favourable, propitious 730 *prosperous*.

not bad, tolerable, so-so, passable, respectable, fair; all right, okay, OK; indifferent, middle-of-the-road, middling, mediocre, ordinary, fifty-fifty, average 30 *median*.

Vb. *be good*, be sound, etc. (see adj.); have merit, deserve well 915 *deserve*; stand the test, pass muster 635 *suffice*; equal the best 28 *be equal*; excel, transcend, take the prize 34 *be superior*; exceed expectations *or* requirements, punch above one's weight.

do good, have a good effect, improve, edify; do a world of good; be the making of, make a man of 654 *make better*; help 615 *benefit*; do a favour, do a good turn.

645 Badness

N. *badness*, obnoxiousness, nastiness, beastliness, foulness, grossness, rottenness; unworthiness, worthlessness; second-rateness, inferiority; flaw 647 *imperfection*; shoddiness 641 *uselessness*; unsoundness, decay, corruption 655 *deterioration*; disruption; morbidity 651 *disease*; harmfulness, hurtfulness, ill, hurt, harm, injury, detriment, damage, mischief 616 *evil*; noxiousness, poisonousness, deadliness, virulence 653 *unhealthiness*; poison, blight, canker, cancer 659 *bane*; pestilence, sickness 651 *plague*; contamination, plague spot, trouble spot, hotbed 651 *infection*; affair, scandal 867 *slur*; abomination, filth 649 *uncleanness*; sewer 649 *sink*; bitterness, painfulness, sting, ache, pang, thorn in the flesh 377 *pain*; angst, anguish 825 *suffering*; maltreatment, oppression, persecution; unkindness, cruelty, malignancy, spitefulness, spite 898 *malevolence*; depravity, vice 934 *wickedness*; sin 936 *guilt*; bad influence, evil genius; ill wind; black magic, evil eye, jettatura, hoodoo, jinx, gremlin 983 *sorcery*; curse 899 *curse*; snake in the grass 663 *troublemaker*.

Adj. *bad*, vile, base, evil; gross, black; irredeemable; poor, mean, wretched, grotty, gungy, gruesome, measly, execrable, awful, low-grade, second-rate 35 *inferior*; cringe-making, cringeworthy, buttock-clenching, thudding; worthless, shoddy, tacky, naff, crummy, ropy, punk, pathetic 641 *useless*; unsatisfactory, faulty, flawed 647 *imperfect*; incompetent, inefficient; mangled, spoiled 695 *bungled*; scruffy, filthy, mangy, manky 649 *dirty*; foul; gone bad, rank, tainted; corrupt, decaying, rotten to the core; infected, poisoned, septic 651 *diseased*; incurable; depraved, vicious, villainous, accursed 934 *wicked*; heinous, sinful 936 *guilty*; mean, wrongful, unjust 914 *wrong*; sinister 616 *evil*; contemptible; shameful, scandalous, disgraceful 867 *discreditable*; lamentable, deplorable, grievous, heavy, burdensome; too bad 827 *annoying*.

harmful, hurtful, injurious, damaging, detrimental, prejudicial, disadvantageous 643 *inexpedient*; deleterious, corrosive, destructive; pernicious, fatal 362 *deadly*; disastrous, ruinous, calamitous 731 *adverse*; degenerative, noxious, malign, malignant, unhealthy, unwholesome, infectious 653 *unhealthy*; polluting, poisonous, risky 661 *dangerous*; sinister, ominous, dire, dreadful, accursed, devilish 616 *evil*; mischievous, spiteful, malicious, malevolent, ill-disposed; mischief-making; inhuman 898 *cruel*; outrageous, rough, harsh, intolerant, persecuting 735 *oppressive*; monstrous 32 *exorbitant*.

not nice, obnoxious, nasty, beastly, horrid, horrific, horrible, terrible, gruesome, grim, ghastly, awful, dreadful, from hell; foul, rotten, lousy, putrid, putrefying, stinking, sickening, revolting, nauseous, nauseating; loathsome, detestable, abominable, scurvy 888 *hateful*; vulgar, sordid, low, indecent, improper, gross, filthy, pornographic, obscene 951 *impure*; shocking, disgusting, reprehensible, monstrous, horrendous.

damnable, damn, damned, darn, darned, dashed, dratted, blasted, bloody, blinking, blankety-blank, confounded, perishing, fucking (vulg), effing (vulg), frigging (vulg); execrable, accursed, cursed, hellish, infernal, devilish, diabolical.

Vb. *harm*, do harm to, do one a mischief; disagree with, make one ill, make one sick; injure, damage, pollute 655 *impair*; corrupt 655 *pervert*; play havoc with 63 *disarrange*; do no good; have a deleterious effect on, disimprove, worsen; molest; plague; land one in trouble, queer one's pitch, do for; be unkind 898 *be malevolent*.

ill-treat, maltreat, abuse 675 *misuse*; ill-use, put upon, tyrannize, trample on, victimize, prey upon; persecute 735 *oppress*; wrong, distress 827 *torment*; outrage, violate, force; savage, maul, bite, scratch, tear 655 *wound*; stab 263 *pierce*; batter, bruise, buffet 279 *strike*; crucify 963 *torture*; take one's spite out on; crush 165 *destroy*.

Adv. *badly*, amiss, wrong, ill.

646 Perfection

N. *perfection*, sheer perfection; finish; the ideal; immaculateness, faultlessness, flawlessness, mint condition; correctness, irreproachability; impeccability, infallibility; transcendence 34 *superiority*; quintessence, essence; peak, zenith, pinnacle 213 *summit*; height of perfection, acme of perfection, peak of perfection; ne plus ultra, last word; chef d'oeuvre, flawless performance 694 *masterpiece*.

paragon, nonpareil, flower, prince of 644 *exceller*; ideal, dream team, knight in shining armour, saint, plaster saint; classic, pattern of perfection, model, shining example 23 *prototype*; superman, superwoman, wonderwoman, demigod 864 *prodigy*.

Adj. perfect, picture-perfect, perfected, finished; just right, ideal, flawless, faultless, impeccable, infallible, correct, irreproachable; immaculate, spotless, blemish-free, without a stain; uncontaminated, pure 44 *unmixed*; sound as a bell, right as rain, in perfect condition; one hundred per cent, A1; complete 52 *intact*; consummate, unsurpassable 34 *supreme*; brilliant, masterly 694 *skilful*; model, classical.

undamaged, safe and sound, unhurt, unscathed, no harm done; unmarked; without blemish, unspoilt; without loss, intact; in the pink 650 *healthy*.

Vb. perfect, consummate, bring to perfection; put the finishing touch 213 *crown*; complete, leave nothing to be desired 725 *carry through*.

647 Imperfection

N. imperfection, imperfectness; room for improvement; faultiness, erroneousness, fallibility 495 *error*; patchiness, unevenness, curate's egg 17 *non-uniformity*; defectiveness, bit *or* piece missing 55 *incompleteness*; deficiency, inadequacy 636 *insufficiency*; unsoundness 661 *vulnerability*; failure, weakness 307 *shortfall*; second best, third rate, makeshift 150 *substitute*; mediocrity; adulteration 43 *mixture*.

defect, fault 495 *error*; flaw, rift, leak, loophole, crack lacuna 201 *gap*; deficiency, limitation 307 *shortfall*; kink, foible, screw loose 503 *eccentricity*; weak point, soft spot, tragic flaw, chink in one's armour, Achilles's heel, soft underbelly 661 *vulnerability*; feet of clay, weak link in the chain, weakest link 163 *weakness*; stain, blot, spot, smudge 845 *blemish*; snag.

Adj. imperfect, not quite right, less than perfect, fallible, uneven, patchy, good in parts, like the curate's egg 17 *non-uniform*; faulty, botched 695 *bungled*; flawed, cracked; leaky; wobbly, rickety 163 *flimsy*; unsound 661 *vulnerable*; shop-soiled, tainted, stained, spotted, marked, scratched; below par, off form; unfit, not good enough, not up to the mark, inadequate, deficient, wanting, lacking 636 *insufficient*; defective 55 *incomplete*; broken 53 *fragmentary*; crippled; half-finished 55 *unfinished*; perfunctory 456 *inattentive*; warped, twisted, distorted 246 *deformed*; mutilated, maimed, lame 163 *weakened*; undeveloped, makeshift, jerry-built, rough and ready, provisional 150 *substituted*; second-rate, third-rate

35 *inferior*; unimpressive, underwhelming, no great shakes, nothing to boast of, nothing to write home about.

Vb. be imperfect, fall short of perfection, be flawed; not bear inspection, not pass muster, fail the test, dissatisfy 636 *be insufficient*; not make the grade 924 *incur blame*; have feet of clay.

648 Cleanness

N. cleanness, immaculateness 950 *purity*; freshness, whiteness; spit and polish; cleanliness, daintiness 862 *fastidiousness*; smokeless zone.

cleansing, clean, spring-cleaning, dry-cleaning; washing, cleaning up, mopping up, washing up, wiping up, scrubbing; refining, purification, desalination; purgation; washing out, flushing, dialysis; defecation, purging, enema, colonic irrigation 302 *excretion*; airing, ventilation, fumigation 338 *vaporization*; deodorization 395 *odourlessness*; sterilization, disinfection, decontamination, delousing; sanitation, drainage, sewerage, plumbing 652 *hygiene*; water closet, flush 649 *toilet*.

washing, ablutions; hygiene, oral hygiene; douche, flush; wash, lick and a promise; soaking, bathing, dipping; soaping, lathering, scrubbing, sponging, rinsing, shampoo; dip 313 *plunge*; bath, tub; bathtub, hipbath, bidet; washbasin, wash-hand basin, washstand; Turkish bath, sauna, Jacuzzi (tdmk), whirlpool bath, hot tub; shower; bathroom, washroom 183 *room*; public baths; swimming bath, swimming pool; wash, laundry; washtub, washboard, dolly; copper, boiler, washing machine, washer, twin tub, launderette.

cleanser, purifier; disinfectant, carbolic, deodorant; detergent, soap, soap flakes; washing powder, soap powder, washing-up liquid, water, soap and water, shampoo; mouth wash, gargle; cleansing cream; toothpaste; pumice stone; furniture polish, boot polish, blacking; wax, varnish; whitewash, paint; blacklead; aperient 658 *purgative*; carbon sink.

cleaning utensil, broom, besom, mop, sponge, swab, scourer; loofah; duster, feather duster; brush, scrubbing brush, nailbrush, toothbrush, toothpick, dental floss; comb, hair brush, clothes brush; dustpan and brush, waste bin, dustbin, wastepaper basket, litter bin, waste disposal unit, compactor; poopscoop, pooper-scooper; carpet sweeper, vacuum cleaner, Hoover (tdmk); doormat, foot-scraper; pipe cleaner, windscreen wiper; sieve, riddle; filter; dishwasher.

cloth, cleaning cloth, duster; dishcloth, tea towel; wash-leather; chamois, shammy; flannel, face flannel, facecloth, towel, bath towel, hand towel; handkerchief, paper handkerchief, tissue; toilet tissue, toilet paper, lavatory paper, toilet roll.

cleaner, laundryman, laundress, washer-woman; washer-up, dish-washer; charwoman, char, charlady, cleaner, help, daily help, daily, home help; Mrs Mop; dustman, refuse collector; lavatory attendant, sanitary engineer; chimneysweep, window cleaner; bootblack.

Adj. *clean*, dirt-free; snowy 427 *white*; polished, clean, shining 417 *undimmed*; cleanly; fresh; bright as a new pin, fresh as a daisy; cleaned, scrubbed, polished, etc. (see vb.); cleaned up, laundered; spruce, spick and span, well-groomed 60 *orderly*; deodorized, disinfected, hygienic, sterilized; purified, immaculate, spotless, clean as a whistle 646 *perfect*; ritually clean, kosher, halal 301 *edible*.

Vb. *clean*, spring-clean, clean up, clear up; groom, valet, spruce; wash, wipe, wipe clean, wash up, sponge, mop, mop up, swab, wash down; scrub, scour; scrape 333 *rub*; do the washing, launder; bleach, dry-clean; soap, lather, shampoo; bathe, dip, dunk, rinse, swill down, sluice, douche, shower 341 *drench*; dust, sweep, sweep up, beat, vacuum, hoover; brush, brush up; buff, polish; blacklead 417 *make bright*; whitewash 427 *whiten*; erase 550 *obliterate*; clean out, clear out, make a clean sweep 300 *eject*.

purify, purge, clean up; bowdlerize, censor, blue-pencil, expurgate; elevate 654 *make better*; cleanse, freshen, ventilate, deodorize, fumigate; desalinate; decontaminate, disinfect, sterilize, chlorinate, pasteurize 652 *make sanitary*; refine, distil, clarify, skim, scum, decarbonize; strain, filter, percolate, leach; sift, sieve; dialyse, catheterize, clean out, wash out, drain.

649 Uncleanness

N. *uncleanness*, uncleanliness; soiling, dirtiness (see also *dirt* below); muckiness; scruffiness, grottiness, filthiness; lousiness; squalor; untidiness, sluttishness, slovenliness 61 *disorder*; pigsty; stink 397 *stench*; pollution, defilement; corruption, taint, putrefaction 51 *decomposition*; contamination 651 *infection*; unwashed body.

dirt, filth, stain, blot; crud, yuk, gunge, gunk, muck, mud, sludge, slime; bog 347 *marsh*; dung, droppings, ordure, faeces 302 *excrement*; snot, mucus; dust, mote 332 *powder*; cobweb, grime, smut, smudge, soot, smoke; grounds, dregs; scourings 41 *leavings*; sediment, deposit, precipitate, residuum, fur; scum, dross, froth; ashes, cinders, ash; drainage, sewerage; slough; scurf, dandruff; tartar,

plaque; pus, matter, refuse, garbage, litter 641 *rubbish*; rot, rust, mildew, mould, fungus 51 *decay*; vermin.

toilet, lavatory, bathroom, smallest room, latrine, privy, heads, jakes, bog, john, loo; closet, earth closet, water closet, WC; cloakroom, powder room, rest room, washroom, little boys' room, urinal, public convenience, comfort station, Ladies, Gents; toilet bowl, lavatory bowl, commode, bedpan, room pot, potty 302 *defecation*.

sink, kitchen sink, draining board; cesspit, cesspool, sump, septic tank; gutter, sewer 351 *drain*; dunghill, midden, tip, rubbish heap, dust-heap, compost-heap; dustbin, trashcan 194 *vessel*; pigsty; slum, spittoon.

dirty person, sloven, slattern, slut; litterbug, litter lout; street arab; scavenger 648 *cleaner*; pig, ratbag, fleabag.

Adj. *unclean*, smutty, obscene, corrupt 951 *impure*; coarse, unpurified; septic, festering; non-sterile 653 *infectious*; sordid, squalid, slummy, insanitary, unhygienic 653 *unhealthy*; foul, offensive, nasty, grotty, manky, yukky; disgusting, repulsive 645 *not nice*; nauseous, nauseating, stinking, ponging; uncleanly; grubby, scruffy, scabby, mangy; flea-ridden, lousy, crawling; faecal, rotting, tainted, high; flyblown, maggoty.

dirty, filthy; dusty, grimy, sooty, smoky, fuggy; polluted, littered; untidy, unkempt, slatternly, sleazy, slovenly, sluttish, bedraggled; unwashed; black, dingy, tarnished, stained, soiled; greasy, oily; caked, matted, muddied; messy, mucky, muddy, slimy 347 *marshy*; turbid; furred up, scummy; musty, fusty, cobwebby; mouldy, rotten 655 *dilapidated*.

Vb. *be unclean*, be dirty, etc. (see adj.); collect dust, foul up, clog; rust, mildew, moulder, rot, go bad, go off 51 *decompose*; smell 397 *stink*.

make unclean, foul, dirty, soil; stain, blot, sully, tarnish; muck up, make a mess, untidy 61 *be disordered*; besmirch, smudge, blur, smoke 419 *dim*; spot, streak, smear, besmear, grease, cake, clog, muddy, bespatter, splash; taint, infect, pollute, contaminate 655 *impair*; defile, profane, desecrate.

650 Health

N. *health*, rude health, good health; healthiness, iron constitution, health and strength 162 *vitality*; fitness, good condition, pink of condition; bloom, rosy cheeks, ruddy complexion; well-being, physical well-being; soundness; clean bill of health; health warning.

Adj. *healthy*, wholesome, sanitary 652

healthy; in good health, bursting with health, blooming, ruddy, rosy; lusty, bouncing, strapping, hale, hearty, hale and hearty, sound, fit, well, full of beans 174 *vigorous*; robust, hardy, strong, vigorous 162 *stalwart*; fighting fit, in peak condition, in tip-top condition, in the pink, in good nick, in good shape, in fine fettle; feeling great; sound in wind and limb, sound as a bell, fit as a fiddle *or* as a flea, strong as a horse, A1; a picture of health, feeling good; getting well, convalescent, on the mend, on the up and up, up and about.

Vb. *be healthy*, be well, etc. (see adj.); look after oneself, take care of oneself; feel fine, bloom, thrive, flourish, enjoy good health; be in the pink, have never felt better; wear well, be well-preserved; keep fit, keep well, have a clean bill of health.

get healthy, get fit, etc. (see adj.); recuperate, return to health, recover one's health, get the colour back in one's cheeks; mend, convalesce, get back on one's feet, take a fresh lease of life, become a new man *or* woman 656 *revive*.

651 Ill health. Disease

N. *ill health*, poor health, delicate health; weak constitution; unhealthiness, weakliness, infirmity, debility 163 *weakness*; seediness; indisposition; allergy; chronic ill health, invalidism, valetudinarianism, hypochondria; nerves 503 *neurosis*; health warning.

illness, loss of health 655 *deterioration*; affliction, disability, handicap, infirmity, lameness, spasticity 163 *weakness*; dysfunction; sickness, indisposition, ailment, complaint, virus, viral infection, complication; healthcare-associated infection, hospital-acquired infection, HAI; immune deficiency disorder, human immuno-deficiency virus, HIV, acquired immune deficiency syndrome, AIDS; condition, history of; bout of sickness, attack; spasm, stroke, seizure, apoplexy, fit; shock; poisoning, food poisoning, blood poisoning (see also *infection* below); nausea, queasiness, vomiting, airsickness, carsickness, seasickness; dizziness, vertigo; headache, migraine 377 *pain*; symptom, syndrome 547 *indication*; temperature, feverishness, fever, ague, shivers, shakes 318 *spasm*; hypothermia, hyperthermia; pyrexia; delirium 503 *frenzy*; breakdown, collapse; fainting 375 *insensitivity*; prostration, coma; terminal disease, fatal illness 361 *decease*. (See also 655 *wound*.)

disease, malady, disorder; epidemic disease, endemic disease; infectious disease, contagious disease, communicable disease, notifiable disease, debilitating disease, killer disease; congenital disease, occupational disease, industrial disease; alcoholism, drug addiction; obesity; malnutrition, anorexia nervosa, bulimia nervosa, avitaminosis, kwashiorkor, beri-beri, pellagra, rickets, scurvy; degenerative disease, wasting disease, atrophy; trauma; organic disease; neurological disease, nervous disease, epilepsy; heart disease, cardiac disease; diabetes, late-onset diabetes; venereal disease; cancer; respiratory disease, gastro-intestinal disease, bacterial disease; virus, viral infection; fibrosis; chronic fatigue syndrome, ME, myalgic encephalomyelitis; Gulf War Syndrome, desert fever; brain disease, post-traumatic stress disorder 503 *mental disorder*; caisson disease, the bends.

plague, pest, scourge 659 *bane*; pestilence, infection, contagion; epidemic; bubonic plague, Black Death.

infection, contagion, bug, pollution; infectiousness, infectivity, contagiousness 653 *unhealthiness*; disease party; suppuration, maturation, estering, purulence, gangrene; toxicity, sepsis, poisoning 659 *poison*; vector, carrier, host; parasite, worm, toxocara canis 659 *bane*; virus, parvovirus, retrovirus, lentivirus, bacillus, bacterium, germ, pathogen; Coxsackie virus, corona virus; superbug, MRSA; blood-poisoning, toxaemia, septicaemia; necrotizing fasciitis, flesh-eating bug; food-poisoning, botulism, salmonella, E coli, campylobacter, helicobacter pylori; gastroenteritis, cholera; winter vomiting bug, small round structured virus; parasitical disease, toxocariasis, toxoplasmosis, bilharzia (see also *tropical disease* below); infectious disease, common cold, influenza, flu, Asian flu, bird flu, SARS, severe acute respiratory disease; diphtheria, pneumonia, viral pneumonia; infective hepatitis; tuberculosis, consumption; measles, German measles, rubella; whooping-cough, pertussis, mumps; chickenpox, smallpox, variola; scarlet fever, scarlatina, roseola; fever, malaria (see also *tropical disease* below); typhus; typhoid; glandular fever, infectious mononucleosis; poliomyelitis, polio; encephalitis, meningitis; sleepy sickness, sleeping sickness; tetanus, lockjaw; rabies, hydrophobia.

tropical disease, malaria; cholera; yellow fever, blackwater fever, Lassa fever, dengue; green monkey disease; kala-azar, leishmaniasis; sleeping sickness; bilharzia; hookworm; trachoma, glaucoma, river blindness 439 *blindness*; yaws; leprosy; beri-beri, kwashiorkor.

digestive disorder, indigestion, dyspepsia, liverishness; biliousness, nausea, sickness, vomiting, retching; winter vomiting *or* winter vomiting disease; colic, gripes; stomach ache; stomach upset, tummy upset, collywobbles, gippy tummy, irritable bowel syndrome, diarrhoea, diarrhoea and vomiting, D and V; travellers' diarrhoea, holiday tummy, Spanish tummy, dreaded lurgy, Montezuma's revenge, Aztec two-step, Delhi belly, the runs, the trots 302 *defecation*; gastroenteritis; dysentery, cholera, typhoid; food poisoning, botulism; flatulence, wind, belching 300 *clearing*; acidosis, heartburn; hiatus hernia; ulcer, peptic ulcer, gastric ulcer, duodenal ulcer; gastritis, enteritis, colitis, peritonitis, appendicitis, diverticulitis, diverticulosis; jaundice, hepatitis, cirrhosis, cystitis, nephritis; gallstones, kidney stones; haemorrhoids, piles; constipation; stomach cancer, bowel cancer;.

respiratory disease, cough, cold, common cold, a cold in the head, coryza; sore throat, catarrh, rhinitis, allergic rhinitis, sinusitis, adenoids, tonsillitis, pharyngitis; laryngitis, tracheitis, croup, bronchitis; emphysema, asthma; pleurisy, pneumonia, legionnaire's disease, sick building syndrome; pneumoconiosis, silicosis, asbestosis; anthrax; diphtheria; whooping-cough, pertussis; lung cancer; smoker's cough; cystic fibrosis; tuberculosis, consumption.

cardiovascular disease, cardiac disease; angina; chest-pain; bradycardia, tachycardia; palpitation; heart murmur; enlarged heart; heart condition, bad heart, weak heart, heart trouble; congenital heart disease, hole in the heart; rheumatic heart disease, coronary heart disease; heart failure, cardiac arrest; heart attack, coronary thrombosis, coronary; cerebral thrombosis, brain haemorrhage, stroke; blood pressure, hypertension, high blood pressure, hypotension, low blood pressure; vascular disease, atheroma, aneurysm; arteriosclerosis; phlebitis, varicose veins; thrombosis, embolism, pulmonary embolism, infarction, myocardial infarction; deep vein thrombosis, DVT, economy-class syndrome.

blood disease, anaemia, aplastic anaemia, pernicious anaemia, sickle-cell anaemia, thalassaemia; leukaemia, Hodgkin's disease; haemophilia, AIDS; haemorrhage.

cancer, neoplasm, growth; primary growth, secondary growth, tumour, malignant tumour, brain tumour, cancerous growth; carcinoma, sarcoma, melanoma; benign tumour, innocent tumour.

skin disease, skin lesion; mange; yaws; leprosy; erythema, prickly heat; erysipelas; impetigo, herpes, herpes zoster, shingles; dermatitis, eczema; serpigo, ringworm; pruritis, itch 378 *formication*; hives, urticaria, nettlerash; thrush; athlete's foot; rash, eruption, acne, rosacea, spots, blackheads; pustule,

papula, pimple; goitre, cyst, sebaceous cyst, blister, wart, verruca 253 *swelling*; macula, mole, freckle, birthmark, pockmark 845 *blemish*; skin cancer, melanoma.

venereal disease, VD, sexually-transmitted disease, social disease, pox; syphilis, gonorrhoea, the clap; chlamydia; herpes.

ulcer, ulceration, gathering, festering, purulence; inflammation, lesion 655 *wound*; scald, burn, first-degree burn; sore, boil, abscess, fistula; cyst; chilblain, corn 253 *swelling*; gangrene.

Inflammation

adenitis (inflammation of a gland), appendicitis (appendix), arteritis (artery), arthritis (joint), balanitis (glans penis), blepharitis (eyelid), bronchitis (bronchial tubes), bursitis (sac-like membrane in shoulder, foot, etc), carditis (heart), colitis (colon), conjunctivitis (membrane of the eye), cystitis (bladder), dermatitis (skin), diverticulitis (sacs in the wall of the intestine), duodenitis (duodenum), encephalitis (brain), endocarditis (lining of the heart), endometritis (lining of the uterus), enteritis (intestine), fasciitis (plantar fasciitis: inflammation of a ligament in the sole of the foot; necrotizing fasciitis: inflammation of the sheath of tissue around a muscle or organ accompanied by destruction of tissue), fibrositis (fibrous tissue), gastritis (lining of the stomach), gastroenteritis (lining of the stomach and the intestine), gingivitis (gums), hepatitis (liver), laryngitis (larynx), mastitis (breast), meningitis (membranes surrounding brain and spinal cord), myelitis (spinal cord or bone marrow), myocarditis (heart muscle), nephritis (kidney), neuritis (nerve), oophoritis (ovary), ophthalmitis (eye, especially the membrane of the eye), orchitis (testicle), osteoarthritis (arthritis with damage to bone and cartilage), otitis (ear), pericarditis (sac around the heart), peritonitis (abdominal membrane), pharyngitis (pharynx), phlebitis (vein), pleuritis (inflammation of the membrane around the lungs; = pleurisy), poliomyelitis (nerve cells of the spinal cord), retinitis (retina of the eye), rhinitis (mucous membrane of the nose), salpingitis (Fallopian tube), sinusitis (sinus), spondylitis (joint in the backbone), tendonitis (tendon), tonsillitis (tonsils), tracheitis (windpipe), tympanitis (membrane of the ear), urethritis (urinary tract).

rheumatism, rheumatics; rheumatic fever; fibrositis; frozen shoulder, tennis elbow, housemaid's knee, pulled muscle; arthritis, rheumatoid arthritis; gout 377 *pang*; osteoarthritis; lumbago, sciatica; slipped disc.

nervous disorder, nervous breakdown 503 *psychopathy*; brain tumour; cerebral haemorrhage, stroke, cerebrovascular accident, CVA, seizure; general paralysis, atrophy 375 *insensitivity*; partial paralysis, paresis; cerebral palsy, spasticity; tic 318 *spasm*; petit mal, grand mal, epilepsy; poliomyelitis, polio; spina bifida; Parkinson's disease; chorea, Huntington's chorea, St Vitus's dance 318 *spasm*; multiple sclerosis, MS; muscular dystrophy.

animal disease, distemper, foot-and-mouth disease, swine fever, swine vesicular disease; BSE, bovine spongiform encephalopathy, mad cow disease, myxomatosis; rinderpest, murrain; anthrax, sheeprot, bloat; liver fluke, worms; megrims, staggers; glanders, farcy, sweeny, spavin, thrush; Newcastle disease, fowl pest; psittacosis; hard pad, Kennel cough; mange; rabies; parapox.

sick person, patient, in-patient, out-patient; medical *or* health *or* surgical *or* transplant tourist; stretcher case, hospital case; mental case 504 *madman*; invalid, chronic invalid; valetudinarian, hypochondriac, cyberchondriac, malingerer, lead-swinger, martyr to ill health; consumptive, asthmatic, bronchitic, dyspeptic, diabetic; haemophiliae, bleeder; person with AIDS, PWA; insomniac; addict, alcoholic; spastic, arthritic, paralytic; paraplegic, disabled person; crock, old crock, cripple 163 *weakling*; sick list; sick room, sick bay.

Adj. *unhealthy*, sickly; infirm, weakly 163 *weak*; delicate, of weak constitution, in poor health, out of kilter, in poor condition; anorexic, malnourished 636 *underfed*; peaky, emaciated, skin and bones; sallow, pale, anaemic 426 *colourless*; bilious 434 *green*; jaundiced 433 *yellow*.

sick, ill, unwell, indisposed, out of sorts, under the weather, off-colour, below par, one degree under, out of kilter; queasy, nauseated, nauseous, green around the gills, acidotic; in a bad way, poorly, seedy, squeamish, groggy, grotty, queer, ailing; sickening for; feverish, headachy, off one's food, off one's oats; confined, laid up, bedridden, on one's back, in bed, in hospital, on the sick list, invalided, hospitalized; run down, exhausted 684 *fatigued*; taken ill, taken bad; prostrate, collapsed; in a coma 375 *insensitive*; on the danger list, in intensive care; critical, serious; chronic, incurable, inoperable; terminally ill 361 *dying*.

diseased, pathological; infected, contaminated, tainted, rotten, gangrenous; morbid, pathogenic; iatrogenic; psychosomatic 447 *mental*; infectious, contagious; poisonous, festering, purulent 653 *toxic*; degenerative, consumptive, tubercular; diabetic, hydrocephalic; anaemic; bloodless, leukaemic, haemophilic; arthritic, rheumatic, rheumatoid; palsied, paralysed, spastic, epileptic; leprous; cancerous, oncogenic, carcinogenic; syphilitic, venereal; swollen, oedematous, gouty; bronchial, bronchitic, asthmatic; allergic; pyretic, febrile, fevered, shivering, feverish, delirious; ulcerated, inflamed; erythematous, erysipelatous.

Vb. *be ill*, be sick, etc. (see adj.); enjoy poor health; ail, suffer, undergo treatment; have a complaint *or* an affliction, be a chronic invalid; not feel well, complain of; feel queer, etc. (see adj.), come over all queer; feel sick 300 *vomit*; sicken, fall sick, fall ill; become infected, catch a bug, contract a disease; go down with; be seized, be stricken, be taken bad, not feel so good; have a stroke, collapse; be laid up, take to one's bed; be invalided out; go into a decline; fail, sink, weak 163 *be weak*.

652 Healthiness,

N. *healthiness*, salubrity; state of health; well-being 650 *health*; salubriousness, wholesomeness; fresh air.

hygiene, sanitation, cleanliness 648 *cleanness*; quarantine, cordon sanitaire, biosecurity zone 660 *protection*; pasteurization; antisepsis, sterilization, disinfection, chlorination.

Adj. *healthy*, healthful, salubrious, wholesome; pure, fresh 648 *clean*; ventilated; hygienic, sanitary, disinfected, chlorinated, pasteurized, sterilized, aseptic, antiseptic; good for, salutary, what the doctor ordered 644 *beneficial*; nutritious, nourishing, high-fibre, low-calory, low-fat, low-salt, non-fattening, slimline, body-building, health-giving.

make sanitary, disinfect, boil, sterilize, chlorinate, pasteurize; put in quarantine; ventilate 340 *aerate*; decontaminate 648 *purify*; cleanse 648 *clean*.

653 Unhealthiness

N. *unhealthiness*, insalubrity, unwholesomeness; uncleanliness, lack of hygiene, dirty habits 649 *uncleanness*; slum; bad air, fug, smog; infectiousness, infectivity, contagiousness; sewer 649 *sink*; contagion 651 *infection*; pollution, radioactivity, fallout; poisonousness 659 *bane*.

Adj. *unhealthy*, insalubrious, unwholesome; insanitary, unhygienic 649 *unclean*; noxious; injurious 645 *harmful*; radioactive, carcinogenic; verminous, rat-infested, flea-ridden, flyblown; stagnant, polluted, undrinkable, inedible; unnutritious; stale, gone bad, gone off; unventilated; stuffy; overheated, underheated.

infectious, pathogenic; infective, germ-carrying; contagious, catching, communicable; pestilent, plague-stricken; epidemic, pandemic, endemic; infected 649 *dirty*.

toxic, poisonous, germ-laden; venomous, poisoned; festering, septic, purulent, suppurating; lethal 362 *deadly*.

654 Improvement

N. *improvement*, betterment, amelioration, kaizen, uplift, regeneration; good influence, the making of 178 *influence*; a turn for the better, change for the better, sea change, step change, transfiguration 143 *transformation*; conversion, new leaf 939 *penitence*; revival, recovery, economic recovery, green shoots, dead cat bounce 656 *restoration*; evolution; enrichment; advance, progress, learning curve 285 *progression*; development, personal development; promotion, uptitling, rise, lift; upturn, upward mobility, upswing 310 *elevation*; enhancement 36 *increase*; no pain, no gain.

amendment, mending, etc. (see vb.); renovation 656 *repair*; reorganization 62 *arrangement*; reformation, reform; rectification; correction, revision, red ink, blue pencil; emendation, revised edition, new edition, improved version 589 *edition*; revise, proof; second thoughts, review; polish, finishing touch 725 *completion*.

reformer, repairer, restorer 656 *mender*; emender, corrector, editor, proofreader, reviser; progressive, gradualist, Fabian 625 *moderate*; liberal, radical, feminist, masculinist; extremist, revolutionary 738 *agitator*; socialist, communist, Marxist, Red; reformist; idealist, Utopian 513 *visionary*; egalitarian 16 *uniformist*; champagne socialist; sociologist, social worker 901 *philanthropist*.

Adj. *improving*, reformatory, remedial; reforming, reformist, progressive, radical; civilizing, cultural; idealistic, perfectionistic, Utopian; perfectionist 862 *fastidious*.

Vb. *get better*, improve, mend, take a turn for the better, turn the corner; pick up, rally, revive, recover 656 *be restored*; make progress, make headway, advance, develop, evolve 285 *progress*; mellow, ripen 669 *mature*; bear fruit 171 *be fruitful*; rise 308 *ascend*; graduate 727 *succeed*; rise in the world, prosper; better oneself, be upwardly mobile, mend one's ways, reform, turn over a new leaf, go straight 939 *be penitent*; improve oneself, learn by experience 536 *learn*; raise one's game.

make better, better, improve, refine, ameliorate, reform; make improvements, improve upon, polish, enrich, enhance; work a miracle on, do one a power of good 644 *do good*; improve out of all recognition, transfigure 147 *transform*; make, be the making of, have a good influence, leaven 178 *influence*; uplift, regenerate; refine, elevate, sublimate 648 *purify*; civilize, socialize, teach manners; mend 656 *repair*; restore 656 *cure*; revive, infuse fresh blood into 685 *refresh*; forward, advance, upgrade 285 *promote*; foster, encourage, hype, bring to fruition 669 *mature*; make the most of, get the best out of 673 *use*; develop, open up; tidy up, make shipshape, neaten 62 *arrange*; spruce up, freshen up 648 *clean*; do

up, vamp up, rationalize; renovate, refurbish, renew, give a face lift; bring up to date 126 *modernize*; touch up 841 *beautify*; improve on nature, gild the lily, make up, titivate 843 *primp*; embellish, adorn, ornament 844 *decorate*; sex up.

rectify, put right, set right, straighten, straighten out 24 *adjust*; mend, patch 656 *repair*; correct, debug, decontaminate, blue-pencil, proofread; revise, edit, subedit, amend, emend; rewrite, redraft; remould, refashion, remodel, reform; reorganize 62 *regularize*; streamline, finetune, rationalize; review; have second thoughts.

655 Deterioration

N. *deterioration*, debasement; cheapening, devaluation; retrogression, losing ground 286 *regression*; decline, ebb 37 *decrease*; twilight, fading 419 *dimness*; falling off, downturn, slump, depression, recession; impoverishment 801 *poverty*; exhaustion 634 *waste*; corruption, perversion, prostitution, depravation, degeneration, degeneracy, decadence, depravity 934 *wickedness*; downward course, primrose path 309 *descent*; setback 657 *relapse*.

dilapidation, collapse, ruination 165 *destruction*; planning blight; inner city deprivation, sink estate; disrepair, neglect 458 *negligence*; slum 801 *poverty*; ravages of time, wear and tear, erosion, corrosion, rust, rot, canker, corruption, putrefaction, cancer, concrete cancer 51 *decay*; mouldiness, mildew 659 *blight*; decrepitude, senility 131 *old age*; atrophy 651 *disease*; ruin, wreck.

impairment, spoiling 675 *misuse*; detriment, damage, spoilage, waste 772 *loss*; discoloration; pollution, contamination, defilement 649 *uncleanness*; adulteration; ruination, demolition 165 *destruction*; injury, mischief, harm; disablement, crippling, laming, nobbling, disabling, mutilation, weakening 163 *weakness*; sprain, strain, pulled muscle, dislocation; sabotage.

wound, injury, trauma; sore, running sore 651 *ulcer*; laceration, lesion; cut, gash, incision, abrasion, nick, scratch 46 *splitting*; stab, prick, jab, puncture; contusion, bruise, bump, discoloration, black eye, shiner, cauliflower ear 253 *swelling*; burn, scald; rupture, hernia, hiatus hernia; broken bones, fracture; scar, mark, scab, proud flesh; repetitive strain injury, RSI; brain injury, brain damage, shaken baby syndrome.

wounded person, casualty, fatality, victim, basket case; the injured, the wounded, the walking wounded; collateral damage.

Adj. *dilapidated*, the worse for wear, falling

to pieces, in disrepair, in ruins; broken, kaput, cracked, leaking; battered, weather-beaten, storm-tossed; decrepit, ramshackle, tottery, wonky, shaky, rickety, tumbledown, run-down, on its last legs 163 *weakened*; condemned; worn, well-worn, frayed, shabby, tatty, dingy, in tatters, in rags, out-at-elbows; worn out, done for 641 *useless*; seedy, down at heel, down and out 801 *poor*; rusty, rotten, mildewed, mouldering, moth-eaten, dog-eared.

Vb. *deteriorate*, worsen, get worse, go from bad to worse, take a turn for the worse; slip, slide, go downhill, disimprove; have seen better days; fall off, slump, decline, wane, ebb, sink, fail 37 *decrease*; revert 286 *regress*; lapse; degenerate, let oneself go, go to pieces, run to seed; tread the primrose path, go to the bad 934 *be wicked*; disintegrate, fall apart, collapse, break down, fall, totter, droop 309 *tumble*; contract, shrink 198 *become small*; wear out, age; fade, wither, wilt, shrivel, perish, crumble, moulder, mildew; go to rack and ruin; weather, rust, rot, decay 51 *decompose*; spoil, go flat, go off, go sour, turn 391 *be unpalatable*; go bad, smell, pong 397 *stink*; corrupt, putrefy, rankle, fester, suppurate, maturate 51 *decompose*; sicken 651 *be ill*; make things worse, jump from the frying pan into the fire.

pervert, deform, warp, twist 246 *distort*; prostitute 675 *misuse*; deprave 951 *debauch*; corrupt 934 *make wicked*; lower, degrade, debase 311 *abase*; brutalize, dehumanize; brainwash.

impair, damage, make inoperative, hurt, injure 645 *harm*; mess up, muck up 63 *jumble*; play havoc with 63 *disarrange*; disorganize; spoil, mar, botch, cock up, make a balls-up of 695 *be clumsy*; tinker, tamper, meddle with, fool with, monkey with 678 *meddle*; deteriorate, disimprove; degrade, devalue, debase 812 *cheapen*; stain; scar, mark; deface, disfigure, deform, warp 246 *distort*; mutilate, maim, lame, cripple 161 *disable*; cramp, hamper 702 *hinder*; castrate 161 *unman*; curtail; adulterate; deactivate 679 *make inactive*; subvert, sap, undermine, demoralize 163 *weaken*; erode, corrode, rust, rot, mildew 51 *decompose*; blight, blast; ravage, rape, waste, scorch; vandalize, wreck, ruin 165 *destroy*; crumble 332 *grind*; dilapidate, wear out; exhaust, deplete, drain; infect, contaminate; taint, pollute 649 *make unclean*; defile, desecrate, profane 980 *be impious*.

wound, draw blood; tear, lacerate, slit, mangle, rip 46 *disunite*; maul, savage, traumatize; black one's eye, bloody one's nose; bite, scratch, claw; slash, gash, hack, incise 46 *cut*;

scarify, score 262 *groove*; nick 260 *notch*; sting, prick, stab, puncture 263 *pierce*; bruise, contuse; crush, grind 332 *grind*; chafe 333 *rub*; smash 46 *break*; graze, wing.

656 Restoration

N. *restoration*, giving back 787 *restitution*; redress, amends, reparation 941 *atonement*; retrieval, recovery, re-establishment, recall, replacement, reinstatement; rehabilitation; reclamation, gentrification, recycling; rescue, salvage, redemption, ransom, salvation 668 *rescue*; reconstitution, rebuilding, reformation, reconstruction, reorganization; nation building; readjustment; remodelling 654 *amendment*; resumption.

repair, reparation, repairs, running repairs, service, servicing, renovation, renewal, reconditioning; overhauling; DIY; rectification, emendation; restoration, mending, invisible mending, darning, patching; cobbling, tinkering, etc. (see vb.); reinforcement; new look, face-lift 843 *beauty treatment*.

revival, recovery 685 *refreshment*; renewal, reawakening, resurgence, rally, comeback; economic recovery, green shoots, economic miracle, boom 730 *prosperity*; reactivation, resuscitation, rejuvenation; face-lift, new look; rebirth, renaissance; regeneration; new life, resurrection.

recuperation, recovery, pulling through, rallying, perking up, taking a turn for the better, turning the corner, cure; healing, mending; healing over; convalescence 658 *remedy*; easing 831 *relief*; curability; recovering alcoholic.

mender, repairer, renovator, painter, decorator, interior decorator, DIYer; mechanic; restorer; cobbler, shoe-repairer; plumber, handyman; healer, bone-setter, osteopath 658 *doctor*.

Vb. *be restored*, recover, come round, come to, revive, pick up, rally 685 *be refreshed*; pull through, get over, get well, convalesce, recuperate; turn the corner 654 *get better*; weather the storm, survive, live through; come to life again, arise from the dead, return from the grave; reappear, make a comeback, take on a new lease of life; be oneself again, bounce back, snap out of it, come up smiling; pick oneself up, find one's feet again; return to normal, get back to normal; regroup.

restore, give back, hand back, yield up 787 *make restitution*; make amends 941 *atone*; replace, recall, reappoint, reinstall, re-establish, rehabilitate; reconstitute, reconstruct, reform, reorganize 654 *make better*; renovate, renew, rebuild, remake, redo; overhaul, service, refit, refurbish, make like new 126 *modernize*; make whole; reclaim; recycle; build up one's strength 162 *strengthen*; rally, reassemble 74 *bring together*; redeem, rescue, salvage 668 *rescue*.

revive, revitalize, resuscitate, regenerate, resurrect, rekindle; breathe fresh life into, give a new lease of life, rejuvenate; freshen 685 *refresh*.

cure, heal, make well, cure of, break of; nurse; bandage, put a plaster on, nurse through, work a cure, snatch from the grave, restore to health, set on one's feet again; set (a bone); heal over; knit together; right itself.

repair, do repairs; amend, emend, right, set to rights, put right, put back into operation, remedy, sort 654 *rectify*; overhaul, DIY, mend, fix; cobble, resole, heel; recover, resurface, thatch 226 *cover*; reline 227 *line*; darn, patch, fill (teeth); make over, do up, touch up, freshen up, retouch, revamp, fill in the cracks, paper over; seal, plug a hole 350 *staunch*; caulk 264 *close*; splice, bind 45 *tie*; piece together, reassemble, cannibalize 45 *join*; give a face-lift, upgrade, gentrify, refurbish, recondition, renovate, renew, remodel, reform.

retrieve, get back, recover, regain, retake, recapture; find again, reclaim, claim back, compensate oneself 31 *recoup*; make up for, make up time, make up leeway.

657 Relapse

N. *relapse*, lapse, falling back; throwback, return 148 *reversion*; retrogression 286 *regression*; sinking, falling off, fall 655 *deterioration*; back-sliding; reinfection, recurrence, fresh outbreak.

Vb. *relapse*, slip back, slide back, sink back, fall back, lose ground; return, retrogress 286 *regress*; degenerate 655 *deteriorate*; backslide, lapse, fall from grace 603 *apostatize*; revert to 148 *revert*; have a relapse, suffer a recurrence.

658 Remedy

N. *remedy*, succour, help 703 *aid*; oil on troubled waters 177 *moderator*; corrective 654 *amendment*; redress, amends 787 *restitution*; expiation 941 *atonement*; cure 656 *recuperation*; healing quality *or* property; sovereign remedy, specific, answer, solution; prescription, recipe, formula, nostrum; quack remedy, patent medicine; panacea, cure-all, elixir; hair of the dog.

medicine, medication, medicament, patent medicine, proprietary drug, generic drug, ethical drug, wonderdrug, pharmaceutical, nutraceutical; herbal remedy, medicinal herb; balm, balsam; placebo; pill, bolus, tablet, capsule, caplet, lozenge; draught, potion, elixir; homoeopathic medicine, nosode; infusion; dose, booster dose; drops, drip; injection, jab, shot; preparation, mixture, powder, linctus; plaster, etc. (see also *surgical dressing* below); pessary, suppository; spray, inhaler; pharmacopoeia; inappropriate use of drugs: off-label use, off-labelling.

diagnosis, symptom, syndrome; e-health, telemedicine, dot-com doctor; sample, urine sample, semen sample; battery of tests, test, laboratory test, lab test, blood test, serotests, sputum test, stool test, eye test, hearing test; breath test; pregnancy test; amniocentesis, alphafetoprotein test, chorionic villus sampling; cervical smear, smear test, Pap test, liquid-based cytology; mammogram, angiogram, arteriogram, cardiogram, ECG, hysterogram, lymphogram, pyelogram, venogram; radiograph; chest X-ray; barium meal, barium enema; diagnostic radiology, ultrasound, screening, scanning, CAT scanning, body scanning, brain scanning, EEG; MRI, magnetic resonance imaging; biopsy, cone biopsy; stethoscope, bronchoscope, ophthalmoscope, auriscope; endoscope, colposcope, ureteroscope, bronchoscopy, colonoscopy, endoscopy, gastroscopy, laparoscopy; forensic test; DNA fingerprinting, genetic fingerprinting.

preventive, prophylactic; cordon sanitaire, quarantine 652 *hygiene*; prophylaxis, immunization, inoculation, vaccination, chemoprevention; vaccine, triple vaccine, MMR, BCG, TAB; quinine; antisepsis, disinfection, sterilization; antiseptic, disinfectant, iodine, carbolic, boric acid, boracic acid; bactericide, germicide, insecticide, acaricide 659 *poison*; fumigant; fluoridation, fluoride; contraceptive 172 *contraception*.

antidote, counterirritant, antihistamine; antiserum, antitoxin; antiemetic; febrifuge, quinine; vermifuge, anthelmintic; antigen, antibody, interferon; antibiotic; immunosuppressant; antispasmodic, anticonvulsant; sedative; anticoagulant; antacid, analgesic, painkiller; antidepressant.

purgative, purge, cathartic, laxative, aperient; castor oil, Epsom salts, health salts, aloes, senna pods; cascara, milk of magnesia; diuretic; expectorant, emetic, nauseant, ipecacuanha; carminative, digestive, liquorice, dill water; douche, enema.

tonic, restorative; tonic wine; reviver, refresher, pick-me-up 174 *stimulant*; caffeine, nicotine, alcohol; spirits, smelling salts, sal volatile; infusion, tisane, herb tea; betel, betel nut, ginseng, royal jelly; vitamin tablet, iron pill.

drug, medicinal drug, wonderdrug, etc. (see *medicine* above); antibiotic, sulphonamide;

penicillin; aureomycin, streptomycin, insulin, cortisone; hormone, steroid; progesterone, oestrogen; HRT; Viagra; contraceptive pill 172 *contraception*; tamoxifen; analgesic, aspirin, codeine, paracetamol, 375 *anaesthetic*; tranquillizer, diazepam, Valium (tdmk), temazepan, antidepressant, Prozac (tdmk), sedative; barbiturate, sleeping pill; narcotic, dope, morphia, morphine, opium, cocaine, heroin; stimulant 949 *drug-taking*; AZT; Aricept; Ritalin; Viagra (tdmk).

balm, balsam oil, emollient, antipruritic 177 *moderator*; salve, ointment; cream 843 *cosmetic*; lanolin, liniment, embrocation; lotion, wash; eyewash.

surgical dressing, dressing, lint, gauze; swab; bandage, sling, splint, cast, plaster of Paris; tourniquet; fingerstall; patch; plaster, sticking plaster, Elastoplast (tdmk), Band-Aid (tdmk) corn plaster; fomentation, poultice, compress; tampon, pessary.

medical art, therapeutics; medical advice, medical practice; medical care, health care, managed care, primary care, integrated care; triage; telemedicine; homeopathy, naturopathy; medicine, clinical medicine, preventive medicine, fringe medicine, alternative medicine, complementary medicine, holistic medicine, unorthodox medicine, folk medicine; biomedicine; iridology, reflexology, radiesthesia; acupuncture, acupressure; radiography, radiology, tomography; diagnosis, prognosis; healing, laying on of hands, faith healing, Christian Science; sexology; obstetrics, gynaecology, midwifery 167 *obstetrics*; reproductive medicine 167 *propagation*; gerontology, geriatrics, paediatrics; orthopaedics, orthotics, ophthalmology, orthoptics, neurology, dermatology, otology, otolaryngology, otorhinolaryngology, ear, nose and throat, ENT, cardiology, oncology; nuclear medicine; radiotherapy; psychopathology, bacteriology, microbiology, virology, immunology; pharmaceutics, pharmacology; veterinary medicine.

surgery, general surgery, keyhole surgery, telesurgery, laser surgery, brain surgery, neurosurgery, heart surgery, cardiac surgery, angioplasty, balloon angioplasty, open-heart surgery, by-pass surgery, transplant surgery, xenotransplantation; cryosurgery; plastic surgery, cosmetic surgery, nip-and-tuck, bus-stop surgery, rhinoplasty, prosthesis, prosthetics; liposuction; chiropractic; operation, surgical operation, op; phlebotomy, venesection, sinonoplasty; tranfusion; dialysis; D and C, dilatation and curettage, transplant, xenotransplant; cauterization; amputation, trephination, trepanning; colostomy.

Surgical Operations: -ectomies and -otomies
adenectomy (removal of a gland), appendectomy *or* appendicectomy (appendix), craniotomy (skull), cystectomy *and* cystotomy (bladder, or gall bladder), episiotomy (opening of the vagina), gastrectomy (stomach), hysterectomy (uterus), keratectomy *and* keratotomy (cornea), laparotomy (abdomen), laryngectomy *and* laryngotomy (larynx), leucotomy (nerve fibres in the brain), lithotomy (stone from the bladder, kidney or urinary tract), lobectomy (lobe of lung, brain, etc), lobotomy (lobe of brain), lumpectomy (lump in the breast), mastectomy (breast), radical mastectomy (breast, pectoral muscles and lymph nodes), nephrectomy (kidney), neurotomy (nerve), oophorectomy (ovary), orchidectomy (testicle), ovariectomy *or* ovariotomy (ovary), pharyngotomy (pharynx), phlebotomy (vein), pneumonectomy (lung), rhytidectomy (wrinkles; = a facelift), salpingectomy (Fallopian tube), splenectomy (spleen), sympathectomy (sympathetic nerve), tenotomy (tendon), thoracotomy (chest), tonsillectomy (tonsils), tracheotomy (windpipe), tubectomy (Fallopian tube), varicotomy (varicose vein), vasectomy (vas deferens).

---

dentistry, dental care; extracting, filling, scaling, bridgework, root canal treatment; orthodontics, periodontics, cosmetic dentistry; dental hygiene, oral health; dental tourism.

therapy, therapeutics; medical care treatment, medical treatment, clinical treatment; medical tourism, health tourism, surgical tourism, transplant tourism, cosmetic holiday; scalpel safari; nursing, bedside manner; first aid, aftercare; cure, faith cure, faith healing; hydrotherapy; thalassotherapy; regimen; bonesetting, orthopaedics, osteopathy, osteotherapy; hormone therapy, hormone replacement therapy, HRT, HRT patch; immunotherapy; chemotherapy, photodynamic therapy; gene therapy; physiotherapy, occupational therapy; radiotherapy; heat treatment; electrotherapy, ECT, shock treatment; clinical psychology; child psychology; hypnotherapy, psychotherapy; psychiatry, psychoanalysis, counselling, genetic counselling 447 *psychology*; group therapy, behaviour therapy, cognitive behaviour therapy, cognitive therapy, Neuro-Linguistic Programming, aversion therapy, Gestalt therapy, primal therapy; self-analysis, enneagram; speech therapy, speech pathology and therapeutics; acupuncture, acupressure; catheterization; intravenous injection, dripfeed; fomentation, poulticing; retail therapy, shopping therapy.

alternative therapy, complementary therapy, supplementary therapy, homeopathy, holistic medicine; folk medicine, traditional medicine, traditional Chinese medicine, TCM, fringe medicine, herbal medicine, Chinese herbal medicine, CHM, ayurveda, ayurvedic medicine; macrobiotics; naturopathy; acupuncture, acupressure, shiatsu, craniosacral therapy, reiki; osteopathy, chiropractic manipulative therapy; faith healing, laying on of hands; relaxation therapy, stress-busting, destresser; massage, Swedish massage, Thai massage, hot stone therapy; Hopi ear candles; autogenic therapy, autogenics, autogenic training; meditations; aromatherapy, crystal healing, crystal therapy; Bach flower remedies; colonic irrigation; reflexology; iridology; kinesiology; bodywork, therapeutic massage, Alexander technique, Rolfing *or* structural integration, Hellerwork, Tui Na; breathwork, vivation, rebirthing; sensory deprivation, flotation tank.

hospital, infirmary, general hospital, foundation hospital, hospital trust, NHS trust, hospital manager; maternity hospital, children's hospital 503 *mental hospital*; dispensary, clinic, antenatal clinic; nursing home, convalescent home; hospice; hospital ship, hospital train; stretcher, ambulance; ward, hospital ward, casualty ward, isolation ward, sick bay, sickroom, sick-bed; hospital bed; bed-blocking; oxygen tent, iron lung; respirator, life-support system, life-support machine, heart-lung machine, kidney machine; incubator, intensive care unit; X-ray machine, scanner, body scanner, brain scanner, head scanner, CAT scanner; first-aid station; casualty department, crash team; operating theatre, operating table; consulting room, surgery, clinic, one-stop clinic, community health centre; sanatorium, spa, hydro; pump room, baths, hot springs, thermae.

doctor, physician; quack; veterinary surgeon, vet, horse-doctor; herbalist; faith healer, Christian Scientist; homeopath, naturopath; acupuncturist, acupressurist; hakim, barefoot doctor, flying doctor; witchdoctor, medicine man 983 *sorcerer*; medic, medical student; houseman, house officer, intern, registrar; medical practitioner, general practitioner, GP, family doctor; locum tenens, locum; clinician, therapeutist; surgeon, general surgeon, plastic surgeon; dot-com doctor; neurosurgeon; medical officer, environmental health officer, sanitary inspector; medical adviser, consultant, specialist; diagnostician, pathologist; alienist; psychiatrist, psychoanalyst, shrink, neurologist, radiographer; physiotherapist, occupational therapist, speech therapist; paediatrician, geriatrician; obstetrician, midwife; gynaecologist; sexologist; dermatologist, haematologist; biochemist, microbiologist; radiotherapist; orthopaedist, orthotist, osteopath, chiropractor, podiatrist, chiropodist; ophthalmologist, optician, ophthalmic optician, oculist, orthoptist; ear, nose and throat

specialist, aurist, otologist, audiologist 415 *ear*; dentist, dental surgeon, orthodontist; dietician; medical profession, private medicine, Harley Street, National Health Service; Red Cross, Red Crescent, St John Ambulance, St Andrew's Ambulance Association; Hippocratic oath.

pharmacist, druggist, apothecary, chemist; dispenser, pharmacologist; herbalist; chemist's, pharmacy.

nurse, male nurse, student nurse, staff nurse; charge nurse, sister, night sister, ward sister, theatre sister, nursing officer, senior nursing officer; matron; state-enrolled nurse, SEN, state-registered nurse, SRN; special nurse, day nurse, night nurse; district nurse, community nurse, Diana nurse, Macmillan nurse, Marie Curie nurse, palliative care nurse; health visitor; nursing auxiliary, ward orderly; dental nurse, dental hygienist; paramedic, ambulanceman *or* -woman; almoner, hospital social worker, medical social worker 901 *social care*; caring profession; Florence Nightingale, the lady with the lamp, ministering angel.

Adj. *remedial*, corrective, curative, restorative; helpful 644 *beneficial*; therapeutic, medicinal, healing, curing; soothing, emollient, palliative; anodyne, analgesic, narcotic, hypnotic, anaesthetic 375 *insensitive*; digestive; purging; cathartic, emetic, laxative; antidotal; prophylactic, disinfectant, antiseptic; antibiotic, anticoagulant, anticonvulsant, antidepressant, anti-emetic, anti-inflammatory, antipsychotic, antispasmodic, antitussive, antiviral; antipyretic, febrifugal; tonic; nutritional.

medical, pathological, homeopathic, herbal; surgical, rhinoplastic, orthopaedic, orthotic; obstetric, obstetrical; clinical; operable, curable.

Vb. *remedy*, fix, put right, correct 656 *restore*; help 703 *aid*; treat, heal; soothe 831 *relieve*.

practise medicine, doctor; treat, prescribe; attend 703 *minister to*; tend, nurse; give first aid, give the kiss of life 656 *revive*; hospitalize, medicate; inject, give a jab, give a shot; dress, bandage, put a plaster on; apply a tourniquet 350 *staunch*; poultice, plaster; set, put in splints; drug, anaesthetize; operate, amputate; trepan, trephine; curette; cauterize; bleed, phlebotomize; transfuse; manipulate; extract, pull, fill; immunize, vaccinate, inoculate; sterilize.

659 Bane

N. *bane*, plague, curse, scourge, ruin 616 *evil*; malady 651 *disease*; bad habit, besetting sin 934 *vice*; hell, affliction 731 *adversity*; woe, funeral 825 *sorrow*; cross, cross to bear, trial; bore 838 *tedium*; bugbear, bête noire 827 *annoyance*; burden, imposition, white elephant; thorn in the flesh, stone round one's neck; stress, strain, perpetual worry, constant anxiety, angst, torment, nagging pain 825 *worry*; running sore 651 *ulcer*; bitterness 393 *sourness*; bite, sting, poison dart, fang, nettle 256 *sharp point*; trouble spot, flash point, hornet's nest 663 *pitfall*; viper, adder, serpent 365 *reptile*; snake, snake in the grass 663 *troublemaker*; parasite, tapeworm 365 *insect, creepy-crawly*; mosquito, mozzie, wasp; locust 168 *destroyer*; oppressor 735 *tyrant*.

blight, rot, dry rot, wet rot; mildew, mould, rust, fungus; moth, woodworm, canker, cancer 51 *decay*; nuclear winter; visitation 651 *plague*; frost 380 *coldness*, drought 342 *drying*.

poison, poisonousness, virulence, venomousness, toxicity; pollution; bacterium, salmonella, bacillus, germ, virus 651 *infection*; teratogen, carcinogen, oncogen; biological weapon; venom, toxin, neurotoxin, genotoxin; deadly poison, snake poison, rat poison, warfarin, slug pellet; germicide; insecticide, carbofuran; pesticide, organo-phosphate; fungicide, herbicide, weed-killer, defoliant, dioxin, paraquat, derris, DDT; hemlock, arsenic, strychnine, cyanide, prussic acid, vitriol; asphyxiant, poison gas, nerve gas, mustard gas, tear gas, CS gas; carbon monoxide, carbon dioxide; CFC, chlorofluorocarbon; miasma, sewer gas 653 *unhealthiness*; atmospheric pollution, acid rain, smog; lead pollution; uranium, depleted uranium, DU, plutonium; radioactivity, nuclear fallout, strontium 90 417 *radiation*; heroin 658 *drug*, 949 *drug-taking*; lethal dose, overdose; toxicology.

poisonous plant, hemlock, deadly nightshade, belladonna, datura, henbane, monkshood, aconite, hellebore; nux vomica, upas tree.

660 Safety

N. safety, safeness, security; immunity; safety in numbers 104 *multitude*; secure position, safe job; social security, welfare state 901 *social care*; safe distance, wide berth 620 *avoidance*; all clear, the coast is clear; guarantee, warrant 473 *certainty*; sense of security, assurance, confidence, false sense of security 855 *courage*; safety valve 667 *means of escape*; rescue 668 *rescue*.

protection, conservation 666 *preservation*; insurance, surety 858 *caution*; patronage, care, sponsorship, good offices, auspices, aegis, fatherly eye 703 *aid*; protectorate, guardianship, wardenship, wardship, tutelage, custody,

protective custody, care in the community, community care, caring profession; surrogacy 747 *restraint*; safekeeping, keeping, charge, safe hands; ward, watch, electronic surveillance, Big Brother, vetting, positive vetting 457 *surveillance*; safeguard, precaution, security system, alarm system, preventive measure 713 *defence*; fire door; firewall; safety cage; panic room; immunization, prophylaxis, quarantine, cordon sanitaire, biosecurity zone 652 *hygiene*; cushion, buffer; screen, cover; sun screen, suntan cream, sun protection factor, protection factor; umbrella 662 *shelter*; deterrent 723 *weapon*; safe-conduct, passport, pass 756 *permit*; escort, convoy, guard 722 *armed force*; defence, bastion, bulwark, tower of strength 713 *defences*; haven, sanctuary, asylum 662 *refuge*; anchor 662 *safeguard*; moat, ditch, palisade, stockade 235 *fence*; shield, breastplate, armour plate 713 *armour*; human shield.

protector, protectress, guardian; guardian angel, patron saint, liege lord, feudal lord, fairy godmother 707 *patron*; defender, preserver, shepherd; bodyguard, minder, lifeguard, strongarm man, bouncer; vigilante 713 *defender*; custodian, curator, warden; warder, guard, security guard, coastguard; chaperon, duenna, governess, nursemaid, nanny, babysitter, au pair, care assistant, buddy, carer, minder 457 *carer*, 749 *keeper*; caring profession; lookout, watch, watchman, night watchman 664 *warner*; firewatcher, fire fighter, fireman; policeman *or* -woman, police constable, community policeman *or* -woman, police sergeant, sheriff, copper, cop 955 *police*; private eye 459 *detective*; sentry, sentinel, garrison, security forces 722 *soldiers*; sky marshal, air marshal; animal liberationist, animal protectionist, antivivisectionist; anti-abortionist, pro-lifer; watchdog, guard dog, police dog, Cerberus 365 *dog*.

Adj. safe, secure, sure; safe and sound, spared 666 *preserved*; intact, unharmed 646 *undamaged*; garrisoned, well-defended; insured; immunized, vaccinated, inoculated; disinfected; in safety, on sure ground, home and dry, on home ground, on the home stretch, on terra firma; in harbour; out of the wood, out of danger, out of harm's way; clear, in the clear, sheltered, shielded, screened, protected, etc. (see vb.); under the protection of, under the wing of; in safe hands, in custody, behind bars, under lock and key 747 *imprisoned*; reliable, guaranteed; harmless 615 *good*.

invulnerable, immune, impregnable, sacrosanct; unassailable, untouchable, unbreakable; tenable 162 *strong*; proof, foolproof; weatherproof, waterproof, showerproof, leakproof, gasproof, fireproof, bulletproof, bombproof, shatterproof; seaworthy, airworthy; shrink-wrapped, vacuum-packed, vacuum-sealed, hermetically sealed; armoured.

Vb. *be safe*, be invulnerable, etc. (see adj.); reach safety; come through, save one's bacon 667 *escape*; land on one's feet, keep one's head above water, weather the storm, ride it out; bear a charmed life, have nine lives; have a roof over one's head; be under cover 523 *lurk*; keep a safe distance, give a wide berth 620 *avoid*.

safeguard, keep safe, guard, protect; stand surety for, go bail for 713 *defend*; shield; grant asylum, afford sanctuary; keep, conserve 666 *preserve*; hoard 632 *store*; keep in custody 747 *imprison*; ward, watch over, care for, mother, take under one's wing; nurse, foster, cherish; have charge of, keep an eye on, chaperon 457 *look after*; hide, put in a safe place, squirrel away 525 *conceal*; cushion, cocoon 218 *support*; insulate; cover, shade 421 *screen*; keep under cover, garage, lock up; take in, house, shelter; enfold, make safe, secure, fortify 162 *strengthen*; entrench, fence in, fence round 232 *encircle*; arm, armour; shepherd, convoy, escort; flank, support; garrison, mount guard; immunize, inoculate, vaccinate; pasteurize, chlorinate, fluoridate, fluoridize, disinfect; give assurances, warrant, guarantee 473 *make certain*; keep order, police, patrol.

661 Danger

N. *danger*, peril; dangerousness, perilousness, shadow of death, jaws of death, lion's mouth, dragon's lair; dangerous situation, parlous state, dire straits, forlorn hope 700 *predicament*; emergency 137 *crisis*; jeopardy, risk, hazard, banana skin, precariousness, razor's edge 474 *uncertainty*; black spot, snag 663 *pitfall*; trap, death trap 527 *ambush*; endangerment, imperilment, hazarding, dangerous course; daring, overdaring 857 *rashness*; venture 672 *undertaking*; leap in the dark 618 *gambling*; slippery slope, road to ruin 655 *deterioration*; sword of Damocles, menace, rod in pickle 900 *threat*; cause for alarm, rocks ahead, storm brewing, gathering clouds, gathering storm 665 *danger signal*; tip of the iceberg; narrow escape, close shave, near thing 667 *escape*.

vulnerability, danger of 180 *liability*; security risk; exposure, nakedness, defencelessness, naivety 161 *helplessness*; insecurity 152 *changeableness*; easy target, sitting duck; chink in the armour, Achilles's heel 163 *weakness*; soft underbelly 327 *softness*; feet of clay, human error, flaw, tragic flaw, fatal flaw 647 *imperfection*; weaker brethren, weaker sex.

Adj. *dangerous*, perilous, fraught with danger, treacherous, beset with perils; risky, hazardous, venturesome, dicey, dodgy, chancy 618 *speculative*; serious, nasty, critical; at stake; menacing, ominous, foreboding, alarming; toxic, poisonous 645 *harmful*; unhealthy, infectious 653 *unhealthy*; inflammable, flammable, explosive, radioactive.

unsafe, slippery, treacherous, untrustworthy 474 *unreliable*; insecure, precarious, dicky; unsteady; shaky, tottering, crumbling, ramshackle, rickety, frail 655 *dilapidated*; jerry-built, gimcrack, crazy 163 *weak*; built on sand; critical, touch and go, hanging by a thread, trembling in the balance, teetering on the edge, on the edge, on the brink, on the verge.

vulnerable, in danger of 180 *liable*; exposed, naked, bare 229 *uncovered*; undefended, unprotected, at the mercy of; shelterless, helpless; unguarded, unescorted; unsupported, out on a limb; off one's guard 508 *inexpectant*.

endangered, in danger, in peril, etc. (see n.); in a bad way; on the rocks, on slippery ground, on thin ice; in a tight corner, surrounded, trapped, under fire; in the lion's den, be thrown to the lions, on the razor's edge; out of the frying pan into the fire; between the devil and the deep blue sea, between Scylla and Charybdis; on the run, not out of the wood; at bay, with one's back to the wall, awaiting execution 961 *condemned*.

Vb. *be in danger*, run the risk of 180 *be liable*: enter the lion's den, walk into a trap, tread on dangerous ground, skate on thin ice, get out of one's depth, sail too near the wind, play with fire, sit on a powder barrel, sleep on a volcano; lean on a broken reed, feel the ground give way, be up against it, have to run for it; hang by a thread, tremble in the balance, hover on the brink, teeter on the edge 474 *be uncertain*.

face danger, dice with death, have one's back to the wall; take one's life in one's hands 855 *be courageous*; lay oneself open to; bell the cat, look danger in the face, look down a gun barrel; face heavy odds, have the odds against one; engage in a forlorn hope, be on a hiding to nothing, tempt providence, court disaster; take a tiger by the tail, put one's head in the lion's mouth 857 *be rash*; run the gauntlet, come under fire; take a chance, stick one's neck out 618 *gamble*.

endanger, be dangerous, spell danger, expose to danger, put at risk, put in jeopardy; imperil, jeopardize; risk 618 *gamble*; run on the rocks, drive dangerously, drive without due care and attention, put one in fear of his or her life; loom, forebode, bode ill, menace 900 *threaten*.

662 Refuge. Safeguard

N. *refuge*, sanctuary, asylum, retreat, safe house; traffic island, green man, zebra crossing, pedestrian crossing, etc. 305 *traffic control*; last resort, bolthole, burrow; trench, dugout, air-raid shelter, fallout shelter; earth, hole, den, lair; hearth 192 *home*; sanctum 194 *room*; cloister, ivory tower 192 *retreat*; sanctum sanctorum, temple; bastion; stronghold 713 *fort*; keep; secret place 527 *hiding-place*; tower of strength, mainstay 218 *prop*.

shelter, cover, roof, roof over one's head; earth, hole; fold, sheepfold; lee; windbreak, hedge 235 *fence*; camp, stockade 235 *enclosure*; shield; fireguard, fender, bumper, mudguard, windscreen, windshield (US) 263 *window*, 421 *screen*; umbrella, gamp, oilskins; sunglasses, goggles, ear muffs, ear plugs; shinguard, pads; protective clothing, overalls; haven, harbour, port; harbourage, anchorage, quay, jetty, marina, dock 192 *stable*; doss-house 192 *inn*; halfway house, sheltered housing; old people's home, eventide home, children's home, hospice; dogs' home, cat and dog home; Welfare State, nanny state.

safeguard, protection 660 *safety*; precautions 702 *hindrance*; crush barrier, guardrail, railing; safety cage; mail 713 *armour*; arms, deterrent, anti-missile defence system, Star Wars, SDI 723 *weapon*; respirator, gas mask; air-bag, dead man's handle, safety catch, safety valve; crash helmet, safety helmet 228 *headgear*; seat belt, safety belt, safety harness; ejector-seat, parachute; safety net; lifeboat, rubber dinghy, life raft; life belt, life jacket, lifeline, breeches buoy; reins, brake 748 *fetter*; bolt, lock 264 *stopper*; ballast; breakwater, sea wall, embankment; lighthouse, lightship 269 *sailing aid*; spare parts 40 *extra*.

Vb. *seek refuge*, take refuge; take to the hills; shelter under the wing of, pull the blankets over one's head; seek political asylum; clasp the knees of, hide behind the skirts of; reach safety, find shelter; let down the portcullis, raise the drawbridge, batten down the hatches.

663 Pitfall: source of danger

N. *pitfall*, pit, trap for the unwary, banana skin, catch, Catch-22; snag 702 *obstacle*; booby trap, death trap, minefield 542 *trap*; lying in wait 527 *ambush*; sleeping dog; thin ice; quagmire 347 *marsh*; quicksands; reef, coral reef, rock; chasm, abyss, crevasse, precipice 209 *high land*; rapids, crosscurrent, undertow 350 *current*; vortex, maelstrom, whirlpool 350 *eddy*; tidal wave, flash flood; volcano 383 *furnace*; dynamite, time bomb, powder keg 723 *explo-*

sive; trouble spot 661 *danger*; hotbed 651 *infection*; hornet's nest, hazard 659 *bane*.

troublemaker, mischiefmaker, agent provocateur 738 *agitator*; ugly customer, vandal, delinquent 904 *ruffian*; nigger in the woodpile, snake in the grass, viper in the bosom; a wolf in sheep's clothing; yellow peril.

664 Warning

N. *warning*, caution, caveat; example, lesson, object lesson; notice, advance notice 524 *information*; word, word in the ear, word to the wise, tip, tip-off, wink, nudge 524 *hint*; whistle-blowing 528 *publication*; final warning, final notice, ultimatum 737 *demand*; admonition, admonishment 924 *reprimand*; deterrent 613 *dissuasion*; warning shot, shot across the bows; foreboding, premonition 511 *prediction*; warning voice 917 *conscience*; alarm, siren, foghorn, red alert 665 *danger signal*; bird of ill omen, stormy petrel 511 *omen*; gathering cloud, war cloud 661 *danger*; writing on the wall, symptom, sign, wake-up call 547 *indication*; death knell 364 *funeral rites*; beacon.

warner, prophet, Cassandra 511 *diviner*; signaller; lighthouse-keeper; watchman, lookout, security man *or* woman, watch 457 *surveillance*; scout, spy; picket, sentinel, sentry 660 *protector*; advanced guard, rearguard; watchdog.

Adj. *warning*, cautionary, monitory, admonitory; protesting, deprecatory; premonitory, ill-omened, ominous; threatening, menacing, minatory; deterrent 854 *frightening*.

Vb. *warn*, caution; give fair warning, give notice, notify 524 *inform*; drop a hint, tip off, blow the whistle on 524 *hint*; admonish 924 *reprove*; forewarn 511 *predict*; forearm, put someone on their guard, alert 669 *prepare*; lour, menace 900 *threaten*; issue a caveat; sound the alarm 665 *raise the alarm*.

665 Danger signal

N. *danger signal*, warning; writing on the wall, evil omen 511 *omen*; gale warning; alarm bell, burglar alarm, fire alarm, foghorn, motor horn, bicycle bell, police whistle; alarm, curfew, siren, red alert; war cry, battle cry, rallying cry; fiery cross; warning light, red light, beacon; red flag, SOS 547 *signal*.

false alarm, cry of 'wolf', scare, hoax; hoax call; bad dream 854 *intimidation*; flash in the pan 4 *lacking substance*; scaremonger 854 *alarmist*.

Vb. *raise the alarm*, sound the alarm, give the alarm, dial 999, alert, arouse, scare, startle 854 *frighten*; sound one's horn, honk, toot; turn out the guard, call the police, raise a hue

and cry, cry blue murder 528 *proclaim*; give a
false alarm, cry wolf, cry too soon; sound a
warning, toll, knell.

666 Preservation

N. *preservation*, safekeeping; safe conduct 660
protection; saving, salvation 668 *rescue*; conservation, conservancy; conservation of the environment, ecotage, tree-hugging, tree-sitting,
tree-spiking, tree-house, twigloo; energy-
saving, energy audit; perpetuation 144 *permanence*; support 633 *provision*; self-preservation
932 *selfishness*; game reserve, nature reserve,
bird sanctuary, conservation area, green belt,
listed building; protected species; taxidermy,
mummification, embalming 364 *interment*;
cold storage, deep-freezing, freeze-drying 382
refrigeration; UHT, dehydration 342 *drying*; canning, processing; preventive medicine, quarantine, cordon sanitaire, biosecurity zone.

preserver, life-saver, saviour, rescuer, deliv-
erer 668 *rescue*; preservative, ice, formalde-
hyde; camphor, mothball; pickle, marinade,
brine 389 *condiment*; freezer 384 *refrigerator*;
vacuum flask, Thermos (tdmk) flask; canning
factory, bottling plant; safety device, seat belt,
airbag, gas mask 662 *safeguard*; incubator, respirator, iron lung, life support system;
embalmer, mummifier; canner, bottler; preser-
vationist, conservationist, environmentalist,
green, eco-activist, ecowarrior, tree-hugger;
green movement, green peace movement.

Adj. *preserved*, well-preserved, long-life; frozen, deep-frozen, on ice; pickled, marinated,
salted, canned, bottled; mummified,
embalmed; mothballed; conserved, protected
660 *safe*.

Vb. *preserve*, conserve, freeze, freeze-dry,
keep on ice 382 *refrigerate*; embalm, mummify,
stuff; pickle, salt 388 *season*; marinate; cure,
smoke, kipper, dehydrate 342 *dry*; bottle, tin,
can, process; protect, varnish, creosote, waterproof; maintain, keep in good repair, service
656 *repair*; prop up, shore up 218 *support*; sustain; keep safe; hold 778 *retain*; prolong; save,
rescue 668 *rescue*.

667 Escape

N. *escape*, leak, leakage; extrication, delivery,
rescue 668 *rescue*; riddance, good riddance 831
relief; getaway, breakout; decampment, flight,
flit, moonlight flit, French leave 296 *departure*;
withdrawal, retreat, hasty retreat 286 *regression*; disappearing trick 446 *disappearance*;
elopement; evasion, truancy, bunking off, tax-
dodging, black economy, moonlighting 620
avoidance; narrow escape, close shave, narrow
squeak, near thing 661 *danger*; let-off, dis-

charge, reprieve 960 *acquittal*; setting free 746
liberation; immunity, exemption 919 *non-
liability*; escapology, escapism.

means of escape, exit, emergency exit, way
out, back door, secret passage 298 *going out*;
ladder, fire escape, escape hatch; drawbridge
624 *bridge*; vent, safety valve 662 *safeguard*;
dodge; loophole, escape clause, technicality,
let-out, get-out; escape route; exit strategy.

escaper, escapee, runaway; truant, escaped
prisoner, prison-breaker; fugitive, refugee,
asylum-seeker; survivor; escapist; escapologist,
Houdini.

Vb. *escape*, find *or* win freedom 746 *achieve
liberty*; make good one's escape, make a getaway, vamoose, break gaol, break out of prison;
abscond, jump bail, flit, elope, skip, take
flight, take French leave, go AWOL 620 *run
away*; steal away, sneak off, duck and run,
make oneself scarce, beat a hasty retreat 296
walk out; slip through, break through, break
out, break loose, break away, get free, break
one's chains, go over the wall, slip one's lead,
shake off one's yoke; get out, bluff one's way
out, sneak out 298 *emerge*; get away, slip
through one's fingers; get off, get off lightly,
go scot-free; get off on a
technicality, save one's bacon, weather the
storm, survive; get away with it, secure
exemption, wriggle out of 919 *be exempt*; rid
oneself, be well rid of; leak.

elude, evade, welsh, abscond, dodge 620
avoid; lie low 523 *lurk*; give one the slip, shake
off, throw off the scent, throw dust in one's
eye, draw a red herring, give one a run for
one's money; escape notice, be found to be
missing 190 *be absent*.

668 Rescue

N. *rescue*, deliverance, delivery, extrication
304 *extraction*; riddance 831 *relief*; liberation,
life-saving; salvage, retrieval 656 *restoration*;
salvation, redemption 965 *divine function*;
ransom, buying off 792 *purchase*; release,
amnesty; discharge, reprieve 960 *acquittal*; day
of grace, respite 136 *delay*; truce; way out, let-
out 667 *escape*; dispensation, exemption 919
non-liability.

Vb. *rescue*, deliver, save, come to the rescue, save by the bell, snatch from the jaws of
death, throw a lifeline; get one out of 304
extract; extricate; untie, unbind 46 *disunite*; rid,
save from 831 *relieve*; release; free, set free 746
liberate; let one off, get one off 960 *acquit*;
deliver oneself 667 *escape*; save one's skin, rid
oneself, get rid of; snatch a brand from the
burning, be the salvation of; redeem, ransom,

buy off 792 *purchase*; salvage, retrieve, recover; spare, excuse, dispense from 919 *exempt*.

669 Preparation

N. preparation, preparing, making ready; premedication; clearing the decks; preliminaries, priming; mobilization 718 *war measures*; trial run, trial, trials 461 *experiment*; practice, rehearsal, dress rehearsal; brief, briefing; training 534 *teaching*; prep, homework 536 *learning*; spadework 682 *labour*; groundwork, foundation 218 *basis*; planning, blue-sky planning, first draft, outline, blueprint, prototype, pilot scheme 623 *plan*; advance factory; prearrangement, premeditation 608 *predetermination*; consultation 691 *advice*; precautions 510 *foresight*; bottom drawer, nest egg 632 *store*.

ripening, maturation, bringing to a head; seasoning, acclimatization; brewing, hatching, gestation, incubation 167 *propagation*; nurture; cultivation, tillage, sowing, planting 370 *agriculture*; bloom, efflorescence; fruition 725 *completion*.

Adj. preparatory, preparing, etc. (see adj.); precautionary, preliminary 64 *preceding*; provisional, stopgap 150 *substituted*; marinating, brewing, cooking; brooding, hatching, incubating, maturing; in embryo; in preparation, afoot, on the stocks; in store, in the offing, forthcoming 155 *impending*; under consideration, at the committee stage, mooted 623 *planned*; under training.

prepared, ready, alert 457 *vigilant*; made ready, in readiness, at the ready; mobilized, standing by, on call; all set, ready to go, raring to go; teed up, keyed up, psyched up, spoiling for; trained, qualified, well-prepared, practised, in practice, at concert pitch, word-perfect; primed, briefed, instructed 524 *informed*; forewarned, forearmed; saddled; battened down; groomed, in one's best bib and tucker, dressed to kill, in full war-paint; accoutred, armed, in harness, armed to the teeth 718 *warring*, 723 *armed*; rigged, rigged out, equipped, furnished, fully furnished, well-appointed, provided; in store, in hand; in reserve, to hand, ready for use; ready for anything; in working order, operational.

matured, ripened, cooked, hatched, etc. (see vb.); ripe, mellow, mature, seasoned, weathered, hardened; tried, experienced, veteran 694 *expert*; adult, full-grown, full-fledged 134 *grown-up*; out, in flower, florescent, flowering, fruiting; overripe; elaborated, worked up, laboured, smelling of the lamp; perfected 725 *completed*.

ready-made, ready-mixed, cut and dried, ready to use, ready-to-wear, off the peg; prefabricated; processed, oven-ready; precooked, instant.

Vb. prepare, take steps, take measures; make preparations, make ready, pave the way, show the way, bridge, build a bridge, lead up to, pioneer 64 *come before*; choose one's ground, lay the foundations, do the groundwork, provide the basis; soften up; prepare the ground, sow the seed 370 *cultivate*; set to work, address oneself to 68 *begin*; cut out, block out; sketch, outline, blueprint 623 *plan*; plot, prearrange 608 *predetermine*; prepare for, forearm, insure, take precautions, prepare for a rainy day; anticipate 507 *expect*.

make ready, ready, prepare, prep; set in order, make operational, weaponize; batten down the hatches; put in commission; put one's house in order, put in working order, bring up to scratch, wind up, tune, adjust 62 *arrange*; set the stage; clear the decks; mobilize 74 *bring together*; whet the knife, shuffle the cards, tee up; set, cock, prime, load; warm up, crank up, rev up, get into gear; equip, man; fit out, furnish, kit out, rig out, dress; arm 633 *provide*; rehearse, drill, groom, exercise, lick into shape 534 *train*; inure, acclimatize 610 *accustom oneself*; coach, brief, bring one up to date 524 *inform*.

mature, mellow, ripen, bring to fruition 646 *perfect*; force, bring on 174 *invigorate*; bring to a head 725 *climax*; brew 301 *cook*; gestate, hatch, incubate 369 *breed stock*; grow, farm 370 *cultivate*; nurture; elaborate, work out 725 *carry through*; season, weather, smoke, dry, cure; temper, harden, season.

prepare oneself, brace oneself; serve an apprenticeship; study, brief oneself, do one's homework; train, exercise, go for the burn, rehearse, practise 536 *learn*; gird up one's loins, roll up one's sleeves; limber up, warm up, gear oneself up, psych oneself up, flex one's muscles; buckle on one's armour, take up one's sword, take sword in hand, shoulder arms; be prepared, get ready for action, stand by, hold oneself in readiness, keep one's powder dry.

Adv. in preparation, in hand, in train, under way, under construction.

670 Non-preparation

N. non-preparation, potluck; unpreparedness, unreadiness; lack of practice, rustiness; unfitness; rawness, immaturity, greenness, unripeness 126 *newness*; belatedness 136 *lateness*; neglect 458 *negligence*; hastiness; improvisation 609 *spontaneity*; imperfection 55 *incompleteness*.

undevelopment, virgin soil; untilled ground

458 *negligence*; raw material, unlicked cub, rough diamond; late developer; rough copy; embryo, abortion.

Adj. unprepared, not ready, behindhand 136 *late*; unorganized; unpremeditated, without preparation, ad hoc, ad lib, extemporized, improvised, impromptu, snap, off the top of one's head, off the cuff 609 *spontaneous*; careless 458 *negligent*; overhasty 680 *hasty*; unguarded, with one's trousers down 661 *vulnerable*; caught unawares, taken off guard, caught napping, on the wrong foot 508 *inexpectant*; at sixes and sevens; scratch, untrained 491 *uninstructed*; unrehearsed 611 *unaccustomed*; untilled, virgin.

immature, half-grown, unripe, green, underripe; unseasoned; unfledged, callow, bumfluffed, wet behind the ears; adolescent, juvenile, childish, puerile, boyish, girlish 130 *young*; undeveloped, half-baked, raw 647 *imperfect*; underdeveloped, backward, retarded 136 *late*; unhatched, unborn, embryonic, rudimentary 68 *beginning*; half-formed, unformed, rough-hewn, uncut, unpolished, half-finished, unfinished; premature, abortive, at half-cock 728 *unsuccessful*; untrained, apprentice 695 *unskilled*; crude; forced.

uncooked, raw, rare, underdone; cold; ungarnished.

unequipped, unrigged, undressed 229 *uncovered*; unfurnished, ill-provided 307 *deficient*; unfitted, unqualified.

Vb. be unprepared, be unready, etc. (see adj.); want practice; make no preparations, offer potluck, extemporize 609 *improvise*; live from day to day, take one day at a time, let tomorrow take care of itself; be premature, go off at half-cock 135 *be early*; take no precautions, drop one's guard 456 *be inattentive*; catch unawares 508 *surprise*.

Adv. unreadily, extempore, off the cuff, ad hoc.

671 Attempt

N. attempt, essay, bid; step, move, gambit 676 *deed*; endeavour, effort 682 *exertion*; tackle, try, some attempt; good try; valiant effort; one's level best, best one can do; catch-as-catch-can; determined effort, dead set 712 *attack*; trial, probation 461 *experiment*; go at, shot at, stab at, crack at, bash at; first attempt, first go, first shot, first offence, first strike 68 *debut*; final attempt, swan song, last bid, last throw; venture; speculation; aim, goal 617 *objective*; straining after, high endeavour.

Vb. attempt, essay, try; seek to, aim, make it one's aim 617 *intend*; angle for, fish for, seek 459 *search*; offer, bid, make a bid; make an

attempt, make shift to, make the effort, do something about, not just stand there; endeavour, struggle, strive, try hard, try and try again 599 *be resolute*; do one's best, do one's damnedest, go all out, redouble one's efforts 682 *exert oneself*; push hard, strain, sweat 682 *work*; tackle, take on, try one's hand at, have a go, give it a try, give it a whirl, have a shot at, have a crack at, have a stab at 672 *undertake*; take the bull by the horns; chance one's arm, try one's luck, venture, speculate 618 *gamble*; put out a feeler, dip in a toe, put a toe in the water, fly a kite 461 *be tentative*; bite off more than one can chew; die in the attempt 728 *fail*.

Int. here goes!, nothing ventured, nothing gained.

672 Undertaking

N. undertaking, job, task, assignment; self-imposed task, labour of love, pilgrimage 597 *voluntary work*; contract, engagement, obligation, subcontract 764 *promise*; operation, exercise; programme, project, design 623 *plan*; tall order, big undertaking 700 *hard task*; enterprise, quest, search, adventure 459 *enquiry*; venture, speculation 618 *gambling*; occupation, matter in hand 622 *business*; campaign 671 *attempt*.

Adj. enterprising, pioneering, adventurous, venturesome, daring; go-ahead, go-go, progressive, innovative; opportunist, with an eye to the main chance; ambitious.

Vb. undertake, engage in, apply oneself to, address oneself to, take up, go in for, devote oneself to; venture on, take on, tackle 671 *attempt*; go about, take in hand, turn or put or set one's hand to; set going 68 *initiate*; proceed to, embark on, launch into, plunge into, fall to, set to, get one's head down, buckle to, put one's best foot forward, set one's shoulder to the wheel, set one's hand to the plough 68 *begin*; grasp the nettle 855 *be courageous*; assume responsibility, take charge of 689 *manage*; execute 725 *carry out*; set up shop, have irons in the fire 622 *busy oneself*; shoulder, take on one's shoulders, take upon oneself 917 *incur a duty*; commit oneself 764 *promise*; get involved, let oneself in for, volunteer 597 *be willing*; take on too much, bite off more than one can chew, have too many irons in the fire 678 *be busy*.

673 Use

N. use, utilization, exploitation; employment, application, appliance; exercise 610 *practice*; usage; treatment, proper treatment 457 *carefulness*; ill-treatment; misuse; abuse; wear, wear and tear 655 *dilapidation*; exhaustion, consumption 634 *waste*; reuse, recycling; usefulness, benefit, service 642 *good policy*; practicality, applicability 640 *utility*.

Adj. *used*, applied, employed, etc. (see vb.); in service, in use, in constant use, in practice; used up, consumed, worn, thread-bare, down-at-heel, second-hand, well-used, well-thumbed, dog-eared, well-worn 655 *dilapidated*; beaten, well-trodden 490 *known*; hackneyed, stale; available, usable, employable, utilizable, convertible 640 *useful*; at one's service, consumable, disposable.

Vb. *use*, employ, exercise, practise, put into practice, put into operation; apply, exert, bring to bear, administer; spend on, give to, devote to, dedicate to; assign to, allot; utilize, make use of, convert, convert to use 640 *find useful*; reuse, recycle, exploit, get a lot of mileage out of, use to the full, get the best out of, make the most of, maximize, exhaust the possibilities; milk, drain 304 *extract*; put to good use, turn to good account, capitalize on, make capital out of, use to advantage, profit by; play on, trade on, cash in on; play off against; make a pawn *or* cat's-paw of, take advantage of; put to use, wear, wear out, use up, eat into, consume 634 *waste*; work, manipulate 173 *operate*; wield, ply, brandish; overwork, tax 684 *fatigue*.

avail oneself of, take up, adopt, try; resort to, have recourse to, fall back on, turn to, draw on; impose on, presume on; press into service, enlist in one's service.

dispose of, have at one's disposal, control, have at one's command, do what one likes with; allot, assign 783 *allocate*; requisition; call into play, set in motion, set going, deploy 612 *motivate*; enjoy 773 *possess*; consume, expend, absorb, use up 634 *waste*.

674 Non-use

N. *non-use*, abeyance, suspension 677 *inaction*; non-availability 190 *absence*; stagnation, unemployment 679 *inactivity*; abstinence 620 *avoidance*; disuse, obsolescence 611 *disuse*; redundancy, dismissal 300 *ejection*; surrender, throwing in the towel 621 *relinquishment*; withdrawal, cancellation 752 *annulment*; unsuitability 643 *inexpediency*; uselessness, write-off 641 *uselessness*.

Adj. *disused*, derelict, discarded, cast-off, jettisoned, scrapped, written off; sacked, discharged, laid off, etc. (see vb.); laid up, mothballed, put on the back burner, out of commission, rusting; in limbo 458 *neglected*; worn out; on the shelf, retired; out of use, superseded, superannuated, obsolete, discredited 127 *antiquated*.

Vb. *not use*, not utilize, hold in abeyance; not touch, have no use for; abstain, forbear, hold off, do without 620 *avoid*; dispense with; reserve, keep in hand 632 *store*.

stop using, leave off 145 *cease*; outgrow 611 *disaccustom*; lay up, put in mothballs, put on the back burner, put out of commission; have done with, lay aside, put on the shelf; pension off, put out to grass; discard, dump, ditch, scrap, write off; jettison, throw away, throw overboard 300 *eject*; slough, cast off; give up, relinquish, resign 779 *not retain*; suspend, withdraw, cancel, unsubscribe 752 *annul*; discharge, lay off, pay off, make redundant 300 *dismiss*; drop, supersede, replace 150 *substitute*.

675 Misuse

N. *misuse*, abuse, wrong use, alcohol abuse, drug abuse, substance abuse, inhalant abuse, steroid abuse, solvent abuse, volatile substance abuse, VSA; misapplication; mismanagement, maladministration 695 *bungling*; misappropriation, malpractice 788 *peculation*; perversion 246 *distortion*; prostitution, violation; desecration 980 *impiety*; commercialization, commodification; malapropism 565 *bad grammar*; pollution 649 *uncleanness*; overuse, overgrazing, overfishing; extravagance 634 *waste*; misusage, mishandling, mistreatment, maltreatment, ill-treatment.

Vb. *misuse*, abuse; use wrongly, misemploy, put to bad use, misdirect; manipulate, misappropriate 788 *defraud*; commercialize, commodify; violate, desecrate, take in vain 980 *profane*; prostitute 655 *pervert*; pollute 649 *make unclean*; do violence to 176 *force*; take advantage of, exploit 673 *use*; manhandle, knock about 645 *ill-treat*; maltreat 735 *oppress*; misgovern, misrule, mishandle, mismanage 695 *be unskilful*; squander, fritter away 634 *waste*; misapply, use a sledgehammer to crack a nut 641 *waste effort*.

SECTION THREE

Voluntary action

676 Action

N. *action*, doing, performance; steps, measures, move 623 *policy*; transaction, enactment, commission; execution, accomplishment 725 *completion*; procedure, routine 610 *practice*; behaviour 688 *conduct*; movement, play, swing 265 *motion*; operation, working, interaction 173 *agency*; force, pressure 178 *influence*; work, labour 682 *exertion*; militancy, activeness;

effort, endeavour, campaign, crusade, battle 671 *attempt*; implementation, administration, handling 689 *management*.

deed, act; action, piece of the action, exploit, feat, achievement 855 *prowess*; crime; stunt, tour de force, stroke of genius 875 *ostentation*; gesture, measure, step, move 623 *policy*; manoeuvre 688 *tactics*; stroke, blow, coup, coup d'état 623 *contrivance*; job, task, operation, exercise 672 *undertaking*; proceeding, transaction, deal, doings, dealings 154 *affairs*; work, handiwork.

doer, man *or* woman of action, go-getter, activist, movers and shakers 638 *bigwig*, 678 *busy person*; practical person; achiever; hero, heroine 855 *brave person*; practitioner 696 *expert*; stunt man *or* woman, player 594 *actor*; executant, performer; perpetrator, committer; mover, controller, manipulator 612 *motivator*; operator 686 *agent*; contractor, undertaker, entrepreneur, intrapreneur; campaigner, canvasser; executor, executive, administrator, manager 690 *director*; hand, workman, operative 686 *worker*;

Vb. *do*, act, perform, get in on the act; be in action, come into operation 173 *operate*; militate, act upon 178 *influence*; manipulate 612 *motivate*; use tactics, manoeuvre 698 *be cunning*; do something, lift a finger; proceed, proceed with, get on with, get going, move, take action, take steps; try 671 *attempt*; tackle, take on 672 *undertake*; adopt a measure, enact, legislate 953 *make legal*; do the deed, perpetrate, commit, achieve, accomplish, complete, have been there, done that 725 *carry through*; do the needful, take care of, dispatch, execute, implement, fulfil, put into practice 725 *carry out*; do great deeds, make history, win renown 866 *have a reputation*; practise, exercise, carry on, discharge, prosecute, pursue, wage, ply, ply one's trade, employ oneself 622 *busy oneself*; officiate, do one's stuff 622 *function*; transact, proceed 622 *do business*; administer, administrate, manage, control 689 *direct*; have to do with 688 *deal with*; sweat, labour, campaign, canvass 682 *work*; exploit 673 *use*; have a hand in, be active in, play a part in 775 *participate*; deal in, have a finger in, get mixed up in 678 *meddle*; conduct oneself, indulge in 688 *behave*.

677 Inaction

N. *inaction*, nothing doing, inertia 175 *inertness*; impotence; failure to act, neglect 458 *negligence*; abstention, refraining 620 *avoidance*; passive resistance 711 *defiance*; suspension, abeyance, dormancy 674 *non-use*; deadlock, stalemate, logjam, gridlock 145 *stop*;

immobility, paralysis, impassivity 375 *insensitivity*; passivity, stagnation, vegetation, doldrums, stillness, quiet, calm 266 *state of rest*; time on one's hands, idle hours 681 *leisure*; rest 683 *rest*; non-employment, underemployment, unemployment, joblessness; no work, sinecure; loafing, idleness, indolence, twiddling one's thumbs 679 *inactivity*; Fabian policy, Fabian tactics 136 *delay*; lack of progress 655 *deterioration*; non-interference, non-intervention 860 *indifference*; head in the sand, defeatism 856 *cowardice*.

Adj. *non-active*, inoperative, idle, suspended, in abeyance 679 *inactive*; passive, dull, sluggish 175 *inert*; unoccupied, leisured 681 *leisurely*; do-nothing, unprogressive, ostrich-like; Fabian, cunctative, delaying, procrastinating; stationary, motionless, immobile, becalmed 266 *at rest*; cold, extinct; not stirring, without a sign of life, dead-and-alive 361 *dead*; laid off, unemployed, jobless, out of work, on the dole, without employment; incapable of action 161 *impotent*; benumbed, paralysed 375 *insensitive*; apathetic, phlegmatic 820 *impassive*.

Vb. *not act*, hang fire 598 *be unwilling*; refrain, abstain, pass the buck 620 *avoid*; look on, stand by 441 *watch*; let the world go by, wait and see, bide one's time 136 *wait*; procrastinate 136 *put off*; let things take their course, laissez-faire, let sleeping dogs lie, let well alone, mind one's own business, butt out; hold no brief for, stay neutral, not take sides, sit on the fence 860 *be indifferent*; do nothing, turn a blind eye 458 *disregard*; sit tight, not move, not budge, not lift a finger, not even attempt 175 *be inert*; rest on one's oars, rest on one's laurels; drift, slide, coast, free-wheel; have no hope 853 *despair*; let pass, let go by, leave alone, let alone, give it a miss 458 *neglect*; stet; stay still, keep quiet 266 *be at rest*; sit back, relax 683 *rest*; have no function; have nothing to do, kick one's heels, twiddle one's thumbs, sit on one's hands; pause, desist 145 *cease*; rust, rust in idle, lie idle, stay on the shelf, lie fallow 674 *not use*; have no life, lie dead 361 *die*.

678 Activity

N. *activity*, activeness, activism, militancy 676 *action*; scene; interest, active interest 775 *participation*; social activity, group activity 882 *sociability*; activation 612 *motive*; excitation 174 *simulation*; agitation, movement, mass movement 738 *sedition*; life, stir 265 *motion*; nimbleness, briskness, smartness, alacrity, promptitude 597 *willingness*; readiness 135 *punctuality*; quickness, dispatch, expedition 277 *velocity*; spurt *or* spirt, burst, fit 318 *spasm*;

hurry, flurry, hurry-skurry, hustle, bustle 680 *haste*; hussle, fuss, bother, botheration, ado, to-do, tumult, frenzy 61 *turmoil*; whirl, scramble, mad scramble, rat race, life in the fast lane, maelstrom 315 *whirl*; drama, much ado, thick of things, thick of the action, the fray; plenty to do, a piece of the action, irons in the fire 622 *business*; call on one's time; pressure of work, no sinecure; hum, hive of industry 687 *workshop*.

restlessness, fiddling; fidgets, fidgetiness 318 *agitation*; fret 503 *frenzy*; energy, dynamism, aggressiveness, militancy, enterprise, initiative, push, drive, go, get-up-and-go, pep 174 *vigorousness*; vivacity, spirit, animation, liveliness, vitality 360 *life*; watchfulness, wakefulness, vigilance 457 *carefulness*; sleeplessness, insomnia.

assiduousness, assiduity, application, concentration, intentness, sedulity, sedulousness 455 *attention*; industriousness, industry, laboriousness; determination, earnestness, empressement 599 *resolution*; tirelessness, indefatigability 600 *perseverance*; studiousness, painstaking, diligence; whole-heartedness, devotedness.

overactivity, overextension, overexpansion, excess 637 *redundancy*; Parkinson's law; displacement activity; chasing one's own tail 641 *wasted effort*; song and dance 318 *commotion*; hyperthyroidism, overexertion; officiousness, interference, finger in every pie.

busy person, new broom, enthusiast, hustler, jet-setter; workaholic 686 *worker*; factotum, jack-of-all-trades, maid-of-all-work, galley slave, Trojan; eager beaver, busy bee, workhorse, willing horse; man *or* woman of action, activist, militant 676 *doer*; live wire, human dynamo; powerhouse, whiz kid, go-getter, pusher, careerist.

meddler, stirrer, interferer, trouble-maker, busybody; nosy parker, curtain-twitcher; backseat driver 691 *adviser*.

Adj. *active*, stirring, kicking 265 *moving*; going, working, incessant; expeditious; able, able-bodied, abled 162 *strong*; quick, brisk, nippy, spry, smart 277 *speedy*; nimble, energetic, forceful, proactive 174 *vigorous*; pushing, go-getting, up-and-coming 672 *enterprising*; frisky, sprightly, mettlesome, live, alive and kicking, full of beans, animated, bright-eyed and bushy-tailed, vivacious 819 *lively*; eager 818 *fervent*; enthusiastic, zealous, prompt, on one's toes 597 *willing*; awake, alert, watchful, wakeful, on the qui vive 457 *vigilant*; sleepless, restless, feverish, fretful, tossing, fidgety, jumpy, nervy, like a cat on hot bricks, like a hen on a hot griddle; frantic 503 *frenzied*;

hyperactive, overactive 822 *excitable*; involved; aggressive, militant, up in arms 718 *warlike*.

busy, bustling, humming, lively, eventful; coming and going, rushing to and fro; up and doing, stirring, astir, afoot, on the move, on the go, on the trot, in full swing; rushed off one's feet, hard at it, up to one's eyes; timepoor; at work, at one's desk; occupied, fully occupied, employed; busy as a bee.

industrious, studious, sedulous, assiduous; hardworking; slogging 682 *laborious*; tireless, indefatigable, burning the candle at both ends, efficient, workman-like.

Vb. *be active*, interest oneself in, join in 775 *participate*; be stirring, rush to and fro 265 *move*; run riot 61 *rampage*; rouse oneself, bestir oneself, stir one's stumps, rub the sleep from one's eyes, be up and doing; hum, thrive 730 *prosper*; make progress 285 *progress*; keep moving, keep on the go, keep the pot boiling 146 *go on*; push, shove, thrust, drive 279 *impel*; elbow one's way, thrust oneself forward 174 *be vigorous*; rush, surge 350 *flow*; roar, rage, bluster 352 *blow*; explode, burst; dash, fly, run 277 *move fast*; make the effort, do one's best 671 *attempt*; take pains 455 *be attentive*; buckle to, put one's shoulder to the wheel, put one's hand to the tiller 682 *exert oneself*; persist, beaver away 600 *persevere*; polish off, dispatch, make short work of, not let the grass grow under one's feet; rise to the occasion, work wonders 727 *be successful*; jump to it, show willing, make things hum 676 *do*; be on one's toes, anticipate 457 *be careful*; seize the opportunity, take one's chance, take the bull by the horns 137 *profit by*; assert oneself, not take it lying down, be up in arms, react, react sharply, show fight 711 *defy*; protest, agitate, demonstrate, kick up a shindy, raise the dust 762 *deprecate*; be busy, keep busy; have irons in the fire 622 *busy oneself*; be always on the go, bustle, hurry, hassle, scurry 680 *hasten*; live in a whirl, join the rat race, run round in circles; chase one's own tail 641 *waste effort*; not know which way to turn 700 *be in difficulty*; have one's hands full, be rushed off one's feet, have not a moment to spare *or* to call one's own, have no time to lose, burn the midnight oil, burn the candle at both ends; stamp with impatience 822 *be excitable*; have other fish to fry 138 *be engaged*; slave, slog 682 *work*; never stop, improve the shining hour.

meddle, intervene, interfere, be officious, not mind one's own business, have a finger in every pie; pry into, poke one's nose in, shove *or* put *or* stick one's oar in, butt in 297 *intrude*; pester, bother, annoy 827 *trouble*; be bossy, boss, boss one around, tyrannize 735 *oppress*; tinker, tamper.

Adv. *actively*, on the go, on one's toes; full tilt, full belt, whole hog, like a bomb, on all cylinders; with might and main, for all one is worth, for dear life, as if one's life depended on it.

679 Inactivity

N. *inactivity*, inactiveness 677 *inaction*; inertia, torpor 175 *inertness*; lull, suspension 145 *cessation*; immobility, stillness, slack period, doldrums, morgue 266 *state of rest*; logjam, putting off till tomorrow, stagnation 655 *deterioration*; rustiness 674 *non-use*; slump, recession 37 *decrease*; unemployment, shutdown; absenteeism 598 *unwillingness*; procrastination, laissez-faire, mañana 136 *delay*; idleness, indolence, loafing, slacking, cyberslacking.

sluggishness, lethargy, laziness, indolence, sloth; dawdling 278 *slowness*; debility 163 *weakness*; lifelessness; languor, listlessness 820 *moral insensibility*; stupor, torpor 375 *insensitivity*; apathy 860 *indifference*; phlegm, impassivity 823 *inexcitability*; supineness, line of least resistance 721 *submission*.

sleepiness, tiredness, weariness, lassitude 684 *fatigue*; drowsiness, heaviness, nodding; yawning; tired eyes, heavy lids, sand in the eyes; dreaminess 513 *fantasy*.

sleep, slumber, kip, bye-byes; beauty sleep; sleep of the just; drowse; nap, catnap, power-nap, forty winks, shut-eye, snooze, doze, siesta 683 *rest*; hibernation; unconsciousness, coma, oblivion, trance, catalepsy, hypnosis 375 *insensitivity*; sleepwalking, somnambulism; sleepy sickness, sleeping sickness 651 *disease*; dreams; Land of Nod.

sleeping draught, soporific, nightcap, sleeping pill, sedative, barbiturate; opiate, opium, morphine 375 *anaesthetic*; lullaby, cradlesong, bedtime story.

idler, drone, lazybones, loafer, sloucher, couch potato, mouse potato, sluggard; slacker, skiver, clock-watcher; sleepyhead; dawdler 278 *slowcoach*; hobo, bum, tramp 268 *wanderer*; mendicant 763 *beggar*; parasite, cadger, sponger, scrounger, moocher, freeloader; layabout, good-fornothing, ne'er-do-well; drifter, free-wheeler; lotus-eater; passenger, sleeping partner; Sloane Ranger, society girl; idle rich, leisured classes, ladies who lunch; dreamer.

Adj. *inactive*, motionless, stationary, at a standstill, still 266 *at rest*; suspended, discontinued, not working, not operating, not in use, laid up, out of commission 674 *disused*; inanimate, lifeless 175 *inert*; torpid, unconscious, drugged 375 *insensitive*; sluggish, rusty 677 *non-active*;

listless, lackadaisical 834 *dejected*; tired, faint, languid, languorous 684 *fatigued*; dull, heavy, leaden, lumpish, stolid 820 *impassive*; unresisting, supine, submissive 721 *submitting*; uninterested 454 *incurious*; apathetic 860 *indifferent*; lethargic 823 *inexcitable*; non-participating, sleeping 190 *absent*; idle, unoccupied 681 *leisurely*; on strike, out, locked out.

lazy, bone-lazy; slothful, sluggish, workshy, indolent, idle, bone-idle, parasitical; idling, loafing 681 *leisurely*; dawdling 278 *slow*; tardy, procrastinating 136 *late*; slack 458 *negligent*.

sleepy, ready for bed, tired 684 *fatigued*; half-awake, half-asleep; somnolent, heavy-eyed; drowsy, dozy, dopey, groggy, nodding, yawning; napping, dozing; asleep, dreaming, snoring, fast asleep, sound asleep, dead to the world; unconscious, out, out cold; dormant, hibernating, comatose; in dreamland, in the land of Nod, in the arms of Morpheus, in bed.

Vb. *be inactive*, do nothing, relax, hang out, chill out, veg out; rust, stagnate, vegetate, veg, smoulder, hang fire 677 *no act*; let the grass grow under one's feet, let the world go by, delay 136 *put off*; not bother, take it easy, let things go, laissez-faire 458 *be neglectful*; hang about, kick one's heels 136 *wait*; slouch, lag, loiter, dawdle 278 *move slowly*; dally, drag one's feet 136 *be late*; stand, sit, lie, loll, lounge, laze, rest, take it easy 683 *rest*; lie down on the job, slack, skive, shirk 620 *avoid*; not work, fold one's arms, sit around; have nothing to do, loaf, idle, mooch about, moon about, while away the time, kill time, sit on one's hands, twiddle one's thumbs; waste time, trifle, dabble, fritter away the time, piddle, potter 641 *waste effort*; come to a standstill 278 *slow down*; dilly-dally, hesitate 474 *be uncertain*; droop, faint, fail, languish, slacken 266 *come to rest*; slump 37 *decrease*; be still, be hushed 266 *be at rest*; discontinue, stop, come to an end 145 *cease*; strike, come out, take industrial action.

sleep, slumber, snooze, nap, catnap, power-nap; hibernate; sleep like a log, sleep like a top, sleep the sleep of the just; dream; snore, drive pigs to market; go to sleep, nod off, drop off, fall asleep, take a nap, have a kip, have forty winks; close one's eyes, feel sleepy, yawn, nod, doze, drowse; go to bed, turn in, doss down, kip down, shake down, hit the hay; settle down, bed down.

make inactive, put to sleep; send to sleep, lull, rock, cradle; soothe 177 *assuage*; deaden, paralyse, benumb, anaesthetize, dope, drug 375 *make insensitive*; cramp, immobilize 747 *fetter*; lay up, put out of commission 674 *stop using*; dismantle 641 *make useless*; lay off 300 *dismiss*.

680 Haste

N. *haste*, hurry, scurry, hurry-scurry, hustle, bustle, hassle, flurry, whirl, scramble 678 *activity*; flap, flutter, fidget, fuss 318 *agitation*; rush, rush job 670 *non-preparation*; feverish haste, tearing hurry, race against time, no time to lose 136 *lateness*; immediacy, urgency 638 *importance*; push, drive, expedition, dispatch 277 *velocity*; hastening, acceleration, forced march, dash, rush, etc. 277 *spurt*; precipitateness, impetuosity 857 *rashness*; hastiness, impatience 822 *excitability*; the more haste, the less speed.

Adj. *hasty*, impetuous, impulsive, hot-headed 857 *rash*; feverish, impatient; pushing, shoving, elbowing, boisterous, furious 176 *violent*; precipitate, headlong, breakneck 277 *speedy*; without delay; hastening, making speed; in haste, in all haste, hotfoot, running, racing; in a hurry, unable to wait, pressed for time, hard-pressed, driven; done in haste, hurried, scamped, slapdash, cursory 458 *negligent*; rough and ready, forced, rushed, rush, last-minute 670 *unprepared*; rushed into, railroaded; stampeded; allowing no time, brooking no delay, urgent, immediate 638 *important*.

Vb. *hasten*, expedite; urge, drive, stampede, spur, goad, whip, lash, flog 612 *incite*; bundle off, hustle away; rush, allow no time, railroaded, brook no delay; be hasty, be precipitate, rush headlong 857 *be rash*; haste, make haste; race, run, dash off, tear off 277 *move fast*; make up for lost time, overtake 277 *outstrip*; spurt *or* spirt, dash, make a forced march 277 *accelerate*; hurry, scurry, hustle, bustle, fret, fume, fidget, rush to and fro, dart to and fro 678 *be active*; be in a hurry, have no time to spare, have no time to lose, act without ceremony, cut short the preliminaries, brush aside; cut corners, rush one's fences; rush through, dash through, make short work of; be pressed for time, work against time *or* to a deadline, work under pressure, think on one's feet; do at the last moment 136 *be late*; lose no time, lose not a moment, make every minute count; hasten away, cut and run, make oneself scarce, not be seen for dust 296 *walk out*.

Int. *hurry up!*, be quick!, buck up!, look lively!, look sharp!, get a move on!, step on it!, quick march!, at the double!

681 Leisure

N. *leisure*, spare time, free time; idle moments; time on one's hands, time to kill; sinecure; idleness, breathing space, off duty, time off, day off, holiday, half-holiday, half-day, break, gap year, vacation, leave, sabbatical, furlough 679 *inactivity*; time to spare, no hurry, ample time, all the time in the world; rest, ease, relaxation 683 *rest*; redundancy, retirement 753 *resignation*.

Adj. *leisurely*, unhurried 278 *slow*; at one's convenience, in one's own time, at any odd moment; leisured, at leisure, unoccupied 683 *restful*; at a loose end; off duty, on holiday, on vacation, on leave, on furlough, on sabbatical; retired, in retirement, redundant; labour-saving.

682 Exertion

N. *exertion*, effort, struggle 671 *attempt*; strain, stress, might and main; tug, pull, stretch, heave, lift, throw; drive, force, pressure, applied energy 160 *energy*; ergonomics; ado, hassle, trouble, the hard way; muscle, elbow grease, sweat of one's brow; pains 678 *assiduousness*; overwork 678 *overactivity*.

exercise, practice, drill, training, cross-training, work-out, the bar (ballet) 669 *preparation*; physical education, PE, keeping fit, jogging, jarming, cycling, constitutional, daily dozen; gymnastics 162 *athletics*; weight-lifting, body-building; yoga, isometrics, eurhythmics, Medau, callisthenics, aerobics, step, body pump, body combat, qigong *or* qi gong *or* ch'i kung, tai ji *or* tai ji quan *or* t'ai chi *or* t'ai chi ch'uan, Tae Bo (tdmk); games, sports, races 837 *sport*.

exercise equipment, exercise bike, rowing machine, stepper, treadmill, multigym, weights; Indian clubs, medicine ball, Swiss ball, skipping rope.

labour, industry, work, hard work, long haul; spadework, donkeywork; legwork; manual labour, sweat of one's brow; housework, chores, daily grind, toil, drudgery, slavery, sweat, fag, grind, strain, treadmill, grindstone, blood, sweat and tears; hack work; bull; hard labour 963 *penalty*; forced labour, fatigue, spell of duty 917 *duty*; piecework, taskwork, homework, homeworking, out-work, telecommuting; task, chore, job, job of work, operation, exercise 676 *deed*; shift, stint, stretch, bout, spell of work 110 *period*; stroke of work, hand's turn; working life, working week, working day, man-hours, woman-hours; work ethic, Protestant work ethic.

Adj. *labouring*, horny-handed; working, drudging, etc. (see vb.); on the go, hard at it 678 *busy*; hardworking, laborious 678 *industrious*; slogging, plodding, strenuous, energetic 678 *active*; painstaking.

laborious, backbreaking; gruelling, punishing, unremitting, exhausting; weary, wearisome, painful, burdensome; heroic, Herculean;

arduous, hard, heavy, uphill 700 *difficult*; hard-fought, hard-won; thorough, painstaking, laboured; effort-wasting 641 *useless*.

Vb. *exert oneself*, apply oneself, put one's best foot forward, make an effort, try 671 *attempt*; struggle, strain, strive, sweat blood; trouble oneself, put oneself out, bend over backwards; spare no effort, turn every stone, leave no stone unturned, do one's utmost, try one's best, use one's best endeavours, do all one can, go to any lengths, move heaven and earth; go all out, pull out all the stops, put one's heart and soul into it, put one's back into it, strain every nerve 678 *be active*; force one's way, elbow one's way, drive through, wade through; hammer at, slog at 600 *persevere*; take action 676 *do*.

work, labour, toil, drudge, grind, slog, sweat, work up a sweat, work up a lather; sweat blood; pull, haul, tug, shove, hump, heave, ply the oar; dig, lumber; get down to it, set to, roll up one's sleeves 68 *begin*; keep at it, plod 600 *persevere*; work hard, work overtime, moonlight, work all hours, be firing on all cylinders, burn the midnight oil 678 *be busy*; work at home, be self-employed, telecommute; job-share; slave away, beaver away, work one's fingers to the bone, work like a galley slave, work like a horse, work like a Trojan; work oneself to death; overdo it; work for, serve 703 *minister to*; put to work, tax 684 *fatigue*.

exercise, drill, practise, train; do one's daily dozen, do physical jerks, go for the burn, pump iron; cycle, jog, power-walk, run, swim, walk, work out.

683 Rest

N. *rest*, repose 679 *inactivity*; restfulness, ease, comfort 376 *euphoria*; peace and quiet, tranquillity 266 *state of rest*; happy dreams 679 *sleep*; relaxation, breathing space, breather 685 *refreshment*; pause, respite, let-up, recess, break 145 *lull*; interval; holiday, vacation, leave, furlough, day off, sabbatical, sabbatical year 681 *leisure*; day of rest, Sabbath, Lord's Day.

Adj. *restful*, reposeful, relaxing; carefree, relaxed, laid-back, at ease 828 *content*; peaceful, quiet 266 *tranquil*; leisured, holiday 681 *leisurely*.

Vb. *rest*, take a rest, repose, take it easy, take one's ease, sit back, put one's feet up; recline, lie down, loll, lounge, laze, sprawl 216 *be horizontal*; perch, roost 311 *sit down*; go to bed, kip down, go to sleep 679 *sleep*; relax, unwind, unbend; take a breather 685 *be refreshed*; slack off, let up, slow down; rest on one's oars 266 *come to rest*; take time off *or* out.

684 Fatigue

N. *fatigue*, tiredness, weariness, lassitude, languor, lethargy; exhaustion, collapse, prostration; sleep-deprivation; strain, stress, mental fatigue, overwork, burn-out, karoshi 682 *exertion*; donor fatigue, charity fatigue, compassion fatigue, disaster fatigue, election fatigue.

Adj. *fatigued*, tired, ready for bed 679 *sleepy*; exhausted, asleep on one's feet, tired out, spent, done, done up, done in, all in, pooped, fagged out, zonked, knocked up, washed out, worn to a frazzle, dog-tired, bone-weary, tired to death, ready to drop, on one's last legs, dead beat, whacked, knackered, flaked out, flat out; sleep-deprived; stressed, strained, overworked, overtired, burned out, stressed out; more dead than alive, prostrate; stiff, aching, sore, footsore, walked off one's feet; heavy-eyed, hollow-eyed; tired-looking, haggard, worn; drooping, flagging.

Vb. *be fatigued*, be fagged, etc. (see adj.); tire oneself out, overdo it, overtax one's strength; get weary, ache in every muscle *or* limb, gasp, pant, puff, blow, grunt 352 *breathe*; languish, droop, drop, sink, flag, fail 163 *be weak*; stagger, faint, swoon, feel giddy; yawn, nod, drowse 679 *sleep*; succumb, drop, collapse, flake out, crack up, pack up; be at the end of one's tether; can go no further; overwork, need a rest, need a break; be burned out.

fatigue, tire, tire out, wear, wear out, exhaust, do up, fag, whack, knock up, prostrate; wind; tax, strain, stress, overwork, overtax, overtask, overburden, overstrain, burn out; enervate, drain, take it out of; tire to death, weary 838 *be tedious*.

685 Refreshment

N. *refreshment*, breather, breath of air 683 *rest*; break, screen break, recess, etc. 145 *lull*; recreation, recuperation 656 *restoration*; revival; easing 831 *relief*; refresher, reviver, stimulant, refreshments.

Adj. *refreshing*, thirst-quenching; comforting; bracing, reviving.

Vb. *refresh*, freshen, freshen up 648 *clean*; air, fan, ventilate 340 *aerate*; cool, cool off, cool one down 382 *refrigerate*; brace, stimulate 174 *invigorate*; revive; offer food 301 *feed*.

be refreshed, draw breath, get one's breath back, regain *or* recover one's breath; clear one's head; come to, perk up, get one's second wind, feel like a new man *or* woman; revive 656 *be restored*; mop one's brow, stretch one's legs, refresh oneself, take a breather, sleep it off.

686 Agent

N. *agent*, operator, actor, performer, player, executant, practitioner; perpetrator 676 *doer*;

minister, tool 628 *instrument*; functionary 741 *officer*; representative 754 *delegate*; spokesman 755 *deputy*; proxy 150 *substitute*; executor, executrix, executive, administrator, dealer, factor; middleman 794 *merchant*; subcontractor.

worker, voluntary worker 597 *volunteer*; social worker 901 *philanthropist*; freelance, freelancer, e-lancer, self-employed person; home-worker, teleworker, telecommuter; organization man 83 *conformist*; trade unionist 775 *participator*; toiler, drudge, dogsbody, fag, hack; flunkey, menial, factotum, maid-of-all-work, domestic servant 742 *servant*; hewer of wood and drawer of water, beast of burden 742 *slave*; professional person, business man, business woman, career woman, executive; breadwinner, wage earner, salary earner, wage slave, employee; boffin; clerical worker, desk worker, white-collar worker, black-coat worker; office worker, girl Friday, man Friday; shop assistant 793 *seller*; charwoman, dustman 648 *cleaner*; labourer, casual labourer, agricultural labourer, farm worker 370 *farmer*; pieceworker, manual worker, blue-collar worker; working man *or* woman, working girl, workman, hand, operative, factory worker, factory hand; navvy, roadman; ganger, plate-layer; docker, stevedore, packer; porter.

artisan, tradesman; skilled worker, semi-skilled worker, master 696 *proficient person*; journeyman, apprentice 538 *learner*; craftsman *or* -woman, potter, turner, joiner, cabinet-maker, carpenter, carver, woodworker, cooper; wheelwright; coach-builder; shipwright, boat-builder; builder, architect, master mason, mason, housebuilder, bricklayer, plasterer, tiler, thatcher, dyker, painter, decorator; cowboy; forger, metalworker, smith, blacksmith, tinsmith, goldsmith, silversmith, gunsmith, locksmith; tinker, knife-grinder; collier, miner, face-worker, steelworker, foundryman; mechanic, machinist, fitter; engineer, civil engineer, mining engineer, computer engineer, television engineer; plumber, welder, electrician, gas-fitter; weaver, spinner, tailor, needlewoman 228 *clothier*; watchmaker, clockmaker; jeweller; glass-blower.

personnel, staff, force, company, team, gang, squad, crew; dramatis personae 594 *actor*; workpeople, hands, men, payroll; labour; workforce, labour force, manpower, human resources, liveware, peopleware; personnel management, human resource management; staff turnover, churn, churn rate.

687 Workshop
N. workshop, studio; workroom, study, den, library; laboratory; works, factory; workshop,

yard; mill, loom; sawmill, paper mill; foundry, metalworks; steelyard, steelworks, smelter; blast furnace, forge, smithy 383 *furnace*; power station, gasworks 160 *energy*; quarry, mine 632 *store*; colliery, coalmine, pit, coalface; tin mine; mint; arsenal, armoury; dockyard, shipyard, slips; wharf, dock, dry dock 192 *stable*; construction site, building site; refinery, distillery, brewery, shop, shopfloor, bench, production line; nursery 370 *farm*; dairy, creamery 369 *stock farm*; kitchen, laundry; office, bureau, call centre; workstation.

688 Conduct
N. conduct, behaviour, deportment; bearing, comportment, carriage; demeanour, attitude, posture 445 *mien*; aspect, look 445 *appearance*; tone of voice, delivery 577 *voice*; motion, action, gesticulation 547 *gesture*; mode of behaviour, fashion, style; manner, guise, air; poise, savoir-faire, dignity, presence; breeding, graciousness, good manners, one's p's and q's 848 *etiquette*, 884 *courtesy*; good behaviour 933 *virtue*; ungraciousness, boorishness, rudeness, bad manners 885 *discourtesy*; pose, role-playing 850 *affectation*; outlook 485 *opinion*; mood 818 *feeling*; misbehaviour, misconduct 934 *wickedness*; abnormal behaviour, aberration 495 *error*, 934 *vice*, 936 *guilty act*; past behaviour, track record, history; reward of conduct: deserts 915 *what is due*; way of life, ethos, morals, principles, ideals, customs, mores, manners, lifestyle 610 *habit*; line of action 623 *policy*; career, course, race, walk, walk of life 622 *vocation*; observance, routine 610 *practice*; procedure, process, method, modus operandi 624 *way*; organization, orchestration, treatment, handling, manipulation, direction, masterminding 689 *management*; gentle handling, kid gloves, velvet glove 736 *leniency*; rough handling, putting the boot in, jackboot, iron hand 735 *severity*; dealings, transactions 154 *affairs*; deeds 676 *deed*; behaviourism.

tactics, strategy, campaign, plan of campaign, logistics; programme 623 *plan*; line, party line 623 *policy*; politics, statesmanship, diplomacy 733 *governing*; shuttle diplomacy, gunboat diplomacy; lifemanship, gamesmanship, one-upmanship 698 *cunning*; brinkmanship, generalship, seamanship 694 *skill*; jockeying for position; tactical advantage, vantage ground 34 *advantage*; playing for time 136 *delay*; manoeuvre; move, gambit 676 *deed*; stratagem.

Vb. behave, act 676 *do*; behave well, mind one's p's and q's, play the game 933 *be virtuous*; behave badly, forget oneself, break all the rules, misbehave, try it on 934 *be wicked*; keep out of mischief, be on one's best behaviour, keep a low profile; gesture 547 *gesticulate*; posture, pose, affect 850 *be affected*; conduct oneself, behave oneself, acquit oneself, comport oneself; set an example; conduct one's affairs 622 *busy oneself*; follow a course, steer a course 281 *steer for*; paddle one's own canoe, be master of one's own ship, shift for oneself 744 *be free*; employ tactics; behave towards, treat.

deal with, have on one's plate, have to do with 676 *do*; handle, manipulate 173 *operate*; carry on, conduct, run 689 *manage*; see to, cope with, do the needful; transact, enact, execute, dispatch, carry through, put into practice 725 *carry out*; work out 623 *plan*; work at, work through, wade through, plough through 682 *work*; go through, read 536 *study*.

689 Management

N. *management*, conduct of affairs, running handling; managership, agency 751 *commission*; care, charge, control 733 *authority*; superintendence, oversight 457 *surveillance*; art of management, tact 694 *skill*; business management, work study, management study, time and motion study; organization, masterminding, decision-making, adhocracy 623 *policy*, housekeeping, husbandry; the economy, national economy, stakeholder economy; economics, political economy, Keynesianism, neo-liberalism; statesmanship; government 733 *governing*; ménage, regime *or* régime; regulation, law-making 953 *legislation*; reins of government, ministry, cabinet; administration; bureaucracy.

directorship, direction, responsibility, control 737 *command*; dictatorship, leadership, premiership, chairmanship, captaincy 34 *superiority*; guidance.

Vb. *manage*, organize; influence; handle, conduct, run, carry on; administer; supervise, superintend, oversee, caretake 457 *keep watch*; have charge of; hold the purse strings, hold the reins 612 *motivate*; keep order, police; legislate; control, govern, rule.

direct, lead; boss, dictate 737 *command*; be in charge, head up, wear the trousers; hold office; mastermind, have overall responsibility; assume command; preside, take the chair, be in the chair; head, captain, skipper; steer, take the helm, show the way 547 *indicate*; guide, conduct, compère; channel.

690 Director

N. *director*, governing body 741 *governor*; steering committee, quango, select committee; cabinet, inner cabinet 692 *council*; board of directors, board, chair; staff, top brass, VIPs; management, suits, men in suits *or* in grey suits; manager, line manager, controller; legislator; employer, boss 741 *master*; headman, chief, head of state 34 *superior*; principal, head, headmaster *or* -mistress, rector, moderator, dean, vice-chancellor, chancellor; president; chairperson *or* -man *or* -woman, speaker, presiding officer; premier, prime minister, first minister, captain, skipper; master 270 *mariner*; pilot 520 *guide*; director of studies 537 *teacher*; backseat driver 691 *adviser*; organizer, planner, control freak 623 *planner*; fashion police, food police, etc.

leader, -meister; judge (Old Testament) 741 *governor*; messiah; ayatollah, guru; leader of the House, leader of the opposition; spearhead, centre forward; shepherd, drover 369 *herdsman*; bell-wether; pacemaker, pacesetter; master of ceremonies, MC; high priest; chorusleader; conductor, leader of the orchestra, first violin, drum major; Führer, Caudillo, Duce 741 *autocrat*; ringleader; captain; patrol leader, sixer; alpha male *or* female.

manager, line manager (see also *director* above); man *or* woman in charge, key person, kingpin, tsar 638 *bigwig*; administrator, executive, executor 676 *doer*; statesman *or* -woman, politician; housekeeper, chatelaine, housewife, house husband; steward, bailiff, farm manager, agent, factor 754 *nominee*; superintendent, supervisor, inspector, overseer, foreman *or* -woman, ganger, gaffer; warden, matron, senior nursing officer; party manager, whip, chief whip; custodian, caretaker, curator 749 *keeper*; master of hounds; ringmaster; compère.

official, office-bearer; steward; shop steward; Member of Parliament, MP, Euro-MP, MEP, MSP, AM, MLA, MHK, TD; constituency member, additional member, list member; public servant, civil servant, apparatchik; minister, cabinet minister, secretary of state; secretary-general; permanent secretary; bureaucrat, Eurocrat, suit (see also *director* above); magistrate 733 *position of authority*; commissioner, prefect; consul, praetor; first secretary; alderman, mayor 692 *councillor*; party official.

691 Advice

N. *advice*, word of advice, piece of advice, counsel, counsel of perfection; words of wisdom, counselling, marriage counselling, debt counselling, genetic counselling 658 *therapy*; criticism 480 *estimate*; didacticism, prescription 693 *precept*; caution 664 *warning*; recommendation, proposition, proposal, motion 512 *supposition*; suggestion; tip, word to the wise

524 *hint*; guidance, briefing, instruction 524 *information*; taking counsel, consultation, huddle, heads together, tête-à-tête, powwow, parley 584 *conference*.

adviser, counsellor, consultant, troubleshooter; referee, arbiter, arbitrator 480 *estimator*; advocate, prompter 612 *motivator*; medical adviser, therapist 658 *doctor*; legal adviser, advocate, counsel 958 *lawyer*; expert witness; guide, mentor, confidant(e) 537 *teacher*; life coach, personal trainer 537 *trainer*; family therapist; agony aunt; Dutch uncle; oracle, wise man 500 *sage*; backseat driver; public enquiry, consultative body 692 *council*; focus group; information bureau, information centre, information desk, help desk, call centre.

Vb. *advise*, give advice, counsel; recommend, prescribe, advocate, commend; propose, move, submit, suggest 512 *propound*; prompt 524 *hint*; urge, exhort 612 *incite*; advise against 613 *dissuade*; admonish 664 *warn*.

consult, seek advice, refer; call in, call on; refer to arbitration, ask for a second opinion, hold a public enquiry; confide in, be closeted with; take advice; take one's cue from, follow advice; sit in conclave, put heads together, hold a council of war, have a powwow with, parley, sit round a table.

692 Council

N. *council*, round table; council room; board room; court 956 *tribunal*; Privy Council; ecclesiastical council, general assembly, General Synod, Bench of Bishops, vestry, etc. 985 *synod*; cabinet; panel, quango, think tank, board, advisory board, consultative body, Royal Commission; assembly, conventicle, congregation 74 *assembly*; conclave, convocation 985 *synod*; convention, congress, meeting, top-level meeting, summit; League of Nations, UNO, Security Council; municipal council, county council, regional council, district council, town council, parish council; residents association, community council; soviet; council of elders; sitting, session, séance.

parliament, Mother of Parliaments, Westminster, Upper House, House of Lords, Privy Council, Lower House, House of Commons; European Parliament; senate, senatus; legislative assembly; loya jirga; quorum, division.

Parliaments

Althing or Althingi (Iceland); Assembly of the Republic (Portugal); Bundestag, Bundesrat, (Germany; *formerly* Reichstag, Reichsrat); Bundesrat, Nationalrat (Austria); Room of Deputies, Senate (Italy); Chief Pleas (Sark); Congress, House of Representatives, Senate (United States); Cortes, Congress of Deputies, Senate (Spain); Diet, House of Representatives, House of Councillors (Japan); Eduskunta/Riksdag (Finland); Federal Assembly, Federal Council, State Duma (Russia; Duma *also* pre-1917 parliament); Folketing (Danish; *formerly* Rigsdag); Great Hural (Mongolia); House of Commons, Senate (Canada); House of Representatives (New Zealand); House of Representatives, Senate (Australia); Knesset (Israel); Lok Sabha, Rajya Sabha (India); Majlis (Iran); Majlis as-Shoora, Senate (Pakistan); National Assembly, National Council of Provinces (South Africa); National Assembly/Chambre des Députés, Senate (France); National Assembly, Sejm, Senate (Poland); Nationalrat, Ständerat (Switzerland); Oireachtas, Dáil Éireann, Seanad Éireann (Republic of Ireland); Riksdag (Sweden); Sabor (Croatia); States (Alderney, Guernsey, Jersey); States-General (Netherlands); Storting (Norway); Supreme Rada (Ukraine); Supreme Soviet (parliament of the former USSR); Tynwald, House of Keys, Legislative Council (Isle of Man).

councillor, privy councillor; senator, peer; Lords Spiritual, Lords Temporal; representative, deputy, congressman *or* -woman; member of Parliament, MP, etc. 690 *official*, 754 *delegate*; backbencher, parliamentarian; mayor, alderman 690 *official*.

693 Precept

N. *precept*, firm advice 691 *advice*; direction, instruction; instructions, directions for use, care label, user's manual; injunction, charge 737 *command*; commission 751 *mandate*; order, writ 737 *warrant*; prescription, ordinance, regulation 737 *decree*; canon, form, formula, formulary; guidelines 81 *rule*; principle, rule, golden rule, moral 496 *maxim*; recipe, receipt 658 *remedy*; commandment, statute, enactment, act, code, penal code 953 *legislation*; tenet, article, set of rules, constitution; ticket, party line; Ten Commandments, Decalogue, Twelve Tables; canon law, common law, unwritten law 953 *law*; habit and repute, convention 610 *practice*.

694 Skill

N. *skill*, skilfulness, dexterity, handiness, ambidexterity; style 575 *elegance*; deftness, adroitness; ease 701 *easiness*; proficiency, competence; faculty, capability, capacity 160 *ability*; versatility; adaptability, flexibility; mastery, wizardry, virtuosity, excellence, prowess 644 *goodness*; strong point, métier, forte; attainment, accomplishment, skills; seamanship, airmanship, horsemanship, marksmanship; experience, expertise, professionalism; specialism; know-how, technique 490 *knowledge*; deft fingers; craftsmanship, art, artistry; finish, execution 646 *perfection*; ingenuity, resourcefulness, craft, craftiness 698 *cunning*; cleverness, sharpness, worldly wisdom; savoir-faire, finesse 463 *discrimination*; feat of skill, trick, dodge 623 *contrivance*; sleight of hand.

aptitude, innate ability, good head for; bent, natural bent 179 *tendency*; faculty, endowment, gift, flair; knack, green fingers; talent, natural talent, genius, genius for; aptness, fitness.

masterpiece, chef-d'oeuvre, a beauty, a creation; pièce de résistance, masterwork, magnum opus; stroke of genius, masterstroke, coup, feat, exploit, hat trick 676 *deed*; smash hit; tour de force; ace, trump 644 *exceller*; work of art, objet d'art, collector's piece *or* item.

Adj. *skilful*, good, good at, adept, top-flight, top-notch, first-rate, ace 644 *excellent*; skilled, crack; handy, dexterous, ambidextrous, deft, slick, adroit, agile, nimble; nimble-fingered, green-fingered; sure-footed; cunning, clever, quick, quickwitted, shrewd, smart, ingenious 498 *intelligent*; politic, diplomatic, statesman-like 498 *wise*; flexible, resourceful; versatile; sound, able, competent; wizard, masterly, accomplished.

gifted, of many parts, talented, endowed, well-endowed.

expert, experienced, veteran, seasoned, tried, versed in, up in, well up in, au fait; skilled, trained, practised, well-practised 669 *prepared*; finished, specialized 669 *matured*; proficient, adept, qualified, competent, up to the mark; professional; computer-literate.

Vb. *be skilful*, be deft, etc. (see adj.); be good at, do well 644 *be good*; shine, excel 34 *be superior*; have a gift for, show aptitude, show a talent for; have the knack; be on form, be in good *or* top form, have one's eye *or* hand in, play one's cards well, not put a foot wrong, know what one is about; live by one's wits, know all the answers, know what's what, have one's wits about one 498 *be wise*.

be expert, be at the top of one's profession, be good at one's job, be a top-notcher, know one's stuff *or* one's onions, have the know-how; have experience, be an old hand, know the ropes, know all the ins and outs, know backwards; display one's skill.

Adv. *skilfully*, craftily, artfully, etc. (see adj.); well, with skill, with aplomb; knowledgeably, expertly; faultlessly, as to the manner born.

695 Lack of skill

N. *lack of skill*, unskilfulness, lack of practice, rustiness 674 *non-use*; inexperience, inexpertness 491 *ignorance*; inability, incompetence, inefficiency; lack of proficiency; clumsiness, awkwardness, gaucherie (see also *bungling* below); backwardness, slowness 499 *unintelli-*

gence; booby prize, wooden spoon.

bungling, botching, half-measures, pale imitation, travesty 726 *non-completion*; bungle, botch, dog's breakfast *or* dinner, pig's ear, cock-up, balls-up, shambles; off day, poor show, bad job, flop 728 *failure*; hamhandedness, dropped catch, butter-fingers, fumble, muff, fluff, miss, mishit, slice, misfire, own goal, friendly fire 495 *mistake*; tactlessness, heavy-handedness, indiscretion 464 *lack of discrimination*; mishandling, misapplication 675 *misuse*; too many cooks; mismanagement, misrule, misgovernment, maladministration 481 *misjudgment*; wild-goose chase 641 *wasted effort*.

Adj. *unskilful*, talentless, unendowed, unaccomplished; unversatile 679 *inactive*; unfit, inept 25 *unapt*; unable, incapable 161 *impotent*; incompetent, inefficient, ineffectual; unpractical, unbusinesslike, stupid, foolish 499 *unwise*; feckless; not up to scratch, failed 728 *unsuccessful*; inadequate 636 *insufficient*.

unskilled, raw, green, undeveloped 670 *immature*; uninitiated, under training, untrained, apprentice, half-skilled, semi-skilled 670 *unprepared*; unqualified, inexpert, inexperienced, ignorant, unversed 491 *uninstructed*; non-professional, ham, amateurish, amateur, self-taught; unsound, quack.

clumsy, awkward, uneasy, gauche, gawky, boorish, uncouth 885 *discourteous*; stuttering; tactless, indiscreet, thudding 464 *undiscriminating*; bumbling, bungling; maladroit, all thumbs, butter-fingered, handless; cackhanded, heavy-handed, ham-handed, hamfisted, heavy-footed; ungainly, lumbering, hulking, gangling, shambling; out of practice, out of training 611 *unaccustomed*; slovenly, slatternly, slapdash 458 *negligent*; fumbling, groping, tentative 461 *experimental*; graceless 576 *inelegant*; top-heavy, lopsided 29 *unequal*; cumbersome, ungainly.

bungled, botched, messed up, fouled up, screwed up, mismanaged, mishandled, etc. (see vb.); ill-considered; ill-prepared 670 *unprepared*; ill-contrived, ill-devised, cobbled together; crude, rough and ready, inartistic, amateurish, jerry-built, slapdash, perfunctory 458 *neglected*; half-baked 726 *uncompleted*.

Vb. *be unskilful*, be inept, be unqualified, etc. (see adj.); not know how 491 *not know*; show one's ignorance, be handless, be clueless, on the wrong way about it; paper over the cracks 726 *not complete*; burn one's fingers, catch a Tartar 508 *not expect*; mismanage, misgovern; misapply 675 *misuse*; misdirect 495 *blunder*; forget one's words, fluff one's lines, miss one's cue 506 *forget*; ham; go rusty, get out of practice 611 *disaccustom*.

act foolishly, not know what one is about, cut one's own throat, cut off one's nose to spite one's face, throw out the baby with the bath water, make a fool of oneself, make an ass of oneself, lose face, be left with egg all over one's face 497 *be absurd*; bite the hand that feeds one, kill the goose that lays the golden eggs; spoil the ship for a ha'porth of tar; bring one's house about one's ears, knock one's head against a brick wall, put the cart before the horse; have too many eggs in one basket; bite off more than one can chew, have too many irons in the fire; put a square peg in a round hole, put new wine into old bottles 495 *blunder*; labour in vain 470 *attempt the impossible*; go on a fool's errand 641 *waste effort*; strain at a gnat and swallow a camel.

be clumsy, lumber, bumble, galumph, hulk, get in the way, be de trop, stand in the light; trip, trip over, stumble, blunder, boob; not look where one is going 456 *be inattentive*; stutter 580 *stammer*; fumble, grope, flounder 461 *be tentative*; muff, fluff; slice, mishit, misthrow, misfire; spill, slop, drop, drop a catch, drop a sitter 311 *let fall*; catch a crab; let the cat out of the bag, bungle, drop a brick, put one's foot in it, make a faux pas, get egg on one's face 495 *blunder*; botch, spoil, mar, blot 655 *impair*; fool with 678 *meddle*; make a mess of it, make a hash of it 728 *miscarry*; do a bad job, make a poor fist at 728 *fail*.

696 Proficient person

N. *proficient person*, sound player, expert, adept, dab hand, dabster; do-it-yourself type, all-rounder, Jack of all trades, handyman, admirable Crichton 646 *paragon*; Renaissance man, person of many parts; maître, maître, past master, graduate, cordon bleu; intellectual, mastermind 500 *sage*; genius, wizard, gifted child 864 *prodigy*; magician; maestro, virtuoso; -meister; bravura player 413 *musician*; prima donna, first fiddle, top sawyer, prize-winner, gold-medallist, champion, title-holder, cup-holder, dan, black belt, sensei, ace 644 *exceller*; picked man, capped player, star player, seeded player, seed, white hope; crack shot; acrobat, gymnast 162 *athlete*.

expert, professional, pro, specialist; authority, doyen, professor 537 *teacher*; pundit, guru, walking encyclopaedia 492 *scholar*; veteran, old hand, old stager, old dog, old soldier, war-horse, sea dog; practised hand, practised eye; man *or* woman of the world, businessman *or* -woman, career woman, careerist; tactician, strategist, politician; diplomat, diplomatist; artist, craftsman *or* -woman; technician, skilled worker 686 *artisan*; experienced hand, right person for the job, key man *or* -woman; consultant 691 *adviser*; boffin 623 *planner*; cognoscente, connoisseur; anorak, freak, geek, wonk 504 *enthusiast*.

697 Bungler

N. *bungler*, failure 728 *loser*; the despair of —; incompetent, botcher; bumbler, blunderer; fumbler, muffer, butterfingers; clumsy lout; hulk, bull in a china shop; duffer, buffoon, booby, galoot, clot, clod, hick, oaf, ass, plonker, big girl's blouse 501 *fool*; slob, sloven, slattern 61 *slut*; hack, dauber; poor shot; amateur, ham, cowboy; Jack of all trades and master of none; novice, greenhorn, raw recruit 538 *beginner*; landlubber; muggle; fish out of water, square peg in a round hole 25 *misfit*.

698 Cunning

N. *cunning*, craft 694 *skill*; know-how; resourcefulness, inventiveness, ingenuity 513 *imagination*; guile, gamesmanship, cunningness, craftiness, artfulness, subtlety, wiliness, slyness; stealthiness, stealth 523 *latency*; cageyness 525 *concealment*; slipperiness; sleight of hand 542 *sleight of hand*; cheating, monkey business 542 *deception*; double-dealing, imposture, sleight 541 *duplicity*; wheeling and dealing, manoeuvring 688 *tactics*; diplomacy, Machiavellism, realpolitik; smoke-filled room; gerrymandering 930 *improbity*; underhand dealing, under-the-counter dealing, sharp practice.

stratagem, ruse, wile, artifice, device, ploy, dodge 623 *contrivance*; machination, game, little game 623 *plot*; subterfuge, evasion; excuse 614 *pretext*; white lie; cheat 542 *deception*; trick, old trick, box of tricks, tricks of the trade, rules of the game 542 *trickery*; feint; ambush, Greek gift, Trojan horse, stalking horse 542 *trap*; ditch, pit 663 *pitfall*; Parthian shot; web of cunning, web of deceit; blind, dust thrown in the eyes, red herring; thin end of the wedge, tip of the iceberg; manoeuvre, move 688 *tactics*.

wily person, slyboots, artful dodger, serpent, snake, fox; fraud, wolf in sheep's clothing, double-crosser 545 *deceiver* cheat, sharper 545 *trickster*; juggler; smoothie 925 *flatterer*; Machiavelli, intriguer, plotter, schemer 623 *planner*; strategist, tactician, manoeuvrer, wheeler-dealer.

Adj. *cunning*, crafty, disingenuous, artful, sly, wily, subtle; tricksy; scheming, plotting, intriguing, Machiavellian; knowing, fly, slick, smart, sophisticated, urbane; canny, pawky, sharp, astute, shrewd, acute; too clever for, too clever by half, too smart for his *or* her own good, up to everything, not to be caught napping, no flies on, not born yesterday 498 *intelligent*; not to be drawn, cagey 525 *reticent*; experienced 694 *skilful*; resourceful, ingenious; tactical; insidious 930 *perfidious*; shifty, slippery 518 *equivocal*; deceitful, crooked, devious 930 *dishonest*.

Vb. be cunning. be sly, etc. (see adj.); dodge, juggle, manoeuvre, jockey, double-cross; intrigue, scheme, weave a plot, have an ulterior motive, have an axe to grind, have an eye to the main chance 623 *plot*; contrive, wangle, devise 623 *plan*; monkey about with, gerrymander; pull a fast one, steal a march on, trick, cheat 542 *deceive*; sweet-talk 925 *flatter*; play for time; be too clever for, box clever, be one up on, outsmart, outwit, go one better, know a trick worth two of that 306 *outdo*; be too quick for, snatch from under one's nose, pip at the post; waylay, dig a pit for, undermine, bait the trap 527 *ambush*; get one's foot in the door; have a card up one's sleeve, have a shot in one's locker; know all the answers, live by one's wits.

699 Artlessness

N. *artlessness*, simplicity, simple-mindedness; naivety, ingenuousness, guilelessness 935 *innocence*; inexperience, unworldliness; unaffectedness, unsophistication, naturalness 573 *plainness*; sincerity, candour, frankness; truth, honesty 929 *probity*.

Adj. *artless*, without artifice; unstudied; uncomplicated, uncontrived 44 *simple*; unadorned, unvarnished 573 *plain*; native, natural, unartificial, homespun, homemade; do-it-yourself 695 *unskilled*; in a state of nature, primitive; unsophisticated, ingenuous, naive, childlike 935 *innocent*; green, unworldly, simple-minded, callow, wet behind the ears; guileless, unsuspicious, confiding; unaffected 609 *spontaneous*; candid, frank, open, undissembling, straightforward 540 *truthful*; true, honest, sincere 929 *honourable*; above-board, on the level; transparent; shy, unassuming, unpretentious 874 *modest*.

Vb. be artless, be natural, etc. (see adj.); have no guile 935 *be innocent*; have no affectations; wear one's heart upon one's sleeve; look one in the face, look one straight in the eyes, call a spade a spade, say what is in one's mind, speak one's mind 573 *speak plainly*; not mince one's words 540 *be truthful*.

Antagonism

700 Difficulty

N. *difficulty*, hardness, arduousness, laboriousness 682 *exertion*; impracticability, no go, non-starter 470 *impossibility*; intricacy, perplexity, inextricability, involvement 61 *complexity*; complication 832 *aggravation*; obscurity, impenetrability 517 *unintelligibility*; rocket science; inconvenience, awkwardness 643 *inexpediency*; difficult terrain, rough ground, hard going, bad patch 259 *roughness*; quagmire, slough 347 *marsh*; knot, Gordian knot 251 *coil*; problem, knotty problem, thorny problem, problematics, crux, hard nut to crack, poser, teaser, puzzle, the sixty-four-thousand-dollar question, headache 530 *enigma*; impediment, handicap, obstacle, snag, rub, where the shoe pinches 702 *hindrance*; teething troubles 702 *hitch*; maze, crooked path 251 *convolution*; cul-de-sac, dead end, impasse, no-go area, blank wall 264 *closure*; deadlock, standstill, logjam, stoppage 145 *stop*; stress, brunt, burden 684 *fatigue*; trial, ordeal, temptation, tribulation, vexation 825 *suffering*; trouble, sea of troubles 731 *adversity*; bad time, bad day, bad hair day, annus horribilis, mauvais quart d'heure; difficult person, handful, one's despair, hot potato.

***hard task*,** test, trial of strength; Herculean task, superhuman task; thankless task, never-ending task, Sisyphean labour; work cut out, hard row to hoe, hard furrow to plough, no picnic; handful, tall order, tough assignment, impossible task, hard work, uphill struggle 682 *labour*.

***predicament*,** embarrassment, delicate situation; quandary, dilemma, cleft stick; catch-22 situation; fix, jam, hole, scrape, hot water, trouble, a pretty *or* fine kettle of fish, pickle, shtook, stew, soup, imbroglio, mess, muddle, straits, a pretty pass 61 *complexity*; slippery slope, sticky wicket, tight corner, painting oneself into a corner, diplomatic incident, ticklish situation, tricky situation, hot seat 661 *danger*; emergency 137 *crisis*.

Adj. *difficult*, hard, tough, formidable; steep, arduous, uphill; inconvenient, onerous, burdensome, irksome 682 *laborious*; exacting, demanding, high maintenance; insuperable, impracticable 470 *impossible*; problematic *or* problematical; delicate, ticklish, tricky;

unwieldy, unmanageable; intractable, refractory 738 *disobedient*; recalcitrant, stubborn, unyielding, perverse 602 *obstinate*; ill-behaved, naughty 934 *wicked*; perplexing, obscure 517 *unintelligible*; knotty, complex, complicated, inextricable, labyrinthine 251 *intricate*; impenetrable, impassable, unnavigable; thorny, rugged, craggy 259 *rough*; sticky, critical 661 *dangerous*.

in difficulties, hampered 702 *hindered*; labouring under difficulties; in a quandary, in a dilemma, in a cleft stick, between two stools, between Scylla and Charybdis, between the devil and the deep blue sea 474 *doubting*; baffled, clueless, nonplussed 517 *puzzled*; in a jam, in a fix, on the hook, up a gum tree, up the creek, up shit creek without a paddle (vulg), in a spot, in a hole, in a scrape, in hot water, in the soup, in a pickle; in deep water, out of one's depth, under fire, not out of the wood, in danger, on the danger list, on a hit list, in the hot seat 661 *endangered*; worried, beset with difficulties 825 *suffering*; under pressure, up against it, in a catch-22 situation, harassed, hard pressed, sore pressed, hard put to it, driven to extremities; in dire straits, in distressed circumstances; left holding the baby, left in the lurch; at one's wits end, at the end of one's tether, cornered, at bay, with one's back against the wall; down on one's luck 731 *unfortunate*, 801 *poor*; stuck, stuck fast, aground.

Vb. *be difficult*, be hard, etc. (see adj.); complicate matters 63 *throw into confusion*; put one on the spot, inconvenience, bother, irk, try one's patience, lead one a merry dance, be a thorn in one's flesh, be one's bête noire, go against the grain 827 *trouble*; present difficulties, set one a problem, pose, perplex, baffle, nonplus, stump 474 *puzzle*; hamper, obstruct 702 *hinder*; make things worse 832 *aggravate*; lead to an impasse, create deadlock 470 *make impossible*; come to or reach a pretty pass.

be in difficulty, have a problem; walk or tread on eggs or eggshells 457 *be careful*, 461 *be tentative*; have one's hands full 678 *be busy*; not know which way to turn, be at a loss 474 *be uncertain*; have difficulties, have one's work cut out, be hard put to it, have trouble with; run into trouble, strike a bad patch; be asking for trouble, fish in troubled waters; let oneself in for, cop it, catch it, catch a packet, catch a Tartar, have a tiger by the tail, stir up a hornet's nest; have a hard time of it 731 *have trouble*; bear the brunt, feel the pinch 825 *suffer*; sink under the burden 684 *be fatigued*; bring it on oneself, make heavy weather of, flounder; come unstuck 728 *miscarry*; do it the

hard way, swim upstream, fight 716 *contend*; live dangerously 661 *face danger*; labour under difficulties, be disadvantaged, labour under a disadvantage, have one hand tied behind one's back, be handicapped by.

Adv. *with difficulty*, with much ado; the hard way, uphill, against the stream, against the wind, against the grain; in the teeth of; at a pinch.

701 Easiness

N. *easiness*, facility, ease, convenience, comfort; flexibility, pliancy 327 *softness*; capability, capacity, feasibility 469 *possibility*; comprehensibility 516 *intelligibility*; facilitation, easing, making easy, simplification, dumbing down, smoothing, disentanglement 746 *liberation*; free hand, full scope, blank cheque, clean slate 744 *scope*; facilities, provision for 703 *aid*; leave 756 *permission*; simplicity, no complication, not rocket science 44 *simpleness*; straightforwardness, no difficulty, no competition; an open-and-shut case; no friction, easy going, calm seas 258 *smoothness*; fair wind, clear coast, clear road 137 *opportunity*; straight road.

easy thing, no trouble, no sweat, a pleasure, child's play, kid's stuff, no-brainer; soft option, short work, light work, cushy number, sinecure 679 *inactivity*; picnic, doddle 837 *amusement*; chickenfeed, peanuts, piece of cake, money for jam or old rope; easy money, fast buck; smooth sailing, plain sailing, easy ride; nothing to it, easy target, sitting duck; easy meat, soft touch; pushover, walkover 727 *victory*; cinch, sure thing, dead cert 473 *certainty*.

Adj. *easy*, facile, undemanding, cushy; effortless, painless; light, -light or -lite; uncomplicated, user-friendly 44 *simple*; not hard, not difficult, easy as pie, easily done, no sooner said than done; as easy as falling off a log, as simple as ABC; feasible 469 *possible*; facilitating 703 *helping*; downhill, with the current, with the tide, with the crowd; convenient 376 *comfortable*; approachable, within reach, within easy reach 289 *accessible*; open to all 263 *open*; comprehensible 516 *intelligible*.

manageable, tractable 597 *willing*; submissive 721 *submitting*; yielding, malleable, pliant 327 *flexible*; manoeuvrable.

Vb. *be easy*, be simple, etc. (see adj.); be trouble-free, require no effort, present no difficulties, give no trouble, make no demands; be one's for the asking; be easily solved, have a simple answer 516 *be intelligible*; go like clockwork.

do easily, have no trouble; make light of, make no bones about, make short work of, do it standing on one's head, do it with one hand tied behind one's back; have it all one's own way, carry all before one, have it in the bag, hold all the trumps, win hands down, have a walk-over 727 *win*; sail home, coast home, free-wheel; be at ease, be at home, be in one's element, take in one's stride, take to like a duck to water; not strain oneself, drift with the tide, swim with the stream 721 *submit*; take the easy way out, take the line of least resistance.

facilitate, make easy, ease; iron out 258 *smooth*; oil 334 *lubricate*; explain, gloss, simplify, dumb down 520 *interpret*; enable; make way for, allow 756 *permit*; put one in the way of 469 *make possible*; help, speed, accelerate, expedite 703 *aid*; clear the way, blaze a trail 64 *come before*; pave the way, bridge the gap; make an opening for 744 *give scope*.

disencumber, free, set free, liberate, unshackle, unfetter 668 *rescue*; clear, clear the ground, declutter, clear away, weed, unclog 648 *clean*; derestrict, cut through red tape; disentangle, extricate; untie 46 *disunite*; cut the knot *or* the Gordian knot 46 *cut*; ease, lighten, unload, unhamper, unburden, ease the burden, alleviate, obviate 831 *relieve*.

Adv. *easily*, smoothly, like clockwork; swimmingly; effortlessly, with one's eyes closed, with one hand tied behind one's back, just like that; without a hitch.

702 Hindrance

N. *hindrance*, let or hindrance, impediment; inhibition, block, emotional baggage; stalling, thwarting, obstruction, frustration; hampering, shackling, clogging, etc. (see vb.); blockage, logjam, blocking, bed-blocking 264 *closure*; blockade, siege 712 *attack*; limitation, restriction, control, squeeze 747 *restraint*; arrest 747 *detention*; check, retardation, deceleration 278 *slowness*; drag 333 *friction*; interference, meddling 678 *overactivity*; interruption, interception, intervention 231 *betweenness*; obtrusion 303 *insertion*; objection 762 *deprecation*; obstructiveness, dog in a manger; picketing, secondary picketing, sabotage, Not in My Back Yard, NIMBY, Build Absolutely Nothing Anywhere Near Anything, BANANA 704 *opposition*; lockout 182 *counteraction*; defence 715 *resistance*; discouragement, disincentive 613 *dissuasion*; hostility 924 *disapprobation*; blacking, boycott 620 *avoidance*; forestalling, prevention; prophylaxis 652 *hygiene*; sterilization, birth control 172 *contraception*; ban, embargo, no-no 757 *prohibition*; nuisance value.

obstacle, impediment, hindrance, nuisance, drawback, inconvenience, handicap 700 *difficulty*; hazard; bottleneck, blockage, roadblock, rolling roadblock, contraflow, traffic jam, logjam, gridlock; a hindrance, wheel clamp, tie, tether 47 *bond*; previous engagement 138 *untimeliness*; red tape, regulations; gatekeeper; snag, block; stumbling block, tripwire, hurdle, hedge, ditch, moat; water-jump; something in the way, barrier, bulkhead, wall, brick wall, stone wall, sea wall, dam, weir, dike, embankment 662 *safeguard*; bulwark, buffer, parapet, portcullis, barbed wire, razor wire 713 *defences*; fence, blockade 235 *enclosure*; curtain, Iron Curtain, Bamboo Curtain 231 *partition*; stile, gate, turnstile, tollgate; crosswind, headwind, crosscurrent; impasse, deadlock, stalemate, vicious circle, catch-22; cul-de-sac, blind alley, dead end, blank wall.

hitch, unexpected obstacle, snag, catch; contretemps; teething troubles; technical hitch, breakdown, engine failure; puncture, flat; leak, burst pipe; fuse, short circuit; stoppage, holdup, setback 145 *stop*; something wrong, computer malfunction, screw loose, spanner in the works, fly in the ointment.

encumbrance, handicap; drag, shackle, chain 748 *fetter*; trammels; impedimenta, cross, millstone, albatross round one's neck, weight on one's shoulders, dead weight 322 *gravity*; burden, overload, last straw; onus, the Old Man of the Sea; family commitments; mortgage, debts 803 *debt*.

Adj. *hindered*, waterlogged, handicapped, disadvantaged, encumbered, burdened with, lumbered with, saddled with, stuck with; frustrated, thwarted, stymied, etc. (see vb.); up against a brick wall; held up, delayed, stuck, becalmed, fogbound, snowbound, snowed-up 747 *restrained*; stopped, prevented 757 *prohibited*; heavy-laden, overburdened 684 *fatigued*; marooned, stranded, left high and dry, up the creek.

Vb. *hinder*, hamper, obstruct, impede; delay, use Fabian tactics; inconvenience 827 *trouble*; upset 63 *disarrange*; trip up, get under one's feet; entangle 542 *ensnare*; get in the way; come between, intervene, interpose 678 *meddle*; intercept, head off, undermine, stop one in the act, cut the ground from under one's feet, pull the rug from under one's feet; nip in the bud, stifle, choke; gag, muzzle 578 *make mute*; suffocate, repress 165 *suppress*; quell; hamper, burden, encumber; hang like a millstone round one's neck 322 *weigh*; load with, saddle with 193 *load*; handicap; shackle, trammel, tie one's hands, tie hand and foot 747 *fetter*; put under house arrest, put under curfew; restrict 236 *limit*; check, brake, be a drag on, hold back 747 *restrain*; hold up, slow down, set one back 278 *retard*; lame, cripple, hobble, hamstring, paralyse 161 *disable*; wing 655 *wound*; clip the wings, cramp the style of, take the wind out of one's sails; deter 854 *frighten*; damp down, throw cold water on.

obstruct, intervene, interfere 678 *meddle*; obtrude 297 *intrude*; stymie, snooker, stand in the way 231 *lie between*; buzz, jostle, crowd, elbow, squeeze; sit on one's tail 284 *follow*; stop, intercept, occlude, stop up, block, block up, wall up 264 *close*; jam, jam tight, foul up, cause a stoppage, bring to a standstill; bind 350 *staunch*; dam, dam up; divert 495 *mislead*; fend off, stave off; barricade 235 *enclose*; fence, hedge in, blockade 232 *encircle*; deny access, keep out 57 *exclude*; prevent, inhibit, ban, bar, debar 757 *prohibit*.

be obstructive, make it hard for, play up 700 *be difficult*; put off, stall, stonewall; not play ball 598 *be unwilling*; baffle, foil, stymie, balk, be a dog in the manger; counter 182 *counteract*; thwart, frustrate; object, raise objections 704 *oppose*; interrupt, heckle, barrack; shout down 400 *be loud*; take evasive action 620 *avoid*; filibuster 581 *be talkative*; play for time, use Fabian tactics, protract; strike 145 *halt*; picket; sabotage, throw a spanner in the works, gum up the works, spike the guns, put a spoke in one's wheel; take the wind out of one's sails.

703 Aid

N. aid, assistance, help, customer service, helping hand, leg-up, lift, boost; succour, rescue 668 *rescue*; support, backing, seconding; abetment, encouragement; reinforcement; helpfulness 706 *cooperation*; service, ministration; good offices, patronage, auspices; sponsorship, favour 178 *influence*, 660 *protection*; good will, charity 897 *benevolence*; intercession 981 *prayers*; championship; good advice, constructive criticism 691 *advice*; spoonfeeding, featherbedding; first aid, medical assistance 658 *medical art*; favourable circumstances 730 *prosperity*; fair wind; self-help.

monetary help, financial assistance, economic aid, donation, subvention 781 *gift*; charity 901 *philanthropy*; social security, welfare benefit, unemployment benefit, jobseeker's allowance, sickness benefit, supplementary benefit, child benefit; loan 802 *credit*; subsidy, hand-out, bounty, grant, allowance, expense account; stipend, bursary, scholarship 962 *reward*; maintenance, alimony, aliment, support, keep, upkeep 633 *provision*; dependency culture.

helper, help, assistant, aider, lieutenant, henchman, aide, right-hand man *or* woman, man Friday, girl Friday, amanuensis; personal assistant, PA 586 *shorthand writer*; backing group; stand-by, support, mainstay; tower of strength, rock 660 *protector*; problem-solver, troubleshooter; agent, spokesperson 720 *mediator*; district nurse, community nurse, etc. 658 *nurse*; social worker; Child Support Agency, CSA; helpline, helpdesk, information bureau, information centre, information desk, call centre; counsellor 691 *adviser*; farm hand 370 *farmer*; good neighbour, Good Samaritan, ally, brother-in-arms 707 *collaborator*; reinforcements 707 *auxiliary*; fairy godmother 903 *benefactor*; sponsor 707 *patron*; abettor.

Adj. helping, helpful, aiding, obliging 706 *cooperative*; kind 897 *benevolent*; supporting, seconding, abetting; supportive, encouraging; of service, of help, of great assistance 640 *useful*; constructive, well-meant; morale-boosting; assistant, auxiliary, subsidiary, ancillary; contributory, assisting 628 *instrumental*.

Vb. aid, help, assist, lend a hand, give a helping hand 706 *cooperate*; render assistance; be there for, hold out a hand to, take under one's wing, take in tow, give a lift to; hold one's hand, spoonfeed, featherbed; be kind to, do one a good turn, give a leg up, help a lame duck, help a lame dog over a stile; help one out, tide one over, see one through; oblige, accommodate, lend money to 784 *lend*; put up the money, finance, subsidize; pitch in, chip in, pass *or* send the hat round; facilitate, boost 285 *promote*; abet, fan the flame 612 *induce*; contribute to, be accessory to; lend support to, boost one's morale, back up, stand by, bolster, prop up 218 *support*; comfort, sustain, hearten, encourage, rally 855 *give courage*; succour, send help to, bail out, help out 668 *rescue*; step into the breach, reinforce; set one on his *or* her feet 656 *restore*; solve a problem, troubleshoot.

patronize, sponsor, back, guarantee, go bail for, stand surety for; recommend, put up for; propose, second; contribute to, subscribe to 488 *endorse*; take an interest in 880 *befriend*; champion, take up the cudgels for, stick up for, stand up for, stand by 713 *defend*; canvass for, root for, vote for 605 *vote*; bestow one's custom, buy from 792 *purchase*.

minister to, wait on, do for, help, oblige 742 *serve*; give first aid to, nurse 658 *doctor*; squire, valet, mother; be of service to, make oneself useful to; anticipate the wishes of 597 *be willing*; pander to, toady, humour, be a cat's paw to, scratch one's back, suck up to 925 *flatter*; slave, do all one can for, wait hand and foot on, do everything for 682 *work*; be assistant to, make oneself the tool of 628 *be instrumental*.

704 Opposition

N. opposition, antagonism, hostility 881 *enmity*; conflict, friction, office politics 709 *dissension*; non-cooperation 598 *unwillingness*; negative attitude, negativeness, negativity, negativism, nihilism; Not in My Back Yard, NIMBY, Build Absolutely Nothing Anywhere Near Anything, BANANA; luddism, neoluddism, new luddism; contrariness, recalcitrance 602 *obstinacy*; counterargument 479 *confutation*; contradiction, denial 533 *negation*; challenge 711 *defiance*; stout opposition, stand 715 *resistance*; infringement 738 *revolt*; going against, siding against, voting against, canvassing against 924 *disapprobation*; headwind, crosscurrent 702 *obstacle*; cross purposes, tug of war, tug of love, battle of wills; faction, rivalry, emulation, competition 716 *contention*; political opposition, the Opposition, Her Majesty's Opposition, the other side.

opposites, contraries, extremes, opposite poles 14 *contrariety*; rivals, duellists, competitors 716 *contender*; opposite parties, factions; black and white, cat and dog, chalk and cheese, day and night, Democrat and Republican, east and west, fire and water, good and evil, haves and have-nots, hot and cold, Labour and Conservative, light and darkness, male and female, management and workers, Mars and Venus, north and south, positive and negative, right and left, them and us, town and gown, Unionist and Confederate, nationalist and loyalist, yin and yang.

Adj. *opposing*, opposed; in opposition; anti, against, agin; antagonistic, hostile, unfriendly, antipathetic, unsympathetic, Eurosceptic 881 *hostile*; unfavourable, unpropitious 731 *adverse*; cross, thwarting; contradictory 14 *nonidentical*; cussed, bloody-minded, bolshie 602 *obstinate*; refractory, recalcitrant 738 *disobedient*; resistant; clashing, conflicting, at variance, at odds with 709 *quarrelling*; militant, up in arms, at daggers drawn; face to face, eyeball to eyeball, man to man 237 *frontal*; at opposite extremes 240 *opposite*; rival, competitive 911 *jealous*.

Vb. *oppose*, go against, militate against 14 *have nothing in common*; side against, stand against, hold out against, fight against, dig one's heels in, refuse to budge, stand one's ground 715 *resist*; set one's face against, make a dead set against 607 *reject*; object, kick, protest, protest against 762 *deprecate*; vote against 924 *disapprove*; canvass against, dissociate oneself; contradict, belie 533 *negate*; counter 479 *confute*; work against 182 *counteract*; countermine, thwart, baffle, foil 702 *be obstructive*; be at cross purposes; stand up to, challenge, dare 711 *defy*; vie with, compete with, bid against 716 *contend*.

withstand, confront, face, stand against, stand up to 661 *face danger*; rise against 738 *revolt*; take on, meet, encounter, cross swords with 716 *fight*; struggle against, breast the tide, stem the tide, swim against the stream; cope with, grapple with, wrestle with 678 *be active*; not be beaten 599 *stand firm*; hold one's own, bear the brunt 715 *resist*.

Adv. *in opposition*, against, versus, v, agin; in conflict with, against the crowd, against the tide, against the wind, against the grain, in the teeth of, in the face of, in defiance of.

705 Opponent

N. *opponent*, opposer, adversary, challenger, antagonist, foe 881 *enemy*; assailant 712 *attacker*; opposing party, opposition party, the opposition, opposite camp; cross benches; objector, Eurosceptic, withdrawalist 489 *objector*; resister, dissident, refusenik 829 *malcontent*; challenger, rival, competitor, combatant, contestant, duellist; entrant, the field, all comers 716 *contender*; sparring partner.

706 Cooperation

N. *cooperation*, helpfulness 597 *willingness*; interaction; duet, tandem; collaboration, joint effort, combined operation; team work, working together, concerted effort; relay race; team spirit, esprit de corps; unanimity, agreement 710 *harmony*; clannishness, party spirit, cliquishness, partisanship; connivance, collusion, abetment 612 *inducement*; conspiracy 623 *plot*; complicity, participation, worker participation; sympathy 880 *friendliness*; fraternity, sorority, solidarity, fellowship, freemasonry, fellow feeling, comradeship, fellow-travelling; common cause, mutual assistance, networking, back-scratching, aiding and abetting; reciprocity, give and take, mutual concession 770 *compromise*.

association, co-ownership, partnership 775 *participation*; nationalization 775 *joint possession*; pool, kitty; affiliation 78 *inclusion*; tie-up 9 *relation*; combination 45 *union*; solidarity 52 *whole*; unification 88 *unity*; amalgamation, fusion, merger; coalition, alliance, league, federation, confederacy, umbrella organization; united front, people's front, popular front 708 *political party*; an association, fellowship, club, fraternity, sorority 708 *community*; set, clique, coterie, cell 708 *party*; workers' association, trade union, chapel; business association, company, joint-stock company, private company, public company, public limited company, PLC, Ltd, Limited Liability Partnership, LLP; syndicate, combine consortium, trust, cartel, ring 708 *corporation*; workers' cooperative, commune 708 *community*.

Adj. *cooperative*, helpful 703 *helping*; collaborating, married, associating, associated, in league, back-scratching, hand in glove with; bipartisan; federal 708 *corporate*.

Vb. *cooperate*, collaborate, work together, pull together, work as a team; hunt in pairs, run in double harness; team up, join forces, pool resources, go into partnership 775 *participate*; show willing, play ball, reciprocate, respond; join in, take part, enter into, pitch in; rally round 703 *aid*; stand shoulder to shoulder, stand by each other, sink or swim together; be in league with, be in cahoots with, make common cause with; network, band together, gang up, associate, ally; coalesce, merge, unite; combine, make common cause, club together; conspire 623 *plot*; collude, connive, negotiate 766 *make terms*.

707 Auxiliary

N. *auxiliary*, reinforcement; back-up; second line 722 *soldiers*; paramedic, auxiliary nurse; assistant, helper 703 *helper*; right-hand man; adjutant, lieutenant, aide-de-camp; amanuensis, secretary, girl Friday; dogsbody 742 *servant*; acolyte; best man, bridesmaid; henchman, follower 742 *dependant*; disciple, adherent 978 *sectarian*; loyalist, flunkey, stooge, cat's-paw, puppet 628 *instrument*; shadow.

collaborator, cooperator, co-author, co-worker, fellow worker; team-mate; fellow traveller, fifth column, fifth columnist, quisling, traitor, mole, conspirator, conniver.

colleague, associate, fellow-worker, peer, brother, sister; co-director, partner 775 *participator*; comrade, companion, boon companion, playmate; alter ego, faithful companion; mate, chum, pal, buddy, oppo, crony 880 *friend*; helpmate, better half 894 *spouse*; stalwart; ally, confederate; accomplice, accessory, abettor, aider and abettor, fellow conspirator, partner in crime.

patron, guardian angel 660 *protector*; champion, friend at court; supporter, sponsor, backer, angel, guarantor; fan 887 *lover*; good friend, friend in need, deus ex machina; fairy godmother, rich uncle, sugar daddy 903 *benefactor*; promoter, founder; customer, client 792 *purchaser*.

708 Party

N. *party*, group, class 77 *classification*; denomination, church 978 *sect*; faction, cabal, cave, splinter group, breakaway movement 489 *objector*; circle, inner circle, charmed circle, kitchen cabinet; set, clique, in-crowd, loop, coterie; caucus, committee, quango, club, cell, cadre; ring, closed shop; eight,

eleven, fifteen; crew, team, complement 686 *personnel*; troupe, company 594 *actor*; gang, outfit 74 *band*; side, camp.

political party, right, left, centre; Conservative, Tories, Unionists, Ulster Unionists, Democratic Unionists; British National Party, National Front; Liberals, Radicals, Whigs, Liberal Democrats; Socialists, Labour, New Labour; Social Democrats, SDP; Social Democratic and Labour Party; Nationalists, Mebyon Kernow, Mec Vannin, Plaid Cymru, Scottish National Party, SNP, Sinn Fein, United Kingdom Independence Party, UKIP; Ecologists, Greens; Alliance Party; Fianna Fáil, Fine Gael; Democrats, Republicans, GOP; Militant Tendency, Scottish Socialist Party, Socialist Labour Party, Workers' Revolutionary Party, International Socialists, Trotskyists, Marxists, Maoists, Communists, Bolsheviks, Mensheviks; Fascists, Nazis; Monster Raving Loony Party; coalition, popular front, people's front, bloc; comrade; socialist, Fabian; anarchist 738 *rebel*; right-winger, true blue, neo-conservative; left-winger, leftist, leftie, pinko; populist, democrat; moderate; wet, dry; extremist, fundamentalist, fundie; party worker, canvasser, party member, politician; militant, activist 676 *doer*.

society, partnership, coalition, combination, combine 706 *association*; league, alliance; federation, confederacy; cooperative, union, EEC, European Community, European Union, EU, Euroland, Eurozone, Common Market, free trade area, single market; club 76 *focus*; secret society, Freemasonry, lodge, cell; trades union; chapel; youth movement, Scouts, Boy Scouts, Beavers, Cubs, Rovers; Girl Guides, Rainbows, Brownies, Rangers; Boys' Brigade, Life Boys, Girls' Brigade, Church Lads' and Church Girls' Brigade; Women's Institute, Mother's Union; fellow, associate, member, associate member; party member, paid-up member, card-carrying member; trade unionist.

community, fellowship, brotherhood, congregation, fraternity, sorority, sisterhood; clique, coterie; guild; Ummah; race, tribe, clan, sect 11 *family*; order 77 *classification*; social class 371 *social group*; state, nation; planet, world, global village; plant community, biome.

corporation, body; company, private company, joint-stock company, limited liability company, public limited company, holding company, dot com company, dotcom; multinational company, transnational corporation; firm, concern; partnership; business house; establishment, organization, institute; trust, combine, monopoly, cartel, syndicate, conglomerate 706 *association*; trade association, room of commerce, guild, cooperative society; consumers' association.

Vb. *join a party*, subscribe; join, swell the ranks, become one of, become a member, take out membership; sign on, enlist, enrol oneself, get elected; align oneself, side with, range oneself with, team up with 706 *cooperate*; associate, ally.

709 Dissension

N. *dissension*, disagreement 489 *dissent*; non-cooperation 704 *opposition*; disharmony, jar, jangle, jarring note, discordant note 411 *discord*; wrangling, quarrelling, bickering, sniping, cat-and-dog life; differences, odds, variance, friction, tension, unpleasantness, scenes, aggro; hostility 888 *hatred*; disunity, internal dissension, muttering in the ranks, house divided against itself 25 *disagreement*; office politics; rift, cleavage, parting of the ways, separation 294 *divergence*; split 978 *schism*; cross purposes 481 *misjudgment*; breach, rupture, severance of relations; declaration of war 718 *war*.

quarrelsomeness, factiousness, litigiousness; aggressiveness, combativeness, pugnacity, belligerence, warlike behaviour 718 *aggressiveness*; provocativeness, inviting trouble, trailing one's coat 711 *defiance*; contentiousness 716 *contention*; rivalry 911 *jealousy*; apple of discord.

quarrel, feud, blood feud, vendetta 910 *revenge*; blood on the carpet; war 718 *warfare*; strife 716 *contention*; conflict, clash 279 *collision*; legal battle 959 *litigation*; controversy, dispute, wrangle, argy-bargy; paper war 475 *argument*; words, war of words, raised voices, stormy exchange, confrontation, altercation, set-to, slanging match 899 *scurrility*; spat, tiff, squabble, wrangle, barney, hassle, squall, storm in a teacup; rumpus, dustup, disturbance, hubbub, racket, row, shindig, stramash, commotion, scrimmage, fracas, brawl, fisticuffs, breach of the peace 61 *turmoil*; gang warfare, turf war, street fighting, riot 716 *fight*; coat-trailing.

Adj. *quarrelling*, clashing, conflicting 14 *non-identical*; on bad terms, feuding, at odds, at loggerheads, at variance, at daggers drawn, up in arms 881 *hostile*; divided, factious, schismatic 489 *dissenting*; mutinous, rebellious 738 *disobedient*; cantankerous 892 *irascible*; litigious; quarrelsome, bellicose 718 *warlike*; pugnacious, combative, spoiling for a fight, trailing one's coat, inviting trouble, asking for it, belligerent, aggressive, militant; argumentative, contentious, disputatious, wrangling; kick-ass.

Vb. *quarrel*, clash, conflict 279 *collide*; cross swords with, be at one another's throats; be at cross purposes, be at variance, have differences, have a bone to pick 15 *differ*; fall out, go one's separate ways, part company, split, break with; break away; break off relations, break off diplomatic relations, declare war 718 *go to war*; go to law, take it to court 959 *litigate*; squabble, row with, go at it hammer and tongs, brawl; have a feud with, carry on a vendetta 910 *be vengeful*.

make quarrels, pick quarrels, pick a fight; look for trouble, ask for it, be spoiling for a fight, trail one's coat, challenge 711 *defy*; rub up the wrong way, tread on one's toes, get up one's nose, provoke 891 *enrage*; have a bone to pick; estrange, set at odds, set at variance, set by the ears; sound a discordant note 411 *discord*; sow dissension, stir it, make mischief, make trouble, kick up a shindy, disturb the peace; put the cat among the pigeons; come between, drive a wedge between 46 *break up*; widen the breach, fan the flame 832 *aggravate*; set against.

710 Harmony

N. *harmony*, concord, 410 *melody*; unison, unity, duet 24 *agreement*; unanimity, bipartisanship 488 *consensus*; understanding, mutual understanding, rapport; solidarity, team spirit 706 *cooperation*; reciprocity 12 *correlation*; sympathy, fellow feeling 887 *love*; compatibility, coexistence 880 *friendship*; détente, reunion, reconciliation, conciliation, conflict resolution, peacemaking 719 *pacification*; arbitration 720 *mediation*; entente cordiale, happy family, picture of content, the best of friends, sweetness and light, love and peace 717 *peace*; goodwill, honeymoon period.

Vb. *bring into harmony*, concord 410 *harmonize*; bring into concord 719 *pacify*; agree 24 *accord*; hit it off, see eye to eye, sing from the same song *or* hymn sheet, play a duet, chime in with, pull together 706 *cooperate*; reciprocate, respond, run parallel 181 *concur*; fraternize 880 *be friendly*; keep the peace, remain at peace 717 *be at peace*.

711 Defiance

N. *defiance*, dare, daring, challenge, gage, gauntlet, hat in the ring; bold front, belling the cat, brave face 855 *courage*; war dance, war cry, war whoop, war song, battle cry, declaration of war 900 *threat*; brazenness 878 *insolence*; demonstration, display, bravura 875 *ostentation*.

Adj. *defiant*, defying, challenging, provocative; in-your-face, belligerent, bellicose, militant 718 *warlike*; saucy, insulting 878 *insolent*;

mutinous, rebellious 738 *disobedient*; greatly daring 855 *courageous*; stiff-necked 871 *proud*; reckless, trigger-happy 857 *rash*.

Vb. defy, challenge, take one up on 489 *dissent*; stand up to 704 *oppose*; caution 664 *warn*; throw in one's teeth, throw down the gauntlet, throw one's hat in the ring; demand satisfaction, call out, send one's seconds; dare, outdare, beard; brave, run the gauntlet 661 *face danger*; laugh to scorn, laugh in one's face, laugh in one's beard, set at naught, snap one's fingers at 922 *hold cheap*; bid defiance to, set at defiance, hurl defiance; call one's bluff, double the bid; show fight, bare one's teeth, show one's fangs, double one's fist, clench one's fist, shake one's fist 900 *threaten*; refuse to bow down to 871 *be proud*; look big, throw out one's chest, beat one's chest, show a bold front; wave a banner 317 *brandish*; march, demonstrate, hold a demonstration, stage a sit-in, not be moved; cock a snook 878 *be insolent*; ask for trouble 709 *make quarrels*; crow over, shout 727 *triumph*; crow, bluster, brag 877 *boast*.

Adv. defiantly, challengingly, in defiance of, in one's teeth, to one's face, under the very nose of; in open rebellion.

Int. do your worst!, come on if you dare!

712 Attack

N. attack, hostile attack, best method of defence; pugnacity, combativeness, aggressiveness 718 *aggressiveness*; belligerence, aggression, unprovoked aggression 914 *injustice*; blood on the carpet; stab in the back; mugging, -bashing, assault, assault and battery, actual bodily harm, ABH, grievous bodily harm, GBH 176 *violence*; armed attack, offensive, charm offensive, drive, push, thrust, pincer movement 688 *tactics*; dead set at; onslaught, onset, rush, charge; sally, sortie, breakthrough; counterattack 714 *retaliation*; shock tactics, blitzkrieg, surprise; infringement 306 *overstepping*; invasion, incursion, overrunning 297 *entering*; raid, ram raid, foray 788 *brigandage*; blitz, air raid; taking by storm, boarding; siege, blockade 230 *surroundings*.

terror tactics, guerrilla warfare, sniping, war of attrition, war of nerves 854 *intimidation*; shot across the bows; bloodbath 362 *slaughter*; laying waste.

bombardment, cannonade, barrage, strafe, blitz; broadside, volley, salvo; bomb-dropping, bombing, saturation bombing, carpet bombing; firing, shooting, gunfire, drumfire, fusillade, cross-fusillade; anti-aircraft fire, flak; sniping.

attacker, assailant, aggressor, mugger,

-basher; storm troops, strike force; fighter pilot, bomber 722 *armed force*; sniper; terrorist, guerrilla; invader, raider; besieger; Ku Klux Klan.

Vb. attack, be spoiling for a fight; start a fight, declare war 718 *go to war*; strike the first blow, open fire on, fire the first shot; assault, go for, set on, pounce upon, fall upon, pitch into, sail into; attack tooth and nail, savage, maul, draw blood 655 *wound*; launch out at, let fly at, let one have it, lay into, tear into, lace into, round on; take by surprise, blitz, overwhelm; invade 306 *encroach*; raid, foray, overrun, infest; take the offensive; make a sortie; board, grapple; take by storm, capture 727 *overcome*; ravage, make havoc; harry, drive 619 *hunt*; take up the cudgels 716 *fight*.

besiege, lay siege to, beleaguer, surround, beset, blockade 235 *enclose*.

strike at, raise one's hand against; lay about one, swipe, flail, hammer 279 *strike*; go berserk, run amok; lash out at; beat up, mug; lunge; grapple with, fight hand to hand, cut and thrust; push, butt, thrust, poke at, thrust at; stab, spear, lance, bayonet, run through, cut down 263 *pierce*; lay low, bring down 311 *abase*.

fire at, shoot at; fire a shot at, take a potshot, snipe, pick off 287 *shoot*; shoot down; torpedo; strafe, bombard, blitz, shell, pepper; bomb, drop bombs; open fire; rake; take aim, pull the trigger, level, draw a bead on 281 *aim*.

713 Defence

N. defence, the defensive, self-defence 715 *resistance*; art of self-defence, boxing 716 *boxing*; kick-boxing, Thai boxing; judo, jujitsu, karate 716 *wrestling*; parry, warding off 182 *counteraction*; defensiveness 854 *nervousness*; guard; self-protection 660 *protection*; a defence, rampart, bulwark, screen, buffer, fender, bumper, bull bars 662 *safeguard*.

defences, lines, entrenchment; earthwork, embankment, mound; boom; wall, barricade, fence 235 *barrier*; palisade, paling, stockade; moat, ditch, dike; trench, dugout; tripwire, booby trap 542 *trap*; barbed wire; spike; anti-tank obstacles, Maginot Line, Siegfried Line, Hadrian's Wall, Antonine Wall, Great Wall of China, peace wall; air raid shelter, fallout shelter, bunker 662 *shelter*; barrage, anti-aircraft fire, flak; barrage balloon; minefield, mine; smokescreen 421 *screen*.

fortification (see also *fort* below); bulwark, rampart, wall; parapet, battlement, emplacement; escarp; bastion; outwork; buttress, abutment.

fort, fortress, stronghold, fastness, citadel,

capitol, acropolis 662 *refuge*; castle, keep, tower, turret; portcullis, drawbridge; gate, postern; Martello tower, pillbox; laager, encampment 235 *enclosure*; broch; Roman camp.

armour, panoply; mail, chain mail; breastplate; cuirass; hauberk, coat of mail, corslet; helmet, casque, visor, beaver; steel helmet, tin hat; bearskin 228 *headgear*; gauntlet; shield, buckler; protective clothing, body armour, riot shield, gas mask 662 *safeguard*; exoskeleton, power armour.

defender, champion; patron 703 *helper*; knight errant; loyalist, patriot; bodyguard, lifeguard 722 *soldier*; watch, sentry, sentinel; vigilante; patrol, patrolman; security man *or* woman; garrison, picket, guard, escort, rearguard; Home Guard, Territorials, Territorial Army, militia, thin red line 722 *soldiers*; fireman, firewoman, firefighter; Civil Defence; guardian, warden 660 *protector*; warder, custodian 749 *keeper*.

Vb. *defend*, guard, protect, keep, watch 660 *safeguard*; fence, hedge 232 *encircle*; barricade 235 *enclose*; block 702 *obstruct*; cushion, pad, shield, curtain, cover 421 *screen*; cloak 525 *conceal*; arm 669 *make ready*; armour, reinforce, fortify 162 *strengthen*; entrench, dig in 599 *stand firm*; stand in front, stand by; garrison, man, stop the gap; plead for, hold a brief for, argue for, take up the cause of, champion 927 *vindicate*; fight for, take up arms for, take up the cudgels for, rescue.

714 Retaliation

N. *retaliation*, reprisal 910 *revenge*; requital, recompense, comeuppance 962 *reward*; deserts, just deserts 915 *what is due*; punitive action, poetic justice, retribution, Nemesis 963 *punishment*; reaction, boomerang, backlash 280 *recoil*; counterstroke, counterblast, counterplot, countermine 182 *counteraction*; counterattack, sally, sortie 712 *attack*; recrimination, answering back, rispote, retort 460 *rejoinder*; heaping coals of fire; reciprocation, like for like, tit for tat, quid pro quo, measure for measure, blow for blow, an eye for an eye and a tooth for a tooth, a taste of one's own medicine, a Roland for an Oliver, the biter bit, a game two can play at; what is coming to one; deterrent 854 *intimidation*.

Vb. *retaliate*, exact compensation 31 *recoup*; take reprisals 963 *punish*; counter, riposte; pay off old scores, square the account, be quits, get even with, get upsides with, get one's own back 910 *avenge*; teach one a lesson; reciprocate, give and take, return like for like; return the compliment, give as good as one got, pay one in his own coin, get one's pound of flesh;

retort, cap, answer back 460 *answer*; round on, kick back, hit back, not take it lying down 715 *resist*; turn the tables on, hoist one with his *or* her own petard, make one laugh on the other side of his face, make one take back his *or* her own words, have the last laugh.

715 Resistance

N. *resistance*, stand, brave front 704 *opposition*; intractability 602 *obstinacy*; objection, demur 468 *qualification*; recalcitrance, protest 762 *deprecation*; non-cooperation, passive resistance, civil disobedience, electronic civil disobedience, hacktivism; rising, insurrection, backlash 738 *revolt*; self-defence 713 *defence*; repulsion, rebuff 760 *refusal*.

Adj. *resisting*, opposing; protesting, reluctant 598 *unwilling*; recalcitrant, mutinous 738 *disobedient*; stubborn 602 *obstinate*; unyielding, indomitable; resistant, tough, proofed, bulletproof, waterproof, showerproof.

Vb. *resist*, offer resistance, stand against 704 *withstand*; obstruct 702 *hinder*; challenge, stand out against 711 *defy*; confront 661 *face danger*; struggle against, contend with, stem the tide 704 *oppose*; kick against the pricks, protest 762 *deprecate*; demur, object 468 *qualify*; down tools, vote with one's feet, walk out, come out 145 *cease*; call out 145 *halt*; mutiny, rise, not take it lying down 738 *revolt*; make a stand, fight off, keep at arm's length, keep at bay, hold off; make a fight of it 716 *contend*; hold out, not submit, stand one's ground, not give way 599 *stand firm*; endure 825 *suffer*; repel, rebuff 760 *refuse*; resist temptation, not be tempted.

716 Contention

N. *contention*, strife, tussle, conflict, clash, running battle 709 *dissension*; combat, fighting, war 718 *warfare*; debate, dispute, controversy, polemics, ink-slinging 475 *argument*; altercation, words, war of words 709 *quarrel*; bone of contention; competition, rivalry, price war, emulation 911 *jealousy*; competitiveness, gamesmanship; survival of the fittest, rat race; turf war; cut-throat competition, war to the knife, no holds barred; feeding frenzy; sports, athletics 837 *sport*.

contest, trial, trial of strength, marathon, biathlon, triathlon, pentathlon, decathlon, tug-of-war, tug of love 682 *exertion*; tussle, struggle 671 *attempt*; match, boxing match, football match, cricket match, Test match, needle match, benefit match; nothing in it, close finish, photo finish 200 *short distance*; competition, free-for-all; pro-am, knockout competition, tournament; prize competition, stakes, Ashes; rally; event, handicap, run-off; heat, final, semifinal, quarterfinal, Cup tie, Cup final; set, game, rubber; sporting event, wager, bet 837 *sport*; field day 837 *amusement*; Derby day (see also *racing* below); athletics, gymnastics; gymkhana, horseshow, rodeo; games, Highland Games, Commonwealth Games, Olympic Games, Olympics, Winter Olympics, Paralympics; Wimbledon, Wembley, Lord's 724 *arena*.

racing, races, race, foot race, flat race, sprint; racewalking, road race, marathon, fun run; long-distance race, cross-country race, orienteering; slalom, obstacle race; hare and hounds race, treasure hunt; sack race, egg and spoon race; relay race, team race; the Turf, horse racing, sport of kings; the Derby, the Oaks; point-to-point, steeplechase, hurdles, sticks 312 *leap*; motor race, motor rally, dirt-track racing, stockcar racing, speedway, motocross; cycle race, Tour de France, cyclocross; dog racing, the dogs; boat race, bumping race, yacht race; regatta, eights, Ascot, racecourse, track, dog track, stadium 724 *arena*.

boxing, pugilism, noble art of self-defence, sparring, jabbing, socking, slugging, pummeling, lambasting, fisticuffs; fighting, prize-fighting; target boxing, kick-boxing, Thai boxing; boxing match, prizefight; round, bout; the ring, the fancy 837 *sport*; Queensberry rules.

wrestling, all-in wrestling, catch-as-catch-can, no holds barred; catch, hold; wrestle, grapple, wrestling match; absolute *or* extreme *or* ultimate fighting, cage fighting.

martial arts, aikido, ba gua *or* pa kua, budo, capoeira, iaido, jeet kune do, judo, jujitsu, karate, kendo, kung fu, ninjutsu, tae kwon do, tai ji quan *or* t'ai chi ch'uan, tang soo do, tukido, wu shu; kick-boxing (see also *boxing* above).

duel, affair of honour, seconds out; jousting, tilting, tournament; fencing, iaido, swordplay, kendo (see also *martial arts* above); hand-to-hand fighting; bullfight, corrida; cockfight; bullring, cockpit, lists 724 *arena*.

fight, hostilities, blow-up, appeal to arms, alarums and excursions 718 *warfare*; battle royal, free fight, free-for-all, showdown, rough and tumble, roughhouse, horseplay, shindig, stramash, scuffle, scrum, scrimmage, scramble, dogfight, mêlée, fracas, uproar, rumpus, ruction 61 *turmoil*; gang warfare, street fight, aggro, riot, brawl, broil 709 *quarrel*; fisticuffs, blows, hard knocks; give and take, cut and thrust; affray, set-to, tussle; running fight, hand-to-hand fighting; combat, fray, clash, conflict 279 *collision*; encounter, dustup, scrap,

brush; skirmish; engagement, action, pitched battle, stand-up fight, shoot-out 718 *battle*; campaign, struggle; war to the knife, fight to the death; Armageddon.

contender, fighter; gladiator, bullfighter, matador, toreador; boxer, prizefighter 722 *boxer*; dueller, duellist; candidate, entrant, examinee; competitor, rival; challenger, front runner, favourite, top seed; the field, all comers; contestant; racer, runner, marathoner 162 *athlete*; sprinter.

Vb. *contend*, combat, strive, struggle, battle, fight, tussle, wrestle, grapple 671 *attempt*; oppose, put up a fight 715 *resist*; argue for, stick out for, insist 532 *emphasize*; contest, compete, challenge, stake, wager, bet; play, play against, match oneself, vie with, race, run a race; emulate, rival; outrival 306 *outdo*; enter, enter for, take on, enter the lists, descend into the arena, take up the challenge, pick up the gauntlet; cross swords with; take on, grapple with, lock horns with 712 *strike at*; have a hard fight, fight to a finish.

fight, scuffle, row, scrimmage, scrap, set to; pitch into, sail into 712 *attack*; lay about one 712 *strike at*; mix it, join in the mêlée; square up to, come to blows, exchange blows, put up one's fists; box, spar, pummel, jostle, hit, kick, scratch, bite 279 *strike*; quarrel; duel; encounter, have a brush with, scrap with, skirmish; take on, engage, fight a pitched battle; come to grips, close with, grapple, lock horns; fence, cross swords; fight hand to hand, combat, campaign, fight the good fight 718 *wage war*; fight it out, fight to the last man 599 *be resolute*.

717 Peace

N. *peace*, peacefulness, peace and quiet, a quiet life, the line of least resistance 266 *state of rest*; harmony 710 *harmony*; peacetime; law and order 60 *order*; truce, armistice 145 *lull*; peace dividend; coexistence; neutrality, non-alignment; non-involvement 860 *indifference*; non-intervention 620 *avoidance*; peaceableness, non-aggression 177 *moderation*; cordial relations 880 *friendship*; pacifism, peace at any price, peace in our time, non-violence; disarmament, decommissioning, peacemaking, peace process 719 *pacification*; pipe of peace; peace treaty, burying the hatchet 506 *amnesty*.

pacifist, man *or* woman of peace, peace women, peace-lover, peacemonger, dove; peace camp, CND 177 *moderator*; neutral, non-combatant; passive resister, conscientious objector, conchie; peacemaker 720 *mediator*.

Adj. *peaceful*, quiet, halcyon 266 *tranquil*; bloodless; harmless, dovelike 935 *innocent*;

easy-going 884 *amiable*; uncompetitive; peaceable, law-abiding, peace-loving, pacific, unaggressive, pacifist, non-violent; unarmed, noncombatant; passive, submissive 721 *submitting*; peacemaking, conciliatory; without enemies, at peace; not at war, neutral; postwar, prewar, interwar; peacetime.

Vb. *be at peace*, stay at peace, observe neutrality, keep out of trouble; mean no harm, forget one's differences, be pacific 935 *be innocent*; keep the peace, make peace 720 *mediate*; beat swords into plough-shares, make the lion lie down with the lamb, smoke the pipe of peace.

718 War

N. *war*, arms, the sword; ground war, air war, cold war, armed neutrality; paper war, war of words, polemic 709 *quarrel*; war of nerves, sabre-rattling, gunboat diplomacy 854 *intimidation*; uneasy peace, phoney war; armed intervention, police action; civil war, war of revolution, war of independence; wars of religion, holy war, crusade; war of expansion; all-out war; world war, total war, blitzkrieg, atomic war, nuclear war; price war, predatory pricing; war of attrition, war to the death, no holds barred; war to end all wars, Armageddon; the panoply of war, martial music; call to arms, bugle call 547 *call*; battle cry, rallying cry; god or goddess of war: Ares, Mars, Bellona. (See also *warfare* below.)

state of war, hostilities, wartime; belligerency; declaration of war, militancy.

aggressiveness, bellicosity, war fever; pugnacity, combativeness, hawkishness, militancy 709 *quarrelsomeness*; militarism, expansionism; jingoism, chauvinism, gung-ho 481 *prejudice*.

war measures, war preparations, arming 669 *preparation*; call to arms, clarion call, fiery cross 547 *call*; war effort, war work, call-up, rally, mobilization, recruitment, conscription; national service, military duty; volunteering, doing one's duty, for king *or* queen and country, joining up, enlisting.

warfare, war, open war, warpath, waging war; bloodshed, battles, sieges 176 *violence*; fighting, campaigning, soldiering, active service; military service, naval service, air service; bombing, saturation bombing, carpet bombing 712 *bombardment*; raiding; besieging, blockading 235 *enclosure*; aerial warfare, naval warfare, chemical warfare, gas warfare, germ warfare, atomic warfare, nuclear warfare, electronic warfare; economic warfare, blockade, attrition, scorched earth policy; psychological warfare, propaganda; cyberwar, cyberwarfare, information warfare; offensive warfare 712

attack; defensive warfare 713 *defence*; asymmetric warfare; trench warfare, desert warfare, jungle warfare; bush-fighting, guerrilla warfare, sniping; campaign, expedition; operations; incursion, invasion, raid; order, orders 737 *command*; battle cry; plan of campaign, strategy 623 *plan*.

battle, pitched battle, battle royal 716 *fight*; line of battle, array; line, firing line, front line, front, battle front, battle station; armed conflict, action, scrap, skirmish, brush, collision, clash, shoot-out, gun battle, firefight; offensive, blitz 712 *attack*; defensive battle, stand 713 *defence*; engagement, naval engagement, sea fight, air fight, dogfight; battlefield, theatre of war 724 *battleground*.

Adj. *warring*, on the warpath; campaigning, battling, etc. (see vb.); at war; belligerent, aggressive, bellicose, militant, mobilized, under arms, in the army, at the front, on active service; militant, up in arms; armed, sword in hand 669 *prepared*, 723 *armed*; arrayed, embattled; engaged, at loggerheads 709 *quarrelling*; on the offensive.

warlike, militaristic, bellicose, hawkish, militant, aggressive, belligerent, pugnacious, pugilistic, combative; war-loving, warmongering; bloodthirsty, war-fevered; military, paramilitary, martial, battle-scarred.

Vb. *go to war*, resort to arms; declare war, open hostilities, let slip the dogs of war; appeal to arms, unsheathe the sword, throw away the scabbard, whet the sword, take up the cudgels 716 *fight*; fly to arms, rise, rebel 738 *revolt*; raise one's banner, call to arms, send round the fiery cross; arm, militarize, mobilize, put on a war footing; rally, call up, call to the colours, recruit, conscript; join the army, join up, enlist; make war, go on the warpath, march to war, engage in hostilities, war against; go on active service; open a campaign, take the offensive, invade 712 *attack*; act on the defensive 713 *defend*; march, countermarch; blockade, besiege 230 *surround*; shed blood, put to the sword 362 *slaughter*; ravage, burn, scorch; give battle; cross swords with, take issue with; join battle, engage, stage a shoot-out, call for a show-down, combat, confront, fight it out 716 *fight*; beat the drum, go over the top; open fire 712 *fire at*.

719 Pacification

N. *pacification*, peacemaking, pacifying, conflict resolution; conciliation, appeasement, mollification 177 *moderation*; reconciliation, reconcilement, détente, rapprochement; accommodation, adjustment 24 *agreement*; good offices 720 *mediation*; peace process, peace talks; entente, understanding, peace treaty, non-aggression pact, SALT 765 *treaty*; truce, armistice, cease-fire 145 *lull*; disarmament, decommissioning, CND, peace movement, demobilization, disbanding; nuclear-free zone, peace camp.

peace offering, appeasement 736 *leniency*; dove of peace, olive branch, overture, hand of friendship, outstretched hand 880 *friendliness*; flag of truce, white flag, pipe of peace 717 *peace*; blood money, compensation 787 *restitution*; plea for peace 506 *amnesty*.

Vb. *pacify*, make peace between; allay, tranquillize, mollify, soothe 177 *assuage*; smooth one's ruffled feathers, pour balm into one's wounds, heal 656 *cure*; hold out the olive branch, hold out one's hand, coo like a dove 880 *be friendly*; conciliate, propitiate, disarm, reconcile, placate, appease, satisfy 828 *content*; pour oil on troubled waters 266 *bring to rest*; restore harmony 410 *harmonize*; win over, meet halfway 770 *compromise*; settle differences; bring together 720 *mediate*; grant peace 766 *give terms*; keep the peace 717 *be at peace*.

make peace, stop fighting, cry quits, break it up 145 *cease*; bury the hatchet, let bygones be bygones, forgive and forget 506 *forget*; shake hands, make it up, make friends, kiss and make up, patch up a quarrel, come to an understanding, agree to differ; lay down one's arms, sheathe the sword, put up one's sword, beat swords into ploughshares; make a truce, suspend hostilities, demilitarize, disarm, decommission, demobilize, civilianize; smoke the pipe of peace.

720 Mediation

mediation, good offices, mediatorship, intercession; arbitration, refereeship, umpirage; intervention, stepping-in, diplomacy; parley, negotiation 584 *conference*.

mediator, mutual friend, middleman, matchmaker, marriage bureau, dating agency, introduction agency, speed dating, computer dating, lonely hearts column; go-between, pander, Pandarus, negotiator 231 *intermediary*; arbitrator, umpire, referee, assistant referee, linesman *or* -woman, fourth official 480 *estimator*; diplomat, diplomatist, representative, agent, spokesperson 754 *delegate*; pacifier, troubleshooter, ombudsman, ACAS; marriage guidance counsellor, family conciliation service 691 *adviser*; peace movement, peace-maker, peace-keeping force 177 *moderator*.

Vb. *mediate*, intervene 678 *meddle*; step in, interpose; proffer one's good offices, intercede for, propitiate; run messages for, be a go-between, act as a pander for; bring together, negotiate, act as agent; arbitrate, umpire 480 *judge*.

721 Submission

N. *submission*, submissiveness 739 *obedience*; subservience 745 *servitude*; acquiescence, compliance, consent 488 *assent*; supineness, peace at any price, line of least resistance, non-resistance, passiveness, resignation, fatalism 679 *inactivity*; yielding, giving way, giving in, white flag, capitulation, surrender, unconditional surrender 621 *relinquishment*; deference 872 *humility*; homage 739 *loyalty*; genuflexion, prostration 311 *bow*.

Adj. *submitting*, surrendering, etc. (see vb.); meek, unresisting, law-abiding 717 *peaceful*; submissive 739 *obedient*; fatalistic, resigned, acquiescent 488 *assenting*; pliant, accommodating, malleable 327 *soft*; crawling, cringing, supine, prostrate; boot-licking, bowing and scraping; kneeling, on bended knees, sycophantic, Uriah Heepish, toadying 872 *humble*.

Vb. *submit*, yield, give in; defer to; bow to, make a virtue of necessity, admit defeat 728 *be defeated*; be resigned, bite the bullet 488 *acquiesce*; accept 488 *assent*; shrug one's shoulders 860 *be indifferent*; withdraw, make way for, draw in one's horns 286 *turn back*; not contest 679 *be inactive*; stop fighting, have no fight left, have all the fight knocked out of one, give up, cry quits, have had enough, throw up the sponge, throw in the towel, surrender, hold up one's hands, show the white flag, ask for terms; surrender, capitulate; throw oneself on another's mercy; give oneself up, throw down one's arms, hand over one's sword, hang up one's sword, haul down the flag, strike one's colours.

knuckle under, succumb, cave in, collapse; show no fight, take the line of least resistance, bow before the inevitable, bow before the storm; be submissive, bow one's neck to the yoke, do homage 745 *be subject*; take one's medicine, swallow the pill 963 *be punished*; eat humble pie, eat dirt 872 *be humble*; take it, take it from one, take it lying down, grin and bear it, stomach, put up with 825 *suffer*; bend, bow, kneel, kowtow, toady, crouch, cringe, crawl, bow and scrape 311 *stoop*; grovel, lick the dust, lick the boots of, kiss the rod; fall on one's knees, throw oneself at the feet of, clasp someone's knees, beg for mercy, cry *or* howl for mercy.

722 Combatant. Army. Navy. Air Force

N. *combatant*, fighter 716 *contender*; aggressor, assailant, mugger 712 *attacker*; besieger, stormtroops; belligerent, fighting man, man-at-arms, warrior, brave; bodyguard 713 *defender*;

gunman, strongarm man, hitman 362 *killer*; bully, rough, rowdy, bovver boy, boot boy 904 *ruffian*; duellist; swordsman, fencer; gladiator 162 *athlete*; fighting cock; bull-fighter, toreador, matador, picador; wrestler, jujitsuist, judoist, karate expert 716 *wrestling*; competitor 716 *contender*; jouster, knight; wrangler; barrister, advocate 959 *litigant*.

boxer, pugilist, champion, champ, sparring partner; flyweight, bantamweight, featherweight, welterweight, middleweight, cruiserweight, heavyweight; slogger, pummeler 716 *boxing*.

militarist, jingoist, chauvinist, gung-ho, expansionist, militant, warmonger, hawk; crusader, jihadi 979 *zealot*; mercenary; soldier of fortune; freebooter, pirate, buccaneer 789 *robber*.

soldier, army man, military man, regular; soldiery, troops (see also *armed force, soldiers* below); fighting man, warrior, brave; man-at-arms, redcoat, legionnaire, centurion; standard-bearer, colour sergeant, ensign; rifleman, sharpshooter, sniper; territorial, Home Guard, militiaman; yeomanry, yeoman; irregular troops; raider, guerrilla, partisan, freedom fighter; resistance fighter, Maquis; guards 660 *protector*; enlisted man; reservist; volunteer; mercenary; conscript, recruit, rookie; serviceman, Tommy, Jock, GI, Anzac, sepoy, Gurkha; old soldier, old campaigner, veteran, Chelsea pensioner; female warrior: Amazon, Boadicea; Valkyrie; Wren, WRAF, WRAC.

soldiers, soldiery, cannon fodder, gallant company, heroes; rank and file, other ranks; private, common soldier, man-at-arms; archer, crossbowman; spearman, pike-man, halberdier, lancer; musketeer, fusilier, rifleman, grenadier, bombardier, gunner, artilleryman; sapper, engineer; signalman; corporal, sergeant, lieutenant, etc. 741 *army officer*.

army, host; legion; cohorts, big battalions; horde 104 *multitude*; National Guard, Home Guard; militia, yeomanry, vigilantes; regular army, standing army, professional army, mercenary army, territorial army, draft; the services, the military, armed forces.

armed force, forces, ground forces, troops, ground troops, contingents, men, personnel; armada; guards; Household Cavalry, Life Guards, crack troops; reconnaissance party, expeditionary force, flying column; paratroops, Commandos, Special Air Service, SAS, Special Boat Service, SBS, task force, raiding party, guerrilla force; combat troops, field army, line, thin red line, front line; vanguard, rearguard; reserves, recruits, reinforcements, draft, levy 707 *auxiliary*; detachment, party,

detail; patrol; sentry; garrison, army of occupation.

formation, line; legion; column, file; unit, detachment, corps, division, armoured division; brigade, light brigade; battery; regiment, cavalry regiment, squadron, troop; battalion, company, platoon, section, squad, detail, party 74 *band*.

infantry, foot regiment, infantryman, foot soldier; light infantry.

cavalry, yeomanry; cavalry regiment; horseman; mounted troops, mounted police, cavalryman, yeoman; trooper; knight; man-at-arms, hussar, dragoon; Cossack; armoured car; tank, Panzer; charger.

navy, admiralty; senior service, sail; fleet arm, armada; fleet, flotilla, squadron; argosy; merchant marine.

naval man, admiral, Sea Lord 741 *naval officer*; sailor 270 *mariner*; able seaman, rating; cabin boy; swabbie; marine, limey; submariner 270 *nautical personnel*; Royal Navy, RN, WRNS; Royal Marines; Royal Naval Reserve, RNR.

warship, galleon 275 *ship*; pirate ship; man-o'-war, privateer, ship of the line, battleship, dreadnought, destroyer, cruiser; frigate, corvette; gunboat, E-boat; fire ship, minesweeper; submarine, nuclear submarine, U-boat; Q-ship; aircraft carrier; landing craft, troopship; hospital ship; flagship.

air force, RAF, WRAF; flying corps; fleet air arm; squadron, flight, group, wing; warplane 276 *aircraft*; battle plane, bomber, fighter; troop-carrier; Zeppelin, barrage balloon 276 *airship*; paratroopers; ground staff; fighter pilot, navigator, observer, air crew.

723 Arms

N. *arms* armament, munitions; armaments, arms race; nuclear deterrent, anti-missile defence system, Star Wars, Strategic Defence Initiative, SDI, Son of Star Wars 713 *defence*; gun-running; ballistics, rocketry, missilery, gunnery, musketry, archery 287 *propulsion*. (See also *weapon* below.)

arsenal, armoury, gun room; magazine, powder keg; caisson; cartridge belt, bandolier; quiver; scabbard, sheath; holster 194 *receptacle*.

weapon, deterrent; conventional weapon, nuclear weapon (see also *throwing weapons, projectiles and missiles* and *bomb* below); stand-off weapon; weapon of mass destruction, WMD, weapon of mass effect; secret weapon, death ray, laser, directed-energy weapon, particle-beam weapon; germ warfare, chemical warfare; electronic warfare; poison gas, mustard gas, nerve gas 659 *poison*; teeth, claws, nails 256 *sharp point*.

throwing weapons, projectiles and missiles, missile weapons, javelin, harpoon, dart, throwing star; lasso; boomerang; arrow, poisoned arrow, shaft, bolt; arrowhead, barb; stone, brick; shot, ball, bullet, pellet, shell, shrapnel 287 *missile*; rocket, MIRV (see also *ammunition* below); bow, longbow, crossbow, catapult, sling; blowpipe; bazooka, rocket-thrower; guided missile, nuclear missile, ballistic missile, intercontinental ballistic missile, ICBM, surface-to-air missile, cruise missile, Exocet (tdmk); Star Wars, etc. (see *arms* above); depleted uranium, DU; nuclear winter.

club, mace, hammer; battering ram 279 *ram*; bat, staff, stave, stick, switch; life-preserver, bludgeon, truncheon, cosh, cudgel, shillelagh, blackjack, nunchaku, sandbag, bicycle chain, blunt instrument; knuckle-duster.

spear, harpoon, gaff; lance, javelin, pike, assegai; halberd, pikestaff 256 *sharp point*; throwing stick (see also *throwing weapons, projectiles and missiles* above).

axe, battleaxe, tomahawk, hatchet; bill, halberd, poleaxe, chopper 256 *sharp edge*.

side arms, sword; broadsword, claymore; cutlass, swordstick; sabre, scimitar; blade, trusty blade; rapier; épée, foil; dagger, bayonet, dirk, skean, skean-dhu, poniard, dudgeon, stiletto 256 *sharp point*; machete, kukri, kris, parang, panga; knife, bowie knife, flick knife 256 *sharp edge*; Excalibur.

firearm, small arms, hand gun; matchlock, flintlock, fusil, musket; blunder-buss, carbine; rifle, Winchester; fowling piece, shotgun, sawn-off shotgun, double-barrelled gun, elephant gun; Enfield rifle, bore, calibre; muzzle; trigger, lock; magazine; breech, butt; sight, ramrod.

pistol, duelling pistol; six-shooter, colt, revolver, repeater, rod, shooting iron, automatic; stun gun, Taser *or* Tazer (tdmk).

gun, guns, cannonry, artillery; battery, broadside; cannon, bombard, carronade; mortar; field gun; great gun; Big Bertha; howitzer, minethrower, trench gun; anti-aircraft gun; Bofors gun, bazooka; Gatling gun, Lewis gun, machine gun, Bren gun, submachine gun, tommy gun; flamethrower; caisson; gun emplacement, rocket site, launching pad, silo.

ammunition, live ammunition, ammo; round of ammunition; shot, grape shot, buckshot; cannonball, bullet, soft-nosed bullet, dumdum bullet, rubber bullet, plastic bullet, baton round; projectile 287 *missile*; slug, stone, pellet; shell, shrapnel; flak, ack-ack; wad, cartridge; spent cartridge, dud; blank cartridge, blank; cartridge belt, cartridge case.

explosive, gunpowder; saltpetre; high explosive, plastic explosive, lyddite, melinite, cordite, gun cotton, dynamite, gelignite, Semtex (tdmk), TNT, nitroglycerine; cap, detonator, fuse; priming, charge, warhead, atomic warhead; fissionable material; fireworks, banger, squib, rocket, catherine wheel, roman candle, jumping jack, sparkler.

bomb, shell, bombshell; grenade, hand grenade, rocket-propelled grenade; Molotov cocktail, petrol bomb, acid bomb; megaton bomb, atom bomb, A-bomb, nuclear bomb, hydrogen bomb, H-bomb, neutron bomb, enhanced radiation bomb; battlefield nuclear weapon, mini-nuke; dirty bomb; smart bomb, dumb bomb; mushroom cloud, fallout; blockbuster, bunker buster, daisy-cutter bomb; cluster bomb, fragmentation bomb, bomblet; fuel-air bomb, fuel-air explosive, thermobaric weapon, vacuum bomb; firebomb, incendiary bomb, napalm bomb; letter bomb, nail bomb, parcel bomb, pipe bomb, blast bomb, car bomb, truck bomb; mine, landmine, anti-personnel mine, anti-tank mine; minefield, minelaying; booby trap 542 *trap*; depth charge, torpedo; flying bomb, doodlebug; time bomb; ethnic bomb, gene bomb; unexploded bomb, UXB, unexploded ordnance, UXO; bomb disposal, mine detection, mine-clearing, demining, deminer; e-bomb, electronic bomb, electromagnetic bomb.

Adj. *armed*, fully armed, well armed, armed to the teeth, accoutred, sword in hand, tooled up, packing heat 669 *prepared*, 718 *warring*.

724 Arena

N. *arena*, field; ground, terrain; centre, scene, stage, theatre; hustings, platform, floor; amphitheatre, coliseum, stadium, stand, grandstand; campus, parade ground, training ground; forum, marketplace 76 *focus*; hippodrome, circus, course, racecourse, turf; racetrack, track, running track, cinder track, indoor track, dog track; ring, bullring, boxing ring, ropes; rink, skating rink, ice rink; gymnasium, gym, exercise room, work-out range; range, shooting range, rifle range, butts; playground, beach, swimming complex, lido, marina, pier, fairground 837 *place of amusement*; leisure centre, recreation ground, playing field, football field, pitch, football pitch, cricket pitch; AstroTurf (tdmk); court, tennis court, badminton court, squash court; putting green, bowling green, bowling alley, skittle alley; snooker club; beargarden; chessboard; bridge table; snooker table, pool table; auction room.

battleground, battlefield, field of conflict, scene of action, theatre of war, combat zone, battle arena, front, front line, firing line, trenches, no-man's-land 718 *battle*; no-go area; disputed territory.

SECTION FIVE

Results of action

725 Completion

N. *completion*, finish, termination, conclusion, end of the matter 69 *end*; terminus 295 *goal*; issue, upshot 154 *event*; result, end result, final result, end product 157 *effect*; fullness 54 *completeness*; fulfilment 635 *sufficiency*; maturity, maturation, fruition, readiness; consummation, culmination, ne plus ultra 646 *perfection*; exhaustiveness, thoroughness 455 *attention*; elaboration, rounding off, finishing off, mopping up, winding up; topping out; top, crown 213 *summit*; missing link 627 *requirement*; last touch, crowning glory, final stroke, coup de grâce; the icing on the cake, achievement; fait accompli, a done deal; finished product; boiling point, danger point, breaking point, last straw 236 *limit*; climax, payoff; resolution, solution, dénouement, catastrophe, last act, final curtain, swansong, finale, finis 69 *finality*; execution, implementation, accomplishment, achievement.

Adj. *completed*, full 54 *complete*; accomplished, etc. (see vb.); elaborate 646 *perfect*; sewn up, buttoned up, done and dusted, in the can, in the bag, under one's belt, secured 727 *successful*.

Vb. *carry through*, follow through, follow up; drive home, clinch, seal, set the seal on; clear up, mop up, wipe up, finish off, polish off; dispose of, dispatch; complete, consummate, put the finishing touch, put the icing on the cake, top out 54 *make complete*; elaborate, hammer out, work out 646 *perfect*; ripen, bring to a head, bring to the boil 669 *mature*; sit out, see out, see it through; get through, get shot of, dispose of, bring to its close drive a nail into the coffin 69 *terminate*; set at rest 266 *bring to rest*.

carry out, see through, effect, enact 676 *do*; dispatch, execute, discharge, implement, realize, bring about, accomplish, fulfil, consummate, achieve 727 *succeed*; make short work of; leave no loose ends, leave no stone unturned, not do by halves, go the whole hog, be in at the death; deliver the goods, bring home the bacon, be as good as one's word, fill the bill.

climax, cap, crown all 213 *crown*; culminate, peak, reach its peak; reach the zenith, reach a climax, scale the heights, conquer Everest;

have an orgasm, come; reach boiling point, come to a crisis; reach the limit, put the lid on; come to fruition, achieve one's goal 295 *arrive*.

726 Non-completion

N. *non-completion*, neglect 458 *negligence*; non-fulfilment 636 *insufficiency*; deficit 307 *shortfall*; lack 55 *incompleteness*; immaturity 670 *undevelopment*; never-ending task, painting the Forth Bridge, a woman's work, Sisyphean labour *or* labour of Sisyphus, going round in circles, recurring decimal 71 *continuity*; continuation 146 *continuance*; superficiality, a lick and a promise 456 *inattention*; work undone, job half-done, loose ends; no result, drawn game, draw; stalemate, deadlock.

Adj. *uncompleted*, fragmentary 55 *incomplete*; unaccomplished; unrealized, half-done, half-finished, scamped 458 *neglected*; unripe 670 *immature*; superficial; left hanging, left in the air; lacking finish, not worked out, not thought through, sketchy 647 *imperfect*; unprocessed.

Vb. *not complete*, leave undone, leave in the air, leave hanging 458 *neglect*; skip, skive, scamp, do by halves, scotch the snake not kill it 655 *wound*; give up, not follow through; fall out, drop out, not stay the course; fall short of one's goal, fall down on 728 *fail*; defer, postpone.

727 Success

N. *success*, sweet smell of success, coming up roses, glory 866 *fame*; happy ending; success story, progress 285 *progression*; breakthrough, quantum leap; one's day, landing on one's feet, run of luck, good fortune 730 *prosperity*; lead 34 *advantage*; flash in the pan; feat, achievement 676 *deed*; accomplishment, goal 725 *completion*; a success, feather in one's cap, triumph, hit, smash hit, box-office hit; top of the charts, chart-topper, top twenty, hit parade, the charts; best-seller; sell-out, howling success, succès fou, rave reviews; good shot 694 *skill*; beginner's luck, lucky stroke, fluke 618 *non-design*; hat trick, stroke of genius, coup, tour de force, masterstroke 694 *masterpiece*; trump, trump card; pass, qualification.

victory, beating, licking, trouncing 728 *defeat*; conquest; taking by storm 712 *attack*; the best of it; win, game, set and match; outright win, checkmate; narrow win, Pyrrhic victory; runaway victory, love game, walkover, pushover, picnic 701 *easy thing*; crushing victory, slam, grand slam; knockout, KO; upper hand, whip hand, advantage, edge, pole position; triumph, ovation, standing ovation, bouquets.

victor, winner, champion, medallist, prize-winner, dux, first, double first 644 *exceller*; winning side, the winners; conquering hero; conqueror, vanquisher; master *or* mistress of the field, master *or* mistress of the situation; a success, man *or* woman to watch, whiz kid, high flier, rising star 730 *prosperous person*.

Adj. *successful*, effective, efficacious; fruitful 640 *profitable*; felicitous 694 *skilful*; foolproof; home and dry 725 *completed*; prizewinning, victorious, world-beating, chart-topping 644 *excellent*; winning, leading; on top, in the ascendant, rising, on the up and up, going places, sitting pretty 730 *prosperous*; triumphant; triumphal, victorious; crowned with success, flushed with victory.

Vb. *succeed*, succeed in, effect, accomplish, achieve; be successful, make out, win one's spurs; be a success of, make a go of, make short work of, rise to the occasion; make good, rise, do well, pull oneself up by one's bootstraps, become a self-made man *or* woman, get promotion, work one's way up the ladder, come to the top 730 *prosper*; pass, make the grade, qualify, graduate, come off well, land on one's feet, give a good account of oneself, come well out of it, come off with flying colours, come out on top, have the best of it 34 *be superior*; advance, break through, make a breakthrough 285 *progress*; reach one's goal, obtain one's objective; pull it off, bring it off, be as good as one's word, bring home the bacon; have a success, score a success, make the big time, make a hit, top the charts, make a kill, go over big; hit the jackpot, break the bank; score *or* win a point, carry a point; carry the day; arrive, be a success, make one's mark, click.

be *successful*, do the trick, fill the bill; turn up trumps, rise to the occasion; do the job, do wonders, do marvels, work miracles; work, work like magic, act like a charm 173 *operate*; take effect 178 *influence*; turn out well, pay off, pay dividends, bear fruit 171 *be fruitful*; hit it, hit the nail on the head, find the mot juste; play one's hand well, not put a foot wrong, never go wrong, not be wrong-footed; keep on the right side of; have the ball at one's feet, hold all the trumps; have the world in his *or* her hand; be irresistible, not know the meaning of failure, brush obstacles aside 701 *do easily*; not know when one is beaten, land on one's feet, come up smiling, come up smelling of roses 599 *be resolute*; hold one's own 599 *stand firm*.

triumph, have one's day, be crowned with success, wear the laurels of victory 876 *celebrate*; crow, crow over 877 *boast*; score, score

off, be one up on; triumph over difficulties, manage, make it, win through; overcome obstacles; find a loophole, find a way out, find a way round 667 *escape*; make headway against, stem the tide, weather the storm 715 *resist*; reap the fruits 771 *gain*.

go well, go like a bomb, go gangbusters *or* like gangbusters, sell like hot cakes.

overcome, master, overpower, overthrow, overturn, override 306 *outdo*; be more than a match for, be too much for, overmaster, dominate 34 *be superior*, 733 *dominate*; have the advantage, seize the advantage, prevail 34 *predominate*; have one on the hip, have someone where one wants him *or* her, have one by the short hairs hairs *or* by the short and curlies; have at one's mercy; checkmate, trump; conquer, vanquish, quell, subdue, subject, suppress, put down, crush 745 *subjugate*; capture, take by storm.

defeat, discomfit, dash, put another's nose out of joint, settle one's hash, cook one's goose; repulse, rebuff 292 *repel*; best, be too good for, be too much for, get the upper hand, get the whip hand 34 *be superior*; worst, outplay, outpoint, outflank, outmanoeuvre, outclass, outwit, outshine 306 *outdo*; pip at the post; disconcert, cut the ground from under one's feet, lay by the heels 702 *obstruct*; baffle, nonplus 474 *puzzle*; knock spots off, wipe the floor with; beat, lick, thrash, trounce, crush, give a drubbing, trample underfoot, beat hollow, rout, put to flight, scatter 75 *disperse*; silence, put the lid on 165 *suppress*; flatten, knock the stuffing out of, put out for the count, knock out; knock *or* hit for six; bowl out; drive to the wall, check, put in check 661 *endanger*; put an end to, wipe out, do for, settle, fix, dish 165 *destroy*; sink; break, bankrupt, beggar 801 *impoverish*.

win, win the match, get a result; win the battle, carry the day, achieve victory, defeat the enemy; be victorious; claim the victory; come off best, come off with flying colours; win hands down, carry all before one, have it all one's own way, romp home, have a walk-over, walk off with, waltz away with, walk it 701 *do easily*; win on points, win by a short head, win by a whisker, scrape home; win the last battle, win the last round; win the match, take the prize, gain the palm, wear the laurel wreath; become champion, beat all comers, sweep the board, rule OK 34 *be superior*.

728 Failure

N. *failure*, lack of success; no luck, off day 731 *misfortune*; non-fulfilment, close but no cigar 726 *non-completion*; frustration 702 *hindrance*; vain attempt, abortive attempt, wild-goose chase, futile effort, no result, no-win situation 641 *wasted effort*; bungle 695 *bungling*; abortion, miscarriage 172 *unproductiveness*; impotence, brewer's droop, premature ejaculation; damp squib, washout, fiasco, flop; slip, omission, faux pas 495 *mistake*; no go, halt 145 *stop*; engine failure, electrical fault, computer fault, machine malfunction, gremlin, bug, breakdown 702 *hitch*; collapse, fall 309 *descent*; losses 772 *loss*; bankruptcy 805 *insolvency*.

defeat, bafflement 474 *uncertainty*; deadlock, stalemate 145 *stop*; repulse, rebuff, bloody nose, check, reverse; checkmate; the worst of it, discomfiture, stick, flak, beating, drubbing, hiding, licking, thrashing, trouncing; retreat; flight 290 *movement away*; stampede; rout, landslide; fall, downfall, collapse, débâcle; lost cause, losing battle; deathblow, nail in the coffin, quietus; Waterloo; Pyrrhic victory.

loser, also-ran, non-starter; has-been, history; dud, failure, flop, no-hoper, lemon; born loser 731 *unlucky person*; underdog 35 *inferior*; dropout 25 *misfit*; bankrupt 805 *non-payer*; losing side.

Adj. *unsuccessful*, vain, fruitless; dud, misfired; miscarried, stillborn, aborted, abortive; ditched; manqué, failed, bombed, ploughed, flunked; out of one's depth, losing one's grip 474 *uncertain*; down on one's luck 731 *unfortunate*, 801 *poor*.

defeated, beaten, bested, worsted, done for; baffled, thwarted, foiled 702 *hindered*; dashed, discomfited, hoist with one's own petard; outmanoeuvred, outplayed, outvoted; outwitted, outclassed, outshone 35 *inferior*; thrashed, licked; on the losing side, out of the running; in retreat; routed, put to flight; sunk; overthrown, had it, knocked out, kaput, brought low, fallen; captured.

Vb. *fail*, have no success; be unsuccessful, be beaten, etc. (see adj.); bomb, flop, die the death; flatline; fall down on, botch, bungle 495 *blunder*; flunk, not make the grade, be found wanting 636 *be insufficient*; miss the boat 138 *lose a chance*; go wide, miss, hit the wrong target, fall between two stools, miss an opportunity 282 *deviate*; get nothing out of it, get no change out of it, draw a blank, back the wrong horse, return empty-handed, labour in vain, have shot one's bolt 641 *waste effort*; kiss goodbye to 772 *lose*; overreach oneself; bite off more than one can chew, come a cropper, fall, collapse, slide 309 *tumble*; break down, malfunction, come to pieces, fall to bits, come unstuck; falter, stall, seize up, pack

up, conk out; stop, come to a dead stop, come up against a blank wall, come to a dead end; stick, get bogged down 145 *cease*; come to a sticky end, come to a bad end 655 *deteriorate*; go on the rocks, hit the buffers, run aground, be left high and dry, make a loss, crash, go bust, go bankrupt, go belly-up 805 *not pay*.

miscarry, be stillborn, abort; misfire; crash 309 *tumble*; not come off, come to naught, come to nothing, go by the board; fall flat, come to grief; blow up, go up in smoke; flop, bomb, prove a fiasco; go wrong, go awry, gang agley, take a turn for the worse, take an ugly turn; do no good, make things worse 832 *aggravate*.

be defeated, lose, lose out, suffer defeat, take a beating, lose the day, lose the battle, lose the match; lose the election, concede defeat, lose one's seat, lose the vote, be outvoted; lose by a whisker, get pipped at the post; be in a catch-22 situation; be on a hiding to nothing; get the worst of it, come off second best, go off with one's tail between one's legs, lick one's wounds; be taken to the cleaner's; lose hands down, come in last; bite the dust; fall; be captured, fall a prey to; retreat, lose ground 290 *recede*; take to flight 620 *run away*; admit defeat, had enough, cry quits 721 *submit*; have not a leg to stand on, have the ground cut from under one's feet; go to the wall, be history.

729 Trophy

N. *trophy*, spoils of war, captives 790 *booty*; scalp, battle, scars, wounds 655 *wound*; memorial, war memorial; memento 505 *reminder*; triumphal arch 548 *monument*; triumph, ovation, standing ovation 876 *celebration*; plum, glittering prizes; benefit match; prize, consolation prize, booby prize, wooden spoon 962 *reward*; sports trophy, Ashes, cup, shield; award, Academy Award, Oscar, Tony, Emmy; silver disc, gold disc, platinum disc, double platinum; laurels, crown, garland, wreath, palm of victory; pat on the back; bouquet; feather in one's cap.

decoration, battle honours, spurs 866 *honours*; citation, mention in dispatches; rosette, ribbon, sash, cordon bleu; blue, oar, cap; medal, gong, cross, garter, order; service stripe, long-service medal, war medal, campaign medal; Victoria Cross, VC, Military Cross, MC, Croix de Guerre, Iron Cross; Distinguished Service Cross, DSC, Congressional Medal, Medal of Honour; George Cross, GC, Legion of Honour *or* Légion d'honneur, civic crown; honours list.

730 Prosperity

N. *prosperity*, thriving, health and wealth; well-being, welfare; social inclusion; economic prosperity, boom, booming economy, sunrise economy; roaring trade, seller's market, bullish market, luxury, affluence, Easy Street 800 *wealth*; golden touch, Midas touch; fleshpots, fat of the land, milk and honey 635 *plenty*; auspiciousness, good fortune; bonanza, winning streak, luck, run of luck, good luck, break, lucky break, lucky gamble, lucky shot, luck of the draw 159 *chance*.

heyday, palmy days, prime, peak, zenith, halcyon days, summer, fair weather, Indian summer; life of Riley, place in the sun, clover, velvet, bed of roses, roses all the way 376 *euphoria*; Golden Age 824 *happiness*.

prosperous person, man *or* woman of substance *or* of property, fat cat 800 *rich person*; whiz kid; entrepreneur, nouveau riche, profiteer; celebrity.

Adj. *prosperous*, thriving, flourishing, booming 727 *successful*; rising, doing well, up and coming, on the up and up, in the ascendant, going up in the world; on the make, profiteering; well set-up, established, well-to-do, well-off, well-heeled, rolling in it, affluent, comfortable, comfortably off 800 *moneyed*; riding on the crest of a wave, buoyant, bullish; fortunate, lucky, born with a silver spoon in one's mouth, born under a lucky star; in clover, on velvet; on easy street, in the money, fat.

bringing prosperity, get-rich-quick.

halcyon, palmy, balmy, golden, rosy; blissful; providential, favourable, promising, auspicious, propitious, cloudless, clear, fine, fair, set fair; glorious, euphoric.

Vb. *prosper*, thrive, flourish, do well, have a good time of it 376 *enjoy*; bask in sunshine, make hay, live in clover, lie on velvet, have it easy, live on easy street, have it made, live on milk and honey, live on the fat of the land, 'never have had it so good'; be in the money, be rolling in it; be well-heeled, batten on, grow fat; blossom, bloom, flower 171 *be fruitful*; boom, drive a roaring trade, enjoy a seller's market; profiteer 771 *gain*; get on, go far, rise in the world, work one's way up, make it, arrive 727 *succeed*; make money, make a fortune, strike it rich, make one's pile, feather one's nest, line one's pockets 800 *get rich*; run smoothly; go on swimmingly.

have luck, have all the luck, have a stroke of luck, have a lucky break, have a run of luck, luck out, strike lucky, strike oil, be on to a good thing, get on the gravy train; fall on one's feet, bear a charmed life, be born under a lucky star, be born with a silver spoon in one's mouth, have the ball at one's feet.

be auspicious, be propitious, etc. (see adj.);

promise well, augur well, set fair; look kindly on, smile on, bless.

Int. *good luck!*, all the best!, best of British!

731 Adversity

N. *adversity*, adverse circumstances, misfortune; continual struggle; hardship, hard life, tough time 825 *suffering*; travail 377 *pain*; hard times, hell upon earth, vale of sorrows 616 *evil*; burden, load, pressure, pressure of the times; ups and downs of life, rollercoaster, slings and arrows, vicissitude 154 *event*; troubles, sea of troubles, trials, cares, worries 825 *worry*; wretchedness, misery, despondency, Slough of Despond 834 *dejection*; bitter pill 872 *humiliation*; cross 825 *sorrow*; curse, blight, plague, scourge, infliction, visitation 659 *bane*; bleakness, cold wind, draught, chill, cold, winter 380 *coldness*; gloom 418 *darkness*; ill wind; blow, hard blow 704 *opposition*; setback, check, rebuff, reverse 728 *defeat*; pinch, plight, poor lookout, trouble ahead; trough, bad patch, rainy day 655 *deterioration*; slump, recession, depression 679 *inactivity*; storm clouds, gathering clouds 900 *threat*; decline, downfall 165 *ruin*; want, need, distress, extremity 801 *poverty*.

misfortune, bad luck, hard luck, ill luck, a bad hair day, annus horribilis; no luck 728 *failure*; evil star 645 *badness*; raw deal; hard lines, sod's *or* Sod's law, Murphy's law; ill hap, mishap, misadventure, contretemps, accident, casualty 159 *chance*; disaster, calamity, catastrophe, the pits.

unlucky person, no-hoper, poor risk; star-crossed lover, plaything of the gods, Jonah; down-and-out 728 *loser*; underdog 35 *inferior*; lame dog, lame duck 163 *weakling*; scapegoat, victim.

Adj. *adverse*, hostile, ominous, sinister, inauspicious, unfavourable; disadvantageous, antipathetic, bleak, cold, hard; opposed, contrary, opposing; malign 645 *harmful*; ruinous 165 *destructive*; disastrous, calamitous, catastrophic.

not prosperous, unprosperous, in poor shape, out of kilter; not doing well, badly off 801 *poor*; in trouble, up against it, in adverse circumstances, with one's back to the wall, declining, on the wane, on the down grade, on the slippery slope, on the road to ruin; in a bad way, in dire straits.

unfortunate, ill-fated, unlucky, ill-starred, star-crossed; luckless, hapless, poor, wretched, forlorn, miserable, unhappy; stricken, doomed, accursed; out of luck, down on one's luck 801 *poor*; born under an evil star; accident-prone.

Vb. *have trouble*, be in trouble; have no luck, get more kicks than ha'pence; get more bricks than bouquets; be in for it, go through it, be hard pressed, be up against it, strike a bad patch 825 *suffer*; come to grief 728 *miscarry*; feel the pinch, feel the draught, fall on evil days, have seen better days 801 *be poor*; go downhill, go down in the world, decline 655 *deteriorate*; sink 313 *go down*; come to a bad end 728 *fail*; go to rack and ruin, go to the dogs 165 *be destroyed*.

732 Averageness

N. *averageness*, mediocrity 30 *average*; golden mean, neither too much nor too little; middle class; suburbia, common man, everyman, man in the street, the average punter, Joe Bloggs, Joe Public, Joe Soap 869 *commoner*; hoi polloi.

Adj. *middling*, average, mediocre; neither good nor bad, ordinary, commonplace 30 *median*; middle-of-the-road 177 *moderate*; undistinguished, nothing special, fair, fair to middling; so-so, comme ci, comme ça, adequate; tolerable, passable, fifty-fifty, much of a muchness; medium, middle, grey 625 *neutral*.

Vb. *be middling*, be mediocre, etc. (see adj.); jog on, manage well enough, never *or* not set the Thames on fire, never *or* not set the heather on fire.

5.2
Social Volition

SECTION ONE

General social volition

733 Authority

N. *authority*, power; powers that be, 'they', the Establishment, ruling classes, Big Brother 741 *master*; the Government, the Administration, Whitehall 690 *director*; right, divine right, divine right of kings, prerogative, royal prerogative; law, rightful power; legislative assembly 692 *parliament*; regency, committee 751 *commission*; office, place; portfolio 955 *jurisdiction*; power behind the throne, éminence grise, etc. 178 *influence*; credit; leadership 689 *directorship*; ascendance, supremacy 34 *superiority*; pride of place, seniority, priority 64 *precedence*; majesty, royalty, crown 868 *nobility*; authoritativeness.

governing, governance, rule, sway, reins of government, direction, command 689 *directorship*; control; hold, grip, clutches 778 *retention*; domination, control freakery, mastery, whip hand, long arm; ascendancy, dominion, sovereignty, raj, overlordship, presidency, supremacy 34 *superiority*; reign, regency, dynasty; foreign rule, empire 745 *subjection*; imperialism, colonialism, white supremacy, black power; regime *or* régime, regiment, regimen; state control, paternalism; bureaucracy, apparat, civil service, officialism, beadledom, bumbledom, red tape, bumf; Parkinson's law 197 *expansion*.

government, direction 689 *management*; politics; constitutionalism, rule of law 953 *legality*; misgovernment 734 *anarchy*; theocracy, papal rule, hierocracy, clericalism 985 *clericalism*; monarchy, constitutional monarchy; republicanism, federalism; tribal system, tribalism, clan system; patriarchy, matriarchate; feudalism; benevolent despotism, paternalism; aristocracy, meritocracy, oligarchy, elitism; gynocracy, pornocracy, regiment of women 373 *womankind*; gerontocracy; triumvirate; kleptocracy; plutocracy; representative government, parliamentary government, government by the ballot box, party system 605 *vote*, 708 *political party*; democracy, direct democracy, egalitarianism, government of the people, by the people, for the people; demagogy, vox populi, vox pop; majority rule, one man one vote, proportional representation; pluralism, collectivism, proletarianism; communism, Marxism, Leninism, Bolshevism, Maoism; Fascism, Nazism, Third Position; neo-conservatism; Westminster, Whitehall, White House, Pentagon, Kremlin; committee rule, sovietism; military government, martial law; mob rule, anarchy; socialism, Fabianism; bureaucracy, technocracy; self-government, autonomy, home rule 744 *independence*; puppet government 628 *instrument*; caretaker government, regency, interregnum; mandate; change of government, regime change.

position of authority, high office, kingship, tsardom, royalty, regency, protectorship; chieftainship, sheikhdom, emirate, lordship, sultanate, caliphate, governorship, viceroyalty; consulate, consulship, proconsulate, prefecture, tribunate, magistracy; mayoralty, aldermanship; headship, presidency, premiership, chairmanship 689 *directorship*; overlordship, superintendency, inspectorship; mastership; Big Brother; government post, Cabinet seat; seat of government.

despotism, paternalism; tyranny; dictatorship, Caesarism, tsarism, Stalinism; autocracy, absolute monarchy; totalitarianism; police state, rule of terror 735 *brute force*.

political organization, body politic; state, commonwealth, superstate; country, realm, kingdom, republic, city state, city; federation, confederation; principality, duchy, archduchy, dukedom; empire, dominion, colony, dependency, protectorate, mandate, mandated territory 184 *territory*; communist bloc, Third World, Fourth World 184 *region*; superpower, hyperpower 34 *superiority*; banana republic 35 *inferiority*; buffer state 231 *betweenness*; province, county 184 *district*; welfare state.

Adj. *authoritative*, empowered, sanctioned, approved, competent; in office, in authority, magisterial, official, ex officio; ex cathedra; mandatory, binding, compulsory 740 *compelling*; magistral, masterful, domineering; commanding, lordly, dignified, majestic; overruling, imperious, bossy; peremptory, arbitrary, absolute, autocratic, tyrannical, dictatorial, totalitarian 735 *authoritarian*; powerful 162 *strong*; leading 178 *influential*; preeminent, preponderant, predominant, dominant, paramount 34 *supreme*; Big Brotherish.

ruling, reigning; sovereign, on the throne; royal, regal, majestic, kinglike, kingly, queenly, princely, lordly; imperial; magisterial; governing, controlling, dictating, etc. (see vb.).

governmental, gubernatorial, political, constitutional; administrative, ministerial, official, bureaucratic, centralized; technocratic; matriarchal, patriarchal; monarchical, feudal, aristocratic, oligarchic, plutocratic, democratic; popular, classless, republican; self-governing, autonomous, autarchic, autocephalous 744 *independent*; anarchy.

Vb. *rule*, hold sway, reign, reign supreme, wear the crown, wield the sceptre; govern, control 737 *command*; manage, hold the reins, hold office 689 *direct*; be in power, have authority, wield power, exercise authority, exert authority, use one's authority; rule absolutely, tyrannize 735 *oppress*; dictate, lay down the law; keep order, police.

take authority, ascend the throne, succeed to the throne, take office, assume command; take over the reins; assume authority, form a government; gain power, take control; seize power, usurp.

dominate, turn the scale, hold all the aces, hold all the cards 34 *predominate*; lord it over, boss, rule the roost, be queen bee, wear the trousers, be in the driving seat, be in the saddle 737 *command*; have the upper hand, have the whip hand, call the tune, call the shots 727 *overcome*; have in one's power, have over a barrel; lead by the nose, twist round one's little finger, have under one's thumb, have one by the short hairs *or* by the short and curlies, bend to one's will, hold in the palm of one's hand 178 *influence*; drive 735 *be severe*; dictate,

coerce 740 *compel*; hold down, ride roughshod over 745 *subjugate*; override, overrule, have it all one's own way.

734 Laxity: absence of authority

N. *laxity*, laxness, slackness, remissness, indifference 458 *negligence*; laissez-faire 744 *scope*; informality, lack of ceremony 769 *nonobservance*; looseness, relaxation, derestriction, loose cannon 746 *liberation*; decentralization 46 *disunion*; indulgence, toleration, licence, permissiveness 736 *leniency*; line of least resistance 721 *submission*; weak will, feeble grasp, weak administration, crumbling power 163 *weakness*; no drive, no push, inertia 175 *inertness*; no control, policy of non-intervention, abdication of authority, surrender of control 753 *resignation*; renunciation 621 *relinquishment*.

anarchy, breakdown of law and order; free-for-all, every man for himself, dog-eat-dog; disorder, disorganization, chaos 61 *turmoil*; anarchism 769 *non-observance*; mob rule, mob law, lynch law 954 *lawlessness*.

Adj. *lax*, loose, slack; disorganized; feeble, soft, wet, wimpish 163 *weak*; slipshod, remiss 458 *negligent*; relaxed, informal, free-and-easy; permissive, tolerant, undemanding 736 *lenient*; unassertive.

Vb. *be lax*, give one his *or* her head, give rope enough 744 *give scope*; waive the rules, stretch a point; tolerate, put up with; laissez-faire, laissez-aller 756 *permit*; let one get away with, not say boo to a goose; spoonfeed, featherbed, indulge, spoil 736 *be lenient*; make concessions 770 *compromise*; relax 46 *disunite*; lose control, reduce to chaos 63 *disarrange*.

735 Severity

N. *severity*, rigorousness, strictness, stringency; formalism; rigidity, inflexibility 326 *hardness*; discipline, strong hand, iron hand, tight grasp 733 *authority*; rod of iron, heavy hand, zero tolerance, Draconian laws; harshness, rigour, extremity, extremes; letter of the law, pound of flesh; intolerance, rigorism; censorship; puritanism 950 *prudery*; infliction, visitation, inquisition, persecution, exploitation, sexploitation; droit du seigneur; harassment, oppression; callousness, inclemency, mercilessness, pitilessness; harsh treatment, the hard way, tender mercies, cruelty 898 *inhumanity*; austerity 945 *asceticism*.

brute force, show of force 176 *violence*; big battalions, gunboat diplomacy 160 *power*; coercion, bludgeoning 740 *compulsion*; violence; subjugation 745 *subjection*; autocracy, dictatorship 733 *despotism*; tyranny; Fascism,

Nazism, totalitarianism; Prussianism, militarism; martial law, iron rule, iron hand, mailed fist, jackboot, bludgeon.

tyrant, petty tyrant; disciplinarian, martinet, sergeant major; militarist, jackboot; hanging judge; heavy father, Dutch uncle; Big Brother, authoritarian, despot, dictator 741 *autocrat*; boss, inquisitor, persecutor; Ku Klux Klan; oppressor, bully, taskmaster, slave-driver; bloodsucker; ogre, brute 938 *monster*.

Adj. *severe*, austere, Spartan 945 *ascetic*; strict, rigorous, extreme; straitlaced, puritanical, prudish, old-maidish; donnish, pedagogic, hide-bound; formalistic, pedantic; bigoted, fanatical; hypercritical 862 *fastidious*; intolerant, censorious 924 *disapproving*; unbending, stiff-necked, rigid 326 *hard*; hard as nails, hard-headed, hard-boiled, flinty, dour; inflexible, obdurate, uncompromising 602 *obstinate*; inexorable, relentless, merciless, unsparing, implacable, unforgiving 906 *pitiless*; heavy, stern, stiff; punitive; stringent, Draconian, drastic, savage.

authoritarian, masterful, domineering, lordly, arrogant, haughty 878 *insolent*; despotic, absolute, arbitrary; totalitarian, Fascist; dictatorial, Big Brotherish, autocratic; undemocratic; coercive, compulsive 740 *compelling*; bossy, nannyish.

oppressive, hard on 914 *unjust*; tyrannical, despotic; tyrannous, harsh, exigent, exacting, extortionate, persecuting, inquisitorial, unsparing; high-handed, overbearing, domineering; heavy-handed, Draconian, brutal, ogreish 898 *cruel*.

Vb. *be severe*, be harsh, be strict, etc. (see adj.), be cruel to be kind; bear hard on; keep a tight rein on 747 *restrain*; be down on, have a down on; come down on, come down like a ton of bricks, crack down on, stamp on, put a stop to, clamp down on 165 *suppress*; persecute, hunt down 619 *pursue*; ill-treat, mishandle, abuse 675 *misuse*; get tough with, play hardball with, pull no punches; take off the gloves, rule with an iron hand, inflict; mete out stern punishment; have one's pound of flesh; harden one's heart, show no mercy, take Draconian measures 906 *be pitiless*; give no quarter, put to the sword 362 *slaughter*.

oppress, tyrannize, play the tyrant, be despotic, abuse one's authority; domineer, lord it; overawe, intimidate, terrorize 854 *frighten*; bludgeon 740 *compel*; boss around, put upon; bully, be always on one's back, harass, plague, hassle 827 *torment*; persecute, victimize 898 *be malevolent*; break, crush the spirit, take the heart out of, tame 369 *break in*; tax 684 *fatigue*; overtax, exploit, extort, suck, squeeze,

grind, grind the faces of the poor; trample, tread down, tread underfoot, stamp on, hold down 165 *suppress*; enslave 745 *subjugate*; ride roughshod, inflict injustice 914 *do wrong*; rule with an iron hand, rule with a rod of iron; take Draconian measures; whip, scourge, put the screws on 963 *torture*; shed blood 362 *murder*; be heavy, weigh on, burden, crush 322 *weigh*.

736 Leniency

N. *leniency*, lenience; mildness, gentleness, tenderness; forbearance, easygoingness, long-suffering 823 *patience*; pardon 909 *forgiveness*; quarter, mercy, lenity, clemency, mercifulness, compassion 905 *pity*; humanity, kindness 897 *benevolence*; indulgence, toleration; moderation; light rein, velvet glove, kid gloves.

Adj. *lenient*, soft, gentle, mild; indulgent, tolerant; moderate, easy, easy-going, undemanding 734 *lax*; longsuffering 823 *patient*; clement, merciful; soft on; tender 905 *pitying*.

Vb. *be lenient*, make few demands; go easy, handle with kid gloves 177 *moderate*; featherbed, spoonfeed, spoil, indulge, play the fond parent, humour 889 *pet*; stretch a point; forbear 823 *be patient*; pity, spare, give quarter 905 *show mercy*; pardon 909 *forgive*; relax.

737 Command

N. *command*, royal command, tablets of stone; summons; commandment, ordinance; injunction, imposition; dictation, bidding, behest; dictum, say-so 532 *affirmation*; charge, commission, appointment 751 *mandate*; instructions, manifesto, rules, regulations, code of practice, CAT standard (for ISAs and mortgages); brief 524 *information*; directive, order, order of the day, marching orders; word of command, word; beck, nod, sign 547 *gesture*; signal, bugle call, trumpet call 547 *call*; whip, three-line whip; dictate 740 *compulsion*; ban, embargo; counterorder 752 *annulment*.

decree, edict, ipse dixit; law, canon, prescript 693 *precept*; bull, papal decree; circular, encyclical; ordinance; decree nisi, decree absolute; decision 480 *judgment*; enactment, act 953 *legislation*; plebiscite, manifesto, electoral mandate 605 *vote*; dictate, diktat.

demand, claim, requisition 761 *request*; notice, warning notice, final notice, final demand, ultimatum; blackmail 900 *threat*; imposition, exaction, levy, tax demand 809 *tax*.

warrant, search warrant, authorization, written authority, passport 756 *permit*; writ, summons, subpoena, citation, habeas corpus 959 *legal process*.

Adj. commanding, imperative, categorical, dictatorial; mandatory, obligatory, peremptory, compulsive, written on tablets of stone 740 *compelling*; authoritative; decisive, conclusive, final; demanding, insistent, hectoring.

Vb. command, bid, invite; order, tell, issue a command, give an order, lay down the law; signal, call, nod, beck, motion, sign, make a sign 547 *gesticulate*; wink, give a cue, tip the wink 524 *hint*; direct, give a directive, instruct, brief, circularize; rule, lay down, enjoin; give a mandate, charge, call upon 751 *commission*; impose, lay upon, set a task, make obligatory 917 *impose a duty*; detail; call together, rally, convene 74 *bring together*; send for, summon; cite, subpoena, issue a writ 959 *litigate*; remand; dictate, take a strong line, put one's foot down 740 *compel*; countermand 752 *annul*; lay an embargo, ban, impose a ban, taboo, declare taboo, proscribe 757 *prohibit*.

decree, promulgate 528 *proclaim*; declare, say so, lay down the law 532 *affirm*; signify one's will and pleasure, prescribe, ordain 608 *predetermine*; enact, pass a law, legislate, decriminalize 953 *make legal*; pass judgment, give judgment, give a ruling 480 *judge*.

demand, require, requisition 627 *require*; order, indent 761 *request*; make demands on, send a final demand, issue a final warning, give final notice, present an ultimatum, demand with threats, blackmail 900 *threaten*; present one's claim, make claims upon, demand payment, dun, sue, bill, invoice; charge 809 *price*; exact, levy 809 *tax*.

738 Disobedience

N. disobedience, indiscipline, recalcitrance, refractoriness 598 *unwillingness*; naughtiness, misbehaviour, mischief-making, monkey tricks; delinquency 934 *wickedness*; insubordination, mutinousness, mutineering; defiance; non-compliance 769 *non-observance*; disloyalty, defection, desertion 918 *undutifulness*; infraction, infringement, criminality, crime, sin 936 *guilty act*; civil disobedience, passive resistance, electronic civil disobedience, hacktivism 715 *resistance*; conscientious objection 704 *opposition*; obstructionism 702 *hindrance*; seditiousness; wildness 954 *lawlessness*.

revolt, mutiny; strike; faction 709 *dissension*; breakaway, secession 978 *schism*; defection 603 *change of mind*; restiveness 318 *agitation*; sabotage 165 *destruction*; breach of the peace, riot, street riot, rioting, gang warfare, streetfighting, tumult 61 *turmoil*; rebellion, insurrection, rising, uprising, intifada 176 *outbreak*; putsch, coup d'état; resistance movement, insurgency 715 *resistance*; subversion 149 *revolution*; terrorism, bioterrorism, cyberterrorism, narcoterrorism 954 *lawlessness*; civil war 718 *war*; anarchy; regicide, tyrannicide 362 *homicide*.

sedition, seditiousness; intrigue 623 *plot*; agitprop, subversion, infiltration, fifth-columnism; spying, espionage, underground activities 523 *latency*; terrorism, anarchism, nihilism; treason, high treason, lese-majesty 930 *perfidiousness*.

rebel, revolter, mutineer; demonstrator, striker, picketer 705 *opponent*; secessionist, seceder, splinter group, rebel group 978 *schismatic*; dissident, refusenik 829 *malcontent*; blackleg, scab 84 *nonconformist*; maverick, lone wolf; seditionary, seditionist; traitor, Guy Fawkes, Quisling, fifth columnist, infiltrator, spy, industrial spy 603 *recanter*; insurrectionist, insurgent; guerrilla, urban guerrilla, partisan, strugglista; resistance, underground, Maquis; Black Panther, Black Muslim, Rastafarian; Provisional, Provo; extremist, Jacobin, Bolshevist, Trotskyist, red; terrorist, bioterrorist, cyberterrorist; sleeper, clean skin; anarchist, nihilist 149 *revolutionary*, 708 *political party*; counter-revolutionary, reactionary, monarchist, White Russian, capitalist roader; mafia.

agitator, agent provocateur; agitprop, protester, demonstrator, marcher; soap-box orator, tub-thumper, ranter, rabble-rouser; firebrand, mischief-maker 663 *troublemaker*; seditionist; ringleader.

rioter, street rioter, urban guerrilla, bovver boy, boot boy, brawler, rowdy 904 *ruffian*; saboteur, Luddite.

Adj. disobedient, undisciplined; naughty, mischievous, misbehaving; unbiddable, difficult, self-willed, wayward, unruly, unmanageable 176 *violent*; intractable, ungovernable 598 *unwilling*; insubordinate, mutinous, rebellious, contumacious, bolshie, bloody-minded; contrary 704 *opposing*; nonconformist 84 *unconformable*; uncompliant 769 *non-observant*; recalcitrant 715 *resisting*; challenging 711 *defiant*; refractory, perverse 602 *obstinate*; subversive, revolutionary, reactionary; seditious, traitorous, treasonous; untamed.

Vb. disobey, be disobedient, misbehave, get into mischief; flout authority, not comply with 769 *not observe*; not do as one is told, disobey orders, show insubordination 711 *defy*; defy the whip; cock a snook, snap one's fingers, fly in the face of 704 *oppose*; break the law, commit a crime 954 *be illegal*; violate, infringe, transgress, trespass 306 *encroach*; kick, chafe, fret, champ at the bit, play up; take the bit between one's teeth, kick over the traces, take the law into one's own hands, be a law unto oneself; bolt, take French leave, go AWOL, go walkabout 190 *be absent*, 446 *disappear*.

revolt, rebel, mutiny; down tools, strike, take industrial action, come out 145 *cease*; sabotage 702 *obstruct*; undermine, work underground; secede, break away; betray 603 *change one's mind*; agitate, demonstrate, protest 762 *deprecate*; create, create a row, kick up a stink, raise Cain, start a riot, stage a revolt, lead a rebellion 715 *resist*; rise up, rise in arms, throw off the yoke, throw off one's shackles, overthrow.

739 Obedience

N. obedience, compliance 768 *observance*; meekness, biddability, tractability, pliancy, malleability 327 *softness*; willingness; non-resistance, submissiveness, acquiescence 721 *submission*; passiveness 679 *inactivity*; dutifulness, discipline 917 *duty*; deference, obsequiousness, slavishness 879 *servility*; tameness, docility.

loyalty, constancy, devotion, fidelity, faithfulness, good faith 929 *probity*; allegiance, fealty.

Adj. obedient, compliant, cooperating, conforming 768 *observant*; loyal, faithful, steadfast, constant; devoted, dedicated, sworn; submissive 721 *submitting*; law-abiding 717 *peaceful*; amenable, docile; good, well-behaved; daughterly; acquiescent, passive 679 *inactive*; meek, sheep-like, biddable, like putty in one's hands, dutiful; at one's beck and call, on a string, on a lead, puppet-like, under one's thumb, under control; disciplined, regimented 917 *obliged*; trained, manageable, tame; obsequious 879 *servile*.

Vb. obey, comply, act upon 768 *observe*; do the needful, sign on the dotted line, toe the line, come to heel 83 *conform*; assent 758 *consent*; listen, heed, obey orders, do as one is told; put oneself at one's service 597 *be willing*; obey the whip, follow the party line; do one's bidding, wait upon, follow, follow like a sheep, follow to the world's end 742 *serve*; be loyal, bear allegiance, pay homage 768 *keep faith*; pay tribute 745 *be subject*; make oneself useful, do sterling service 703 *minister to*; defer to, be submissive 721 *submit*.

740 Compulsion

N. compulsion, needs must 596 *necessity*; law of nature 953 *law*; act of God; moral compulsion 917 *conscience*; Hobson's choice 606 *no choice*; carrot and stick; coercion, regimentation; arm-twisting, blackmail 900 *threat*; sanctions 963 *penalty*; constraint, duress, force,

physical force; big stick, strongarm tactics 735 *brute force*; force-feeding; pressgang, conscription, call-up, draft 718 *war measures*; extortion; slavery, forced labour.

Adj. compelling, compulsive, of necessity, unavoidable, inevitable 596 *necessary*; imperative 737 *commanding*; compulsory, mandatory, binding 917 *obligatory*; urgent, pressing; coercive; forceful, cogent.

Vb. compel, constrain, coerce 176 *force*; enforce, put into force; dictate, necessitate, oblige, bind; order 737 *command*; impose 917 *impose a duty*; make one, leave no option; leave no escape, pin down, tie down; impress, draft, conscript; drive, dragoon, regiment, discipline; force one's hand, apply pressure, bulldoze, steamroller, railroad, stampede, pressgang, bully into, drag kicking and screaming, bludgeon 735 *oppress*; take by force, requisition, commandeer, extort, exact, wring from, drag from 786 *take*; apply pressure, lean on, squeeze, take the gloves off, turn the heat on, put the screws on, twist one's arm 963 *torture*; blackmail, hijack, hold to ransom 900 *threaten*; be peremptory, insist, make a point of, press, urge 532 *emphasize*; brook no denial, not take no for an answer 532 *affirm*; force upon, ram down one's throat, inflict, foist, fob off on; force-feed; hold back 747 *restrain*.

Adv. by force, under pressure, under protest, under duress; forcibly, willy-nilly, at gunpoint, at knifepoint.

741 Master

N. master, mistress; master *or* mistress of, captor, possessor 776 *owner*; sire, lord, lady, dame; liege, lord, overlord; protector 707 *patron*; seigneur, lord *or* lady of the manor, squire, laird 868 *aristocrat*; lord and master, man of the house 372 *male*; lady of the house, landlady 373 *lady*; senator; sir, madam 870 *title*; patriarch, matriarch 169 *parentage*; senior, head, principal, provost 34 *superior*; schoolmaster *or* -mistress 537 *teacher*; president, chairman *or* -woman, chairperson, speaker 690 *director*; employer, captain of industry, boss, governor, guvnor, guv 690 *manager*; -meister, the main man; leader, Duce, Caudillo, Führer (see also *autocrat* below); bigwig 638 *bigwig*; ruling class, ruling party, vested interest, the Establishment; the authorities, the powers that be, 'them', Big Brother, Westminster, the Government, Whitehall, White House, Pentagon, Kremlin 733 *government*.

autocrat, absolute ruler, despot, tyrant, dictator, Duce, Führer, Caudillo, Big Brother; tycoon, boss, shogun, VIP, big gun, big shot

638 *bigwig*; petty tyrant, tin god, little Hitler 690 *official*.

sovereign, crowned head, anointed king *or* queen; Majesty, Highness, Royal Highness, Serene Highness, Excellence *or* Excellency; dynasty, house, royal line, royal blood; royalty, monarch, king, queen, rex, regina; divine king, Pharaoh; emperor, empress; Caesar; Kaiser, Kaiserin; Tsar *or* Czar, Tsarina *or* Czarina, Tsarevitch *or* Czarevich; prince, princess, Infante, Infanta; Dauphin; Prince of Wales, Princess Royal; Crown Prince *or* Princess; King of Kings, Shah; khan; Mikado; Mogul, sultan, sultana; pope, pontiff, Dalai Lama, Aga Khan; caliph.

potentate, ruler; chief, chieftain, headman, sheikh; prince, princeling, rajah, rani, maharajah, maharani; emir, sherif; nawab, begum; archduke, archduchess, duke, duchess; Elector, Electress; regent, Prince Regent.

governor, military governor, High Commissioner, Governor-General, Crown Representative, viceroy, vicereine, khedive; proconsul; grand vizier, bey, pasha, bashaw; ecclesiastical governor, Prince Bishop; patriarch, archbishop, cardinal 986 church dignitary; ayatollah 690 *leader*.

officer, person in authority; functionary, mandarin, nabob, bureaucrat, apparatchik 690 *official*; civil servant, public servant 742 *servant*; commissar; prime minister, premier, first minister; grand vizier, chancellor, vice-chancellor; Pooh-bah; constable, marshal, warden; mayor, lord mayor, lady mayor, mayoress, alderman, provost, lord provost, bailie, city father, councillor; dignitary, local worthy 866 *person of repute*; sheriff, bailiff; justice of the peace, judge; magistrate, chief magistrate, president, doge; consul; prefect, district officer; commissioner, deputy commissioner; headman; mace-bearer, beadle, sexton, verger 986 *church officer*; party official, whip, chief whip; powers that be.

naval officer, Sea Lord; admiral, vice-admiral, rear-admiral, commodore, captain, commander, lieutenant-commander, lieutenant, sub-lieutenant, petty officer, leading seaman.

army officer, staff, High Command, staff officer, brass hat; commissioned officer; marshal, field marshal, commander-in-chief, general, lieutenant-general, major-general; brigadier, colonel, lieutenant-colonel, major, captain, lieutenant, second lieutenant, subaltern; ensign; warrant officer, non-commissioned officer, NCO, sergeant major, regimental sergeant major, staff sergeant, colour sergeant, sergeant, corporal, lance corporal; adjutant, aide-de-camp, quartermaster; war minister, warlord, commanding officer, commander, commandant.

air officer, air marshal, air commodore, group captain, wing commander, squadron leader, flight lieutenant, flying officer, pilot officer, warrant officer, flight sergeant 722 *air force*.

742 Servant

N. servant, public servant, civil servant 690 *official*; fag, slave, lapdog; general servant, factotum, gyp, skivvy, maid of all work, chief cook and bottle washer 678 *busy person*; humble servant, menial; orderly, attendant; verger 986 *church officer*; subordinate, underling 35 *inferior*; subaltern, helper, assistant, right-hand man, man Friday, girl Friday, amanuensis 703 *helper*; mercenary, hireling, employee, hand, hired man; odd-job man, handyman, worker, labourer; hewer of wood and drawer of water, hack, drudge, dogsbody; farm hand 370 *farmer*; shepherd, cowherd, milkmaid 369 *herdsman*; shop assistant, salesperson, etc. 793 *seller*; steward, stewardess, air hostess, cabin personnel, cabin boy; waiter, waitress, head waiter, wine waiter; bartender, barman, barmaid, pot boy, tapster 192 *tavern*; barista; stableman, ostler, groom, stable boy *or* lad, postilion; errand boy, messenger, runner 529 *courier*; doorman, commissionaire, janitor, concierge 264 *doorkeeper*; porter, night porter; caddy; callboy, page boy, bellboy, bellhop, buttons; boots, sweeper 648 *cleaner*; caretaker, house-minder, house-sitter, housekeeper; help, daily, daily help, char, charwoman, cleaning lady; universal aunt; baby-sitter, baby-minder; nurse, nursemaid, nanny 749 *keeper*; companion, confidante.

domestic, domestic servant, general servant, manservant, man, serving man; footman, flunkey, lackey; servant girl, maid, maidservant, handmaid, parlour maid, housemaid, roommaid; maid of all work, tweeny, skivvy, slavey; kitchen maid, scullery maid, dairy maid, laundry maid; scullion, washer-up, dishwasher, housekeeper, butler, cook; steward, governess, tutor, nurse, nanny, nursemaid, doula; personal servant, page, valet, gentlemen's gentleman, batman; lady's maid, waiting woman; mother's help, ayah, amah, au pair, doula; scout, bed-maker; gardener, under-gardener, groom; coachman, chauffeur 268 *driver*.

retainer, follower, train, cortege 67 *retinue*; court, courtier; attendant, usher, gillie; bodyguard, henchman, squire, page, train-bearer; majordomo, roomlain, equerry, steward, bailiff; chatelaine, housekeeper, butler, cup-bearer;

chaplain, beadsman; lady's maid, lady-in-waiting, companion, confidante; governess, nurse, nursemaid, mother's help, nanny 749 *keeper*.

dependant, hanger-on, parasite, satellite, camp follower, groupie, creature, jackal 284 *follower*; stooge, puppet 628 *instrument*; minion, lackey, flunkey; henchman, vassal; apprentice, protégé(e), ward, charge.

subject, national, citizen, patrial 191 *native*; liege, vassal; people, citizenry 869 *common people*.

slave, bondman, bondmaid, slave girl; serf, villein; galley slave, wage slave, sweated labour 686 *worker*; eunuch; chattel, puppet, pawn; captive, chaingang 750 *prisoner*.

Adj. serving, ministering 703 *helping*; in service, in domestic service, menial; working, in employment, on the payroll; on the staff; at one's beck and call 739 *obedient*; in servitude, in slavery, in captivity 745 *subject*.

Vb. serve, be in service, wait upon, wait on hand and foot 703 *minister to*; live in 89 *accompany*; follow 739 *obey*; tend, squire, valet; char, do chores, do housework, clean for, do for, oblige; fag for, do service; be part of the workforce, work for 622 *function*.

743 Badge of office

N. regalia, insignia of royalty; crown, orb, sceptre; coronet, tiara, diadem; sword of state 733 *authority*; coronation robes, royal robe; ermine, royal purple; throne, seat of kings; ensign 547 *flag*; royal standard, royal arms 547 *heraldry*; lion, eagle, fleur-de-lis; Prince of Wales's feathers.

badge of office, chain of office, badge of rule; emblem of authority, staff, wand, verge, rod, Black Rod, baton, truncheon, gavel; signet, seal, privy seal, keys, ring; sword of state, sword of justice, mace; crosier; woolsack, chair, bench; triple crown, mitre, bishop's hat, cardinal's hat, biretta; bishop's apron, gaiters 989 *clerical dress*; judge's cap, black cap 961 *condemnation*; robe, mantle, toga.

badge of rank, sword, belt, sash, spurs, cocked hat, epaulette, tab 547 *badge*; uniform; brass, star, pips, crown, gold braid; chevron, stripe, anchor, armlet; garter, order 729 *decoration*.

744 Freedom

N. freedom, liberty; freedom of action, Liberty Hall; free will 595 *will*; free speech, freedom of the press, academic freedom, the four freedoms; civil rights, equal rights, women's rights 915 *what is due*; privilege, prerogative, exemption, immunity, diplomatic immunity

919 *non-liability*; liberalism; licence, poetic licence; free love 951 *illicit love*; laissez-faire, non-intervention; neutralism 860 *indifference*; latitudinarianism 977 *heterodoxy*; non-alignment, cross benches; isolationism; emancipation 746 *liberation*; women's liberation, women's lib; gay lib; enfranchisement.

independence, freedom of action; freedom of choice 605 *choice*; floating vote, don't know; freedom of thought, emancipation 84 *nonconformity*; bachelorhood 895 *celibacy*; self-expression, individuality 80 *speciality*; self-determination, national status 371 *nation*; autonomy, self-regulation, self-government, self-rule, home rule; self-sufficiency 635 *sufficiency*; freehold 777 *property*; independent means, private means.

scope, free play, full play 183 *range*; swing, rope; manoeuvrability, leverage; field, room, lebensraum, living space, elbowroom, room to swing a cat, wide berth, leeway, margin, clearance 183 *room*; latitude, liberty; permissive society; informality; fling, licence, excess 734 *laxity*; one's head, one's own way, nothing in one's way; a free hand, ball at one's feet 137 *opportunity*; the run of, free hand, blank cheque, carte blanche; room to manoeuvre, wriggle room; free-for-all, free enterprise, free trade, free port, free market.

free person, freeman, citizen, free citizen, patrial; freedman *or* -woman; ex-convict; escapee 667 *escaper*; free agent, freelance, free spirit; independent, cross-bencher; neutral 625 *moderate*; free-trader; freethinker, libertarian, bohemian, individualist, eccentric 84 *nonconformist*; loose cannon.

freedom fighter, partisan 722 *soldier*; nationalist 901 *patriot*; anarchist 61 *anarchist*; animal liberationist 660 *protector*.

Adj. free, freeborn, enfranchised; heart-whole, fancy-free, unattached; scot-free 960 *acquitted*; on the loose, at large; released, freed; free as air, free as the wind, free as a bird; footloose, go-as-you-please; privileged; exempt, immune; free-speaking 573 *plain*; freethinking, emancipated, broadminded; independent, uninfluenced 913 *just*; free and easy 882 *sociable*; loose, licentious, unbridled, at leisure, retired; relaxed, at ease 681 *leisurely*; free of cost, gratis, freebie, on the house, for free, unpaid for 812 *free of charge*; going begging 860 *unwanted*; free for all, unreserved, vacant, unoccupied, up for grabs 289 *accessible*.

independent, uncontrolled; unilateral 609 *spontaneous*; unforced, uninfluenced; unattached 860 *indifferent*; uncommitted, uninvolved; unaffiliated 625 *neutral*; isolationist

883 *unsociable*; unconquered, unbowed, irrepressible; autonomous, self-governing, autarchic, autocephalous; self-sufficient, self-supporting, self-contained, self-motivated; self-reliant; anarchic; self-employed, one's own boss, freelance; unofficial, cowboy, wildcat; free-minded, free-spirited, maverick; single, bachelor; individualistic, unconventional 84 *unconformable*; breakaway 489 *dissenting*.

Vb. *be free*, enjoy liberty; go free, save oneself 667 *escape*; take French leave 738 *disobey*; have the run of, have the freedom of, range, have scope, have room to swing a cat, have room to breathe, have a free hand, have elbowroom; have plenty of rope, have one's head; feel at home, make oneself at home; feel free, let oneself go, let it all hang out, let one's hair down 683 *rest*; have one's fling, have one's way, have it one's own way, cut loose, drop out, follow one's bent, do one's own thing; go as you please, roam 282 *stray*; go one's own way, go it alone, be one's own boss, shift for oneself, fend for oneself, paddle one's own canoe, stand alone; have a will of one's own 595 *will*; be independent, call no man master, be one's own man; stand up for one's rights, defy the whip 711 *defy*; stand on one's own feet, be self-sufficient; take liberties, make free with, go too far, presume on 878 *be insolent*; dare, make bold to.

give scope, give one his *or* her head, allow full play, give free rein to, allow enough rope 734 *be lax*; give a free hand, not cramp one's style, give the run of 701 *facilitate*; release, set free 746 *liberate*; live and let live, laissez-aller, laissez-faire.

745 Subjection

N. *subjection*, subordination; inferior rank, inferior status 35 *inferiority*; dependence, tutelage, guardianship, wardship, apron strings, leading strings; apprenticeship 536 *learning*; mutual dependence, symbiosis 12 *correlation*; allegiance; subjugation, conquest; loss of freedom, disfranchisement, bondage, enslavement 721 *submission*; constraint 747 *restraint*; oppression 735 *severity*; yoke 748 *fetter*; slavishness 879 *servility*.

servitude, slavery; captivity, bondage, yoke; serfdom.

Adj. *subjected*, dominated, etc. (see vb.); subjugated, overwhelmed 728 *defeated*; subdued; taken prisoner, in chains 747 *restrained*; discriminated against, disadvantaged, disfranchised; colonized, reduced to slavery, sold into slavery; in harness 742 *serving*; under the yoke, under the heel; oppressed, brought to one's knees, downtrodden; treated like dirt,

henpecked, browbeaten; the sport of, the plaything of, kicked around like a football; brought to heel, quelled; eating out of one's hand, like putty in one's hands, submissive 721 *submitting*; subservient, slavish 879 *servile*.

subject, satellite; tributary; liege, vassal, feudal 739 *obedient*; subordinate, of lower rank, junior, cadet 35 *inferior*; dependent, in chancery; tied to one's apron strings; subject to, liable to, exposed to 180 *liable*; a slave to 610 *accustomed to*; in the hands of, in the clutches of, under the control of, in the power of, at the mercy of, under the sway of, under one's thumb; not able to call one's soul one's own; puppet-like, like a puppet on a string; having no say in; parasitical, hanging on 879 *servile*; in the pay of; mortgaged 917 *obliged*.

Vb. *be subject*, pay tribute 739 *obey*; obey the whip; depend on 35 *be inferior*; be a doormat, let oneself be trampled on, let oneself be kicked around, be the stooge of; serve, be a slave; lose one's independence 721 *submit*; sacrifice one's freedom, have no will of one's own, be unable to stand on one's own two feet, be a cat's-paw, be a tool 628 *be instrumental*.

subjugate, subdue 727 *overcome*; colonize, annex; take captive, drag at one's chariot wheels 727 *triumph*; take, capture, lead captive, sell into slavery; fetter, bind, hold in bondage 747 *imprison*; disfranchise; trample on, tread on, treat like dirt, treat like scum 735 *oppress*; keep under, hold down, repress, sit on, stamp out 165 *suppress*; enthral, captivate 821 *impress*; enchant 983 *bewitch*; dominate, lead by the nose 178 *influence*; tame, quell 369 *break in*; have eating out of one's hand, bring to heel, bring one to his *or* her knees, have at one's beck and call; make one's plaything, make a stooge of, do what one likes with 673 *dispose of*.

746 Liberation

N. *liberation*, setting free, release, discharge 960 *acquittal*; abreaction, catharsis 818 *feeling*; unravelling, disentanglement, extrication, disinvolvement 46 *separation*; riddance, good riddance 831 *relief*; rescue, redemption, salvation 668 *rescue*; emancipation, enfranchisement; parole, bail, police bail; liberalization, relaxation (of control); derationing, deregulation, derestriction 752 *annulment*; demobilization 75 *dispersion*; absolution 909 *forgiveness*; acquittance.

Vb. *liberate*, rescue, save 668 *rescue*; pardon 909 *forgive*; discharge, absolve, let off the hook 960 *acquit*; make free, emancipate; enfranchise, give the vote; grant equal rights; introduce positive discrimination, adopt a policy of affirmative action, release, free, set free, set at liberty, let out; bail, parole 766 *give terms*; unfetter, unshackle, unchain; unlock 263 *open*; loosen, unloose, loose, unbind, untie, disentangle, extricate, disengage, clear; unstop, unplug, uncork; unleash, let off the lead; let loose, turn adrift; give play to, give free rein 744 *give scope*; give vent to 300 *empty*; leave hold, let go 779 *not retain*; relax 734 *be lax*; lift 831 *relieve*; decontrol, deregulate, deration 752 *annul*; demobilize, disband 75 *disperse*; unyoke, unharness, unload 701 *disencumber*.

achieve liberty, gain one's freedom; free oneself, shake oneself free; stand on one's own two feet; break loose, burst one's bonds, throw off the yoke, cast off one's shackles, throw off one's ball and chain, slip the collar, kick over the traces, get away 667 *escape*.

747 Restraint

N. restraint, self-restraint, self-control 942 *temperance*; reserve, shyness, inhibitions; suppression, repression, coercion, constraint, straitjacket 740 *compulsion*; cramp, check, obstacle, stumbling-block 702 *hindrance*; curb, drag; brake, disc brake, anti-lock braking system, ABS; lamp, bridle 748 *fetter*; arrest, retardation, deceleration 278 *slowness*; prevention, veto, ban, bar, embargo 757 *prohibition*; legal restraint, Official Secrets Act, D-notice 953 *law*; control, discipline 733 *authority*; censorship 550 *obliteration*; press laws 735 *severity*.

restriction, limitation, ceiling, glass ceiling 236 *limit*, 481 *prejudice*; keeping within limits 232 *encircling*; rut, rat-trap; speed limit, restricted area; exclusion order, no-go area, exclusion zone; curfew; constriction, squeeze 198 *compression*; duress, pressure 740 *compulsion*; control, rationing; restrictive practice, exclusive rights, exclusivity 57 *exclusion*; monopoly, price ring, cartel, closed shop; charmed circle; protectionism, intervention, interventionism, tariff wall; retrenchment, cuts 814 *economy*; economic pressure, freeze, price freeze, price control, credit squeeze; rate-capping; blockade.

detention, custody, protective custody 660 *protection*; arrest, house arrest, curfew; custodianship, keeping, guarding, keep care, charge, ward; quarantine, internment; remand; captivity, duress; bondage, slavery 745 *servitude*; entombment, burial 364 *interment*; immurement, confinement, solitary confinement, incarceration, imprisonment; sentence, time, a stretch, bird, lag, porridge; penology, penologist.

Adj. restraining, checking, etc. (see vb.); restrictive, conditional; limiting, custodial;

cramping, hidebound; unbending, unyielding, strict 735 *severe*; stiff 326 *rigid*; tight 206 *narrow*; confining, close 198 *compressive*; confined, poky; coercive; repressive, inhibiting; monopolistic, protectionist, mercantilist.

restrained, self-controlled 942 *temperate*; pent up, bottled up; reserved, shy; disciplined, controlled, under control 739 *obedient*; kept on a leash, under the thumb; pinned down, kept under 745 *subjected*; on parole 917 *obliged*; protected, rationed; limited, restricted; cramped, hampered, trammelled, shackled 702 *hindered*; tied, bound, gagged; held up, weatherbound, fogbound, snowbound, housebound, bedridden, confined to bed.

imprisoned, confined, detained, kept in; landlocked; entombed, confined; quarantined, in quarantine; interned, in internment; under detention, under house arrest, incommunicado; under arrest, in custody; on remand; behind bars, incarcerated, locked up 750 *captive*; inside, in jug, in clink, in quod, in the slammer, in stir, in the cooler, in a cell; gated, confined to barracks; corralled, penned up, impounded; in irons, fettered, shackled; pilloried, in the stocks; serving a sentence, doing time, doing bird, doing porridge; caged, in captivity, trapped.

Vb. restrain, hold back; arrest, check, curb, rein in, brake, put a brake on, put clamps on, act as a brake 278 *retard*; cramp, clog, hamper 702 *hinder*; bind, tie hand and foot 45 *tie*; call a halt, stop, put a stop to 145 *halt*; inhibit, veto, ban, bar, embargo 757 *prohibit*; bridle, discipline, control 735 *be severe*; subdue 745 *subjugate*; restrain oneself, keep one's cool, keep one's hair *or* shirt on 823 *keep calm*; grip, hold, pin, keep a tight hold *or* rein on, hold in check 778 *retain*; hold in, keep in, fight back, bottle up, choke back; restrict, tighten, hem in, limit, keep within bounds, cordon off, declare a no-go area, draw the line 232 *encircle*; damp down, pour water on 177 *moderate*; hold down, clamp down on, crack down on, keep under, sit on, jump on, repress 165 *suppress*; muzzle, gag, silence 578 *make mute*; censor, black out 550 *obliterate*; debar from, rope off, keep out 57 *exclude*; withhold, keep back, stint; ration, be sparing, cut back, retrench 814 *economize*; resist 704 *oppose*; police, patrol, keep order.

arrest, make an arrest, apprehend, lay by the heels, catch, cop, nab, collar, pinch, nick, pick up; haul in, run in; fetter, handcuff, put the handcuffs on; take, make a prisoner, take prisoner, capture, lead captive; kidnap, seize, snatch, take hostage; put under arrest, run in, take into custody, clap in jail, hold.

fetter, manacle, bind, pinion, tie up, handcuff, put in irons; pillory, put in the stocks, tether 45 *tie*; shackle, trammel, hobble; chain up, put a ball and chain on.

imprison, confine, immure, quarantine, intern; hold, detain, keep in, gate; keep in detention, keep under arrest, hold incommunicado; cloister 883 *seclude*; entomb, bury 364 *inter*; wall up, seal up; coop up, cage, impound, corral, pen up, box up, shut up, shut in, trap 235 *enclose*; put in a straitjacket; incarcerate, throw into prison, send to prison, commit to prison, remand, run in; lock up; turn the key on, keep under lock and key, keep behind bars, clap in irons; keep prisoner, keep in captivity, keep in custody; hold hostage.

748 Prison

N. *prison*, prison-house, jail-house, jail, gaol, house of correction; quod, clink, jug, can, stir, slammer, cooler; glasshouse, brig; open prison, prison without bars, halfway house; penitentiary, reformatory, Borstal; boot camp; approved school, List D school, remand home, community home; assessment centre, detention centre; sin bin; dungeon, oubliette; Bastille, Tower; debtor's prison; Newgate, Wormwood Scrubs, Barlinnie, Holloway, Sing Sing, Alcatraz, Château d'If; Black Hole of Calcutta; criminal lunatic asylum, Broadmoor, Carstairs.

lockup, choky, calaboose, nick, police station; guardroom, guardhouse; cooler, slammer; peter, cell, prison cell, condemned cell, Death Row; dungeon, oubliette, torture room; prison van, Black Maria; dock, bar; pound, pen, cage, coop, kennel 235 *enclosure*; reserve; stocks, pillory.

prison camp, detention camp, internment camp, Stalag, Colditz; concentration camp, extermination camp, Belsen, Auschwitz, Buchenwald, Dachau, Treblinka; labour camp, Gulag; penal settlement *or* colony, Botany Bay, Devil's Island.

fetter, shackle, trammel, bond, chain, ball and chain, irons, hobble; manacle, pinion, handcuff; straitjacket; muzzle, gag, bit, bridle, halter; rein, bearing rein, check-rein, leading rein, reins, traces; yoke, collar, harness; curb, brake, clamp 702 *hindrance*; lead, tether, rope, leading string, apron strings.

749 Keeper

N. *keeper*, custodian, curator; archivist, record keeper 549 *recorder*; officer in charge; caretaker, house-minder, janitor, concierge, housekeeper; chatelaine, warden; ranger, gamekeeper; guard,

escort; garrison 713 *defender*; watchdog, sentry, sentinel, lookout, watchman, night watchman, security man *or* woman, security officer, watch, house-minder, house-sitter, vigilante, coastguard, lighthouse keeper 660 *protector*; invigilator, tutor, chaperon, duenna, governess, nurse, foster nurse, wet nurse, nanny, nursemaid, baby-sitter, baby-minder 742 *domestic*; foster parent, adoptive parent, guardian, legal guardian; appropriate person; probation officer 901 *philanthropist*.

gaoler, jailer, turnkey, warder, wardress, prison guard, prison officer, screw; prison governor.

750 Prisoner

N. *prisoner*, captive, prisoner of war, POW, battlefield detainee, unlawful combatant; ticket-of-leave man; political prisoner, prisoner of conscience; detainee; prisoner at the bar, defendant, accused 928 *accused person*; persistent offender, old lag, jailbird 904 *offender*; guest of Her Majesty; condemned prisoner, convict; lifer; galley slave 742 *slave*; hostage, kidnap victim 767 *security*.

Adj. *captive*, imprisoned, in chains, in irons, behind bars, under lock and key; jailed, in jail, in prison, inside 747 *imprisoned*; in custody, under arrest, remanded; under detention, detained at Her Majesty's pleasure; held hostage.

751 Commission: vicarious authority

N. *commission*, vicarious authority (see also *mandate* below); committal, delegation; devolution, decentralization; deputation, legation, mission, embassy 754 *envoy*; regency 733 *authority*; representation, proxy; card vote; agency, factorage, trusteeship, executorship 689 *management*; clerkship.

mandate, trust, charge 737 *command*; commission, roving commission, assignment, appointment, office, task, errand, mission; enterprise 672 *undertaking*; nomination, return, election 605 *vote*; posting, translation, transfer 272 *transference*; investment, induction, inauguration, ordination, coronation; power of attorney, written authority, charter, writ 737 *warrant*; diploma 756 *permit*; terms of reference 766 *conditions*; responsibility, care, cure (of souls); ward, charge.

Vb. *commission*, empower, authorize, charge, sanction, charter, license 756 *permit*; post, appoint, detail, assign, nominate; engage, hire, staff 622 *employ*; subcontract, contractorize, outsource; invest, induct, install, ordain; crown, anoint; commit, turn over to, leave it to; consign, entrust, trust with, grant powers of attorney; delegate, depute, send on a mission, send on an errand, send out, return, elect, give a mandate 605 *vote*.

752 Annulment

N. *annulment*, abrogation, invalidation; nullification; cancellation, suppression; repeal, revocation, rescinding; abolition, dissolution; repudiation 533 *negation*; recantation; suspension, discontinuance, disuse, undoing 148 *reversion*; counterorder.

deposing, deposal, deposition, dethronement; demotion, degradation; disestablishment, discharge, congé, dismissal, sack, redundancy, decruitment, downsizing, outplacement, removal, garden leave *or* gardening leave 300 *ejection*; unfrocking 963 *punishment*; ousting, deprivation, divestment 786 *expropriation*.

Vb. *annul*, abrogate, cancel; scrub, wipe out 550 *obliterate*; invalidate, abolish, dissolve, nullify, void, make null and void, declare null and void; quash, set aside, reverse, overrule; repeal, revoke, recall; rescind, tear up; undo 148 *revert*; countermand, counterorder; disclaim, disown, deny 533 *negate*; repudiate, retract 603 *recant*; ignore 458 *disregard*; call off, call a halt 747 *restrain*; suspend, discontinue, write off, unsubscribe 674 *stop using*.

depose, dethrone; unseat; divest 786 *deprive*; unfrock; disbar, strike off the register, strike off 57 *exclude*; disestablish; suspend 300 *dismiss*; ease out, edge out, elbow out, oust 300 *eject*; demote, degrade, reduce to the ranks, take down a peg or two, kick upstairs; remove 272 *transfer*.

753 Resignation

N. *resignation*, retirement, retiral; leaving, withdrawal 296 *departure*; pension, compensation, golden handshake 962 *reward*; waiver, surrender, abandonment, abdication, renunciation 621 *relinquishment*; abjuration, disclaimer 533 *negation*; state of retirement 681 *leisure*.

Vb. *resign*, tender one's resignation, hand in one's notice, give notice; hand over, vacate office; apply for the Chiltern Hundreds; stand down, stand aside, make way for; sign off, declare (cricket); scratch, withdraw, back out, give a walkover, retire from the contest, throw in one's hand, surrender, give up 721 *submit*; quit, throw up, chuck it; ask for one's cards; sign away, give away 780 *assign*; abdicate, abandon, renounce 621 *relinquish*; retire, go into retirement, take early retirement, accept redundancy, be superannuated, be put out to grass; be pensioned off.

754 Nominee

N. *nominee*, consignee, licensee; trustee, executor 686 *agent*; factor, agent, one's man of business, bailiff, steward 690 *manager*; caretaker, curator 749 *keeper*; representative; legal representative, attorney, counsel, advocate 958 *law agent*; proxy, surrogate 755 *deputy*; negotiator, middleman, broker, stockbroker 231 *intermediary*; committee, steering committee, panel, quango 692 *council*; counsellor, team of experts, think tank, brains trust, working party 691 *adviser*; underwriter, insurer; purser, bursar 798 *treasurer*; rent collector, tax collector, revenue collector, income-tax officer; officebearer, secretary of state 741 *officer*; functionary 690 *official*.

delegate, shop steward; representative, nominee (see also *nominee* above); correspondent, special correspondent 588 *correspondent*; emissary, special messenger 529 *messenger*; delegation, mission.

envoy, emissary, legate, papal nuncio, representative, ambassador, ambassadress, High Commissioner, chargé d'affaires; ambassador at large; diplomatic corps; minister, diplomat; consul, vice-consul; attaché; embassy, legation, mission, consulate, High Commission; diplomatist, negotiator.

755 Deputy

N. *deputy*, surrogate, alternate, proxy; scapegoat, substitute, locum tenens, locum, understudy, stand-in, temp 150 *substitution*; viceroy, vice-president, vice-chairman, vice-chancellor, vice-admiral, vice-captain, vice-consul; vicar; second-in-command, number two 741 *officer*; right-hand man, lieutenant, secretary 703 *helper*; alter ego, power behind the throne, éminence grise 612 *motivator*; caretaker government; heir, heir apparent 776 *beneficiary*; spokesperson, spokesman or -woman, mouthpiece, herald 529 *messenger*; second, advocate, champion 707 *patron*; agent, factor, attorney 754 *nominee*.

Vb. *deputize*, act for 622 *function*; act on behalf of, represent, hold a proxy for, appear for, speak for, answer for, hold a brief for; hold in trust, be executor 689 *manage*; negotiate, act as go-between for, be broker for, replace, stand in for, understudy, do duty for 150 *substitute*; act as scapegoat.

SECTION TWO

Special social volition

756 Permission

N. *permission*, liberty 744 *freedom*; leave, sanction, clearance; grant; licence, authorization, warrant; allowance, sufferance, tolerance, indulgence 736 *leniency*; acquiescence 758 *consent*; blessing, approval 923 *approbation*; grace and favour 897 *benevolence*; concession, dispensation, exemption 919 *non-liability*; release 746 *liberation*.

permit, written permission; authority, law 737 *warrant*; commission 751 *mandate*; charter, pass, password; passport, pet passport, animal passport, passbook, visa, safe-conduct; ticket, chit; licence, driving licence; free hand, carte blanche, blank cheque 744 *scope*; leave, compassionate leave, sick leave, leave of absence, furlough, holiday, vacation, sabbatical; parole; clearance, all clear, green light, go-ahead; imprimatur.

Adj. *permitting*, permissive, indulgent, complaisant, laissez-faire, easy-going.

Vb. *permit*, let 469 *make possible*; give permission, grant leave, accord, vouchsafe 781 *give*; nod, say yes 758 *consent*; give one's blessing; sanction 923 *approve*; entitle, authorize, warrant, charter, patent, license, enable; ratify, legalize, decriminalize 953 *make legal*; decontrol; lift a ban, raise an embargo, dispense, release 919 *exempt*; clear, give clearance 746 *liberate*; give the go-ahead, give the all clear, give the green light, green-light, tip the wink, let off the hook; recognize, concede, allow 488 *assent*; give one a chance, let one try; leave the way open, open the door to 263 *open*; suffer, tolerate, put up with, brook 736 *be lenient*; connive at, close *or* shut one's eyes to, turn a blind eye, wink at 734 *be lax*; laissez-faire, laissez-aller, allow a free hand, give carte blanche, issue a blank cheque 744 *give scope*; permit oneself, allow oneself, take the liberty.

ask leave, beg leave, ask if one may, ask one's blessing; ask to be excused; petition 761 *request*.

757 Prohibition

N. *prohibition*, inhibition, injunction; counterorder; intervention, interference; interdict, veto, ban, embargo, restriction, curfew 747 *restraint*; proscription, taboo; rejection, red light, thumbs down 760 *refusal*; intolerance 924 *disapprobation*; licensing laws 942 *temperance*; censorship, press laws, repression, suppression 735 *severity*; abolition, cancellation, suspension 752 *annulment*; blackout 550 *obliteration*; forbidden fruit.

Adj. *prohibited*, forbidden, verboten; barred, banned, under ban; censored, blue-pencilled, blacked-out; contraband, illicit, unlawful, outlawed, against the law 954 *illegal*; taboo; frowned on, not done; unmentionable, unprintable; out of bounds; blackballed, ostracized.

Vb. *prohibit*, forbid; disallow, veto, withhold permission, refuse leave, give the thumbs down, give the red light, forbid the banns 760 *refuse*; withdraw permission, cancel leave; countermand, counterorder, revoke, suspend 752 *annul*; prevent 702 *hinder*; restrict, stop 747 *restrain*; ban, taboo, proscribe, outlaw; black; impose a ban, place out of bounds; bar, debar, warn off, shut the door on, blackball, ostracize 57 *exclude*; excommunicate 300 *eject*; repress, stifle, kill 165 *suppress*; censor, blue-pencil 550 *obliterate*; put one's foot down 735 *be severe*; frown on, not countenance, not brook 924 *disapprove*; discourage, crack down on 613 *dissuade*; cramp 232 *encircle*; draw the line; intervene, interfere.

758 Consent

N. *consent*, willingness; agreement 488 *assent*; compliance 768 *observance*; accord; acquiescence, acceptance 756 *permission*; sanction, endorsement, ratification, confirmation.

Vb. *consent*, say yes, nod; give consent, give the go-ahead, give the green light, set one's seal on, ratify, confirm 488 *endorse*; sanction, pass 756 *permit*; give one's approval 923 *approve*; tolerate, recognize, allow, connive 736 *be lenient*; agree, fall in with, go along with, accede 488 *assent*; have no objection 488 *acquiesce*; be persuaded, come round; yield, give way 721 *submit*; comply; grant, concede 781 *give*; go halfway to meet 597 *be willing*; do all one is asked 828 *content*; accept, take up an offer, jump at; clinch a deal, seal a bargain 766 *make terms*.

759 Offer

N. *offer*, fair offer, proffer; bribe 612 *inducement*; tender, bid, takeover bid, green mail, buy-out, merger, proposal; motion, proposition, proposal; approach, overture, advance, invitation; feeler; final offer; present, presentation, offering, sacrifice 781 *gift*; dedication.

Vb. *offer*, proffer, hold out, make an offer, bid, tender; set out one's stall; present, lay at one's feet 781 *give*; dedicate, consecrate; sacrifice to; introduce, broach, move, propose, make a proposition, put forward, suggest 512 *propound*; make overtures, leave the door open, keep one's offer open; bribe; invite, send an invitation, ask one in 882 *be hospitable*; hawk, invite tenders, put up for sale 793 *sell*; auction; make a present of 469 *make possible*.

offer oneself, stand, be a candidate, compete, run for, be in the running for, enter 716 *contend*; volunteer, come forward 597 *be willing*; apply, put in for 761 *request*.

760 Refusal

N. refusal, non-acceptance, declining, turning down, thumbs down, red light 607 *rejection*; denial, no, nay 533 *negation*; disclaimer, flat refusal 711 *defiance*; repulse, rebuff, slap in the face 292 *repulsion*; withholding 778 *retention*; recalcitrance 738 *disobedience*; non-compliance 769 *non-observance*; recusancy 598 *unwillingness*; objection, protest 762 *deprecation*; renunciation, abnegation 621 *relinquishment*.

Vb. refuse, say no, shake one's head; excuse oneself, send one's apologies; disagree 489 *dissent*; deny, repudiate, disclaim 533 *negate*; decline, turn down, pass up, opt out; spurn 607 *reject*; repulse, rebuff 292 *repel*; turn away 300 *dismiss*; dig one's heels in, be unmoved, harden one's heart 602 *be obstinate*; not hear, not listen, turn a deaf ear 416 *be deaf*; close one's purse; turn one's back on; hang fire, hang back 598 *be unwilling*; beg off, back down; turn from, have nothing to do with, shy at, jib at 620 *avoid*; debar, keep out, shut the door 57 *exclude*; not allow 757 *prohibit*; set one's face against 715 *resist*; oppose 704 *withstand*; kick, protest 762 *deprecate*; not comply 769 *not observe*; grudge, begrudge, withhold, keep from 778 *retain*.

Int. *thanks but no thanks.*

761 Request

N. request, asking, first time of asking; canvassing, hawking 793 *sale*; requisition; final demand, last time of asking, ultimatum 737 *demand*; blackmail 900 *threat*; claim, counterclaim 915 *what is due*; consumer demand, seller's market 627 *requirement*; postulate 475 *premise*; proposition, proposal, motion; overture, approach 759 *offer*; bid, application; petition, round robin; prayer, appeal, plea; insistence 740 *compulsion*; cri de coeur; importunity; invitation, temptation; soliciting, accosting, mendicancy, begging, aggressive begging, busking, bumming; begging letter, flag day, bazaar, charity performance, benefit match.

entreaty, imploring, begging, beseeching; submission, clasped hands, bended knees; supplication, prayer 981 *prayers*; appeal 583 *address*; solemn entreaty, imprecation.

Adj. supplicatory, entreating, suppliant, on bended knees, with folded hands, cap in hand; imploring, beseeching.

Vb. request, ask, invite, solicit; make overtures, approach, accost 759 *offer*; woo, pop the question 889 *court*; seek, look for 459 *search*; fish for, angle for; need, call for, clamour for 627 *require*; crave, make a request, ask *or* beg a favour, have a request to make, make bold to ask, trouble one for 859 *desire*; apply, make application, put in for, bid, bid for, make a bid for; apply to, call on, appeal to, run to, address oneself to, go cap in hand to; tout, hawk, doorstep, canvass, solicit orders 793 *sell*; petition, press a suit, press a claim, expect 915 *claim*; make demands 737 *demand*; blackmail, put the bite on 900 *threaten*; coax, wheedle, cajole; importune, dun; touch 785 *borrow*; requisition 786 *take*; send an ultimatum 766 *give terms*.

beg, cadge, crave, sponge, freeload; bum, scrounge, mooch; thumb a lift, hitchhike; hold out one's hand, go from door to door, doorstep, knock at doors; appeal for funds, pass *or* send the hat round, launch an appeal 786 *levy*.

entreat, supplicate, be a suppliant; pray, implore, beseech, appeal, invoke, appeal to, call on 583 *speak to*; address one's prayers to, pray to 981 *offer worship*; kneel to, go down on one's knees, go down on bended knee, fall at one's feet.

762 Deprecation: negative request

N. deprecation, dissuasion; plea for mercy; intercession, mediation 981 *prayers*; counterclaim 761 *request*; murmur, complaint 829 *discontent*; exception, demur, expostulation, remonstrance, protest 704 *opposition*; reaction, backlash 182 *counteraction*; tut-tut, raised eyebrows, groans, jeers, sniffs of disapproval 924 *disapprobation*; petition, open letter, round robin; demonstration, march, protest march, hunger march, hunger strike, industrial action, sit-in, protest meeting, indignation meeting; non-compliance 760 *refusal*.

Vb. deprecate, ask one not to, advise against, have a better idea, make a counterproposal 613 *dissuade*; touch wood, knock on wood, cross one's fingers, keep one's fingers crossed; beg off, intercede 720 *mediate*; pray, appeal 761 *entreat*; cry for mercy 905 *ask for mercy*; tut-tut, shake one's head, raise one's eyebrows, sniff 924 *disapprove*; remonstrate, expostulate 924 *reprove*; jeer, groan, stamp 926 *detract*; murmur, beef, complain 829 *be discontented*; object, take exception to; demur, jib, kick, squeak, protest against, appeal against, petition against, lobby against, campaign against, raise one's voice against, cry out against 704 *oppose*; demonstrate, organize a protest march, hold a protest meeting, go on hunger strike; strike, take industrial action, come out, walk out 145 *cease*.

763 Petitioner

N. petitioner, suppliant, supplicant; appealer, appellant; claimant, pretender; postulant, aspirant; solicitor, asker, seeker, enquirer, advertiser; customer, bidder, tenderer; suitor, courter, wooer; canvasser, hawker, tout, barker; dunner; pressure group, ginger group, lobby, lobbyist; applicant, candidate, entrant; competitor 716 *contender*.

beggar, busker, mendicant; tramp, bum 268 *wanderer*; cadger, borrower, moocher, scrounger, hitch-hiker; sponger, freeloader, ligger, parasite 879 *toady*.

SECTION THREE

Conditional social volition

764 Promise

N. *promise*, offer; undertaking, commitment; affiance, betrothal, engagement 894 *marriage*; troth, plight, word, word of honour, vow, marriage vow 532 *oath*; declaration 532 *affirmation*; declared intention 617 *intention*; profession, fair words; assurance, pledge, warranty, guarantee, insurance 767 *security*; bargain, gentlemen's agreement, unwritten agreement, mutual agreement 765 *pact*; covenant, bond, promise to pay 803 *debt*; debt of honour 917 *duty*.

promised, covenanted, guaranteed, secured; bespoke, reserved; betrothed, affianced; committed, bound 917 *obliged*.

Vb. *promise*, say one will 532 *affirm*; hold out, proffer 759 *offer*; make a promise, give one's word, pledge one's word; vow, take one's oath on it 532 *swear*; vouch for, go bail for, warrant, guarantee, assure, insure, underwrite 767 *give security*; pledge, stake; pledge one's honour, stake one's credit; engage, enter into an engagement 672 *undertake*; make a gentleman's agreement, strike a bargain, sign on the dotted line, shake on it, commit oneself, bind oneself, be bound, covenant 765 *contract*; take on oneself, accept responsibility 917 *incur a duty*; accept a liability, promise to pay, incur a debt of honour 785 *borrow*; plight one's troth, exchange vows 894 *wed*.

take a pledge, demand security 473 *make certain*; put on oath, swear, make one swear 466 *testify*; exact a promise; take one's word 485 *believe*; rely on, expect 473 *be certain*.

Adv. *as promised*, according to contract, as agreed, duly.

765 Pact

N. *pact*, agreement, bargain, compact, concordat, mutual undertaking 672 *undertaking*; gentleman's agreement, unwritten agreement; debt of honour 764 *promise*; contract;

exchange of vows; engagement, betrothal 894 *marriage*; covenant, bond 767 *security*; league, alliance, cartel 706 *cooperation*; understanding, private understanding, something between them 24 *agreement*; conspiracy 623 *plot*; negotiation 766 *conditions*; deal 770 *compromise*; arrangement, settlement; seal, signature, countersignature; deed of agreement, indenture 767 *title deed*; Magna Carta.

treaty, international agreement; Treaty of Rome, Warsaw Pact; peace treaty, non-aggression pact 719 *pacification*; convention, concordat; Geneva Convention.

signatory, signer, countersigner, subscriber, the undersigned; swearer, attestor 466 *witness*; endorser, ratifier; adherent, consenting party 488 *assenter*; covenanter, contractor, contracting party; treaty-maker, negotiator 720 *mediator*.

Adj. *contractual*, bilateral, multilateral; agreed to, negotiated, signed, countersigned, sworn, ratified; covenanted, signed, signed on the dotted line, signed, sealed and delivered.

Vb. *contract*, enter into a contract, engage 672 *undertake*; promise; covenant, strike a bargain, sign a pact, shake hands on, do a deal, clinch a deal; ally 706 *cooperate*; treat, negotiate 791 *bargain*; agree, come to terms 766 *make terms*; conclude, close, settle; indent, execute, sign, sign on the dotted line, subscribe, ratify, attest, confirm 488 *endorse*; insure, underwrite 767 *give security*.

766 Conditions

N. *conditions*, terms, formula, terms for agreement; part of the bargain, set of terms; basis for negotiation, frame of reference, articles of agreement; provision, clause, escape clause, let-out clause, proviso, limitation, strings, reservation, exception, small print 468 *qualification*; stipulation, sine qua non, essential clause 627 *requirement*; ultimatum, time limit 900 *threat*; rule 693 *precept*; terms of reference 751 *mandate*; treaty-making, diplomacy, summitry, negotiation, bargaining, collective bargaining; hard bargaining, trade-off, horse-trading 791 *barter*.

Adj. *conditional*, with strings attached, stipulatory, qualificatory, provisory 468 *qualifying*; limiting, subject to terms, contingent, provisional.

Vb. *give terms*, propose conditions; attach strings; hold out for, insist on, make demands 737 *demand*; stipulate, make it a sine qua non 627 *require*; allow no exception 735 *be severe*; insert a proviso, leave a loophole 468 *qualify*; fix the terms, impose the conditions, write the articles, draft the clauses; add a let-out clause, write in; keep one's options open, hedge one's bets.

make terms, negotiate, be in treaty, parley, powwow, hold conversations 584 *confer*; deal with, treat with, negotiate with; make overtures, throw out a feeler 461 *be tentative*; haggle 791 *bargain*; make proposals 759 *offer*; compromise; negotiate a treaty, hammer out a formula, work something out, do a deal 765 *contract*; plea-bargain.

Adv. *on terms*, on one's own terms; conditionally, provisionally, subject to, with a reservation.

767 Security

N. *security*, guarantee, warranty, authorization, writ 737 *warrant*; word of honour 764 *promise*; sponsorship, patronage 660 *protection*; surety, bail, police bail, parole; gage, pledge, pawn, hostage; stake, deposit, earnest, handsel, token, instalment; colour of one's money, earnest money; down payment 804 *payment*; indemnity, insurance, underwriting 660 *safety*; transfer of security, mortgage 780 *transfer*; collateral.

title deed, deed, instrument; deed poll; indenture; charter, covenant, bond, bearer bond; receipt, IOU, voucher, counterfoil, certificate, authentication, marriage lines; verification, seal, stamp, signature, endorsement, acceptance 466 *credential*; banknote, treasury note, promissory note, note of hand, bill, treasury bill, bill of exchange; blue chip, gilt-edged security; portfolio, scrip, share, debenture; insurance policy; will, last will and testament, living will, codicil, certificate of probate; archives 548 *record*.

Vb. *give bail*, go bail, bail one out, go surety; take bail, release on bail; hold in pledge, keep in pawn 764 *take a pledge*.

give security, offer collateral, mortgage; pledge, pawn, pop, hock 785 *borrow*; guarantee, act as guarantor, stand surety for, warrant 473 *make certain*; authenticate, verify 466 *corroborate*; execute, endorse, seal, stamp, sign, sign on the dotted line, countersign, subscribe, give one's signature 488 *endorse*; vouch for 764 *promise*; secure, indemnify, insure, assure, underwrite 660 *safeguard*.

768 Observance

N. *observance*, practice; fulfilment 635 *sufficiency*; diligence, conscientiousness; adherence to, attention to; acknowledgment; performance, discharge 676 *action*; compliance 739 *obedience*; conformance 83 *conformity*; fidelity; dependability, reliability 929 *probity*.

Adj. *observant*, practising; heedful, watchful, careful of, attentive to 455 *attentive*; conscientious, diligent, religious, punctilious; meticulous; exact 494 *accurate*; responsible, reliable, dependable 929 *trustworthy*; loyal 739 *obedient*; adhering to, sticking to 83 *conformable*; faithful 929 *honourable*.

Vb. *observe*, heed, respect, regard, have regard to, pay respect to, acknowledge, pay attention to, attend to 455 *be attentive*; keep, practise, adhere to, stick to, cling to, follow, hold by, abide by, be loyal to 83 *conform*; comply 739 *obey*; fulfil, discharge, perform, execute, carry out, carry out to the letter 676 *do*; satisfy 635 *suffice*.

keep faith, be faithful or loyal to, discharge one's functions 917 *do one's duty*; honour one's obligations, meet one's obligations, be as good as one's word, make good one's promise, keep one's promise, fulfil one's engagement, come up to scratch, 'it does exactly or just what it says on the tin or box or packet'; be true to the spirit of, stand by; pay one's debt, pay up 804 *pay*; give one his due.

769 Non-observance

N. *non-observance*, informality, indifference 734 *laxity*; inattention, omission 458 *negligence*; non-adherence 84 *nonconformity*; non-performance; non-fulfilment, shortcoming 726 *non-completion*; infringement, violation; non-compliance, disloyalty 738 *disobedience*; protest 762 *deprecation*; disregard, discourtesy 921 *disrespect*; breach of faith, repudiation, denial 533 *negation*.

Adj. *non-observant*, non-practising, lapsed; nonconforming, blacklegging, non-adhering, nonconformist 84 *unconformable*; inattentive to, disregarding, neglectful 458 *negligent*; informal 734 *lax*; non-compliant 738 *disobedient*; infringing, unlawful 954 *law- breaking*; disloyal 918 *undutiful*; unfaithful 930 *perfidious*.

Vb. *not observe*, not practise; not conform, not adhere, stand out 84 *be unconformable*; discard 674 *stop using*; set aside 752 *annul*; omit, ignore 458 *neglect*; disregard, show no respect for, cock a snook, snap one's fingers at 921 *not respect*; stretch a point 734 *be lax*; violate, do violence to, drive a coach and horses through, ride roughshod over, trample underfoot 176 *force*; transgress 306 *overstep*; not comply with 738 *disobey*; desert 918 *fail in duty*; fail, not qualify, not come up to scratch 636 *be insufficient*; break one's word; renege on, go back on, back out, cancel; give the go-by, cut, shirk, dodge, parry, evade, elude 620 *avoid*.

770 Compromise

N. *compromise*, mutual concession, give and take, trade-off, adjustment; commutation; second best, half a loaf 35 *inferiority*; working arrangement 624 *way*; splitting the difference 30 *average*; halfway 625 *middle way*; balancing act, swings and roundabouts.

Vb. compromise, find a formula; make mutual concessions, strike a balance, find a happy medium, steer a middle course, give and take, meet one halfway; live and let live, stretch a point 734 *be lax*; take the mean, go half and half, go Dutch, split the difference 30 *average out*; commute 150 *substitute*; compose differences, go to arbitration; patch up 719 *pacify*; take the good with the bad, take what is offered, make a virtue of necessity, make the best of a bad job; sit on the fence.

SECTION FOUR

Possessive relations

771 Acquisition

N. acquisition, getting, winning; earning; acquirement, obtainment, procurement; collection 74 *assemblage*; realization, profit-taking 793 *sale*; encashment 780 *transfer*; fund-raising; exploitation, profiteering; money-grubbing 816 *avarice*; heap, stack, pile, mountain, pool, scoop, jackpot 74 *accumulation*; finding 484 *discovery*; recovery, retrieval, recoupment 656 *restoration*; redemption 792 *purchase*; appropriation; theft 788 *stealing*; inheritance, patrimony; find, windfall, treasure trove; something for nothing, free gift, freebie, giveaway 781 *gift*; legacy, bequest; gratuity, baksheesh 962 *reward*; benefit match, prize 729 *trophy*; gravy 615 *benefit*; easy money 701 *easiness*; lucre 797 *money*; plunder 790 *booty*.

earnings, income, earned income, wage, minimum wage, salary, screw, pay packet, take-home pay, productivity bonus, performance-related pay 804 *pay*; rate for the job, pay scale, differential; fee for service, honorarium; pension, superannuation, compensation, golden handshake; remuneration, emolument 962 *reward*; allowance, expense account; pickings, perquisite, perks, fringe benefits, extras; commission, rake-off 810 *discount*; return, receipts, proceeds, turnover, takings, revenue, taxes 807 *receipt*; harvest, crop, gleanings.

gain, savings 814 *economy*; credit side, profit, net profit, capital gain, winnings; dividend, share-out 775 *participation*; usury, interest, high interest, compound interest, simple interest 36 *increment*; profitable transaction; pay increase, rise, raise 36 *increase*; advantage, benefit.

Adj. acquiring, acquisitive, accumulative;

on the make, gold-digging, getting, winning 730 *prosperous*.

gainful, paying, money-making, money-spinning, lucrative, remunerative; advantageous 640 *profitable*; fruitful.

Vb. acquire, get, come by; earn, gain, obtain, procure, beg, borrow or steal; find, strike, come across, come by, pick up, light or *or* upon 484 *discover*; get hold of, get possession of, lay one's hands on, make one's own, annex 786 *appropriate*; win, secure, capture, catch, land, net, bag 786 *take*; pick, glean, fill one's pockets; gather, reap, crop, harvest; derive, draw, tap, milk, mine 304 *extract*; collect, accumulate, heap, pile up 74 *bring together*; scrape together, rake together; collect funds, launch an appeal, raise, levy, raise the wind; save, save up, hoard 632 *store*; buy, pre-empt 792 *purchase*; reserve, book, engage 135 *be early*; earn a living, turn an honest penny, keep the wolf from the door 622 *busy oneself*; make money, draw a salary, draw a pension, receive one's wages; have an income, be in receipt of, have a turnover, gross, take 782 *receive*; convert, cash, encash, realize, clear, make; get back, recover, salvage, recycle, regain, redeem, recapture, reconquer 656 *retrieve*; take back, resume, reclaim; recover one's losses 31 *recoup*; recover one's costs, break even, balance the books, practise creative accounting, balance accounts 28 *equalize*; attain, reach; come in for, catch, incur.

inherit, come into, be left, be willed, be bequeathed, fall heir to, come by, come in for, receive a legacy; succeed, succeed to, step into the shoes of, be the heir of.

gain, make a profit, earn a dividend; make; make money, coin money, coin it, line one's pockets 730 *prosper*; make a fortune, make a killing, make one's pile, rake in the shekels, rake it in, turn a pretty penny 800 *get rich*; make a scoop, win, win the jackpot, break the bank; sell at a profit.

be profitable, profit, repay, be worthwhile; pay, pay well; yield 164 *produce*; bring in a return, pay a dividend, show a profit 730 *prosper*.

772 Loss

N. loss, deprivation, privation, bereavement; dispossession, eviction 786 *expropriation*; sacrifice, forfeit, lapse 963 *penalty*; dead loss, irretrievable loss, perdition 165 *ruin*; depreciation 655 *deterioration*; diminishing returns; setback, check, reverse; loss of profit, loss leader; overdraft, bankruptcy 805 *insolvency*; consumption 806 *expenditure*; non-recovery, spilt milk, wastage, wear and tear, leakage 634 *waste*; dissipation, evaporation, drain 37 *decrease*; good riddance 746 *liberation*; losing battle 728 *defeat*.

Adj. *lost*, long lost, gone, gone for ever; gone by the board, out of sight, out of mind, consigned to oblivion 458 *neglected*; vanished, flown out of the window; missing, astray, adrift, mislaid; untraceable, lost, stolen or strayed 190 *absent*; lacking 307 *deficient*; irrecoverable, irretrievable, irredeemable, unsalvageable, non-returnable, non-recyclable; spent, gone down the drain, squandered; forfeited.

Vb. *lose*, be unable to find, look in vain for; mislay 188 *misplace*; miss, let slip through one's fingers, kiss *or* say goodbye to 138 *lose a chance*; meet one's Waterloo; squander, throw away 634 *waste*; deserve to lose, forfeit, sacrifice; spill; fritter away, throw good money after bad, sink 806 *expend*; be a loser, draw a blank, burn one's fingers 731 *have trouble*; lose one's bet, pay out; be out of pocket; be set back, incur losses, sell at a loss; be unable to pay, go broke, go bankrupt 805 *not pay*; be overdrawn, be in the red, be minus.

be lost, be missing, be declared missing 190 *be absent*; go down the drain, go down the spout, go up in smoke, go to pot 165 *be destroyed*.

773 Possession

N. *possession*, ownership, proprietorship, lawful possession, enjoyment; occupancy, nine points of the law, bird in the hand; mastery, hold, grasp, grip 778 *retention*; haves and have-nots 776 *possessor*; a possession 777 *property*; tenancy, holding 777 *estate*; tenure, feu, fief; monopoly, ring; preoccupancy, preemption, squatting; expectations, inheritance, heritage, patrimony, taking possession, appropriation, laying claim to.

Adj. *possessed*, held, etc. (see vb.); in the possession of, in one's hand, in one's grasp, in the bag; in the bank, to one's name; at one's disposal, on hand; one's own, exclusive; monopolized by, engrossed by, taken up by; booked, reserved, engaged, occupied; included in, attaching.

Vb. *possess*, be possessed of, be the proud possessor of, number among one's possessions, own, have; hold, have and hold, hold in one's grasp, grip 778 *retain*; have at one's command, have absolute disposal of; call one's own, boast of 915 *claim*; contain, include 78 *comprise*; fill, occupy; squat, settle upon, inhabit; enjoy, have for one's own 673 *use*; monopolize, have exclusive rights to, hog, corner the market; get, take possession, make one's own 786 *take*; preoccupy; reserve, engage 135 *be early*.

belong, be vested in, belong to; go with, be included in.

774 Non-ownership

N. *non-ownership*, non-possession, vacancy; tenancy, temporary lease; pauperism 801 *poverty*; deprivation 772 *loss*; no-man's-land, debatable territory 190 *emptiness*.

Adj. *not possessed*, unpossessed, unattached; masterless, ownerless, nobody's, no man's; common; unclaimed; disowned; up for grabs, anybody's; unoccupied, untenanted; vacant 190 *empty*; abandoned 779 *not retained*; untaken, free, going begging 860 *unwanted*.

775 Joint possession. Joint activity

N. *joint possession*, joint tenancy; joint ownership; common land, common; public property, public domain 777 *property*; condominium 733 *political organization*; joint stock, pool, kitty 632 *store*; cooperative system; nationalization, public ownership, state ownership, socialism, communism, collectivism; collective farm, collective, commune, kolkhoz, kibbutz 370 *farm*; time-sharing.

participation, membership, affiliation 78 *inclusion*; partnership, profit-sharing, timesharing 706 *association*; sharing facilities, hotdesking; Dutch treat, bottle party, byob, shareout; involvement, sympathy; fellow feeling, empathy, sympathetic strike, joint action.

participator, member, associate member, founder member; partner, joint heir; shareholder, stockholder 776 *possessor*; co-tenant, flat-mate, room-mate, housing association; cooperator; trade unionist; collectivist, socialist, communist; commune-dweller, communitarian, kolkhoznik, kibbutznik; sympathizer, contributor 707 *patron*.

participant, joiner, joiner-in; the usual suspects.

Vb. *participate*, have a hand in, have a say in, join in, pitch in, sit in, be in on, have a finger in the pie 706 *cooperate*; partake in, share in, come in for a share; share, go shares, go halves, go fifty-fifty, pull one's weight, share and share alike 783 *allocate*; share expenses, go Dutch 804 *pay for*; job-share.

776 Possessor

N. *possessor*, holder, taker, captor, hostagetaker;conqueror; squatter; monopolizer, dog in the manger; occupant, lodger, occupier, incumbent; mortgagee; renter, hirer, lessee, leaseholder, rent-payer; tenantry, tenant; house-owner, owner-occupier, householder, freeholder.

owner, monarch, monarch of all one surveys; master, mistress, proprietor, proprietress, proprietrix; purchaser, buyer 792 *purchaser;* lord, lord *or* lady of the manor, landed gentry, landed interest; squire, laird 868 *aristocracy;* man *or* woman of property, property-holder, shareholder, stockholder, landowner, landlord, landlady; mortgagor; testator, testatrix, bequeather 781 *giver.*

beneficiary, grantee; incumbent 986 *cleric;* legatee; inheritor, successor, successor apparent; next of kin 11 *kinsman;* son and heir, etc. 119 *previousness;* heir *or* heiress; heir apparent, heir presumptive; crown prince 741 *sovereign.*

777 Property

N. *property*, possession, possessions, one's all; stake; personal property, public property, common property, church property; chattel, immovables; movables, personal estate, goods and chattels, worldly goods, appurtenances, belongings, paraphernalia, accoutrements, effects, personal effects, impedimenta, baggage, bag and baggage, things, gear, what one stands up in; goods, stock 795 *merchandise;* plant, fixtures, furniture.

estate, estate and effects, assets, frozen assets, liquid assets, assets and liabilities; circumstances, what one is worth, resources 629 *means;* substance, capital, one's money, one's fortune 800 *wealth;* revenue, income 807 *receipt;* valuables, securities, stocks and shares, portfolio; stake, holding, investment; intellectual property; debts; title, interest; living 985 *benefice;* lease, tenure, freehold, copyhold, fee.

lands, land, acres, broad acres, acreage, tract, grounds; estate, property, landed property; real estate, realty; holding, tenure, freehold, copyhold, fief, manor; lordship, domain; plot 184 *territory;* farm, home farm, manor farm, homestead, plantation, ranch, hacienda; crown lands, common land, common 775 *joint possession;* dependency, dominion 733 *political organization.*

dowry, dower, marriage portion, jointure, marriage settlement; allowance, pin money; alimony, aliment, maintenance, palimony; patrimony, birthright 915 *what is due;* heritage; inheritance, legacy, bequest; heirloom; expectations, entail.

Adj. *proprietary,* branded, patented; landed, feudal, freehold, leasehold, copyhold; hereditary, heritable, entailed; endowed.

Vb. *endow,* endow with, bless with 781 *give;* bequeath; grant, allot 780 *assign;* put in possession, install 751 *commission;* found.

778 Retention

N. *retention,* prehensility, tenacity; stickiness 354 *glutinousness;* tenaciousness, retentiveness, holding on, hanging on, clinging to, handhold, foothold, toehold 218 *support;* beachhead 34 *advantage;* clutches, grip, vice-like grip, grasp, hold, firm hold, stranglehold, half-nelson; squeeze 198 *compression;* clinch, lock; hug, bear hug, embrace, clasp, cuddle 889 *endearment;* keeping in 747 *detention;* finders keepers 760 *refusal;* containment 235 *enclosure.*

pincers, nippers; tweezers, pliers, snub-nosed pliers, wrench, tongs, forceps, vice, clamp 47 *fastening;* talon, claw, nails 256 *sharp point;* tentacle, hook, tendril 378 *feeler;* teeth, fangs 256 *tooth;* paw, hand, fingers 378 *finger;* fist, clenched fist, duke.

Adj. *retentive,* tenacious, prehensile; vice-like, retaining 747 *restraining;* clinging, adhesive, sticky, gummy, gluey, gooey 48 *cohesive;* firm, unshakable 45 *tied;* tight, strangling.

Vb. *retain,* hold; grab, buttonhole, hold back 702 *obstruct;* hold up, catch, steady 218 *support;* hold on, hold fast, hold tight, keep a firm hold of, maintain one's hold, not let go; cling to, hang on to, freeze on to, stick to, adhere; fasten on, grip, grasp, grapple, clench, clinch, lock; hug, clasp, clutch, embrace; pin, pin down, hold down; have by the throat, throttle, strangle, keep a stranglehold on, get a half-nelson on, tighten one's grip 747 *restrain;* dig one's nails in, dig one's toes in, hang on like a bulldog, hang on with all one's might, hang on for dear life; keep in, detain 747 *imprison;* contain, keep within limits, draw the line 235 *enclose;* keep to oneself, keep in one's own hands, keep back, keep to one side, withhold 525 *keep secret;* not dispose of 632 *store;* save, keep 666 *preserve;* not part with, keep back, withhold 760 *refuse.*

779 Non-retention

N. *non-retention,* parting with, disposal, alienation 780 *transfer;* selling off 793 *sale;* letting go, leaving hold of, release 746 *liberation;* dispensation; dissolution (of a marriage) 896 *divorce;* abandonment, renunciation 621 *relinquishment;* cancellation 752 *annulment;* disuse 611 *disuse,* leak 298 *outflow;* incontinence.

derelict, jetsam, flotsam 641 *rubbish;* castoff; waif, stray, foundling, orphan, outcast, pariah; down-and-out, vagrant.

Adj. *not retained,* under notice to quit; alienated, disposed of, sold off; left behind 41 *remaining;* dispensed with, abandoned; released; fired, made redundant, given the sack *or* the chop, given the heave-ho; derelict, unclaimed; disowned, divorced, disinherited; for sale 793 *saleable.*

Vb. *not retain,* part with, alienate, transfer 780 *assign;* sell off, dispose of 793 *sell;* be open-handed 815 *be prodigal*; free, let go, let slip, unhand, leave hold of, relax one's grip, release one's hold; unlock, unclench 263 *open*; unbind, untie, disentangle 46 *disunite*; forgo, dispense with, do without, spare, give up, waive, abandon, cede, yield 621 *relinquish*; renounce, abjure 603 *recant*; cancel, revoke 752 *annul*; lift restrictions, derestrict, raise an embargo, decontrol, deregulate, deration 746 *liberate*; supersede, replace 150 *substitute*; wash one's hands of, turn one's back on, disown, disclaim 533 *negate*; dissolve (a marriage) 896 *divorce*; disinherit, cut off without a penny, cut off with a shilling 801 *impoverish*; marry off 894 *marry*; get rid of, cast off, ditch, jettison, throw overboard 300 *eject*; cast away, abandon, maroon; pension off, put out to grass, invalid out, retire; discharge, give notice to quit, declare redundant, give the heave-ho, ease out, edge out, elbow out, kick out 300 *dismiss*; lay off; drop, discard 674 *stop using*; withdraw, abandon one's position 753 *resign*; estrange; leak 300 *emit*.

780 Transfer (of property)

N. transfer, transmission, consignment, delivery, handover 272 *transference*; settlement; conveyancing; bequeathal; assignment; bequest 781 *gift*; lease, let, rental, hire; buying 793 *sale*; trade, trade-off 791 *barter*; conversion, exchange 151 *interchange*; nationalization, privatization, mutualization, demutualization, change of hands, changeover 150 *substitution*; devolution, delegation 751 *commission*; succession, inheritance; pawn.

Vb. assign, convey; transfer by will; grant, sign away, give away 781 *give*; let, rent, hire 784 *lease*; sell; negotiate, barter 791 *trade*; change over 150 *substitute*; exchange, convert 151 *interchange*; confer ownership, put in possession, invest with; devolve, delegate, entrust 751 *commission*; give away, marry off 894 *marry*; deliver, transmit, hand over, unload on, pass to, pass the buck 272 *transfer*; pawn 784 *lend*; transfer ownership, nationalize, privatize.

bequeath, will; grant, assign; leave, leave by will, make a bequest, leave a legacy; make a will, make one's last will and testament, put in one's will, add a codicil; leave a fortune.

change hands, be under new management; change places, be transferred, pass, shift; revert to, devolve upon; pass from hand to hand, circulate, go the rounds 314 *circle*.

781 Giving

N. giving, bestowal, donation; alms-giving, charity 901 *philanthropy*; liberality; contribution, subscription; prize-giving, presentation; award 962 *reward*; delivery, consignment, conveyance 780 *transfer*; endowment, settlement 777 *dowry*; grant, conferment; investment, investiture; bequeathal.

gift, souvenir, memento, keepsake, token; gift token, gift voucher; present, birthday present, Christmas present, stocking filler; good-luck present, handsel; Christmas box, whip-round, tip, fee, honorarium, baksheesh, gratuity, pourboire, trinkgeld 962 *reward*; token, consideration; bribe, sweetener, douceur, slush fund 612 *inducement*; prize, award, presentation 729 *trophy*; benefit, benefit match, benefit performance; alms, maundy money, dole, charity 901 *philanthropy*; food parcel, free meal; freebie, giveaway; bounty, manna from heaven; largesse, donation, hand-out; bonus; extras, perks, perquisites, expense account; grant, allowance, subsidy, aid 703 *subvention*; boon, grace, favour, service, labour of love 597 *voluntary work*; free gift, ex gratia payment; piece of luck, windfall 771 *acquisition*; conscience money 804 *payment*; tribute 809 *tax*; bequest, legacy 780 *transfer*.

offering, dedication, consecration; peace offering, offertory, collection, sacrifice 981 *religious offering*; Peter's pence; widow's mite; contribution, subscription, flag day, appeal; stake.

giver, donor, bestower; rewarder, tipper, briber; grantor; presenter, awarder, prize-giver; bequeather; subscriber, contributor; sacrificer 981 *worshipper*; almsgiver, blood donor, kidney donor, organ donor 903 *benefactor*; Lady Bountiful, fairy godmother, rich uncle, sugar daddy, Santa Claus, Father Christmas 813 *good giver*; backer, angel.

Adj. given, gratuitous, gratis, for nothing, free, freebie, giveaway 812 *free of charge*; concessional.

Vb. give, bestow, lend, render; afford, provide; vouchsafe, honour with; grant, accord 756 *permit*; gift, donate, make a present of; leave 780 *bequeath*; endow; present, award 962 *reward*; confer, bestow upon, invest with; dedicate, consecrate; offer; devote, offer up, sacrifice 981 *offer worship*; make time for; give a present, tip, remember, cross someone's palm with silver; grease the palm 612 *bribe*; bestow alms, give to charity 897 *do good*; give freely, open one's purse, put one's hand in one's pocket, lavish, pour out, shower upon 813 *be liberal*; spare, give away; stand, treat 882 *be hospitable*; give out, dispense, dole out, allot, deal out 783 *allocate*; contribute, subscribe, subsidize, help 703 *aid*; have a whip-round, pass round the hat, launch an appeal; pay one's share *or* whack, chip in 775 *participate*;

part with, fork out, shell out 804 _pay_; impart 524 _communicate_; pay tribute; yield 621 _relinquish_; hand over, give over, deliver 780 _assign_; commit, entrust 751 _commission_; dispatch 272 _send_.

782 Receiving

N. receiving, admittance 299 _reception_; getting 771 _acquisition_; acceptance; inheritance; collection; a receipt, windfall 781 _gift_; toll, tribute, dues, receipts, proceeds, winnings, takings 771 _earnings_; receiving end.

recipient, acceptor, receiver, taker; trustee 754 _nominee_; addressee 588 _correspondent_; buyer 792 _purchaser_; grantee, assignee, licensee, patentee, lessee; legatee, inheritor, heir, successor 776 _beneficiary_; payee, earner, wage-earner; pensioner, old-age pensioner, remittance man 742 _dependant_; winner, prize-winner, exhibitioner; one at the receiving end 825 _sufferer_.

receiver, official receiver, liquidator 798 _treasurer_, payee, collector, debt-collector, rent-collector, tax-collector, publican; income-tax officer, excise officer, customs officer; booking clerk.

Vb. receive, be given, have from; get 771 _acquire_; collect, take up; gross, net, clear, pocket, be in receipt of, get one's share; accept, take in 299 _admit_; accept from, draw, encash, be paid; have an income, draw a pension; inherit, come into, come in for, be left.

783 Allocation

N. allocation, apportionment, assignment, allotment, earmarking; division, sharing out, parcelling out, divvying up, doing out; shares, distribution, deal; job-sharing, job-splitting; stakeholder economy; dispensing, administration; demarcation, delimitation 236 _limit_; assigned place, seat 27 _degree_.

portion, share, share-out, split; dividend, interim dividend, final dividend, divvy, divi; allocation, allotment; lot; proportion, ratio; quota; halves 53 _part_; deal, hand (at cards); modicum, pittance, allowance; ration, iron rations; dose, dosage, measure, dollop, whack, helping, slice, slice of the cake, piece of the action 53 _piece_; rake-off, cut, commission 810 _discount_; stake, ante; task, stint 682 _labour_.

Vb. allocate, apportion, allot, earmark; appoint, assign; cast; assign a place, detail, billet; partition, zone; demarcate, delimit 236 _limit_; divide up, subdivide, carve up, split, cut; halve 92 _divide_; go shares 775 _participate_; share out, divvy up, distribute, spread around; dispense, administer, serve, deal out, dole out, parcel out, dish out 781 _give_; mete out, measure, ration.

Adv. pro rata, to each according to his share; proportionately, respectively, each to each; per capita.

784 Lending

N. lending, hiring, leasing, farming out; letting, subletting, renting out, lending at interest, on-lending, usury, giving credit 802 _credit_; investment; mortgage, bridging loan; advance, loan; pawnbroking; lease; let, sublet.

pawnshop, pawnbroker's, one's uncle's, pop-shop, hock shop; bank, credit company, building society, International Monetary Fund, IMF, World Bank.

lender, creditor; investor, financier, banker; moneylender, usurer, Shylock; pawnbroker, uncle; mortgagee, lessor, hirer, renter, letter; backer, angel; tallyman; hire-purchase dealer.

Vb. lend, loan, on-lend; advance, accommodate, give one a loan 802 _credit_; lend on security, lend on collateral; put up the money, back, finance; invest, risk one's money, play the stockmarket 791 _speculate_.

lease, let, hire out, rent out, farm out; sublet; outsource.

785 Borrowing

N. borrowing, touching; request for credit, mortgage 803 _debt_; credit account, credit card, plastic money, plastic; hire purchase, HP, tick, instalment plan, the never-never; pawning; loan, bank loan; forced loan, Morton's fork or crutch; infringement, plagiarism, piracy, copying, hot-plating 20 _imitation_; borrowed plumes 542 _deception_.

Vb. borrow, cadge from, scrounge from, bum from, mooch from, touch for 761 _request_; mortgage, pawn, pop, hock; provide collateral 767 _give security_; take a loan, exact a forced loan; use a credit card, use plastic money, use plastic, get credit, take on loan, take on credit, take on tick; buy in instalments, buy on hire purchase _or_ the never-never 792 _purchase_; ask for credit, apply for a loan, raise a loan, raise the wind; issue debentures; beg, borrow or steal 771 _acquire_; crib, plagiarize, pirate, infringe 20 _copy_.

hire, charter, lease, outsource, rent.

786 Taking

N. taking, snatching; seizure, capture, rape; taking hold, grasp, apprehension 778 _retention_; taking possession, appropriation, assumption 916 _unjustifed claim_; requisition, earmarking, commandeering, compulsory purchase 771 _acquisition_; exaction, taxation, levy 809 _tax_; cash back, withdrawal 39 _subtraction_; taking away, removal 188 _displacement_; stealing; cadging, scrounging, mooching, bumming, touching one for money, abduction, kidnapping, dognapping; hijacking, piracy; raid; hostage, take, haul, catch, bag, prize, plum 790 *booty*; receipts, takings, winnings, pickings, ill-gotten gains, gleanings 771 *earnings*.

expropriation, dispossession; attachment, foreclosure; eviction 300 *ejection*; takeover, deprivation; hiving off, asset-stripping; disinheritance 780 *transfer*; confiscation; extortion; swindle, rip-off; impounding, sequestration.

rapacity, rapaciousness, avidity, thirst 859 *hunger*; greed, insatiability 816 *avarice*; extortion, blackmail.

taker, appropriator, remover; seizer, snatcher, grabber; raider, pillager, marauder, ransacker, sacker, looter 789 *robber*; kidnapper, hijacker, abductor, press gang; captor, capturer, hostage-taker; usurper, extortioner, extortionist, blackmailer; devourer 168 *destroyer*; bloodsucker, leech, parasite, vampire, harpy, vulture, wolf, shark; beast *or* bird of prey, predator; confiscator, sequestrator 782 *receiver*; expropriator, asset-stripper.

Vb. *take*, accept, be given 782 *receive*; take over, take back, claw back (see also *appropriate* below); take in, let in 299 *admit*; take up; anticipate 135 *be early*; take hold, fasten on, stick to, clutch, grip, cling 778 *retain*; lay hands on, seize, snatch, grab, pounce on; snatch at, reach out for, make a long arm; grasp at, clutch at, grab at, make a grab, scramble for, rush for; capture, rape, storm, take by storm 727 *overcome*; conquer, captive 745 *subjugate*; catch, overtake, intercept 277 *outstrip*; apprehend, take into custody, make an arrest, run in, nab, nobble, collar, lay by the heels 747 *arrest*; make sure of, fasten, pinion 747 *fetter*; hook, trap, snare, lime 542 *ensnare*; net, land, bag, pocket; gross, have a turnover 771 *acquire*; gather, accumulate, amass, collect 74 *bring together*; cull, pick, pluck; reap, crop, harvest, glean 370 *cultivate*; scrounge, cadge, mooch, bum, ransack 459 *search*; pick up, snap up, snaffle; knock off, help oneself 788 *steal*; pick clean, strip 229 *uncover*; remove; deduct 39 *subtract*; draw off, milk, tap, mine 304 *extract*.

appropriate, take to *or* for oneself, make one's own, annex; pirate, plagiarize 20 *copy*; take possession, lay claim to, stake one's claim; take over, assume ownership, possess; enter into, come into, succeed 771 *inherit*; install oneself, seat oneself 187 *place oneself*; overrun, occupy, settle, colonize; win, conquer; recover 656 *retrieve*; reclaim 915 *claim*; earmark, commandeer, requisition 737 *demand*; usurp, trespass, squat 916 *be undue*; treat as one's own, make free with; mono-

polize, hog, engulf, swallow up 299 *absorb*; devour, eat up.

levy, raise, extort, exact, wrest from 304 *extract*; compel to lend 785 *borrow*; exact tribute, extort protection money, raise taxes 809 *tax*; fleece; wring, squeeze dry, squeeze till the pips squeak 735 *oppress*; sequestrate.

take away, remove, shift, unload, disburden 188 *displace*; hive off, relieve of 788 *steal*; escort 89 *accompany*; kidnap, shanghai, pressgang, abduct, take hostage, hijack, carry off; run away with, elope with 296 *walk out*.

deprive, bereave, orphan, widow; divest, denude, strip 229 *uncover*; unfrock 752 *depose*; dispossess, usurp 916 *disentitle*; oust, elbow out, evict, expel 300 *eject*; confiscate, sequester, foreclose; disinherit, cut out of one's will, cut off with a shilling.

fleece, pluck, skin, shear, clip; strip, denude 229 *uncover*; take to the cleaners, rip off; take one for a ride, swindle, bilk, welsh, con, cheat 542 *deceive*; blackmail, bleed, bleed white, sponge, suck dry; soak, sting; mulct 788 *defraud*; devour, eat out of house and home 301 *eat*; rook, bankrupt, leave one without a penny *or* cent 801 *impoverish*.

787 Restitution

N. *restitution*, giving back, return, reversion; bringing back, repatriation; reinstatement; rehabilitation 656 *restoration*; ransom, rescue 668 *rescue*; recuperation, recovery; compensation, repayment, recoupment; refund, reimbursement; indemnity, damages 963 *penalty*; amends, reparation 941 *atonement*.

Vb. *make restitution*, restitute 656 *restore*; return, give back 779 *not retain*; refund, repay, give one one's money back, recoup, reimburse; indemnify, compensate, make it up to; pay compensation, make reparation, make redress, make amends 941 *atone*; repatriate; redeem 668 *rescue*; reinstate, rehabilitate, restore one to favour; recover 656 *retrieve*.

788 Stealing

N. *stealing*, thieving, lifting, robbing, etc. (see vb.); theft, larceny, petty larceny; inside job; pilfering, snitching, swiping, nicking, filching, putting one's fingers in the till, pickpocketing, shoplifting, kleptomania; burglary, housebreaking, breaking and entering; safe-breaking, robbery, highway robbery, robbery with violence, stickup, holdup, bag-snatching, mugging, phone-jacking, jumping, smash and grab raid, ram raid; poaching, cattle-rustling; rape, gang-rape, etc. 951 *rape*; abduction, kidnapping, dognapping, hijack, skyjack, yachtjacking; body-snatching; cribbing, plagiarism, pirating 20 *imitation*; autocrime, autotheft, joyride, twoc (taken without consent), etc. 274 *car*, 785 *borrowing*; thievery, job, fiddle.

plundering, looting, pillage, sacking ravaging; banditry, outlawry, piracy buccaneering; raiding, foray 712 *attack*

swindling, embezzlement, misappropriation; blackmail, extortion, protection racket; daylight robbery, rip-off moonlighting, tax evasion, black economy, fraud, computer fraud, computer crime, white-coller crime, fiddle, swindle, cheating; confidence trick; identity theft, identity fraud, shoulder surfing; car clocking.

thievishness, thievery, light-fingeredness, sticky fingers, kleptomania; dishonesty, crookedness 930 *improbity*.

Adj. *thieving*, light-fingered, sticky-fingered; kleptomaniac; larcenous, predatory, raptorial; piratical, buccaneering, raiding, marauding; scrounging, foraging; fraudulent, on the fiddle 930 *dishonest*.

Vb. *steal*, lift, thieve, pilfer, shoplift, help oneself; be light-fingered, be sticky-fingered, pick pockets, have a finger in the till; pick locks, blow a safe; burgle, burglarize, housebreak; rob, relieve of; rifle, sack, clean out; swipe, nobble, nick, pinch, pocket, snaffle, snitch, trouser, knock off 786 *take*; forage, scrounge; rustle, make off with; abduct, kidnap, shanghai; purloin, filch; walk off with, spirit away; crib, copy, lift, plagiarize, pirate 20 *copy*; smuggle, bootleg, poach, hijack, skyjack.

defraud, embezzle, misappropriate, purloin, fiddle, cook the books, practise creative accounting, obtain money on false pretences; commit a computer crime; con, swindle, cheat, diddle, do out of, bilk, shaft 542 *deceive*; rook, gull, dupe; rip off 786 *fleece*.

rob, mug; hold up, stick up; maraud, raid; foray, forage, ransack, rifle; plunder, pillage, loot, sack, despoil, ravage; blackmail, demand money with menaces; extort protection money, screw, squeeze 735 *oppress*.

789 Thief

N. *thief*, den of thieves; crook, Artful Dodger; light fingers, sticky fingers; kleptomaniac, stealer, lifter, filcher, purloiner, pilferer, petty thief, larcenist; sneak thief, shoplifter; pickpocket, cutpurse, bag-snatcher; cattle thief, rustler; burglar, cat burglar, house-breaker, safe-breaker, safe-blower, picklock, poacher, bootlegger, smuggler, gun runner, abductor, kidnapper 786 *taker*; hijacker, skyjacker, yachtjacker; body-snatcher, resurrectionist; fence, plagiarist, pirate.

robber, forty thieves; brigand, bandit, outlaw, Robin Hood; footpad, highwayman, Dick

Turpin, mugger, phone-mugger, thug, gangster, racketeer; gunman; terrorist; pirate, buccaneer; raider, reaver *or* reiver, freebooter, plunderer, pillager, sacker, ravager; kleptocrat, kleptocracy.

defrauder, embezzler, fiddler, creative accountant, diddler, defaulter, welsher; fraudster, swindler, sharper, cheat, computer criminal, shark, con man, hustler 545 *trickster*; forger, counterfeiter.

790 Booty

N. *booty*, spoils; spoils of war, plunder, loot, pillage; find, strike, prize, haul, catch 771 *gain*; pickings, gleanings, stolen goods, swag; contraband; ill-gotten gains, graft, blackmail.

791 Barter

N. *barter*, exchange, fair exchange, swap 151 *interchange*; payment in kind, traffic, trading, dealing, trade-off, buying and selling; factorage, brokerage, agiotage, jobbing; insider trading *or* dealing; negotiation, bargaining, hard bargaining, haggling, horse-trading.

trade, trading, exporting 272 *transference*; visible trade, invisible trade; protection, trade restrictions, intervention, interventionism 747 *restriction*; free trade, open market, single market, economic zone, European Economic Community, EEC, European Community, EC, European Union, EU, European Free Trade Association, EFTA, Organization of Petroleum Exporting Countries, OPEC 796 *market*; traffic, drug traffic, slave traffic, white slave trade; smuggling, black market, gun-running, drug-trafficking; retail trade 793 *sale*; capitalism, free enterprise, laissez-faire 744 *scope*; boom and bust 317 *fluctuation*; commerce 622 *business*; private enterprise, Private Finance Initiative, PFI, Public Private Partnership, PPP, privatization, nationalization; private sector, public sector; business venture 672 *undertaking*; speculation, day-trading 618 *gambling*; transaction, commercial transaction, deal, business deal, bargain, trade-off, negotiation 765 *pact*.

Vb. *trade*, exchange 151 *interchange*; barter, haggle, swap, do a swap; traffic in; vend, buy and sell, export and import; drive a trade, peddle, do business; trade in, deal in, handle; deal in stolen property, fence; turn over 793 *sell*; commercialize, put on a business footing; trade with, do business with, deal with, have dealings with, open an account with.

speculate, venture, risk 618 *gamble*; invest, sink one's capital in, put one's money to work, make one's money work for one; profiteer; deal in the black market, sell under the counter; play the market.

bargain, negotiate, push up, beat down; haggle, argy-bargy 766 *make terms*; bid for, make a takeover bid, propose a merger, act as white knight; raise the bid, outbid 759 *offer*; underbid 483 *underestimate*; stick out for, hold out for, ask for, charge 766 *give terms*; settle for, drive a hard bargain, do a deal, shake hands on, sign on the dotted line 765 *contract*; plea-bargain.

792 Purchase

N. *purchase*, buying; buying up, takeover, buy-out, green mail, cornering, pre-emption; hire purchase, HP, the never-never, tick 785 *borrowing*; shopping, retail therapy, shopping therapy, spending, shopping spree, compulsive shopping disorder, binge-shopping; one-stop shopping; ethical shopping 806 *expenditure*; shopping by post, mail order, home shopping, teleshopping, tele-ordering, electronic shopping, e-shopping, cybershopping, virtual shopping, virtual storefront, virtual mall; consumer demand, consumerism 627 *requirement*; bid, take-over bid 759 *offer*; buy, purchase on appro, on approval, good buy, bargain, real bargain; shopping list, shopping basket, reward card, loyalty card; shop rage *or* shopping rage, trolley rage; window shopping.

purchaser, buyer, consignee; shopper, personal shopper; customer, patron, client, clientele, consumer; bidder; bargainer, haggler; share-buyer, bull, stag, corporate raider; user, end user.

Vb. *purchase*, make a purchase, complete a purchase; buy 771 *acquire*; shop, market, be in the market for, go shopping, purchase by mail order, purchase by tele-ordering, teleshop; get one's money's worth; buy outright, pay cash for, pay on the spot; buy on credit, buy on hire purchase; buy on the never-never, buy on an instalment plan, pay by instalment, buy on tick 785 *borrow*; pay by cheque *or* by Giro, pay by credit card, buy in 632 *store*; buy up; buy out, make a take-over bid, propose a merger, act as a white knight; buy over, bribe; buy back, redeem; pay for, bear the cost of 804 *pay for*; buy oneself in, invest in, sink one's money in 791 *speculate*; rent; bid for 759 *offer*; buy shares.

793 Sale

N. *sale*, selling, putting on sale, putting on the market, marketing, mass marketing, niche marketing, telemarketing, phone message marketing, undercover marketing, viral marketing; distribution, disposal 779 *non-retention*; sell-out; clearance sale, stock-taking sale, end-of-

season sale, closing-down sale, white sale, jumble sale, sale of work, charity sale, car boot sale, garage sale, bazaar; monopoly; auction, sale by auction, roup, Dutch auction, good market, market for; boom 730 *prosperity*; salesmanship, sales talk, pitch, sales patter, spiel; hard sell, soft sell 528 *advertisement*; market research 459 *enquiry*; saleability, marketability.

seller, vendor, share-seller, bear; auctioneer; market trader, barrow boy, costermonger, hawker 794 *pedlar*; shopkeeper, dealer 633 *caterer*; wholesaler, retailer 794 *tradespeople*; sales representative, rep, door-to-door salesman, door-stepper; traveller, commercial traveller, travelling salesman *or* -woman; agent, canvasser, tout; shop assistant, salesman *or* -woman, salesperson; booking clerk, ticket agent; roundsman.

Adj. *saleable or* salable, sellable, marketable, on sale, for sale; in demand, sought after; on the market, up for sale; bearish, up for grabs; on auction, under the hammer.

Vb. *sell*, make a sale; flog, dispose of; market, put on sale, offer for sale, have for sale, have on offer, vend; hawk, peddle, push; cross-sell, upsell; canvass, tout; put up for sale, auction, auction off, sell by auction, bring under the hammer, sell to the highest bidder, knock down to; wholesale; retail, sell under the counter, sell on the black market; turn over one's stock 791 *trade*; sell at a profit 771 *gain*; sell at a loss 772 *lose*; undercut 812 *cheapen*; sell off, remainder; sell up, sell out, wind up 145 *cease*; hold a sale.

be sold, be on sale, come under the hammer 780 *change hands*; sell, have a market, meet a demand, sell well, go *or* sell like hot cakes; be a best-seller, be a loss-leader.

794 Merchant

N. *merchant*, guild, room of commerce, firm 708 *corporation*; business person, man *or* woman of business; entrepreneur, cyberpreneur, e-preneur, speculator, operator 618 *gambler*; trafficker, fence, importer, exporter; wholesaler; retailer, merchandiser, dealer; middleman, broker, stockbroker; estate agent, house agent; financier, banker 784 *lender*.

tradespeople, tradesman, retailer, middleman, tallyman; shopkeeper 793 *seller*; ironmonger, haberdasher, grocer, greengrocer, butcher, tobacconist, newsagent, etc. 633 *provider*.

pedlar, seller; hawker, tinker, gipsy, bagman; costermonger, barrow boy; market trader, stall-keeper.

795 Merchandise

N. *merchandise*, line, staple; article, commodity, stock, range 632 *store*; freight, cargo 193 *contents*; wares, goods, consumer durables; perishable goods, dry goods, white goods, sundries.

796 Market
N. *market*, mart; free trade area. Common Market, EEC, OPEC, etc. 791 *trade*; free market, single market, economic zone 791 *trade*; black market, black economy, grey economy; grey market; seller's market, buyer's market; market-place, market cross; street market, flea market, Petticoat Lane; farmers' market; auction room, Christie's, Sotheby's; fair, world fair, international fair, trade fair; exhibition, exposition, shop window 522 *exhibit*; exchange, corn exchange, stock exchange, bourse; share shop, bucket shop; Wall Street.

emporium, free port; warehouse 632 *storage*; trading centre, trading post; bazaar, arcade, covered market, shopping mall, pedestrian precinct, shopping centre; virtual storefront, virtual mall 792 *purchase*.

shop, retailer's, store, multiple store, department store, chain store, emporium, bazaar, boutique, bargain basement, supermarket, hypermarket, superstore, cash and carry, warehouse club; Naafi; trading house; corner shop, convenience store, stall, booth, stand, newsstand, kiosk, barrow, vending machine, slot machine.

797 Money
N. *money*, Lsd, pounds, shillings and pence; wealth; lucre, filthy lucre, mammon, the root of all evil; currency, unit of currency, decimal currency, hard currency, soft currency; legal tender; money of account, sterling, pound sterling; single currency, euro; precious metal, gold, bullion, gold bar, ingot; silver; e-cash, e-money; ready money, the ready, cash, spot cash, hard cash, petty cash; change, small change, coppers 33 *small quantity*; pocket money, pin money, allowance; spending money; paltry sum, chickenfeed, peanuts; shekels, brass, dough, lolly, bread, dosh, moolah; loot, gravy; toy money, Monopoly money.

funds, hot money; liquidity, bank account, current account, deposit account, savings account; ISA, PEP etc. 629 *means*; money in the bank, liquid assets; wherewithal, the needful 629 *means*; ready money, the ready, finances, exchequer, cash flow, monies, treasure 633 *provision*; financial control, Private Finance Initiative, PFI, Public Private Partnership, PPP 791 *trade*; remittance 804 *payment*; withdrawal, cash back; capital; reserves, balances; sum of money, amount, figure, sum,

round sum, lump sum; quid, smacker, oncer, buck; fiver, tenner, pony, monkey, ton, century, grand; mint of money, wads, scads, pile, packet, stacks, heaps, mountains, etc., millions, billions, zillions, etc. 32 *great quantity*.

finance, high finance, International Monetary Fund, IMF; financial control, purse strings, almighty dollar; investment, ethical investment, zaitech; money market, Eurodollar market, Eurozone, Euroland; exchange, stock exchange, Big Bang 796 *market*; share index, FT Index, FTSE, Footsie, Dow-Jones average, Nikkei average, EASDAQ, NASDAQ; exchange rate, bank rate, minimum lending rate, effective rate, sterling effective rate; APR, annual percentage rate; agio, agiotage, snake; floating pound; cash transaction; devaluation; depreciation; strong pound, rallying 654 *improvement*; gold standard; green pound; managed currency, sinking fund, inflation, deflation, stagflation, reflation; arbitrageur, bear, bull, etc. 618 *gambler*.

coinage, minting, issue; metallic currency, stamped coinage, gold coinage, silver coinage, electrum coinage, copper coinage, nickel coinage, billon coinage, bronze coinage; specie, minted coinage, coin, piece, coin of the realm; guinea, sovereign, half sovereign; pound, quid, nicker; crown, half crown, florin, shilling, bob, sixpence, tanner, threepenny bit, penny, bun penny, copper, halfpenny, ship halfpenny; farthing; decimal coinage, pound coin, fifty p, twenty p, etc.; dollar, buck; half dollar, quarter, dime, nickel, jitney, cent; ten-dollar piece, eagle; napoleon, louis d'or; franc, new franc, mark, Deutschmark, drachma, peseta; obol, talent, shekel, solidus, bezant, ducat, angel, noble, real, pistole, piece of eight; change, small change, groat, bawbee, obolus, centime, sou, pfennig, piastre, kopek; cash 33 *small quantity*; Eurocurrency, ecu, euro, single currency; petrodollar; shell money, cowrie, wampum; coin collecting, numismatics, numismatology.

Some Currency Units
afghani (Afghanistan), baht (Thailand), balboa (Panama), birr (Ethiopia), bolívar (Venezuela), boliviano (Bolivia), cedi (Ghana), colón (Costa Rica, El Salvador), córdoba (Nicaragua), dalasi (The Gambia), denar (Macedonia), dinar (Algeria, Bahrain, Iraq and other countries), dirham (Morocco, United Arab Emirates), dobra (São Tomé and Príncipe), dollar (Australia, Canada, New Zealand, United States, and other countries), dong (Vietnam), dram (Armenia), escudo (Cape Verde), euro (Austria, Belgium, Finland, France, Germany, Greece, Ireland, Italy, Luxembourg, Netherlands, Portugal, Spain + Andorra, Monaco, San Marino), forint (Hungary), franc (Switzerland, Mali, and other countries), gourde (Haiti), guaraní (Paraguay), guilder or gulden (Suriname), hryvnia or hryvna

(Ukraine), kina (Papua New Guinea), kip (Laos), koruna (Czech Republic, Slovakia), krona (Sweden), króna (Iceland), krone (Denmark, Norway), kroon (Estonia), kuna (Croatia), kwacha (Malawi, Zambia), kyat (Myanmar), lari (Georgia), lat (Latvia), lek (Albania), lempira (Honduras), leone (Sierra Leone), leu (Romania), lev (Bulgaria), lilangeni (Swaziland), lira (Malta, Turkey), litas (Lithuania), loti (Lesotho), manat (Azerbaijan, Turkmenistan), marka (Bosnia-Hercegovina), metical (Mozambique), naira (Nigeria), nakfa (Eritrea), new kwanza (Angola), new sol (peru), new zaire (Democratic Republic of Congo), ngultrum (Bhutan), ouguiya (Mauritania), pa'anga (Tonga), pataca (Macau), peso (Argentina, Chile, Colombia, Mexico and other countries), pound (Egypt, Lebanon, United Kingdom), pula (Botswana), quetzal (Guatemala), rand (South Africa), real (Brazil), rial (Iran), riel (Cambodia), ringgit (Malaysia), riyal (Oman, Qatar, Saudi Arabia, Yemen), rouble or ruble (Belarus, Russia), rufiyaa (Maldives), rupee (India, Nepal, Pakistan, Seychelles, Sri Lanka), rupiah (Indonesia), shekel (Israel), shilling (Kenya, Somalia, Tanzania, Uganda), som (Kyrgyzstan), somoni (Tajikistan), soum or sum (Uzbekistan), sucre (Ecuador), taka (Bangladesh), tala (Samoa), tenge (Kazakhstan), tolar (Slovenia), tugrik (Mongolia), vatu (Vanuatu), won (Korea), yen (Japan), yuan (China), zloty (Poland).

paper money, fiduciary currency; bankroll, wad; note, banknote, treasury note, pound note, five-pound note, ten-pound note, etc., bill, dollar bill, greenback, buck, ten-dollar bill, etc.; bill of exchange; draft, money order, postal order, cheque, certified cheque, giro cheque, traveller's cheque, Eurocheque, letter of credit; promissory note, note of hand, IOU; standing order, direct debit; scrip, premium bond 767 *security*.

Adj. monetary, numismatic; pecuniary, financial, fiscal, budgetary; coined, stamped, minted, issued; fiduciary; gold-based, sterling, solvent 800 *rich*; inflationary, deflationary, floating; devalued, depreciated.

Vb. mint, coin, stamp; issue, circulate; forge, counterfeit.

draw money, cash, encash, realize, draw upon, cash a cheque, endorse a cheque, write a cheque 804 *pay*.

798 Treasurer

N. treasurer, honorary treasurer; bursar, purser; cashier, teller, croupier; trustee, steward 754 *nominee*; liquidator 782 *receiver*; book-keeper 808 *accountant*; banker, financier; keeper of the purse, paymaster, controller, comptroller, Chancellor of the Exchequer, Secretary of the Treasury, Governor of the Bank of England.

799 Treasury

N. treasury, exchequer, fisc, public purse; reserves, fund 632 *store*; counting house; bursary; bank, the Bank of England, the Old Lady of Threadneedle Street; savings bank, Post Office savings bank, building society, friendly society; mutualization, demutualization 780 *transfer*; credit union; coffer, chest 194 *box*; treasure chest, depository 632 *storage*; strong-room, strongbox, safe, safe deposit, cash box, moneybox, piggybank, stocking, mattress; till, cash register, cash desk, slot machine; cash dispenser, cashpoint, automated teller machine, ATM, hole in the wall; personal identification number, PIN, PIN number; box office, gate, turnstile; purse 194 *pocket*; wallet, pocket book, billfold.

800 Wealth

N. wealth, lucre, brass 797 *money*; moneymaking, golden touch, Midas touch, philosopher's stone; riches, fleshpots 635 *plenty*; luxury 637 *superfluity*; opulence, affluence 730 *prosperity*; ease, comfort, easy street 376 *euphoria*; solvency, creditworthiness 802 *credit*; substance 3 *having substance*; independence, competence, self-sufficiency 635 *sufficiency*; high income; gains 771 *gain*; resources, well-lined pockets, capital 629 *means*; liquid assets, bank account, building society account, Post Office savings account, ISA, Individual Savings Account, TESSA, Tax-Exempt Special Savings Account, TOISA, Tessa-only ISA, bottomless purse, goose that lays golden eggs; nest egg 632 *store*; fortune, small fortune, tidy sum, pots of money, pile, heap, mountain, scads, wads, packet, megabucks, cool million, zillions, etc. 32 *great quantity*; fortune; broad acres 777 *property*; bonanza, gold mine; El Dorado, pot of gold, the end of the rainbow, riches of Solomon, king's ransom; sudden wealth syndrome.

rich person, wealthy person, well-to-do person, man *or* woman of means; baron, tycoon, magnate, moneybags, millionaire, multimillionaire, millionairess, billionaire; Croesus, Midas, Dives, Loadsamoney; moneymaker, fat cat, capitalist, plutocrat, bloated plutocrat; heir, heiress, poor little rich girl 776 *beneficiary*; the haves, the privileged, moneyed class, propertied class, leisured class, the well-to-do, the well-off, the well-heeled, jet set, glitterati 848 *fashionable society*; Dinkies, dual income no kids, Woofs, well-off older folk; new rich, nouveau riche, self-made man 730 *prosperous person*; stockbroker belt.

Adj. rich, cash-rich; richly endowed, lush, fertile 171 *prolific*; abundant 635 *plentiful*; luxurious, upholstered, plush, ritzy; glittering, glitzy 875 *ostentatious*; wealthy, well-endowed, born in the purple, born with a silver spoon in one's mouth; opulent, affluent 730 *prosperous*; well-off, well-to-do, well-heeled, in easy circumstances, comfortably off, well-paid.

moneyed, propertied, worth a packet, worth millions; made of money, rolling in money, rolling in it, dripping, loaded; stinking rich, filthy rich; rich as Croesus; on easy street, in clover, in funds, in cash, in credit, in the black; well-heeled, flush, in the money; quids in, doing nicely thank you; creditworthy, solvent.

Vb. *be rich*, have money, have means; be rolling in money, wallow in riches; be in clover, be on easy street, be on velvet, be born in the purple, be born with a silver spoon in one's mouth; be sitting on a goldmine, be raking it in; be flush, be in funds, etc. (see adj.); have money to burn.

afford, have the means, have the wherewithal, be solvent, make both ends meet, keep one's head above water, keep the wolf from the door, keep up with the Joneses 635 *have enough*.

get rich, come into money 771 *inherit*; do all right for oneself 730 *prosper*; make a profit, make money, coin it, rake in the shekels, rake it in, laugh all the way to the bank; make a packet, make a pile, make a bomb, make a fortune, make a mint, make a killing, clean up, feather one's nest, line one's pocket, strike it rich, hit the jackpot, turn up trumps, win the pools, have one's ship come home, find one's Eldorado, find the pot of gold at the end of the rainbow 771 *gain*.

801 Poverty

N. *poverty*, ascetism; financial embarrassment, difficulties, Queer Street 805 *insolvency*; impoverishment, beggary, penury, pennilessness, pauperism, social exclusion, destitution; privation, indigence, neediness, necessity, dire necessity, need, want, pinch 627 *requirement*; empty larder 636 *scarcity*; wolf at the door, famine 946 *fasting*; empty purse, slender means, straitened circumstances, insufficiency, dire straits, belt-tightening 825 *suffering*; grinding poverty, subsistence level, breadline, poverty line, poverty trap, hand-to-mouth existence; poorness, meagreness, shabbiness, seediness, raggedness; recession, slump, depression 655 *deterioration*; squalor, slum, shanty town; workhouse, poorhouse.

poor person, broken man *or* woman, bankrupt, insolvent 805 *non-payer*; pauper, indigent, beggar, vagrant, tramp, bum, down-and-out 763 *beggar*; the poor, new poor, the have-nots, the disadvantaged, the underprivileged 869 *lower classes*; Cinderella; poor relation 35 *inferior*.

Adj. *poor*, as poor as a church-mouse; not well-off, badly off, hard up; low-paid, low-income, underprivileged; hard up, impecunious, short of cash, out of pocket, in the red; skint, cleaned out, bust, broke, flat broke, stony broke, bankrupt, insolvent 805 *non-paying*; on the breadline, below the poverty line, in the poverty trap, on the dole; impoverished, beggared; deprived, robbed; poverty-stricken; needy, indigent, in want, in need 627 *necessitous*; homeless; hungry 636 *underfed*; in distress, hard put to it, down at heel, down and out, down on one's luck, out at elbow, on one's uppers, on one's beam ends, on the rocks, up against it, not knowing which way to turn 700 *in difficulties*; unable to make both ends meet, unable to pay one's way, unable to keep the wolf from the door; unprovided for, penniless, destitute; down to one's last penny, without a bean, without a cent, without a sou.

Vb. *be poor*, live on a pittance, eke out a livelihood, scratch a living, live from hand to mouth; feel the pinch, fall on hard times, be in dire straits, be on one's uppers, be on the breadline, be below the poverty line, be caught in the poverty trap, have to watch the pennies; sing for one's supper; starve 859 *be hungry*; want, lack 627 *require*; not have a penny, not have two halfpennies to rub together; have no prospects; go broke 805 *not pay*; lose one's money, come down in the world 655 *deteriorate*; go on the dole, claim supplementary benefit.

impoverish, reduce to poverty, leave destitute, beggar, ruin 165 *destroy*; rob, strip 786 *fleece*; disinherit, cut off without a penny 786 *deprive*.

802 Credit

N. *credit*, repute, reputation 866 *prestige*; creditworthiness, white information; borrowing capacity, tick; letter of credit, credit card, charge card, plastic card, plastic money, plastic, affinity card, store card, loyalty card 804 *payment*; phonecard; credit note, the black; APR, annual percentage rate (of charge); credits, balances, credit balance 807 *receipt*; unpaid bill, account, budget account, score, tally, bill 808 *accounts*; trading deficit, floating debt 803 *debt*; loan, mortgage.

Vb. *credit*, give *or* furnish credit, extend credit; credit one's account; grant, vote; charge to one's account, charge to one's budget account; sell on tick, take credit, open an account, run up an account, run up a bill 785 *borrow*.

803 Debt

N. *debt*, indebtedness 785 *borrowing*; liability, obligation, commitment; mortgage 767 *security*; debit, charge; debts, bills, hire-purchase debt; national debt, floating debt; debt of honour, unsecured debt 764 *promise*; gearing, leverage; bad debt, write-off 772 *loss*; tally, account; deficit, negative equity, overdraft 307 *shortfall*; insolvency, frozen assets, black information 805 *non-payment*; deferred payment 802 *credit*; arrears, back pay; foreclosure; debt counselling.

interest, simple interest, compound interest, usury, pound of flesh; premium, rate of interest, minimum lending rate, discount rate, bank rate.

Vb. *be in debt*, owe, owe money; be debited with; get credit, overdraw (one's account); get on tick, buy on hire purchase *or* the never-never 785 *borrow*; use a credit card, use a charge card, use plastic money, use plastic, keep an account with, have charged to one's account; charge to one's budget account, run up an account, run into debt; be in the red, be overdrawn; leave one's bills unpaid, bilk, welsh.

804 Payment

N. *payment*, bearing the cost; defraying the cost, paying off, satisfaction, liquidation, clearance, settlement, settlement on account; cheque; receipt; cash, cash payment, down payment, ready money 797 *money*; EFTPOS, electronic funds transfer at point of sale, Switch card, smart card, swipe card, credit card, plastic, etc. 802 *credit*; earnest money, deposit, instalment, bank draft, standing order, direct debit; deferred payment, hire purchase 785 *borrowing*; subscription, tribute 809 *tax*; contribution, whip-round, appeal, collection 781 *offering*; compensation, indemnity 787 *restitution*; remittance 806 *expenditure*.

pay, payout, payoff, pay packet, pay cheque, take-home pay, pay day, wages, salary 771 *earnings*; grant, subsidy 703 *subvention*; salary, pension, annuity, remuneration, emolument, fee, honorarium, bribe, bonus, overtime pay, performance-related pay 962 *reward*; cut, commission 810 *discount*; contribution, subscription, collection, tribute 809 *tax*; damages, indemnity 963 *penalty*; back pay, compensation, redundancy pay, severance pay, golden handshake, ex gratia payment.

Vb. *pay*, disburse 806 *expend*; contribute 781 *give*; negotiate a trade-off, barter 791 *trade*; pay out, shell out, fork out, dole out, dish out, stump up, cough up; come across, do the needful, put one's hand in one's pocket, open one's wallet; pay a high price, pay an exorbitant price, pay through the nose 811 *pay too much*; pay back, repay, reimburse, compensate 787 *make restitution*; grease the palm, cross

one's palm with silver 612 *bribe*; pay wages, remunerate, tip 962 *reward*; pay in advance, put money up front, ante up, pay on sight, pay on delivery, cash on delivery, C.O.D., pay on demand; pay by cheque *or* by giro; pay by banker's order *or* by standing order *or* by direct debit; pay on the nail, pay cash; honour (a bill), pay up, meet, discharge, get a receipt; settle an account, square accounts with 808 *account*; settle accounts with, settle a score.

pay for, bear the cost, defray, put up funds; pay one's way, pay one's share; foot the bill, pick up the tab, pay the piper; stand a round, treat 781 *give*; go Dutch 775 *participate*.

805 Non-payment

N. *non-payment*, default; deduction 963 *penalty*; moratorium, embargo, freeze; refusal to pay, repudiation 760 *refusal*; tax avoidance, tax evasion, creative accounting, black economy 620 *avoidance*; deferred payment, hire purchase 785 *borrowing*; dishonoured cheque, dud cheque, cheque that bounces.

insolvency, inability to pay, failure to meet one's obligations; crash; failure of credit, cash-flow crisis; bankruptcy; nothing in the kitty, overdraft 636 *insufficiency*.

non-payer, defaulter, embezzler, tax dodger 789 *defrauder*; bilker, welsher, bankrupt.

Adj. *non-paying*, in arrears; insolvent, bankrupt, in administration; up to one's ears in debt, ruined 801 *poor*.

Vb. *not pay*, default; fall into arrears, get behindhand; withhold payment, freeze; refuse payment; fiddle one's income tax, practise tax evasion, moonlight, be part of the black economy 930 *be dishonest*; divert, sequester 786 *deprive*; have one's cheque bounce, dishonour; have a cashflow crisis, become insolvent, go bankrupt, go to the wall; sink, fail, go bust, crash, wind up, go into liquidation; welsh, bilk 542 *deceive*, be unable to pay 801 *be poor*.

806 Expenditure

N. *expenditure*, spending, disbursement 804 *payment*; cost of living; outgoings, overheads, costs, expenses, out-of-pocket expenses, extras, expense account; expense, outlay, investment, spending spree 815 *prodigality*.

Vb. *expend*, spend; buy 792 *purchase*; lay out, invest, sink money; be out of pocket, incur expenses; afford, stand, bear the cost, defray the cost, bankroll, meet charges, disburse, pay out 804 *pay*; draw on one's savings; open one's wallet, put one's hand in one's pocket; donate 781 *give*; spare no expense, go on a spree, do one proud, be lavish 813 *be liberal*; fling money around, splash out, blow,

blow one's cash 815 *be prodigal*; use up, consume, eat into, get through 634 *waste*.

807 Receipt
N. *receipt*, voucher, counterfoil; credits, revenue, royalty, rents, rates, dues; customs, taxes 809 *tax*; turnover, takings, proceeds, returns, receipts, gross receipts, net receipts, box-office receipts, gate money; income, private income, privy purse; emolument, regular income, pay, half pay, salary, wages 771 *earnings*; remuneration 962 *reward*; pension, annuity; allowance, personal allowance, pin money, pocket money, spending money; alimony, aliment, palimony, maintenance; bursary, scholarship 771 *acquisition*; interest, return, rake-off, cut; winnings, profits, gross profits, net profits, capital gain 771 *gain*; bonus, premium 40 *extra*; legacy, inheritance 777 *dowry*.
Vb. acquire, receive, take, etc. 771 *acquire*, 782 *receive*, 786 *take*.

808 Accounts
N. *accounts*, accountancy, accounting; book-keeping, entry; audit; account, profit and loss account, balance sheet, debit and credit; budgeting, budget, zero-based budgeting; current account, cash account, deposit account, savings account, expense account; account rendered, statement, bill, invoice 87 *list*; account settled 804 *payment*; reckoning, computation, score, tally, facts and figures 86 *numbering*; creative accounting 805 *non-payment*.
accountant, chartered accountant, book-keeper; cashier 798 *treasurer*; auditor; actuary, statistician; beancounter.
Adj. *accounting*, actuarial, computing, inventorial, budgetary.
Vb. *account*, keep the books, keep accounts; make up an account, budget, prepare a budget; cost, value, write up, write down 480 *estimate*; enter, carry over, debit, credit 548 *register*; prepare a cashflow forecast, prepare a balance sheet, balance accounts; settle accounts, square accounts, finalize accounts, wind up accounts; prepare a statement, present an account, charge, bill, invoice; practise creative accounting, cook the accounts *or* the books, falsify the accounts, fiddle, doctor 788 *defraud*; audit, go through the books; take stock.

809 Price
N. *price*, selling price, market price, retail price, wholesale price, discount price, list price; rate, going rate, rate for the job, fee for service; piece rate, flat rate; price control, fixed price 747 *restraint*; price-cutting, predatory

pricing; value, face value; worth, what it will fetch; premium, scarcity value; price list, tariff; quoted price, quotation; amount, figure, sum asked for; ransom, fine 963 *penalty*; demand, dues, charge; surcharge, supplement 40 *extra*; rip-off; fare, flat fare, hire, rental, rent, ground rent, peppercorn rent; fee, top-up fees; entrance *or* admission fee; refresher, commission, cut, rake-off; charges, freightage, wharfage; postage; cover charge, service charge, corkage.
cost, purchase price; damage, costs, expenses 806 *expenditure*; running costs, overheads; wage bill, salary bill; legal costs, damages 963 *penalty*; cost of living.
tax, taxes, dues; taxation self-assessment, council tax; Inland Revenue, tax return, tax form, tax demand 737 *demand*; rating, assessment, rateable value; rates, community charge *or* tax, poll tax, capitation tax; rate-capping; water rate; tartan tax; green taxes, carbon tax; stealth tax; levy, toll, duty; imposition; charge; exaction, forced loan, Morton's fork *or* crutch; punitive tax 963 *penalty*; tribute, danegeld, blackmail, protection money, ransom 804 *payment*; ecclesiastical tax, Peter's pence, tithe, zakat; national insurance; estate duty, death duty, inheritance tax; direct taxation, income tax, PAYE, surtax, supertax, company tax, corporation tax; capital levy, capital gains tax 786 *expropriation*; tax rebate, tax concession; tax credit, tax break, windfall tax; indirect taxation, excise, customs, tariff; local tax, purchase tax, sales tax, value-added tax, VAT, zero-rated goods; road tax, vehicle excise duty.
Vb. *price*, cost, assess, value, rate 480 *estimate*; put a price on; place a value on, fix a price for; raise *or* lower a price; fix the price; ask a price, charge 737 *demand*.
cost, be worth, fetch, bring in; amount to, come to, mount up to; be priced at, be valued at; bear a price; sell for, go for, set one back, change hands for, realize.
tax, impose a tax; fix a tariff, levy a rate, assess for tax, value; subject to duty, raise taxes, collect taxes, levy taxes.

810 Discount
N. *discount*, something off, reduction, rebate, cut, markdown; concession, special price; cut price, cut rate, special offer, loss leader 612 *incentive*; bargain price, knock-down price, bargain sale 812 *cheapness*; one's cut, commission, rake-off.
Vb. *discount*, deduct 39 *subtract*; allow a margin, reduce, depreciate, give a rebate; offer a discount; mark down, take off, cut, slash

812 *cheapen*; take a discount, take one's cut, take one's percentage.

811 Dearness

N. *dearness*, costliness, expensiveness; value, pricelessness; scarcity value, rarity; exorbitance, extortion, rack rents, rip-off; overcharge, daylight robbery; bad bargain, high price, fancy price; cost, high cost, pretty penny; ruinous charge; rising costs, sellers' market, bull market, soaring prices; inflation.

Adj. *dear*, high-priced, pricy, expensive, exclusive, ritzy, upmarket; costly, multi-million; extravagant, dearly-bought; dear at the price, overpriced, overpaid; exorbitant, excessive, extortionate; steep, stiff, sky-high; beyond one's means, prohibitive; dear at any price 641 *useless*; rising in price, soaring, mounting, going through the ceiling, inflationary; bullish.

of value, of worth 644 *valuable*; priceless, beyond price; invaluable 640 *useful*; inestimable, worth a king's ransom, worth its weight in gold, worth a fortune; precious, rare, scarce, like gold dust 140 *infrequent*; at a premium, not to be had for love or money.

Vb. *be dear*, cost a lot, cost a packet, cost a pretty penny, be high-priced, hurt one's pocket, make a hole in one's pocket; rise in price, harden; go up, appreciate, escalate, soar, go through the ceiling; be out of one's price range, price itself out of the market; prove expensive, cost one dear, cost a fortune, cost the earth.

overcharge, overprice, sell dear, ask too much; profiteer, soak, sting, bleed, skin, extort, charge rack rents, rip off, do, short-change, hold to ransom 786 *fleece*; put up prices, inflate prices, mark up; bull, raise the price, raise the bid.

pay too much, pay through the nose, be stung, be ripped off, be had, be done; pay dear, buy a white elephant; achieve a Pyrrhic victory; ruin oneself.

812 Cheapness

N. *cheapness*, inexpensiveness, affordability; good value, value for money, snip, steal, bargain, sale goods, seconds, rejects; low price; cheap rate, off-peak rate, off-season rate, concessional rate, excursion fare, railcard 810 *discount*; reduced price, knock-down price, cut price, bargain price, budget price, competitive price, sale price, giveaway price, rockbottom price, loss leader; peppercorn rent, easy terms; buyers' market, sluggish market; Dutch auction; falling prices, bearishness; depreciation, fall, slump; deflation; glut, drug on the market

635 *plenty*; happy hour.

no charge, nominal charge 781 *gift*; gratuitousness, labour of love 597 *voluntary work*; free trade, free port; free entry, free admission, free seats, free pass, free ticket, freebie, complimentary ticket; free quarters, grace and favour; free board, free service, free delivery; everything for nothing.

Adj. *cheap*, inexpensive, reasonable; affordable, within one's means, easy on the pocket; low-budget; substandard; economical, economy, economy size; not dear, worth the money; low-priced, cheap at the price; dirt-cheap, going cheap, going for a song, for peanuts; cheap and cheerful; bargain-rate, bargain-basement, downmarket, cut-price, concessional, sale-price, reduced, reduced to clear, marked down, half-price; low-rent; tourist-class, off-season; two-a-penny; cheapjack, jerry-built; cheapening, bearish, falling; underpaid, underpriced.

free of charge, uncharged, gratuitous, complimentary, courtesy; gratis, for nothing, for love, for kicks, for the asking; costing nothing, free, scot-free, for free, giveaway; zero-rated, untaxed, tax-free, rent-free, post-free; given away, as a gift 781 *given*; free, gratis and for nothing.

Vb. *be cheap*, be inexpensive, etc. (see adj.); cost little, be economical, be within anyone's reach, be easy on the pocket; be cheap at the price; be bought for a song, go dirt-cheap; cost nothing, be free, be had for the asking; cheapen, get cheaper, fall in price, depreciate.

cheapen, lower or reduce the price; keep cheap, lower one's charges, trim one's prices, mark down, cut, slash; undercharge, let go for a song, give away 781 *give*; beat down, haggle, undercut, undersell.

Adv. *cheaply*, on the cheap; at cost price, at wholesale prices, at a discount, for a song.

813 Liberality

N. *liberality*, bountifulness, munificence, generosity 931 *disinterestedness*; open-handedness, open hand, open purse, hospitality, open house 882 *sociability*; free hand, blank cheque, carte blanche 744 *scope*; lavishness 815 *prodigality*; bounty, largesse 781 *gift*; charity.

good giver, generous giver; donor, blood donor, organ donor, kidney donor; good tipper; fairy godmother, Lady Bountiful, Father Christmas, Santa Claus, sugar daddy, rich uncle 903 *benefactor*.

Adj. *liberal*, free-spending, open-handed, lavish 815 *prodigal*; bountiful, charitable 897 *benevolent*; hospitable 882 *sociable*; handsome, generous, munificent, slap-up; lordly, princely, royal, right royal; unstinting, unsparing; in liberal quantities, abundant, ample, overwhelming, bounteous, profuse, full, plenteous; overflowing 637 *redundant*.

Vb. *be liberal*, be generous, etc. (see adj.); lavish, shower largesse, shower upon 781 *give*; put one's hand in one's pocket, open one's wallet; give generously, give one's last penny, give the shirt off one's back; pay well, tip well; keep open house 882 *be hospitable*; do one proud, spare no expense; give carte blanche, give a blank cheque 744 *give scope*; spend freely, not ask for the change, throw money about like water, throw one's money around 815 *be prodigal*.

814 Economy

N. *economy*, thrift, thriftiness, frugality; prudence, care, carefulness; husbandry, good housekeeping, sound stewardship, good management; terotechnology; credit squeeze 747 *restriction*; economy drive, economy measures; time-saving, labour-saving, time and motion study, management study; husbanding of resources, economizing, saving, sparing, pinching, cheese-paring; retrenchment, economies, cuts, cutbacks; savings 632 *store*; conservation, energy-saving.

Adj. *economical*, time-saving, labour-saving, energy-saving, money-saving, cost-cutting; money-conscious, counting every penny 816 *parsimonious*; thrifty, careful, prudent, canny, frugal, cheese-paring, saving, sparing; meagre, Spartan.

Vb. *economize*, be economical, be sparing, etc. (see adj.); husband one's resources, keep costs down, waste nothing, recycle, reuse; keep within one's budget, cut one's coat according to one's cloth, make both ends meet; cut costs, trim expenditure, cut back, make economies, retrench, tighten one's belt; pinch, scrape, scrimp and save, look after the pennies 816 *be parsimonious*; save 632 *store*; make one's money work for one.

815 Prodigality

N. *prodigality*, lavishness, profusion, profuseness 637 *redundancy*; extravagance; wastefulness, profligacy, dissipation, squandering, spending spree, splurge 634 *waste*; conspicuous consumption, consumerism; improvidence; misuse of funds 675 *misuse*; money burning a hole in one's pocket.

prodigal, prodigal son, big spender; wastrel, profligate, spendthrift, spendaholic, squanderer.

Adj. *prodigal*, lavish 813 *liberal*; profuse, extravagant, wasteful, squandering, profligate;

uneconomic, uneconomical, thriftless, spendthrift, improvident, reckless, dissipated.

Vb. *be prodigal*, blow one's money, blue one's money; overspend, pour out money, splash money around, throw one's money around, flash pound notes; splurge, go on a spending spree, spend money like water; burn one's money, run through one's savings, exhaust one's resources, spend up to the hilt, splurge out, lash out, blow everything, waste one's inheritance, squander 634 *waste*; burn the candle at both ends, fritter away, throw away, dissipate, scatter to the winds, pour down the drain; not count the cost, have no money sense, think money grows on trees; misspend, throw good money after bad; have no thought for the morrow, overdraw; eat up one's capital; put nothing by, have no nest-egg, have nothing to fall back on, keep nothing for a rainy day.

Int. *hang the expense!*, a short life and a merry one!, easy come, easy go!, you can't take it with you.

816 Parsimony

N. *parsimony*, parsimoniousness; false economy; cheese-paring, scrimping, pinching, scraping, penny-pinching; tightfistedness, niggardliness, meanness, minginess, stinginess, miserliness; uncharitableness; moths in one's wallet 932 *selfishness*.

avarice, cupidity, acquisitiveness, covetousness, green-eyed monster, possessiveness; money-grubbing, itching palm; rapacity, avidity, greed 859 *desire*; mercenariness.

skinflint, niggard, penny pincher, cheese-parer, tightwad, meanie; miser, money-grubber, cadger; hoarder, magpie; Scrooge.

Adj. *parsimonious*, careful 814 *economical*; money-conscious, pennywise, miserly, mean, mingy, stingy, near, close, tight; tight-fisted, close-fisted 778 *retentive*; grudging, cheese-paring, ungenerous, uncharitable; sparing, pinching, scraping, scrimping.

avaricious, grasping, monopolistic 932 *selfish*; possessive, acquisitive 771 *acquiring*; hoarding; penny-pinching; miserly; money-grubbing, money-mad, covetous 859 *greedy*; rapacious; mercenary,

Vb. *be parsimonious*, be niggardly, etc. (see adj.); begrudge; stint, skimp; scrape, scrimp, scrimp and save, pinch 814 *economize*; fleece; be penny-wise, spoil the ship for a ha'porth of tar; starve oneself, live on a shoestring, live like a pauper; grudge every farthing, haggle 791 *bargain*; sit on, keep for oneself 932 *be selfish*.

Emotion, religion and morality

General

817 Mental state

N. mental state, qualities, instincts, affections; passions, feelings, inner feelings, emotions; chemistry; nature, disposition 5 *character*; spirit, temper, mettle 5 *temperament*; cast of mind, trait 7 *state*; personality, psychology, psyche, mentality, outlook, inherited characteristics 5 *heredity*; being, innermost being, breast, bosom, heart, soul, core, inmost soul, inner man, cockles of the heart, heart of hearts 5 *essential part*, 447 *spirit*; animus, attitude, frame of mind, state of mind, vein, strain, humour, mood; predilection, predisposition, inclinations, turn, bent, bias 179 *tendency*; passion, ruling passion; prejudice; heartstrings 818 *feeling*; personality testing, Rorschach *or* inkblot test, phrenology.

Adj. having a certain mental state, affected, characterized, formed, moulded, shaped, cast, tempered, framed; imbued with, permeated with, devoured with; obsessed with, hung up about; ingrained, inborn, inbred, congenital 5 *hereditary*; deep-rooted, deep-set; emotional, demonstrative 818 *feeling*.

818 Feeling

N. feeling, experience, emotional life, sensation, sense of 374 *sense*; emotion, sentiment; sincerity 540 *truthfulness*; impulse 609 *spontaneity*; intuition, instinct; responsiveness, response, reaction, fellow feeling, sympathy, involvement, personal involvement 880 *friendliness*; vibrations, vibes, bad vibes, good vibes; empathy, appreciation, understanding 490 *knowledge*; impression, deep feeling, deep sense of 819 *moral sensibility*; religious feeling, piety; finer feelings 897 *benevolence*; tender feelings 887 *love*; hard feelings 891 *resentment*; thrill, kick 318 *spasm*; shock, turn 508 *lack of expectation*; pathos 825 *suffering*; catharsis, abreaction; animus, emotionalism 822 *excit-*

ability; sob-stuff 821 *excitation*; sentimentality, romanticism; show of feeling, demonstration, demonstrativeness; expression, facial expression, play of features 547 *gesture*; blush, reddening, going pink, flush, hectic flush, suffusion; tingling, gooseflesh, creeps, tremor, trembling, nervous tension, quiver, flutter, flurry, palpitation, pulsation, heaving, panting, throbbing 318 *agitation*; ferment 318 *commotion*; lump in one's throat, tears in one's eyes; stoicism, endurance, stiff upper lip 823 *patience*.

warm feeling, glow; cordiality, effusiveness, heartiness; hot head, impatience; unction, earnestness 834 *seriousness*; eagerness, keenness, fervour, ardour, vehemence, enthusiasm, dash, fire 174 *vigorousness*; vigour, zeal 678 *activity*; fanaticism, mania 481 *prejudice*; emotion, passion, ecstasy, inspiration, hwyl, transports of delight 822 *excitable state*.

Adj. feeling, sensory 374 *sentient*; spirited, vivacious, lively 819 *sensitive*; sensuous 944 *sensual*; intuitive, sensitive, vibrant, responsive; involved, sympathetic, empathetic; tenderhearted 819 *impressible*; emotional, passionate red-blooded, full of feeling; touchy-feely; unctuous, soulful; intense, tense 821 *excited*; cordial, hearty; gushing, effusive; sentimental, romantic; mawkish, maudlin; schmaltzy, soppy, cutesy; thrilling, tingling, throbbing.

impressed, affected, influenced; stirred, aroused, moved, touched 821 *excited*; struck, awed, awestruck, overwhelmed, struck all of a heap; imbued with, aflame with, consumed with, devoured by, inspired by; rapt, enraptured, enthralled, ecstatic; lyrical, raving 822 *excitable*.

fervent, fervid, passionate, red-blooded, ardent, tense, intense; eager, breathless, panting, throbbing, pulsating, palpitating; impassioned, vehement, earnest, zealous; enthusiastic, exuberant, happy-clappy, bubbling, bubbly; hot-headed, warm-blooded, impetuous, impatient 822 *excitable*; warm, fiery, glowing, burning, red-hot, flaming, white-hot, boiling 379 *hot*; frenzied; strong, uncontrollable, overwhelming, furious 176 *violent*.

Vb. feel, sense, receive an impression, get the feeling, have a funny feeling, feel in one's bones, have a hunch; entertain feelings, have feelings, cherish feelings, harbour feelings, feel deeply, take to heart 819 *be sensitive*; know the feeling, experience, live, live through, go through, pass through, taste; bear, endure, undergo, smart under 825 *suffer*; sympathize, empathize, share 775 *participate*; respond, react, tingle, warm to, fire, kindle, catch.

show feeling, show signs of emotion; be demonstrative, not hide one's feelings 522 *manifest*; enthuse, rhapsodize, go into ecstasies, go into transports of delight 824 *be pleased*; fly into a passion, fly off the handle 891 *get angry*; change colour, colour up; go purple 428 *blacken*; blench, turn pale, go white, look ashen 427 *whiten*; colour, blush, flush, go pink, turn red, turn crimson, go red in the face 431 *redden*; quiver, tremble, shudder, wince; shake, quake 318 *be agitated*; tingle, thrill, vibrate, throb, pulsate, beat faster 317 *oscillate*; palpitate, pant, heave, draw a deep breath 352 *breathe*; reel, lurch, stagger; stutter 580 *stammer*.

819 Sensibility

N. moral sensibility, sensitivity, sensitiveness, soul; self-awareness, emotional intelligence, EI, EQ; over-sensitivity, touchiness, prickliness, irritability 892 *irascibility*; thin skin, soft spot, Achilles' heel; sore point, where the shoe pinches 891 *resentment*; susceptibility; finer feelings, sentiments, sentimentality, mawkishness; tenderness, affection 887 *love*; spirit, spiritedness, vivacity, vivaciousness, liveliness, verve 571 *vigour*; emotionalism, over-emotionalism, ebullience, effervescence 822 *excitability*; fastidiousness, finickiness, fikiness, aestheticism 463 *discrimination*; temperament, mood, changeability 152 *changeableness*.

Adj. impressible, malleable, plastic, puttylike 327 *soft*; sensible, aware, conscious of, mindful of, awake to, alive to, responsive 374 *sentient*; impressed with, touched, moved, moved to tears, touched to the quick 818 *impressed*; impressionable 822 *excitable*; susceptible; romantic, sentimental; mawkish, maudlin, schmaltzy, soppy, wet, sentimentalizing, gushing; emotional; tender-hearted, softhearted, compassionate 905 *pitying*.

sensitive, sensitized; tingling, sore, raw, tender 374 *sentient*; aesthetic, fastidious 463 *discriminating*; oversensitive, hypersensitive, with

one's heart on one's sleeve 822 *excitable*; touchy, irritable, thin-skinned.

lively, vital, vivacious, animated, fun-loving; irrepressible, ebullient, effervescent, bubbly; spirited, high-spirited; alert, on one's toes 455 *attentive*; highly-strung; expressive, racy 571 *forceful*.

Vb. be sensitive, be sentimental, etc. (see adj.); be tender-hearted, have a soft heart, take it to heart, weep for, break one's heart for 905 *pity*; tingle 318 *be agitated*.

820 Insensibility

N. moral insensibility, insensitiveness; numbness, stupor 375 *insensitivity*; inertia 175 *inertness*; lethargy 679 *inactivity*; stagnation, vegetation 266 *state of rest*; woodenness, blockishness, obtuseness, stupidity, dullness; slowness, delayed reaction 456 *inattention*; uninterest 454 *lack of curiosity*; nonchalance, insouciance, unconcern, lack of care, detachment, apathy 860 *indifference*; phlegm, stolidness, calmness, steadiness, coolness, imperturbability, sangfroid 823 *inexcitability*; aloofness, impassivity, repression, stoicism, stiff upper lip 823 *patience*; inscrutability, poker face, deadpan expression 834 *seriousness*; insensitivity, coarseness, Philistinism 699 *artlessness*; thick skin, rhinoceros hide, elephant hide; frigidity; dourness; unsentimentality, cynicism; callousness 326 *hardness*; lack of feeling, dry eyes, no heart, heart of stone, brutishness, brutality 898 *inhumanity*.

unfeeling person, iceberg, icicle, cold fish; stoic, ascetic; vegetable, stone, block.

Adj. impassive, unconscious 375 *insensitive*; unsusceptible, insensitive, unimaginative, uninspired; unresponsive, unimpressionable; phlegmatic, stolid, vegetable-like; wooden, blockish; bovine; dull, slow, slow-witted 499 *unintelligent*; unemotional, passionless; proof against, stoical, with stiff upper lip, ascetic, controlled, undemonstrative; aloof, distant, detached 860 *indifferent*; unaffected, calm 266 *tranquil*; steady, unruffled, unshaken, unshockable; imperturbable, without a nerve in one's body; cool; inscrutable, blank, expressionless, deadpan, poker-faced; unseeing 439 *blind*; unhearing 416 *deaf*; unsentimental, cynical; impersonal, dispassionate, reserved, unforthcoming, stony, frigid, frozen, icy, cold; unfeeling, heartless, soulless, inhuman; fancy-free, heart-whole; undemonstrative.

apathetic, unenthusiastic, unambitious; unimpassioned, uninspired, unexcited, unmoved; half-hearted, luke-warm, Laodicean; uninterested 454 *incurious*; insouciant, neglectful 458 *negligent*; spiritless, lackadaisical, couldn't care less; stagnant, bovine, cow-like 266 *at rest*; sluggish, supine 679 *inactive*; passive 175 *inert.*

thick-skinned, impenetrable, impervious, impermeable; blind to, deaf to, dead to, closed to; obtuse, unimaginative, insensitive, uninspired; callous, insensate, tough, hard, case-hardened, hard-bitten, hard-boiled, inured 669 *matured*; shameless, brazen.

Vb. *be insensitive*, be impassive, etc. (see adj.); have no feelings; miss the point of, be blind to 439 *be blind*; lack animation, lack spirit; steel oneself, harden one's heart against, be pitiless; feel indifference; feel no emotion, have no finer feelings, be a Philistine; show no regard for 922 *despise*; take no interest 454 *be incurious*; ignore 458 *disregard*; keep a stiff upper lip 942 *be temperate*; stagnate, vegetate 679 *be inactive*; not turn a hair, not bat an eyelid 599 *be resolute.*

821 Excitation

N. *excitation*, rousing, arousal, stirring up, waking up, working up, whipping up; igniting, galvanization, electrification 174 *stimulation*; inspiration, muse, exhilaration, intoxication, headiness; evocation, calling forth; encouragement, animation, incitement, invitation, appeal 612 *inducement*; provocation, irritation; impact 178 *influence*; enchantment 983 *sorcery*; rapture 824 *joy*; sentiment, sob-stuff, pathos; sensationalism; excitement, tension 160 *energy*; perturbation, effervescence, ebullience 318 *agitation*; shock, thrill, kicks 318 *spasm*; ferment, tizzy, flurry, furore 318 *commotion*; fever pitch, orgasm 503 *frenzy*; sexual arousal 376 *sexual pleasure*; climax 137 *crisis*, passion, emotion, enthusiasm 818 *feeling*; fuss, hassle, drama 822 *excitable state*; temper, fury, rage, etc. 891 *anger*; amazement 864 *wonder*; awe 854 *fear.*

stimulator, excitant; fillip, ginger, tonic, pick-me-up 174 *stimulant*; upper, pep pill 949 *drug-taking*; sting, prick, goad, spur, whip, lash, stick, carrot and stick 612 *incentive*; agent provocateur, rabble-rouser, tub-thumper 738 *agitator*; sensationalist, sob sister, muck-raker, chequebook journalist; headline, banner headline 528 *publicity*; watercooler TV; fan; irritant, gadfly.

Adj. *excited*, activated, stimulated, stung, etc. (see vb.); busy, astir, bustling, rushing 678 *active*; ebullient, effervescent, boiling, seething 355 *bubbly*; tense, wrought up, uptight, strung up, keyed up, wound up; feverish, frantic 503 *frenzied*; flushed 379 *hot*; violent 176 *furious*; hot under the collar, hot and bothered; seeing red, wild, mad, livid, fuming, foaming at the mouth, frothing, roaring, raging 891 *angry*; avid, eager, itching, agog, watering at the mouth; tingling 818 *feeling*; flurried, atwitter, all of a flutter, all of a doodah; restless, restive, overexcited, overwrought, distraught, distracted, distrait(e); freaked out, on a high, on a trip, on an ego-trip; beside oneself, hysterical, out of control, uncontrollable, running amok, carried away; turned on, hyped up; crazy about 887 *in love*; possessed, impassioned, enthusiastic.

exciting, stimulating, intoxicating, heady, exhilarating, sexy, kicking, mad; provocative, teasing, piquant, tantalizing; spicy, appetizing; alluring; evocative, emotive, suggestive; cliff-hanging, hair-raising, spine-chilling; thrilling, agitating; moving, affecting, inspiring; rousing, stirring; sensational, dramatic, melodramatic, mind-boggling; gripping; happening.

impressive, imposing, grand, stately; dignified, august, lofty, majestic, regal, royal, kingly, queenly 868 *noble*; awe-inspiring, overwhelming, overpowering; picturesque, scenic; cool, striking, arresting, dramatic; telling, forceful 178 *influential.*

Vb. *excite*, affect, infect 178 *influence*; cheer; touch, move; touch the heart-strings, strike a chord; quicken the pulse, startle, electrify, galvanize; raise to fever pitch 381 *heat*; inflame, set on fire, light the touchpaper 381 *burn*; sting, goad, pique, irritate 891 *enrage*; tease 827 *torment*; cut to the quick; work up, whip up 612 *incite*; enthuse; stir, rouse, arouse, wake, awaken, kindle, turn on (see also *animate* below); touch off, evoke, elicit, summon up, call forth; thrill, exhilarate, intoxicate; send into ecstasies 826 *delight.*

animate, enliven, breathe life into, quicken 360 *vitalize*; revive, resuscitate; inspire; encourage, hearten, buoy up 855 *give courage*; give an edge, put teeth into, whet 256 *sharpen*; urge, nag, egg on, spur, goad, lash 277 *accelerate*; jolt, jog, shake up; buck up, pep up, give a fillip to, stimulate, ginger 174 *invigorate*; cherish, foster, foment 162 *strengthen*; fuel, intensify, fan the flame, blow on the coals, add fuel to the fire, stir the embers.

impress, sink in, leave an impression; project *or* present an image; interest, hold, grip, absorb; intrigue, rouse curiosity, make one sit up; claim attention 455 *attract notice*; affect 178 *influence*; let sink in, bring home to, drive home 532 *emphasize*; penetrate, pierce 516 *be intelligible*; amaze, astound, arrest, shake, stagger, stupefy, dazzle, flabbergast, sock it to, take one's breath away 508 *surprise*, 864 *be wonderful*; overwhelm, overpower; upset, unsettle, distress, worry 827 *trouble.*

be excited, lose one's cool, lose control of oneself; flare up, burn 379 *be hot*; sizzle, seethe, simmer, boil, explode 318 *effervesce*; thrill to 818 *feel*; tingle, tremble 822 *be excitable*; quiver, flutter, palpitate, pulsate 318 *be agitated*; squirm, writhe 251 *wriggle*; dance; jump, leap up and down with excitement 312 *leap*; toss and turn.

822 Excitability

N. excitability, excitableness, inflammability; instability, emotionalism; hot temper, irritability, touchiness 892 *irascibility*; impatience, impetuosity, recklessness 857 *rashness*; effervescence, turbulence; restlessness, fidgets, nerves, butterflies in the stomach, social phobia, collywobbles, flap 318 *agitation*.

excitable state, exhilaration, elation, euphoria, intoxication; thrill, trip, high, ecstasy; fever, fret, perturbation, trepidation, bother, fuss, hassle, flurry, whirl 318 *agitation*; ferment, pother, stew; storm, tempest 352 *gale*; effervescence, outburst, explosion, scene, song and dance 318 *commotion*; hysterics, fit, apoplectic fit, frenzy; madness 503 *mental disorder*; passion, rage, towering rage, fury 176 *violence*; temper, tantrums, rampage 891 *anger*.

Adj. excitable, passionate, emotional; inflammable, like tinder, like touchpaper; unstable, impressionable; temperamental, moody, mercurial, volatile 152 *changing*; fitful 604 *capricious*; restless, nervy, fidgety, edgy, on edge, agitated; nervous, skittish 819 *lively*; irritable, fiery, hot-tempered, hot-headed 892 *irascible*; impatient, trigger-happy 680 *hasty*; impetuous, impulsive, madcap 857 *rash*; tempestuous, turbulent, stormy 176 *violent*; restive; effervescent, seething, boiling; volcanic, explosive; unbalanced; rabid 176 *furious*; feverish, hysterical 503 *frenzied*; like a cat on hot bricks *or* on a hot tin roof, like a hen on a hot girdle *or* griddle; tense, electric; elated.

Vb. be excitable, be impatient, etc. (see adj.); drum one's fingers, tap one's foot, fret, fume, stamp; shuffle, fidget, champ at the bit; be itching to, be dying to; be on edge, be in a stew, flap 318 *be agitated*; start, jump 854 *be nervous*; be on the verge of a breakdown; have a temper; fume, foam, froth, throw fits, have hysterics 503 *go mad*; throw a tantrum, have a hissy fit, go wild, run riot, run amok, go berserk, see red; rush about 61 *rampage*; rage, rant; fly into a temper, fly off the handle, explode; kindle; flare up 821 *be excited*.

823 Inexcitability

N. inexcitability, imperturbability, calmness, steadiness, composure, the zone; coolness,

cool, sangfroid, nonchalance; frigidity; tranquillity 266 *quietness*; serenity, placidity 828 contentment; equanimity, poise, equilibrium; self-control 942 *temperance*; stoicism 945 *asceticism*; detachment, dispassionateness 860 *indifference*; staidness, sobriety 834 *seriousness*; lack of fire.

patience, patience of Job; forbearance, endurance, longsuffering, tolerance, stoicism; resignation 721 *submission*.

Adj. inexcitable, dispassionate, cold, frigid, impassive; stable 153 *unchangeable*; cool, imperturbable, unflappable; level-headed; composed, controlled, grounded; moderate 942 *temperate*; inscrutable, deadpan, poker-faced; unhurried; equable 16 *uniform*; even-tempered, easy-going; staid, sedate, reserved, grave 834 *serious*; placid, unruffled, calm, peaceful, serene 266 *tranquil*; spiritless, lackadaisical, torpid, passive, vegetable-like 175 *inert*; earthbound 593 *prosaic*.

patient, meek, like patience on a monument, tolerant, longsuffering, forbearing, enduring; stoic, stoical, philosophic *or* philosophical, uncomplaining.

Vb. keep calm, compose oneself, keep cool, keep a cool head, swallow one's resentment, control one's temper, keep one's cool, not rise to the bait, keep one's hair *or* shirt on; not turn a hair, not bat an eyelid 820 *be insensitive*; relax, not excite oneself, not worry, stop worrying, take things easy, take things as they come 683 *rest*; resign oneself, take in good part, take philosophically, have patience, be resigned 721 *submit*; cool it 266 *come to rest*.

be patient, show patience, show forbearance; show restraint, put up with, stand, tolerate, bear, endure, support, suffer, abide; resign oneself, grin and bear it, accept the situation with good grace, put a brave face on it; brook, take, take it from, swallow, digest, stomach, pocket 721 *knuckle under*; turn the other cheek 909 *forgive*; be tolerant, live and let live, condone 736 *be lenient*; turn a blind eye, overlook 734 *be lax*; allow 756 *permit*; not rise to the bait, coexist 770 *compromise*.

calm, steady, moderate, assuage, tranquillize; lull 266 *bring to rest*; cool down, compose 719 *pacify*; set one's mind at rest 831 *relieve*; control, restrain.

SECTION TWO

Personal emotion

824 Joy

N. joy 376 *pleasure*; enjoyment, thrill, kick 826 *pleasurableness*; joyfulness 835 *rejoicing*;

delight, gladness, rapture, exaltation, exhilaration, transports of delight; abandonment, euphoria, ecstasy; gloating; life of pleasure, joys of life, roses all the way; halcyon days, days of wine and roses.

happiness, felicity, good fortune, well-being, ease, feel-good factor 376 *euphoria*; golden age, age of Aquarius 730 *prosperity*; blessedness, bliss; seventh heaven, cloud nine, nirvana, Paradise, Elysium, the happy hunting-ground in the sky, Garden of Eden, Isles of the Blessed, Arcadia 513 *fantasy*; happy valley, bower of bliss, home sweet home.

enjoyment, gratification, satisfaction, fulfilment 828 *contentment*; delectation, relish, lip-smacking, zest, gusto; indulgence, luxuriation, wallowing 943 *intemperance*; full life, hedonism, Epicureanism 944 *sensualism*; merrymaking, merriment; fun, treat, excursion, outing 837 *amusement*; feast, bean-feast, thrash; refreshment, good cheer, cakes and ale, beer and skittles 301 *eating*.

happy person, happy camper; smiler.

Adj. *pleased*, well-pleased, glad, welcoming; satisfied, happy 828 *content*; gratified, flattered, chuffed, pleased as Punch *or* as a dog with two tails; over the moon, on top of the world; enjoying, loving it, tickled to death, tickled pink; exhilarated 833 *merry*; euphoric, walking on air, with feet not touching the ground; euphoric, elated, overjoyed 833 *jubilant*; delighted, transported; approving; ravished, in raptures, in transports, in the seventh heaven, on cloud nine; captivated, charmed, enchanted 818 *impressed*; gloating.

happy, happy as a king *or* as a sandboy *or* as a lark *or* as Larry *or* as a pig in muck, happy as the day is long; over the moon, blissed out; blithe, joyful, joyous, gladsome 833 *merry*; beaming, smiling 835 *laughing*; radiant, starryeyed; felicitous, lucky, fortunate 730 *prosperous*; blissful, blessed; in paradise; unduly happy, pronoid, starry-eyed, looking through rose-coloured *or* rose-tinted spectacles.

Vb. *be pleased*, be glad, etc. (see adj.); hug oneself, congratulate oneself, pat oneself on the back, purr with pleasure, be like a cat with a dish of cream, be like a dog with two tails, jump *or* dance for joy 833 *be cheerful*; laugh, smile 835 *rejoice*; get pleasure from, get a kick out of, take pleasure in, delight in, rejoice in; go into ecstasies, be in a state of euphoria, rave about, enthuse over, rhapsodize about 818 *show feeling*; luxuriate in, bask in, wallow; enjoy; have fun 837 *amuse oneself*; gloat; savour, relish, smack one's lips 386 *taste*; take a fancy to, like 887 *love*; think well of 923 *approve*.

825 Suffering

N. *suffering*, heartache, weltschmerz 834 *melancholy*; longing, homesickness, nostalgia 859 *desire*; discontent, weariness 684 *fatigue*; nightmare, waking nightmare, pain, affliction, distress, dolour, anguish, angst, agony, torture, torment, mental torment; twinge, stab, smart, sting, thorn 377 *pang*; painfulness; Passion, Crucifixion, Calvary, martyrdom; rack, the stake 963 *punishment*; purgatory, hell, damnation, eternal damnation 961 *condemnation*; bed of nails, bed of thorns 700 *difficulty*; bad time, bad day, bad hair day, mauvais quart d'heure, annus horribilis; unpleasantness, setback, inconvenience, disagreeableness, discomfort, malaise; the hard way, trial, ordeal; shock, trauma, blow, infliction, visitation, tribulation 659 *bane*; extremity, death's door 651 *illness*; living death, fate worse than death 616 *evil*; evil days, unhappy times.

sorrow, grief, sadness, mournfulness, gloom 834 *dejection*; woe, wretchedness, misery, depths of misery; prostration, despair, despondency, desolation 853 *hopelessness*; unhappiness, tale of woe 731 *adversity*; heavy heart, broken heart; displeasure, dissatisfaction 829 *discontent*; vexation, bitterness, mortification, chagrin, fretting, remorse 830 *regret*.

worry, worrying, worriedness, uneasiness, disquiet, fretting 318 *agitation*; dismay, distress 63 *disarrangement*; phobia, hang-up, obsession; something on one's mind, weight on one's mind, anxiety, health anxiety, performance anxiety; concern, solicitude, care; responsibility, load, burden; strain, stress, tension; a worry, worries, business worries, cares, cares of the world; trouble, troubles 616 *evil*; bother, annoyance, irritation, bête noire, pest, thorn in the flesh, the limit *or* giddy limit; headache, teaser, puzzle, problem 530 *enigma*.

sufferer, victim, scapegoat, sacrifice; prey; martyr; patient 651 *sick person*.

worrier, neurotic, obsessive, worryguts (inf); control freak.

Adj. *suffering*, ill, indisposed 651 *sick*; writhing, aching, in pain, on a bed of pain, in agony, bleeding, harrowed, on the rack, in torment, in hell; inconvenienced, uncomfortable, ill at ease; distressed, anxious, unhappy about, worried, troubled, apprehensive, dismayed 854 *nervous*; anguished, tormented, angst-ridden; sick with worry, out of one's mind with worry, cut up about, in a state 316 *agitated*; discomposed, disconcerted; ill-used, maltreated, abused; longsuffering, downtrodden 745 *subjected*; martyred, victimized, sacrificed; stricken, wounded; heavy-laden, crushed, prostrate 684 *fatigued*; careworn; woeful, woebegone, haggard; suffering from, plagued by, sick with, riddled with, lousy with, possessed by, -ridden, -stricken.

unhappy, infelicitous, unlucky, accursed 731 *unfortunate*; despairing 853 *hopeless*; doomed 961 *condemned*; pitiable, poor, wretched, miserable; sad, melancholy, despondent, disconsolate; cut up, heart-broken, broken-hearted, heavy-hearted, sick at heart; sorrowful, sorrowing, grieved, grieving, grief-stricken, woebegone 834 *dejected*; sunk in misery, weeping, weeping buckets, sobbing, tearful, in tears, in buckets of tears 836 *lamenting*; disappointed 829 *discontented*; offended, vexed, peeved, miffed, annoyed, pained 924 *disapproving*; piqued, mortified, humiliated 891 *resentful*; sickened, disgusted, nauseated; sorry, remorseful, regretful 830 *regretting*.

Vb. suffer, undergo, endure, go through, experience 818 *feel*; bear, put up with, grin and bear it; suffer torments, bleed; hurt oneself, be hurt, do harm to oneself, smart, chafe, ache 377 *feel pain*; wince, flinch, writhe, squirm 251 *wriggle*; take up one's cross, become a martyr, sacrifice oneself; take one's punishment, take it on the chin 599 *stand firm*; have a thin time, have a bad time, go through it, have trouble enough 731 *have trouble*; distress oneself, fuss, hassle, worry, worry to death, fret, be on pins and needles, be on tenterhooks, agonize 318 *be agitated*; mind, be upset, take it badly, take it ill, take it to heart; sorrow, grieve, weep, sigh 836 *lament*.

826 Pleasurableness

N. pleasurableness, the pleasures of —, pleasantness, niceness, delectableness, delectability, delightfulness, amenity, sunny side, bright side; attractiveness, appeal, sex appeal, it, come-hither look 291 *attraction*; winning ways 925 *flattery*; amiability, winsomeness, charm, fascination, enchantment, witchery, loveliness, sight for sore eyes 841 *beauty*; joyfulness, honeymoon 824 *joy*; a real tonic, a little of what one fancies, a delight, a treat, a joy; novelty, pastime, fun 837 *amusement*; melody, harmony 412 *music*; tastiness, deliciousness 390 *savouriness*; spice, zest, relish, je ne sais quoi; dainty, titbit, sweet 392 *sweetness*; manna in the wilderness, balm 685 *refreshment*; land flowing with milk and honey 635 *plenty*; peace, peace and quiet, tranquillity 266 *quietness*, 681 *leisure*; idyll; pipedream 513 *fantasy*.

Adj. pleasurable, pleasant, nice, good; pleasure-giving 837 *amusing*; pleasing, agreeable, gratifying; acceptable, welcome, welcome as the flowers in May; well-liked, to one's taste, to one's liking, just what the doctor ordered; wonderful, marvellous, fabulous,

splendid 644 *excellent*; easeful, refreshing 683 *restful*; peaceful, quiet 266 *tranquil*; luxurious, voluptuous 376 *sensuous*; genial, warm, sunny; delightful, delectable, delicious, exquisite, choice; luscious, juicy; delicate, tasty 390 *savoury*; sugary 392 *sweet*; dulcet, musical, harmonious 410 *melodious*; picturesque, scenic, lovely 841 *beautiful*; amiable, dear, winning, disarming, endearing; attractive, fetching, appealing, alluring, interesting; seductive, enticing, inviting, captivating; charming, enchanting, bewitching, ravishing; haunting, thrilling, heart-melting, heart-warming 821 *exciting*; homely, cosy; pastoral, idyllic; heavenly, out of this world; beatific, blessed, blissful 824 *happy*.

Vb. please, give pleasure, agree with; lull, soothe, calm 177 *assuage*; comfort 833 *cheer*; put at ease, make comfortable 831 *relieve*; give a golden hello to, give a sweetener to, sugar, gild *or* sugar the pill 392 *sweeten*; stroke, pat, pet, baby, coddle, nurse, cuddle 889 *caress*; indulge, pander to 734 *be lax*; charm, interest 837 *amuse*; rejoice, gladden, make happy; gratify, satisfy, leave one walking on air, leave nothing more to be desired 828 *content*; raise to the seventh heaven.

delight, rejoice, exhilarate, elate, elevate, uplift; rejoice one's heart, warm the cockles of one's heart, do one's heart good, bring tears of joy *or* happiness; thrill, intoxicate, ravish; transport, turn on, send, send one into raptures *or* ecstasies 821 *excite*; be music to one's ears 925 *flatter*; take one's fancy, tickle one's fancy; tickle one's palate 390 *make appetizing*; regale, refresh; tickle, tickle one to death, titillate; entrance, enrapture; enchant, charm 983 *bewitch*; take one's breath away 821 *impress*; allure, seduce 291 *attract*.

827 Painfulness

N. painfulness, harshness, roughness, abuse, child abuse, sexual abuse, harassment, sexual harassment, persecution 735 *severity*; hurtfulness, harmfulness 645 *badness*; disagreeableness, unpleasantness; loathsomeness, hatefulness, beastliness 616 *evil*; grimness 842 *ugliness*; friction, chafing, irritation, ulceration, inflammation, exacerbation 832 *aggravation*; soreness, tenderness 377 *pain*; irritability, inflammability 822 *excitability*; sore point; sore, running sore, ulcer, thorn in the flesh, pinprick, where the shoe pinches 659 *bane*; shock 508 *lack of expectation*; unpalatability, disgust, nausea, sickener 391 *unsavouriness*; sharpness, bitterness, bitter pill, gall and wormwood, vinegar 393 *sourness*; affliction, adversity; tribulation, trials and tribulations, ordeal, cross 825 *suffering*; trouble, care 825 *worry*; pathos, poignancy; sorry sight, sad spectacle, object of pity 731 *unlucky person*; sorrow.

annoyance, vexation, the death of —, pest, bête noire, curse, plague, pain in the neck, bugger 659 *bane*; botheration, hassle, embarrassment 825 *worry*; nuisance, pinprick; burden, drag 702 *encumbrance*; grievance, complaint; hardship, troubles 616 *evil*; last straw, limit, the end; offence, affront, insult, provocation 921 *indignity*; molestation, infestation, persecution, malignity 898 *malevolence*; displeasure, mortification 891 *resentment*.

annoying person, menace, troublemaker, awkward squad; enfant terrible; pain, pain in the neck, pain in the arse; bugger, fart, fucker (vulg), arse (vulg), arsehole (vulg), tosser (vulg), wanker (vulg).

Adj. *causing pain*, painful, paining, hurting, aching, sore, tender; agonizing 377 *painful*; searing, scalding, burning, sharp, shooting, biting, nipping, gnawing, throbbing; caustic, corrosive, vitriolic; harsh, hard, rough, cruel 735 *severe*; grinding, gruelling, punishing, excruciating, extreme; hurtful, harmful, poisonous.

unpleasant, unpleasing, disagreeable; uncomfortable, comfortless, joyless, dreary, dreich, dismal, depressing 834 *cheerless*; unattractive; hideous 842 *ugly*; unwelcome, unacceptable 860 *unwanted*; thankless, unpopular, displeasing; disappointing, unsatisfactory; distasteful, unpalatable, off 391 *unsavoury*; foul, nasty, beastly, horrible, ghastly 645 *not nice*; malodorous, stinking 397 *fetid*; bitter, sharp 393 *sour*; invidious, obnoxious, offensive, objectionable, undesirable, odious, hateful, loathsome, nauseous, slimy, disgusting, revolting, repellent; execrable, accursed 645 *damnable*.

annoying, too bad; troublesome, embarrassing, discomfiting, worrying; bothersome, wearisome, irksome, tiresome, boring, balls-aching, buttock-clenching 838 *tedious*; burdensome, onerous, oppressive 322 *weighty*; disappointing, unlucky, unfortunate, untoward 731 *adverse*; awkward, unaccommodating, impossible, harassing, hassling; importunate, pestering; trying, irritating, aggravating, provoking, maddening, infuriating; galling, mortifying.

distressing, afflicting, crushing, prostrating, grievous, traumatic; moving, affecting, poignant, touching; harrowing, heartbreaking, heart-rending, tear-jerking; pathetic, tragic, tragical, sad, woeful, rueful, mournful, pitiful, lamentable, deplorable; ghastly, grim, dreadful, shocking, appalling, horrifying,

horrific 854 *frightening*.

intolerable, insufferable, impossible, insupportable, unbearable 32 *exorbitant*; past enduring, not to be borne; balls-aching, buttock-clenching, thudding; extreme, beyond the limits of tolerance, more than flesh and blood can stand, enough to make a parson swear, enough to try the patience of Job, enough to provoke a saint; a bridge too far.

Vb. *hurt*, injure 645 *harm*; pain, cause pain 377 *give pain*; bite, cut, tear, rend 655 *wound*; hurt the feelings, gall, pique, nettle, mortify 891 *huff*; rub up the wrong way, tread on one's corns; cut to the quick, pierce the heart, rend the heartstrings, bring tears to one's eyes, draw tears, grieve, afflict, cause trauma, distress 834 *sadden*; plant a thorn in one's side; corrode, embitter, exacerbate, make matters worse, rub salt in the wound, gnaw, chafe, rankle, fester 832 *aggravate*; offend, aggrieve (see also *displease* below); insult, affront 921 *not respect*.

torment, martyr; harrow, rack, put to the rack, break on the wheel 963 *torture*; give the third degree, give one the works; put one through it, put through the hoop, give one a bad time, maltreat, abuse, bait, bully, rag, bullyrag, persecute 735 *oppress*; be offensive, snap at, bark at 885 *be rude*; importune, dun, doorstep, beset, besiege 737 *demand*; haunt, obsess; annoy; tease, wind up, pester, plague, nag, henpeck, badger, worry, try, chivvy, harass, hassle, harry, heckle; molest, bother, vex, provoke, peeve, miff, ruffle, irritate, wind up, needle, sting, chafe, fret, bug, gall, irk, roil, rile 891 *enrage*.

trouble, disquiet, disturb, agitate, discompose, disconcert, discomfit, put one out, upset, incommode 63 *disarrange*; worry, embarrass, perplex 474 *puzzle*; tire 684 *fatigue*; weary, bore 838 *be tedious*; obsess, haunt, bedevil; weigh upon one, prey on the mind, weigh on the spirits, act as a damper, deject 834 *depress*; infest, get in one's hair, dog one's footsteps, get under one's feet, get in one's way, thwart 702 *obstruct*.

displease, find no favour 924 *incur blame*; disagree with, grate on, jar on, strike a jarring note, get on one's nerves, set the teeth on edge, go against the grain, give one the pip, give one a pain, get one's goat, get on one's wick, get up one's nose, get under one's skin; disenchant, disillusion 509 *disappoint*; dissatisfy, aggrieve 829 *cause discontent*; offend, shock, horrify, scandalize, disgust, revolt, repel, put one off, turn one off, sicken, nauseate, fill one with loathing, stick in the throat, make one's gorge rise, turn one's stomach, make one sick, make one sick to one's stomach, make one vomit, make one throw up 861 *cause dislike*; make one's hair curl, make one's flesh creep, make one's blood run cold, curdle the blood, make one's hair stand on end, appal 854 *frighten*.

828 Contentment

N. contentment, content, satisfaction, complacency; self-complacency, self-satisfaction, smugness 873 *vanity*; half-smile, purr of content, feel-good factor, ray of comfort; serenity, tranquillity 266 *quietness*; peace of mind, heart's ease 376 *euphoria*; reconciliation 719 *pacification*; snugness, cosiness, comfort, sitting pretty; dreams come true 730 *prosperity*.

Adj. content, contented, satisfied 824 *happy*; appeased, pacified 717 *peaceful*; cosy, snug 376 *comfortable*; at ease 683 *restful*; smiling 833 *cheerful*, pleased; with nothing left to wish for, having nothing to grumble at 863 *satiated*; uncomplaining, with no regrets, without complaints; philosophic *or* philosophical, resigned 721 *submitting*; easily pleased, easygoing, easyosy 736 *lenient*; secure 660 *safe*; untroubled, blessed with contentment.

Vb. be content, be satisfied, etc. (see adj.); purr with content 824 *be pleased*; rest and be thankful, count one's blessings; be thankful, have much to be thankful for 907 *be grateful*; have all one could ask for, have one's wish, make one's dreams come true, fulfil one's ambition 730 *prosper*; congratulate oneself, rejoice; be at ease, be in one's element, sit pretty 376 *enjoy*; be reconciled 719 *make peace*; get over it, take comfort; rest content; take things as they come, make the best of, have no complaints, have nothing to grumble about, have no regrets; acquiesce 721 *submit*.

content, satisfy, make one's day 826 *please*; meet with approval, go down well, go down a treat; make happy, bless with contentment; grant a boon 781 *give*; make one's dreams come true, comfort 833 *cheer*; bring comfort to; lull, set at ease, set at rest; propitiate, reconcile, conciliate, appease 719 *pacify*.

829 Discontent

N. discontent, discontentment; displeasure, pain, dissatisfaction, feel-bad factor 924 *disapprobation*; cold comfort 509 *disappointment*; irritation, chagrin, pique, mortification, bitterness, spleen 891 *resentment*; uneasiness, disquiet 825 *worry*; grief 825 *sorrow*; unrest, state of unrest, winter of discontent, restiveness 738 *disobedience*; agitation 318 *commotion*; finickiness, faddiness, fikiness, hypercriticism, nitpicking 862 *fastidiousness*; querulousness 709

quarrelsomeness; chip on one's shoulder, grievance, grouse, grudge, complaint 709 *quarrel*; weariness, world-weariness, weltschmerz, melancholy, ennui 834 *dejection*; sulkiness, sulks, the hump, dirty look, grimace, scowl, frown 893 *sullenness*; groan, curse 899 *curse*; murmuring, whispering campaign, smear campaign 762 *deprecation*.

malcontent, grumbler, grouch, grouser, sniper, complainer, whiner, bleater, bellyacher, Jonah 834 *moper*; plaintiff 763 *petitioner*; faultfinder, nit-picker, critic, censurer; person with a grievance, someone with a chip on their shoulder, angry young man; dissident, dropout, refusenik 738 *rebel*; seditionist 738 *agitator*; protest meeting, sit-in; conscientious objector.

Adj. discontented, displeased, not best pleased; dissatisfied 924 *disapproving*; frustrated 509 *disappointed*; defeated 728 *unsuccessful*; malcontent, dissident 489 *dissenting*; restive 738 *disobedient*; disgruntled, dischuffed, weary, browned off, cheesed off, hacked off, gutted, fed up to the back teeth 825 *unhappy*, 838 *bored*; sad, disconsolate 834 *dejected*; illdisposed, grudging, jealous, envious; embittered, soured 393 *sour*; peevish, testy, crabbed, crabbit, cross, sulky, sulking, pouting 893 *sullen*; grouchy, grumbling, grousing, whining, swearing 899 *cursing*; protesting; smarting, mortified, insulted, affronted, piqued, vexed, miffed, put out, annoyed 891 *resentful*; fretful, querulous, petulant, complaining; difficult, hard to please, never satisfied, exigent, exacting 862 *fastidious*; fault-finding, critical, hypercritical, censorious; resisting 704 *opposing*.

Vb. be discontented, be dissatisfied, etc. (see adj.); carp, criticize, give flak, find fault 862 *be fastidious*; lack, miss 627 *require*; jeer 924 *disapprove*; take offence, take amiss, take ill, take to heart, take on, be offended, be miffed 891 *resent*; get the hump, sulk; look blue, look glum; moan, whine, whinge, winge, bleat, beef, protest, complain, object 762 *deprecate*; bellyache, grumble, grouse, grouch, gripe; wail 836 *lament*; be aggrieved, have a grievance, nurse a grudge, harbour a grudge, have a chip on one's shoulder; join the opposition 704 *oppose*; rise up, be up in arms about 738 *revolt*; grudge 912 *envy*; quarrel; not know when one is well off, look a gift horse in the mouth; ask for one's money back, demand a refund, return 607 *reject*.

cause discontent, dissatisfy 636 *be insufficient*; leave room for complaint 509 *disappoint*; spoil one's pleasure, get one down 834 *depress*; dishearten, discourage 613 *dissuade*; sour, embitter, disgruntle, dischuff; upset, miff, chafe, niggle, put out of humour, irritate 891 *huff*; mortify 872 *humiliate*; offend, cause resentment 827 *displease*; disgust, gross out 861 *cause dislike*; sow the seeds of discontent, make trouble, stir up trouble, mix it, agitate 738 *revolt*.

830 Regret

N. *regret*, regretfulness; mortification 891 *resentment*; harking back, crying over spilt milk; soul-searching, remorse, contrition, repentance, compunction, qualms, pangs of conscience, regrets, apologies 939 *penitence*; disillusion, second thoughts 67 *sequel*; longing, homesickness, nostalgia 859 *desire*; sense of loss 737 *demand*; matter of regret, pity of it.

Adj. *regretting*, homesick, nostalgic; regretful, remorseful, rueful, conscience-stricken, sorry, apologetic, penitent, contrite 939 *repentant*; disillusioned, sadder and wiser.

Vb. *regret*, rue, deplore, rue the day; curse one's folly, never forgive oneself, blame oneself, reproach oneself, kick oneself, bite one's tongue; wish undone, wring one's hands, cry over spilt milk, spend time in vain regrets 836 *lament*; want one's time over again, sigh for the good old days, fight one's battles over again, relive the past, reopen old wounds, hark back; look back, look over one's shoulder; miss, sadly miss, regret the loss; long for, hanker after, be homesick 859 *desire*; express regrets, apologize, be full of remorse, feel contrite, feel remorse, be sorry 939 *be penitent*; ask for another chance 905 *ask for mercy*; lament 924 *disapprove*; feel mortified, gnash one's teeth 891 *resent*; have cause for regret, have had one's lesson 963 *be punished*.

831 Relief

N. *relief*, welcome relief, rest 685 *refreshment*; easing, alleviation, mitigation, palliation, abatement 177 *moderation*; good riddance; exemption 668 *rescue*; solace, consolation, comfort, ray of comfort, crumb of comfort; silver lining, break in the clouds 852 *hope*; load off one's mind, sense of relief 656 *revival*; lulling; soothing, salve 658 *balm*; painkiller, analgesic 375 *anaesthetic*; sedative, tranquilliser.

Vb. *relieve*, ease, soften, cushion; relax, lessen the strain; temper 177 *moderate*; lift, raise, take off, lighten, relieve the burden, take a load off one's mind 701 *disencumber*; spare, exempt from 919 *exempt*; save 668 *rescue*; console, solace, comfort, bring comfort, offer a crumb of comfort; cheer up, buck up, encourage, hearten 833 *cheer*; refresh; restore, repair 656 *cure*; put a plaster on, bandage, bind up,

apply a tourniquet, poultice, kiss it better 658 *practise medicine*; calm, soothe, palliate, mitigate, moderate, alleviate 177 *assuage*; smooth the brow, take out the wrinkles, iron out the difficulties 258 *smooth*; lull; kill the pain 375 *make insensitive*; take pity on, put one out of one's misery.

832 Aggravation

N. *aggravation*, exacerbation, exasperation, irritation; enhancement, augmentation 36 *increase*; intensification; heightening, deepening, adding to 482 *overestimate*; making worse 655 *deterioration*; complication 700 *difficulty*.

Vb. *aggravate*, intensify 162 *strengthen*; enhance, heighten, deepen; increase 36 *augment*; worsen, make things worse, disimprove, not improve matters 655 *deteriorate*; add insult to injury, rub salt in the wound, rub it in, rub one's nose in it, exacerbate, inflame 821 *excite*; exasperate, irritate 891 *enrage*; add fuel to the flame, fan the embers; complicate, make bad worse, escalate the war, go from bad to worse, jump from the frying pan into the fire.

833 Cheerfulness

N. *cheerfulness*, alacrity 597 *willingness*; optimism, hopefulness 852 *hope*; happiness 824 *joy*; geniality, smiles, good humour; vitality, high spirits, youthful high spirits, joie de vivre 360 *life*; light-heartedness, spring in one's step, optimistic outlook 828 *contentment*; liveliness, sparkle, vivacity, animation, elation, euphoria, exhilaration, elevation 822 *excitable state*; life and soul of the party, party spirit, conviviality 882 *sociability*.

merriment, good cheer; high spirits, gay abandon; jollity, joviality, jocularity, gaiety, glee, mirth, hilarity 835 *laughter*; levity, frivolity 499 *folly*; merrymaking, fun, fun and games, amusement; jubilation, jubilee 876 *celebration*.

Adj. *cheerful*, cheery, blithe 824 *happy*; hearty, genial, convivial 882 *sociable*; sanguine, optimistic, pronoid, rose-coloured; smiling, sunny, bright, beaming, radiant 835 *laughing*; breezy, of good cheer, in high spirits, in a good humour; in good heart, optimistic, upbeat, hopeful, buoyant; irrepressible; carefree, light-hearted, happy-go-lucky; bouncing; pert, jaunty, bright-eyed and bushy-tailed, perky, chirpy, chipper, spry, spirited, peppy, sprightly, vivacious, animated, vital, sparkling, all lit up, full of beans, on the top of one's form 819 *lively*.

merry, joyful, happy as a sandboy *or* as a king *or* as Larry, etc. 824 *happy*; ebullient, effervescent, bubbly, sparkling, laughter-loving, jocular 839 *witty*; gay, frivolous 456 *lacking concentration*; playful, sportive, frisky, frolicsome, kittenish 837 *amusing*; roguish, arch, sly; merrymaking, mirthful, jovial, jolly, joking, dancing, laughing, singing, drinking; hilarious, uproarious, rip-roaring, rollicking, splitting one's sides, helpless with laughter, tickled pink.

jubilant, overjoyed, gleeful, delighted 824 *pleased*; chuffed, elated, euphoric, flushed, exultant, triumphant, cock-a-hoop, dancing on air 727 *successful*; celebratory.

Vb. *be cheerful*, be in good spirits, be in good humour, be in a good mood, be in good heart; keep cheerful, look on the bright side, keep one's spirits up 852 *hope*; keep one's pecker up, grin and bear it, make the best of it, put a good face upon it 599 *be resolute*; take heart, snap out of it, cheer up, perk up, buck up; brighten, liven up, grow animated, let oneself go, let one's hair down, abandon oneself; radiate good humour, smile, grin from ear to ear, beam, sparkle; dance, sing, carol, lilt, chirrup, chirp, whistle, laugh 835 *rejoice*; whoop, cheer 876 *celebrate*; have fun, frisk, frolic, rollick, romp, gambol, sport, disport oneself, enjoy oneself, have a good time, large it 837 *amuse oneself*; throw a party, make whoopee 882 *be sociable*.

cheer, gladden, warm the cockles of the heart 828 *content*; comfort, console 831 *relieve*; rejoice the heart, put in a good humour 826 *please*; enliven 821 *animate*; exhilarate, elate 826 *delight*; encourage, uplift, hearten, raise the spirits, buck up, perk up, jolly along, bolster up 855 *give courage*; act like a tonic, put new life into 174 *invigorate*.

834 Dejection. Seriousness

N. *dejection*, joylessness, unhappiness, cheerlessness, dreariness, dejectedness, low spirits, blues, dumps, doldrums; dispiritedness, low spirits, feet-bad factor, sinking heart; disillusion 509 *disappointment*; defeatism, pessimism, cynicism, depression, despair, death wish, suicidal tendency 853 *hopelessness*; weariness, oppression, enervation, exhaustion 684 *fatigue*; oppression of spirit, heartache, heaviness, sadness, misery, wretchedness, disconsolateness, dolefulness 825 *sorrow*; despondency, prostration; Slough of Despond, grey dawn; gloom; glumness, long face, face as long as a fiddle; funereal aspect, lacklustre eye; gloom and doom, trouble 825 *worry*.

melancholy, melancholia, depression, clinical depression, endogenous depression, exogenous depression, reactive depression, SAD,

seasonal affective disorder, black mood, blues, moping, sighing, sigh; vapours, spleen 829 *discontent*; weariness of life, world-weariness, taedium vitae, Weltschmerz, angst, nostalgia, homesickness 825 *suffering*.

seriousness, earnestness; gravity, solemnity, sobriety, demureness, staidness, grimness 893 *sullenness*; primness, humourlessness; straight face, poker face, dead pan; sternness; no laughing matter, no cause for mirth.

moper, complainer, Jonah 829 *malcontent*; sourpuss, crosspatch, grouch, bear with a sore head; pessimist, damper, wet blanket, killjoy, faceache, spoilsport; Job's comforter; misery, sad-sack, sobersides, sourpuss; death's-head, skeleton at the feast, gloom and doom merchant, prophet of doom, doomwatcher, doomster, ecodoomster; hypochondriac, malade imaginaire, cyberchondriac.

Adj. *dejected*, joyless, dreary, dreich, cheerless, unhappy, sad; gloomy, despondent, downbeat, unhopeful, pessimistic, defeatist, despairing 853 *hopeless*; discouraged, disheartened; dispirited; troubled, worried 825 *suffering*; downcast, downhearted, low, down, down in the mouth, low-spirited, depressed; out of sorts, not oneself, out of spirits; sluggish, listless, spiritless, lackadaisical 679 *inactive*; lacklustre 419 *dim*; crestfallen 509 *disappointed*; browned off, cheesed off, pissed off, hacked off, gutted, sick as a parrot 829 *discontented*; down in the dumps, in the doldrums; sadder and wiser 830 *regretting*; subdued, disillusioned 509 *disappointed*.

melancholic, hypochondriacal; blue, down in the dumps; jaundiced, sour, pensive, deep in thought; melancholy, sad, triste; saddened, cut up, heavy-hearted, sick at heart, heart-sick 825 *unhappy*; sorry, rueful 830 *regretting*; mournful, doleful, woeful, tearful 836 *lamenting*; cheerless, joyless, dreary, comfortless; forlorn, miserable, broken up, wretched, disconsolate; self-pitying; moody, sulky 893 *sullen*; dismal, gloomy, morose, glum, sunk in gloom; down in the mouth, woebegone.

serious, sober, sober as a judge, sober-sided, solemn, sedate, stolid, staid, demure, muted, grave, stern, Puritanical 735 *severe*; dour, grim, forbidding 893 *sullen*; unsmiling; inscrutable, straight-faced, po-faced, poker-faced, deadpan; prim; humourless; unfunny, heavy-going, dull, solid 838 *tedious*.

cheerless, comfortless; uncongenial, unwelcoming; depressing, dreary, dreich, dull 838 *tedious*; dismal, lugubrious, funereal, gloomy, dark, forbidding; drab, grey, sombre; ungenial.

Vb. *be dejected*, become despondent, lose heart, admit defeat 853 *despair*; succumb 728 *be defeated*; languish, sink, droop, sag, wilt, flag, give up 684 *be fatigued*; look downcast, look down in the mouth, look blue, hang one's head, pull a long face, laugh on the wrong side of one's face; mope, brood 449 *think*; take to heart, sulk; eat one's heart out, sigh, grieve 829 *be discontented*; groan 825 *suffer*; weep 836 *lament*.

be serious, keep a straight face, keep one's countenance, maintain one's gravity; look grave; lack humour, not see the joke, have no sense of humour, take oneself seriously, be a bore 838 *be tedious*.

sadden, grieve; turn one's hair grey, break one's heart, pluck at one's heartstrings, make one's heart bleed; draw tears, bring tears to one's eyes, bring tears to a glass eye, touch the heart, leave not a dry eye 821 *impress*; pain, spoil one's pleasure 829 *cause discontent*; drive to despair; prostrate.

depress, deject, get one down; cause alarm and despondency, dishearten, discourage, dispirit, take the heart out of, unman, unnerve 854 *frighten*; spoil the fun, take the joy out of, cast a shadow, cast a gloom over 418 *darken*; damp, dampen, damp the spirits, put a damper on, be a wet blanket, throw cold water, frown upon 613 *dissuade*; dash one's hopes 509 *disappoint*; weigh heavy on one's heart; make the heart sick, weary 684 *fatigue*; sober 534 *teach*.

835 Rejoicing

N. *rejoicing*, jubilation, exultation 876 *celebration*; congratulations, felicitation, pat on the back, bouquets, self-congratulation, mutual congratulation 886 *congratulation*; plaudits, clapping, applause, shout, cheers, rousing cheers, three cheers, huzza, hurrah, high-five, hosannah, hallelujah 923 *praise*; thanksgiving 907 *thanks*; paean; raptures, elation, euphoria 824 *joy*; revelling 837 *revel*; merrymaking, gay abandon 833 *merriment*.

laughter, risibility; loud laughter, hearty laughter, shout of laughter, peal of laughter, shrieks of laughter, hoots of laughter, gales of laughter, cachinnation; derision 851 *ridicule*; laugh, belly laugh, horse laugh, guffaw, chuckle, chortle, gurgle, cackle, crow, coo; giggle, snigger, snicker, titter, tee-hee; fit of laughing, the giggles; forced laugh; smile, simper, smirk, grin, broad grin, grin from ear to ear, Cheshire cat grin; twinkle, half-smile, enigmatic smile, Gioconda smile; humour, sense of humour 839 *wit*; laughableness, laughing matter, comedy, farce 497 *absurdity*.

Adj. *rejoicing*, revelling, cheering, shouting, etc. (see vb.); exultant, elated, euphoric 833 *jubilant*; lyrical, ecstatic 923 *approving*.

laughing, guffawing, etc. (see vb.); splitting one's sides, laughing one's head off, creased, doubled up, convulsed with laughter, dying with laughter, shrieking with mirth, rolling in the aisles; humorous; mocking; laughable, risible, derisory 849 *ridiculous*; comic, comical, funny, farcical 497 *absurd*.

Vb. *rejoice*, be joyful, jump for joy, dance for joy, dance, skip 312 *leap*; clap, clap one's hands, throw one's cap in the air, whoop, cheer, huzza, hurrah 923 *applaud*; shout 408 *shout*; carol 413 *sing*; sing paeans, shout hosannas, sound the trumpet 923 *praise*; exult, crow 876 *celebrate*; felicitate 886 *congratulate*; give thanks, thank one's lucky stars 907 *thank*; abandon oneself, let oneself go, loosen up, let one's hair down, paint the town red, go mad for joy, dance in the streets; make merry 833 *be cheerful*; have a good time, frolic, frisk 837 *revel*; have a party, go on a spree, celebrate 882 *be sociable*; feel pleased, congratulate oneself, hug oneself, give oneself a pat on the back, rub one's hands, smack one's lips, gloat 824 *be pleased*; purr, coo, gurgle; sigh for pleasure, cry for joy.

laugh, burst out laughing, crack up, break up, get the giggles, get a fit of the giggles; hoot, chuckle, chortle, cackle; giggle, snigger, snicker, titter, tee-hee, ha-ha, haw-haw; laugh at, laugh in one's sleeve *or* one's beard, mock, deride 851 *ridicule*; cachinnate; shake with mirth, fall about, split one's sides, be in stitches, double up, shriek with laughter, hoot with laughter, roar with laughter, nearly die laughing, kill oneself laughing, laugh fit to burst, laugh one's head off.

smile, break into a smile, grin, grin from ear to ear, grin like a Cheshire cat; give a half-smile, smirk; twinkle, beam, flash a smile.

Int. *cheers!*, three cheers!, huzza!, hurrah!, hooray!, hosanna!, hallelujah!, glory be!, hail the conquering hero!

836 Lamentation

N. *lamentation*, lamenting, ululation, wail, groaning, weeping, wailing, keening; weeping and wailing, beating the breast, tearing one's hair, wringing one's hands; mourning 364 *funeral rites*; sackcloth and ashes; widow's weeds, crepe, black; Wailing Wall; crying, sobbing, sighing, blubbering, whimpering, whining, snivelling, etc. (see vb.); tears, tearfulness, dolefulness 834 *dejection*; tears of pity 905 *pity*; red eyes, eyes swimming *or* brimming with tears; floods of tears, hysterics; cry, good cry; tear, teardrop; heaving breast, sob, sigh, groan, moan, bawl, boo-hoo.

lament, plaint, dirge, knell, requiem, elegy, swansong, funeral oration 364 *funeral rites*; keen, wake 905 *condolence*; howl 409 *howling*; tears of grief; tale of woe; show of grief, crocodile tears 542 *sham.*

Adj. lamenting, crying, etc. (see vb.); in tears, bathed in tears; tearful, lachrymose; red-eyed, with moist eyes; close to tears, on the verge of tears, ready to cry; mournful, doleful, lugubrious 825 *unhappy*; woeful, woebegone, wringing one's hands, beating one's breast 834 *dejected*; plaintive, singing the blues; elegiac, dirgelike 364 *funereal*; in mourning, in black, in widow's weeds, in sackcloth and ashes; at half-mast; with a tale of woe; pathetic, pitiful, lamentable, tear-jerking.

Vb. lament, grieve, sorrow, sigh, heave a sigh 825 *suffer*; deplore 830 *regret*; condole, commiserate 905 *pity*; grieve for, sigh for, weep over, cry over, bewail, bemoan, elegize; sing the dirge, sing a requiem, toll the knell 364 *inter*; mourn, wail, weep and wail, keen; express grief, go into mourning; put on sackcloth and ashes, wring one's hands, beat one's breast, tear one's hair; take on, carry on, take it badly; tell one's tale of woe 829 *be discontented.*

weep, wail, greet; shed tears, burst into tears, dissolve in tears, give way to tears, break down, cry, cry like a baby, boo-hoo, bawl, cry one's eyes out; howl, yell, scream, shriek 409 *howl*; sob, sigh, moan, groan 825 *suffer*; snivel, grizzle, blubber, pule, mewl, whine, whinge, whimper; be on the verge of tears; cry out before one is hurt.

837 Amusement

N. amusement, pleasure, delight 826 *pleasurableness*; game (see also *indoor game*, *ball game*, etc. below); diversion, divertissement, entertainment, light entertainment, popular entertainment; dramatic entertainment 594 *drama*; radio, television 531 *broadcasting*; video, video game; pop music, personal stereo, ghetto blaster; karaoke; pastime, hobby, labour of love 597 *voluntary work*; solace, recreation 685 *refreshment*; relaxation 683 *rest*; holiday, Bank holiday 681 *leisure*; April Fool's Day, rag day, gala day, red-letter day 876 *special day*; play, sport, fun, good clean fun, high jinks, merriment; do, show, thrash, junket, Gaudy night 876 *celebration*; outing, excursion, jaunt, day out, pleasure trip; treat, Sunday school treat, picnic; social gathering, get-together, at-home, conversazione, garden party, bunfight, bean-feast, fête, flower show, gymkhana, jamboree 74 *assembly*; whist drive, bridge party (see also *card game* below); party games (see also *indoor game* below).

festivity, holiday-making, vacationing; visiting 882 *social round*; fun 835 *laughter*; beer and skittles 824 *enjoyment*; social whirl, round of pleasure; high life, night life; good time; living it up, painting the town red, burning the candle at both ends, a short life and a merry one 943 *intemperance*; festival, fair, funfair, fun of the fair, carnival, fiesta, gala; masque; festivities, fun and games, merrymaking, revels, Mardi Gras 833 *merriment*; feast day, special day; carousal, wassail 301 *feasting*; conviviality, house-warming, party, bottle party, byob (= bring your own bottle) party 882 *social gathering*; drinking bout, spree, bender, booze-up 301 *drinking*; orgy, carouse 949 *drunkenness*; binge, beano, thrash, blowout; barbecue, bean-feast, bunfight, dinner, annual dinner, banquet 301 *meal.*

revel, rave-up, knees-up, jollification, whoopee, fun, high old time; fun fast and furious, high jinks, spree, junket, junketing; night out, night on the tiles; bonfire; play, game, romp, frolic, lark, skylarking, escapade, antic, prank, rag, trick, monkey trick 497 *foolery.*

pleasure ground, park, theme park, adventure park, deer park, wildlife park, safari park, national park, grouse moor; village green, gardens, pleasure gardens, winter gardens 192 *park*; beach, seaside, Riviera, lido, marina, bathing beach, holiday camp; playground, adventure playground, recreation ground, playing field, links, golf course, golf links, putting green; rink, skating rink, ice rink; tennis court, petanque court, bowling green, croquet lawn 724 *arena*; circus, fair.

place of amusement, fairground, funfair, amusement park, shooting gallery, amusement arcade; skittle alley, bowling alley, billiard room, pool room; concert hall, music hall, cinema, movie theatre; theatre, ballroom; dance hall, discothèque, disco; cabaret, night club, strip joint, clip joint; bingo hall, casino 618 *gambling den.*

sport, outdoor life; sportsmanship, gamesmanship 694 *skill*; sports, field sports, track events; games, gymnastics 162 *athletics*, 312 *leap*, 716 *contest*, *racing*, *boxing*, *wrestling*; weight-lifting, snatch, clean and jerk; weight-training, pumping iron, going for the burn; trampolining; outdoor sports, cycling, hiking, rambling, orienteering, trail-running, speed-walking, camping, picnicking; running, jogging, trail-running, speed-walking, race-walking, marathon; riding, pony-trekking; archery, shooting, clay-pigeon shooting; hunting, shooting and fishing 619 *chase*; watersports, swimming, bathing, snorkelling, surf-riding, wind-surfing, boardsailing, body-surfing; water skiing, aqua-planing, boating, rowing, yachting, sailing, diving, skin diving, subaqua, free diving, scuba diving, deep-sea diving 269 *watersports*; bog-snorkelling; rock-climbing, mountaineering, hill-walking, etc. 308 *ascent*; exploring, caving, speleology, pot-holing 309 *descent*; winter sports, skiing, snow-boarding, ski-jumping, bobsleighing, tobogganing, skeleton-bob, skating, ice skating, ice hockey; curling; flying, microlighting, gliding, hang-gliding, paragliding, parasailing, parascending 271 *aeronautics*; extreme sports, base jumping, bungee-jumping, cliff jumping, skydiving, whitewater rafting; mind sports.

ball game, bat and ball game; cricket, French cricket; baseball, rounders; tennis, lawn tennis, mini tennis, real tennis, table tennis, pingpong; badminton; squash, rackets, racketball; handball, volleyball, beach volleyball; fives, pelota; netball, basketball; football, Association football, soccer, the beautiful game, five-a-side, fantasy football, rugby, Rugby football, Rugby Union, Rugby League, rugger, seven-a-side, sevens, Gaelic football, Australian Rules football, Rules; lacrosse; hockey, ice hockey, shinty, hurling; polo, water polo; croquet; quidditch; golf, clock golf, crazy golf, putting; pitch and putt; skittles, ninepins, bowling, ten-pin bowling, five-pin bowling, bowls, carpet bowling, crown-green bowling, petanque, boules; marbles; billiards, snooker, pool; bagatelle, pinball. (See also 287 *missile*.)

throwing game, quoits, deck quoits, hoop-la, horseshoes; tossing the caber, throwing the hammer, putting the shot *or* shot-putting *or* shot-put, discus, javelin; shove ha'penny, curling. (See also 287 *missile*.)

indoor game, parlour game, panel game, party game; musical bumps, musical chairs, hunt the thimble, hunt the slipper, pass the parcel, postman's knock, kiss in the ring, oranges and lemons, nuts in May; sardines, rabbits, murder; forfeits, guessing game; quiz, twenty questions; charades; parson's *or* minister's cat, I-spy; word game, spelling bee, riddles, crosswords, acrostics, pangrams; paper game, consequences, noughts and crosses, battleships, hangman; darts, dominoes, mah jong(g), tiddlywinks, jigsaw puzzle; computer game, etc. 86 *computing*.

board game, chess; draughts, checkers, Chinese checkers, halma; backgammon; Scrabble (tdmk), ludo, snakes and ladders, Monopoly (tdmk), Trivial Pursuit (tdmk), go.

children's games, ring-a-ring-o'-roses; leap-frog, hopscotch, peever 312 *leap*; touch, tag, tig, he, hide-and-seek, follow-my-leader, Simon says, blind man's buff, hares and hounds, cowboys and Indians, cops and robbers.

outdoor amusements, climbing frame, helter-skelter, roundabout, seesaw, slide, swings; sandpit, tree house, Wendy house; paddling, building sandcastles.

card game, cards, game of cards, rubber of whist, rubber of bridge; whist, solo whist, auction whist; auction bridge, contract bridge; nap, napoleon; picquet, cribbage, bezique; rummy, gin rummy, canasta, hearts, Newmarket, speculation, solitaire, patience; snap, beggar-my-neighbour, old maid, Happy Families; lotto, housey-housey, bingo, vingt-et-un, pontoon, black jack; poker, strip poker, stud poker; banker, baccarat, chemin de fer, chemmy.

gambling game, dice game, roulette, rouge et noir; roulette wheel; coin-spinning, heads and tails, raffle, tombola, sweepstake, lottery, National Lottery, football pool 618 *gambling*; raffle ticket, lottery ticket, scratch card.

dancing, dance, ball; masquerade; fancy dress dance; thé dansant, tea dance, ceilidh, square dance, hoe-down; hop, disco, rave; disco dancing, breakdancing, body-popping; ballet dancing, ballet enthusiast, balletomane 504 *enthusiast*; tap dancing, clog dancing, folk dancing, country dancing, Scottish country dancing, Highland dancing, Irish dancing, morris dancing, old-time dancing, sequence dancing, ballroom dancing, line dancing; table dancing, lap dancing, pole dancing; choreography; eurhythmics, aerobics, step.

dance, war dance, sword dance, corroboree; soft-shoe shuffle, cakewalk; clog dance, step dance, tap dance, toe dance; fan dance, dance of the seven veils, hula-hula; high kicks, can-can; belly dance; country dance, morris dance, barn dance, square dance, dance round a maypole; sailor's dance, hornpipe; folk dance, polonaise, mazurka, czardas; jig, Irish jig; Highland fling; reel, eightsome reel, foursome reel, strathspey; Gay Gordons, Petronella, Duke of Perth, Strip the Willow, Dashing White Sergeant, Sir Roger de Coverley; tarantella, bolero, fandango, galliard, écossaise, gavotte, quadrille, cotillion, minuet, pavane, allemande, schottische, polka; progressive dance *or* progressive; waltz, last waltz, Viennese waltz, hesitation waltz, St Bernard waltz, valeta; Lancers; foxtrot, turkey trot, quickstep, Charleston, black bottom, blues, one-step, two-step, Boston two-step, military two-step; flamenco, paso-doble, tango, rumba, samba, mambo, bossa nova, limbo, beguine, cerok, conga, conga line, cha-cha, lambada, macarena, salsa, mosh; boomps-a-daisy, hokey-cokey, Lambeth Walk, Palais Glide; stomp, bop, bebop, shimmy, jive, breakdancing, bodypopping, disco dancing, Lindy-hopping, rock 'n' roll, twist, shake, locomotion; excuse-me dance, Paul Jones, snowball.

plaything, toy 639 *bauble*; children's toy, rattle, bricks, building bricks, Meccano (tdmk), Lego (tdmk); Jack-in-the-box, teddy bear, puppet, glove puppet, golliwog, doll, china doll, rag doll, Cabbage Patch (tdmk) doll, Cindy (tdmk) doll, Barbie (tdmk) doll, Action Man (tdmk), Power Ranger (tdmk), Teletubbies (tdmk), Furby (tdmk), Pokémon; doll's house, Wendy house, bouncy castle; doll's pram; top, whipping top, yo-yo; marbles; ball, balloon 252 *sphere*; hoop, Hula-Hoop (tdmk), skipping rope, stilts, pogo stick, rocking horse, hobby horse, tricycle; scooter, microscooter; roller skates, Roller Blades (tdmk), blades, skateboard, mountain board, snowboard, surfboard; popgun, airgun, water pistol; toy soldier, tin soldier, lead soldier; kite; model, model aeroplane, clockwork train, model railway; magic lantern, toy theatre 522 *exhibit*; puppet show, marionettes, Punch and Judy 551 *image*; billiard table; cards; domino, tile; draught, counter, chip; tiddly-wink; chess piece, pawn, knight, bishop, castle *or* rook, queen, king.

player, sportsman *or* -woman, sportsperson; competitor 716 *contender*; seed, seeded player; all-rounder; ball-player, footballer, forward, centre forward, back, striker, winger, defence, sweeper, libero, playmaker, midfield, engine room, goal-keeper; cricketer, batsman, fielder, wicket-keeper, bowler; hockey-player, tennis-player; marksman, archer; shot-putter; gambler; card-player, chess-player.

Adj. *amusing*, entertaining, diverting, etc. (see vb.); fun-making, full of fun 833 *merry*; pleasant 826 *pleasurable*; recreational 685 *refreshing*.

Vb. *amuse*, entertain, divert, tickle, make one laugh, take one out of oneself; tickle the fancy, titillate, please 826 *delight*; enliven 833 *cheer*; raise a smile, convulse with laughter, have them rolling in the aisles, wow, slay, be the death of 849 *be ridiculous*; humour, keep amused, put in a good humour, put in a cheerful mood; give a party, have a get-together, play the host *or* hostess 882 *be hospitable*.

amuse oneself, relax, hang out; kill time, while away the time, pass the time, pursue one's hobby, dabble in; play, play at; have fun, enjoy oneself, get one's jollies, large it 833 *be cheerful*; take a holiday, have a break, go on vacation, go on an outing, have a field day,

have a ball; disport oneself; take one's pleasure; frolic, romp, gambol, caper, play tricks, play pranks, lark around, fool about, play the fool 497 *be absurd*; jest 839 *be witty*; play cards; game, dice 618 *gamble*; play games, be a fitness freak; live the outdoor life, camp, caravan, take a holiday home, timeshare; picnic; sail, yacht, surf, windsurf, sailboard, fly; hunt, shoot, fish; play golf; ride, trek, hike, ramble; run, jog, race, jump; bathe, swim, dive; skate, roller-skate, ski, toboggan; work out, pump iron.

dance, go dancing; tap-dance, waltz, foxtrot, quickstep, Charleston, tango, rumba, jive, jitterbug, stomp, bop, twist, rock 'n' roll, disco-dance, breakdance, bodypop; whirl 315 *rotate*; cavort, caper, jig about, bob up and down; shuffle, hoof, tread a measure, trip the light fantastic 312 *leap*.

revel, make merry, make whoopee, have a ball, celebrate 835 *rejoice*; drive dull care away, make it a party, have a good time; let oneself go, let one's hair down, let off steam; go on a bender, go on a spree, have a night out, have a night on the tiles, live it up, paint the town red; junket, roister; feast, banquet, carouse, make the rafters ring; go on a binge, go pub-crawling 301 *drink*; drown one's sorrows 949 *get drunk*; sow one's wild oats, burn the candle at both ends; stay up till all hours, go home in the wee sma' hours, never go home till morning, go home with the cows.

838 Tedium

N. *tedium*, boredom, ennui, world-weariness, Weltschmerz 834 *melancholy*; lack of interest, election fatigue, donor fatigue, compassion fatigue, disaster fatigue 860 *indifference*; weariness, languor 684 *fatigue*; tediousness, irksomeness; dryness, stodginess, heaviness; flatness, staleness 387 *insipidness*; stuffiness 840 *dullness*; prolixity 570 *diffuseness*; sameness 16 *uniformity*; monotony 106 *repetition*; time to kill 679 *inactivity*; doodling, thumb-twiddling.

bore, utter bore, no fun; drag, bind, chore; beaten track, daily round, rut 610 *habit*; grindstone, treadmill 682 *labour*; boring person, drip, anorak, train-spotter, saddo, dweeb, fart (vulg), geek, pain in the neck, pub bore; wet blanket, killjoy, misery 834 *moper*; boring story: ancient history, old hat, old news, Queen Anne's dead.

Adj. *tedious*, uninteresting, unexciting, unentertaining; slow, dragging, leaden, heavy; dry, arid; flat, stale, insipid 387 *tasteless*; bald 573 *plain*; humdrum, soulless, suburban, depressing, dreary, dreich, stuffy, bourgeois

840 *dull*; stodgy, prosaic, uninspired; long-winded, drawn out 570 *long-winded*; soporific, boring, wearisome, tiresome, irksome; wearing; repetitive; unvarying, monotonous 16 *uniform*; cloying, satiating.

bored, twiddling one's thumbs, doodling, kicking one's heels 679 *inactive*; fed up to the back teeth, browned off, cheesed off, hacked off, had it up to here 829 *discontented*; jaded 684 *fatigued*; world-weary 834 *melancholic*; blasé 860 *indifferent*; satiated, cloyed 863 *satiated*; sick of, sick and tired, fed up; been there, done that.

Vb. *be tedious*, pall, lose its novelty, cloy, jade, satiate 863 *satiate*; bore, irk, try, weary 684 *fatigue*; bore to death, bore to tears, bore the pants off, bore stiff; weary to distraction, get one down, get on one's nerves, outstay one's welcome; make one yawn, send one to sleep; drag 278 *move slowly*; go on and on, never end; drone on, bang on, harp on; be prolix 570 *be diffuse*.

Adv. *boringly*, ad nauseam, to death.

839 Wit

N. *wit*, wittiness, pointedness, point; ready wit, badinage, repartee; Attic salt, elegance; sparkle, scintillation, brightness 498 *intelligence*; humour, sense of humour; wry humour, pawkiness, dryness; drollery, pleasantry, waggishness, facetiousness; jocularity 833 *merriment*; comicalness, absurdity 849 *ridiculousness*; flippancy 456 *inattention*; fun, joking, practical joking, jesting, tomfoolery, buffoonery, clowning, funny business 497 *foolery*; comic turn, laugh a minute; broad humour, low humour, vulgarity 847 *bad taste*; farce, broad farce, knockabout comedy, slapstick, custard-pie humour, ham, high camp 594 *dramatic theory*; whimsicality, fancy 604 *whim*; cartoon, comic strip, caricature; biting wit, cruel humour, satire, sarcasm 851 *ridicule*; irony, spoof 850 *affectation*; black comedy, black humour, sick humour; wordplay, play upon words, punning.

witticism, witty remark, wisecrack; sally, mot, bon mot; epigram; pun, play upon words; punch line, throwaway line; banter, chaff, badinage; repartee, quid pro quo, backchat 460 *answer*; sarcasm 851 *satire*; joke, standing joke, private joke, family joke, in-joke; jest, good one, rib-tickler, side-splitter; quip; gag, one-liner; old joke, corny joke, chestnut; practical joke, hoax, spoof, legpull; dirty joke, blue joke, sick joke; story, funny story, shaggy-dog story; limerick, clerihew.

humorist, wit, epigrammatist; life and soul of the party, wag, joker; jokesmith, funny man, gagster, punster; banterer, leg-puller, ragger, teaser; practical joker, hoaxer, spoof artist 545 *deceiver*; satirist, lampooner 926 *detractor*; comedian, comedienne, comic, standup comic, slapstick comic 594 *entertainer*; comic writer, cartoonist, caricaturist; impersonator, parodist 20 *imitator*; raconteur, raconteuse; jester, court jester, clown, zany, buffoon, stooge 501 *fool*.

Adj. *witty*, nimble-witted, quick; elegant; pointed, pithy, epigrammatic; brilliant, sparkling, smart, clever, too clever by half 498 *intelligent*; salty, racy, piquant; fruity, risqué; snappy, biting, pungent, keen, sharp, sarcastic; ironic, dry, sly, pawky; facetious, flippant 456 *lacking concentration*; jocular, joking, jokey, waggish, roguish; comic, funny ha-ha, rib-tickling 849 *funny*; comical, humorous, droll; whimsical 604 *capricious*; playful, sportive, fooling 497 *absurd*.

Vb. *be witty*, scintillate, sparkle; jest, joke, crack a joke, quip, wisecrack; tell a good story, raise a laugh, have the audience in stitches 837 *amuse*; pun, make a pun, play upon words; pull one's leg, have one on, put one on, make fun of, poke fun at, get a rise out of 851 *ridicule*; caricature 851 *satirize*.

840 Dullness

N. *dullness*, heaviness 834 *dejection*; stuffiness, dreariness, deadliness; monotony, boringness 838 *tedium*; colourlessness, drabness, dreichness; lack of sparkle, lack of fire, lack of inspiration, lack of originality; stodginess, turgidity; staleness, flatness 387 *insipidness*; banality; lack of humour, prosaicness.

Adj. *dull*, uninteresting, uninspiring; deadly dull, dull as ditchwater; stuffy, dreary, deadly; boring, tedious; colourless, drab, dreich; flat, bland, vapid, insipid 387 *tasteless*; unimaginative, uninventive, unoriginal, derivative; stupid 499 *unintelligent*; humourless, frumpish 834 *serious*; inelegant; heavy, heavy-footed, clod-hopping, ponderous, sluggish 278 *slow*; stodgy, turgid, prosaic, matter-of-fact, pedestrian; stale, banal, common-place, hackneyed, trite, platitudinous 610 *usual*.

841 Beauty

N. *beauty*, pulchritude; perfection; the sublime, splendour, gorgeousness; radiance; transfiguration 843 *beautification*; polish, gloss, ornament 844 *ornamentation*; scenic beauty, picturesqueness, scenery, view, landscape, seascape, snowscape, cloudscape 445 *spectacle*; regular features, classic features 245 *symmetry*; physical beauty, loveliness, comeliness, fairness, handsomeness, bonniness, prettiness, chocolate-box prettiness, picture-postcard prettiness; attraction, attractiveness, agreeableness, charm 826 *pleasurableness*; appeal, glamour, glitz, sex appeal, it, cuteness, attractions, physical attractions, charms; good looks, pretty face, beaux yeux; eyes of blue, ruby lips, schoolgirl complexion, peaches and cream complexion; shapeliness, trim figure, curves, curvaceousness, vital statistics, the body beautiful; gracefulness, grace 575 *elegance*; chic, style, dress sense 848 *fashion*; delicacy, refinement 846 *good taste*; aesthetics.

a beauty, thing of beauty, work of art; garden, beauty spot; masterpiece 644 *exceller*; bijou, jewel, jewel in the crown, pearl, treasure 646 *paragon*; peacock, swan, flower, rosebud, rose, lily; belle, raving beauty, toast of the tour, idol 890 *favourite*; dream girl; jolie laide; beauty queen, Miss World, bathing beauty, bathing belle, pin-up girl, cover girl, page 3 girl, centre-fold girl, sweater girl, pin-up, cheesecake; English rose; beefcake, hunk, über-hunk, muscleman, Mr Universe; fine figure of a man *or* woman, spunk (Aust & NZ); blond(e), brunette, redhead; dream, a dream walking, vision, poem, picture, sight for sore eyes; angel, charmer, dazzler; knockout, eyeful, good-looker, looker; doll, dolly bird, bimbo; glamour puss, glamour girl *or* boy, It girl; heartthrob, dreamboat; enchantress, femme fatale, vamp, seductress, siren, witch 983 *sorceress*; smasher, stunner, lovely, cutie, honey, beaut, peach, dish, arm candy, eye candy, über-babe, sex on a stick; beautiful woman: Venus, Aphrodite, Helen of Troy; handsome man: Adonis, Narcissus.

Adj. beautiful, beauteous, pulchritudinous; lovely, fair, radiant, comely, bonny, pretty; pretty-pretty, pretty in a chocolate box way, picture-postcard, good enough to eat; pretty as a picture, photogenic; handsome, good-looking; well-built, husky, manly; tall, dark and handsome; statuesque, Junoesque; godlike, goddess-like, divine, pleasing to the eye, lovely to behold; picturesque, scenic, ornamental; aesthetic 846 *tasteful*; exquisite, perfect, picture-perfect.

splendid, superb, fine 644 *excellent*; grand 868 *noble*; glorious, rich, gorgeous; resplendent, magnificent.

shapely, well-proportioned, of classic proportions 245 *symmetrical*; well-formed, well-turned; well-rounded, well-stacked, well-endowed, buxom, bosomy, curvaceous 248 *curved*; slinky; clean-limbed, straight, slender, slim, lissom, svelte, willowy 206 *lean*; graceful, elegant, chic; petite, dainty, delicate; perfect.

personable, attractive, prepossessing, agreeable; buxom, sonsy; dishy, phat, fetching, appealing 826 *pleasurable*; fanciable, sexy, foxy, cute; charming, entrancing, alluring, enchanting, glamorous; winsome; fresh-faced, clean-cut, wholesome, blooming; rosy-cheeked, apple-cheeked, cherry-lipped, fresh-complexioned, bright-eyed; sightly, becoming, easy on the eye; presentable, natty, trim; spruce, dapper, glossy, sleek; well-dressed, well turned out, smart, stylish, classy, chic, soigné(e) 848 *fashionable*; elegant, dainty, delicate, refined 846 *tasteful*.

Vb. be beautiful, be splendid, etc. (see adj.); be entrancing 983 *bewitch*; take one's breath away, beggar all description; be photogenic, photograph well; have good looks, bloom, dazzle 417 *shine*; be dressed to kill.

beautify, trim, improve; prettify, decorate; ornament; set off, grace, suit, become, go well, show one off, flatter; bring out the highlights, enhance one's looks, glamorize, transfigure; give a face-lift, smarten up; prink, titivate, do oneself up, do one's face, powder, rouge 843 *primp*.

842 Ugliness

N. ugliness, unsightliness, hideousness, repulsiveness; gracelessness, lumpishness, clumsiness 576 *inelegance*; asymmetry 246 *distortion*; unshapeliness 246 *deformity*; disfigurement 845 *blemish*; defacement; squalor, filth, grottiness, yuk 649 *uncleanness*; homeliness, plainness, ugly face; not much to look at, no beauty, no oil painting, wry face, forbidding countenance, haggardness; fading beauty, dim eyes, wrinkles, crow's-feet, hand of time, ravages of time 131 *age*.

eyesore, hideosity; blemish; offence to the eyes; blot on the landscape, architectural monstrosity, satanic mills; ugly person, fright, sight, faceache, frump; scarecrow, horror, death's-head, gargoyle; monster; harridan, witch; toad, gorilla, baboon, crow; plain Jane, ugly duckling; satyr, Caliban; Gorgon, Medusa; Beast. (See also 938 *monster*.)

Adj. ugly, ugly as sin, butt-ugly, hideous, foul 649 *unclean*; frightful, shocking, monstrous; repulsive, repellent, odious, loathsome; beastly; not much to look at, short on looks, unprepossessing, homely, plain, plain-looking, without any looks; mousy, frumpish; ill-favoured, saturnine 893 *sullen*.

unsightly, ravaged, wrinkled 131 *ageing*; not fit to be seen, unseemly; marred; shapeless, formless 244 *formless*; grotesque, twisted, deformed, disfigured 246 *distorted*; defaced, vandalized, litter-strewn; ill-proportioned, misshapen; dumpy, squat 196 *dwarfish*; bloated 195 *fat*; ghastly; gruesome.

graceless, ungraceful 576 *inelegant*; unaesthetic; unattractive; badly dressed; tawdry; crude, uncouth 699 *artless*; clumsy, awkward, ungainly, cumbersome, hulky, hulking, slouching, clodhopping 195 *unwieldy*.

Vb. *be ugly*, be short on looks, lose one's looks; show one's age; look a wreck, look a mess, look a fright.

make ugly, uglify; sully 649 *make unclean*; deface, disfigure, mar, blemish; grimace; twist 246 *distort*; mutilate, vandalize 655 *impair*.

843 Beautification

N. *beautification*, beautifying 844 *ornamentation*; make-over, transfiguration 143 *transformation*; landscape gardening, garden design 844 *ornamental art*.

beauty treatment, beauty therapy; plastic surgery, cosmetic surgery, bus-stop surgery; cosmetic holiday; nose-job, skin-grafting, face-lift 658 *surgery*; rhinoplasty, browlift, ear tuck, eyelift, genoplasty, abdominoplasty, tummy tuck; breast enlargement, breast implant, breast lift, face-lifting, eyebrow-plucking, waxing, bikini wax, sugaring, electrolysis; face mask, mud pack, facial, facial scrub; skin peel, acid peel, AHA peel, chemical peel, microdermabrasion, lunchtime peel, particle resurfacing, laser resurfacing; Botox (tdmk), gel-filler *or* filler-gel; cellulite, orange peel; liposuction, lipo (inf), microsuction, lipoplasty, lipectomy; body wrap; massage, body massage, Swedish massage, Thai massage; manicure, buffing; pedicure, chiropody; tattooing 844 *ornamental art*; body-piercing, ear-piercing, eyebrow-piercing, navel-piercing, nose-piercing, tongue-piercing; suntanning; sun lamp, sun bed; toilet, grooming, make-up, cosmetology; cleansing, moisturizing, toning, creaming, rouging, painting, dyeing, powdering; soaping, shampooing; wash and brush up 648 *washing*.

hairdressing, trichology; shaving, clipping, trimming, thinning, singeing; depilation; cutting, haircut, bobbing, shingling; shave, hair cut, razor cut, clip, trim, singe, short back and sides; hair style, coiffure, crop, Eton crop, bob, shingle, pageboy, crewcut, buzz cut, urchin cut, bouffant cut, coupe sauvage, spike; styling, hair-styling, curling, frizzing, waving, setting, hair-straightening, defrizzing; hairdo, restyle, shampoo and set, set; blow-dry, finger-dry, scrunching; wave, blow wave, marcel wave, cold wave; permanent wave, perm; curl 251 *coil*; bang, fringe, ponytail, bunches, pigtail, plaits, chignon, bun; pompadour, beehive, Afro 259 *hair*; hairpiece, toupee, switch, hair extension, hair weaving, hair implant;

curling iron, tongs, curl papers, curlers, rollers, heated rollers; bandeau, Alice band; comb, hairpin, hairgrip, bobby pin, Kirbigrip (tdmk), slide; hairnet, snood 228 *headgear*.

hairwash, shampoo, conditioner, rinse, highlights, bleach, tint, dye, henna, peroxide; hair mousse, hair gel, setting lotion, hair spray, lacquer, volumizer; hair-cream, brilliantine; hair-restorer.

cosmetic, beauty aid, beauty spot; make-up, stick make-up; greasepaint, warpaint, rouge, blusher, highlighter, concealer; cream, face cream, cold cream, cleansing cream, vanishing cream, moisturizing cream, night cream, lanolin 357 *ointment*; lipstick, lip gloss; nail polish, nail varnish, powder, face powder, talcum powder, talc; eye make-up, kohl, mascara, eye shadow, eyeliner, eyebrow pencil; hand lotion, skin toner, aftershave lotion, suntan lotion; bath salts, bath oil, bath essence, bubble bath, foam bath 648 *cleanser*; antiperspirant, deodorant; scent, perfume, essence, cologne, eau de cologne, lavender water, toilet water; false eyelashes; powder puff, compact; vanity case, manicure set, nail file, nail scissors, clippers; shaver, razor, electric razor, depilatory, strip wax; toiletry, toiletries.

beautician, beauty specialist, beauty therapist; plastic surgeon; make-up artist; cosmetician; barber, hairdresser, hair stylist, coiffeur, coiffeuse; trichologist; manicurist, pedicurist, chiropodist; beauty salon, nail bar.

Vb. *primp*, prettify, doll up, do up, dress up, ornament 844 *decorate*; prink, trick out; preen; titivate, make up, apply cosmetics, rouge, paint, powder; shave, pluck one's eyebrows, wax one's eyebrows, varnish one's nails, dye *or* tint one's hair; curl, wave, perm; have a hairdo, have a facial, have a manicure 841 *beautify*.

844 Ornamentation

N. *ornamentation*, decoration, adornment, garnish; ornateness 574 *ornament*; art deco, art nouveau, baroque, rococo; chinoiserie; richness, gilt, gaudiness 875 *ostentation*; enhancement, enrichment, embellishment; table decoration, tablecloth, runner, centrepiece; silver, china, glass; floral decoration, flower arrangement, wreath, garland, bouquet, nosegay, posy, buttonhole; objet d'art, bric-a-brac, curio, bibelot.

ornamental art, landscape gardening, topiary *or* topiarism; architecture; interior decoration; statuary 554 *sculpture*; frieze, dado, triglyph; figurehead; boss, cornice, gargoyle; astragal, moulding, beading, fluting, fretting, tracery; varnishing 226 *facing*; veneering, panelling; ormolu, gilt, gold leaf; illumination, illustration, sign-painting, graphic art 551 *art*; stained glass; tie-dyeing, batik; heraldic art 547 *heraldry*; tattooing, body-piercing, ear-piercing, etc. 843 *beauty treatment*; etching 555 *engraving*; handiwork, handicraft, fancywork, woodwork, fretwork, open-work, filigree; whittling, carving, embossing, chasing, intaglio; inlay, inset, enamelling, mosaic, marquetry 437 *variegation*; metalwork; gem-cutting, setting; cut glass, engraved glass; wrought iron.

pattern, motif, print, design, composition 331 *structure*; detail; geometrical style, rose window, spandrel, cyma, ogee, fleuron, cusp, trefoil, fleur-de-lis; tracery, scrollwork, arabesque, flourish, curlicue 251 *coil*; weave 331 *texture*; argyle, Arran, paisley 222 *textile*; chevron; tartan, check 437 *chequer*; pin-stripe 437 *stripe*; spot, dot, polka dot 437 *maculation*; herringbone, zigzag, dogtooth, hound's tooth 220 *obliqueness*; watermark, logo 547 *identification*.

needlework, cross-stitch; patchwork, appliqué; open work, drawn-thread work; embroidery, smocking; crochet, lace, broderie anglaise; tatting, knitting 222 *network*; stitch, purl, plain, stocking stitch, garter stitch, moss stitch; gros point, petit point, needlepoint; chain stitch, cable stitch, hem stitch, stem stitch, blanket stitch, feather stitch, back stitch, satin stitch, herringbone stitch, French knot, lazy-daisy.

trimming, piping, valance, border, fringe, frieze, frill, flounce 234 *edging*; binding 589 *bookbinding*; trappings; braid, frog, lapel, epaulette, star, rosette, cockade 547 *badge*; bow 47 *fastening*; bobble, pompom; tassel, bead; ermine, fur 259 *hair*; feather, ostrich feather, osprey, plume 259 *plumage*; streamer, ribbon.

finery, togs, gear, glad rags, Sunday best, best bib and tucker 228 *clothing*; frippery, frills and furbelows, ribbons, froufrou; trinket, knick-knack, gewgaw *or* geegaw, fandangle; tinsel, spangle, sequin, diamante, costume jewellery, glass, paste, marcasite, rhinestone 639 *bauble*.

jewellery, bijouterie, bling *or* bling-bling; crown jewels, diadem, tiara 743 *regalia*; costume jewellery; drop, pendant, locket 217 *hanging object*; crucifix; amulet, charm 983 *talisman*; rope, string, necklet, necklace, beads, pearls, choker, lariat, chain, watch chain 250 *loop*; armlet, anklet, bracelet, bangle; earring, drop earring; ring, signet ring, wedding ring, eternity ring, engagement ring, dress ring 250 *circle*; keeper; cameo, brooch, clasp, badge; crest; stud, pin, gold pin, tie pin, collar stud; cufflinks 47 *fastening*; medal, medallion, bindi. (See also *finery* above.)

gem, jewel, bijou; stone, precious stone, semiprecious stone; uncut gem, cut gem, cabochon; diamond, rock, ice; solitaire; ruby, pearl, cultured pearl, seed pearl; opal, black opal, fire opal; sapphire, turquoise, emerald, beryl, aquamarine; quartz, cairngorm, garnet, amethyst, topaz, chalcedony, cornelian *or* carnelian, jasper, agate, onyx; heliotrope, bloodstone, moonstone, cat's-eye, zircon, jacinth, hyacinth, chrysolite, obsidian; coral, ivory, mother of pearl, jet, amber, jade, lapis lazuli.

Adj. *ornamental*, decorative, decorated, patterned, fancy, arty-crafty; intricate, elaborate; picturesque, pretty-pretty, chocolate-box pretty; scenic; geometric; Doric, Ionic, Corinthian, Moresque, Romanesque, Decorated; baroque, rococo; gimmicky, with bells and whistles, all singing, all dancing.

Vb. *decorate*, adorn, embellish, enhance, enrich; set off 574 *ornament*; paint, bejewel; tart up, glamorize; garnish, trim; array, bedeck 228 *dress*; deck out, trick out, preen, titivate 843 *primp*; add the finishing touches; freshen, smarten, spruce up, furbish, burnish 648 *clean*; stud, beribbon; bespangle 437 *variegate*; whitewash, varnish, japan, lacquer 226 *coat*; enamel, gild, silver; emblazon, illuminate, illustrate 553 *paint*, 425 *colour*; trim 234 *hem*; work, pick out, embroider; inlay, engrave; encrust, emboss, bead, mould; fret, carve 262 *groove*, 260 *notch*; wreathe.

845 Blemish

N. *blemish*, scar, cicatrice, weal, welt, mark, pockmark; flaw, crack, defect 647 *imperfection*; disfigurement, deformity 246 *distortion*; stigma, blot, blot on the landscape 842 *eyesore*; graffiti; blotch, splotch, smudge 550 *obliteration*; smut, patch, smear, stain, tarnish, rust, patina 649 *dirt*; spot, speck, speckle, macula, spottiness 437 *maculation*; freckle, mole, birthmark, strawberry mark; excrescence, pimple, plook, zit, blackhead, whitehead, carbuncle, sebaceous cyst, wen, wart 253 *swelling*; acne, rosacea, eczema 651 *skin disease*; harelip, cleft palate; cast, squint; scratch, bruise, black eye, shiner, cauliflower ear, broken nose 655 *wound*.

Vb. *blemish*, flaw, crack, injure, damage 655 *impair*; blot, smudge, stain, smear, sully, soil 649 *make unclean*; stigmatize, brand 547 *mark*; scar, pit, pockmark; mar, spoil, spoil the look of 842 *make ugly*; deface, vandalize, disfigure, scratch 244 *deform*.

846 Good taste

N. *good taste*, tastefulness, taste; simplicity 573 *plainness*; refinement, delicacy 950 *purity*;

discernment, palate 463 *discrimination*; daintiness, finickiness, fikiness, kid gloves 862 *fastidiousness*; decency, seemliness 848 *etiquette*; tact, consideration, dignity, manners, table manners, breeding, civility, social graces 884 *courtesy*; propriety, decorum; grace, polish, finish, sophistication, gracious living 575 *elegance*; cultivation, culture, connoisseurship; epicureanism, epicurism; aesthetics 480 *judgment*; artistry, virtuosity.

person of taste, connoisseur, cognoscente; epicurean, epicure, gourmet; aesthete, art critic 480 *estimator*; arbiter of taste; purist.

Adj. *tasteful*, in good taste, in the best of taste; exquisite 644 *excellent*; simple 573 *plain*; graceful, classical 575 *elegant*; refined, delicate 950 *pure*; aesthetic, artistic 819 *sensitive*; discerning, epicurean 463 *discriminating*; nice, dainty 862 *fastidious*; decent, seemly, becoming 24 *apt*; proper, correct, comme il faut 848 *fashionable*; mannerly 848 *well-bred*.

Vb. *have taste*, show good taste, reveal fine feelings 463 *discriminate*; appreciate, value 480 *judge*; settle for nothing less than the best, be a perfectionist 862 *be fastidious*.

847 Bad taste

N. *bad taste*, tastelessness, poor taste 645 *badness*; no taste; kitsch; commercialization, commodification; yellow press, gutter press; unrefinement, coarseness, barbarism, vulgarism, philistinism 699 *artlessness*; vulgarity, gaudiness, garishness, loudness; tawdriness, shoddiness; paste, ersatz, imitation 639 *bauble*; insensitivity, crassness, grossness, coarseness; tactlessness, indelicacy, impropriety, unseemliness; bad joke, sick joke, obscenity 951 *impurity*; dowdiness.

ill-breeding, vulgarity, commonness; loudness; provinciality, suburbanism, unfashionableness; bad form, lack of etiquette; bad manners, boorishness, impoliteness 885 *discourtesy*; ungentlemanliness; unladylikeness; misbehaviour, indecorum; rowdyism, ruffianism, yob culture 61 *disorder*.

Adj. *vulgar*, unrefined 576 *inelegant*; tasteless, in bad taste, in the worst possible taste; gross, crass, coarse; philistine, yobbish, barbarian 699 *artless*; commercial, commercialized; tawdry, cheap, cheap and nasty, naff, kitschy, ersatz; flashy; blatant, loud, gaudy, garish; flaunting, shameless; excessive; schmaltzy; overdressed; common, common as muck, low, gutter, sordid 867 *disreputable*; improper, indelicate, indecorous; beyond the pale, scandalous, indecent, ribald 951 *impure*.

ill-bred, badly brought up; unpresentable, not to be taken anywhere; ungentlemanly, unladylike; hoydenish; ungenteel, non-U 869 *plebeian*; loud; tactless, insensitive, blunt; impolite, unmannerly, ill-mannered 885 *discourteous*; provincial, gone native; crude, rude, boorish, churlish, yobbish, loutish, clodhopping, uncouth, uncultured, unrefined 491 *ignorant*; unsophisticated, knowing no better 699 *artless*; uncivilized, barbaric; gauche 695 *clumsy*; rowdy 61 *disorderly*.

Vb. *vulgarize*, cheapen, coarsen, debase, lower, lower the tone; commercialize, commodify, popularize.

848 Fashion. Etiquette

N. *fashion*, style, mode, cut 243 *form*; method 624 *way*; vogue, cult 610 *habit*; prevailing taste, current fashion, trend 126 *modernism*; rage, fad, craze; new look, the latest, latest fashion, what's new, New Look 126 *newness*; retro, retro fashion; retro style; Gothic look; grunge; dernier cri, last word, ne plus ultra, height of fashion; dash 875 *ostentation*; fashionableness; stylishness, flair, chic, anti-chic; dress sense; fashion show, mannequin parade 522 *exhibit*; modelling; model, fashion model; haute couture, elegance; foppery 850 *affectation*.

etiquette, point of etiquette 875 *formality*; protocol, convention, custom, conventionality, netiquette 610 *practice*; done thing, good form, what is expected; proprieties, appearances, Mrs Grundy; decorum, propriety, right note, correctness 846 *good taste*; courtesy; breeding, good breeding; gentility, gentlemanliness, ladylike behaviour; manners, table manners, good manners; best behaviour, one's p's and q's; savoir-faire, savvy 688 *conduct*.

fashionable society, society, high society, café society, beau monde; civilization; Mayfair, St James's, court; top drawer, the right people, the smart set, the upper ten 868 *nobility*; upper crust, cream of society 644 *elite*; the beautiful people, glitterati, jet set; yuppy; man *or* woman about town, man *or* woman of the world, socialite, playboy 882 *sociable person*; fashionable person, man *or* woman of fashion, metrosexual, Sloane Ranger, Sloane, dolly bird, society girl; trend-setter; slave to fashion, dedicated follower of fashion, fashion victim, fashionista; fashion police.

dandy, fop, buck, beau, Beau Brummel, popinjay, peacock, clothes-horse, fashion plate; coxcomb; swell, toff, dude, nob, His Nibs, Lady Muck; lounge lizard, gigolo, gallant; ladykiller.

Adj. *fashionable*, modish, stylish, voguish; in, the new —, in vogue, in fashion, à la mode, chichi; chic, elegant, colour-supplement, well-dressed, well-groomed 846 *tasteful*; clothes-conscious, foppish, dressy; dashing, snazzy, flashy 875 *showy*; smart, classy, ritzy, swanky, swish; posh; up-to-the-minute, bang up-to-date, ultrafashionable, new-fangled, all the rage 126 *modern*; cool, hip, hep, groovy, trendy, with it, happening; dressed up to the nines, dressed to kill; from the top drawer, moving in the best circles, knowing the right people; in the swim 83 *conformable*.

well-bred, thoroughbred, blue-blooded 868 *noble*; civilized, urbane; well brought up, house-trained; U, gentlemanly, ladylike 868 *genteel*; civil, well-mannered, well-spoken 884 *courteous*; courtly 875 *formal*; poised; correct, conventional, decorous, proper; considerate 884 *amiable*; punctilious 929 *honourable*.

Vb. be in fashion, be done, catch on 610 *be in the habit of*; be all the rage, be the latest, be the latest craze, be trendy 126 *modernize*; get with it, follow the fashion, jump on the band wagon, change with the times 83 *conform*; move in the best circles, be seen in the right places; keep up with the Joneses, keep up appearances; cut a dash, be a trend-setter, set the tone; have style.

849 Ridiculousness

N. ridiculousness, ludicrousness, risibility, laughability, height of nonsense, height of absurdity 497 *absurdity*; funniness, priceless-ness, drollery 839 *wit*; quaintness, oddness, queerness, eccentricity 84 *nonconformity*; bathos, anticlimax 509 *disappointment*; extravagance, bombast 546 *exaggeration*; light relief, comic relief; light verse, comic verse, nonsense verse, doggerel, limerick 839 *witticism*; spoonerism, malapropism, bull; comic turn, comedy, farce, burlesque, slapstick, knockabout, clowning, buffoonery 594 *stage play*.

Adj. ridiculous, ludicrous, preposterous, monstrous, grotesque, fantastic, inappropriate 497 *absurd*; clownish 695 *clumsy*; silly 499 *foolish*; derisory 639 *unimportant*; laughable, risible; bizarre, rum, quaint, odd, queer 84 *unusual*; Heath Robinson; strange, outlandish 59 *extraneous*; stilted 850 *affected*; bombastic, extravagant, outré; crazy, crackpot, Pythonesque.

funny, funny-peculiar 84 *abnormal*; funny-ha-ha, good for a laugh 837 *amusing*; comical, droll, humorous, zany 839 *witty*; rich, price-less, side-splitting, wildly amusing, hilarious, a real hoot, a scream, too funny for words; light, comic; ironical, satirical; burlesque; dog-gerel; farcical, slapstick, clownish, custard-pie, knockabout.

Vb. be ridiculous, make one laugh, excite laughter, raise a laugh; tickle, make one fall about, give one the giggles; entertain 837 *amuse*; look silly, be a figure of fun, cut a ridiculous figure, be a laughing stock, fool, play the fool 497 *be absurd*; pass from the sub-lime to the ridiculous; make an exhibition of oneself 695 *act foolishly*.

850 Affectation

N. affectation, fad 848 *fashion*; affectedness, pretentiousness 875 *ostentation*; putting on airs, grand airs 873 *airs*; posing, posturing, attitudinizing; pose, public image, façade; arti-ficiality, mannerism, literary affectation, gran-diloquence; preciosity, euphuism 574 *ornament*; foppery, foppishness, dandyism 873 *vanity*; euphemism, mock modesty 874 *mod-esty*; theatricality, camp, histrionics, breast-beating.

pretension, pretensions, false pretensions; artifice, sham, humbug, quackery, charlatan-ism, fraud 542 *deception*; superficiality; stilted-ness; pedantry 735 *severity*; prudery; sanctimony, sanctimoniousness 979 *show of piety*.

Adj. affected, self-conscious; studied, man-nered, euphuistic, precious, chichi 574 *ornate*; artificial, unnatural, stilted 875 *formal*; prim, priggish, prudish, goody-goody, mealy-mouthed, euphemistic, sanctimonious, self-righteous, holier than thou, smug, demure 979 *pietistic*; arch, sly, nudging, winking 833 *merry*; coquettish, coy, cute, cutesy, twee, too-too, namby-pamby, mincing, simpering; hypo-critical, tongue-in-cheek, ironical; bluffing; shallow, hollow, specious, pretentious, high-sounding; gushing, fulsome, stagy, theatrical, camp, overdramatized 875 *ostentatious*; dandi-fied, foppish, poncy, camp; conceited, la-di-da, giving oneself airs, putting on airs, showing off, swanking, posturing, posing, striking poses, attitudinizing 873 *vain*; stuck up 871 *proud*; name-dropping, keeping up appear-ances 847 *ill-bred*; bogus 541 *false*; for effect, assumed, put on, insincere, phoney; overdone.

Vb. be affected, affect, put on, assume; pre-tend, feign, go through the motions, make a show of, bluff 541 *dissemble*; make as if 20 *imitate*; act a part, play-act, role-play 594 *act*; overact, ham, barnstorm 546 *exaggerate*; do for effect, camp it up, play to the gallery; drama-tize oneself, attitudinize, strike attitudes, pos-ture, strike a posture, prance, mince, ponce about 875 *be ostentatious*; put on airs, give oneself airs, put on side, swank, show off, make an exhibition of oneself 873 *be vain*; air one's knowledge 490 *know*; euphuize.

851 Ridicule

N. *ridicule*, derision, derisiveness, poking fun; mockery, mimicry, scoffing; sniggering, grinning 835 *laughter*; teasing, making fun of, ribbing, banter, badinage, leg-pulling, chaff, leg-pull; buffoonery, horseplay, clowning, practical joke 497 *foolery*; snigger, scoff, mock; irony, sarcasm, barbed shaft, backhanded compliment; catcall, hoot, hiss 924 *censure*; ribaldry 839 *witticism*.

satire, parody, burlesque, travesty, caricature, cartoon 552 *misrepresentation*; skit, spoof, send-up, take-off 20 *mimicry*; lampoon 926 *detraction*.

laughing stock, object of ridicule, figure of fun, butt; sport, game, fair game; Aunt Sally; April fool, silly fool, buffoon, clown, zany 501 *fool*; stooge, foil, feed, straight man; guy, caricature, travesty, mockery of, apology for; eccentric 504 *crank*; original, card, caution, queer fish, odd fish; fall guy, victim 728 *loser*.

Vb. *ridicule*, deride, pour scorn on, laugh at, smirk at; snigger, laugh in *or* up one's sleeve; banter, chaff, twit, rib, tease, rag, pull one's leg, poke fun, make fun of, make sport of, make game of, take the mickey out of, have one on, put one on, kid, fool, make a fool of, make a laughing-stock of, take the piss out of (vulg.), make an April fool of; mock, scoff, jeer 926 *detract*; make a joke of 922 *hold cheap*; take down, deflate, debunk, take the wind out of one's sails, make one look silly, make one laugh on the other side of his face 872 *humiliate*.

satirize, lampoon 921 *not respect*; mock; mimic, send up, take off 20 *imitate*; parody, travesty, spoof, burlesque, caricature 552 *misrepresent*; pillory 928 *accuse*.

852 Hope

N. *hope*, hopes, expectations, presumption 507 *expectation*; high hopes, conviction 485 *belief*; reliance, trust, confidence, faith, assurance 473 *certainty*; reassurance 831 *relief*; security, anchor, mainstay, staff 218 *support*; last hope, ray of hope, glimmer of hope 469 *possibility*; good omen, favourable auspices, promise, bright prospect 511 *omen*; blue sky, silver lining, a break in the clouds; hopefulness; buoyancy, optimism 833 *cheerfulness*; wishful thinking, self-deception; rose-coloured spectacles, rosy picture.

aspiration, ambition, purpose 617 *intention*; pious hope, fond hope; vision, pipe dream, heart's desire; castles in the air, castles in Spain, El Dorado, fool's paradise 513 *fantasy*; the end of the rainbow, promised land, utopia, millennium, the day 617 *objective*.

hopeful person, hoper, aspirant, candidate, young hopeful, wannabe; optimist; utopian 513 *visionary*; Micawber.

Adj. *hoping*, aspiring, starry-eyed; ambitious, go-getting, would-be; dreaming, day-dreaming 513 *imaginative*; hopeful, in hopes 507 *expectant*; happy in the hope, in sight of, on the verge of; sanguine, confident 473 *certain*; buoyant, optimistic; hoping for the best, everhoping.

promising, full of promise, favourable, auspicious, propitious 730 *prosperous*; bright, fair, golden, rosy; hopeful, encouraging; likely 471 *probable*; utopian, millennial; visionary 513 *imaginary*.

Vb. *hope*, trust, have faith; rest assured, feel confident, put one's trust in, rely, bank on, count on, pin one's hopes on, hope and believe 485 *believe*; assume; look forward 507 *expect*; hope for, dream of, aspire, promise oneself, aim high 617 *intend*; have hopes, have high hopes, have expectations, live in hopes, keep one's fingers crossed; nurse hope; take hope, recover hope, see light at the end of the tunnel; refuse to give up hope, see no cause for despair, hope against hope, keep hope alive, never say die; catch at straws, keep one's spirits up, look on the bright side, hope for the best 833 *be cheerful*; keep smiling 600 *persevere*; see life through rose-coloured spectacles; delude oneself 477 *reason badly*; anticipate, count one's chickens before they are hatched 135 *be early*; indulge in wishful thinking, dream 513 *imagine*.

Int. *never say die!*, nil desperandum!, while there's life there's hope!, hope springs eternal!

853 Hopelessness

N. *hopelessness*, no hope, defeatism, despondency 834 *dejection*; pessimism, cynicism, despair, desperation, no way out, last hope gone; dashed hopes, hope extinguished 509 *disappointment*; resignation 508 *lack of expectation*; not a hope 470 *impossibility*; vain hope, forlorn hope 513 *fantasy*; poor lookout, no prospects; hopeless case, dead duck; hopeless situation, catch-22, bad business 700 *predicament*; Job's comforter.

Adj. *hopeless*, bereft of hope, devoid of hope, despairing, in despair, desperate, suicidal; unhopeful, pessimistic, cynical, looking on the black side; defeatist, fearing the worst, sunk in despair, inconsolable, disconsolate 834 *dejected*; wringing one's hands 836 *lamenting*; disappointed; desolate, forlorn; ruined, undone 731 *unfortunate*.

unpromising, hopeless 834 *cheerless*; desperate 661 *dangerous*; unpropitious, inauspicious

731 *adverse*; ill-omened, ominous; irremediable, incurable, inoperable, terminal; beyond hope, past recall, despaired of; incorrigible, irreparable, irrecoverable, irrevocable, irreversible, inevitable; out of the question 470 *impossible*.

Vb. *despair*, lose heart, lose hope; become despondent, give way to despair, wring one's hands 834 *be dejected*; have shot one's last bolt, have no cards up one's sleeves, give up hope; abandon hope, hope for nothing more from, write off 674 *stop using*; give up, turn one's face to the wall 721 *submit*.

cause to despair, drive to despair, dishearten, discourage 834 *sadden, depress*.

854 Fear

N. *fear*, healthy fear, dread, awe 920 *respect*; abject fear 856 *cowardice*; fright, stage fright; wind-up, funk, blue funk; terror, mortal terror; state of terror, intimidation, trepidation, alarm, false alarm; shock, flutter, flap, flat spin 318 *agitation*; fit, fit of terror, scare, stampede, panic, panic attack 318 *spasm*; flight, sauve qui peut; the creeps, horror, one's hair on end, cold sweat; dismay 853 *hopelessness*; defence mechanism, fight or flight.

nervousness, lack of confidence 856 *cowardice*; diffidence 874 *modesty*; timidity, timorousness, fearfulness, hesitation 620 *avoidance*; loss of nerve, cold feet, second thoughts, fears, suspicions, misgivings, qualms, mistrust, apprehension, apprehensiveness, uneasiness, disquiet, anxiety, angst, care 825 *worry*; perturbation, trepidation, fear and trembling, flutter, tremor, palpitation, trembling, quaking, shaking, shuddering, shivering, stuttering; nerves, willies, butterflies, collywobbles, creeps, shivers, jumps, jitters, heebie-jeebies 318 *agitation*; social phobia, performance anxiety; health anxiety; gooseflesh, hair on end, knees knocking, teeth chattering.

phobia, fear, hatred, prejudice, hang-up, thing; fear of technology: technofear, technophobia, PC paranoia; financial phobia; anti-Semitism, racial prejudice, race hatred 888 *hatred*; McCarthyism, Reds under the beds, spy mania, witch-hunting; prejudice 481 *prejudice*.

Some Common Phobias

acarophobia (mites and small insects), achluophobia (darkness), acrophobia (heights), aerophobia (draughts), agoraphobia (open spaces), aichmophobia (sharp or pointed objects), ailurophobia (cats), algophobia (pain), androphobia (men), Anglophobia (England or Britain, the English or British, English or British culture, etc.), anthophobia (flowers), anthropophobia (people), antlophobia (floods), apiphobia (bees), aquaphobia (water), arachnophobia (spiders), astraphobia (thunder and lightning),

astrophobia (stars, space), autophobia (being alone, loneliness), bacillophobia (microbes), bacteriophobia (bacteria), bathophobia (depths), batophobia (heights, or being close to high buildings, mountains, etc), batrachophobia (frogs, toads, etc), belonephobia (pins and needles), bibliophobia (books), brontophobia (thunder), canophobia (dogs), claustrophobia (enclosed places), cyberphobia (computers), cynophobia (dogs), dendrophobia (trees), doraphobia (fur or animal skins), entomophobia (insects), ergophobia (work), erythrophobia (blushing), Francophobia (France, the French, French culture, etc), frigophobia (cold or cold things), Gallophobia (= Francophobia), gynophobia (women), haemophobia / haemaphobia / haematophobia (blood), halitophobia (= unwarranted anxiety about having bad breath), herpetophobia (reptiles), hippophobia (horses), homophobia (homosexuality or homosexual people), hydrophobia (water), iatrophobia (doctors, or going to the doctor), ichthyophobia (fish), monophobia (being alone, loneliness), murophobia / musophobia (mice), myrmecophobia (ants), mysophobia (germs, dirt or contamination), necrophobia (death or corpses), nyctophobia (darkness, night), ochlophobia (crowds), ophiophobia / ophidiophobia (snakes), ornithophobia (birds), panphobia / pantophobia (everything), pathophobia (disease), phobophobia (fear), photophobia (light), pogonophobia (beards), pyrophobia (fire), sciophobia (shadows), siderophobia (stars), Sinophobia (China, the Chinese, Chinese culture, etc), technophobia (technology), thalassophobia (sea), thanatophobia (death), tocophobia or tokophobia (childbirth), triskaidekaphobia (the number 13), xenophobia (foreigners, strangers), zoophobia (animals).

intimidation, deterrence, war of nerves, sabre-rattling, arms build up, fee faw fum; threatening 900 *threat*; caution 664 *warning*; terror, terrorism, reign of terror 735 *severity*; alarmism, scaremongering; sword of Damocles, suspended sentence 963 *punishment*; deterrent 723 *weapon*; object of terror, goblin, hobgoblin 970 *demon*; spook, spectre 970 *ghost*; Gorgon, Medusa, scarecrow, tattie bogle, nightmare; bugbear, ogre 938 *monster*; skeleton, death's head, skull and crossbones.

alarmist, scaremonger, doom merchant, gloom and doom merchant, doom-watcher, doomster, ecodoomster, Cassandra, Calamity Jane; pessimist; terrorist; sabre-rattler.

Adj. *afraid*, fearing, frightened, funky, panicky; overawed 920 *respectful*; intimidated, terrorized; panic-stricken; stampeding, scared, alarmed, startled; hysterical, having fits, in hysterics, in the grip of a panic attack; in mortal fear, in trepidation, in a cold sweat, in a flap, in a flat spin, in a panic, in a frenzy, in a funk *or* blue funk; shitting bricks (vulg); dismayed; frozen, petrified, stunned; aghast, horror-struck, unmanned, scared out of one's wits, trembling with fear, paralysed by fear, rooted to the spot with fear, frightened to death, white as a sheet, ashen-faced.

nervous, tense, uptight; waiting for the axe

to fall; timid, timorous, shy, diffident, self-conscious 874 *modest*; wary, shrinking, treading warily 858 *cautious*; doubtful, distrustful, suspicious 474 *doubting*; windy, faint-hearted 601 *irresolute*; disturbed; apprehensive, uneasy, fearful, dreading, anxious, worried, angsty 825 *unhappy*; a prey to fears; highly-strung, afraid of one's own shadow, jittery, jumpy, nervy, rattled, on edge; shaking, trembling, quaking, cowering, cringing 856 *cowardly*; with one's heart in one's mouth, shaking like a leaf *or* a jelly; on pins and needles, palpitating, breathless.

frightening, shocking, startling, alarming, etc. (see vb.); formidable, redoubtable; hazardous, hairy 661 *dangerous*; dreadful, awe-inspiring, fearsome, awesome 821 *impressive*; grim, grisly, hideous, ghastly, lurid, frightful, revolting, petrifying, horrifying, horrific, horrible, terrible, awful; mind-boggling, mind-blowing; hair-raising, flesh-creeping, blood-curdling; weird, eerie, creepy, scary, ghoulish, nightmarish, gruesome, macabre, sinister; portentous, ominous; intimidating, sabre-rattling, bullying, hectoring 735 *oppressive*; menacing; nerve-racking 827 *distressing*.

Vb. *fear*, funk, be afraid, be frightened, etc. (see adj.); stand in fear *or* awe, go in fear and trembling, dread 920 *respect*; flap, be in a flap, etc. (see also *afraid* above), be in a bit of a state, have the wind up, have the willies; get the wind up, take fright, take alarm; shit oneself (vulg), shit a brick *or* bricks (vulg); panic, fall into panic, have a panic attack, press the panic button, stampede, take to flight, fly 620 *run away*; start, jump 318 *be agitated*; faint, collapse.

quake, shake, tremble, quiver, shiver, shudder, stutter, quaver; quake in one's shoes, shake like a jelly, fear for one's life, be frightened to death, be scared out of one's wits; change colour, blench, pale, go white as a sheet, turn ashen; wince, flinch, shrink, shy, jib 620 *avoid*; quail, cower, crouch; stand aghast, be horrified, be petrified, be chilled with fear, freeze, freeze with horror, be rooted to the spot with terror, feel one's blood run cold, feel one's hair stand on end.

be nervous, be apprehensive, etc. (see adj.); have misgivings; shrink, quail, funk it, put off the evil day; be anxious, dread, have qualms; hesitate, get cold feet, think twice, have second thoughts, think better of it, not dare 858 *be cautious*; get the wind up, start at one's own shadow, be on edge, be all of a doodah 318 *be agitated*.

frighten, scare, panic, stampede; intimidate, menace 900 *threaten*; hang over 155 *impend*;

alarm, cause alarm, raise the alarm, press the panic button, cry wolf; frighten to death, scare the living daylights out of, scare stiff, scare half to death; make one jump, give one a fright, give one a turn, startle, make one all of a doodah 318 *agitate*; disquiet, disturb, perturb, prey on the mind 827 *trouble*; put the wind up, make nervous, set on edge, rattle, shake, unnerve; play on one's nerves, throw into a nervous state; unman, make a coward of; put the fear of God into, overawe 821 *impress*; cow 727 *overcome*; disconcert 63 *disarrange*; frighten off, daunt, deter; terrorize 735 *oppress*; browbeat, bully 827 *torment*; terrify; chill, freeze, paralyse, petrify, turn to stone, mesmerize 375 *make insensitive*; make one's blood run cold; make one's hair stand on end *or* curl, make one's flesh creep, make one's knees knock, make one's teeth chatter, frighten out of one's wits, reduce one to a quivering jelly; frighten the horses.

855 Courage

N. *courage*, bravery, valour, derring-do; courage of one's convictions 929 *probity*; courage in the face of the enemy, heroism, gallantry, chivalry; fearlessness, intrepidity, daring, nerve, bottle; boldness, audacity 857 *rashness*; spirit; mettle, dash, go, élan, panache 174 *vigorousness*; enterprise 672 *undertaking*; tenacity, survivability, bulldog courage 600 *perseverance*; stoutness of heart, resoluteness 599 *resolution*; gameness, pluck, smeddum, spunk, guts, heart, stout heart, heart of oak, backbone, grit 600 *stamina*; Dutch courage; courage of despair; brave face, bold front 711 *defiance*; fresh courage, new heart, encouragement 612 *inducement*.

manliness, manhood, machismo 929 *probity*; chivalry; manly spirit; endurance, stiff upper lip 599 *resolution*.

prowess, derring-do, chivalry, heroism, act of courage, courage in the face of the enemy; feat, exploit, bold stroke, coup de grâce 676 *deed*; desperate venture 857 *rashness*; heroics.

brave person, hero, heroine; knight; brave, warrior 722 *soldier*; man *or* woman of mettle, man *or* woman of spirit, plucky fellow, bulldog, braveheart, daredevil, stunt man *or* woman; fire-eater; Galahad, Lancelot, Lionheart; Joan of Arc, Boadicea *or* Boudicca, Amazon; knight-errant; the bravest of the brave; Victoria Cross, VC, George Cross, GC, Croix de Guerre, Légion d'honneur *or* Legion of Honour, Iron Cross; Dickin Medal; band of heroes, gallant company, SAS, Foreign Legion; forlorn hope 644 *elite*; lion, tiger, fighting cock, bulldog.

Adj. *courageous*, brave, valiant, gallant, heroic; chivalrous, knightly; soldierly, martial, Amazonian 718 *warlike*; stout, manly, tough, macho, Ramboesque, red-blooded; aggressive, fire-eating; fierce; bold 711 *defiant*; audacious, daring, venturesome, bold as brass 857 *rash*; adventurous 672 *enterprising*; mettlesome, spirited, stouthearted, brave-hearted, braveheart, lion-hearted, bold as a lion; full of courage, spunky; unbowed, firm, indomitable, never say die; determined 599 *resolute*; game, plucky, sporting; ready for the fray, ready for anything, unflinching 597 *willing*.

unafraid, intrepid, with nerves of steel; danger-loving; sure of oneself, confident, self-confident, self-reliant; fearless, dauntless, unshrinking, untrembling, unblenching, undismayed, undaunted, nothing daunted, unabashed, unawed, unalarmed, unconcerned, unapprehensive, unappalled, unshaken, unshakable.

Vb. *be courageous*, be bold, etc. (see adj.); have what it takes, have guts, come up to scratch, show spirit, show one's mettle 716 *fight*; venture, bell the cat, take the plunge, take the bull by the horns 672 *undertake*; dare 661 *face danger*; show fight, brave, face, outface, outdare, beard, defy; confront, look straight in the face, look in the eyes, be eyeball to eyeball with, eyeball; speak out, speak one's mind, speak up, stand up and be counted 532 *affirm*; face the music, stick one's neck out, show a bold front 599 *stand firm*; laugh at danger, mock at danger 857 *be rash*; grin and bear it, take one's medicine 825 *suffer*.

take courage, pluck up courage, muster courage, nerve *or* steel oneself, take one's courage in both hands; put a brave face on it, screw up one's courage 599 *be resolute*.

give courage, infuse courage; put heart into, hearten, make a man of; embolden 612 *incite*; buck up, rally 833 *cheer*; raise morale, bolster up, give confidence.

856 Cowardice

N. *cowardice*, abject fear, funk, blue funk 854 *fear*; cowardliness, no guts 601 *irresolution*; timidity; faintheartedness, chicken-heartedness; unmanliness, defeatism 853 *hopelessness*; leaving the sinking ship, desertion, quitting, shirking 918 *undutifulness*; white feather, yellow streak, faint heart, chicken liver; Dutch courage; cowering, skulking; overcaution 858 *caution*; moral cowardice.

coward, funk, poltroon, craven, lily-liver, chickenheart, wheyface; scaredy-cat, fraidy-cat, cowardy custard; coward at heart; sissy, milk-

sop, mummy's boy, baby, big baby, cry-baby, big girl's blouse 163 *weakling*; quitter, shirker, deserter; surrender monkey; cur, chicken, rabbit, mouse, jellyfish, invertebrate, doormat; scaremonger.

Adj. *cowardly*, coward, craven, poltroonish; pusillanimous, timid, timorous, fearful, afraid of one's own shadow, unable to say boo to a goose, of a nervous disposition 854 *nervous*; soft, womanish, babyish, unmanly, sissy 163 *weak*; spiritless, spunkless, without grit, without guts, lacking smeddum, with no backbone, faint-hearted, chicken-livered, yellow-livered, lily-livered, chicken; cowering, quailing; yellow, abject, base; unwarlike, cowed, defeatist 853 *hopeless*; unheroic, uncourageous 858 *cautious*; shy, coy 874 *modest*; infirm of purpose 601 *irresolute*.

Vb. *be cowardly*, lack courage, have no fight, have no pluck, have no grit, have no guts, lack smeddum, have no backbone, have no heart *or* stomach for, not dare 601 *be irresolute*; lose one's nerve, get the jitters, have cold feet 854 *be nervous*; shrink, funk, shy from, back out, chicken out 620 *avoid*; hide, skulk, quail, cower, cringe 721 *knuckle under*; show a yellow streak, show the white feather, show fear, turn tail, cut and run, run for cover, panic, press the panic button, stampede, scuttle, show one's back, desert 620 *run away*; lead from behind, keep well to the rear 858 *be cautious*.

857 Rashness

N. *rashness*, lack of caution, incautiousness, unwariness, heedlessness 456 *inattention*; carelessness, neglect 458 *negligence*; imprudence, improvidence, indiscretion 499 *folly*; lack of consideration, irresponsibility; wildness, indiscipline 738 *disobedience*; daredevilry, recklessness, foolhardiness, temerity, audacity, presumption, over-confidence; hotheadedness, impatience 822 *excitability*; rushing into things, impetuosity, precipitance, hastiness, overhastiness 680 *haste*; quixotry; playing with fire, brinkmanship, game of chicken; desperation, courage of despair 855 *courage*; needless risk, leap in the dark 661 *danger*; too many eggs in one basket, underinsurance, counting one's chickens before they are hatched 661 *vulnerability*; reckless gamble, last throw 618 *gambling*; reckless expenditure 815 *prodigality*.

desperado, daredevil, madcap, hothead, adventurer, inveterate gambler 618 *gambler*; harum-scarum, ne'er-do-well; one who sticks at nothing, gunman, terrorist, contra, guerrilla; bully 904 *ruffian*.

Adj. rash, ill-considered, ill-conceived, ill-advised, harebrained, foolhardy, mad, wildcat, injudicious, indiscreet, imprudent 499 *unwise*; careless, hit-and-miss, slapdash, free-and-easy 458 *negligent*; uncircumspect, lemming-like, incautious, unwary, heedless, thoughtless, inconsiderate, uncalculating 456 *inattentive*; frivolous, flippant, giddy, devil-may-care, harum-scarum, slaphappy, trigger-happy 456 *lacking concentration*; irresponsible, reckless, regardless, couldn't-care-less, don't-care, damning the consequances, lunatic, wanton, wild, cavalier; bold, daring, audacious; overdaring, madcap, daredevil, do-or-die, breakneck, suicidal; overambitious, over the top, oversanguine, oversure, overconfident 852 *hoping*; overweening, presumptuous, arrogant 878 *insolent*; precipitate, headlong, hell-bent, desperate 680 *hasty*; unchecked, headstrong 491 *ignorant*, 602 *wilful*; impulsive, impatient, hot-blooded, hot-headed 822 *excitable*; venturesome 618 *speculative*; adventurous, thrill-seeking, risk-taking 672 *enterprising*; improvident 815 *prodigal*.

Vb. be rash, be reckless, etc. (see adj.); lack caution, want judgment, lean on a broken reed; expose oneself, drop one's guard, stick one's neck out, take unnecessary risks, put one's head in the lion's cage, ride the tiger; go bull-headed at, charge at, rush at, rush into, rush one's fences 680 *hasten*; take a leap in the dark, leap before one looks, buy a pig in a poke, take something on trust, buy something sight unseen; ignore the consequences, damn the consequences; gamble, put all one's eggs into one basket, underinsure; not care 456 *be inattentive*; play fast and loose 634 *waste*; spend to the hilt 815 *be prodigal*; play the fool, play with fire, burn one's fingers; go out on a limb, risk one's neck, dice with death 661 *face danger*; play a desperate game, court disaster, ask for trouble, tempt providence, push one's luck, rush in where angels fear to tread; count one's chickens before they are hatched, aim too high 695 *act foolishly*.

Adv. rashly, incautiously; headlong, recklessly, like Gadarene swine, like lemmings.

858 Caution

N. caution, cautiousness, wariness, heedfulness, care, heed 457 *carefulness*; hesitation, doubt, second thoughts 854 *nervousness*; instinct of self-preservation 932 *selfishness*; looking before one leaps, looking twice, looking round, circumspection; guardedness, secretiveness, reticence 525 *secrecy*; calculation, counting the risk, safety first; nothing left to chance 669 *preparation*; deliberation, due

deliberation, mature consideration 480 *judgment*; sobriety, balance, level-headedness 834 *seriousness*; prudence, discretion, worldly wisdom 498 *wisdom*; insurance, precaution 662 *safeguard*; forethought 510 *foresight*; Fabian policy 823 *patience*; going slow, taking one's time, watching one's step, one step at a time, festina lente 278 *slowness*; wait-and-see policy, waiting game, cat-and-mouse 136 *delay*.

Adj. cautious, wary, watchful 455 *attentive*; heedful 457 *careful*; hesitating, doubtful, suspicious 854 *nervous*; taking no risks, insured, hedging; guarded, secret, secretive, incommunicative, cagey 525 *reticent*; experienced, taught by experience, been there, done that, once bitten, twice shy 669 *prepared*; on one's guard, circumspect, looking round, looking all ways, gingerly, stealthy, feeling one's way, taking one's time, watching one's step, tentative 461 *experimental*; conservative 660 *safe*; responsible 929 *trustworthy*; prudent, discreet 498 *wise*; non-committal 625 *neutral*; frugal, counting the cost 814 *economical*; canny; timid, slow-moving, overcautious, unenterprising, unadventurous; slow, deliberate, Fabian 823 *patient*; sober, cool-headed, level-headed, cool; cold-blooded, calm, self-possessed 823 *inexcitable*.

Vb. be cautious, beware 457 *be careful*; take no risks, play it by the book, play safe, play a waiting game, play a cat-and-mouse game 498 *be wise*; ca' canny, go slow, festina lente 278 *move slowly*; cover up, cover one's tracks 525 *conceal*; not talk 525 *keep* secret; keep under cover, keep on the safe side, keep in the rear, keep in the background, keep out of the limelight, hide 523 *lurk*; look out, see how the land lies 438 *scan*; see how the wind blows, feel one's way, play it by ear, put a toe in the water 461 *be tentative*; be on one's guard, tread warily, watch one's step, pussyfoot 525 *be stealthy*; think twice 455 *be mindful*; calculate, reckon 480 *judge*; consider the risk factor, count the cost, cut one's coat according to one's cloth 814 *economize*; know when to stop, take one's time; let well alone, let sleeping dogs lie, keep well out of 620 *avoid*; consider the consequences 511 *predict*; take precautions; look a gift horse in the mouth 480 *estimate*; make sure 473 *make certain*; cover oneself, insure, hedge; leave nothing to chance 669 *prepare*.

Adv. cautiously, gingerly; softly softly.

859 Desire

N. desire, wish, will and pleasure 595 *will*; summons, call, cry 737 *command*; demand; wanting, want, need, exigency 627 *requirement*; shopping list, wish list; claim 915 *what* *is due*; nostalgia, nostalgie de la boue, home-sickness 830 *regret*; wistfulness, longing, han-kering, yearning, sheep's eyes; wishing, thinking, daydreaming, daydream, castles in the air 513 *fantasy*; ambition, aspiration 852 *hope*; yen, urge 279 *impulse*; itch; thrill-seeking, rubbernecking, curiousness, thirst for knowledge, intellectual curiosity 453 *curiosity*; avidity, eagerness, zeal 597 *willingness*; pas-sion, ardour, warmth, impetuosity, impatience 822 *excitability*; rage, fury 503 *frenzy*; mania 503 *personality disorder*; craving, lust for, appe-tite, hunger, thirst; expansionism, a place in the sun; covetousness, cupidity, itching palm 816 *avarice*; luxury fever; graspingness, greedi-ness, greed 786 *rapacity*; voracity, wolfishness, insatiability 947 *gluttony*; concupiscence, lust (see also *sexual urge* below); incontinence 943 *intemperance*.

hunger, starvation, famine, famished condi-tion, empty stomach, snack attack 946 *fasting*; appetite, good appetite, keen appetite, vora-cious appetite, edge of appetite; thirst, thirsti-ness 342 *dryness*; dipsomania 949 *alcoholism*.

liking, fancy, fondness, infatuation 887 *love*; stomach, appetite, zest, craving; relish, tooth, sweet tooth 386 *taste*; leaning, penchant, pro-pensity, trend 179 *tendency*; weakness, partial-ity; affinity; sympathy, involvement 775 *participation*; inclination, mind 617 *intention*; predilection, favour 605 *choice*; whim, whimsy 604 *caprice*; hobby, craze, fad, mania 481 *bias*; fascination, allurement, attraction, tempta-tion, titillation, seduction 612 *inducement*.

sexual urge, sexual desire, carnal desire, libido, passion, rut, heat, concupiscence, oestrus; erotism, eroticism; erogenous zone, G-spot, Gräfenberg spot; mating season; libidi-nousness, prurience, lust, lecherousness, letch, the hots 951 *unchastity*; nymphomania, pria-pism, satyriasis 84 *abnormality*.

desired object, one's heart's desire, wish, desire 627 *requirement*; catch, prize, plum 729 *trophy*; cynosure 890 *favourite*; forbidden fruit, torment of Tantalus; envy, temptation; mag-net, lure, draw 291 *attraction*; the unattain-able; aim, goal, star, ambition, aspiration, dream 617 *objective*; ideal, dream team 646 *perfection*; height of one's ambition.

Adj. *greedy*, acquisitive 932 *selfish*; ambi-tious, status-seeking; voracious, omnivorous, open-mouthed 947 *gluttonous*; unsated, unsat-isfied, unslaked; insatiable, rapacious, grasp-ing, retentive 816 *avaricious*.

hungry, hungering, unfilled, empty, supper-less, dinnerless 946 *fasting*; half-starved, starv-ing, famished 636 *underfed*; peckish, ready for, ravenous, hungry as a hunter, ready to eat a horse; thirsty, dry, drouthy, parched, dehy-drated.

desired, wanted, liked; likable, desirable, worth having, enviable, coveted, to die for, in demand; acceptable, welcome; appetizing 826 *pleasurable*; fetching, catchy, attractive, appeal-ing; wished, self-sought, invited 597 *voluntary*.

Vb. *desire*, want, miss, feel the lack of 627 *require*; ask for, cry out for, clamour for 737 *demand*; call, summon, send for, ring for 737 *command*; invite 882 *be hospitable*; wish, make a wish, pray; wish otherwise, unwish 830 *regret*; covet 912 *envy*; have a mind to, set one's heart on, set one's mind on, have designs on, set one's sights on, aim at, have at heart 617 *intend*; plan for, angle for, fish for 623 *plan*; aspire, dream of, dream, daydream 852 *hope*; aim high; look for, expect 915 *claim*; wish in vain, whistle for, cry for the moon 695 *act foolishly*; pray for, intercede, invoke, wish on, call down on; wish ill 899 *curse*; wish one well; welcome, be glad of, jump at, catch at, grasp at, clutch at 786 *take*; lean towards 179 *tend*; favour, prefer, select 605 *choose*; crave, itch for, hanker after, have a yen for, long for; long, yearn, pine, languish; pant for, gasp for, burn for, die for, be dying for 636 *be unsatisfied*; have a heart for; thirst for, hunger for; can't wait, must have; like, have a liking, have a taste for, care for 887 *love*; take to, warm to, take a fancy to, fall in love with, dote, dote on, be infatuated with, moon after, be in love, ogle, make eyes at, make passes, solicit, woo 889 *court*; set one's cap at, make a dead set at, run after, chase 619 *pursue*; lust, lust for, lust after, lech after, have the hots for 951 *be impure*; rut, be on heat.

be hungry, hunger, famish, starve, be raven-ous, have an empty stomach, have an aching void, be ready to eat a horse 636 *be unsatisfied*; have a good appetite, lick one's chops, sali-vate, water at the mouth 301 *eat*; thirst, be dry, be dying for a drink, be parched, be dehy-drated.

860 Indifference

N. *indifference*, unconcern, uninterestedness 454 *lack of curiosity*; lack of interest, half-heartedness, lack of zeal, lukewarmness 598 *unwillingness*; coolness, coldness, faint praise; lovelessness, mutual indifference, nothing between them; anorexia, no appetite, loss of appetite; no desire for; inertia, apathy 679 *inactivity*; nonchalance, insouciance 458 *negli-gence*; perfunctoriness, carelessness 456 *inatten-tion*; don't-care attitude 734 *laxity*; recklessness, heedlessness 857 *rashness*; pro-miscuousness 464 *lack of discrimination*; amo-rality; open mind, unbiased attitude, impartiality, equity 913 *justice*; neutrality 625 *middle way*; nothing to choose between, six of one and half a dozen of the other, all one 28 *equivalent*.

Adj. indifferent, unconcerned, uninterested 454 *incurious*; lukewarm, Laodicean, half-hearted 598 *unwilling*; impersonal, uninvolved, phlegmatic 820 *impassive*; unimpressed, blasé; calm, cool, cold 823 *inexcitable*; nonchalant, insouciant, careless, perfunctory 458 *negligent*; supine, lackadaisical, listless 679 *inactive*; unambitious, unaspiring; don't-care, easy-going 734 *lax*; unresponsive, unmoved, insensible to; fancy-free, uninvolved; disenchanted, disillusioned, out of love, cooling off; impartial; non-committal 625 *neutral*.

unwanted, unwelcome, de trop, in the way; unwished for, unasked, uninvited; unvalued 458 *neglected*; on the shelf; unattractive, undesirable.

Vb. be indifferent, be unconcerned, etc. (see adj.); be uninvolved, take no interest 456 *be inattentive*; not mind, care little for, not lose any sleep over, damn with faint praise; care nothing for, not give a fig *or* a thank-you for, not care a straw about, couldn't care less, take it or leave it; not think twice about, not care, not give a hoot, shrug off, dismiss, let go, make light of 922 *hold cheap*; not defend, hold no brief for, take neither side, sit on the fence 606 *be neutral*; grow indifferent, fall out of love, lose interest, cool off.

Int. never mind!, what does it matter?, who cares?, so what?

861 Dislike

N. dislike, disinclination, no inclination for, no fancy for, no stomach for; reluctance, backwardness 598 *unwillingness*; displeasure 891 *resentment*; dissatisfaction 829 *discontent*; disagreement 489 *dissent*; shyness, aversion 620 *avoidance*; sudden *or* instant dislike, antipathy, allergy; rooted dislike, distaste, repugnance, repulsion, disgust, abomination, abhorrence, detestation, loathing; shuddering, horror, mortal horror 854 *fear*; xenophobia 854 *phobia*; prejudice 481 *bias*; animosity, bad blood, ill feeling, mutual hatred, common hatred 888 *hatred*; nausea, queasiness, turn, heaving stomach, vomit 300 *clearing*; object of dislike: not one's type, bête noire, pet aversion, pet hate, a red rag to a bull.

Vb. dislike, find not to one's taste; not care for, have no liking for, have no desire for; have no stomach for, have no heart for 598 *be unwilling*; not choose, prefer not to 607 *reject*; object 762 *deprecate*; mind 891 *resent*; take a dislike to, feel an aversion for, have a down

on, have one's knife in, have it in for 481 *be biased*; react against 280 *recoil*; feel sick at 300 *vomit*; shun, turn away, shrink from, have no time for 620 *avoid*; look askance at 924 *disapprove*; turn up the nose at, sniff at, sneer at 922 *despise*; make a face, grimace; be unable to abide, not endure, can't stand, can't bear, detest, loathe, abominate, abhor 888 *hate*; not like the look of, shudder at 854 *fear*; unwish, wish undone 830 *regret*.

cause dislike, disincline, deter 854 *frighten*; go against the grain, rub the wrong way, antagonize, put one's back up 891 *enrage*; set against, set at odds, make bad blood; satiate, pall, jade 863 *satiate*; disagree with, upset 25 *disagree*; put off, revolt 292 *repel*; offend, grate, jar 827 *displease*; get one's goat, get up one's nose, get on one's nerves 827 *torment*; suck; disgust, stick in one's throat, nauseate, sicken, make one's gorge rise, turn one's stomach, make one sick; shock, scandalize, make a scandal 924 *incur blame*.

862 Fastidiousness

N. fastidiousness, niceness, nicety, daintiness, finicalness, finicality, fikiness, pernicketiness, delicacy; discernment, perspicacity, sublety 463 *discrimination*; refinement 846 *good taste*; connoisseurship, epicurism; meticulousness, preciseness 457 *carefulness*; idealism, over-developed conscience 917 *conscience*; perfectionism, fussiness, nit-picking, over-refinement, hypercriticalness, pedantry, hair-splitting; prudishness, Puritanism 950 *prudery*.

perfectionist, idealist, purist, rigorist, fusspot, pedant, nit-picker, stickler, hard taskmaster; picker and chooser, gourmet, epicure.

Adj. fastidious, nice, dainty, delicate, epicurean; perspicacious, discerning 463 *discriminating*; particular, demanding, choosy, finicky, finical, fiky; overnice, over-particular, scrupulous, meticulous, squeamish 455 *attentive*; punctilious, painstaking, conscientious, over-conscientious, critical, hypercritical, overcritical, fussy, pernickety, hard to please, fault-finding, censorious 924 *disapproving*; pedantic, donnish, precise, rigorous, exacting, difficult 735 *severe*; prim, puritanical 950 *prudish*.

Vb. be fastidious, be choosy, etc. (see adj.); settle for nothing less than the best; pick and choose 605 *choose*; over-refine, split hairs, mince matters 475 *argue*; draw distinctions 463 *discriminate*; find fault 924 *dispraise*; fuss, turn up one's nose, wrinkle one's nose; look a gift horse in the mouth, feel superior, disdain 922 *despise*; keep oneself to oneself.

863 Satiation

N. satiation, satiety, jadedness, fullness, repletion 54 *fullness*; overfullness, plethora, overabundance, stuffing, engorgement, saturation,

saturation point 637 *redundancy*; glut, surfeit, too much of a good thing 838 *tedium*; overdose, excess 637 *superfluity*; spoiled child, spoilt brat.

Adj. *satiated*, sated, satisfied, replete, saturated, brimming 635 *filled*; overfull, surfeited, gorged, glutted, cloyed, sick of; jaded, blasé 838 *bored*.

Vb. *satiate*, sate; satisfy, quench, slake 635 *suffice*; fill up, overfill, saturate 54 *fill*; soak 341 *drench*; stuff, gorge, glut, surfeit, cloy, jade, pall; overdose, overfeed; sicken 861 *cause dislike*; spoil, overindulge, kill with kindness; bore, weary 838 *be tedious*.

864 Wonder

N. *wonder*, state of wonder, wonderment, raptness; admiration; hero worship 887 *love*; awe, fascination; cry of wonder, gasp of admiration, whistle, wolf whistle, exclamation, exclamation mark; shocked silence 399 *silence*; open mouth, popping eyes, eyes on stalks; shock, surprise, surprisal 508 *lack of expectation*; astonishment, amazement; stupor, stupefaction; bewilderment, bafflement 474 *uncertainty*; consternation 854 *fear*.

***miracle-working*,** wonder-working, spellbinding, magic 983 *sorcery*; stroke of genius, feat, exploit 676 *deed*; transformation scene, coup de théâtre 594 *dramatic theory*.

***prodigy*,** quite something, phenomenon, miracle, marvel, wonder; portent, sign, eye-opener 511 *omen*; drama, sensation, cause célèbre, nine-days' wonder; object of wonder or admiration, wonderland, fairyland 513 *fantasy*; seven wonders of the world; sight 445 *spectacle*; infant prodigy, genius, man or woman of genius 696 *proficient person*; miracle-worker, thaumaturge, wizard, witch, fairy godmother 983 *sorcerer*; hero, heroine, wonder boy, superman, dream girl, superwoman, whiz kid 646 *paragon*; freak, sport, curiosity, oddity, guy, monster, monstrosity; puzzle 530 *enigma*.

Adj. *wonderful*, to wonder at, wondrous, marvellous, miraculous, monstrous, prodigious, phenomenal; stupendous, fearful 854 *frightening*; admirable, exquisite 644 *excellent*; record-breaking 644 *best*; striking, overwhelming, awesome, awe-inspiring, breathtaking 821 *impressive*; dramatic, sensational; shocking, scandalizing; rare, exceptional, extraordinary, unprecedented 84 *unusual*; remarkable, noteworthy; strange, passing strange, odd, very odd, outré, weird, weird and wonderful, unaccountable, mysterious, enigmatic 517 *puzzling*; exotic, outlandish, unheard of 59 *extraneous*; fantastic 513 *imaginary*; impossible, hardly possible, too good or bad to be true 472

improbable; unbelievable, incredible, inconceivable, unimaginable, indescribable; unutterable, unspeakable, ineffable 517 *inexpressible*; surprising 508 *unexpected*; mind-boggling, mind-blowing, astounding, amazing, shattering, bewildering, etc. (see vb.); wonder-working; magic, like magic 983 *magical*.

Vb. *wonder*, marvel, admire, whistle; hold one's breath, gasp, gasp with admiration; stare, goggle at, gawk, open one's eyes wide, rub one's eyes, not believe one's eyes; gape, gawp, open one's mouth, stand in amazement, look aghast 508 *not expect*; be awestruck, be overwhelmed 854 *fear*; have no words to express, not know what to say, be reduced to silence, be struck dumb 399 *be silent*.

***be wonderful*,** be marvellous, etc. (see adj.); do wonders, work miracles, achieve marvels; surpass belief, stagger belief, beggar belief, boggle the mind 486 *cause doubt*; beggar all description, baffle description, beat everything; spellbind, enchant 983 *bewitch*; dazzle, strike with admiration, turn one's head; strike dumb, awe, electrify 821 *impress*; make one's eyes open, make one sit up and take notice, take one's breath away; bowl over, stagger; blow one's mind, stun, daze, stupefy, petrify, dumbfound, confound, astound, astonish, amaze, flabbergast 508 *surprise*; baffle, bewilder 474 *puzzle*; startle 854 *frighten*; shock, scandalize 924 *incur blame*.

865 Lack of wonder

N. *lack of wonder*, irreverence, refusal to be impressed, blankness, stony indifference 860 *indifference*; composure, calmness, serenity, tranquillity 266 *quietness*; imperturbability, impassiveness, cold blood 820 *moral insensibility*; taking for granted 610 *habituation*; lack of imagination, unimaginativeness; disbelief 486 *unbelief*; matter of course, just what one thought, nothing to wonder at, nothing to write home about, nothing in it.

Vb. *not wonder*, see nothing remarkable 820 *be insensitive*; treat as a matter of course, not raise an eyebrow, take for granted, take as one's due; see it coming 507 *expect*.

866 Repute

N. *repute*, good repute, high repute; reputation, good reputation; report, good report; title to fame, name, great name, good name, fair name, character, good character, high character, reputability, respectability 802 *credit*; regard, esteem 920 *respect*; opinion, good opinion, good odour, favour, high favour, popular favour, good books; popularity, vogue

848 *fashion*; acclaim, applause, approval, stamp of approval, seal of approval, cachet **923** *approbation*.

prestige, aura, mystique, magic; glamour, glitz, dazzle, éclat, lustre, splendour; brilliance, prowess; illustriousness, glory, honour, honour and glory, kudos, claim to fame, succès d'estime (see also *fame* below); esteem, estimation, izzat, account, high account, worship **638** *importance*; face, caste; degree, rank, ranking, standing, footing, status, honorary status; condition, position, position in society; top of the ladder *or* the tree, precedence **34** *superiority*; conspicuousness, prominence, eminence **443** *visibility*; distinction, greatness, high rank, exaltedness, majesty **868** *nobility*; impressiveness, dignity, stateliness, solemnity, grandeur, sublimity, awesomeness; name to conjure with **178** *influence*; paramountcy, ascendancy, hegemony, primacy **733** *authority*; leadership, acknowledged leadership **689** *directorship*; prestigiousness, snob value; status symbol, trophy wife.

fame, famousness, title to fame, celebrity, notability, remarkability; illustriousness, renown, stardom, fame, name, note; household name, synonym for; glory **727** *success*; notoriety **867** *disrepute*; talk of the town **528** *publicity*; claim to fame, place in history, posthumous fame **505** *memory*; undying name, immortal name, immortality, deathlessness; remembrance, commemoration, niche in the hall of fame.

honours, honour, blaze of glory, crown of glory; crown, martyr's crown; halo, aureole, nimbus, glory; blushing honours, battle honours; laurels, bays, wreath, garland, favour; feather, feather in one's cap **729** *trophy*; order, star, garter, ribbon, medal **729** *decoration*; spurs, sword, shield, arms **547** *heraldry*; an honour, signal honour, distinction, accolade, award **962** *reward*; compliment, bouquet, flattery, incense, laud, eulogy **923** *praise*; memorial, statue, bust, picture, portrait, niche, plaque, temple, monument **505** *reminder*; title of honour, dignity, handle **870** *title*; patent of nobility, knighthood, baronetcy, peerage **868** *nobility*; academic honour, baccalaureate, doctorate, degree, academic degree, honours degree, pass degree, ordinary degree, aegrotat degree, honorary degree, diploma, certificate **870** *academic title*; sports trophy, cup, cap, blue; source of honour, fount of honour; honours list, birthday honours, roll of honour **87** *list*; College of Arms.

person of repute, honoured sir *or* madam, gentle reader; worthy, sound person, good citizen, loyal subject, pillar of society, pillar of the church, pillar of the state; man *or* woman of honour; knight, dame, peer, people's peer **868** *person of rank*; somebody, great man, great woman, big shot, big noise, big gun, big name, big wheel, VIP **638** *bigwig*; top dog, queen bee; someone of mark, notable, celebrity, notability, figure, public figure; champion **644** *exceller*; lion, star, rising star, luminary; man *or* woman of the hour, heroine of the hour, hero of the day, popular hero, icon; pop singer, idol **890** *favourite*; cynosure, model, mirror **646** *paragon*; cream, cream of society, crème de la crème **644** *elite*; choice spirit, master spirit, leading light **690** *leader*; grand old man, GOM **500** *sage*; noble army, great company, bevy, galaxy, constellation **74** *band*.

Adj. *reputable*, reputed, of repute, of good *or* sound reputation, of credit; creditworthy **929** *trustworthy*; gentlemanly **929** *honourable*; worthy, creditable, meritorious, prestigious **644** *excellent*; esteemed, respectable, regarded, well-regarded, well thought of; edifying, moral **933** *virtuous*; in good odour, in the good books, in favour, in high favour **923** *approved*; popular, modish **848** *fashionable*; sanctioned, allowed, admitted.

worshipful, reverend, honourable; admirable **864** *wonderful*; heroic **855** *courageous*; imposing, dignified, august, stately, grand, sublime **821** *impressive*; lofty, high; high and mighty, mighty **32** *great*; lordly, princely, kingly, queenly, majestic, royal, regal **868** *noble*; aristocratic, well-born, high-caste, heaven-born; glorious, in glory, full of glory, full of honours, honoured, titled, ennobled; time-honoured, ancient, age-old **127** *immemorial*; sacrosanct, sacred, holy **979** *sanctified*; honorific, dignifying.

noteworthy, notable, remarkable, extraordinary **84** *unusual*; wonderful, of mark, of distinction, distinguished, distingué(e) **638** *important*; conspicuous, prominent, public, in the public eye, in the limelight, famous for fifteen minutes **443** *obvious*; eminent, pre-eminent, supereminent; peerless, nonpareil, foremost, in the forefront **34** *superior*; ranking, starring, leading, commanding; brilliant, bright, lustrous **417** *luminous*; illustrious, splendid, glorious **875** *ostentatious*.

renowned, celebrated, acclaimed; of renown, of glorious name, of fame; famous, fabled, legendary, famed, far-famed; historic, illustrious, great, noble, glorious **644** *excellent*; notorious **867** *disreputable*; known as, well-known, on the map **490** *known*; of note, noted (see also *noteworthy* above); talked of, resounding, on all lips, on every tongue, in the news; lasting, unfading, never-fading, evergreen, imperishable, deathless, immortal, eternal **115** *perpetual*.

Vb. *have a reputation*, enjoy a reputation, wear a halo; have a good name; rank, stand high, have status *or* standing, be looked up to, have a name for, be praised for 920 *command respect*; stand well with, do oneself credit, win honour, win renown, gain prestige, gain recognition, build a reputation, earn a name; be somebody, make one's mark, set the heather on fire 730 *prosper*; win one's spurs, gain one's laurels, take one's degree, graduate 727 *succeed*; cut a figure, cut a dash, cover oneself with glory 875 *be ostentatious*; rise to fame, get to the top of the ladder *or* tree, flash to stardom; shine, excel 644 *be good*; outshine, eclipse, steal the show, throw into the shade, overshadow 34 *be superior*; have precedence, play first fiddle, take the lead, play the lead, star 64 *come before*; bask in glory, have fame, have a great name, hand down one's name to posterity; make history, live in history, be sure of immortality, carve a niche for oneself in the hall of fame 505 *be remembered*.

honour, revere, regard, look up to, hold in respect, hold in reverence, hold in honour 920 *respect*; stand in awe of 854 *fear*; bow down to, recognize as superior 981 *worship*; know how to value, appreciate, prize; value, tender, treasure 887 *love*; show honour, pay respect, pay due regard, pay one's respects to 920 *show respect*; be polite to 884 *be courteous*; compliment 925 *flatter*; grace with, honour with, dedicate to, inscribe to; praise, sing the praises, laud, glorify, acclaim 923 *applaud*; crown, grant the palm, deck with laurels, make much of, eulogize, lionize, chair, ask for one's autograph; credit, give credit, honour for 907 *thank*; glorify, immortalize, eternize, commemorate, memorialize 505 *remember*; celebrate, renown, blazon 528 *proclaim*; reflect honour, redound to one's honour *or* one's credit, lend distinction *or* lustre to, do credit to, be a credit to.

dignify, glorify, exalt; canonize, beatify, deify, consecrate, dedicate 979 *sanctify*; install, enthrone, crown 751 *commission*; signalize, mark out, distinguish 547 *indicate*; aggrandize, advance, upgrade 285 *promote*; honour, delight to honour, confer an honour; bemedal, beribbon 844 *decorate*; bestow a title, create, elevate, raise to the peerage, ennoble; confer a knighthood, dub, knight, give the accolade; give one his *or* her title, sir, bemadam 561 *name*; take a title, take a handle to one's name, accept a knighthood.

867 Disrepute

N. *disrepute*, disreputableness, bad reputation, bad name, bad character, shady reputation,

past; disesteem 921 *disrespect*; notoriety, infamy, ill repute, ill fame, succès de scandale; no reputation, no standing, ingloriousness, obscurity; bad odour, ill favour, disfavour, bad books, discredit, black books, bad light; derogation, dishonour, disgrace, shame (see also *slur* below), smear campaign 926 *detraction*; ignominy, loss of honour, loss of reputation, faded repuation, withered laurels, tarnished honour; departed glory, Ichabod; loss of face, loss of rank, demotion, degradation, reduction to the ranks, dishonourable discharge; debasement, abasement, comedown 872 *humiliation*; abjectness, baseness, vileness, turpitude 934 *wickedness*.

slur, reproach 924 *censure*; imputation, brick-bat, aspersion, reflection, slander, opprobrium, abuse 926 *calumny*; slight, insult, put-down 921 *indignity*; scandal, shocking scandal, disgrace, shame, burning shame, crying shame; defilement, pollution 649 *uncleanness*; stain, smear, smudge 649 *dirt*; stigma, brand, mark, black mark, spot, blot, tarnish, taint 845 *blemish*; dirty linen; bar sinister, blot on one's scutcheon, badge of infamy, scarlet letter, mark of Cain.

Adj. *disreputable*, not respectable, disrespectable, louche, shifty, shady; notorious, infamous, of ill fame *or* ill repute, nefarious; arrant 645 *bad*; doubtful, dubious, questionable, objectionable 645 *not nice*; risqué, ribald, improper, indecent, obscene 951 *impure*; not thought much of, held in contempt, despised 922 *contemptible*; characterless, without references, of no repute *or* reputation; petty, pitiful 639 *unimportant*; outcast; down-and-out, degraded, base, abject, despicable, odious 888 *hateful*; mean, cheap, low 847 *vulgar*; shabby, squalid, dirty, scruffy 649 *unclean*; poor, down at heel, out at elbows 655 *dilapidated*; in a bad light, under a cloud, in one's bad *or* black books, in the doghouse, in Coventry, unable to show one's face; discredited, disgraced, in disgrace (see also *inglorious* below); reproached; unpopular.

discreditable, no credit to, bringing discredit, reflecting upon one, damaging, compromising; ignoble, unworthy; improper, unbecoming 643 *inexpedient*; dishonourable 930 *dishonest*; despicable 922 *contemptible*; censurable 924 *blameworthy*; shameful, shame-making, disgraceful, infamous, scandalous, shocking, outrageous, unmentionable, disgusting; too bad 645 *not nice*.

degrading, lowering, demeaning, ignominious, opprobrious, mortifying, humiliating; derogatory, hurting one's dignity; beneath one, beneath one's dignity, infra dig.

inglorious, without repute, without prestige, without note; without a name, nameless 562 *anonymous*; unheroic 879 *servile*; unaspiring, unambitious 874 *modest*; unnoted, unremarked, unnoticed, unmentioned 458 *neglected*; unrenowned, unknown to fame, unheard of, obscure 491 *unknown*; unseen, unheard 444 *invisible*; unhymned, unsung, unglorified, unhonoured, undecorated; titleless 869 *plebeian*; deflated, put down, cut down to size, debunked, humiliated, mortified; sunk low, shorn of glory, faded, withered, tarnished; stripped of reputation, discredited, creditless, disgraced, dishonoured, out of favour, in the bad *or* black books, in eclipse; degraded, demoted, reduced to the ranks.

Vb. *have no repute*, have no reputation, have no character, have no name to lose, have a past; have no credit, rank low, stand low in estimation, have no standing, have little status, be a nobody, cut no ice; be out of favour, be in the bad *or* black books, be in bad odour, be unpopular, be discredited, be in disgrace, stink in the nostrils; play second fiddle, take a back seat, stay in the background 35 *be inferior*; blush unseen, hide one's light 444 *be unseen*.

lose repute, fall *or* go out of fashion, pass from the public eye, fall out of favour; come down in the world, fall, sink 309 *descend*; fade, wither; fall into disrepute, incur discredit *or* dishonour *or* disgrace, achieve notoriety, get a bad name for oneself 924 *incur blame*; spoil one's record, blot one's copybook, disgrace oneself, compromise one's name, risk one's reputation, lose one's reputation, outlive one's reputation; tarnish one's glory, forfeit one's honour, lose one's halo, lose one's good name, earn no credit, earn no honour, win no glory 728 *fail*; come down in the eyes of, forfeit one's good opinion, sink in estimation, suffer in reputation, lose prestige, lose face, lose rank; admit defeat, slink away, crawl, crouch 721 *knuckle under*; look silly, look foolish, be a laughing-stock, cut a sorry figure, blush for shame, laugh on the wrong side of one's mouth 497 *be absurd*; be exposed, be brought to book 963 *be punished*.

demean oneself, lower oneself, degrade oneself; condescend, stoop, marry beneath one; make oneself cheap, cheapen oneself, disgrace oneself, behave unworthily, have no sense of one's position; sacrifice one's pride, forfeit self-respect; have no pride, feel no shame, think no shame.

shame, put to shame, hold up to shame; pillory, expose, show up, post; scorn, mock 851 *ridicule*; snub, put down, take down a peg or two 872 *humiliate*; discompose, disconcert, discomfit, put out of countenance, put one's nose out of joint, deflate, cut down to size, debunk; strip of one's honours, strip of rank, deplume, degrade, downgrade, demote, disrate, reduce to the ranks, cashier, disbar, defrock, deprive, strip 963 *punish*; blackball, ostracize 57 *exclude*; vilify, malign, disparage 926 *defame*; destroy one's reputation, take away one's good name, ruin one's credit; put in a bad light, reflect upon, taint; sully, mar, blacken, tarnish, stain, blot, besmear, smear, bespatter 649 *make unclean*; debase, defile, desecrate, profane 980 *be impious*; stigmatize, brand, cast a slur upon, tar 547 *mark*; dishonour, disgrace, discredit, give a bad name, bring into disrepute, bring shame upon, scandalize, be a public scandal 924 *incur blame*; heap shame upon, dump on, heap dirt upon, drag through the mire *or* mud; trample, tread underfoot, ride roughshod over, outrage 735 *oppress*; contemn, disdain 922 *despise*; make one blush, outrage one's modesty 951 *debauch*; not spare one's blushes, eulogize, overpraise.

868 Nobility

N. *nobility*, nobleness, distinction, rank, high rank, titled rank, station, order 27 *degree*; royalty, kingliness, queenliness, princeliness, majesty, prerogative 733 *authority*; birth, high birth, gentle birth, gentility, noblesse; descent, high descent, noble descent, ancestry, long ancestry, line, unbroken line, lineage, pedigree, ancient pedigree 169 *genealogy*; noble family, noble house, ancient house, royal house, dynasty, royal dynasty 11 *family*; blood, blue blood, best blood; bloodstock, caste, high caste; badge of rank, patent of nobility, coat of arms, crest 547 *heraldry*.

aristocracy, patriciate, patrician order; nobility, hereditary nobility, lesser nobility, noblesse, ancien régime; lordship, lords, peerage, House of Lords, lords spiritual and temporal; dukedom, earldom, viscountcy, baronetcy; baronage, knightage; landed interest, squirearchy, squiredom; county family, county set, gentry, landed gentry, gentlefolk; the great, great folk, the high and the mighty, notables; life peerage.

upper class, upper classes, upper ten, upper crust, top layer, top drawer; first families, the quality, best people, better sort, chosen few 644 *elite*; high society, social register, high life, fashionable world 848 *fashionable society*; ruling class, the twice-born, the Establishment 733 *authority*; high-ups, Olympians; the haves 800 *rich person*; salaried class, salariat.

aristocrat, patrician, nobleman *or* -woman;

person of high caste, Brahman; bloodstock, thoroughbred; senator, magnifico, magnate, dignitary; don, grandee, caballero, hidalgo; gentleman, gentlewoman; squire, laird; boyar, Junker; emperor, king, queen, prince 741 *sovereign*; nob, swell, gent, toff 848 *dandy*; panjandrum, superior person 638 *bigwig*.

person of rank, titled person, noble, nobleman *or* -woman, noble lord *or* lady, seigneur; princeling, lordling, aristo; lordship, milord; ladyship, milady; peer, hereditary peer, life peer, people's peer, peer of the realm, peeress; Prince of Wales, Princess Royal, duke, grand duke, archduke, duchess; marquis, marquess, marquise, marchioness, margrave, margravine, count, countess, contessa; earl, belted earl; viscount, viscountess, baron, baroness, thane, baronet, knight, banneret, knight-bachelor; knight-banneret; rajah, bey, nawab, begum, emir, khan, sheikh, doge 741 *potentate*, *governor*.

Adj. *noble*, chivalrous, knightly; gentlemanly, gentlemanlike, ladylike (see also *genteel* below); majestic, royal, regal, every inch a king *or* queen; kingly, queenly, princely, lordly; ducal, baronial, seigneurial; of royal blood, of high *or* gentle birth, of good family, pedigreed, well-born, high-born, born in the purple, born with a silver spoon in one's mouth; thoroughbred, blue-blooded; of rank, ennobled, titled, in Debrett, in Burke's Peerage; haughty, high, exalted, high-up, grand 32 *great*.

genteel, patrician, senatorial; aristocratic; superior, top-drawer, upper-crust, high-class, upper-class, cabin-class, classy, posh, U, highly respectable, comme il faut; of good breeding 848 *well-bred*.

869 Commonalty

N. *common people*, common folk, commonalty, commonality, commons, people at large, populace, the people, third estate, bourgeoisie, middle classes, lower classes; plebs, plebeians; citizenry, democracy; townsfolk, country-folk; silent majority, grass roots; the public, general public, Joe Public, etc. (see *commoner* below); vulgar herd, great unwashed; the many, the multitude, hoi polloi; the masses, mass of society, mass of the people, admass, proletariat; the general, rank and file, rag, tag and bobtail, Tom, Dick and Harry 79 *everyman*.

rabble, mob, horde 74 *crowd*; riffraff, scum, off-scourings, dregs of society, the flotsam and jetsam, canaille, cattle, vermin; clamjamphrie, rout, rabble rout, varletry.

lower classes, lower orders, one's inferiors 35 *inferior*; common sort, small fry, humble folk; working class, blue-collar workers, wage earners, servant class; steerage class, lower deck; second-class citizens, the have-nots, the under-privileged, the disadvantaged; proletariat, proles; down-and-outs, depressed class, outcasts, outcasts of society, poor whites, white trash; demi-monde, under-world, low company, low life.

middle classes, bourgeoisie 732 *averageness*; professional classes, salaried classes, white-collar workers; Brown, Jones and Robinson; Middle England, Middle America.

commoner, bourgeois(e), plebeian, pleb; untitled person, plain Mr *or* Mrs; citizen, mere citizen, John Citizen, Joe Bloggs, Joe Public, Joe Soap; one of the people, man *or* woman of the people, democrat, republican; proletarian, prole; working man *or* woman 686 *worker*; town-dweller, country-dweller 191 *native*; little man, man *or* woman in the street, everyman, everywoman, common type, average type, the average punter 30 *common man*, 371 *social group*; common person, groundling, pittite; galleryite 35 *inferior*; backbencher, private; underling 742 *servant*; ranker, upstart, parvenu, social climber, arriviste, nouveau riche, Philistine; a nobody, nobody one knows, nobody knows who 639 *nonentity*; low-caste person, outcaste; Untouchable, dalit, harijan; villein, serf 742 *slave*.

country-dweller, countryman *or* -woman, yeoman, rustic, swain, gaffer, peasant, son *or* daughter of the soil, tiller of the soil, ploughman, teuchter 370 *farmer*; boor, churl, bog-trotter; yokel, hind, clod, clodhopper, rube, redneck, hayseed, hick, backwoodsman; bumpkin, country bumpkin, Tony Lumpkin, country cousin, provincial, hillbilly; village idiot 501 *ninny*.

low fellow, fellow, varlet 938 *cad*; slum-dweller 801 *poor person*; guttersnipe, mudlark, street arab, gamin, ragamuffin; down-and-out, tramp, bag lady, bum, vagabond, trailer trash 268 *wanderer*; gaberlunzie, panhandler 763 *beggar*; low type, rough type, bully, ugly customer, plug-ugly, low-life, ruffian, rowdy, rough, bit of rough, boot boy, bovver boy, roughneck 904 *ruffian*; rascal 938 *knave*; gangster, hood, crook; criminal, delinquent, juvenile delinquent 904 *offender*; barbarian, savage, Goth, Vandal, Yahoo.

Adj. *plebeian*, common, simple, untitled, unennobled, without rank, titleless; ignoble, below the salt; below-stairs, servant-class; lower-deck, rank and file 732 *middling*; mean, low, low-down, street-corner 867 *disreputable*; lowly, base-born, low-born, low-caste, of low birth, of low origin, of mean parentage, of mean extraction; slave-born, servile; humble, of low estate, of humble condition 35 *inferior*; unaristocratic, middle-class, lower middle-class, working-class, cloth-cap, non-U, proletarian; homely, homespun 573 *plain*; obscure 867 *inglorious*; coarse, brutish, uncouth, unpolished 847 *ill-bred*; unfashionable, cockney, bourgeois, Main Street, suburban, provincial, rustic; parvenu, risen from the ranks 847 *vulgar*; boorish, churlish, loutish, yobbish.

   barbaric, barbarous, barbarian, wild, savage, brutish, yobbish; uncivilized, uncultured, without arts, philistine, primitive, neolithic 699 *artless*.

870 Title

N. *title*, title to fame, entitlement, claim 915 *what is due*; title of honour, courtesy title, handle, handle to one's name; honour, distinction, order, knighthood 866 *honours*; royal we, editorial we 875 *formality*; mode of address, style of address, Royal Highness, Serene Highness, Excellency, Grace, Lordship, Ladyship, noble, most noble, my liege, my lord, my lady, dame; the Honourable, Right Honourable; Reverend, Very Reverend, Right Reverend, Most Reverend, Monsignor, His Holiness; dom, padre; your reverence, your honour, your worship; sire, esquire, sir, dear sir, madam, ma'am, master, mister, Mr, mistress, Mrs, miss, Ms; monsieur, madame, mademoiselle; don, señor, señora, señorita; dom, senhor, senhora, senhorita, signor *or* signore, signora, signorina; Herr, Frau, Fräulein; mynheer *or* mijnheer *or* meneer, mevrouw, mejuffrouw; babu, Sri *or* Shri, sahib, memsahib; bwana, effendi, mirza; san; citoyen, comrade, tovarich.

   academic title, degree, diploma, baccalaureate, licentiate, doctorate; ordinary degree, honours degree; first-, second- *or* third-class honours; first, double first, congratulatory first, second, upper second, lower second, third; doctor, doctor honoris causa; doctor of divinity, DD; doctor of laws, LLD; doctor of letters *or* literature, DLitt, LittD; doctor of medicine, MD; doctor of music, MusD; doctor of philosophy, DPhil, PhD; doctor of science, DSc; master of arts, MA; master of education, MEd; master of letters *or* literature, MLitt, master of philosophy, MPhil; master of sacred theology, STM; master of science, MSc; bachelor of architecture, BArch; bachelor of arts, BA; bachelor of dental surgery, BDS; bachelor of divinity, BD; bachelor of education, BEd; bachelor of letters *or* literature, BLitt; bachelor of medicine and surgery, MBChB, MBBS; bachelor of law, BL, bachelor of laws, LLB; bachelor

of music, MusB, BMus; bachelor of science, BSc; bachelor of veterinary medicine and surgery, BVMS, BVM&S; diploma of art, DA; diploma in education, DipEd; diploma of higher education, DipHE; diploma in social work, DipSW; lecturer, reader, professor, professor emeritus.

871 Pride

N. *pride*, self-esteem, amour propre; self-respect, self-confidence; conceit, self-conceit, swelled *or* swollen head, swank, side 873 *vanity*; snobbery, inverted snobbery 850 *affectation*; false pride, touchiness 819 *moral sensibility*; dignity, reputation 866 *prestige*; stateliness, loftiness; condescension, hauteur, haughtiness, uppitiness, unapproachability, disdain 922 *contempt*; overweening pride, bumptiousness, arrogance, attitude, hubris 878 *insolence*; swelling pride, pomp, pomposity, grandiosity, show, display 875 *ostentation*; egoism, self-praise, vainglory 877 *boasting*; class-consciousness, race-prejudice, sexism 481 *prejudice*.

   proud person, vain person, snob, parvenu; swelled *or* swollen head, swank; Lady Muck, queen bee, lord of creation 638 *bigwig*; fine gentleman, grande dame 848 *dandy*; peacock, turkey cock, cock of the walk, swaggerer, bragger; purse-proud plutocrat 800 *rich person*; class-conscious person 868 *aristocrat*.

   Adj. *proud*, elevated, haughty, lofty, sublime 209 *high*; plumed, crested 875 *showy*; fine, grand 848 *fashionable*; grandiose, dignified, stately, statuesque 821 *impressive*; majestic, royal, kingly, queenly, lordly, aristocratic 868 *noble*; self-respecting, self-confident, pronoid, proud-hearted, high-souled 855 *courageous*; high-stepping, high-spirited 819 *lively*; stiff-necked 602 *obstinate*; mighty, overmighty 32 *great*; imperious, commanding 733 *authoritative*; high-handed 735 *oppressive*; overweening, overbearing, hubristic, arrogant, with attitude 878 *insolent*; puffed-up, inflated, swelling, swollen, big-headed; overproud, high and mighty, stuck-up, toffee-nosed, snobbish, nose-in-the-air, snooty; upstage, uppish, uppity; on one's dignity, on one's high horse; haughty, disdainful, superior, holier than thou, supercilious, hoity-toity, high-hat, patronizing, condescending; standoffish, aloof; taking pride in, house-proud; proud of, bursting with pride, inches taller; strutting, swaggering, vainglorious; pleased with oneself, pleased as Punch, pleased as a dog with two tails, like the cat that got the cream; cocky, bumptious, conceited 873 *vain*; pretentious 850 *affected*; swanky, swanking, pompous 875 *showy*; proud as Lucifer, proud as a peacock.

Vb. *be proud*, have one's pride, have one's self-respect, be jealous of one's honour, guard one's reputation, hold one's head high, stand erect, refuse to stoop, bow to no one, stand on one's dignity, mount one's high horse; give oneself airs, toss one's head, hold one's nose in the air, think it beneath one, be too proud to, be too grand to; be stuck-up, be snooty, swank, show off, swagger, strut 875 *be ostentatious*; condescend, patronize; look down on, disdain 922 *despise*; display hauteur 878 *be insolent*; lord it, queen it, come it over, throw one's weight about, pull rank, overween 735 *oppress*.

872 Humility. Humiliation

N. *humility*, humbleness, humble spirit 874 *modesty*; abasement, lowness, lowliness; unpretentiousness, quietness; harmlessness, inoffensiveness 935 *innocence*; meekness, resignation, submissiveness, servility 721 *submission*; self-depreciation, self-effacement, self-abasement, mortification 931 *disinterestedness*; condescension, stooping 884 *courtesy*; mouse, violet, shrinking violet.

humiliation, abasement, humbling, letdown, climbdown, comedown, slap in the face 921 *indignity*; crushing retort; rebuke 924 *reprimand*; shame, disgrace 867 *disrepute*; scandal, Watergate, -gate; sense of shame, sense of disgrace, blush, suffusion, confusion; shamefaced look, hangdog expression, tail between the legs; chastening thought, mortification, hurt pride, injured pride, offended dignity 891 *resentment*.

Adj. *humble*, humble-minded, self-deprecating, poor in spirit, lowly; meek, submissive, resigned, unprotesting, servile 721 *submitting*; self-effacing 931 *disinterested*; self-abasing, stooping, condescending 884 *courteous*; mouselike, harmless, inoffensive, unoffending 935 *innocent*; unassuming, unpretentious, without airs, without side 874 *modest*; mean, low 639 *unimportant*; of lowly birth 869 *plebeian*.

Vb. *be humble*, be lowly, etc. (see adj.); have no sense of pride, have no self-conceit, humble oneself 867 *demean oneself*; play second fiddle, take a back seat 874 *be modest*; put others first, not think of oneself 931 *be disinterested*; condescend, unbend 884 *be courteous*; stoop, bow down, crawl, be a sycophant, sing small, eat humble pie, eat crow 721 *knuckle under*; turn the other cheek.

be humbled, be humiliated, etc. (see adj.); receive a snub, be cold-shouldered, get a slap in the face, be put in one's place, be taken

down a peg; be ashamed, be ashamed of oneself, feel shame; blush, colour up 431 *redden*; feel small, hide one's face, hang one's head, avert one's eyes, have nothing to say for oneself, wish to sink through the floor, wish the earth would swallow one up; stop swanking, come off it.

humiliate, humble, chasten, abash, disconcert, put to the blush; lower, take down a peg, put down, debunk, deflate; make one feel small, make one sing small, make one feel this high, teach one his place, make one crawl, rub one's nose in the dirt, rub one's nose in it; snub, cut, crush, squash, sit on, send away with a flea in their ear 885 *be rude*; slight 921 *not respect*; mortify, hurt one's pride, offend one's dignity, lower in all men's eyes, put to shame 867 *shame*;

score off, put one's nose out of joint, make a fool of, make one look silly; put in the shade 306 *outdo*; outstare, outfrown, frown down, daunt 854 *frighten*; get the better of, gain the upper hand, triumph over, crow over 727 *overcome*.

873 Vanity

N. *vanity*, emptiness 4 *lacking substance*; empty pride 871 *pride*; immodesty, conceit, conceitedness, self-importance, megalomania; swank, side, puffed-up chest, swelled *or* swollen head; know-it-allness; cockiness, bumptiousness, assurance, self-assurance; good opinion of oneself, self-conceit, self-esteem, amour propre; self-satisfaction, smugness; self-love, self-admiration, narcissism; self-complacency, self-approbation, self-praise, self-applause, self-flattery, self-congratulation, self-glorification, vainglory 877 *boasting*; self-sufficiency, self-centredness, egotism, egocentrism, egocentricity, egomania, me-ism 932 *selfishness*; exhibitionism, showing off, self-display 875 *ostentation*; vanity domain, vanity publishing;.

airs, fine airs, airs and graces, mannerisms, pretensions, absurd pretensions 850 *affectation*; swank, side, pompousness 875 *ostentation*; coxcombry, priggishness, foppery.

vain person, self-admirer, Narcissus, popinjay; self-centred person, me generation, egotist, coxcomb 848 *dandy*; exhibitionist, peacock, turkey cock, show-off; know-all, bighead, God's gift to women; smarty-pants, smart alec, smart ass, cleverstick, clever dick, Mr Clever, Miss Clever 500 *wiseacre*; stuffed shirt, pompous twit 4 *thing that lacks substance*.

Adj. *vain*, conceited, overweening, stuck-up, snooty, proud 871 *proud*; egotistic, egocentric, self-centred, self-satisfied, self-complacent, full of oneself, self-important 932 *selfish*; smug, pleased with oneself; self-loving, narcissistic, stuck on oneself; wise in one's own conceit, dogmatic, opinionated, oversubtle, overclever, clever clever, too clever by half, too smart for one's own good 498 *intelligent*; swollen-headed, puffed-up, too big for one's boots, bigheaded, bumptious, cocky, perky, smart-ass 878 *insolent*; immodest, blatant; showing off, swaggering, vainglorious, selfglorious; pompous 875 *ostentatious*; pretentious, soi-disant, so-called, self-styled; coxcombical, fantastical, putting on airs 850 *affected*.

Vb. *be vain*, be conceited, etc. (see adj.); have a swelled head, have one's head turned; have a high opinion of oneself, set a high value on oneself, think a lot of oneself, think too much of oneself, think oneself the cat's pyjamas, think oneself God Almighty, regard oneself as God's gift (to —); exaggerate one's own merits, blow one's own trumpet 877 *boast*; admire oneself, hug oneself, flatter oneself, give oneself a pat on the back; plume oneself, preen oneself, pride oneself; swank, strut, show off, put on airs, put on side, show one's paces, display one's talents, talk for effect, talk big, not hide one's light under a bushel, push oneself forward 875 *be ostentatious*; lap up flattery, fish for compliments; get above oneself, have pretentions, give oneself airs 850 *be affected*; play the fop, be overconcerned with one's appearance, dress up, doll oneself up, dandify 843 *primp*.

874 Modesty

N. *modesty*, lack of ostentation, shyness, retiring disposition; diffidence, timidness, timidity 854 *nervousness*; overmodesty, prudishness 950 *prudery*; bashfulness, blushing, blush; shamefacedness, shockability; chastity 950 *purity*; deprecation, self-deprecation, selfdepreciation, self-effacement, hiding one's light 872 *humility*; unobtrusiveness, unpretentiousness, unassuming nature; demureness, reserve; shrinking violet, mouse.

Adj. *modest*, without vanity, free from pride; self-effacing, unobtrusive, unseen, unheard 872 *humble*; self-deprecating, unboastful; unassertive, unpushing, unthrustful, unambitious; quiet, unassuming, unpretentious, unpretending; unimposing, unimpressive, moderate, mediocre, underwhelming 639 *unimportant*; shy, retiring, shrinking, timid, mouse-like, diffident, unselfconfident, unsure of oneself 854 *nervous*; overshy, awkward, constrained, embarrassed, inarticulate; deprecating, demurring; bashful,

blushing, rosy; shamefaced, sheepish; reserved, demure, coy; shockable, overmodest, prudish 850 *affected*; chaste 950 *pure*.

Vb. *be modest*, show moderation; not blow one's trumpet, not push oneself forward, efface oneself, yield precedence 872 *be humble*; play second fiddle, keep in the background, merge into the background, take a back seat, be a back-room boy *or* girl, know one's place; blush unseen, shun the limelight, shrink from the public gaze, hide one's light under a bushel 456 *escape notice*; not look for praise, do good by stealth and blush to find it fame; retire, creep into one's shell, shrink, hang back, be coy 620 *avoid*; show bashfulness, blush, colour, go red, crimson 431 *redden*; preserve one's modesty 933 *be virtuous*.

875 Ostentation. Formality. Pageant.

N. *ostentation*, demonstration, display, parade, show 522 *manifestation*; unconcealment, blatancy, flagrancy, shamelessness, brazenness, exhibitionism 528 *publicity*; ostentatiousness, showiness, magnificence, bling *or* bling-bling; delusions of grandeur, grandiosity; splendour, brilliance; selfconsequence, self-importance 873 *vanity*; pomposity, fuss, swagger, showing off, pretension, pretensions, airs and graces 873 *airs*; swank, side, thrown-out chest, strut; machismo, bravado, heroics 877 *boast*; theatricality, camp, histrionics, dramatization, dramatics, sensationalism 546 *exaggeration*; demonstrativeness, back-slapping, bonhomie 882 *sociability*; showmanship, effect, window-dressing; solemnity; grandeur, dignity, stateliness, impressiveness; declamation, rhetoric 574 *grandiloquence*; flourish, flourish of trumpets, fanfaronade, big drum 528 *publication*; pageantry, pomp, circumstance, pomp and circumstance, bravery, pride, panache, waving plumes, fine feathers, flying colours, dash, splash, splurge 844 *finery*; frippery, gaudiness, glitter, tinsel 844 *ornamentation*; idle pomp, idle show, false glitter, unsubstantial pageant, mummery, mockery, idle mockery, hollow mockery, solemn mockery 4 *lacking substance*; tomfoolery 497 *foolery*; travesty 20 *mimicry*; exterior, gloss, veneer, polish, varnish 223 *exteriority*; pretence, profession 614 *pretext*; insincerity, lip service, tokenism 542 *deception*; formality, state, stateliness, dignity; ceremoniousness, stiffness, starchiness; royal we, editorial we 870 *title*; ceremony, ceremonial 988 *ritual*; drill, smartness, spit and polish, military bull; correctness, correctitude, protocol, form, good form, right form 848 *etiquette*; punctilio, punctiliousness, preciseness 455 *attention*; routine, fixed routine 610 *practice*; solemnity, formal occasion, ceremonial occasion, state occasion, function, grand function, official function, red carpet 876 *celebration*; full dress, court dress, robes, regalia, finery, black tie 228 *formal dress*; correct dress 228 *uniform*.

pageant, show 522 *exhibit*; fete, gala, gala performance, tournament, tattoo; field day, great doings 876 *celebration*; son et lumière 445 *spectacle*; set piece, tableau, scene, transformation scene, stage effect 594 *stage set*; display, bravura, stunt; pyrotechnics; carnival, Lord Mayor's Show 837 *festivity*, *revel*; procession, promenade, march-past, fly-past; changing the guard, trooping the colour; turnout, review, grand review, parade, array, Orange Walk 74 *assembly*, 267 *marching*.

Adj. *ostentatious*, showy, pompous; done for effect; window-dressing, for show, for the sake of appearance; for prestige, for the look of the thing; specious, seeming, hollow 542 *spurious*; consequential, self-important; pretentious, would-be 850 *affected*; showing off, swanking, swanky 873 *vain*; inflated, turgid, orotund, pontificating, windy, magniloquent, declamatory, high-sounding, high-flown; grand, highfalutin, splendiferous, splendid, brilliant, magnificent, grandiose, posh; superb, royal 813 *liberal*; sumptuous, diamond-studded, luxurious, de luxe, plushy, ritzy, glitzy, costly, expensive, expense-account 811 *dear*; painted, glorified, tarted up.

showy, flashy, dressy, dressed to kill, all dolled up, foppish 848 *fashionable*; colourful, lurid, gaudy, gorgeous 425 *florid*; tinsel, glittering, garish, tawdry 847 *vulgar*; flaming, flaring, flaunting, flagrant, blatant, public; brave, dashing, gallant, gay, jaunty, rakish, sporty; spectacular, scenic, dramatic, histrionic, theatrical, camp, stagy; sensational, daring; exhibitionist, stunting.

formal, dignified, solemn, stately, majestic, grand, fine; ceremonious, standing on ceremony, punctilious, stickling, correct, precise, stiff, starchy; black-tie, white-tie, full-dress; — of state, public, official; ceremonial, ritual 988 *ritualistic*; for a special occasion, for a gala occasion.

Vb. *be ostentatious*, be showy, etc. (see adj.); observe the formalities, stand on ceremony; splurge, splash out, cut a dash, make a splash, make a figure; glitter, dazzle 417 *shine*; flaunt, sport 228 *wear*; dress up 843 *primp*; wave, flourish 317 *brandish*; blazon, trumpet, sound the trumpet, beat the big drum 528 *proclaim*; stage a demonstration, wave banners 711 *defy*; demonstrate, exhibit 522 *show*; act the showman, make a display, put on a show; make the most of, put on a front, window-dress, stage-manage; see to the outside, paper the cracks, polish, veneer 226 *coat*; intend for effect, strive for effect, sensationalize, camp up; talk for effect, shoot a line 877 *boast*; take the centre of the stage, grab *or* hog the limelight 455 *attract notice*; put oneself forward, advertise oneself, dramatize oneself; play to the gallery, fish for compliments 850 *be affected*; show off, flaunt oneself, show one's paces, prance, promenade, swan around; parade, march, march past, fly past; peacock, strut, swank, put on side 873 *be vain*; make an exhibition of oneself, make a public spectacle of oneself, make people stare.

876 Celebration

N. *celebration*, performance, solemnization 676 *action*; commemoration 505 *remembrance*; observance, solemn observance 988 *ritual*; ceremony, ceremonial, function, occasion, do; formal occasion, coronation, enthronement, inauguration, installation, presentation 751 *commission*; debut, coming out 68 *beginning*; reception, welcome, hero's welcome, ticker-tape welcome, red-carpet treatment 875 *formality*; official reception 923 *applause*; festive occasion, fete, jubilee, diamond jubilee 837 *festivity*; jubilation, cheering, high-five, ovation, standing ovation, triumph, salute, salvo, tattoo, roll, roll of drums, fanfare, fanfaronade, flourish of trumpets, flying colours, flag waving, mafficking 835 *rejoicing*; flags, banners, bunting, streamers, decorations, Chinese lanterns, illuminations; firework display; bonfire 379 *fire*; triumphal arch 729 *trophy*; harvest home, thanksgiving, Te Deum 907 *thanks*; paean, hosannah, hallelujah 886 *congratulation*; health, toast.

special day, day to remember, great day, red-letter day, gala day, flag day, field day; saint's day, feast day, fast day 988 *holy day*; Armistice Day, D-Day, Remembrance Sunday; Fourth of July, Independence Day, Republic Day, Bastille Day; birthday, name-day; wedding anniversary, silver wedding, golden wedding, diamond wedding, ruby wedding, centenary, bicentenary, sesquicentenary 141 *anniversary*.

Vb. *celebrate*, solemnize; hallow, keep holy, keep sacred 979 *sanctify*; commemorate 505 *remember*; honour, observe; make it an occasion, mark the occasion; make much of, welcome, kill the fatted calf, do one proud 882 *be hospitable*; do honour to, fete; chair, carry shoulder-high 310 *elevate*; mob, rush 61 *rampage*; garland, deck with flowers, wreathe, crown 962 *reward*; lionize, give a hero's welcome, fling wide the gates, roll out the red carpet, hang out the flags, put out the bunting, push the boat out, beat a tattoo, blow the trumpets, clash the cymbals, fire a salute, fire a salvo, fire a feu de joie 884 *pay one's respects*; cheer, jubilate, triumph, rejoice; make holiday 837 *revel*.

toast, pledge, clink glasses; drink to, raise one's glass to, drink a health 301 *drink*.

877 Boasting

N. *boasting*, bragging, boastfulness, fanfaronade; ostentation; self-glorification, swagger, swank 873 *vanity*; advertisement, hype, spam 528 *publicity*; puffery 482 *overestimation*; grandiloquence, fine talk 515 *empty talk*; swaggering, swashbuckling, heroics, bravado; flagwagging *or* -waving, chauvinism, jingoism 481 *bias*; defensiveness, blustering, bluster 854 *nervousness*; sabre-rattling, intimidation 900 *threat*.

boast, brag; hype, spam 528 *advertisement*; flourish, fanfaronade, bravado, bombast, rant, tall talk 546 *exaggeration*; hot air, gas, bunkum 515 *empty talk*; bluff 542 *deception*; big talk, bluster, hectoring, idle threat 900 *threat*.

Vb. *boast*, brag, crow, vaunt, talk big, have a big mouth, shoot one's mouth, shoot a line, bluff, huff and puff, bluster, hector, shout; bid defiance 711 *defy*; vapour, prate, rant, gas 515 *mean nothing*; enlarge, magnify, lay it on thick, draw the longbow 546 *exaggerate*; trumpet, parade, flaunt, show off 528 *publish*; puff, crack up, cry one's wares 528 *advertise*; sell oneself, advertise oneself, be a self-publicist, blow one's own trumpet, blow hard, sing one's own praises, bang the big drum 875 *be ostentatious*; flourish, wave 317 *brandish*; play the jingo, rattle the sabre 900 *threaten*; show off, strut, swagger, prance, swank, throw out one's chest 873 *be vain*; gloat, pat oneself on the back, hug oneself 824 *be pleased*; boast of, plume oneself on 871 *be proud*; glory in, crow over 727 *triumph*; exult 835 *rejoice*.

878 Insolence

N. *insolence*, arrogance, haughtiness, attitude, loftiness 871 *pride*; domineering, tyranny 735 *severity*; bravado 711 *defiance*; bluster 900 *threat*; disdain 922 *contempt*; sneer, sneering 926 *detraction*; contumely 899 *scurrility*; assurance, self-assurance, self-assertion, bumptiousness, cockiness, brashness; presumption 916 *unjustifed claim*; audacity, hardihood, boldness, effrontery, chutzpah, shamelessness, brazenness, brass neck, blatancy, flagrancy; face, front, hardened front, brazen face.

sauciness, disrespect, impertinence, impudence, pertness, freshness, sassiness, flippancy,

nerve, gall, brass, cheek, cool cheek, neck; lip, mouth, sauce, crust, sass, snook, V-sign 547 *gesture*; taunt, personality, insult, affront 921 *indignity*; rudeness, incivility, throwaway manner 885 *discourtesy*; petulance, defiance, answer, provocation, answering back, backtalk, backchat 460 *rejoinder*; raillery, banter 851 *ridicule*.

insolent person, minx, hussy, baggage, madam; whippersnapper, pup, puppy; upstart, Jack-in-office, tin god 639 *nonentity*; blusterer, swaggerer, braggart; bantam-cock; bratpack; bully, swashbuckler; loudmouth.

Adj. *insolent*, rebellious 711 *defiant*; sneering; insulting 921 *disrespectful*; injurious, scurrilous 899 *cursing*; lofty, supercilious, disdainful, contemptuous; undemocratic, snobbish, haughty, snooty, up-stage, high-hat, high and mighty 871 *proud*; arrogant, presumptuous, assuming; with attitude; brash, bumptious, bouncing 873 *vain*; flagrant, blatant; shameless, brazen, brazen-faced, brassnecked, bold as brass; bold, hardy, audacious 857 *rash*; overweening, overbearing, domineering, imperious, lordly, dictatorial, arbitrary, high-handed, harsh, tyrannical 735 *oppressive*.

impertinent, pert, forward, fresh; impudent, saucy, sassy, cheeky, smart-mouth, cool, cocky, cocksure, flippant, flip; cavalier, offhand, presumptuous, out of line, familiar, overfamiliar, free-and-easy 921 *disrespectful*; impolite, rude, uncivil, ill-mannered 885 *discourteous*; defiant, answering back, offensive; loudmouthed, gobby.

Vb. *be insolent*, be arrogant, etc. (see adj.); forget one's manners, get personal 885 *be rude*; have a nerve, cheek, sauce, sass, give lip, taunt, provoke 891 *enrage*; have the audacity to, have the brass neck to, have the cheek to; retort, answer back 460 *answer*; shout down 479 *confute*; get above oneself, get above one's station, teach one's grandmother to suck eggs; not know one's place, presume, be out of line, arrogate, assume, take on oneself, make bold to, make free with, get fresh; put on airs, hold one's nose in the air, look one up and down 871 *be proud*; look down on, sneer at 922 *despise*; banter, rally 851 *ridicule*; express contempt, sniff, snort; not give a fig 860 *be indifferent*; cock a snook, put one's tongue out, give the V-sign 711 *defy*; outstare, outface, brazen it out, brave it out; take a high tone, lord it, queen it, lord it over; lay down the law, throw one's weight around; hector, bully, browbeat, grind down, trample on, ride roughshod over, treat with a high hand 735 *oppress*; swank, swagger, swell, look big 873 *be vain*; brag, talk big 877 *boast*; be a law unto oneself 738 *disobey*; tempt providence *or* fate.

879 Servility

N. *servility*, slavishness, no pride, lack of self-respect 856 *cowardice*; subservience 721 *submission*; submissiveness, obsequiousness, compliance, pliancy 739 *obedience*; time-serving 603 *change of mind*; abasement 872 *humility*; prostration, genuflexion, stooping, bent back, bow, scrape, bowing and scraping, duck, bob 311 *bow*; cringing, crawling, fawning, bootlicking, bumsucking, toadyism, sycophancy, ingratiation, soft soap 925 *flattery*; flunkeyism; servile condition, slavery 745 *servitude*.

toady, collaborator, Uncle Tom; yes-man, rubber stamp 488 *assenter*; lickspittle, bootlicker, backscratcher, bumsucker, apple-polisher, kowtower, groveller, crawler, creep, brown-nose; hypocrite, creeping Jesus, Uriah Heep; spaniel, fawner, courtier, fortune-hunter, lion-hunter 925 *flatterer*; sycophant, parasite, leech, sponger, freeloader; jackal, hanger-on, gigolo 742 *dependant*; flunkey, lackey 742 *retainer*; born slave, slave; doormat, footstool, lapdog, poodle; tool, creature, puppet, dupe, cat's-paw 628 *instrument*.

Adj. *servile*, not free, dependent 745 *subject*; slavish 856 *cowardly*; mean-spirited, mean, abject, base, tame 745 *subjected*; subservient, submissive, deferential 721 *submitting*; pliant, putty-like, compliant, supple 739 *obedient*; time-serving; bowed, stooping, prostrate, bootlicking, backscratching, bumsucking, grovelling, kowtowing, bowing, scraping, cringing, cowering, crawling, sneaking, fawning; begging, whining; toadying, toadyish, sycophantic, parasitical; creepy, obsequious, unctuous, soapy, oily, slimy, overattentive, soft-soaping, ingratiating 925 *flattering*.

Vb. *be servile*, forfeit one's self-respect, stoop to anything 867 *demean oneself*; crawl, grovel, kiss the hands of, kiss the feet of, kiss the hem of one's garment, lick the boots of 721 *knuckle under*; bow and scrape, bend, kowtow, touch the forelock, make obeisance, kneel 311 *stoop*; swallow insults 872 *be humble*; make-up to, cosy up to, toady to, suck up to, fawn, ingratiate oneself, soft-soap, pay court to, curry favour, worm oneself into favour 925 *flatter*; squire, attend, dance attendance on, fetch and carry for 742 *serve*; comply 739 *obey*; be the tool of, do one's dirty work, pander to, stooge for 628 *be instrumental*; let oneself be walked all over, be a doormat, act as a footstool; beg for favours, beg for crumbs 761 *beg*; play the parasite, batten on, sponge, sponge

on; jump on the band wagon, run with the hare and hunt with the hounds 83 *conform*; serve the times 603 *change one's mind*.

SECTION THREE

Interpersonal emotion

880 Friendship

N. *friendship*, bonds of friendship, amity 710 *harmony*; compatibility, mateyness, chumminess, palliness; friendly relations, social intercourse, hobnobbing 882 *fellowship*; companionship, belonging, togetherness; chemistry; alignment, fellowship, comradeship, sodality, freemansonry, brotherhood, sisterhood 706 *association*; solidarity, mutual support 706 *cooperation*; acquaintanceship, acquaintance, mutual acquaintance, familiarity, intimacy 490 *knowledge*; close friendship 887 *love*; bonding, male bonding.

friendliness, amicability, kindliness, kindness, neighbourliness 884 *courtesy*; heartiness, cordiality, warmth 897 *benevolence*; fraternization, camaraderie, palliness, mateyness; hospitality 882 *sociability*; greeting, welcome, open arms, handclasp, handshake, hand-kissing, kissing, peck on the cheek, hug, rubbing noses 884 *courteous act*; regard, mutual regard 920 *respect*; goodwill, mutual goodwill, fellow feeling, sympathy, response 775 *participation*; understanding, same wavelength, entente, entente cordiale, hands across the sea.

friend, girlfriend, boyfriend 887 *loved one*; friends and acquaintances, circle of friends, acquaintance, intimate acquaintance; friend of the family, lifelong friend, mutual friend, friend of a friend; crony, old crony (see also *chum* below); neighbour, good neighbour, fellow townsman *or* -woman, fellow countryman *or* -woman; cousin, clansman 11 *kinsman*; well-wisher, backer, angel 707 *patron*; second 660 *protector*; fellow, sister, brother, partner, associate 707 *colleague*; ally, brother-in-arms 707 *auxiliary*; collaborator, helper, friend in need 703 *helper*; guest, welcome guest, frequent visitor, persona grata; young friend, protégé(e); host, kind host 882 *sociable person*; former friend, fairweather friend 603 *recanter*.

close friend, best friend; soul mate, kindred spirit; best man, bridesmaid 894 *bridal party*; dear friend, good friend, close friend, friend in need; intimate, bosom friend, bosom pal, confidant(e), alter ego, other self, shadow; comrade, companion, boon companion, drinking companion; good friends all, happy family; mutual friends, inseparables, band of brothers *or* sisters, Three Musketeers, David and

Jonathan, Ruth and Naomi, Castor and Pollux; two minds with but a single thought, birds of a feather.

chum, crony; pal, mate, amigo, cobber, buddy, butty, marrow, sidekick, oppo; fellow, comrade, shipmate, messmate, roommate, stable companion 707 *colleague*; teammate, playmate, classmate, schoolmate, schoolfellow; pen friend, pen pal.

Adj. *friendly*, non-hostile, amicable, devoted 887 *loving*; loyal, faithful, staunch, fast, firm, tried and true 929 *trustworthy*; fraternal, brotherly, sisterly, cousinly; natural, unstrained, easy, harmonious; compatible, congenial, sympathetic, understanding; well-wishing, well-meaning, well-intentioned, philanthropic 897 *benevolent*; hearty, cordial, warm, welcoming, hospitable 882 *sociable*; effusive, demonstrative, back-slapping, hail-fellow-well-met; comradely, chummy, pally, matey, buddy-buddy, palsy-walsy; friendly with, good friends with, at home with; acquainted 490 *knowing*; free and easy, on familiar terms, on visiting terms, on intimate terms, on the best of terms, well in with, intimate, inseparable, thick, thick as thieves, hand in glove.

Vb. *be friendly*, be friends with, get on well with, be on friendly terms with; have dealings with, rub along with, be palsy-walsy with, be buddy-buddy with; fraternize, hobnob, keep company with, keep up with, keep in with, cosy up to, go about together, be inseparable 882 *be sociable*; have friends, make friends, win friends, have a wide circle of friends, have a large acquaintance; shake hands, clasp hands, embrace 884 *greet*; welcome, entertain 882 *be hospitable*; sympathize 516 *understand*; like, warm to, become fond of 887 *love*; mean well, have the best intentions, have the friendliest feelings.

befriend, take up, take in tow, protect 703 *patronize*; gain one's friendship; extend the right hand of fellowship, make welcome; strike an acquaintance, scrape an acquaintance; break the ice, make overtures 289 *approach*; seek one's friendship, cultivate one's friendship, pay one's addresses to 889 *court*; take to, warm to, click with, hit it off; fraternize with, frat, hobnob, get pally *or* matey *or* chummy with, chum up with, make friends with.

881 Enmity

N. *enmity*, inimicality, hostility, antagonism 704 *opposition*; no love lost, unfriendliness, incompatibility, antipathy 861 *dislike*; loathing 888 *hatred*; animosity, spite, grudge, ill feeling,

ill will, bad blood, intolerance, persecution 898 *malevolence*; jealousy 912 *envy*; coolness, coldness 380 *ice*; estrangement, alienation, strain, tension, dissension; bitterness, hard feelings, rancour, soreness 891 *resentment*; unfaithfulness, disloyalty 930 *perfidiousness*; breach, open breach, breach of friendship 709 *quarrel*; hostile act; conflict, hostilities, breaking off of diplomatic relations, state of war 718 *state of war*; vendetta, feud, blood feud.

enemy, no friend; ex-friend 603 *recanter*; traitor, viper in one's bosom 663 *troublemaker*; bad neighbour, ill-wisher; antagonist, opposite side, other side, them 705 *opponent*; competitor, rival 716 *contender*; open enemy, foe, foeman, hostile force 722 *combatant*; aggressor 712 *attacker*; enemy within the gates, fifth column, Trojan Horse; public enemy; sworn enemy, bitter enemy, arch enemy; misanthropist, misogynist 902 *misanthropist*; xenophobe, Anglophobe, Francophobe, racialist, anti-Semite 481 *narrow mind*; persona non grata, pet aversion, bête noire 888 *hateful object*.

Adj. *hostile*, inimical, unfriendly, ill-disposed, disaffected; disloyal, unfaithful 930 *perfidious*; aloof, distant, unwelcoming 883 *unsociable*; cool, chilly, frigid, icy 380 *cold*; antipathetic, incompatible, unsympathetic; loathing; hostile, antagonistic, warring, conflicting, actively opposed, Eurosceptic 704 *opposing*; antagonized, estranged, alienated, unreconciled, irreconcilable; bitter, embittered, rancorous 891 *resentful*; jealous, grudging 912 *envious*; spiteful 898 *malevolent*; bad friends with, on bad terms, not on speaking terms; at variance, at loggerheads, at daggers drawn 709 *quarrelling*; aggressive, militant, belligerent, at war with 718 *warring*; intolerant, persecuting 735 *oppressive*; dangerous, venomous, virulent, deadly, fell.

Vb. *be hostile*, be unfriendly, etc. (see adj.); show hostility; harden one's heart, bear ill will, bear malice 898 *be malevolent*; grudge, harbour *or* nurse a grudge 912 *envy*; hound, persecute 735 *oppress*; chase, hunt down 619 *hunt*; battle 716 *fight*; make war 718 *wage war*; take offence, take something the wrong way, take umbrage 891 *resent*; fall out, come to blows 709 *quarrel*; be incompatible, have nothing in common, be on different wavelengths, conflict, collide, clash 14 *have nothing in common*; withstand 704 *oppose*.

882 Sociality

N. *fellowship*, membership, membership of society, intercommunity, consociation 706 *association*; making one of, being one of, belonging; team spirit, esprit de corps; comradeship, companionship, society; camaraderie, fraternization, hobnobbing; social intercourse, familiarity, intimacy, palliness, mateyness, togetherness 880 *friendship*; social circle, home circle, family circle, one's friends and acquaintances 880 *friend*; social ambition, social climbing; society, the world.

sociability, group activity; compatibility 83 *conformity*; sociableness, gregariousness, sociable disposition 880 *friendliness*; social success, popularity; street credibility, street cred, social tact; social graces, savoir-vivre, good manners, easy manners 884 *courtesy*; urbanity 846 *good taste*; clubbability; affability 584 *conversation*; acceptability, welcome, smiling reception, open door; greeting, glad hand, handshake, hand-clasp, embrace 884 *courteous act*; entertaining, hospitality, corporate hospitality; home from home, open house, Liberty Hall, pot luck 813 *liberality*; good company, good fellowship, geniality, cordiality, heartiness, back-slapping, bonhomie; conviviality, joviality, jollity, merrymaking 824 *enjoyment*; gaiety 837 *revel*; good cheer 301 *food*; festive board, the cup that cheers.

social gathering, forgathering, meeting 74 *assembly*; reunion, get-together, social; reception, at home, soirée, levee; entertainment 837 *amusement*; singsong, camp fire; party, do, shindig, thrash, hen party, stag party, tête-à-tête; housewarming, house party, weekend party, birthday party, coming-out party; feast, banquet, orgy 301 *feasting*; communion, love feast 988 *ritual act*; coffee morning, tea party, bun fight, drinks, cocktail party, dinner party, supper party, garden party, picnic, barbecue, bottle party, byob (= bring your own bottle *or* booze) party, booze-up 837 *festivity*; dance, ball, ceilidh, hop, disco 837 *dancing*; pyjama party, sleepover.

social round, social activities, social whirl, season, social season, social entertainment; social calls, round of visits; seeing one's friends, visiting, calling, dropping in; weekending, stay, visit, formal visit, call, courtesy call; visiting terms, haunting 880 *friendship*; social demands, engagement, something on; dating, trysting, rendezvous, assignation, date, blind date; meeting place, club, pub, local 76 *focus*.

sociable person, active member, keen member; caller, visitor, dropper-in, frequenter, haunter, habitué; convivial person, bon vivant, bon viveur; good mixer, good company, life and soul of the party; social success, catch, lion 890 *favourite*; boon companion, hobnobber, clubman, club woman; good neighbour 880 *friend*; hostess, host, mine host; guest, welcome guest, one of the family; parasite, freeloader, ligger, gatecrasher; gadabout,

social butterfly; socialite, social climber 848 *fashionable society*.

Adj. *sociable*, gregarious, social, sociably disposed, extrovert, outgoing, fond of company, party-minded; companionable, fraternizing, affable, conversable, chatty, gossipy; clubbable; couthie, cosy, folksy; neighbourly, matey, chummy, pally, palsy-walsy, buddy-buddy 880 *friendly*; hospitable, welcoming, smiling, cordial, warm, hearty, back-slapping, hail-fellow-well-met; convivial, jolly, jovial 833 *merry*; lively, witty 837 *amusing*; urbane 884 *courteous*; easy, free-and-easy.

Vb. *be sociable*, be gregarious, etc. (see adj.); like company, have friends, make friends easily, hobnob, fraternize, socialize, mix with 880 *be friendly*; mix well, be a good mixer, get around, mix in society, go out, dine out; freeload, lig, gate-crash; have fun, live it up, be the life and soul of the party 837 *amuse oneself*; join in, get together, make it a party, club together, go Dutch, share, go shares 775 *participate*; take pot luck 301 *eat*; join in a bottle, crack a bottle 301 *drink*; toast; carouse 837 *revel*; make oneself at home, become one of the family; relax, unbend 683 *rest*; chat to 584 *converse*; make engagements, date, make a date; make friends, make friendly overtures 880 *befriend*; introduce oneself, exchange names, exchange telephone numbers; enlarge one's circle of acquaintances; keep up with, keep in touch with, write to 588 *correspond*.

visit, go visiting, pay a visit, be one's guest, sojourn, stay, weekend; see one's friends; go and see, look one up, call, call in, look in, drop in; leave a card; exchange visits, be on visiting terms.

be hospitable, keep open house 813 *be liberal*; invite, have round, ask in, be at home to, receive, open one's home to, keep open house; welcome, welcome with open arms; act the host, do the honours, preside; do one proud, kill the fatted calf 876 *celebrate*; have company, entertain 301 *feed*; give a party, throw a party 837 *revel*; cater for, provide entertainment 633 *provide*.

883 Unsociability. Seclusion

N. *unsociability*, unsociableness, unsocial habits, shyness 620 *avoidance*; introversion, autism; keeping one's own company, keeping oneself to oneself; staying at home; inhospitality 816 *parsimony*; standoffishness, unapproachability, distance, aloofness 871 *pride*; unfriendliness, coolness, coldness, moroseness 893 *sullenness*; silence, lack of conversation 582 *uncommunicativeness*; ostracism, boycott

57 *exclusion*; blacklist 607 *rejection*; singledom, singleness 895 *celibacy*.

seclusion, privacy, private world, world of one's own; island universe 321 *star*; peace and quiet 266 *quietness*; home life, domesticity; loneliness, solitariness, solitude; retreat, retirement, withdrawal; hiddenness 523 *latency*; confinement, solitary confinement, purdah 525 *concealment*; isolation, splendid isolation 744 *independence*; division, estrangement 46 *separation*; renunciation 621 *relinquishment*; renunciation of the world, monasticism; self-exile, expatriation; sequestration, segregation, ghettoization, rustication, excommunication, house arrest, quarantine, deportation, banishment, exile 57 *exclusion*; reserve, reservation, ghetto, harem; gaol 748 *prison*; sequestered nook, godforsaken hole, the back of beyond, the sticks; island, desert, wilderness; hideout, hideaway 527 *hiding-place*; den, study, sanctum, inner sanctum, cloister, cell, hermitage 192 *retreat*; ivory tower, private quarters, shell; backwater.

unsocial person, solitary, iceberg; loner, lone wolf, rogue elephant; isolationist; introvert; stay-at-home, home-body; ruralist, recluse, anchorite, anchoress *or* ancress, hermit, stylite; maroon, castaway 779 *derelict*; Robinson Crusoe; lonely heart, Norman No-Mates.

outcast, pariah, leper, outsider; outcaste, untouchable; expatriate, alien 59 *foreigner*; exile, evictee, deportee, evacuee, refugee, political refugee, asylum-seeker, displaced person, homeless person, rough sleeper, skell; stateless person; non-person, unperson; proscribed person, outlaw, bandit; reject, flotsam and jetsam, the dregs 641 *rubbish*.

Adj. unsociable, unsocial, antisocial, introverted, morose; unassimilated, foreign 59 *extraneous*; unclubbable, stay-at-home, domestic; inhospitable, unwelcoming, forbidding, hostile, unneighbourly, unfriendly, uncongenial, unaffable, misanthropic; distant, aloof, unbending, stiff; stand-offish, haughty 871 *proud*; unwelcoming, frosty, icy, cold 893 *sullen*; unforthcoming, in one's shell; unconversational, uncommunicative, close, silent 582 *uncommunicative*; cool, impersonal 860 *indifferent*; solitary, lonely, lone 88 *alone*; shy, reserved, retiring, withdrawn; wild, feral; celibate, unmarried; by the world forgot.

secluded, private, sequestered, cloistered, shut away, hidden, buried, tucked away 523 *latent*; veiled, in purdah; quiet, lonely, isolated, enisled, marooned; remote, out of the way; godforsaken, unfrequented, unexplored, unseen, unfamiliar, off the beaten track, far from the madding crowd 491 *unknown*; uninhabited, deserted 190 *empty*.

Vb. seclude, sequester, isolate, quarantine, segregate, ghettoize; keep in purdah; confine, shut up 747 *imprison*.

884 Courtesy

N. courtesy, chivalry, knightliness, gallantry; common courtesy, deference 920 *respect*; consideration, condescension 872 *humility*; graciousness, politeness, civility, urbanity, mannerliness, manners, good manners, good behaviour; good breeding, gentlemanliness, ladylikeness, gentility 846 *good taste*; tactfulness, diplomacy; courtliness, correctness, correctitude, etiquette 875 *formality*; amiability, niceness, obligingness, kindness, kindliness 897 *benevolence*; gentleness, mildness 736 *leniency*; agreeableness, affability, social tact 882 *sociability*.

courteous act, act of courtesy, graceful gesture, courtesy, common courtesy, civility, favour, kindness, compliment, bouquet 886 *congratulation*; kind words, fair words, sweet words 889 *endearment*; introduction 880 *friendliness*; welcome, reception, invitation; acknowledgment, recognition, nod, salutation, salute, greeting, smile, kiss, kiss on the cheek, air-kiss, air-kissing, hug, squeeze, handclasp, hand-shake 920 *respects*; salaam, kowtow, bow, curtsy, namaste, namaste 311 *bow*; respects, regards, kind regards, best regards, remembrances, love, best wishes; love and kisses; farewell 296 *farewell*.

Adj. courteous, chivalrous, knightly, generous 868 *noble*; courtly, gallant, old-world, correct 875 *formal*; polite, civil, urbane, gentle, gentlemanly, ladylike, dignified, well-mannered, fine-mannered 848 *well-bred*; gracious, mannerly 920 *respectful*; on one's best behaviour, minding one's p's and q's 455 *attentive*; obliging, kind 897 *benevolent*; agreeable, suave; well-spoken.

amiable, nice, sweet, winning; affable, friendly, amicable 882 *sociable*; considerate, kind 897 *benevolent*; inoffensive, harmless 935 *innocent*; gentle, easy, mild, soft-spoken 736 *lenient*; good-tempered, sweet-tempered, good-natured, unruffled 823 *inexcitable*; well-behaved, good 739 *obedient*; peaceable 717 *peaceful*.

Vb. be courteous, be on one's best behaviour, mind one's p's and q's; mind one's manners; show courtesy; make time for 455 *be attentive*; not forget one's manners, keep a civil tongue in one's head, make oneself agreeable, be all things to all men; take no offence, take in good part 823 *be patient*; mend one's manners.

pay one's respects, give one's regards, send

one's regards, send one's compliments, do one the honour; pay compliments 925 *flatter*; drink to, toast; pay homage, show one's respect, kneel, kiss hands 920 *show respect*; honour 876 *celebrate*.

greet, send greetings (see also *pay one's respects* above); acknowledge, recognize, hold out one's hand 455 *notice*; shout or call out one's greeting, hail 408 *shout*; nod, wave, smile, kiss one's fingers, blow a kiss; say hallo, bid good morning 583 *speak to*; salute, raise one's hat; touch one's cap, tug one's forelock; bow, bob, curtsy, salaam, make obeisance, kiss hands, prostrate oneself, kowtow 311 *stoop*; shake hands, clasp hands, shake the hand, press or squeeze or wring or pump the hand; escort 89 *accompany*; make a salute, fire a salute, present arms, parade 876 *celebrate*; receive, do the honours, be mother; welcome 882 *be sociable*; welcome with open arms 824 *be pleased*; embrace, hug, kiss, kiss on both cheeks 889 *caress*; usher in, present, introduce 299 *admit*.

885 Discourtesy

N. *discourtesy*, impoliteness, bad manners, disgraceful table manners; no manners, lack of courtesy, lack of politeness, lack of manners, incivility; churlishness, uncouthness, boorishness, yobbishness, yob culture 847 *ill-breeding*; unpleasantness, nastiness, misbehaviour, misconduct, unbecoming conduct; tactlessness, lack of consideration, stepping on one's toes.

rudeness, ungraciousness, gruffness, bluntness; sharpness, tartness, acerbity, acrimony, asperity; roughness, harshness 735 *severity*; off-handedness 456 *inattention*; shortness; sarcasm 851 *ridicule*; unparliamentary language, bad language, rude words, virulence 899 *scurrility*; rebuff, insult 921 *indignity*; impertinence, pertness, sauce, sassiness, lip, cheek, truculence 878 *insolence*; interruption, shouting 822 *excitability*; black look, sour look, scowl, frown, pulling faces, sticking out the tongue 893 *sullenness*; act of discourtesy, display of bad manners.

rude person, no gentleman, no lady; savage, barbarian, brute, lout, boor, yob, oik, loud-mouth, white van man; bratpack; crab, bear; sourpuss, crosspatch, grouch, grouser, fault-finder, bellyacher, beefer, sulker 829 *malcontent*.

Adj. *discourteous*, unchivalrous; unceremonious, ungentlemanly, unladylike; impolite, uncivil, rude; mannerless, unmannerly, ill-mannered, bad-mannered, boorish, loutish, yobbish, uncouth, brutish, beastly, savage, barbarian 847 *ill-bred*; insolent, impudent;

cheeky, saucy, sassy, pert, forward, loud-mouthed, gobby 878 *impertinent*; unpleasant, disagreeable; unaccommodating 860 *indifferent*; offhanded, cavalier, tactless, inconsiderate 456 *inattentive*.

Vb. *be rude*, be mannerless, etc. (see adj.); have no manners, flout etiquette; know no better 699 *be artless*; forget one's manners, show discourtesy 878 *be insolent*; show no thought for others, step on everyone's toes, ride roughshod over everyone 921 *not respect*; have no time for 456 *be inattentive*; treat rudely, snub, turn one's back on, cold-shoulder, hand one the frozen mitt, cut, ignore, look right through, cut dead; show one the door, send away with a flea in their ear 300 *eject*; cause offence, miff, ruffle one's feelings 891 *huff*; insult, abuse; take liberties, make free with, make bold; stare, ogle 438 *gaze*; make one blush 867 *shame*; lose one's temper, shout, interrupt 891 *get angry*; curse, swear; snarl, growl, frown, scowl, lour, pout, sulk.

886 Congratulation

N. *congratulation*, congratulations, felicitations, compliments, bouquets, compliments of the season; good wishes, best wishes; salute, toast; welcome, hero's welcome, official reception 876 *celebration*; thanks 907 *gratitude*.

Vb. *congratulate*, compliment, proffer bouquets; offer one's congratulations, wish one joy, wish many happy returns, wish a merry Christmas, wish a happy New Year, offer the season's greetings; send one's congratulations, send one's compliments 884 *pay one's respects*; give one a hero's welcome, give a standing ovation, give three cheers, clap 923 *applaud*; fete, lionize 876 *celebrate*; congratulate oneself, give oneself a pat on the back, pat oneself on the back.

887 Love

N. *love*, affection, friendship, charity; brotherly love, sisterly love, Christian love, agape; true love, real thing; parental affection, paternal affection, maternal affection, mother-love; possessiveness 911 *jealousy*; conjugal love, uxoriousness; closeness, intimacy; sentiment 818 *feeling*; tenderness 897 *benevolence*; Platonic love 880 *friendship*; two hearts that beat as one, mutual love, mutual affection, mutual attraction, compatibility, sympathy, fellow feeling, understanding; fondness, liking, predilection, inclination 179 *tendency*; preference 605 *choice*; fancy 604 *caprice*; attachment, sentimental attachment; devotion, patriotism 739 *loyalty*; courtly love, gallantry; sentimentality, susceptibility, amorousness 819 *moral sensibility*; power of love, fascination, enchantment, bewitchment 983 *sorcery*; lovesickness, yearning, longing 859 *desire*; eroticism, eros, lust 859 *sexual urge*; regard 920 *respect*; admiration, hero-worship, worship from afar 864 *wonder*; first love, calf love, puppy love, young love, love's young dream; crush, pash, infatuation; cupboard love; worship 982 *idolatry*; romantic love, love at first sight, coup de foudre, passion, tender passion, flames of love, enthusiasm, rapture, ecstasy, transports of love 822 *excitable state*; narcissism, Oedipus complex, Electra complex; love-hate; Cupid, Eros, Venus.

love affair, romantic affair, affair of the heart, affaire de coeur; romance, love and the world well lost; flirtation, amour, entanglement, relationship; free love; liaison, intrigue, seduction, adultery 951 *illicit love*; falling in love, something between them; course of love, the old old story; betrothal, engagement, wedding bells 894 *marriage*; relationship, serial monogamy.

lovemaking, flirting, spooning, canoodling, necking, billing and cooing 889 *endearment*; courting, walking out, going with, going steady, pressing one's suit, laying siege 889 *wooing*; pursuit of love, flirting, flirtation, cyberflirtation, coquetry, philandering; dalliance.

lover, love, true love, sweetheart; squeeze; young man, boyfriend, Romeo; young woman, girlfriend, girl, bird, squeeze; swain, beau, gallant, cavalier, squire, escort, date; steady, fiancé(e); wooer, courter, suitor, follower, admirer, hero-worshipper, adorer, votary, worshipper; aficionado, fan, groupie, devoted following, fan club; sugar daddy; gigolo, ladies' man, lady-killer, seducer, Lothario, Don Juan, Casanova; paramour, flirt, coquette, philanderer; gold-digger, vamp; cohabitee, common-law husband *or* wife, partner, man, woman, live-in, bidie-in, POSSLQ (= person of opposite sex sharing living quarters). (See also 894 *spouse*.)

loved one, beloved, love, true love, soul mate, heart's desire, light of one's life, one's own 890 *darling*; intimate 880 *close friend*; lucky man, intended, betrothed, affianced, fiancé(e), bride-to-be 894 *spouse*; conquest, inamorata, lady-love, girlfriend, girl, bird, bit, honey, baby, sweetie, squeeze; angel, princess, goddess; sweetheart, valentine, flame, old flame; idol; hero; heartthrob, maiden's prayer, dream man, Alpha man, dream girl 859 *desired object*; favourite, mistress, concubine 952 *kept woman*; femme fatale.

Adj. *loving*, brotherly, sisterly; loyal, patriotic 931 *disinterested*; wooing; courting, cuddling, making love; affectionate, demonstrative; tender, motherly, wifely, conjugal; lover-like, gallant, romantic, sentimental, lovesick; mooning, moping, lovelorn, languishing 834 *dejected*; attached to, fond of, fond, mad about, uxorious, doting; possessive 911 *jealous*; admiring, adoring, devoted, enslaved (see also *in love* below); flirtatious, coquettish 604 *capricious*; amorous, ardent, passionate 818 *fervent*; yearning; lustful, libidinous 951 *lecherous*.

in love, enamoured, inclined to, sweet on, soft on, keen on, set on, stuck on, gone on, sold on; struck with, taken with, smitten, bitten, caught, hooked; charmed, enchanted, fascinated 983 *bewitched*; mad on, infatuated, besotted, crazy about, wild about, head over heels in love 503 *crazy*; loved up 949 *drugged*.

erotic, sexy, titillating; adult, hard-core, page 3, pornographic, top-shelf 951 *impure*; aphrodisiac, erogenous.

Vb. *love*, like, care, rather care for, quite like, take pleasure in, be partial to, take an interest in; sympathize with, feel with, be fond of, have a soft spot for; be susceptible, have a heart, have a warm heart; bear love towards, hold in affection, hold dear, care for, have a heart for, cherish, cling to, embrace; appreciate, value, prize, treasure, think the world of, regard, admire, revere 920 *respect*; adore, worship, idolize, only have eyes for; live for, live only for; burn with love, be on fire with passion (see also *be in love* below); make love, bestow one's favours 45 *unite with*; make much of, spoil, indulge, pet, fondle, drool over, slobber over 889 *caress*.

be in love, burn with love, dote 503 *be insane*; take a fancy to, take a shine to, cotton on to, take to, warm to, be taken with, be sweet on, dig, have a crush on, have a pash for; carry a torch for 859 *desire*; form an attachment, fall for, fall in love, get infatuated, get hooked on, have it bad; go crazy over, be nuts on 503 *go mad*; set one's heart on, lose one's heart, bestow one's affections; declare one's love, offer one's heart to, woo, sue, sigh, press one's suit, make one's addresses 889 *court*; set one's cap at, chase 619 *pursue*; enjoy one's favours; honeymoon 894 *wed*; have an affair; play away *or* play away from home.

888 Hatred

N. *hatred*, hate, no love lost; love-hate; disillusion; aversion, antipathy, allergy, nausea 861 *dislike*; intense dislike, repugnance, detestation, loathing, abhorrence, abomination; disfavour, displeasure; disaffection, estrangement, alienation 709 *dissension*; hostility, antagonism 881 *enmity*; animosity, ill feeling, bad blood, bitterness, acrimony, rancour 891 *resentment*; malice, ill will, spite, grudge, ancient grudge 898 *malevolence*; evil eye, jettatura 983 *spell*; jealousy 912 *envy*; wrath 891 *anger*; execration 899 *curse*; scowl, black looks, snap, snarl, baring one's fangs 893 *sullenness*; phobia, xenophobia, Anglophobia 854 *phobia*; anti-Semitism, racialism, racism, institutional racism, race hatred, racial prejudice, colour prejudice, white supremacy 481 *prejudice*; misogyny 902 *misanthropy*, odium, disfavour, unpopularity 924 *disapprobation*; discredit, bad odour, bad books, black books 867 *disrepute*; odiousness, hatefulness, loathsomeness, beastliness, obnoxiousness; despicability, despisedness 922 *contemptibility*.

hateful object, anathema; unwelcome necessity, bitter pill; abomination; object of one's hate 881 *enemy*; not one's type, pet aversion, pet hate, bête noire, bugbear, Dr Fell, nobody's darling; pest, menace, public nuisance, good riddance 659 *bane*; blackleg.

Adj. *hateful*, odious, unlovable, unloved; invidious, antagonizing, obnoxious, pestilential; beastly, nasty, horrid, — from hell 645 *not nice*; abhorrent, loathsome, abominable; accursed, execrable; offensive, repulsive, repellent, nauseous, nauseating, revolting, disgusting; bitter, sharp 393 *sour*; unwelcome 860 *unwanted*.

Vb. *hate*, bear hatred, have no love for; hate one's guts; loathe, abominate, detest, abhor; turn away from, shrink from 620 *avoid*; revolt from, recoil at 280 *recoil*; can't bear, can't stand, can't stomach 861 *dislike*; reject; spurn 922 *despise*; denounce 899 *curse*; bear malice, have a down on 898 *be malevolent*; bear a grudge, nurse resentment, have it in for 910 *be vengeful*, 891 *resent*; conceive a hatred for, fall out of love, become disenchanted with, turn to hate.

889 Endearment

N. *endearment*, blandishments, compliments, bouquets 925 *flattery*; loving words, pretty speeches, pet name; sweet nothings, lovers' vows; billing and cooing, holding hands, slap and tickle, footsie; fondling, cuddling, canoodling, lovemaking, petting, necking, smooching, snogging, kissing, French kissing, tonsil hockey *or* tonsil tennis; caress, embrace, clasp, hug, bear hug, cuddle, squeeze; salute, kiss, butterfly kiss, French kiss, smacker; nibble, bite, love bite; stroke, tickle, pat.

wooing, courting, spooning, flirting; loveplay, lovemaking; flirtation, philandering,

coquetry; courtship, suit, love suit, addresses, advances 887 *lovemaking*; serenade, love song, love lyric, amorous ditty; love letter, billet-doux; love poem, sonnet; proposal, engagement, betrothal 894 *marriage*.

love token, true lover's knot, favour, ribbon, glove; ring, engagement ring, wedding ring, eternity ring; valentine, love letter, billet-doux; love spoon; language of flowers, posy, red roses; arrow, heart; tattoo.

Vb. *pet*, pamper, spoil, indulge, over-indulge, spoonfeed, featherbed, mother, smother, kill with kindness; cosset, coddle; make much of, be all over one; nurse, rock, cradle, baby; sing to, croon over; coax, wheedle 925 *flatter*.

caress, fondle, dandle, take in one's lap; play with, stroke, smooth, pat, paw, pinch one's cheek, pat one on the head, chuck under the chin; kiss, brush one's cheek; embrace, enfold, fold in one's arms, press to one's bosom, hang on one's neck, fly into the arms of; open one's arms, clasp, hug, hold one tight, cling 778 *retain*; squeeze, cuddle; snuggle, nestle, nuzzle, nibble, give love bites; play, romp, wanton, toy, trifle, dally, spark; make love, carry on, canoodle, spoon, bill and coo, hold hands, pet, neck, snog, smooch; play footsie; touch up.

court, make advances, give the glad eye; make eyes, make sheep's eyes, ogle, leer, eye 438 *gaze*; get off with, try to get off with, get fresh, make a pass, make passes, chat up, come on to, hit on, pat one's bottom, goose; philander, flirt, coquette; be sweet on 887 *be in love*; set one's cap at, run after, do all the running, chase 619 *pursue*; squire, escort 89 *accompany*; hang round, wait on 284 *follow*; date, make a date, take out; walk out with, go steady, go out with, go with; sue, woo, go a-wooing, go courting, pay court to, pay one's addresses to, pay suit to, press one's suit; lay siege to one's affections, whisper sweet nothings; serenade; sigh, pine, languish 887 *love*; offer one's heart, offer one's hand; ask for the hand of, propose, propose marriage, pop the question, plight one's troth, become engaged, announce one's engagement, publish the banns, make a match 894 *wed*.

890 Darling. Favourite

N. *darling*, dear, my dear; dear friend; dearest, dear one, only one; one's own, one's all; truelove, love, beloved 887 *loved one*; heart, dear heart; sweetheart, fancy, valentine; sweeting, sweetie, sugar, honeybaby, honeybunch; flower, precious, jewel, treasure; chéri(e), chou, mavourneen; angel, angel child, cherub; poppet, popsy, moppet, mopsy; pet, lamb, precious lamb, chick, chicken, duck, ducks, ducky, hen, dearie, lovey.

favourite, spoiled darling, spoiled child, mother's darling, teacher's pet; jewel, jewel in the crown, apple of one's eye, blue-eyed boy; persona grata, someone after one's own heart, one of the best, Mr *or* Miss Right; flavour of the month, the tops, salt of the earth, diamond geezer; first choice, front runner, top seed, only possible choice 644 *exceller;* someone to be proud of, pride and joy; favourite son, man *or* woman of the hour 866 *person of repute;* idol, pop idol, hero, heroine, golden girl *or* boy, icon; screen goddess, media personality, star, film star; universal favourite, toast of the town; world's sweetheart, pin-up girl 841 *a beauty;* centre of attraction, cynosure 291 *attraction;* catch, lion 859 *desired object.*

891 Resentment. Anger

N. resentment, dissatisfaction 829 *discontent;* huffiness, ill humour, the hump, sulks 893 *sullenness;* sternness 735 *severity;* rankling, rancour, soreness, painful feelings; growing impatience; indignation (see also *anger* below); umbrage, offence, taking offence, huff, tiff, pique; bile, spleen, gall; acerbity, acrimony, bitterness, bitter resentment, smouldering resentment, hard feelings, daggers drawn; virulence, hate 888 *hatred;* animosity, grudge, ancient grudge, bone to pick 881 *enmity;* vindictiveness, revengefulness, spite 910 *revenge;* malice 898 *malevolence;* impatience, fierceness, hot blood 892 *irascibility;* cause of offence, red rag to a bull, sore point; pinprick, irritation 827 *annoyance;* provocation, aggravation, insult, affront, last straw 921 *indignity;* wrong, injury 914 *injustice.*

anger, wrathfulness, irritation, exasperation, vexation, indignation; dudgeon, high dudgeon, wrath, ire; rage, air rage, desk rage *or* office rage, parking rage, rail rage, road rage, shop rage *or* shopping rage, sports rage, trolley rage; red mist; fury, raging fury, passion, towering passion 822 *excitable state;* crossness, temper, tantrum, tizzy, paddy, fume, fret, pet, hissy fit, fit of temper, burst of anger, outburst, explosion, storm, stew, ferment, taking, paroxysm, tears of rage 318 *agitation;* rampage, fire and fury, gnashing the teeth, stamping the foot; shout, roar 400 *loudness;* fierceness, angry look, glare, frown, scowl, black look; growl, snarl, bark, bite, snap, snappishness, asperity 892 *irascibility;* warmth, heat, words, high words, angry words 709 *quarrel;* box on the ear, rap on the knuckles, slap in the face 921 *indignity;* blows, fisticuffs 716 *fight.*

Adj. resentful, piqued, stung, galled, huffed,

miffed; hurt, sore, smarting 829 *discontented;* surprised, pained, hurt, offended; warm, indignant; unresigned, reproachful 924 *disapproving;* acidulous, bitter, embittered, acrimonious, full of hate, rancorous, virulent; splenetic, spiteful 898 *malevolent;* full of revenge, vindictive; jealous, green with envy 912 *envious;* grudging 598 *unwilling.*

angry, displeased, not amused, stern, frowning 834 *serious;* impatient, cross, crabbit, waxy, ratty, wild, mad, livid; wroth, wrathy, wrathful, ireful, irate; peeved, nettled, rattled, annoyed, irritated, vexed, provoked, stung; worked up, wrought up, het up, hot, hot under the collar; angry with, mad at; indignant, angered, incensed, infuriated, beside oneself with rage, leaping up and down in anger; shirty, in a temper, in a paddy, in a wax, in a huff, in a rage, in a boiling rage, in a fury, in a taking, in a passion; warm, fuming, boiling, burning; speechless, stuttering, gnashing, spitting with fury, crying with rage, stamping one's foot in rage; raging, foaming, savage, violent 176 *furious;* apoplectic, rabid, foaming at the mouth, mad as a hornet, hopping mad, dancing, rampaging, rampageous 503 *frenzied;* seeing red, berserk; roaring, ramping, rearing; snarling, snapping, glaring, glowering 893 *sullen;* red with anger, flushed with rage, purple with rage, red-eyed, bloodshot 431 *red;* blue in the face; pale with anger; dangerous, fierce 892 *irascible.*

Vb. resent, be piqued, be offended, etc. (see adj.); find intolerable, not bear, be unable to stomach 825 *suffer;* mind, have a chip on one's shoulder, feel resentment, smart under 829 *be discontented;* take amiss, take ill, take the wrong way, not see the joke; feel insulted, take offence, take on the nose, take umbrage, take exception to 709 *quarrel;* jib, take in ill *or* bad part, get sore, cut up rough; burn, smoulder, sizzle, simmer, boil with indignation; express resentment, vent one's spleen, indulge one's spite 898 *be malevolent;* take to heart, let it rankle, remember an injury, cherish a grudge, nurse resentment, bear malice 910 *be vengeful;* go green with envy 912 *envy.*

get angry, get cross, get wild, get mad; get peeved, get sore, get in a pet, go spare; kindle, grow warm, grow heated, colour, redden, go purple, flush with anger; take fire, flare up, start up, rear up, ramp; bridle, bristle, raise one's hackles, arch one's back; lose patience, lose one's temper, lose control of one's temper, forget oneself; throw a tantrum, stamp, shout, throw things; get one's dander up, get one's monkey up, fall into a passion, fly into a temper, fly off the handle; let fly, burst out, let off steam, boil over, blow up, flip one's lid, blow one's top, explode; see red, go berserk, go mad, go apeshit (vulg), foam at the mouth 822 *be excitable*.

be angry, be impatient, etc. (see adj.); show impatience, interrupt, chafe, fret, fume, fuss, flounce, dance, ramp, stamp, champ, champ the bit, paw the ground; carry on, create, perform, make a scene, make an exhibition of oneself, make a row, go on the warpath 61 *rampage*; turn nasty, cut up rough, raise Cain; rage, rant, roar, bellow, bluster, storm, thunder, fulminate 400 *be loud*; look like thunder, look black, look daggers, glare, glower, frown, scowl, growl, snarl; spit, snap, lash out; gnash *or* grind one's teeth, weep with rage, boil with rage, quiver with rage, shake with passion, swell with fury, burst with indignation, stamp with rage, dance with fury, lash one's tail 821 *be excited*; breathe fire and fury, out-Lear Lear; let fly, express one's feelings, vent one's spleen.

huff, miff, pique, sting, nettle, rankle, smart; ruffle the dignity, ruffle one's feathers, wound, wound the feelings 827 *hurt*; antagonize, put one's back up, rub up the wrong way, get across, give umbrage, offend, cause offence, cause lasting offence, put one's nose out of joint, embitter; stick in the throat, raise one's gorge 861 *cause dislike*; affront, insult, outrage 921 *not respect*.

enrage, upset, discompose, ruffle, disturb one's equanimity, ruffle one's temper, irritate, wind up, rile, push one's buttons, peeve, miff; annoy, vex, pester, bug, bother 827 *trouble*; get on one's nerves, get under one's skin, get up one's nose, get one's goat, give one the pip; do it to annoy, tease, bait, pinprick, needle 827 *torment*; bite, fret, nag, gnaw; put in an ill humour, try one's patience, exasperate; push too far, make one lose one's temper, put into a temper, work into a passion; anger, incense, infuriate, madden, drive mad; goad, sting, taunt, trail one's coat, invite a quarrel, throw down the gauntlet; drive into a fury, lash into fury, whip up one's anger, rouse one's ire, kindle one's wrath, excite indignation, stir the blood, stir one's bile, make one's gorge rise, raise one's hackles, get one's dander up; make one's blood boil, make one see red; cause resentment, embitter, poison; exasperate, add fuel to the fire *or* flame, fan the flame 832 *aggravate*; embroil, set at loggerheads, set by the ears 709 *make quarrels*.

892 Irascibility

N. *irascibility*, irritability, impatience 822 *excitability*; grumpiness, gruffness 883 *unsocia-*

bility; sharpness, tartness, asperity, gall 393 *sourness*; sensitivity 819 *moral sensibility*; huffiness, touchiness, prickliness, readiness to take offence, pugnacity, bellicosity 709 *quarrelsomeness*; temperament, testiness, pepperiness, peevishness, petulance; captiousness, uncertain temper, doubtful temper, sharp temper, short temper, quick temper; hot temper, fierce temper, fiery temper; limited patience, snappishness, fierceness, dangerousness, hot blood, fieriness, inflammable nature; bad temper, dangerous temper, foul temper, nasty temper, evil temper.

irascible person, hotspur; crosspatch, etc. 834 *moper*.

Adj. *irascible*, impatient, choleric, irritable, peppery, testy, crusty, peevish, crotchety, cranky, cross-grained; short-tempered, hot-tempered, sharp-tempered; prickly, touchy, tetchy, huffy, thin-skinned 819 *sensitive*; inflammable, like tinder; hot-blooded, fierce, fiery, passionate 822 *excitable*; quick, warm, hasty, overhasty, trigger-happy 857 *rash*; quick-tempered, easily roused 709 *quarrelling*; scolding, shrewish, vixenish; sharp-tongued 899 *cursing*; petulant, cantankerous, crabbed, crabbit, snarling, querulous; captious, bitter, vinegary 393 *sour*; splenetic, liverish; snappy, waspish; tart, sharp, short, acidulous; uptight, edgy; fractious, fretful, moody, temperamental, changeable; gruff, grumpy, ratty, like a bear with a sore head 829 *discontented*; ill-humoured, cross, stroppy 893 *sullen*.

893 Sullenness

N. *sullenness*, sternness, grimness 834 *seriousness*; sulkiness, ill humour, pettishness; morosity, surliness, churlishness, crabbedness, crustiness, unsociableness 883 *unsociability*; vinegar 393 *sourness*; grumpiness, grouchiness, pout, grimace 829 *discontent*; gruffness 885 *discourtesy*; crossness, peevishness, ill temper, bad temper, savage temper, shocking temper 892 *irascibility*; spleen, bile, liver; sulks, fit of the sulks, the hump, the pouts, mulligrubs, dumps, grouch, bouderie, moodiness, temperament; cafard, the blues, blue devils 834 *melancholy*; black look, hangdog look; glare, glower, lour, frown, scowl; snort, growl, snarl, snap, bite.

Adj. *sullen*, forbidding, ugly; gloomy, saturnine, overcast, cloudy, sunless 418 *dark*; glowering, scowling; stern, frowning, unsmiling, grim 834 *serious*; sulky, sulking, cross, cross as two sticks, out of temper, out of humour, out of sorts, misanthropic 883 *unsociable*; surly, morose, dyspeptic, crabbed, crabbit, crusty, cross-grained, difficult; snarling, snapping, snappish, shrewish, vixenish, cantankerous, quarrelsome, stroppy 709 *quarrelling*; refractory, jibbing 738 *disobedient*; grouchy, grumbling, grousing, belly-aching, beefing, grumpy 829 *discontented*; acid, tart, vinegary 393 *sour*; gruff, rough, abrupt, brusque 885 *discourteous*; temperamental, moody, up and down 152 *changing*; jaundiced, dyspeptic; blue, down, down in the dumps, depressed, melancholy 834 *melancholic*; petulant, pettish, peevish, shirty, ill-tempered, bad-tempered 892 *irascible*; smouldering, sultry.

894 Marriage

N. *marriage*, matrimony, holy matrimony, sacrament of matrimony, one flesh; wedlock, wedded state, married state, state of matrimony, wedded bliss; match, union, alliance, partnership; conjugality, conjugal knot, nuptial bond, marriage tie, marriage bed, bed and board, cohabitation, living as man and wife, living together by habit and repute, living together, life together; banns, marriage certificate, marriage lines; prenuptial agreement, prenup.

type of marriage, matrimonial arrangement, monogamy, serial monogamy, monandry, bigamy, polygamy, Mormonism, polygyny, polyandry; digamy, deuterogamy, second marriage, remarriage, levirate; endogamy, exogamy; arranged match, marriage of convenience, mariage de convenance, mariage blanc; love-match; mixed marriage, intermarriage, miscegenation 43 *mixture*; mismarriage, mésalliance, misalliance, morganatic marriage, left-handed marriage; civil partnership, same-sex marriage; companionate marriage, temporary marriage, trial marriage, open marriage, common-law marriage, marriage by habit and repute; free union, free love, concubinage; compulsory marriage, forcible wedlock, shotgun wedding; abduction, Sabine rape.

wedding, getting married, match, matchmaking, betrothal, engagement; nuptial vows, marriage vows, ring, wedding ring; bridal, nuptials; leading to the altar, tying the knot, getting spliced, getting hitched; marriage rites, marriage ceremony; wedding march; wedding service, nuptial mass, nuptial benediction 988 *Christian rite*; church wedding, white wedding, civil marriage, registry-office marriage; Gretna Green marriage, run-away match, elopement; solemn wedding, quiet wedding; wedding day, wedding bells; confetti; marriage feast, wedding breakfast, reception; honeymoon; silver wedding, golden wedding, wedding anniversary 876 *special day*.

bridal party, best man, groomsman, brides-maid, maid *or* matron of honour, best maid, page, train-bearer; attendant, usher.

spouse, one's promised, one's betrothed 887 *loved one*; man, wife; spouses, man and wife, Mr and Mrs, Darby and Joan; married couple, young marrieds, bridal pair, newlyweds, honeymooners; bride, blushing bride; bridegroom, consort, partner, mate, helpmate *or* helpmeet, better half, soul-mate; married man, husband, hubbie, man, old man, lord and master; much-married man, henpecked husband; injured husband; new man; married woman, wife, wedded wife, lawful wife, lady, matron, feme covert, partner of one's bed and board, wife of one's bosom, woman, old woman, missus, wifey, better half, old dutch, rib, trouble and strife, squaw, her indoors, she who must be obeyed; common-law husband *or* wife 887 *lover*.

Vb. *marry*, marry off, find a husband *or* wife for, match, mate; matchmake, make a match, arrange a match, arrange a marriage; betroth, affiance, publish the banns, announce the engagement; give in marriage, give away; join in marriage, declare man and wife; join, couple, splice, hitch, tie the knot.

wed, marry; take a wife, find a husband; ask for the hand of 889 *court*; give up one's freedom, renounce bachelorhood, take the plunge, get married, get hitched, get spliced, mate with, marry oneself to, unite oneself with, give oneself in marriage, bestow one's hand, accept a proposal, plight one's troth, become engaged, put up the banns; lead to the altar, walk down the aisle, say 'I do', take for better or worse, be made one 45 *unite with*; pair off, mate, couple; honeymoon, cohabit, live together, set up house together, share bed and board, live as man and wife; marry well, make a good match, make a marriage of convenience; mismarry, make a bad match, repent at leisure; make a love match 887 *be in love*; marry in haste, run away, elope; contract marriage, make an honest woman of, go through a form of marriage; marry again, remarry; commit bigamy; intermarry, miscegenate.

895 Celibacy

N. *celibacy*, singleness, singledom, single state, unmarried state, single blessedness 744 *independence*; bachelorhood, bachelorship, bachelordom; misogamy, misogyny 883 *unsociability*; spinsterhood, spinsterdom, the shelf; monkhood, the veil 985 *monasticism*; maidenhood, virginity 950 *purity*.

celibate, unmarried man, single man, bachelor; confirmed bachelor, born bachelor, old bachelor, gay bachelor, not the marrying kind; misogamist, misogynist 902 *misanthropist*; monk; hermit 883 *unsocial person*.

spinster, unmarried woman, bachelor girl; maid, maiden, virgo intacta; maiden aunt, old maid; Vestal Virgin 986 *nun*.

896 Divorce. Widowhood

N. divorce, dissolution of marriage, putting away, repudiation; divorce decree, decree nisi, decree absolute; separation, legal separation, judicial separation; annulment; non-consummation; nullity, impediment, prohibited degree, consanguinity, affinity; desertion, living apart; alimony, aliment, palimony; marriage on the rocks, breakup, split-up, broken marriage, broken engagement, forbidding the banns; divorce court, divorce case; divorced person, divorcee, divorcé(e); co-respondent; single parent.

Vb. divorce, separate, split up, break up, go one's separate ways, live separately, live apart, desert 621 *relinquish*; untie the knot 46 *disunite*; put away, sue for divorce, file a divorce suit; bring a charge of adultery; get a divorce, revert to bachelorhood, revert to the single state, regain one's freedom; put asunder, dissolve marriage, annul a marriage, grant a decree of nullity, grant a divorce, pronounce a decree absolute.

897 Benevolence

N. benevolence, good will, helpfulness 880 *friendliness*; ahimsa, harmlessness 935 *innocence*; benignity, kindly disposition, heart of gold; amiability, bonhomie 882 *sociability*; milk of human kindness, goodness of nature, warmth of heart, warm-heartedness, kind-heartedness, kindliness, kindness, loving-kindness, goodness and mercy, charity, Christian charity 887 *love*; godly love, brotherly love, brotherliness, fraternal feeling 880 *friendship*; tenderness, consideration 736 *leniency*; understanding, responsiveness, caring, concern, fellow feeling, empathy, sympathy, overflowing sympathy 818 *feeling*; condolence 905 *pity*; decent feeling, humanity, humaneness, humanitarianism 901 *philanthropy*; utilitarianism 901 *social care*; charitableness, hospitality, unselfishness, generosity, magnanimity 813 *liberality*; gentleness, softness, mildness, tolerance, toleration 734 *laxity*; placability, mercy 909 *forgiveness*; God's love, grace of God; blessing, benediction.

Adj. benevolent, well meant, well-intentioned, with the best intentions, for the best 880 *friendly*; out of kindness, to oblige; out of charity, eleemosynary; kind of one,

good of one, so good of; sympathetic, wishing well, well-wishing, favouring, praying for; kindly disposed, benign, benignant, kindly, kind-hearted, overflowing with kindness, full of the milk of human kindness, warm-hearted, large-hearted, golden-hearted; kind, good, human, decent, Christian; affectionate 887 *loving*; fatherly, paternal; motherly, maternal; brotherly, fraternal; sisterly, cousinly; good-humoured, good-natured, easy, sweet, gentle 884 *amiable*; placable, merciful; tolerant, indulgent 734 *lax*; humane, considerate 736 *lenient*; soft-hearted, tender; pitiful, sympathizing, condolent 905 *pitying*; genial, hospitable 882 *sociable*; bounteous, bountiful 813 *liberal*; generous, magnanimous, unselfish, selfless, unenvious, unjealous, altruistic 931 *disinterested*; beneficent, charitable, humanitarian, doing good 901 *philanthropic*; obliging, accommodating, helpful 703 *helping*; tactful, complaisant, gracious, gallant, chivalrous, chivalric 884 *courteous*.

Vb. do good, philanthropize, do good works, be a caring person, have a social conscience, serve the community, show public spirit, be a good Samaritan, do a good turn, do one a favour, render a service; care; get involved 678 *be active*; reform; relieve the poor, visit, nurse 703 *minister to*; mother 889 *pet*.

898 Malevolence

N. malevolence, ill will 881 *enmity*; truculence, cussedness, bitchiness, beastliness, evil intent, bad intention, worst intentions, cloven hoof; spite, gall, spitefulness, viciousness, despite, malignity, malignancy, malice, malice aforethought; bad blood, hate 888 *hatred*; venom, virulence, deadliness, balefulness 659 *bane*; bitterness, acrimony, acerbity 393 *sourness*; mordacity 388 *pungency*; rancour, spleen 891 *resentment*; gloating, unholy joy 912 *envy*; evil eye, jettatura 983 *spell*.

inhumanity, misanthropy; inconsiderateness, lack of concern; uncharitableness; intolerance, persecution 735 *severity*; harshness, mercilessness, implacability, hardness of heart, obduracy, heart of stone 906 *pitilessness*; cold feelings, unkindness; callousness 326 *hardness*; cruelty, barbarity, bloodthirstiness; barbarism, savagery, ferocity, barbarousness, savageness, ferociousness; outrageousness; sadism, fiendishness, devilishness 934 *wickedness*; truculence, brutality, ruffianism; destructiveness, vandalism 165 *destruction*.

cruel act, brutality; ill-treatment, ill usage 675 *misuse*; abuse, child abuse, elder abuse, sexual abuse; disservice, ill turn; victimization, bullying, harassment, sexual harassment, stalking, e-stalking 735 *severity*; foul play, bloodshed 176 *violence*; act of inhumanity, atrocity, outrage; cruelty, torture, barbarities; cannibalism, murder 362 *homicide*; mass murder, genocide 362 *slaughter*.

Adj. malevolent, ill-wishing, ill-willed, evil-intentioned, ill-disposed, meaning harm 661 *dangerous*; ill-natured, churlish 893 *sullen*; nasty, bloody-minded, bitchy, cussed 602 *wilful*; malicious, catty, spiteful; mischievous, mischief-making; baleful, squint-eyed, malign, malignant 645 *harmful*; vicious, viperous, venomous 362 *deadly*; black-hearted, full of spite; jealous 912 *envious*; disloyal, treacherous 930 *perfidious*; bitter, rancorous 891 *resentful*; implacable, unforgiving, merciless 906 *pitiless*; vindictive, gloating; hostile, fell 881 *hostile*; intolerant, persecuting 735 *oppressive*.

unkind, ill-natured 893 *sullen*; unkindly; unchristian; cold, unfriendly, hostile, misanthropic 881 *hostile*; inhospitable 883 *unsociable*; unhelpful, disobliging; uncharitable; mean, nasty; unsympathetic, unmoved 820 *impassive*; stern 735 *severe*; inhuman.

cruel, grim, fell; hard-hearted, flint-hearted, stony-hearted; callous, cold-blooded; heartless, ruthless, merciless 906 *pitiless*; tyrannical 735 *oppressive*; sadistic; blood-thirsty, cannibalistic 362 *murderous*; bloody 176 *violent*; atrocious, outrageous, feral, tigerish, wolfish; unnatural, subhuman, dehumanized, brutalized, brutish; brutal, rough, fierce, ferocious; savage, barbarous, wild, untamed; inhuman, ghoulish, fiendish, devilish, diabolical, demoniacal, satanic, hellish, infernal.

Vb. be malevolent, bear malice, cherish a grudge, nurse resentment, have it in for 888 *hate*; show ill will, spite, do one a bad turn; do one's worst, wreak one's spite, break a butterfly on a wheel, have no mercy 906 *be pitiless*; take one's revenge, exact revenge, victimize; take it out of one, bully, maltreat, abuse 645 *ill-treat*; molest, hurt, injure, annoy 645 *harm*; malign, run down, throw stones at 926 *detract*; tease, harass, harry, hound, persecute, tyrannize, torture 735 *oppress*; thirst for blood 362 *slaughter*; rankle, fester, poison, be a thorn in the flesh; create havoc, blight; blast, cast the evil eye 983 *bewitch*.

899 Malediction: cursing

N. curse, malediction, imprecation, anathema; evil eye, jettatura 983 *spell*; ill wishes, execration, denunciation; fulmination, thunder; ban, proscription, ex-communication; exorcism, bell, book and candle.

scurrility, ribaldry, vulgarity; profanity, cursing, swearing, profane swearing, cursing and swearing, blasting, effing and blinding, effing and ceeing; bad language, foul language, filthy language, blue language, shocking language, strong language, unparliamentary language, Limehouse, Billingsgate; naughty word, four-letter word, expletive, swearword, oath, swear, damn, curse, cuss, tinker's cuss; invective, vituperation, abuse, volley of abuse; mutual abuse, slanging match, stormy exchange; vain abuse, empty curse, more bark than bite 900 *threat*; no compliment, aspersion, reflection, vilification, slander 926 *calumny*; cheek, sauce 878 *sauciness*; personal remarks, epithet, insult 921 *indignity*; contumely, scorn 922 *contempt*; scolding, rough edge of one's tongue, lambasting, tongue-lashing 924 *reproach*.

Adj. cursing, evil-speaking, swearing, damning, blasting; profane, foul-mouthed, foul-tongued, foul-spoken, unparliamentary, scurrilous, scurrile, ribald 847 *vulgar*; blue; vituperative, abusive, vitriolic, injurious; scornful.

Vb. curse, cast the evil eye 983 *bewitch*; accurse, wish ill 898 *be malevolent*; wish on, call down on; wish one joy of; curse with bell, book and candle, curse up hill and down dale; anathematize, imprecate, invoke curses on, execrate, hold up to execration; fulminate, thunder against, rant and rail against, inveigh 924 *reprove*; denounce 928 *accuse*; excommunicate, damn 961 *condemn*; round upon, confound, send to the devil, send to blazes; abuse, vituperate, revile, rail, chide, heap abuse, pour vitriol 924 *reproach*.

curse and swear, curse, cuss, swear, damn, blast; blaspheme 980 *be impious*; swear like a trooper, use expletives, use Billingsgate, use four-letter words, eff and blind, eff and cee, turn the air blue; slang, abuse; rail at, scold, lash out at, give the rough edge of one's tongue, slag off.

Int. blast!, bugger!, damn!, darn!, drat!, fuck!; confound it!, damn it!, drat it!, fuck it!, hang it!, sod it!; damn —, fuck —, curse —!, a curse on —!, devil take —!, a plague on —!, woe to —!, woe betide —!, ill betide —!; the deuce!, the dickens!

900 Threat

N. threat, menace; fulmination 899 *curse*; minacity, ominousness; challenge, dare 711 *defiance*; blackmail 737 *demand*; battle cry, war cry, war whoop, sabre-rattling, war of nerves 854 *intimidation*; deterrent, big stick, weapon of mass effect 723 *weapon*; rod in pickle; clenched fist; black cloud, gathering clouds 511 *omen*; hidden fires, secret weapon 663 *pitfall*; impending danger, sword of Damocles

661 *danger*; danger signal, fair warning, writing on the wall 664 *warning*; bluster, idle threat, hollow threat 877 *boast*; bark, growl, snarl, bared teeth 893 *sullenness*; aggressive begging; prowler, stalker.

Vb. threaten, menace, use threats, hold out threats, utter threats; demand with menaces, blackmail 737 *demand*; hijack, hold to ransom, take hostage; frighten, deter, intimidate, bully, wave the big stick 854 *frighten*; roar, bellow 408 *shout*; fulminate, thunder 899 *curse*; bark, talk big, bluster, hector 877 *boast*; shake, wave, flaunt 317 *brandish*; rattle the sabre, clench the fist, draw one's sword 711 *defy*; bare the fangs, snarl, growl, mutter; bristle, spit, look daggers, grow nasty 891 *get angry*; pull a gun on, hold at gunpoint; draw a bead on, cover, have one covered, keep one covered 281 *aim*; gather, mass, lour, hang over, hover 155 *impend*; bode ill, presage, disaster, mean no good, promise trouble, spell danger 511 *predict*; serve notice, caution, forewarn 664 *warn*; breathe revenge, threaten reprisals 910 *be vengeful*.

901 Philanthropy

N. philanthropy, humanitarianism, humanity, humaneness, the golden rule 897 *benevolence*; humanism, cosmopolitanism, internationalism; altruism 931 *disinterestedness*; idealism, ideals 933 *virtue*; the greatest happiness of the greatest number, utilitarianism, Benthamism; common good, socialism, communism; reformism; chivalry, knight-errantry; dedication, crusading spirit, missionary spirit, social conscience, corporate social responsibility, CSR; good works, mission; Holy War, jihad, crusade, campaign, cause, good cause.

social care, social security, benefit, dole, poor relief; social services, Welfare State; social inclusion; social planning, social engineering; dependency culture; community service, social service, social work, good works; care in the community, community care; social inclusion; sociology, social science.

patriotism, civic ideals, good citizenship, public spirit, concern for the community, love of one's country; parochialism; nationalism, chauvinism, gung-hoism, my country right or wrong.

philanthropist, humanitarian, do-gooder, benefactor, social worker; community service worker, VSO, Peace Corps 597 *volunteer*; paladin, champion, crusader, knight, knight errant; Messiah 690 *leader*; missionary; idealist, altruist, flower people 513 *visionary*; reformist 654 *reformer*; utilitarian, Benthamite; Utopian, millenarian; humanist.

patriot, lover of one's country; nationalist, chauvinist.

Adj. philanthropic, humanitarian, humane, human 897 *benevolent*; charitable, aid-giving 703 *helping*; enlightened, humanistic, liberal; idealistic, altruistic 931 *disinterested*; visionary, dedicated; socialistic, communistic; utilitarian.

patriotic, public-spirited, community-minded; nationalistic, chauvinistic; loyal, true, true-blue.

902 Misanthropy

N. misanthropy, cynicism 883 *unsociability*; misandry, misogyny; moroseness 893 *sullenness*; inhumanity.

misanthropist, misanthrope, man-hater, woman-hater, misandrist, misogynist; cynic, Diogenes; world-hater.

903 Benefactor

N. benefactor, benefactress 901 *philanthropist*; Lady Bountiful, Father Christmas, Santa Claus 781 *giver*; fairy godmother, guardian angel, good genius 660 *protector*; founder, foundress, supporter, angel, backer 707 *patron*; protector of the people 901 *patriot*; saviour, redeemer, rescuer 668 *rescue*; champion 713 *defender*; Good Samaritan; good neighbour 880 *friend*; helper, present help in time of trouble 703 *helper*; saint 937 *good person*.

904 Evildoer

N. evildoer, malefactor, wrongdoer, sinner 934 *wickedness*; villain, blackguard, bad lot, baddy; one up to no good, mischief-maker 663 *trouble-maker*; slanderer 926 *detractor*; snake in the grass, viper in the bosom, traitor 545 *deceiver*; saboteur; despoiler, wrecker, defacer, vandal, Hun, iconoclast 168 *destroyer*; terrorist, nihilist, anarchist 738 *rebel*; incendiary, arsonist 381 *incendiarism*; disturber of the peace 738 *rioter*.

ruffian, blackguard, rogue, scoundrel 938 *knave*; lout, lager lout, hooligan, casual, football hooligan, football casual, hoodlum, boot boy, bovver boy, larrikin, Hell's Angel, skinhead, yob, yobbo, punk 176 *violent creature*, 869 *low fellow*; white van man; bully, terror, terror of the neighbourhood; rough, tough, rowdy, ugly customer, hard man, plug-ugly, bruiser, thug, bravo, desperado, assassin, hired assassin; cutthroat, hatchet man, gunman, hit man, contract man, killer, butcher 362 *murderer*; genocide, mass murderer; plague, scourge, scourge of the human race, Attila 659 *bane*; petty tyrant; molester, brute, savage brute, beast, savage, barbarian; homicidal maniac 504 *madman*.

offender, sinner, black sheep 938 *bad person*; suspect; culprit, guilty person, law-breaker; criminal, archcriminal, master criminal, villain, crook, malefactor, wrongdoer, felon; delinquent, juvenile delinquent, first offender; recidivist, backslider, old offender, hardened offender, lag, old lag, convict, ex-convict, jailbird; lifer, gallowsbird, parolee, probationer, ticket-of-leave man; mafioso, mobster, gangster, racketeer; housebreaker 789 *thief, robber*; forger 789 *defrauder*; blackmailer, bloodsucker; poisoner 362 *murderer*; outlaw, public enemy, most wanted 881 *enemy*; intruder, trespasser; criminal world, underworld, Mafia 934 *wickedness*.

905 Pity

N. *pity*, ruth; remorse, compunction 830 *regret*; charity, compassion, compassionateness, humanity 897 *benevolence*; soft heart, tender heart, bleeding heart; gentleness, softness 736 *leniency*; commiseration, touched feelings, melting mood, tears of sympathy 825 *sorrow*; Weltschmerz 834 *dejection*; sympathy, empathy, understanding, fellow feeling; self-pity.

condolence, commiseration, sympathy, fellow feeling 775 *participation*; consolation, comfort 831 *relief*; keen, coronach, wake 836 *lament*.

mercy, tender mercies, quarter, grace; second chance; mercifulness, clemency, lenity, placability, forbearance, longsuffering 909 *forgiveness*; light sentence 963 *penalty*; let-off, pardon 960 *acquittal*.

Adj. *pitying*, compassionate, sympathetic, understanding, commiserating; sorry for, feeling for; merciful, clement, full of mercy 736 *lenient*; tender, tender-hearted, soft, softhearted 819 *impressible*; disposed to mercy; humane, charitable 897 *benevolent*; forbearing 823 *patient*.

Vb. *pity*, feel pity; show compassion, show pity, take pity on; sympathize, sympathize with, empathize, feel for, feel with, share the grief of 775 *participate*; sorrow, grieve, bleed for, feel sorry for, weep for, lament for, commiserate, condole, express *or* offer one's condolences, send one's condolences; yearn over 836 *lament*; console, comfort, offer consolation, wipe away one's tears 833 *cheer*; have pity, have compassion.

show mercy, have mercy, spare, spare the life of, give quarter; commute (a sentence), pardon, grant a pardon; forget one's anger 909 *forgive*; be slow to anger, forbear; give one a break, give one a second chance 736 *be lenient*; relent, not be too hard upon, go easy on, let one down gently; put out of their misery.

ask for mercy, plead for mercy, appeal for mercy, pray for mercy, beg for mercy, throw oneself upon another's mercy, fall at one's feet, cry mercy, ask for quarter, plead for one's life.

906 Pitilessness

N. *pitilessness*, lack of pity, heartlessness, ruthlessness, mercilessness; inclemency, intolerance, rigour, zero tolerance 735 *severity*; callousness, hardness of heart, compassion fatigue, disaster fatigue 898 *inhumanity*; inflexibility 326 *hardness*; inexorability, relentlessness, remorselessness, unforgivingness 910 *vengefulness*; letter of the law, pound of flesh; no pity, no heart, no feelings, short shrift, no quarter.

Adj. *pitiless*, unfeeling 820 *impassive*; unsympathetic; unmoved, dry-eyed; hardhearted, stony-hearted; callous 326 *hard*; harsh, rigorous, intolerant, persecuting 735 *severe*; brutal, sadistic 898 *cruel*; merciless, ruthless, heartless; inclement, unmerciful, unrelenting, relentless, remorseless, inflexible, inexorable, implacable.

Vb. *be pitiless*, be ruthless, etc. (see adj.); have no heart, have no compassion, have no pity; not be moved, turn a deaf ear; show no pity, show no mercy, give no quarter; harden one's heart, be deaf to appeal; stand on the letter of the law, insist on one's pound of flesh 735 *be severe*; take one's revenge 910 *avenge*.

907 Gratitude

N. *gratitude*, gratefulness, thankfulness, grateful heart, sense of obligation; appreciativeness, appreciation.

thanks, hearty thanks, grateful thanks; vote of thanks, thank-you; thanksgiving, eucharist, benediction, blessing; praises, Te Deum 876 *celebration*; grace; thank-you letter, bread-and-butter letter, Collins; credit, credit title, acknowledgment, due acknowledgment, grateful acknowledgment, recognition, grateful recognition; tribute 923 *praise*; parting present, leaving present, recognition of one's services, golden handshake, token of one's gratitude, tip 962 *reward*.

Adj. *grateful*, thankful, appreciative; thanking; crediting, giving credit; obliged, under obligation, in one's debt, owing a favour, beholden, indebted.

Vb. *be grateful*, thank one's lucky stars; feel an obligation; accept gratefully, receive with open arms, not look a gift horse in the mouth.

thank, give thanks, express thanks;

acknowledge, credit, give credit, give due credit, give full credit 158 *attribute*; show appreciation, tip 962 *reward*; return a favour.

Int. *thanks!*, many thanks!, much obliged!, thank you!, ta!, cheers!, thank goodness!, thank heavens!, Heaven be praised!

908 Ingratitude

N. *ingratitude*, lack of appreciation, ungratefulness; grudging thanks; thanklessness; taking everything as one's due, thankless task; ingrate.

Adj. *ungrateful*, unthankful 885 *discourteous*; unbeholden; unmindful of favours.

Vb. *be ungrateful*, take for granted, take as one's due; omit to thank; not give a thank-you for, look a gift horse in the mouth; forget a kindness, return evil for good.

Int. *thank you for nothing!*, no thanks to.

909 Forgiveness

N. *forgiveness*, pardon, free pardon, full pardon, reprieve 506 *amnesty*; indemnity, grace, indulgence, plenary indulgence 905 *mercy*; cancellation, remission, absolution 960 *acquittal*; justification, exculpation, exoneration, excuse 927 *vindication*; conciliation, reconciliation 719 *pacification*; mercifulness, placability, lenity 905 *pity*; longsuffering, forbearance 823 *patience*.

Vb. *forgive*, pardon, reprieve, forgive and forget, think no more of, not give another thought 506 *forget*; remit, absolve, shrive; cancel, blot out, wipe the slate clean 550 *obliterate*; relent, unbend, accept an apology 736 *be lenient*; be merciful, not be too hard upon, let one down gently, let one off the hook 905 *show mercy*; bear with, put up with, forbear, tolerate, make allowances 823 *be patient*; take no offence, bear no malice, take in good part, pocket, stomach, not hold it against one; forget an injury, ignore a wrong, overlook, pass over, not punish, leave unavenged, turn the other cheek; return good for evil; connive, wink at, condone, not make an issue of, turn a blind eye 458 *disregard*; excuse, find excuses for 927 *justify*; intercede 720 *mediate*; exculpate, exonerate 960 *acquit*; be ready to forgive, make the first move, bury the hatchet, let bygones be bygones, make it up, extend the hand of forgiveness, shake hands, kiss and be friends, kiss and make up, be reconciled 880 *be friendly*; restore to favour, kill the fatted calf 876 *celebrate*.

910 Revenge

N. *vengefulness*, revengefulness, thirst for revenge; vindictiveness, spitefulness, spite 898

malevolence; ruthlessness 906 *pitilessness*; remorselessness, relentlessness, implacability, irreconcilability, unappeasability; resentment.

revenge, sweet revenge; crime passionel 911 *jealousy*; vengeance, day of reckoning 963 *punishment*; reprisal, reprisals, punitive expedition 714 *retaliation*; tit for tat, a Roland for an Oliver, measure for measure, eye for an eye, tooth for a tooth; vendetta, feud, blood feud 881 *enmity*.

Vb. *avenge*, avenge or revenge oneself, take one's revenge, exact revenge, take vengeance, wreak vengeance, take the law into one's own hands; exact retribution, get one's own back, repay, pay out, pay off or settle old scores, square an account, give someone what was coming to them, give someone his or her comeuppance; get back at, give tit for tat 714 *retaliate*; enjoy one's revenge, gloat.

be vengeful, be revengeful, get one's knife into 898 *be malevolent*; bear malice, promise vengeance 888 *hate*; nurse one's revenge, harbour a grudge, carry on a feud, conduct a blood feud, have a rod in pickle, have a bone to pick, have a score or accounts to settle 881 *be hostile*; let it rankle, remember an injury, refuse to forget 891 *resent*.

911 Jealousy

N. *jealousy*, pangs of jealousy, jealousness; jaundiced eye, green-eyed monster; sour grapes; distrust, mistrust 486 *doubt*; resentment; enviousness 912 *envy*; hate 888 *hatred*; inferiority complex, emulation, competitiveness, competitive spirit, competition, rivalry, jealous rivalry 716 *contention*; possessiveness 887 *love*; sexual jealousy, eternal triangle, crime passionel 910 *revenge*; competitor, rival, hated rival, the other man or woman; Othello.

Adj. *jealous*, green-eyed, yellow-eyed, jaundiced, envying 912 *envious*; devoured with jealousy, consumed with jealousy, eaten up with jealousy; possessive 887 *loving*; suspicious, mistrusting, distrustful 474 *doubting*; emulative, competitive, rival, competing.

912 Envy

N. *envy*, envious eye, enviousness, covetousness 859 *desire*; rivalry 716 *contention*; jealousy; ill will, spite, spleen; mortification, unwilling admiration, grudging praise.

Adj. *envious*, envying, envious-eyed, green with envy 911 *jealous*; greedy, unsatisfied 829 *discontented*; covetous, longing; grudging.

Vb. *envy*, view with envy, cast envious or covetous looks, turn green with envy, resent; covet, crave, lust after, must have for oneself, long to change places with 859 *desire*.

SECTION FOUR

Morality

913 Right

N. right, rightfulness, rightness, fitness, what is fitting, what ought to be, what should be; obligation 917 *duty*; fittingness, seemliness, propriety, decency 848 *etiquette*; normality 83 *conformity*; rules, rules and regulations 693 *precept*; ethicalness, ethicality, morality, moral code, good morals 917 *morals*; righteousness 933 *virtue*; rectitude, uprightness, honour 929 *probity*; one's right, one's due, one's prerogative, deserts, merits, claim 915 *what is due*.

justice, freedom from wrong, justifiability; righting wrong, redress; reform 654 *reformism*; even-handed justice, impartial justice; scales of justice, justice under the law, process of law, McNaghten rules 953 *legality*; retribution, retributive justice, poetic justice 962 *reward*; give and take, retaliation; fair-mindedness, objectivity, lack of bias, disinterestedness, detachment, impartiality, equalness 28 *equality*; equity, equitableness, reasonableness, fairness; fair deal, square deal, fair treatment, fair play; no discrimination, equal opportunity; fair society; good law, Queensberry rules.

Adj. right, rightful, proper, right and proper, fitting, suitable, appropriate 24 *fit*; good 917 *ethical*; put right, redressed, reformed; normal, standard, classical 83 *conformable*.

just, upright, righteous, right-minded, high-principled, on the side of the angels 933 *virtuous*; fair-minded, disinterested, unprejudiced, unbiased, unswerving, undeflected 625 *neutral*; detached, impersonal, dispassionate, objective, open-minded; equal, egalitarian, impartial, even-handed; fair, square, fair and square, equitable, reasonable, fair enough; in the right, justifiable, justified, unchallengeable, unchallenged, unimpeachable; above-board, legitimate, according to law 953 *legal*; sporting, sportsmanlike 929 *honourable*; deserved, well-deserved, earned, merited, well-merited 915 *due*; overdue, demanded, claimed, rightly claimed, claimable 627 *required*.

914 Wrong

N. wrong, wrongness, something wrong, something amiss, oddness, queerness 84 *abnormality*; something rotten, curse, bane, scandal 645 *badness*; disgrace, shame, crying shame, dishonour 867 *slur*; impropriety, indecorum 847 *bad taste*; wrongheadedness, unreasonableness 481 *misjudgment*; unjustifiability, what ought not to be, what must not be 916 *what is not due*; inexcusability, culpability, guiltiness

936 *guilt*; immorality, vice, sin 934 *wickedness*; dishonesty, unrighteousness 930 *improbity*; irregularity, illegitimacy, criminality, crime, lawlessness 954 *illegality*; wrongfulness, misdoing, transgression, trespass, encroachment; misdeed, offence, arrestable offence 936 *guilty act*; a wrong, injustice, mischief, outrage, foul; sense of wrong, complaint, charge 928 *accusation*; grievance, just grievance 891 *resentment*; wrong-doer, unjust judge 938 *bad person*.

injustice, no justice; miscarriage of justice, wrong verdict 481 *misjudgment*; warped judgment, packed jury 481 *bias*; one-sidedness, inequity, unfairness; sweetheart deal; discrimination, race discrimination, sex discrimination, racism, institutional racism, sexism, heterosexism, ageism, classism, ableism; partiality, leaning, favouritism, favour, nepotism; preferential treatment, positive discrimination, affirmative action; partisanship, party spirit, old school tie 481 *prejudice*; unlawfulness, no law 954 *illegality*; justice denied, right withheld, privilege curtailed 916 *what is not due*; unfair advantage, 'heads I win, tails you lose'; no equality, the wolf and the lamb, asymmetric warfare 29 *inequality*; not cricket; imposition, robbing Peter to pay Paul.

Adj. wrong, not right 645 *bad*; odd, queer, suspect 84 *abnormal*; unfitting, inappropriate, unseemly, improper 847 *vulgar*; wrongheaded, unreasonable; wrong from the start, out of court, inadmissible; irregular, against the rules, foul, unauthorized, unwarranted 757 *prohibited*; wrongful, illegitimate, illicit, felonious, criminal 954 *illegal*; condemnable, culpable, in the wrong, offside 936 *guilty*; unwarrantable, inexcusable, unpardonable, unforgivable, unjustifiable (see also *unjust* below); open to objection, objectionable, reprehensible, scandalous; injurious, mischievous 645 *harmful*; unrighteous 930 *dishonest*; iniquitous, sinful, vicious, immoral 934 *wicked*.

unjust, unjustifiable; uneven, weighted 29 *unequal*; inequitable, iniquitous, unfair; hard, hard on 735 *severe*; foul, not playing the game, not keeping to the rules, below the belt, unsportsmanlike; discriminatory, favouring, one-sided, leaning to one side, partial, partisan, prejudiced 481 *biased*; selling justice 930 *corruptible*; wresting the law 954 *illegal*.

Vb. do wrong, wrong, hurt, injure, do an injury 645 *harm*; be hard on, have a down on 735 *be severe*; not play the game, not play cricket, hit below the belt; break the rules, commit a foul; commit a crime, break the law, pervert the course of justice, be illegal; transgress, infringe, trespass 306 *encroach*; wink at, connive at, turn a blind eye; do less than justice, withhold justice, deny justice, deny one his *or* her rights; weight, load the scales, pack the jury, rig the jury; lean, lean to one side, discriminate against, show partiality, show favouritism, discriminate 481 *be biased*; favour 703 *patronize*; go too far, overcompensate, lean over backwards; commit, perpetrate.

915 Dueness

N. *what is due*, dueness, what is owing; accountability, responsibility, obligation 917 *duty*; from each according to his ability and to each according to his need; the least one can do, bare minimum; what one looks for, expectations; dues 804 *payment*; something owed, indebtedness 803 *debt*; tribute, credit 158 *attribution*; recognition, acknowledgment 907 *thanks*; something to be said for, something in favour of, case for; qualification, merits, deserts, just deserts 913 *right*; justification 927 *vindication*; entitlement, claim, title 913 *right*; birthright, patriality, patrimony 777 *dowry*; interest, vested interest, prescriptive right, absolute right, inalienable right; legal right, prescription, ancient lights; human rights, social justice, women's rights, equal opportunity, gay rights 744 *freedom*; animal rights, antivivisectionism 365 *animal life*; constitutional right, civil rights, bill of rights, Magna Carta; privilege, exemption, immunity 919 *non-liability*; prerogative, privilege; charter, warrant, licence 756 *permit*; liberty, franchise; bond, security 767 *title deed*; patent, copyright; intellectual property; recovery of rights, restoration, compensation 787 *restitution*; owner, title-holder 776 *possessor*; heir 776 *beneficiary*; claimant, plaintiff, pursuer, appellant; person with a grievance 763 *petitioner*.

Adj. *due*, owing, payable; ascribable, attributable, assignable; merited, well-merited, deserved, well-deserved, richly-deserved, earned, well-earned, coming to one; admitted, allowed, sanctioned, warranted, licit, lawful; constitutional, entrenched, untouchable, uninfringeable, unchallengeable, unimpeachable, inviolable; privileged, sacrosanct; confirmed, vested, prescriptive, inalienable, imprescriptible; secured by law, legalized, legitimate, rightful, of right, de jure, by habit and repute 953 *legal*; claimable, heritable, inheritable, earmarked, reserved, set aside; expected, fit, fitting, befitting 913 *right*; proper, en règle 642 *advisable*.

Vb. *claim*, claim as a right, lay claim to, stake a claim, take possession 786 *appropriate*; claim unduly, arrogate; demand one's rights, assert one's rights, stand up for one's rights, vindicate one's rights, insist on one's rights, stand on one's rights; draw on, come down on

for, take one's toll 786 *levy*; call in (debts), reclaim 656 *retrieve*; publish one's claims, declare one's right; sue, demand redress 761 *request*; enforce a claim, exercise a right; establish a right, patent, copyright.

deserve, merit, be worthy, be found worthy, have a claim on; have a right to, have right on one's side; earn, receive one's due, meet with one's deserts, get one's deserts; have it coming to one, get one's comeuppance, have only oneself to thank; sow the wind and reap the whirlwind.

916 Undueness

N. *what is not due*, undueness, not what one expects *or* would expect 508 *lack of expectation*; not the thing, not quite the thing, impropriety, unseemliness, indecorum 847 *bad taste*; inappropriateness, unfittingness 643 *inexpediency*; unworthiness, demerit 934 *vice*; illicitness, illegitimacy, bastardy 954 *illegality*; no thanks to 908 *ingratitude*; absence of right, lack of title, failure of title, non-entitlement; no claim, no right, no title, false title, courtesy title; gratuitousness, gratuity, bonus, grace marks, unearned increment; inordinacy, excessiveness, too much, overpayment 637 *redundancy*; imposition, exaction 735 *severity*; unfair share, lion's share; violation, breach, infraction, infringement, encroachment 306 *overstepping*; profanation, desecration 980 *impiety*.

unjustified claim, unjustified assumption, assumption, arrogation, presumption, unwarranted presumption; pretendership, usurpation, tyranny; misappropriation 786 *expropriation*; encroachment, inroad, trespass 306 *overstepping*.

loss of right, disentitlement, disfranchisement, disqualification; denaturalization, detribalization 147 *conversion*; forfeiture 772 *loss*; deportation, dismissal, deprivation, dethronement 752 *deposing*; ouster, dispossession 786 *expropriation*; seizure, forcible seizure, robbery 788 *stealing*; cancellation 752 *annulment*; waiver, abdication 621 *relinquishment*.

usurper, pretender 545 *impostor*; desecrator; violator, infringer, encroacher, trespasser, squatter, cuckoo in the nest.

Adj. *unwarranted*, unwarrantable; unauthorized, unsanctioned, unlicensed, unchartered, unconstitutional; unrightful, unlegalized, illicit, illegitimate, ultra vires 954 *illegal*; arrogated, usurped, stolen, borrowed; excessive, presumptuous, assuming 878 *insolent*; unjustified, unjustifiable 914 *wrong*; undeserved, unmerited, unearned; overpaid, underpaid; invalid, weak; forfeited, forfeit;

false, bastard 542 *spurious*; fictitious, would-be, self-styled 850 *affected*.

Vb. *disentitle*, uncrown, dethrone 752 *depose*; disqualify, unfrock, disfranchise, alienize, denaturalize, detribalize, denationalize; invalidate 752 *annul*; disallow 757 *prohibit*; dispossess, expropriate 786 *deprive*; forfeit, declare forfeit; defeat a claim, mock the claims of; make illegitimate, illegalize, criminalize 954 *make illegal*; bastardize, debase 655 *impair*.

917 Duty

N. *duty*, what ought to be done, what is up to one, the right thing, the proper thing, the decent thing; one's duty, bounden duty, inescapable duty; obligation, liability, onus, responsibility, accountability 915 *what is due*; fealty, allegiance, loyalty 739 *obedience*; sense of duty, dutifulness, duteousness 597 *willingness*; discharge of duty, performance, acquittal, discharge 768 *observance*; call of duty, claims of conscience, case of conscience; bond, tie, engagement, commitment, word, pledge 764 *promise*; task, office, charge 751 *commission*; walk of life, station, profession 622 *vocation*.

conscience, tender conscience, inner voice, 'still small voice'.

code of duty, code of honour, unwritten code, professional code; Ten Commandments, Decalogue, Hippocratic oath 693 *precept*.

morals, morality 933 *virtue*; honour 929 *probity*; moral principles, high principles, ideals, high ideals, standards, high standards, professional standards; moral high ground, moral majority; ethics, religious ethics, humanist ethics, professional ethics; Protestant work ethic; ethical investment, socially responsible investment, SRI, ethical shopping, ethology, deontology, casuistry, ethical philosophy, moral philosophy, moral science, idealism, humanism, utilitarianism, behaviourism 449 *philosophy*.

Adj. *obliged*, duty-bound, on duty, bound by duty, called by duty; under duty, in duty bound, in the line of duty; obligated, beholden, under obligation; tied, bound, sworn, pledged, committed, engaged; unexempted, liable, chargeable, answerable, responsible, accountable; in honour bound, bound in conscience, answerable to God; plagued by conscience, conscience-stricken 939 *repentant*; conscientious, punctilious 768 *observant*; duteous, dutiful 739 *obedient*; vowed, under a vow.

obligatory, incumbent, imposed, behoving, up to one; binding, de rigueur, compulsory, mandatory, peremptory, operative 740 *compelling*; inescapable, unavoidable; strict, unconditional, categorical.

ethical, moral, principled 933 *virtuous*; honest, decent 929 *honourable*; moralistic, ethological, casuistical; moralizing; humanistic, idealistic; utilitarian.

Vb. *be one's duty*, be incumbent, behove, become, befit 915 *be due*; devolve on, belong to, be up to, pertain to, fall to, arise from one's functions, be part of the job; lie with, lie at one's door, rest with, rest on one's shoulders.

incur a duty, make it one's duty, take on oneself, accept responsibility, shoulder one's responsibility; make oneself liable, commit oneself, pledge oneself, engage for 764 *promise*; assume one's functions, enter upon one's office, receive a posting; have the office, have the function, have the charge, have the duty; owe it to oneself, feel it up to one, feel it incumbent upon one; feel duty's call, accept the call, answer the call, submit to one's vocation.

do one's duty, fulfil one's duty 739 *obey*; discharge, acquit, perform, do the needful 676 *do*; do one's bit, play one's part; perform one's office, discharge one's functions 768 *observe*; be on duty, stay at one's post, go down with one's ship; come up to what is expected of one, come up to expectation, not be found wanting; keep faith with one's conscience, meet one's obligations, discharge an obligation, make good one's promise, redeem a pledge, be as good as one's word; honour, meet, pay up 804 *pay*.

impose a duty, require, oblige, look to, call upon; devolve, call to office, swear one in, offer a post, post 751 *commission*; assign a duty, saddle with, detail, order, enjoin, decree 737 *command*; tax, overtax, task, overtask 684 *fatigue*; exact 735 *be severe*; demand obedience, expect it of one, expect too much of one 507 *expect*; bind, condition 766 *give terms*; bind over, take security 764 *take a pledge*.

Adv. *on duty*, at one's post; under an obligation; in the line of duty, as in duty bound; with a clear conscience; for conscience' sake.

918 Undutifulness

N. *undutifulness*, default, dereliction of duty, want of duty; neglect, wilful neglect, culpable negligence 458 *negligence*; disrespect; malingering, swinging the lead, evasion of duty, cop-out 620 *avoidance*; non-practice, non-performance 769 *non-observance*; idleness, laziness 679 *sluggishness*; forgetfulness 506 *no memory*; non-cooperation, lack of alacrity 598 *unwillingness*; truancy, absenteeism 190 *absence*; absconding 667 *escape*; infraction, violation, breach of orders, indiscipline, mutiny, rebellion 738 *disobedience*; incompetence, mismanagement 695 *bungling*; obstruction, sabotage 702 *hindrance*; desertion, defection 603 *change of mind*; disloyalty, treachery, treason 930 *perfidiousness*; secession, breakaway 978 *schism*; irresponsibility, escapism; truant, absentee, malingerer, defaulter, lead-swinger 620 *avoider*; slacker 679 *idler*; deserter, absconder 667 *escaper*; betrayer, traitor 603 *recanter*; saboteur; mutineer, rebel 738 *rebel*; seceder, splinter group 978 *schismatic*.

Adj. undutiful, wanting in duty, uncooperative 598 *unwilling*; unfilial, un-daughterly 921 *disrespectful*; mutinous, rebellious, seceding, breakaway 738 *disobedient*; disloyal, treacherous, treasonous 930 *perfidious*; irresponsible, unreliable; truant, absentee 190 *absent*; absconding.

Vb. fail in duty, neglect one's duty, be wilfully negligent 458 *neglect*; ignore one's obligations 458 *disregard*; oversleep, sleep in 679 *sleep*; default, let one down, leave one in the lurch 509 *disappoint*; mismanage, bungle 495 *blunder*; not remember 506 *forget*; shirk, evade, wriggle out of, malinger, swing the lead 620 *avoid*; wash one's hands of, pass the buck 919 *be exempt*; play truant, overstay leave 190 *be absent*; abscond 667 *escape*; quit, scuttle, scarper 296 *walk out*; abandon, abandon one's post, desert, desert the colours 621 *relinquish*; break orders, disobey orders, violate orders, exceed one's instructions 738 *disobey*; mutiny, rebel 738 *revolt*; be disloyal, prove treacherous, betray, commit treason 603 *change one's mind*; sabotage 702 *obstruct*; non-cooperate, withdraw, walk out, break away, form a splinter group, secede.

919 Non-liability

N. non-liability, non-responsibility, exemption, dispensation; conscience clause, escape clause, let-out clause, force majeure 468 *qualification*; immunity, impunity, privilege, special treatment, special case, benefit of clergy; extraterritoriality, diplomatic immunity; franchise, charter 915 *what is due*; independence, liberty, the four freedoms 744 *freedom*; licence, leave 756 *permission*; compassionate leave, aegrotat, certificate of exemption 756 *permit*; excuse, exoneration, exculpation 960 *acquittal*; absolution, pardon, amnesty 909 *forgiveness*; discharge, release 746 *liberation*; renunciation 621 *relinquishment*; evasion of responsibility, escapism, self-exemption, washing one's hands, passing the buck 753 *resignation*.

Vb. exempt, set apart, set aside; eliminate, count out, rule out 57 *exclude*; excuse, exonerate, exculpate 960 *acquit*; grant absolution, absolve, pardon 909 *forgive*; spare 905 *show mercy*; grant immunity, privilege, charter 756 *permit*; license, dispense, give dispensation, grant impunity; amnesty, declare an amnesty 506 *forget*; enfranchise, set free, set at liberty, release 746 *liberate*; pass over, stretch a point 736 *be lenient*.

be exempt, be exempted, etc. (see adj.); owe no responsibility, be free from responsibility, have no liability, not come within the scope of; enjoy immunity, enjoy diplomatic immunity, enjoy impunity, enjoy a privileged position, enjoy independence 744 *be free*; spare oneself the necessity, exempt oneself, excuse oneself, absent oneself, take leave, go on leave 190 *go away*; transfer the responsibility, pass the buck, shift the blame 272 *transfer*; evade *or* escape liability, get away with 667 *escape*; own *or* admit no responsibility, wash one's hands of 918 *fail in duty*.

920 Respect

N. respect, regard, consideration, esteem 923 *approbation*; high standing, honour, favour 866 *repute*; polite regard, attention, attentions, flattering attentions 884 *courtesy*; due respect, respectfulness, deference, humbleness 872 *humility*; obsequiousness 879 *servility*; devotion 739 *loyalty*; admiration, awe 864 *wonder*; terror 854 *fear*; reverence, veneration, adoration 981 *worship*.

respects, regards, duty, kind regards, kindest regards, greetings 884 *courteous act*; red carpet, guard of honour, address of welcome, illuminated address, salutation, salaam; nod, bob, duck, bow, scrape, curtsy, genuflexion, prostration, kowtow 311 *bow*; reverence, homage; salute, presenting arms; honours of war, flags flying.

Adj. respectful, deferential, knowing one's place 872 *humble*; obsequious, boot-licking, kowtowing 879 *servile*; submissive 721 *submitting*; reverent, reverential, admiring, awestruck; polite 884 *courteous*; ceremonious, at the salute, saluting, cap in hand, bare-headed, forelock-tugging; kneeling, on one's knees, prostrate; bobbing, bowing, scraping, bowing and scraping, bending; showing respect, rising, standing, on one's feet, all standing.

Vb. respect, hold in respect, hold in honour, hold in high regard, hold in high esteem, think well of, rank high, place high, look up to, esteem, regard, value; admire 864 *wonder*; reverence, venerate, exalt 866 *honour*; adore 981 *worship*; idolize; think the world of; revere, stand in awe of, have a wholesome respect for 854 *fear*; know one's place, defer to, take a back seat to 721 *submit*; pay tribute to, take one's hat off to 923 *praise*; do homage to, make much of, lionize, chair, carry shoulder-high 876 *celebrate*.

show respect, render honour, pay homage, do the honours 884 *pay one's respects*; make way for, leave room for, keep one's distance, take a back seat to, know one's place; welcome, hail, salute, present arms, turn out the guard, roll out the red carpet, put out the bunting 884 *greet*; cheer, drink to 876 *toast*; bob, bow, bow and scrape, curtsy, kneel, kowtow, prostrate oneself 311 *stoop*; observe decorum, stand on ceremony, stand, rise, rise to one's feet, rise from one's seat, uncover, remove one's hat *or* cap, stand bareheaded; humble oneself, condescend 872 *be humble*.

command respect, inspire respect, awe, strike with awe, overawe, impose 821 *impress*; enjoy a reputation, rank high, stand high, stand well in the eyes of all 866 *have a reputation*; compel respect, demand respect, command admiration 864 *be wonderful*; dazzle, bedazzle 875 *be ostentatious*; receive respect, gain honour, gain a reputation, receive bouquets 923 *be praised*.

921 Disrespect

N. *disrespect*, lack of respect, scant respect, disrespectfulness, irreverence, impoliteness, incivility, discourtesy 885 *rudeness*; dishonour, disfavour 924 *disapprobation*; neglect, undervaluation 483 *underestimation*; low esteem 867 *disrepute*; depreciation, disparagement 926 *detraction*; scorn 922 *contempt*; mockery 851 *ridicule*; desecration 980 *impiety*.

indignity, humiliation, mortification, affront, insult, slight, snub, slap in the face, outrage 878 *insolence*; snook, V-sign, Harvey Smith salute 878 *sauciness*; gibe, taunt, jeer 922 *contempt*; quip, sarcasm, mock, flout 851 *ridicule*; hiss, hoot, boo, catcall, brickbat, rotten eggs 924 *disapprobation*.

Adj. *disrespectful*, wanting in respect, slighting, neglectful 458 *negligent*; insubordinate 738 *disobedient*; irreverent, irreverential, aweless; sacrilegious 980 *profane*; outspoken, overcandid 573 *plain*; rude, impolite 885 *discourteous*; airy, breezy, offhand, offhanded, cavalier, familiar, cheeky, saucy 878 *impertinent*; insulting, outrageous 878 *insolent*; flouting, jeering, gibing, scoffing, mocking, satirical, cynical, sarcastic; injurious, contumelious, scurrilous 899 *cursing*; denigratory, depreciative, pejorative; snobbish, supercilious, disdainful, scornful; unflattering, uncomplimentary 924 *disapproving*.

Vb. *not respect*, be disrespectful; have no respect for, have no regard for, have no use for

924 *disapprove*; misprize, undervalue, underrate 483 *underestimate*; look down on, have a low opinion of, marginalize, disdain, scorn 922 *despise*; run down, denigrate, disparage 926 *defame*; spit on, toss aside 607 *reject*; show disrespect, show no respect, lack courtesy, remain seated, remain covered, keep one's hat on, push *or* shove *or* elbow aside, crowd, jostle 885 *be rude*; marginalize, ignore, turn one's back 458 *disregard*; snub, slight, insult, affront, outrage 872 *humiliate*; dishonour, disgrace, put to shame, drag in the mud 867 *shame*; trifle with, treat lightly 922 *hold cheap*; cheapen, lower, degrade; have no awe, not reverence, desecrate, profane 980 *be impious*; call names, abuse 899 *curse*; taunt, twit, cock a snook 878 *be insolent*; laugh at, guy, scoff, mock, flout, deride 851 *ridicule*; make mouths at, make faces at, jeer, hiss, hoot, heckle, boo, point at, spit at 924 *reproach*; mob, hound, chase 619 *pursue*; pelt, stone, heave a brick.

922 Contempt

N. *contempt*, utter contempt; scorn, disdain, disdainfulness, superiority, loftiness 871 *pride*; contemptuousness, sniffiness, snootiness, superciliousness, snobbishness 850 *affectation*; superior airs, side, smile of contempt, curl of the lip, snort, sniff; slight, humiliation 921 *indignity*; sneer, dig at 926 *detraction*; derision, scoffing 851 *ridicule*; snub, rebuff 885 *discourtesy*.

contemptibility, unworthiness, despisedness, insignificance, puerility, pitiability, futility 639 *unimportance*; pettiness, meanness, mean streak, littleness, paltriness 33 *smallness*; cause for shame, byword of reproach.

Adj. *contemptible*, despicable, beneath contempt; abject, worthless 645 *bad*; petty, paltry, little, mean 33 *small*; spurned, spat on; scorned, despised, contemned, low in one's estimation; trifling, pitiable, futile, of no account 639 *unimportant*.

Vb. *despise*, hold in contempt, feel utter contempt for, have no use for 921 *not respect*; look down on, consider beneath one, be too good for, be too grand for 871 *be proud*; disdain, spurn, sniff at, snort at 607 *reject*; come it over, turn up one's nose, wrinkle the nose, curl one's lips, toss one's head, snort; snub, turn one's back on 885 *be rude*; scorn, whistle, hiss, boo, give a slow handclap, point at, point the finger of scorn 924 *reproach*; laugh at, have a dig at, laugh to scorn, scoff, scout, flout, gibe, jeer, mock, deride 851 *ridicule*; trample on, ride roughshod over 735 *oppress*; disgrace, roll in the mire 867 *shame*.

hold cheap, have a low opinion of 921 *not*

respect; ignore, dismiss, discount, marginalize, take no account of 458 *disregard*; belittle, disparage, fail to appreciate, underrate, undervalue 483 *underestimate*; decry 926 *detract*; marginalize, set no value on, set no store by, think nothing of, think small beer of, not care a rap for, not care a straw, not give a hoot *or* a damn, not give that for, laugh at, treat as a laughing matter, snap one's fingers at, shrug away, pooh-pooh; slight, trifle with, treat lightly, treat like dirt, denigrate, lower, degrade 872 *humiliate*.

Int. *get lost!*, get stuffed!, in your face!, get a life!

923 Approbation

N. *approbation*, approval, modified rapture; satisfaction 828 *contentment*; appreciation, recognition, acknowledgment 907 *gratitude*; good opinion, golden opinions, kudos, credit 866 *prestige*; regard, admiration, esteem 920 *respect*; good books, good graces, grace, favour, popularity, affection 887 *love*; adoption, acceptance, welcome, favourable reception 299 *reception*; sanction 756 *permission*; nod of approval, seal of approval, blessing; nod, wink, thumbs up, consent 488 *assent*; vote of confidence; countenance, patronage, championship, advocacy, backing 703 *aid*; friendly notice, favourable review, rave review 480 *estimate*; good word, kind word, testimonial, written testimonial, reference, commendation, recommendation 466 *credential*.

praise, loud praise, praise and glory, laudation, benediction, blessing; compliment, eulogy, panegyric, glorification, adulation, idolatry 925 *flattery*; hero worship 864 *wonder*; overpraise 482 *overestimation*; faint praise, two cheers; shout of praise, hosanna, alleluia; praises, song of praise, hymn of praise, paean of praise, Te Deum; tribute, credit, due credit 907 *thanks*; complimentary reference, bouquet, accolade, citation, honourable mention, commendation, glowing terms; official biography, hagiography; self-praise, self-glorification 877 *boasting*; name in lights, letters of gold; puff, blurb 528 *advertisement*.

applause, clamorous applause, acclaim, universal acclaim; enthusiasm, excitement 821 *excitation*; warm reception, hero's welcome 876 *celebration*; acclamation, plaudits, clapping, stamping, whistling, cheering; clap, three cheers, paean, hosannah; thunderous applause, shout of applause, chorus of applause, round of applause, salvo of applause, storm of applause, ovation, standing ovation, shouts of 'encore', shouts of 'more, more'; encore, curtain call; bouquet, pat on the back.

commender, praiser, eulogist, panegyrist; clapper, applauder, shouter; approver, friendly critic, admirer, devoted admirer, hero-worshipper, fan club, supporters' club; advocate, recommender, supporter, speaker for the motion 707 *patron*; Europhile; inscriber, dedicator; advertiser, blurb-writer, puffer, promotions manager, booster; agent, tout, touter, barker 528 *publicizer*; canvasser, electioneer, election agent.

Adj. *approving*, uncensorious, uncomplaining, satisfied 828 *content*; favouring, supporting, advocating 703 *helping*; Europhile; appreciative 907 *grateful*; approbatory, favourable, friendly, well-inclined; complimentary, commendatory, laudatory, eulogistic, panegyrical, lyrical; admiring, hero-worshipping, idolatrous; lavish, generous; fulsome, overpraising, uncritical, undiscriminating; acclamatory, clapping, applauding, thunderous 400 *loud*; ecstatic, rapturous, in raptures 821 *excited*.

approved, passed, tested, tried; uncensured, free from blame, stamped with approval, blessed; popular, big, huge, massive; in favour, in high favour, in one's good books, in the good graces of, in good odour, in high esteem, thought well of 866 *reputable*; praised, etc. (see vb.); commended, highly commended; favoured, backed, odds on 605 *chosen*.

Vb. *approve*, see nothing wrong with, sound pleased, have no fault to find, be unable to fault, have nothing but praise for, think highly of 920 *respect*; like well 887 *love*; think well of, admire, esteem, value, prize, treasure, cherish, set store by 866 *honour*; appreciate, give credit, give full credit, give credit where credit is due, salute, take one's hat off to, hand it to, give full marks; think no worse of, think the better of; count it to one's credit, see the good points, see the good in one, think good, think perfect, think desirable 912 *envy*; think the best, award the palm; pronounce good, mark with approbation, give the seal *or* stamp of approval; accept, pass, tick, give marks for, give points for; nod, wink, nod one's approval, give one's assent 488 *assent*; sanction, bless, give one's blessing 756 *permit*; ratify 488 *endorse*; commend, recommend, advocate, support, back, favour, countenance, stand up for, speak up for, put in a good word for, give one a reference *or* a testimonial, act as referee for 703 *patronize*.

praise, compliment, pay compliments 925 *flatter*; speak well of, speak highly of, big up, swear by; bless 907 *thank*; salute, pay tribute to, hand it to, take one's hat off to; commend, give praise, hand out bouquets to, laud, eulogize, praise to the skies, sound the praises, sing the praises, exalt, extol, glorify, magnify; wax lyrical, get carried away; not spare one's blushes 546 *exaggerate*; puff, inflate, over-praise, overestimate 482 *overrate*; lionize, hero-worship, idolize; trumpet, write up, cry up, puff up, hype up, crack up, boost 528 *advertise*; praise oneself, glorify oneself 877 *boast*.

applaud, welcome, hail; acclaim, receive with acclamation, clap, clap one's hands, give a big hand, stamp, whistle, bring the house down, raise the roof; give a standing ovation; cheer, raise a cheer, give three cheers, give three times three; cheer to the echo, shout for, root for; clap on the back, pat on the back, hand out bouquets to; welcome, congratulate, garland, chair 876 *celebrate*; drink to 876 *toast*.

Int. *bravo!*, well done!, hear hear!, encore!, more, more!, bis!, three cheers!, hurrah!, hosannah!, olé!, way to go!

924 Disapprobation

N. *disapprobation*, disapproval, dissatisfaction 829 *discontent*; non-approval, return 607 *rejection*; refusal; disfavour, displeasure, unpopularity 861 *dislike*; low opinion 921 *disrespect*; bad books, black books 867 *disrepute*; disparagement, decrial, carping, niggling 926 *detraction*; censoriousness, fault-finding 862 *fastidiousness*; hostility 881 *enmity*; Euroscepticism; objection, exception, cavil 468 *qualification*; complaint, clamour, outcry, protest, tut-tut, sniffing 762 *deprecation*; indignation 891 *anger*; hissing, hiss, sibilation, boo, slow handclap, whistle, catcall; brickbats 851 *ridicule*; ostracism, boycott, bar, colour bar, ban, non-admission 57 *exclusion*; blackball, blacklist, Index, Index Expurgatorius, Index Librorum Prohibitorum.

censure, blame, impeachment, inculpation 928 *accusation*; home truth, no compliment, left-handed compliment, back-handed compliment; criticism, stricture; lambasting, hyper-criticism, fault-finding, blame culture; onslaught 712 *attack*; brickbats, bad press, critical review, hostile review, slashing review, slating, panning; open letter, tirade, jeremiad, philippic, diatribe 704 *opposition*; conviction 961 *condemnation*; false accusation 928 *false charge*; slur, slander, aspersions, insinuation, innuendo 926 *calumny*; brand, stigma.

reproach, reproaches; recriminations 709 *quarrel*; home truths, invective, vituperation, calling names, bawling out, shouting down 899 *scurrility*; execration 899 *curse*; personal remarks, aspersion, reflection 921 *indignity*; taunt, sneer 878 *insolence*; sarcasm, irony, satire, biting wit, biting tongue, dig, cut, hit, brickbat 851 *ridicule*; rough side of one's

tongue, tongue-lashing, lambasting, hard words, cutting words, bitter words (see also *reprimand* below); silent reproach, disapproving look, old-fashioned look, dirty look, black look 893 *sullenness*.

reprimand, remonstrance 762 *deprecation*; stricture, animadversion, reprehension, reprobation; censure, rebuke, flea in one's ear, reproof, snub; rocket, raspberry; piece of one's mind, expression of displeasure, mark of displeasure, black mark; castigation, correction, rap over the knuckles, smack *or* slap on the wrist, box on the ears 963 *punishment*; inculpation, admonition, admonishment, tongue-lashing, chiding, talking-to, upbraiding, scolding, slating, strafing, trouncing, lambasting, dressing-down, blowing-up, roasting, wigging, carpeting; lecture, curtain lecture.

disapprover, no admirer, no fan; wet blanket, spoilsport, misery 834 *moper*; puritan, rigorist 950 *prude*; opponent, opposer, attacker 705 *opponent*; critic, hostile critic, knocker, fault-finder, carper, caviller, castigator, censurer, censor; lampooner, mocker 926 *detractor*; grouser, grouch 829 *malcontent*; Eurosceptic.

Adj. *disapproving*, unapproving, not amused; shocked, scandalized; unimpressed; disillusioned 509 *disappointed*; sparing of praise, grudging; silent 582 *uncommunicative*; unfavourable, hostile 881 *hostile*; objecting, protesting, deprecatory; reproachful, chiding, scolding, upbraiding, vituperative, lambasting; critical, unflattering, uncomplimentary; withering, hard-hitting, pulling no punches, strongly worded; overcritical, hypercritical, captious, fault-finding, niggling, carping, cavilling; disparaging, defamatory, damaging; caustic, sharp, bitter, venomous, trenchant, mordant; sarcastic, sardonic, cynical; censorious, holier than thou; blaming, faulting, censuring, reprimanding, recriminative, denunciatory, accusatory, condemning, damning, damnatory.

blameworthy, blamable, open to criticism, censurable, condemnable 645 *bad*; reprehensible, dishonourable, unjustifiable 867 *discreditable*; unpraiseworthy, uncommendable, not to be thought of; reprobate, culpable, to blame.

Vb. *disapprove*, hold no brief for, have no regard for, not think much of, think little of, take a dim view of; think the worse of, think ill of 922 *despise*; not pass, fail, plough; return 607 *reject*; disallow 757 *prohibit*; cancel 752 *annul*; censor 550 *obliterate*; withhold approval, look grave, shake one's head, not hold with 489 *dissent*; disfavour, reprehend, lament, deplore 830 *regret*; abhor, reprobate 861 *dislike*; wash one's hands of, turn one's back on, disown, look askance, avoid, ignore; keep at a distance, draw the line, ostracize, ban, bar, blacklist 57 *exclude*; protest, tut-tut, sniff, remonstrate, object, take exception to, demur 762 *deprecate*; discountenance, show disapproval, exclaim, shout down, bawl down, hoot, boo, bay, heckle, hiss, whistle, give a slow handclap, give the bird, drive off the stage; hand out brickbats, throw mud, throw rotten eggs, throw bricks *or* stones; hound, chase, mob, lynch; make a face, grimace, make a moue, make mouths at, spit; look black; sullen; look daggers 891 *be angry*.

criticize, not recommend, give no marks *or* points to, damn with faint praise, damn 961 *condemn*; fault, find fault, pick holes, niggle, cavil, carp, nitpick, deprecate, run down, belittle 926 *detract*; oppose, tilt at, shoot at, throw the book at 712 *attack*; weigh in, pitch into, hit out at, let fly, lay into, lam into, savage, maul, slash, slate, lambast, scourge, flay, put the boot in; inveigh, thunder, fulminate, storm against, rage against 61 *rampage*; shout down, cry shame, slang, call names; gird, rail, revile, abuse, heap abuse, pour vitriol, objurgate, execrate 899 *curse*; vilify, blacken, denigrate 926 *defame*; stigmatize, brand, pillory; expose, denounce, recriminate 928 *accuse*; sneer, twit, taunt 921 *not respect*.

reprove, reprehend, reproach, rebuke, administer a rebuke, snub, rebuff, send away with a flea in the ear; call to order, caution, wag one's finger, read the Riot Act 664 *warn*; book, give one a black mark; censure, reprimand, take to task, rap over the knuckles, smack *or* slap the wrist, box the ears; tick off, tell off, have one's head for, carpet, have on the carpet, haul over the coals, send before the beak; remonstrate, expostulate, admonish, castigate, chide, correct; lecture, read one a lecture, give one a talking to, give one a wigging, give one a dressing-down, lambast, trounce, roast, browbeat, blow up, tear strips off, come down hard on, come down on like a ton of bricks, chastise 963 *punish*.

blame, find fault, carp, cavil, nitpick, pick holes in; get at, henpeck; reprehend, hold to blame, pick on, put the blame on, hold responsible; throw the first stone, inculpate, incriminate, complain against, impute, impeach, charge, criminate 928 *accuse*; round on, return the charge, recriminate 714 *retaliate*; think the worst of 961 *condemn*.

reproach, heap reproaches on; upbraid, slate, rate, berate, rail, slag, strafe, shend, lambast, revile, abuse, denigrate, blackguard 899 *curse*; go for, inveigh against, bawl out, scold, tongue-lash, lash, give the rough edge of one's

tongue, rail in good set terms against, give one a piece of one's mind, give one what for, give it to one straight from the shoulder, give to one straight, not mince matters, not pull one's punches, let it rip.

incur blame, take the blame, take the rap, carry the can, catch it; be held responsible, have to answer for; be open to criticism, blot one's copy book, get a bad name 867 *lose repute*; be up on a charge, be carpeted, be up before the beak, be court-martialled, stand accused; stand corrected; be an example, be a scandal, scandalize, shock, revolt 861 *cause dislike*.

925 Flattery

N. *flattery*, cajolery, wheedling, getting round, blarney, blandishments, sweet talk; flannel, soft soap; adulation; voice of the charmer, honeyed words, sweet nothings 889 *endearment*; compliment, pretty speeches, bouquets; coquetry, winning ways; fawning, backscratching; obsequiousness, flunkeyism, sycophancy, toadying 879 *servility*; unctuousness, smarminess, euphemism, insincerity, hypocrisy, tongue in cheek, lip-homage 542 *sham*.

flatterer, adulator, cajoler, wheedler; coquette, charmer; tout, puffer, hyper, promoter, booster, claqueur, claque 923 *commender*; courtier, yes-man 488 *assenter*; creep, fawner, backscratcher, sycophant, parasite, minion, hanger-on 879 *toady*; fair-weather friend, hypocrite 545 *deceiver*.

Adj. *flattering*, overpraising, overdone; boosting, puffing, hyping, overpromoting; complimentary, overcomplimentary, full of compliments; fulsome, adulatory; sugary, saccharine; cajoling, wheedling, coaxing, blarneying, mealy-mouthed, glozing, canting; smooth-tongued, honey-tongued, bland; smooth, oily, unctuous, soapy, slimy, smarmy; obsequious, all over one, courtly, fawning, crawling, back-scratching, sycophantic 879 *servile*; specious, plausible, beguiling, ingratiating, insinuating; lulling, soothing; vote-catching, vote-snatching; false, insincere, tongue-in-cheek, unreliable 541 *hypocritical*.

Vb. *flatter*, deal in flattery, have kissed the Blarney Stone; compliment, hand out bouquets 923 *praise*; overpraise, overdo it, lard it on, lay it on thick, lay it on with a trowel, not spare one's blushes; puff, hype, promote, boost, cry up 482 *overrate*; adulate, burn incense to, assail with flattery, turn one's head; butter up, soften up, soft-soap; blarney, flannel; sweet-talk, sugar; wheedle, coax, cajole, coo; lull, soothe, beguile 542 *deceive*; humour, jolly along, pander to; gild the pill, sugar the pill, make things pleasant, tell people what they want to hear; blandish, smooth, smarm; make much of, be all over one 889 *caress*; fawn, fawn on, cultivate, court, pay court to, play the courtier, massage one's ego; smirk 835 *smile*; scratch one's back, backscratch, curry favour, make up to, suck up to; toady to, pander to 879 *be servile*; insinuate oneself, worm oneself into favour, get on the right side of, creep into one's good graces; flatter oneself, have a swollen *or* swelled head 873 *be vain*.

926 Detraction

N. detraction, faint praise, two cheers, understatement 483 *underestimation*; criticism, hostile criticism; destructive criticism, bad review, slating review, bad press 924 *disapprobation*; onslaught 712 *attack*; hatchet job; impeachment 928 *accusation*; exposure, bad light 867 *disrepute*; decrial, disparagement, depreciation, running down; sour grapes; lowering, derogation; slighting language, scorn 922 *contempt*; vilification, abuse, invective 899 *scurrility*; defamation 543 *untruth*; backbiting, cattiness, spite 898 *malevolence*; aspersion, reflection, snide remark; whisper, innuendo, insinuation, imputation, whispering campaign; smear campaign, mud-slinging, smirching, denigration, character assassination; brand, stigma; muck-raking, scandalmongering; disillusionment, cynicism 865 *lack of wonder*.

calumny, aspersion, slander, libel; false report 543 *untruth*; a defamation, defamatory remark, damaging report; smear, smear-word, dirty word 867 *slur*; offensive remark, personal remark, insult, taunt, dig at, brickbat 921 *indignity*; scoff, sarcasm 851 *ridicule*; sneer, sniff; caricature 552 *misrepresentation*; skit, lampoon 851 *satire*; scandal, scandalous talk, malicious gossip, bad mouth.

detractor, decrier, disparager, slighter; debunker, deflater, cynic; mocker, scoffer, satirizer, satirist, lampooner; castigator, denouncer, reprover, censurer, censor; no respecter of persons, no flatterer, candid friend, candid critic; critic, hostile critic, destructive critic, attacker; archcritic, chief accuser, impeacher 928 *accuser*; captious critic, knocker, fault-finder, carper, caviller, niggler, nit-picker, hair-splitter; heckler, barracker; Philistine; defamer, destroyer of reputations; hatchet man; smircher, smearer, slanderer, libeller; backbiter, gossiper, scandal-monger, muck-raker; gossip columnist, gutter press, chequebook journalist; denigrator, mudslinger; brander, stigmatizer; vituperator;

reviler; scold, poison pen.

Vb. detract, deprecate, disparage, run down, sell short; debunk, deflate, puncture, cut down to size 921 *not respect*; minimize 483 *underestimate*; belittle, slight, diss 922 *hold cheap*; sneer at, sniff at 922 *despise*; decry, cry down, rubbish, damn with faint praise, fail to appreciate 924 *disapprove*; find nothing to praise, criticize, knock, bad mouth, slam, fault, find fault, pick holes in, slate, pull to pieces, tear to ribbons 924 *criticize*; caricature, guy 552 *misrepresent*; lampoon, dip one's pen in gall 851 *satirize*; scoff, mock 851 *ridicule*; make catty remarks, get in a dig at; whisper, insinuate, cast aspersions.

defame, dishonour, damage, compromise, scandalize, degrade, lower, put to shame 867 *shame*; give a dog a bad name, lower *or* lessen one's reputation, destroy one's good name; denounce, expose, pillory, stigmatize, brand 928 *accuse*; libel, slander, traduce, malign; vilify, denigrate, blacken, tarnish, sully; reflect upon, put in a bad light; speak ill of, speak evil, gossip, badmouth, make scandal, talk about, backbite, talk behind one's back; discredit 486 *cause doubt*; smear, start a smear campaign, besmear, smirch, besmirch, spatter, bespatter, throw mud, fling dirt, drag in the gutter 649 *make unclean*; hound, witch-hunt 619 *hunt*; look for scandal, smell evil, muck-rake, rake about in the gutter 619 *pursue*.

927 Vindication

N. vindication, restoration, rehabilitation 787 *restitution*; triumph of justice, wrong righted; exoneration, exculpation, clearance 960 *acquittal*; justification, good grounds, just cause, every excuse; apologetics, self-defence, apologia, defence, legal defence, good defence; alibi, plea, excuse, whitewash, gloss 614 *pretext*; fair excuse, good excuse 494 *truth*; extenuation, palliation, mitigation, mitigating circumstance, extenuating circumstance, palliative 468 *qualification*; counterargument 479 *confutation*; reply, reply for the defence, rebuttal 460 *rejoinder*; recrimination, countercharge; accusation; bringing to book, poetic justice, just punishment 963 *punishment*.

Vb. vindicate, revenge 910 *avenge*; do justice to, give the devil his due; set right, restore, rehabilitate 787 *make restitution*; maintain, speak up for, argue for, contend for, advocate 475 *argue*; undertake to prove, bear out, confirm, make good, prove the truth of, prove 478 *demonstrate*; champion, stand up for, stick up for 713 *defend*; support, offer moral support 703 *patronize*.

justify, warrant, justify by the event, give

grounds for, provide justification, furnish an excuse, give one cause; put one in the right, put one in the clear, clear, clear one's name, free from blame, exonerate, exculpate, acquit; whitewash, varnish, gloss; salve one's conscience, justify oneself, defend oneself 614 *plead*; plead one's own cause, say in defence, rebut the charge, plead ignorance.

extenuate, excuse, make excuses for, make allowances; palliate, mitigate, soften, mince one's words, soft-pedal, slur, slur over, play down, downplay, gloss, gloss over, varnish, whitewash; take the will for the deed 736 *be lenient*.

928 Accusation

N. accusation, complaint, charge, home truth; censure, blame, stricture 924 *reproach*; challenge 711 *defiance*; counishcharge, recrimination 460 *rejoinder*; twit, taunt 921 *indignity*; imputation, allegation, information, denunciation; plaint, suit, action 959 *litigation*; prosecution, impeachment, arraignment, indictment, citation, summons; bill of indictment, true bill; gravamen, substance of a charge; case, case to answer, case for the prosecution 475 *reasons*; evidence.

false charge, trumped-up charge, put-up job, frame-up; false information, perjured testimony, false evidence; counterfeit evidence, plant; illegal prosecution; lie, libel, slander, scandal, stigma 926 *calumny*.

accuser, complainant, plaintiff, pursuer, petitioner, appellant, libellant, litigant; challenger, denouncer, charger; grass, supergrass, nark, copper's nark 524 *informer*; common informer, delator, relator, impeacher, indicter, prosecutor, public prosecutor, procurator fiscal; libeller, slanderer, calumniator, stigmatizer; hostile witness 881 *enemy*; the finger of suspicion.

accused person, the accused, prisoner, prisoner at the bar; defendant, respondent, co-respondent; culprit; suspect, victim of suspicion, marked man; slandered person, libellee, victim.

Vb. accuse, challenge 711 *defy*; taunt; point a finger at, finger, cast the first stone, throw in one's teeth, reproach 924 *reprove*; stigmatize, brand, pillory, cast a slur on, cast aspersions, defame; impute, charge with, saddle with, tax with, hold against, lay to one's charge, lay at one's door, hold responsible, make responsible; pick on, fix on, hold to blame, put the blame on, pin on, stick on, bring home to 924 *blame*; point at, expose, show up, name, name names 526 *divulge*; denounce, inform against, tell, tell on, clype, blab, squeal, sing, rat on,

split on, turn Queen's evidence 524 *inform*; involve, implicate, incriminate; countercharge, rebut the charge, turn the tables upon 479 *confute*; make one a scapegoat, shift the blame; admit the charge, plead guilty 526 *confess*; implicate oneself, lay oneself open.

indict, impeach, arraign, inform against, lodge a complaint, lay information against; complain, charge, bring a charge, file charges, swear an indictment 959 *litigate*; book, cite, summon, serve with a writ, prosecute, sue; bring an action, bring a suit, bring a case; haul up, send before the beak, have up, put on trial, put in the dock; throw the book at 712 *attack*; charge falsely, lie against 541 *be false*; frame, trump up a charge, use false evidence, cook the evidence, fake the evidence, plant the evidence 541 *fake*.

Adv. accusingly, censoriously.

929 Probity

N. probity, rectitude, uprightness, goodness, sanctity 933 *virtue*; stainlessness 950 *purity*; good character, moral fibre, honesty, soundness, incorruptibility, integrity; high character, nobleness, nobility, honourableness, decent feelings, finer feelings, tender conscience; honour, personal honour, sense of honour, honour among thieves, omertà, principles, high principles; conscientiousness 768 *observance*; scrupulousness, scrupulosity, punctiliousness, meticulousness 457 *carefulness*; ingenuousness, single-heartedness; trustworthiness, reliability, sense of responsibility; truthfulness 540 *truthfulness*; candour, plain-speaking 573 *plainness*; sincerity, good faith 494 *truth*; fidelity, faith, troth, faithfulness, trustiness, constancy 739 *loyalty*; clean hands, clear conscience 935 *innocence*; impartiality, fairness, sportsmanship 913 *justice*; respectability 866 *repute*; gentlemanliness, ladylikeness, chivalry; principle, point of honour, punctilio, code, code of honour, bushido 913 *right*; court of justice, court of honour, field of honour.

Adj. honourable, upright, erect, of integrity, of honour 933 *virtuous*; correct, strict; law-abiding, honest, on the level; principled, high-principled, above-board, on the up-and-up; scrupulous, conscientious, soul-searching; incorruptible, not to be bought off; incorrupt, immaculate 935 *innocent*; stainless, unstained, untarnished, unsullied 648 *clean*; noble, high-minded, pure-minded 950 *pure*; ingenuous, unworldly 699 *artless*; good, straight, straight as a die, square, on the square, one hundred per cent; fair, fair-dealing, equitable, impartial 913 *just*; sporting, sportsmanlike, playing the game; gentlemanly, chivalrous, knightly, jealous of one's honour; careful of one's reputation, respectable 866 *reputable*; saintly 979 *pious*.

trustworthy, creditworthy, reliable, dependable, tried, tested, proven; trusty, true-hearted, true-blue, true to the core, sure, staunch, single-hearted, constant, unchanging, faithful, loyal 739 *obedient*; responsible, duteous, dutiful 768 *observant*; conscientious, religious, scrupulous, meticulous, punctilious 457 *careful*; candid, frank, open, open and above-board, open-hearted, transparent, ingenuous, without guile, guileless 494 *true*; straightforward, truthful, truth-speaking, as good as one's word 540 *truthful*; unperjured, unperfidious, untreacherous.

930 Improbity

N. *improbity*, dishonesty; lack of principle; laxity; unconscientiousness 456 *inattention*; unscrupulousness, opportunism; insincerity, disingenuousness, unstraightforwardness, untrustworthiness, unreliability, undependability, untruthfulness 541 *falsehood*; unfairness, partiality, bias 914 *injustice*; shuffling, slipperiness, artfulness; suspiciousness, shadiness, deviousness, crookedness; corruption, sleaze, sleaze factor, corruptibility, venality, bribability, graft, palm-greasing, nepotism, simony, baseness, shabbiness, abjectness, debasement, shamefulness, disgrace, dishonour, shame 867 *disrepute*; worthlessness, good-for-nothingness, villainousness, villainy, knavery, roguery, rascality, spivvery, skulduggery, racketeering, black market, under-the-counter dealings; criminality, crime, complicity, aiding and abetting 954 *lawbreaking*; turpitude, moral turpitude 934 *wickedness*.

perfidiousness, perfidy, faithlessness, unfaithfulness, infidelity, unfaith 543 *untruth*; bad faith, divided allegiance, wavering loyalty, sitting on the fence, disloyalty 738 *disobedience*; running with the hare and hunting with the hounds, double-dealing, double-crossing, Judas kiss 541 *duplicity*; volte face, U-turn 603 *change of mind*; defection, desertion 918 *undutifulness*; betrayal, treachery, stab in the back, sell-out; treason, high treason 738 *sedition*; fifth column, Trojan horse; breach of faith, broken word, broken promise, breach of promise, cry of treason, dirty trick, stab in the back; not playing the game, foul, hitting below the belt 914 *wrong*; professional foul 623 *contrivance*; trick, shuffle, chicanery 542 *trickery*; sharp practice, 'heads I win, tails you lose'; dirty work, job, deal, racket; under-the-counter dealing, fiddle, wangle, manipulation, gerrymandering, hanky-panky, monkey business; tax evasion 620 *avoidance*; malversation 788 *peculation*; crime, felony 954 *lawbreaking*.

Adj. *dishonest*, not on the level 914 *wrong*; lying, economical with the truth; unprincipled, unscrupulous; shameless, dead to honour, lost to shame; unethical, immoral 934 *wicked*; untrustworthy, unreliable, undependable, not to be trusted; disingenuous, economical with the truth, untruthful 543 *untrue*; two-faced, insincere 541 *hypocritical*; creeping, crawling; artful, dodging, opportunist, slippery, foxy 698 *cunning*; shifty, shuffling, prevaricating 518 *equivocal*; designing, scheming; sneaking, underhand 523 *latent*; up to something, on the fiddle, wangling; not straight, bent, crooked, devious, tortuous, winding; insidious, dark, sinister; shady, fishy, suspicious, doubtful, questionable; fraudulent 542 *spurious*; illicit 954 *illegal*; foul 645 *bad*; unclean 649 *dirty*; mean, shabby, dishonourable, infamous 867 *disreputable*; derogatory, unworthy, undignified; inglorious, ignominious 867 *degrading*; ignoble, unchivalrous, ungentlemanly; unsporting, unsportsmanlike, unfair.

corruptible, venal, bribable, mercenary; palm-greasing, corrupt, grafting, nepotistic.

perfidious, treacherous, unfaithful, inconstant, faithless 541 *false*; double-dealing, double-crossing; disloyal; false-hearted, traitorous, treasonous, untrue 738 *disobedient*; plotting, scheming, intriguing; Machiavellian; cheating; fraudulent 542 *spurious*.

Vb. *be dishonest*, have no morals, yield to temptation, be lost to shame; lack honesty, live by one's wits, lead a life of crime 954 *be illegal*; fiddle, finagle, wangle, gerrymander, racketeer; defraud; cheat, swindle 542 *deceive*; betray, play false, do the dirty on, stab in the back; run with the hare and hunt with the hounds, double-cross 541 *dissemble*; fawn 925 *flatter*; break faith, break one's word, go back on one's promises, tell lies 541 *be false*; shuffle, dodge, prevaricate 518 *be equivocal*; sell out, sell down the river 603 *apostatize*; sink into crime, sell one's honour 867 *lose repute*; smack of dishonesty, smell fishy.

931 Disinterestedness

N. *disinterestedness*, impartiality, lack of bias 913 *justice*; selflessness, self-effacement 872 *humility*; self-sacrifice, martyrdom; loftiness of purpose, idealism; magnanimity; quixotry; purity of motive, labour of love; altruism, thought for others; charity 887 *love*.

Adj. *disinterested*, impartial, without self-interest, without bias 913 *just*; incorruptible, uncorrupted; unselfish, selfless, self-sacrificing; altruistic, philanthropic; undesigning; sacrificial, unmercenary, for love, non-profitmaking; idealistic, quixotic, lofty, elevated; magnanimous.

Vb. *be disinterested*, be unselfish, etc. (see adj.); sacrifice, sacrifice oneself; think of others, put oneself last, take a back seat 872 *be humble*; rise above petty considerations; have no axe to grind, have nothing to gain, have no ulterior motive, do for its own sake.

932 Selfishness

N. *selfishness*, self-love, self-admiration, narcissism, self-worship, self-praise 873 *vanity*; self-pity, self-indulgence, ego trip 943 *intemperance*; egocentrism, egocentricity, egomania; egoism, egotism; self-preservation, everyone for themselves; axe to grind, personal considerations, personal motives, private ends, personal advantage; self-seeking, self-aggrandizement, self-interest, looking after number one; no thought for others, 'I'm all right, Jack'; charity that begins at home, cupboard love; meanness 816 *parsimony*; greed, acquisitiveness, luxury fever 816 *avarice*; possessiveness 911 *jealousy*; 'heads I win, tails you lose' 914 *injustice*; selfish ambition; power politics.

egotist, self-centred person, egoist, narcissist 873 *vain person*; self-seeker; go-getter, adventurer; monopolist, dog in the manger, hog, road hog; opportunist.

Adj. *selfish*, egocentric, self-centred, wrapped up in oneself; egoistic, egotistic, egotistical; personal, concerned with number one; self-interested, self-seeking; self-indulgent 943 *intemperate*; narcissistic 873 *vain*; not altruistic; uncharitable, mean, acquisitive, mercenary 816 *avaricious*; covetous 912 *envious*; hogging, monopolistic 859 *greedy*; possessive, dog-in-the-manger; designing, axe-grinding; go-getting, on the make, on the gravy train, opportunist; materialistic.

Vb. *be selfish*, be egoistic, etc. (see adj.); put oneself first, think only of oneself, take care of number one; indulge oneself, spoil oneself; have only oneself to please; feather one's nest, look out for oneself, have an eye to the main chance, know on which side one's bread is buttered; keep for oneself, hog, monopolize, be a dog in the manger 778 *retain*; have personal motives, have an axe to grind; pursue one's interests, advance one's own interests, sacrifice the interests of others.

933 Virtue

N. *virtue*, virtuousness; goodness; saintliness, holiness, spirituality, odour of sanctity 979 *sanctity*; righteousness 913 *justice*; uprightness, rectitude, moral rectitude, character, integrity, principles, high principle, honour, etc. 929 *probity*; guiltlessness 935 *innocence*; morality,

ethics 917 *morals*; temperance, chastity 950 *purity*; straight and narrow path, virtuous conduct, christian conduct, good behaviour, well-spent life, duty done; clear conscience.

virtues, cardinal virtues, moral virtues; theological virtues: faith, hope, charity; natural virtues: prudence, justice, temperance, fortitude; qualities, saving grace; merits; perfections 646 *perfection*; nobleness, magnanimity.

Adj. *virtuous*, moral 917 *ethical*; good, good as gold 644 *excellent*; stainless 950 *pure*; guiltless 935 *innocent*; irreproachable, above reproach, impeccable, above temptation 646 *perfect*; saint-like, seraphic, angelic, saintly, holy 979 *sanctified*; high-principled, right-minded, on the side of the angels 913 *right*; righteous 913 *just*; upright, honest 929 *honourable*; dutiful 739 *obedient*; generous, magnanimous, philanthropic 897 *benevolent*; sober 942 *temperate*; chaste, virginal; proper, exemplary; meritorious, worthy, praiseworthy, commendable 923 *approved*.

Vb. *be virtuous*, be good, etc. (see adj.); have all the virtues, be a shining light 644 *be good*; behave, be on one's good *or* best behaviour; resist temptation 942 *be temperate*; have a soul above; keep to the straight and narrow path, follow one's conscience, fight the good fight; discharge one's obligations 917 *do one's duty*; go straight; hear no evil, see no evil, speak no evil; set a good example, be a shining example, shame the devil 644 *do good*.

934 Wickedness

N. *wickedness*, principle of evil 645 *badness*; Devil, cloven hoof 969 *Satan*; fallen nature, Old Adam; iniquity, sinfulness, sin 914 *wrong*; loss of innocence 936 *guilt*; ungodliness 980 *impiety*; amorality 860 *indifference*; hardness of heart 898 *malevolence*; naughtiness, bad behaviour 738 *disobedience*; immorality, turpitude, moral turpitude; loose morals, profligacy 951 *impurity*; degeneracy, degradation 655 *deterioration*; vice, corruption, depravity 645 *badness*; heinousness, flagrancy; bad character, viciousness, unworthiness, baseness, vileness; villainy; dishonesty 930 *improbity*; crime, criminality 954 *lawbreaking*; devilry, hellishness 898 *inhumanity*; devil worship 982 *idolatry*; scandal, abomination, enormity, infamy 867 *disrepute*; infamous conduct, misbehaviour, delinquency, wrongdoing, evil-doing, transgression, wicked ways, career of crime; primrose path, slippery slope; low life, criminal world, underworld, demi-monde; den of vice, sink of iniquity 649 *sink*.

vice, fault, demerit, unworthiness; human weakness, moral weakness, infirmity, frailty, human frailty, foible 163 *weakness*; imperfection, shortcoming, defect, deficiency, limitation, failing, flaw, fatal flaw, weak point, weakness of the flesh; transgression, trespass, injury, outrage, enormity 914 *wrong*; sin, besetting sin, deadly sin; seven deadly sins, pride, covetousness, lust, anger, gluttony, envy, sloth; venial sin, small fault, slight transgression, peccadillo, scrape; impropriety, indecorum 847 *bad taste*; offence 936 *guilty act*; crime, felony, deadly crime, capital crime, hanging matter 954 *illegality*.

Adj. wicked, unvirtuous, immoral; amoral, amoralistic 860 *indifferent*; unprincipled, unscrupulous 930 *dishonest*; callous; ungodly, irreligious, profane 980 *impious*; iniquitous 914 *unjust*; evil 645 *bad*; evil-minded, black-hearted 898 *malevolent*; evil-doing; misbehaving, bad, naughty 738 *disobedient*; erring, sinning, transgressing; sinful 936 *guilty*; unworthy; not in a state of grace, reprobate; unredeemed, irredeemable, accursed, godforsaken; hellish, infernal, devilish, fiendish, Mephistophelian, satanic 969 *diabolic*.

villainous, miscreant; vicious, steeped in vice, sunk in iniquity; good-for-nothing, ne'er-do-well; past praying for; unworthy, graceless; improper, indecent 847 *vulgar*; immoral; unvirtuous, intemperate 951 *unchaste*; profligate, dissolute, abandoned; corrupt, debauched, depraved, perverted, degenerate, sick, rotten, rotten to the core; brutalized, brutal 898 *cruel*.

morally weak, weak, frail, feeble 163 *weak*; having foibles, having a touch of human frailty, human, only human; easily tempted 661 *vulnerable*; not above temptation, not perfect, fallen 647 *imperfect*; slipping, sliding, recidivous.

heinous, grave, serious, deadly; abysmal, hellish, infernal; sinful, immoral, wicked 914 *wrong*; criminal, nefarious, felonious 954 *law-breaking*; monstrous, flagrant, scandalous, shocking, outrageous, obscene; gross, foul, rank; base, vile, abominable, accursed; despicable 645 *bad*; blameworthy, culpable; reprehensible, indefensible, unjustifiable 916 *unwarranted*; atrocious, brutal 898 *cruel*; unforgivable, unpardonable, inexcusable.

Vb. be wicked, be vicious, be sinful, etc. (see adj.); not be in a state of grace; fall from grace, spoil one's record, blot one's copybook, lapse, relapse, backslide; fall into evil ways, go to the bad *or* to the dogs 655 *deteriorate*; do wrong, transgress, misbehave, carry on, be naughty, sow one's wild oats, kick over the traces; trespass, offend, sin, commit sin; leave *or* stray from the straight and narrow, deviate

from the paths of virtue, err, stray, slip, trip, stumble, fall.

make wicked, corrupt, deform one's character, brutalize 655 *pervert*; mislead, lead astray, seduce 612 *tempt*; set a bad example, dehumanize.

935 Innocence

N. innocence, guiltlessness, clean hands; clear conscience, irreproachability; nothing to confess; blamelessness, freedom from blame, every excuse; declared innocence 960 *acquittal*; inexperience, unworldliness 699 *artlessness*; playfulness, harmlessness, inoffensiveness; freedom from sin, unfallen state, saintliness, purity of heart, state of grace 933 *virtue*; undefilement 950 *purity*; incorruptibility 929 *probity*; impeccability 646 *perfection*; days of innocence, golden age 824 *happiness*.

innocent, Holy Innocents, babe, newborn babe, babe unborn, babes and sucklings; child, ingénue; lamb, dove; angel, pure soul; milk-sop, goody-goody; one in the right, innocent party, injured party.

Adj. innocent, pure, unspotted, stainless, unblemished, spotless, immaculate 648 *clean*; uncorrupted, undefiled; unfallen, free from sin, unerring, impeccable 646 *perfect*; green, inexperienced, callow, naive, unversed in crime 491 *ignorant*; unworldly, guileless 699 *artless*; innocuous, harmless, inoffensive, playful, gentle, lamb-like, dove-like, child-like, angelic, saintly; wide-eyed, looking as if butter would not melt in one's mouth; innocent as a lamb *or* a dove *or* a child *or* a babe unborn; Arcadian.

guiltless, free from guilt, not responsible, not guilty, squeaky-clean 960 *acquitted*; more sinned against than sinning; falsely accused, wrongly accused, misunderstood; clean-handed, bloodless; blameless, faultless, unblameworthy, not culpable; irreproachable, above reproach, above suspicion; unobjectionable, unexceptionable, unimpeachable; pardonable, forgivable, excusable, venial.

Vb. be innocent, know no wrong; live in a state of grace, not fall from grace 933 *be virtuous*; have every excuse, have no need to blush, have clean hands, have a clear conscience, have nothing to be ashamed of, have nothing to confess; know no better.

936 Guilt

N. guilt, guiltiness, red-handedness; culpability; criminality, delinquency 954 *illegality*; sinfulness, original sin 934 *wickedness*; involvement, complicity, aiding and abetting; liability, one's fault; burden of guilt 702 *encumbrance*; blame, censure 924 *reproach*; guilt complex 503 *eccentricity*; guilty feelings, guilty conscience, bad conscience; guilty behaviour, suspicious conduct, blush, stammer, embarrassment; confession 526 *disclosure*; twinge of conscience, remorse, shame 939 *penitence*.

guilty act, sin, deadly sin, venial sin 934 *vice*; misdeed, wicked deed, misdoing, sinning, transgression, trespass, offence, arrestable offence, crime 954 *illegality*; misdemeanour, felony; misconduct, misbehaviour, malpractice; unprofessional conduct; indiscretion, impropriety, peccadillo; naughtiness, scrape; lapse, slip, faux pas, blunder 495 *mistake*; omission, sin of omission 458 *negligence*; fault, failure, dereliction of duty 918 *undutifulness*; injustice, injury 914 *wrong*; enormity, atrocity, outrage 898 *cruel act*.

Adj. guilty, found guilty, convicted 961 *condemned*; suspected, blamed, censured 924 *disapproved*; responsible 180 *liable*; in the wrong, at fault, to blame, culpable, chargeable; reprehensible, censurable 924 *blameworthy*; deadly 934 *heinous*; trespassing, transgressing, sinful 934 *wicked*; criminal 954 *illegal*; red-handed, caught in the act, flagrante delicto, caught with one's pants *or* trousers down; caught with one's hand in the till, caught bang to rights; hangdog, sheepish, shamefaced, blushing, ashamed.

Vb. be guilty, be at fault, be in the wrong, be to blame; have crimes to answer for, have blood on one's hands; be caught in the act, etc. (see adj.); have nothing to say for oneself, plead guilty 526 *confess*; have no excuse, stand condemned; trespass, transgress, sin 934 *be wicked*.

find guilty, blame 924 *blame*, 928 *accuse*; condemn, convict, judge, sentence, pass *or* pronounce judgment on 961 *condemn*; catch in the act, catch red-handed, catch with one's hand in the till, catch *or* have one bang to rights.

937 Good person

N. good person, sterling character; pillar of society, model of virtue, salt of the earth, shining light 646 *paragon*; Christian, true Christian; saint 979 *pious person*; angel 935 *innocent*; heart of gold; good neighbour, Good Samaritan 903 *benefactor*; one of the best, one in a million, the tops 890 *favourite*; hero, heroine 855 *brave person*; goody, good guy, good sort, good old boy, stout fellow, brick, trump, sport.

938 Bad person

N. bad person, no saint, sinner, hardened sinner, limb of Satan, Antichrist 904 *evildoer*;

fallen angel, lost sheep, lost soul; reprobate, scapegrace, good-for-nothing, ne'er-do-well, black sheep, the despair of; scallywag, scamp; rake, roué, profligate 952 *libertine*; wanton, hussy 952 *loose woman*; wastrel, waster, prodigal son 815 *prodigal*; scum; nasty type, ugly customer, undesirable, bad 'un, wrong 'un, thug, bully, boot boy, bovver boy, hitman, terrorist, roughneck 904 *ruffian*; bad lot, bad egg, bad hat, bad character, bad guy, baddy, villain; rotten apple; bad influence, bad example; bad child, naughty child, terror, holy terror, enfant terrible, monkey, little devil 663 *troublemaker*; knave, wretch, rascal, low-life 869 *low fellow*; rogue, criminal 904 *offender*; thief, pirate, freebooter 789 *robber*; villain, blackguard, scoundrel, miscreant; cheat, liar, crook, impostor, twister, conman 545 *trickster*; sneak, grass, supergrass, squealer, canary, rat 524 *informer*; renegade, recreant 603 *recanter*; betrayer, traitor, Quisling, Judas.

cad, utter cad, nasty bit of work, scoundrel, blackguard; rotter, out-and-out rotter, blighter, bastard, bounder, oik, jerk, heel, shit (vulg), slob, scab, sod, son of a bitch; stinker, skunk, dirty dog, filthy beast; pervert, degenerate; swine, rat, worm; louse, insect, vermin; pig, beast, cat, bitch.

monster, unspeakable villain; brute, savage, sadist; ogre 735 *tyrant*; fiend, demon, ghoul 969 *devil*; hellhound, fury; devil incarnate, ape-man, King Kong, Frankenstein *or* Frankenstein's monster, bogy *or* bogey. (See also 842 *eyesore*.)

939 Penitence

N. penitence, repentance, contrition, attrition, compunction, remorse, self-reproach 830 *regret*; confession 988 *Christian rite*; weight on one's mind, voice of conscience, uneasy conscience, guilty conscience, bad conscience, twinge of conscience 936 *guilt*; deathbed repentance, sackcloth and ashes, hair shirt, stool of repentance 941 *penance*; apology 941 *atonement*.

penitent, confessor; returned prodigal, a sadder and a wiser man; reformed character.

Adj. repentant, contrite, remorseful, regretful, sorry, apologetic 830 *regretting*; ashamed; weeping 836 *lamenting*; conscience-stricken, plagued by conscience; self-condemned; confessing; penitent, doing penance 941 *atoning*; chastened, sobered; reclaimed, reformed, converted, born again.

Vb. be penitent, repent, show compunction, feel remorse, feel shame, blush for shame, feel sorry, say one is sorry, express regrets, apologize; reproach oneself, blame oneself; go to confession 526 *confess*; do penance, repent in sackcloth and ashes 941 *atone*; bewail one's sins; beat one's breast, prostrate oneself; eat humble pie 721 *knuckle under*; rue, have regrets, wish undone 830 *regret*; have second thoughts, think better of; learn one's lesson, find out from bitter experience 536 *learn*; reform, be reformed, be a reformed character, be reclaimed, turn over a new leaf 654 *get better*; see the light, see the error of one's ways, be converted, return to the straight and narrow 147 *be turned to*.

940 Impenitence

N. *impenitence*, lack of contrition; refusal to recant, obduracy, stubbornness 602 *obstinacy*; hardness of heart 326 *hardness*; no apologies, no regrets, no remorse, no compunction 906 *pitilessness*; hardened sinner, despair of 938 *bad person*.

Adj. *impenitent*, unregretting; obdurate, inveterate, stubborn 602 *obstinate*; unrepentant; without regrets; unrelenting, relentless; without compunction, without remorse, remorseless, heartless 898 *cruel*; hard, hardened; conscienceless, unashamed, unblushing, brazen; incorrigible, irreclaimable, irredeemable, hopeless, despaired of, lost 934 *wicked*; unshriven; unreformed, unreconciled; unconverted.

Vb. *be impenitent*, make no excuses, offer no apologies, have no regrets, not wish things otherwise, would do it again; not see the light, not see the error of one's ways, refuse to recant 602 *be obstinate*; make no confession; stay unreconciled, want no forgiveness; feel no compunction, feel no remorse, harden one's heart, steel one's heart 906 *be pitiless*.

941 Atonement

N. *atonement*, making amends, amends, apology, satisfaction; reparation, compensation, indemnity, indemnification, blood money, conscience money 787 *restitution*; repayment, quits.

propitiation, expiation, satisfaction, reconciliation, conciliation 719 *pacification*; reclamation, redemption; sacrifice, offering, burnt offering, peace offering 981 *religious offering*; scapegoat, whipping boy 150 *substitute*.

penance, shrift, confession, acknowledgment 939 *penitence*; sacrament of penance, fasting, flagellation 945 *asceticism*; purgation; purgatory; penitent form, stool of repentance, cutty stool, corner 964 *pillory*; sackcloth and ashes, hair shirt, breast-beating 836 *lamentation*.

Adj. *atoning*, making amends 939 *repentant*; reparatory, compensatory, indemnificatory; conciliatory, apologetic; expiatory, purgatorial; sacrificial; penitential, penitentiary, doing penance 963 *punitive*.

Vb. *atone*, salve one's conscience, make amends, make reparation, indemnify, compensate, pay compensation, make it up to; apologize, make apologies, offer one's apologies; propitiate, conciliate 719 *pacify*; give satisfaction, offer satisfaction 787 *make restitution*; make up for, make *or* put matters right; sacrifice to, offer sacrifice; expiate, pay the penalty, pay the forfeit, pay the cost; become the whipping boy, make oneself the scapegoat 931 *be disinterested*.

do penance, undergo penance; pray, fast, flagellate oneself, scourge oneself; suffer purgatory; put on sackcloth and ashes, don a hair shirt, rend one's garments, stand in the corner, sit on the stool of repentance; take one's punishment, swallow one's medicine 963 *be punished*; salve one's conscience, go to confession 526 *confess*.

942 Temperance

N. *temperance*, temperateness, nothing in excess 177 *moderation*; self-denial, asceticism, puritanism, Pleasure Deficiency Syndrome 931 *disinterestedness*, 945 *asceticism*; self-restraint, self-control, self-discipline, keeping a stiff upper lip, stoicism 747 *restraint*; continence, chastity 950 *purity*; soberness 948 *sobriety*; forbearance 620 *avoidance*; renunciation 621 *relinquishment*; abstemiousness, abstinence, abstention, total abstinence, teetotalism; prohibition, prohibitionism 747 *restriction*; vegetarianism, veganism, rawism; dieting 301 *dieting*, 946 *fasting*; frugality 814 *economy*; plain living, simple life, self-sufficiency, getting away from it all; frugal diet 945 *asceticism*.

abstainer, total abstainer, teetotaller, nondrinker 948 *sober person*; prohibitionist; non-smoker; vegetarian, veggie, demi-vegetarian, demi-veg, lacto-vegetarian, lacto-ovo-vegetarian, vegan, rawist; dropout; dieter, faster, slimmer, weight-watcher; Spartan 945 *ascetic*.

Adj. *temperate*, not excessive, within bounds, within reasonable limits; tempered, understated 177 *moderate*; plain, Spartan, sparing 814 *economical*; frugal 816 *parsimonious*; forbearing, abstemious, abstinent; dry, teetotal 948 *sober*; vegan, vegetarian, not self-indulgent, self-controlled, self-disciplined, continent 747 *restrained*; chaste 950 *pure*; self-denying 945 *ascetic*.

Vb. *be temperate*, be moderate, etc. (see adj.); moderate, temper, keep within bounds, avoid excess, know when one has had enough, know when to stop; keep sober 948 *be sober*; forbear, refrain, abstain 620 *avoid*; control oneself, contain oneself 747 *restrain*; deny oneself 945 *be ascetic*; take the pledge, go on the wagon; give up, swear off; ration oneself, restrict oneself, tighten one's belt, draw in one's belt 946 *starve*; diet, go on a diet 206 *make thin*.

943 Intemperance

N. *intemperance*, immoderation, abandon; excess, excessiveness, luxury 637 *redundancy*; too much 637 *superfluity*; wastefulness, extravagance, profligacy, waste, consumerism 815 *prodigality*; indiscipline, incontinence 734 *laxity*; indulgence, self-indulgence, overindulgence; addiction, bad habit 610 *habit*; drug habit 949 *drug-taking*; high living, dissipation, licentiousness, debauchery 944 *sensualism*; overeating, binge-eating 947 *gluttony*; excessive drinking, binge-drinking, intoxication.

Adj. *intemperate*, immoderate, excessive 637 *redundant*; unlimited 635 *plentiful*; wasteful, extravagant, profligate, spendthrift 815 *prodigal*; luxurious 637 *superfluous*; hedonistic, indulgent, self-indulgent, overindulgent, denying oneself nothing; unrestrained, uncontrolled, lacking self-control, undisciplined; incontinent 951 *unchaste*.

Vb. *be intemperate*, be immoderate, etc. (see adj.); roll in, luxuriate, wallow; lack self-control, want discipline, lose control 734 *be lax*; deny oneself nothing, indulge oneself, give oneself up to; kick over the traces, have one's fling, sow one's wild oats 815 *be prodigal*; run to excess, run riot, exceed 306 *overstep*; observe no limits, go to any lengths, stick at nothing, not know when to stop, overindulge, burn the candle at both ends 634 *waste*; live it up, go on a spree, go on a binge, go on a bender 837 *revel*; drink like a fish, drink to excess, be a heavy drinker 949 *get drunk*; eat to excess, gorge, overeat, binge, binge-eat, make oneself sick 947 *eat to excess*; be incontinent, grow dissipated 951 *be impure*.

944 Sensualism

N. *sensualism*, earthiness, materialism 319 *materiality*; sensuality, carnality, sexuality, the flesh; grossness, beastliness, bestiality, wallowing; craze for excitement 822 *excitability*; love of pleasure, search for pleasure, hedonism, epicurism, epicureanism 376 *pleasure*; voluptuousness, voluptuosity, softness, luxuriousness, dolce vita; luxury, lap of luxury 637 *superfluity*; full life, life of pleasure, high living, fast living, wine, women and song 824 *enjoyment*;

dissipation, abandon 943 *intemperance*; licentiousness, dissoluteness, debauchery 951 *impurity*; indulgence, self-indulgence, overindulgence, greediness 947 *gluttony*; eating and drinking 301 *feasting*; bingeing, orgy, Bacchanalia 837 *revel*.

sensualist, hedonist, playboy or -girl, pleasure-lover, thrill-seeker; luxury-lover, epicurean, bon vivant, bon viveur; epicure, gourmet, gourmand 947 *glutton*; hard drinker 949 *drunkard*; loose liver, profligate, rake 952 *libertine*; drug addict 949 *drug-taking*; degenerate, decadent; pig, swine, hog, wallower.

Adj. *sensual*, earthy, gross, unspiritual 319 *material*; fleshly, carnal, bodily; sexual, venereal 887 *erotic*; bestial, beastly, brutish, swinish, hoggish, wallowing; pleasure-giving 826 *pleasurable*; voluptuous, pleasure-loving, thrill-seeking, living for kicks; hedonistic, epicurean, luxury-loving, luxurious; pampered, indulged, spoilt, self-indulged, overindulged, featherbedded; overfed 947 *gluttonous*; high-living, fast-living, incontinent 943 *intemperate*; licentious, dissipated, debauched 951 *impure*; riotous, orgiastic, bingeing, Bacchanalian 949 *drunken*.

Vb. *be sensual*, be voluptuous, etc. (see adj.); live for pleasure, wallow in luxury, live off the fat of the land 730 *prosper*; indulge oneself, pamper oneself, spoil oneself, do oneself proud; run riot, live in the fast lane, burn the candle at both ends 943 *be intemperate*.

945 Asceticism

N. *asceticism*, ascesis, austerity, mortification, flagellation 941 *penance*; ascetic practice, yoga; anchoritism 883 *seclusion*; holy poverty 801 *poverty*; plain living, simple fare, Spartan fare 946 *fasting*; fast day 946 *fast*; self-denial, Pleasure Deficiency Syndrome 942 *temperance*; frugality 814 *economy*; Puritanism, sackcloth, hair shirt.

ascetic, yogi, fakir, dervish, fire-walker; hermit, anchorite, recluse 883 *unsocial person*; flagellant 939 *penitent*; faster 942 *abstainer*; Puritan; Spartan.

Adj. *ascetic*, yogic, self-mortifying, fasting, flagellating; hermit-like, anchoretic; puritanical; austere, rigorous 735 *severe*; Spartan.

Vb. *be ascetic*, live like a Spartan, live the simple life; fast 946 *starve*; live like a hermit, wear a hair shirt, put on sackcloth; lie on nails, walk through fire.

946 Fasting

N. *fasting*, abstinence from food; no appetite, anorexia, anorexia nervosa 651 *ill health*; cutting down 301 *dieting*; strict fast, hunger strike; lenten fare, bread and water, meagre diet, starvation diet; iron rations, short commons 636 *scarcity*; no food, starvation 859 *hunger*.

fast, fast day, Good Friday, Lent, Ramadan; day of abstinence; hunger strike 145 *strike*.

Adj. *fasting*, not eating, off one's food; abstinent 942 *temperate*; on hunger strike; without food, unfed, empty, with an empty stomach, supperless; poorly fed, half-starved 636 *underfed*; starved, starving, famished, famishing, ravenous, wasting away 206 *lean*; wanting food 859 *hungry*.

Vb. *starve*, famish 859 *be hungry*; waste with hunger, be a bag of bones; have no food, have nothing to eat, live on water, live on air 801 *be poor*; fast, go without food, abstain from food, eat no meat; keep Lent, keep Ramadan; give up eating, refuse one's food, go on hunger strike; eat less, diet, go on a diet, go on a crash diet, reduce, take off weight 37 *lessen*; tighten one's belt, go on short commons, live on iron rations; eat sparingly, make a little go a long way, control one's appetite 942 *be temperate*; keep a poor table 816 *be parsimonious*.

947 Gluttony

N. *gluttony*, greediness, greed, insatiability, voracity, voraciousness, wolfishness, hoggishness, piggishness; insatiable appetite 859 *hunger*; good living, high living, indulgence, overindulgence, overeating, binge-eating, overfeeding 943 *intemperance*; guzzling, gorging, bingeing, gormandizing, gluttonizing, epicureanism, epicurism, foodism, pleasures of the table 301 *gastronomy*; bust, binge, blowout, masses of food, groaning table 301 *feasting*.

glutton, glutton for food, guzzler, gormandizer, bolter, gorger, crammer, stuffer, binger; locust, wolf, vulture, cormorant, pig, hog; trencherman *or* -woman, good eater, hearty eater 301 *eater*; greedy-guts, greedy pig; gourmand, gastronome, gourmet, epicure, bon vivant, bon viveur.

Adj. *gluttonous*, greedy; devouring, voracious, wolfish; omnivorous 464 *undiscriminating*; insatiable, never full 859 *hungry*; eating one's fill 301 *feeding*; guzzling, gorging, bingeing, stuffing, cramming, licking one's lips, licking one's chops, drooling, watering at the mouth; gastronomic, epicurean.

Vb. *eat to excess*, gluttonize, guzzle, bolt, wolf, gobble, gobble up, devour, gulp down; fill oneself, gorge, cram, stuff, binge; overeat, binge-eat 301 *eat*; eat one's head off, eat out of house and home; have a good appetite, be a good trencherman *or* -woman; eat like a trooper, eat like a horse, eat like a pig, have

eyes bigger than one's stomach; make oneself sick; tickle one's palate; lick one's lips, lick one's chops, water at the mouth, drool at the sight of food; keep a good table; like one's food, live to eat, not eat to live, live only for eating.

948 Sobriety

N. *sobriety*, soberness 942 *temperance*; teetotalism; clear head, unfuddled brain, no hangover; dry area.

sober person, moderate drinker; non-drinker, teetotaller, total abstainer 942 *abstainer*; temperance society, Alcoholics Anonymous; prohibitionist.

Adj. *sober*, abstinent, abstemious; off drink, drying out, on the wagon; teetotal, strictly TT, prohibitionist, dry; clearheaded, with a clear head, sober as a judge, stone-cold sober, sobered up, without a hangover; dried out, off the bottle.

Vb. *be sober*, be abstemious, etc. (see adj.); not drink, never touch drink, drink moderately 942 *be temperate*; give up drinking, dry out, come off (drugs), go on the wagon, give up alcohol, become teetotal, sign the pledge; go dry; hold one's liquor, keep a clear head, be sober as a judge; sober up, clear one's head, sleep it off.

949 Drunkenness. Drug-taking

N. *drunkenness*, excessive drinking, binge-drinking 943 *intemperance*; insobriety; weakness for liquor, fondness for the bottle; Dutch courage 855 *courage*; intoxication, inebriation; thick speech, slurred speech 580 *speech defect*; tipsiness, wooziness, staggering 317 *oscillation*; one for the road, deoch an doris *or* doch an dorris; getting drunk, one over the eight, one too many, drop too much, hard drinking; libations; hair of the dog that bit one; booze, liquor 301 *alcoholic drink, wine*; drinking bout, jag, lush, blind, binge, spree, bender, pub-crawl; Bacchus, Dionysos.

hangover; morning after the night before, thick head, sick headache, crapulence, crapulousness.

alcoholism, alcoholic addiction, alcohol abuse, dipsomania; delirium tremens, dt's, the horrors, heebie-jeebies, jimjams, pink elephants.

drug-taking, drug abuse, drug addiction, drug dependence, drug habit, habit, substance abuse 943 *intemperance*; smoking, snorting, freebasing, sniffing, glue-sniffing, hitting up, shooting up, injecting, main-lining; pill-popping, chasing the dragon.

drugs, drug, hard drug, soft drug, controlled

drug, recreational drug, substance, illegal substance; joint, reefer, spliff, roach; line, wrap; shot, fix; narcotic, dope, designer drug; nicotine 388 *tobacco*; cannabis, marijuana, ganja, hemp, hashish, hash, bhang, kef, pot, grass, whacky baccy, Acapulco gold, sinsemilla; cocaine, coke, basuco *or* basuko, snow, crack, rock, free-base, heroin, horse, junk, smack, scag, black tar, candy, nose candy, dogfood, gumball, Mexican mud, tootsie roll; methadone; downers; barbiturates, barbs, morphia, morphine, opium 658 *drug*; stimulant, pep pill, amphetamine, speed, purple hearts, dexies, uppers 821 *stimulator*; performance-enhancing drug; intoxicant, hallucinogen, LSD, lysergic acid diethylamide, acid, Ecstasy, Yaba, MDHA, phencyclidine, PCP, angel dust, mescalin, peyote, magic mushroom, drug addiction (see also *drug-taking* above); trip (see also *drug experience* below); drug-selling, cannabis café, drug-pushing (see also *drug-peddler* below); gateway substance; lifestyle drug, Viagra (tdmk); date rape drug, Rohypnol; drug rehabilitation, rehab; drug tsar.

drug-taker, drug-user, user, drug addict, dope fiend, freak, head, acid-head, coke-head, base-head, junkie, mainliner, acid-scorer, drug-scorer, stoner.

drug-peddler, drug-dealer, drug-pusher, pusher, dope-peddler, drug-baron, drug-carrier, mule, drug mule, stuffer; narcoterrorist; drug-peddling, drug-pushing, drug traffic; narcoterrorism.

drug experience, trip, acid trip, bad trip, freak-out; drying-out, withdrawal symptoms, cold turkey, bogue.

drunkard, drunk, sot, lush; slave to drink, wino, alcoholic, recovering alcoholic, dipsomaniac, dipso; drinker, social drinker, hard drinker, secret drinker; tippler, toper, boozer, swiller, old soak; tosspot, barfly; pub-crawler.

Adj. *drunk*, inebriated, intoxicated, under the influence, having had a drop too much; in one's cups, in liquor, the worse for liquor; half-seas over, three sheets to the wind, one over the eight; boozed up, ginned up, liquored up, lit up, flushed, merry, happy, high; full, fou, tanked up, bevvied up.

tipsy, tiddly, squiffy, tight, half-cut, pissed, Brahms and Liszt; well-oiled, pickled, canned, bottled, stewed, well-lubricated; pixilated, fuddled; maudlin; tired and emotional, drunken, boozy, muzzy, woozy, pie-eyed; reeling, staggering; hiccupping.

dead drunk, smashed, sloshed, sozzled, soaked, soused, plastered, stinko, stoned, out of it; blind drunk, blind, blotto; legless, paralytic, stocious; shit-faced (vulg); in a drunken stupor; under the table; drunk as a lord; pissed as a newt, fou as a coot *or* a wulk (Scots) ; roaring drunk, drunk and disorderly 61 *disorderly*.

hung over, with a hangover, crapulous, crapulent, with a thick head; dizzy, giddy, sick.

drugged, doped, high, zonked, spaced out, freaked out, in a trance; stoned 375 *insensitive*; loved up, turned on, hooked on drugs, addicted.

drunken, never sober; gin-sodden; boozy, beery; fond of a drink, having a drink problem; tippling, boozing, toping, swilling, hard-drinking; pub-crawling; gouty, given to drink, a slave to drink, addicted to drink, on the bottle, alcoholic, dipsomaniac.

intoxicating, inebriating; exhilarating, going to the head, heady, winy, like wine 821 *exciting*; stimulant, intoxicant; opiate, narcotic; hallucinatory, psychedelic, psychotropic, mind-bending, mind-blowing; addictive, habit-forming; alcoholic, spirituous, vinous, beery; hard, potent, double-strength, over-proof 162 *strong*; neat 44 *unmixed*.

Vb. *be drunk*, be tipsy, etc. (see adj.); be under the influence of liquor, be under the influence, have had too much, have had one too many; have a weak head, not hold one's liquor, not walk straight, lurch, stagger, reel 317 *oscillate*.

get drunk, have too much, have one over the eight, drink like a fish; liquor up, tank up, crack a bottle, knock back a few, bend one's elbow, lush, bib, tipple, fuddle, booze, tope, swill, souse, hit the bottle 301 *drink*; go on the spree, go on a blind *or* a bender, go pub-crawling; drown one's sorrows; quaff, carouse, wassail.

drug oneself, take drugs, smoke, sniff, snort, inject oneself, shoot, shoot up, mainline; turn on, take a trip, blow one's mind; freak out.

950 Purity

N. *purity*, faultlessness 646 *perfection*; innocence; moral purity, morals, morality 933 *virtue*; decency, propriety, delicacy 846 *good taste*; shame, bashfulness 874 *modesty*; chastity 942 *temperance*; frigidity 820 *moral insensibility*; honour, one's honour; virginity, maidenhood, maidenhead 895 *celibacy*; prudery, prudishness; false modesty 874 *modesty*; demureness, gravity 834 *seriousness*; priggishness, primness, coyness 850 *affectation*; sanctimoniousness 979 *show of piety*; Puritanism; euphemism, Grundyism, genteelism, mealy-mouthedness; censorship, expurgation, bowdlerization 550 *obliteration*.

virgin, maiden, vestal virgin, virgo intacta, maid, old maid, spinster 895 *celibate*; religious celibate 986 *monk, nun*; virtuous woman.

prude, prig, Victorian, euphemist; Puritan, wowser; guardian of morality, censor, Watch Committee, Mrs Grundy.

Adj. pure, faultless 646 *perfect*; undefiled, unfallen 935 *innocent*; maidenly, virgin, virginal, vestal, untouched; modest; coy, shy; chaste 942 *temperate*; impregnable, incorruptible 929 *honourable*; frigid 380 *cold*; immaculate, spotless, snowy 427 *white*; good, moral 933 *virtuous*; Platonic, purified; decent, decorous, delicate, refined 846 *tasteful*; censored, bowdlerized, expurgated.

prudish, squeamish, shockable, Victorian; prim 850 *affected*; straitlaced, narrow-minded, puritan, priggish; holy, sanctimonious 979 *pietistic*.

951 Impurity

N. impurity, impure thoughts, filthiness, defilement 649 *uncleanness*; indelicacy 847 *bad taste*; indecency, immodesty, shamelessness, exhibitionism; coarseness, grossness, nastiness; ribaldry, bawdiness, salaciousness; blue joke; double entendre; smut, dirt, filth, obscenity, obscene literature, adult literature, erotic literature, erotica; explicit lyrics; pornography, hard-core pornography, porn, soft porn, page 3, girlie magazine; blue film, skin flick, video nasty, hentai; prurience.

unchastity, promiscuity, wantonness; easy virtue, amorality; permissive society 734 *laxity*; vice, immorality; prurience, lust 859 *sexual urge*; carnality, sexuality, eroticism, the flesh 944 *sensualism*; sexiness, lasciviousness, lewdness, salacity, lubricity; dissoluteness, dissipation, debauchery, licentiousness, licence, libertinism; seduction, defloration; lechery, fornication, womanizing, whoring, screwing around, sleeping around; harlotry, whorishness.

illicit love, unlawful desires, forbidden fruit; extramarital relations; incest; perversion, pederasty, buggery, anal intercourse, sodomy, bestiality; satyriasis, priapism, nymphomania; paedophilia, grooming; masturbation, onanism, etc. 376 *sexual pleasure*; adultery, unfaithfulness, infidelity, marital infidelity, cuckolding, cuckoldry; eternal triangle, liaison, intrigue, amour, seduction 887 *love affair*; free love, living together; wife-swapping, sharing, swinging, dogging.

rape, ravishment, violation, indecent assault, grope; date rape, acquaintance rape, stranger rape, drug rape; date rape drug, Rohypnol; gang rape, gang bang; sexual abuse, sex crime.

social evil, prostitution, harlotry, hooking, sex industry, soliciting, streetwalking, survival sex, whoredom, the oldest profession, Mrs Warren's profession; pimping, pandering, brothel-keeping, living on immoral earnings; white slave traffic; sex tourism; vice squad; indecent exposure, exposing oneself, flashing.

brothel, bordello, whorehouse, bawdyhouse, cathouse, disorderly house, house of ill fame *or* ill repute; knocking-shop; red-light district, tolerance zone.

Adj. impure, defiled, unclean; unwholesome 653 *unhealthy*; vulgar, coarse, gross; ribald, loose; strong, racy, bawdy, Rabelaisian; uncensored, unexpurgated, unbowdlerized, explicit; suggestive, Freudian, provocative, piquant, titillating, near the knuckle, near the bone; spicy; immoral, risqué, nudge-nudge wink-wink; naughty, wicked, blue; unmentionable, unquotable, unprintable; smutty, filthy, scatological, offensive; indecent, obscene, lewd, salacious; licentious, pornographic, adult, top-shelf; prurient, erotic, priapic; sexual, sexy, hot.

unchaste, unvirtuous 934 *villainous*; fallen, seduced; of easy virtue, of loose morals, amoral, immoral; light, wanton, loose, fast, naughty; wild, rackety; immodest, daring, revealing; unblushing, shameless, brazen, flaunting, scarlet, meretricious, whorish, tarty; promiscuous, sleeping around, screwing around; street-walking, on the game.

lecherous, carnal; libidinous, lustful, goatish; prurient; on *or* in heat, rutting; turned-on, hot, horny, randy; oversexed, sex-mad, sex-crazy, nymphomaniac; perverted, bestial; lewd, licentious, libertine; depraved, debauched, dissolute, dissipated, profligate 934 *villainous*.

Vb. be impure, be unchaste, etc. (see adj.); have no morals; be unfaithful, commit adultery, cuckold; be dissipated 943 *be intemperate*; fornicate, womanize, whore, keep a mistress, have a lover; lech, lust, rut, be on heat, be hot, have the hots 859 *desire*; be promiscuous, sleep around, screw around; become a prostitute, become a hooker, become a rent-boy, street-walk, be on the streets; pimp, pander, procure, keep a brothel.

debauch, defile, smirch 649 *make unclean*; proposition, seduce, lead astray; have one's way with; dishonour, deflower, disgrace 867 *shame*; prostitute, make a whore of; lay, screw, knock off, bed, go to bed with, lie with, sleep with 45 *unite with*; rape, ravish, violate, molest, abuse, interfere with, assault, indecently assault, sexually abuse.

952 Libertine

N. libertine, philanderer, flirt; free-lover, fast man *or* woman, gay dog, rip, rake, roué, debauchee 944 *sensualist*; lady-killer, gallant; fancy man, gigolo, sugar daddy; seducer, deceiver, gay deceiver, Lothario; co-respondent, adulterer; cuckolder, bed-hopper, wife-swapper, sharer, swinger; Don Juan, Casanova; wolf, kerb-crawler; woman-izer, fornicator, stud; whoremonger, whore-master; voyeur, lecher, flasher, satyr, goat, dirty old man, DOM; sex maniac; rapist; male prostitute, rent-boy; paedophile, pederast, sodomite, pervert 84 *nonconformist*.

loose woman, wanton, easy lay, anybody's; fast woman, sexpot, hot stuff; woman of easy virtue, one no better than she should be; flirt, bit, bint, wench, floozy, jade, hussy, minx, nymphet, sex kitten, Lolita, groupie; baggage, trash, trollop, slut; tart, chippy, scrubber, slap-per, pickup; vamp, adventuress, temptress; seductress, femme fatale, scarlet woman, painted woman, Jezebel, Delilah; adulteress, other woman; nymphomaniac, nympho.

kept woman, fancy woman, mistress, para-mour, concubine; bit of fluff, bit on the side, floozie, doxy, moll.

prostitute, pro; white slave, fallen woman; harlot, trollop, whore, strumpet, ho; street-walker, woman of the streets, broad, hustler, hooker, scrubber, slapper, pickup, callgirl; courtesan; male prostitute, rent-boy, gigolo.

pimp, go-between, ponce, pander, procurer, procuress, bawd, brothel-keeper, madam; white slaver.

953 Legality

N. *legality*, due process 959 *litigation*; letter of the law, four corners of the law; respect for law, constitutionalism; judgment according to the law 480 *judgment*; keeping within the law, lawfulness, legitimateness, legitimacy, validity.

legislation, legislature, legislatorship, law-giving, law-making, constitution-making; legalization, legitimization, validation, ratifica-tion, confirmation 532 *affirmation*; passing into law, enacting, enactment, regulation; plebiscite 605 *vote*; law, statute, ordinance, order, bylaw 737 *decree*; canon, rule, edict 693 *precept*.

law, the law; body of law, constitution, writ-ten constitution, unwritten constitution; char-ter, institution; statute book, legal code; Ten Commandments, Decalogue; penal code, civil code, Napoleonic code; written law, common law, unwritten law, natural law; canon law, ecclesiastical law; international law, law of nations, law of the sea, law of the air; cyber-law; law of commerce, commercial law, law of contract, criminal law, civil law, constitutional law, law of the land; arm of the law, legal

process 955 *jurisdiction*; writ, summons, law-suit 959 *legal trial*.

Adj. *legal*, lawful 913 *just*; law-abiding 739 *obedient*; legitimate, competent; licit, licensed, permissible, allowable; within the law, sanc-tioned by law, according to law, legally sound; statutory, constitutional; law-giving, legisla-tive; legislated, enacted, passed, voted, made law, ordained, decreed, ordered, by order; legalized, legitimized, decriminalized, brought within the law; actionable; pertaining to law, jurisprudential.

Vb. *be legal*, be legitimate, etc. (see adj.); stand up in law *or* court; come within the law, keep within the law, stay the right side of the law.

make legal, legalize, legitimize, decriminal-ize, validate, confirm, ratify, formalize 488 *endorse*; vest, establish 153 *stabilize*; legislate, make laws, give laws; pass, enact, ordain, enforce 737 *decree*.

954 Illegality

N. *illegality*, legal flaw, loophole, let-out, irregularity, error of law; wrong verdict, bad judgment 481 *misjudgment*; contradictory law; miscarriage of justice 914 *injustice*; wrong side of the law, unlawfulness; incompetence, illicit-ness, illegitimacy 757 *prohibition*.

lawbreaking, breach of the law, violation of the law, transgression, contravention, infringe-ment, encroachment 306 *overstepping*; trespass, offence, offence against the law, civil wrong; malpractice; dishonesty 930 *improbity*; crimi-nality 936 *guilt*; criminal activity, criminal offence, indictable offence, crime, capital crime, misdemeanour, felony; wrongdoing 914 *wrong*; computer crime 531 *Internet*; car crime 274 *car*; criminology.

lawlessness, outlawry; breakdown of law and order, crime wave 734 *anarchy*; summary justice, vigilantism; kangaroo court, gang rule, mob law, lynch law; riot, race riot, rioting, hooliganism, ruffianism, rebellion 738 *revolt*; coup d'état, usurpation 916 *unjustifed claim*; arbitrary rule, abolition of law; martial law; mailed fist, jackboot 735 *brute force*.

illegitimacy; bastardy, bastardization; bas-tard, illegitimate child, natural child, love child, by-blow; bar *or* bend *or* baton sinister.

Adj. *illegal*, illegitimate, illicit; contraband, black-market, hot; impermissible, verboten 757 *prohibited*; unauthorized, incompetent, without authority, unwarrantable, informal, unofficial; unlawful, wrongful 914 *wrong*; unlegislated, exceeding the law; unchartered, unconstitutional, unstatutory; suspended, null and void, nullified, annulled; irregular; extra-judicial; on the wrong side of the law, against the law; outside or outwith the law, outlawed, out of bounds; actionable, punishable.

lawbreaking, trespassing, transgressing, infringing, encroaching; sinning 934 *wicked*; offending 936 *guilty*; criminal, felonious; fraudulent, shady 930 *dishonest*.

lawless, chaotic; ungovernable, licentious; violent, summary; arbitrary, irresponsible, unanswerable, unaccountable; without legal backing, unofficial, cowboy; above the law; despotic, tyrannical 735 *oppressive*.

illegitimate, bastard, spurious; born out of wedlock, born on the wrong side of the blanket; without a father, without a name, without benefit of clergy; bastardized.

Vb. *be illegal*, be against the law, break the law; circumvent the law; be lawless, defy the law, drive a coach and horses through the law 914 *do wrong*; take the law into one's own hands, exceed one's authority, encroach; stand above the law; stand outside the law.

make illegal, make unlawful, etc. (see adj.); outlaw; criminalize 757 *prohibit*; forbid by law, penalize 963 *punish*; bastardize; suspend, annul, cancel, make the law a dead letter 752 *annul*.

955 Jurisdiction

N. *jurisdiction*, portfolio 622 *function*; judicature, magistracy, commission of the peace; mayoralty; competence, legal competence, legal authority, arm of the law 733 *authority*; administration of justice, legal administration, Home Office; local authority, corporation, municipality, county council, regional council, district council, parish council, community council, bailiwick 692 *council*; vigilance committee, watch committee 956 *tribunal*; office, bureau, secretariat 687 *workshop*; legal authority, competence, cognizance 751 *mandate*.

law officer, legal administrator, Lord Chancellor, Attorney General, Lord Advocate, Solicitor General, Queen's Proctor; Crown Counsel, public prosecutor; judge advocate, procurator fiscal, district attorney 957 *judge*; mayor, lord mayor, provost, lord provost, sheriff 733 *position of authority*; court officer, clerk of the court, bailiff; summoner, Bow Street runner; beadle, mace-bearer 690 *official*.

police, forces of law and order, long arm of the law; police force, the force, the fuzz, Old Bill, the boys in blue; Scotland Yard; constabulary, gendarmerie, Garda, military police, transport police; police officer, limb of the law, policeman or -woman, constable, community policeman, special constable, copper, cop, traffic cop, patrolman or -woman; bobby, flatfoot, rozzer, pig, smokey bear, flic; sergeant,

police sergeant, inspector, police inspector, chief inspector, superintendent, super, police superintendant, chief superintendant, commissioner of police, commander, chief constable; military police, provost marshal; watch, posse comitatus; special patrol group, SPG; plain-clothes man, CID, dick 459 *detective*. (See also 459 *police enquiry*.)

956 Tribunal

N. *tribunal*, seat of justice, woolsack, throne; judgment seat, bar; confessional, Judgment Day; forum 692 *council*; public opinion, vox populi, electorate; judicatory, bench, board, bench of judges, panel of judges, judge and jury; judicial assembly; Justices of the Peace.

lawcourt, court, open court; court of law, court of justice, criminal court, civil court; Federal Court, High Court, Court of Justiciary; Sheriff Court, District Court, County Court; Supreme Court, appellate court, Court of Appeal; Court of Exchequer, Star Room; House of Lords 692 *parliament*; High Court of Justice, Queen's Bench, Queen's Bench Division, Court of Criminal Appeal; Admiralty Division; Probate Court, Divorce Court; Court of Chancery, court of equity, court of arbitration; Court of Common Pleas; circuit court; assizes; Court of Session, sessions, quarter sessions, petty sessions; Central Criminal Court, Old Bailey; magistrate's court, juvenile court, police court; coroner's court; court of record, feudal court, manorial court, Stannary Court, court baron, court leet; guild court, hustings; court-martial, summary court.

957 Judge

N. *judge*, justice, your Lordship, my lud or m'lud; justiciary, Lord Chancellor, Lord Chief Justice, Master of the Rolls, Lords of Appeal; military judge, Judge Advocate General; chief justice, puisné judge, county court judge, recorder, Common Serjeant, sessions judge, assize judge, circuit judge; district judge, subordinate judge; hanging judge; sheriff, sheriff substitute; magistrate, district magistrate, city magistrate, police magistrate, stipendiary magistrate; the beak, his or her Worship, his or her Honour, his or her nibs; coroner; honorary magistrate, justice of the peace, JP; bench, judiciary, magistracy; arbiter, umpire, referee, assessor, arbitrator, Ombudsman 480 *estimator*; Recording Angel 549 *recorder*; Solomon, a Daniel come to judgment.

jury, twelve good men and true; grand jury, special jury, common jury, petty jury, trial jury, coroner's jury; rigged jury; hung jury; juror's panel, jury list; juror, juryman or

-woman, jurat; foreman *or* forewoman of the jury.

958 Lawyer

N. *lawyer*, legal practitioner, solicitor, member of the legal profession, man *or* woman of law, legal eagle; civil lawyer, criminal lawyer; one called to the bar, barrister, barrister-at-law, devil, advocate, counsel, learned counsel; junior barrister, junior counsel; senior barrister, bencher, bencher of the Inns of Court; silk, leading counsel, King's Counsel, K.C., Queen's Counsel, Q.C.; serjeant, serjeant-at-law; circuit barrister; Philadelphia lawyer 696 *expert*; shyster, pettifogger, crooked lawyer; ambulance chaser.

law agent, attorney, public aattorney, attorney at law, proctor, procurator; Writer to the Signet, solicitor before the Supreme Court; solicitor, legal adviser; legal representative, legal agent, pleader, advocate; conveyancer.

notary, notary public, commissioner for oaths; scrivener, petition-writer; clerk of the court 955 *law officer*; solicitor's clerk, barrister's clerk, barrister's devil.

jurist, legal adviser, legal expert; pundit, legalist; student of law.

bar, civil bar, criminal bar, English bar, Scottish bar, junior bar, senior bar; Inns of Chancery, Inns of Court, Gray's Inn, Lincoln's Inn, Inner Temple, Middle Temple; barristership, advocacy.

Vb. *do law*, study law, go in for law, take up law; be called to the bar; take silk; practise at the bar, accept a brief, take a case, advocate, plead; practise law; devil.

959 Litigation

N. *litigation*, going to law, litigiousness 709 *quarrelsomeness*; legal dispute 709 *quarrel*; issue, legal issue; lawsuit, suit at law, suit, case, cause, action; prosecution, arraignment, impeachment, charge 928 *accusation*; test case 461 *experiment*; claim, counter claim 915 *what is due*; plea, petition 761 *request*; affidavit, written statement, averment, pleading, demurrer 532 *affirmation*.

legal process, proceedings, legal procedure, arm of the law 955 *jurisdiction*; citation, subpoena, summons, search warrant 737 *warrant*; arrest, apprehension, detention, committal 747 *restraint*; habeas corpus, bail, police bail, surety, security; injunction; writ.

legal trial, trial, justice seen to be done; trial by law, trial by jury, trial at the bar, trial in court, assize, sessions 956 *lawcourt*; inquest, inquisition, examination 459 *enquiry*; hearing, prosecution, defence; hearing of evidence, tak-

ing of evidence, recording of evidence 466 *evidence*; examination, cross-examination; objection sustained, objection overruled 466 *testimony*; pleadings, arguments 475 *reasoning*; counterargument, rebutter, rebuttal 460 *rejoinder*; proof 478 *demonstration*; disproof 479 *confutation*; summing-up, charge to the jury; ruling, finding, decision, verdict 480 *judgment*; majority verdict, hung jury; favourable verdict 960 *acquittal*; unfavourable verdict 961 *condemnation*; execution of judgment 963 *punishment*; appeal, motion of appeal; successful appeal, reversal of judgment, retrial; precedent, case law; law reports; case record, dossier 548 *record*.

litigant, litigator, party, party to a suit, suitor 763 *petitioner*; claimant, plaintiff, pursuer, defendant, appellant, respondent, objector, intervener; accused, prisoner at the bar 928 *accused person*; prosecutor 928 *accuser*.

Vb. *litigate*, go to law, appeal to law, set the law in motion, institute legal proceedings, bring a suit, file a suit, petition 761 *request*; prepare a brief, brief counsel; file a claim, contest at law 915 *claim*; have the law on one, take one to court, haul before the court, have one up, sue, arraign, impeach, accuse, charge, prefer charges, press charges 928 *indict*; cite, summon, serve notice on; prosecute, put on trial, bring to justice, bring to trial; call evidence 475 *argue*.

try a case, put down for hearing; call witnesses, examine, cross-examine, take statements; sit in judgment, rule, find, decide, adjudicate 480 *judge*; sum up, charge the jury; bring in a verdict, pronounce sentence; commit for trial.

stand trial, come up for trial, be put on trial, stand in the dock; plead guilty, plead not guilty; submit to judgment, hear sentence; defend an action.

960 Acquittal

N. *acquittal*, favourable verdict, verdict of not guilty, verdict of not proven, benefit of the doubt; clearance, exculpation, exoneration 935 *innocence*; absolution, discharge; let-off, thumbs up 746 *liberation*; white-washing, justification, compurgation 927 *vindication*; successful defence; case dismissed; no case, withdrawal of the charge, quashing, quietus; reprieve, pardon 909 *forgiveness*; nonprosecution, exemption, impunity 919 *non-liability*.

Adj. *acquitted*, not guilty, not proven 935 *guiltless*; clear, cleared, in the clear, exonerated, exculpated, vindicated; immune, exempted, exempt; let off, let off the hook, discharged, without a stain on one's character; reprieved; recommended for mercy.

Vb. *acquit*, find *or* pronounce not guilty *or* not proven, prove innocent, find that the case is not proven, justify, whitewash, get one off 927 *vindicate*; clear, absolve, exonerate, exculpate; find there is no case to answer, not press charges, not prosecute 919 *exempt*; discharge, let go, let off 746 *liberate*; reprieve, respite, pardon, remit the penalty 909 *forgive*; quash, quash the conviction, set aside the sentence, allow an appeal 752 *annul*.

961 Condemnation

N. *condemnation*, unfavourable verdict; conviction; successful prosecution; damnation, perdition; blacklist, Index 924 *disapprobation*; excommunication 899 *curse*; doom, judgment, sentence 963 *punishment*; writing on the wall 511 *omen*; outlawry, price on one's head, proscription, attainder; death warrant, condemned cell, execution room, electric chair, Death Row; black cap, thumbs down.

Adj. *condemned*, found guilty, made liable; convicted, sentenced; sentenced to death; proscribed, outlawed, with a price on one's head; having no case, without a leg to stand on; damned, in hell.

Vb. *condemn*, prove guilty, bring home the charge; find liable, find against; find guilty, pronounce guilty, convict, sentence; sentence to death, put on the black cap, sign one's death warrant; reject one's defence, reject one's appeal 607 *reject*; proscribe, outlaw, bar, put a price on one's head 954 *make illegal*; blacklist 924 *disapprove*; damn, excommunicate 899 *curse*; stand condemned out of one's own mouth 936 *be guilty*; plead guilty, sign a confession, be verballed 526 *confess*.

962 Reward

N. *reward*, remuneration, recompense; meed, deserts, just deserts 913 *justice*; recognition, due recognition, acknowledgment, thanks 907 *gratitude*; tribute, bouquets, brownie points 923 *praise*; prize-giving, award, presentation, prize; Nobel Prize, Turner Prize, Booker Prize, Pulitzer Prize; crown, cup, shield, certificate, medal 729 *trophy*; consolation prize, booby prize; honour 729 *decoration*; birthday honours 866 *honours*; letters after one's name, peerdom 870 *title*; prize money, cash prize, jackpot; prize fellowship, scholarship, bursary, stipend, exhibition 703 *subvention*; reward for service, fee, retainer, refresher, honorarium, payment, payment in kind, remuneration, emolument, pension, salary, wage, wages, increment 804 *pay*; productivity bonus, performance-related

pay, overtime pay 612 *incentive*; perquisite, perks, expense account, fringe benefits; Green Shield Stamps, Air Miles; income, turnover 771 *earnings*; return, profit, margin of profit, bottom line 771 *gain*; compensation, indemnification, satisfaction; consideration, quid pro quo; comeuppance 714 *retaliation*; reparation 787 *restitution*; bounty, gratuity, golden handshake, golden parachute, redundancy money; commission, rake-off; golden handcuffs; tip, douceur, sweetener, pourboire, trinkgeld, baksheesh 781 *gift*; tempting offer 759 *offer*; golden hello, bait, lure, bribe 612 *incentive*; slush fund, hush money, protection money, blackmail.

Vb. *reward*, recompense; award, give a prize, offer a reward; bestow a medal, honour with a title 866 *honour*; recognize, acknowledge, pay tribute, hand out bouquets, thank, show one's gratitude 907 *be grateful*; remunerate 804 *pay*; satisfy, tip 781 *give*; repay, requite 714 *retaliate*; compensate, indemnify, make reparation 787 *make restitution*; offer a bribe, grease the palm, win over 612 *bribe*.

be rewarded, win a prize, get a medal, receive a title; be given an honorarium, get paid, draw a salary, earn an income, have a gainful occupation 771 *acquire*; accept payment 782 *receive*; take a bribe, have one's palm greased; have one's reward, get one's deserts, receive one's due 915 *deserve*; get one's comeuppance; reap a profit 771 *gain*.

963 Punishment

N. *punishment*, sentence 961 *condemnation*; execution of sentence; chastisement, heads rolling, zero tolerance; castigation, carpeting 924 *reprimand*, disciplinary action; dose, pill, bitter pill, infliction, trial, visitation, carrying the can 731 *adversity*; just deserts, meet reward, comeuppance 915 *what is due*; doom, judgment, day of judgment, day of reckoning, divine justice 913 *justice*; poetic justice, retribution, Nemesis; reckoning, repayment 787 *restitution*; requital, reprisal 714 *retaliation*; penance 941 *atonement*; hara-kiri, seppuku 362 *suicide*; penology.

corporal punishment, spanking, smacking, slapping, trouncing, hiding, beating, thrashing, licking, leathering, kicking, dusting, pasting, bashing, hammering, caning, whipping, flogging, birching, scourging, flagellation, punishment beating; ducking, keel-hauling; slap, smack, rap over the knuckles, box on the ear; drubbing, blow, buffet, cuff, clout, stroke, stripe 279 *knock*; kick; third degree, torture, breaking on the wheel.

capital punishment, death penalty, extreme

penalty, ultimate penalty 361 *death*; death sentence, death warrant; execution 362 *killing*; decapitation, beheading, guillotining; hanging, drawing and quartering; strangulation, garrotte; hanging, the long drop; electrocution, electric chair, hot seat; lethal injection; stoning; crucifixion, impalement, flaying alive; burning, burning at the stake; drowning, noyade; massacre, mass murder, mass execution, purge, genocide 362 *slaughter*; martyrdom, martyrization; lynching, lynch law, contract; judicial murder.

penalty, injury, damage 772 *loss*; imposition, task, lines, punishment exercise; sentence, tariff, three strikes and you are out, penalization; penal code, penology; community service, community service order, community punishment order, community sentence, community penalties; devil to pay, liability, legal liability 915 *what is due*; damages, costs, compensation, restoration 787 *restitution*; fining, fine, compulsory payment 804 *payment*; ransom 809 *price*; forfeit, forfeiture, sequestration, confiscation, deprivation 786 *expropriation*; keeping in, gating, imprisonment 747 *detention*; suspension, rustication; binding over 747 *restraint*; penal servitude, hard labour; transportation; expulsion, deportation 300 *ejection*; ostracism, sending to Coventry, banishment, exile, proscription, ban, outlawing, blackballing 57 *exclusion*; reprisal 714 *retaliation*.

Adj. *punitive*, penal, punitory; castigatory, disciplinary, corrective; vindictive, retributive; in reprisal; penalizing, fining; confiscatory, expropriatory; scourging, flagellatory, torturing 377 *painful*.

Vb. *punish*, afflict 827 *hurt*; persecute, victimize, make an example of 735 *be severe*; inflict punishment, take disciplinary action; give *or* teach one a lesson, discipline, correct, chastise, castigate; reprimand, rebuke, tell off, rap across the knuckles, smack on the wrist; throw the book at, come down hard on, come down on like a ton of bricks, give one what for; penalize, impose a penalty, sentence 961 *condemn*; exact retribution, settle with, get even with, pay one out *or* back 714 *retaliate*; settle, fix, bring to book, give one what was coming to him, give one his/her comeuppance; fine, forfeit, deprive, sequestrate, confiscate 786 *take away*; unfrock, demote, degrade, downgrade, reduce to the ranks, suspend 867 *shame*; stand in a corner, send out of the room; tar and feather, pillory, set in the stocks; duck, keelhaul; lock up 747 *imprison*; transport.

spank, slap, smack; cuff, clout, box on the

ears, rap over the knuckles, smack on the wrist; drub, trounce, beat, belt, strap, leather, lather, wallop, tan, cane, birch, whack, tan one's hide, give one a hiding, beat black and blue 279 *strike*.

flog, whip, horsewhip, thrash, hide, give a hiding, cudgel 279 *strike*; scourge, give one the cat; lash, birch, give one the birch, flay; flagellate.

torture, give the third degree; put on the rack, break on the wheel, kneecap, persecute, martyrize 827 *torment*.

execute, put to death 362 *kill*; lynch 362 *murder*; tear limb from limb; crucify; stone to death; shoot, fusillade; burn at the stake, send to the stake; necklace, give one a necklace; garrotte, strangle; hang, hang by the neck, string up, bring to the gallows; hang, draw and quarter; send to the scaffold, behead, decapitate, guillotine; electrocute, send to the chair, send to the hot seat; gas, put in the gas room; commit genocide, hold mass executions, purge, massacre, decimate 362 *slaughter*.

be punished, suffer punishment, take the consequences, be for the high jump, have it coming to one, get one's comeuppance, catch it, catch *or* get it in the neck; take the rap, face the music; take one's medicine; get what one was asking for, get one's deserts; kiss the gunner's daughter; pay the ultimate price; lay one's head on the block; come to the gallows, swing; die the death.

964 Means of punishment

N. *scourge*, birch, switch, cat, cat-o'-nine-tails, knout, quirt, rope's end, sjambok *or* shambok, whip, horsewhip; lash, strap, tawse, thong, belt; cane, rattan; paddle, stick, big stick, rod, ferule, ruler; bastinado; cudgel, cosh 723 *club*; a rod in pickle; rubber hose, bicycle chain, sandbag.

pillory, stocks, whipping post, ducking stool; corner, dunce's cap; stool of repentance, cutty stool; chain, ball and chain, irons 748 *fetter*; prison house 748 *prison*; home detention curfew, tagging.

instrument of punishment or torture, rack, thumbscrew, iron boot; scavenger's daughter, Iron Maiden, wheel; treadmill; torture room.

means of execution, scaffold, block, gallows, gibbet; cross; stake; breaking on the wheel; hemlock 659 *poison*; bullet; axe, guillotine, maiden, widow-maker; rope, noose; garrotte; necklace; impalement; electric chair, hot seat; death room, gas chamber, lethal injection; condemned cell, Death Row 961 *condemnation*.

Religion

965 Divineness

N. *divineness*, divinity, deity; godhead; divine principle, Brahma; mana; divine essence, the Good, the True and the Beautiful; love, Fatherhood; Brahmahood, nirvana; world soul; divine nature, God's ways, Providence; assumption, glorification; deification, apotheosis.

divine attribute, omnipresence 189 *presence*; omniscience, wisdom 490 *knowledge*; omnipotence, almightiness 160 *power*; timelessness, eternity 115 *perpetuity*; changelessness 153 *stability*; truth, sanctity, holiness, goodness, justice, mercy; transcendence, sublimity, supremacy, sovereignty, majesty, glory, light; glory of the Lord.

the Deity, God, Supreme Being, Alpha and Omega; the Almighty; the All-holy, the All-merciful; Ruler of Heaven and Earth, Judge of all men, Maker of all things, Creator, Preserver; name of God, ineffable name, Elohim, Yahweh, Jehovah, Adonai, I AM, Allah, Jah; Tetragrammaton; God of Abraham, God of Moses, Lord of Hosts, God of our fathers; God the Father, our Father; All-Father, Great Spirit; Krishna.

Jesus, Jesus Christ, Jesus of Nazareth, Jesu; God the Son, Son of God; the Only Begotten; Messiah, Son of David, the Lord's Anointed, Christ; Immanuel; Lamb of God, Son of Man; Son of Mary, Holy Infant, Christ Child, Child of Bethlehem; the Good Shepherd, Saviour, Redeemer, Friend; Lord, Master; Rock of Ages, Bread of Life; the Way, the Truth and the Life; Light of the World, Sun of Righteousness; King of Kings, Prince of Peace.

Saviour, Redeemer, Jesus (see also *Jesus* above); bodhisattva, Amitabha, Amida.

Holy Spirit, Holy Ghost, Paraclete, Comforter.

Adj. *divine*, holy, hallowed, sanctified, sacred, sacrosanct, heavenly, celestial; transcendental, sublime, ineffable; mystical, religious, spiritual, superhuman, supernatural, unearthly, not of this world.

godlike, divine, superhuman; omnipresent 189 *present everywhere*; immortal 115 *perpetual*; immutable, changeless 144 *permanent*; almighty, all-powerful, omnipotent 160 *powerful*; creative 160 *dynamic*; all-wise, all-seeing, all-knowing, omniscient 490 *knowing*; all-merciful, merciful; compassionate 905 *pitying*; holy, all-holy, worshipped 979 *sanctified*; sovereign 34 *supreme*; incarnate, in the image of God, deified; messianic, anointed; Christly, Christlike.

966 Deities in general

N. *deity*, god, goddess, deva, devi; the gods, the immortals; Olympian 967 *Olympian deity*; false god, idol; minor god, petty god, inferior god; demigod, half-god, divine hero, divine king; fetish, totem 982 *idol*; mumbo jumbo.

mythical deity, nature god *or* goddess, Pan, Flora; earth goddess, Gaia; mother earth, mother goddess, earth mother; fertility god, Adonis, Marduk, Atys; god of the underworld, Pluto, Dis 967 *underworld deity*; sky god, Zeus, Jupiter; storm god, Indra, wind god, Aeolus; sun god, Apollo, Hyperion, Helios, Ra, Mithras; river god, sea god, Poseidon, Neptune; war god *or* goddess, Mars, Ares, Bellona; god *or* goddess of love, Cupid, Eros, Venus, Aphrodite; household gods, Lares, Penates; the Fates 596 *fate*.

967 Pantheon: classical and non-classical deities

N. *classical deities*, gods and goddesses of Greece and Rome, Graeco-Roman pantheon; Homeric deities, Hesiodic theogony; primeval deities, Erebus, Nox; Ge, Gaia, Tellus, Uranus, Cronus, Saturn, Rhea, Ops; Pontus, Oceanus, Tethys; Helios, Sol, Hyperion, Phaethon; Titan, Atlas, Prometheus; Giant, Enceladus; the Fates, Parcae, Clotho, Lachesis, Atropos.

Olympian deity, Olympian, Zeus, Jupiter, Jove, president of the immortals; Pluto, Hades; Poseidon, Neptune; Apollo, Phoebus; Hermes, Mercury; Ares, Mars; Hephaestus, Vulcan; Dionysus, Bacchus; Hera, Juno; Demeter, Ceres; Persephone, Proserpina; Athena, Minerva; Aphrodite, Venus; Artemis, Diana; Eros, Cupid; Iris; Hebe.

underworld deity, chthonian deity, Ge, Gaia, Dis Pater, Orcus, Hades, Pluto, Persephone; Erectheus, Trophonius, Pytho; Eumenides, Erinyes, Furies.

lesser deity, Pan, Silvanus, Flora, Faunus, Silenus; Aurora, Eos; Luna, Selene; Aeolus, Boreas 352 *wind*; Triton, Nereus, Proteus, Glaucus; Ate, Eris, Bellona, Nike; Astraea; Muses, tuneful Nine, Erato, Euterpe, Terpsichore, Polyhymnia, Clio, Calliope, Melpomene, Thalia, Urania; Asclepius, Aesculapius; Hypnos, Somnus, Morpheus; Hymen; Hestia, Vesta; household gods, Lares, Penates; local god, genius loci.

nymph, wood nymph, tree nymph, dryad, hamadryad; mountain nymph, oread; water nymph, river nymph, naiad, water spirit, Undine; sea nymph, nereid, Oceanid; Thetis, Calypso, Callisto; Pleiades, Maia; Latona, Leto; siren 970 *mythical being*.

demigod, divine offspring, divine hero;

Heracles *or* Hercules; Dioscuri, Castor and Pollux *or* Polydeuces; Perseus, Achilles, Aeneas,
Memnon.

Hindu deities, Brahmanic deities, Vedic deities; Dyaus Pitar, Prithivi; Varuna (sky), Mitra
(light), Indra (thunder), Agni (fire), Surya
(sun); Trimurti, Brahma, Siva, Vishnu; Sakti,
Uma *or* Parvat, Kali *or* Durga; Ganesha (luck-
bringer), Karttikeya (fertility), Sarasvati (learning), Hanuman (monkey-god), Sitala
(smallpox), Manasa (snakes), Lakshmi (wealth
and fortune).

Egyptian deities, Nun, Atum; Shu (air), Tef-
nut (moisture), Nut (sky), Geb (earth), Osiris,
Isis, Set, Nephthys; Ra *or* Re, Amon-Ra *or*
Amun-Ra, Atum-ra, Aton; Horus, elder Horus,
Ra-Harakhte, Khepera; Amon, Min (all-father),
Hathor (all-mother), Neith, Anata; Ptah (creator), Ma'at (truth), Imhotep (peace), Bes (dancing), Serapis (underworld); theriomorphic
deity, theriocephalous deity; Apis (sacred bull),
Thoth (ibis), Anubis (jackal), Sekhmet (lioness), Sebek (crocodile), Bast (cat), Setekh
(hound), Uadjit (cobra), Taurt (hippopotamus).

Semitic deities, Nammu, Anu, Enlil, Enki *or*
Ea; Shamash, Sin, Adad; Bel, Marduk; El, Baal,
Aleyan-Baal; Moloch, Rimmon, Asshur; great
mother, Ishtar, Ashtoreth, Astarte, Asherah,
Inanna, Anat; fertility god, Tammuz, Atys;
Mot, Allatu.

Nordic deities, Aesir, Vanir; Odin *or* Wotan,
Frigg his wife; Thor (thunder god), his wife
Sif, his son Ull; Tiu *or* Tyr (war), Heimdall, Bal-
der the beautiful, Vidar the silent, Hoder the
blind, Bragi (god of poetry), Hermoder (messenger), Vali (youngest son of Odin); Frey *or*
Freyr (peace, fertility), Freya *or* Freyja (goddess
of love), Njord *or* Nerthus (wealth and ships),
Hoenir, Odmir; Skadi; Loki (evil and strife),
Hel (goddess of the dead); Aegir (ocean), his
wife Ran, Mimir (guardian of the spring of
wisdom), Ymir (father of the Giants).

Celtic deities, Dagda, Math, Magog, Oengus
or Dwyn; Ogma, Belinus, Esos, Teutates, Tara-
nis; Mabon, Borvo *or* Bormo; Epona; Bilé *or*
Beli, Govannon *or* Goibniu (smith), Diancecht
(medecine), Lludd *or* Nudd *or* Nuada (sun);
Gwydion, Amaethon; Lleu *or* Lug (light),
Dylan (darkness); sea gods: Ler *or* Llyr, Bran *or*
Branwen, Manannan *or* Manawydan; Dana *or*
Don, Morrigan (war), Brigit, Blathnat, Arian-
rod, Blodeuwedd, Creirwy (love), Keridwen
(poetry), Rhiannon (underworld).

Aztec deities, Nahuan deities; Cipactli (earth
dragon); Coatlicue (ancient earth goddess);
Red Tezcatlipoca, Black Tezcatlipoca, White
Tezcatlipoca, Blue Tezcatlipoca, Xipe Topec
(spring), Quetzalcoatl (culture), Huitzilopochtli

(warrior); god and goddess of creation: Tona-
catecuhtli, Tonicacihuatl; deities of fertility,
Cihuacoatl, Chicomecoatl, Centeotl, Tlazolte-
otl, Xochipilli; Tlaloc (rain), Chalcihuitlicue
(water); Xiuhtecuhtli (fire), Tonatiuh (sun),
Teccuciztecutl, Metztli (moon), Mixcoatl (sky),
Mictlantecuhtli (death).

968 Angel. Saint. Madonna

N. *angel*, archangel, heavenly host; seraph,
seraphim, cherub, cherubim; Michael, Gabriel,
Raphael, Uriel, Zadkiel, Israfel, Azrael, angel of
death; guardian angel.

saint, patron saint, the blessed —.

Madonna, Our Lady, Blessed Virgin Mary,
BVM, Mother of God, Mater Dolorosa, Queen
of Heaven; Mariolatry.

Adj. *angelic*, seraphic, cherubic; saintly.

969 Devil

N. *Satan*, Lucifer, fallen angel; Archfiend,
Prince of Darkness; serpent, Tempter, Adversary, Antichrist, Common Enemy, Enemy of
mankind, the foul fiend, the Devil, the Evil
One, the Wicked One, cloven hoof, Mephisto,
Mephistopheles, His Satanic Majesty, the old
one, the Old Gentleman, Old Nick *or* Auld
Nick, Old Harry, Old Scratch, Auld Hornie,
Clootie; evil genie, Shaitan, Eblis; King of Hell,
angel of the bottomless pit, Apollyon, Abaddon; Ahriman, Angra Mainyu.

devil, fiend; familiar, imp of Satan 938 *bad
person*; Tutivillus, Asmodeus, Azazel 970
demon; malevolent spirit; powers of darkness;
fallen angel, lost soul, sinner, dweller in Pandemonium, denizen of Hell; Mammon, Belial,
Beelzebub, Lord of the Flies; horns, cloven
hoof.

devil worship, demonism, demonolatry;
diabolism, devilry, demonry, diablerie 898
inhumanity; Satanism, devilism; demonomania, demoniac possession; witchcraft, the craft,
black magic, Black Mass 983 *sorcery*; Satanol-
ogy, demonology; demonization.

devil-worshipper, diabolist, Satanist, demon-
olater, demonist; demonologist, demonologer.

Adj. *diabolic*, diabolical, devil-like, satanic,
Mephistophelean, fiendish, demonic, demoniacal, devilish 898 *malevolent*; infernal, hellish, hell-born; devil-worshipping; demoniac,
possessed; demonological.

970 Fairy

N. *fairy*, elfland, fairyland, faerie; fairy folk,
little people; fay, peri; good fairy, fairy godmother 903 *benefactor*; bad fairy, witch 983
sorceress; fairy queen, Mab, Queen Mab, Tita-
nia; fairy king, Oberon, Erl King; Puck, Robin

Goodfellow; spirit of air, Ariel; sylph, sylphid; fairy ring; fairy tales; A Midsummer Night's Dream, The Faerie Queene.

elf, elves, elfin folk, pixie, brownie; gnome, dwarf, Nibelung; troll, trow; orc, goblin, flibbertigibbet; imp, sprite, hobgoblin; changeling; leprechaun; poltergeist, gremlin; Puck, Hob, Robin Goodfellow.

ghost, spirit, departed spirit; shades, souls of the dead, Manes; zombie; revenant, haunter, poltergeist; spook, spectre, apparition, phantom, shade, wraith, presence, doppelganger 440 *visual fallacy*; White Lady, Grey Lady.

demon, imp, flibbertigibbet, familiar 969 *devil*; she-demon, banshee; water horse, kelpie, troll; ogre, ogress, giant, giantess; bugbear, bugaboo, bogle, bogy, bogyman 938 *monster*; afreet *or* afrit, ghoul, vampire, lycanthrope, werewolf; incubus, succubus, nightmare; fury, harpy; Gorgon.

mythical being 968 *angel*, 969 *devil*; demon, genie, jinn; houri; Valkyrie; centaur, satyr, faun; sea nymph, river nymph, water spirit, etc. 967 *nymph*; kelpie, nix, nixie; merman, mermaid; Lorelei, siren; the Lady of the Lake, the Old Man of the Sea; Merlin, Morgan le Fay 983 *sorcerer*; Wayland Smith, the Green Man, Wodwose; Gorgon, Cyclops; Snark, Jabberwocky, hobbit 513 *fantasy*. (See also 365 *mythical animal*.)

Adj. *fairylike*, fairy, sylph-like 206 *lean*; dwarf-like 196 *dwarfish*; elf-like, elfin, elvish, impish, Puckish; magic 983 *magical*.

spooky, ghostly, ghoulish; haunted, hagridden; nightmarish, macabre 854 *frightening*; weird, uncanny, unearthly, eldritch 84 *abnormal*; eerie, supernatural; spectral, wraith-like; disembodied 320 *non-material*; spiritualistic 984 *psychical*.

Vb. *haunt*, visit, walk.

971 Heaven

N. *heaven*, abode of God, heavenly kingdom, kingdom come; Paradise, abode of the saints, land of the leal, gates of St Peter; Abraham's bosom, eternal home, happy home; next world, afterworld, world to come 155 *destiny*; eternal rest, blessed state; nirvana, seventh heaven; earthly Paradise, Shangri-la, the Millennium, kingdom of God, kingdom of heaven, heaven on earth, Zion, Land of Beulah, New Jerusalem, Holy City, Celestial City; afterlife, the hereafter, eternal life, eternity 124 *future state*; Pure Land; resurrection; assumption, glorification; deification, apotheosis.

mythical heaven, Olympus; Valhalla, Asgard; Elysium, Elysian fields, happy hunting grounds, the happy hunting grounds in the skies; Earthly Paradise, Eden, Garden of Eden, garden of the Hesperides, Islands of the Blest, the Happy Isles, Isle of Avalon, Tir nan Og 513 *fantasy*.

972 Hell

N. *hell*, place of the dead, nether regions, underworld; grave, limbo, Hades; purgatory; perdition, place of the damned, abode of evil spirits, inferno, Pandemonium; abyss, bottomless pit, Abaddon; place of torment, Gehenna, lake of fire and brimstone; hellfire.

mythical hell, Hel, Niflheim; realm of Pluto, Hades, Tartarus, Avernus, Erebus; river of hell, Acheron, Styx, Cocytus, Phlegethon, Lethe; Stygian Ferryman, Charon; infernal watchdog, Cerberus; infernal judge, Minos, Rhadamanthus; nether gods, Chthonians, Pluto, Osiris 967 *underworld deity*.

973 Religion

N. *religion*, religious belief, creed, dogma; deism; primitive religion; paganism 982 *idolatry*; neo-paganism, Wicca; dharma, revealed religion, incarnational religion, sacramental religion; mystery religion, mysticism, Sufism; yoga, hatha yoga, etc. 981 *worship*; Eightfold Path; theosophy 449 *philosophy*; theolatry 981 *worship*; religious cult, state religion 981 *cult*; atheism 974 *lack of religion*.

theism, belief in a god, deism; animism; pantheism, panentheism, polytheism, henotheism, monotheism, dualism; gnosticism.

religious faith, faith 485 *belief*; Christianity, the Cross; Judaism; Islam, Muhammedanism, the Crescent; Baha'ism *or* Baha'i; Ahmaddiya; Zoroastrianism, Mazdaism; Vedic religion, Dharma; Hinduism, Brahmanism, Vedantism, Tantrism; Vaishnavism 978 *sectarianism*; Sikhism; Jainism; Buddhism, Theravada, Hinayana, Mahayana, Jodo, Nichiren, Pure Land, Zen; Shintoism; Taoism, Confucianism; Falun Gong; Theosophy; Scientology, Aetherius Society, Raëlians.

theology, natural theology, revealed theology; religious knowledge, religious learning, divinity; scholastic theology, scholasticism, Scotism, Thomism; Rabbinism; demythologization; Christology; eschatology; hagiology, hagiography, iconology; dogmatics; symbolics, credal theology; deposit of faith; religious doctrine, received doctrine, defined doctrine; definition, canon; doxy, dogma, tenet; articles of faith, credo, shahada 485 *creed*; confession, Thirty-nine Articles, Westminster Confession of Faith, Augsburg Confession, Apostles' Creed, Nicene Creed, Athanasian Creed; fundamentalism 976 *strictness of belief*; Bible study, Bibliology; comparative religion.

theologian, divinity student, divine; rabbi, scribe, mufti, mullah; schoolman, scholastic, scholastic theologian, Thomist, Talmudist, canonist; theogonist, hagiologist, hagiographer, iconologist; psalmist, hymnographer, hymnwriter; textualist; scripturalist, fundamentalist, rabbinist.

religious teacher, prophet, rishi, inspired writer; guru, maharishi 500 *sage*; evangelist, apostle, missionary; reformer, religious reformer; expected leader, Messiah, Mahdi, Invisible Imam, twelfth avatar of Vishnu, future Buddha, Maitreya; founder of Christianity, Christ, Jesus Christ 965 *Jesus*; Prophet of God, Muhammad *or* Mohammed *or* Mahomet; Zoroaster *or* Zarathustra; Ramakrishna, Baha'ullah; Buddha, Gautama; Confucius, Laotzu; Joseph Smith, Mary Baker Eddy, Madame Blavatsky; expounder, hierophant, gospeller, catechist 520 *interpreter*.

religionist, deist, theist; monotheist, polytheist, pantheist; animist, fetishist; pagan, gentile 974 *heathen*; adherent, believer, orthodoxist; believer 979 *zealot*; Christian, Nazarene, messianic Jew; Jew; Muslim, Moslem, Islamite, Mussulman, Muhammedan; Sunnite, Shi'ite 978 *non-Christian sect*; Sufi, dervish, Druze, Mandaean *or* Mandean, Manichaean *or* Manichean, Yezidi, Baha'i; Parsee, Zoroastrian; Hindu, gymnosophist, Brahmanist; Sikh; Jain; Buddhist, Zen Buddhist; Tantrist; Taoist; Confucianist; Shintoist; Theosophist; Mormon 978 *sect*; Rosicrucian 984 *occultist*; gnostic 977 *heretic*.

Adj. *religious*, divine, holy, sacred, spiritual, sacramental, deistic, theistic, pantheistic, monotheistic, dualistic; Christian, Islamic, Moslem, Jewish, Judaistic, Mosaic; Baha'i, Zoroastrian, Avestan; Confucian, Taoistic; Buddhistic, Hinduistic, Vedic, Brahminical, Upanashadic, Vedantic; yogic, mystic, Sufic; devotional, devout, practising.

974 Lack of religion

N. *lack of religion*, irreligion, profaneness, ungodliness 980 *impiety*; heathenism 982 *idolatry*; atheism, disbelief 486 *unbelief*; humanism; agnosticism, scepticism; lack of faith; lapse from faith, recidivism, backsliding 603 *change of mind*; paganization; apathy 860 *indifference*.

heathen, non-Christian, pagan, paynim; unbeliever, misbeliever, infidel, giaour; gentile, the uncircumcised, the unbaptized, the unconverted; apostate, backslider, lapsed Christian 603 *recanter*.

Adj. *irreligious*, godless, profane 980 *impi-*

ous; atheistic, atheistical; humanistic; agnostic, doubting, sceptical, Pyrrhonic; free-thinking, rationalistic, non-practising; ungodly 934 *wicked*; amoral 860 *indifferent*; secular, worldly, materialistic, Mammonistic 944 *sensual*; lacking faith, backsliding, recidivous, lapsed, paganized; unchristian, non-Christian; anti-clerical.

heathenish, unholy, unhallowed, unsanctified, unblest, unconsecrated 980 *profane*; unchristian, unbaptized, unconfirmed; gentile, uncircumcised; heathen, pagan, infidel; pre-Christian, unconverted, in darkness 491 *uninstructed*.

Vb. *be irreligious*, be atheistic, etc. (see adj.); have no religion, lack faith; serve Mammon; lose one's faith, suffer a lapse of faith, give up the Church 603 *apostatize*; deny God, blaspheme 980 *be impious*; rationalize, demythologize.

975 Revelation

N. *revelation*, divine revelation, apocalypse 526 *disclosure*; illumination 417 *light*; inspiration, divine inspiration; prophecy, word of knowledge; intuition, mysticism; Mosaic Law, Ten Commandments; God's word, gospel; God revealed, theophany, burning bush, epiphany, incarnation, Word made flesh; avatar, emanation, divine emanation.

scripture, word of God, sacred writings; Holy Scripture, Holy Writ, Bible, Holy Bible, the Book, the Good Book, the Word; Wyclif's Bible, Geneva *or* Breeches Bible, King James's Bible, Authorized Version, Revised Version, Revised Standard Version, Jerusalem Bible, New English Bible, Good News Bible, New International Version; Itala, Italic Version, Vulgate, Douai Version, Greek version, Septuagint; canonical writings, canonical books, canon; Old Testament, Pentateuch, Hexateuch, Heptateuch, Octateuch, Major Prophets, Minor Prophets; Torah, the Law and the Prophets, Hagiographa; New Testament, Gospels, Synoptic Gospels, Epistles, Pastoral Epistles, Pauline Epistles, Johannine Epistles, Petrine Epistles; Acts of the Apostles, Revelation, Apocalypse; non-canonical writings, Apocrypha, agrapha, logia, sayings, pseudepigrapha, non-canonical gospel; patristic writings; psalter, psalmbook, breviary, missal; prayer book, Book of Common Prayer 981 *prayers*; hymnbook, etc. 988 *hymnbook*; Bible study, Bibliology 973 *theology*; textual commentary, Masorah, Higher Criticism; fundamentalism, scripturalism.

Scriptures

Christian scriptures: Bible, Old Testament, New Testament; Apocrypha; Book of Mormon, Science and

Health with Key to the Scriptures.
Jewish scriptures: Torah, Targum, Talmud, Mishnah, Gemara.
Muslim scriptures: Koran or Qur'an, the Glorious Koran; Hadith, Sunna or Sunnah.
Baha'i scriptures: Kitab-i-Aqdas (Most Holy Book), Kitab-i-Iqan (Book of Certitude), Kalimat-i-Maknunih (The Hidden Words), Haft Vadi (The Seven Valleys), Epistle to the Son of the Wolf.
Hindu scriptures: Veda, the Four Vedas, Rigveda, Yajurveda, Samaveda, Atharvaveda; Brahmana, Upanishad, Purana; Bhagavad Gita.
Buddhist scriptures: Pitaka, Tripitaka / Tipitaka, Dhammapada, Lotus Sutra, Nikaya.
Sikh scriptures: Granth, Adi Granth, Guru Granth Sahib, Dasam Granth, Japji.
Taoist scriptures: Tao Te Ching or Lao-tzu, Chuang-tzu, Lieh-tzu.
Zoroastrian scriptures: Avesta, Zend-Avesta.

non-Biblical scripture, sruti, smriti, shastra, sutra, tantra; Book of the Dead (Egyptian).

Adj. *revelational*, inspirational, mystic; inspired, prophetic, revealed; visional; apocalyptic; prophetic, evangelical.

scriptural, sacred, holy; hierographic; revealed, inspired, prophetic; canonical 733 *authoritative*; biblical, Mosaic; gospel, evangelistic, apostolic; patristic, homiletic; Talmudic, Mishnaic; Koranic, uncreated; Vedic, Upanishadic, Puranic; textuary, textual, Masoretic.

976 Orthodoxy

N. *orthodoxy*, orthodoxness, correct opinion; sound theology, religious truth, gospel truth, pure Gospel 494 *truth*; scripturality, canonicity; the Faith, the true faith; early Church, Apostolic age; ecumenicalism, catholicity, Catholicism; formulated faith, credo 485 *creed*; Apostles' Creed, Nicene Creed, Athanasian Creed; Thirty-nine Articles, Westminster Confession of Faith, Augsburg Confession, Tridentine decrees; textuary, catechism, Church Catechism.

strictness of belief, strictness of interpretation, strict interpretation, orthodoxism; scripturalism, textualism, fundamentalism, literalism, precisionism; Karaism (Jewish); traditionalism, institutionalism, ecclesiasticism, churchianity 985 *the church*; sound churchmanship 83 *conformity*; Christian practice 768 *observance*; intolerance, heresy-hunting, persecution; suppression of heresy, extermination of error, Counter-Reformation; religious censorship, Holy Office 956 *tribunal*; Inquisition 459 *interrogation*; Index, Index Expurgatorius, Index Librorum Prohibitorum 924 *disapprobation*; guaranteed orthodoxy, imprimatur 923 *approbation*.

Christendom, Christian world, the Church; undivided Church; Holy Church, Mother Church; Bride of Christ; Body of Christ, universal Church; Church Militant, Church on earth, visible Church; invisible Church, Church Triumphant; established church, recognized church, denominational church; Orthodox Church, Eastern Orthodox Church, Greek Orthodox Church, Russian Orthodox Church; Armenian Church, Coptic Church; Church of Rome, Roman Catholic Church; Catholic Apostolic Church; Anglican Church, Anglican Communion, Church of England, Episcopalian or Episcopal Church; Protestant Church, Lutheran Church, Calvinist Church, Reformed Church, Church of Scotland, United Free Church, Free Church; Church of South India; Ecumenical Council, World Council of Churches.

Catholicism, Roman Catholicism, Romanism, popery, papistry, ultramontanism, Scarlet Woman; Counter-Reformation; Old Catholicism; Anglicanism, Episcopalianism, prelacy; Anglo-Catholicism, High Church; Tractarianism, Oxford Movement; Orthodoxy, Eastern Orthodoxy.

Protestantism, the Reformation, Anglicanism, Lutheranism, Zwinglianism, Calvinism; Presbyterianism, Congregationalism, United Reformed Church, Baptists; Quakerism, Society of Friends; Wesleyanism, Methodism, Primitive Methodism 978 *sect*.

Catholic, Roman Catholic, Romanist, papist, ultramontanist; Old Catholic, Anglo-Catholic, Anglican, Episcopalian, High-Churchman, Tractarian; Orthodox, Eastern Orthodox; Greek Orthodox, Russian Orthodox; Coptic.

Protestant, reformer, Anglican, Lutheran, Zwinglian, Calvinist, Huguenot, Anabaptist; Presbyterian, Wee Free, Congregationalist, United Reformist, Baptist, Wesleyan, Methodist, Wesleyan Methodist, Primitive Methodist; Quaker, Friend; Plymouth Brother.

Adj. *orthodox*, right-minded; non-heretical, unschismatical 488 *assenting*; undivided 52 *whole*; unswerving, undeviating, loyal, devout 739 *obedient*; practising, conforming, conventional 83 *conformable*; churchy 979 *pietistic*; strict, pedantic; holier than thou, bible-thumping or -bashing; intolerant, witch-hunting, inquisitional 459 *enquiring*; correct 494 *accurate*; doctrinal 485 *credal*; authoritative, defined, canonical, biblical, scriptural, evangelical, gospel 494 *genuine*; textual, literal, fundamentalist, fundamentalistic; fundie; Trinitarian; Athanasian; catholic, ecumenical, universal; accepted, held, widely held, believed, generally believed 485 *credible*; traditional, customary 610 *usual*.

Roman Catholic, Catholic, Roman, Romish, Romanist, Romanizing, ultramontanist; popish, papistic.

Anglican, episcopalian; tractarian, Anglo-Catholic, High-Church, high; Low-Church; Broad-Church, Latitudinarian.

Protestant, reformed; denominational 978 *sectarian*; Lutheran, Zwinglian, Calvinist, Calvinistic; Presbyterian, Congregational, United Reformed, Baptist, Methodist, Wesleyan, Quaker; bishopless, non-episcopal.

977 Heterodoxy

N. heterodoxy, unorthodoxy; erroneous opinion, wrong belief, false creed, superstition 495 *error*; new teaching; perversion of the truth; heretical tendency, latitudinarianism, modernism, Higher Criticism; unscripturality, non-catholicity, partial truth; heresy, rank heresy (see also *heresy* below).

heresy, heathen theology, Gnosticism; Monarchianism, Arianism; Socinianism; Unitarianism; Apollinarianism, Nestorianism; Monophysitism, Monothelitism; Pelagianism, Semi-Pelagianism; Montanism, Donatism, Manichaeism, Albigensianism, Antinomianism; Lollardy; Erastianism, antipapalism.

heretic, arch-heretic, heresiarch; Ebionite; Monarchian, Unitarian; Sabellius, Sabellian; Arius, Arian; Nestorius, Nestorian; Eutyches, Eutychian; Apollinaris, Apollinarian; Monophysite, Monothelite; Pelagius, Pelagian, Semi-Pelagian; Montanus, Montanist, millenarian; Donatus, Donatist; Gnostic, Basilidian, Marcionist *or* Marcionite, Ophite, Valentinian; Mani, Manichaean *or* Manichean *or* Manichee, Paulician, Bogomil, Albigensian, Cathar; antinomian; Wycliffite, Lollard, Hussite; Socinus, Socinian; Waldenses.

Adj. heretical, heretic; heathen, Gnostic, Manichean, Monarchian, Unitarian, Socinian; Arian, Eutychian, Apollinarian, Nestorian; Monophysitic, Monothelite; Pelagian; Montanist; Manichaean, Albigensian; Antinomian, Waldensian, Wycliffite, Lollard, Hussite.

978 Sectarianism

N. sectarianism, exclusiveness, clannishness, cliqueishness, sectionalism 481 *prejudice*; bigotry 481 *bias*; party spirit, factiousness 709 *quarrelsomeness*; separatism, schismatical tendency 738 *disobedience*; denominationalism, nonconformism, nonconformity 489 *dissent*; Lutheranism, Calvinism, Anabaptism, Pietism, Moravianism, Puritanism 976 *Protestantism*; Puseyism, Tractarianism 976 *Catholicism*.

schism, division, differences 709 *quarrel*; dissociation, breakaway, splintering, secession, withdrawal 46 *separation*; non-recognition, mutual excommunication 883 *seclusion*; recusancy 769 *non-observance*; religious schism, Great Schism.

sect, division, off-shoot, branch, group, faction, splinter group 708 *party*; order, religious order, brotherhood, sisterhood 708 *community*; nonconformist sect, chapel, conventicle 976 *Protestantism*; Society of Friends, Friends, Quakers; Unitarians, Universalists; Moravians; Plymouth Brethren; Churches of Christ; Sabbatarians, Seventh-day Adventists; Church of Christ Scientist; Church of Jesus Christ of the Latter-Day Saints, Mormons; Jehovah's Witnesses; Salvation Army, Salvationists; Oxford Group, Moral Rearmament.

non-Christian sect, Jewish sect: Pharisees, Sadducees, Karaites; Nazarites, Essenes; Hasidim, Rabbinists; Orthodox Judaism, Conservative Judaism, Reform Judaism; paganochristian sect: Gnostics, Mandaeans, Euchites; Islamic sect: Sunnis, Shi'ites, Sufis, Wahhabis; Druze, Yezidis; Black Muslims; Rastafarians, Rastas; Hindu sect: Vedantists, Vaishnavas, Saivas, Shaktas; Brahmoists, Hare Krishna sect; Buddhist sect: Tantrists, Pure Land, Zen, Jodo, Nichiren; Falun Gong 973 *religious faith*; Aetherius Society, Raëlians.

sectarian, particularist; follower, adherent, devotee; Sectary, Nonconformist, Independant; Puritan, Shaker; Quaker, Friend; Pentecostalist; Presbyterian, Wee Free, Covenanter 976 *Protestant*; Salvationist, Christian Scientist, Christadelphian, Jehovah's Witness, Seventh-day Adventist, Mennonite, Unitarian, Universalist; Mormon; Moonie; Scientologist; Gnostic 977 *heretic*.

schismatic, separated brother; schismatics, separated brethren; separatist, separationist; seceder, secessionist; splinter group; factionary, factionist; rebel, mutineer 738 *rebel*; recusant, non-juror; dissident, dissenter, nonconformist 489 *objector*; wrong believer 977 *heretic*; apostate 603 *recanter*.

Adj. sectarian, particularist; party-minded, partisan 481 *biased*; clannish, exclusive; Judaizer, Ebionite; Gallican; Erastian; High-Church, episcopalian 976 *Anglican*; Low-Church, evangelical 976 *Protestant*; Puritan, Independant, Presbyterian, Covenanting; revivalist, Pentecostalist; Vaishnavite, Saiva, Shakta, Tantrist; Ramakrishna; Rastafarian; Sunni, Shi'ite, Sufic; Essene, Pharisaic, Sadducean, Hasidic; Gnostic.

schismatical, schismatic, secessionist, seceding, breakaway; divided, separated 46 *separate*; excommunicated, excommunicable 977 *heretical*; dissentient, nonconformist 489 *dissenting*; recusant 769 *non-observant*; rebellious, rebel, contumacious 738 *disobedient*; apostate.

979 Piety

N. piety, piousness, goodness 933 *virtue*; reverence, veneration, honour, decent respect 920 *respect*; dutifulness, attendance at worship, regular churchgoing 768 *observance*; churchmanship 976 *orthodoxy*; religiousness, religion, theism 973 *theism*; religious feeling; fear of God 854 *fear*; pious belief, faith, trust in God 485 *belief*; devotion, dedication 931 *disinterestedness*; devoutness, sincerity, earnestness, unction; enthusiasm, fervour, zeal; inspiration, exaltation, word of knowledge, charisma, speaking in tongues, glossolalia, xenoglossia, charismatic movement 821 *excitation*; adoration, prostration 981 *worship*; meditation, retreat; contemplation, mysticism, communion with God, mystic communion 973 *religion*; faith healing 656 *restoration*; act of piety; good works; pilgrimage, hajj.

sanctity, sanctitude, holiness, hallowedness, sacredness, sacrosanctity; goodness, cardinal virtues 933 *virtue*; state of grace, odour of sanctity 950 *purity*; godliness, saintliness; spirituality, unworldliness, otherworldliness; spiritual life; sainthood, blessedness, blessed state; enlightenment, Buddhahood, satori; conversion, regeneration, rebirth, new birth 656 *revival*; sanctification; canonization, beatification, consecration, dedication.

show of piety, pietism, sanctimony; sanctimoniousness, unction, cant 542 *sham*; religionism, religiosity, religious mania; bible-thumping *or* -bashing; tender conscience; austerity 945 *asceticism*; formalism, Puritanism 481 *narrow mind*; literalness, fundamentalism, Bible-worship, bibliolatry 494 *accuracy*; sabbatarianism 978 *sectarianism*; churchiness, sacerdotalism, ritualism 985 *clericalism*; preachiness, unctuousness; bigotry, fanaticism 481 *prejudice*; persecution, witch-hunting, heresy-hunting 735 *severity*. (See also 980 *false piety*.)

pious person, pietist, real saint 937 *good person*; children of God, children of light; the good, the righteous, the just; conformist 488 *assenter*; practising Christian, communicant 981 *worshipper*; confessor, martyr; saint, bodhisattva, marabout; man *or* woman of prayer, contemplative, mystic, sufi; holy man, sadhu, sannyasi, bhikshu *or* bhikku, fakir, dervish 945 *ascetic*; hermit, anchorite 883 *unsocial person*; monk, nun, religious 986 *clergy*; devotee; convert, neophyte, catechumen, ordinand 538 *learner*; believer, the faithful; the chosen people, the elect; pilgrim, palmer, hajji; votary.

zealot, religionist, enthusiast, wowser, fanatic, bigot, image-breaker, iconoclast; formalist, precisian, Puritan; Pharisee, scribe, scribes and Pharisees; the unco guid, goody-goody; fundamentalist, fundie; inerrantist,

Bible-worshipper, bibliolater, Sabbatarian 978 *sectarian*; bible-puncher *or* -thumper *or* -basher; pulpiteer 537 *preacher*; evangelical, salvationist, hot-gospeller; missionary 901 *philanthropist*; revivalist, speaker in tongues, faith healer; militant Christian: champion of the faith, crusader 722 *militarist*; militant Muslim: ghazi, Islamist, fedayee, jihadi *or* jihadist, al Qaeda *or* al Qaida; Red Guard; persecutor 735 *tyrant*.

Adj. *pious*, good 933 *virtuous*; decent, reverent 920 *respectful*; faithful 739 *obedient*; conforming; believing 976 *orthodox*; sincere; pure, pure in heart, holy-minded; unworldly, otherworldly, spiritual; godly, God-fearing, religious, devout; praying, psalm-singing; happy-clappy; in retreat, meditative, contemplative, mystic; holy, saintly, saintlike; Christian.

pietistic, ardent, fervent, seraphic; enthusiastic, inspired; austere 945 *ascetic*; hermit-like, anchoretic 883 *unsociable*; earnest, pi, religiose, overreligious, overpious, self-righteous, holier than thou; overstrict, precise, Puritan; formalistic, Pharisaic, ritualistic 978 *sectarian*; priest-ridden, churchy; psalm-singing, hymn-singing; preachy, bible-thumping *or* -bashing, sanctimonious, canting 850 *affected*; goody-goody, too good to be true 933 *virtuous*; crusading, evangelical, missionary-minded.

sanctified, consecrated, dedicated, enshrined; reverend, holy, sacred, solemn, sacrosanct 866 *worshipful*; haloed, sainted, canonized, beatified; chosen; saved, redeemed, ransomed; renewed, reborn, born again.

Vb. *be pious*, be religious, etc. (see adj.); have one's mind on higher things; fear God 854 *fear*; have faith 485 *believe*; keep the faith, fight the good fight 162 *be strong*; walk humbly with one's God; go to church, be a regular churchgoer; pray, say one's prayers 981 *worship*; kneel, genuflect, bow 311 *stoop*; cross oneself, make the sign of the cross; make offering, sacrifice, devote 759 *offer*; give alms and oblations, lend to God 781 *give*; give to charity; glorify God 923 *praise*; give God the glory 907 *thank*; revere, show reverence 920 *show respect*; sermonize, preach at 534 *teach*; set a good example.

become pious, be converted, get religion; see the light, see the error of one's ways 603 *recant*; mend one's ways, reform, repent, repent of one's evil ways, receive Christ 939 *be penitent*; enter the church, become ordained, take holy orders, take vows, take the veil 986 *take orders*.

make pious, bring religion to, proselytize, convert 485 *convince*; Christianize, win for Christ, baptize, receive into the church 299 *admit*; Islamize, Judaize; spiritualize 648 *purify*; confirm in the faith 162 *strengthen*; inspire, fill with grace; redeem 656 *restore*.

sanctify, hallow, make holy, keep holy 866 *honour*; consecrate, dedicate, enshrine 866 *dignify*; make a saint of, canonize, beatify, invest with a halo; bless, make the sign of the cross.

980 Impiety

N. impiety, impiousness; irreverence; godlessness 974 *lack of religion*; scoffing, mockery, derision 851 *ridicule*; scorn, pride 922 *contempt*; sacrilegiousness, profanity; blasphemy, cursing, swearing 899 *curse*; sacrilege, desecration, violation, profanation, perversion, abuse 675 *misuse*; immorality, sin, pervertedness 934 *wickedness*; lapse of faith, backsliding, apostasy; profaneness, unholiness, worldliness, materialism 319 *materiality*; paganism, heathenism.

false piety, sham piety 541 *falsehood*; sanctimoniousness, Pharisaism 979 *show of piety*; hypocrisy, lip service 541 *duplicity*; cant 850 *affectation*.

impious person, blasphemer, curser, swearer 899 *curse*; defamer 926 *detractor*; desecrator, violator, profaner 904 *offender*; gentile, pagan, infidel, unbeliever 974 *heathen*; atheist, sceptic; materialist, immoralist 944 *sensualist*; sinner, reprobate, children of darkness 938 *bad person*; recidivist, backslider, apostate; fallen angel 969 *Satan*.

Adj. impious, ungodly, anti-Christian; dissenting 977 *heretical*; unbelieving, nonbelieving, atheistical, godless 974 *irreligious*; non-practising 769 *non-observant*; scoffing, mocking, deriding; blasphemous, swearing 899 *cursing*; irreligious, irreverent; sacrilegious, profaning, desecrating, violating, iconoclastic 954 *lawless*; sinning, sinful, impure, perverted, reprobate 934 *wicked*; lapsing, backsliding, apostate.

profane, unholy, unhallowed, unsanctified, unblest; accursed; unconsecrated; infidel, pagan.

Vb. be impious, be sacrilegious, etc. (see adj.); sin 934 *be wicked*; swear, blaspheme, take the name of the Lord in vain 899 *curse*; profane, desecrate, violate 675 *misuse*; commit sacrilege, defile, sully 649 *make unclean*; worship false gods; play false 541 *dissemble*; lapse, backslide 603 *apostatize*.

981 Worship

N. worship, honour, reverence, homage 920 *respect*; awe 854 *fear*; veneration, adoration; humbleness 872 *humility*; devotion, devotedness 979 *piety*; prayer, one's devotions, one's prayers; retreat, meditation, contemplation, communion with God, yoga.

Words Associated with Yoga and Meditation
bhakti yoga, jnana yoga, karma yoga; dharma yoga; astanga yoga, dru yoga, hatha yoga, Iyengar yoga, raja yoga, tantric yoga; asana, dhyana, mantra; chakra, kundalini; zen, zazen, koan; enlightenment, bodhi, moksha, samadhi, satori.

---

cult, mystique; service of God, supreme worship, latria; inferior worship, dulia, hyperdulia; Christolatry, Mariolatry; iconolatry, imageworship; false worship 982 *idolatry*.

act of worship, rites; praises; glorification; hymn-singing, psalm-singing, psalmody, plainsong, chanting 412 *vocal music*; thanksgiving, blessing, benediction 907 *thanks*; offering, oblation, almsgiving, sacrifice, offering (see also *religious offering* below); praying, saying one's prayers, reciting the rosary; self-examination 939 *penitence*; self-denial, self-discipline 945 *asceticism*; keeping fast 946 *fasting*; hajj, pilgrimage.

prayers, orisons, devotions; retreat, contemplation 449 *meditation*; prayer, salat; petition, petitionary prayer 761 *request*; invocation, invocatory prayer 583 *address*; intercession, intercessory prayer, arrow prayer 762 *deprecation*; suffrage, prayers for the dead, vigils; special prayer, intention; rogation, supplication, solemn supplication, litany, solemn litany; comminatory prayer, commination, denunciation 900 *threat*; imprecation, imprecatory prayer 899 *curse*; excommunication, ban 883 *seclusion*; exorcism 300 *ejection*; benediction, benedicite, benison, grace 907 *thanks*; prayer for the day, collect; liturgical prayer, the Lord's Prayer, Paternoster, Our Father; Ave, Ave Maria, Hail Mary; Kyrie Eleison, Sursum Corda, Sanctus, Angelus; Nunc Dimittis; dismissal, blessing; rosary, beads, bead-roll; prayer-wheel; prayer book, missal, breviary, book of hours; call to prayer, muezzin's cry 547 *call*; e-prayer.

hymn, song, psalm, metrical psalm; religious song, worship song, spiritual; processional hymn, recessional; introit; plainsong, Gregorian chant, Ambrosian chant, descant 412 *vocal music*; anthem, cantata, motet; antiphon, response; canticle, Te Deum, Benedicite; song of praise, paean, Magnificat; doxology, Gloria; greater doxology, Gloria in Excelsis; lesser doxology, Gloria Patri; paean, Hallelujah, Hosanna; Homeric hymn; Vedic hymn; hymn-singing, hymnody; psalm-singing, psalmody; hymnbook, psalm-book, etc. 988 *hymn book*; Vedic hymns, Rigveda, Samaveda; hymnology, hymnography.

religious offering, offering, offertory, collection, oblation, alms and oblations 781 *offering*;

pew rent, pewage; libation, incense; dedication, consecration; votive offering; scapegoat 150 *substitute*; burnt offering, holocaust; sacrifice, devotion; immolation, hecatomb 362 *slaughter*; human sacrifice 362 *homicide*; self-sacrifice 931 *disinterestedness*; self-immolation, suttee 362 *suicide*; expiation, propitiation 941 *atonement*; a humble and a contrite heart 939 *penitence*.

   public worship, common prayer, intercommunion; agape, love-feast; service, divine service, divine office, mass, matins, evensong, benediction 988 *church service*; psalm-singing, psalmody, hymn-singing 412 *vocal music*; church, church-going, chapel-going 979 *piety*; meeting for prayer, gathering for worship 74 *assembly*; prayer meeting, revival meeting; open-air service, mission service, street evangelism, revivalism; temple worship, state religion 973 *religion*; e-prayer.

   worshipper, fellow worshipper, coreligionist; adorer, venerator, votary, devotee, oblate 979 *pious person*; glorifier, hymner, praiser, idolizer, admirer, ardent admirer, humble admirer 923 *commender*; follower, server 742 *servant*; image-worshipper, iconolater; sacrificer, offerer 781 *giver*; invocator, invoker, caller 583 *address*; supplicator, supplicant, suppliant 763 *petitioner*, man *or* woman of prayer, beadsman, intercessor; contemplative, mystic, sufi, visionary; dervish, marabout, enthusiast, revivalist, prophet 973 *religious teacher*; celebrant, officiant 986 *clergy*; communicant, churchgoer, chapelgoer, temple worshipper; congregation, the faithful; psalm-singer, hymn-singer, psalmodist, chanter, cantor; psalmist, hymnwriter, hymnologist; pilgrim, palmer, hajji 268 *traveller*.

   Vb. *worship*, honour, revere, venerate, adore 920 *respect*; honour and obey 854 *fear*; pay homage to, acknowledge 917 *do one's duty*; make a god of, deify; bow down before, kneel to, genuflect, prostrate oneself, lift up one's heart; extol, laud, magnify, glorify, give glory to, lift up 923 *praise*; celebrate 413 *sing*; light candles to, burn incense before, offer sacrifice to; pray, say a prayer, say one's prayers, recite the rosary; commune with God, be slain in the Spirit 979 *be pious*.

   offer worship, celebrate, officiate, minister, administer the sacraments 988 *perform ritual*; lead the congregation, lead in prayer; sacrifice, make sacrifice, offer up 781 *give*; sacrifice to, propitiate, appease 719 *pacify*; vow, make vows 764 *promise*; dedicate, consecrate 979 *sanctify*; take vows, enter holy orders 986 *take orders*; go to church, go to chapel, go to meeting, meet for prayer 979 *be pious*; go to service,

hear Mass, take the sacraments, receive the Eucharist, take Holy Communion; observe Lent 946 *starve*; deny oneself 945 *be ascetic*; go into retreat 449 *meditate*; chant psalms, sing hymns, sing praises.

982 Idolatry

N. *idolatry*, idolatrousness, false worship, superstition 981 *worship*; heathenism, paganism 973 *religion*; fetishism, anthropomorphism, zoomorphism; iconolatry, image worship; mumbo jumbo, hocus-pocus 983 *sorcery*; cult; sacrifice, human sacrifice 981 *religious offering*; heliolatry, sun worship; star worship, Sabaism; pyrolatry, fire worship; zoolatry, animal worship; ophiolatry, snake worship; necrolatry, worship of the dead, demonolatry, devil worship 969 *devil worship*; Mammonism, worship of wealth.

   idol, image, graven image, fetish, totem pole; lingam, yoni; golden calf 966 *deity*; godling, joss; teraphim, lares and penates, totem; mumbo jumbo, Juggernaut, Baal, Moloch.

983 Sorcery

N. *sorcery*, witchery, magic arts, enchantments; witchcraft, the craft; magic lore 490 *knowledge*; wizardry; wonder-working, thaumaturgy 864 *miracle-working*; magic, jugglery, illusionism 542 *sleight of hand*; white magic; black magic, black art, necromancy; witch-doctoring, shamanism; obeah, obi, voodooism, voodoo, hoodoo, macumba, muti; spirit-raising 511 *divination*, 984 *occultism*; spirit-laying, ghost-laying, exorcism 988 *rite*; magic rite, incantation; coven, witches' sabbath, witches' coven; Walpurgisnacht, Hallowe'en; witching hour.

   spell, charm, enchantment, cantrip, hoodoo, curse; evil eye, jettatura, jinx, hex, influence; bewitchment, fascination 291 *attraction*; obsession, possession, demoniacal possession; incantation; magic sign; magic word, magic formula, abraxas, open sesame, abracadabra; hocus pocus, mumbo jumbo, fee faw fum 515 *lack of meaning*; philtre, love potion.

   talisman, charm, countercharm; cross, phylactery; St Christopher medal 662 *safeguard*; juju, obeah, mojo, fetish 982 *idol*; periapt, amulet, mascot, lucky charm; rabbit's foot, four-leaf clover, horseshoe, black cat; pentacle, pentagram 547 *indication*; swastika, fylfot, gammadion; scarab; birthstone; emblem; relic, holy relic.

   magic instrument, bell, book and candle, broomstick; witches' brew, hellbroth, witches' cauldron; philtre, potion, moly; wand, magic wand, fairy wand; magic ring, wishing cap;

Aladdin's lamp, flying carpet, magic carpet; seven-league boots; Excalibur; wishing well, wishbone, merrythought.

sorcerer, wise man, seer, soothsayer; astrologer, alchemist 984 *occultist*; Druid, magus, the Magi; thaumaturgist, wonder-worker, miracle-worker 864 *miracle-working*; shaman, witchdoctor, medicine man, angekok, fetishist, obiman, voodooist, houngan, hoodooist, spiritraiser 984 *occultist*; conjuror, exorcist, minister of deliverance, ghost-buster; snake-charmer; juggler, illusionist; enchanter, wizard, warlock; magician, theurgist; necromancer 969 *devilworshipper*; familiar, imp, evil spirit 969 *devil*; sorcerer's apprentice; Merlin, Prospero, Gandalf, Faust, Pied Piper.

sorceress, wise woman, Sibyl 511 *diviner*; Druidess; enchantress, witch, weird sister; hag, hellcat; succubus, succuba; lamia; fairy godmother, wicked fairy, Morgan le Fay 970 *fairy*; Witch of Endor, Hecate, Circe, Medea; three witches in 'Macbeth'.

Adj. *magical*, otherworldly, supernatural, uncanny, eldritch, weird 970 *fairy-like*; spelllike; voodooistic; talismanic, phylacteric; magic, charmed, enchanted 178 *influential*.

bewitched, enchanted, charmed, fey; hypnotized, fascinated, spellbound, under the evil eye; under a curse, cursed; blighted, blasted, withered; hag-ridden, haunted.

Vb. *bewitch*, charm, enchant, fascinate 291 *attract*; hypnotize; magic; spellbind, cast a spell on, weave a spell over, lay under a spell; put a voodoo on; cast the evil eye, blight, blast 898 *be malevolent*; put a curse on, lay under a curse 899 *curse*; taboo, make taboo 757 *prohibit*; hag-ride.

984 Occultism

N. *occultism*, esotericism, hermeticism, mysticism, transcendentalism 973 *religion*; cabbalism, cabbala, gematria; theosophy, reincarnationism; yogism; sciosophy, hyperphysics, metapsychics; supernaturalism, psychicism, pseudopsychology; secret art, esoteric science, occult lore, alchemy, astrology, psychomancy, spiritualism, magic 983 *sorcery*; sortilege, fortune-telling, crystal-gazing, palmistry *or* palm-reading, chiromancy, tea-leaf reading, etc. 511 *divination*; clairvoyance, feyness, second sight 438 *vision*; sixth sense 476 *intuition*; animal magnetism, mesmerism, hypnotism; hypnosis, hypnotic trance 375 *insensitivity*.

psychics, parapsychology, psychism 447 *psychology*; psychic science, psychical research; paranormal perception, extrasensory perception, ESP; telaesthesia, clairvoyance, feyness,

second sight 476 *intuition*; psychokinesis, forkbending; telepathy, telergy; thought-reading, mind-reading, thought transference; precognition, psi faculty; déjà vu.

spiritualism, spiritism; spirit communication, psychomancy 983 *sorcery*; sciomancy 511 *divination*; mediumism; séance; astral body, spirit body, ethereal body 320 *non-materiality*; spirit manifestation, materialization, ectoplasm 319 *materiality*; apport, telekinesis; poltergeists; spirit-rapping, table-tapping, tableturning; automatism, automatic writing, spirit writing, psychography 586 *writing*; spirit message, psychogram; spiritualistic apparatus, psychograph, planchette, ouija board; control 970 *ghost*; ghost-hunting; psychical research; exorcism.

occultist, mystic; cabbalist; theosophist, yogi; spiritualist; astrologer, fortune-teller, spaewife *or* man, crystalgazer, palmist 511 *diviner*.

psychic, clairvoyant; telepathist; mindreader, thought-reader; mesmerist, hypnotist; medium, spirit-rapper, automatist, psychographer, spirit-writer; seer, prophet 511 *oracle*.

Adj. *psychical*, psychic, fey, second-sighted; prophetic 511 *predicting*; telepathic, clairvoyant; thought-reading, mind-reading; spiritualistic, mediumistic; ectoplasmic, telekinetic, spirit-rapping; mesmeric, hypnotic.

paranormal, parapsychological, metapsychological, supernatural, preternatural, supranormal, supranatural.

985 The Church

N. *the church*, theocracy 733 *authority*, church government, Canterbury, the Vatican 733 *government*; ecclesiastical order; papalism, papacy, popedom; popishness, ultramontanism; prelatism, prelacy; episcopacy, episcopalianism; presbytery, presbyterianism, congregationalism, ecclesiology.

clericalism, ecclesiasticism, sacerdotalism; priestliness, priesthood, brahminhood; priestdom, priestcraft; Brahminism; benefit of clergy 919 *non-liability*; Holy Office, Index Expurgatorious 757 *prohibition*.

monasticism, monastic life, monachism 895 *celibacy*; cenobitism 883 *seclusion*; monkhood, monkishness 945 *asceticism*.

holy orders, orders, minor orders 986 *cleric*; apostolic succession, ordination, consecration; induction, reading in; installation, enthronement; nomination, presentation, appointment 751 *commission*; preferment, translation, elevation 285 *progression*.

church office 689 *management*; ecclesiastical rank; priesthood; apostolate, apostleship; pontificate, papacy, Holy See, Vatican; cardinalate, cardinalship; patriarchate, exarchate, metropolitanate; primacy, primateship; archiepiscopate, archbishopric; see, bishopric, episcopate, episcopacy, prelacy, prelature; abbotship, abbacy, abbotric; priorate, priorship; archdeaconry, archdeaconate, archdeaconship; deanery, deanship; canonry, canonicate; prebendaryship; deaconate, deaconship; diaconate, subdiaconate; presbyterate, presbytership, eldership, moderatorship, ministership, pastorship, pastorate; rectorship, vicarship, vicariate; curacy, cure of souls; chaplainship, chaplaincy, chaplainry; incumbency, tenure; benefice 773 *possession.*

parish, deanery; presbytery; diocese, bishopric, see, archbishopric; metro-politanate, patriarchate, province 184 *district.*

benefice, incumbency, tenure; living, rectorship, parsonage; glebe, tithe; prebend, prebendal stall, canonry; temporalities, church lands, church endowments 777 *property;* patronage, advowson, right of presentation.

synod, provincial synod, convocation, general council, ecumenical council 692 *council;* college of cardinals, curia; consistory, conclave; House of Bishops, House of Clergy, House of Laity, General Synod, bench of bishops, episcopal bench; chapter, vestry; congregational board, deacons court, session, kirk session, presbytery, synod, general assembly; Sanhedrim 956 *tribunal;* consistorial court, Court of Arches.

Adj. *ecclesiastical,* ecclesiastic, churchly, ecclesiological, theocratic; infallible 733 *authoritative;* priest-ridden, ultramontane 976 *orthodox;* apostolic; hierarchical, pontifical, papal 976 *Roman Catholic;* patriarchal, metropolitan; episcopa , prelatic; episcopalian, presbyterian, Wee Free 978 *sectarian;* prioral, abbatial; conciliar, synodic, presbyteral, capitular; sanhedral, consistorial; provincial, diocesan, parochial.

986 Clergy

N. *clergy,* hierarchy; clerical order, parsondom, the cloth, the pulpit, the ministry; sacerdotal order, priesthood, secular clergy, regular clergy, religious.

cleric, clerk in holy orders, priest, deacon, subdeacon, acolyte, exorcist, lector, ostiary; churchman *or* -woman, ecclesiastic, divine; Doctor of Divinity; clergyman *or* -woman, man *or* woman of the cloth, minister of the Gospel, servant of God; reverend, father, father in God; padre, sky pilot, Holy Joe; beneficed clergyman, beneficiary, pluralist, parson, minister, rector, incumbent, residentiary 776 *possessor;* hedgepriest, priestling 639 *non-*

entity; ordinand, seminarist 538 *learner.*

pastor, shepherd, father in God, minister, woman minister, parish priest, rector, vicar, perpetual curate, curate, abbé; chaplain; confessor, father confessor, penitentiary; spiritual director, spiritual adviser; pardoner; friar; preaching order, predicant; pulpiteer, lay preacher 537 *preacher;* field preacher, missioner, missionary 901 *philanthropist;* evangelist, revivalist, salvationist, hot-gospeller.

church dignitary, dignitary, ecclesiarch, ecclesiastical potentate, hierarch 741 *governor;* pope, Supreme Pontiff, Holy Father, Vicar of Christ, Bishop of Rome, servant of the servants of God, servus servorum Dei; cardinal, prince of the church; patriarch, exarch, metropolitan, primate, archbishop; prelate, diocesan, bishop; suffragan, assistant bishop, 'episcopal curate'; bench of bishops, episcopate, Lords Spiritual; episcopi vagantes; archpriest, archpresbyter; archdeacon, deacon, subdeacon; dean, subdean, rural dean; canon, canon regular, canon secular, residentiary; prebendary, capitular; archimandrite; Superior, Mother Superior; abbot, abbess; prior, prioress, Grand Prior; elder, presbyter, moderator.

monk, monastic 895 *celibate;* hermit, cenobite, Desert Father 883 *unsocial person;* Orthodox monk, caloyer; Islamic monk, santon, marabout; sufi 979 *pious person;* dervish, fakir 945 *ascetic;* Buddhist monk, pongye, bonze; brother, regular, conventual; superior, archimandrite, abbot, prior; novice, lay brother; friar, begging friar, mendicant friar, discalced friar, barefoot friar; monks, religious; fraternity, brotherhood, lay brotherhood, friary; order, religious order 708 *community;* Black Monk, Benedictine, Cistercian, Bernardine, Trappist; Carthusian; Cluniac; Gilbertine; Premonstratensian, Mathurin, Trinitarian; Dominicans, Friars Majors, Black Friars; Franciscans, Poverelli, Grey Friars, Friars Minors, Capuchins; Augustines, Austin Friars; Carmelites, White Friars; Crutched Friars; Beghards; teaching order, missionary order, Society of Jesus, Jesuits; crusading order, Templars, Knights Templars; Hospitallers, Knights Hospitallers, Knights of the Hospital of St John of Jerusalem, Knights of Malta.

nun, clergywoman; anchoress, recluse; religious, bride of Christ; sister, mother; novice, postulant; lay sister; Superioress, Mother Superior, abbess, prioress, canoness, deaconess; sisterhood, lay sisterhood, beguinage, Beguine; Carmelites, Ursulines. Poor Clares, Little Sisters of the Poor, Sisters of Mercy.

church officer, elder, presbyter, deacon 741 *officer;* priest, chantry priest, chaplain; curate in charge, minister; lay preacher; lay reader; acolyte, server, altar boy; crucifer, thurifer; chorister, choirboy, precentor, succentor, cantor 413 *choir*; sidesman *or* -woman; churchwarden; clerk, vestry clerk, parish clerk, session clerk; beadle, verger, pew-opener; sacristan, sexton; grave digger, bellringer.

priest, chief priest, high priest, archpriest, hierophant; priestess, Vestal, Pythia, Pythoness, prophetess, prophet 511 *oracle*; Levite; rabbi; imam, mufti; Brahmin; bonze, lama, Dalai Lama, Panchen Lama, Karmapa Lama; pontifex, pontiff, flamen, archflamen; Druid, Druidess; shaman, witch doctor.

church title, Holy Father; Eminence; Monsignor, Monseigneur; Lordship, Lord Spiritual; the Reverend —; Most Reverend, Right Reverend, Very Reverend; parson, rector, vicar; father, brother, Dom; mother, sister.

monastery, friary, priory, abbey; monkery; bonzery, lamasery; cloister, convent, nunnery, beguinage; ashram, hermitage 192 *retreat*; community house 192 *abode*; theological college, seminary; cell 194 *room*.

parsonage, presbytery, rectory, vicarage; manse; deanery, archdeaconry 192 *abode*; palace, bishop's palace; patriarchate; Lambeth, Vatican; close, cathedral close, precincts 235 *enclosure*.

Adj. *monastic*, cloistered, enclosed; monkish, celibate; contemplative, in retreat; cowled, veiled; tonsured, shaven and shorn.

Vb. *take orders*, take holy orders, be ordained, enter the church, enter the ministry, become a minister *or* vicar, wear the cloth; take vows, take the tonsure, take the cowl; take the veil, become a nun; enter a monastery *or* a nunnery, renounce the world.

987 Laity

N. *laity*, lay people, temporalty, people, civilians 869 *common people*; cure, charge, parish; flock, sheep, fold; diocesans, parishioners; brethren, congregation, society; lay brethren, lay sisterhood, lay community 708 *community*.

lay person, laic; lay rector, lay deacon; lay brother, lay sister; catechumen, ordinand, seminarist, novice, postulant 538 *learner*; lay preacher, lay reader; elder, deacon, deaconess 986 *church officer*; parishioner, diocesan, member of the flock; laicizer, secularizer.

988 Ritual

N. *ritual*, procedure, way of doing things, method, routine 624 *way*; prescribed procedure, due order 60 *order*; form, order, liturgy 610 *practice*; ceremonial, ceremony 875 *formality*.

rite, mode of worship 981 *cult*; observance, ritual practice 610 *practice*; form, order, ordinance, rubric, formula, formulary 693 *precept*; ceremony, solemnity, sacrament, mystery 876 *celebration*; rites, mysteries 551 *representation*; initiatory rite, rite of passage, circumcision, female circumcision, initiation, initiation rites, baptism 299 *reception*; christening; bar mitzvah, bat mitzvah; salat, puja.

ministration, functioning, officiation, performance 676 *action*; administration, celebration, solemnization; the pulpit, sermon, address, preaching 534 *teaching*; homily 534 *lecture*; homiletics 579 *oratory*; pastoral care, cure of souls; pastoral epistle, pastoral letter; confession, auricular confession; shrift, absolution, penance.

Christian rite, rites of the Church; sacrament, the seven sacraments; baptism, christening, adult baptism, believer's baptism, infant baptism, paedobaptism 299 *reception*; immersion, total immersion 303 *immersion*; laying on of hands, confirmation, First Communion; Holy Communion, Eucharist, reservation of the sacraments; penitential rites 941 *penance*; absolution 960 *acquittal*; Holy Matrimony 894 *marriage*; Holy Orders 985 *the church*; Holy Unction, chrism; visitation of the sick, extreme unction, last rites, viaticum; burial of the dead; requiem mass; liturgy, order of service, order of baptism, marriage service, solemnization of matrimony, nuptial mass; churching of women; ordination, ordering of deacons, ordering of priests; consecration, consecration of bishops; exorcism 300 *ejection*; excommunication, ban, bell, book and candle; canonization, beatification; dedication, undedication.

Holy Communion, Eucharist Blessed Eucharist; mass, high mass, missa solemnis; sung mass, missa cantata; low mass; public mass, private mass; communion, the Lord's Supper; preparation, confession, asperges; service of the book, introit, the Kyries, the Gloria, the Lesson, the Gradual, the Collects, the Gospel, the creed; service of the Altar, the offertory, offertory sentence, offertory prayers, the biddings; the blessing, the thanksgiving, Sursum Corda, Preface, Sanctus, Great Amen; the breaking of the bread, the commixture; the Pax; consecration; elevation of the Host; Angus Dei; the Communion; kiss of peace; prayers of thanksgiving, the dismissal; the blessing.

the sacrament, the Holy Sacrament, the Blessed Eucharist; Corpus Christi, body and blood of Christ; real presence, transubstantiation, consubstantiation, impanation; the elements, bread and wine, altar bread;

consecrated bread, host; reserved sacrament; viaticum.

church service, office, duty, service 981 *act of worship*; liturgy, celebration, concelebration; canonical hours, matins, lauds, prime, terce, sext, none *or* nones, vespers, compline; the little hours; morning prayer, matins; evening prayer, evensong, benediction; Tenebrae; vigil, midnight mass, watchnight service; devotional service, three-hour service; novena.

ritual act, symbolical act, sacramental, symbolism 551 *representation*; lustration, purification; thurification, incense-burning 338 *vaporization*; sprinkling, aspersion, asperges; circumambulation 314 *circuitous motion*; procession 285 *progression*; stations of the cross 981 *act of worship*; obeisance, bowing, kneeling, genuflexion, prostration, homage, Toronto blessing 920 *respects*; crossing oneself, signation, sign of the cross 547 *gesture*; eucharistic rite, breaking the bread; intinction; elevating of the Host; kiss of peace; sacrifice.

ritual object, cross, rood, Holy Rood, crucifix; altar, Lord's table, communion table; altar furniture, altar cloth, candle, candlestick; communion wine, communion bread; cup, chalice, grail, Holy Grail, Sangrail; cruet; paten, ciborium, pyx, pyx chest, tabernacle; monstrance, chrism, chrismatory; collection plate, salver; incense, incensory, censer, thurible; holy water; aspergillum; aspersorium; piscina; sacring bell, Sanctus bell; font, baptismal font, baptistery; baptismal garment, chrisom, christening gown; wedding garment, wedding dress, bridal veil, wedding ring; devotional object, relics, sacred relics; reliquary, shrine, casket 194 *box*; icon, Pietà, Holy Sepulchre, stations of the cross 551 *image*; osculatory, pax; Agnus Dei, rosary, beads, beadroll 981 *prayers*; votive candle; non-Christian objects, Ark of the Covenant, Mercy-seat; sevenbranched candlestick; shewbread; laver; hyssop; sackcloth and ashes; libation dish, patina; joss stick; prayer wheel; altar of incense; urim, thummim; temple veil.

hymnbook, hymnal, hymnary; psalm-book, book of psalms, psalter 981 *hymn*.

holy day, feast, feast day, festival 837 *festivity*; fast day, meatless day 946 *fast*; high day, day of observance, day of obligation 876 *celebration*; sabbath, sabbath day, day of rest 681 *leisure*; Lord's Day, Sunday; saint's day 141 *anniversary*.

Religious Festivals and Holy Days

Christian: Advent; Christmas, Christmastide, Yuletide, Noel, Nativity; Epiphany, Twelfth Night; Lent, Shrove Tuesday, Ash Wednesday, Passion Sunday; Easter, Eastertide, Holy Week, Passion Week, Palm Sunday, Maundy Thursday, Good Friday, Easter Sunday; Ascension Day; Whitsuntide, Whitsun, Pentecost; Corpus Christi; Trinity Sunday; All Saints, All Souls, Lady Day, Feast of the Annunciation; Candlemas, Feast of the Purification; Feast of the Assumption; Lammas, Martinmas, Michaelmas.

Jewish: Hanukkah *or* Chanukkah *or* Chanukah, Feast of Dedication, Feast of Lights; Pesach *or* Pesah, Passover; Purim, Feast of Lots; Rosh Hashanah, New Year, Feast of Trumpets; Shavuot *or* Shavuoth *or* Shabuoth, Feast of Weeks, Pentecost; Sukkot *or* Sukkoth *or* Succoth, Feast of Tabernacles, Feast of Ingathering; Yom Kippur, Day of Atonement.

Muslim: Ashura; Bairam, Lesser Bairam, Greater Bairam; Eid *or* Id al-Adha, Feast of Sacrifice; Eid *or* Id al-Fitr, Feast of the Breaking of the Fast; Mawlid an-Nabi, the Birthday of the Prophet Muhammad; Moharram *or* Muharram, New Year; Ramadan.

Hindu: Diwali *or* Divali *or* Dewali, Festival of Lights; Durga Puja; Holi, Festival of Fire; Maha Shivaratri; Mela, Kumbh Mela, Maha Kumbh Mela; Navaratri; Ramnavami.

Buddhist: Bodhi Day; Dharma Day; Sangha Day; Paranirvana Day; Wesak *or* Vesak, Buddha Day.

Sikh: Baisakhi, Diwali *or* Divali *or* Dewali, Festival of Lights; gurpurb; Hola Mohalla; Maghi.

Wiccan: Beltane, Imbolc, Lughnasadh, Samhain.

Adj. *ritual*, procedural; formal, solemn, ceremonial, liturgical; processional, recessional; symbolic, symbolical.

ritualistic, ceremonious, ceremonial, formulistic.

Vb. *perform ritual*, perform the rites, say office, celebrate, concelebrate, officiate; take the service, lead worship 981 *offer worship*; baptize, christen, confirm, ordain, lay on hands; minister, administer the sacraments, give communion; sacrifice, offer sacrifice, make sacrifice; offer prayers, bless, give benediction; anathematize, ban, ban with bell, book and candle; excommunicate, unchurch, unfrock; dedicate, consecrate, deconsecrate; purify, lustrate, asperge; cense, burn incense; anoint, give extreme unction; confess, absolve, pronounce absolution, shrive; take communion, partake of Holy Communion, receive the sacraments; bow, kneel, genuflect, prostrate oneself; sign oneself, cross oneself, make the sign of the cross; take holy water; tell one's beads, say one's rosary; make one's stations; process, go in procession; circumambulate; fast, flagellate oneself, do penance.

989 Clerical dress

N. *clerical dress*, clericals, canonicals, cloth, clerical black 228 *dress*; frock, soutane, cassock, scapular; cloak, gown, Geneva gown 228 *cloak*; robe, cowl, hood, capuche; lappet, bands, Geneva bands, preaching bands; clerical collar, dog collar; chimere, lawn sleeves; apron, gaiters, shovel hat; cardinal's hat, priest's cap, biretta, black biretta, purple biretta, red biretta; skullcap, calotte, zucchetto;

Salvation Army bonnet 228 *headgear*; tonsure, shaven crown 229 *bareness*; prayer-cap; tallith.

vestments, ephod, priestly vesture, canonical robes; pontificalia, pontificals; cassock, surplice, rochet; cope, tunicle, dalmatic, alb 228 *robe*; amice, chasuble; stole, deacon's stole; scarf, tippet, pallium; cingulum; maniple, fanon; mitre, tiara, triple crown 743 *regalia*; papal vestment, orale; crosier, crook, staff, pastoral staff 743 *badge of rank*; pectoral 222 *cross*; episcopal ring; orphrey *or* orfray, ecclesiastical embroidery 844 *ornamentation*.

990 Temple
N. *temple*, pantheon; shrine; place of worship; joss house; house of God, tabernacle, the Temple, House of the Lord; house of prayer; pagoda, stupa, tope, dagoba, ziggurat 164 *building*; torii, toran, gopuram 263 *doorway*. (See also *church* below.)

holy place, holy ground, sacred ground; sanctuary, adytum, cella, naos; Ark of the Covenant, Mercy-seat, Sanctum, Holy of Holies, oracle; martyry, sacred tomb, marabout, sepulchre, Holy Sepulchre; graveyard, God's Acre 364 *cemetery*; place of pilgrimage; Holy City, Zion, Jerusalem; Mecca, Benares.

church, God's house; parish church, mother church, daughter church, chapel of ease; cathedral, minster, procathedral; basilica; abbey; kirk, chapel, tabernacle, temple, bethel, ebenezer; conventicle, meeting house, prayer house; house of prayer, oratory, chantry, chantry chapel; synagogue, mosque, masjid, gurdwara.

altar, high altar, sacrarium, sanctuary, bema; altar stone, altar slab; altar table, Lord's table, communion table; altar bread 988 *the sacrament*; altar pyx; prothesis, credence, credence table 988 *ritual object*; canopy, baldachin, altarpiece, diptych, triptych, altar screen, reredos; altar cloth, altar frontal, antependium; predella, altar rails.

church utensil, font, baptistry; ambry, stoup, piscina; chalice, paten 988 *ritual object*; pulpit, lectern; bible, chained bible, hymnal, hymnary, prayer book 981 *prayers*; hassock, kneeler; salver, collection plate, offertory bag; organ, harmonium; bell, church bell, carillon.

church interior, nave, aisle, apse, ambulatory, transept; chancel, chevet, choir, sanctuary; hagioscope, squint; chancel screen, rood screen, jube, rood loft, gallery, organ loft; stall, choir stall, sedile, sedilia, misericorde; pew, box pew; pulpit, ambo; lectern; chapel, side chapel, Lady chapel, feretory; confessional; clerestory, triforium; spandrel; stained glass, stained-glass window, rose window, jesse window; calvary, stations of the cross, Easter sepulchre; baptistry, font; aumbry, sacristy, vestry; undercroft, crypt, vault; rood, cross, crucifix.

church exterior, porch, narthex, galilee; tympanum 263 *doorway*; tower, steeple, spire 209 *high structure*; bell tower, bellcote, belfry, campanile; buttress, flying buttress 218 *prop*; cloister, ambulatory; chapterhouse, presbytery 692 *council*; churchyard, kirkyard, lychgate; close 235 *enclosure*.

Adj. *churchlike*, churchy, basilican, cathedral-like, cathedralesque; cruciform 222 *crossed*; apsidal 248 *curved*; architectural style: Romanesque, Norman, Gothic, Early English, Decorated, Perpendicular, baroque, Puginesque, Gothic revival 192 *architectural*.

Index

For a note on how to use the index, see p. xii

917 vb.
justify 927 vb.
acquit 960 vb.
acquittal
duty 917 n.
acquittal 960 n.
acreage
measure 183 n.
lands 777 n.
acres
measure 183 n.
land 344 n.
lands 777 n.
acrid
keen 174 adj.
pungent 388 adj.
unsavoury
391 adj.
fetid 397 adj.
acrimonious
keen 174 adj.
resentful 891 adj.
acrimony
edge 234 n.
rudeness 885 n.
hatred 888 n.
resentment 891 n.
malevolence
898 n.
acrobat
athlete 162 n.
entertainer 594 n.
proficient person
696 n.
acrobatics
athletics 162 n.
acronym
word 559 n.
across-the-board
extensive 32 adj.
comprehensive
52 adj.
inclusive 78 adj.
general 79 adj.
act
imitate 20 vb.
operate 173 vb.
duplicity 541 n.
act 594 n.
dramatic theory
594 n.
stage show 594 n.
function 622 vb.
be instrumental
628 vb.
deed 676 n.
do 676 vb.
behave 688 vb.
precept 693 n.
decree 737 n.
act for
substitute 150 vb.

deputize 755 vb.
acting
substituted
150 adj.
acting 594 n.
action
dramatic theory
594 n.
action 676 n.
deed 676 n.
conduct 688 n.
fight 716 n.
battle 718 n.
accusation 928 n.
litigation 959 n.
actionable
legal 953 n.
illegal 954 n.
action replay
repetition 106 n.
activate
operate 173 vb.
invigorate 174 vb.
active
active 678 adj.
active service
warfare 718 n.
activist
doer 676 n.
busy person 678 n.
political party
708 n.
activity
activity 678 n.
act of God
ruin 165 n.
necessity 596 n.
compulsion 740 n.
actor
imitator 20 n.
actor 594 n.
agent 686 n.
actress
actor 594 n.
actual
real 1 adj.
substantial 3 adj.
present 121 adj.
true 494 adj.
actuality
reality 1 n.
truth 494 n.
actuary
accountant 808 n.
actuate
operate 173 vb.
influence 178 vb.
move 265 vb.
motivate 612 vb.
acuity
sharpness 256 n.
sound judgment

498 n.
acumen
discrimination
463 n.
sound judgment
498 n.
acute
keen 174 adj.
violent 176 adj.
sharp 256 adj.
sentient 374 adj.
strident 407 adj.
intelligent 498 adj.
cunning 698 adj.
acuteness
sharpness 256 n.
sound judgment
498 n.
adage
maxim 496 n.
phrase 563 n.
adamant
hardness 326 n.
obstinate 602 adj.
adapt
adjust 24 vb.
modify 143 vb.
translate 520 vb.
adaptable
conformable
83 adj.
adaptation
adaptation 24 n.
conformity 83 n.
transformation
143 n.
musical piece
412 n.
translation 520 n.
edition 589 n.
add
add 38 vb.
added
additional 38 adj.
addendum
addition 38 n.
adjunct 40 n.
extra 40 n.
adder
reptile 365 n.
bane 659 n.
**add fuel to the
fire/flames**
augment 36 vb.
kindle 381 vb.
animate 821 vb.
aggravate 832 vb.
enrage 891 vb.
addict
enthusiast 504 n.
creature of habit
610 n.

sick person 651 n.
addiction
habit 610 n.
intemperance
943 n.
addictive
influential
178 adj.
intoxicating
949 adj.
**add insult to
injury**
aggravate 832 vb.
addition
addition 38 n.
adjunct 40 n.
additive
addition 38 n.
additional 38 adj.
adjunct 40 n.
extra 40 n.
component 58 n.
dieting 301 n.
food content
301 n.
add on
place after 65 vb.
add-on
addition 38 n.
adjunct 40 n.
join 45 vb.
exaggerate 546 vb.
address
place 185 n.
situation 186 n.
locality 187 n.
abode 192 n.
send 272 vb.
name 561 vb.
orate 579 vb.
oration 579 n.
speech 579 n.
address 583 n.
speak to 583 vb.
way 624 n.
ministration
988 n.
addressee
resident 191 n.
recipient 782 n.
add up
add 38 vb.
be intelligible
516 vb.
add up to
number 86 vb.
mean 514 vb.
adenoids
swelling 253 n.
respiratory disease
651 n.
adept
skilful 694 adj.

expert 694 adj.
proficient person
696 n.
adequate
powerful 160 adj.
sufficient 635 adj.
useful 640 adj.
middling 732 adj.
adhere
unite with 45 vb.
cohere 48 vb.
be contiguous
202 vb.
transfer 272 vb.
retain 778 vb.
adherent
cohesive 48 adj.
follower 284 n.
auxiliary 707 n.
signatory 765 n.
religionist 973 n.
sectarian 978 n.
adhere to
observe 768 vb.
adhesive
connective 45 adj.
adhesive 47 n.
cohesive 48 adj.
retentive 778 adj.
ad hoc
specially 80 adv.
extempore
609 adv.
spontaneity 609 n.
spontaneous
609 adj.
unprepared
670 adj.
unreadily 670 adv.
ad infinitum
infinitely 107 adv.
adjacent
near 200 adj.
adjective
adjunct 40 n.
part of speech
564 n.
adjoin
be contiguous
202 vb.
adjourn
put off 136 vb.
pause 145 vb.
adjudicate
judge 480 vb.
try a case 959 vb.
adjudicator
estimator 480 n.
adjunct
adjunct 40 n.
adjust
adjust 24 vb.

portion 783 n.
money 797 n.
receipt 807 n.
due 915 adj.
allowing
thus 8 adv.
allowing for
provided 468 adv.
qualifying 468 adj.
alloy
a mixture 43 n.
mix 43 vb.
compound 50 n.
mineral 359 n.
all right
not bad 644 adj.
all-rounder
athlete 162 n.
proficient person
696 n.
player 837 n.
All Saints
holy day 988 n.
**all-singing,
  all-dancing**
comprehensive
52 adj.
ornamental
844 adj.
all set
prepared 669 adj.
all sorts
medley 43 n.
everyman 79 n.
All Souls
holy day 988 n.
all talk
thing that lacks
substance 4 n.
all the same
nevertheless
468 adv.
all the time
while 108 adv.
**all the time in
  the world**
slowness 278 n.
leisure 681 n.
all the way
throughout 54 adv.
all together
collectively 52 adv.
together 74 adv.
all told
completely 54 adv.
all to the good
well 615 adv.
allude
imply 523 vb.
hint 524 vb.
all up with, be
be destroyed

165 vb.
allure
attract 291 vb.
attraction 291 n.
tempt 612 vb.
delight 826 vb.
alluring
exciting 821 adj.
pleasurable
826 adj.
personable
841 adj.
allusion
act of referring
9 n.
metaphor 519 n.
alluvium
leavings 41 n.
soil 344 n.
ally
join 45 vb.
combine 50 vb.
assenter 488 n.
helper 703 n.
cooperate 706 vb.
colleague 707 n.
join a party
708 vb.
contract 765 vb.
friend 880 n.
almanac
directory 87 n.
chronology 117 n.
almighty
powerful 160 adj.
godlike 965 adj.
Almighty, the
the Deity 965 n.
almoner
nurse 658 n.
almost
almost 33 adv.
on the whole
52 adv.
nearly 200 adv.
alms
gift 781 n.
almshouse
retreat 192 n.
aloes
unsavouriness
391 n.
alone
alone 88 adj.
singly 88 adv.
along
lengthwise
203 adv.
alongside
near 200 adv.
along with
in addition

38 adv.
with 89 adv.
aloof
distant 199 adj.
incurious 454 adj.
impassive 820 adj.
proud 871 adj.
hostile 881 adj.
unsociable
883 adj.
aloud
loudly 400 adv.
alp
high land 209 n.
alphabet
beginning 68 n.
list 87 n.
letter 558 n.
lettering 586 n.
alphanumeric
computerized
86 adj.
already
before 119 adv.
at present
121 adv.
also
in addition
38 adv.
also-ran
inferior 35 n.
loser 728 n.
altar
ritual object
988 n.
altar 990 n.
altar boy
church officer
986 n.
altarpiece
altar 990 n.
alter
adjust 24 vb.
change 143 vb.
modify 143 vb.
qualify 468 vb.
alteration
difference 15 n.
change 143 n.
transition 147 n.
altercation
quarrel 709 n.
contention 716 n.
alter ego
identity 13 n.
analogue 18 n.
colleague 707 n.
deputy 755 n.
close friend 880 n.
alternate
correlate 12 vb.
correlative 12 adj.

come after 65 vb.
sequential 65 adj.
be discontinuous
72 vb.
discontinuous
72 adj.
periodical 141 adj.
substitute 150 n.
vary 152 vb.
fluctuate 317 vb.
deputy 755 n.
alternately
correlatively
12 adv.
alternating
correlative 12 adj.
sequential 65 adj.
discontinuous
72 adj.
periodical 141 adj.
alternative
changeable
143 adj.
substitute 150 n.
choice 605 n.
contrivance 623 n.
**alternative
  reading**
interpretation
520 n.
alternator
electronics 160 n.
although
although 182 adv.
provided 468 adv.
altitude
quantity 26 n.
degree 27 n.
height 209 n.
alto
vocalist 413 n.
altogether
completely 54 adv.
altruism
philanthropy
901 n.
disinterestedness
931 n.
altruistic
benevolent
897 adj.
philanthropic
901 adj.
disinterested
931 adj.
alumnus
student 538 n.
always
while 108 adv.
**Alzheimer's
  disease**
old age 131 n.

helplessness
161 n.
mental disorder
503 n.
a.m.
o'clock 117 adv.
morning 128 n.
amalgam
a mixture 43 n.
compound 50 n.
amalgamation
mixture 43 n.
combination 50 n.
association 706 n.
amass
join 45 vb.
bring together
74 vb.
store 632 vb.
take 786 vb.
amateur
ignorance 491 n.
beginner 538 n.
unskilled 695 adj.
bungler 697 n.
amateurish
ignorant 491 adj.
bungled 695 adj.
unskilled 695 adj.
amaze
surprise 508 vb.
disappoint 509 vb.
impress 821 vb.
be wonderful
864 vb.
amazing
prodigious 32 adj.
unexpected
508 adj.
wonderful 864 adj.
Amazon
violent creature
176 n.
female 373 n.
soldier 722 n.
brave person
855 n.
ambassador
messenger 529 n.
envoy 754 n.
amber
resin 357 n.
brownness 430 n.
orange 432 n.
yellow 433 adj.
yellowness 433 n.
gem 844 n.
ambidextrous
dual 90 adj.
double 91 adj.
skilful 694 adj.
ambience
surroundings

230 n.
painting 553 n.
ambiguity
disagreement 25 n.
uncertainty 474 n.
connotation 514 n.
unintelligibility
517 n.
equivocalness
518 n.
obscurity 568 n.
ambition
motive 612 n.
intention 617 n.
aspiration 852 n.
desire 859 n.
desired object
859 n.
ambivalence
contrariety 14 n.
disagreement 25 n.
uncertainty 474 n.
equivocalness
518 n.
falsehood 541 n.
amble
gait 265 n.
walking 267 n.
ride 267 vb.
wander 267 vb.
move slowly
278 vb.
slowness 278 n.
ambulance
conveyance 267 n.
vehicle 274 n.
hospital 658 n.
ambush
surprise 508 vb.
ambush 527 n.
ambush 527 vb.
stratagem 698 n.
ameliorate
make better
654 vb.
amen
amen 488 int.
assent 488 n.
amenable
credulous 487 adj.
willing 597 adj.
obedient 739 adj.
amend
rectify 654 vb.
repair 656 vb.
amendment
amendment 654 n.
amends
compensation
31 n.
restoration 656 n.
remedy 658 n.

restitution 787 n.
atonement 941 n.
amenity
pleasurableness
826 n.
amiable
pleasurable
826 adj.
friendliness 880 n.
amiable 884 adj.
amicable
friendly 880 adj.
amiable 884 adj.
amid
among 43 adv.
between 231 adv.
amidst
among 43 adv.
between 231 adv.
amiss
amiss 616 adv.
badly 645 adv.
ammunition
means 629 n.
ammunition
723 n.
amnesia
no memory 506 n.
amnesty
amnesty 506 n.
forget 506 vb.
rescue 668 n.
exempt 919 vb.
non-liability
919 n.
among
among 43 adv.
between 231 adv.
amongst
among 43 adv.
between 231 adv.
amoral
wicked 934 adj.
unchaste 951 adj.
irreligious 974 adj.
amorous
loving 887 adj.
amorphous
abnormal 84 adj.
formless 244 adj.
amount
quantity 26 n.
funds 797 n.
price 809 n.
ampere
electricity 160 n.
amphibious
dual 90 adj.
double 91 adj.
animal 365 adj.
amphitheatre
theatre 594 n.

arena 724 n.
ample
great 32 adj.
many 104 adj.
spacious 183 adj.
fat 195 adj.
large 195 adj.
broad 205 adj.
diffuse 570 adj.
plentiful 635 adj.
liberal 813 adj.
amplification
increase 36 n.
expansion 197 n.
diffuseness 570 n.
amplifier
megaphone 400 n.
music player
414 n.
hearing aid 415 n.
amplify
augment 36 vb.
enlarge 197 vb.
be diffuse 570 vb.
amplitude
degree 27 n.
largeness 32 n.
fullness 54 n.
range 183 n.
size 95 n.
breadth 205 n.
amputate
subtract 39 vb.
break up 46 vb.
practise medicine
658 vb.
amulet
jewellery 844 n.
talisman 983 n.
amuse
amuse 837 vb.
amusement
merriment 833 n.
amusement 837 n.
**amusement
arcade**
gambling den
618 n.
place of amuse-
ment 837 n.
amusing
amusing 837 adj.
an
one 88 adj.
anachronism
anachronism
118 n.
anaemia
blood 335 n.
colourlessness
426 n.
blood disease

651 n.
anaemic
colourless 426 adj.
diseased 651 adj.
unhealthy 651 adj.
anaesthesia
insensitivity
375 n.
anaesthetic
anaesthetic 375 n.
remedial 658 adj.
anagram
equivocalness
518 n.
enigma 530 n.
anal
back 238 adj.
analgesic
anaesthetic 375 n.
antidote 658 n.
drug 658 n.
remedial 658 adj.
relief 831 n.
analogous
relative 9 adj.
correlative 12 adj.
similar 18 adj.
equal 28 adj.
symmetrical
245 adj.
analogue
analogue 18 n.
computerized
86 adj.
analogy
relativeness 9 n.
similarity 18 n.
comparison 462 n.
analyse
break up 46 vb.
decompose 51 vb.
class 62 vb.
enquire 459 vb.
experiment
461 vb.
argue 475 vb.
analysis
separation 46 n.
decomposition
51 n.
arrangement 62 n.
enquiry 459 n.
experiment 461 n.
grammar 564 n.
compendium
592 n.
analyst
psychologist
447 n.
enquirer 459 n.
experimenter
461 n.

mental disorder
503 n.
anarchism
anarchy 734 n.
sedition 738 n.
anarchist
anarchist 61 n.
revolutionary
149 n.
destroyer 168 n.
political party
708 n.
rebel 738 n.
evildoer 904 n.
anarchy
government 733 n.
governmental
733 adj.
anarchy 734 n.
revolt 738 n.
anathema
hateful object
888 n.
curse 899 n.
anatomy
structure 331 n.
biology 358 n.
ancestor
precursor 66 n.
source 156 n.
paternity 169 n.
ancestral
parental 169 adj.
ancestry
heredity 5 n.
kinship 11 n.
origin 68 n.
source 156 n.
genealogy 169 n.
nobility 868 n.
anchor
affix 45 vb.
place 187 vb.
place oneself
187 vb.
live 192 vb.
come to rest
266 vb.
sailing aid 269 n.
protection 660 n.
badge of rank
743 n.
hope 852 n.
ancient
great 32 adj.
past 125 adj.
olden 127 adj.
worshipful
866 adj.
ancient history
repetition 106 n.
ancillary
inferior 35 adj.

apologize
change one's mind
603 vb.
recant 603 vb.
regret 830 vb.
be penitent
939 vb.
atone 941 vb.
apology
recantation 603 n.
pretext 614 n.
penitence 939 n.
atonement 941 n.
apoplectic fit
excitable state
822 n.
apoplexy
helplessness
161 n.
insensitivity
375 n.
illness 651 n.
apostasy
change of mind
603 n.
impiety 980 n.
apostle
messenger 529 n.
preacher 537 n.
religious teacher
973 n.
apostolic
scriptural 975 adj.
ecclesiastical
985 adj.
apostrophe
punctuation
547 n.
address 583 n.
soliloquy 585 n.
appal
displease 827 vb.
appalling
distressing
827 adj.
apparatchik
official 690 n.
officer 741 n.
apparatus
tool 630 n.
apparel
clothing 228 n.
apparent
visible 443 adj.
appearing 445 adj.
certain 473 adj.
manifest 522 adj.
apparition
visual fallacy
440 n.
manifestation
522 n.

ghost 970 n.
appeal
attract 291 vb.
attraction 291 n.
affirm 532 vb.
negation 533 n.
address 583 n.
motivate 612 vb.
entreat 761 vb.
entreaty 761 n.
request 761 n.
deprecate 762 vb.
offering 781 n.
payment 804 n.
excitation 821 n.
pleasurableness
826 n.
beauty 841 n.
legal trial 959 n.
appeal against
negate 533 vb.
deprecate 762 vb.
appealing
pleasurable
826 adj.
personable
841 adj.
desired 859 adj.
appeal to
speak to 583 vb.
entreat 761 vb.
request 761 vb.
appear
begin 68 vb.
happen 154 vb.
arrive 295 vb.
appear 445 vb.
appearance
form 243 n.
arrival 295 n.
appearance 445 n.
appearances
circumstance 8 n.
appearance 445 n.
etiquette 848 n.
appear for
deputize 755 vb.
appease
assuage 177 vb.
pacify 719 vb.
content 828 vb.
offer worship
981 vb.
appellant
petitioner 763 n.
appellant
petitioner 763 n.
what is due 915 n.
accuser 928 n.
litigant 959 n.
appellation
name 561 n.
nomenclature
561 n.

appendage
addition 38 n.
adjunct 40 n.
limb 53 n.
sequel 67 n.
concomitant 89 n.
appendix
addition 38 n.
adjunct 40 n.
sequel 67 n.
extremity 69 n.
hanging object
217 n.
edition 589 n.
appertain
be related 9 vb.
be included 78 vb.
appertaining
relative 9 adj.
appetite
eating 301 n.
taste 386 n.
desire 859 n.
hunger 859 n.
liking 859 n.
appetizer
prelude 66 n.
stimulant 174 n.
hors-d'oeuvres
301 n.
savouriness 390 n.
appetizing
tasty 386 adj.
savoury 390 adj.
exciting 821 adj.
desired 859 adj.
applaud
applaud 923 vb.
applause
rejoicing 835 n.
repute 866 n.
applause 923 n.
appliance
instrument 628 n.
tool 630 n.
use 673 n.
applicable
relevant 9 adj.
apt 24 adj.
useful 640 adj.
advisable 642 adj.
applicant
respondent 460 n.
petitioner 763 n.
application
act of referring
9 n.
relevance 9 n.
meditation 449 n.
attention 455 n.
connotation 514 n.
study 536 n.

perseverance
600 n.
use 673 n.
assiduousness
678 n.
request 761 n.
apply
relate 9 vb.
use 673 vb.
offer oneself
759 vb.
request 761 vb.
apply for
require 627 vb.
apply oneself
think 449 vb.
study 536 vb.
exert oneself
682 vb.
apply to
request 761 vb.
appoint
select 605 vb.
employ 622 vb.
commission
751 vb.
allocate 783 vb.
appointment
choice 605 n.
job 622 n.
command 737 n.
mandate 751 n.
holy orders 985 n.
apportion
allocate 783 vb.
apposite
relevant 9 adj.
appraise
appraise 465 vb.
estimate 480 vb.
appreciate
grow 36 vb.
appraise 465 vb.
be dear 811 vb.
have taste 846 vb.
honour 866 vb.
love 887 vb.
approve 923 vb.
appreciation
discrimination
463 n.
measurement
465 n.
estimate 480 n.
interpretation
520 n.
feeling 818 n.
gratitude 907 n.
approbation
923 n.
appreciative
grateful 907 adj.

approving 923 adj.
apprehend
know 490 vb.
understand
516 vb.
arrest 747 vb.
take 786 vb.
apprehension
idea 451 n.
knowledge 490 n.
expectation 507 n.
taking 786 n.
nervousness 854 n.
legal process
959 n.
apprehensive
suffering 825 adj.
nervous 854 adj.
apprentice
beginner 538 n.
immature 670 adj.
artisan 686 n.
unskilled 695 adj.
dependant 742 n.
apprise
inform 524 vb.
approach
doorway 263 n.
approach 289 n.
approach 289 vb.
speak to 583 vb.
policy 623 n.
way 624 n.
offer 759 n.
request 761 n.
request 761 vb.
approachable
accessible 289 adj.
possible 469 adj.
easy 701 adj.
approaching
relative 9 adj.
approaching
289 adj.
approbation
approbation
923 n.
appropriate
circumstantial
8 adj.
relevant 9 adj.
apt 24 adj.
special 80 adj.
appropriate
786 vb.
right 913 adj.
approval
assent 488 n.
permission 756 n.
repute 866 n.
approbation
923 n.

peace 717 n.
pacification 719 n.
Armistice Day
special day 876 n.
armlet
loop 250 n.
badge of rank
743 n.
jewellery 844 n.
armorial
heraldic 547 adj.
armory
heraldry 547 n.
armour
safeguard 660 vb.
armour 713 n.
defend 713 vb.
armoured
hard 326 adj.
resolute 599 adj.
invulnerable
660 adj.
armoured car
war chariot 274 n.
cavalry 722 n.
armoury
accumulation 74 n.
storage 632 n.
workshop 687 n.
arsenal 723 n.
arms
article of clothing
228 n.
(See also **sleeve**.)
vocation 622 n.
safeguard 662 n.
war 718 n.
arms 723 n.
(See also
weapon.)
honours 866 n.
arm's length
measurement of
length 203 n.
arms race
arms 723 n.
army
army 722 n.
aroma
odour 394 n.
fragrance 396 n.
aromatic
pungent 388 adj.
savoury 390 adj.
fragrant 396 adj.
around
nearly 200 adv.
around 230 adv.
arouse
cause 156 vb.
cause feeling
374 vb.

have or give sexual
pleasure 376 vb.
raise the alarm
665 vb.
excite 821 vb.
arraign
indict 928 vb.
litigate 959 vb.
arrange
arrange 62 vb.
compose music
413 vb.
predetermine
608 vb.
arranged
arranged 62 adj.
musical 412 adj.
arrangement
medley 43 n.
arrangement 62 n.
musical piece
412 n.
pact 765 n.
arranger
musician 413 n.
arrant
consummate
32 adj.
prodigious 32 adj.
arras
hanging object
217 n.
array
medley 43 n.
order 60 n.
arrange 62 vb.
arrangement 62 n.
series 71 n.
multitude 104 n.
place 187 vb.
dress 228 vb.
dressing 228 n.
battle 718 n.
decorate 844 vb.
pageant 875 n.
arrears
debt 803 n.
arrest
cessation 145 n.
halt 145 vb.
hindrance 702 n.
arrest 747 vb.
detention 747 n.
restrain 747 vb.
restraint 747 n.
impress 821 vb.
legal process
959 n.
arrival
outsider 59 n.
arrival 295 n.
arrive
arrive 295 vb.

flourish 615 vb.
succeed 727 vb.
prosper 730 vb.
arrogant
authoritarian
735 adj.
rash 857 adj.
proud 871 adj.
insolent 878 adj.
arrow
sharp point 256 n.
missile 287 n.
indicator 547 n.
throwing weapons,
projectiles and
missiles 723 n.
love token 889 n.
arrowhead
sharp point 256 n.
throwing weapons,
projectiles and
missiles 723 n.
arrowroot
powder 332 n.
thickening 354 n.
arsenal
storage 632 n.
workshop 687 n.
arsenal 723 n.
arsenic
poison 659 n.
arson
destruction 165 n.
fire 379 n.
arson 381 n.
art
art 551 n.
skill 694 n.
artefact
product 164 n.
artery
essential part 5 n.
tube 263 n.
water channel
351 n.
life 360 n.
road 624 n.
artful
deceiving 542 adj.
cunning 698 adj.
dishonest 930 adj.
artfulness
deception 542 n.
cunning 698 n.
improbity 930 n.
art gallery
collection 632 n.
arthritic
impotent 161 adj.
crippled 163 adj.
diseased 651 adj.
sick person 651 n.

arthritis
pang 377 n.
rheumatism
651 n.
arthropod
animal 365 n.
article
unit 88 n.
product 164 n.
object 319 n.
part of speech
564 n.
article 591 n.
precept 693 n.
merchandise
795 n.
articled clerk
beginner 538 n.
articles
creed 485 n.
**articles of
agreement**
conditions 766 n.
articles of faith
creed 485 n.
theology 973 n.
articulate
join 45 vb.
intelligible
516 adj.
phrase 563 vb.
voice 577 vb.
speak 579 vb.
speaking 579 adj.
articulation
pronunciation
577 n.
voice 577 n.
speech 579 n.
artifact
product 164 n.
artifice
contrivance 623 n.
stratagem 698 n.
pretension 850 n.
artificer
producer 164 n.
artificial
simulating 18 adj.
imitative 20 adj.
spurious 542 adj.
untrue 543 adj.
inelegant 576 adj.
affected 850 adj.
**artificial intelli-
gence**
computing 86 n.
artificiality
inelegance 576 n.
affectation 850 n.
artillery
loudness 400 n.

gun 723 n.
artisan
artisan 686 n.
artist
artist 556 n.
entertainer 594 n.
expert 696 n.
artiste
musician 413 n.
entertainer 594 n.
artistic
elegant 575 adj.
tasteful 846 adj.
artistry
touch 378 n.
imagination 513 n.
painting 553 n.
skill 694 n.
good taste 846 n.
artless
artless 699 adj.
**art-master *or*
-mistress**
artist 556 n.
art museum
collection 632 n.
arts, the
culture 490 n.
artwork
representation
551 n.
arty-crafty
ornamental
844 adj.
as
similarly 18 adv.
as agreed
as promised
764 adv.
as arranged
purposely 617 adv.
ascend
ascend 308 vb.
ascendance
authority 733 n.
ascendancy
superiority 34 n.
power 160 n.
influence 178 n.
governing 733 n.
prestige 866 n.
ascending order
series 71 n.
ascension
ascent 308 n.
ascent
incline 220 n.
ascent 308 n.
ascertain
make certain
473 vb.

at this time
at present
121 adv.
attic
attic 194 n.
at times
sometimes
139 adv.
attire
dress 228 vb.
dressing 228 n.
attitude
state 7 n.
situation 186 n.
form 243 n.
idea 451 n.
opinion 485 n.
conduct 688 n.
mental state
817 n.
pride 871 n.
insolence 878 n.
attitudinize
be affected 850 vb.
attorney
nominee 754 n.
deputy 755 n.
law agent 958 n.
Attorney General
law officer 955 n.
attract
attract 291 vb.
attraction
attraction 291 n.
incentive 612 n.
beauty 841 n.
liking 859 n.
attractions
beauty 841 n.
attractive
influential
178 adj.
pleasurable
826 adj.
personable
841 adj.
desired 859 adj.
attractiveness
attraction 291 n.
inducement 612 n.
pleasurableness
826 n.
beauty 841 n.
attributable
due 915 adj.
attribute
essential part 5 n.
speciality 80 n.
concomitant 89 n.
attribute 158 vb.
attribution 158 n.

ability 160 n.
attributed to
caused 157 adj.
attributive
grammatical
564 adj.
attrition
powderiness
332 n.
friction 333 n.
warfare 718 n.
penitence 939 n.
attune
adjust 24 vb.
harmonize 410 vb.
at variance
disagreeing 25 adj.
opposing 704 adj.
quarrelling
709 adj.
hostile 881 adj.
at war
disagreeing 25 adj.
warring 718 adj.
at work
operative 173 adj.
busy 678 adj.
atypical
non-uniform
17 adj.
dissimilar 19 adj.
inimitable 21 adj.
abnormal 84 adj.
auburn
brown 430 adj.
red 431 adj.
auction
offer 759 vb.
sale 793 n.
sell 793 vb.
auctioneer
seller 793 n.
audacious
courageous
855 adj.
rash 857 adj.
insolent 878 adj.
audacity
courage 855 n.
rashness 857 n.
insolence 878 n.
audibility
sound 398 n.
loudness 400 n.
hearing 415 n.
audible
making sound
398 adj.
loud 400 adj.
auditory 415 adj.
intelligible
516 adj.

speaking 579 adj.
audience
listener 415 n.
listening 415 n.
onlookers 441 n.
publicity 528 n.
conference 584 n.
theatregoer 594 n.
audio
sound 398 n.
making sound
398 adj.
audiovisual
making sound
398 adj.
auditory 415 adj.
educational
534 adj.
audit
number 86 vb.
enquire 459 vb.
enquiry 459 n.
account 808 vb.
accounts 808 n.
audition
hearing 415 n.
listening 415 n.
exam 459 n.
experiment 461 n.
dramatic theory
594 n.
auditorium
listener 415 n.
onlookers 441 n.
theatre 594 n.
auger
sharp point 256 n.
piercer 263 n.
augment
augment 36 vb.
augmentation
increase 36 n.
increment 36 n.
expansion 197 n.
aggravation 832 n.
augur
predict 511 vb.
augury
divination 511 n.
august
great 32 adj.
notable 638 adj.
impressive
821 adj.
worshipful
866 adj.
auld lang syne
past time 125 n.
aunt
kinsman 11 n.
female 373 n.
auntie
kinsman 11 n.

female 373 n.
Aunt Sally
laughing stock
851 n.
au pair
resident 191 n.
domestic 742 n.
aura
surroundings
230 n.
prestige 866 n.
aural
auditory 415 adj.
aureole
light 417 n.
honours 866 n.
auricular
auditory 415 adj.
aurora
glow 417 n.
auspices
protection 660 n.
aid 703 n.
auspicious
opportune 137 adj.
predicting 511 adj.
halcyon 730 adj.
promising 852 adj.
austere
plain 573 adj.
severe 735 adj.
ascetic 945 adj.
pietistic 979 adj.
austerity
unsavouriness
391 n.
plainness 573 n.
insufficiency
636 n.
severity 735 n.
asceticism 945 n.
show of piety
979 n.
authentic
genuine 494 adj.
authenticate
testify 466 vb.
make certain
473 vb.
endorse 488 vb.
give security
767 vb.
title deed 767 n.
authenticity
authenticity
494 n.
author
cause 156 n.
author 589 n.
planner 623 n.
authoritarian
authoritarian

735 adj.
tyrant 735 n.
authoritative
evidential 466 adj.
certain 473 adj.
credal 485 adj.
authoritative
733 adj.
commanding
737 adj.
orthodox 976 adj.
authorities, the
master 741 n.
authority
credential 466 n.
sage 500 n.
informant 524 n.
expert 696 n.
authority 733 n.
permit 756 n.
authorization
warrant 737 n.
permission 756 n.
security 767 n.
authorize
endorse 488 vb.
commission
751 vb.
permit 756 vb.
authorship
composition 56 n.
causation 156 n.
production 164 n.
writing 586 n.
autism
introversion 224 n.
learning disability
503 n.
unsociability
883 n.
autistic
inward-looking
224 adj.
*having a learning
disability*
503 adj.
autobiography
biography 590 n.
autocrat
autocrat 741 n.
autocratic
volitional 595 adj.
authoritative
733 adj.
authoritarian
735 adj.
autograph
no imitation 21 n.
reminder 505 n.
identification
547 n.
label 547 n.

sign 547 vb.
script 586 n.
automated
dynamic 160 adj.
mechanical
630 adj.
automatic
inherent 5 adj.
computerized
86 adj.
involuntary
596 adj.
spontaneous
609 adj.
instrumental
628 adj.
mechanical
630 adj.
pistol 723 n.
automatic pilot
navigation 269 n.
aeronaut 271 n.
aircraft 276 n.
spontaneity 609 n.
automatic
reflex
spontaneity 609 n.
automation
uniformity 16 n.
electronics 160 n.
instrumentality
628 n.
automatism
spiritualism 984 n.
automaton
image 551 n.
machine 630 n.
automobile
car 274 n.
automotive
moving 265 adj.
autonomous
governmental
733 adj.
independent
744 adj.
autonomy
government 733 n.
independence
744 n.
autopsy
death 361 n.
inquest 364 n.
inspection 438 n.
enquiry 459 n.
autosuggestion
sense 374 n.
insensitivity
375 n.
misjudgment
481 n.
fantasy 513 n.

autumn
period 110 n.
autumn 129 n.
auxiliary
inferior 35 adj.
additional 38 adj.
helping 703 adj.
auxiliary 707 n.
avail
benefit 615 vb.
utility 640 n.
available
accessible 289 adj.
possible 469 adj.
useful 640 adj.
used 673 adj.
avalanche
revolution 149 n.
descent 309 n.
snow 380 n.
redundancy 637 n.
avant-garde
precursor 66 n.
modern 126 adj.
modernist 126 n.
front 237 n.
preceding 283 n.
dramatic 594 adj.
avarice
avarice 816 n.
avaricious
avaricious
816 adj.
avatar
transformation
143 n.
revelation 975 n.
avenge
avenge 910 vb.
avenue
housing 192 n.
park 192 n.
path 624 n.
road 624 n.
aver
affirm 532 vb.
average
average 30 n.
average out 30 vb.
median 30 adj.
general 79 adj.
typical 83 adj.
not bad 644 adj.
middling 732 adj.
averageness
averageness 732 n.
averages
statistics 86 n.
averment
affirmation 532 n.
litigation 959 n.
averse
unwilling 598 adj.

aversion
unwillingness
598 n.
dislike 861 n.
hatred 888 n.
avert
deflect 282 vb.
avian
animal 365 adj.
aviary
nest 192 n.
cattle pen 369 n.
zoo 369 n.
aviation
aeronautics 271 n.
aviator
aeronaut 271 n.
avid
excited 821 adj.
avidity
rapacity 786 n.
avarice 816 n.
desire 859 n.
avoid
avoid 620 vb.
disapprove 924 vb.
avoidance
avoidance 620 n.
avoirdupois
finite quantity
26 n.
bulk 195 n.
weights and meas-
ures 465 n.
avow
testify 466 vb.
assent 488 vb.
confess 526 vb.
affirm 532 vb.
avowal
disclosure 526 n.
affirmation 532 n.
avuncular
akin 11 adj.
await
await 507 vb.
awake
attentive 455 adj.
active 678 adj.
awaken
cause 156 vb.
cause feeling
374 vb.
have feeling
374 vb.
excite 821 vb.
awake to
attentive 455 adj.
discover 484 vb.
impressible
819 adj.
award
judge 480 vb.

judgment 480 n.
trophy 729 n.
gift 781 n.
give 781 vb.
giving 781 n.
honours 866 n.
reward 962 n.
reward 962 vb.
aware
sentient 374 adj.
attentive 455 adj.
knowing 490 adj.
intelligent 498 adj.
impressible
819 adj.
awareness
sensitivity 374 n.
intellect 447 n.
knowledge 490 n.
sound judgment
498 n.
away
absent 190 adj.
distant 199 adj.
away 199 adv.
awe
excitation 821 n.
fear 854 n.
be wonderful
864 vb.
wonder 864 n.
command respect
920 vb.
respect 920 n.
worship 981 n.
awesome
great 32 adj.
excellent 644 adj.
frightening
854 adj.
wonderful 864 adj.
awful
bad 645 adj.
not nice 645 adj.
frightening
854 adj.
awfully
extremely 32 vb.
awkward
young 130 adj.
unwieldy 195 adj.
inelegant 576 adj.
inexpedient
643 adj.
clumsy 695 adj.
annoying 827 adj.
graceless 842 adj.
modest 874 adj.
awl
sharp point 256 n.
piercer 263 n.
tool 630 n.

awning
canopy 226 n.
screen 421 n.
awry
unequal 29 adj.
lacking order
61 adj.
distorted 246 adj.
amiss 616 adv.
evil 616 adj.
awry, be
be oblique 220 vb.
axe
destroy 165 vb.
shorten 204 vb.
sharp edge 256 n.
dismiss 300 vb.
fell 311 vb.
tool 630 n.
axe 723 n.
means of execution
964 n.
axe to grind
affairs 154 n.
objective 617 n.
selfishness 932 n.
axiom
premise 475 n.
axiom 496 n.
axiomatic
certain 473 adj.
undisputed
473 adj.
rational 475 adj.
proverbial 496 adj.
axis
pivot 218 n.
centre 225 n.
rotator 315 n.
gauge 465 n.
axle
pivot 218 n.
rotator 315 n.
aye
assent 488 vb.
ayes, the
assenter 488 n.
A-Z
list 87 n.
itinerary 267 n.
guidebook 524 n.
azure
blue 435 adj.
blueness 435 n.
heraldic 547 adj.
heraldry 547 n.

B

baa
howl 409 vb.

lake 346 n.
seclusion 883 n.
backwoods
district 184 n.
backwoodsman
absence 190 n.
country-dweller
869 n.
backyard
place 185 n.
bacon
meat 301 n.
bacteria
infection 651 n.
poison 659 n.
bacteriology
medical art 658 n.
bad
inferior 35 adj.
fetid 397 adj.
evil 616 adj.
bad 645 adj.
wicked 934 adj.
bad blood
dislike 861 n.
enmity 881 n.
hatred 888 n.
malevolence
898 n.
bad books
disrepute 867 n.
hatred 888 n.
disapprobation
924 n.
baddy
evildoer 904 n.
bad person 938 n.
bad form
not customary
611 adj.
ill-breeding 847 n.
badge
badge 547 n.
heraldry 547 n.
jewellery 844 n.
badger
mammal 365 n.
interrogate 459 vb.
torment 827 vb.
bad language
rudeness 885 n.
scurrility 899 n.
badly
slightly 33 adv.
badly 645 adv.
badly brought
up
ill-bred 847 adj.
bad manners
conduct 688 n.
ill-breeding 847 n.
discourtesy 885 n.

badminton
ball game 837 n.
bad mouth
news 529 n.
calumny 926 n.
detract 926 vb.
badness
badness 645 n.
bad patch
difficulty 700 n.
adversity 731 n.
bad person
evildoer 904 n.
bad person 938 n.
bad press
censure 924 n.
detraction 926 n.
bad reputation
disrepute 867 n.
bad-tempered
sullen 893 adj.
baffle
puzzle 474 vb.
be difficult
700 vb.
be obstructive
702 vb.
oppose 704 vb.
defeat 727 vb.
be wonderful
864 vb.
bag
bunch 74 n.
bag 194 n.
acquire 771 vb.
take 786 vb.
taking 786 n.
bag and bag-
gage
all 52 n.
property 777 n.
bagatelle
trifle 639 n.
ball game 837 n.
bagful
finite quantity
26 n.
store 632 n.
baggage
young person
132 n.
box 194 n.
transport 272 n.
female 373 n.
property 777 n.
insolent person
878 n.
loose woman
952 n.
baggy
spacious 183 adj.
large 195 adj.

broad 205 adj.
bag lady
nonconformist
84 n.
displaced person
188 n.
wanderer 268 n.
low fellow 869 n.
bagman
pedlar 794 n.
bag of tricks
trickery 542 n.
means 629 n.
tool 630 n.
collection 632 n.
bagpipes
flute 414 n.
bail
liberate 746 vb.
liberation 746 n.
security 767 n.
legal process
959 n.
bailie
officer 741 n.
bailiff
farmer 370 n.
manager 690 n.
officer 741 n.
retainer 742 n.
nominee 754 n.
law officer 955 n.
bail one out
give bail 767 vb.
bail out
transpose 272 vb.
empty 300 vb.
aid 703 vb.
Bairam
holy day 988 n.
bait
attract 291 vb.
attraction 291 n.
ensnare 542 vb.
trap 542 n.
trickery 542 n.
incentive 612 n.
chase 619 n.
torment 827 vb.
enrage 891 vb.
reward 962 n.
bake
cook 301 vb.
harden 326 vb.
dry 342 vb.
be hot 379 vb.
baked
dry 342 adj.
baker
cookery 301 n.
bakery
cookery 301 n.

baking
cookery 301 n.
hot 379 adj.
heating 381 n.
baking-powder
raising agent
323 n.
balance
relate 9 vb.
correlate 12 vb.
adjust 24 vb.
equality 28 n.
equalize 28 vb.
equilibrium 28 n.
average 30 n.
remainder 41 n.
number 86 vb.
stability 153 n.
stabilize 153 vb.
symmetry 245 n.
scales 322 n.
weigh 322 vb.
compare 462 vb.
gauge 465 n.
measure 465 n.
sound judgment
498 n.
elegance 575 n.
be irresolute
601 vb.
middle way 625 n.
superfluity 637 n.
caution 858 n.
balanced
adjusted 24 adj.
equal 28 adj.
fixed 153 adj.
symmetrical
245 adj.
elegant 575 adj.
balance of
power
equilibrium 28 n.
balance of trade
equilibrium 28 n.
balancing act
compromise 770 n.
balcony
lobby 194 n.
projection 254 n.
theatre 594 n.
bald
hairless 229 adj.
smooth 258 adj.
feeble 572 adj.
plain 573 adj.
tedious 838 adj.
bale
bunch 74 n.
cultivate 370 vb.
baleful
malevolent

898 adj.
bale out
fly 271 vb.
emerge 298 vb.
balk
beam 218 n.
disappoint 509 vb.
disappointment
509 n.
be obstructive
702 vb.
balk at
avoid 620 vb.
ball
sphere 252 n.
missile 287 n.
throwing weapons,
projectiles and
missiles 723 n.
dancing 837 n.
plaything 837 n.
social gathering
882 n.
ballad
vocal music 412 n.
narrative 590 n.
poem 593 n.
ball and chain
fetter 748 n.
ballast
compensate 31 vb.
stabilizer 153 n.
gravity 322 n.
safeguard 662 n.
balled up
complex 61 adj.
crossed 222 adj.
ballerina
entertainer 594 n.
ballet
ballet 594 n.
ball game
ball game 837 n.
ball game, new
or different
variant 15 n.
ballistics
propulsion 287 n.
arms 723 n.
balloon
expand 197 vb.
encircling 232 n.
sphere 252 n.
airship 276 n.
lightness 323 n.
gas 336 n.
plaything 837 n.
ballot
affirmation 532 n.
vote 605 n.
ballot box
electorate 605 n.

vote 605 n.
ballroom
place of amuse-
ment 837 n.
balls-up
mistake 495 n.
bungling 695 n.
ballyhoo
loudness 400 n.
overestimation
482 n.
advertisement
528 n.
publicity 528 n.
exaggeration
546 n.
balm
herb 301 n.
scent 396 n.
balm 658 n.
medicine 658 n.
pleasurableness
826 n.
balmy
warm 379 adj.
fragrant 396 adj.
halcyon 730 adj.
balsam
balm 658 n.
medicine 658 n.
balustrade
handle 218 n.
barrier 235 n.
fence 235 n.
bamboo
grass 366 n.
bamboo curtain
exclusion 57 n.
partition 231 n.
obstacle 702 n.
bamboozle
puzzle 474 vb.
keep secret 525 vb.
deceive 542 vb.
fool 542 vb.
ban
exclude 57 vb.
exclusion 57 n.
hindrance 702 n.
obstruct 702 vb.
command 737 n.
command 737 vb.
restrain 747 vb.
restraint 747 n.
prohibit 757 vb.
prohibition 757 n.
curse 899 n.
disapprobation
924 n.
disapprove 924 vb.
penalty 963 n.
prayers 981 n.

Christian rite
988 n.
perform ritual
988 vb.
banal
proverbial 496 adj.
usual 610 adj.
dull 840 adj.
banana
fruit and vegeta-
bles 301 n.
banana republic
political organiza-
tion 733 n.
banana skin
rubbish 641 n.
danger 661 n.
pitfall 663 n.
band
bond 47 n.
ligature 47 n.
band 74 n.
strip 208 n.
loop 250 n.
orchestra 413 n.
musical instrument
414 n.
stripe 437 n.
class 538 n.
bandage
tie 45 vb.
ligature 47 n.
make smaller
198 vb.
strip 208 n.
support 218 n.
support 218 n.
cover 226 vb.
wrapping 226 n.
blind 439 vb.
cure 656 vb.
practise medicine
658 vb.
surgical dressing
658 n.
relieve 831 vb.
**Band-Aid
(tdmk)**
adhesive 47 n.
substitute 150 n.
covering 226 n.
bandanna
headgear 228 n.
bandeau
hairdressing
843 n.
bandit
robber 789 n.
outcast 883 n.
bandleader
living model 23 n.
orchestra 413 n.

bandstand
pavilion 192 n.
band together
combine 50 vb.
congregate 74 vb.
cooperate 706 vb.
bandy about
publish 528 vb.
bandy-legged
deformed 246 adj.
curved 248 adj.
bandy words
interchange
151 vb.
argue 475 vb.
converse 584 vb.
bane
bane 659 n.
wrong 914 n.
bang
impel 279 vb.
impulse 279 n.
knock 279 n.
strike 279 vb.
bang 402 n.
bang 402 vb.
hairdressing
843 n.
bangle
jewellery 844 n.
bang on
be tedious 838 vb.
banish
exclude 57 vb.
displace 188 vb.
eject 300 vb.
banisters
handle 218 n.
support 218 n.
fence 235 n.
banjo
stringed instrument
414 n.
bank
high land 209 n.
seat 218 n.
be oblique 220 vb.
incline 220 n.
edge 234 n.
laterality 239 n.
shore 344 n.
storage 632 n.
store 632 vb.
pawnshop 784 n.
treasury 799 n.
bank account
funds 797 n.
wealth 800 n.
banker
lender 784 n.
merchant 794 n.
treasurer 798 n.

card game 837 n.
Bank holiday
amusement 837 n.
banknote
title deed 767 n.
paper money
797 n.
bank on
be certain 473 vb.
believe 485 vb.
expect 507 vb.
hope 852 vb.
bank rate
finance 797 n.
interest 803 n.
bankroll
paper money
797 n.
expend 806 vb.
bankrupt
defeat 727 vb.
loser 728 n.
fleece 786 vb.
poor 801 adj.
poor person 801 n.
non-payer 805 n.
non-paying
805 adj.
bankruptcy
insufficiency
636 n.
failure 728 n.
loss 772 n.
insolvency 805 n.
banner
flag 547 n.
bannock
bread, pastries
and cakes
301 n.
banns
marriage 894 n.
banquet
eat 301 vb.
feed 301 vb.
plenty 635 n.
festivity 837 n.
revel 837 vb.
social gathering
882 n.
banshee
demon 970 n.
bantam
dwarf 196 n.
poultry 365 n.
banter
conversation
584 n.
witticism 839 n.
ridicule 851 n.
ridicule 851 vb.
be insolent

878 vb.
sauciness 878 n.
bap
bread, pastries
and cakes
301 n.
baptism
reception 299 n.
nomenclature
561 n.
Christian rite
988 n.
rite 988 n.
baptism of fire
debut 68 n.
Baptist
Protestant 976 adj.
Protestant 976 n.
baptistry
church interior
990 n.
church utensil
990 n.
baptize
inaugurate 68 vb.
admit 299 vb.
immerse 303 vb.
drench 341 vb.
name 561 vb.
make pious
979 vb.
perform ritual
988 vb.
bar
degree 27 n.
fastening 47 n.
exclude 57 vb.
exclusion 57 n.
exclusive of
57 adv.
tavern 192 n.
room 194 n.
line 203 n.
support 218 n.
barrier 235 n.
close 264 vb.
stopper 264 n.
notation 410 n.
stripe 437 n.
heraldry 547 n.
obstruct 702 vb.
restrain 747 vb.
restraint 747 n.
lockup 748 n.
prohibit 757 vb.
disapprobation
924 n.
disapprove 924 vb.
tribunal 956 n.
bar 958 n.
condemn 961 vb.
barb
filament 208 n.

bastion
protection 660 n.
refuge 662 n.
fortification 713 n.
bat
velocity 277 n.
strike 279 vb.
propel 287 vb.
mammal 365 n.
club 723 n.
batch
finite quantity
26 n.
bunch 74 n.
group 74 n.
bated breath
faintness 401 n.
voicelessness
578 n.
bath
vessel 194 n.
water 339 n.
washing 648 n.
bath chair
pushcart 274 n.
bathe
swim 269 vb.
immerse 303 vb.
be wet 341 vb.
drench 341 vb.
clean 648 vb.
amuse oneself
837 vb.
bathing suit
beachwear 228 n.
bathos
absurdity 497 n.
ridiculousness
849 n.
bathrobe
informal dress
228 n.
bathroom
room 194 n.
toilet 648 n.
washing 648 n.
bath salts
cosmetic 843 n.
bathtub
washing 648 n.
batik
textile 222 n.
printing 555 n.
ornamental art
844 n.
batman
clothier 228 n.
domestic 742 n.
baton
support 218 n.
badge of office
743 n.

bat one's eye-
lashes
gesticulate 547 vb.
batsman
player 837 n.
battalion(s)
multitude 104 n.
formation 722 n.
batten
fastening 47 n.
strip 208 n.
batten down
the hatches
close 264 vb.
seek refuge 662 vb.
make ready
669 vb.
batten on
eat 301 vb.
prosper 730 vb.
be servile 879 vb.
batter
demolish 165 vb.
deform 244 vb.
distort 246 vb.
collide 279 vb.
strike 279 vb.
pulpiness 356 n.
ill-treat 645 vb.
battering ram
ram 279 n.
club 723 n.
battery
accumulation
74 n.
electronics 160 n.
stable 192 n.
stock farm 369 n.
exam 459 n.
storage 632 n.
formation 722 n.
gun 723 n.
battle
slaughter 362 n.
action 676 n.
contend 716 vb.
battle 718 n.
trophy 729 n.
be hostile 881 vb.
battleaxe
violent creature
176 n.
sharp edge 256 n.
axe 723 n.
battle cry
call 547 n.
danger signal
665 n.
defiance 711 n.
war 718 n.
warfare 718 n.
threat 900 n.

battlement
notch 260 n.
fortification 713 n.
battleship
warship 722 n.
bauble
thing that lacks
substance 4 n.
bauble 639 n.
bawdy
impure 951 adj.
bawl
cry 408 n.
shout 408 vb.
lamentation
836 n.
weep 836 vb.
bawl out
reproach 924 vb.
bay
compartment
194 n.
curve 248 n.
cavity 255 n.
horse 273 n.
gulf 345 n.
tree 366 n.
howl 409 n.
brown 430 adj.
disapprove 924 vb.
bayonet
pierce 263 vb.
kill 362 vb.
strike at 712 vb.
side arms 723 n.
bayou
gulf 345 n.
bazaar
request 761 n.
sale 793 n.
emporium 796 n.
shop 796 n.
bazooka
flute 414 n.
gun 723 n.
throwing weapons,
projectiles and
missiles 723 n.
be
be 1 vb.
be situated
186 vb.
be present 189 vb.
beach
edge 234 n.
land 295 vb.
shore 344 n.
arena 724 n.
beachcomber
wanderer 268 n.
beacon
signal light 420 n.

signal 547 n.
warning 664 n.
danger signal
665 n.
bead
sphere 252 n.
decorate 844 vb.
trimming 844 n.
beading
ornamental art
844 n.
beadle
officer 741 n.
law officer 955 n.
church officer
986 n.
beads
jewellery 844 n.
prayers 981 n.
ritual object
988 n.
beak
protuberance
254 n.
teacher 537 n.
beaker
cup 194 n.
be-all and end-
all
all 52 n.
important matter
638 n.
beam
beam 218 n.
laterality 239 n.
direction 281 n.
flash 417 n.
radiate 417 vb.
communicate
524 vb.
be cheerful
833 vb.
smile 835 vb.
beaming
luminous 417 adj.
happy 824 adj.
cheerful 833 adj.
bear
reproduce itself
167 vb.
be fruitful 171 vb.
support 218 vb.
carry 273 vb.
mammal 365 n.
acquiesce 488 vb.
heraldry 547 n.
gambler 618 n.
seller 793 n.
feel 818 n.
be patient 823 vb.
suffer 825 vb.
rude person 885 n.

bear a grudge
hate 888 vb.
beard
filament 208 n.
prickle 256 n.
hair 259 n.
print-type 587 n.
defy 711 vb.
be courageous
855 vb.
bearded
hairy 259 adj.
bear down on
approach 289 vb.
bear fruit
reproduce itself
167 vb.
get better 654 vb.
be successful
727 vb.
beargarden
turmoil 61 n.
arena 724 n.
bear hug
retention 778 n.
endearment 889 n.
bear ill will
be hostile 881 vb.
bearing
relation 9 n.
pivot 218 n.
support 218 n.
direction 281 n.
expression 445 n.
meaning 514 n.
heraldry 547 n.
conduct 688 n.
bear in mind
think 449 vb.
be mindful
455 vb.
bearish
animal 365 adj.
saleable 793 adj.
cheap 812 adj.
bear out
corroborate
466 vb.
demonstrate
478 vb.
vindicate 927 vb.
bearskin
headgear 228 n.
armour 713 n.
bear the brunt
stand firm 599 vb.
busy oneself
622 vb.
be in difficulty
700 vb.
withstand 704 vb.
bear the mark
of
be inherent 5 vb.

bear up
support 218 vb.
elevate 310 vb.
bear upon
be related 9 vb.
influence 178 vb.
bear with
forgive 909 vb.
bear witness
testify 466 vb.
affirm 532 vb.
beast
inferior 35 n.
violent creature
176 n.
animal 365 n.
eyesore 842 n.
ruffian 904 n.
cad 938 n.
beastly
animal 365 adj.
not nice 645 adj.
unpleasant
827 adj.
ugly 842 adj.
discourteous
885 adj.
hateful 888 adj.
sensual 944 adj.
beast of burden
beast of burden
273 n.
animal 365 n.
worker 686 n.
beat
be superior 34 vb.
periodic recurrence
141 n.
territory 184 n.
place 185 n.
impulse 279 n.
strike 279 vb.
cook 301 vb.
pass 305 vb.
oscillate 317 vb.
oscillation 317 n.
agitate 318 vb.
be agitated
318 vb.
grind 332 vb.
roll 403 vb.
tempo 410 n.
play music
413 vb.
prosody 593 n.
chase 619 vb.
hunt 619 vb.
clean 648 vb.
defeat 727 vb.
spank 963 vb.
**beat about the
bush**
use sophistry

477 vb.
be equivocal
518 vb.
dissemble 541 vb.
be diffuse 570 vb.
beat a tattoo
roll 403 vb.
celebrate 876 vb.
beat down
demolish 165 vb.
bargain 791 vb.
cheapen 812 vb.
beaten
inferior 35 adj.
used 673 adj.
defeated 728 adj.
beaten track
habit 610 n.
bore 838 n.
beater
hunter 619 n.
beatific
pleasurable
826 adj.
beatify
dignify 866 vb.
sanctify 979 vb.
beating
periodical 141 adj.
impulse 279 n.
knock 279 n.
victory 727 n.
defeat 728 n.
corporal punish-
ment 963 n.
beatnik
nonconformist
84 n.
unconformable
84 adj.
**beat one's
breast**
lament 836 vb.
be penitent
939 vb.
**beat one's head
against a
brick wall**
waste effort
641 adj.
**beat the big
drum**
proclaim 528 vb.
be ostentatious
875 vb.
beat the record
be superior 34 vb.
beat time
time 117 vb.
play music
413 vb.
beat up
force 176 vb.

strike 279 vb.
thicken 354 vb.
strike at 712 vb.
beau
male 372 n.
dandy 848 n.
lover 887 n.
beautician
beautician 843 n.
beautiful
beautiful 841 adj.
beautify
ornament 574 vb.
beautify 841 vb.
beauty
beauty 841 n.
beauty, a
masterpiece 694 n.
beauty queen
a beauty 841 n.
beauty spot
a beauty 841 n.
cosmetic 843 n.
beaver
headgear 228 n.
hair 259 n.
mammal 365 n.
armour 713 n.
beaver away
be active 678 vb.
work 682 vb.
becalmed
at rest 266 adj.
still 266 adj.
non-active
677 adj.
hindered 702 adj.
because
hence 158 adv.
beck
stream 350 n.
gesture 547 n.
command 737 n.
command 737 vb.
beckon
gesticulate 547 vb.
become
become 1 vb.
be turned to
147 vb.
happen 154 vb.
beautify 841 vb.
be one's duty
917 vb.
become one of
join a party
708 vb.
**become one of
the family**
be sociable
882 vb.
**become public
knowledge**
be disclosed

526 vb.
becoming
agreeing 24 adj.
converted 147 adj.
personable
841 adj.
tasteful 846 adj.
bed
have sexual inter-
course with
45 vb.
place 187 vb.
layer 207 n.
base 214 n.
basis 218 n.
bed 218 n.
garden 370 n.
debauch 951 vb.
**bed and break-
fast**
inn 192 n.
provision 633 n.
bedazzle
shine 417 vb.
command respect
920 vb.
bedclothes
coverlet 226 n.
bedding
bed 218 n.
coverlet 226 n.
bed down
place 187 vb.
sleep 679 vb.
bedevil
throw into confu-
sion 63 vb.
trouble 827 vb.
bedlam, Bedlam
disorder 61 n.
turmoil 61 n.
loudness 400 n.
discord 411 n.
mental hospital
503 n.
bed linen
coverlet 226 n.
bed of nails
suffering 825 n.
bed of roses
heyday 730 n.
bedouin
inhabitant 191 n.
wanderer 268 n.
bed out
implant 303 vb.
cultivate 370 vb.
bedpan
vessel 194 n.
toilet 649 n.
bedraggled
dirty 649 adj.

bedridden
sick 651 adj.
restrained 747 adj.
bedrock
reality 1 n.
permanence 144 n.
fixture 153 n.
source 156 n.
base 214 n.
basis 218 n.
chief thing 638 n.
important 638 adj.
bedroom
room 194 n.
bedside manner
therapy 658 n.
bed-sitter
flat 192 n.
bedspread
coverlet 226 n.
bedtime
clock time 117 n.
evening 129 n.
bee
insect 365 n.
beef
meat 301 n.
deprecate 762 vb.
be discontented
829 vb.
beefiness
vitality 162 n.
bulk 195 n.
beef up
strengthen 162 vb.
beefy
stalwart 162 adj.
fat 195 adj.
thick 205 adj.
beehive
nest 192 n.
dome 253 n.
stock farm 369 n.
hairdressing
843 n.
**bee in one's
bonnet**
prejudgment
481 n.
eccentricity 503 n.
whim 604 n.
beeline
short distance
200 n.
straightness 249 n.
direction 281 n.
beer
alcoholic drink
301 n.
**beer and skit-
tles**
enjoyment 824 n.

boarding house
inn 192 n.
quarters 192 n.
board of exam-
iners
enquirer 459 n.
board out
live 192 vb.
board room
council 692 n.
boards
wrapping 226 n.
bookbinding
589 n.
stage set 594 n.
theatre 594 n.
boast
comprise 78 vb.
boast 877 n.
boast 877 vb.
boastfulness
boasting 877 n.
boasting
overestimation
482 n.
boasting 877 n.
boast of
possess 773 vb.
boast 877 vb.
boat
go to sea 269 vb.
row 269 vb.
water travel
269 n.
boat 275 n.
ship 275 n.
boat-builder
artisan 686 n.
boating
watersports 269 n.
water travel
269 n.
sport 837 n.
boatman
boatman 270 n.
boat race
racing 716 n.
boatswain
mariner 270 n.
navigator 270 n.
bob
shorten 204 vb.
shortness 204 n.
hang 217 vb.
hanging object
217 n.
bow 311 n.
stoop 311 vb.
leap 312 vb.
oscillate 317 vb.
oscillation 317 n.
be agitated

318 vb.
coinage 797 n.
hairdressing
843 n.
servility 879 n.
greet 884 vb.
respects 920 n.
show respect
920 vb.
bobble
hanging object
217 n.
trimming 844 n.
bobsled
sled 274 n.
bobsleigh
sled 274 n.
bob up
ascend 308 vb.
bob up and
down
leap 312 vb.
oscillate 317 vb.
dance 837 vb.
bode
predict 511 vb.
bode ill
endanger 661 vb.
threaten 900 vb.
bodice
article of clothing
228 n.
bodily
violently 176 adv.
material 319 adj.
sensuous 376 adj.
sensual 944 adj.
bodkin
sharp point 256 n.
piercer 263 n.
body
quantity 26 n.
chief part 52 n.
band 74 n.
matter 319 n.
object 319 n.
structure 331 n.
corpse 363 n.
person 371 n.
savouriness 390 n.
print-type 587 n.
corporation 708 n.
body blow
knock 279 n.
body-builder
athlete 162 n.
body-building
athletics 162 n.
nourishing
301 adj.
healthy 652 adj.
exercise 682 n.

body double
substitute 150 n.
actor 594 n.
bodyguard
concomitant 89 n.
protector 660 n.
defender 713 n.
combatant 722 n.
retainer 742 n.
body heat
heat 379 n.
body language
gesture 547 n.
voicelessness
578 n.
speech 579 n.
body-piercing
perforation 263 n.
body-snatcher
thief 789 n.
body stocking
suit 228 n.
underwear 228 n.
body-suit
suit 228 n.
boffin
sage 500 n.
planner 623 n.
worker 686 n.
expert 696 n.
bog
moisture 341 n.
marsh 347 n.
dirt 649 n.
toilet 649 n.
bogey
fantasy 513 n.
bogged down
late 136 adj.
boggle
puzzle 474 vb.
doubt 486 vb.
dissent 489 vb.
disappoint 509 vb.
be unwilling
598 vb.
be wonderful
864 vb.
boggy
soft 327 adj.
humid 341 adj.
marshy 347 adj.
bogle
demon 970 n.
bog standard
simple 44 adj.
plain 573 adj.
bogus
erroneous 495 adj.
false 541 adj.
spurious 542 adj.
untrue 543 adj.

affected 850 adj.
bogy
monster 938 n.
demon 970 n.
Bohemian
nonconformist
84 n.
unconformable
84 adj.
free person 744 n.
boil
swelling 253 n.
cook 301 vb.
be agitated
318 vb.
effervesce 318 vb.
bubble 355 vb.
be hot 379 vb.
ulcer 651 n.
make sanitary
652 adj.
be excited 821 vb.
boil down
lessen 37 vb.
make smaller
198 vb.
shorten 204 vb.
boil down to
be inherent 5 vb.
mean 514 vb.
boil dry
be hot 379 vb.
burn 381 vb.
boiler
pot 194 n.
poultry 365 n.
heater 383 n.
washing 648 n.
boiler suit
suit 228 n.
boiling
furious 176 adj.
commotion 318 n.
hot 379 adj.
heating 381 n.
fervent 818 adj.
excited 821 adj.
excitable 822 adj.
angry 891 adj.
boiling point
heat 379 n.
completion 725 n.
boil over
effervesce 318 vb.
get angry 891 vb.
boisterous
disorderly 61 adj.
violent 176 adj.
windy 352 adj.
hasty 680 adj.
bold
projecting 254 adj.

forceful 571 adj.
written 586 adj.
print-type 587 n.
courageous
855 adj.
rash 857 adj.
insolent 878 adj.
boldface
print-type 587 n.
boldness
courage 855 n.
insolence 878 n.
bole
chief part 52 n.
soil 344 n.
tree 366 n.
bolero
jacket 228 n.
dance 837 n.
boll
receptacle 194 n.
sphere 252 n.
bollard
fastening 47 n.
traffic control
305 n.
boloney
empty talk 515 n.
falsehood 541 n.
Bolsheviks
political party
708 n.
bolshie
opposing 704 adj.
disobedient
738 adj.
bolster
cushion 218 n.
support 218 vb.
aid 703 vb.
bolster up
support 218 vb.
cheer 833 vb.
give courage
855 vb.
bolt
affix 45 vb.
fastening 47 n.
bunch 74 n.
textile 222 n.
barrier 235 n.
sharp point 256 n.
close 264 vb.
stopper 264 n.
move fast 277 vb.
walk out 296 vb.
eat 301 vb.
cultivate 370 vb.
run away 620 vb.
safeguard 662 n.
tool 630 n.
throwing weapons,

boot boy
violent creature
176 n.
combatant 722 n.
rioter 738 n.
low fellow 869 n.
ruffian 904 n.
bad person 938 n.
bootees
legwear 228 n.
booth
small house
192 n.
compartment
194 n.
shop 796 n.
bootlegger
thief 789 n.
boot-licking
submitting
721 adj.
respectful 920 adj.
bootmaker
clothier 228 n.
boot out
repel 292 vb.
eject 300 vb.
boots
footwear 228 n.
servant 742 n.
booty
booty 790 n.
booze
alcoholic drink
301 n.
drink 301 vb.
drunkenness
949 n.
get drunk 949 vb.
bop
strike 279 vb.
music 412 n.
dance 837 n.
dance 837 vb.
border
entrance 68 n.
contiguity 202 n.
encircle 232 vb.
edge 234 n.
edging 234 n.
hem 234 n.
marginal 234 adj.
limit 236 n.
limit 236 vb.
flank 239 vb.
garden 370 n.
trimming 844 n.
borderline
marginal 234 adj.
uncertain 474 adj.
bore
enlarge 197 vb.

breadth 205 n.
make concave
255 vb.
pierce 263 vb.
pass 305 vb.
current 350 n.
wave 350 n.
be talkative
581 vb.
bane 659 n.
firearm 723 n.
trouble 827 vb.
be tedious 838 vb.
bore 838 n.
satiate 863 vb.
borehole
excavation 255 n.
water 339 n.
borer
piercer 263 n.
insect 365 n.
boring
tunnel 263 n.
long-winded
570 adj.
feeble 572 adj.
annoying 827 adj.
tedious 838 adj.
dull 840 adj.
born
born 360 adj.
born again
converted 147 adj.
repentant 939 adj.
sanctified 979 adj.
borough
district 184 n.
electorate 605 n.
borrow
copy 20 vb.
borrow 785 vb.
**borrowed
plumes**
sham 542 n.
borrowing 785 n.
Borstal
school 539 n.
prison 748 n.
bosh
silly talk 515 n.
bosom
receptacle 194 n.
insides 224 n.
interiority 224 n.
article of clothing
228 n.
bosom 253 n.
spirit 447 n.
mental state
817 n.
boss
superior 34 n.

roughen 259 vb.
meddle 678 vb.
direct 689 vb.
director 690 n.
dominate 733 vb.
tyrant 735 n.
autocrat 741 n.
master 741 n.
ornamental art
844 n.
boss-eyed
dim-sighted
440 adj.
bossy
authoritative
733 adj.
authoritarian
735 adj.
bosun
mariner 270 n.
**botanical gar-
den**
botany 368 n.
garden 370 n.
botanist
botany 368 n.
botany
botany 368 n.
botch
distort 246 vb.
neglect 458 vb.
blunder 495 vb.
misrepresent
552 vb.
misrepresentation
552 vb.
impair 655 vb.
be clumsy 695 vb.
bungling 695 vb.
fail 728 vb.
botch-up
mistake 495 vb.
Botox (tdmk)
beauty treatment
843 n.
both
dual 90 adj.
bother
commotion 318 n.
be attentive
455 vb.
distract 456 vb.
activity 678 n.
meddle 678 vb.
be difficult
700 vb.
excitable state
822 n.
worry 825 n.
torment 827 vb.
enrage 891 vb.
bottle
vessel 194 n.

drink 301 n.
store 632 n.
preserve 666 vb.
courage 855 n.
bottleneck
contraction 198 n.
narrowness 206 n.
play music
413 n.
obstacle 702 n.
bottle party
participation
775 n.
festivity 837 n.
social gathering
882 n.
bottle up
remember 505 vb.
conceal 525 vb.
restrain 747 vb.
bottom
extremity 69 n.
lowness 210 n.
depth 211 n.
base 214 n.
support 218 vb.
buttocks 238 n.
ship 275 n.
bottom dollar
extremity 69 n.
bottom drawer
store 632 n.
preparation 669 n.
bottomless
deep 211 adj.
bottomless pit
depth 211 n.
hell 972 n.
bottom line
event 154 n.
utility 640 n.
important matter
638 n.
reward 962 n.
bottom out
decrease 37 vb.
become small
198 vb.
be horizontal
216 vb.
descend 309 vb.
bottoms up
cheers 301 int.
botulism
digestive disorder
651 n.
infection 651 n.
bouclé
rough 259 adj.
boudoir
room 194 n.
bouffant
convex 253 adj.

bough
branch 53 n.
foliage 366 n.
tree 366 n.
boulder
bulk 195 n.
sphere 252 n.
hardness 326 n.
rock 344 n.
boules
ball game 837 n.
boulevard
park 192 n.
path 624 n.
bounce
recoil 280 n.
eject 300 vb.
ascend 308 vb.
ascent 308 n.
leap 312 vb.
oscillate 317 vb.
agitation 318 n.
be agitated
318 vb.
elasticity 328 n.
bounce back
regress 286 vb.
be restored 656 vb.
bouncer
protector 660 n.
bouncing
vigorous 174 adj.
healthy 650 adj.
cheerful 833 adj.
insolent 878 adj.
bouncy castle
elasticity 328 n.
plaything 837 n.
bound
tied 45 adj.
hem 234 vb.
limit 236 vb.
move fast 277 vb.
spurt 277 n.
leap 312 n.
leap 312 vb.
certain 473 adj.
restrained 747 adj.
promised 764 n.
obliged 917 adj.
bound, be
affirm 532 vb.
boundaries
region 184 n.
boundary
extremity 69 n.
edge 234 n.
limit 236 n.
bounder
cad 938 n.
bound for
directed 281 adj.

restrain 747 vb.
restraint 747 n.
fetter 748 n.
get angry 891 vb.
brief
small 33 adj.
brief 114 adj.
short 204 adj.
inform 524 vb.
concise 569 adj.
description 590 n.
compendium
592 n.
function 622 n.
make ready
669 vb.
preparation 669 n.
command 737 n.
command 737 n.
briefcase
box 194 n.
case 194 n.
briefing
information
524 n.
preparation 669 n.
advice 691 n.
briefs
underwear 228 n.
brigade
bring together
74 vb.
group 74 n.
formation 722 n.
brigadier
army officer
741 n.
brigand
robber 789 n.
bright
modernist 126 n.
luminous 417 n.
undimmed
417 adj.
light 420 n.
florid 425 adj.
white 427 adj.
yellow 433 adj.
green 434 adj.
intelligent 498 adj.
contrivance 623 n.
active 678 adj.
cheerful 833 adj.
promising 852 adj.
noteworthy
866 adj.
brighten
make bright
417 vb.
be cheerful
833 vb.
brightness
light 417 n.

intelligence 498 n.
wit 839 n.
brilliance
light 417 n.
hue 425 n.
intelligence 498 n.
prestige 866 n.
ostentation 875 n.
brilliant
luminous 417 adj.
florid 425 adj.
intelligent 498 adj.
perfect 646 adj.
witty 839 adj.
noteworthy
866 adj.
ostentatious
875 adj.
brim
fill 54 vb.
edge 234 n.
abound 635 vb.
brim over
be overabundant
637 vb.
brine
water 339 n.
ocean 343 n.
pungency 388 n.
preserver 666 n.
bring
happen 154 vb.
cause 156 vb.
produce 164 vb.
carry 273 vb.
manifest 522 vb.
induce 612 vb.
carry out 725 vb.
divorce 896 vb.
indict 928 vb.
bring down
fell 311 vb.
strike at 712 vb.
bring forth
reproduce itself
167 vb.
manifest 522 vb.
bring in
admit 299 vb.
cost 809 vb.
bring it off
succeed 727 vb.
bring on
cause 156 vb.
mature 669 vb.
bring out
cause 156 vb.
manifest 522 vb.
print 587 vb.
bring round
assuage 177 vb.
convince 485 vb.

induce 612 vb.
bring to
bring to rest
266 vb.
bring to bear
use 673 vb.
bring to book
punish 963 vb.
bring together
bring together
74 vb.
compare 462 vb.
pacify 719 vb.
mediate 720 vb.
bring to light
discover 484 vb.
manifest 522 vb.
bring up
produce 164 vb.
generate 167 vb.
vomit 300 vb.
manifest 522 vb.
educate 534 vb.
brink
extremity 69 n.
nearness 200 n.
edge 234 n.
brinkmanship
tactics 688 n.
rashness 857 n.
brisk
brief 114 adj.
vigorous 174 adj.
speedy 277 adj.
concise 569 adj.
active 678 adj.
bristle
be vertical 215 vb.
prickle 256 n.
be rough 259 vb.
hair 259 n.
roughness 259 n.
elevate 310 vb.
get angry 891 vb.
threaten 900 vb.
bristle with
be many 104 vb.
be sharp 256 vb.
abound 635 vb.
be overabundant
637 vb.
brittle
brittle 330 adj.
broach
initiate 68 vb.
cause 156 vb.
piercer 263 n.
empty 300 vb.
publish 528 vb.
offer 759 vb.
broad
general 79 adj.

spacious 183 adj.
broad 205 adj.
female 373 n.
inexact 495 adj.
dialectal 560 adj.
prostitute 952 n.
broadcast
disperse 75 vb.
generalize 79 vb.
let fall 311 vb.
communicate
524 vb.
publication 528 n.
publish 528 vb.
broadcast 531 n.
oration 579 n.
broadcasting
dispersion 75 n.
publication 528 n.
broadcasting
531 n.
broaden
augment 36 vb.
generalize 79 vb.
enlarge 197 vb.
expand 197 vb.
broadminded
free 744 adj.
broadside
laterality 239 n.
bombardment
712 n.
gun 723 n.
Broadway
drama 594 n.
broccoli
fruit and vegeta-
bles 301 n.
brochure
the press 528 n.
book 589 n.
compendium
592 n.
broil
cook 301 vb.
be hot 379 vb.
fight 716 n.
broke
poor 801 adj.
broken
fragmentary
53 adj.
discontinuous
72 adj.
imperfect 647 adj.
dilapidated
655 adj.
broken-hearted
unhappy 825 adj.
broken in
accustomed to
610 adj.

broker
intermediary
231 n.
nominee 754 n.
merchant 794 n.
brokerage
barter 791 n.
bromide
moderator 177 n.
maxim 496 n.
print 587 n.
bronchitis
respiratory disease
651 n.
bronze
a mixture 43 n.
brown 430 adj.
brown 430 vb.
brownness 430 n.
sculpture 554 n.
brooch
fastening 47 n.
jewellery 844 n.
brood
group 74 n.
child 132 n.
young creature
132 n.
posterity 170 n.
meditate 449 vb.
be dejected
834 vb.
brood upon
meditate 449 vb.
brook
stream 350 n.
permit 756 vb.
be patient 823 vb.
broom
cleaning utensil
648 n.
broomstick
thinness 206 n.
magic instrument
983 n.
broth
hors-d'oeuvres
301 n.
brothel
brothel 951 n.
brother
peer 28 n.
male 372 n.
colleague 707 n.
friend 880 n.
church title 986 n.
monk 986 n.
brotherhood
family 11 n.
group 74 n.
community 708 n.
friendship 880 n.

sanctify 979 vb.
canoodle
caress 889 vb.
canopy
canopy 226 n.
screen 421 vb.
altar 990 n.
cant
be oblique 220 vb.
obliqueness 220 n.
propel 287 vb.
duplicity 541 n.
falsehood 541 n.
dialectal 560 adj.
slang 560 adj.
show of piety
979 n.
false piety 980 n.
cantankerous
quarrelling
709 adj.
irascible 892 adj.
sullen 893 adj.
cantata
vocal music 412 n.
hymn 981 n.
canteen
café 192 n.
box 194 n.
room 194 n.
canter
gait 265 n.
ride 267 vb.
cantilever
support 218 n.
canton
district 184 n.
flag 547 n.
heraldry 547 n.
cantor
choir 413 n.
worshipper 981 n.
church officer
986 n.
canvas
textile 222 n.
canopy 226 n.
sail 275 n.
picture 553 n.
canvass
enquire 459 vb.
enquiry 459 n.
divulge 526 vb.
publish 528 vb.
vote 605 vb.
do 676 vb.
request 761 vb.
sell 793 vb.
canyon
gap 201 n.
high land 209 n.
valley 255 n.

water channel
351 n.
cap
be superior 34 vb.
culminate 34 vb.
crown 213 vb.
apex 213 n.
cover 226 vb.
covering 226 n.
headgear 228 n.
close 264 vb.
stopper 264 n.
badge 547 n.
letter 558 n.
retaliate 714 vb.
explosive 723 n.
climax 725 vb.
decoration 729 n.
honours 866 n.
capable
fit 24 adj.
powerful 160 adj.
possible 469 adj.
intelligent 498 adj.
capacious
great 32 adj.
spacious 183 adj.
large 195 adj.
capacity
largeness 32 n.
fullness 54 n.
ability 160 n.
room 183 n.
size 195 n.
limit 236 n.
possibility 469 n.
intelligence 498 n.
function 622 n.
means 629 n.
utility 640 n.
easiness 701 n.
cape
cloak 228 n.
caper
ride 267 vb.
leap 312 n.
leap 312 vb.
amuse oneself
837 vb.
dance 837 vb.
capers
spice 301 n.
foolery 497 n.
capillary
narrow 206 adj.
narrowness 206 n.
filament 208 n.
tube 263 n.
cap in hand
supplicatory
761 adj.
respectful 920 adj.

capital
supreme 34 adj.
city 184 n.
summit 213 n.
topmost 213 adj.
deadly 362 adj.
means 629 n.
store 632 n.
important 638 adj.
super 644 adj.
estate 777 n.
funds 797 n.
wealth 800 n.
capitalist
rich person 800 n.
capitalize
profit by 137 vb.
capitalize on
use 673 vb.
**capital punish-
ment**
capital punishment
963 n.
capitals
print-type 587 n.
capitation
numbering 86 n.
statistics 86 n.
capitulate
submit 721 vb.
capon
poultry 365 n.
male animal
372 n.
caprice
musical piece
412 n.
caprice 604 n.
whim 604 n.
capricious
capricious 604 adj.
capsize
be unequal 29 vb.
disarrange 63 vb.
be inverted
221 vb.
invert 221 vb.
navigate 269 vb.
descent 309 n.
tumble 309 vb.
capsule
receptacle 194 n.
covering 226 n.
fruit 366 n.
medicine 658 n.
captain
navigate 269 vb.
nautical personnel
270 n.
direct 689 vb.
director 690 n.
leader 690 n.

army officer
741 n.
naval officer
741 n.
**captain of
industry**
bigwig 638 n.
master 741 n.
caption
commentary
520 n.
indication 547 n.
label 547 n.
record 548 n.
name 561 n.
phrase 563 n.
script 586 n.
edition 589 n.
description 590 n.
captious
irascible 892 adj.
disapproving
924 adj.
captivate
motivate 612 vb.
subjugate 745 vb.
captive
slave 742 n.
captive 750 adj.
prisoner 750 n.
take 786 vb.
captivity
servitude 745 n.
detention 747 n.
captor
master 741 n.
possessor 776 n.
taker 786 n.
capture
imagine 513 vb.
represent 551 vb.
describe 590 vb.
attack 712 vb.
overcome 727 vb.
subjugate 745 vb.
arrest 747 vb.
acquire 771 vb.
take 786 vb.
taking 786 n.
car
conveyance 267 n.
car 274 n.
airship 276 n.
carafe
vessel 194 n.
caramel
sweets 301 n.
brownness 430 n.
carapace
covering 226 n.
carat
weighing 322 n.

caravan
small house
192 n.
cart 274 n.
follower 284 n.
traction 288 n.
amuse oneself
837 vb.
caravan site
station 187 n.
caraway
spice 301 n.
carbohydrates
food content
301 n.
carbolic
cleanser 648 n.
preventive 658 n.
carbonate
gasify 336 vb.
bubble 355 vb.
carbonated
gaseous 336 adj.
carbuncle
swelling 253 n.
blemish 845 n.
carcass
structure 331 n.
corpse 363 n.
carcinogenic
diseased 651 adj.
unhealthy 653 adj.
carcinoma
growth 157 n.
swelling 253 n.
cancer 651 n.
card
nonconformist
84 n.
smoother 258 n.
sailing aid 269 n.
male 372 n.
label 547 n.
record 548 n.
correspondence
588 n.
contrivance 623 n.
paper 631 n.
laughing stock
851 n.
cardamom
spice 301 n.
cardboard
paper 631 n.
card game
card game 837 n.
cardiac arrest
cardiovascular dis-
ease 651 n.
cardigan
jersey 228 n.
cardinal
inherent 5 adj.

244 n.
anarchy 734 n.
chaotic
lacking order
61 adj.
formless 244 adj.
lawless 954 adj.
chap
gap 201 n.
roughen 259 vb.
roughness 259 n.
person 371 n.
male 372 n.
coldness 380 n.
chapel
association 706 n.
society 708 n.
sect 978 n.
church 990 n.
church interior
990 n.
chaperon
accompany 89 n.
concomitant 89 n.
look after 457 n.
surveillance 457 n.
protector 660 n.
safeguard 660 vb.
keeper 749 n.
chaplain
retainer 742 n.
church officer
986 n.
pastor 986 n.
chaplaincy
church office
985 n.
chapped
rough 259 adj.
chapter
subdivision 53 n.
topic 452 n.
edition 589 n.
synod 985 n.
**chapter and
verse**
evidence 466 n.
accuracy 494 n.
chapterhouse
church exterior
990 n.
char
soft drink 301 n.
burn 381 vb.
blacken 428 vb.
brown 430 vb.
cleaner 648 n.
servant 742 n.
serve 742 vb.
charabanc
carriage 274 n.
character
character 5 n.

mode 7 n.
composition 56 n.
nonconformist
84 n.
number 85 n.
person 371 n.
credential 466 n.
letter 558 n.
acting 594 n.
repute 866 n.
virtue 933 n.
characteristic
characteristic
5 adj.
inherent 5 adj.
special 80 adj.
speciality 80 n.
tendency 179 n.
identification
547 n.
characteristics
character 5 n.
**characteriza-
tion**
representation
551 n.
description 590 n.
dramatic theory
594 n.
characterize
make uniform
16 vb.
represent 551 vb.
describe 590 vb.
characters
lettering 586 n.
actor 594 n.
charade
enigma 530 n.
gesture 547 n.
representation
551 n.
drama 594 n.
charades
indoor game
837 n.
charcoal
fuel 385 n.
black thing 428 n.
charge
fill 54 vb.
energy 160 n.
be violent 176 vb.
load 193 vb.
move fast 277 vb.
collision 279 n.
make heavy
322 vb.
heraldry 547 n.
ornament 574 vb.
job 622 n.
protection 660 n.

management
689 n.
precept 693 n.
attack 712 n.
explosive 723 n.
command 737 n.
command 737 vb.
demand 737 vb.
dependant 742 n.
detention 747 n.
commission
751 vb.
mandate 751 n.
bargain 791 vb.
debt 803 n.
account 808 vb.
price 809 n.
price 809 vb.
tax 809 n.
wrong 914 n.
duty 917 n.
blame 924 vb.
accusation 928 n.
indict 928 vb.
litigate 959 vb.
litigation 959 n.
laity 987 n.
charge at
be rash 857 vb.
charge card
credit 802 n.
charged
weighty 322 adj.
**chargé
d'affaires**
envoy 754 n.
charger
plate 194 n.
horse 273 n.
cavalry 722 n.
accuser 928 n.
charges
price 809 n.
charge with
attribute 158 vb.
accuse 928 vb.
chariot
carriage 274 n.
charisma
power 160 n.
influence 178 n.
charismatic
influential
178 adj.
charitable
liberal 813 adj.
benevolent
897 adj.
philanthropic
901 adj.
pitying 905 adj.
charity
aid 703 n.

monetary help
703 n.
gift 781 n.
giving 781 n.
liberality 813 n.
love 887 n.
benevolence 897 n.
pity 905 n.
disinterestedness
931 n.
virtues 933 n.
charlatan
dabbler 493 n.
impostor 545 n.
charlatanism
superficial know-
ledge 491 n.
duplicity 541 n.
pretension 850 n.
charley
ninny 501 n.
charlotte
dessert 301 n.
charm
attract 291 vb.
attraction 291 n.
incentive 612 n.
inducement 612 n.
motivate 612 vb.
delight 826 vb.
please 826 vb.
pleasurableness
826 n.
beauty 841 n.
jewellery 844 n.
bewitch 983 vb.
spell 983 n.
talisman 983 n.
charmer
attraction 291 n.
exceller 644 n.
a beauty 841 n.
flatterer 925 n.
charming
pleasurable
826 adj.
personable
841 adj.
charm offensive
inducement 612 n.
attack 712 n.
charms
beauty 841 n.
chart
statistics 86 n.
list 87 n.
situation 186 n.
itinerary 267 n.
sailing aid 269 n.
guidebook 524 n.
map 551 n.
represent 551 vb.

charter
record 548 n.
commission
751 vb.
mandate 751 n.
permit 756 n.
permit 756 vb.
title deed 767 n.
hire 785 vb.
what is due 915 n.
exempt 919 vb.
non-liability
919 n.
law 953 n.
charwoman
cleaner 648 n.
worker 686 n.
servant 742 n.
chase
park 192 n.
move fast 277 vb.
follow 284 vb.
grassland 348 n.
wood 366 n.
sculpt 554 vb.
chase 619 n.
pursue 619 vb.
desire 859 vb.
be hostile 881 vb.
be in love 887 vb.
court 889 vb.
not respect 921 vb.
disapprove 924 vb.
chasing
ornamental art
844 n.
chasm
disunion 46 n.
gap 201 n.
depth 211 n.
cavity 255 n.
pitfall 663 n.
chassis
base 214 n.
frame 218 n.
support 218 n.
carrier 273 n.
structure 331 n.
chaste
plain 573 adj.
modest 874 adj.
virtuous 933 adj.
temperate 942 adj.
pure 950 adj.
chasten
moderate 177 vb.
humiliate 872 vb.
chastened
repentant 939 adj.
chastise
reprove 924 vb.
punish 963 vb.

chastity
contraception
172 n.
modesty 874 n.
virtue 933 n.
temperance 942 n.
purity 950 n.
chat
cry 408 n.
speech 579 n.
chat 584 n.
converse 584 vb.
conversation
584 n.
chateau
house 192 n.
chatelaine
resident 191 n.
manager 690 n.
retainer 742 n.
keeper 749 n.
chat show
broadcast 531 n.
chattel
slave 742 n.
property 777 n.
chattels
equipment 630 n.
chatter
oscillate 317 vb.
be cold 380 vb.
roll 403 n.
roll 403 vb.
howl 409 n.
empty talk 515 n.
speak 579 vb.
be talkative
581 vb.
chatter 581 n.
chatterbox
chatterer 581 n.
chat to
be sociable
882 vb.
chattering
classes
informant 524 n.
chatterer 581 n.
chatty
talkative 581 adj.
sociable 882 adj.
chat up
court 889 vb.
chauffeur
driver 268 n.
domestic 742 n.
chauvinism
nation 371 n.
prejudice 481 n.
exaggeration
546 n.
aggressiveness

718 n.
boasting 877 n.
patriotism 901 n.
chauvinist
narrow mind
481 n.
militarist 722 n.
patriot 901 n.
cheap
cheap 812 adj.
vulgar 847 adj.
disreputable
867 adj.
cheapen
be cheap 812 vb.
cheapen 812 vb.
vulgarize 847 vb.
not respect 921 vb.
cheapen oneself
demean oneself
867 vb.
cheat
deceive 542 vb.
deception 542 n.
trickery 542 n.
trickster 545 n.
be cunning
698 vb.
wily person 698 n.
stratagem 698 n.
fleece 786 vb.
defraud 788 vb.
defrauder 789 n.
be dishonest
930 vb.
bad person 938 n.
cheating
duplicity 541 n.
false 541 adj.
deceiving 542 adj.
deception 542 n.
cunning 698 n.
swindling 788 n.
perfidious 930 adj.
check
number 86 vb.
halt 145 vb.
stop 145 vb.
moderate 177 vb.
moderation 177 n.
counteraction
182 n.
retard 278 vb.
chequer 437 n.
pied 437 adj.
enquire 459 vb.
enquiry 459 n.
experiment 461 n.
measurement
465 n.
certainty 473 n.
make certain

473 vb.
hinder 702 vb.
hindrance 702 n.
defeat 727 vb.
defeat 728 n.
adversity 731 n.
restrain 747 vb.
restraint 747 n.
loss 772 n.
pattern 844 n.
checking
measurement
465 n.
restraining
747 adj.
checklist
list 87 n.
comparison 462 n.
checkmate
halt 145 vb.
stop 145 n.
overcome 727 vb.
victory 727 n.
defeat 728 n.
check on
enquire 459 vb.
checkout
recording instru-
ment 549 n.
checkup
attention 455 n.
enquiry 459 n.
check with
compare 462 vb.
cheek
laterality 239 n.
be insolent
878 vb.
sauciness 878 n.
rudeness 885 n.
scurrility 899 n.
cheeky
impertinent
878 adj.
discourteous
885 adj.
disrespectful
921 adj.
cheep
howl 409 vb.
howling 409 n.
cheer
cry 408 n.
cry 408 vb.
shout 408 vb.
gesture 547 n.
excite 821 vb.
be cheerful
833 vb.
cheer 833 vb.
rejoice 835 vb.
celebrate 876 vb.

show respect
920 vb.
applaud 923 vb.
cheerful
cheerful 833 adj.
cheerio
goodbye 296 int.
cheerleader
cry 408 n.
cheerless
cheerless 834 adj.
dejected 834 adj.
melancholic
834 adj.
cheers
cheers 301 int.
cheers 835 int.
rejoicing 835 n.
thanks 907 int.
cheer up
relieve 831 vb.
be cheerful
833 vb.
cheery
cheerful 833 adj.
cheese
dairy products and
eggs 301 n.
cheesecake
bread, pastries
and cakes
301 n.
a beauty 841 n.
cheesed off
discontented
829 adj.
dejected 834 adj.
bored 838 adj.
cheetah
big cat 365 n.
chef
cookery 301 n.
caterer 633 n.
chef d'oeuvre
perfection 646 n.
masterpiece 694 n.
chemise
dress 228 n.
underwear 228 n.
chemist
union 45 n.
experimenter
461 n.
pharmacist 658 n.
mental state
817 n.
chemistry
conversion 147 n.
physics 319 n.
cheque
paper money
797 n.

chequebook
record 548 n.
chequer
chequer 437 n.
variegate 437 vb.
chequered
changeable
143 adj.
pied 437 adj.
cherish
look after 457 vb.
safeguard 660 vb.
animate 821 vb.
love 887 vb.
approve 923 vb.
cherry
fruit and vegeta-
bles 301 n.
redness 431 n.
cherub
child 132 n.
image 551 n.
darling 890 n.
angel 968 n.
chess
board game 837 n.
chessboard
chequer 437 n.
arena 724 n.
chess piece
plaything 837 n.
chest
box 194 n.
insides 224 n.
bosom 253 n.
treasury 799 n.
chestnut
repetition 106 n.
horse 273 n.
fruit and vegeta-
bles 301 n.
brown 430 adj.
witticism 839 n.
chest of draw-
ers
cabinet 194 n.
chevron
obliqueness 220 n.
angularity 247 n.
heraldry 547 n.
badge of rank
743 n.
pattern 844 n.
chew
chew 301 vb.
chewing
eating 301 n.
chewing gum
mouthful 301 n.
sweets 301 n.
elasticity 328 n.
chewy
tough 329 adj.

circle
continuity 71 n.
assembly 74 n.
group 74 n.
region 184 n.
encircle 232 vb.
encircling 232 n.
circle 250 n.
fly 271 vb.
circle 314 vb.
onlookers 441 n.
informant 524 n.
theatre 594 n.
party 708 n.
circuit
continuity 71 n.
periodic recurrence 141 n.
regular return 141 n.
revolution 149 n.
electricity 160 n.
region 184 n.
surroundings 230 n.
outline 233 n.
circle 250 n.
orbit 250 n.
land travel 267 n.
circle 314 vb.
circuitous motion 314 n.
circuit 626 n.
circuit 626 vb.
circuitous
circuitous 314 adj.
roundabout 626 adj.
circular
continuous 71 adj.
round 250 adj.
information 524 n.
publication 528 n.
correspondence 588 n.
reading matter 589 n.
decree 737 n.
circularity
circularity 250 n.
circularize
publish 528 vb.
correspond 588 vb.
command 737 vb.
circulate
disperse 75 vb.
pass 305 vb.
circle 314 vb.
be published 528 vb.
publish 528 vb.

change hands 780 vb.
mint 797 vb.
circulation
dispersion 75 n.
orbit 250 n.
circuitous motion 314 n.
rotation 315 n.
blood 335 n.
publication 528 n.
publicity 528 n.
circumcision
splitting 46 n.
rite 988 n.
circumference
region 184 n.
size 195 n.
distance 199 n.
exteriority 223 n.
surroundings 230 n.
outline 233 n.
enclosure 235 n.
limit 236 n.
circle 250 n.
circuit 626 n.
circumflex
curved 248 adj.
punctuation 547 n.
circumlocution
obliqueness 220 n.
figure of speech 519 n.
phrase 563 n.
diffuseness 570 n.
circumnavigate
navigate 269 vb.
circle 314 vb.
circumscribe
encircle 232 vb.
circumspect
vigilant 457 adj.
cautious 858 adj.
circumstance
circumstance 8 n.
concomitant 89 n.
event 154 n.
ostentation 875 n.
circumstances
circumstance 8 n.
particulars 80 n.
estate 777 n.
circumstances beyond one's control
necessity 596 n.
circumstantial
circumstantial 8 adj.
circumvent
avoid 620 vb.

circus
medley 43 n.
housing 192 n.
circle 250 n.
zoo 369 n.
stage show 594 n.
theatre 594 n.
arena 724 n.
pleasure ground 837 n.
cissy
see **sissy**
cist
interment 364 n.
tomb 364 n.
cistern
vat 194 n.
storage 632 n.
citadel
fort 713 n.
citation
act of referring 9 n.
evidence 466 n.
exhibit 522 n.
decoration 729 n.
warrant 737 n.
praise 923 n.
accusation 928 n.
legal process 959 n.
cite
specify 80 vb.
exemplify 83 vb.
repeat 106 vb.
manifest 522 vb.
command 737 vb.
indict 928 vb.
litigate 959 vb.
citizen
native 191 n.
subject 742 n.
free person 744 n.
commoner 869 n.
city
city 184 n.
abode 192 n.
political organiza-tion 733 n.
City
region 184 n.
business 622 n.
city centre
focus 76 n.
city father
officer 741 n.
civic
national 371 adj.
civil
well-bred 848 adj.
courteous 884 adj.
Civil Defence
defender 713 n.

civilians
laity 987 n.
civility
good taste 846 n.
courteous act 884 n.
courtesy 884 n.
civilization
culture 490 n.
fashionable society 848 n.
civilize
make better 654 vb.
civilized
well-bred 848 adj.
civilized world
humankind 371 n.
civil law
law 953 n.
civil rights
freedom 744 n.
what is due 915 n.
civil servant
official 690 n.
officer 741 n.
servant 742 n.
civvies
non-uniform 17 adj.
informal dress 228 n.
cladding
facing 226 n.
claim
territory 184 n.
enclosure 235 n.
affirm 532 vb.
plead 614 vb.
pretext 614 n.
require 627 vb.
requirement 627 n.
demand 737 n.
request 761 n.
desire 859 n.
title 870 n.
right 913 n.
claim 915 vb.
what is due 915 n.
litigation 959 n.
claimant
petitioner 763 n.
what is due 915 n.
litigant 959 n.
claim back
retrieve 656 vb.
claim to fame
goodness 644 n.
fame 866 n.
prestige 866 n.
clairvoyant
intuitive 476 adj.

foreseeing 510 adj.
oracle 511 n.
predicting 511 adj.
psychic 984 n.
psychical 984 n.
clam
marine life 365 n.
uncommunicative-ness 582 n.
clamber
climb 308 vb.
clamlike
reticent 525 adj.
clamour
loudness 400 n.
cry 408 n.
shout 408 vb.
disapprobation 924 n.
clamp
affix 45 vb.
fastening 47 n.
moderator 177 n.
restraint 747 n.
fetter 748 n.
pincers 778 n.
clamp down on
suppress 165 vb.
be severe 735 vb.
restrain 747 vb.
clan
family 11 n.
race 11 n.
group 74 n.
breed 77 n.
genealogy 169 n.
native 191 n.
community 708 n.
clandestine
occult 523 adj.
concealed 525 adj.
stealthy 525 adj.
clang
be loud 400 vb.
loudness 400 n.
roll 403 n.
roll 403 vb.
resonance 404 n.
clank
resound 404 vb.
rasp 407 vb.
clannish
ethnic 11 adj.
excluding 57 adj.
biased 481 adj.
sectarian 978 adj.
clansman
kinsman 11 n.
friend 880 n.
clap
knock 279 n.
be loud 400 vb.

clubfoot
deformity 246 n.
clubhouse
meeting place
192 n.
club together
cooperate 706 vb.
be sociable
882 vb.
cluck
howl 409 vb.
howling 409 n.
clue
answer 460 n.
evidence 466 n.
knowledge 490 n.
interpretation
520 n.
hint 524 n.
indication 547 n.
clueless
doubting 474 adj.
ignorant 491 adj.
in difficulties
700 adj.
clump
bunch 74 n.
walk 267 vb.
solid body 324 n.
wood 366 n.
clumsy
inelegant 576 adj.
clumsy 695 adj.
graceless 842 adj.
clunk
resound 404 vb.
cluster
congregate 74 vb.
crowd 74 n.
group 74 n.
clutch
group 74 n.
young creature
132 n.
retain 778 vb.
take 786 vb.
clutch at
take 786 vb.
desire 859 vb.
clutches
governing 733 n.
retention 778 n.
clutter
disorder 61 n.
be many 104 vb.
coach
conveyance 267 n.
bus 274 n.
carriage 274 n.
train 274 n.
educate 534 vb.
train 534 vb.

teacher 537 n.
trainer 537 n.
make ready
669 vb.
coach-builder
artisan 686 n.
coaching
teaching 534 n.
coachman
driver 268 n.
domestic 742 n.
coagulate
cohere 48 vb.
be dense 324 vb.
thicken 354 vb.
coal
propellant 287 n.
heater 383 n.
coal 385 n.
fuel 385 n.
black thing 428 n.
coalesce
be identical 13 vb.
combine 50 vb.
cooperate 706 vb.
coalface
store 632 n.
workshop 687 n.
coalfield
coal 385 n.
store 632 n.
coalition
union 45 n.
association 706 n.
political party
708 n.
society 708 n.
coarse
rough 259 adj.
textural 331 adj.
undiscriminating
464 adj.
inelegant 576 adj.
unclean 649 adj.
vulgar 847 adj.
plebeian 869 adj.
impure 951 adj.
coarseness
roughness 259 n.
lack of discrimina-
tion 464 n.
plainness 573 n.
inelegance 576 n.
moral insensibility
820 n.
bad taste 847 n.
impurity 951 n.
coast
edge 234 n.
flank 239 vb.
laterality 239 n.
be in motion

265 vb.
ride 267 vb.
travel 267 vb.
voyage 269 vb.
pass 305 vb.
shore 344 n.
be neglectful
458 vb.
not act 677 vb.
coastal
marginal 234 adj.
coaster
stand 218 n.
merchant ship
275 n.
coastguard
nautical personnel
270 n.
protector 660 n.
keeper 749 n.
coast home
do easily 701 vb.
coasting
water travel
269 n.
coastline
outline 233 n.
shore 344 n.
coat
layer 207 n.
coat 226 vb.
skin 226 n.
wrapping 226 n.
jacket 228 n.
overcoat 228 n.
coating
layer 207 n.
covering 226 n.
facing 226 n.
lining 227 n.
coat of arms
heraldry 547 n.
nobility 868 n.
coat-tail(s)
extremity 69 n.
hanging object
217 n.
article of clothing
228 n.
coax
tempt 612 vb.
request 761 vb.
pet 889 vb.
flatter 925 vb.
cobble
paving 226 n.
building material
631 n.
repair 656 vb.
cobbler
clothier 228 n.
mender 656 n.

cobblestone
paving 226 n.
cobble together
produce 164 vb.
cobra
reptile 365 n.
cobweb
weak thing 163 n.
filament 208 n.
network 222 n.
lightness 323 n.
dirt 649 n.
cocaine
anaesthetic 375 n.
drug 658 n.
drugs 949 n.
coccyx
buttocks 238 n.
cock
poultry 365 n.
male animal
372 n.
make ready
669 vb.
cockade
trimming 844 n.
cock-and-bull
story
thing that lacks
substance 4 n.
fable 543 n.
cock a snook
defy 711 vb.
disobey 738 vb.
not observe
769 vb.
be insolent
878 vb.
not respect 921 vb.
cockerel
poultry 365 n.
male animal
372 n.
cock-eyed
distorted 246 adj.
erroneous 495 adj.
absurd 497 adj.
cockfight
duel 716 n.
cockle
fish as food 301 n.
marine life 365 n.
cockles of the
heart
mental state
817 n.
Cockney, cock-
ney
native 191 n.
dialect 560 adj.
dialectal 560 adj.
plebeian 869 adj.

cockpit
room 194 n.
aircraft 276 n.
duel 716 n.
cockroach
insect 365 n.
cocktail
a mixture 43 n.
alcoholic drink
301 n.
drink 301 n.
cocky
proud 871 adj.
vain 873 adj.
impertinent
878 adj.
cocoa
milk 301 n.
soft drink 301 n.
cocoon
young creature
132 n.
source 156 n.
receptacle 194 n.
wrapping 226 n.
safeguard 660 vb.
C.O.D.
pay 804 vb.
coda
adjunct 40 n.
sequel 67 n.
end 69 n.
rear 238 n.
melody 410 n.
musical piece
412 n.
coddle
cook 301 vb.
please 826 vb.
pet 889 vb.
code
arrangement 62 n.
rule 81 n.
latency 523 n.
secrecy 525 n.
enigma 530 n.
writing 586 n.
precept 693 n.
probity 929 n.
codicil
adjunct 40 n.
sequel 67 n.
title deed 767 n.
codification
arrangement 62 n.
coeducational
educational
534 adj.
coefficient
numerical element
85 n.
coerce
dominate 733 vb.

collector
collector 492 n.
receiver 782 n.
collector's item
exhibit 522 n.
exceller 644 n.
masterpiece 694 n.
college
building 164 n.
academy 539 n.
collide
disagree 25 vb.
collide 279 vb.
meet 295 vb.
be hostile 881 vb.
collier
merchant ship 275 n.
artisan 686 n.
colliery
excavation 255 n.
store 632 n.
workshop 687 n.
collision
collision 279 n.
battle 718 n.
collocate
arrange 62 vb.
bring together 74 vb.
place 187 vb.
collocation
assemblage 74 n.
location 187 n.
phrase 563 n.
colloid
semiliquidity 354 n.
glutinousness 354 n.
colloquial
linguistic 557 adj.
dialectal 560 adj.
collusion
concurrence 181 n.
duplicity 541 n.
deception 542 n.
cooperation 706 n.
cologne
cosmetic 843 n.
colon
insides 224 n.
tube 263 n.
punctuation 547 n.
colonel
army officer 741 n.
colonial
foreigner 59 n.
settler 191 n.
colonize
place oneself

187 vb.
be present 189 vb.
live 192 vb.
subjugate 745 vb.
appropriate 786 vb.
colonnade
series 71 n.
pavilion 192 n.
path 624 n.
colony
crowd 74 n.
descendant 170 n.
territory 184 n.
station 187 n.
*political organiza-
 tion* 733 n.
colophon
sequel 67 n.
rear 238 n.
label 547 n.
edition 589 n.
coloration
colour 425 n.
hue 425 n.
colorize
colour 425 vb.
colossal
enormous 32 adj.
stalwart 162 adj.
huge 195 adj.
tall 209 adj.
colossus
giant 195 n.
high structure 209 n.
tall creature 209 n.
image 551 n.
colour
character 5 n.
tincture 43 n.
sort 77 n.
colour 425 n.
colour 425 vb.
blackness 428 n.
redden 431 vb.
expression 445 n.
qualify 468 vb.
use sophistry 477 vb.
heraldry 547 n.
ornament 574 n.
plead 614 vb.
pretext 614 vb.
show feeling 818 vb.
be modest 874 vb.
get angry 891 vb.
colour bar
exclusion 57 n.
prejudice 481 n.

disapprobation 924 n.
colour-blind
dim-sighted 440 adj.
undiscriminating 464 adj.
**colour blind-
 ness**
blindness 439 n.
dim sight 440 n.
coloured
black 428 adj.
blackish 428 adj.
blackness 428 n.
colourful
luminous 417 adj.
florid 425 adj.
variegated 437 adj.
descriptive 590 adj.
showy 875 adj.
colouring
hue 425 n.
qualification 468 n.
qualifying 468 adj.
identification 547 n.
painting 553 n.
**colouring mat-
 ter**
pigment 425 n.
colourless
colourless 426 adj.
feeble 572 adj.
dull 840 adj.
colours
badge 547 n.
flag 547 n.
colt
young creature 132 n.
horse 273 n.
male animal 372 n.
beginner 538 n.
pistol 723 n.
column
high structure 209 n.
pillar 218 n.
cylinder 252 n.
article 591 n.
formation 722 n.
columnist
informant 524 n.
author 589 n.
coma
helplessness 161 n.

insensitivity 375 n.
illness 651 n.
sleep 679 n.
comatose
impotent 161 adj.
insensitive 375 adj.
sleepy 679 adj.
comb
tooth 256 n.
smooth 258 vb.
smoother 258 n.
notch 260 n.
organ 414 n.
search 459 vb.
cleaning utensil 648 n.
hairdressing 843 n.
combat
contend 716 vb.
contention 716 n.
fight 716 n.
fight 716 vb.
go to war 718 vb.
combatant
opponent 705 n.
combatant 722 n.
combination
combination 50 n.
association 706 n.
society 708 n.
combinations
underwear 228 n.
combine
combine 50 vb.
association 706 n.
cooperate 706 vb.
corporation 708 n.
society 708 n.
combine with
accrue 38 vb.
combings
leavings 41 n.
combustible
fuel 385 n.
combustion
burning 381 n.
come
arrive 295 vb.
climax 725 vb.
come about
be 1 vb.
happen 154 vb.
come across
acquire 771 vb.
pay 804 vb.
**come across
 with**
confess 526 vb.
come and go
fluctuate 317 vb.

come apart
separate 46 vb.
comeback
recurrence 106 n.
revival 656 n.
come between
interfere 231 vb.
lie between 231 vb.
hinder 702 vb.
make quarrels 709 vb.
come by
acquire 771 vb.
inherit 771 vb.
come clean
confess 526 vb.
be truthful 540 vb.
speak 579 vb.
**comedian,
 comedienne**
actor 594 n.
entertainer 594 n.
humorist 839 n.
come down
decrease 37 vb.
descend 309 vb.
raw 350 vb.
comedown
descent 309 n.
disrepute 867 n.
humiliation 872 n.
come down on
be severe 735 vb.
comedy
stage play 594 n.
laughter 835 n.
ridiculousness 849 n.
come forward
offer oneself 759 vb.
**come-hither
 look**
glance 438 n.
pleasurableness 826 n.
come home
arrive 295 vb.
come in
be included 78 vb.
approach 289 vb.
enter 297 vb.
come into
inherit 771 vb.
receive 782 vb.
appropriate 786 vb.
come it over
be proud 871 vb.
despise 922 vb.
comely
beautiful 841 adj.

utility 640 n.
merchandise
   795 n.
commodore
nautical personnel
   270 n.
naval officer
   741 n.
common
general 79 adj.
typical 83 adj.
frequent 139 adj.
plain 348 n.
proverbial 496 adj.
linguistic 557 adj.
usual 610 adj.
not possessed
   774 adj.
joint possession
   775 n.
lands 777 n.
vulgar 847 adj.
plebeian 869 adj.
common cold
excretion 302 n.
coldness 380 n.
infection 651 n.
respiratory disease
   651 n.
common
   denominator
relation 9 n.
numerical element
   85 n.
common factor
numerical element
   85 n.
common know-
   ledge
knowledge 490 n.
information
   524 n.
publicity 528 n.
common law
tradition 127 n.
precept 693 n.
law 953 n.
common man
common man
   30 n.
averageness 732 n.
Common Mar-
   ket
society 708 n.
market 796 n.
common or
   garden
typical 83 adj.
commonplace
median 30 adj.
general 79 adj.
typical 83 adj.

topic 452 n.
known 490 adj.
proverbial 496 adj.
maxim 496 n.
phrase 563 n.
plain 573 adj.
usual 610 adj.
trivial 639 adj.
middling 732 adj.
dull 840 adj.
commonplace
   book
reminder 505 n.
record 548 n.
anthology 592 n.
common prayer
public worship
   981 n.
commonsense
intelligence 498 n.
sanity 502 n.
commonwealth
territory 184 n.
nation 371 n.
political organiza-
   tion 733 n.
commotion
commotion 318 n.
quarrel 709 n.
communal
national 371 adj.
commune
district 184 n.
communicate
   524 vb.
association 706 n.
joint possession
   775 n.
commune with
converse 584 vb.
communicable
infectious 653 adj.
communicant
pious person
   979 n.
worshipper 981 n.
communicate
connect 45 vb.
communicate
   524 vb.
communication
union 45 n.
transference 272 n.
information
   524 n.
disclosure 526 n.
message 529 n.
conversation
   584 n.
correspondence
   588 n.
communica-
   tions
access 624 n.

communicative
informative
   524 adj.
talkative 581 adj.
communion
conversation
   584 n.
social gathering
   882 n.
Holy Communion
   988 n.
communiqué
report 524 n.
news 529 n.
communism
government 733 n.
joint possession
   775 n.
philanthropy
   901 n.
communist
revolutionary
   149 n.
community
subdivision 53 n.
district 184 n.
housing 192 n.
social group
   371 n.
community 708 n.
community care
protection 660 n.
social care 901 n.
community
   centre
focus 76 n.
meeting place
   192 n.
commutation
compensation
   31 n.
substitution 150 n.
interchange 151 n.
compromise 770 n.
commute
interchange
   151 vb.
travel 267 vb.
compromise
   770 vb.
show mercy
   905 vb.
commuter
inhabitant 191 n.
traveller 268 n.
transport 272 n.
compact
small 33 adj.
case 194 n.
little 196 adj.
make smaller
   198 vb.

short 204 adj.
be dense 324 vb.
dense 324 adj.
concise 569 adj.
pact 765 n.
cosmetic 843 n.
compact disc
rotator 315 n.
music player
   414 n.
recording instru-
   ment 549 n.
compaction
cohesiveness 48 n.
compression
   198 n.
companion
analogue 18 n.
concomitant 89 n.
window 263 n.
colleague 707 n.
retainer 742 n.
servant 742 n.
close friend 880 n.
companionship
accompaniment
   89 n.
friendship 880 n.
fellowship 882 n.
companionway
doorway 263 n.
ascent 308 n.
company
component 58 n.
assembly 74 n.
band 74 n.
accompaniment
   89 n.
actor 594 n.
personnel 686 n.
association 706 n.
corporation 708 n.
party 708 n.
formation 722 n.
comparable
relative 9 adj.
equivalent 28 adj.
compared 462 adj.
comparative
relative 9 adj.
distinctive 15 adj.
comparative 27 n.
compared 462 adj.
grammatical
   564 adj.
compare
relate 9 vb.
graduate 27 vb.
compare 462 vb.
comparison
comparison 462 n.
compartment
subdivision 53 n.

compartment
   194 n.
train 274 n.
compass
degree 27 n.
range 183 n.
region 184 n.
distance 199 n.
surroundings
   230 n.
outline 233 n.
sailing aid 269 n.
navigator 270 n.
direction 281 n.
gauge 465 n.
signpost 547 n.
compassion
leniency 736 n.
pity 905 n.
compassionate
impressible
   819 adj.
pitying 905 adj.
godlike 965 adj.
compatibility
adaptation 24 n.
harmony 710 n.
friendship 880 n.
sociability 882 n.
love 887 n.
compatriot
kinsman 11 n.
compeer
peer 28 n.
compel
compel 740 vb.
compendium
compendium
   592 n.
compensate
be equal 28 vb.
compensate 31 vb.
make restitution
   787 vb.
pay 804 vb.
atone 941 vb.
reward 962 vb.
compensation
compensation
   31 n.
peace offering
   719 n.
resignation 753 n.
earnings 771 n.
restitution 787 n.
pay 804 n.
payment 804 n.
what is due 915 n.
atonement 941 n.
reward 962 n.
penalty 963 n.
compere
broadcaster 531 n.

community 708 n.
worshipper 981 n.
laity 987 n.
congress
union 45 n.
convergence 293 n.
council 692 n.
parliament 692 n.
congruent
identical 13 adj.
agreeing 24 adj.
equal 28 adj.
symmetrical
245 adj.
congruity
similarity 18 n.
conformance 24 n.
symmetry 245 n.
conical
convergent
293 adj.
conjecture
attribution 158 n.
assume 471 vb.
estimate 480 vb.
conjecture 512 n.
suppose 512 vb.
conjugal
loving 887 adj.
conjugate
verbal 559 adj.
conjugation
differentiation
15 n.
arrangement 62 n.
grammar 564 n.
conjunction
union 45 n.
concurrence 181 n.
contiguity 202 n.
part of speech
564 n.
conjunctive
additional 38 adj.
connective 45 adj.
grammatical
564 adj.
conjure
deceive 542 vb.
conjure up
remember 505 vb.
imagine 513 vb.
conjuror
sorcerer 983 n.
conk out
die 361 vb.
fail 728 vb.
con man
impostor 545 n.
trickster 545 n.
defrauder 789 n.
bad person 938 n.

connect
relate 9 vb.
connect 45 vb.
connection
relation 9 n.
kinship 11 n.
union 45 n.
bond 47 n.
cohesiveness 48 n.
connivance
cooperation 706 n.
connive
concur 181 vb.
cooperate 706 vb.
consent 758 vb.
forgive 909 vb.
connive at
disregard 458 vb.
permit 756 vb.
do wrong 914 adj.
connoisseur
eater 301 n.
collector 492 n.
enthusiast 504 n.
expert 696 n.
person of taste
846 n.
connotation
connotation 514 n.
connote
mean 514 vb.
imply 523 vb.
indicate 547 vb.
conquer
climb 308 vb.
overcome 727 vb.
appropriate
786 vb.
take 786 vb.
conqueror
victor 727 n.
possessor 776 n.
conquest
victory 727 n.
subjection 745 n.
loved one 887 n.
consanguinity
kinship 11 n.
divorce 896 n.
conscience
knowledge 490 n.
necessity 596 n.
motive 612 n.
conscience 917 n.
conscientious
careful 457 adj.
observant 768 adj.
fastidious 862 adj.
obliged 917 adj.
honourable
929 adj.
trustworthy

929 adj.
**conscientious
objector**
objector 489 n.
pacifist 717 n.
malcontent 829 n.
conscious
sentient 374 adj.
attentive 455 adj.
knowing 490 adj.
conscript
go to war 718 vb.
soldier 722 n.
compel 740 vb.
consecrate
offer 759 vb.
dignify 866 vb.
sanctify 979 vb.
offer worship
981 vb.
perform ritual
988 vb.
consecutive
relative 9 adj.
sequential 65 adj.
continuous 71 adj.
subsequent
120 adj.
consensus
concurrence 181 n.
consensus 488 n.
consent
agreement 24 n.
submission 721 n.
consent 758 n.
consent 758 vb.
approbation
923 n.
consequence
conformance 24 n.
sequence 65 n.
sequel 67 n.
event 154 n.
effect 157 n.
importance 638 n.
consequential
caused 157 adj.
ostentatious
875 adj.
conservation
permanence 144 n.
storage 632 n.
protection 660 n.
preservation
666 n.
economy 814 n.
conservationist
preserver 666 n.
Conservative
political party
708 n.

conservative
antiquated
127 adj.
permanent
144 adj.
cautious 858 adj.
conservatoire
music 412 n.
academy 539 n.
conservatory
arbour 194 n.
garden 370 n.
conserve
sweet thing 392 n.
store 632 vb.
safeguard 660 vb.
preserve 666 vb.
consider
meditate 449 vb.
notice 455 vb.
estimate 480 vb.
considerable
substantial 3 adj.
great 32 adj.
many 104 adj.
large 195 adj.
important 638 adj.
considerate
thoughtful
449 adj.
attentive 455 adj.
careful 457 adj.
well-bred 848 adj.
amiable 884 adj.
benevolent
897 adj.
consideration
meditation 449 n.
attention 455 n.
qualification
468 n.
estimate 480 n.
importance 638 n.
gift 781 n.
good taste 846 n.
courtesy 884 n.
benevolence 897 n.
respect 920 n.
reward 962 n.
**consider
beneath one**
despise 922 vb.
consign
send 272 vb.
commission
751 n.
consignment
transport 272 n.
transfer 780 n.
giving 781 n.
**consign to
oblivion**
forget 506 vb.

consistency
uniformity 16 n.
conformance 24 n.
density 324 n.
consistent
uniform 16 adj.
agreeing 24 adj.
dense 324 adj.
rational 475 adj.
consist of
contain 56 vb.
comprise 78 vb.
consolation
relief 831 n.
condolence 905 n.
console
cabinet 194 n.
shelf 218 n.
relieve 831 vb.
cheer 833 vb.
pity 905 vb.
consolidate
bring together
74 vb.
centralize 225 vb.
be dense 324 vb.
consonant
speech sound
398 n.
harmonious
410 adj.
consort
concomitant 89 n.
spouse 894 n.
consortium
agreement 24 n.
association 706 n.
conspectus
combination 50 n.
whole 52 n.
generality 79 n.
compendium
592 n.
conspicuous
obvious 443 adj.
manifest 522 adj.
notable 638 adj.
noteworthy
866 adj.
conspiracy
assemblage 74 n.
concurrence 181 n.
secrecy 525 n.
plot 623 n.
cooperation 706 n.
pact 765 n.
conspirator
deceiver 545 n.
planner 623 n.
collaborator
707 n.
conspire
combine 50 vb.

240 n.
current 350 n.
pitfall 663 n.
obstacle 702 n.
opposition 704 n.
cross-dresser
nonconformist
84 n.
crossed
mixed 43 adj.
crossed 222 adj.
crossed lines
misinterpretation
521 n.
cross-examine
interrogate 459 vb.
try a case 959 vb.
cross-eyed
crossed 222 adj.
dim-sighted
440 adj.
**cross-
  fertilization**
mixture 43 n.
cross-fire
interchange 151 n.
crossing
crossed 222 adj.
crossing 222 n.
water travel
269 n.
passage 305 n.
access 624 n.
road 624 n.
cross-legged
crossed 222 adj.
crossness
anger 891 n.
sullenness 893 n.
cross off
register 548 vb.
**cross one's
  fingers**
deprecate 762 vb.
cross out
subtract 39 vb.
exclude 57 vb.
mark 547 n.
obliterate 550 n.
cross over
cross 222 vb.
pass 305 vb.
apostatize 603 vb.
crossover
railway 624 n.
crosspatch
moper 834 n.
rude person 885 n.
cross-purposes
error 495 n.
misinterpretation
521 n.

opposition 704 n.
dissension 709 n.
cross-question
interrogate 459 vb.
cross-reference
act of referring
9 n.
class 62 vb.
sorting 62 n.
crossroads
juncture 8 n.
joint 45 n.
focus 76 n.
crossing 222 n.
divergence 294 n.
road 624 n.
cross-section
example 83 n.
cross swords
collide 279 vb.
argue 475 vb.
withstand 704 vb.
quarrel 709 vb.
contend 716 vb.
fight 716 vb.
go to war 718 vb.
**cross the Rubi-
  con**
overstep 306 vb.
be resolute 599 vb.
cross to bear
bane 659 n.
crosswind
wind 352 n.
obstacle 702 n.
cross with
*have sexual inter-
  course with*
45 vb.
crossword
enigma 530 n.
indoor game
837 n.
crotch
angularity 247 n.
crotchet
angularity 247 n.
notation 410 n.
punctuation
547 n.
crotchety
crazy 503 adj.
capricious 604 adj.
irascible 892 adj.
crouch
stoop 311 vb.
knuckle under
721 vb.
quake 854 vb.
lose repute 867 vb.
croupier
treasurer 798 n.

croûton
*bread, pastries
  and cakes*
301 n.
crow
bird 365 n.
black thing 428 n.
defy 711 vb.
triumph 727 vb.
laughter 835 n.
rejoice 835 vb.
eyesore 842 n.
boast 877 vb.
crowbar
tool 630 n.
crowd
congregate 74 vb.
crowd 74 n.
be many 104 vb.
be contiguous
202 vb.
be dense 324 vb.
violin 414 n.
onlookers 441 n.
obstruct 702 vb.
not respect 921 vb.
crowded
firm 45 adj.
multitudinous
104 adj.
printed 587 adj.
crowds
great quantity
32 n.
crowd together
make smaller
198 vb.
crown
completeness 54 n.
crown 213 vb.
head 213 n.
summit 213 n.
apex 213 n.
headgear 228 n.
loop 250 n.
strike 279 vb.
badge 547 n.
heraldry 547 n.
objective 617 n.
completion 725 n.
trophy 729 n.
authority 733 n.
badge of rank
743 n.
regalia 743 n.
commission
751 n.
coinage 797 n.
dignify 866 vb.
honour 866 vb.
honours 866 n.
celebrate 876 vb.

reward 962 n.
crown all
culminate 34 vb.
climax 725 vb.
crowning
complete 54 adj.
final 69 adj.
topmost 213 adj.
crow over
defy 711 vb.
triumph 727 vb.
humiliate 872 vb.
boast 877 vb.
crow's feet
fold 261 n.
ugliness 842 n.
crow's nest
high structure
209 n.
apex 213 n.
view 438 n.
crucial
circumstantial
8 adj.
crucial 137 adj.
fundamental
156 adj.
crossed 222 adj.
important 638 adj.
crucial moment
juncture 8 n.
crisis 137 n.
important matter
638 n.
crucible
vessel 194 n.
heater 383 n.
crucifix
cross 222 n.
jewellery 844 n.
ritual object
988 n.
church interior
990 n.
crucifixion
killing 362 n.
pain 377 n.
suffering 825 n.
capital punishment
963 n.
cruciform
crossed 222 adj.
churchlike
990 adj.
crucify
give pain 377 vb.
ill-treat 645 vb.
execute 963 vb.
crud
dirt 649 n.
crude
incomplete 55 adj.

florid 425 adj.
inelegant 576 adj.
immature 670 adj.
bungled 695 adj.
graceless 842 adj.
ill-bred 847 adj.
cruel
causing pain
827 adj.
cruel 898 adj.
cruelty
badness 645 n.
severity 735 n.
cruel act 898 n.
inhumanity 898 n.
cruet
small box 194 n.
condiment 389 n.
ritual object
988 n.
cruise
be in motion
265 vb.
go to sea 269 vb.
voyage 269 vb.
water travel
269 n.
cruiser
warship 722 n.
crumb
small thing 33 n.
piece 53 n.
*bread, pastries
  and cakes*
301 n.
powder 332 n.
crumble
lessen 37 vb.
break 46 vb.
decompose 51 vb.
be weak 163 vb.
be destroyed
165 vb.
dessert 301 n.
grind 332 vb.
deteriorate 655 vb.
impair 655 vb.
crumbling
decrease 37 n.
unsafe 661 adj.
crumbly
fragmentary
53 adj.
brittle 330 adj.
powdery 332 adj.
crumbs
leavings 41 n.
rubbish 641 n.
crummy
inferior 35 adj.
bad 645 adj.
crumpet
head 213 n.

bread, pastries
and cakes
301 n.
female 373 n.
crumple
jumble 63 vb.
make smaller
198 vb.
distort 246 vb.
crinkle 251 vb.
roughen 259 vb.
crunch
rend 46 vb.
chew 301 vb.
grind 332 vb.
rasp 407 vb.
crusade
action 676 n.
war 718 n.
philanthropy
901 n.
crusader
militarist 722 n.
philanthropist
901 n.
zealot 979 n.
crush
jumble 63 vb.
crowd 74 n.
demolish 165 vb.
force 176 vb.
make smaller
198 vb.
make concave
255 vb.
abase 311 vb.
lower 311 vb.
grind 332 vb.
touch 378 vb.
confute 479 vb.
ill-treat 645 vb.
wound 655 vb.
defeat 727 vb.
overcome 727 vb.
oppress 735 vb.
humiliate 872 vb.
love 887 n.
crush barrier
safeguard 662 n.
crushing
destruction 165 n.
destructive
165 adj.
distressing
827 adj.
crushing blow
ruin 165 n.
crust
piece 53 n.
exteriority 223 n.
covering 226 n.
skin 226 n.

bread, pastries
and cakes
301 n.
be dense 324 vb.
hardness 326 n.
sauciness 878 n.
crustacean
animal 365 n.
marine life 365 n.
crusty
irascible 892 adj.
sullen 893 adj.
crutch
support 218 n.
article of clothing
228 n.
crux
crisis 137 n.
cross 222 n.
chief thing 638 n.
difficulty 700 n.
cry
cry 408 n.
cry 408 vb.
howl 409 vb.
howling 409 n.
lamentation
836 n.
weep 836 vb.
desire 859 vb.
cry down
underestimate
483 vb.
detract 926 vb.
crying
lamentation
836 n.
crying shame
evil 616 n.
slur 867 n.
wrong 914 n.
cry out
cry 408 vb.
shout 408 vb.
cry out against
deprecate 762 vb.
cry out for
require 627 vb.
desire 859 vb.
crypt
cellar 194 n.
depth 211 n.
tomb 364 n.
hiding-place
527 n.
church interior
990 n.
cryptic
uncertain 474 adj.
unintelligible
517 adj.
occult 523 adj.

concealed 525 adj.
cryptogram
enigma 530 n.
cryptologist
interpreter 520 n.
crystal
minuteness 196 n.
covering 226 n.
solid body 324 n.
transparency
422 n.
transparent
422 adj.
crystal ball
sphere 252 n.
oracle 511 n.
crystal-gazing
divination 511 n.
prediction 511 n.
occultism 984 n.
crystalline
dense 324 adj.
hard 326 adj.
transparent
422 adj.
crystallize
be dense 324 vb.
harden 326 vb.
sweeten 392 vb.
cry wolf
be false 541 vb.
raise the alarm
665 vb.
frighten 854 vb.
cub
young creature
132 n.
young person
132 n.
reproduce itself
167 vb.
cubbyhole
retreat 192 n.
compartment
194 n.
cube
three 93 n.
treble 94 vb.
angular figure
247 n.
cubic
metrical 465 adj.
cubicle
room 194 n.
compartment
194 n.
cuckold
fool 542 vb.
be impure 951 vb.
cuckoo
resident 191 n.
bird 365 n.

roll 403 n.
howling 409 n.
fool 501 n.
crazy 503 adj.
**cuckoo in the
nest**
unrelatedness
10 n.
outsider 59 n.
impostor 545 n.
usurper 916 n.
cuddle
surround 230 vb.
enclose 235 vb.
retention 778 n.
please 826 vb.
caress 889 vb.
endearment 889 n.
cuddly
fat 195 adj.
cudgel
hammer 279 n.
strike 279 vb.
club 723 n.
flog 963 vb.
scourge 964 n.
cue
ram 279 n.
remind 505 vb.
reminder 505 n.
hint 524 n.
dramatic theory
594 n.
cue in
act 594 vb.
cuff
article of clothing
228 n.
sleeve 228 n.
fold 261 n.
fold 261 vb.
knock 279 n.
corporal punish-
ment 963 n.
spank 963 vb.
cufflinks
jewellery 844 n.
cuisine
cookery 301 n.
cul-de-sac
stopping place
145 n.
closure 264 n.
road 624 n.
difficulty 700 n.
obstacle 702 n.
culinary
culinary 301 adj.
cull
killing 362 n.
select 605 vb.
take 786 vb.

culminate
culminate 34 vb.
be complete 54 vb.
be high 209 vb.
crown 213 vb.
ascend 308 vb.
climax 725 vb.
culottes
skirt 228 n.
culpable
wrong 914 adj.
blameworthy
924 adj.
heinous 934 adj.
guilty 936 adj.
culprit
offender 904 n.
accused person
928 n.
cult
fashion 848 n.
cult 981 n.
idolatry 982 n.
cultivate
cultivate 370 vb.
train 534 vb.
flatter 925 vb.
cultivation
causation 156 n.
agriculture 370 n.
learning 536 n.
ripening 669 n.
good taste 846 n.
cultural
educational
534 adj.
improving 654 adj.
culture
breed stock
369 vb.
culture 490 n.
learning 536 n.
good taste 846 n.
cultured
spurious 542 adj.
culvert
drain 351 n.
cumbersome
unwieldy 195 adj.
weighty 322 adj.
inexpedient
643 adj.
clumsy 695 adj.
graceless 842 adj.
cummerbund
belt 228 n.
loop 250 n.
cumulative
increasing 36 adj.
cumulus
accumulation
74 n.

cut a dash
be in fashion
848 vb.
have a reputation
866 vb.
be ostentatious
875 vb.

assent 488 n.
declaration of war
dissension 709 n.
defiance 711 n.
state of war 718 n.
declare
believe 485 vb.
mean 514 vb.
divulge 526 vb.
proclaim 528 vb.
affirm 532 vb.
indicate 547 vb.
speak 579 vb.
decree 737 vb.
declare (cricket)
resign 753 vb.
declare oneself
disclose 526 vb.
declare war
quarrel 709 vb.
attack 712 vb.
go to war 718 vb.
declassify
disarrange 63 vb.
declension
differentiation 15 n.
decrease 37 n.
change 143 n.
deviation 282 n.
descent 309 n.
grammar 564 n.
decline
inferiority 35 n.
decrease 37 n.
decrease 37 vb.
be old 127 vb.
oldness 127 n.
be weak 163 vb.
weakness 163 n.
contraction 198 n.
be oblique 220 vb.
regress 286 vb.
regression 286 n.
recede 290 vb.
descend 309 vb.
descent 309 n.
negate 533 vb.
reject 607 vb.
deteriorate 655 vb.
deterioration 655 n.
adversity 731 n.
have trouble 731 vb.
refuse 760 vb.
declining
small 33 adj.
decreasing 37 adj.
ageing 131 adj.

sloping 220 adj.
not prosperous 731 adj.
refusal 760 n.
declivity
incline 220 n.
descent 309 n.
declutter
arrange 62 vb.
decode
decipher 520 vb.
décolleté
bareness 229 n.
uncovered 229 adj.
decolorant
bleacher 426 n.
decommission
disable 161 vb.
decompose
decompose 51 vb.
deconsecrate
perform ritual 988 vb.
decontaminate
purify 648 vb.
make sanitary 652 adj.
rectify 654 vb.
decontrol
liberate 746 vb.
permit 756 vb.
not retain 779 vb.
decor
spectacle 445 n.
stage set 594 n.
decorate
beautify 841 vb.
decorate 844 vb.
decoration
spectacle 445 n.
ornament 574 n.
decoration 729 n.
ornamentation 844 n.
decorations
celebration 876 n.
decorative
painted 553 adj.
ornamental 844 adj.
decorator
mender 656 n.
artisan 686 n.
decorous
fit 24 adj.
orderly 60 adj.
well-bred 848 adj.
pure 950 adj.
decorum
good taste 846 n.
etiquette 848 n.
decoy
attract 291 vb.

attraction 291 n.
ambush 527 n.
ensnare 542 vb.
trap 542 n.
trickster 545 n.
incentive 612 n.
decrease
lessen 37 vb.
decrease 37 n.
decrease 37 vb.
subtract 39 vb.
contraction 198 n.
decree
judge 480 vb.
judgment 480 n.
predetermination 608 n.
decree 737 n.
decree 737 vb.
impose a duty 917 vb.
decree absolute, decree nisi
judgment 480 n.
decree 737 n.
divorce 896 n.
decrepit
ageing 131 adj.
weak 163 adj.
dilapidated 655 adj.
decrier
detractor 926 n.
decriminalize
decree 737 vb.
permit 756 vb.
make legal 953 vb.
decry
lessen 37 vb.
hold cheap 922 vb.
detract 926 vb.
dedicate
offer 759 vb.
give 781 vb.
dignify 866 vb.
sanctify 979 vb.
offer worship 981 vb.
perform ritual 988 vb.
dedicated
willing 597 adj.
resolute 599 adj.
obedient 739 adj.
philanthropic 901 adj.
sanctified 979 adj.
dedicate to
use 673 vb.
honour 866 vb.

dedication
edition 589 n.
willingness 597 n.
resolution 599 n.
offer 759 n.
offering 781 n.
philanthropy 901 n.
piety 979 n.
sanctity 979 n.
religious offering 981 n.
Christian rite 988 n.
deduce
assume 471 vb.
reason 475 vb.
demonstrate 478 vb.
interpret 520 vb.
deducible
evidential 466 adj.
deduction
diminution 37 n.
subtraction 39 n.
deduction 42 n.
reasoning 475 n.
demonstration 478 n.
non-payment 805 n.
deed
testimony 466 n.
deed 676 n.
title deed 767 n.
deed poll
title deed 767 n.
deeds
conduct 688 n.
deejay
broadcaster 531 n.
deem
be of the opinion that 485 vb.
deep
spacious 183 adj.
deep 211 adj.
ocean 343 n.
hoarse 407 adj.
florid 425 adj.
wise 498 adj.
deep down
inherent 5 adj.
inside 224 adv.
deepen
augment 36 vb.
enlarge 197 vb.
be deep 211 vb.
aggravate 832 vb.
deep-freeze
refrigerate 382 vb.
refrigerator 384 n.

storage 632 n.
deep in thought
melancholic 834 adj.
deeply
greatly 32 vb.
inside 224 adv.
deepness
quantity 26 n.
interiority 224 n.
deep-rooted
inherent 5 adj.
lasting 113 adj.
fixed 153 adj.
deep 211 adj.
interior 224 adj.
remembered 505 adj.
habitual 610 adj.
having a certain mental state 817 adj.
deep-sea
deep 211 adj.
deep-seated
inherent 5 adj.
lasting 113 adj.
fixed 153 adj.
deep 211 adj.
interior 224 adj.
habitual 610 adj.
deep water
depth 211 n.
deer
mammal 365 n.
deer stalking
chase 619 n.
de-escalation
decrease 37 n.
diminution 37 n.
deface
destroy 165 vb.
deform 244 vb.
obliterate 550 vb.
make useless 641 adj.
impair 655 vb.
make ugly 842 vb.
blemish 845 vb.
defamation
detraction 926 n.
defame
defame 926 vb.
accuse 928 vb.
default
be incomplete 55 vb.
deficit 55 n.
negligence 458 n.
be insufficient 636 vb.
non-payment

prestige 866 n.
academic title
870 n.
dehumanize
pervert 655 vb.
make wicked
934 vb.
dehumidify
dry 342 vb.
dehydrate
make smaller
198 vb.
dry 342 vb.
preserve 666 vb.
dehydrated
dry 342 adj.
hungry 859 adj.
dehydration
drying 342 n.
preservation
666 n.
deification
heaven 971 n.
deity
divineness 965 n.
deity 966 n.
Deity, the
the Deity 965 n.
déjà vu
remembrance
505 n.
psychics 984 n.
dejected
dejected 834 adj.
dejection
dejection 834 n.
delay
delay 136 n.
put off 136 vb.
be irresolute
601 vb,
be inactive
679 vb.
hinder 702 vb.
delayed
late 136 adj.
hindered 702 adj.
delaying
non-active
677 adj.
delectable
savoury 390 adj.
pleasurable
826 adj.
delectation
enjoyment 824 n.
delegate
transfer 272 vb.
commission
751 vb.
delegate 754 n.
assign 780 vb.

delegation
decomposition
51 n.
dispersion 75 n.
commission 751 n.
delegate 754 n.
transfer 780 n.
delete
subtract 39 vb.
destroy 165 vb.
obliterate 550 vb.
deleterious
harmful 645 adj.
deletion
subtraction 39 n.
obliteration 550 n.
deliberate
slow 278 adj.
predetermined
608 adj.
cautious 858 adj.
deliberateness
intention 617 n.
deliberation
slowness 278 n.
meditation 449 n.
caution 858 n.
delicacy
weakness 163 n.
savouriness 390 n.
discrimination
463 n.
beauty 841 n.
good taste 846 n.
fastidiousness
862 n.
purity 950 n.
delicate
lacking substance
4 adj.
small 33 adj.
flimsy 163 adj.
weak 163 adj.
weakly 163 adj.
narrow 206 adj.
soft-hued 425 adj.
discriminating
463 adj.
accurate 494 adj.
unhealthy 651 adj.
difficult 700 adj.
pleasurable
826 adj.
personable
841 adj.
shapely 841 adj.
tasteful 846 adj.
fastidious 862 adj.
pure 950 adj.
delicatessen
cookery 301 n.
delicious
edible 301 adj.

pleasant 376 adj.
savoury 390 adj.
sweet 392 adj.
super 644 adj.
pleasurable
826 adj.
delight
pleasure 376 n.
joy 824 n.
delight 826 vb.
amusement 837 n.
delighted
willing 597 adj.
pleased 824 adj.
jubilant 833 adj.
delightful
pleasant 376 adj.
pleasurable
826 adj.
delight in
be pleased 824 vb.
delineation
outline 233 n.
representation
551 n.
description 590 n.
delinquent
troublemaker
663 n.
low fellow 869 n.
offender 904 n.
deliquesce
liquefy 337 vb.
delirious
frenzied 503 adj.
diseased 651 adj.
delirium
mental disorder
503 n.
fantasy 513 n.
lack of meaning
515 n.
illness 651 n.
**delirium tre-
mens**
agitation 318 n.
frenzy 503 n.
alcoholism 949 n.
deliver
transfer 272 vb.
propel 287 vb.
affirm 532 vb.
provide 633 vb.
rescue 668 vb.
assign 780 vb.
give 781 vb.
deliverance
rescue 668 n.
deliver a speech
orate 579 vb.
**deliver the
goods**
provide 633 vb.

be expedient
642 vb.
carry out 725 vb.
delivery
obstetrics 167 n.
transference 272 n.
voice 577 n.
speech 579 n.
provision 633 n.
escape 667 n.
rescue 668 n.
conduct 688 n.
transfer 780 n.
giving 781 n.
delivery boy
carrier 273 n.
delta
land 344 n.
plain 348 n.
delude
deceive 542 vb.
deluded
mistaken 495 adj.
crazy 503 adj.
delude oneself
err 495 vb.
hope 852 vb.
deluge
crowd 74 n.
drench 341 vb.
flow 350 vb.
rain 350 n.
be overabundant
637 vb.
delusion
error 495 n.
fantasy 513 n.
deception 542 n.
delusions
psychosis 503 n.
**delusions of
grandeur**
ostentation 875 n.
de luxe
ostentatious
875 adj.
delve into
enquire 459 vb.
demagogy
government 733 n.
demand
enquire 459 vb.
necessitate 596 vb.
requirement 627 n.
demand 737 n.
demand 737 vb.
price 809 n.
desire 859 n.
demanding
difficult 700 adj.
commanding
737 adj.

fastidious 862 adj.
**demand satis-
faction**
defy 711 vb.
demarcation
limit 236 n.
allocation 783 n.
dematerialize
pass away 2 vb.
disappear 446 vb.
demeaning
degrading 867 adj.
demean oneself
demean oneself
867 vb.
demeanour
expression 445 n.
gesture 547 n.
conduct 688 n.
demented
crazy 503 adj.
frenzied 503 adj.
mentally disordered
503 adj.
dementia
helplessness
161 n.
unintelligence
499 n.
mental disorder
503 n.
demerit
what is not due
916 n.
vice 934 n.
demigod
paragon 646 n.
deity 966 n.
demigod 967 n.
demilitarize
disable 161 vb.
make peace
719 vb.
demi-monde
lower classes
869 n.
wickedness 934 n.
demise
decease 361 n.
demobilization
dispersion 75 n.
lack of power
161 n.
pacification 719 n.
liberation 746 n.
democracy
nation 371 n.
government 733 n.
common people
869 n.
democrat
political party

reception 299 n.
eating 301 n.
digestive
purgative 658 n.
remedial 658 adj.
dig for
search 459 vb.
pursue 619 vb.
digger
excavator 255 n.
dig in
place oneself
187 vb.
defend 713 vb.
**dig in one's
heels**
persevere 600 vb.
be obstinate
602 vb.
refuse 760 vb.
dig into
enquire 459 vb.
digit
number 85 n.
feeler 378 n.
digital
numerical 85 adj.
computerized
86 adj.
statistical 86 adj.
digitize
computerize 86 vb.
dignified
elegant 575 adj.
authoritative
733 adj.
impressive
821 adj.
worshipful
866 adj.
proud 871 adj.
formal 875 adj.
courteous 884 adj.
dignitary
officer 741 n.
aristocrat 868 n.
church dignitary
986 n.
dignity
conduct 688 n.
good taste 846 n.
honours 866 n.
prestige 866 n.
pride 871 n.
ostentation 875 n.
digress
deviate 282 vb.
be inattentive
456 vb.
be diffuse 570 vb.
digression
obliqueness 220 n.

deviation 282 n.
overstepping
306 n.
diffuseness 570 n.
oration 579 n.
digs
quarters 192 n.
dig up
extract 304 vb.
exhume 364 vb.
be curious 453 vb.
dike
nonconformist
84 n.
gap 201 n.
fence 235 n.
furrow 262 n.
water channel
351 n.
female 373 n.
obstacle 702 n.
defences 713 n.
dilapidated
dilapidated
655 adj.
dilatation
distension 197 n.
lack of density
325 n.
surgery 658 n.
dilate
grow 36 vb.
expand 197 vb.
rarefy 325 vb.
blow up 352 vb.
dilatoriness
delay 136 n.
dilatory
late 136 adj.
slow 278 adj.
dilemma
circumstance 8 n.
dubiety 474 n.
choice 605 n.
predicament
700 n.
dilettante
dabbling 491 adj.
collector 492 n.
dabbler 493 n.
diligent
attentive 455 adj.
careful 457 adj.
studious 536 adj.
observant 768 adj.
dilly-dally
be irresolute
601 vb.
be inactive
679 vb.
dilute
lessen 37 vb.

weaken 163 vb.
rarefy 325 vb.
moisten 341 vb.
dim
darken 418 vb.
dim 419 adj.
dim 419 vb.
be dim-sighted
440 vb.
blur 440 vb.
unintelligent
499 adj.
dime
small thing 33 n.
coinage 797 n.
dimension
quantity 26 n.
measure 183 n.
appearance 445 n.
dimensions
quantity 26 n.
largeness 32 n.
size 195 n.
weights and meas-
ures 465 n.
diminish
lessen 37 vb.
subtract 39 vb.
cause to be few
105 vb.
moderate 177 vb.
shorten 204 vb.
diminuendo
contraction 198 n.
adagio 412 adv.
diminution
smallness 33 n.
diminution 37 n.
subtraction 39 n.
diminutive
small 33 adj.
little 196 adj.
word 559 n.
name 561 n.
part of speech
564 n.
diminutiveness
smallness 33 n.
littleness 196 n.
dimple
cavity 255 n.
concavity 255 n.
notch 260 n.
lowering 311 n.
dimwit
dunce 501 n.
fool 501 n.
dim-witted
weak 163 adj.
unintelligent
499 adj.
din
largeness 32 n.

commotion 318 n.
be loud 400 vb.
loudness 400 n.
roll 403 n.
discord 411 n.
dine
eat 301 vb.
feed 301 vb.
dine out
eat 301 vb.
be sociable
882 vb.
diner
café 192 n.
eater 301 n.
ding
resound 404 vb.
dingdong
roll 403 n.
dinghy
boat 275 n.
rowing boat
275 n.
dingy
dim 419 adj.
colourless 426 adj.
dirty 649 adj.
dilapidated
655 adj.
din in
emphasize 532 vb.
educate 534 vb.
dining
eating 301 n.
dining room
room 194 n.
dinner
meal 301 n.
festivity 837 n.
dinosaur
fossil 125 n.
archaism 127 n.
giant 195 n.
animal 365 n.
dint
concavity 255 n.
make concave
255 vb.
notch 260 n.
collide 279 vb.
knock 279 n.
diocese
district 184 n.
parish 985 n.
dip
be oblique 220 vb.
incline 220 n.
cavity 255 n.
valley 255 n.
swim 269 vb.
impel 279 vb.
immerse 303 vb.

descend 309 vb.
descent 309 n.
lower 311 vb.
lowering 311 n.
plunge 313 n.
plunge 313 vb.
be wet 341 vb.
drench 341 vb.
dim 419 vb.
torch 420 n.
colour 425 vb.
clean 648 vb.
washing 648 n.
diphtheria
infection 651 n.
respiratory disease
651 n.
diphthong
speech sound
398 n.
voice 577 n.
dip into
be curious 453 vb.
pay some attention
455 vb.
study 536 vb.
diploma
credential 466 n.
record 548 n.
mandate 751 n.
honours 866 n.
diplomacy
tactics 688 n.
cunning 698 n.
mediation 720 n.
conditions 766 n.
courtesy 884 n.
diplomat
expert 696 n.
mediator 720 n.
envoy 754 n.
diplomatic
hypocritical
541 adj.
skilful 694 adj.
**diplomatic
excuse**
untruth 543 n.
**diplomatic
immunity**
freedom 744 n.
non-liability
919 n.
**diplomatic
incident**
predicament
700 n.
**diplomatic
service**
vocation 622 n.
diplomatist
expert 696 n.

922 vb.
dismissal
exclusion 57 n.
repulsion 292 n.
farewell 296 n.
ejection 300 n.
non-use 674 n.
deposing 752 n.
loss of right 916 n.
prayers 981 n.
dismount
sunder 46 vb.
land 295 vb.
descend 309 vb.
disobedience
disobedience
738 n.
disobedient
disobedient
738 adj.
disobey
disobey 738 vb.
disobliging
unkind 898 adj.
disorder
be disordered
61 vb.
disorder 61 n.
disarrange 63 vb.
roughen 259 vb.
disease 651 n.
anarchy 734 n.
disorderly
disorderly 61 adj.
disorganize
disarrange 63 vb.
impair 655 vb.
disorganized
lacking order
61 adj.
disorientate
disarrange 63 vb.
displace 188 vb.
disorientated
doubting 474 adj.
disown
negate 533 vb.
annul 752 vb.
not retain 779 vb.
disapprove 924 vb.
disparage
lessen 37 vb.
underestimate
483 vb.
shame 867 vb.
not respect 921 vb.
hold cheap
922 vb.
detract 926 vb.
disparaging
disapproving
924 adj.

disparate
unrelated 10 adj.
different 15 adj.
dissimilar 19 adj.
unequal 29 adj.
disparity
unrelatedness
10 n.
difference 15 n.
dissimilarity 19 n.
disagreement 25 n.
inequality 29 n.
dispassionate
judicial 480 adj.
impassive 820 adj.
inexcitable
823 adj.
just 913 adj.
dispatch
displace 188 vb.
move 265 vb.
send 272 vb.
transference 272 n.
velocity 277 n.
eat 301 vb.
kill 362 vb.
report 524 n.
news 529 n.
correspondence
588 n.
do 676 vb.
activity 678 n.
be active 78 vb.
haste 680 n.
deal with 688 vb.
carry out 725 vb.
carry through
725 vb.
give 781 vb.
dispatches
report 524 n.
message 529 n.
news 529 n.
dispel
disunite 46 vb.
disperse 75 vb.
destroy 165 vb.
displace 188 vb.
repel 292 vb.
disappear 446 vb.
dispensable
superfluous
637 adj.
useless 641 adj.
dispensary
hospital 658 n.
dispensation
exclusion 57 n.
rescue 668 n.
permission 756 n.
non-retention
779 n.

non-liability
919 n.
dispense
exclude 57 vb.
disperse 75 vb.
permit 756 vb.
give 781 vb.
allocate 783 vb.
exempt 919 vb.
dispenser
pharmacist 658 n.
dispense with
not use 674 vb.
not retain 779 vb.
dispersal
disunion 46 n.
dispersion 75 n.
transference 272 n.
disperse
be dispersed 75 vb.
disperse 75 vb.
disappear 446 vb.
dispirited
dejected 834 adj.
displace
disunite 46 vb.
substitute 150 vb.
displace 188 vb.
displaced person
outcast 883 n.
display
accumulation
74 n.
appearance 445 n.
spectacle 445 n.
exhibit 522 n.
manifestation
522 n.
show 522 vb.
publicity 528 n.
defiance 711 n.
pride 871 n.
ostentation 875 n.
pageant 875 n.
displeased
discontented
829 adj.
angry 891 adj.
displeasure
sorrow 825 n.
annoyance 827 n.
discontent 829 n.
dislike 861 n.
hatred 888 n.
disapprobation
924 n.
disport oneself
be cheerful
833 vb.
amuse oneself
837 vb.

disposable
ephemeral
114 adj.
used 673 adj.
disposal
arrangement 62 n.
non-retention
779 n.
sale 793 n.
dispose
order 60 vb.
arrange 62 vb.
motivate 612 vb.
disposed
arranged 62 adj.
willing 597 adj.
dispose of
dispose of 673 vb.
carry through
725 vb.
not retain 779 vb.
sell 793 vb.
disposition
temperament 5 n.
state 7 n.
arrangement 62 n.
location 187 n.
will 595 n.
willingness 597 n.
habit 610 n.
mental state
817 n.
dispossess
eject 300 vb.
deprive 786 vb.
disentitle 916 vb.
disproportionate
unrelated 10 adj.
unequal 29 adj.
distorted 246 adj.
disprove
confute 479 vb.
negate 533 vb.
disputable
uncertain 474 adj.
disputation
argument 475 n.
dispute
disagree 25 vb.
argue 475 vb.
quarrel 709 n.
contention 716 n.
disputed territory
battleground
724 n.
disqualify
exclude 57 vb.
disable 161 vb.
make useless
641 adj.

disentitle 916 vb.
disquiet
changeableness
152 n.
agitation 318 n.
worry 825 n.
trouble 827 vb.
discontent 829 n.
frighten 854 vb.
nervousness 854 n.
disquisition
oration 579 n.
dissertation 591 n.
disregard
exclude 57 vb.
be inattentive
456 vb.
inattention 456 n.
disregard 458 vb.
negligence 458 n.
non-observance
769 n.
not observe
769 vb.
disregarding
negligent 458 adj.
non-observant
769 adj.
disrepair
dilapidation
655 n.
disreputable
disreputable
867 adj.
disrepute
disrepute 867 n.
disrespect
sauciness 878 n.
undutifulness
918 n.
disrespect 921 n.
disrespectful
disrespectful
921 adj.
disruption
separation 46 n.
discontinuity 72 n.
destruction 165 n.
badness 645 n.
dissatisfaction
incompleteness
55 n.
dissent 489 n.
sorrow 825 n.
discontent 829 n.
dislike 861 n.
resentment 891 n.
disapprobation
924 n.
dissatisfied
dissenting 489 adj.
discontented

829 adj.
dissatisfy
disappoint 509 vb.
be imperfect
647 vb.
displease 827 vb.
cause discontent
829 vb.
dissect
sunder 46 vb.
decompose 51 vb.
class 62 vb.
enquire 459 vb.
dissection
splitting 46 n.
separation 46 n.
decomposition
51 n.
enquiry 459 n.
dissemblance
dissimilarity 19 n.
dissemble
make unlike
19 vb.
dissemble 541 vb.
disseminate
disperse 75 vb.
communicate
524 vb.
publish 528 vb.
dissemination
dispersion 75 n.
publication 528 n.
dissension
dissension 709 n.
enmity 881 n.
dissent
dissent 489 n.
dissent 489 vb.
dissenting
non-uniform
17 adj.
disagreeing 25 adj.
dissenting 489 adj.
impious 980 adj.
dissertation
dissertation 591 n.
disservice
evil 616 n.
cruel act 898 n.
dissidence
disagreement 25 n.
nonconformity
84 n.
dissent 489 n.
dissident
misfit 25 n.
nonconformist
84 n.
unconformable
84 adj.
objector 489 n.

dissenting 489 adj.
opponent 705 n.
rebel 738 n.
discontented
829 adj.
malcontent 829 n.
schismatic 978 n.
dissimilar
dissimilar 19 adj.
dissimulate
dissemble 541 vb.
dissipate
disperse 75 vb.
destroy 165 vb.
disappear 446 vb.
waste 634 vb.
be prodigal
815 vb.
dissipated
weakened 163 adj.
prodigal 815 adj.
sensual 944 adj.
lecherous 951 adj.
dissipation
dispersion 75 n.
pleasure 376 n.
disappearance
446 n.
waste 634 n.
loss 772 n.
prodigality 815 n.
intemperance
943 n.
sensualism 944 n.
unchastity 951 n.
dissociate
disunite 46 vb.
**dissociate one-
self**
negate 533 vb.
oppose 704 vb.
dissolute
villainous 934 adj.
lecherous 951 adj.
dissolution
disunion 46 n.
separation 46 n.
decomposition
51 n.
finality 69 n.
destruction 165 n.
liquefaction 337 n.
disappearance
446 n.
annulment 752 n.
dissolve
pass away 2 vb.
be dispersed 75 vb.
destroy 165 vb.
liquefy 337 vb.
disappear 446 vb.
annul 752 vb.

dissonant
discordant
411 adj.
dissuade
dissuade 613 vb.
distaff
weaving 222 n.
distance
distance 199 n.
progress 285 vb.
invisibility 444 n.
unsociability
883 n.
distant
distant 199 adj.
muted 401 adj.
incurious 454 adj.
impassive 820 adj.
hostile 881 adj.
unsociable
883 adj.
distasteful
unpleasant
827 adj.
distemper
coat 226 vb.
facing 226 n.
colour 425 vb.
pigment 425 n.
animal disease
651 n.
distend
augment 36 vb.
enlarge 197 vb.
expand 197 vb.
distil
exude 298 vb.
extract 304 vb.
vaporize 338 vb.
purify 648 vb.
distillation
essential part 5 n.
extraction 304 n.
vaporization
338 n.
distillery
vaporizer 338 n.
workshop 687 n.
distinct
different 15 adj.
separate 46 adj.
definite 80 adj.
making sound
398 adj.
obvious 443 adj.
intelligible
516 adj.
distinction
differentiation
15 n.
speciality 80 n.
discrimination

463 n.
reasoning 475 n.
importance 638 n.
honours 866 n.
prestige 866 n.
nobility 868 n.
title 870 n.
distinctive
distinctive 15 adj.
special 80 adj.
distinctness
difference 15 n.
visibility 443 n.
distinguish
differentiate 15 vb.
make unlike
19 vb.
set apart 46 vb.
see 438 vb.
discriminate
463 vb.
understand
516 vb.
dignify 866 vb.
distinguishable
separate 46 adj.
intelligible
516 adj.
distinguished
different 15 adj.
remarkable 32 adj.
superior 34 adj.
notable 638 adj.
noteworthy
866 adj.
distinguishing
distinctive 15 adj.
discriminating
463 adj.
distort
distort 246 vb.
distorted
distorted 246 adj.
imperfect 647 adj.
distract
distract 456 vb.
distracted
distracted 456 adj.
excited 821 adj.
distraction
abstractedness
456 n.
inattention 456 n.
frenzy 503 n.
distrait(e)
abstracted
456 adj.
excited 821 adj.
distraught
frenzied 503 adj.
excited 821 adj.
distress
give pain 377 vb.

pain 377 n.
evil 616 n.
ill-treat 645 vb.
adversity 731 n.
impress 821 vb.
suffering 825 n.
worry 825 n.
hurt 827 vb.
distressing
distressing
827 adj.
distribute
arrange 62 vb.
publish 528 vb.
provide 633 vb.
allocate 783 vb.
distribution
arrangement 62 n.
dispersion 75 n.
transference 272 n.
provision 633 n.
allocation 783 n.
sale 793 n.
distributor
electronics 160 n.
district
district 184 n.
land 344 n.
distrust
doubt 486 n.
doubt 486 vb.
jealousy 911 n.
distrustful
doubting 474 adj.
nervous 854 adj.
jealous 911 adj.
disturb
decompose 51 vb.
disarrange 63 vb.
mistime 138 vb.
displace 188 vb.
agitate 318 vb.
distract 456 vb.
trouble 827 vb.
frighten 854 vb.
disturbance
turmoil 61 n.
disarrangement
63 n.
untimeliness
138 n.
commotion 318 n.
quarrel 709 n.
disturbed
violent 176 adj.
nervous 854 adj.
disunity
disagreement 25 n.
dissension 709 n.
disuse
disuse 611 n.
relinquishment

621 n.
non-use 674 n.
annulment 752 n.
non-retention
779 n.
ditch
gap 201 n.
partition 231 n.
fence 235 n.
cavity 255 n.
furrow 262 n.
fly 271 vb.
water channel
351 n.
drain 351 n.
cultivate 370 vb.
change one's mind
603 vb.
reject 607 vb.
relinquish 621 vb.
protection 660 n.
stop using 674 vb.
stratagem 698 n.
obstacle 702 n.
defences 713 n.
not retrain 779 vb.
dither
be agitated
318 vb.
be uncertain
474 vb.
be irresolute
601 vb.
ditto
be identical 13 vb.
identically 13 adv.
identity 13 n.
do likewise 20 vb.
accord 24 vb.
again 106 vb.
repeat 106 vb.
repetition 106 n.
diuretic
purgative 658 n.
diurnal
seasonal 141 adj.
diva
vocalist 413 n.
actor 594 n.
divan
bed 218 n.
seat 218 n.
dive
tavern 192 n.
navigate 269 vb.
swim 269 vb.
fly 271 vb.
move fast 277 vb.
spurt 277 n.
descend 309 vb.
descent 309 n.
tumble 309 vb.

plunge 313 n.
plunge 313 vb.
amuse oneself
837 vb.
diver
diver 313 n.
bird 365 n.
diverge
disagree 25 vb.
be oblique 220 vb.
diverge 294 vb.
diverge from
differ 15 vb.
divergence
difference 15 n.
non-uniformity
17 n.
dissimilarity 19 n.
disagreement 25 n.
divergence 294 n.
divergent
non-uniform
17 adj.
divergent 294 adj.
divers
existing in many
forms 82 adj.
many 104 adj.
diverse
different 15 adj.
non-uniform
17 adj.
dissimilar 19 adj.
existing in many
forms 82 adj.
diversification
variegation 437 n.
diversify
modify 143 vb.
variegate 437 vb.
diversion
irrelevance 10 n.
change 143 n.
deviation 282 n.
traffic control
305 n.
pleasure 376 n.
inattention 456 n.
trickery 542 n.
circuit 626 n.
amusement 837 n.
diversity
unrelatedness
10 n.
difference 15 n.
non-uniformity
17 n.
medley 43 n.
existence in many
forms 82 n.
variegation 437 n.
divert
deflect 282 vb.

distract 456 vb.
obstruct 702 vb.
not pay 805 vb.
amuse 837 vb.
diverting
amusing 837 adj.
divert one's
attention
distract 456 vb.
divest
subtract 39 vb.
uncover 229 vb.
relinquish 621 vb.
depose 752 vb.
deprive 786 vb.
divide
sunder 46 vb.
part 53 vb.
class 62 vb.
divide 92 vb.
partition 231 n.
limit 236 n.
mete out 465 vb.
divided
fragmentary
53 adj.
quarrelling
709 adj.
schismatical
978 adj.
divided alle-
giance
perfidiousness
930 n.
dividend
part 53 n.
numerical element
85 n.
gain 771 n.
portion 783 n.
dividers
gauge 465 n.
divide up
sunder 46 vb.
allocate 783 vb.
dividing
separate 46 adj.
lying between
231 adj.
divination
intuition 476 n.
divination 511 n.
divine
foresee 510 vb.
divine 511 vb.
beautiful 841 adj.
divine 965 adj.
godlike 965 adj.
religious 973 adj.
theologian 973 n.
cleric 986 n.
diviner
diviner 511 n.

divine right
authority 733 n.
diving
depth 211 n.
divining rod
detector 484 n.
divinity
divineness 965 n.
theology 973 n.
divisible
numerical 85 adj.
division
splitting 46 n.
decomposition
51 n.
subdivision 53 n.
arrangement 62 n.
discontinuity 72 n.
classification 77 n.
district 184 n.
partition 231 n.
vote 605 n.
formation 722 n.
allocation 783 n.
seclusion 883 n.
schism 978 n.
sect 978 n.
divisor
numerical element
85 n.
divorce
disunite 46 vb.
separate 46 vb.
divorce 896 n.
divorce 896 vb.
divorcé(e)
divorce 896 n.
divorced
separate 46 vb.
not retained
779 adj.
divot
piece 53 n.
divulge
manifest 522 vb.
divulge 526 vb.
DIY
repair 656 n.
repair 656 vb.
dizzy
unequal 29 adj.
changing 152 adj.
high 209 adj.
with one's head
spinning 315 adj.
crazy 503 adj.
hung over 949 adj.
DJ
broadcaster 531 n.
DNA
heredity 5 n.
organism 358 n.

D notice
restraint 747 n.
do
accord 24 vb.
have sexual inter-
course with
45 vb.
feasting 301 n.
study 536 vb.
deceive 542 vb.
suffice 635 vb.
be expedient
642 vb.
do 676 vb.
overcharge 811 vb.
amusement 837 n.
celebration 876 n.
social gathering
882 n.
do a favour
do good 644 vb.
do away with
destroy 165 vb.
kill 362 vb.
docile
willing 597 adj.
obedient 739 adj.
dock
subtract 39 vb.
cut 46 vb.
sunder 46 vb.
place 187 vb.
live 192 vb.
stable 192 n.
shorten 204 vb.
edge 234 n.
navigate 269 vb.
arrive 295 vb.
storage 632 n.
shelter 662 n.
workshop 687 n.
lockup 748 n.
docker
displacement
188 n.
boatman 270 n.
worker 686 n.
docket
list 87 n.
list 87 vb.
credential 466 n.
label 547 n.
mark 547 n.
record 548 n.
abstract 592 vb.
dockyard
workshop 687 n.
doctor
mix 43 vb.
modify 143 vb.
sage 500 n.
be false 541 vb.

incentive 612 n.
monetary help
703 n.
gift 781 n.
giving 781 n.
done
past 125 adj.
caused 157 adj.
usual 610 adj.
fatigued 684 adj.
done, be
be duped 544 vb.
pay too much
811 vb.
be in fashion
848 vb.
done for
dead 361 adj.
dying 361 adj.
dilapidated
655 adj.
defeated 728 adj.
done thing
practice 610 n.
etiquette 848 n.
Don Juan
lover 887 n.
libertine 952 n.
donkey
beast of burden
273 n.
mammal 365 n.
fool 501 n.
donkey's years
long duration
113 n.
donor
propagation 167 n.
provider 633 n.
giver 781 n.
good giver 813 n.
don't care
rash 857 adj.
indifferent
860 adj.
don't know
changeable thing
152 n.
uncertainty 474 n.
moderate 625 n.
neutral 625 adj.
independence
744 n.
doodle
be inattentive
456 vb.
picture 553 n.
doom
finality 69 n.
ruin 165 n.
death 361 n.
judge 480 vb.

fate 596 n.
necessitate 596 vb.
condemnation
961 n.
punishment 963 n.
doomed
dying 361 adj.
fated 596 adj.
unfortunate
731 adj.
unhappy 825 adj.
doomsday
future state 124 n.
doomwatch
surveillance 457 n.
expect 507 vb.
door
threshold 234 n.
barrier 235 n.
doorway 263 n.
way in 297 n.
access 624 n.
doorbell
signal 547 n.
do-or-die
rash 857 adj.
doorkeeper
doorkeeper 264 n.
doorknob
opener 263 n.
doorknocker
signal 547 n.
doorman
doorkeeper 264 n.
servant 742 n.
doormat
weakling 163 n.
floor-cover 226 n.
cleaning utensil
648 n.
coward 856 n.
toady 879 n.
doorpost
pillar 218 n.
doorstep
stand 218 n.
threshold 234 n.
doorway 263 n.
beg 761 vb.
request 761 vb.
torment 827 vb.
doorstepping
vote 605 n.
doorway
doorway 263 n.
do out of
deceive 542 vb.
defraud 788 vb.
dope
anaesthetic 375 n.
make insensitive
375 vb.

ninny 501 n.
information
524 n.
drug 658 n.
make inactive
679 vb.
drugs 949 n.
dope addict
the maladjusted
504 n.
drug-taker 949 n.
doppelgänger
analogue 18 n.
ghost 970 n.
Doppler effect
displacement
188 n.
dorm
quarters 192 n.
dormant
inert 175 adj.
at rest 266 adj.
latent 523 adj.
sleepy 679 adj.
dormitory
quarters 192 n.
room 194 n.
dosage
measurement
465 n.
portion 783 n.
dose
finite quantity
26 n.
piece 53 n.
measurement
465 n.
medicine 658 n.
portion 783 n.
punishment 963 n.
doss down
live 192 vb.
be at rest 266 vb.
sleep 679 vb.
doss-house
inn 192 n.
shelter 662 n.
dossier
bunch 74 n.
testimony 466 n.
information
524 n.
record 548 n.
legal trial 959 n.
dot
small thing 33 n.
place 185 n.
mottle 437 n.
mark 547 vb.
punctuation
547 n.
lettering 586 n.

pattern 844 n.
dotage
old age 131 n.
folly 499 n.
dote
be foolish 499 vb.
desire 859 vb.
be in love 887 vb.
dote on
desire 859 vb.
doting
foolish 499 adj.
loving 887 adj.
**dot one's i's and
cross one's t's**
be careful 457 vb.
emphasize 532 vb.
dotted line
discontinuity 72 n.
dotty
foolish 499 adj.
crazy 503 adj.
double
identity 13 n.
analogue 18 n.
augment 36 vb.
double 91 adj.
double 91 vb.
substitute 150 n.
vary 152 vb.
invigorate 174 vb.
enlarge 197 vb.
fold 261 vb.
move fast 277 vb.
spirit 447 n.
representation
551 n.
double agent
secret service
459 n.
deceiver 545 n.
double back
turn back 286 vb.
**double-
barrelled**
dual 90 adj.
double bass
violin 414 n.
double-check
make certain
473 vb.
double chin
bulk 195 n.
protuberance
254 n.
double-cross
deceive 542 vb.
be cunning
698 vb.
be dishonest
930 vb.
double-dealing
duplicity 541 n.

hypocritical
541 adj.
cunning 698 n.
perfidious 930 adj.
perfidiousness
930 n.
double Dutch
lack of meaning
515 n.
unintelligibility
517 n.
double entendre
equivocalness
518 n.
impurity 951 n.
double figures
over five 99 n.
double-glazing
lining 227 n.
barrier 235 n.
screen 421 n.
double-jointed
flexible 327 adj.
double life
existence as two
90 n.
duplicity 541 n.
double meaning
connotation 514 n.
double take
inspection 438 n.
doublet
substitute 150 n.
word 559 n.
doubletalk
lack of meaning
515 n.
equivocalness
518 n.
falsehood 541 n.
neologism 560 n.
double up
laugh 835 vb.
double vision
vision 438 n.
dim sight 440 n.
**double
whammy**
existence as two
90 n.
disappointment
509 n.
doublethink
error 495 n.
doubly
greatly 32 vb.
doubt
improbability
472 n.
dubiety 474 n.
doubt 486 n.
doubt 486 vb.

drag up
  elevate 310 vb.
drain
  receptacle 194 n.
  base 214 n.
  outflow 298 n.
  empty 300 vb.
  drink 301 vb.
  dry 342 vb.
  drain 351 n.
  cultivate 370 vb.
  storage 632 n.
  waste 634 vb.
  purify 648 vb.
  impair 655 vb.
  use 673 vb.
  fatigue 684 vb.
  loss 772 n.
drainage
  outflow 298 n.
  clearing 300 n.
  drying 342 n.
  waste 634 n.
  cleansing 648 n.
  dirt 649 n.
drained
  weakened 163 adj.
  dry 342 adj.
draining
  outflow 298 n.
  drying 342 n.
dram
  drink 301 n.
  *weights and meas-
  ures* 465 n.
drama
  drama 594 n.
  stage play 594 n.
  activity 678 n.
  excitation 821 n.
  prodigy 864 n.
dramatic
  dramatic 594 adj.
  exciting 821 adj.
  impressive
  821 adj.
  wonderful 864 adj.
  showy 875 adj.
dramatics
  dramatic theory
  594 n.
  ostentation 875 n.
dramatist
  dramatist 594 n.
dramatize
  exaggerate 546 vb.
  dramatize 594 vb.
**dramatize one-
self**
  be affected 850 vb.
  be ostentatious
  875 vb.

drape
  hang 217 vb.
  suspension 217 n.
  dress 228 vb.
draper
  clothier 228 n.
drapes
  hanging object
  217 n.
  covering 226 n.
  curtain 421 n.
drastic
  severe 735 adj.
drat
  curse 899 int.
dratted
  damnable 645 adj.
draught
  transport 272 n.
  drink 301 n.
  gravity 322 n.
  ventilation 352 n.
  wind 352 n.
  anaesthetic 375 n.
  medicine 658 n.
  adversity 731 n.
  plaything 837 n.
draughtboard
  chequer 437 n.
draughts
  board game 837 n.
**draughtsman or
-woman**
  artist 556 n.
draughty
  windy 352 adj.
draw
  be equal 28 vb.
  draw 28 n.
  compose 56 vb.
  bring together
  74 vb.
  displace 188 vb.
  make thin 206 vb.
  outline 233 vb.
  form 243 vb.
  draw 288 vb.
  attraction 291 n.
  cook 301 vb.
  descend 309 vb.
  blow 352 vb.
  be hot 379 vb.
  smoke 388 vb.
  demonstrate
  478 vb.
  represent 551 vb.
  paint 553 vb.
  describe 590 vb.
  gambling 618 n.
  non-completion
  726 n.
  acquire 771 vb.

  receive 782 vb.
  desired object
  859 n.
draw a blank
  forget 506 vb.
  fail 728 vb.
  lose 772 vb.
**draw a red
herring**
  be unrelated
  10 vb.
  deflect 282 vb.
  distract 456 vb.
  avoid 620 vb.
  elude 667 vb.
draw back
  regress 286 vb.
  recede 290 vb.
  avoid 620 vb.
drawback
  evil 616 n.
  obstacle 702 n.
drawbridge
  doorway 263 n.
  bridge 624 n.
  means of escape
  667 n.
  fort 713 n.
drawer
  compartment
  194 n.
  artist 556 n.
drawers
  underwear 228 n.
draw in
  become small
  198 vb.
  make smaller
  198 vb.
  draw 288 vb.
drawing
  copy 22 n.
  representation
  551 n.
  painting 553 n.
  picture 553 n.
  plan 623 n.
drawing pin
  fastening 47 n.
  sharp point 256 n.
drawing room
  room 194 n.
**draw in one's
horns**
  submit 721 vb.
drawl
  lengthen 203 vb.
  move slowly
  278 vb.
  pronunciation
  577 n.
  voice 577 vb.

  speech defect
  580 n.
  stammer 580 vb.
draw lots
  gamble 618 vb.
drawn
  equal 28 adj.
  lean 206 adj.
drawn out
  tedious 838 adj.
draw on
  avail oneself of
  673 vb.
  claim 915 vb.
draw out
  cause 156 vb.
  displace 188 vb.
  enlarge 197 vb.
  lengthen 203 vb.
  extract 304 vb.
  be diffuse 570 vb.
drawstring
  fastening 47 n.
  ligature 47 n.
draw the line
  exclude 57 vb.
  discriminate
  463 vb.
  restrain 747 vb.
  prohibit 757 vb.
  retain 778 vb.
  disapprove 924 vb.
draw up
  compose 56 vb.
  be in order 60 vb.
  cease 145 vb.
  come to rest
  266 vb.
  arrive 295 vb.
  plan 623 vb.
draw upon
  draw money
  797 vb.
dread
  expect 507 vb.
  expectation 507 n.
  be nervous 854 vb.
  fear 854 n.
  fear 854 vb.
dreadful
  prodigious 32 adj.
  harmful 645 adj.
  not nice 645 adj.
  distressing
  827 adj.
  frightening
  854 adj.
dreading
  expectant 507 adj.
  nervous 854 adj.
dream
  thing that lacks

  substance 4 n.
  visual fallacy
  440 n.
  be inattentive
  456 vb.
  error 495 n.
  fantasy 513 n.
  imagine 513 vb.
  objective 617 n.
  sleep 679 vb.
  a beauty 841 n.
  hope 852 vb.
  desire 859 vb.
  desired object
  859 n.
dreamer
  visionary 513 n.
  avoider 620 n.
  idler 679 n.
dreaming
  imaginative
  513 adj.
  sleepy 679 adj.
  hoping 852 adj.
dreamlike
  shadowy 419 adj.
  appearing 445 adj.
dreams
  sleep 679 n.
**dreams come
true**
  contentment
  828 n.
dream up
  imagine 513 vb.
dreamy
  thoughtful
  449 adj.
  abstracted
  456 adj.
  imaginary
  513 adj.
dreary
  unpleasant
  827 adj.
  cheerless 834 adj.
  dejected 834 adj.
  melancholic
  834 adj.
  tedious 838 adj.
  dull 840 adj.
dredge
  extract 304 vb.
  let fall 311 vb.
dredger
  ship 275 n.
dredge up
  bring together
  74 vb.
  extract 304 vb.
  elevate 310 vb.
dregs
  leavings 41 n.

728 adj.
dude
dupe 544 n.
dandy 848 n.
dudgeon
side arms 723 n.
anger 891 n.
duds
clothing 228 n.
due
future 124 adj.
impending
155 adj.
due 915 adj.
duel
existence as two
90 n.
duel 716 n.
fight 716 vb.
duenna
protector 660 n.
keeper 749 n.
dues
receiving 782 n.
receipt 807 n.
price 809 n.
tax 809 n.
what is due 915 n.
duet
existence as two
90 n.
cooperation 706 n.
harmony 710 n.
due to
caused 157 adj.
duffer
ignoramus 493 n.
dunce 501 n.
bungler 697 n.
dugout
concave 255 adj.
excavation 255 n.
furrow 262 n.
rowing boat
275 n.
refuge 662 n.
defences 713 n.
duke
potentate 741 n.
pincers 778 n.
person of rank
868 n.
dukedom
*political organiza-
tion* 733 n.
aristocracy 868 n.
dulcet
melodious 410 adj.
pleasurable
826 adj.
dull
assuage 177 vb.

blunt 257 vb.
make insensitive
375 vb.
mute 401 vb.
muted 401 adj.
dim 419 adj.
colourless 426 adj.
grey 429 adj.
ignorant 491 adj.
unintelligent
499 adj.
feeble 572 adj.
non-active
677 adj.
inactive 679 adj.
impassive 820 adj.
cheerless 834 adj.
serious 834 adj.
dull 840 adj.
dullard
dunce 501 n.
duly
as promised
764 adv.
dumb
ignorant 491 adj.
uninstructed
491 adj.
unintelligent
499 adj.
voiceless 578 adj.
dumbfound
surprise 508 vb.
disappoint 509 vb.
make mute
578 vb.
be wonderful
864 vb.
dumb show
gesture 547 n.
representation
551 n.
drama 594 n.
dummy
copy 22 n.
prototype 23 n.
substituted
150 adj.
moderator 177 n.
sham 542 n.
image 551 n.
dump
accumulation
74 n.
computerize 86 vb.
small house
192 n.
storage 632 n.
store 632 vb.
rubbish 641 n.
stop using 674 vb.
dumpling
bulk 195 n.

*bread, pastries
and cakes*
301 n.
dumps
dejection 834 n.
sullenness 893 n.
dumpy
fat 195 adj.
dwarfish 196 adj.
short 204 adj.
thick 205 adj.
unsightly 842 adj.
dun
horse 273 n.
dim 419 adj.
grey 429 adj.
brown 430 adj.
demand 737 vb.
request 761 vb.
torment 827 vb.
dunce
dunce 501 n.
dunderhead
dunce 501 n.
dung
fertilizer 171 n.
excrement 302 n.
stench 397 n.
dirt 649 n.
dungarees
suit 228 n.
trousers 228 n.
dungeon
cellar 194 n.
depth 211 n.
lockup 748 n.
prison 748 n.
dunghill
sink 649 n.
dunk
drench 341 vb.
clean 648 vb.
duo
existence as two
90 n.
dupe
deceive 542 vb.
fool 542 vb.
dupe 544 n.
defraud 788 vb.
toady 879 n.
duplex
dual 90 adj.
double 91 adj.
flat 192 n.
duplicate
identity 13 n.
copy 20 vb.
duplicate 22 n.
augment 36 vb.
double 91 adj.
double 91 vb.

repeat 106 vb.
reproduce 166 vb.
label 547 n.
be superfluous
637 vb.
duplicity
duplicity 541 n.
durable
lasting 113 adj.
perpetual 115 adj.
permanent
144 adj.
unchangeable
153 adj.
tough 329 adj.
duration
time 108 n.
course of time
111 n.
permanence 144 n.
duress
compulsion 740 n.
detention 747 n.
restriction 747 n.
during
while 108 adv.
dusk
evening 29 n.
darkness 418 n.
dim 419 adj.
half-light 419 n.
dusky
dark 418 adj.
dim 419 adj.
blackish 428 adj.
dust
minuteness 196 n.
let fall 311 vb.
lightness 323 n.
powder 332 n.
soil 344 n.
trifle 639 n.
rubbish 641 n.
clean 648 vb.
dirt 649 n.
sink 649 n.
dustbin
vessel 194 n.
cleaning utensil
648 n.
sink 649 n.
dustbowl
desert 172 n.
duster
overcoat 228 n.
cloth 648 n.
cleaning utensil
648 n.
dusting
knock 279 n.
powderiness
332 n.

dust jacket
wrapping 226 n.
bookbinding
589 n.
dustman
cleaner 648 n.
worker 686 n.
**dust thrown in
the eyes**
pretext 614 n.
stratagem 698 n.
dustup
turmoil 61 n.
quarrel 709 n.
fight 716 n.
dusty
powdery 332 adj.
dry 342 adj.
dirty 649 adj.
Dutch auction
sale 793 n.
cheapness 812 n.
Dutch courage
courage 855 n.
cowardice 856 n.
drunkenness
949 n.
Dutch treat
participation
775 n.
Dutch uncle
adviser 691 n.
tyrant 735 n.
duteous
obliged 917 n.
trustworthy
929 adj.
dutiful
obedient 739 adj.
obliged 917 adj.
trustworthy
929 adj.
virtuous 933 adj.
duty
function 622 n.
job 622 n.
tax 809 n.
duty 917 n.
respects 920 n.
church service
988 n.
duty-bound
obliged 917 adj.
duvet
bed 218 n.
coverlet 226 n.
dux
victor 727 n.
DVD
computing 86 n.
dwarf
lessen 37 vb.

dwarf 196 n.
dwarfish 196 adj.
make smaller
198 vb.
star 321 n.
elf 970 n.
dwell
live 192 vb.
dwelling
dwelling 192 n.
house 192 n.
dwell on
emphasize 532 vb.
devil 969 n.
dwindle
decrease 37 vb.
be weak 163 vb.
become small
198 vb.
dye
mix 43 vb.
tincture 43 n.
modify 143 vb.
colour 425 vb.
hue 425 n.
pigment 425 n.
hairwash 843 n.
dyed in the
wool
consummate
32 adj.
permanent
144 adj.
habitual 610 adj.
dying
death 361 n.
(See also
decease.)
dying 361 adj.
dying for, be
desire 859 vb.
dying to
willing 597 adj.
dyke
nonconformist
84 n.
partition 231 n.
rock 344 n.
female 373 n.
dynamic
dynamic 160 adj.
dynamics
motion 265 n.
impulse 279 n.
dynamism
energy 160 n.
vigorousness
174 n.
restlessness 678 n.
dynamite
destroyer 168 n.
propellant 287 n.

pitfall 663 n.
explosive 723 n.
dynamo
electronics 160 n.
machine 630 n.
dynasty
continuity 71 n.
governing 733 n.
sovereign 741 n.
nobility 868 n.
dysentery
digestive disorder
651 n.
dyslexia
learning difficulty
536 n.
dyspepsia
digestive disorder
651 n.
dyspeptic
sick person 651 n.
sullen 893 adj.

E

each
correlation 12 n.
universal 79 adj.
severally 80 adv.
each one
everyman 79 n.
each other
correlation 12 n.
correlatively
12 adv.
each to each
correlatively
12 adv.
pro rata 783 adv.
eager
willing 597 adj.
active 678 adj.
fervent 818 adj.
excited 821 adj.
eager beaver
busy person 678 n.
eagerness
willingness 597 n.
warm feeling
818 n.
desire 859 n.
eagle
bird 365 n.
eye 438 n.
flag 547 n.
heraldry 547 n.
regalia 743 n.
coinage 797 n.
eagle-eyed
seeing 438 adj.
vigilant 457 adj.

ear
growth 157 n.
handle 218 n.
ear 415 n.
medical art 658 n.
earache
pang 377 n.
eardrum
ear 415 n.
earl
person of rank
868 n.
earlier
before 64 adv.
before 119 adv.
prior 119 adj.
early
beginning 68 adj.
past 125 adj.
primal 127 adj.
early 135 adv.
early 135 adj.
early bird
earliness 135 n.
early warning
system
detector 484 n.
earmark
identification
547 n.
label 547 n.
mark 547 vb.
select 605 vb.
intend 617 vb.
allocate 783 vb.
appropriate
786 vb.
earn
busy oneself
622 vb.
acquire 771 vb.
deserve 915 vb.
earnest
part 53 n.
attentive 455 adj.
affirmative
532 adj.
resolute 599 adj.
security 767 n.
fervent 818 adj.
pietistic 979 adj.
earnest money
security 767 n.
payment 804 n.
earnings
earnings 771 n.
earn one's liv-
ing
busy oneself
622 vb.
do business
622 vb.

earpiece
hearing aid 415 n.
ear plugs
stopper 264 n.
shelter 662 n.
earring
hanging object
217 n.
jewellery 844 n.
earshot
short distance
200 n.
hearing 415 n.
earth
connect 45 vb.
cable 47 n.
electricity 160 n.
dwelling 192 n.
base 214 n.
element 319 n.
planet 321 n.
world 321 n.
land 344 n.
refuge 662 n.
shelter 662 n.
earthbound
native 191 adj.
inexcitable
823 adj.
earthenware
product 164 n.
pottery 381 n.
earthling
humankind 371 n.
earth mother
mythical deity
966 n.
earthquake
destroyer 168 n.
outbreak 176 n.
oscillation 317 n.
earth-shaking
revolutionary
149 adj.
influential
178 adj.
important 638 adj.
notable 638 adj.
earthwork
earthwork 253 n.
defences 713 n.
earthworm
creepy-crawly
365 n.
earthy
sensual 944 adj.
ear trumpet
megaphone 400 n.
hearing aid 415 n.
earwig
creepy-crawly
365 n.

ease
decrease 37 vb.
assuage 177 vb.
lighten 323 vb.
elegance 575 n.
leisure 681 n.
rest 683 n.
skill 694 n.
disencumber
701 vb.
facilitate 701 vb.
easiness 701 n.
wealth 800 n.
happiness 824 n.
relieve 831 vb.
easel
frame 218 n.
ease off
slow down 278 vb.
ease up
slow down 278 vb.
east and west
polarity 14 n.
Easter
holy day 988 n.
easy
easy 701 adj.
lenient 736 adj.
friendly 880 adj.
sociable 882 adj.
amiable 884 adj.
benevolent
897 adj.
easy come, easy
go
hang the expense
815 int.
easy-going
tranquil 266 adj.
willing 597 adj.
peaceful 717 adj.
lenient 736 adj.
permitting
756 adj.
inexcitable
823 adj.
content 828 adj.
indifferent
860 adj.
easy money
easy thing 701 n.
acquisition 771 n.
easy-osy
content 828 adj.
Easy Street
prosperity 730 n.
wealth 800 n.
easy terms
cheapness 812 n.
eat
eat 301 vb.
eatable
edible 301 adj.

86 adj.
dynamic 160 adj.
instrumental
 628 adj.
mechanical
 630 adj.
electronic mail
message 529 n.
telecommunication
 531 n.
electronics
electronics 160 n.
electronic tag
label 547 n.
electroplate
coat 226 vb.
elegance
elegance 575 n.
wit 839 n.
fashion 848 n.
elegant
stylistic 566 adj.
elegant 575 adj.
witty 839 adj.
personable
 841 adj.
shapely 841 adj.
fashionable
 848 adj.
elegiac
funereal 364 adj.
poetic 593 adj.
lamenting 836 adj.
elegy
funeral rites
 364 n.
poem 593 n.
lament 836 n.
element
tincture 43 n.
part 53 n.
component 58 n.
source 156 n.
filament 208 n.
element 319 n.
person 371 n.
elemental
inherent 5 adj.
simple 44 adj.
fundamental
 156 adj.
elementary
simple 44 adj.
beginning 68 adj.
elephant
giant 195 n.
tall creature
 209 n.
beast of burden
 273 n.
mammal 365 n.
elevate
elevate 310 vb.

purify 648 vb.
make better
 654 vb.
delight 826 vb.
dignify 866 vb.
elevated
proud 871 adj.
disinterested
 931 adj.
elevation
height 209 n.
verticality 215 n.
elevation 310 n.
feature 445 n.
map 551 n.
cheerfulness
 833 n.
holy orders 985 n.
elevator
conveyance 267 n.
ascent 308 n.
eleven
band 74 n.
over five 99 n.
party 708 n.
eleventh hour
late 136 adj.
lateness 136 n.
crisis 137 n.
elf
elf 970 n.
elfin
little, 196 adj.
fairylike 970 adj.
elicit
cause 156 vb.
extract 304 vb.
discover 484 vb.
manifest 522 vb.
excite 821 vb.
eligible
included 78 adj.
eliminate
cause to be few
 105 vb.
eject 300 vb.
empty 300 vb.
extract 304 vb.
obliterate 550 vb.
exempt 919 vb.
elision
contraction 198 n.
prosody 593 n.
elite
elite 644 n.
elitism
government 733 n.
elixir
medicine 658 n.
remedy 658 n.
ellipse
arc 250 n.

ellipsis
punctuation
 547 n.
grammar 564 n.
obscurity 568 n.
conciseness 569 n.
elliptic
round 250 adj.
concise 569 adj.
elocution
pronunciation
 577 n.
eloquence 579 n.
oratory 579 n.
speech 579 n.
elongate
lengthen 203 vb.
elope
walk out 296 vb.
run away 620 vb.
escape 667 vb.
wed 894 vb.
eloquence
eloquence 579 n.
eloquent
intelligible
 516 adj.
stylistic 566 adj.
eloquent 579 adj.
else
in addition
 38 adv.
elucidate
be intelligible
 516 vb.
interpret 520 vb.
elude
elude 667 vb.
not observe
 769 vb.
elusive
impracticable
 470 adj.
puzzling 517 adj.
emaciated
lean 206 adj.
underfed 636 adj.
unhealthy 651 adj.
e-mail
telecommunication
 531 n.
Internet 531 n.
emanate
happen 154 vb.
result 157 vb.
emerge 298 vb.
be plain 522 vb.
emanation
going out 298 n.
excretion 302 n.
appearance 445 n.
revelation 975 n.

emancipated
free 744 adj.
emancipation
freedom 744 n.
independence
 744 n.
liberation 746 n.
emasculated
impotent 161 adj.
feeble 572 adj.
embalm
inter 364 vb.
preserve 666 vb.
embankment
support 218 n.
earthwork 253 n.
railway 624 n.
safeguard 662 n.
embargo
exclusion 57 n.
state of rest 266 n.
hindrance 702 n.
command 737 n.
restrain 747 vb.
restraint 747 n.
prohibition 757 n.
non-payment
 805 n.
embark
voyage 269 vb.
start out 296 vb.
embarkation
start 68 n.
departure 296 n.
embark on
begin 68 vb.
undertake 672 vb.
embarrass
trouble 827 vb.
embarrassment
predicament
 700 n.
annoyance 827 n.
guilt 936 n.
embassy
house 192 n.
commission 751 n.
envoy 754 n.
embed
place 187 vb.
implant 303 vb.
embellish
add 38 vb.
make better
 654 vb.
decorate 844 vb.
embers
coal 385 n.
embezzle
defraud 788 vb.

embittered
discontented
 829 adj.
hostile 881 adj.
resentful 891 adj.
emblazon
colour 425 vb.
mark 547 vb.
decorate 844 vb.
emblem
badge 547 n.
indication 547 n.
talisman 983 n.
emblematic
lacking substance
 4 adj.
heraldic 547 adj.
embody
combine 50 vb.
contain 56 vb.
comprise 78 vb.
materialize
 319 vb.
represent 551 vb.
embolism
interjection 231 n.
closure 264 n.
*cardiovascular dis-
ease* 651 n.
emboss
mark 547 vb.
sculpt 554 vb.
decorate 844 vb.
embrace
join 45 vb.
unite with 45 vb.
cohere 48 vb.
contain 56 vb.
comprise 78 vb.
surround 230 vb.
encircle 232 vb.
enclose 235 vb.
choose 605 vb.
be in the habit of
 610 vb.
retain 778 vb.
retention 778 n.
be friendly 880 vb.
sociability 882 n.
greet 884 vb.
love 887 vb.
caress 889 vb.
endearment 889 n.
embrasure
window 263 n.
embrocation
ointment 357 n.
balm 658 n.
embroider
variegate 437 vb.
fake 541 vb.
exaggerate 546 vb.

decorate 844 vb.

embroidery
adjunct 40 n.
exaggeration
546 n.
art 551 n.
ornament 574 n.
needlework 844 n.

embroil
*throw into confu-
sion* 63 vb.
enrage 891 vb.

embryo
young creature
132 n.
source 156 n.
undevelopment
670 n.

embryonic
beginning 68 adj.
converted 147 adj.
impending
155 adj.
formless 244 adj.
immature 670 adj.

emend
rectify 654 vb.
repair 656 vb.

emendation
amendment 654 n.
repair 656 n.

emerald
green 434 adj.
greenness 434 n.
gem 844 n.

emerge
begin 68 vb.
emerge 298 vb.

emergence
beginning 68 n.
going out 298 n.

emergency
crisis 137 n.
event 154 n.
needfulness 627 n.
danger 661 n.
predicament
700 n.

emeritus
prior 119 adj.
former 125 adj.

emersion
going out 298 n.

emery board
smoother 258 n.
roughness 259 n.
grinder 332 n.

emetic
purgative 658 n.
remedial 658 adj.

emigrant
foreigner 59 n.

wanderer 268 n.
leaver 298 n.

emigrate
travel 267 vb.
recede 290 vb.
depart 296 vb.
emerge 298 vb.

emigration
movement away
290 n.
departure 296 n.
going out 298 n.

émigré
foreigner 59 n.
wanderer 268 n.
leaver 298 n.

eminence
largeness 32 n.
superiority 34 n.
height 209 n.
high land 209 n.
prominence 254 n.
elevation 310 n.
importance 638 n.
goodness 644 n.
prestige 866 n.

eminent
remarkable 32 adj.
high 209 adj.
notable 638 adj.
noteworthy
866 adj.

eminently
eminently 34 adv.

emir
potentate 741 n.
person of rank
868 n.

emissary
messenger 529 n.
delegate 754 n.
envoy 754 n.

emission
outflow 298 n.
ejection 300 n.

emit
emit 300 vb.
publish 528 vb.

emollient
soft 327 adj.
lubricant 334 n.
balm 658 n.
remedial 658 adj.

emolument
earnings 771 n.
pay 804 n.
receipt 807 n.
reward 962 n.

emotion
feeling 818 n.
warm feeling
818 n.

excitation 821 n.

emotional
*having a certain
mental state*
817 adj.
feeling 818 adj.
impressible
819 adj.
excitable 822 adj.

emotions
mental state
817 n.

emotive
descriptive
590 adj.
exciting 821 adj.

empathy
bond 47 n.
attraction 291 n.
imagination
513 n.
participation
775 n.
feeling 818 n.
benevolence 897 n.
pity 905 n.

emperor
sovereign 741 n.
aristocrat 868 n.

emphasis
figure of speech
519 n.
affirmation 532 n.
vigour 571 n.
pronunciation
577 n.
importance 638 n.

emphasize
emphasize 532 vb.

emphatic
strong 162 adj.
florid 425 adj.
expressive 516 adj.
assertive 532 adj.
forceful 571 adj.

empire
territory 184 n.
governing 733 n.
*political organiza-
tion* 733 n.

empirical
enquiring 459 adj.
experimental
461 adj.

empiricism
philosophy 449 n.
empiricism 461 n.

emplacement
place 185 n.
situation 186 n.
location 187 n.
station 187 n.

stand 218 n.
fortification 713 n.

employ
employ 622 vb.
job 622 vb.
use 673 vb.

employee
worker 686 n.
servant 742 n.

employer
director 690 n.
master 741 n.

employment
business 622 n.
job 622 n.
utility 640 n.
use 673 n.

**employment
agency**
job 622 n.

emporium
emporium 796 n.
shop 796 n.

empowered
powerful 160 adj.
authoritative
733 adj.

empress
sovereign 741 n.

emptiness
emptiness 190 n.
lack of meaning
515 n.
vanity 873 n.

empty
empty 190 adj.
empty 300 vb.
meaningless
515 adj.
untrue 543 adj.
feeble 572 adj.
hungry 859 adj.
fasting 946 adj.

empty-headed
mindless 448 adj.
ignorant 491 adj.

emulate
do likewise 20 vb.
imitate 20 vb.
contend 716 vb.

emulsify
thicken 354 vb.

emulsion
coat 226 n.
facing 226 n.
semiliquidity
354 n.
glutinousness
354 n.

enable
make possible
469 vb.

facilitate 701 vb.
permit 756 vb.

enact
show 522 vb.
represent 551 vb.
act 594 vb.
do 676 vb.
deal with 688 vb.
carry out 725 vb.
decree 737 vb.
make legal
953 vb.

enactment
representation
551 n.
dramatic theory
594 n.
action 676 n.
precept 693 n.
decree 737 n.
legislation 953 n.

enamel
coat 226 vb.
facing 226 n.
smoother 258 n.
colour 425 vb.
decorate 844 vb.

enamoured
in love 887 adj.

encampment
station 187 n.
abode 192 n.
fort 713 n.

encapsulate
comprise 78 vb.
cover 226 vb.
abstract 592 vb.

encase
cover 226 vb.
encircle 232 vb.

enchant
convert 147 vb.
subjugate 745 vb.
delight 826 vb.
be wonderful
864 vb.
bewitch 983 vb.

enchanted
pleased 824 adj.
in love 887 adj.
bewitched 983 adj.
magical 983 adj.

enchantress
a beauty 841 n.
sorceress 983 n.

encircle
comprise 78 vb.
surround 230 vb.
encircle 232 vb.
circuit 626 vb.

enclave
region 184 n.

enclose
encircle 232 vb.
enclose 235 vb.
close 264 vb.
enclosure
contents 193 n.
enclosure 235 n.
correspondence
588 n.
encode
translate 520 vb.
conceal 525 vb.
encompass
comprise 78 vb.
extend 183 vb.
surround 230 vb.
encircle 232 vb.
limit 236 vb.
circuit 626 vb.
encore
double 91 vb.
duplication 91 n.
again 106 vb.
repetition 106 n.
dramatic theory
594 n.
applause 923 n.
bravo 923 int.
encounter
synchronize
123 vb.
event 154 n.
meet with 154 vb.
contiguity 202 n.
collide 279 vb.
collision 279 n.
arrival 295 n.
meet 295 vb.
discover 484 vb.
withstand 704 vb.
fight 716 n.
fight 716 vb.
encourage
incite 612 vb.
make better
654 vb.
aid 703 vb.
animate 821 vb.
relieve 831 vb.
cheer 833 vb.
encouragement
causation 156 n.
impulse 279 n.
inducement 612 n.
aid 703 n.
excitation 821 n.
courage 855 n.
encroach
encroach 306 vb.
be illegal 954 vb.
encroachment
progression 285 n.

overstepping
306 n.
wrong 914 n.
unjustified claim
916 n.
what is not due
916 n.
lawbreaking
954 n.
encrust
coat 226 vb.
line 227 vb.
decorate 844 vb.
encumbrance
gravity 322 n.
encumbrance
702 n.
encyclopaedia
erudition 490 n.
reference book
589 n.
encyclopaedic
general 79 adj.
knowing 490 adj.
end
end 69 n.
end 69 vb.
extremity 69 n.
cease 145 vb.
destroy 165 vb.
ruin 165 n.
apex 213 n.
objective 617 n.
endangered
endangered
661 adj.
endearment
endearment 889 n.
endeavour
power 160 n.
production 164 n.
attempt 671 n.
attempt 671 vb.
action 676 n.
endemic
interior 224 adj.
infectious 653 adj.
ending
adjunct 40 n.
end 69 n.
finality 69 n.
final 69 adj.
endless
multitudinous
104 adj.
infinite 107 adj.
perpetual 115 adj.
**end of one's
tether**
limit 236 n.
**end of the mat-
ter**
finality 69 n.

**end of the
world**
finality 69 n.
(See also **not
the end of the
world**.)
endogenous
interior 224 adj.
endorse
testify 466 vb.
endorse 488 vb.
give security
767 vb.
endow
endow 777 vb.
give 781 vb.
endowment
aptitude 694 n.
giving 781 n.
endpaper
edition 589 n.
end-product
product 164 n.
completion 725 n.
endurance
durability 113 n.
perpetuity 115 n.
permanence 144 n.
power 160 n.
strength 162 n.
perseverance
600 n.
stamina 600 n.
feeling 818 n.
patience 823 n.
manliness 855 n.
endure
be 1 vb.
continue 108 vb.
last 113 vb.
stay 144 vb.
go on 146 vb.
meet with 154 vb.
support 218 vb.
acquiesce 488 vb.
be resolute 599 vb.
stand firm 599 vb.
persevere 600 vb.
resist 715 vb.
feel 818 vb.
be patient 823 vb.
suffer 825 vb.
enema
insertion 303 n.
cleansing 648 n.
purgative 658 n.
enemy
enemy 881 n.
energetic
dynamic 160 adj.
vigorous 174 adj.
forceful 571 adj.

resolute 599 adj.
active 678 adj.
labouring 682 adj.
energy
energy 160 n.
strength 162 n.
vigorousness
174 n.
resolution 599 n.
restlessness 678 n.
enervate
weaken 163 vb.
fatigue 684 vb.
enfant terrible
firearm 723 n.
annoyance 827 n.
bad person 938 n.
enfold
cover 226 vb.
dress 228 vb.
encircle 232 vb.
enclose 235 vb.
fold 261 vb.
safeguard 660 vb.
caress 889 vb.
enforce
motivate 612 vb.
compel 740 vb.
make legal
953 vb.
enfranchise
liberate 746 vb.
exempt 919 vb.
engage
unite with 45 vb.
be early 135 vb.
induce 612 vb.
employ 622 vb.
fight 716 vb.
go to war 718 vb.
commission
751 vb.
promise 764 vb.
contract 765 vb.
acquire 771 vb.
possess 773 vb.
engage in
busy oneself
622 vb.
do business
622 vb.
undertake 672 vb.
engagement
undertaking
672 n.
fight 716 n.
battle 718 n.
promise 764 n.
pact 765 n.
social round
882 n.
love affair 887 n.

wooing 889 n.
wedding 894 n.
duty 917 n.
**engagement
book**
list 87 n.
**engagement
ring**
jewellery 844 n.
love token 889 n.
engender
generate 167 vb.
engine
strengthen 162 vb.
machine 630 n.
engine driver
driver 268 n.
engineer
cause 156 vb.
produce 164 vb.
producer 164 n.
plan 623 vb.
machinist 630 n.
artisan 686 n.
soldiers 722 n.
engineering
production 164 n.
engorgement
satiation 863 n.
engrave
memorize 505 vb.
sculpt 554 vb.
engrave 555 vb.
decorate 844 vb.
engraving
engraving 555 n.
engross
absorb 299 vb.
absorb 449 vb.
engulf
consume 165 vb.
destroy 165 vb.
absorb 299 vb.
be overabundant
637 vb.
appropriate
786 vb.
enhance
augment 36 vb.
manifest 522 vb.
emphasize 532 vb.
exaggerate 546 vb.
make better
654 vb.
aggravate 832 vb.
decorate 844 vb.
enigma
unknown thing
491 n.
enigma 530 n.
enigmatic
uncertain 474 adj.

entrée
entering 297 n.
reception 299 n.
entrench
stabilize 153 vb.
safeguard 660 vb.
defend 713 vb.
entrench one-
self
place oneself
187 vb.
entrepreneur
gambler 618 n.
doer 676 n.
prosperous person
730 n.
merchant 794 n.
entropy
decomposition
51 n.
entrust
transfer 272 vb.
commission
751 vb.
assign 780 vb.
give 781 vb.
entry
doorway 263 n.
entering 297 n.
way in 297 n.
accounts 808 n.
entwine
unite with 45 vb.
twine 251 vb.
enumerate
specify 80 vb.
number 86 vb.
list 87 vb.
enunciate
affirm 532 vb.
voice 577 vb.
envelop
comprise 78 vb.
consume 165 vb.
dress 228 vb.
encircle 232 vb.
envelope
receptacle 194 n.
cover 226 n.
covering 226 n.
enclosure 235 n.
correspondence
588 n.
envelopment
encircling 232 n.
enviable
desired 859 adj.
envious
discontented
829 adj.
envious 912 adj.
environment
circumstance 8 n.

relation 9 n.
locality 187 n.
surroundings
230 n.
environmental
external 6 adj.
circumstantial
8 adj.
environmental-
ist
preserver 666 n.
environs
locality 187 n.
surroundings
230 n.
envisage
imagine 513 vb.
envoi
adjunct 40 n.
sequel 67 n.
end 69 n.
verse form 593 n.
envoy
envoy 754 n.
envy
desired object
859 n.
envy 912 n.
envy 912 vb.
vice 934 n.
enzyme
raising agent
323 n.
organism 358 n.
epaulette
badge 547 n.
badge of rank
743 n.
trimming 844 n.
ephemeral
ephemeral
114 adj.
dying 361 adj.
epic
film 445 n.
long-winded
570 adj.
narrative 590 n.
poem 593 n.
epicene
abnormal 84 adj.
epicentre
centre 225 n.
epicure
eater 301 n.
person of taste
846 n.
perfectionist
862 n.
sensualist 944 n.
glutton 947 n.
epicurean
culinary 301 adj.

sensuous 376 adj.
savoury 390 adj.
person of taste
846 n.
tasteful 846 adj.
fastidious 862 adj.
sensual 944 adj.
sensualist 944 n.
gluttonous
947 adj.
epidemic
extensive 32 adj.
comprehensive
52 adj.
generality 79 n.
universal 79 adj.
plague 651 n.
infectious 653 adj.
epigram
maxim 496 n.
figure of speech
519 n.
phrase 563 n.
conciseness 569 n.
witticism 839 n.
epilepsy
spasm 318 n.
frenzy 503 n.
disease 651 n.
nervous disorder
651 n.
epileptic
diseased 651 adj.
epileptic fit
frenzy 503 n.
epilogue
sequel 67 n.
extremity 69 n.
dramatic theory
594 n.
epiphany
revelation 975 n.
holy day 988 n.
episcopacy
church office
985 n.
the church 985 n.
episcopal
ecclesiastical
985 adj.
episcopalian
Anglican 976 adj.
sectarian 978 adj.
ecclesiastical
985 adj.
episcopalianism
the church 985 n.
episcopate
church office
985 n.
church dignitary
986 n.

episode
event 154 n.
interjection 231 n.
narrative 590 n.
episodic
unrelated 10 adj.
discontinuous
72 adj.
lying between
231 adj.
long-winded
570 adj.
epistemology
knowledge 490 n.
epistle
script 586 n.
correspondence
588 n.
epitaph
farewell 296 n.
funeral rites
364 n.
indication 547 n.
phrase 563 n.
description 590 n.
epithet
name 561 n.
scurrility 899 n.
epitome
miniature 196 n.
contraction 198 n.
conciseness 569 n.
compendium
592 n.
epitomize
shorten 204 vb.
abstract 592 vb.
epoch
era 110 n.
chronology 117 n.
eponym
name 561 n.
nomenclature
561 n.
equable
uniform 16 adj.
equal 28 adj.
inexcitable
823 adj.
equal
be equal 28 vb.
peer 28 n.
equal 28 adj.
just 913 adj.
equality
equality 28 n.
equalize
equalize 28 vb.
equal opportu-
nity
equality 28 n.
justice 913 n.

equanimity
inexcitability
823 n.
equate
treat as identical
13 vb.
equalize 28 vb.
equation
equalization 28 n.
equivalence 28 n.
number 85 n.
numerical result
85 n.
equator
middle 70 n.
dividing line 92 n.
limit 236 n.
circle 250 n.
equatorial
middle 70 adj.
astronomy 321 n.
warm 379 adj.
equerry
retainer 742 n.
equestrian
rider 268 n.
equidistant
equal 28 adj.
middle 70 adj.
equilateral
equal 28 adj.
symmetrical
245 adj.
equilibrium
equilibrium 28 n.
state of rest 266 n.
inexcitability
823 n.
equine
equine 273 adj.
animal 365 adj.
equinoctial
celestial 321 adj.
equip
dress 228 vb.
provide 633 vb.
make ready
669 vb.
equipage
carriage 274 n.
equipment
contents 193 n.
means 629 n.
equipment 630 n.
provision 633 n.
equipoise
equilibrium 28 n.
weighing 322 n.
equitable
equal 28 adj.
just 913 adj.
honourable

everyone
all 52 n.
everyman 79 n.
everyone for themselves
selfishness 932 n.
everywhere
widely 183 adv.
everywoman
common man
30 n.
everyman 79 n.
person 371 n.
commoner 869 n.
evict
displace 188 vb.
eject 300 vb.
deprive 786 vb.
eviction
exclusion 57 n.
ejection 300 n.
loss 772 n.
expropriation
786 n.
evidence
evidence 466 n.
evidence 466 vb.
accusation 928 n.
evident
certain 473 adj.
manifest 522 adj.
evil
evil 616 adj.
evil 616 n.
bad 645 n.
wicked 934 adj.
evildoer
evildoer 904 n.
evil eye
eye 438 n.
badness 645 n.
hatred 888 n.
malevolence
898 n.
spell 983 n.
evince
evidence 466 vb.
demonstrate
478 vb.
manifest 522 vb.
eviscerate
weaken 163 vb.
empty 300 vb.
extract 304 vb.
evocative
remembering
505 adj.
descriptive
590 adj.
exciting 821 adj.
evoke
cause 156 vb.

describe 590 vb.
incite 612 vb.
excite 821 vb.
evolution
existence 1 n.
conversion 147 n.
progression 285 n.
evolution 316 n.
biology 358 n.
improvement
654 n.
evolve
generate 167 vb.
evolve 316 vb.
get better 654 vb.
evolve into
be turned to
147 vb.
ewe
sheep 365 n.
female animal
373 n.
ewer
vessel 194 n.
water 339 n.
exacerbate
augment 36 vb.
exaggerate 546 vb.
hurt 827 vb.
aggravate 832 vb.
exact
lifelike 18 adj.
definite 80 adj.
careful 457 adj.
accurate 494 adj.
truthful 540 adj.
concise 569 adj.
demand 737 vb.
compel 740 vb.
observant 768 adj.
levy 786 vb.
impose a duty
917 vb.
exacting
difficult 700 adj.
oppressive 735 adj.
discontented
829 adj.
fastidious 862 adj.
exactitude
carefulness 457 n.
accuracy 494 n.
truthfulness
540 n.
exactly
truly 494 adv.
exactness
accuracy 494 n.
clarity 567 n.
exaggerate
exaggerate 546 vb.
exaggeration
exaggeration

546 n.
exaltation
elevation 310 n.
joy 824 n.
piety 979 n.
exalted
great 32 adj.
high 209 adj.
notable 638 adj.
noble 868 adj.
exaltedness
prestige 866 n.
examination
inspection 438 n.
attention 455 n.
enquiry 459 n.
exam 459 n.
experiment 461 n.
dissertation 591 n.
legal trial 959 n.
**examination
paper**
question 459 n.
examine
scan 438 vb.
enquire 459 vb.
interrogate 459 vb.
try a case 959 vb.
examiner
listener 415 n.
spectator 441 n.
enquirer 459 n.
estimator 480 n.
example
example 83 n.
warning 664 n.
exasperate
aggravate 832 vb.
enrage 891 vb.
excavate
make concave
255 vb.
extract 304 vb.
search 459 vb.
excavation
antiquity 125 n.
excavation 255 n.
search 459 n.
discovery 484 n.
excavator
excavator 255 n.
exceed
be great 32 vb.
be superior 34 vb.
grow 36 vb.
outdo 306 vb.
overstep 306 vb.
be intemperate
943 vb.
exceedingly
extremely 32 vb.
excel
be superior 34 vb.

be good 644 vb.
be skilful 694 vb.
have a reputation
866 vb.
excellence
superiority 34 n.
precedence 64 n.
goodness 644 n.
skill 694 n.
Excellency
title 870 n.
excellent
great 32 adj.
supreme 34 adj.
excellent 644 adj.
except
thus 8 adv.
lessen 37 vb.
subtract 39 vb.
exclude 57 vb.
exclusive of
57 adv.
excepting
exclusive of
57 adv.
qualifying 468 adj.
exception
non-uniformity
17 n.
exclusion 57 n.
speciality 80 n.
nonconformity
84 n.
qualification
468 n.
deprecation 762 n.
conditions 766 n.
disapprobation
924 n.
exceptional
remarkable 32 adj.
extraneous 59 adj.
abnormal 84 adj.
qualifying 468 adj.
wonderful 864 adj.
exceptionally
greatly 32 vb.
excerpt
part 53 n.
abstract 592 vb.
excess
largeness 32 n.
superiority 34 n.
exaggeration
546 n.
redundancy 637 n.
superfluity 637 n.
overactivity 678 n.
scope 744 n.
satiation 863 n.
intemperance
943 n.

excessive
exorbitant 32 adj.
violent 176 adj.
diffuse 570 adj.
redundant
637 adj.
superfluous
637 adj.
dear 811 adj.
vulgar 847 adj.
unwarranted
916 adj.
intemperate
943 adj.
excessively
extremely 32 vb.
exchange
correlate 12 vb.
correlation 12 n.
equivalence 28 n.
union 45 n.
focus 76 n.
substitute 150 vb.
substitution 150 n.
interchange 151 n.
interchange
151 vb.
conversation
584 n.
stock exchange
618 n.
assign 780 vb.
transfer 780 n.
barter 791 n.
trade 791 vb.
market 796 n.
finance 797 n.
exchequer
storage 632 n.
funds 797 n.
treasury 799 n.
excise
subtract 39 vb.
extract 304 vb.
tax 809 n.
excise officer
receiver 782 n.
excision
subtraction 39 n.
extraction 304 n.
excitable
excitable 822 adj.
excitation
increase 36 n.
activity 678 n.
excitation 821 n.
excite
cause feeling
374 vb.
have or give sexual
pleasure 376 vb.
excite 821 vb.

**fairy god-
mother**
protector 660 n.
helper 703 n.
patron 707 n.
giver 781 n.
good giver 813 n.
prodigy 864 n.
benefactor 903 n.
fairy 970 n.
sorceress 983 n.
fairyland
fantasy 513 n.
prodigy 864 n.
fairy 970 n.
fairylike
fairylike 970 adj.
fairy queen
fairy 970 n.
fairy tale
conception 513 n.
fable 543 n.
narrative 590 n.
fairy 970 n.
fait accompli
reality 1 n.
certainty 473 n.
completion 725 n.
faith
belief 485 n.
hope 852 n.
probity 929 n.
virtues 933 n.
religious faith
  973 n.
piety 979 n.
faithful
lifelike 18 adj.
conformable
  83 adj.
accurate 494 adj.
true 494 adj.
interpretative
  520 adj.
obedient 739 adj.
observant 768 adj.
friendly 880 adj.
trustworthy
  929 adj.
pious 979 adj.
faithful, the
pious person
  979 n.
worshipper 981 n.
faithfulness
conformity 83 n.
loyalty 739 n.
probity 929 n.
faith healing
medical art 658 n.
piety 979 n.
faithless
perfidious 930 adj.

fake
imitation 20 n.
copy 22 n.
erroneous 495 adj.
duplicity 541 n.
fake 541 vb.
false 541 adj.
sham 542 n.
spurious 542 adj.
impostor 545 n.
faked
spurious 542 adj.
fakir
ascetic 945 n.
pious person
  979 n.
monk 986 n.
falcon
bird 365 n.
heraldry 547 n.
falconry
chase 619 n.
fall
decrease 37 n.
decrease 37 vb.
period 110 n.
autumn 129 n.
be weak 163 vb.
be destroyed
  165 vb.
reproduce itself
  167 vb.
depth 211 n.
incline 220 n.
deviation 282 n.
regress 286 n.
regression 286 n.
descend 309 vb.
descent 309 n.
tumble 309 vb.
flow 350 vb.
rain 350 vb.
deteriorate 655 vb.
relapse 657 n.
be defeated
  728 vb.
defeat 728 n.
fail 728 vb.
failure 728 n.
cheapness 812 n.
lose repute 867 vb.
be wicked 934 vb.
fall about
laugh 835 vb.
fallacious
illogical 477 adj.
erroneous 495 adj.
fallacy
sophism 477 n.
error 495 n.
deception 542 n.
fall apart
separate 46 vb.

deteriorate 655 vb.
fall away
separate 46 vb.
become small
  198 vb.
fall back
regress 286 vb.
recede 290 vb.
relapse 657 vb.
fall back on
avail oneself of
  673 vb.
fall behind
be inferior 35 vb.
be dispersed 75 vb.
move slowly
  278 vb.
regress 286 vb.
fall short 307 vb.
fall below
be inferior 35 vb.
be insufficient
  636 vb.
**fall between
  two stools**
fail 728 vb.
fall by the way
fall short 307 vb.
fall down
descend 309 vb.
fallen
pregnant 167 adj.
defeated 728 adj.
morally weak
  934 adj.
unchaste 951 adj.
fallen, the
death roll 361 n.
fallen angel
bad person 938 n.
devil 969 n.
Satan 969 n.
impious person
  980 n.
fall flat
miscarry 728 vb.
fall for
be credulous
  487 vb.
be duped 544 vb.
be in love 887 vb.
fall foul of
collide 279 vb.
fall from grace
relapse 657 vb.
be wicked 934 vb.
fall guy
dupe 544 n.
laughing stock
  851 n.
fallible
unreliable 474 adj.

illogical 477 adj.
misjudging
  481 adj.
erroneous 495 adj.
imperfect 647 adj.
fall in
be uniform 16 vb.
descend 309 vb.
plunge 313 vb.
falling
unequal 29 adj.
sloping 220 adj.
descent 309 n.
cheap 812 adj.
fall in love
be in love 887 vb.
fall into
be turned to
  147 vb.
enter 297 vb.
fall into line
conform 83 vb.
fall into place
be in order 60 vb.
fall in with
conform 83 vb.
consent 758 vb.
fall off
separate 46 vb.
descend 309 vb.
tumble 309 vb.
deteriorate 655 vb.
**fall on one's
  feet**
have luck 730 vb.
fall out
disagree 25 vb.
be dispersed 75 vb.
happen 154 vb.
result 157 vb.
fall short 307 vb.
quarrel 709 n.
not complete
  726 vb.
be hostile 881 vb.
fallout
sequel 67 n.
nuclear physics
  160 n.
radiation 417 n.
unhealthiness
  653 n.
bomb 723 n.
**fall out of
  favour**
lose repute 867 vb.
fall out of love
be indifferent
  860 vb.
hate 888 vb.
fallow
unproductive

172 adj.
inert 175 adj.
farm 370 n.
fall prostrate
tumble 309 vb.
falls
waterfall 350 n.
fall short
be unequal 29 vb.
be inferior 35 vb.
fall short 307 vb.
fall through
fall short 307 vb.
fall to
eat 301 vb.
undertake 672 vb.
be one's duty
  917 vb.
fall under
be included 78 vb.
fall upon
surprise 508 vb.
attack 712 vb.
false
substituted
  150 adj.
illogical 477 adj.
false 541 adj.
spurious 542 adj.
unwarranted
  916 adj.
flattering 925 adj.
false alarm
false alarm 665 n.
fear 854 n.
false dawn
misjudgment
  481 n.
error 495 n.
disappointment
  509 n.
false-hearted
perfidious 930 adj.
falsehood
falsehood 541 n.
false name
misnomer 562 n.
falseness
error 495 n.
falsehood 541 n.
deception 542 n.
false pregnancy
error 495 n.
**false preten-
  sions**
pretension 850 n.
falsetto
stridency 407 n.
voicelessness
  578 n.
falsify
mislead 495 vb.

way 624 n.
conduct 688 n.
fashion 848 n.
fashionable
fashionable
848 adj.
fashionable
person
fashionable society
848 n.
fashionable
society
fashionable society
848 n.
fashion
designer
clothier 228 n.
fashion victim
imitator 20 n.
conformist 83 n.
fast
firm 45 adj.
tied 45 adj.
fixed 153 adj.
speedy 277 adj.
inexact 495 adj.
friendly 880 adj.
do penance
941 vb.
be ascetic 945 vb.
fast 946 n.
starve 946 vb.
unchaste 951 adj.
perform ritual
988 vb.
fast buck
easy thing 701 n.
fast day
special day 876 n.
asceticism 945 n.
fast 946 n.
holy day 988 n.
fasten
affix 45 vb.
join 45 vb.
tighten 45 vb.
close 264 vb.
take 786 vb.
fastener
fastening 47 n.
fastening
fastening 47 n.
fasten on
retain 778 vb.
take 786 vb.
faster
abstainer 942 n.
ascetic 945 n.
fastidious
sensitive 819 adj.
fastidious 862 adj.
fasting
penance 941 n.

ascetic 945 adj.
fasting 946 adj.
fasting 946 n.
fast lane
progression 265 n.
road 624 n.
activity 678 n.
fast one
trickery 542 n.
fast-track
speedy 277 adj.
fat
prolific 171 adj.
fat 195 adj.
food content
301 n.
fat 357 n.
fatty 357 adj.
plentiful 635 adj.
plenty 635 n.
prosperous
730 adj.
(See also **fat**
person.)
fatal
deadly 362 adj.
fated 596 adj.
evil 616 adj.
harmful 645 adj.
fatalistic
submitting
721 adj.
fatality
death roll 361 n.
decease 361 n.
necessity 596 n.
evil 616 n.
wounded person
655 n.
fat cat
prosperous person
730 n.
rich person 800 n.
fate
futurity 124 n.
cause 156 n.
fate 596 n.
fated
future 124 adj.
fated 596 adj.
fateful
important 638 adj.
fate worse than
death
suffering 825 n.
fathead
dunce 501 n.
fool 501 n.
father
be akin 11 vb.
kinsman 11 n.
cause 156 n.

generate 167 vb.
paternity 169 n.
male 372 n.
church title 986 n.
cleric 986 n.
Father Christ-
mas
giver 781 n.
good giver 813 n.
benefactor 903 n.
father confessor
pastor 986 n.
fathered
born 360 adj.
father figure
substitute 150 n.
paternity 169 n.
fatherhood
family 11 n.
parentage 169 n.
paternity 169 n.
father-in-law
paternity 169 n.
fatherland
paternity 169 n.
territory 184 n.
home 192 n.
fatherlike
parental 169 adj.
fatherly
parental 169 adj.
benevolent
897 adj.
fatherly eye
protection 660 n.
father upon
attribute 158 vb.
fathom
measurement of
length 203 n.
be deep 211 vb.
enquire 459 vb.
measure 465 vb.
understand
516 vb.
fathomless
deep 211 adj.
fatigue
labour 682 n.
fatigue 684 n.
fatigue 684 vb.
fatigued
fatigued 684 adj.
fatigues
uniform 228 n.
fat in the fire
turmoil 61 n.
fatness
bulk 195 n.
fat person
bulk 195 n.
fatten
grow 36 vb.

enlarge 197 vb.
feed 301 vb.
breed stock
369 vb.
fatten on
eat 301 vb.
fatten up
feed 301 vb.
fattiness
greasiness 357 n.
fatty
bulk 195 n.
fatty 357 adj.
fatuity
lacking substance
4 n.
thing that lacks
substance 4 n.
absence of thought
450 n.
absurdity 497 n.
folly 499 n.
fatuous
absurd 497 adj.
foolish 499 adj.
meaningless
515 adj.
fatuousness
folly 499 n.
faucet
stopper 264 n.
outlet 298 n.
water 339 n.
fault
discontinuity 72 n.
weakness 163 n.
gap 201 n.
blunder 495 vb.
defect 647 n.
criticize 924 vb.
detract 926 vb.
vice 934 n.
guilty act 936 n.
fault-finding
discontented
829 adj.
fastidious 862 adj.
censure 924 n.
disapprobation
924 n.
disapproving
924 adj.
faultless
perfect 646 adj.
guiltless 935 adj.
pure 950 adj.
faultlessness
perfection 646 n.
purity 950 n.
faulty
inexact 495 adj.
bad 645 adj.

imperfect 647 adj.
faun
mythical being
970 n.
fauna
animal life 365 n.
faux pas
mistake 495 n.
failure 728 n.
guilty act 936 n.
favour
resemble 18 vb.
advantage 34 n.
influence 178 n.
promote 285 vb.
be biased 481 vb.
badge 547 n.
choice 605 n.
choose 605 vb.
benefit 615 n.
aid 703 n.
gift 781 n.
desire 859 vb.
liking 859 n.
honours 866 n.
repute 866 n.
courteous act
884 n.
love token 889 n.
do wrong 914 adj.
injustice 914 n.
respect 920 n.
approbation
923 n.
approve 923 vb.
favourable
opportune 137 adj.
predicting 511 adj.
beneficial 644 adj.
halcyon 730 adj.
promising 852 adj.
approving 923 adj.
favourably
well 615 adv.
favourite
chosen 605 adj.
contender 716 n.
loved one 887 n.
favourite 890 n.
favouritism
prejudice 481 n.
injustice 914 n.
fawn
young creature
132 n.
mammal 365 n.
brown 430 adj.
be servile 879 vb.
flatter 925 vb.
be dishonest
930 vb.
fawn on
flatter 925 vb.

irrigator 341 n.
extinguisher
382 n.
fire escape
ascent 308 n.
means of escape
667 n.
**fire extin-
guisher**
extinguisher
382 n.
firefighter
extinguisher
382 n.
protector 660 n.
defender 713 n.
firefly
insect 365 n.
flash 417 n.
fireguard
furnace 383 n.
shelter 662 n.
firelight
light 417 n.
fire-lighter
lighter 385 n.
fireman
extinguisher
382 n.
protector 660 n.
defender 713 n.
fireplace
home 192 n.
furnace 383 n.
fireproof
strong 162 adj.
coat 226 vb.
invulnerable
660 adj.
fire-raiser
arson 381 n.
fire ship
lighter 385 n.
warship 722 n.
fireside
focus 76 n.
place 185 n.
home 192 n.
fire station
extinguisher
382 n.
firewatcher
protector 660 n.
firewood
fuel 385 n.
fireworks
explosive 723 n.
firing
propulsion 287 n.
bang 402 n.
bombardment
712 n.

firing line
battle 718 n.
battleground
724 n.
firm
firm 45 adj.
fixed 153 adj.
dense 324 adj.
rigid 326 adj.
resolute 599 adj.
obstinate 602 adj.
corporation 708 n.
retentive 778 adj.
merchant 794 n.
courageous
855 adj.
friendly 880 adj.
firmament
heavens 321 n.
firmness
permanence 144 n.
stability 153 n.
hardness 326 n.
resolution 599 n.
**firmness of
purpose**
will 595 n.
first
original 21 adj.
supreme 34 adj.
first 68 adj.
initially 68 adv.
prior 119 adj.
victor 727 n.
first aid
therapy 658 n.
aid 703 n.
**first and fore-
most**
initially 68 adv.
firstborn
precursor 66 n.
prior 119 adj.
previousness
119 n.
older 131 adj.
first-class
supreme 34 adj.
first-hand
original 21 adj.
new 126 adj.
**first-hand
impression**
beginning 68 n.
firstly
initially 68 adv.
first minister
director 690 n.
first night
debut 68 n.
dramatic theory
594 n.

first of all
initially 68 adv.
first principles
beginning 68 n.
first-rate
supreme 34 adj.
notable 638 adj.
best 644 adj.
excellent 644 adj.
skilful 694 adj.
first-rater
exceller 644 n.
first secretary
official 690 n.
first strike
attempt 671 n.
first thing
early 135 adv.
firth
gulf 345 n.
fiscal
monetary 797 adj.
fish
fish as food 301 n.
animal 365 n.
fish 365 n.
search 459 vb.
hunt 619 vb.
amuse oneself
837 vb.
fisherman
hunter 619 n.
**fisherman's
yarn**
improbability
472 n.
fable 543 n.
fishery
extraction 304 n.
fish for
search 459 vb.
be tentative
461 vb.
pursue 619 vb.
attempt 671 vb.
request 761 vb.
desire 859 vb.
**fish for compli-
ments**
be vain 873 vb.
be ostentatious
875 vb.
fishing
chase 619 n.
fishing net
receptacle 194 n.
fishing tackle
chase 619 n.
fishnet
network 222 n.
**fish out of
water**
unrelatedness

10 n.
misfit 25 n.
nonconformist
84 n.
displacement
188 n.
bungler 697 n.
fish tank
stock farm 369 n.
fish up
elevate 310 vb.
fishy
animal 365 adj.
improbable
472 adj.
puzzling 517 adj.
dishonest 930 adj.
fissile
brittle 330 adj.
fission
separation 46 n.
decompose 51 vb.
decomposition
51 n.
nuclear physics
160 n.
fissure
disunion 46 n.
gap 201 n.
fist
pincers 778 n.
fistful
contents 193 n.
fisticuffs
turmoil 61 n.
violence 176 n.
knock 279 n.
quarrel 709 n.
fight 716 n.
boxing 716 n.
anger 891 n.
fistula
tube 263 n.
ulcer 651 n.
fit
accord 24 vb.
adjust 24 vb.
fit 24 vb.
equalize 28 vb.
join 45 vb.
cohere 48 vb.
make conform
83 vb.
violence 176 n.
spasm 318 n.
frenzy 503 n.
whim 604 n.
be expedient
642 vb.
healthy 650 adj.
illness 651 n.
activity 678 n.

excitable state
822 n.
fear 854 n.
due 915 adj.
fit for
useful 640 adj.
fit for nothing
useless 641 adj.
fitful
fitful 142 adj.
capricious 604 adj.
excitable 822 adj.
fit in
accord 24 vb.
conform 83 vb.
make conform
83 vb.
load 193 vb.
insert 303 vb.
fitness
suitability 24 n.
vitality 162 n.
good policy 642 n.
health 650 n.
aptitude 694 n.
right 913 n.
fit out
dress 228 vb.
provide 633 vb.
make ready
669 vb.
fits and starts
fitfulness 142 n.
agitation 318 n.
fitter
machinist 630 n.
artisan 686 n.
fitting
relevant 9 adj.
adaptation 24 n.
adjusted 24 adj.
fit 24 adj.
opportune 137 adj.
advisable 642 adj.
right 913 adj.
due 915 adj.
five
five 99 n.
five o'clock
evening 129 n.
**five o'clock
shadow**
hair 259 n.
roughness 259 n.
five-pound note
coinage 797 n.
paper money
797 n.
fiver
funds 797 n.
fix
circumstance 8 n.

flimsy 163 adj.
rarefied 325 adj.
brittle 330 adj.
poorly reasoned
477 adj.
flinch
recoil 280 vb.
recede 290 vb.
feel pain 377 vb.
avoid 620 vb.
suffer 825 vb.
quake 854 vb.
fling
move 265 vb.
impel 279 vb.
impulse 279 n.
propel 287 vb.
propulsion 287 n.
scope 744 n.
fling out
emerge 298 vb.
eject 300 vb.
reject 607 vb.
flint
hardness 326 n.
soil 344 n.
lighter 385 n.
tool 630 n.
building material
631 n.
flinty
hard 326 adj.
severe 735 adj.
flip
impel 279 vb.
knock 279 n.
touch 378 n.
touch 378 vb.
impertinent
878 adj.
flip one's lid
get angry 891 vb.
flippant
lacking concentra-
tion 456 adj.
witty 839 adj.
rash 857 adj.
impertinent
878 adj.
flipper
limb 53 n.
propeller 269 n.
feeler 378 n.
flip side
rear 238 n.
music player
414 n.
flip through
pay some attention
455 vb.
study 536 vb.
flirt
be capricious

604 vb.
lover 887 n.
court 889 vb.
libertine 952 n.
loose woman
952 n.
flirtation
whim 604 n.
love affair 887 n.
wooing 889 n.
flirtatious
loving 887 adj.
flit
elapse 111 vb.
be transient
114 vb.
vary 152 vb.
be in motion
265 vb.
fly 271 vb.
move fast 277 vb.
walk out 296 vb.
depart 296 vb.
run away 620 vb.
escape 667 n.
escape 667 vb.
flitting
transient 114 adj.
transference 272 n.
float
vary 152 vb.
stabilize 153 vb.
fly 271 vb.
lorry 274 n.
pushcart 274 n.
be light 323 vb.
be uncertain
474 vb.
floating
unrelated 10 adj.
watersports 269 n.
light 323 adj.
monetary 797 adj.
floating popula-
tion
wanderer 268 n.
floating pound
finance 797 n.
floating vote
dubiety 474 n.
irresolution 601 n.
independence
744 n.
flock
group 74 n.
be many 104 vb.
filament 208 n.
hair 259 n.
animal 365 n.
laity 987 n.
flock together
congregate 74 vb.

floe
ice 380 n.
flog
give pain 377 vb.
incite 612 vb.
hasten 680 vb.
sell 793 vb.
flog 963 vb.
flog a dead
horse
waste effort
641 adj.
flogging
knock 279 n.
corporal punish-
ment 963 n.
flog on
impel 279 vb.
flood
increase 36 vb.
congregate 74 vb.
crowd 74 n.
be dispersed 75 vb.
be many 104 vb.
destroyer 168 n.
outbreak 176 n.
progression 285 n.
entering 297 n.
outflow 298 n.
encroach 306 vb.
drench 341 vb.
irrigate 341 vb.
moisten 341 vb.
flow 350 vb.
plenty 635 n.
be overabundant
637 vb.
floodgate
outlet 298 n.
water channel
351 n.
flooding
flowing 350 adj.
redundant
637 adj.
floodlight
light 417 n.
lamp 420 n.
floodlit
luminous 417 adj.
floods
great quantity
32 n.
floor
compartment
194 n.
layer 207 n.
lowness 210 n.
base 214 n.
flatten 216 vb.
basis 218 n.
paving 226 n.

strike 279 vb.
fell 311 vb.
puzzle 474 vb.
confute 479 vb.
arena 724 n.
floorboards
paving 226 n.
floored by, be
not understand
517 vb.
flooring
base 214 n.
basis 218 n.
paving 226 n.
floor show
spectacle 445 n.
stage show 594 n.
flop
close 264 vb.
descend 309 vb.
be agitated
318 vb.
dramatic theory
594 n.
bungling 695 n.
fail 728 vb.
failure 728 n.
loser 728 n.
miscarry 728 vb.
floppy
weak 163 adj.
soft 327 adj.
flora
plant life 366 n.
flora and fauna
organism 358 n.
florid
florid 425 adj.
red 431 adj.
ornate 574 adj.
florin
coinage 797 n.
floss
fibre 208 n.
flotilla
shipping 275 n.
navy 722 n.
flotsam
transport 272 n.
derelict 779 n.
flotsam and
jetsam
rabble 869 n.
outcast 883 n.
flounce
edging 234 n.
fold 261 n.
trimming 844 n.
be angry 891 vb.
flounder
be agitated
318 vb.

be uncertain
474 vb.
be clumsy 695 vb.
be in difficulty
700 vb.
flour
cereals 301 n.
powder 332 n.
thickening 354 n.
white thing 427 n.
flourish
grow 36 vb.
be fruitful 171 vb.
coil 251 n.
brandish 317 vb.
agitate 318 vb.
blow 352 vb.
loudness 400 n.
figure of speech
519 n.
show 522 vb.
call 547 n.
ornament 574 n.
elegance 575 n.
lettering 586 n.
flourish 615 vb.
be healthy 650 vb.
prosper 730 vb.
pattern 844 n.
be ostentatious
875 vb.
ostentation 875 n.
boast 877 n.
boast 877 vb.
flourishing
prosperous
730 adj.
flourish of
trumpets
publication 528 n.
ostentation 875 n.
celebration 876 n.
floury
powdery 332 adj.
flout
indignity 921 n.
not respect 921 vb.
despise 922 vb.
flow
quantity 26 n.
continuity 71 n.
elapse 111 vb.
continuance
146 n.
hang 217 vb.
motion 265 n.
current 350 n.
flow 350 vb.
diffuseness 570 n.
abound 635 vb.
flow chart
statistics 86 n.

freeze
halt 145 vb.
come to rest
266 vb.
state of rest 266 n.
stop 266 int.
be dense 324 vb.
harden 326 vb.
make insensitive
375 vb.
be cold 380 vb.
wintriness 380 n.
refrigerate 382 vb.
preserve 666 vb.
restriction 747 n.
non-payment
805 n.
not pay 805 vb.
frighten 854 vb.
quake 854 vb.
freeze-dry
dry 342 vb.
refrigerate 382 vb.
preserve 666 vb.
freezer
cabinet 194 n.
refrigerator 384 n.
storage 632 n.
preserver 666 n.
freezing
contraction 198 n.
cold 380 adj.
refrigeration
382 n.
freezing point
coldness 380 n.
freight
fill 54 vb.
contents 193 n.
load 193 vb.
transport 272 n.
gravity 322 n.
merchandise
795 n.
French dressing
hors-d'oeuvres
301 n.
sauce 389 n.
French fries
fruit and vegeta-
bles 301 n.
French horn
horn 414 n.
French kiss
endearment 889 n.
French leave
absence 190 n.
escape 667 n.
French letter
contraception
172 n.
frenetic
furious 176 adj.

frenzied 503 adj.
frenzied
frenzied 503 adj.
fervent 818 adj.
frenzy
turmoil 61 n.
violence 176 n.
frenzy 503 n.
activity 678 n.
excitable state
822 n.
frequency
degree 27 n.
frequency 139 n.
periodic recurrence
141 n.
electricity 160 n.
oscillation 317 n.
frequency band
oscillation 317 n.
frequency wave
radiation 417 n.
frequent
frequent 139 adj.
recur 139 vb.
go on 146 vb.
be present 189 vb.
live 192 vb.
be in the habit of
610 vb.
frequently
often 139 adv.
fresco
picture 553 n.
fresh
original 21 adj.
lasting 113 adj.
new 126 adj.
airy 340 adj.
humid 341 adj.
windy 352 adj.
cold 380 adj.
remembered
505 adj.
unaccustomed
611 adj.
clean 648 adj.
healthy 652 adj.
impertinent
878 adj.
fresh air
air 340 n.
healthiness 652 n.
freshen
invigorate 174 vb.
aerate 340 vb.
purify 648 vb.
revive 656 vb.
refresh 685 vb.
decorate 844 vb.
freshen up
make better

654 vb.
repair 656 vb.
refresh 685 vb.
fresh-faced
personable
841 adj.
freshness
originality 21 n.
newness 126 n.
youth 130 n.
coldness 380 n.
cleanness 648 n.
sauciness 878 n.
fret
rend 46 vb.
rub 333 vb.
give pain 377 vb.
cry 408 vb.
stringed instrument
414 n.
restlessness 678 n.
hasten 680 vb.
disobey 738 vb.
be excitable
822 vb.
excitable state
822 n.
suffer 825 vb.
torment 827 vb.
decorate 844 vb.
anger 891 n.
be angry 891 vb.
enrage 891 vb.
fretful
capricious 604 adj.
active 678 adj.
discontented
829 adj.
irascible 892 adj.
fretwork
network 222 n.
ornamental art
844 n.
friable
brittle 330 adj.
powdery 332 adj.
friar
monk 986 n.
pastor 986 n.
friary
monastery 986 n.
monk 986 n.
fricassee
dish 301 n.
fricative
speech sound
398 n.
friction
counteraction
182 n.
friction 333 n.
opposition 704 n.

dissension 709 n.
painfulness 827 n.
fridge
refrigerator 384 n.
storage 632 n.
friend
friend 880 n.
friend at court
influence 178 n.
latency 523 n.
patron 707 n.
friendly
pleasant 376 adj.
friendly 880 adj.
amiable 884 adj.
approving 923 adj.
friendly fire
mistake 495 n.
bungling 695 n.
friendship
friendship 880 n.
love 887 n.
frieze
textile 222 n.
ornamental art
844 n.
trimming 844 n.
frigate
sailing ship 275 n.
warship 722 n.
fright
eyesore 842 n.
fear 854 n.
frighten
frighten 854 vb.
threaten 900 vb.
frightened
afraid 854 adj.
frightening
frightening
854 adj.
frightful
prodigious 32 adj.
ugly 842 adj.
frightening
854 adj.
frigid
cold 380 adj.
impassive 820 adj.
inexcitable
823 adj.
hostile 881 adj.
pure 950 adj.
frigidity
coldness 380 n.
moral insensibility
820 n.
inexcitability
823 n.
purity 950 n.
frill
edging 234 n.

plumage 259 n.
fold 261 n.
fold 261 vb.
trimming 844 n.
fringe
adjunct 40 n.
extremity 69 n.
contiguity 202 n.
filament 208 n.
edge 234 n.
edging 234 n.
hem 234 vb.
hair 259 n.
unimportant
639 adj.
hairdressing
843 n.
trimming 844 n.
fringe benefits
earnings 771 n.
reward 962 n.
frippery
clothing 228 n.
bauble 639 n.
finery 844 n.
ostentation 875 n.
frisk
be in motion
265 vb.
move fast 277 vb.
leap 312 vb.
search 459 vb.
be cheerful
833 vb.
rejoice 835 vb.
frisky
active 678 adj.
merry 833 adj.
frisson
agitation 318 n.
fritter away
waste 634 vb.
misuse 675 vb.
lose 772 vb.
be prodigal
815 vb.
fritters
dish 301 n.
frivolous
changing 152 adj.
lacking concentra-
tion 456 adj.
capricious 604 adj.
trivial 639 adj.
merry 833 adj.
rash 857 adj.
frizzy
undulatory
251 adj.
hairy 259 adj.
frock
dress 228 n.

862 vb.
ostentation 875 n.
be angry 891 vb.
fusspot
perfectionist
862 n.
fussy
narrow-minded
481 adj.
fastidious 862 adj.
fusty
fetid 397 adj.
dirty 649 adj.
futile
absurd 497 adj.
foolish 499 adj.
useless 641 adj.
contemptible
922 adj.
futon
bed 218 n.
seat 218 n.
future
future 124 adj.
futurity 124 n.
expected 507 adj.
future tense
futurity 124 n.
futuristic
modern 126 adj.
literary 557 adj.
futurologist
oracle 511 n.
fu yung
dish 301 n.
fuzz
hair 259 n.
fuzzy
formless 244 adj.
hairy 259 adj.
dim 419 adj.
shadowy 419 adj.
indistinct 444 adj.

G

gabardine
textile 222 n.
overcoat 228 n.
gabble
howl 409 vb.
empty talk 515 n.
lack of meaning
515 n.
mean nothing
515 vb.
speak 579 vb.
stammer 580 vb.
be talkative
581 vb.
chatter 581 n.

gabbling
talkative 581 adj.
gable
apex 213 n.
gable end
extremity 69 n.
apex 213 n.
gad
wander 267 vb.
gadabout
sociable person
882 n.
gadfly
insect 365 n.
stimulator 821 n.
gadget
object 319 n.
contrivance 623 n.
instrument 628 n.
tool 630 n.
Gael
native 191 n.
gaff
sharp point 256 n.
spear 723 n.
gaffe
mistake 495 n.
gaffer
old man 133 n.
male 372 n.
manager 690 n.
country-dweller
869 n.
gag
stopper 264 n.
vomit 300 vb.
silence 399 vb.
make mute
578 vb.
act 594 vb.
hinder 702 vb.
restrain 747 vb.
fetter 748 n.
witticism 839 n.
gaga
ageing 131 adj.
impotent 161 adj.
foolish 499 adj.
crazy 503 adj.
mentally disordered
503 adj.
gage
defiance 711 n.
security 767 n.
gagging order
silence 399 n.
gaggle
group 74 n.
howl 409 vb.
gaiety
merriment 833 n.
sociability 882 n.

gain
grow 36 vb.
progress 285 vb.
progression 285 n.
arrive 295 vb.
err 495 vb.
benefit 615 vb.
acquire 771 vb.
gain 771 n.
gain 771 vb.
gainful
gainful 771 adj.
gain on
outstrip 277 vb.
progress 285 vb.
gains
wealth 800 n.
gainsay
negate 533 vb.
gait
gait 265 n.
way 624 n.
gaiters
legwear 228 n.
badge of office
743 n.
clerical dress
989 n.
gala
festivity 837 n.
pageant 875 n.
galactic
cosmic 321 adj.
gala day
amusement 837 n.
special day 876 n.
**gala perform-
ance**
pageant 875 n.
galaxy
group 74 n.
star 321 n.
light 420 n.
person of repute
866 n.
gale
velocity 277 n.
gale 352 n.
windy 352 adj.
gall
swelling 253 n.
give pain 377 vb.
sourness 393 n.
hurt 827 vb.
torment 827 vb.
sauciness 878 n.
resentment 891 n.
irascibility 892 n.
malevolence
898 n.
gallant
dandy 848 n.

courageous
855 adj.
showy 875 adj.
courteous 884 adj.
lover 887 n.
loving 887 adj.
benevolent
897 adj.
libertine 952 n.
gallantry
courage 855 n.
courtesy 884 n.
love 887 n.
galleon
merchant ship
275 n.
warship 722 n.
gallery
lobby 194 n.
tunnel 263 n.
listener 415 n.
onlookers 441 n.
exhibit 522 n.
theatregoer 594 n.
theatre 594 n.
collection 632 n.
church interior
990 n.
galley
room 194 n.
rowing boat
275 n.
cookery 301 n.
heater 383 n.
galley slave
boatman 270 n.
busy person 678 n.
slave 742 n.
prisoner 750 n.
galling
annoying 827 adj.
gallivant
wander 267 vb.
gallon
*weights and meas-
ures* 465 n.
gallons
great quantity
32 n.
gallop
be transient
114 vb.
gait 265 n.
ride 267 vb.
move fast 277 vb.
spurt 277 n.
gallows
hanger 217 n.
means of execution
964 n.
gallstones
digestive disorder

651 n.
**Gallup poll
(tdmk)**
statistics 86 n.
enquiry 459 n.
vote 605 n.
galoot
ninny 501 n.
bungler 697 n.
galore
great quantity
32 n.
many 104 adj.
plenty 635 n.
galumph
be clumsy 695 vb.
galvanize
invigorate 174 vb.
move 265 vb.
incite 612 vb.
excite 821 vb.
gambit
debut 68 n.
attempt 671 n.
tactics 688 n.
gamble
empiricism 461 n.
uncertainty 474 n.
conjecture 512 n.
gamble 618 vb.
gambling 618 n.
be rash 857 vb.
gambler
gambler 618 n.
player 837 n.
gambling
gambling 618 n.
gambling den
gambling den
618 n.
gambol
leap 312 n.
leap 312 vb.
be cheerful
833 vb.
amuse oneself
837 vb.
game
crippled 163 adj.
meat 301 n.
animal 365 n.
trickery 542 n.
resolute 599 adj.
persevering
600 adj.
objective 617 n.
chase 619 n.
plot 623 n.
stratagem 698 n.
contest 716 n.
amusement 837 n.
amuse oneself

gasworks
gas 336 n.
workshop 687 n.
gate
barrier 235 n.
doorway 263 n.
onlookers 441 n.
obstacle 702 n.
fort 713 n.
imprison 747 vb.
treasury 799 n.
gateau
*bread, pastries
and cakes*
301 n.
gate-crash
intrude 297 vb.
be sociable
882 vb.
gated
imprisoned
747 adj.
gatekeeper
doorkeeper 264 n.
gate money
receipt 807 n.
gateway
entrance 68 n.
doorway 263 n.
gather
join 45 vb.
bring together
74 vb.
congregate 74 vb.
expand 197 vb.
fold 261 n.
fold 261 vb.
meet 295 vb.
cultivate 370 vb.
assume 471 vb.
store 632 vb.
acquire 771 vb.
take 786 vb.
threaten 900 vb.
gathering
assemblage 74 n.
assembly 74 n.
conference 584 n.
storage 632 n.
ulcer 651 n.
**gathering
clouds**
omen 511 n.
danger 661 n.
adversity 731 n.
threat 900 n.
gathering storm
danger 661 n.
**gather momen-
tum**
accelerate 277 vb.
gather round
congregate 74 vb.

gather speed
accelerate 277 vb.
gather together
converge 293 vb.
gating
penalty 963 n.
gauche
inelegant 576 adj.
clumsy 695 adj.
ill-bred 847 adj.
gaudy
florid 425 adj.
manifest 522 adj.
spurious 542 adj.
vulgar 847 adj.
showy 875 adj.
gauge
breadth 205 n.
appraise 465 vb.
gauge 465 n.
gauge 465 vb.
gaunt
unproductive
172 adj.
lean 206 adj.
gauntlet
glove 228 n.
defiance 711 n.
armour 713 n.
gauze
textile 222 n.
transparency
422 n.
semitransparency
424 n.
surgical dressing
658 n.
gavel
hammer 279 n.
badge of office
743 n.
gawky
clumsy 695 adj.
gawp
gaze 438 vb.
scan 438 vb.
not expect 508 vb.
wonder 864 vb.
gay
nonconformist
84 n.
unconformable
84 adj.
luminous 417 adj.
florid 425 adj.
merry 833 adj.
showy 875 adj.
gay abandon
merriment 833 n.
rejoicing 835 n.
gay lib
freedom 744 n.

gaze
gaze 438 vb.
glance 438 n.
gazebo
arbour 194 n.
gazelle
mammal 365 n.
gazette
journal 528 n.
record 548 n.
gazetteer
directory 87 n.
guidebook 524 n.
reference book
589 n.
gear
accumulation
74 n.
sort 77 n.
box 194 n.
clothing 228 n.
dressing 228 n.
form 243 n.
equipment 630 n.
property 777 n.
finery 844 n.
gearing
machine 630 n.
debt 803 n.
gear oneself up
prepare oneself
669 vb.
gears
machine 630 n.
geegaw
bauble 639 n.
finery 844 n.
geek
fool 501 n.
enthusiast 504 n.
bore 838 n.
Internet 531 n.
Geiger counter
radiation 417 n.
meter 465 n.
detector 484 n.
gel
be dense 324 vb.
harden 326 vb.
thicken 354 vb.
glutinousness
354 n.
gelatine
thickening 354 n.
geld
subtract 39 vb.
unman 161 vb.
gelding
horse 273 n.
male animal
372 n.
gelignite
explosive 723 n.

gem
gem 844 n.
gen
information
524 n.
gender
classification 77 n.
grammar 564 n.
gene
heredity 5 n.
organism 358 n.
genealogy
genealogy 169 n.
general
general 79 adj.
national 371 adj.
army officer
741 n.
general council
synod 985 n.
generality
generality 79 n.
generalization
whole 52 n.
generality 79 n.
reasoning 475 n.
inexactness 495 n.
**general know-
ledge**
erudition 490 n.
generally
generally 79 adv.
often 139 adv.
**general practi-
tioner**
doctor 658 n.
general public
social group
371 n.
common people
869 n.
generalship
tactics 688 n.
generate
generate 167 vb.
generation
sexual intercourse
45 n.
era 110 n.
generations
long duration
113 n.
generator
electronics 160 n.
generic
general 79 adj.
generosity
liberality 813 n.
benevolence 897 n.
generous
great 32 adj.
many 104 adj.

liberal 813 adj.
courteous 884 adj.
benevolent
897 adj.
approving 923 adj.
virtuous 933 adj.
genesis
origin 68 n.
source 156 n.
genetic
hereditary 5 adj.
**genetic engi-
neering**
heredity 5 n.
biology 358 n.
**genetic finger-
printing**
evidence 466 n.
identification
547 n.
diagnosis 658 n.
**genetic modifi-
cation**
heredity 5 n.
genetics
heredity 5 n.
biology 358 n.
**Geneva Conven-
tion**
treaty 765 n.
genial
pleasant 376 adj.
warm 379 adj.
pleasurable
826 adj.
cheerful 833 adj.
benevolent
897 adj.
genie
mythical being
970 n.
**genitals, genita-
lia**
genitals 167 n.
genius
identity 13 n.
analogue 18 n.
tendency 179 n.
intellect 447 n.
spirit 447 n.
intellectual 492 n.
intelligence 498 n.
sage 500 n.
exceller 644 n.
aptitude 694 n.
proficient person
696 n.
prodigy 864 n.
genned-up
informed 524 adj.
genocide
destruction 165 n.

be stealthy
525 vb.

glider
aeronaut 271 n.
aircraft 276 n.

glimmer
flash 417 n.
shine 417 vb.
be dim 419 vb.

glimpse
glance 438 n.
see 438 vb.
knowledge 490 n.
superficial know-
ledge 491 n.
hint 524 n.

glint
flash 417 n.
shine 417 vb.
glance 438 n.

glisten
flash 417 n.
reflection 417 n.
shine 417 vb.

glitter
flash 417 n.
shine 417 vb.
be ostentatious
875 vb.
ostentation 875 n.

glitzy
rich 800 adj.
ostentatious
875 adj.

gloat
be pleased 824 vb.
rejoice 835 vb.
boast 877 vb.
avenge 910 vb.

global
extensive 32 adj.
comprehensive
52 adj.
inclusive 78 adj.
universal 79 adj.
spacious 183 adj.
broad 205 adj.
rotund 252 adj.
indiscriminate
464 adj.

globe
whole 52 n.
sphere 252 n.
universe 321 n.
world 321 n.
map 551 n.

globe-trotter
traveller 268 n.
spectator 441 n.

globule
sphere 252 n.

glockenspiel
gong 414 n.

gloom
darkness 418 n.
dimness 419 n.
adversity 731 n.
sorrow 825 n.
dejection 834 n.

**gloom and
doom**
dejection 834 n.

gloomy
dark 418 adj.
black 428 adj.
cheerless 834 adj.
dejected 834 adj.
melancholic
834 adj.
sullen 893 adj.

glorified
ostentatious
875 adj.

glorify
augment 36 vb.
dignify 866 vb.
honour 866 vb.
praise 923 vb.
worship 981 vb.

glorious
great 32 adj.
excellent 644 adj.
super 644 adj.
halcyon 730 adj.
splendid 841 adj.
noteworthy
866 adj.
renowned 866 adj.
worshipful
866 adj.

glory
success 727 n.
fame 866 n.
honours 866 n.
prestige 866 n.
divine attribute
965 n.

gloss
smoothness 258 n.
light 417 n.
reflection 417 n.
maxim 496 n.
commentary
520 n.
interpret 520 vb.
sham 542 n.
untruth 543 n.
facilitate 701 vb.
beauty 841 n.
ostentation 875 n.
extenuate 927 vb.
justify 927 vb.
vindication 927 n.

glossary
word list 87 n.

commentary
520 n.
dictionary 559 n.

gloss over
neglect 458 vb.
use sophistry
477 vb.
mislead 495 vb.
conceal 525 vb.
fake 541 vb.
plead 614 vb.
extenuate 927 vb.

glossy
luminous 417 adj.
personable
841 adj.

glove
glove 228 n.
love token 889 n.

glow
be hot 379 vb.
heat 379 n.
glow 417 n.
shine 417 vb.
hue 425 n.
redden 431 vb.
vigour 571 n.
warm feeling
818 n.

glower
gaze 438 vb.
be angry 891 vb.
sullenness 893 n.

glowering
angry 891 adj.
sullen 893 adj.

glucose
food content
301 n.
sweet thing 392 n.

glue
join 45 vb.
adhesive 47 n.
glutinousness
354 n.

glue-sniffing
drug-taking 949 n.

glum
melancholic
834 adj.

glut
productiveness
171 n.
redundancy 637 n.
be overabundant
637 vb.
superfluity 637 n.
cheapness 812 n.
satiate 863 vb.
satiation 863 n.

gluten
glutinousness

354 n.

glutton
glutton 947 n.

gluttony
vice 934 n.
gluttony 947 n.

glycerine
lubricant 334 n.
fat 357 n.

gnarled
distorted 246 adj.
rough 259 adj.
dense 324 adj.

gnash
rub 333 vb.

**gnash one's
teeth**
gesticulate 547 vb.
regret 830 vb.
be angry 891 vb.

gnat
small thing 33 n.
insect 365 n.

gnaw
lessen 37 vb.
rend 46 vb.
chew 301 vb.
give pain 377 vb.
hurt 827 vb.
enrage 891 vb.

gnome
elf 970 n.

gnostic
religionist 973 n.
heretic 977 n.
heretical 977 adj.
sectarian 978 adj.
sectarian 978 n.

gnu
mammal 365 n.

go
pass away 2 vb.
period 110 n.
periodic recurrence
141 n.
operate 173 vb.
vigorousness
174 n.
be in motion
265 vb.
travel 267 vb.
walk 267 vb.
recede 290 vb.
excrete 302 vb.
disappear 446 vb.
vigour 571 n.
function 622 vb.
restlessness 678 n.
board game 837 n.
courage 855 n.

go about
undertake 672 vb.

goad
stimulant 174 n.
sharp point 256 n.
impel 279 vb.
incentive 612 n.
incite 612 vb.
hasten 680 vb.
animate 821 vb.
stimulator 821 n.
excite 821 vb.
engage 891 vb.

go against
counteract 182 vb.
oppose 704 vb.

**go against the
grain**
be difficult
700 vb.
displease 827 vb.
cause dislike
861 vb.

go-ahead
vigorous 174 adj.
progressive
285 adj.
assent 488 n.
enterprising
672 adj.
permit 756 vb.

goal
limit 236 n.
goal 295 n.
objective 617 n.
attempt 671 n.
success 727 n.
desired object
859 n.

go along with
concur 181 vb.
assent 488 vb.
consent 758 vb.

goat
goat 365 n.
libertine 952 n.

go back
revert 148 vb.
turn round
282 vb.
turn back 286 vb.
recede 290 vb.

go back on
recant 603 vb.
not observe
769 vb.

gobbet
small thing 33 n.

gobbledygook
lack of meaning
515 n.
neologism 560 n.
slang 560 adj.

gobble (up)
consume 165 vb.

discord 411 vb.
cause dislike
861 vb.
grateful
grateful 907 adj.
grater
roughness 259 n.
porousness 263 n.
grinder 332 n.
gratification
pleasure 376 n.
enjoyment 824 n.
gratify
please 826 vb.
grating
disagreeing 25 adj.
network 222 n.
strident 407 adj.
discordant
411 adj.
inelegant 576 adj.
gratis
free 744 adj.
given 781 adj.
free of charge
812 adj.
gratitude
gratitude 907 n.
gratuitous
voluntary 597 adj.
given 781 adj.
free of charge
812 adj.
gratuity
extra 40 n.
incentive 612 n.
acquisition 771 n.
gift 781 n.
what is not due
916 n.
reward 962 n.
grave
great 32 adj.
place 185 n.
excavation 255 n.
tomb 364 n.
engrave 555 vb.
forceful 571 adj.
important 638 adj.
inexcitable
823 adj.
serious 834 adj.
heinous 934 adj.
hell 972 n.
gravedigger
interment 364 n.
church officer
986 n.
gravel
paving 226 n.
powder 332 n.
soil 344 n.

confute 479 vb.
building material
631 n.
graveyard
cemetery 364 n.
holy place 990 n.
gravitate
descend 309 vb.
gravitation
tendency 179 n.
gravity 322 n.
gravity
gravity 322 n.
vigour 571 n.
importance 638 n.
seriousness 834 n.
purity 950 n.
gravy
sauce 389 n.
acquisition 771 n.
money 797 n.
graze
be contiguous
202 vb.
shallowness
212 n.
collide 279 vb.
collision 279 n.
eat 301 vb.
feed 301 vb.
graze 301 vb.
friction 333 n.
rub 333 vb.
give pain 377 vb.
touch 378 n.
touch 378 vb.
wound 655 vb.
grazing
eating 301 n.
feeding 301 adj.
grassland 348 n.
stock farm 369 n.
tactile 378 adj.
grease
adhesive 47 n.
coat 226 vb.
smooth 258 vb.
smoother 258 n.
soften 327 vb.
softness 327 n.
lubricant 334 n.
lubricate 334 vb.
fat 357 n.
grease 357 vb.
make unclean
649 vb.
greasepaint
stage set 594 n.
cosmetic 843 n.
greasy
smooth 258 adj.
dirty 649 adj.

great
great 32 adj.
excellent 644 adj.
super 644 adj.
renowned 866 adj.
great day
important matter
638 n.
special day 876 n.
greatest
great 32 adj.
supreme 34 adj.
greatest, the
exceller 644 n.
great man *or*
woman
bigwig 638 n.
person of repute
866 n.
greatness
largeness 32 n.
prestige 866 n.
greed
rapacity 786 n.
avarice 816 n.
desire 859 n.
selfishness 932 n.
gluttony 947 n.
greedy
greedy 859 adj.
envious 912 adj.
gluttonous
947 adj.
green
new 126 adj.
young 130 adj.
park 192 n.
vomiting 300 n.
grassland 348 n.
sour 393 adj.
green 434 adj.
credulous 487 adj.
ignorant 491 adj.
remembered
505 adj.
unaccustomed
611 adj.
preserver 666 n.
immature 670 adj.
unskilled 695 adj.
artless 699 adj.
innocent 935 adj.
green belt
space 183 n.
district 184 n.
plain 348 n.
preservation
666 n.
greenery
foliage 366 n.
greenness 434 n.
green fingers
agriculture 370 n.

aptitude 694 n.
greengrocer
tradespeople
794 n.
greenhorn
ignoramus 493 n.
ninny 501 n.
beginner 538 n.
dupe 544 n.
bungler 697 n.
greenhouse
arbour 194 n.
brittleness 330 n.
garden 370 n.
heater 383 n.
green light
signal light 420 n.
assent 488 n.
signal 547 n.
permit 756 n.
green man
traffic control
305 n.
refuge 662 n.
greet
meet 295 vb.
weep 836 vb.
greet 884 vb.
greeting
arrival 295 n.
address 583 n.
friendliness 880 n.
sociability 882 n.
courteous act
884 n.
gregarious
sociable 882 adj.
gremlin
badness 645 n.
failure 728 n.
elf 970 n.
grenade
bomb 723 n.
grey
median 30 adj.
horse 273 n.
dim 419 adj.
dimness 419 n.
grey 429 adj.
greyness 429 n.
neutral 625 adj.
middling 732 adj.
cheerless 834 adj.
grey area
uncertainty 474 n.
grid
correlation 12 n.
electronics 160 n.
network 222 n.
griddle
cook 301 vb.
gridiron
horizontality

216 n.
network 222 n.
bicycle 274 n.
gridlock
cessation 145 n.
state of rest 266 n.
inaction 677 n.
grief
evil 616 n.
sorrow 825 n.
discontent 829 n.
grievance
evil 616 n.
annoyance 827 n.
discontent 829 n.
wrong 914 n.
grieve
farmer 370 n.
suffer 825 vb.
hurt 827 vb.
be dejected
834 vb.
sadden 834 vb.
lament 836 vb.
pity 905 vb.
grievous
bad 645 adj.
distressing
827 adj.
grievous bodily
harm
attack 712 n.
grill
cook 301 vb.
be hot 379 vb.
heater 383 n.
interrogate 459 vb.
grille
network 222 n.
window 263 n.
grim
resolute 599 adj.
obstinate 602 adj.
not nice 645 adj.
distressing
827 adj.
serious 834 adj.
frightening
854 adj.
sullen 893 adj.
cruel 898 adj.
grimace
distort 246 vb.
distortion 246 n.
agitation 318 n.
glance 438 n.
gesticulate 547 vb.
gesture 547 n.
discontent 829 n.
make ugly 842 vb.
dislike 861 vb.
sullenness 893 n.

rejoicing 835 n.
celebration 876 n.
hymn 981 n.
hallmark
label 547 n.
hallowed
divine 965 adj.
Hallowe'en
sorcery 983 n.
hallucination
lacking substance
4 n.
appearance 445 n.
error 495 n.
fantasy 513 n.
deception 542 n.
hallway
access 624 n.
halo
loop 250 n.
light 417 n.
honours 866 n.
halt
end 69 n.
be discontinuous
72 vb.
cease 145 vb.
halt 145 vb.
stop 145 n.
stopping place
145 n.
be weak 163 vb.
crippled 163 adj.
state of rest 266 n.
stop 266 int.
goal 295 n.
railway 624 n.
failure 728 n.
halter
fetter 748 n.
halting
incomplete 55 adj.
fitful 142 adj.
slow 278 adj.
inelegant 576 adj.
halve
sunder 46 vb.
divide 92 vb.
allocate 783 vb.
halves
portion 783 n.
ham
leg 267 n.
meat 301 n.
ignorant 491 adj.
act 594 vb.
actor 594 n.
be unskilful
695 vb.
unskilled 695 adj.
bungler 697 n.
wit 839 n.

be affected 850 vb.
hamburger
dish 301 n.
meal 301 n.
hamlet
district 184 n.
housing 192 n.
hammer
hammer 279 n.
strike 279 vb.
missile 287 n.
be loud 400 vb.
tool 630 n.
strike at 712 vb.
club 723 n.
**hammer and
tongs**
be violent 176 vb.
knock 279 n.
**hammer away
at**
persevere 600 vb.
hammer in
affix 45 vb.
hammering
recurrence 106 n.
repeated 106 adj.
impulse 279 n.
knock 279 n.
hammock
hanging object
217 n.
bed 218 n.
hamper
basket 194 n.
impair 655 vb.
be difficult
700 vb.
hinder 702 vb.
restrain 747 vb.
hamster
animal 365 n.
hamstring
disable 161 vb.
hinder 702 vb.
hand
limb 53 n.
bunch 74 n.
timekeeper 117 n.
measurement of
length 203 n.
laterality 239 n.
pass 305 vb.
person 371 n.
feeler 378 n.
identification
547 n.
indicator 547 n.
instrument 628 n.
doer 676 n.
worker 686 n.
servant 742 n.

pincers 778 n.
hand (at cards)
group 74 n.
portion 783 n.
hand back
restore 656 vb.
handbag
bag 194 n.
handbook
guidebook 524 n.
handcuff
tie 45 vb.
bond 47 n.
arrest 747 n.
fetter 747 vb.
fetter 748 n.
hand down
transfer 272 vb.
handful
small quantity
33 n.
bunch 74 n.
contents 193 n.
difficulty 700 n.
hard task 700 n.
handicap
equalize 28 vb.
advantage 34 n.
inferiority 35 n.
retard 278 vb.
illness 651 n.
difficulty 700 n.
encumbrance
702 n.
hinder 702 vb.
obstacle 702 n.
contest 716 n.
handicapped
crippled 163 adj.
hindered 702 adj.
handicraft
business 622 n.
ornamental art
844 n.
**hand in glove
(with)**
cooperative
706 adj.
friendly 880 adj.
hand in hand
with 89 adv.
hand it to
be inferior 35 vb.
approve 923 vb.
praise 923 vb.
handiwork
effect 157 n.
product 164 n.
deed 676 n.
ornamental art
844 n.
handkerchief
cloth 648 n.

handle
handle 218 n.
opener 263 n.
touch 378 vb.
name 561 n.
dissertate 591 vb.
deal with 688 vb.
manage 689 vb.
trade 791 vb.
honours 866 n.
title 870 n.
handless
crippled 163 adj.
clumsy 695 adj.
hand-made
non-uniform
17 adj.
hand-me-downs
clothing 228 n.
hand on
transfer 272 vb.
hand out
provide 633 vb.
handout
report 524 n.
advertisement
528 n.
news 529 n.
incentive 612 n.
monetary help
703 n.
gift 781 n.
hand over
transfer 272 vb.
pass 305 vb.
relinquish 621 vb.
resign 753 vb.
assign 780 vb.
give 781 vb.
hand over fist
swiftly 277 adv.
handsel
initiate 68 vb.
security 767 n.
gift 781 n.
handshake
arrival 295 n.
gesture 547 n.
friendliness 880 n.
sociability 882 n.
courteous act
884 n.
handsome
liberal 813 adj.
beautiful 841 adj.
hand's turn
labour 682 n.
**hand-to-mouth
existence**
poverty 801 n.
handwriting
lettering 586 n.

writing 586 n.
handy
little 196 adj.
near 200 adj.
light 323 adj.
useful 640 adj.
skilful 694 adj.
handyman
mender 656 n.
proficient person
696 n.
servant 742 n.
hang
hang 217 vb.
suspension 217 n.
kill 362 vb.
curse 899 int.
execute 963 vb.
hang (a picture)
show 522 vb.
hang about
wait 136 vb.
be in motion
265 vb.
be inactive
679 vb.
hangar
stable 192 n.
air travel 271 n.
hang around
expect 507 n.
hang back
be late 136 vb.
avoid 620 vb.
refuse 760 vb.
be modest 874 vb.
**hang by a
thread**
be uncertain
474 vb.
be in danger
661 vb.
hangdog
guilty 936 adj.
hang down
hang 217 vb.
descend 309 vb.
hanger
hanger 217 n.
hanger-on
successor 67 n.
concomitant 89 n.
follower 284 n.
dependant 742 n.
toady 879 n.
flatterer 925 n.
hang fire
wait 136 vb.
pause 145 vb.
move slowly
278 vb.

heartstrings
mental state
817 n.
heartthrob
a beauty 841 n.
loved one 887 n.
heart-warming
pleasant 376 adj.
pleasurable
826 adj.
hearty
vigorous 174 adj.
healthy 650 adj.
feeling 818 adj.
cheerful 833 adj.
friendly 880 adj.
sociable 882 adj.
heat
part 53 n.
heat 379 n.
heat 381 vb.
contest 716 n.
sexual urge 859 n.
anger 891 n.
heated
hot 379 adj.
heated 381 adj.
heater
heater 383 n.
heath
desert 172 n.
plain 348 n.
wood 366 n.
heathen
unbeliever 486 n.
heathen 974 n.
heathenish
974 adj.
heresy 977 n.
heretical 977 adj.
heather
plant 366 n.
purpleness 436 n.
Heath Robinson
imaginative
513 adj.
heating
heating 381 adj.
heating 381 n.
heave
carry 273 vb.
impel 279 vb.
impulse 279 n.
propel 287 vb.
draw 288 vb.
vomit 300 vb.
oscillate 317 vb.
breathe 352 vb.
exertion 682 n.
work 682 vb.
show feeling
818 vb.

heaven
summit 213 n.
heaven 971 n.
mythical heaven
971 n.
heavenly
celestial 321 adj.
super 644 adj.
pleasurable
826 adj.
divine 965 adj.
heaven-sent
opportune 137 adj.
good 615 adj.
heave to
bring to rest
266 vb.
navigate 269 vb.
heavy
substantial 3 adj.
great 32 adj.
strong 162 adj.
inert 175 adj.
alcoholic drink
301 n.
weighty 322 adj.
dense 324 adj.
the press 528 n.
forceful 571 adj.
bad 645 adj.
inactive 679 adj.
laborious 682 adj.
severe 735 adj.
tedious 838 adj.
dull 840 adj.
heavy-going
serious 834 adj.
heavy-handed
violent 176 adj.
weighty 322 adj.
oppressive 735 adj.
heavy-hearted
unhappy 825 adj.
melancholic
834 adj.
heavyweight
athlete 162 n.
weighty 322 adj.
bigwig 638 n.
boxer 722 n.
heavy with
impending
155 adj.
pregnant 167 adj.
prolific 171 adj.
hecatomb
religious offering
981 n.
heckle
interrogate 459 vb.
be obstructive
702 vb.

torment 827 vb.
not respect 921 vb.
disapprove 924 vb.
hector
boast 877 vb.
be insolent
878 vb.
threaten 900 vb.
hedge
partition 231 n.
edge 234 n.
fence 235 n.
wood 366 n.
screen 421 n.
avoid 620 vb.
shelter 662 n.
obstacle 702 n.
defend 713 vb.
be cautious
858 vb.
hedgehog
mammal 365 n.
hedonism
pleasure 376 n.
philosophy 449 n.
enjoyment 824 n.
sensualism 944 n.
heed
attention 455 n.
be attentive
455 vb.
be careful 457 vb.
carefulness 457 n.
obey 739 vb.
observe 768 vb.
caution 858 n.
heedless
inattentive
456 adj.
negligent 458 adj.
forgetful 506 adj.
rash 857 adj.
heel
foot 214 n.
be oblique 220 vb.
rear 238 n.
repair 656 vb.
cad 938 n.
hefty
stalwart 162 adj.
heifer
young creature
132 n.
cattle 365 n.
female animal
373 n.
height
height 209 n.
high land 209 n.
*weights and meas-
ures* 465 n.
heighten
augment 36 vb.

enlarge 197 vb.
make higher
209 vb.
elevate 310 vb.
exaggerate 546 vb.
aggravate 832 vb.
heinous
bad 645 adj.
heinous 934 adj.
heir
successor 67 n.
descendant 170 n.
deputy 755 n.
recipient 782 n.
rich person 800 n.
what is due 915 n.
heir apparent
deputy 755 n.
beneficiary 776 n.
heiress
descendant 170 n.
rich person 800 n.
heirloom
archaism 127 n.
dowry 777 n.
held
credible 485 adj.
orthodox 976 adj.
held up
late 136 adj.
hindered 702 adj.
restrained 747 adj.
helical
coiled 251 adj.
helicopter
aircraft 276 n.
heliograph
signal 547 n.
signal 547 vb.
helix
coil 251 n.
circuitous motion
314 n.
hell
pain 377 n.
bane 659 n.
suffering 825 n.
hell 972 n.
hell-bent
volitional 595 adj.
rash 857 adj.
hellish
damnable 645 adj.
cruel 898 adj.
heinous 934 adj.
wicked 934 adj.
diabolic 969 adj.
helm
sailing aid 269 n.
tool 630 n.
helmet
headgear 228 n.

heraldry 547 n.
armour 713 n.
help
concur 181 vb.
benefit 615 vb.
be instrumental
628 vb.
instrument 628 n.
utility 640 n.
be expedient
642 vb.
do good 644 vb.
cleaner 648 n.
remedy 658 n.
remedy 658 vb.
facilitate 701 vb.
aid 703 n.
aid 703 vb.
helper 703 n.
minister to
703 vb.
servant 742 n.
give 781 vb.
helper
helper 703 n.
auxiliary 707 n.
servant 742 n.
friend 880 n.
benefactor 903 n.
helpful
willing 597 adj.
good 615 adj.
instrumental
628 adj.
useful 640 adj.
remedial 658 adj.
helping 703 adj.
cooperative
706 adj.
benevolent
897 adj.
helpfulness
willingness 597 n.
aid 703 n.
cooperation 706 n.
benevolence 897 n.
helping
meal 301 n.
provisions 301 n.
provision 633 n.
portion 783 n.
helpless
impotent 161 adj.
vulnerable
661 adj.
help-line
helper 703 n.
help oneself
take 786 vb.
steal 788 vb.
helter-skelter
swiftly 277 adv.

hotel
inn 192 n.
hotelier
caterer 633 n.
hotfoot
hasty 680 adj.
hot-headed
hasty 680 adj.
fervent 818 adj.
excitable 822 adj.
rash 857 adj.
hothouse
invigorate 174 vb.
arbour 194 n.
garden 370 n.
heater 383 n.
hot line
telecommunication
531 n.
hotpot
dish 301 n.
hot potato
difficulty 700 n.
hot seat
predicament
700 n.
hot under the
collar
excited 821 adj.
angry 891 adj.
hot up
heat 381 vb.
hot water
heat 379 n.
predicament
700 n.
hound
dog 365 n.
hunter 619 n.
be hostile 881 vb.
be malevolent
898 vb.
not respect 921 vb.
disapprove 924 vb.
defame 926 vb.
hour
juncture 8 n.
period 110 n.
hourglass
timekeeper 117 n.
contraction 198 n.
curved 248 adj.
house
race 11 n.
genealogy 169 n.
place 187 vb.
abode 192 n.
house 192 n.
music 412 n.
onlookers 441 n.
class 538 n.
theatregoer 594 n.

safeguard 660 vb.
sovereign 741 vb.
house arrest
detention 747 n.
seclusion 883 n.
house-breaking
stealing 788 n.
household
family 11 n.
group 74 n.
home 192 n.
known 490 adj.
usual 610 adj.
household name
fame 866 n.
housekeeper
resident 191 n.
caterer 633 n.
manager 690 n.
domestic 742 n.
retainer 742 n.
servant 742 n.
keeper 749 n.
housekeeping
management
689 n.
housemaid
domestic 742 n.
houseman
doctor 658 n.
house of cards
weak thing 163 n.
housetop
apex 213 n.
roof 226 n.
housewarming
start 68 n.
festivity 837 n.
social gathering
882 n.
housewife
resident 191 n.
case 194 n.
female 373 n.
caterer 633 n.
manager 690 n.
housework
labour 682 n.
housing
housing 192 n.
frame 218 n.
dressing 228 n.
hover
vary 152 vb.
impend 155 vb.
be high 209 vb.
hang 217 vb.
be in motion
265 vb.
wander 267 vb.
fly 271 vb.
move slowly

278 vb.
approach 289 vb.
be light 323 vb.
be uncertain
474 vb.
be irresolute
601 vb.
threaten 900 vb.
how-do-you-do
complexity 61 n.
howl
blow 352 vb.
be loud 400 vb.
loudness 400 n.
cry 408 n.
cry 408 vb.
howl 409 n.
lament 836 n.
weep 836 vb.
howler
mistake 495 n.
absurdity 497 n.
hoydenish
ill-bred 847 adj.
hub
middle 70 n.
focus 76 n.
centre 225 n.
wheel 250 n.
chief thing 638 n.
hubbub
turmoil 61 n.
commotion 318 n.
loudness 400 n.
quarrel 709 n.
huddle
congregate 74 vb.
crowd 74 n.
make smaller
198 vb.
conference 584 n.
advice 691 n.
hue
character 5 n.
hue 425 n.
hue and cry
cry 408 n.
call 547 n.
chase 619 n.
huff
breathe 352 vb.
huff 891 vb.
resentment 891 n.
huffy
irascible 892 adj.
hug
cohere 48 vb.
make smaller
198 vb.
surround 230 vb.
enclose 235 vb.
gesture 547 n.

retain 778 vb.
retention 778 n.
friendliness 880 n.
courteous act
884 n.
greet 884 vb.
caress 889 vb.
endearment 889 n.
huge
huge 195 adj.
hugely
greatly 32 vb.
hulk
chief part 52 n.
bulk 195 n.
ship 275 n.
be clumsy 695 vb.
bungler 697 n.
hulking
stalwart 162 adj.
unwieldy 195 adj.
clumsy 695 adj.
graceless 842 adj.
hull
chief part 52 n.
skin 226 n.
uncover 229 vb.
ship 275 n.
hullabaloo
turmoil 61 n.
loudness 400 n.
cry 408 n.
hullo
welcome 295 int.
hum
rotate 315 vb.
blow 352 vb.
stink 397 vb.
faintness 401 n.
sound faint
401 vb.
roll 403 n.
roll 403 vb.
resound 404 vb.
shrill 407 vb.
howl 409 n.
howling 409 n.
sing 413 vb.
voice 577 n.
activity 678 n.
be active 678 vb.
human
animal 365 adj.
benevolent
897 adj.
philanthropic
901 adj.
morally weak
934 adj.
human being
humankind 371 n.
person 371 n.

hum and haw
stammer 580 vb.
be irresolute
601 vb.
humane
benevolent
897 adj.
philanthropic
901 adj.
pitying 905 adj.
humanism
anthropology
371 n.
philosophy 449 n.
philanthropy
901 n.
morals 917 n.
lack of religion
974 n.
humanitarian
benevolent
897 adj.
philanthropic
901 adj.
philanthropist
901 n.
humanities
culture 490 n.
literature 557 n.
humanity
humankind 371 n.
leniency 736 n.
benevolence 897 n.
philanthropy
901 n.
pity 905 n.
humankind
humankind 371 n.
humble
inconsiderable
33 adj.
abase 311 vb.
plebeian 869 adj.
humble 872 adj.
humiliate 872 vb.
humbug
empty talk 515 n.
falsehood 541 n.
fable 543 n.
impostor 545 n.
pretension 850 n.
humdrum
tedious 838 adj.
humid
humid 341 adj.
humidifier
air 340 n.
humidify
moisten 341 vb.
humidity
water 339 n.
moisture 341 n.

humiliate
humiliate 872 vb.
humiliation
humiliation 872 n.
indignity 921 n.
contempt 922 n.
humility
humility 872 n.
humming
multitudinous
104 adj.
fetid 397 adj.
howling 409 n.
busy 678 adj.
humorist
humorist 839 n.
humorous
laughing 835 adj.
witty 839 adj.
funny 849 adj.
humour
temperament 5 n.
state 7 n.
composition 56 n.
tendency 179 n.
fluid 335 n.
whim 604 n.
minister to
703 vb.
be lenient 736 vb.
mental state
817 n.
laughter 835 n.
amuse 837 vb.
wit 839 n.
flatter 925 vb.
humourless
serious 834 adj.
dull 840 adj.
hump
camber 253 n.
carry 273 vb.
work 682 vb.
humpback
obliqueness 220 n.
camber 253 n.
hunch
intuition 476 n.
spontaneity 609 n.
hundred
hundred 99 n.
district 184 n.
hung
appearing 445 adj.
hunger
be hungry 859 vb.
desire 859 n.
hunger 859 n.
hunger strike
deprecation 762 n.
fast 946 n.
fasting 946 n.

hungry
poor 801 adj.
hungry 859 adj.
hungry for
inquisitive
453 adj.
hunk
piece 53 n.
bulk 195 n.
a beauty 841 n.
hunkers
buttocks 238 n.
hunt
rider 268 n.
search 459 n.
chase 619 n.
hunt 619 vb.
pursue 619 vb.
amuse oneself
837 vb.
hunter
timekeeper 117 n.
horse 273 n.
hunter 619 n.
hunting
killing 362 n.
chase 619 n.
pursuit 619 n.
hurdle
bed 218 n.
fence 235 n.
vehicle 274 n.
leap 312 vb.
obstacle 702 n.
hurl
propel 287 vb.
hurl oneself
be violent 176 vb.
hurly-burly
turmoil 61 n.
commotion 318 n.
hurrah
cry 408 n.
cry 408 vb.
shout 408 vb.
cheers 835 int.
rejoice 835 vb.
rejoicing 835 n.
bravo 923 int.
hurricane
turmoil 61 n.
storm 176 n.
velocity 277 n.
gale 352 n.
hurry
move fast 277 vb.
velocity 277 n.
activity 678 n.
be active 678 vb.
haste 680 n.
hasten 680 vb.
hurt
weaken 163 vb.

give pain 377 vb.
pain 377 n.
evil 616 n.
badness 645 n.
impair 655 vb.
hurt 827 vb.
resentful 891 adj.
be malevolent
898 vb.
do wrong 914 adj.
hurtful
harmful 645 adj.
causing pain
827 adj.
hurtle
be violent 176 vb.
move fast 277 vb.
**hurt the feel-
ings**
hurt 827 vb.
husband
male 372 n.
store 632 vb.
spouse 894 n.
husbandry
agriculture 370 n.
management
689 n.
economy 814 n.
hush
assuage 177 vb.
bring to rest
266 vb.
quietness 266 n.
hush 399 int.
silence 399 n.
silence 399 vb.
mute 401 vb.
make mute
578 vb.
hush-hush
occult 523 adj.
concealed 525 adj.
important 638 adj.
husk
remainder 41 n.
skin 226 n.
grass 366 n.
husky
stalwart 162 adj.
beast of burden
273 n.
dog 365 n.
hoarse 407 adj.
beautiful 841 adj.
hussy
female 373 n.
insolent person
878 n.
bad person 938 n.
loose woman
952 n.

hustings
publicity 528 n.
vote 605 n.
arena 724 n.
lawcourt 956 n.
hustle
move 265 vb.
accelerate 277 vb.
impel 279 vb.
propel 287 vb.
activity 678 n.
haste 680 n.
hasten 680 vb.
hustler
trickster 545 n.
busy person 678 n.
defrauder 789 n.
prostitute 952 n.
hut
dwelling 192 n.
small house
192 n.
hutch
stable 192 n.
receptacle 194 n.
cattle pen 369 n.
hyacinth
plant 366 n.
gem 844 n.
hybrid
hybrid 43 n.
mixed 43 adj.
abnormal 84 adj.
neologism 560 n.
hydrant
water 339 n.
water channel
351 n.
extinguisher
382 n.
hydro
inn 192 n.
hospital 658 n.
hydrolysis
decomposition
51 n.
hyena
eater 301 n.
mammal 365 n.
hygiene
washing 648 n.
hygiene 652 n.
hygrometer
weather 340 n.
meter 465 n.
recording instru-
ment 549 n.
hymn
hymn 981 n.
hymnal
musical 412 adj.
scripture 975 n.

hymnbook 988 n.
church utensil
990 n.
hymnary
hymnbook 988 n.
church utensil
990 n.
hymnbook
vocal music 412 n.
hymn 981 n.
hymnbook 988 n.
hype
overestimate
482 vb.
overestimation
482 n.
advertisement
528 n.
publicity 528 n.
exaggeration
546 n.
make better
654 vb.
boast 877 n.
boasting 877 n.
flatter 925 vb.
hyperactive
psychotic 503 adj.
active 678 adj.
hyperbola
curve 248 n.
hyperbole
expansion 197 n.
figure of speech
519 n.
exaggeration
546 n.
grandiloquence
574 n.
hypercritical
narrow-minded
481 adj.
severe 735 adj.
discontented
829 adj.
fastidious 862 adj.
disapproving
924 adj.
hype up
advertise 528 vb.
exaggerate 546 vb.
praise 923 vb.
hyphen
bond 47 n.
punctuation
547 n.
hypnosis
insensitivity
375 n.
sleep 679 n.
occultism 984 n.
hypnotism
influence 178 n.

820 vb.
be rude 885 vb.
not respect 921 vb.
hold cheap
   922 vb.
disapprove 924 vb.
iguana
reptile 365 n.
ilk
sort 77 n.
ill
evil 616 n.
badly 645 adv.
badness 645 n.
sick 651 adj.
suffering 825 adj.
ill-assorted
disagreeing 25 adj.
ill at ease
suffering 825 adj.
ill-bred
ill-bred 847 adj.
ill-conceived
rash 857 adj.
ill-defined
formless 244 adj.
shadowy 419 adj.
illegal
illegal 954 adj.
illegible
unintelligible
   517 adj.
illegitimate
wrong 914 adj.
unwarranted
   916 adj.
illegitimate
   954 adj.
illegal 954 adj.
ill-fated
unfortunate
   731 adj.
ill-gotten gains
taking 786 n.
booty 790 n.
illicit
prohibited 757 adj.
wrong 914 adj.
unwarranted
   916 adj.
dishonest 930 adj.
illegal 954 adj.
ill-informed
uninstructed
   491 adj.
mistaken 495 adj.
illiterate
ignorance 491 n.
uninstructed
   491 adj.
ignoramus 493 n.
ill-mannered
ill-bred 847 adj.

impertinent
   878 adj.
discourteous
   885 adj.
ill-natured
malevolent
   898 adj.
unkind 898 adj.
illness
illness 651 n.
illogical
irrelevant 10 adj.
illogical 477 adj.
illogicality
sophistry 477 n.
folly 499 n.
ill repute
disrepute 867 n.
ill-spent
profitless 641 adj.
ill-treat
ill-treat 645 vb.
be severe 735 vb.
illuminate
make bright
   417 vb.
colour 425 vb.
interpret 520 vb.
paint 553 vb.
decorate 844 vb.
illumination
light 417 n.
lighting 420 n.
discovery 484 n.
knowledge 490 n.
interpretation
   520 n.
art 551 n.
painting 553 n.
ornamental art
   844 n.
revelation 975 n.
illusion
appearance 445 n.
error 495 n.
deception 542 n.
sleight of hand
   542 n.
illusory
erroneous 495 adj.
imaginary
   513 adj.
deceiving 542 adj.
illustrate
exemplify 83 vb.
interpret 520 vb.
represent 551 vb.
decorate 844 vb.
illustration
example 83 n.
interpretation
   520 n.

representation
   551 n.
picture 553 n.
edition 589 n.
ornamental art
   844 n.
illustrator
artist 556 n.
illustrious
noteworthy
   866 adj.
renowned 866 adj.
ill will
badness 645 n.
adversity 731 n.
enmity 881 n.
hatred 888 n.
malevolence
   898 n.
envy 912 n.
image
copy 22 n.
appearance 445 n.
conception 513 n.
show 522 vb.
indication 547 n.
image 551 n.
idol 982 n.
imagery
imagination
   513 n.
metaphor 519 n.
imaginary
imaginary
   513 adj.
**imaginary
animal**
mythical animal
   365 n.
**imaginary
being**
mythical being
   970 n.
imagination
imagination
   513 n.
imaginative
imaginative
   513 adj.
imagine
perceive 447 adj.
imagine 513 vb.
imbalance
inequality 29 n.
changeableness
   152 n.
distortion 246 n.
imbecile
weak 163 adj.
foolish 499 adj.
unintelligent
   499 adj.

fool 501 n.
*having a learning
   disability*
   503 adj.
imbibe
absorb 299 vb.
drink 301 vb.
imbue
mix 43 vb.
combine 50 vb.
pervade 189 vb.
drench 341 vb.
colour 425 vb.
educate 534 vb.
accustom oneself
   610 vb.
imitate
imitate 20 vb.
imitation
imitation 20 n.
imitative 20 adj.
substituted
   150 adj.
false 541 adj.
sham 542 n.
spurious 542 adj.
bad taste 847 n.
imitative
imitative 20 adj.
imitator
imitator 20 n.
immaculate
perfect 646 adj.
clean 648 adj.
honourable
   929 adj.
innocent 935 adj.
pure 950 adj.
immanent
inherent 5 adj.
immaterial
irrelevant 10 adj.
non-material
   320 adj.
unimportant
   639 adj.
immature
immature 670 adj.
immeasurable
infinite 107 adj.
immediacy
instantaneousness
   116 n.
punctuality 135 n.
haste 680 n.
immediate
instantaneous
   116 adj.
early 135 adj.
impending
   155 adj.
speedy 277 adj.

hasty 680 adj.
immemorial
great 32 adj.
immense
enormous 32 adj.
infinite 107 adj.
huge 195 adj.
immerse
immerse 303 vb.
plunge 313 vb.
immersion
entering 297 n.
plunge 313 n.
Christian rite
   988 n.
immigrant
extraneous 59 adj.
foreigner 59 n.
settler 191 n.
incomer 297 n.
immigrate
travel 267 vb.
enter 297 vb.
immigration
entering 297 n.
imminent
future 124 adj.
early 135 adj.
impending
   155 adj.
approaching
   289 adj.
immobile
permanent
   144 adj.
fixed 153 adj.
still 266 adj.
non-active
   677 adj.
immobilize
bring to rest
   266 vb.
make inactive
   679 vb.
immoderate
violent 176 adj.
redundant
   637 adj.
intemperate
   943 adj.
immodest
vain 873 adj.
unchaste 951 adj.
immolate
kill 362 vb.
immoral
wrong 914 adj.
dishonest 930 adj.
heinous 934 adj.
villainous 934 adj.
wicked 934 adj.
impure 951 adj.

admit 299 vb.
reception 299 n.
meaning 514 n.
importance 638 n.
importance
importance 638 n.
important
necessary 596 adj.
important 638 adj.
importation
transference 272 n.
entering 297 n.
reception 299 n.
importer
carrier 273 n.
merchant 794 n.
importunate
annoying 827 adj.
importune
request 761 vb.
torment 827 vb.
impose
place 187 vb.
print 587 vb.
necessitate 596 vb.
command 737 vb.
compel 740 vb.
command respect
  920 vb.
imposing
notable 638 adj.
impressive
  821 adj.
worshipful
  866 adj.
imposition
addition 38 n.
bane 659 n.
command 737 n.
demand 737 n.
tax 809 n.
injustice 914 n.
what is not due
  916 n.
penalty 963 n.
impossible
impossible
  470 adj.
annoying 827 adj.
intolerable
  827 adj.
wonderful 864 adj.
impostor
impostor 545 n.
bad person 938 n.
imposture
duplicity 541 n.
deception 542 n.
cunning 698 n.
impotent
impotent 161 adj.
powerless 161 adj.

unproductive
  172 adj.
impound
imprison 747 vb.
impoverished
weakened 163 adj.
poor 801 adj.
impracticable
unapt 25 adj.
impracticable
  470 adj.
useless 641 adj.
difficult 700 adj.
impractical
misjudging
  481 adj.
imaginative
  513 adj.
imprecation
entreaty 761 n.
curse 899 n.
prayers 981 n.
imprecise
inexact 495 adj.
unclear 568 adj.
impregnable
strong 162 adj.
invulnerable
  660 adj.
pure 950 adj.
impregnation
mixture 43 n.
propagation 167 n.
impresario
exhibitor 522 n.
stage manager
  594 n.
impress
effect 157 n.
make concave
  255 vb.
mark 547 vb.
engrave 555 vb.
compel 740 vb.
impress 821 vb.
impressible
soft 327 adj.
impressible
  819 adj.
impression
copy 22 n.
concavity 255 n.
sense 374 n.
spectacle 445 n.
idea 451 n.
opinion 485 n.
indication 547 n.
label 547 n.
representation
  551 n.
printing 555 n.
print 587 n.

edition 589 n.
feeling 818 n.
impressionable
sentient 374 adj.
impressible
  819 adj.
excitable 822 adj.
impressive
appearing 445 adj.
impressive
  821 adj.
impress on
emphasize 532 vb.
imprimatur
assent 488 n.
permit 756 n.
strictness of belief
  976 n.
imprint
copy 22 n.
concavity 255 n.
identification
  547 n.
label 547 n.
mark 547 vb.
imprison
imprison 747 vb.
improbable
improbable
  472 adj.
impromptu
musical piece
  412 n.
extempore
  609 adv.
spontaneity 609 n.
spontaneous
  609 adj.
unprepared
  670 adj.
improper
unapt 25 adj.
unwise 499 adj.
inexpedient
  643 adj.
not nice 645 adj.
vulgar 847 adj.
discreditable
  867 adj.
disreputable
  867 adj.
wrong 914 adj.
villainous 934 adj.
impropriety
inaptitude 25 n.
inelegance 576 n.
inexpediency
  643 n.
bad taste 847 n.
wrong 914 n.
what is not due
  916 n.

vice 934 n.
guilty act 936 n.
improve
grow 36 vb.
flourish 615 vb.
do good 644 vb.
get better 654 vb.
make better
  654 vb.
beautify 841 vb.
improvement
improvement
  654 n.
improve on
be superior 34 vb.
make better
  654 vb.
improvident
negligent 458 adj.
prodigal 815 adj.
rash 857 adj.
improvise
compose music
  413 vb.
play music
  413 vb.
improvise 609 vb.
imprudent
inexpedient
  643 adj.
rash 857 adj.
impudent
impertinent
  878 adj.
discourteous
  885 adj.
impugn
negate 533 vb.
impulse
impulse 279 n.
intuition 476 n.
necessity 596 n.
whim 604 n.
spontaneity 609 n.
motive 612 n.
feeling 818 n.
impulsive
intuitive 476 adj.
involuntary
  596 adj.
spontaneous
  609 adj.
hasty 680 adj.
excitable 822 adj.
rash 857 adj.
impunity
non-liability
  919 n.
acquittal 960 n.
impure
impure 951 adj.
impious 980 adj.

impurity
impurity 951 n.
impute
attribute 158 vb.
blame 924 vb.
accuse 928 vb.
in
inside 224 adv.
usual 610 adj.
fashionable
  848 adj.
inability
lack of power
  161 n.
uselessness 641 n.
lack of skill 695 n.
inaccessible
impracticable
  470 adj.
inaccurate
negligent 458 adj.
undiscriminating
  464 adj.
inexact 495 adj.
inactive
inactive 679 adj.
inactivity
weakness 163 n.
inactivity 679 n.
inadequate
unequal 29 adj.
incomplete 55 adj.
powerless 161 adj.
deficient 307 adj.
insufficient
  636 adj.
imperfect 647 adj.
unskilful 695 adj.
inadmissible
unapt 25 adj.
extraneous 59 adj.
inexpedient
  643 adj.
wrong 914 adj.
inadvertent
inattentive
  456 adj.
unintentional
  618 adj.
inadvisable
inexpedient
  643 adj.
inalienable
due 915 adj.
inane
lacking substance
  4 adj.
empty 190 adj.
foolish 499 adj.
meaningless
  515 adj.
feeble 572 adj.

inanimate
mindless 448 adj.
inactive 679 adj.
in a nutshell
proverbially
496 adv.
concisely 569 adv.
inapplicable
irrelevant 10 adj.
unapt 25 adj.
useless 641 adj.
inapposite
irrelevant 10 adj.
inappreciable
unimportant
639 adj.
inappropriate
unrelated 10 adj.
unapt 25 adj.
inexpedient
643 adj.
ridiculous 849 adj.
wrong 914 adj.
inaptitude
inaptitude 25 n.
in arrears
non-paying
805 adj.
inarticulate
voiceless 578 adj.
uncommunicative
582 adj.
modest 874 adj.
inartistic
bungled 695 adj.
inasmuch
concerning 9 adv.
inattentive
inattentive
456 adj.
inaudible
silent 399 adj.
muted 401 adj.
deaf 416 adj.
unintelligible
517 adj.
voiceless 578 adj.
inaugural
precursory 66 adj.
beginning 68 adj.
inaugurate
inaugurate 68 vb.
inauguration
debut 68 n.
mandate 751 n.
celebration 876 n.
inauspicious
inopportune
138 adj.
predicting 511 adj.
evil 616 adj.
adverse 731 adj.

unpromising
853 adj.
**in black and
white**
written 586 adj.
inborn
hereditary 5 adj.
*having a certain
mental state*
817 adj.
inbred
hereditary 5 adj.
external 6 adj.
ethnic 11 adj.
combined 50 adj.
*having a certain
mental state*
817 adj.
incalculable
multitudinous
104 adj.
infinite 107 adj.
casual 159 adj.
incandescent
fiery 379 adj.
luminous 417 adj.
incantation
sorcery 983 n.
spell 983 n.
incapable
powerless 161 adj.
unskilful 695 adj.
incapacitated
impotent 161 adj.
crippled 163 adj.
incarcerate
imprison 747 vb.
incarnate
material 319 adj.
materialize
319 vb.
alive 360 adj.
manifest 522 vb.
godlike 965 adj.
incarnation
essential part 5 n.
materiality 319 n.
manifestation
522 n.
representation
551 n.
revelation 975 n.
incendiary
destructive
165 adj.
violent 176 adj.
violent creature
176 n.
arson 381 n.
heating 381 adj.
evildoer 904 n.
incense
odourlessness

395 n.
scent 396 n.
honours 866 n.
enrage 891 vb.
religious offering
981 n.
ritual object
988 n.
incentive
incentive 612 n.
inception
beginning 68 n.
incessant
continuous 71 adj.
repeated 106 adj.
perpetual 115 adj.
active 678 adj.
incest
illicit love 951 n.
inch
small quantity
33 n.
short distance
200 n.
*measurement of
length* 203 n.
shortness 204 n.
move slowly
278 vb.
island 349 n.
inchworm
creepy-crawly
365 n.
incidence
event 154 n.
incident
event 154 n.
incidental
external 6 adj.
circumstantial
8 adj.
irrelevance 10 n.
irrelevant 10 adj.
unrelated 10 adj.
casual 159 adj.
liable 180 adj.
incinerate
destroy 165 vb.
inter 364 vb.
burn 381 vb.
incinerator;
furnace 383 n.
incipient
beginning 68 adj.
incise
cut 46 vb.
groove 262 vb.
wound 655 vb.
incisive
assertive 532 adj.
concise 569 adj.
incisor
tooth 256 n.

incite
cause 156 vb.
incite 612 vb.
inclement
pitiless 906 adj.
inclination
tendency 179 n.
obliqueness 220 n.
will 595 n.
willingness 597 n.
choice 605 n.
liking 859 n.
love 887 n.
incline
tend 179 vb.
be oblique 220 vb.
incline 220 n.
be curved 248 vb.
approach 289 vb.
choose 605 vb.
motivate 612 vb.
include
join 45 vb.
contain 56 vb.
comprise 78 vb.
possess 773 vb.
including
in addition
38 adv.
including 78 adv.
inclusive 78 adj.
including out
exclusion 57 n.
exclusive of
57 adv.
inclusive
in addition
38 adv.
inclusive 78 adj.
incognito
concealment
525 n.
disguised 525 adj.
secretly 525 adv.
anonymous
562 adj.
incoherent
lacking order
61 adj.
discontinuous
72 adj.
frenzied 503 adj.
meaningless
515 adj.
long-winded
570 adj.
income
means 629 n.
earnings 771 n.
estate 777 n.
receipt 807 n.
reward 962 n.

incomer
incomer 297 n.
income tax
tax 809 n.
incoming
entering 297 n.
incommode
trouble 827 vb.
**incommunica-
ble**
inexpressible
517 adj.
incommunicado
imprisoned
747 adj.
**incommunica-
tive**
uncommunicative
582 adj.
cautious 858 adj.
incomparable
inimitable 21 adj.
supreme 34 adj.
incompatible
unrelated 10 adj.
non-identical
14 adj.
disagreeing 25 adj.
hostile 881 adj.
incompetent
unapt 25 adj.
powerless 161 adj.
unintelligent
499 adj.
fool 501 n.
insufficient
636 adj.
useless 641 adj.
bad 645 adj.
unskilful 695 adj.
bungler 697 n.
illegal 954 adj.
incomplete
incomplete 55 adj.
**incomprehensi-
ble**
infinite 107 adj.
unintelligible
517 adj.
inconceivable
impossible
470 adj.
improbable
472 adj.
unintelligible
517 adj.
wonderful 864 adj.
inconclusive
poorly reasoned
477 adj.
incongruous
different 15 adj.

innocent 935 n.
ingenuous
truthful 540 adj.
artless 699 adj.
honourable
929 adj.
trustworthy
929 adj.
ingest
absorb 299 vb.
eat 301 vb.
inglenook
home 192 n.
inglorious
inglorious 867 adj.
dishonest 930 adj.
ingrained
inherent 5 adj.
combined 50 adj.
fixed 153 adj.
habitual 610 adj.
*having a certain
mental state*
817 adj.
ingrate
ingratitude 908 n.
**ingratiate one-
self**
be servile 879 vb.
ingratitude
ingratitude 908 n.
ingredient
adjunct 40 n.
tincture 43 n.
part 53 n.
component 58 adj.
component 58 n.
element 319 n.
ingredients
contents 193 n.
ingress
entering 297 n.
ingrown
firm 45 adj.
interior 224 adj.
inhabit
be present 189 vb.
live 192 vb.
possess 773 vb.
inhabitant
inhabitant 191 n.
inhalation
reception 299 n.
breathing 352 n.
inhale
absorb 299 vb.
breathe 352 vb.
smoke 388 vb.
smell 394 vb.
inharmonious
discordant
411 adj.

in heat
lecherous 951 adj
inherent
inherent 5 adj.
component 58 adj.
included 78 adj.
inherit
be inherent 5 vb.
come after 65 vb.
reproduce 166 vb.
inherit 771 vb.
receive 782 vb.
inheritance
sequel 67 n.
posterity 170 n.
acquisition 771 n.
possession 773 n.
dowry 777 n.
transfer 780 n.
receiving 782 n.
receipt 807 n.
inhibit
counteract 182 vb.
obstruct 702 vb.
restrain 747 vb.
inhibition
hindrance 702 n.
prohibition 757 n.
inhospitable
unsociable
883 adj.
unkind 898 adj.
inhuman
harmful 645 adj.
impassive 820 adj.
cruel 898 adj.
unkind 898 adj.
inhumanity
inhumanity 898 n.
misanthropy
902 n.
inimical
hostile 881 adj.
inimitable
inimitable 21 adj.
iniquitous
evil 616 adj.
unjust 914 adj.
wrong 914 adj.
wicked 934 adj.
initial
beginning 68 n.
first 68 adj.
sign 547 vb.
spell 558 vb.
initials
label 547 n.
initiate
inaugurate 68 vb.
initiate 68 vb.
admit 299 vb.
train 534 vb.

learner 538 n.
initiative
beginning 68 n.
vigorousness
174 n.
willingness 597 n.
restlessness 678 n.
inject
pierce 263 vb.
irrigate 341 vb.
practise medicine
658 vb.
injection
insertion 303 n.
medicine 658 n.
injudicious
unwise 499 adj.
inexpedient
643 adj.
rash 857 adj.
injunction
requirement 627 n.
precept 693 n.
command 737 n.
prohibition 757 n.
legal process
959 n.
injure
weaken 163 vb.
harm 645 vb.
impair 655 vb.
hurt 827 vb.
blemish 845 vb.
be malevolent
898 vb.
do wrong 914 adj.
injury
evil 616 n.
badness 645 n.
impairment 655 n.
wound 655 n.
resentment 891 n.
vice 934 n.
guilty act 936 n.
penalty 963 n.
injustice
injustice 914 n.
wrong 914 n.
guilty act 936 n.
ink
blacken 428 vb.
black thing 428 n.
inkblot test
enquiry 459 n.
inkling
knowledge 490 n.
hint 524 n.
inky
dark 418 adj.
black 428 adj.
inlaid work
chequer 437 n.

inland
interior 224 adj.
interiority 224 n.
land 344 n.
inlay
line 227 vb.
insert 303 vb.
chequer 437 n.
variegate 437 vb.
decorate 844 vb.
ornamental art
844 n.
inlet
entrance 68 n.
gap 201 n.
cavity 255 n.
way in 297 n.
gulf 345 n.
inmate
resident 191 n.
inn
inn 192 n.
innards
insides 224 n.
innate
hereditary 5 adj.
inner
interior 224 adj.
inner being
essence 1 n.
spirit 447 n.
inner city
housing 192 n.
innermost
interior 224 adj.
innings
period 110 n.
innkeeper
caterer 633 n.
innocence
ignorance 491 n.
innocence 935 n.
purity 950 n.
innocuous
moderate 177 adj.
innocent 935 adj.
innovation
originality 21 n.
beginning 68 n.
newness 126 n.
change 143 n.
production 164 n.
innovative
modern 126 adj.
new 126 adj.
enterprising
672 adj.
innuendo
latency 523 n.
hint 524 n.
censure 924 n.
detraction 926 n.

innumerable
many 104 adj.
multitudinous
104 adj.
infinite 107 adj.
innumerate
uninstructed
491 adj.
inoculate
combine 50 vb.
implant 303 vb.
practise medicine
658 vb.
safeguard 660 vb.
inoffensive
humble 872 adj.
amiable 884 adj.
innocent 935 adj.
inoperable
deadly 362 adj.
sick 651 adj.
unpromising
853 adj.
inoperative
powerless 161 adj.
unproductive
172 adj.
at rest 266 adj.
useless 641 adj.
non-active
677 adj.
inopportune
inopportune
138 adj.
inexpedient
643 adj.
inordinate
exorbitant 32 adj.
input
computing 86 n.
record 548 n.
requirement 627 n.
inquest
inquest 364 n.
enquiry 459 n.
legal trial 959 n.
inquisition
enquiry 459 n.
interrogation
459 n.
severity 735 n.
legal trial 959 n.
inquisitive
inquisitive
453 adj.
inquisitor
questioner 459 n.
tyrant 735 n.
inroad
entering 297 n.
unjustifed claim
916 n.

inrush
entering 297 n.
insalubrious
unhealthy 653 adj.
ins and outs of,
the
particulars 80 n.
insane
mentally disordered
503 adj.
insanitary
unclean 649 adj.
unhealthy 653 adj.
insanity
absence of intellect
448 n.
mental disorder
503 n.
insatiable
greedy 859 adj.
gluttonous
947 adj.
inscription
funeral rites
364 n.
indication 547 n.
monument 548 n.
record 548 n.
phrase 563 n.
script 586 n.
description 590 n.
inscrutable
unintelligible
517 adj.
impassive 820 adj.
inexcitable
823 adj.
serious 834 adj.
insect
animal 365 n.
insect 365 n.
cad 938 n.
insecticide
killer 362 n.
preventive 658 n.
poison 659 n.
insectivorous
feeding 301 adj.
insecure
unsafe 661 adj.
insemination
propagation 167 n.
insensate
thick-skinned
820 adj.
insensible
insensitive
375 adj.
insensitive
insensitive
375 adj.
unfeeling 375 adj.

undiscriminating
464 adj.
inelegant 576 adj.
impassive 820 adj.
thick-skinned
820 adj.
ill-bred 847 adj.
insentient
insensitive
375 adj.
inseparable
inherent 5 adj.
firm 45 adj.
cohesive 48 adj.
indivisible 52 adj.
concomitant 89 n.
near 200 adj.
friendly 880 adj.
insert
interjection 231 n.
insert 303 vb.
insertion 303 n.
the press 528 n.
insertion
adjunct 40 n.
piece 53 n.
insertion 303 n.
advertisement
528 n.
inset
insert 303 vb.
insertion 303 n.
edition 589 n.
ornamental art
844 n.
inshore
near 200 adj.
inside
contents 193 n.
inside 224 adv.
interior 224 adj.
interiority 224 n.
imprisoned
747 adj.
captive 750 adj.
inside job
plot 623 n.
stealing 788 n.
insider trading
or dealing
plot 623 n.
barter 791 n.
insides
component 58 n.
insides 224 n.
insidious
occult 523 adj.
deceiving 542 adj.
evil 616 adj.
cunning 698 adj.
dishonest 930 adj.
insight
intellect 447 n.

discrimination
463 n.
intuition 476 n.
knowledge 490 n.
imagination
513 n.
interpretation
520 n.
insignia
badge 547 n.
(See also **her-**
aldry.)
insignificant
inconsiderable
33 adj.
meaningless
515 adj.
unimportant
639 adj.
insincere
hypocritical
541 adj.
affected 850 adj.
flattering 925 adj.
dishonest 930 adj.
insinuate
introduce 231 vb.
imply 523 vb.
hint 524 vb.
inform 524 vb.
detract 926 vb.
insinuate one-
self
enter 297 vb.
flatter 925 vb.
insipid
weak 163 adj.
tasteless 387 adj.
feeble 572 adj.
tedious 838 adj.
dull 840 adj.
insist
emphasize 532 vb.
be resolute 599 vb.
be obstinate
602 vb.
contend 716 vb.
compel 740 vb.
insistent
assertive 532 adj.
forceful 571 adj.
resolute 599 adj.
commanding
737 adj.
insist on
qualify 468 vb.
give terms 766 vb.
insolent
insolent 878 adj.
discourteous
885 adj.
insoluble
indissoluble

324 adj.
impracticable
470 adj.
puzzling 517 adj.
insolvent
poor 801 adj.
poor person 801 n.
non-paying
805 adj.
insomnia
restlessness 678 n.
inspect
scan 438 vb.
inspection
inspection 438 n.
surveillance 457 n.
inspector
spectator 441 n.
enquirer 459 n.
estimator 480 n.
manager 690 n.
inspiration
causation 156 n.
influence 178 n.
breathing 352 n.
intuition 476 n.
intelligence 498 n.
imagination
513 n.
diffuseness 570 n.
spontaneity 609 n.
contrivance 623 n.
warm feeling
818 n.
excitation 821 n.
revelation 975 n.
piety 979 n.
inspire
cause 156 vb.
influence 178 vb.
incite 612 vb.
animate 821 vb.
make pious
979 vb.
instability
changeableness
152 n.
weakness 163 n.
excitability 822 n.
install
place 187 vb.
commission
751 vb.
dignify 866 vb.
installation
location 187 n.
celebration 876 n.
holy orders 985 n.
instance
example 83 n.
exemplify 83 vb.
instant
instant 116 n.

instantaneous
116 adj.
present 121 adj.
impending
155 adj.
ready-made
669 adj.
instantaneous
instantaneous
116 adj.
instead
instead 150 adv.
instigate
incite 612 vb.
induce 612 vb.
instil
mix 43 vb.
combine 50 vb.
educate 534 vb.
instinct
intellect 447 n.
absence of thought
450 n.
empiricism 461 n.
intuition 476 n.
necessity 596 n.
spontaneity 609 n.
habit 610 n.
non-design 618 n.
feeling 818 n.
instinctive
inherent 5 adj.
intuitive 476 adj.
involuntary
596 adj.
spontaneous
609 adj.
institute
cause 156 vb.
produce 164 vb.
academy 539 n.
corporation 708 n.
institution
beginning 68 n.
practice 610 n.
law 953 n.
institutionalize
make uniform
16 vb.
instruct
inform 524 vb.
educate 534 vb.
command 737 vb.
instruction
culture 490 n.
information
524 n.
teaching 534 n.
advice 691 n.
precept 693 n.
instructions
command 737 n.

instructive
influential
178 adj.
informative
524 adj.
educational
534 adj.
instrument
instrument 628 n.
title deed 767 n.
instrumental
musical 412 adj.
instrumental
628 adj.
instrumentalist
instrumentalist
413 n.
instrumenta-
tion
composition 56 n.
melody 410 n.
music 412 n.
musical piece
412 n.
instrumentality
628 n.
insubordinate
disobedient
738 adj.
disrespectful
921 adj.
insubstantial
lacking substance
4 adj.
insufferable
intolerable
827 adj.
insufficient
insufficient
636 adj.
insular
unrelated 10 adj.
separate 46 adj.
alone 88 adj.
narrow-minded
481 adj.
insulate
set apart 46 vb.
cover 226 vb.
line 227 vb.
be hot 379 vb.
heat 381 vb.
safeguard 660 vb.
insulated
heated 381 adj.
insulation
lining 227 n.
insult
annoyance 827 n.
hurt 827 vb.
slur 867 n.
sauciness 878 n.

be rude 885 vb.
rudeness 885 n.
huff 891 vb.
resentment 891 n.
scurrility 899 n.
indignity 921 n.
not respect 921 vb.
calumny 926 n.
insuperable
impracticable
470 adj.
difficult 700 adj.
insurance
protection 660 n.
promise 764 n.
security 767 n.
caution 858 n.
insurance
policy
title deed 767 n.
insure
prepare 669 vb.
promise 764 vb.
contract 765 vb.
give security
767 vb.
be cautious
858 vb.
insurgent
rebel 738 n.
insurmountable
impracticable
470 adj.
insurrection
resistance 715 n.
revolt 738 n.
intact
intact 52 adj.
undamaged
646 adj.
safe 660 adj.
intake
size 195 n.
entering 297 n.
reception 299 n.
requirement 627 n.
intangible
unreal 2 adj.
non-material
320 adj.
integer
whole 52 n.
number 85 n.
unit 88 n.
integral
inherent 5 adj.
whole 52 adj.
complete 54 adj.
numerical 85 adj.
numerical element
85 n.
integrate
combine 50 vb.

make complete
54 vb.
integration
mixture 43 n.
combination 50 n.
whole 52 n.
completeness 54 n.
inclusion 78 n.
unity 88 n.
integrity
whole 52 adj.
probity 929 n.
virtue 933 n.
intellect
intellect 447 n.
intellectual
mental 447 adj.
intellectual 492 n.
wise 498 adj.
proficient person
696 n.
intelligence
secret service
459 n.
intelligence 498 n.
information
524 n.
news 529 n.
intelligent
intelligent 498 adj.
intelligentsia
intellectual 492 n.
intelligible
intelligible
516 adj.
intemperate
violent 176 adj.
villainous 934 adj.
intemperate
943 adj.
intend
intend 617 vb.
intended
impending
155 adj.
expected 507 adj.
volitional 595 adj.
loved one 887 n.
intense
great 32 adj.
vigorous 174 adj.
florid 425 adj.
feeling 818 adj.
fervent 818 adj.
intensify
augment 36 vb.
invigorate 174 vb.
enlarge 197 vb.
animate 821 vb.
aggravate 832 vb.
intensity
degree 27 n.

largeness 32 n.
vigorousness
174 n.
light 417 n.
hue 425 n.
intensive
increasing 36 adj.
word 559 n.
part of speech
564 n.
intent
attentive 455 adj.
intention 617 n.
intention
motive 612 n.
intention 617 n.
prayers 981 n.
intentional
volitional 595 adj.
intent upon
resolute 599 adj.
inter
correlative 12 adj.
inter 364 vb.
interact
correlate 12 vb.
inter alia
among 43 adv.
intercede
interfere 231 vb.
deprecate 762 vb.
desire 859 vb.
forgive 909 vb.
intercede for
mediate 720 vb.
intercept
interfere 231 vb.
converge 293 vb.
hear 415 vb.
screen 421 vb.
be curious 453 vb.
hinder 702 vb.
obstruct 702 vb.
take 786 vb.
intercession
aid 703 n.
mediation 720 n.
deprecation 762 n.
prayers 981 n.
interchange
interchange 151 n.
interchange
151 vb.
crossing 222 n.
interchangeable
correlative 12 adj.
identical 13 adj.
equivalent 28 adj.
substituted
150 adj.
intercom
telecommunication

531 n.
intercommuni-
cation
union 45 n.
contiguity 202 n.
conversation
584 n.
intercourse
union 45 n.
interdict
prohibition 757 n.
interest
be related 9 vb.
relation 9 n.
extra 40 n.
product 164 n.
topic 452 n.
curiosity 453 n.
attention 455 n.
attract notice
455 vb.
motivate 612 vb.
benefit 615 n.
importance 638 n.
activity 678 n.
gain 771 n.
estate 777 n.
interest 803 n.
receipt 807 n.
impress 821 vb.
please 826 vb.
what is due 915 n.
interesting
pleasurable
826 adj.
interest oneself
in
be active 678 vb.
interests
affairs 154 n.
interface
contiguity 202 n.
interfere
disarrange 63 vb.
counteract 182 vb.
interfere 231 vb.
be curious 453 vb.
meddle 678 vb.
obstruct 702 vb.
prohibit 757 vb.
interfere with
debauch 951 vb.
interior
component 58 n.
interior 224 n.
interiority 224 n.
land 344 n.
art subject 553 n.
interior decora-
tion
ornamental art
844 n.

interject
add 38 vb.
discontinue 72 vb.
interjection
addition 38 n.
interjection 231 n.
reception 299 n.
part of speech
564 n.
speech 579 n.
address 583 n.
interlaced
crossed 222 adj.
interleave
mix 43 vb.
interlocking
correlative 12 adj.
union 45 n.
interloper
outsider 59 n.
interjector 231 n.
interlude
adjunct 40 n.
lull 145 n.
intermarry
wed 894 vb.
intermediary
lying between
231 adj.
intermediary
231 n.
intermediate
median 30 adj.
middle 70 adj.
lying between
231 adj.
interment
interment 364 n.
intermezzo
adjunct 40 n.
musical piece
412 n.
interminable
infinite 107 adj.
perpetual 115 adj.
long 203 adj.
intermingle
mix 43 vb.
intermission
interval 201 n.
dramatic theory
594 n.
intermittent
discontinuous
72 adj.
infrequent 140 adj.
periodical 141 adj.
fitful 142 adj.
intern
doctor 658 n.
imprison 747 vb.
internal
inherent 5 adj.

interior 224 adj.
international
correlative 12 adj.
comprehensive
52 adj.
universal 79 adj.
national 371 adj.
internecine
destructive
165 adj.
murderous
362 adj.
Internet
computing 86 n.
information
524 n.
Internet 531 n.
internment
detention 747 n.
interplay
correlate 12 vb.
correlation 12 n.
interchange 151 n.
interpolation
adjunct 40 n.
mixture 43 n.
interjection 231 n.
insertion 303 n.
interpose
add 38 vb.
discontinue 72 vb.
insert 303 vb.
hinder 702 vb.
mediate 720 vb.
interpret
play music
413 vb.
interpret 520 vb.
interpretation
interpretation
520 n.
acting 594 n.
interregnum
transience 114 n.
government 733 n.
interrogation
interrogation
459 n.
**interrogation
mark**
question 459 n.
punctuation
547 n.
interrupt
be incomplete
55 vb.
disarrange 63 vb.
discontinue 72 vb.
cease 145 vb.
halt 145 vb.
interfere 231 vb.
intrude 297 vb.

distract 456 vb.
be obstructive
702 vb.
be rude 885 vb.
be angry 891 vb.
interruption
inaptitude 25 n.
disarrangement
63 n.
discontinuity 72 n.
stop 145 n.
interval 201 n.
interjection 231 n.
hindrance 702 n.
rudeness 885 n.
intersection
joint 45 n.
crossing 222 n.
passage 305 n.
access 624 n.
road 624 n.
intersperse
mix 43 vb.
interstice
gap 201 n.
intertwine
mix 43 vb.
tie 45 vb.
interval
degree 27 n.
disunion 46 n.
discontinuity 72 n.
period 110 n.
lull 145 n.
interval 201 n.
space 201 vb.
opening 263 n.
musical note
410 n.
notation 410 n.
dramatic theory
594 n.
rest 683 n.
intervene
discontinue 72 vb.
interfere 231 vb.
lie between
231 vb.
meddle 678 vb.
hinder 702 vb.
obstruct 702 vb.
mediate 720 vb.
prohibit 757 vb.
intervention
discontinuity 72 n.
betweenness
231 n.
passage 305 n.
instrumentality
628 n.
hindrance 702 n.
mediation 720 n.

restriction 747 n.
prohibition 757 n.
trade 791 n.
interview
hear 415 vb.
listening 415 n.
exam 459 n.
interrogate 459 vb.
conference 584 n.
intestinal
interior 224 adj.
intestines
insides 224 n.
in the clear
safe 660 adj.
acquitted 960 adj.
in the flesh
material 319 adj.
alive 360 adj.
in the red
poor 801 adj.
in the red, be
lose 772 vb.
be in debt 803 vb.
**in the running
for, be**
offer oneself
759 vb.
**in the same
boat**
with 89 adv.
in the teeth of
with difficulty
700 adv.
in opposition
704 adv.
in the thick of
between 231 adv.
in the way
near 200 adv.
unwanted
860 adv.
intimacy
relation 9 n.
sexual intercourse
45 n.
knowledge 490 n.
friendship 880 n.
fellowship 882 n.
love 887 n.
intimate
connective 45 adj.
private 80 adj.
near 200 adj.
interior 224 adj.
knowing 490 adj.
known 490 adj.
hint 524 n.
inform 524 vb.
close friend 880 n.
friendly 880 adj.
loved one 887 n.

intimation
knowledge 490 n.
hint 524 n.
information
524 n.
news 529 n.
intimidate
oppress 735 vb.
frighten 854 vb.
threaten 900 vb.
intimidation
fear 854 n.
intimidation
854 n.
boasting 877 n.
into
obsessed 455 adj.
intolerable
intolerable
827 adj.
intolerant
biased 481 adj.
harmful 645 adj.
severe 735 adj.
hostile 881 adj.
malevolent
898 adj.
pitiless 906 adj.
orthodox 976 adj.
intonation
sound 398 n.
voice 577 n.
intoxicate
invigorate 174 vb.
excite 821 vb.
delight 826 vb.
intoxication
excitation 821 n.
excitable state
822 n.
intemperance
943 n.
drunkenness
949 n.
intractable
rigid 326 adj.
wilful 602 adj.
difficult 700 adj.
disobedient
738 adj.
intransigent
strong 162 adj.
rigid 326 adj.
resolute 599 adj.
obstinate 602 adj.
intravenous
interior 224 adj.
intrepid
unafraid 855 adj.
intricacy
complexity 61 n.
crossing 222 n.

convolution 251 n.
enigma 530 n.
difficulty 700 n.
intricate
tied 45 adj.
complex 61 adj.
intricate 251 adj.
ornamental
844 adj.
intrigue
latency 523 n.
motivate 612 vb.
plot 623 n.
plot 623 vb.
be cunning
698 vb.
sedition 738 n.
impress 821 vb.
love affair 887 n.
illicit love 951 n.
intriguing
cunning 698 adj.
perfidious 930 adj.
intrinsic
inherent 5 adj.
introduce
add 38 vb.
come before 64 vb.
initiate 68 vb.
introduce 231 vb.
precede 283 vb.
admit 299 vb.
insert 303 vb.
offer 759 vb.
greet 884 vb.
introduction
prelude 66 n.
beginning 68 n.
reception 299 n.
insertion 303 n.
teaching 534 n.
courteous act
884 n.
introspective
inherent 5 adj.
thoughtful
449 adj.
introverted
inward-looking
224 adj.
unsociable
883 adj.
intrude
intrude 297 vb.
insert 303 vb.
intruder
unrelatedness
10 n.
outsider 59 n.
interjector 231 n.
offender 904 n.
intrusion
interjection 231 n.

entering 297 n.
overstepping
306 n.
intrusive
unrelated 10 adj.
extraneous 59 adj.
lying between
231 adj.
intuition
intuition 476 n.
feeling 818 n.
revelation 975 n.
in two minds
irresolute 601 adj.
inundate
drench 341 vb.
flow 350 vb.
be overabundant
637 vb.
inure
train 534 vb.
accustom oneself
610 vb.
make ready
669 vb.
invade
congregate 74 vb.
interfere 131 vb.
encroach 306 vb.
attack 712 vb.
go to war 718 vb.
invader
outsider 59 n.
incomer 297 n.
attacker 712 n.
invalid
helplessness
161 n.
powerless 161 adj.
weakling 163 n.
illogical 477 adj.
useless 641 adj.
sick person 651 n.
unwarranted
916 adj.
invalidate
disable 161 vb.
weaken 163 vb.
destroy 165 vb.
confute 479 vb.
negate 533 vb.
annul 752 vb.
disentitle 916 vb.
invalided
sick 651 adj.
invalidity
lack of power
161 n.
lack of meaning
515 n.
invaluable
profitable 640 adj.

valuable 644 adj.
of value 811 adj.
invariable
identical 13 adj.
uniform 16 adj.
unchangeable
153 adj.
usual 610 adj.
invasion
crowd 74 n.
entering 297 n.
attack 712 n.
warfare 718 n.
invective
oration 579 n.
oratory 579 n.
scurrility 899 n.
reproach 924 n.
detraction 926 n.
inveigh
curse 899 vb.
criticize 924 vb.
inveigle
ensnare 542 vb.
tempt 612 vb.
invent
initiate 68 vb.
cause 156 vb.
produce 164 vb.
perceive 447 adj.
think 449 vb.
discover 484 vb.
imagine 513 vb.
manifest 522 vb.
be false 541 vb.
fake 541 vb.
plan 623 vb.
invention
beginning 68 n.
causation 156 n.
production 164 n.
idea 451 n.
discovery 484 n.
falsehood 541 n.
fable 543 n.
untruth 543 n.
contrivance 623 n.
inventive
original 21 adj.
new 126 adj.
imaginative
513 adj.
inventor
precursor 66 n.
cause 156 n.
producer 164 n.
detector 484 n.
planner 623 n.
inventory
all 52 n.
arrangement 62 n.
number 86 vb.

list 87 n.
list 87 vb.
contents 193 n.
inverse
contrariety 14 n.
non-identical
14 adj.
oppositeness
240 n.
opposite 240 adj.
invert
invert 221 vb.
invertebrate
animal 365 adj.
animal 365 n.
coward 856 n.
invest
place 187 vb.
dress 228 vb.
encircle 232 vb.
store 632 vb.
commission
751 vb.
lend 784 vb.
speculate 791 vb.
expend 806 vb.
investigate
enquire 459 vb.
investigation
enquiry 459 n.
police enquiry
459 n.
search 459 n.
study 536 n.
investiture
dressing 228 n.
giving 781 n.
investment
dressing 228 n.
store 632 n.
mandate 751 n.
estate 777 n.
giving 781 n.
lending 784 n.
expenditure 806 n.
inveterate
lasting 113 adj.
permanent
144 adj.
habitual 610 adj.
accustomed to
610 adj.
impenitent
940 adj.
invidious
unpleasant
827 adj.
hateful 888 adj.
invigilate
keep watch
457 vb.
invigilator
spectator 441 n.

keeper 749 n.
invigorate
invigorate 174 vb.
invincible
strong 162 adj.
inviolable
certain 473 adj.
due 915 adj.
invisible
invisible 444 adj.
invitation
reception 299 n.
inducement 612 n.
offer 759 n.
request 761 n.
excitation 821 n.
courteous act
884 n.
invite
admit 299 vb.
incite 612 vb.
command 737 vb.
offer 759 vb.
request 761 vb.
desire 859 vb.
be hospitable
882 vb.
inviting
accessible 289 adj.
pleasurable
826 adj.
invocation
address 583 n.
prayers 981 n.
invoice
list 87 n.
demand 737 vb.
account 808 vb.
accounts 808 n.
invoke
entreat 761 vb.
desire 859 vb.
involuntary
intuitive 476 adj.
involuntary
596 adj.
spontaneous
609 adj.
involution
convolution 251 n.
involve
be inherent 5 vb.
throw into confu-
sion 63 vb.
comprise 78 vb.
evidence 466 vb.
make likely
471 vb.
mean 514 vb.
imply 523 vb.
indicate 547 vb.
accuse 928 vb.

involvement
relation 9 n.
union 45 n.
complexity 61 n.
affairs 154 n.
difficulty 700 n.
participation
775 n.
feeling 818 n.
liking 859 n.
guilt 936 n.
invulnerable
invulnerable
660 adj.
inward
inherent 5 adj.
interior 224 adj.
inward-looking
inward-looking
224 adj.
inwardness
introversion 224 n.
in-your-face
defiant 711 adj.
iodine
preventive 658 n.
element 319 n.
ion
element 319 n.
ionizer
air 340 n.
iota
small quantity
33 n.
IOU
title deed 767 n.
paper money
797 n.
IQ
intellect 447 n.
intelligence 498 n.
irascible
irascible 892 adj.
irate
angry 891 adj.
ire
anger 891 n.
iridescence
light 417 n.
variegation 437 n.
iris
circle 250 n.
plant 366 n.
eye 438 n.
irksome
difficult 700 adj.
annoying 827 adj.
tedious 838 adj.
iron
flatten 216 vb.
flattener 216 n.
smooth 258 vb.

smoother 258 n.
food content
301 n.
hard 326 adj.
hardness 326 n.
rub 333 vb.
heater 383 n.
resolute 599 adj.
resolution 599 n.
materials 631 n.
iron curtain
exclusion 57 n.
partition 231 n.
obstacle 702 n.
iron hand in a
velvet glove
latency 523 n.
iron out
flatten 216 vb.
straighten 249 vb.
smooth 258 vb.
facilitate 701 vb.
iron rations
provisions 301 n.
insufficiency
636 n.
portion 783 n.
fasting 946 n.
irons
support 218 n.
fetter 748 n.
pillory 964 n.
irons in the fire
affairs 154 n.
business 622 n.
activity 678 n.
irony
underestimation
483 n.
figure of speech
519 n.
wit 839 n.
ridicule 851 n.
reproach 924 n.
irradiation
light 417 n.
radiation 417 n.
lighting 420 n.
irrational
numerical 85 adj.
illogical 477 adj.
unwise 499 adj.
irreconcilable
unrelated 10 adj.
hostile 881 adj.
irrecoverable
lost 772 adj.
unpromising
853 adj.
irredeemable
bad 645 adj.
lost 772 adj.

wicked 934 adj.
impenitent
940 adj.
irrefutable
undisputed
473 adj.
irregular
unequal 29 adj.
lacking order
61 adj.
discontinuous
72 adj.
abnormal 84 adj.
unconformable
84 adj.
fitful 142 adj.
distorted 246 adj.
rough 259 adj.
grammatical
564 adj.
wrong 914 adj.
illegal 954 adj.
irregularity
non-uniformity
17 n.
inequality 29 n.
disorder 61 n.
discontinuity 72 n.
nonconformity
84 n.
fitfulness 142 n.
changeableness
152 n.
wrong 914 n.
illegality 954 n.
irrelevant
irrelevant 10 adj.
illogical 477 adj.
irreligious
wicked 934 adj.
irreligious 974 adj.
irremovable
fixed 153 adj.
irreparable
unpromising
853 adj.
irrepressible
violent 176 adj.
independent
744 adj.
lively 819 adj.
cheerful 833 adj.
irreproachable
perfect 646 adj.
virtuous 933 adj.
guiltless 935 adj.
irresistible
powerful 160 adj.
strong 162 adj.
influential
178 adj.
necessary 596 adj.

irresolute
irresolute 601 adj.
irrespective
unrelated 10 adj.
irresponsible
changing 152 adj.
capricious 604 adj.
rash 857 adj.
undutiful 918 adj.
lawless 954 adj.
irretrievable
lost 772 adj.
irreverent
disrespectful
921 adj.
impious 980 adj.
irreversible
unchangeable
153 adj.
unpromising
853 adj.
irrevocable
certain 473 adj.
unpromising
853 adj.
irrigation
agriculture 370 n.
(See also **irriga-**
tor.)
irritable
sensitive 819 adj.
excitable 822 adj.
irascible 892 adj.
irritant
stimulator 821 n.
irritate
give pain 377 vb.
excite 821 vb.
torment 827 vb.
cause discontent
829 vb.
aggravate 832 vb.
enrage 891 vb.
irritation
excitation 821 n.
worry 825 n.
painfulness 827 n.
discontent 829 n.
aggravation 832 n.
anger 891 n.
resentment 891 n.
irruption
entering 297 n.
Islam
religious faith
973 n.
island
region 184 n.
traffic control
305 n.
island 349 n.
seclusion 883 n.

islander
inhabitant 191 n.
isle
land 344 n.
island 349 n.
-ism
prejudice 481 n.
isobar
weather 340 n.
isolate
set apart 46 vb.
seclude 883 vb.
isolation
unrelatedness 10 n.
disunion 46 n.
unity 88 n.
seclusion 883 n.
isotope
element 319 n.
I-spy
indoor game
837 n.
issue
kinsman 11 n.
subdivision 53 n.
child 132 n.
event 154 n.
happen 154 vb.
effect 157 n.
result 157 vb.
posterity 170 n.
going out 298 n.
emerge 298 vb.
outflow 298 n.
flow 350 vb.
topic 452 n.
publish 528 vb.
the press 528 n.
edition 589 n.
reading matter
589 n.
completion 725 n.
coinage 797 n.
mint 797 vb.
litigation 959 n.
isthmus
bond 47 n.
contraction 198 n.
narrowness 206 n.
land 344 n.
bridge 624 n.
it
identity 13 n.
attraction 291 n.
authenticity 494 n.
inducement 612 n.
pleasurableness
826 n.
beauty 841 n.
IT
information
524 n.

917 vb.
keep fit
be healthy 650 vb.
keep going
go on 146 vb.
persevere 600 vb.
keep in
surround 230 vb.
imprison 747 vb.
restrain 747 vb.
retain 778 vb.
keep in step
conform 83 vb.
**keep in touch
with**
correspond 588 vb.
be sociable
882 vb.
keep off
be distant 199 vb.
screen 421 vb.
avoid 620 vb.
keep on
recur 139 vb.
stay 144 vb.
sustain 146 vb.
progress 285 vb.
persevere 600 vb.
**keep oneself to
oneself**
be fastidious
862 vb.
keep order
order 60 vb.
safeguard 660 vb.
manage 689 vb.
rule 733 vb.
restrain 747 vb.
keep out
exclude 57 vb.
screen 421 vb.
obstruct 702 vb.
restrain 747 vb.
refuse 760 vb.
keepsake
reminder 505 vb.
gift 781 n.
keep time
time 117 vb.
synchronize
123 vb.
keep up
stay 144 vb.
sustain 146 vb.
persevere 600 vb.
keep up with
be equal 28 vb.
be friendly 880 vb.
be sociable
882 vb.
**keep up with
the Joneses**
conform 83 vb.

afford 800 vb.
be in fashion
848 vb.
keg
vat 194 n.
ken
know 490 vb.
knowledge 490 n.
kennel
group 74 n.
stable 192 n.
lockup 748 n.
kept woman
kept woman
952 n.
kerb
edge 234 n.
limit 236 n.
road 624 n.
kerfuffle
commotion 318 n.
kernel
essential part 5 n.
middle 70 n.
focus 76 n.
centre 225 n.
chief thing 638 n.
kerosene
oil 357 n.
fuel 385 n.
ketchup
sauce 389 n.
kettle
pot 194 n.
heater 383 n.
key
degree 27 n.
crucial 137 adj.
reason why 156 n.
influential
178 adj.
opener 263 n.
stopper 264 n.
island 349 n.
key 410 n.
answer 460 n.
interpretation
520 n.
translation 520 n.
indication 547 n.
write 586 vb.
print 587 vb.
instrument 628 n.
important 638 adj.
keyboard
computerize 86 vb.
computing 86 n.
musical note
410 n.
organ 414 n.
piano 414 n.
keyed up
expectant 507 adj.

prepared 669 adj.
excited 821 adj.
keyhole
circle 250 n.
aperture 263 n.
window 263 n.
key in
computerize 86 vb.
keynote
prototype 23 n.
rule 81 n.
musical note
410 n.
chief thing 638 n.
keystone
summit 213 n.
support 218 n.
KGB
secret service
459 n.
khaki
textile 222 n.
uniform 228 n.
brown 430 adj.
kibbutz
farm 370 n.
joint possession
775 n.
kick
vigorousness
174 n.
impulse 279 n.
knock 279 n.
recoil 280 n.
propel 287 vb.
propulsion 287 n.
leap 312 n.
be agitated
318 vb.
pungency 388 n.
hint 524 n.
gesticulate 547 vb.
gesture 547 n.
indication 547 n.
rejection 607 n.
oppose 704 vb.
fight 716 vb.
disobey 738 vb.
refuse 760 vb.
deprecate 762 vb.
feeling 818 n.
joy 824 n.
corporal punish-
ment 963 n.
kick oneself
regret 830 vb.
kick one's heels
not act 677 vb.
be inactive
679 vb.
kick out
repel 292 vb.

eject 300 vb.
reject 607 vb.
not retain 779 vb.
kicks
excitation 821 n.
kick-start
initiate 68 vb.
kick the habit
disaccustom
611 vb.
kick upstairs
displace 188 vb.
ejection 300 n.
reject 607 vb.
depose 752 vb.
kid
child 132 n.
young creature
132 n.
skin 226 n.
deceive 542 vb.
fool 542 vb.
ridicule 851 vb.
kid gloves
discrimination
463 n.
conduct 688 n.
leniency 736 n.
good taste 846 n.
kidnap
ensnare 542 vb.
arrest 747 vb.
take away 786 vb.
steal 788 vb.
kidney
sort 77 n.
meal 301 n.
kidology
deception 542 n.
kids' stuff
easy thing 701 n.
kill
kill 362 vb.
prohibit 757 vb.
killer
destroyer 168 n.
killer 362 n.
murderer 362 n.
ruffian 904 n.
killjoy
moderator 177 n.
dissuasion 613 n.
moper 834 n.
bore 838 n.
kill oneself
kill oneself
362 vb.
kill time
pass time 108 vb.
be inactive
679 vb.
amuse oneself

837 vb.
kiln
furnace 383 n.
kilo
weighing 322 n.
kilometre
measurement of
length 203 n.
kilt
shorten 204 vb.
skirt 228 n.
kimono
robe 228 n.
kin
kinsman 11 n.
breed 77 n.
genealogy 169 n.
kind
degree 27 n.
sort 77 n.
form 243 n.
helping 703 adj.
amiable 884 adj.
courteous 884 adj.
benevolent
897 adj.
kindergarten
tender age 130 n.
school 539 n.
kind-hearted
benevolent
897 adj.
kindle
cause 156 vb.
invigorate 174 vb.
be hot 379 vb.
kindle 381 vb.
incite 612 vb.
feel 818 vb.
excite 821 vb.
be excitable
822 vb.
get angry 891 vb.
kindliness
friendliness 880 n.
courtesy 884 n.
benevolence 897 n.
kindly
benevolent
897 adj.
kindness
leniency 736 n.
friendliness 880 n.
courteous act
884 n.
courtesy 884 n.
benevolence 897 n.
kindred
relative 9 adj.
akin 11 adj.
kinship 11 n.
kinsman 11 n.

866 n.
sociable person
882 n.
favourite 890 n.
lioness
big cat 365 n.
female animal
373 n.
lionize
honour 866 vb.
celebrate 876 vb.
congratulate
886 vb.
respect 920 vb.
praise 923 vb.
lion's share
chief part 52 n.
redundancy 637 n.
what is not due
916 n.
lip
edge 234 n.
projection 254 n.
sauciness 878 n.
rudeness 885 n.
liposuction
fat 357 n.
surgery 658 n.
beauty treatment
843 n.
lip-reading
listening 415 n.
interpretative
520 adj.
lip service
duplicity 541 n.
sham 542 n.
ostentation 875 n.
false piety 980 n.
liquefy
liquefy 337 vb.
liqueur
alcoholic drink
301 n.
liquid
formless 244 adj.
liquid 335 adj.
fluid 335 n.
transparent
422 adj.
liquidate
destroy 165 vb.
murder 362 vb.
slaughter 362 vb.
liquidator
receiver 782 n.
treasurer 798 n.
liquidity
fluidity 335 n.
funds 797 n.
liquidize
cook 301 vb.

liquefy 337 vb.
liquidizer
liquefaction 337 n.
liquor
stimulant 174 n.
drunkenness
949 n.
liquorice
sweets 301 n.
purgative 658 n.
lisp
voice 577 vb.
speech defect
580 n.
stammer 580 vb.
lissom
flexible 327 adj.
shapely 841 adj.
list
be unequal 29 vb.
list 87 n.
list 87 vb.
be oblique 220 vb.
obliqueness 220 n.
navigate 269 vb.
hear 415 vb.
listed building
archaism 127 n.
preservation
666 n.
listen
hear 415 vb.
be curious 453 vb.
be attentive
455 vb.
obey 739 vb.
listener
listener 415 n.
listen in
hear 415 vb.
be curious 453 vb.
listless
weakly 163 adj.
inactive 679 adj.
dejected 834 adj.
indifferent
860 adj.
lit
fiery 379 adj.
luminous 417 adj.
litany
prayers 981 n.
literacy
culture 490 n.
literal
narrow-minded
481 adj.
accurate 494 adj.
true 494 adj.
mistake 495 n.
semantic 514 adj.
interpretative

520 adj.
verbal 559 adj.
orthodox 976 adj.
literally
truly 494 adv.
literal-minded
narrow-minded
481 adj.
accurate 494 adj.
literary
linguistic 557 adj.
literary 557 adj.
stylistic 566 adj.
literature
erudition 490 n.
information
524 n.
literature 557 n.
reading matter
589 n.
lithe
flexible 327 adj.
lithography
printing 555 n.
print 587 n.
litigant
accuser 928 n.
litigant 959 n.
litigation
litigation 959 n.
litigious
quarrelling
709 adj.
litmus paper
testing agent
461 n.
litre
*weights and meas-
ures* 465 n.
litter
leavings 41 n.
disorder 61 n.
group 74 n.
be dispersed 75 vb.
young creature
132 n.
reproduce itself
167 vb.
posterity 170 n.
bed 218 n.
vehicle 274 n.
waste 634 n.
rubbish 641 n.
dirt 649 n.
litter lout
slut 61 n.
dirty person 649 n.
little
slightly 33 adv.
few 105 adj.
seldom 140 adv.
little 196 adj.

contemptible
922 adj.
little by little
by degrees 27 adv.
slightly 33 adv.
slowly 278 adv.
littleness
inferiority 35 n.
littleness 196 n.
contemptibility
922 n.
liturgy
Christian rite
988 n.
church service
988 n.
ritual 988 n.
live
be 1 vb.
at present
121 adv.
stay 144 vb.
be situated
186 vb.
live 192 vb.
alive 360 adj.
be alive 360 vb.
dramatic 594 adj.
active 678 adj.
feel 818 vb.
live and let live
give scope 744 vb.
compromise
770 vb.
be patient 823 vb.
lived in
occupied 191 adj.
live in
live 192 vb.
be alive 360 vb.
live-in
lover 887 n.
live in the past
remember 505 vb.
live it up
revel 837 vb.
be sociable
882 vb.
be intemperate
943 vb.
livelihood
vocation 622 n.
livelong
lasting 113 adj.
lively
speedy 277 adj.
imaginative
513 adj.
busy 678 adj.
feeling 818 adj.
lively 819 adj.
sociable 882 adj.

liven up
liven 360 vb.
be cheerful
833 vb.
live on
eat 301 vb.
be remembered
505 vb.
liver
insides 224 n.
meat 301 n.
sullenness 893 n.
livery
clothing 228 n.
uniform 228 n.
hue 425 n.
livestock
animal 365 n.
cattle 365 n.
live together
wed 894 vb.
live with
unite with 45 vb.
accompany 89 vb.
livid
colourless 426 adj.
blackish 428 adj.
grey 429 adj.
blue 435 adj.
excited 821 adj.
angry 891 adj.
living
existing 1 adj.
alive 360 adj.
life 360 n.
linguistic 557 adj.
vocation 622 n.
aware 777 n.
benefice 985 n.
lizard
reptile 365 n.
load
finite quantity
26 n.
addition 38 n.
fill 54 vb.
bunch 74 n.
contents 193 n.
load 193 vb.
transport 272 n.
gravity 322 n.
weigh 322 vb.
store 632 n.
make ready 669 vb.
adversity 731 n.
worry 825 n.
loaded
weighty 322 adj.
moneyed 800 adj.
loads
great quantity
32 n.

multitude 104 n.
loadstone
traction 288 n.
load the dice
deceive 542 vb.
load with
hinder 702 vb.
loaf
head 213 n.
*bread, pastries
and cakes*
301 n.
intelligence 498 n.
be inactive
679 vb.
loam
soil 344 n.
loan
monetary help
703 n.
lend 784 vb.
lending 784 n.
borrowing 785 n.
credit 802 n.
loath
dissenting 489 adj.
unwilling 598 adj.
loathe
dislike 861 vb.
hate 888 vb.
loathsome
unsavoury
391 adj.
not nice 645 adj.
unpleasant
827 adj.
ugly 842 adj.
hateful 888 adj.
lob
strike 279 vb.
propel 287 vb.
propulsion 287 n.
elevate 310 vb.
lobby
influence 178 n.
influence 178 vb.
lobby 194 n.
incite 612 vb.
motivator 612 n.
petitioner 763 n.
lobbyist
motivator 612 n.
petitioner 763 n.
lobe
hanging object
217 n.
ear 415 n.
lobster
fish as food 301 n.
marine life 365 n.
local
focus 76 n.

native 191 n.
provincial 192 adj.
tavern 192 n.
near 200 adj.
dialectal 560 adj.
social round
882 n.
locality
region 184 n.
place 185 n.
locality 187 n.
localize
place 187 vb.
locally
near 200 adv.
locate
specify 80 vb.
place 187 vb.
orientate 281 vb.
discover 484 vb.
location
place 185 n.
situation 186 n.
location 187 n.
lock
join 45 vb.
fastening 47 n.
all 52 n.
filament 208 n.
close 264 vb.
stopper 264 n.
water channel
351 n.
access 624 n.
safeguard 662 n.
firearm 723 n.
retain 778 vb.
retention 778 n.
lock and key
fastening 47 n.
locker
box 194 n.
compartment
194 n.
locket
jewellery 844 n.
lockout
exclusion 57 n.
strike 145 n.
hindrance 702 n.
locksmith
artisan 686 n.
**lock, stock and
barrel**
finite quantity
26 n.
lock up
conceal 525 vb.
safeguard 660 vb.
imprison 747 vb.
punish 963 vb.
lockup
lockup 748 n.

locomotive
dynamic 160 adj.
moving 265 adj.
locomotive 274 n.
locum
substitute 150 n.
doctor 658 n.
deputy 755 n.
locust
destroyer 168 n.
eater 301 n.
insect 365 n.
bane 659 n.
glutton 947 n.
lodge
place 187 vb.
place oneself
187 vb.
live 192 vb.
house 192 n.
small house
192 n.
society 708 n.
lodger
resident 191 n.
possessor 776 n.
lodgings
quarters 192 n.
loft
attic 194 n.
apex 213 n.
propel 287 vb.
elevate 310 vb.
storage 632 n.
lofty
great 32 adj.
high 209 adj.
impressive
821 adj.
worshipful
866 adj.
proud 871 adj.
insolent 878 adj.
disinterested
931 adj.
log
sailing aid 269 n.
velocity 277 n.
fuel 385 n.
gauge 465 n.
record 548 n.
record 548 vb.
register 548 vb.
log-book
chronology 117 n.
record 548 n.
logic
conformance 24 n.
reasoning 475 n.
logical
rational 475 adj.
logistics
transference 272 n.

tactics 688 n.
logjam
equilibrium 28 n.
stop 145 n.
impossibility
470 n.
inaction 677 n.
inactivity 679 n.
difficulty 700 n.
hindrance 702 n.
obstacle 702 n.
logo
label 547 n.
pattern 844 n.
log off
computerize 86 vb.
log on
computerize 86 vb.
loins
source 156 n.
genitals 167 n.
parentage 169 n.
loiter
be late 136 vb.
be stealthy
525 vb.
be inactive
679 vb.
loll
be horizontal
216 vb.
hang 217 vb.
be inactive
679 vb.
rest 683 vb.
lollipop
sweets 301 n.
sweet thing 392 n.
**lollipop man or
lady**
traffic control
305 n.
lone
non-uniform
17 adj.
alone 88 adj.
one 88 adj.
unsociable
883 adj.
lonely
separate 46 adj.
alone 88 adj.
empty 190 adj.
secluded 883 adj.
unsociable
883 adj.
loner
nonconformist
84 n.
unit 88 n.
unsocial person
883 n.

lonesome
alone 88 adj.
lone wolf
unit 88 n.
rebel 738 n.
unsocial person
883 n.
long
for a long time
113 adv.
long 203 adj.
desire 859 vb.
longevity
long duration
113 n.
old age 131 n.
life 360 n.
long for
regret 830 vb.
desire 859 vb.
longing
suffering 825 n.
regret 830 n.
desire 859 n.
love 887 n.
envious 912 adj.
longitude
quantity 26 n.
length 203 n.
world 321 n.
longlasting
perpetual 115 adj.
long-legged
long 203 adj.
narrow 206 adj.
tall 209 adj.
long odds
fair chance 159 n.
improbability
472 n.
long shot
propulsion 287 n.
improbability
472 n.
long sight
vision 438 n.
dim sight 440 n.
long standing
durability 113 n.
permanence 144 n.
longstanding
lasting 113 adj.
permanent
144 adj.
longsuffering
leniency 736 n.
lenient 736 adj.
patience 823 n.
patient 823 adj.
suffering 825 adj.
mercy 905 n.
forgiveness 909 n.

luggage
box 194 n.
transport 272 n.
lugubrious
cheerless 834 adj.
lamenting 836 adj.
lukewarm
median 30 adj.
warm 379 adj.
unwilling 598 adj.
irresolute 601 adj.
neutral 625 adj.
apathetic 820 adj.
indifferent
860 adj.
lull
lull 145 n.
assuage 177 vb.
bring to rest
266 vb.
silence 399 n.
silence 399 vb.
inactivity 679 n.
make inactive
679 vb.
calm 823 vb.
please 826 vb.
content 828 vb.
relieve 831 vb.
flatter 925 vb.
lullaby
moderator 177 n.
musical piece
412 n.
vocal music 412 n.
sleeping draught
679 n.
lumbago
pang 377 n.
rheumatism
651 n.
lumber
leavings 41 n.
disorder 61 n.
walk 267 vb.
move slowly
278 vb.
wood 366 n.
rubbish 641 n.
work 682 vb.
be clumsy 695 vb.
lumbered with
hindered 702 adj.
lumbering
unwieldy 195 adj.
clumsy 695 adj.
luminary
light 420 n.
sage 500 n.
person of repute
866 n.
luminous
luminous 417 adj.

lump
great quantity
32 n.
piece 53 n.
bulk 195 n.
convexity 253 n.
swelling 253 n.
gravity 322 n.
solid body 324 n.
hardness 326 n.
lump in one's
throat
feeling 818 n.
lumpish
inert 175 adj.
unwieldy 195 adj.
inactive 679 adj.
lump sum
funds 797 n.
lump together
join 45 vb.
combine 50 vb.
bring together
74 vb.
lumpy
unwieldy 195 adj.
thick 205 adj.
convex 253 adj.
rough 259 adj.
dense 324 adj.
lunacy
folly 499 n.
mental disorder
503 n.
lunar
curved 248 adj.
celestial 321 adj.
lunatic
mentally disordered
503 adj.
madman 504 n.
rash 857 adj.
lunch
eat 301 vb.
meal 301 n.
lunch box
genitals 167 n.
small box 194 n.
luncheon
meal 301 n.
lunge
move fast 277 vb.
impulse 279 n.
strike at 712 vb.
lunge at
strike 279 vb.
lungs
insides 224 n.
breathing 352 n.
voice 577 n.
lurch
obliqueness 220 n.

walk 267 vb.
move slowly
278 vb.
descent 309 n.
fluctuation 317 n.
oscillate 317 vb.
be agitated
318 vb.
show feeling
818 vb.
be drunk 949 vb.
lurching
fitfulness 142 n.
lure
attract 291 vb.
attraction 291 n.
ensnare 542 vb.
trap 542 n.
incentive 612 n.
tempt 612 vb.
desired object
859 n.
reward 962 n.
lurid
luminous 417 adj.
florid 425 adj.
frightening
854 adj.
showy 875 adj.
lurk
lurk 523 vb.
lurking
invisible 444 adj.
latent 523 adj.
stealthy 525 adj.
luscious
sweet 392 adj.
pleasurable
826 adj.
lush
prolific 171 adj.
vigorous 174 adj.
plentiful 635 adj.
rich 800 adj.
drunkard 949 n.
drunkenness
949 n.
get drunk 949 vb.
lust
desire 859 n.
desire 859 vb.
sexual urge 859 n.
love 887 n.
vice 934 n.
be impure 951 vb.
unchastity 951 n.
lust after
desire 859 n.
envy 912 vb.
lustful
loving 887 adj.
lecherous 951 adj.

lustre
light 417 n.
reflection 417 n.
prestige 866 n.
lustrous
luminous 417 adj.
noteworthy
866 adj.
lusty
strong 162 adj.
vigorous 174 adj.
fat 195 adj.
healthy 650 adj.
lute
stringed instrument
414 n.
luxuriant
prolific 171 adj.
dense 324 adj.
ornate 574 adj.
plentiful 635 adj.
luxuriate
abound 635 vb.
be overabundant
637 vb.
be intemperate
943 vb.
luxurious
comfortable
376 adj.
superfluous
637 adj.
rich 800 adj.
pleasurable
826 adj.
ostentatious
875 adj.
intemperate
943 adj.
sensual 944 adj.
luxury
plenty 635 n.
superfluity 637 n.
prosperity 730 n.
wealth 800 n.
intemperance
943 n.
sensualism 944 n.
lying
erroneous 495 adj.
false 541 adj.
falsehood 541 n.
deceiving 542 adj.
untrue 543 adj.
lymph
blood 335 n.
fluid 335 n.
lymphatic
bloody 335 adj.
watery 339 adj.
lynch
kill 362 vb.

disapprove 924 vb.
execute 963 vb.
lynx
big cat 365 n.
eye 438 n.
lyre
stringed instrument
414 n.
lyric
musical 412 adj.
vocal music 412 n.
poetic 593 adj.
lyrical
melodious 410 adj.
poetic 593 adj.
impressed 818 adj.
rejoicing 835 adj.
approving 923 adj.
lyrics
vocal music 412 n.
reading matter
589 n.

M

ma'am
female 373 n.
title 870 n.
mac
overcoat 228 n.
macabre
frightening
854 adj.
spooky 970 adj.
macadam
road 624 n.
macaroni
dish 301 n.
macaroon
bread, pastries
and cakes
301 n.
mace
spice 301 n.
badge 547 n.
club 723 n.
badge of office
743 n.
macerate
soften 327 vb.
drench 341 vb.
machete
sharp edge 256 n.
side arms 723 n.
Machiavellian
hypocritical
541 adj.
cunning 698 adj.
perfidious 930 adj.
machination
deception 542 n.

plot 623 n.
stratagem 698 n.
machine
produce 164 vb.
print 587 vb.
machine 630 n.
machinery
component 58 n.
machine 630 n.
machinist
machinist 630 n.
artisan 686 n.
machismo
male 372 n.
manliness 855 n.
ostentation 875 n.
macho
manly 162 adj.
male 372 adj.
male 372 n.
courageous
855 adj.
mackerel
fish as food 301 n.
mackintosh
overcoat 228 n.
macramé
network 222 n.
macrocosm
generality 79 n.
universe 321 n.
macroscopic
large 195 adj.
macula
mottle 437 n.
skin disease
651 n.
blemish 845 n.
mad
furious 176 adj.
absurd 497 adj.
mentally disordered
503 adj.
capricious 604 adj.
excited 821 adj.
rash 857 adj.
angry 891 adj.
mad about
loving 887 adj.
madam
female 373 n.
master 741 n.
title 870 n.
insolent person
878 n.
pimp 952 n.
madame
female 373 n.
title 870 n.
madcap
foolish 499 adj.
excitable 822 adj.

desperado 857 n.
rash 857 adj.
madden
make mad
503 vb.
enrage 891 vb.
maddening
annoying 827 adj.
made-to-
measure
tailored 228 adj.
madhouse
disorder 61 n.
turmoil 61 n.
mental hospital
503 n.
madly
extremely 32 vb.
(See also **mad**.)
madman
madman 504 n.
madrigal
vocal music 412 n.
maelstrom
whirl 315 n.
eddy 350 n.
pitfall 663 n.
activity 678 n.
maestro
orchestra 413 n.
proficient person
696 n.
mafia
rebel 738 n.
offender 904 n.
magazine
accumulation
74 n.
journal 528 n.
book 589 n.
reading matter
589 n.
storage 632 n.
arsenal 723 n.
firearm 723 n.
maggot
creepy-crawly
365 n.
Magi
sage 500 n.
magic
influence 178 n.
sleight of hand
542 n.
super 644 adj.
miracle-working
864 n.
wonderful 864 adj.
prestige 866 n.
fairylike 970 adj.
bewitch 983 vb.
magical 983 adj.

sorcery 983 n.
occultism 984 n.
magic carpet
airship 276 n.
magic instrument
983 n.
magician
proficient person
696 n.
sorcerer 983 n.
magic lantern
lamp 420 n.
visual fallacy
440 n.
camera 442 n.
plaything 837 n.
magistrate
official 690 n.
officer 741 n.
judge 957 n.
magnanimous
benevolent
897 adj.
disinterested
931 adj.
virtuous 933 adj.
magnate
bigwig 638 n.
rich person 800 n.
aristocrat 868 n.
magnet
incentive 612 n.
desired object
859 n.
magnetic
dynamic 160 adj.
magnetic field
energy 160 n.
attraction 291 n.
magnetic tape
computing 86 n.
rotator 315 n.
hearing aid 415 n.
record 548 n.
magnetism
influence 178 n.
traction 288 n.
attraction 291 n.
inducement 612 n.
magnetize
attract 291 vb.
magneto
electronics 160 n.
magnification
largeness 32 n.
vision 438 n.
exaggeration
546 n.
magnificent
large 195 adj.
excellent 644 adj.
splendid 841 adj.

ostentatious
875 adj.
magnify
augment 36 vb.
enlarge 197 vb.
overestimate
482 vb.
exaggerate 546 vb.
boast 877 vb.
praise 923 vb.
worship 981 vb.
magnifying
glass
enlarger 197 n.
transparency
422 n.
magnitude
degree 27 n.
largeness 32 n.
size 195 n.
light 417 n.
importance 638 n.
magnum opus
product 164 n.
book 589 n.
masterpiece 694 n.
magpie
bird 365 n.
niggard 816 n.
maharajah
potentate 741 n.
maharishi
religious teacher
973 n.
mahatma
sage 500 n.
mahogany
tree 366 n.
brown 430 adj.
brownness 430 n.
maid
young person
132 n.
domestic 742 n.
spinster 895 n.
virgin 950 n.
maiden
first 68 adj.
new 126 adj.
young person
132 n.
female 373 n.
spinster 895 n.
virgin 950 n.
means of execution
964 n.
maidenhead
purity 950 n.
maidenhood
celibacy 895 n.
purity 950 n.
maid of honour
bridal party 894 n.

mail
covering 226 n.
send 272 vb.
postal communica-
tions 531 n.
correspondence
588 n.
safeguard 662 n.
armour 713 n.
mailing list
information
524 n.
correspondence
588 n.
mail order
send 272 vb.
purchase 792 n.
maim
disable 161 vb.
impair 655 vb.
main
great 32 adj.
supreme 34 adj.
ocean 343 n.
important 638 adj.
mainland
land 344 n.
mainly
greatly 32 vb.
on the whole
52 adv.
generally 79 adv.
mainstay
support 218 n.
chief thing 638 n.
refuge 662 n.
helper 703 n.
hope 852 n.
maintain
stay 144 vb.
sustain 146 vb.
support 218 vb.
vitalize 360 vb.
believe 485 vb.
affirm 532 vb.
persevere 600 vb.
provide 633 vb.
preserve 666 vb.
vindicate 927 vb.
maintenance
continuance
146 n.
provisions 301 n.
perseverance
600 n.
provision 633 n.
monetary help
703 n.
dowry 777 n.
receipt 807 n.
maize
cereals 301 n.

food 301 n.
majestic
elegant 575 adj.
authoritative
733 adj.
ruling 733 adj.
impressive
821 adj.
worshipful
866 adj.
noble 868 adj.
proud 871 adj.
formal 875 adj.
majesty
largeness 32 n.
superiority 34 n.
authority 733 n.
prestige 866 n.
nobility 868 n.
divine attribute
965 n.
major
great 32 adj.
first 68 adj.
older 131 adj.
important 638 adj.
army officer
741 n.
majority
finite quantity
26 n.
degree 27 n.
chief part 52 n.
plurality 101 n.
adultness 134 n.
make
have sexual inter-
course with
45 vb.
compose 56 vb.
constitute 56 vb.
sort 77 n.
convert 147 vb.
cause 156 vb.
produce 164 vb.
form 243 vb.
arrive 295 vb.
structure 331 n.
estimate 480 vb.
make better
654 vb.
compel 740 vb.
acquire 771 vb.
gain 771 vb.
**make a beeline
for**
steer for 281 vb.
**make a break
for it**
walk out 296 vb.
**make a clean
sweep (of)**
revolutionize

149 vb.
empty 300 vb.
clean 648 vb.
**make a come-
back**
recoup 31 vb.
be restored 656 vb.
make advances
court 889 vb.
make a face
dislike 861 vb.
disapprove 924 vb.
make a fool of
be absurd 497 vb.
fool 542 vb.
ridicule 851 vb.
humiliate 872 vb.
make a go of
succeed 727 vb.
make a killing
gain 771 vb.
get rich 800 vb.
**make altera-
tions**
differ 15 vb.
make a man of
do good 644 vb.
give courage
855 vb.
make amends
compensate 31 vb.
restore 656 vb.
make restitution
787 vb.
atone 941 vb.
make an aside
voice 577 vb.
soliloquize 585 vb.
make a pass
court 889 vb.
make a point of
compel 740 vb.
make a show of
show 522 vb.
dissemble 541 vb.
be affected 850 vb.
make a stand
resist 715 vb.
make believe
imitate 20 vb.
imagine 513 vb.
be false 541 vb.
be untrue 543 vb.
make-believe
fantasy 513 n.
imaginary
513 adj.
hypocritical
541 adj.
sham 542 n.
spurious 542 adj.
untrue 543 adj.

**make capital
out of**
plead 614 vb.
find useful
640 adj.
use 673 vb.
make do with
substitute 150 vb.
make ends meet
vitalize 360 vb.
make fast
tighten 45 vb.
stabilize 153 vb.
make for
congregate 74 vb.
navigate 269 vb.
promote 285 vb.
make free with
be free 744 vb.
appropriate
786 vb.
be insolent
878 vb.
be rude 885 vb.
make fun of
fool 542 vb.
be witty 839 vb.
ridicule 851 vb.
make good
compensate 31 vb.
succeed 727 vb.
vindicate 927 vb.
**make hay while
the sun shines**
profit by 137 vb.
make headway
progress 285 vb.
get better 654 vb.
**make inroads
on**
encroach 306 vb.
make into
convert 147 vb.
make it
triumph 727 vb.
prosper 730 vb.
make it up
make peace
719 vb.
forgive 909 vb.
make light of
underestimate
483 vb.
do easily 701 vb.
be indifferent
860 vb.
make love
have sexual inter-
course with
45 vb.
have or give sexual
pleasure 376 vb.

love 887 vb.
caress 889 vb.
make money
flourish 615 vb.
prosper 730 vb.
acquire 771 vb.
gain 771 vb.
get rich 800 vb.
make one jump
surprise 508 vb.
frighten 854 vb.
make one sit up
impress 821 vb.
make or mar
cause 156 vb.
make out
see 438 vb.
understand
516 vb.
decipher 520 vb.
succeed 727 vb.
make over
transfer 272 vb.
repair 656 vb.
make-over
change 143 n.
transformation
143 n.
beautification
843 n.
make overtures
approach 289 vb.
offer 759 vb.
request 761 vb.
make terms
766 vb.
befriend 880 vb.
make peace
make peace
719 vb.
make public
publish 528 vb.
make sense
be intelligible
516 vb.
makeshift
inferior 35 adj.
substitute 150 n.
substituted
150 adj.
flimsy 163 adj.
spontaneous
609 adj.
imperfect 647 adj.
imperfection
647 n.
make shipshape
make better
654 vb.
**make short
work of**
destroy 165 vb.

eat 301 vb.
be active 678 vb.
hasten 680 vb.
do easily 701 vb.
carry out 725 vb.
succeed 727 vb.
make sure
stabilize 153 vb.
make certain
473 vb.
be cautious
858 vb.
make terms
make terms
766 vb.
**make the best
of**
be content 828 vb.
make the grade
be equal 28 vb.
suffice 635 vb.
succeed 727 vb.
**make the most
of**
overestimate
482 vb.
make better
654 vb.
use 673 vb.
be ostentatious
875 vb.
**make the run-
ning**
outstrip 277 vb.
**make things
worse**
deteriorate 655 vb.
be difficult
700 vb.
miscarry 728 vb.
**make to meas-
ure**
adjust 24 vb.
**make too much
of**
overestimate
482 vb.
exaggerate 546 vb.
make up
compensate 31 vb.
combine 50 vb.
make complete
54 vb.
compose 56 vb.
constitute 56 vb.
produce 164 vb.
imagine 513 vb.
be false 541 vb.
make better
654 vb.
make-up
character 5 n.

decree 737 n.
manifold
*existing in many
forms* 82 adj.
many 104 adj.
**man in the
street**
common man
30 n.
everyman 79 n.
social group
371 n.
commoner 869 n.
manipulate
touch 378 vb.
fake 541 vb.
fool 542 vb.
motivate 612 vb.
plot 623 vb.
practise medicine
658 vb.
use 673 vb.
misuse 675 vb.
do 676 vb.
deal with 688 vb.
mankind
humankind 371 n.
manliness
male 372 n.
manliness 855 n.
manly
grown-up 134 adj.
manly 162 adj.
animal 365 adj.
male 372 adj.
beautiful 841 adj.
courageous
855 adj.
man-made
imitative 20 adj.
spurious 542 adj.
manned
occupied 191 adj.
mannequin
living model 23 n.
exhibitor 522 n.
manner
mode 7 n.
sort 77 n.
style 566 n.
way 624 n.
conduct 688 n.
mannered
stylistic 566 adj.
affected 850 adj.
mannerism
speciality 80 n.
nonconformity
84 n.
identification
547 n.
phrase 563 n.

style 566 n.
habit 610 n.
affectation 850 n.
mannerly
tasteful 846 adj.
courteous 884 adj.
manners
practice 610 n.
conduct 688 n.
good taste 846 n.
etiquette 848 n.
courtesy 884 n.
mannish
male 372 adj.
manoeuvre
be in motion
265 vb.
motion 265 n.
deed 676 n.
do 676 vb.
tactics 688 n.
be cunning
698 vb.
stratagem 698 n.
**man of the
world**
expert 696 n.
fashionable society
848 n.
manor
house 192 n.
lands 777 n.
man of straw
*thing that lacks
substance* 4 n.
changeable thing
152 n.
sham 542 n.
nonentity 639 n.
manpower
band 74 n.
power 160 n.
means 629 n.
personnel 686 n.
manqué
unsuccessful
728 adj.
manse
parsonage 986 n.
mansion
building 164 n.
place 185 n.
house 192 n.
man-size
large 195 adj.
manslaughter
homicide 362 n.
mantelpiece
shelf 218 n.
mantle
sequence 65 n.
cover 226 vb.

wrapping 226 n.
dress 228 vb.
screen 421 n.
badge of office
743 n.
mantra
maxim 496 n.
manual
handed 378 adj.
musical note
410 n.
organ 414 n.
piano 414 n.
guidebook 524 n.
instrumental
628 adj.
manufacture
produce 164 vb.
product 164 n.
production 164 n.
business 622 n.
manufacturer
producer 164 n.
manure
fertilizer 171 n.
excrement 302 n.
cultivate 370 vb.
manuscript
no imitation 21 n.
prototype 23 n.
script 586 n.
written 586 adj.
book 589 n.
many
great 32 adj.
many 104 adj.
many-sided
*existing in many
forms* 82 adj.
plural 101 adj.
lateral 239 adj.
Maoism
government 733 n.
map
outline 233 vb.
gauge 465 vb.
map 551 n.
represent 551 vb.
map out
plan 623 vb.
Maquis
soldier 722 n.
rebel 738 n.
mar
disarrange 63 vb.
impair 655 vb.
be clumsy 695 vb.
make ugly 842 vb.
blemish 845 vb.
shame 867 vb.
marathon
lasting 113 adj.

distance 199 n.
walking 267 n.
contest 716 n.
racing 716 n.
sport 837 n.
marauding
thieving 788 adj.
marble
sphere 252 n.
smooth 258 adj.
smoothness 258 n.
hardness 326 n.
rock 344 n.
white 427 adj.
white thing 427 n.
variegate 437 vb.
sculpture 554 n.
building material
631 n.
marbled
mottled 437 adj.
marbles
ball game 837 n.
plaything 837 n.
march
assembly 74 n.
be in motion
265 vb.
gait 265 n.
motion 265 n.
marching 267 n.
walking 267 n.
walk 267 vb.
progression 285 n.
musical piece
412 n.
route 624 n.
defy 711 vb.
go to war 718 vb.
deprecation 762 n.
be ostentatious
875 vb.
marcher
pedestrian 268 n.
agitator 738 n.
marches
region 184 n.
limit 236 n.
**marching
orders**
ejection 300 n.
command 737 n.
marchioness
person of rank
868 n.
march-past
pageant 875 n.
Mardi Gras
festivity 837 n.
mare
horse 273 n.
moon 321 n.

female animal
373 n.
margarine
fat 357 n.
margin
difference 15 n.
range 183 n.
room 183 n.
interval 201 n.
edge 234 n.
edition 589 n.
superfluity 637 n.
scope 744 n.
marginal
inconsiderable
33 adj.
marginal 234 adj.
uncertain 474 adj.
marginalize
not respect 921 vb.
hold cheap
922 vb.
marijuana
drugs 949 n.
marina
stable 192 n.
shore 344 n.
shelter 662 n.
arena 724 n.
pleasure ground
837 n.
marinade
soften 327 vb.
season 388 vb.
preserver 666 n.
marinate
immerse 303 vb.
drench 341 vb.
preserve 666 vb.
marine
nautical personnel
270 n.
marine 275 adj.
shipping 275 n.
naval man 722 n.
marine creature
marine life 365 n.
mariner
mariner 270 n.
marionette
image 551 n.
maritime
marine 275 adj.
mark
degree 27 n.
serial place 73 n.
sort 77 n.
speciality 80 n.
effect 157 n.
feature 445 n.
perceive 447 adj.
notice 455 vb.

meet halfway
be willing 597 vb.
pacify 719 vb.
meeting
union 45 n.
assembly 74 n.
event 154 n.
contiguity 202 n.
collision 279 n.
approach 289 n.
approaching
289 adj.
convergence 293 n.
arrival 295 n.
conference 584 n.
council 692 n.
social gathering
882 n.
meeting place
union 45 n.
place 185 n.
locality 187 n.
meeting place
192 n.
social round
882 n.
meet one's end
perish 361 vb.
meet with
meet with 154 vb.
megalomania
overestimation
482 n.
psychosis 503 n.
vanity 873 n.
megaphone
megaphone 400 n.
megaton
weighing 322 n.
melancholia
psychosis 503 n.
melancholy 834 n.
melancholy
unhappy 825 adj.
discontent 829 n.
melancholic
834 adj.
melancholy 834 n.
sullen 893 adj.
mélange
a mixture 43 n.
melanoma
cancer 651 n.
skin disease
651 n.
mêlée
turmoil 61 n.
fight 716 n.
mellow
ageing 131 adj.
be turned to
147 vb.

soften 327 vb.
tasty 386 adj.
colour 425 vb.
soft-hued 425 adj.
get better 654 vb.
mature 669 vb.
matured 669 adj.
melodeon
organ 414 n.
melodious
melodious 410 adj.
melodrama
stage play 594 n.
melodramatic
dramatic 594 adj.
exciting 821 adj.
melody
melody 410 n.
tune 412 n.
pleasurableness
826 n.
melt
pass away 2 vb.
come unstuck
49 vb.
decompose 51 vb.
be dispersed 75 vb.
be transient
114 vb.
deform 244 vb.
soften 327 vb.
liquefy 337 vb.
sound faint
401 vb.
waste 634 vb.
meltdown
ruin 165 n.
melting
soft 327 adj.
liquid 335 adj.
liquefaction 337 n.
heating 381 n.
waste 634 n.
melting point
heat 379 n.
member
limb 53 n.
part 53 n.
component 58 n.
society 708 n.
participator 775 n.
Member of
Parliament
official 690 n.
councillor 692 n.
membership
inclusion 78 n.
participation
775 n.
fellowship 882 n.
membrane
layer 207 n.

skin 226 n.
memento
reminder 505 n.
trophy 729 n.
gift 781 n.
memo
reminder 505 n.
record 548 n.
memoir
record 548 n.
memoirs
remembrance
505 n.
reading matter
589 n.
biography 590 n.
memorabilia
remainder 41 n.
remembrance
505 n.
record 548 n.
reading matter
589 n.
memorable
remembered
505 adj.
notable 638 adj.
memorandum
reminder 505 n.
record 548 n.
memorial
tomb 364 n.
reminder 505 n.
monument 548 n.
trophy 729 n.
honours 866 n.
memorize
memorize 505 vb.
memory
computing 86 n.
memory 505 n.
men
component 58 n.
mariner 270 n.
personnel 686 n.
armed force 722 n.
menace
predict 511 vb.
danger 661 n.
endanger 661 vb.
warn 664 vb.
annoyance 827 n.
annoying person
827 n.
frighten 854 vb.
hateful object
888 n.
threat 900 n.
threaten 900 vb.
menacing
dangerous 661 adj.
warning 664 adj.

frightening
854 adj.
ménage
management
689 n.
menagerie
accumulation
74 n.
zoo 369 n.
collection 632 n.
mend
join 45 vb.
get healthy
650 vb.
get better 654 vb.
make better
654 vb.
rectify 654 vb.
repair 656 vb.
mendacious
false 541 adj.
untrue 543 adj.
mendicant
idler 679 n.
beggar 763 n.
mending
amendment 654 n.
recuperation
656 n.
repair 656 vb.
mend one's
ways
change one's mind
603 vb.
get better 654 vb.
become pious
979 vb.
menial
inferior 35 n.
worker 686 n.
servant 742 n.
serving 742 adj.
meningitis
infection 651 n.
menopause
middle age 131 n.
unproductiveness
172 n.
menstrual
seasonal 141 adj.
menstruation
bleeding 302 n.
mental
mental 447 adj.
mentally disordered
503 adj.
mental block
no memory 506 n.
mental disorder
mental disorder
503 n.
mental handi-
cap
unintelligence

499 n.
mental hospital
mental hospital
503 n.
mental illness
mental disorder
503 n.
mentality
intellect 447 n.
mental state
817 n.
mentally defi-
cient
unintelligent
499 adj.
mentally handi-
capped
unintelligent
499 adj.
mentally handi-
capped 503 adj.
mention
act of referring
9 n.
relate 9 vb.
specify 80 vb.
notice 455 vb.
evidence 466 n.
manifest 522 vb.
inform 524 vb.
information
524 n.
speak 579 vb.
mentor
sage 500 n.
teacher 537 n.
adviser 691 n.
menu
computing 86 n.
list 87 n.
mercenary
militarist 722 n.
soldier 722 n.
servant 742 n.
avaricious
816 adj.
corruptible
930 adj.
selfish 932 adj.
merchandise
merchandise
795 n.
merchant
merchant 794 n.
merchant navy
shipping 275 n.
merciful
lenient 736 adj.
benevolent
897 adj.
pitying 905 adj.
godlike 965 adj.

merciless
destructive
165 adj.
resolute 599 adj.
severe 735 adj.
cruel 898 adj.
malevolent
898 adj.
pitiless 906 adj.
mercurial
changing 152 adj.
moving 265 adj.
speedy 277 adj.
lacking concentration 456 adj.
irresolute 601 adj.
capricious 604 adj.
excitable 822 adj.
mercury
changeable thing
152 n.
element 319 n.
mercy
leniency 736 n.
benevolence 897 n.
mercy 905 n.
divine attribute
965 n.
mere
absolute 32 adj.
simple 44 adj.
lake 346 n.
mere nothing
trifle 639 n.
merge
be identical 13 vb.
mix 43 vb.
join 45 vb.
combine 50 vb.
cooperate 706 vb.
merger
relation 9 n.
mixture 43 n.
union 45 n.
combination 50 n.
association 706 n.
offer 759 n.
meridian
noon 128 n.
region 184 n.
summit 213 n.
topmost 213 adj.
meringue
*bread, pastries
and cakes*
301 n.
bubble 355 n.
merit
importance 638 n.
utility 640 n.
goodness 644 n.
deserve 915 vb.

meritocracy
elite 644 n.
government 733 n.
meritorious
excellent 644 adj.
reputable 866 adj.
virtuous 933 adj.
merits
right 913 n.
what is due 915 n.
virtues 933 n.
mermaid
sea nymph 343 n.
mythical being
970 n.
merman
sea god 343 n.
mythical being
970 n.
merriment
enjoyment 824 n.
merriment 833 n.
amusement 837 n.
merry
merry 833 adj.
drunk 949 adj.
merry-go-round
rotator 315 n.
merrymaking
enjoyment 824 n.
merriment 833 n.
merry 833 adj.
rejoicing 835 n.
festivity 837 n.
sociability 882 n.
mesh
unite with 45 vb.
gap 201 n.
space 201 vb.
cross 222 vb.
network 222 n.
mesmerism
influence 178 n.
occultism 984 n.
mesmerize
influence 178 vb.
make insensitive
375 vb.
convince 485 vb.
frighten 854 vb.
mesolithic
primal 127 adj.
mess
disorder 61 n.
jumble 63 vb.
room 194 n.
eat 301 vb.
predicament
700 n.
message
topic 452 n.
message 529 n.

messenger
traveller 268 n.
messenger 529 n.
servant 742 n.
Messiah
philanthropist
901 n.
Jesus 965 n.
religious teacher
973 n.
messiah
leader 690 n.
mess up
jumble 63 vb.
blunder 495 vb.
impair 655 vb.
messy
lacking order
61 adj.
dirty 649 adj.
metabolism
transformation
143 n.
metabolize
modify 143 vb.
metal
hardness 326 n.
mineral 359 n.
heraldry 547 n.
materials 631 n.
metallic
strident 407 adj.
metallurgy
mineralogy 359 n.
metamorphosis
transformation
143 n.
revolution 149 n.
metaphor
analogue 18 n.
assimilation 18 n.
substitute 150 n.
metaphor 519 n.
phrase 563 n.
ornament 574 n.
metaphorical
compared 462 adj.
semantic 514 adj.
figurative 519 adj.
metaphysics
existence 1 n.
philosophy 449 n.
metastasis
transference 272 n.
metathesis
interchange 151 n.
inversion 221 n.
transference 272 n.
figure of speech
519 n.
mete
mete out 465 vb.

meteor
brief span 114 n.
meteor 321 n.
meteoric
brief 114 adj.
speedy 277 adj.
celestial 321 adj.
meteorite
meteor 321 n.
meteorological
airy 340 adj.
meteorology
weather 340 n.
meter
gauge 465 vb.
meter 465 n.
method
uniformity 16 n.
order 60 n.
arrangement 62 n.
regularity 81 n.
way 624 n.
means 629 n.
conduct 688 n.
fashion 848 n.
ritual 988 n.
methodical
orderly 60 adj.
arranged 62 adj.
regular 81 adj.
Methodism
Protestantism
976 n.
methodology
order 60 n.
**methylated
spirit**
fuel 385 n.
meticulous
attentive 455 adj.
careful 457 adj.
accurate 494 adj.
observant 768 adj.
fastidious 862 adj.
trustworthy
929 adj.
metre
*measurement of
length* 203 n.
prosody 593 n.
metric
metrical 465 adj.
metrical
metrical 465 adj.
poetic 593 adj.
metric system
weights and measures 465 n.
metro
tunnel 263 n.
railway 624 n.
metronome
prototype 23 n.

timekeeper 117 n.
oscillation 317 n.
tempo 410 n.
meter 465 n.
metropolis
city 184 n.
metropolitan
inhabitant 191 n.
central 225 adj.
ecclesiastical
985 adj.
church dignitary
986 n.
mettle
vigorousness
174 n.
resolution 599 n.
mental state
817 n.
courage 855 n.
mew
howl 409 vb.
howling 409 n.
mewl
cry 408 vb.
howl 409 vb.
weep 836 vb.
mews
flat 192 n.
stable 192 n.
mezzo-soprano
vocalist 413 n.
miaow
howl 409 vb.
howling 409 n.
miasma
gas 336 n.
stench 397 n.
poison 659 n.
miasmic
gaseous 336 adj.
deadly 362 adj.
fetid 397 adj.
Michaelmas
autumn 129 n.
holy day 988 n.
microbiology
biology 358 n.
medical art 658 n.
microcomputer
counting instrument 86 n.
microcosm
small thing 33 n.
whole 52 n.
miniature 196 n.
universe 321 n.
microfiche
copy 22 n.
miniature 196 n.
record 548 n.
photography

866 n.
mirror image
contrariety 14 n.
mirth
merriment 833 n.
misadventure
event 154 n.
chance 159 n.
misfortune 731 n.
misanthropy
inhumanity 898 n.
misanthropy
902 n.
misapply
use sophistry
477 vb.
waste 634 vb.
misuse 675 vb.
be unskilful
695 vb.
**misapprehen-
sion**
misinterpretation
521 n.
misappropriate
misuse 675 vb.
defraud 788 vb.
misbehave
behave 688 vb.
disobey 738 vb.
be wicked 934 vb.
miscalculate
misjudge 481 vb.
blunder 495 vb.
be foolish 499 vb.
miscarriage
failure 728 n.
**miscarriage of
justice**
misjudgment
481 n.
injustice 914 n.
illegality 954 n.
miscarry
miscarry 728 vb.
miscellaneous
non-uniform
17 adj.
mixed 43 adj.
miscellany
medley 43 n.
accumulation
74 n.
anthology 592 n.
mischief
evil 616 n.
badness 645 n.
impairment 655 n.
wrong 914 n.
mischievous
destructive
165 adj.

capricious 604 adj.
harmful 645 adj.
disobedient
738 adj.
malevolent
898 adj.
wrong 914 adj.
misconception
misjudgment
481 n.
error 495 n.
misconduct
conduct 688 n.
discourtesy 885 n.
guilty act 936 n.
misconstruction
misjudgment
481 n.
error 495 n.
misinterpretation
521 n.
misconstrue
distort 246 vb.
not know 491 vb.
misinterpret
521 vb.
misinterpretation
521 n.
misconstrued
mistaken 495 adj.
miscount
misjudge 481 vb.
blunder 495 vb.
err 495 vb.
miscreant
villainous 934 adj.
bad person 938 n.
misdeed
wrong 914 n.
guilty act 936 n.
misdemeanour
guilty act 936 n.
lawbreaking
954 n.
misdirect
disarrange 63 vb.
deflect 282 vb.
mislead 495 vb.
misuse 675 vb.
be unskilful
695 vb.
miser
niggard 816 n.
miserable
unfortunate
731 adj.
unhappy 825 adj.
melancholic
834 adj.
miserly
careful 457 adj.
insufficient

636 adj.
avaricious
816 adj.
parsimonious
816 adj.
misery
evil 616 n.
adversity 731 n.
sorrow 825 n.
dejection 834 n.
moper 834 n.
bore 838 n.
disapprover 924 n.
misfire
be clumsy 695 vb.
bungling 695 n.
miscarry 728 vb.
misfit
misfit 25 n.
misfortune
adversity 731 n.
misfortune 731 n.
misgiving(s)
doubt 486 n.
nervousness 854 n.
misguided
misjudging
481 adj.
mistaken 495 adj.
mishandle
misuse 675 vb.
be severe 735 vb.
mishap
untimeliness
138 n.
event 154 n.
misfortune 731 n.
mishmash
medley 43 n.
disorder 61 n.
misinform
mislead 495 vb.
be false 541 vb.
misinterpret
misinterpret
521 vb.
misjudge
misjudge 481 vb.
mislay
misplace 188 vb.
lose 772 vb.
mislead
use sophistry
477 vb.
mislead 495 vb.
make wicked
934 vb.
misleading
erroneous 495 adj.
mismanage
misuse 675 vb.
be unskilful

695 vb.
fail in duty
918 vb.
misnomer
misnomer 562 n.
misogyny
hatred 888 n.
celibacy 895 n.
misanthropy
902 n.
misplace
misplace 188 vb.
misprint
blunder 495 vb.
mistake 495 n.
mispronounce
voice 577 vb.
stammer 580 vb.
misquote
blunder 495 vb.
misinterpret
521 vb.
be false 541 vb.
misremember
forget 506 vb.
misrepresent
misinterpret
521 vb.
misrepresent
552 vb.
**misrepresenta-
tion**
falsehood 541 n.
untruth 543 n.
misrepresentation
552 n.
misrule
misuse 675 vb.
bungling 695 n.
miss
be incomplete
55 vb.
young person
132 n.
female 373 n.
blunder 495 vb.
require 627 vb.
be unsatisfied
636 vb.
bungling 695 n.
fail 728 vb.
lose 772 vb.
be discontented
829 vb.
regret 830 vb.
desire 859 vb.
title 870 n.
misshapen
formless 244 adj.
deformed 246 adj.
unsightly 842 adj.
missile
missile 287 n.

missing
non-existent 2 adj.
incomplete 55 adj.
absent 190 adj.
deficient 307 adj.
lost 772 adj.
missing link
deficit 55 n.
incompleteness
55 n.
discontinuity 72 n.
completion 725 n.
mission
job 622 n.
vocation 622 n.
commission 751 n.
mandate 751 n.
delegate 754 n.
envoy 754 n.
philanthropy
901 n.
missionary
preacher 537 n.
philanthropist
901 n.
religious teacher
973 n.
zealot 979 n.
pastor 986 n.
**mission state-
ment**
affirmation 532 n.
objective 617 n.
missive
correspondence
588 n.
miss out
be incomplete
55 vb.
exclude 57 vb.
misspell
misinterpret
521 vb.
misspend
be prodigal
815 vb.
Miss Right
favourite 890 n.
miss the boat
be late 136 vb.
lose a chance
138 vb.
fail 728 vb.
miss the mark
fall short 307 vb.
Miss X
unknown thing
491 n.
mist
thing that lacks
substance 4 n.
moisture 341 n.

textile 222 n.
hair 259 n.
moist
watery 339 adj.
humid 341 adj.
moisten
moisten 341 vb.
moisture
moisture 341 n.
moisturizing
beauty treatment
843 n.
molar
tooth 256 n.
grinder 332 n.
molasses
sweet thing 392 n.
mole
mammal 365 n.
spectator 441 n.
secret service
459 n.
latency 523 n.
informer 524 n.
identification
547 n.
skin disease
651 n.
collaborator
707 n.
blemish 845 n.
molecule
minuteness 196 n.
element 319 n.
molehill
minuteness 196 n.
dome 253 n.
molest
harm 645 vb.
torment 827 vb.
be malevolent
898 vb.
debauch 951 vb.
mollify
assuage 177 vb.
pacify 719 vb.
mollusc
animal 365 n.
marine life 365 n.
moment
juncture 8 n.
small quantity
33 n.
point in time
108 n.
brief span 114 n.
instant 116 n.
cause 156 n.
importance 638 n.
momentary
brief 114 adj.
momentous
crucial 137 adj.

influential
178 adj.
important 638 adj.
momentum
energy 160 n.
impulse 279 n.
monad
existence 1 n.
unit 88 n.
monarch
sovereign 741 n.
owner 776 n.
heretical 977 adj.
monarchist
rebel 738 n.
monarchy
government 733 n.
monastery
monastery 986 n.
monastic
monastic 986 adj.
monk 986 n.
monetary
monetary 797 adj.
money
money 797 n.
moneybox
box 194 n.
storage 632 n.
treasury 799 n.
moneyed
moneyed 800 adj.
**money for jam
or old rope**
easy thing 701 n.
moneylender
lender 784 n.
money-making
gainful 771 adj.
mongrel
hybrid 43 n.
mixed 43 adj.
abnormal 84 adj.
nonconformist
84 n.
dog 365 n.
monies
funds 797 n.
monism
unity 88 n.
monitor
reptile 365 n.
listener 415 n.
look after 457 vb.
enquire 459 vb.
monk
celibate 895 n.
pious person
979 n.
monk 986 n.
monkey
ram 279 n.

mammal 365 n.
be cunning
698 vb.
funds 797 n.
bad person 938 n.
**monkey busi-
ness**
deception 542 n.
cunning 698 n.
perfidiousness
930 n.
monkey tricks
foolery 497 n.
disobedience
738 n.
revel 837 n.
monkey with
impair 655 vb.
mono
one 88 n.
sound 398 n.
making sound
398 adj.
monochrome
uniform 16 adj.
colourlessness
426 n.
painting 553 n.
monogamy
type of marriage
894 n.
monogram
indication 547 n.
label 547 n.
monograph
dissertation 591 n.
monolith
uniformity 16 n.
cohesiveness 48 n.
unit 88 n.
monument 548 n.
monolithic
identical 13 adj.
uniform 16 adj.
simple 44 adj.
cohesive 48 adj.
indivisible 52 adj.
one 88 n.
dense 324 adj.
monologue
uniformity 16 n.
unit 88 n.
oration 579 n.
soliloquy 585 n.
stage play 594 n.
monomania
prejudgment
481 n.
monopolize
prevail 178 vb.
absorb 449 vb.
possess 773 vb.

appropriate
786 vb.
be selfish 932 vb.
monopoly
exclusion 57 n.
corporation 708 n.
restriction 747 n.
possession 773 n.
sale 793 n.
monorail
railway 624 n.
monotheism
unity 88 n.
theism 973 n.
monotheist
religionist 973 n.
monotone
uniform 16 adj.
uniformity 16 n.
musical note
410 n.
painting 553 n.
monotonous
identical 13 adj.
uniform 16 adj.
continuous 71 adj.
repeated 106 adj.
feeble 572 adj.
tedious 838 adj.
monotony
uniformity 16 n.
continuity 71 n.
tedium 838 n.
dullness 840 n.
monsoon
rain 350 n.
wind 352 n.
monster
abnormality 84 n.
nonconformist
84 n.
giant 195 n.
eyesore 842 n.
prodigy 864 n.
monster 938 n.
monstrosity
abnormality 84 n.
deformity 246 n.
prodigy 864 n.
monstrous
exorbitant 32 adj.
unusual 84 adj.
huge 195 adj.
harmful 645 adj.
not nice 645 adj.
ugly 842 adj.
ridiculous 849 adj.
wonderful 864 adj.
heinous 934 adj.
montage
cinema 445 n.
picture 553 n.

month
period 110 n.
monthly
periodic 110 adj.
periodically
141 adv.
seasonal 141 adj.
journal 528 n.
usual 610 adj.
**month of Sun-
days**
neverness 109 n.
long duration
113 n.
monument
monument 548 n.
honours 866 n.
monumental
enormous 32 adj.
large 195 adj.
moo
howl 409 vb.
howling 409 n.
mooch
beg 761 vb.
take 786 vb.
mood
temperament 5 n.
state 7 n.
tendency 179 n.
grammar 564 n.
whim 604 n.
conduct 688 n.
mental state
817 n.
moral sensibility
819 n.
moody
fitful 142 adj.
changing 152 adj.
capricious 604 adj.
excitable 822 adj.
melancholic
834 adj.
irascible 892 adj.
sullen 893 adj.
moon
changeable thing
152 n.
follower 284 n.
moon 321 n.
satellite 321 n.
light 420 n.
be inattentive
456 vb.
moonlight
moon 321 n.
light 417 n.
work 682 vb.
not pay 805 vb.
moonlighting
escape 667 n.

motherhood
family 11 n.
maternity 169 n.
parentage 169 n.
mother-in-law
maternity 169 n.
motherland
territory 184 n.
home 192 n.
motherly
parental 169 adj.
loving 887 adj.
benevolent
897 adj.
mother-of-pearl
variegation 437 n.
gem 844 n.
motif
topic 452 n.
pattern 844 n.
motion
motion 265 n.
move 265 vb.
defecation 302 n.
topic 452 n.
gesticulate 547 vb.
gesture 547 n.
plan 623 n.
conduct 688 n.
advice 691 n.
command 737 vb.
offer 759 n.
request 761 n.
motionless
still 266 adj.
non-active
677 adj.
inactive 679 adj.
motivation
causation 156 n.
motive 612 n.
motive
reason why 156 n.
moving 265 adj.
musical piece
412 n.
motive 612 n.
motiveless
aimless 618 adj.
mot juste
suitability 24 n.
accuracy 494 n.
elegance 575 n.
motley
non-uniformity
17 n.
medley 43 n.
mixed 43 adj.
existing in many
forms 82 adj.
clothing 228 n.
variegated

437 adj.
variegation 437 n.
motor
moving 265 adj.
ride 267 vb.
car 274 n.
machine 630 n.
motoring
land travel 267 n.
motorist
driver 268 n.
motorized
mechanical
630 adj.
motorway
road 624 n.
mottled
mottled 437 adj.
motto
maxim 496 n.
commentary
520 n.
heraldry 547 n.
indication 547 n.
phrase 563 n.
mould
mode 7 n.
uniformity 16 n.
mould 23 n.
decay 51 n.
sort 77 n.
convert 147 vb.
produce 164 vb.
receptacle 194 n.
form 243 n.
form 243 vb.
soil 344 n.
plant 366 n.
educate 534 vb.
represent 551 vb.
sculpt 554 vb.
dirt 649 n.
blight 659 n.
decorate 844 vb.
moulded
formed 243 adj.
having a certain
mental state
817 adj.
mouldering
decay 51 n.
antiquated
127 adj.
dilapidated
655 adj.
moulding
cohesive 48 adj.
formation 243 n.
sculpture 554 n.
ornamental art
844 n.
mouldy
dirty 649 adj.

moulting
uncovering 229 n.
mound
bulk 195 n.
dome 253 n.
defences 713 n.
mount
be great 32 vb.
grow 36 vb.
have sexual inter-
course with
45 vb.
be high 209 vb.
high land 209 n.
support 218 vb.
conveyance 267 n.
ride 267 vb.
horse 273 n.
saddle horse
273 n.
start out 296 vb.
enter 297 vb.
ascend 308 vb.
climb 308 vb.
elevate 310 vb.
break in 369 vb.
dramatize 594 vb.
mountain
great quantity
32 n.
bulk 195 n.
high land 209 n.
storage 632 n.
store 632 n.
acquisition 771 n.
wealth 800 n.
mountaineer
traveller 268 n.
climb 308 vb.
climber 308 n.
mountainous
huge 195 adj.
large 195 adj.
mount guard
keep watch
457 vb.
safeguard 660 vb.
mounting
support 218 n.
ascent 308 n.
dear 811 adj.
mourn
inter 364 vb.
lament 836 vb.
mournful
distressing
827 adj.
melancholic
834 adj.
lamenting 836 adj.
mourning
formal dress

228 n.
funereal 364 adj.
funeral rites
364 n.
black 428 adj.
black thing 428 n.
lamentation
836 n.
mouse
computing 86 n.
mammal 365 n.
hunt 619 vb.
coward 856 n.
humility 872 n.
modesty 874 n.
mousse
dessert 301 n.
bubble 355 n.
pulpiness 356 n.
moustache
hair 259 n.
mousy
colourless 426 adj.
grey 429 adj.
ugly 842 adj.
mouth
entrance 68 n.
stomach 194 n.
threshold 234 n.
aperture 263 n.
way in 297 n.
gulf 345 n.
voice 577 vb.
orate 579 vb.
sauciness 878 n.
mouthful
small quantity
33 n.
mouthful 301 n.
mouth organ
air pipe 353 n.
organ 414 n.
mouthpiece
air pipe 353 n.
flute 414 n.
interpreter 520 n.
informant 524 n.
speaker 579 n.
deputy 755 n.
mouth-watering
tasty 386 adj.
movable
moving 265 adj.
move
displacement
188 n.
be in motion
265 vb.
motion 265 n.
move 265 vb.
transpose 272 vb.
move fast 277 vb.

attract 291 vb.
excrete 302 vb.
be agitated
318 vb.
propound 512 vb.
gesture 547 n.
motivate 612 vb.
attempt 671 n.
action 676 n.
deed 676 n.
do 676 vb.
tactics 688 n.
advise 691 vb.
stratagem 698 n.
offer 759 vb.
excite 821 vb.
moved
impressed 818 adj.
impressible
819 adj.
**move heaven
and earth**
persevere 600 vb.
exert oneself
682 vb.
move in
place oneself
187 vb.
live 192 vb.
enter 297 vb.
move it
come along
267 int.
movement
transition 147 n.
motion 265 n.
melody 410 n.
musical piece
412 n.
action 676 n.
activity 678 n.
movies
film 445 n.
moving
influential
178 adj.
moving 265 adj.
exciting 821 adj.
distressing
827 adj.
mow
cut 46 vb.
shorten 204 vb.
smooth 258 vb.
cultivate 370 vb.
store 632 n.
store 632 vb.
mow down
demolish 165 vb.
slaughter 362 vb.
mower
farm and garden

tools 370 n.

MP
official 690 n.
councillor 692 n.

Mr
male 372 n.
title 870 n.

Mr Average
everyman 79 n.

Mr Right
favourite 890 n.

Mr X
unknown thing
491 n.

Mrs
female 373 n.
title 870 n.

Mrs Average
everyman 79 n.

Mrs Grundy
etiquette 848 n.
prude 950 n.

Mrs Mop
cleaner 648 n.

much
greatly 32 vb.
great quantity
32 n.
many 104 adj.

much of a
muchness
similar 18 adj.
middling 732 adj.

muck
excrement 302 n.
rubbish 641 n.
dirt 649 n.

muck about
be absurd 497 vb.

muck-raking
detraction 926 n.

muck up
jumble 63 vb.
make unclean
649 vb.
impair 655 vb.

mucky
dirty 649 adj.

mucous
glutinous 354 adj.

mucus
excrement 302 n.
fluid 335 n.
semiliquidity
354 n.
dirt 649 n.

mud
moisture 341 n.
marsh 347 n.
semiliquidity
354 n.
dirt 649 n.

muddle
disorder 61 n.
disarrange 63 vb.
jumble 63 vb.
distract 456 vb.
predicament
700 n.

muddled
lacking order
61 adj.
poorly reasoned
477 adj.
unintelligent
499 adj.
unclear 568 adj.

muddy
agitate 318 vb.
humid 341 adj.
marshy 347 adj.
dim 419 adj.
dim 419 vb.
opaque 423 adj.
dirty 649 adj.
make unclean
649 vb.

mudguard
shelter 662 n.

mud-slinging
detraction 926 n.

muesli
cereals 301 n.

muff
glove 228 n.
blunder 495 n.
mistake 495 n.
be clumsy 695 vb.
bungling 695 n.

muffin
bread, pastries
and cakes
301 n.

muffle
weaken 163 vb.
moderate 177 vb.
cover 226 vb.
silence 399 vb.
mute 401 vb.
conceal 525 vb.
make mute
578 vb.

muffler
neckwear 228 n.

mug
be violent 176 vb.
force 176 vb.
cup 194 n.
face 237 n.
strike 279 vb.
credulity 487 n.
ninny 501 n.
study 536 vb.
dupe 544 n.

strike at 712 vb.
rob 788 vb.

mugging
attack 712 n.
stealing 788 n.

muggy
humid 341 adj.
warm 379 adj.

mulch
fertilizer 171 n.
covering 226 n.
cultivate 370 vb.

mule
hybrid 43 n.
footwear 228 n.
beast of burden
273 n.
mammal 365 n.

mulish
equine 273 adj.
animal 365 adj.
obstinate 602 adj.
wilful 602 adj.

mull
textile 222 n.
projection 254 n.
sweeten 392 vb.

mullah
theologian 973 n.

mull over
think 449 vb.

multicoloured
non-uniform
17 adj.
variegated
437 adj.

multifarious
unrelated 10 adj.
different 15 adj.
non-uniform
17 adj.
existing in many
forms 82 adj.
many 104 adj.

multiform
existing in many
forms 82 adj.
plural 101 adj.

multinational
influential
178 adj.
business 622 n.

multiple
quantity 26 n.
existing in many
forms 82 adj.
numerical 85 adj.
numerical element
85 n.
plural 101 adj.
many 104 adj.

multiplication
largeness 32 n.

increase 36 n.
reproduction
166 n.
propagation 167 n.
productiveness
171 n.

multiplicity
existence in many
forms 82 n.
plurality 101 n.
multitude 104 n.

multiply
augment 36 vb.
grow 36 vb.
repeat 106 vb.
produce 164 vb.
reproduce 166 vb.
reproduce itself
167 vb.
be fruitful 171 vb.

multipurpose
general 79 adj.
plural 101 adj.
useful 640 adj.

multiracial
mixed 43 adj.

multitude
multitude 104 n.

multitudes
great quantity
32 n.

mum
maternity 169 n.
voiceless 578 adj.
uncommunicative
582 adj.

mumble
stammer 580 vb.

mumbo jumbo
lack of meaning
515 n.
deity 966 n.
idol 982 n.
idolatry 982 n.
spell 983 n.

mummify
dry 342 vb.
preserve 666 vb.

mummy
maternity 169 n.
corpse 363 n.

mummy's boy
weakling 163 n.
male 372 n.
coward 856 n.

mumps
infection 651 n.

munch
chew 301 vb.

municipality
district 184 n.
jurisdiction 955 n.

munificent
liberal 813 adj.

munitions
arms 723 n.

mural
picture 553 n.

murder
homicide 362 n.
killing 362 n.
murder 362 vb.
indoor game
837 n.
cruel act 898 n.

murderer
murderer 362 n.

murderous
murderous
362 adj.

murky
dense 324 adj.
dark 418 adj.
opaque 423 adj.

murmur
flow 350 n.
faintness 401 n.
sound faint
401 vb.
roll 403 n.
imply 523 vb.
deprecate 762 vb.
deprecation 762 n.

Murphy's law
rule 81 n.
axiom 496 n.
disappointment
509 n.
evil 616 n.

muscle
ligature 47 n.
power 160 n.
vitality 162 n.
exertion 682 n.

muscle in
intrude 297 vb.

muscleman
athlete 162 n.
bulk 195 n.
a beauty 841 n.

muscular
stalwart 162 adj.

muse
meditate 449 vb.
be inattentive
456 vb.
poetry 593 n.
excitation 821 n.

museum
accumulation
74 n.
antiquity 125 n.
exhibit 522 n.
collection 632 n.

mush
face 237 n.
aperture 263 n.
pulpiness 356 n.
mushroom
grow 36 vb.
new 126 adj.
be fruitful 171 vb.
expand 197 vb.
dome 253 n.
fruit and vegetables 301 n.
plant 366 n.
whitish 427 adj.
brown 430 adj.
mushy
soft 327 adj.
music
music 412 n.
broadcast 531 n.
musical
melodious 410 adj.
musical 412 adj.
vocal music 412 n.
film 445 n.
stage play 594 n.
pleasurable
826 adj.
musical instrument
musical instrument
414 n.
musician
musician 413 n.
music to one's ears, be
delight 826 vb.
musk
scent 396 n.
musket
firearm 723 n.
musketeer
soldiers 722 n.
musky
fragrant 396 adj.
Muslim
religionist 973 n.
muslin
textile 222 n.
semitransparency
424 n.
mussel
fish as food 301 n.
marine life 365 n.
must, a
necessity 596 n.
requirement 627 n.
mustang
saddle horse
273 n.
mustard
condiment 389 n.

yellowness 433 n.
muster
bring together
74 vb.
number 86 vb.
statistics 86 n.
musty
fetid 397 adj.
dirty 649 adj.
mutable
changeable
143 adj.
changing 152 adj.
mutant
nonconformist
84 n.
mutation
variant 15 n.
non-uniformity
17 n.
misfit 25 n.
abnormality 84 n.
change 143 n.
conversion 147 n.
deformity 246 n.
mute
silent 399 adj.
mute 401 vb.
non-resonance
405 n.
voiceless 578 adj.
uncommunicative
582 adj.
muted
muted 401 adj.
soft-hued 425 adj.
serious 834 adj.
mutilate
subtract 39 vb.
destroy 165 vb.
deform 244 vb.
impair 655 vb.
make ugly 842 vb.
mutineer
rebel 738 n.
undutifulness
918 n.
schismatic 978 n.
mutinous
quarrelling
709 adj.
defiant 711 adj.
resisting 715 adj.
disobedient
738 adj.
undutiful 918 adj.
mutiny
strike 145 n.
resist 715 vb.
revolt 738 n.
revolt 738 vb.
fail in duty

918 vb.
undutifulness
918 n.
mutter
blow 352 vb.
sound faint
401 vb.
roll 403 n.
cry 408 vb.
voice 577 n.
stammer 580 vb.
threaten 900 vb.
mutton
meat 301 n.
mutual
relative 9 adj.
correlative 12 adj.
muzzle
disable 161 vb.
protuberance
254 n.
aperture 263 n.
stopper 264 n.
silence 399 vb.
make mute
578 vb.
hinder 702 vb.
firearm 723 n.
restrain 747 vb.
fetter 748 n.
myopia
dim sight 440 n.
myriad
over one hundred
99 n.
many 104 adj.
myrrh
resin 357 n.
interment 364 n.
scent 396 n.
myself
self 80 n.
subjectivity 320 n.
mysterious
unusual 84 adj.
invisible 444 adj.
uncertain 474 adj.
unknown 491 adj.
puzzling 517 adj.
occult 523 adj.
concealed 525 adj.
unclear 568 adj.
wonderful 864 adj.
mystery
invisibility 444 n.
unknown thing
491 n.
latency 523 n.
secrecy 525 n.
enigma 530 n.
secret 530 n.
rite 988 n.

mystic
occult 523 adj.
religious 973 adj.
revelational
975 adj.
pious person
979 n.
pious 979 adj.
worshipper 981 n.
occultist 984 n.
mystical
divine 965 adj.
mysticism
meditation 449 n.
latency 523 n.
religion 973 n.
revelation 975 n.
piety 979 n.
occultism 984 n.
mystify
puzzle 474 vb.
use sophistry
477 vb.
deceive 542 vb.
mystique
prestige 866 n.
cult 981 n.
myth
fantasy 513 n.
fable 543 n.
narrative 590 n.
mythical
erroneous 495 adj.
mythical animal
mythical animal
365 n.
mythical being
mythical being
970 n.
mythology
tradition 127 n.

N

nab
alcoholic drink
301 n.
ensnare 542 vb.
arrest 747 vb.
take 786 vb.
nabob
officer 741 n.
nadir
inferiority 35 n.
extremity 69 n.
zero 103 n.
lowness 210 n.
depth 211 n.
base 214 n.
nag
horse 273 n.

saddle horse
273 n.
incite 612 vb.
animate 821 vb.
torment 827 vb.
enrage 891 vb.
nail
affix 45 vb.
fastening 47 n.
hanger 217 n.
sharp point 256 n.
piercer 263 n.
tool 630 n.
nail file
smoother 258 n.
cosmetic 843 n.
naive
credulous 487 adj.
ignorant 491 adj.
artless 699 adj.
innocent 935 adj.
naked
simple 44 adj.
uncovered 229 adj.
visible 443 adj.
vulnerable
661 adj.
namby-pamby
weak 163 adj.
weakling 163 n.
affected 850 adj.
name
inform 524 vb.
indicate 547 vb.
label 547 n.
name 561 n.
name 561 vb.
fame 866 n.
repute 866 n.
accuse 928 vb.
name-dropping
affected 850 adj.
nameless
anonymous
562 adj.
inglorious 867 adj.
namely
namely 80 adv.
in plain words
520 adv.
namesake
name 561 n.
nancy
nonconformist
84 n.
nanny
protector 660 n.
domestic 742 n.
retainer 742 n.
servant 742 n.
keeper 749 n.
nap
weaving 222 n.

texture 331 n.
sleep 679 n.
sleep 679 vb.
card game 837 n.
nape
rear 238 n.
narcissism
vanity 873 n.
love 887 n.
selfishness 932 n.
narcotic
anaesthetic 375 n.
drug 658 n.
remedial 658 adj.
drugs 949 n.
intoxicating
   949 adj.
narrate
communicate
   524 vb.
describe 590 vb.
narrative
narrative 590 n.
narrator
speaker 579 n.
narrow
become small
   198 vb.
make smaller
   198 vb.
narrow 206 adj.
narrow-minded
   481 adj.
narrow-minded
narrow-minded
   481 adj.
prudish 950 adj.
narrows
narrowness 206 n.
nasal
speech sound
   398 n.
nascent
beginning 68 adj.
nasty
not nice 645 adj.
unclean 649 adj.
dangerous 661 adj.
unpleasant
   827 adj.
hateful 888 adj.
malevolent
   898 adj.
unkind 898 adj.
natal
first 68 adj.
nation
race 11 n.
nation 371 n.
community 708 n.
national
universal 79 adj.

native 191 adj.
native 191 n.
national 371 adj.
subject 742 n.
nationalism
nation 371 n.
patriotism 901 n.
nationalist
patriot 901 n.
nationalistic
biased 481 adj.
patriotic 901 adj.
nationality
kinship 11 n.
nation 371 n.
nationalization
association 706 n.
joint possession
   775 n.
transfer 780 n.
trade 791 n.
national service
war measures
   718 n.
nationwide
universal 79 adj.
native
hereditary 5 adj.
inherent 5 adj.
component 58 adj.
native 191 adj.
native 191 n.
artless 699 adj.
Nativity
holy day 988 n.
nativity
origin 68 n.
propagation 167 n.
life 360 n.
natter
chat 584 n.
converse 584 vb.
natty
personable
   841 adj.
natural
real 1 adj.
substantial 3 adj.
inherent 5 adj.
typical 83 adj.
material 319 adj.
musical note
   410 n.
genuine 494 adj.
person with a
   learning disability
   504 n.
plain 573 adj.
usual 610 adj.
artless 699 adj.
friendly 880 adj.
naturalistic
literary 557 adj.

naturalized
converted 147 adj.
native 191 adj.
accustomed to
   610 adj.
naturalness
plainness 573 n.
artlessness 699 n.
nature
essence 1 n.
character 5 n.
composition 56 n.
sort 77 n.
tendency 179 n.
mental state
   817 n.
nature study
biology 358 n.
naturism
uncovering 229 n.
naturist
stripper 229 n.
naught
lacking substance
   4 n.
zero 103 n.
naughty
difficult 700 adj.
disobedient
   738 adj.
wicked 934 adj.
impure 951 adj.
unchaste 951 adj.
nausea
clearing 300 n.
digestive disorder
   651 n.
illness 651 n.
painfulness 827 n.
dislike 861 n.
hatred 888 n.
nauseate
be unpalatable
   391 vb.
displease 827 vb.
cause dislike
   861 vb.
nauseous
not nice 645 adj.
unclean 649 adj.
unpleasant
   827 adj.
hateful 888 adj.
nautical
marine 275 adj.
naval
marine 275 adj.
nave
middle 70 n.
church interior
   990 n.
navel
middle 70 n.

centre 225 n.
navigate
navigate 269 vb.
navigator
navigator 270 n.
aeronaut 271 n.
air force 722 n.
navvy
worker 686 n.
navy
blue 435 adj.
navy 722 n.
nawab
potentate 741 n.
person of rank
   868 n.
nay
negation 533 n.
refusal 760 n.
Nazism
government 733 n.
brute force 735 n.
Neanderthal
   man
antiquity 125 n.
fossil 125 n.
violent creature
   176 n.
humankind 371 n.
near
akin 11 adj.
be to come
   124 vb.
near 200 adj.
near 200 adv.
approach 289 vb.
parsimonious
   816 adj.
nearby
near 200 adj.
accessible 289 adj.
near-death
   experience
astral travel
   272 n.
death 361 n.
nearly
nearly 200 adv.
near-sighted
dim-sighted
   440 adj.
near thing
short distance
   200 n.
danger 661 n.
escape 667 n.
neat
unmixed 44 adj.
orderly 60 adj.
strong 162 adj.
careful 457 adj.
concise 569 adj.

plain 573 adj.
elegant 575 adj.
intoxicating
   949 adj.
neaten
arrange 62 vb.
make better
   654 vb.
nebula
star 321 n.
nebulous
formless 244 adj.
celestial 321 adj.
cloudy 355 adj.
dim 419 adj.
puzzling 517 adj.
necessarily
necessarily
   596 adv.
necessary
necessary 596 adj.
required 627 adj.
important 638 adj.
necessitate
necessitate 596 vb.
require 627 vb.
compel 740 vb.
necessity
certainty 473 n.
necessity 596 n.
poverty 801 n.
neck
bond 47 n.
contraction 198 n.
narrowness 206 n.
pillar 218 n.
article of clothing
   228 n.
sauciness 878 n.
caress 889 vb.
neck and crop
completely 54 adv.
neck-and-neck
equal 28 adj.
simultaneousness
   123 n.
synchronous
   123 adj.
near 200 adj.
neckband
loop 250 n.
neckerchief
neckwear 228 n.
necking
lovemaking 887 n.
endearment 889 n.
necklace
neckwear 228 n.
loop 250 n.
jewellery 844 n.
execute 963 vb.
means of execution

964 n.
neck of the woods
locality 187 n.
necromancy
sorcery 983 n.
necrophilia
abnormality 84 n.
nectar
drink 301 n.
sweet thing 392 n.
need
be incomplete
55 vb.
deficit 55 n.
shortfall 307 n.
require 627 vb.
requirement 627 n.
scarcity 636 n.
adversity 731 n.
request 761 vb.
poverty 801 n.
desire 859 n.
needful, the
funds 797 n.
needing
incomplete 55 adj.
needle
prickle 256 n.
sharp point 256 n.
piercer 263 n.
sailing aid 269 n.
music player
414 n.
indicator 547 n.
incite 612 vb.
torment 827 vb.
enrage 891 vb.
needless
superfluous
637 adj.
needy
poor 801 adj.
ne'er-do-well
idler 679 n.
desperado 857 n.
villainous 934 adj.
bad person 938 n.
nefarious
disreputable
867 adj.
heinous 934 adj.
negate
negate 533 vb.
negative
reduce to nothing
2 vb.
mould 23 n.
numerical 85 adj.
electricity 160 n.
darkness 418 n.
dissent 489 vb.

negate 533 vb.
negation 533 n.
negative 533 adj.
photography
551 n.
negative equity
shortfall 301 n.
debt 803 n.
neglect
disorder 61 n.
neglect 458 vb.
negligence 458 n.
unwillingness
598 n.
dilapidation
655 n.
non-preparation
670 n.
inaction 677 n.
non-completion
726 n.
rashness 857 n.
undutifulness
918 n.
disrespect 921 n.
neglectful
negligent 458 adj.
non-observant
769 adj.
apathetic 820 adj.
disrespectful
921 adj.
negligee
nightwear 228 n.
negligent
negligent 458 adj.
negligible
inconsiderable
33 adj.
unimportant
639 adj.
negotiable
possible 469 adj.
negotiate
accord 24 vb.
pass 305 vb.
confer 584 vb.
do business
622 vb.
cooperate 706 vb.
mediate 720 vb.
deputize 755 vb.
contract 765 vb.
make terms
766 vb.
assign 780 vb.
bargain 791 vb.
negotiation
adaptation 24 n.
mediation 720 n.
pact 765 n.
conditions 766 n.

barter 791 n.
trade 791 n.
neigh
howl 409 vb.
howling 409 n.
neighbour
friend 880 n.
neighbourhood
district 184 n.
locality 187 n.
nearness 200 n.
surroundings
230 n.
neither
neither 606 adv.
neolithic
primal 127 adj.
barbaric 869 adj.
neologism
word 559 n.
neologism 560 n.
nephew
kinsman 11 n.
male 372 n.
nepotism
kinship 11 n.
injustice 914 n.
nerve
stability 153 n.
vitality 162 n.
courage 855 n.
sauciness 878 n.
nerve-racking
frightening
854 adj.
nerves
neurosis 503 n.
ill health 651 n.
excitability 822 n.
nervousness 854 n.
nervous
excitable 822 adj.
nervous 854 adj.
nervous break-down
neurosis 503 n.
nervous disorder
651 n.
nervous system
sense 374 n.
nervy
active 678 adj.
excitable 822 adj.
nervous 854 adj.
nest
origin 68 n.
group 74 n.
live 192 vb.
nest 192 n.
nest egg
store 632 n.
preparation 669 n.

wealth 800 n.
nestle
live 192 vb.
caress 889 vb.
nestling
young creature
132 n.
net
remaining 41 adj.
bring together
74 vb.
receptacle 194 n.
cross 222 vb.
network 222 n.
textile 222 n.
enclosure 235 n.
semitransparency
424 n.
ensnare 542 vb.
trap 542 n.
hunt 619 vb.
acquire 771 vb.
receive 782 vb.
take 786 vb.
Net, the
information
524 n.
Internet 531 n.
netball
ball game 837 n.
nether
low 210 adj.
netting
network 222 n.
nettle
prickle 256 n.
bane 659 n.
hurt 827 vb.
huff 891 vb.
nettlerash
tingling 378 n.
skin disease
651 n.
network
connect 45 vb.
union 45 n.
bond 47 n.
network 222 n.
broadcasting
531 n.
cooperate 706 vb.
networking
latency 523 n.
cooperation 706 n.
neuralgia
pang 377 n.
neuritis
pang 377 n.
neurology
medical art 658 n.
neurosis
neurosis 503 n.

neurotic
neurotic 503 adj.
neurotic 504 n.
neuter
unman 161 vb.
material 319 adj.
grammatical
564 adj.
neutral
inert 175 adj.
colourless 426 adj.
grey 429 adj.
greyness 429 n.
moderate 625 n.
neutral 625 adj.
pacifist 717 n.
peaceful 717 adj.
free person 744 n.
neutrality
middle point 30 n.
disunion 46 n.
moderation 177 n.
no choice 606 n.
middle way 625 n.
peace 717 n.
indifference 860 n.
neutralize
reduce to nothing
2 vb.
disable 161 vb.
weaken 163 vb.
assuage 177 vb.
counteract 182 vb.
neutron
minuteness 196 n.
element 319 n.
never
never 109 adv.
never-ending
perpetual 115 adj.
long-winded
570 adj.
never-never, the
borrowing 785 n.
purchase 792 n.
nevertheless
nevertheless
468 adv.
new
new 126 adj.
unknown 491 adj.
unaccustomed
611 adj.
new boy
outsider 59 n.
incomer 297 n.
beginner 538 n.
new broom
newness 126 n.
busy person 678 n.
newcomer
outsider 59 n.

glance 438 n.
idea 451 n.
attention 455 n.
maxim 496 n.
affirmation 532 n.
speech 579 n.
observatory
astronomy 321 n.
view 438 n.
observe
be present 189 vb.
scan 438 vb.
see 438 vb.
watch 441 vb.
affirm 532 vb.
observe 768 vb.
celebrate 876 vb.
**observe deco-
rum**
show respect
920 vb.
observer
spectator 441 n.
estimator 480 n.
air force 722 n.
**observe the
formalities**
be ostentatious
875 vb.
obsess
absorb 449 vb.
cause thought
449 vb.
torment 827 vb.
trouble 827 vb.
obsessed
obsessed 455 adj.
positive 473 adj.
misjudging
481 adj.
obstinate 602 adj.
obsessed with
*having a certain
mental state*
817 adj.
obsession
idea 451 n.
attention 455 n.
positiveness 473 n.
prejudgment
481 n.
belief 485 n.
eccentricity 503 n.
neurosis 503 n.
opinionatedness
602 n.
worry 825 n.
spell 983 n.
obsessive
neurotic 504 n.
obsolescent
antiquated

127 adj.
obsolete
extinct 2 adj.
past 125 adj.
antiquated
127 adj.
powerless 161 adj.
useless 641 adj.
disused 674 adj.
obstacle
difficulty 700 n.
obstacle 702 n.
restraint 747 n.
obstetric
pregnant 167 adj.
medical 658 adj.
obstetrics
obstetrics 167 n.
female 373 n.
medical art 658 n.
obstinate
obstinate 602 adj.
obstreperous
violent 176 adj.
obstruct
be difficult
700 vb.
hinder 702 vb.
obstruct 702 vb.
resist 715 vb.
obstruction
disarrangement
63 n.
closure 264 n.
hindrance 702 n.
undutifulness
918 n.
obstructive
dissenting 489 adj.
obtain
be in the habit of
610 vb.
acquire 771 vb.
obtainable
accessible 289 adj.
possible 469 adj.
obtrude
interfere 231 vb.
obstruct 702 vb.
obtrusion
hindrance 702 n.
obtuse
insensitive
375 adj.
undiscriminating
464 adj.
unintelligent
499 adj.
thick-skinned
820 adj.
obtuseness
bluntness 257 n.

insensitivity
375 n.
*lack of discrimina-
tion* 464 n.
unintelligence
499 n.
moral insensibility
820 n.
obverse
face 237 n.
frontal 237 adj.
obviate
counteract 182 vb.
avoid 620 vb.
disencumber
701 vb.
obvious
obvious 443 adj.
intelligible
516 adj.
occasion
occasion 137 n.
happen 154 vb.
cause 156 vb.
reason why 156 n.
instrumentality
628 n.
celebration 876 n.
occasional
infrequent 140 adj.
fitful 142 adj.
occasionally
sometimes
139 adv.
occlude
close 264 vb.
obstruct 702 vb.
occlusion
closure 264 n.
occult
occult 523 adj.
occultism
occultism 984 n.
occupancy
presence 189 n.
possession 773 n.
occupant
resident 191 n.
possessor 776 n.
occupation
presence 189 n.
habit 610 n.
business 622 n.
job 622 n.
undertaking
672 n.
occupied
occupied 191 adj.
busy 678 adj.
possessed 773 adj.
occupier
resident 191 n.

possessor 776 n.
occupy
fill 54 vb.
be present 189 vb.
live 192 vb.
employ 622 vb.
possess 773 vb.
appropriate
786 vb.
occur
be 1 vb.
happen 154 vb.
be present 189 vb.
occurrence
event 154 n.
occur to
dawn upon
449 vb.
ocean
great quantity
32 n.
ocean 343 n.
oceanography
earth sciences
321 n.
oceans
great quantity
32 n.
plenty 635 n.
ochre
brown pigment
430 n.
orange 432 n.
o'clock
o'clock 117 adv.
octagon
over five 99 n.
angular figure
247 n.
octet
over five 99 n.
octogenarian
twenty and over
99 n.
octopus
marine life 365 n.
ocular
seeing 438 adj.
oculist
vision 438 n.
doctor 658 n.
odd
different 15 adj.
disagreeing 25 adj.
unequal 29 adj.
remaining 41 adj.
unusual 84 adj.
numerical 85 adj.
crazy 503 adj.
puzzling 517 adj.
ridiculous 849 adj.
wonderful 864 adj.

wrong 914 adj.
oddball
nonconformist
84 n.
the maladjusted
504 n.
oddity
misfit 25 n.
nonconformist
84 n.
nonconformity
84 n.
eccentricity 503 n.
prodigy 864 n.
odd-job man
servant 742 n.
oddly
remarkably 32 vb.
odd man out
non-uniformity
17 n.
dissimilarity 19 n.
misfit 25 n.
nonconformist
84 n.
objector 489 n.
oddments
piece 53 n.
oddness
inequality 29 n.
eccentricity 503 n.
ridiculousness
849 n.
wrong 914 n.
odds
difference 15 n.
inequality 29 n.
advantage 34 n.
fair chance 159 n.
dissension 709 n.
odds and ends
non-uniformity
17 n.
extra 40 n.
leavings 41 n.
medley 43 n.
piece 53 n.
odds on
fair chance 159 n.
approved 923 adj.
ode
poem 593 n.
odious
unpleasant
827 adj.
ugly 842 adj.
disreputable
867 adj.
hateful 888 adj.
odium
hatred 888 n.
odoriferous
odorous 394 adj.

orders
warfare 718 n.
holy orders 985 n.
ordinal
numerical 85 adj.
ordinance
precept 693 n.
command 737 n.
decree 737 n.
legislation 953 n.
rite 988 n.
ordinary
median 30 adj.
general 79 adj.
typical 83 adj.
heraldry 547 n.
usual 610 adj.
trivial 639 adj.
not bad 644 adj.
middling 732 adj.
ordination
mandate 751 n.
holy orders 985 n.
Christian rite
988 n.
ore
source 156 n.
rock 344 n.
mineral 359 n.
materials 631 n.
organ
limb 53 n.
organ 414 n.
the press 528 n.
instrument 628 n.
church utensil
990 n.
organic
inherent 5 adj.
organism
organism 358 n.
organization
composition 56 n.
order 60 n.
arrangement 62 n.
production 164 n.
structure 331 n.
plan 623 n.
conduct 688 n.
management
689 n.
corporation 708 n.
organize
compose 56 vb.
order 60 vb.
regularize 62 vb.
produce 164 vb.
plan 623 vb.
manage 689 vb.
organizer
planner 623 n.
orgasm
spasm 318 n.

excitation 821 n.
sexual pleasure
376 n.
have or give sexual
pleasure 376 vb.
orgiastic
disorderly 61 adj.
sensual 944 adj.
orgy
feasting 301 n.
plenty 635 n.
festivity 837 n.
social gathering
882 n.
sensualism 944 n.
oriel
compartment
194 n.
window 263 n.
orientate
orientate 281 vb.
orientation
situation 186 n.
direction 281 n.
orienteering
land travel 267 n.
direction 281 n.
racing 716 n.
sport 837 n.
orifice
aperture 263 n.
origami
sculpture 554 n.
origin
origin 68 n.
original
inherent 5 adj.
different 15 adj.
dissimilar 19 adj.
original 21 adj.
prototype 23 n.
special 80 adj.
nonconformist
84 n.
fundamental
156 adj.
imaginative
513 adj.
script 586 n.
volitional 595 adj.
laughing stock
851 n.
originality
originality 21 n.
speciality 80 n.
originally
initially 68 adv.
original sin
heredity 5 n.
guilt 936 n.
originate
initiate 68 vb.

cause 156 vb.
produce 164 vb.
imagine 513 vb.
**originate from
or in**
result 157 vb.
ornament
add 38 vb.
musical note
410 n.
ornament 574 n.
ornament 574 vb.
make better
654 vb.
beautify 841 vb.
beauty 841 n.
primp 843 vb.
ornamental
beautiful 841 adj.
ornamental
844 adj.
ornate
stylistic 566 adj.
ornate 574 adj.
ornithology
zoology 367 n.
orphan
derelict 779 n.
deprive 786 vb.
orphanage
retreat 192 n.
orthodox
credal 485 adj.
orthodox 976 adj.
orthodoxy
orthodoxy 976 n.
orthography
spelling 558 n.
orthopaedics
medical art 658 n.
therapy 658 n.
oscillate
oscillate 317 vb.
oscillator
electronics 160 n.
oscillation 317 n.
osmosis
entering 297 n.
passage 305 n.
ossified
antiquated
127 adj.
hard 326 adj.
ossify
be dense 324 vb.
harden 326 vb.
ostensible
appearing 445 adj.
manifest 522 adj.
ostensible 614 adj.
ostentation
ostentation 875 n.

boasting 877 n.
osteopathy
therapy 658 n.
ostracize
exclude 57 vb.
prohibit 757 vb.
shame 867 vb.
disapprove 924 vb.
ostrich
tall creature
209 n.
bird 365 n.
avoider 620 n.
other
different 15 adj.
other extreme
contrariety 14 n.
other ranks
inferior 35 n.
nonentity 639 n.
soldiers 722 n.
other side
contrariety 14 n.
exteriority 223 n.
rear 238 n.
oppositeness
240 n.
enemy 881 n.
**other way
round, the**
contrarily 14 adv.
otherwise
contrarily 14 adv.
otherworldly
non-material
320 adj.
pious 979 adj.
magical 983 adj.
otter
mammal 365 n.
ounce
small quantity
33 n.
weighing 322 n.
ourselves
self 80 n.
oust
substitute 150 vb.
eject 300 vb.
depose 752 vb.
deprive 786 vb.
out
absent 190 adj.
externally
223 adv.
open 263 adj.
eject 300 vb.
misjudging
481 adj.
matured 669 adj.
inactive 679 adj.
sleepy 679 adj.

out-and-out
revolutionary
149 adj.
outback
space 183 n.
district 184 n.
outbid
outdo 306 vb.
bargain 791 vb.
outboard
exterior 223 adj.
outbreak
disorder 61 n.
outbreak 176 n.
(See also **tur-
moil.**)
outbuilding
small house
192 n.
outburst
outbreak 176 n.
going out 298 n.
excitable state
822 n.
anger 891 n.
outcast
remaining 41 adj.
derelict 779 n.
disreputable
867 adj.
outcast 883 n.
outclass
be unequal 29 vb.
be superior 34 vb.
outstrip 277 vb.
outdo 306 vb.
defeat 727 vb.
outcome
event 154 n.
effect 157 n.
outcrop
layer 207 n.
projection 254 n.
outcry
loudness 400 n.
disapprobation
924 n.
outdated
antiquated
127 adj.
outdistance
be distant 199 vb.
outstrip 277 vb.
progress 285 vb.
outdo 306 vb.
outdo
outdo 306 vb.
outdoor
exterior 223 adj.
outer
exterior 223 adj.
outermost
exterior 223 adj.

pack
fill 54 vb.
bring together
74 vb.
bunch 74 n.
group 74 n.
load 193 vb.
cover 226 vb.
line 227 n.
animal 365 n.
hunter 619 n.
store 632 vb.
pack (a jury)
fake 541 vb.
predetermine
608 vb.
do wrong 914 adj.
package
bring together
74 vb.
bunch 74 n.
inclusion 78 n.
unit 88 n.
load 193 vb.
package deal
inclusion 78 n.
packaging
receptacle 194 n.
wrapping 226 n.
lining 227 n.
enclosure 235 n.
pack a punch
be strong 162 vb.
packed
firm 45 adj.
full 54 adj.
false 541 adj.
predetermined
608 adj.
packer
worker 686 n.
packet
bunch 74 n.
small box 194 n.
ship 275 n.
store 632 n.
funds 797 n.
wealth 800 n.
packhorse
beast of burden
273 n.
packing
lining 227 n.
pack up
walk out 296 vb.
be fatigued
684 vb.
fail 728 vb.
pact
agreement 24 n.
pact 765 n.
pad
abode 192 n.

enlarge 197 vb.
foot 214 n.
seat 218 n.
line 227 vb.
walk 267 vb.
saddle horse
273 n.
softness 327 n.
faintness 401 n.
stationery 586 n.
defend 713 vb.
padded cell
mental hospital
503 n.
padding
increment 36 n.
adjunct 40 n.
lining 227 n.
stopper 264 n.
softness 327 n.
diffuseness 570 n.
superfluity 637 n.
paddle
be in motion
265 vb.
walk 267 vb.
propeller 269 n.
row 269 vb.
swim 269 vb.
propellant 287 n.
be wet 341 vb.
**paddle one's
own canoe**
behave 688 vb.
be free 744 vb.
paddle steamer
ship 275 n.
paddlewheel
propellant 287 n.
paddock
place 185 n.
enclosure 235 n.
amphibian 365 n.
paddyfield
farm 370 n.
padlock
fastening 47 n.
barrier 235 n.
pad out
augment 36 vb.
be diffuse 570 vb.
padre
title 870 n.
cleric 986 n.
paediatrics
medical art 658 n.
pagan
ignorant 491 adj.
religionist 973 n.
heathen 974 n.
heathenish
974 adj.

impious person
980 n.
profane 980 adj.
page
part 53 n.
courier 529 n.
mark 547 vb.
edition 589 n.
domestic 742 n.
retainer 742 n.
a beauty 841 n.
erotic 887 adj.
bridal party 894 n.
impurity 951 n.
pageant
spectacle 445 n.
pageant 875 n.
pageantry
spectacle 445 n.
ostentation 875 n.
pageboy
servant 742 n.
hairdressing
843 n.
pager
telecommunication
531 n.
signal 547 n.
paginate
number 86 vb.
mark 547 vb.
print 587 vb.
pagoda
high structure
209 n.
temple 990 n.
pail
vessel 194 n.
pain
give pain 377 vb.
pain 377 n.
suffering 825 n.
annoying person
827 n.
hurt 827 vb.
discontent 829 n.
sadden 834 vb.
painful
painful 377 adj.
laborious 682 adj.
causing pain
827 adj.
**pain in the
neck**
annoyance 827 n.
annoying person
827 n.
painkiller
anaesthetic 375 n.
antidote 658 n.
relief 831 n.
painless
easy 701 adj.

painstaking
slow 278 adj.
careful 457 adj.
assiduousness
678 n.
laborious 682 adj.
labouring 682 adj.
fastidious 862 adj.
paint
coat 226 vb.
facing 226 n.
pigment 425 n.
imagine 513 vb.
deception 542 n.
(See also **sham**.)
record 548 vb.
paint 553 vb.
describe 590 vb.
cleanser 648 n.
primp 843 vb.
decorate 844 vb.
painter
cable 47 n.
producer 164 n.
artist 556 n.
mender 656 n.
artisan 686 n.
painting
painting 553 n.
picture 553 n.
beauty treatment
843 n.
**painting oneself
into a corner**
predicament
700 n.
**paint the town
red**
rejoice 835 vb.
revel 837 vb.
pair
treat as identical
13 vb.
identity 13 n.
analogue 18 n.
liken 18 vb.
peer 28 n.
adjunct 40 n.
join 45 vb.
*have sexual inter-
course with*
45 vb.
group 74 n.
concomitant 89 n.
existence as two
90 n.
pair 90 vb.
compare 462 vb.
pair off
pair 90 vb.
wed 894 vb.
paisley
textile 222 n.

pattern 844 n.
pakora
hors-d'oeuvres
301 n.
pal
male 372 n.
colleague 707 n.
chum 880 n.
palace
house 192 n.
palaeology
palaeology 125 n.
palatable
edible 301 adj.
pleasant 376 adj.
tasty 386 adj.
savoury 390 adj.
palate
taste 386 n.
good taste 846 n.
palaver
speech 579 n.
chatter 581 n.
pale
lacking substance
4 adj.
fastening 47 n.
exclusion 57 n.
weak 163 adj.
region 184 n.
barrier 235 n.
fence 235 n.
dim 419 adj.
soft-hued 425 adj.
colourless 426 adj.
lose colour 426 vb.
whiten 427 vb.
whitish 427 adj.
be unseen 444 vb.
heraldry 547 n.
unhealthy 651 adj.
quake 854 vb.
pale imitation
pretext 614 n.
bungling 695 n.
palette
plate 194 n.
colour 425 n.
palindrome
inversion 221 n.
word 559 n.
paling
fence 235 n.
defences 713 n.
palisade
barrier 235 n.
protection 660 n.
defences 713 n.
pall
coverlet 226 n.
funeral 364 n.
be unpalatable

pepper
pierce 263 vb.
shoot 287 vb.
fruit and vegeta-
bles 301 n.
spice 301 n.
pungency 388 n.
season 388 vb.
condiment 389 n.
variegate 437 vb.
fire at 712 vb.
pepper-and-salt
whitish 427 adj.
chequer 437 n.
pied 437 adj.
peppery
pungent 388 adj.
irascible 892 adj.
peppy
dynamic 160 adj.
vigorous 174 adj.
forceful 571 adj.
cheerful 833 adj.
pep talk
stimulant 174 n.
address 583 n.
inducement 612 n.
per
through 628 adv.
perambulator
pushcart 274 n.
per annum
periodically
141 adv.
per capita
pro rata 783 adv.
perceive
have feeling
374 vb.
see 438 vb.
perceive 447 adj.
detect 484 vb.
know 490 vb.
per cent
ratio 85 n.
percentage
increment 36 n.
extra 40 n.
part 53 n.
ratio 85 n.
perceptible
seeing 438 vb.
visible 443 adj.
perception
vision 438 n.
intellect 447 n.
idea 451 n.
discrimination
463 n.
knowledge 490 n.
sound judgment
498 n.

perceptive
sentient 374 adj.
mental 447 adj.
perceptual
sentient 374 adj.
mental 447 adj.
perch
place oneself
187 vb.
live 192 vb.
nest 192 n.
measurement of
length 203 n.
land 295 vb.
descend 309 vb.
sit down 311 vb.
fish 365 n.
gauge 465 n.
rest 683 vb.
perchance
by chance
159 adv.
possibly 469 adv.
percipient
sentient 374 adj.
percolate
infiltrate 297 vb.
exude 298 vb.
pass 305 vb.
be wet 341 vb.
irrigate 341 vb.
flow 350 vb.
purify 648 vb.
percolator
pot 194 n.
percussion
orchestra 413 n.
musical instrument
414 n.
perdition
ruin 165 n.
loss 772 n.
condemnation
961 n.
hell 972 n.
peremptory
assertive 532 adj.
authoritative
733 adj.
commanding
737 adj.
obligatory 917 adj.
perennial
lasting 113 adj.
perpetual 115 adj.
unchangeable
153 adj.
flower 366 n.
perestroika
arrangement 62 n.
revolution 149 n.
perfect
past time 125 n.

perfect 646 adj.
perfect 646 vb.
beautiful 841 adj.
shapely 841 adj.
perfection
perfection 646 n.
beauty 841 n.
perfectionist
careful 457 adj.
improving 654 adj.
perfectionist
862 n.
perfidious
false 541 adj.
perfidious 930 adj.
perfidy
perfidiousness
930 n.
perforate
make concave
255 vb.
pierce 263 vb.
pass 305 vb.
perform
produce 164 vb.
operate 173 vb.
play music
413 vb.
act 594 vb.
be instrumental
628 vb.
do 676 vb.
observe 768 vb.
be angry 891 vb.
do one's duty
917 vb.
performance
effect 157 n.
production 164 n.
representation
551 n.
dramatic theory
594 n.
action 676 n.
observance 768 n.
celebration 876 n.
duty 917 n.
ministration
988 n.
performer
musician 413 n.
interpreter 520 n.
entertainer 594 n.
doer 676 n.
agent 686 n.
perfume
emit 300 vb.
odour 394 n.
fragrance 396 n.
scent 396 n.
cosmetic 843 n.
perfunctory
incomplete 55 adj.

neglected 458 adj.
negligent 458 adj.
unwilling 598 adj.
imperfect 647 adj.
bungled 695 adj.
indifferent
860 adj.
pergola
arbour 194 n.
perhaps
by chance
159 adv.
possibly 469 adv.
peril
danger 661 n.
perilous
dangerous 661 adj.
perimeter
surroundings
230 n.
outline 233 n.
enclosure 235 n.
limit 236 n.
period
end 69 n.
era 110 n.
period 110 n.
periodic 110 adj.
bleeding 302 n.
punctuation
547 n.
periodic
periodic 110 adj.
periodical 141 adj.
fitful 142 adj.
periodical
periodical 141 adj.
journal 528 n.
book 589 n.
periodically
periodically
141 adv.
peripatetic
circuitous 314 adj.
peripheral
irrelevant 10 adj.
distant 199 adj.
exterior 223 adj.
marginal 234 adj.
unimportant
639 adj.
periphery
distance 199 n.
exteriority 223 n.
surroundings
230 n.
outline 233 n.
enclosure 235 n.
limit 236 n.
periphrastic
long-winded
570 adj.

periscope
telescope 442 n.
perish
decompose 51 vb.
perish 361 vb.
deteriorate 655 vb.
perishing
chilly 380 adj.
cold 380 adj.
peritonitis
digestive disorder
651 n.
perjury
falsehood 541 n.
untruth 543 n.
perk
extra 40 n.
perks
incentive 612 n.
earnings 771 n.
gift 781 n.
reward 962 n.
perk up
be refreshed
685 vb.
be cheerful
833 vb.
cheer 833 vb.
perky
cheerful 833 adj.
vain 873 adj.
perm
be curved 248 vb.
crinkle 251 vb.
hairdressing
843 n.
primp 843 vb.
permanence
durability 113 n.
permanence 144 n.
permanent
continuing
108 adj.
lasting 113 adj.
permanent
144 adj.
permeable
porous 263 adj.
permeate
prevail 178 vb.
pervade 189 vb.
infiltrate 297 vb.
pass 305 vb.
permissible
legal 953 adj.
permission
permission 756 n.
permissive
lax 734 adj.
permitting
756 adj.
permissive
society
scope 744 n.

sphere 252 n.
medicine 658 n.
punishment 963 n.
pillage
plundering 788 n.
rob 788 vb.
booty 790 n.
pillar
fixture 153 n.
high structure
209 n.
pillar 218 n.
monument 548 n.
pillar of society
person of repute
866 n.
good person 937 n.
pillbox
headgear 228 n.
cylinder 252 n.
fort 713 n.
pillion
seat 218 n.
pillory
fetter 747 vb.
lockup 748 n.
satirize 851 vb.
shame 867 vb.
criticize 924 vb.
defame 926 vb.
accuse 928 vb.
punish 963 vb.
pillory 964 n.
pillow
cushion 218 n.
support 218 vb.
softness 327 n.
pilot
precursor 66 n.
driver 268 n.
navigate 269 vb.
navigator 270 n.
aeronaut 271 n.
director 690 n.
pilotage
navigation 269 n.
pilot scheme
experiment 461 n.
plan 623 n.
preparation 669 n.
pimp
provide 633 vb.
be impure 951 vb.
pimp 952 n.
pimple
lowness 210 n.
swelling 253 n.
skin disease
651 n.
blemish 845 n.
pimply
convex 253 adj.

PIN
label 547 n.
treasury 799 n.
pin
join 45 vb.
fastening 47 n.
sharp point 256 n.
piercer 263 n.
trifle 639 n.
restrain 747 vb.
retain 778 vb.
jewellery 844 n.
pincers
tool 630 n.
pincers 778 n.
pinch
small quantity
33 n.
make smaller
198 vb.
make thin 206 vb.
notch 260 vb.
give pain 377 vb.
pang 377 n.
touch 378 vb.
refrigerate 382 vb.
adversity 731 n.
arrest 747 vb.
steal 788 vb.
poverty 801 n.
economize 814 vb.
be parsimonious
816 vb.
pinched
lean 206 adj.
narrow 206 adj.
pincushion
receptacle 194 n.
porousness 263 n.
pin down
place 187 vb.
compel 740 vb.
retain 778 vb.
pine
tree 366 n.
desire 859 vb.
court 889 vb.
pineapple
fruit and vegeta-
bles 301 n.
ping
roll 403 n.
roll 403 vb.
resonance 404 n.
resound 404 vb.
pinion
tie 45 vb.
wing 271 n.
fetter 747 vb.
fetter 748 n.
take 786 vb.
pink
moderate 177 adj.

notch 260 vb.
pierce 263 vb.
plant 366 n.
red 431 adj.
pinnacle
superiority 34 n.
crown 213 vb.
summit 213 n.
perfection 646 n.
pin on
affix 45 vb.
accuse 928 vb.
pin one's hopes
on
believe 485 vb.
hope 852 vb.
pinpoint
small thing 33 n.
specify 80 vb.
place 185 n.
place 187 vb.
minuteness 196 n.
orientate 281 vb.
pinprick
small thing 33 n.
shallowness
212 n.
trifle 639 n.
annoyance 827 n.
painfulness 827 n.
enrage 891 vb.
resentment 891 n.
pins-and-
needles
pang 377 n.
tingling 378 n.
pint
weights and meas-
ures 465 n.
pin-up
picture 553 n.
a beauty 841 n.
pioneer
come before 64 vb.
precursor 66 n.
initiate 68 vb.
settler 191 n.
front 237 n.
traveller 268 n.
preceding 283 n.
prepare 669 vb.
pious
pious 979 adj.
pip
timekeeper 117 n.
fruit 366 n.
signal 547 n.
pip at the post
be cunning
698 vb.
defeat 727 vb.
pipe
vat 194 n.

cylinder 252 n.
tube 263 n.
water channel
351 n.
blow 352 vb.
air pipe 353 n.
tobacco 388 n.
howl 409 vb.
play music
413 vb.
sing 413 vb.
flute 414 n.
weights and meas-
ures 465 n.
pipe cleaner
tobacco 388 n.
cleaning utensil
648 n.
pipe down
cease 145 vb.
be at rest 266 vb.
be silent 399 vb.
hush 399 int.
be uncommunica-
tive 582 vb.
pipe dream
thing that lacks
substance 4 n.
fantasy 513 n.
pleasurableness
826 n.
aspiration 852 n.
pipeline
tube 263 n.
transport 272 n.
water channel
351 n.
store 632 n.
provision 633 n.
piper
instrumentalist
413 n.
pipe up
cry 408 vb.
speak 579 vb.
piping
edging 234 n.
hem 234 n.
tube 263 n.
stridency 407 n.
trimming 844 n.
pips
broadcast 531 n.
badge 547 n.
badge of rank
743 n.
piquant
pungent 388 adj.
savoury 390 adj.
exciting 821 adj.
witty 839 adj.
impure 951 adj.

pique
excite 821 vb.
hurt 827 vb.
discontent 829 n.
huff 891 vb.
resentment 891 n.
piracy
imitation 20 n.
copy 22 n.
borrowing 785 n.
taking 786 n.
plundering 788 n.
piranha
fish 365 n.
pirate
copy 20 vb.
imitator 20 n.
mariner 270 n.
militarist 722 n.
borrow 785 vb.
appropriate
786 vb.
steal 788 vb.
robber 789 n.
thief 789 n.
bad person 938 n.
pirouette
rotate 315 vb.
rotation 315 n.
ballet 594 n.
pistol
pistol 723 n.
piston
stopper 264 n.
pit
depth 211 n.
interiority 224 n.
cavity 255 n.
excavation 255 n.
tunnel 263 n.
listener 415 n.
onlookers 441 n.
trap 542 n.
theatregoer 594 n.
theatre 594 n.
pitfall 663 n.
workshop 687 n.
stratagem 698 n.
blemish 845 n.
pit-a-pat
agitation 318 n.
faintness 401 n.
roll 403 n.
pitch
adjust 24 vb.
degree 27 n.
serial place 73 n.
territory 184 n.
place 185 n.
height 209 n.
summit 213 n.
be oblique 220 vb.

obliqueness 220 n.
coat 226 vb.
voyage 269 vb.
propel 287 vb.
fluctuation 317 n.
oscillate 317 vb.
be agitated
  318 vb.
resin 357 n.
sound 398 n.
harmonize 410 vb.
musical note
  410 n.
black thing 428 n.
voice 577 n.
arena 724 n.
sale 793 n.
pitched
adjusted 24 adj.
pitcher
vessel 194 n.
pitchfork
propel 287 vb.
farm and garden
  tools 370 n.
pitch in
aid 703 vb.
cooperate 706 vb.
participate 775 vb.
pitch into
attack 712 vb.
fight 716 vb.
criticize 924 vb.
pitfall
pitfall 663 n.
pith
substance 3 n.
essential part 5 n.
interiority 224 n.
centre 225 n.
pulpiness 356 n.
meaning 514 n.
pithy
substantial 3 adj.
proverbial 496 adj.
meaningful
  514 adj.
concise 569 adj.
witty 839 adj.
pitiable
unhappy 825 adj.
contemptible
  922 adj.
pitiful
distressing
  827 adj.
lamenting 836 adj.
disreputable
  867 adj.
benevolent
  897 adj.
pitiless
pitiless 906 adj.

pits, the
lowness 210 n.
misfortune 731 n.
pittance
small quantity
  33 n.
insufficiency
  636 n.
portion 783 n.
pitted
rough 259 adj.
pitter-patter
oscillation 317 n.
faintness 401 n.
pity
be lenient 736 vb.
pity 905 n.
pity 905 vb.
pivot
pivot 218 n.
pivotal
crucial 137 adj.
central 225 adj.
important 638 adj.
pivot on
depend 157 vb.
pixel
image 551 n.
pixie
elf 970 n.
pizza
dish 301 n.
pizzazz
vigorousness
  174 n.
vigour 571 n.
placard
exhibit 522 n.
advertisement
  528 n.
placate
pacify 719 vb.
place
state 7 n.
grade 73 vb.
serial place 73 n.
place 185 n.
place 187 vb.
house 192 n.
authority 733 n.
placebo
medicine 658 n.
place in the sun
heyday 730 n.
desire 859 n.
placement
location 187 n.
placenta
sequel 67 n.
obstetrics 167 n.
placid
inexcitable

  823 adj.
plagiarize
copy 20 vb.
repeat 106 vb.
fake 541 vb.
borrow 785 vb.
appropriate
  786 vb.
steal 788 vb.
plague
evil 616 n.
harm 645 vb.
plague 651 n.
bane 659 n.
adversity 731 n.
oppress 735 vb.
annoyance 827 n.
torment 827 vb.
ruffian 904 n.
plaice
fish as food 301 n.
plaid
chequer 437 n.
variegated
  437 adj.
plain
complete 54 adj.
plain 348 n.
obvious 443 adj.
manifest 522 adj.
stylistic 566 adj.
plain 573 adj.
ugly 842 adj.
needlework 844 n.
temperate 942 adj.
plain clothes
non-uniform
  17 adj.
plain sailing
navigation 269 n.
easy thing 701 n.
plainsong
vocal music 412 n.
act of worship
  981 n.
hymn 981 n.
plaint
lament 836 n.
accusation 928 n.
plaintiff
malcontent 829 n.
what is due 915 n.
accuser 928 n.
litigant 959 n.
plaintive
lamenting 836 adj.
plait
tie 45 vb.
ligature 47 n.
crossing 222 n.
weave 222 vb.
hair 259 n.

fold 261 n.
plan
itinerary 267 n.
structure 331 n.
guidebook 524 n.
map 551 n.
plan 623 n.
plan 623 vb.
plane
flat 216 adj.
flatten 216 vb.
horizontality
  216 n.
sharp edge 256 n.
smooth 258 vb.
smoother 258 n.
fly 271 vb.
aircraft 276 n.
tree 366 n.
tool 630 n.
planet
rotator 315 n.
planet 321 n.
planetarium
astronomy 321 n.
plank
shelf 218 n.
conceal 525 vb.
materials 631 n.
planning
arrangement 62 n.
production 164 n.
plan 623 n.
preparation 669 n.
plant
cause 156 n.
place 187 vb.
implant 303 vb.
plant 366 n.
vegetate 366 vb.
cultivate 370 vb.
trap 542 n.
equipment 630 n.
property 777 n.
false charge 928 n.
plantation
wood 366 n.
lands 777 n.
planter
producer 164 n.
settler 191 n.
vessel 194 n.
farmer 370 n.
garden 370 n.
plaque
dirt 649 n.
honours 866 n.
plasma
matter 319 n.
blood 335 n.
fluid 335 n.
plaster
adhesive 47 n.

coat 226 vb.
covering 226 n.
facing 226 n.
practise medicine
  658 vb.
medicine 658 n.
surgical dressing
  658 n.
plaster cast
wrapping 226 n.
sculpture 554 n.
(See also **surgi-**
  cal dressing.)
plasterer
artisan 686 n.
plaster of Paris
surgical dressing
  658 n.
plastic
substituted
  150 adj.
changing 152 adj.
flexible 327 adj.
softness 327 n.
spurious 542 adj.
materials 631 n.
borrowing 785 n.
credit 802 n.
payment 805 n.
impressible
  819 adj.
Plasticine
(tdmk)
softness 327 n.
sculpture 554 n.
plasticity
softness 327 n.
plastic money
borrowing 785 n.
credit 802 n.
plastic surgery
surgery 658 n.
beauty treatment
  843 n.
plate
plate 194 n.
coat 226 vb.
covering 226 n.
circle 250 n.
tooth 256 n.
photography
  551 n.
picture 553 n.
print-type 587 n.
edition 589 n.
plateau
high land 209 n.
apex 213 n.
horizontality
  216 n.
plain 348 n.
platform
layer 207 n.

horizontality
216 n.
stand 218 n.
publication 528 n.
publicity 528 n.
policy 623 n.
railway 624 n.
arena 724 n.
platinum
element 319 n.
white thing 427 n.
**platinum
blond(e)**
colourlessness
426 n.
whitish 427 adj.
yellowness 433 n.
platitude
truth 494 n.
maxim 496 n.
lack of meaning
515 n.
Platonic
pure 950 adj.
platoon
band 74 n.
formation 722 n.
platter
plate 194 n.
horizontality
216 n.
music player
414 n.
plaudits
rejoicing 835 n.
applause 923 n.
plausible
plausible 471 adj.
credible 485 adj.
hypocritical
541 adj.
flattering 925 adj.
play
composition 56 n.
operate 173 vb.
influence 178 n.
range 183 n.
ascend 308 vb.
oscillate 317 vb.
flow 350 vb.
play music
413 vb.
act 594 vb.
stage play 594 n.
action 676 n.
contend 716 vb.
amusement 837 n.
amuse oneself
837 vb.
revel 837 n.
caress 889 vb.
play-acting
duplicity 541 n.

hypocritical
541 adj.
acting 594 n.
play at
be inattentive
456 vb.
amuse oneself
837 vb.
playback
repetition 106 n.
music player
414 n.
play ball
cooperate 706 vb.
playboy
fashionable society
848 n.
sensualist 944 n.
play down
moderate 177 vb.
underestimate
483 vb.
extenuate 927 vb.
player
musician 413 n.
interpreter 520 n.
actor 594 n.
gambler 618 n.
doer 676 n.
agent 686 n.
player 837 n.
play for time
be cunning
698 vb.
be obstructive
702 vb.
playful
merry 833 adj.
witty 839 adj.
innocent 935 adj.
play games
amuse oneself
837 vb.
playgirl
fashionable society
848 n.
sensualist 944 n.
playground
arena 724 n.
pleasure ground
837 n.
playgroup
school 539 n.
play havoc with
harm 645 vb.
impair 655 vb.
playing
music 412 n.
playing field
arena 724 n.
pleasure ground
837 n.

**play into one's
hands**
blunder 495 vb.
play it by ear
know intuitively
476 vb.
be cautious
858 vb.
**play it by the
book**
be cautious
858 vb.
play on
use 673 vb.
playmate
colleague 707 n.
chum 880 n.
play safe
be cautious
858 vb.
play the fool
rampage 61 vb.
be absurd 497 vb.
be foolish 499 vb.
amuse oneself
837 vb.
be ridiculous
849 vb.
be rash 857 vb.
play the game
behave 688 vb.
plaything
plaything 837 n.
**play to the
gallery**
act 594 vb.
be affected 850 vb.
be ostentatious
875 vb.
play tricks on
fool 542 vb.
play truant
be absent 190 vb.
disappear 446 vb.
run away 620 vb.
relinquish 621 vb.
fail in duty
918 vb.
play up
overestimate
482 vb.
be obstructive
702 vb.
disobey 738 vb.
play upon
motivate 612 vb.
play with fire
be in danger
661 vb.
be rash 857 vb.
playwright
author 589 n.

dramatist 594 n.
plea
testimony 466 n.
argument 475 n.
pretext 614 n.
request 761 n.
vindication 927 n.
litigation 959 n.
plead
testify 466 vb.
argue 475 vb.
plead 614 vb.
do law 958 vb.
plead guilty
assent 488 vb.
confess 526 vb.
accuse 928 vb.
be guilty 936 vb.
stand trial 959 vb.
condemn 961 vb.
pleasant
pleasant 376 adj.
pleasurable
826 adj.
amusing 837 adj.
pleasantry
wit 839 n.
please
please 826 vb.
amuse 837 vb.
pleased
willing 597 adj.
pleased 824 adj.
content 828 adj.
pleasurable
pleasurable
826 adj.
pleasure
pleasure 376 n.
amusement 837 n.
pleat
article of clothing
228 n.
fold 261 n.
plebeian
commoner 869 n.
plebeian 869 adj.
plebiscite
judgment 480 n.
vote 605 n.
decree 737 n.
legislation 953 n.
pledge
drink 301 vb.
affirm 532 vb.
oath 532 n.
promise 764 n.
promise 764 vb.
give security
767 vb.
security 767 n.
toast 876 vb.

duty 917 n.
plenary
complete 54 adj.
plenitude
largeness 32 n.
fullness 54 n.
plenteous
plentiful 635 adj.
liberal 813 adj.
plentiful
great 32 adj.
plentiful 635 adj.
plenty
plenty 635 n.
plethora
redundancy 637 n.
satiation 863 n.
pliable
flexible 327 adj.
pliant
conformable
83 adj.
flexible 327 adj.
irresolute 601 adj.
manageable
701 adj.
submitting
721 adj.
servile 879 adj.
pliers
tool 630 n.
pincers 778 n.
plight
state 7 n.
circumstance 8 n.
adversity 731 n.
promise 764 n.
plimsolls
footwear 228 n.
plinth
base 214 n.
stand 218 n.
plod
walk 267 vb.
move slowly
278 vb.
persevere 600 vb.
work 682 vb.
plonk
wine 301 n.
non-resonance
405 n.
plop
descend 309 vb.
plunge 313 vb.
non-resonance
405 n.
plot
piece 53 n.
territory 184 n.
place 185 n.
garden 370 n.

sharp 256 adj.
convergent
  293 adj.
obvious 443 adj.
rational 475 adj.
meaningful
  514 adj.
assertive 532 adj.
witty 839 adj.
pointer
dog 365 n.
indication 547 n.
indicator 547 n.
pointless
long-winded
  570 adj.
feeble 572 adj.
useless 641 adj.
point of no
return
juncture 8 n.
limit 236 n.
goal 295 n.
point of view
view 438 n.
idea 451 n.
bias 481 n.
opinion 485 n.
point out
specify 80 vb.
point to 281 vb.
attract notice
  455 vb.
show 522 vb.
inform 524 vb.
indicate 547 vb.
points
advantage 34 n.
divergence 294 n.
railway 624 n.
point the way
come before 64 vb.
indicate 547 vb.
point to
focus 76 vb.
attribute 158 vb.
point to 281 vb.
attract notice
  455 vb.
make likely
  471 vb.
predict 511 vb.
mean 514 vb.
point up
manifest 522 vb.
emphasize 532 vb.
poise
equalize 28 vb.
expression 445 n.
conduct 688 n.
inexcitability
  823 n.

poison
destroy 165 vb.
destroyer 168 n.
alcoholic drink
  301 n.
murder 362 vb.
be unpalatable
  391 vb.
evil 616 n.
badness 645 n.
poison 659 n.
enrage 891 vb.
be malevolent
  898 vb.
poisoner
murderer 362 n.
offender 904 n.
poisonous
destructive
  165 adj.
deadly 362 adj.
unsavoury
  391 adj.
harmful 645 adj.
diseased 651 adj.
toxic 653 n.
dangerous 661 adj.
causing pain
  827 adj.
poison pen
correspondent
  588 n.
detractor 926 n.
poke
bag 194 n.
pierce 263 vb.
touch 378 vb.
gesticulate 547 vb.
poke fun at
be witty 839 vb.
poke one's nose
in
interfere 231 vb.
be curious 453 vb.
meddle 678 vb.
poker
furnace 383 n.
card game 837 n.
poker-faced
still 266 adj.
unintelligible
  517 adj.
reticent 525 adj.
impassive 820 adj.
inexcitable
  823 adj.
serious 834 adj.
poky
little 196 adj.
restraining
  747 adj.
polar
final 69 adj.

topmost 213 adj.
opposite 240 adj.
cold 380 adj.
polarity
polarity 14 n.
tendency 179 n.
counteraction
  182 n.
oppositeness
  240 n.
pole
extremity 69 n.
measurement of
  length 203 n.
high structure
  209 n.
summit 213 n.
verticality 215 n.
pillar 218 n.
pivot 218 n.
centre 225 n.
limit 236 n.
propeller 269 n.
impel 279 vb.
gauge 465 n.
tool 630 n.
poleaxe
kill 362 vb.
slaughter 362 vb.
axe 723 n.
polecat
mammal 365 n.
stench 397 n.
polemics
argument 475 n.
contention 716 n.
pole position
advantage 34 n.
victory 727 n.
poles apart
have nothing in
  common 14 vb.
contrariety 14 n.
non-identical
  14 adj.
different 15 adj.
against 240 adv.
oppositeness
  240 n.
pole vault
ascent 308 n.
leap 312 n.
leap 312 vb.
police
order 60 vb.
safeguard 660 vb.
manage 689 vb.
rule 733 vb.
restrain 747 vb.
police 955 n.
police state
despotism 733 n.

police station
lockup 748 n.
policy
policy 623 n.
polio
infection 651 n.
nervous disorder
  651 n.
polish
facing 226 n.
smooth 258 vb.
smoother 258 n.
smoothness 258 n.
friction 333 n.
rub 333 vb.
light 417 n.
reflection 417 n.
elegance 575 n.
clean 648 vb.
amendment 654 n.
make better
  654 vb.
beauty 841 n.
good taste 846 n.
be ostentatious
  875 vb.
ostentation 875 n.
polished
smooth 258 adj.
luminous 417 adj.
undimmed
  417 adj.
literary 557 adj.
elegant 575 adj.
clean 648 adj.
polish off
be active 678 vb.
carry through
  725 vb.
polite
courteous 884 adj.
respectful 920 adj.
politic
intelligent 498 adj.
wise 498 adj.
advisable 642 adj.
skilful 694 adj.
political
governmental
  733 adj.
political cor-
rectness
conformity 83 n.
political party
political party
  708 n.
politician
planner 623 n.
manager 690 n.
expert 696 n.
political party
  708 n.

politics
tactics 688 n.
government 733 n.
polka
musical piece
  412 n.
dance 837 n.
polka dot
mottle 437 n.
pattern 844 n.
poll
number 86 vb.
numbering 86 n.
statistics 86 n.
head 213 n.
enquiry 459 n.
judgment 480 n.
vote 605 n.
vote 605 n.
pollen
genitals 167 n.
powder 332 n.
flower 366 n.
pollinate
generate 167 vb.
polling
vote 605 n.
polling booth
electorate 605 n.
polls
vote 605 n.
pollster
enquirer 459 n.
pollute
harm 645 vb.
make unclean
  649 vb.
impair 655 vb.
misuse 675 vb.
pollution
uncleanness
  649 n.
infection 651 n.
unhealthiness
  653 n.
impairment 655 n.
poison 659 n.
misuse 675 n.
slur 867 n.
polo
ball game 837 n.
polo neck
jersey 228 n.
neckline 228 n.
shirt 228 n.
poltergeist
elf 970 n.
ghost 970 n.
spiritualism 984 n.
poly
academy 539 n.
polyester
textile 222 n.

polyethylene
materials 631 n.
polygamy
type of marriage
894 n.
polyglot
speaking 579 adj.
polygon
plurality 101 n.
angular figure
247 n.
polymorphous
existing in many
forms 82 adj.
polyp
swelling 253 n.
polystyrene
wrapping 226 n.
lining 227 n.
materials 631 n.
polysyllabic
long 203 adj.
diffuse 570 adj.
polytechnic
academy 539 n.
polythene
wrapping 226 n.
materials 631 n.
polyunsaturate,
polyunsatu-
rated fat
food content
301 n.
fat 357 n.
polyurethane
resin 357 n.
pomade
ointment 357 n.
pomander
scent 396 n.
pomegranate
fruit and vegeta-
bles 301 n.
pommel
handle 218 n.
sphere 252 n.
pomp
pride 871 n.
ostentation 875 n.
pomp and cir-
cumstance
ostentation 875 n.
pompom
trimming 844 n.
pompous
proud 871 adj.
vain 873 adj.
ostentatious
875 adj.
ponce
pimp 952 n.
ponce about
be affected 850 vb.

pond
shallowness
212 n.
lake 346 n.
ponder
meditate 449 vb.
think 449 vb.
estimate 480 vb.
ponderous
weighty 322 adj.
dull 840 adj.
pong
odour 394 n.
smell 394 vb.
stench 397 n.
stink 397 vb.
pontiff
sovereign 741 n.
priest 986 n.
pontificate
dogmatize 473 vb.
affirm 532 vb.
teach 534 vb.
church office
985 n.
pontoon
boat 275 n.
card game 837 n.
pony
twenty and over
99 n.
cup 194 n.
pony 273 n.
funds 797 n.
ponytail
hair 259 n.
hairdressing
843 n.
pony-trekking
sport 837 n.
poodle
dog 365 n.
toady 879 n.
poof
nonconformist
84 n.
pooh-pooh
disregard 458 vb.
underestimate
483 vb.
hold cheap
922 vb.
pool
combine 50 vb.
lake 346 n.
store 632 n.
store 632 vb.
association 706 n.
acquisition 771 n.
joint possession
775 n.

ball game 837 n.
pool resources
cooperate 706 vb.
pools
gambling 618 n.
pool table
arena 724 n.
stand 218 n.
poor
inferior 35 adj.
incomplete 55 adj.
weak 163 adj.
unproductive
172 adj.
feeble 572 adj.
insufficient
636 adj.
bad 645 adj.
unfortunate
731 adj.
poor 801 adj.
unhappy 825 adj.
disreputable
867 adj.
poorhouse
retreat 192 n.
poverty 801 n.
poor lookout
adversity 731 n.
hopelessness
853 n.
poorly
slightly 33 adv.
weakly 163 adj.
sick 651 adj.
poor show
bungling 695 n.
poor turnout
fewness 105 n.
poor visibility
dimness 419 n.
invisibility 444 n.
pop
paternity 169 n.
jut 254 n.
soft drink 301 n.
bang 402 n.
bang 402 vb.
music 412 n.
give security
767 vb.
borrow 785 vb.
popcorn
mouthful 301 n.
pope
sovereign 741 n.
church dignitary
986 n.
pop-eyed
projecting 254 adj.
popgun
plaything 837 n.

pop in
enter 297 vb.
popinjay
dandy 848 n.
poplin
textile 222 n.
pop out
jut 254 vb.
emerge 298 vb.
poppadom
bread, pastries
and cakes
301 n.
popper
fastening 47 n.
poppy
plant 366 n.
redness 431 n.
poppycock
empty talk 515 n.
pop the ques-
tion
interrogate 459 vb.
request 761 vb.
court 889 vb.
populace
social group
371 n.
common people
869 n.
popular
general 79 adj.
native 191 adj.
governmental
733 adj.
reputable 866 adj.
approved 923 adj.
popularity
repute 866 n.
sociability 882 n.
approbation
923 n.
popularize
vulgarize 847 vb.
popular miscon-
ception
error 495 n.
population
social group
371 n.
populous
multitudinous
104 adj.
pop up
happen 154 vb.
arrive 295 vb.
be visible 443 vb.
appear 445 vb.
porcelain
brittleness 330 n.
pottery 381 n.
porch
entrance 68 n.

lobby 194 n.
threshold 234 n.
doorway 263 n.
access 624 n.
church exterior
990 n.
porcupine
mammal 365 n.
pore
cavity 255 n.
aperture 263 n.
outlet 298 n.
pore over
scan 438 vb.
study 536 vb.
pork
meat 301 n.
pornographic
not nice 645 adj.
erotic 887 adj.
impure 951 adj.
pornography
impurity 951 n.
porous
concave 255 adj.
porous 263 adj.
porpoise
mammal 365 n.
porridge
cereals 301 n.
pulpiness 356 n.
detention 747 n.
port
stopping place
145 n.
stable 192 n.
left-handedness
242 n.
window 263 n.
wine 301 n.
redness 431 n.
shelter 662 n.
portable
little 196 adj.
light 323 adj.
broadcasting
531 n.
portal
threshold 234 n.
doorway 263 n.
portcullis
barrier 235 n.
heraldry 547 n.
obstacle 702 n.
fort 713 n.
portent
omen 511 n.
prodigy 864 n.
portentous
predicting 511 adj.
frightening
854 adj.

porter
doorkeeper 264 n.
alcoholic drink
301 n.
worker 686 n.
servant 742 n.

portfolio
bunch 74 n.
list 87 n.
case 194 n.
collection 632 n.
authority 733 n.
title deed 767 n.
estate 777 n.
jurisdiction 955 n.

porthole
window 263 n.

portico
series 71 n.
lobby 194 n.

portion
part 53 n.
piece 53 n.
fate 596 n.
provision 633 n.
portion 783 n.

portion out
mete out 465 vb.

portly
fat 195 adj.

portmanteau
box 194 n.
storage 632 n.

port of call
stopping place
145 n.

portrait
copy 22 n.
composition 56 n.
record 548 n.
picture 553 n.
description 590 n.
honours 866 n.

portray
liken 18 vb.
imitate 20 vb.
represent 551 vb.
paint 553 vb.

portrayal
assimilation 18 n.
representation
551 n.
description 590 n.

pose
be an example
23 vb.
interrogate 459 vb.
represent 551 vb.
behave 688 vb.
conduct 688 n.
be difficult
700 vb.

affectation 850 n.

pose as
represent 551 vb.

poser
living model 23 n.
question 459 n.
enigma 530 n.
difficulty 700 n.

poseur
imitator 20 n.

posh
fashionable
848 adj.
genteel 868 adj.
ostentatious
875 adj.

position
state 7 n.
order 60 n.
arrange 62 vb.
serial place 73 n.
agency 173 n.
place 185 n.
situation 186 n.
place 187 vb.
station 187 n.
opinion 485 n.
job 622 n.
prestige 866 n.

positive
real 1 adj.
absolute 32 adj.
numerical 85 adj.
electricity 160 n.
positive 473 adj.
forceful 571 adj.

**positive dis-
crimination**
equalization 28 n.
injustice 914 n.

posse
band 74 n.

possess
have sexual inter-
course with
45 vb.
make mad 503 vb.
possess 773 vb.
appropriate
786 vb.

possessed
crazy 503 adj.
frenzied 503 adj.
possessed 773 adj.
excited 821 adj.
diabolic 969 adj.

possession
territory 184 n.
possession 773 n.
property 777 n.
spell 983 n.

possessions
land 344 n.

property 777 n.

possessive
avaricious
816 adj.
loving 887 adj.
jealous 911 adj.
selfish 932 adj.

possibility
possibility 469 n.

possible
liable 180 adj.
possible 469 adj.

post
fastening 47 n.
situation 186 n.
place 187 vb.
displace 188 vb.
pillar 218 n.
travel 267 vb.
send 272 vb.
move fast 277 vb.
advertise 528 vb.
postal communica-
tions 531 n.
correspondence
588 n.
employ 622 vb.
job 622 n.
commission
751 vb.
shame 867 vb.
impose a duty
917 vb.

postage
price 809 n.

postal order
paper money
797 n.

postbag
correspondence
588 n.

postbox
postal communica-
tions 531 n.

postcard
message 529 n.
correspondence
588 n.

postcode
postal communica-
tions 531 n.
correspondence
588 n.

post-dated
anachronistic
118 adj.

posted, be
be situated
186 vb.

poster
advertisement
528 n.

picture 553 n.

posterior
sequential 65 adj.
subsequent
120 adj.
future 124 adj.
back 238 adj.
buttocks 238 n.

posterity
posterity 170 n.

postern
rear 238 n.
doorway 263 n.
fort 713 n.

posthumous
subsequent
120 adj.
late 136 adj.

postilion
rider 268 n.
servant 742 n.

posting
location 187 n.
transference 272 n.
mandate 751 n.

post mortem
death 361 n.
inquest 364 n.
enquiry 459 n.

postnatal
subsequent
120 adj.
pregnant 167 adj.

post office
postal communica-
tions 531 n.

postpone
put off 136 vb.
relinquish 621 vb.
not complete
726 vb.

postscript
adjunct 40 n.
sequel 67 n.
extremity 69 n.

postulant
petitioner 763 n.
nun 986 n.
lay person 987 n.

postulate
postulate 475 vb.
premise 475 n.
axiom 496 n.
propound 512 vb.
suppose 512 vb.
supposition 512 n.
request 761 n.

posture
situation 186 n.
form 243 n.
expression 445 n.
behave 688 vb.

conduct 688 n.
be affected 850 vb.

postwar
subsequent
120 adj.
peaceful 717 adj.

posy
bunch 74 n.
ornamentation
844 n.
love token 889 n.

pot
pot 194 n.
vessel 194 n.
shorten 204 vb.
propulsion 287 n.
shoot 287 vb.
insert 303 vb.
pottery 381 n.
abstract 592 vb.
drugs 949 n.

pot belly
stomach 194 n.
swelling 253 n.

potency
power 160 n.
strength 162 n.
influence 178 n.
utility 640 n.

potent
powerful 160 adj.
strong 162 adj.
vigorous 174 adj.
influential
178 adj.
heraldry 547 n.
intoxicating
949 adj.

potentate
potentate 741 n.

potential
quantity 26 n.
possible 469 adj.

pother
turmoil 61 n.
excitable state
822 n.

pothole
depth 211 n.
interiority 224 n.
cavity 255 n.
aperture 263 n.
search 459 n.
discovery 484 n.

pot-holing
depth 211 n.
descent 309 n.
search 459 n.
discovery 484 n.
sport 837 n.

potion
drink 301 n.

medicine 658 n.
magic instrument
  983 n.
potluck
chance 159 n.
meal 301 n.
gambling 618 n.
non-design 618 n.
non-preparation
  670 n.
sociability 882 n.
potpourri
a mixture 43 n.
medley 43 n.
scent 396 n.
musical piece
  412 n.
pot shot
propulsion 287 n.
potted
short 204 adj.
potter
wander 267 vb.
be inactive
  679 vb.
artisan 686 n.
pottery
pottery 381 n.
art 551 n.
potty
crazy 503 adj.
toilet 649 n.
pouch
bag 194 n.
pouffe
seat 218 n.
poultice
pulpiness 356 n.
practise medicine
  658 vb.
surgical dressing
  658 n.
relieve 831 vb.
poultry
meat 301 n.
poultry 365 n.
pounce
move fast 217 vb.
spurt 277 n.
descend 309 n.
descent 309 n.
leap 312 vb.
plunge 313 n.
pounce on
surprise 508 vb.
attack 712 vb.
take 786 vb.
pound
cut 46 vb.
rend 46 vb.
enclosure 235 n.
strike 279 vb.

weighing 322 n.
grind 332 vb.
lockup 748 n.
coinage 797 n.
pound of flesh
severity 735 n.
interest 803 n.
pitilessness 906 n.
pour
emit 300 vb.
let fall 311 vb.
be wet 341 vb.
flow 350 vb.
rain 350 vb.
abound 635 vb.
pouring
prolific 171 adj.
flowing 350 adj.
pour oil on
  troubled
  waters
assuage 177 vb.
pacify 719 vb.
pour out
empty 300 vb.
let fall 311 vb.
give 781 vb.
pour scorn on
ridicule 851 vb.
pour with rain
rain 350 vb.
pout
jut 254 vb.
gesticulate 547 vb.
gesture 547 n.
be rude 885 vb.
sullenness 893 n.
poverty
feebleness 572 n.
poverty 801 n.
POW
prisoner 750 n.
powder
coat 226 vb.
powder 332 n.
grind 332 vb.
medicine 658 n.
beautify 841 vb.
cosmetic 843 n.
primp 843 vb.
powder keg
pitfall 663 n.
arsenal 723 n.
powder puff
cosmetic 843 n.
powder room
toilet 649 n.
powdery
powdery 332 adj.
power
numerical element
  85 n.

power 160 n.
strengthen 162 vb.
operate 173 vb.
influence 178 n.
style 566 n.
vigour 571 n.
means 629 n.
authority 733 n.
power behind
  the throne
cause 156 n.
influence 178 n.
latency 523 n.
authority 733 n.
deputy 755 n.
power cut
scarcity 636 n.
power dressing
dressing 228 n.
influence 178 n.
power-driven
mechanical
  630 adj.
powered
dynamic 160 adj.
mechanical
  630 adj.
powerful
powerful 160 adj.
forceful 571 adj.
notable 638 adj.
authoritative
  733 adj.
powerhouse
busy person 678 n.
powerless
powerless 161 adj.
weak 163 adj.
power station
workshop 687 n.
powers that be
influence 178 n.
authority 733 n.
master 741 n.
officer 741 n.
powwow
confer 584 vb.
conference 584 n.
advice 691 n.
make terms
  766 vb.
pox
venereal disease
  651 n.
PR
publicity 528 n.
practicable
possible 469 adj.
useful 640 adj.
practical
possible 469 adj.
useful 640 adj.

advisable 642 adj.
practicality
use 673 n.
practical joke
foolery 497 n.
trickery 542 n.
witticism 839 n.
ridicule 851 n.
practically
nearly 200 adv.
practice
continuity 71 n.
regularity 81 n.
permanence 144 n.
empiricism 461 n.
practice 610 n.
vocation 622 n.
preparation 669 n.
exercise 682 n.
observance 768 n.
practise
repeat 106 vb.
play music
  413 vb.
train 534 vb.
learn 536 vb.
accustom oneself
  610 vb.
prepare oneself
  669 vb.
use 673 vb.
do 676 vb.
exercise 682 vb.
observe 768 vb.
practised
knowing 490 adj.
accustomed to
  610 adj.
usual 610 adj.
prepared 669 adj.
expert 694 adj.
practise medi-
  cine
practise medicine
  658 vb.
practise on
experiment
  461 vb.
practising
observant 768 adj.
religious 973 adj.
orthodox 976 adj.
practitioner
doer 676 n.
agent 686 n.
pragmatic
useful 640 adj.
advisable 642 adj.
pragmatism
philosophy 449 n.
good policy 642 n.
prairie
space 183 n.

plain 348 n.
praise
honour 866 vb.
praise 923 n.
praise 923 vb.
praises
thanks 907 n.
praise 923 n.
act of worship
  981 n.
praiseworthy
good 615 adj.
excellent 644 adj.
virtuous 933 adj.
pram
pushcart 274 n.
boat 275 n.
prance
ride 267 vb.
walk 267 vb.
leap 312 n.
leap 312 vb.
be affected 850 vb.
be ostentatious
  875 vb.
boast 877 vb.
prang
aeronautics 271 n.
fly 271 vb.
prank
whim 604 n.
revel 837 n.
prating
empty talk 515 n.
prattle
empty talk 515 n.
mean nothing
  515 vb.
speak 579 vb.
speech 579 n.
chatter 581 n.
prawn
fish as food 301 n.
pray
entreat 761 vb.
deprecate 762 vb.
desire 859 vb.
do penance
  941 vb.
be pious 979 vb.
worship 981 vb.
prayer
entreaty 761 n.
request 761 n.
prayers 981 n.
worship 981 n.
prayer book
scripture 975 n.
prayers 981 n.
church utensil
  990 n.
prayer meeting
public worship

981 n.
prayers
prayers 981 n.
praying
pious 979 adj.
act of worship
981 n.
preach
teach 534 vb.
orate 579 vb.
preacher
preacher 537 n.
chatterer 581 n.
**preach to the
converted**
waste effort
641 adj.
preamble
prelude 66 n.
oration 579 n.
prearrange
do before 119 vb.
predetermine
608 vb.
plan 623 vb.
prepare 669 vb.
precarious
unreliable 474 adj.
unsafe 661 adj.
precaution
protection 660 n.
caution 858 n.
precautions
safeguard 662 n.
preparation 669 n.
precede
precede 283 vb.
precedence
precedence 64 n.
prestige 866 n.
precedent
prototype 23 n.
precedence 64 n.
precursor 66 n.
precursory 66 adj.
rule 81 n.
example 83 n.
prior 119 adj.
previousness
119 n.
guide 520 n.
habit 610 n.
legal trial 959 n.
preceding
preceding 64 adj.
preceding 283 n.
precept
precept 693 n.
precinct
place 185 n.
precincts
region 184 n.

surroundings
230 n.
parsonage 986 n.
precious
ornate 574 adj.
valuable 644 adj.
of value 811 adj.
affected 850 adj.
darling 890 adj.
precious metal
mineral 359 n.
money 797 n.
precious stone
rock 344 n.
gem 844 n.
precipice
high land 209 n.
verticality 215 n.
incline 220 n.
descent 309 n.
pitfall 663 n.
precipitance
rashness 857 n.
precipitate
leavings 41 n.
cause 156 vb.
effect 157 n.
speedy 277 adj.
propel 287 vb.
eject 300 vb.
descend 309 vb.
let fall 311 vb.
be dense 324 vb.
solid body 324 n.
dirt 649 n.
hasty 680 adj.
rash 857 adj.
precipitately
violently 176 adv.
precipitation
subtraction 39 n.
velocity 277 n.
propulsion 287 n.
ejection 300 n.
lowering 311 n.
condensing 324 n.
rain 350 n.
precipitous
vertical 215 adj.
sloping 220 adj.
précis
shorten 204 vb.
shortening 204 n.
translate 520 vb.
translation 520 n.
conciseness 569 n.
compendium
592 n.
precise
arranged 62 adj.
definite 80 adj.
accurate 494 adj.

intelligible
516 adj.
fastidious 862 adj.
formal 875 adj.
pietistic 979 adj.
precisely
truly 494 adv.
precision
touch 378 n.
accuracy 494 n.
intelligibility
516 n.
preclude
exclude 57 vb.
precocious
early 135 adj.
precocity
anticipation
135 n.
preconceived
biased 481 adj.
**preconceived
idea**
prejudgment
481 n.
preconception
prejudgment
481 n.
precooked
ready-made
669 adj.
precursor
precursor 66 n.
predator
killer 362 n.
taker 786 n.
predecease
do before 119 vb.
predecessor
precursor 66 n.
paternity 169 n.
predestination
destiny 155 n.
fate 596 n.
predetermination
608 n.
predestined
impending
155 adj.
fated 596 adj.
predetermined
608 adj.
predetermine
necessitate 596 vb.
predetermine
608 vb.
predicament
predicament
700 n.
predicate
part of speech
564 n.

predict
predict 511 vb.
predictable
unchangeable
153 adj.
prediction
prediction 511 n.
predilection
tendency 179 n.
prejudice 481 n.
choice 605 n.
mental state
817 n.
liking 859 n.
love 887 n.
predispose
bias 481 vb.
motivate 612 vb.
predisposition
tendency 179 n.
willingness 597 n.
mental state
817 n.
predominant
powerful 160 adj.
influential
178 adj.
authoritative
733 adj.
predominate
predominate 34 vb.
pre-eminent
supreme 34 adj.
authoritative
733 adj.
noteworthy
866 adj.
pre-empt
exclude 57 vb.
do before 119 vb.
be early 135 vb.
precede 283 vb.
acquire 771 vb.
pre-emptive
excluding 57 adj.
preen
primp 843 vb.
decorate 844 vb.
pre-existence
existence 1 n.
previousness
119 n.
pre-existing
prior 119 adj.
prefabricated
ready-made
669 adj.
preface
add 38 vb.
come before 64 vb.
put in front 64 vb.
prelude 66 n.

front 237 n.
edition 589 n.
prefatory
preceding 64 adj.
precursory 66 adj.
beginning 68 adj.
prior 119 adj.
prefect
official 690 n.
officer 741 n.
prefer
choose 605 vb.
desire 859 vb.
preferable
excellent 644 adj.
prefer charges
litigate 959 vb.
preference
precedence 64 n.
will 595 n.
choice 605 n.
love 887 n.
**preferential
treatment**
injustice 914 n.
preferment
progression 285 n.
holy orders 985 n.
prefigure
predict 511 vb.
indicate 547 vb.
prefix
add 38 vb.
adjunct 40 n.
affix 45 n.
put in front 64 vb.
precursor 66 n.
front 237 n.
part of speech
564 n.
pregnancy
pregnant 167 adj.
propagation 167 n.
prolific 171 adj.
meaningful
514 adj.
important 638 adj.
pregnant with
impending 155 adj.
prehensile
tactile 378 adj.
retentive 778 adj.
prehistoric
prior 119 adj.
past 125 adj.
olden 127 adj.
prejudge
do before 119 vb.
prejudge 481 vb.
prejudgment
prejudgment
481 n.

publication 528 n.
**pressed for
time, be**
hasten 680 vb.
press forward
progress 285 vb.
pressgang
compel 740 vb.
compulsion 740 n.
take away 786 vb.
taker 786 n.
pressing
weighty 322 adj.
record 548 n.
resolute 599 adj.
compelling
740 adj.
**press into serv-
ice**
avail oneself of
673 vb.
press officer
interpreter 520 n.
the press 528 n.
press on
elapse 111 vb.
progress 285 vb.
lower 311 vb.
press one's suit
be in love 887 vb.
court 889 vb.
(See also **press a
suit**.)
press out
extract 304 vb.
press release
report 524 n.
publication 528 n.
news 529 n.
press stud
fastening 47 n.
pressure
quantity 26 n.
energy 160 n.
vigorousness
174 n.
influence 178 n.
compression
198 n.
impulse 279 n.
gravity 322 n.
touch 378 n.
resolution 599 n.
inducement 612 n.
instrumentality
628 n.
action 676 n.
exertion 682 n.
adversity 731 n.
restriction 747 n.
pressure group
influence 178 n.

motivator 612 n.
petitioner 763 n.
pressurize
impel 279 vb.
prestige
largeness 32 n.
prestige 866 n.
prestigious
reputable 866 adj.
presumably
probably 471 adv.
presume
assume 471 vb.
prejudge 481 vb.
*be of the opinion
that* 485 vb.
expect 507 vb.
suppose 512 vb.
be insolent
878 vb.
presume on
avail oneself of
673 vb.
be free 744 vb.
presumption
opinion 485 n.
expectation 507 n.
supposition 512 n.
hope 852 n.
rashness 857 n.
insolence 878 n.
unjustifed claim
916 n.
presumptuous
rash 857 adj.
impertinent
878 adj.
insolent 878 adj.
unwarranted
916 adj.
presuppose
put in front 64 vb.
do before 119 vb.
prejudge 481 vb.
suppose 512 vb.
pretence
*thing that lacks
substance* 4 n.
foolery 497 n.
supposition 512 n.
duplicity 541 n.
sham 542 n.
pretext 614 n.
ostentation 875 n.
pretend
imitate 20 vb.
imagine 513 vb.
dissemble 541 vb.
be untrue 543 vb.
be affected 850 vb.
pretender
impostor 545 n.

petitioner 763 n.
usurper 916 n.
pretensions
pretension 850 n.
airs 873 n.
ostentation 875 n.
pretentious
absurd 497 adj.
ornate 574 adj.
affected 850 adj.
proud 871 adj.
vain 873 adj.
ostentatious
875 adj.
pretext
pretext 614 n.
prettiness
beauty 841 n.
pretty
greatly 32 vb.
beautiful 841 adj.
**pretty kettle of
fish**
circumstance 8 n.
complexity 61 n.
predicament
700 n.
pretty pass
circumstance 8 n.
complexity 61 n.
predicament
700 n.
pretty penny
dearness 811 n.
pretty well
greatly 32 vb.
prevail
be 1 vb.
prevail 178 vb.
overcome 727 vb.
prevailing
powerful 160 adj.
influential
178 adj.
prevail upon
induce 612 vb.
prevalent
existing 1 adj.
extensive 32 adj.
general 79 adj.
universal 79 adj.
powerful 160 adj.
influential
178 adj.
known 490 adj.
prevaricate
be equivocal
518 vb.
dissemble 541 vb.
be dishonest
930 vb.
prevent
counteract 182 vb.

obstruct 702 vb.
prohibit 757 vb.
preventative
counteraction
182 n.
prevention
counteraction
182 n.
avoidance 620 n.
hindrance 702 n.
restraint 747 n.
preventive
excluding 57 adj.
counteraction
182 n.
preventive 658 n.
**preventive
measure**
protection 660 n.
**preventive
medicine**
medical art 658 n.
preservation
666 n.
preview
precursor 66 n.
do before 119 vb.
previousness
119 n.
inspection 438 n.
film 445 n.
manifestation
522 n.
dramatic theory
594 n.
previous
preceding 64 adj.
anachronistic
118 adj.
prior 119 adj.
**previous
engagement**
pretext 614 n.
prewar
prior 119 adj.
antiquated
127 adj.
peaceful 717 adj.
prey
animal 365 n.
objective 617 n.
chase 619 n.
sufferer 825 n.
prey on
eat 301 vb.
**prey on one's
mind**
absorb 449 vb.
trouble 827 vb.
frighten 854 vb.
priapism
sexual urge 859 n.

illicit love 951 n.
price
price 809 n.
price 809 vb.
priceless
profitable 640 adj.
valuable 644 adj.
of value 811 adj.
funny 849 adj.
price war
contention 716 n.
prick
small thing 33 n.
cut 46 vb.
stimulant 174 n.
be sharp 256 vb.
sharp point 256 n.
pierce 263 vb.
give pain 377 vb.
incite 612 vb.
wound 655 n.
wound 655 vb.
stimulator 821 n.
prickle
prickle 256 n.
foliage 366 n.
prickly
sharp 256 adj.
irascible 892 adj.
prick out
implant 303 vb.
cultivate 370 vb.
**prick up (one's
ears)**
elevate 310 vb.
hear 415 vb.
be curious 453 vb.
be attentive
455 vb.
pricy
dear 811 adj.
pride
pride 871 n.
ostentation 875 n.
vice 934 n.
impiety 980 n.
pride and joy
favourite 890 n.
pride of place
precedence 64 n.
preceding 283 n.
authority 733 n.
priest
church officer
986 n.
cleric 986 n.
priest 986 n.
priestess
priest 986 n.
priesthood
church office
985 n.

publicity 528 n.
teaching 534 n.
misteaching
  535 n.
inducement 612 n.
warfare 718 n.
propagandist
publicizer 528 n.
motivator 612 n.
propagate
augment 36 vb.
generate 167 vb.
make fruitful
  171 vb.
publish 528 vb.
propagator
propagation 167 n.
abundance 171 n.
flower 366 n.
garden 370 n.
propel
propel 287 vb.
propellant
propellant 287 n.
propeller
propeller 269 n.
rotator 315 n.
propensity
willingness 597 n.
liking 859 n.
proper
relevant 9 adj.
fit 24 adj.
component 58 adj.
advisable 642 adj.
tasteful 846 adj.
well-bred 848 adj.
right 913 adj.
due 915 adj.
virtuous 933 adj.
**properties (the-
  atrical)**
stage set 594 n.
property
essential part 5 n.
ability 160 n.
lands 777 n.
property 777 n.
prophecy
prediction 511 n.
revelation 975 n.
prophesy
foresee 510 vb.
predict 511 vb.
prophet
sage 500 n.
oracle 511 n.
preacher 537 n.
warner 664 n.
religious teacher
  973 n.
worshipper 981 n.

psychic 984 n.
priest 986 n.
prophetess
oracle 511 n.
priest 986 n.
prophetic
foreseeing 510 adj.
predicting 511 adj.
revelational
  975 adj.
scriptural 975 adj.
psychical 984 n.
**prophet of
  doom**
overestimation
  482 n.
propitiate
pacify 719 vb.
mediate 720 vb.
content 828 vb.
atone 941 vb.
offer worship
  981 vb.
propitious
opportune 137 adj.
beneficial 644 adj.
halcyon 730 adj.
promising 852 adj.
proportion
relativeness 9 n.
correlation 12 n.
adjust 24 vb.
suitability 24 n.
degree 27 n.
part 53 n.
ratio 85 n.
symmetry 245 n.
elegance 575 n.
portion 783 n.
proportional
relative 9 adj.
correlative 12 adj.
agreeing 24 adj.
comparative 27 n.
numerical 85 adj.
**proportional
  representa-
  tion**
vote 605 n.
government 733 n.
proportionate
relative 9 adj.
correlative 12 adj.
agreeing 24 adj.
proportioned
symmetrical
  245 adj.
proportions
measure 183 n.
size 195 n.
proposal
supposition 512 n.

intention 617 n.
plan 623 n.
advice 691 n.
offer 759 n.
request 761 n.
wooing 889 n.
propose
propound 512 vb.
select 605 vb.
intend 617 vb.
advise 691 vb.
patronize 703 vb.
offer 759 vb.
court 889 vb.
**propose mar-
  riage**
court 889 vb.
proposition
topic 452 n.
supposition 512 n.
plan 623 n.
advice 691 n.
offer 759 n.
request 761 n.
debauch 951 vb.
propound
propound 512 vb.
proprietary
proprietary
  777 adj.
proprieties
etiquette 848 n.
**proprietor, pro-
  prietress,
  proprietrix**
owner 776 n.
propriety
relevance 9 n.
suitability 24 n.
elegance 575 n.
good policy 642 n.
good taste 846 n.
etiquette 848 n.
right 913 n.
purity 950 n.
props
stage set 594 n.
propulsion
propulsion 287 n.
prop up
preserve 666 vb.
aid 703 vb.
pro rata
pro rata 783 adv.
prosaic
typical 83 adj.
feeble 572 adj.
plain 573 adj.
prosaic 593 adj.
tedious 838 adj.
dull 840 adj.
pros and cons
reasons 475 n.

proscribe
command 737 vb.
prohibit 757 vb.
condemn 961 vb.
proscription
prohibition 757 n.
curse 899 n.
condemnation
  961 n.
penalty 963 n.
prose
prose 593 n.
prosecute
do 676 vb.
indict 928 vb.
litigate 959 vb.
prosecution
accusation 928 n.
legal trial 959 n.
litigation 959 n.
prosecutor
accuser 928 n.
litigant 959 n.
proselyte
learner 538 n.
prosody
prosody 593 n.
prospect
futurity 124 n.
destiny 155 n.
range 183 n.
view 438 n.
search 459 vb.
be tentative
  461 vb.
expectation 507 n.
prediction 511 n.
art subject 553 n.
intention 617 n.
prospective
future 124 adj.
expected 507 adj.
foreseeing 510 adj.
prospector
enquirer 459 n.
experimenter
  461 n.
detector 484 n.
prospectus
list 87 n.
foresight 510 n.
prediction 511 n.
compendium
  592 n.
policy 623 n.
prosper
grow 36 vb.
get better 654 vb.
prosper 730 vb.
prosperity
prosperity 730 n.
prosperous
prosperous

  730 adj.
prostate
genitals 167 n.
prosthesis
precedence 64 n.
substitute 150 n.
leg 267 n.
surgery 658 n.
prostitute
sexual partner
  45 n.
pervert 655 vb.
misuse 675 vb.
debauch 951 vb.
prostitute 952 n.
prostitution
deterioration
  655 n.
misuse 675 n.
social evil 951 n.
prostrate
disable 161 vb.
low 210 adj.
flatten 216 vb.
flat on one's back
  216 adj.
fell 311 vb.
sick 651 adj.
fatigue 684 vb.
fatigued 684 adj.
submitting
  721 adj.
suffering 825 adj.
sadden 834 vb.
servile 879 adj.
respectful 920 adj.
prostrated
impotent 161 adj.
**prostrate one-
  self**
stoop 311 vb.
greet 884 vb.
show respect
  920 vb.
be penitent
  939 vb.
worship 981 vb.
perform ritual
  988 vb.
prostration
helplessness
  161 n.
weakness 163 n.
lowness 210 n.
lowering 311 n.
illness 651 n.
fatigue 684 n.
submission 721 n.
sorrow 825 n.
dejection 834 n.
servility 879 n.
respects 920 n.

prudish
severe 735 adj.
affected 850 adj.
modest 874 adj.
prudish 950 adj.
prune
subtract 39 vb.
cut 46 vb.
make smaller
198 vb.
shorten 204 vb.
fruit and vegeta-
bles 301 n.
extract 304 vb.
cultivate 370 vb.
prurient
inquisitive
453 adj.
impure 951 adj.
lecherous 951 adj.
pry
scan 438 vb.
be curious 453 vb.
enquire 459 vb.
pry into
search 459 vb.
meddle 678 vb.
P.S.
adjunct 40 n.
psalm
vocal music 412 n.
hymn 981 n.
psalter
vocal music 412 n.
scripture 975 n.
hymn 981 n.
hymnbook 988 n.
pseud
impostor 545 n.
pseudo
simulating 18 adj.
imitative 20 adj.
false 541 adj.
pseudonym
thing that lacks
substance 4 n.
name 561 n.
misnomer 562 n.
psyche
self 80 n.
subjectivity 320 n.
intellect 447 n.
spirit 447 n.
mental state
817 n.
psychedelic
intoxicating
949 adj.
psychiatry
psychology 447 n.
mental disorder
503 n.

therapy 658 n.
psychic
non-material
320 adj.
psychic 984 n.
psychical 984 n.
psychical
psychical 984 n.
psychoanalysis
psychology 447 n.
therapy 658 n.
psychodrama
psychology 447 n.
representation
551 n.
drama 594 n.
psychokinesis
motion 265 n.
psychics 984 n.
**psychological
moment**
crisis 137 n.
psychology
psychology 447 n.
mental state
817 n.
**psych oneself
up**
prepare oneself
669 vb.
psychopath
violent creature
176 n.
killer 362 n.
the maladjusted
504 n.
psychosis
psychosis 503 n.
psychosomatic
diseased 651 adj.
psychotherapy
psychology 447 n.
mental disorder
503 n.
therapy 658 n.
psychotic
psychotic 503 adj.
psychotic 504 n.
psych up
invigorate 174 vb.
prepare oneself
669 vb.
pub
focus 76 n.
tavern 192 n.
social round
882 n.
pub-crawl
drunkenness
949 n.
puberty
propagation 167 n.

pubescence
youth 130 n.
public
social group
371 n.
known 490 adj.
manifest 522 adj.
shown 522 adj.
noteworthy
866 adj.
formal 875 adj.
showy 875 adj.
public, the
common people
869 n.
**public address
system**
megaphone 400 n.
hearing aid 415 n.
publicity 528 n.
publican
caterer 633 n.
receiver 782 n.
publication
publication 528 n.
book 589 n.
public baths
washing 648 n.
**public conven-
ience**
toilet 649 n.
public domain
joint possession
775 n.
public enemy
enemy 881 n.
offender 904 n.
public enquiry
enquiry 459 n.
adviser 691 n.
public eye
publicity 528 n.
public figure
person of repute
866 n.
public house
tavern 192 n.
publicist
exhibitor 522 n.
publicizer 528 n.
dissertator 591 n.
publicity
publicity 528 n.
publicize
attract notice
455 vb.
manifest 522 vb.
communicate
524 vb.
divulge 526 vb.
advertise 528 vb.
public life
vocation 622 n.

**public limited
company**
corporation 708 n.
publicly
remarkably 32 vb.
public nuisance
hateful object
888 n.
public opinion
belief 485 n.
consensus 488 n.
tribunal 956 n.
**public opinion
poll**
enquiry 459 n.
**public prosecu-
tor**
accuser 928 n.
law officer 955 n.
public relations
publicity 528 n.
public speaking
oratory 579 n.
public-spirited
patriotic 901 adj.
**public trans-
port**
vehicle 274 n.
publish
publish 528 vb.
publisher
publicizer 528 n.
book person
589 n.
publishing
publication 528 n.
**publish the
banns**
court 889 vb.
marry 894 vb.
puce
brown 430 adj.
purple 436 adj.
puck
missile 287 n.
pucker
become small
198 vb.
fold 261 n.
fold 261 vb.
pudding
sequel 67 n.
dessert 301 n.
dish 301 n.
puddle
shallowness
212 n.
lake 346 n.
puerile
foolish 499 adj.
trivial 639 adj.
immature 670 adj.

puff
vary 152 vb.
distension 197 n.
enlarge 197 vb.
emit 300 vb.
bread, pastries
and cakes
301 n.
blow 352 vb.
breathe 352 vb.
breeze 352 n.
smoke 388 vb.
overestimate
482 vb.
advertise 528 vb.
advertisement
528 n.
exaggerate 546 vb.
be fatigued
684 vb.
boast 877 n.
praise 923 n.
praise 923 vb.
flatter 925 vb.
puff out
enlarge 197 vb.
puff up
enlarge 197 vb.
elevate 310 vb.
praise 923 vb.
pugilism
boxing 716 n.
sport 837 n.
pugilistic
warlike 718 adj.
pugnacious
quarrelling
709 adj.
warlike 718 adj.
pugnacity
quarrelsomeness
709 n.
attack 712 n.
aggressiveness
718 n.
irascibility 892 n.
pug-nosed
short 204 adj.
puke
clearing 300 n.
vomit 300 vb.
pull
advantage 34 n.
force 176 vb.
influence 178 n.
move 265 vb.
row 269 vb.
transpose 272 vb.
deflect 282 vb.
propel 287 vb.
propulsion 287 n.
draw 288 vb.

execute 963 vb.
put to flight
propel 287 vb.
defeat 727 vb.
defeated 728 adj.
put together
join 45 vb.
combine 50 vb.
compose 56 vb.
bring together
74 vb.
produce 164 vb.
put to rights
regularize 62 vb.
put to shame
shame 867 vb.
humiliate 872 vb.
not respect 921 vb.
defame 926 vb.
put to sleep
kill 362 vb.
make insensitive
375 vb.
make inactive
679 vb.
put to the test
experiment
461 vb.
put to the vote
vote 605 vb.
put to use
use 673 vb.
put to work
initiate 68 vb.
work 682 vb.
**put two and
two together**
reason 475 vb.
putty
adhesive 47 n.
softness 327 n.
pulpiness 356 n.
**putty in one's
hands**
willingness 597 n.
irresolution 601 n.
persuadability
612 n.
put up
place 187 vb.
place oneself
187 vb.
elevate 310 vb.
select 605 vb.
predetermine
608 vb.
provide 633 vb.
put up a fight
contend 716 vb.
put up for
patronize 703 vb.
put up for sale
offer 759 vb.

sell 793 vb.
put-up job
duplicity 541 n.
predetermination
608 n.
plot 623 n.
false charge 928 n.
put upon
ill-treat 645 vb.
oppress 735 vb.
**put up the
banns**
wed 894 vb.
**put up the
shutters**
terminate 69 vb.
cease 145 vb.
close 264 vb.
screen 421 vb.
put up to
incite 612 vb.
put up with
substitute 150 vb.
acquiesce 488 vb.
knuckle under
721 vb.
be lax 734 vb.
permit 756 vb.
be patient 823 vb.
suffer 825 vb.
forgive 909 vb.
puzzle
complexity 61 n.
puzzle 474 vb.
enigma 530 n.
difficulty 700 n.
worry 825 n.
prodigy 864 n.
puzzling
puzzling 517 adj.
PVC
materials 631 n.
pyjamas
nightwear 228 n.
pylon
electronics 160 n.
high structure
209 n.
pyramid
series 71 n.
fixture 153 n.
building 164 n.
bulk 195 n.
high structure
209 n.
angular figure
247 n.
tomb 364 n.
pyre
interment 364 n.
fire 379 n.
pyromania
arson 381 n.

pyrotechnics
fire 379 n.
spectacle 445 n.
pageant 875 n.

Q

Q.C.
lawyer 958 n.
qi
energy 160 n.
strength 162 n.
life 360 n.
quack
howl 409 vb.
howling 409 n.
dabbler 493 n.
false 541 adj.
impostor 545 n.
doctor 658 n.
unskilled 695 adj.
quad
focus 76 n.
existence as four
96 n.
place 185 n.
meeting place
192 n.
print-type 587 n.
quadrangle
existence as four
96 n.
place 185 n.
meeting place
192 n.
angular figure
247 n.
quadrant
angular measure
247 n.
arc 250 n.
sailing aid 269 n.
gauge 465 n.
measurement
465 n.
quadrate
four 96 adj.
multiply by four
97 vb.
quadratic
four 96 adj.
quadrennial
four 96 adj.
seasonal 141 adj.
**quadricenten-
nial**
seasonal 141 adj.
quadrilateral
four 96 adj.
existence as four
96 n.

lateral 239 adj.
angular figure
247 n.
quadrillion
over one hundred
99 n.
quadruped
existence as four
96 n.
horse 273 n.
animal 365 n.
quadruple
fourfold 97 adj.
multiply by four
97 vb.
quadruplet
existence as four
96 n.
child 132 n.
quadruplex
fourfold 97 adj.
quadruplicate
fourfold 97 adj.
multiply by four
97 vb.
quagmire
marsh 347 n.
pitfall 663 n.
difficulty 700 n.
quail
recoil 280 vb.
table bird 365 n.
be nervous 854 vb.
quake 854 vb.
be cowardly
856 vb.
quaint
ridiculous 849 adj.
quake
outbreak 176 n.
be cold 380 vb.
show feeling
818 vb.
quake 854 vb.
qualification
suitability 24 n.
ability 160 n.
qualification
468 n.
success 727 n.
what is due 915 n.
qualified
fit 24 adj.
mixed 43 adj.
qualifying 468 adj.
prepared 669 adj.
expert 694 adj.
qualify
modify 143 vb.
moderate 177 vb.
qualify 468 vb.
train 534 vb.

suffice 635 vb.
succeed 727 vb.
qualitative
characteristic
5 adj.
quality
character 5 n.
sort 77 n.
tendency 179 n.
excellent 644 adj.
goodness 644 n.
qualms
regret 830 n.
nervousness 854 n.
quandary
circumstance 8 n.
dubiety 474 n.
predicament
700 n.
quango
director 690 n.
council 692 n.
party 708 n.
nominee 754 n.
quantify
specify 80 vb.
measure 465 vb.
quantitative
quantitative
26 adj.
quantities
great quantity
32 n.
quantity
quantity 26 n.
great quantity
32 n.
number 85 n.
quantum
finite quantity
26 n.
element 319 n.
quantum leap
progression 285 n.
success 727 n.
quarantine
disunion 46 n.
set apart 46 vb.
exclude 57 vb.
exclusion 57 n.
computing 86 n.
hygiene 652 n.
preventive 658 n.
protection 660 n.
preservation
666 n.
detention 747 n.
imprison 747 vb.
seclude 883 vb.
seclusion 883 n.
quark
minuteness 196 n.

variegate 437 vb.
quin
five 99 n.
quincentennial
seasonal 141 adj.
quinine
antidote 658 n.
preventive 658 n.
quinquennial
periodic 110 adj.
seasonal 141 adj.
quinquennium
period 110 n.
quintessence
essential part 5 n.
goodness 644 n.
perfection 646 n.
quintet
five 99 n.
orchestra 413 n.
quintuplet
five 99 n.
child 132 n.
quip
be witty 839 vb.
witticism 839 n.
indignity 921 n.
quirk
speciality 80 n.
nonconformity
84 n.
eccentricity 503 n.
whim 604 n.
quisling
recanter 603 n.
collaborator
707 n.
rebel 738 n.
bad person 938 n.
quit
separate 46 vb.
depart 296 vb.
relinquish 621 vb.
resign 753 vb.
fail in duty
918 vb.
quite
greatly 32 vb.
slightly 33 adv.
completely 54 adv.
quite something
prodigy 864 n.
quite the
reverse
contrariety 14 n.
inversely 221 adv.
quit one's post
relinquish 621 vb.
quits
equal 28 adj.
equivalence 28 n.
atonement 941 n.

quiver
accumulation
74 n.
case 194 n.
oscillate 317 vb.
agitation 318 n.
be agitated
318 vb.
feel pain 377 vb.
be cold 380 vb.
storage 632 n.
arsenal 723 n.
feeling 818 n.
show feeling
818 vb.
be excited 821 vb.
quake 854 vb.
quixotic
disinterested
931 adj.
quiz
gaze 438 vb.
watch 441 vb.
be curious 453 vb.
interrogate 459 vb.
interrogation
459 n.
broadcast 531 n.
indoor game
837 n.
quizzical
enquiring 459 adj.
quorum
finite quantity
26 n.
fullness 54 n.
electorate 605 n.
sufficiency 635 n.
parliament 692 n.
quota
finite quantity
26 n.
part 53 n.
portion 783 n.
quotable
relevant 9 adj.
quotation
act of referring
9 n.
part 53 n.
repetition 106 n.
evidence 466 n.
exhibit 522 n.
price 809 n.
quotation
marks
punctuation
547 n.
quote
part 53 n.
exemplify 83 vb.
repeat 106 vb.

manifest 522 vb.
quotidian
seasonal 141 adj.
quotient
quantity 26 n.
numerical element
85 n.

R

rabbet
join 45 vb.
furrow 262 n.
rabbi
theologian 973 n.
priest 986 n.
rabbit
mammal 365 n.
beginner 538 n.
coward 856 n.
rabbit on
be diffuse 570 vb.
be talkative
581 vb.
rabbit warren
abundance 171 n.
rabble
rabble 869 n.
rabble-rouser
motivator 612 n.
agitator 738 n.
stimulator 821 n.
rabid
furious 176 adj.
frenzied 503 adj.
excitable 822 adj.
angry 891 adj.
rabies
animal disease
651 n.
infection 651 n.
raccoon
mammal 365 n.
race
race 11 n.
travel 267 vb.
hasten 680 vb.
conduct 688 n.
community 708 n.
contend 716 vb.
racing 716 n.
amuse oneself
837 vb.
race against
time
haste 680 n.
racecourse
meeting place
192 n.
gambling den
618 n.

racing 716 n.
arena 724 n.
racetrack
path 624 n.
arena 724 n.
racial
ethnic 11 adj.
parental 169 adj.
racialism
prejudice 481 n.
hatred 888 n.
racialist
biased 481 adj.
narrow mind
481 n.
enemy 881 n.
racing
speedy 277 adj.
flowing 350 adj.
hasty 680 adj.
racing 716 n.
sport 837 n.
racism
prejudice 481 n.
hatred 888 n.
injustice 914 n.
racist
biased 481 adj.
narrow mind
481 n.
rack
compartment
194 n.
hanger 217 n.
shelf 218 n.
distort 246 vb.
pain 377 n.
suffering 825 n.
torment 827 vb.
instrument of pun-
ishment or torture
964 n.
rack and ruin
ruin 165 n.
racket
turmoil 61 n.
commotion 318 n.
loudness 400 n.
roll 403 n.
discord 411 n.
trickery 542 n.
plot 623 n.
quarrel 709 n.
perfidiousness
930 n.
racketeer
robber 789 n.
offender 904 n.
be dishonest
930 vb.
rack one's
brains
think 449 vb.

remember 505 vb.
raconteur
speaker 579 n.
humorist 839 n.
racy
vigorous 174 adj.
stylistic 566 adj.
forceful 571 adj.
lively 819 adj.
witty 839 adj.
impure 951 adj.
radar
location 187 n.
sailing aid 269 n.
detector 484 n.
telecommunication
531 n.
indicator 547 n.
radially
lengthwise
203 adv.
radiance
glow 417 n.
light 417 n.
beauty 841 n.
radiant
divergent 294 adj.
luminous 417 adj.
happy 824 adj.
cheerful 833 adj.
beautiful 841 adj.
radiate
separate 46 vb.
be dispersed 75 vb.
diverge 294 vb.
radiate 417 vb.
radiation
dispersion 75 n.
divergence 294 n.
radiation 417 n.
radiator
heater 383 n.
radical
numerical 85 adj.
revolutionary
149 adj.
revolutionary
149 n.
fundamental
156 adj.
source 156 n.
important 638 adj.
improving 654 adj.
reformer 654 n.
radio
electronics 160 n.
sound 398 n.
communicate
524 vb.
publicity 528 n.
publish 528 vb.

go to war 718 vb.
war measures
718 n.
command 737 vb.
give courage
855 vb.
be insolent
878 vb.
rallying
recuperation
656 n.
finance 797 n.
rallying cry
call 547 n.
inducement 612 n.
danger signal
665 n.
war 718 n.
rallying point
focus 76 n.
rally round
be in order 60 vb.
cooperate 706 vb.
ram
demolish 165 vb.
collide 279 vb.
ram 279 n.
sheep 365 n.
male animal
372 n.
tool 630 n.
Ramadan
fast 946 n.
holy day 988 n.
ramble
be unrelated
10 vb.
land travel 267 n.
walking 267 n.
wander 267 vb.
stray 282 vb.
be insane 503 vb.
be diffuse 570 vb.
amuse oneself
837 vb.
ramble on
be talkative
581 vb.
rambler
traveller 268 n.
wanderer 268 n.
rambling
lacking order
61 adj.
ram down
fill 54 vb.
close 264 vb.
impel 279 vb.
**ram down one's
throat**
compel 740 vb.
ramekin
bowl 194 n.

ramification
bond 47 n.
branch 53 n.
descendant 170 n.
range 183 n.
filament 208 n.
symmetry 245 n.
divergence 294 n.
ramp
be vertical 215 vb.
incline 220 n.
obliqueness 220 n.
ascend 308 vb.
ascent 308 n.
be agitated
318 vb.
trickery 542 n.
be angry 891 vb.
get angry 891 vb.
rampage
rampage 61 vb.
be violent 176 vb.
excitable state
822 n.
anger 891 n.
rampant
furious 176 adj.
violent 176 adj.
vertical 215 adj.
heraldic 547 adj.
rampart
defence 713 n.
fortification 713 n.
ram raid
attack 712 n.
stealing 788 n.
ramrod
stopper 264 n.
ram 279 n.
firearm 723 n.
ramshackle
flimsy 163 adj.
dilapidated
655 adj.
unsafe 661 adj.
ranch
stock farm 369 n.
cultivate 370 vb.
farm 370 n.
lands 777 n.
rancid
unsavoury
391 adj.
fetid 397 adj.
rancour
enmity 881 n.
hatred 888 n.
resentment 891 n.
malevolence
898 n.
random
non-uniform

17 adj.
mixed 43 adj.
lacking order
61 adj.
casual 159 adj.
indiscriminate
464 adj.
uncertain 474 adj.
aimless 618 adj.
random sample
example 83 n.
equal chance
159 n.
empiricism 461 n.
randy
lecherous 951 adj.
range
medley 43 n.
arrange 62 vb.
series 71 n.
accumulation
74 n.
classification 77 n.
extend 183 vb.
range 183 n.
situation 186 n.
be distant 199 vb.
layer 207 n.
traverse 267 vb.
plain 348 n.
furnace 383 n.
hearing 415 n.
arena 724 n.
be free 744 vb.
merchandise
795 n.
rangefinder
direction 281 n.
telescope 442 n.
**range oneself
with**
join a party
708 vb.
ranger
wanderer 268 n.
keeper 749 n.
rangy
lean 206 adj.
narrow 206 adj.
tall 209 adj.
rank
state 7 n.
relativeness 9 n.
degree 27 n.
graduate 27 vb.
consummate
32 adj.
order 60 n.
arrange 62 vb.
class 62 vb.
grade 73 vb.
serial place 73 n.

classification 77 n.
unsavoury
391 adj.
fetid 397 adj.
estimate 480 vb.
importance 638 n.
bad 645 adj.
have a reputation
866 n.
prestige 866 n.
nobility 868 n.
heinous 934 adj.
rank and file
soldiers 722 n.
common people
869 n.
plebeian 869 adj.
ranking
degree 27 n.
serial place 73 n.
noteworthy
866 adj.
prestige 866 n.
rankle
deteriorate 655 vb.
hurt 827 vb.
huff 891 vb.
be malevolent
898 vb.
ransack
search 459 vb.
take 786 vb.
rob 788 vb.
ransom
restoration 656 n.
rescue 668 vb.
rescue 668 n.
restitution 787 n.
price 809 n.
tax 809 n.
penalty 963 n.
rant
empty talk 515 n.
mean nothing
515 vb.
be diffuse 570 vb.
grandiloquence
574 n.
orate 579 vb.
oratory 579 n.
be excitable
822 vb.
boast 877 n.
boast 877 vb.
be angry 891 vb.
rant and rave
be diffuse 570 vb.
rap
knock 279 n.
strike 279 vb.
bang 402 n.
crackle 402 vb.

classification 77 n.
unsavoury
391 adj.
fetid 397 adj.
estimate 480 vb.

vocal music 412 n.
speak 579 vb.
speech 579 n.
be talkative
581 vb.
chatter 581 n.
chat 584 n.
converse 584 vb.
conversation
584 n.
rapacious
avaricious
816 adj.
greedy 859 adj.
rape
have sexual inter-
course with
45 n.
force 176 vb.
district 184 n.
impair 655 vb.
take 786 vb.
taking 786 n.
stealing 788 n.
debauch 951 vb.
rape 951 n.
rapid
speedy 277 adj.
rapidity
velocity 277 n.
rapids
waterfall 350 n.
pitfall 663 n.
rapier
sharp point 256 n.
side arms 723 n.
rapist
libertine 952 n.
**rap over the
knuckles**
reprimand 924 n.
reprove 924 vb.
corporal punish-
ment 963 n.
spank 963 vb.
rapping
talkative 581 adj.
rapport
relation 9 n.
agreement 24 n.
harmony 710 n.
rapprochement
pacification 719 n.
rapt
attentive 455 adj.
abstracted
456 adj.
impressed 818 adj.
raptorial
thieving 788 adj.
rapture
excitation 821 n.

materials 631 n.
undevelopment
670 n.
ray
small quantity
33 n.
flash 417 n.
rayon
fibre 208 n.
textile 222 n.
raze
demolish 165 vb.
fell 311 vb.
obliterate 550 vb.
razor
sharp edge 256 n.
cosmetic 843 n.
re
concerning 9 adv.
reach
degree 27 n.
range 183 n.
distance 199 n.
length 203 n.
carry 273 vb.
arrive 295 vb.
pass 305 vb.
hearing 415 n.
acquire 771 vb.
**reach new
heights**
culminate 34 vb.
reach out for
take 786 vb.
**reach rock
bottom**
be deep 211 vb.
react
correlate 12 vb.
counteract 182 vb.
recoil 280 vb.
have feeling
374 vb.
be active 678 vb.
feel 818 vb.
reaction
compensation
31 n.
reversion 148 n.
effect 157 n.
counteraction
182 n.
recoil 280 n.
sense 374 n.
answer 460 n.
retaliation 714 n.
deprecation 762 n.
feeling 818 n.
reactionary
permanent
144 adj.
disobedient

738 adj.
rebel 738 n.
read
gauge 465 vb.
decipher 520 vb.
interpret 520 vb.
study 536 vb.
spell 558 vb.
speak 579 vb.
deal with 688 vb.
readable
intelligible
516 adj.
**read between
the lines**
decipher 520 vb.
readdress
send 272 vb.
reader
scholar 492 n.
teacher 537 n.
book person
589 n.
academic title
870 n.
readership
publicity 528 n.
reading
measurement
465 n.
erudition 490 n.
interpretation
520 n.
lecture 534 n.
study 536 n.
oration 579 n.
read into
misinterpret
521 vb.
readjust
adjust 24 vb.
equalize 28 vb.
read one's hand
divine 511 vb.
read out
teach 534 vb.
speak 579 vb.
**read the Riot
Act**
reprove 924 vb.
read through
scan 438 vb.
ready
early 135 adj.
impending
155 adj.
formed 243 adj.
attentive 455 adj.
vigilant 457 adj.
intelligent 498 adj.
expectant 507 adj.
willing 597 adj.

make ready
669 vb.
prepared 669 adj.
ready, the
funds 797 n.
money 797 n.
**ready and will-
ing**
willing 597 adj.
**ready for any-
thing**
prepared 669 adj.
courageous
855 adj.
ready-made
formed 243 adj.
ready-made
669 adj.
ready-mixed
ready-made
669 adj.
ready reckoner
*counting instru-
ment* 86 n.
ready-to-wear
tailored 228 adj.
ready-made
669 adj.
real
real 1 adj.
substantial 3 adj.
material 319 adj.
true 494 adj.
coinage 797 n.
real estate
land 344 n.
lands 777 n.
realism
existence 1 n.
mimicry 20 n.
philosophy 449 n.
accuracy 494 n.
truthfulness
540 n.
representation
551 n.
description 590 n.
realistic
lifelike 18 adj.
true 494 adj.
descriptive
590 adj.
reality
reality 1 n.
realization
existence 1 n.
event 154 n.
materiality 319 n.
discovery 484 n.
knowledge 490 n.
acquisition 771 n.
realize
make external
6 vb.

specify 80 vb.
meet with 154 vb.
materialize
319 vb.
have feeling
374 vb.
perceive 447 adj.
believe 485 vb.
know 490 vb.
understand
516 vb.
carry out 725 vb.
acquire 771 vb.
draw money
797 vb.
cost 809 vb.
real-life
descriptive
590 adj.
really
actually 1 adv.
substantially
3 adv.
truly 494 adv.
realm
territory 184 n.
nation 371 n.
function 622 n.
*political organiza-
tion* 733 n.
real McCoy, the
no imitation 21 n.
realpolitik
cunning 698 n.
real thing
reality 1 n.
identity 13 n.
no imitation 21 n.
authenticity
494 n.
love 887 n.
real-time
computerized
86 adj.
ream
enlarge 197 vb.
paper 631 n.
reap
cultivate 370 vb.
store 632 vb.
acquire 771 vb.
take 786 vb.
reappear
reproduce 166 vb.
be restored 656 vb.
**reap the benefit
of**
find useful
640 adj.
rear
be great 32 vb.
augment 36 vb.

final 69 adj.
produce 164 vb.
generate 167 vb.
be high 209 vb.
be vertical 215 vb.
back 238 adj.
buttocks 238 n.
rear 238 n.
ascend 308 vb.
be agitated
318 vb.
breed stock 369 vb.
educate 534 vb.
rear-end
buttocks 238 n.
rear 238 n.
rearguard
rear 238 n.
warner 664 n.
defender 713 n.
armed force 722 n.
rear its head
be plain 522 vb.
rearrange
arrange 62 vb.
modify 143 vb.
rear up
ascend 308 vb.
elevate 310 vb.
get angry 891 vb.
reason
reason why 156 n.
intellect 447 n.
perceive 447 adj.
thought 449 n.
reason 475 n.
reasoning 475 n.
sanity 502 n.
reasonable
moderate 177 adj.
possible 469 adj.
plausible 471 adj.
rational 475 adj.
credible 485 adj.
true 494 adj.
wise 498 adj.
sane 502 adj.
cheap 812 adj.
just 913 adj.
reasoning
mental 447 adj.
rational 475 adj.
reasoning 475 n.
wise 498 adj.
reason out
think 449 vb.
reassemble
repair 656 vb.
restore 656 vb.
reassure oneself
make certain
473 vb.

sport 837 n.
rocket
grow 36 vb.
rocket 276 n.
missile 287 n.
signal light 420 n.
signal 547 n.
throwing weapons,
projectiles and
missiles 723 n.
reprimand 924 n.
rocketry
aeronautics 271 n.
rocket 276 n.
arms 723 n.
rocklike
permanent
144 adj.
fixed 153 adj.
unchangeable
153 adj.
rock 'n' roll
agitation 318 n.
music 412 n.
dance 837 n.
rocky
weakly 163 adj.
rough 259 adj.
hard 326 adj.
rococo
architectural
192 adj.
ornamental
844 adj.
ornamentation
844 n.
rod
measurement of
length 203 n.
support 218 n.
gauge 465 n.
incentive 612 n.
pistol 723 n.
badge of office
743 n.
scourge 964 n.
rodent
mammal 365 n.
rodeo
contest 716 n.
rod of iron
severity 735 n.
roe
fish as food 301 n.
rogue
trickster 545 n.
ruffian 904 n.
bad person 938 n.
rogue elephant
non-uniformity
17 n.
unsocial person

883 n.
rogues' gallery
record 548 n.
roguish
merry 833 adj.
witty 839 adj.
roister
revel 837 vb.
role
acting 594 n.
function 622 n.
role model
living model 23 n.
role-playing
representation
551 n.
conduct 688 n.
roll
piece 53 n.
bunch 74 n.
list 87 n.
elapse 111 vb.
make smaller
198 vb.
textile 222 n.
coil 251 n.
twine 251 vb.
cylinder 252 n.
smooth 258 vb.
hair 259 n.
fold 261 vb.
be in motion
265 vb.
move 265 vb.
voyage 269 vb.
aeronautics 271 n.
fly 271 vb.
propel 287 vb.
bread, pastries
and cakes
301 n.
rotate 315 vb.
rotation 315 n.
fluctuation 317 n.
oscillate 317 vb.
be agitated
318 vb.
roll 403 n.
roll 403 vb.
record 548 n.
voice 577 vb.
book 589 n.
celebration 876 n.
roll along
travel 267 vb.
rotate 315 vb.
roll back
evolve 316 vb.
roll call
statistics 86 n.
nomenclature
561 n.

roller
flattener 216 n.
wrapping 226 n.
wheel 250 n.
cylinder 252 n.
smoother 258 n.
rotator 315 n.
grinder 332 n.
wave 350 n.
rollercoaster
vehicle 274 n.
fluctuation 317 n.
adversity 731 n.
rollers
hairdressing
843 n.
roller skates
plaything 837 n.
rollicking
merry 833 adj.
roll in
enjoy 376 vb.
be overabundant
637 vb.
be intemperate
943 vb.
rolling
undulatory
251 adj.
motion 265 n.
rotation 315 n.
fluctuation 317 n.
agitation 318 n.
rolling pin
flattener 216 n.
cylinder 252 n.
smoother 258 n.
rolling stone
wanderer 268 n.
rotator 315 n.
roll of honour
list 87 n.
honours 866 n.
roll on
continue 108 vb.
go on 146 vb.
be in motion
265 vb.
**roll out the red
carpet**
celebrate 876 vb.
show respect
920 vb.
roll up
congregate 74 vb.
approach 289 vb.
arrive 295 vb.
rotate 315 vb.
store 632 vb.
**roll up one's
sleeves**
begin 68 vb.

prepare oneself
669 vb.
work 682 vb.
roly-poly
fat 195 adj.
dessert 301 n.
roman
written 586 adj.
print-type 587 n.
**Roman Catholi-
cism**
Catholicism
976 n.
romance
musical piece
412 n.
fantasy 513 n.
conception 513 n.
be false 541 vb.
fable 543 n.
narrative 590 n.
novel 590 n.
love affair 887 n.
romantic
imaginative
513 adj.
visionary 513 n.
literary 557 adj.
feeling 818 adj.
impressible
819 adj.
loving 887 adj.
romanticism
fantasy 513 n.
feeling 818 n.
romanticize
imagine 513 vb.
Romany
wanderer 268 n.
slang 560 adj.
Romeo
lover 887 n.
romp
rampage 61 vb.
leap 312 vb.
be cheerful
833 vb.
amuse oneself
837 vb.
revel 837 n.
caress 889 vb.
rompers
trousers 228 n.
romp home
outstrip 277 vb.
win 727 vb.
rood
cross 222 n.
ritual object
988 n.
church interior
990 n.

roof
home 192 n.
cover 226 vb.
roof 226 n.
shelter 662 n.
rooftop
apex 213 n.
roof 226 n.
rook
bird 365 n.
deceive 542 vb.
fleece 786 vb.
defraud 788 vb.
rookie
beginner 538 n.
soldier 722 n.
room
room 183 n.
room 194 n.
scope 744 n.
rooms
quarters 192 n.
roomy
spacious 183 adj.
roost
live 192 vb.
nest 192 n.
rest 683 vb.
rooster
poultry 365 n.
male animal
372 n.
root
numerical element
85 n.
stabilize 153 vb.
source 156 n.
place 187 vb.
base 214 n.
plant 366 n.
word 559 n.
root about
search 459 vb.
**root and
branch**
completely 54 adv.
revolutionary
149 adj.
destructive
165 adj.
rooted
firm 45 adj.
fixed 153 adj.
habitual 610 adj.
**rooted to the
ground or
spot**
fixed 153 adj.
still 266 adj.
root for
incite 612 vb.
patronize 703 vb.

salvage
restoration 656 n.
restore 656 vb.
rescue 668 vb.
rescue 668 n.
acquire 771 vb.
salvation
restoration 656 n.
preservation
666 n.
rescue 668 n.
liberation 746 n.
salve
lubricant 334 n.
ointment 357 n.
balm 658 n.
relief 831 n.
**salve one's
conscience**
justify 927 vb.
atone 941 vb.
do penance
941 vb.
salver
plate 194 n.
ritual object
988 n.
church utensil
990 n.
salvo
bang 402 n.
qualification
468 n.
bombardment
712 n.
celebration 876 n.
sal volatile
pungency 388 n.
tonic 658 n.
same
identical 13 adj.
uniform 16 adj.
equal 28 adj.
same here
identically 13 adv.
sameness
identity 13 n.
uniformity 16 n.
equivalence 28 n.
tedium 838 n.
same old story
uniformity 16 n.
**same wave-
length**
consensus 488 n.
friendliness 880 n.
samosa
hors-d'oeuvres
301 n.
sample
prototype 23 n.
example 83 n.

taste 386 vb.
enquire 459 vb.
exhibit 522 n.
diagnosis 658 n.
sampler
enquirer 459 n.
sanctify
sanctify 979 vb.
sanctimonious
hypocritical
541 adj.
affected 850 adj.
prudish 950 adj.
pietistic 979 adj.
sanctimony
pretension 850 n.
show of piety
979 n.
sanction
assent 488 n.
assent 488 vb.
endorse 488 vb.
commission
751 vb.
permission 756 n.
permit 756 vb.
consent 758 n.
consent 758 vb.
approbation
923 n.
approve 923 vb.
sanctions
compulsion 740 n.
sanctity
probity 929 n.
divine attribute
965 n.
sanctity 979 n.
sanctuary
retreat 192 n.
reception 299 n.
protection 660 n.
refuge 662 n.
altar 990 n.
church interior
990 n.
holy place 990 n.
sanctum
retreat 192 n.
room 194 n.
refuge 662 n.
seclusion 883 n.
sand
powder 332 n.
dryer 342 n.
soil 344 n.
sandbank
island 349 n.
sandpaper
smoother 258 n.
roughness 259 n.
grinder 332 n.

sands
shore 344 n.
plain 348 n.
sandwich
meal 301 n.
mouthful 301 n.
sandwich board
advertisement
528 n.
sandy
powdery 332 adj.
dry 342 adj.
red 431 adj.
yellow 433 adj.
sane
sane 502 adj.
sangfroid
moral insensibility
820 n.
inexcitability
823 n.
sanguinary
bloody 335 adj.
murderous
362 adj.
sanguine
red 431 adj.
optimistic 482 adj.
expectant 507 adj.
cheerful 833 adj.
hoping 852 adj.
sanitary
healthy 650 adj.
healthy 652 adj.
sanitation
cleansing 648 n.
hygiene 652 n.
sanity
sanity 502 n.
Santa Claus
giver 781 n.
good giver 813 n.
benefactor 903 n.
sap
essential part 5 n.
disable 161 vb.
weaken 163 vb.
fluid 335 n.
moisture 341 n.
semiliquidity
354 n.
ninny 501 n.
dupe 544 n.
impair 655 vb.
sapling
young plant
132 n.
tree 366 n.
sappy
humid 341 adj.
foolish 499 adj.
sarcasm
figure of speech

519 n.
wit 839 n.
witticism 839 n.
ridicule 851 n.
rudeness 885 n.
indignity 921 n.
reproach 924 n.
calumny 926 n.
sarcastic
keen 174 adj.
witty 839 adj.
disrespectful
921 adj.
disapproving
924 adj.
sarcoma
swelling 253 n.
cancer 651 n.
sarcophagus
box 194 n.
interment 364 n.
sardonic
disapproving
924 adj.
sari
robe 228 n.
sarong
skirt 228 n.
sash
frame 218 n.
belt 228 n.
loop 250 n.
window 263 n.
badge 547 n.
decoration 729 n.
badge of rank
743 n.
Sassenach
foreigner 59 n.
sassy
impertinent
878 adj.
discourteous
885 adj.
Satan
Satan 969 n.
satanic
cruel 898 adj.
wicked 934 adj.
diabolic 969 adj.
Satanism
devil worship
969 n.
sated, be
have enough
635 vb.
satellite
successor 67 n.
concomitant 89 n.
follower 284 n.
rotator 315 n.
moon 321 n.

satellite 321 n.
dependant 742 n.
subject 745 adj.
satiated
filled 635 adj.
bored 838 adj.
satiated 863 adj.
satin
textile 222 n.
smoothness 258 n.
satiny
smooth 258 adj.
textural 331 adj.
satire
wit 839 n.
satire 851 n.
reproach 924 n.
satirical
funny 849 adj.
disrespectful
921 adj.
satirist
humorist 839 n.
detractor 926 n.
satirize
satirize 851 vb.
satisfaction
payment 804 n.
enjoyment 824 n.
contentment
828 n.
approbation
923 n.
atonement 941 n.
propitiation 941 n.
reward 962 n.
satisfactory
sufficient 635 adj.
satisfy
fill 54 vb.
have or give sexual
pleasure 376 vb.
demonstrate
478 vb.
convince 485 vb.
suffice 635 vb.
pacify 719 vb.
observe 768 vb.
please 826 vb.
content 828 vb.
satiate 863 vb.
reward 962 vb.
satisfying
pleasant 376 adj.
saturate
fill 54 vb.
pervade 189 vb.
drench 341 vb.
be overabundant
637 vb.
satiate 863 vb.
saturated
full 54 adj.

tasteful 846 adj.
see off
start out 296 vb.
dismiss 300 vb.
see one's way
know 490 vb.
see one through
aid 703 vb.
see out
carry through
725 vb.
seep
infiltrate 297 vb.
be wet 341 vb.
seepage
outflow 298 n.
seep through
exude 298 vb.
pass 305 vb.
seer
sage 500 n.
oracle 511 n.
visionary 513 n.
sorcerer 983 n.
psychic 984 n.
seesaw
correlation 12 n.
correlative 12 adj.
fluctuation 317 n.
oscillate 317 vb.
to and fro
317 adv.
be uncertain
474 vb.
dubiety 474 n.
be irresolute
601 vb.
seethe
congregate 74 vb.
effervesce 318 vb.
bubble 355 vb.
be hot 379 vb.
be excited 821 vb.
see the end of
go on 146 vb.
persevere 600 vb.
see the error of
one's ways
be penitent
939 vb.
become pious
979 vb.
see the last of
cease 145 vb.
see the light
discover 484 vb.
know 490 vb.
understand
516 vb.
be penitent
939 vb.
become pious

979 vb.
seething
hot 379 adj.
heating 381 n.
excited 821 adj.
excitable 822 adj.
see things
be insane 503 vb.
seething with
full 54 adj.
see through
know 490 vb.
understand
516 vb.
carry out 725 vb.
see-through
transparent
422 adj.
see to
be mindful
455 vb.
look after 457 vb.
deal with 688 vb.
segment
break up 46 vb.
part 53 n.
part 53 vb.
piece 53 n.
subdivision 53 n.
component 58 n.
segregate
set apart 46 vb.
exclude 57 vb.
seclude 883 vb.
segregation
disunion 46 n.
separation 46 n.
exclusion 57 n.
prejudice 481 n.
seclusion 883 n.
seismic
revolutionary
149 adj.
violent 176 adj.
seismograph
oscillation 317 n.
meter 465 n.
seize
halt 145 vb.
arrest 747 vb.
take 786 vb.
seize power
take authority
733 vb.
seize the oppor-
tunity
be active 678 vb.
seize up
halt 145 vb.
fail 728 vb.
seizure
spasm 318 n.

illness 651 n.
nervous disorder
651 n.
taking 786 n.
loss of right 916 n.
seldom
seldom 140 adv.
select
abstract 592 vb.
chosen 605 adj.
select 605 vb.
excellent 644 adj.
desire 859 vb.
selection
medley 43 n.
separation 46 n.
accumulation
74 n.
discrimination
463 n.
choice 605 n.
selections
reading matter
589 n.
anthology 592 n.
selective
separate 46 adj.
discriminating
463 adj.
self
identical 13 adj.
self 80 n.
spirit 447 n.
self-assured
positive 473 adj.
assertive 532 adj.
self-centred
vain 873 adj.
selfish 932 adj.
self-complacent
vain 873 adj.
self-confident
positive 473 adj.
resolute 599 adj.
unafraid 855 adj.
proud 871 adj.
self-conscious
affected 850 adj.
nervous 854 adj.
self-contained
complete 54 adj.
reticent 525 adj.
independent
744 adj.
self-control
moderation 177 n.
will 595 n.
resolution 599 n.
restraint 747 n.
inexcitability
823 n.
temperance 942 n.

self-correcting
compensatory
31 adj.
self-deception
sophistry 477 n.
misjudgment
481 n.
credulity 487 n.
error 495 n.
deception 542 n.
hope 852 n.
self-defence
defence 713 n.
resistance 715 n.
vindication 927 n.
self-delusion
lacking substance
4 n.
misjudgment
481 n.
credulity 487 n.
self-denying
temperate 942 adj.
self-destruct
destroy 165 vb.
self-
determination
will 595 n.
independence
744 n.
self-discipline
temperance 942 n.
act of worship
981 n.
self-effacing
humble 872 adj.
modest 874 adj.
self-employed
independent
744 adj.
self-esteem
pride 871 n.
vanity 873 n.
self-evident
certain 473 adj.
manifest 522 adj.
self-explanatory
intelligible
516 adj.
self-governing
governmental
733 adj.
independent
744 adj.
self-government
government 733 n.
independence
744 n.
self-help
aid 703 n.
self-importance
vanity 873 n.

ostentation 875 n.
self-imposed
voluntary 597 adj.
self-indulgent
selfish 932 adj.
intemperate
943 adj.
self-interest
selfishness 932 n.
selfish
selfish 932 adj.
selfless
benevolent
897 adj.
disinterested
931 adj.
self-love
vanity 873 n.
selfishness 932 n.
self-made man
rich person 800 n.
self-opinionated
dogmatist 473 n.
positive 473 adj.
narrow-minded
481 adj.
self-pity
pity 905 n.
selfishness 932 n.
self-possessed
resolute 599 adj.
cautious 858 adj.
self-praise
pride 871 n.
vanity 873 n.
praise 923 n.
selfishness 932 n.
self-
preservation
preservation
666 n.
selfishness 932 n.
self-protection
defence 713 n.
self-regulation
independence
744 n.
self-reliant
resolute 599 adj.
independent
744 adj.
unafraid 855 adj.
self-respect
pride 871 n.
self-restraint
resolution 599 n.
restraint 747 n.
temperance 942 n.
self-righteous
affected 850 adj.
pietistic 979 adj.
self-rule
independence

sense organ
sense 374 n.
instrument 628 n.

senses
intellect 447 n.
sanity 502 n.

sensibility
sensitivity 374 n.
discrimination
463 n.

sensible
sentient 374 adj.
rational 475 adj.
wise 498 adj.
useful 640 adj.
impressible
819 adj.

sensible of
knowing 490 adj.

sensitive
sentient 374 adj.
discriminating
463 adj.
accurate 494 adj.
feeling 818 adj.
sensitive 819 adj.

sensitivity
sensitivity 374 n.
discrimination
463 n.
moral sensibility
819 n.
irascibility 892 n.

sensitized
sentient 374 adj.
sensitive 819 adj.

sensory
sentient 374 adj.
feeling 818 adj.

sensual
sensual 944 adj.

sensuality
materiality 319 n.
pleasure 376 n.
sensualism 944 n.

sensuous
sentient 374 adj.
sensuous 376 adj.
feeling 818 adj.

sentence
part 53 n.
composition 56 n.
period 110 n.
judge 480 vb.
judgment 480 n.
detention 747 n.
find guilty 936 vb.
condemn 961 vb.
condemnation
961 n.
penalty 963 n.
punish 963 vb.

punishment 963 n.

**sentence to
death**
condemn 961 vb.

sententious
judicial 480 adj.
forceful 571 adj.

sentient
sentient 374 adj.

sentiment
opinion 485 n.
feeling 818 n.
excitation 821 n.
love 887 n.

sentimental
feeble 572 adj.
feeling 818 adj.
impressible
819 adj.
loving 887 adj.

sentimentality
feeling 818 n.
moral sensibility
819 n.
love 887 n.

sentiments
moral sensibility
819 n.

sentinel
doorkeeper 264 n.
spectator 441 n.
surveillance 457 n.
protector 660 n.
warner 664 n.
defender 713 n.
keeper 749 n.

sentry
doorkeeper 264 n.
spectator 441 n.
surveillance 457 n.
protector 660 n.
warner 664 n.
defender 713 n.
armed force 722 n.
keeper 749 n.

sentry box
compartment
194 n.

separate
unrelated 10 adj.
subtract 39 vb.
disunite 46 vb.
separate 46 adj.
separate 46 vb.
decompose 51 vb.
disperse 75 vb.
bifurcate 92 vb.
discriminate
463 vb.
select 605 vb.
divorce 896 vb.

separated
divergent 294 adj.

schismatical
978 adj.

separates
suit 228 n.

**separate the
sheep from
the goats**
discriminate
463 vb.

separation
separation 46 n.
dissension 709 n.
divorce 896 n.

separatism
disunion 46 n.
sectarianism
978 n.

sepia
brown pigment
430 n.

sepsis
infection 651 n.

sept
race 11 n.
breed 77 n.

septennial
seasonal 141 adj.

septennium
over five 99 n.

septet
over five 99 n.

septic
bad 645 adj.
unclean 649 adj.
toxic 653 adj.

septicaemia
infection 651 n.

septic tank
stench 397 n.
sink 649 n.

septuagenarian
twenty and over
99 n.

sepulchral
funereal 364 adj.
resonant 404 adj.
hoarse 407 adj.

sepulchre
tomb 364 n.
holy place 990 n.

sequel
sequel 67 n.
reading matter
589 n.

sequence
sequence 65 n.
poem 593 n.

sequential
sequential 65 adj.

sequester
set apart 46 vb.
exclude 57 vb.

deprive 786 vb.
not pay 805 vb.
seclude 883 vb.

sequestered
tranquil 266 adj.
invisible 444 adj.
latent 523 adj.
secluded 883 adj.

sequestrate
levy 786 vb.
punish 963 vb.

sequin
circle 250 n.
finery 844 n.

seraglio
womankind 373 n.

seraph
angel 968 n.

seraphic
virtuous 933 adj.
angelic 968 adj.
pietistic 979 adj.

seraphim
angel 968 n.

serenade
musical piece
412 n.
vocal music 412 n.
sing 413 vb.
court 889 vb.
wooing 889 n.

serendipity
chance 159 n.
discovery 484 n.

serene
tranquil 266 adj.
inexcitable
823 adj.

serenity
inexcitability
823 n.
contentment
828 n.
lack of wonder
865 n.

serf
farmer 370 n.
slave 742 n.
commoner 869 n.

serge
textile 222 n.

sergeant
soldiers 722 n.
army officer
741 n.

sergeant major
tyrant 735 n.
army officer
741 n.

serial
continuous 71 adj.
recurrence 106 n.

periodical 141 adj.
journal 528 n.
reading matter
589 n.
narrative 590 n.

serialize
continue 71 adj.
publish 528 vb.

series
order 60 n.
sequence 65 n.
series 71 n.
number 85 n.
recurrence 106 n.
key 410 n.
broadcast 531 n.
edition 589 n.

serif
print-type 587 n.

serious
great 32 adj.
attentive 455 adj.
resolute 599 adj.
important 638 adj.
sick 651 adj.
dangerous 661 adj.
serious 834 adj.
heinous 934 adj.

sermon
lecture 534 n.
diffuseness 570 n.
oration 579 n.
address 583 n.
dissertation 591 n.
ministration
988 n.

sermonize
teach 534 vb.
be pious 979 vb.

serous
liquid 335 adj.
bloody 335 adj.

serpent
serpent 251 n.
reptile 365 n.
horn 414 n.
deceiver 545 n.
bane 659 n.
wily person 698 n.
Satan 969 n.

serpentine
snaky 251 adj.
animal 365 adj.

serrated
angular 247 adj.
sharp 256 adj.
toothed 256 adj.

serried
cohesive 48 adj.
dense 324 adj.

serried ranks
cohesiveness 48 n.

hinder 702 vb.
fetter 747 vb.
fetter 748 n.
shade
degree 27 n.
small quantity
  33 n.
shade 226 n.
darken 418 vb.
darkness 418 n.
dim 419 vb.
dimness 419 n.
curtain 421 n.
screen 421 vb.
colour 425 vb.
hue 425 n.
qualify 468 vb.
paint 553 vb.
safeguard 660 vb.
ghost 970 n.
shades
shade 226 n.
screen 421 n.
spectacles 442 n.
ghost 970 n.
shadow
thing that lacks
  substance 4 n.
analogue 18 n.
imitation 20 n.
copy 22 n.
peer 28 n.
accompany 89 vb.
concomitant 89 n.
thinness 206 n.
be behind 238 vb.
follow 284 vb.
darkness 418 n.
dim 419 vb.
dimness 419 n.
screen 421 vb.
fantasy 513 n.
hunter 619 n.
pursue 619 vb.
auxiliary 707 n.
close friend 880 n.
shadows
darkness 418 n.
shadowy
non-material
  320 adj.
shadowy 419 adj.
invisible 444 adj.
shady
cold 380 adj.
dark 418 adj.
shadowy 419 adj.
disreputable
  867 adj.
dishonest 930 adj.
lawbreaking
  954 adj.

shaft
have sexual inter-
  course with
  45 vb.
depth 211 n.
handle 218 n.
pillar 218 n.
cavity 255 n.
excavation 255 n.
sharp point 256 n.
tunnel 263 n.
rotator 315 n.
flash 417 n.
tool 630 n.
store 632 n.
throwing weapons,
  projectiles and
  missiles 723 n.
shag
have sexual inter-
  course with
  45 vb.
hair 259 n.
bird 365 n.
tobacco 388 n.
shaggy
hairy 259 adj.
shaggy dog
  story
fable 543 n.
witticism 839 n.
Shah
sovereign 741 n.
shake
mix 43 vb.
come unstuck
  49 vb.
disarrange 63 vb.
vary 152 vb.
be weak 163 vb.
force 176 vb.
wriggle 251 vb.
impel 279 vb.
impulse 279 n.
brandish 317 vb.
fluctuation 317 n.
oscillate 317 vb.
agitate 318 vb.
agitation 318 n.
be agitated
  318 vb.
blow 352 vb.
be cold 380 vb.
roll 403 vb.
musical note
  410 n.
cause doubt
  486 vb.
show feeling
  818 vb.
impress 821 vb.
frighten 854 vb.

quake 854 vb.
threaten 900 vb.
shake hands
meet 295 vb.
make peace
  719 vb.
be friendly 880 vb.
greet 884 vb.
forgive 909 vb.
shake off
outstrip 277 vb.
eject 300 vb.
elude 667 vb.
shake oneself
  free
achieve liberty
  746 vb.
shake one's
  faith
cause doubt
  486 vb.
shake one's fist
defy 711 vb.
shake one's
  head
dissent 489 vb.
negate 533 vb.
gesticulate 547 vb.
refuse 760 vb.
deprecate 762 vb.
disapprove 924 vb.
shake on it
promise 764 vb.
shakes, the
agitation 318 n.
illness 651 n.
shake up
agitate 318 vb.
animate 821 vb.
shake-up
revolution 149 n.
shaking
impulse 279 n.
nervous 854 adj.
nervousness 854 n.
shaky
flimsy 163 adj.
dilapidated
  655 adj.
unsafe 661 adj.
shale
brittleness 330 n.
rock 344 n.
shallow
unproductive
  172 adj.
shallow 212 adj.
dabbling 491 adj.
affected 850 adj.
shallows
shallowness
  212 n.

sham
imitate 20 vb.
imitative 20 adj.
dissemble 541 vb.
false 541 adj.
sham 542 n.
spurious 542 adj.
be untrue 543 vb.
pretension 850 n.
shamble
walk 267 vb.
shambles
disorder 61 n.
turmoil 61 n.
bungling 695 n.
shambolic
lacking order
  61 adj.
shame
evil 616 n.
disrepute 867 n.
shame 867 vb.
slur 867 n.
humiliation 872 n.
wrong 914 n.
improbity 930 n.
guilt 936 n.
purity 950 n.
shamefaced
modest 874 adj.
guilty 936 adj.
shameful
evil 616 adj.
bad 645 adj.
discreditable
  867 adj.
shame into
motivate 612 vb.
shameless
thick-skinned
  820 adj.
vulgar 847 adj.
insolent 878 adj.
dishonest 930 adj.
unchaste 951 adj.
shamming
imitative 20 adj.
shammy
cloth 648 n.
shampoo
rub 333 vb.
clean 648 vb.
cleanser 648 n.
washing 648 n.
hairwash 843 n.
shamrock
three 93 n.
plant 366 n.
heraldry 547 n.
shanghai
ensnare 542 vb.
take away 786 vb.

steal 788 vb.
shanty
small house
  192 n.
vocal music 412 n.
poem 593 n.
shape
mode 7 n.
sort 77 n.
convert 147 vb.
produce 164 vb.
outline 233 n.
form 243 n.
form 243 vb.
appearance 445 n.
feature 445 n.
educate 534 vb.
identification
  547 n.
represent 551 vb.
plan 623 vb.
shapeless
abnormal 84 adj.
formless 244 adj.
unsightly 842 adj.
shapely
shapely 841 adj.
shape of things
  to come
prediction 511 n.
shard
piece 53 n.
share
part 53 n.
divide 92 vb.
mete out 465 vb.
title deed 767 n.
participate 775 vb.
portion 783 n.
feel 818 vb.
be sociable
  882 vb.
share and share
  alike
participate 775 vb.
shareholder
participator 775 n.
owner 776 n.
share in
participate 775 vb.
share out
part 53 vb.
mete out 465 vb.
allocate 783 vb.
share-out
gain 771 n.
participation
  775 n.
portion 783 n.
shares
allocation 783 n.
sharing
equal 28 adj.

shopping centre
meeting place
192 n.
emporium 796 n.
shopping list
requirement 627 n.
purchase 792 n.
shopping mall
meeting place
192 n.
emporium 796 n.
shop-soiled
imperfect 647 adj.
shop steward
official 690 n.
delegate 754 n.
shop window
window 263 n.
exhibit 522 n.
market 796 n.
shore
region 184 n.
support 218 n.
shore 344 n.
shore up
support 218 vb.
preserve 666 vb.
shorn
short 204 adj.
short
incomplete 55 adj.
short 204 adj.
drink 301 n.
deficient 307 adj.
uncommunicative
582 adj.
irascible 892 adj.
shortage
decrease 37 n.
shortfall 307 n.
requirement 627 n.
scarcity 636 n.
short and sweet
brief 114 adj.
concise 569 adj.
shortbread
*bread, pastries
and cakes*
301 n.
shortchange
deceive 542 vb.
overcharge 811 vb.
short-circuit
circuit 626 vb.
shortcoming
shortfall 307 n.
non-observance
769 n.
vice 934 n.
short cut
short distance
200 n.

straightness 249 n.
route 624 n.
shorten
shorten 204 vb.
shortfall
deficit 55 n.
shortfall 307 n.
shorthand
writing 586 n.
shorthanded
unprovided
636 adj.
shorthorn
cattle 365 n.
short leet *or*
short list
list 87 n.
choice 605 n.
short-lived
ephemeral
114 adj.
short measure
shortfall 307 n.
short of
less 35 adv.
incomplete 55 adj.
exclusive of
57 adv.
deficient 307 adj.
short run
brief span 114 n.
shorts
shortness 204 n.
trousers 228 n.
underwear 228 n.
short shrift
pitilessness 906 n.
short-sighted
dim-sighted
440 adj.
misjudging
481 adj.
narrow-minded
481 adj.
unwise 499 adj.
short-staffed
deficient 307 adj.
short step
short distance
200 n.
short supply
scarcity 636 n.
short-tempered
irascible 892 adj.
short-term
brief 114 adj.
short with, be
be concise 569 vb.
short work
easy thing 701 n.
shot
mixed 43 adj.

time 108 n.
period 110 n.
stimulant 174 n.
sphere 252 n.
missile 287 n.
propulsion 287 n.
insertion 303 n.
bang 402 n.
conjecture 512 n.
photography
551 n.
gambling 618 n.
hunter 619 n.
medicine 658 n.
ammunition
723 n.
*throwing weapons,
projectiles and
missiles* 723 n.
drugs 949 n.
shot about
periodic recurrence
141 n.
shotgun
propellant 287 n.
firearm 723 n.
shot in the arm
stimulant 174 n.
shot in the dark
empiricism 461 n.
uncertainty 474 n.
conjecture 512 n.
gambling 618 n.
shot-putter
player 837 n.
shoulder
limb 53 n.
support 218 vb.
carry 273 vb.
impel 279 vb.
propel 287 vb.
meat 301 n.
elevate 310 vb.
print-type 587 n.
undertake 672 vb.
shoulder-length
long 203 adj.
**shoulder one's
responsibility**
incur a duty
917 vb.
**shoulder to
shoulder**
cohesive 48 adj.
shout
be loud 400 vb.
loudness 400 n.
cry 408 n.
shout 408 vb.
affirm 532 vb.
emphasize 532 vb.
call 547 n.

voice 577 vb.
defy 711 vb.
rejoice 835 vb.
rejoicing 835 n.
boast 877 vb.
be rude 885 vb.
anger 891 n.
get angry 891 vb.
shout down
shout 408 vb.
affirm 532 vb.
make mute
578 vb.
be obstructive
702 vb.
be insolent
878 vb.
criticize 924 vb.
disapprove 924 vb.
shout for
applaud 923 vb.
shouting
loud 400 adj.
loudness 400 n.
cry 408 n.
rudeness 885 n.
shove
move 265 vb.
transpose 272 vb.
impel 279 vb.
impulse 279 n.
propel 287 vb.
gesture 547 n.
be active 678 vb.
work 682 vb.
shovel
ladle 194 n.
sharp edge 256 n.
transpose 272 vb.
conveyor 274 n.
furnace 383 n.
shove off
impel 279 vb.
walk out 296 vb.
shoving
hasty 680 adj.
show
point to 281 vb.
be visible 443 vb.
appear 445 vb.
appearance 445 n.
spectacle 445 n.
attract notice
455 vb.
evidence 466 vb.
demonstrate
478 vb.
exhibit 522 n.
show 522 vb.
be disclosed
526 vb.
duplicity 541 n.

stage play 594 n.
amusement 837 n.
pride 871 n.
ostentation 875 n.
pageant 875 n.
show a profit
be profitable
771 vb.
showboat
ship 275 n.
show business
drama 594 n.
showcase
exhibit 522 n.
showdown
disclosure 526 n.
fight 716 n.
shower
crowd 74 n.
propel 287 vb.
descend 309 vb.
descent 309 n.
let fall 311 vb.
water 339 n.
be wet 341 vb.
drench 341 vb.
moisten 341 vb.
rain 350 n.
rain 350 vb.
abound 635 vb.
clean 648 vb.
washing 648 n.
showerproof
strong 162 adj.
dry 342 adj.
invulnerable
660 adj.
resisting 715 adj.
shower upon
give 781 vb.
be liberal 813 vb.
show girl
entertainer 594 n.
show in
admit 299 vb.
showing
obvious 443 adj.
visible 443 adj.
appearing 445 adj.
manifest 522 adj.
shown 522 adj.
dramatic 594 adj.
showing, be
appear 445 vb.
showing off
foolery 497 n.
show interest
be curious 453 vb.
show its face
be visible 443 vb.
be plain 522 vb.
be disclosed

skis
sled 274 n.
skit
stage play 594 n.
satire 851 n.
calumny 926 n.
skitter
be in motion
265 vb.
skittish
capricious 604 adj.
excitable 822 adj.
skittle alley
arena 724 n.
skittles
ball game 837 n.
skive
be absent 190 vb.
be inactive
679 vb.
not complete
726 vb.
skivvy
domestic 742 n.
servant 742 n.
skulduggery
trickery 542 n.
improbity 930 n.
skulk
wander 267 vb.
be stealthy
525 vb.
be cowardly
856 vb.
skull
head 213 n.
dome 253 n.
corpse 363 n.
**skull and cross-
bones**
cross 222 n.
flag 547 n.
heraldry 547 n.
intimidation
854 n.
skullcap
headgear 228 n.
clerical dress
989 n.
skunk
mammal 365 n.
stench 397 n.
cad 938 n.
sky
space 183 n.
height 209 n.
summit 213 n.
propel 287 vb.
heavens 321 n.
skydiving
aeronautics 271 n.
sky-high
enormous 32 adj.

high 209 adj.
dear 811 adj.
skylarking
foolery 497 n.
revel 837 n.
skylight
window 263 n.
skyline
distance 199 n.
horizontality
216 n.
outline 233 n.
edge 234 n.
limit 236 n.
visibility 443 n.
skyscraper
building 164 n.
high structure
209 n.
slab
piece 53 n.
horizontality
216 n.
shelf 218 n.
slack
weak 163 adj.
inert 175 adj.
slow 278 adj.
soft 327 adj.
coal 385 n.
negligent 458 adj.
be inactive
679 vb.
lazy 679 adj.
lax 734 adj.
slacken
decrease 37 vb.
disunite 46 vb.
moderate 177 vb.
slow down 278 vb.
be inactive
679 vb.
slacken off
cease 145 vb.
slow down 278 vb.
slacks
informal dress
228 n.
trousers 228 n.
slag
leavings 41 n.
slut 61 n.
rubbish 641 n.
reproach 924 vb.
slag heap
rubbish 641 n.
slag off
curse and swear
899 vb.
slake
assuage 177 vb.
satiate 863 vb.

**slake one's
thirst**
drink 301 vb.
slalom
racing 716 n.
slam
close 264 vb.
impel 279 vb.
impulse 279 n.
strike 279 vb.
propel 287 vb.
be loud 400 vb.
loudness 400 n.
bang 402 n.
bang 402 vb.
victory 727 n.
detract 926 vb.
slander
slur 867 n.
scurrility 899 n.
censure 924 n.
calumny 926 n.
defame 926 vb.
false charge 928 n.
slang
speciality 80 n.
unintelligibility
517 n.
language 557 n.
slang 560 adj.
curse and swear
899 vb.
criticize 924 vb.
slanging match
conversation
584 n.
quarrel 709 n.
scurrility 899 n.
slant
be oblique 220 vb.
obliqueness 220 n.
appearance 445 n.
idea 451 n.
bias 481 n.
slap
knock 279 n.
strike 279 vb.
bang 402 n.
crackle 402 vb.
*corporal punish-
ment* 963 n.
spank 963 vb.
slap bang
violently 176 vb.
slapdash
negligent 458 adj.
hasty 680 adj.
bungled 695 adj.
clumsy 695 adj.
rash 857 adj.
slap in the face
refusal 760 n.

humiliation 872 n.
anger 891 n.
indignity 921 n.
slapper
loose woman
952 n.
slapstick
dramatic 594 adj.
stage play 594 n.
wit 839 n.
funny 849 adj.
ridiculousness
849 n.
slap-up
liberal 813 adj.
slash
cut 46 vb.
rend 46 vb.
shorten 204 vb.
notch 260 vb.
furrow 262 n.
wound 655 vb.
discount 810 vb.
cheapen 812 vb.
criticize 924 vb.
slat
strip 208 n.
slate
brittleness 330 n.
greyness 429 n.
stationery 586 n.
policy 623 n.
building material
631 n.
criticize 924 vb.
reproach 924 vb.
detract 926 vb.
slating
roof 226 n.
censure 924 n.
reprimand 924 n.
slats
shade 226 n.
slattern
slut 61 n.
dirty person 649 n.
bungler 697 n.
slaughter
slaughter 362 n.
slaughter 362 vb.
slave
instrument 628 n.
be active 678 vb.
minister to
703 vb.
servant 742 n.
slave 742 n.
toady 879 n.
slave away
work 682 vb.
slave-driver
tyrant 735 n.

slavery
labour 682 n.
compulsion 740 n.
servitude 745 n.
detention 747 n.
servility 879 n.
slave to, a
subject 745 adj.
slavish
imitative 20 adj.
conformable
83 adj.
subjected 745 adj.
servile 879 adj.
slay
kill 362 vb.
amuse 837 vb.
sleaze
improbity 930 n.
sled
sled 274 n.
sledge
be in motion
265 vb.
sled 274 n.
sleek
smooth 258 adj.
personable
841 adj.
sleep
sleep 679 n.
sleep 679 vb.
sleep around
*have or give sexual
pleasure* 376 vb.
be impure 951 vb.
sleeper
basis 218 n.
train 274 n.
secret service
459 n.
book 589 n.
sleep in
fail in duty
918 vb.
sleeping dog
latency 523 n.
pitfall 663 n.
sleeping pill
moderator 177 n.
drug 658 n.
sleeping draught
679 n.
**sleeping police-
man**
traffic control
305 n.
sleepless
active 678 adj.
sleep on it
wait 136 vb.
meditate 449 vb.

howl 409 vb.
howling 409 n.
gesticulate 547 vb.
photograph
  551 vb.
photography
  551 n.
picture 553 n.
spontaneous
  609 adj.
unprepared
  670 adj.
card game 837 n.
hatred 888 n.
anger 891 n.
be angry 891 vb.
sullenness 893 n.
snap decision
spontaneity 609 n.
snap one's fin-
gers at
defy 711 vb.
not observe
  769 vb.
hold cheap
  922 vb.
snap out of it
be restored 656 vb.
be cheerful
  833 vb.
snappy
vigorous 174 adj.
speedy 277 adj.
proverbial 496 adj.
witty 839 adj.
irascible 892 adj.
snapshot
photography
  551 n.
snap up
take 786 vb.
snare
ensnare 542 vb.
trap 542 n.
take 786 vb.
snarl
complexity 61 n.
distortion 246 n.
howl 409 vb.
howling 409 n.
be rude 885 vb.
hatred 888 n.
anger 891 n.
be angry 891 vb.
sullenness 893 n.
threat 900 n.
threaten 900 vb.
snarl-up
complexity 61 n.
snatch
small quantity
  33 n.

arrest 747 vb.
take 786 vb.
snatch at
take 786 vb.
snazzy
fashionable
  848 adj.
sneak
informer 524 n.
be stealthy
  525 vb.
bad person 938 n.
sneakers
footwear 228 n.
sneak out
emerge 298 vb.
escape 667 vb.
sneer
insolence 878 n.
contempt 922 n.
criticize 924 vb.
reproach 924 n.
calumny 926 n.
sneer at
dislike 861 vb.
be insolent
  878 vb.
detract 926 vb.
sneeze
breathe 352 vb.
snicker
laugh 835 vb.
laughter 835 n.
snide remark
detraction 926 n.
(See also **cal-**
umny.)
sniff
absorb 299 vb.
breathe 352 vb.
smell 394 vb.
deprecate 762 vb.
be insolent
  878 vb.
contempt 922 n.
disapprove 924 vb.
calumny 926 n.
drug oneself
  949 vb.
sniff at
eat 301 vb.
reject 607 vb.
dislike 861 vb.
despise 922 vb.
detract 926 vb.
sniffle
breathe 352 vb.
sniff out
discover 484 vb.
snigger
cry 408 vb.
laugh 835 vb.

laughter 835 n.
ridicule 851 n.
ridicule 851 vb.
snip
small thing 33 n.
cut 46 vb.
notch 260 n.
notch 260 vb.
cheapness 812 n.
snipe
shoot 287 vb.
table bird 365 n.
fire at 712 vb.
sniper
attacker 712 n.
soldier 722 n.
malcontent 829 n.
snippet
small thing 33 n.
piece 53 n.
snitch
inform 524 vb.
informer 524 n.
steal 788 vb.
snivel
excrete 302 vb.
weep 836 vb.
snob
proud person
  871 n.
snobbish
biased 481 adj.
proud 871 adj.
insolent 878 adj.
disrespectful
  921 adj.
snog
caress 889 vb.
snood
headgear 228 n.
hairdressing
  843 n.
snooker
obstruct 702 vb.
ball game 837 n.
snoop
scan 438 vb.
spectator 441 n.
be curious 453 vb.
enquire 459 vb.
informer 524 n.
be stealthy
  525 vb.
snooper
pedestrian 268 n.
detective 459 n.
snooty
proud 871 adj.
vain 873 adj.
insolent 878 adj.
snooze
sleep 679 n.

sleep 679 vb.
snore
rasp 407 vb.
cry 408 vb.
sleep 679 vb.
snort
drink 301 n.
breathe 352 vb.
hiss 406 vb.
rasp 407 vb.
cry 408 vb.
howl 409 vb.
be insolent
  878 vb.
sullenness 893 n.
contempt 922 n.
despise 922 vb.
drug oneself
  949 vb.
snot
excrement 302 n.
dirt 649 n.
snout
protuberance
  254 n.
tobacco 388 n.
snow
softness 327 n.
rain 350 vb.
snow 380 n.
refrigerator 384 n.
white thing 427 n.
abound 635 vb.
drugs 949 n.
snowball
grow 36 vb.
increase 36 n.
continuity 71 n.
accumulation
  74 n.
expand 197 vb.
missile 287 n.
propel 287 vb.
snow 380 n.
dance 837 n.
snow-boarding
sport 837 n.
snowbound
wintry 129 adj.
snow 380 n.
hindered 702 adj.
restrained 747 adj.
snowdrift
accumulation
  74 n.
snow 380 n.
snowed-up
hindered 702 adj.
snowflake
thing that lacks
  substance 4 n.
softness 327 n.

powder 332 n.
snow 380 n.
snowman
snow 380 n.
image 551 n.
snowplough
vehicle 274 n.
snow 380 n.
snowstorm
storm 176 n.
snow 380 n.
wintriness 380 n.
snow under
be many 104 vb.
snowy
cold 380 adj.
white 427 adj.
clean 648 adj.
pure 950 adj.
snub
short 204 adj.
repel 292 vb.
repulsion 292 n.
shame 867 vb.
humiliate 872 vb.
be rude 885 vb.
indignity 921 n.
not respect 921 vb.
contempt 922 n.
despise 922 vb.
reprimand 924 n.
reprove 924 vb.
snub-nosed
short 204 adj.
snuff
tobacco 388 n.
snuffle
breathe 352 vb.
hiss 406 vb.
snug
retreat 192 n.
tavern 192 n.
room 194 n.
little 196 adj.
marine 275 adj.
comfortable
  376 adj.
warm 379 adj.
content 828 adj.
snuggle
caress 889 vb.
so
thus 8 adv.
similarly 18 adv.
greatly 32 vb.
hence 158 adv.
true 494 adj.
soak
pervade 189 vb.
immerse 303 vb.
drench 341 vb.
fleece 786 vb.

overcharge 811 vb.
satiate 863 vb.
soak in
descend 309 vb.
soaking wet, be
be wet 341 vb.
soak up
absorb 299 vb.
drink 301 vb.
dry 342 vb.
so and so
person 371 n.
no name 562 n.
soap
softness 327 n.
lubricant 334 n.
lubricate 334 vb.
fat 357 n.
clean 648 vb.
cleanser 648 n.
soapbox
publicity 528 n.
oratory 579 n.
soap opera
broadcast 531 n.
narrative 590 n.
soap powder
cleanser 648 n.
soapsuds
bubble 355 n.
soapy
smooth 258 adj.
bubbly 355 adj.
fatty 357 adj.
white 427 adj.
servile 879 adj.
flattering 925 adj.
soar
be great 32 vb.
be high 209 vb.
fly 271 vb.
ascend 308 vb.
be light 323 vb.
be dear 811 vb.
soar above
outdo 306 vb.
sob
breathing 352 n.
rasp 407 vb.
cry 408 n.
cry 408 vb.
voicelessness 578 n.
lamentation 836 n.
weep 836 vb.
sober
moderate 177 vb.
plain 573 adj.
depress 834 vb.
serious 834 adj.
cautious 858 adj.

virtuous 933 adj.
sober 948 adj.
sober up
be sober 948 vb.
sobriety
inexcitability 823 n.
seriousness 834 n.
caution 858 n.
sobriety 948 n.
sob-stuff
feeling 818 n.
excitation 821 n.
so-called
supposed 512 adj.
spurious 542 adj.
untrue 543 adj.
named 561 adj.
vain 873 adj.
soccer
ball game 837 n.
sociable
sociable 882 adj.
social
national 371 adj.
sociable 882 adj.
social gathering 882 n.
social circle
fellowship 882 n.
social class
degree 27 n.
serial place 73 n.
classification 77 n.
community 708 n.
social climber
commoner 869 n.
sociable person 882 n.
social exclusion
poverty 801 n.
social graces
good taste 846 n.
sociability 882 n.
socialism
government 733 n.
joint possession 775 n.
philanthropy 901 n.
socialist
revolutionary 143 n.
socialite
fashionable society 848 n.
sociable person 882 n.
socialize
make better 654 vb.
be sociable

882 vb.
social science
anthropology 371 n.
social care 901 n.
social security
safety 660 n.
monetary help 703 n.
social care 901 n.
social services
social care 901 n.
social whirl
festivity 837 n.
social round 882 n.
social work
social care 901 n.
societal
national 371 adj.
society
accompaniment 89 n.
social group 371 n.
society 708 n.
fashionable society 848 n.
fellowship 882 n.
laity 987 n.
sociology
social care 901 n.
sociopath
the maladjusted 504 n.
sock
strike 279 vb.
drama 594 n.
socket
place 185 n.
receptacle 194 n.
cavity 255 n.
socks
legwear 228 n.
sod
piece 53 n.
soil 344 n.
grass 366 n.
cad 938 n.
sod it
blast! 899 int.
soda
soft drink 301 n.
soda water
soft drink 301 n.
water 339 n.
sodomy
illicit love 951 n.
sod's law
rule 81 n.
axiom 496 n.
disappointment

509 n.
evil 616 n.
sofa
seat 218 n.
soft
small 33 adj.
smooth 258 adj.
soft 327 adj.
hush 399 int.
silent 399 adj.
muted 401 adj.
luminous 417 adj.
soft-hued 425 adj.
foolish 499 adj.
lax 734 adj.
lenient 736 adj.
cowardly 856 adj.
pitying 905 adj.
soften
soften 327 vb.
mute 401 vb.
relieve 831 vb.
extenuate 927 vb.
softening
weakness 163 n.
soft 327 adj.
soften up
weaken 163 vb.
induce 612 vb.
prepare 669 vb.
flatter 925 vb.
soft-hearted
impressible 819 adj.
benevolent 897 adj.
pitying 905 adj.
softly
slightly 33 adv.
softly softly
cautiously 858 adv.
soft on
in love 887 adj.
lenient 736 adj.
soft option
easy thing 701 n.
soft-pedal
moderate 177 vb.
move slowly 278 vb.
silence 399 vb.
mute 401 vb.
underestimate 483 vb.
extenuate 927 vb.
soft sell
advertisement 528 n.
inducement 612 n.
sale 793 n.
soft-soap
be servile 879 vb.

flatter 925 vb.
soft-spoken
speaking 579 adj.
amiable 884 adj.
soft spot
defect 647 n.
moral sensibility 819 n.
soft touch
dupe 544 n.
easy thing 701 n.
software
computing 86 n.
soggy
soft 327 adj.
unsavoury 391 adj.
soil
region 184 n.
soil 344 n.
make unclean 649 vb.
blemish 845 vb.
soirée
evening 129 n.
social gathering 882 n.
sojourn
be present 189 vb.
live 192 vb.
visit 882 vb.
solace
relief 831 n.
relieve 831 vb.
amusement 837 n.
solar
celestial 321 adj.
solarium
arbour 194 n.
heater 383 n.
solar plexus
insides 224 n.
solar system
planet 321 n.
sun 321 n.
solder
join 45 vb.
adhesive 47 n.
soldier
killer 362 n.
soldier 722 n.
soldier on
stand firm 599 vb.
sold on
in love 887 adj.
sold on, be
believe 485 vb.
sole
one 88 adj.
foot 214 n.
fish as food 301 n.
solecism
sophism 477 n.

sophistry
  sophistry 477 n.
soporific
  sleeping draught
    679 n.
  tedious 838 adj.
soppy
  foolish 499 adj.
  feeling 818 adj.
  impressible
    819 adj.
soprano
  stridency 407 n.
  vocalist 413 n.
sorbet
  dessert 301 n.
sorcery
  sorcery 983 n.
sordid
  not nice 645 adj.
  unclean 649 adj.
  vulgar 847 adj.
sore
  sentient 374 adj.
  painful 377 adj.
  evil 616 n.
  ulcer 651 n.
  wound 655 n.
  fatigued 684 adj.
  sensitive 819 adj.
  painfulness 827 n.
  causing pain
    827 adj.
  resentful 891 adj.
sore point
  moral sensibility
    819 n.
  painfulness 827 n.
  resentment 891 n.
sore pressed
  in difficulties
    700 adj.
sorority
  family 11 n.
  association 706 n.
  cooperation 706 n.
  community 708 n.
sorrow
  sorrow 825 n.
  suffer 825 vb.
  painfulness 827 n.
  lament 836 vb.
  pity 905 vb.
sorrowful
  unhappy 825 adj.
sorry
  unhappy 825 adj.
  regretting 830 adj.
  melancholic
    834 adj.
  repentant 939 adj.
sorry, be
  regret 830 vb.

sorry sight
  painfulness 827 n.
sort
  class 62 vb.
  sort 77 n.
sortie
  outbreak 176 n.
  going out 298 n.
  attack 712 n.
  retaliation 714 n.
sorting
  sorting 62 n.
sort of
  partially 33 adv.
sort out
  exclude 57 vb.
  cause to be few
    105 vb.
  discriminate
    463 vb.
  reject 607 vb.
SOS
  signal 547 n.
  danger signal
    665 n.
so-so
  inconsiderable
    33 adj.
  not bad 644 adj.
  middling 732 adj.
so to speak
  similarly 18 adv.
sotto voce
  muted 401 adj.
soufflé
  dessert 301 n.
  dish 301 n.
  bubble 355 n.
sough
  blow 352 vb.
  breeze 352 n.
  faintness 401 n.
  sound faint
    401 vb.
sought after
  saleable 793 adj.
soul
  essence 1 n.
  thing that lacks
    substance 4 n.
  essential part 5 n.
  self 80 n.
  inferiority 224 n.
  life 360 n.
  person 371 n.
  music 412 n.
  spirit 447 n.
  mental state
    817 n.
  moral sensibility
    819 n.
soulful
  feeling 818 adj.

soulless
  impassive 820 adj.
  tedious 838 adj.
soul mate
  close friend 880 n.
  loved one 887 n.
  spouse 894 n.
soul-searching
  regret 830 n.
  honourable
    929 adj.
sound
  firm 45 adj.
  whole 52 adj.
  be deep 211 vb.
  gulf 345 n.
  sound 398 n.
  be loud 400 vb.
  play music
    413 vb.
  enquire 459 vb.
  be tentative
    461 vb.
  measure 465 vb.
  genuine 494 adj.
  wise 498 adj.
  access 624 n.
  healthy 650 adj.
  skilful 694 adj.
sound a retreat
  regress 286 vb.
sound as a bell
  strong 162 adj.
  perfect 646 adj.
  healthy 650 adj.
**sound a warn-
  ing**
  raise the alarm
    665 vb.
sound barrier
  limit 236 n.
  sound 398 n.
soundbite
  publicity 528 n.
  news 529 n.
  broadcast 531 n.
sound effects
  sound 398 n.
  cinema 445 n.
soundless
  still 266 adj.
  silent 399 adj.
soundness
  wisdom 498 n.
  goodness 644 n.
  health 650 n.
  probity 929 n.
sound off
  orate 579 vb.
  speak 579 vb.
sound out
  interrogate 459 vb.

soundproof
  silent 399 adj.
sound recording
  listening 415 n.
**sound the
  alarm**
  signal 547 vb.
  warn 664 vb.
  raise the alarm
    665 vb.
soundtrack
  sound 398 n.
  cinema 445 n.
soup
  a mixture 43 n.
  hors-d'oeuvres
    301 n.
  semiliquidity
    354 n.
  predicament
    700 n.
souped-up
  dynamic 160 adj.
  speedy 277 adj.
sour
  unproductive
    172 adj.
  be sour 393 vb.
  sour 393 adj.
  amiss 616 adv.
  cause discontent
    829 vb.
  melancholic
    834 adj.
source
  source 156 n.
  informant 524 n.
sour grapes
  impossibility
    470 n.
  jealousy 911 n.
  detraction 926 n.
souse
  immerse 303 vb.
  lower 311 vb.
  plunge 313 vb.
  drench 341 vb.
  season 388 vb.
  get drunk 949 vb.
South Pole
  extremity 69 n.
  summit 213 n.
  coldness 380 n.
souvenir
  reminder 505 n.
  gift 781 n.
sovereign
  superior 34 n.
  supreme 34 adj.
  strong 162 adj.
  ruling 733 adj.
  sovereign 741 n.

coinage 797 n.
  godlike 965 adj.
sovereignty
  superiority 34 n.
  governing 733 n.
  divine attribute
    965 n.
sow
  disperse 75 vb.
  cause 156 vb.
  produce 164 vb.
  let fall 311 vb.
  pig 365 n.
  cultivate 370 vb.
  female animal
    373 n.
sow dissension
  make quarrels
    709 vb.
so what
  never mind
    860 int.
**sow one's wild
  oats**
  revel 837 vb.
  be wicked 934 vb.
  be intemperate
    943 vb.
sow the seeds of
  cause 156 vb.
  educate 534 vb.
spa
  inn 192 n.
  hospital 658 n.
space
  disunion 46 n.
  arrange 62 vb.
  time 108 n.
  room 183 n.
  space 183 n.
  interval 201 n.
  space 201 n.
  opening 263 n.
  world 321 n.
  notation 410 n.
  print-type 587 n.
  storage 632 n.
spacecraft
  spaceship 276 n.
space flight
  aeronautics 271 n.
  space travel 271 n.
space lab
  spaceship 276 n.
  satellite 321 n.
**spaceman or
  -woman**
  traveller 268 n.
  aeronaut 271 n.
space out
  grade 73 vb.
  space 201 vb.

commotion 318 n.
gale 352 n.
cry 408 vb.
quarrel 709 n.
squalor
uncleanness
649 n.
poverty 801 n.
ugliness 842 n.
squander
consume 165 vb.
waste 634 vb.
misuse 675 vb.
lose 772 vb.
be prodigal
815 vb.
square
equal 28 adj.
equalize 28 vb.
compensate 31 vb.
double 91 adj.
four 96 adj.
existence as four
96 n.
multiply by four
97 vb.
antiquated
127 adj.
archaism 127 n.
place 185 n.
housing 192 n.
fat 195 adj.
verticality 215 n.
angular figure
247 n.
navigate 269 vb.
be true 494 vb.
bribe 612 vb.
just 913 adj.
honourable
929 adj.
square deal
justice 913 n.
**square peg in a
round hole**
unrelatedness
10 n.
misfit 25 n.
nonconformist
84 n.
displacement
188 n.
bungler 697 n.
square root
numerical element
85 n.
**square the
circle**
*attempt the impos-
sible* 470 vb.
square up to
fight 716 vb.

squash
crowd 74 n.
suppress 165 vb.
make smaller
198 vb.
flatten 216 vb.
*fruit and vegeta-
bles* 301 n.
soft drink 301 n.
abase 311 vb.
lower 311 vb.
soften 327 vb.
pulpiness 356 n.
confute 479 vb.
ball game 837 n.
humiliate 872 vb.
squat
small 33 adj.
place oneself
187 vb.
live 192 vb.
quarters 192 n.
fat 195 adj.
dwarfish 196 adj.
short 204 adj.
thick 205 adj.
low 210 adj.
encroach 306 vb.
sit down 311 vb.
possess 773 vb.
appropriate
786 vb.
unsightly 842 adj.
squatter
outsider 59 n.
resident 191 n.
possessor 776 n.
usurper 916 n.
squaw
female 373 n.
spouse 894 n.
squawk
shrill 407 vb.
stridency 407 n.
cry 408 vb.
howl 409 vb.
howling 409 n.
squeak
faintness 401 n.
sound faint
401 vb.
rasp 407 vb.
stridency 407 n.
cry 408 vb.
howl 409 vb.
howling 409 n.
deprecate 762 vb.
squeaky
strident 407 adj.
squeal
shrill 407 vb.
cry 408 n.

howl 409 vb.
inform 524 vb.
divulge 526 vb.
accuse 928 vb.
squealer
informer 524 n.
bad person 938 n.
squeamish
sick 651 adj.
fastidious 862 adj.
prudish 950 adj.
squeeze
small quantity
33 n.
lessen 37 vb.
diminution 37 n.
crowd 74 n.
compression
198 n.
make smaller
198 vb.
be dense 324 vb.
touch 378 n.
hindrance 702 n.
obstruct 702 vb.
oppress 735 vb.
compel 740 vb.
restriction 747 n.
retention 778 n.
rob 788 vb.
courteous act
884 n.
lover 887 n.
caress 889 vb.
endearment 889 n.
squeeze dry
levy 786 vb.
squeeze in
fill 54 vb.
load 193 vb.
make smaller
198 vb.
squeeze out
extract 304 vb.
squelch
suppress 165 vb.
be wet 341 vb.
moisture 341 n.
hiss 406 vb.
hissing 406 n.
squelchy
soft 327 adj.
humid 341 adj.
marshy 347 adj.
squib
bang 402 n.
squiggle
coil 251 n.
squint
be oblique 220 vb.
obliqueness 220 n.
gaze 438 vb.

glance 438 n.
vision 438 n.
be blind 439 vb.
be dim-sighted
440 vb.
dim sight 440 n.
blemish 845 n.
church interior
990 n.
squint at
scan 438 vb.
squire
accompany 89 vb.
male 372 n.
minister to
703 vb.
master 741 n.
retainer 742 n.
serve 742 vb.
owner 776 n.
aristocrat 868 n.
be servile 879 vb.
lover 887 n.
court 889 vb.
squirm
wriggle 251 vb.
be agitated
318 vb.
feel pain 377 vb.
be excited 821 vb.
suffer 825 vb.
squirt
small quantity
33 n.
dwarf 196 n.
outflow 298 n.
emit 300 vb.
irrigate 341 vb.
irrigator 341 n.
flow 350 vb.
nonentity 639 n.
squish
flatten 216 vb.
hiss 406 vb.
hissing 406 n.
S-shaped
snaky 251 adj.
**St Christopher
medal**
talisman 983 n.
**St Valentine's
Day**
anniversary 141 n.
St Vitus's dance
spasm 318 n.
nervous disorder
651 n.
stab
cut 46 vb.
pierce 263 vb.
kill 362 vb.
give pain 377 vb.

pang 377 n.
ill-treat 645 vb.
wound 655 n.
wound 655 vb.
strike at 712 vb.
suffering 825 n.
stab at
attempt 671 n.
stability
stability 153 n.
stabilize
stabilize 153 vb.
stabilizer
stabilizer 153 n.
stab in the back
attack 712 n.
be dishonest
930 vb.
perfidiousness
930 n.
stable
equal 28 adj.
group 74 n.
lasting 113 adj.
fixed 153 adj.
strong 162 adj.
live 192 vb.
stable 192 n.
horse 273 n.
store 632 vb.
inexcitable
823 adj.
stack
great quantity
32 n.
bring together
74 vb.
bunch 74 n.
rock 344 n.
store 632 n.
store 632 vb.
acquisition 771 n.
stacks
great quantity
32 n.
funds 797 n.
stack the cards
predetermine
608 vb.
stadium
athletics 162 n.
meeting place
192 n.
onlookers 441 n.
theatre 594 n.
racing 716 n.
arena 724 n.
staff
component 58 n.
band 74 n.
support 218 n.
notation 410 n.

sticking
cohesiveness 48 n.
sticking plaster
adhesive 47 n.
substitute 150 n.
surgical dressing
658 n.
sticking point
resolution 599 n.
stick in the
mind
be remembered
505 vb.
stick it out
stand firm 599 vb.
persevere 600 vb.
stickler
narrow mind
481 n.
perfectionist
862 n.
stick on
add 38 vb.
affix 45 vb.
accuse 928 vb.
stick one's neck
out
face danger
661 vb.
be courageous
855 vb.
be rash 857 vb.
stick out
jut 254 vb.
emerge 298 vb.
be visible 443 vb.
stick out for
contend 716 vb.
bargain 791 vb.
stick out like a
sore thumb
disagree 25 vb.
jut 254 vb.
attract notice
455 vb.
sticks
surroundings
230 n.
racing 716 n.
sticks, the
district 184 n.
seclusion 883 n.
stick to
cohere 48 vb.
observe 768 vb.
retain 778 vb.
take 786 vb.
stick together
unite with 45 vb.
concur 181 vb.
stick to one's
guns
be certain 473 vb.

argue 475 vb.
affirm 532 vb.
persevere 600 vb.
be obstinate
602 vb.
stickup
stealing 788 n.
stick up for
patronize 703 vb.
vindicate 927 vb.
stick with it
persevere 600 vb.
sticky
cohesive 48 adj.
tough 329 adj.
glutinous 354 adj.
difficult 700 adj.
retentive 778 adj.
sticky tape
adhesive 47 n.
ligature 47 n.
sticky wicket
predicament
700 n.
stiff
impotent 161 adj.
straight 249 adj.
still 266 adj.
rigid 326 adj.
dead 361 adj.
corpse 363 n.
narrow-minded
481 adj.
ornate 574 adj.
inelegant 576 adj.
fatigued 684 adj.
severe 735 adj.
restraining
747 adj.
dear 811 adj.
formal 875 adj.
unsociable
883 adj.
stiffen
strengthen 162 vb.
harden 326 vb.
stiffener
support 218 n.
hardness 326 n.
stiffen one's
upper lip
strengthen 162 vb.
stiff-necked
obstinate 602 adj.
defiant 711 adj.
severe 735 adj.
proud 871 adj.
stiff upper lip
resolution 599 n.
feeling 818 n.
moral insensibility
820 n.

manliness 855 n.
stiff with
full 54 adj.
stifle
disable 161 vb.
suppress 165 vb.
kill 362 vb.
be hot 379 vb.
heat 381 vb.
extinguish 382 vb.
silence 399 vb.
mute 401 vb.
conceal 525 vb.
make mute
578 vb.
hinder 702 vb.
prohibit 757 vb.
stigma
flower 366 n.
indication 547 n.
blemish 845 n.
slur 867 n.
censure 924 n.
detraction 926 n.
false charge 928 n.
stigmata
indication 547 n.
stigmatize
blemish 845 vb.
shame 867 vb.
criticize 924 vb.
defame 926 vb.
accuse 928 vb.
stile
ascent 308 n.
access 624 n.
obstacle 702 n.
stiletto
footwear 228 n.
sharp point 256 n.
piercer 263 n.
side arms 723 n.
still
assuage 177 vb.
moderate 177 adj.
at rest 266 adj.
still 266 adj.
vaporizer 338 n.
heater 383 n.
silence 399 vb.
silent 399 adj.
nevertheless
468 adv.
photography
551 n.
make mute
578 vb.
inactive 679 adj.
stillborn
dead 361 adj.
unsuccessful
728 adj.

still life
art subject 553 n.
stillroom
room 194 n.
storage 632 n.
stilted
ornate 574 adj.
inelegant 576 adj.
ridiculous 849 adj.
affected 850 adj.
stilts
leg 267 n.
plaything 837 n.
stimulant
stimulant 174 n.
drug 658 n.
refreshment 685 n.
drugs 949 n.
intoxicating
949 adj.
stimulate
augment 36 vb.
cause 156 vb.
invigorate 174 vb.
incite 612 vb.
refresh 685 vb.
animate 821 vb.
stimulator
stimulator 821 n.
stimulus
cause 156 n.
stimulant 174 n.
incentive 612 n.
sting
be sharp 256 vb.
sharpness 256 n.
sharp point 256 n.
give pain 377 vb.
pang 377 n.
pungency 388 n.
duplicity 541 n.
badness 645 n.
wound 655 n.
bane 659 n.
fleece 786 vb.
overcharge 811 vb.
stimulator 821 n.
excite 821 vb.
suffering 825 n.
torment 827 vb.
enrage 891 vb.
huff 891 vb.
stingy
insufficient
636 adj.
parsimonious
816 adj.
stink
odour 394 n.
stench 397 n.
stink 397 vb.
uncleanness

649 n.
stink bomb
stench 397 n.
stinker
cad 938 n.
stinking
unsavoury
391 adj.
fetid 397 adj.
not nice 645 adj.
unclean 649 adj.
unpleasant
827 adj.
stint
degree 27 n.
time 108 n.
period 110 n.
labour 682 n.
restrain 747 vb.
portion 783 n.
be parsimonious
816 vb.
stipend
monetary help
703 n.
reward 962 n.
stipple
variegate 437 vb.
paint 553 vb.
engrave 555 vb.
stipulate
postulate 475 vb.
give terms 766 vb.
stir
mix 43 vb.
stimulation 174 n.
be in motion
265 vb.
motion 265 n.
cook 301 vb.
agitate 318 vb.
be agitated
318 vb.
commotion 318 n.
activity 678 n.
prison 748 n.
excite 821 vb.
stir it
make quarrels
709 vb.
stirring
mixture 43 n.
active 678 adj.
busy 678 adj.
exciting 821 adj.
stirrup
support 218 n.
stir up
move 265 vb.
agitate 318 vb.
stir up a hor-
net's nest
be in difficulty

striped
crossed 222 adj.
mottled 437 adj.

stripes
badge 547 n.

strip joint
place of amusement 837 n.

stripling
young person 132 n.
male 372 n.

stripper
stripper 229 n.

strip-search
search 459 n.
search 459 n.

strip show
stage show 594 n.

striptease
uncovering 229 n.

striptease artist
stripper 229 n.
entertainer 594 n.

strive
attempt 671 vb.
exert oneself 682 vb.
contend 716 vb.

stroke
living model 23 n.
instant 116 n.
helplessness 161 n.
watersports 269 n.
navigate 269 vb.
row 269 vb.
impulse 279 n.
knock 279 n.
propulsion 287 n.
spasm 318 n.
rub 333 vb.
touch 378 n.
touch 378 vb.
gesticulate 547 vb.
indication 547 n.
evil 616 n.
cardiovascular disease 651 n.
illness 651 n.
nervous disorder 651 n.
deed 676 n.
please 826 vb.
caress 889 vb.
endearment 889 n.
corporal punishment 963 n.

stroke of, the
instant 116 n.

stroke of genius
deed 676 n.

masterpiece 694 n.
success 727 n.
miracle-working 864 n.

stroke of luck
non-design 618 n.

stroll
walking 267 n.
wander 267 vb.
move slowly 278 vb.

strong
strong 162 adj.
influential 178 adj.
tasty 386 adj.
pungent 388 adj.
florid 425 adj.
healthy 650 adj.
fervent 818 adj.
impure 951 adj.

strong-arm tactics
violence 176 n.
compulsion 740 n.

strongbox
treasury 799 n.

stronghold
refuge 662 n.
fort 713 n.

strong-minded
resolute 599 n.

strong point
skill 694 n.

strongroom
storage 632 n.
treasury 799 n.

strong-willed
resolute 599 n.

stroppy
irascible 892 adj.
sullen 893 adj.

struck
impressed 818 adj.

struck dumb, be
be mute 578 vb.
wonder 864 vb.

struck with
in love 887 adj.

structure
building 164 n.
structure 331 n.

struggle
be violent 176 vb.
move slowly 278 vb.
attempt 671 vb.
exertion 682 n.
exert oneself 682 vb.
contend 716 vb.

contest 716 n.
fight 716 n.

strum
play music 413 vb.

strung
adjusted 24 adj.

strut
bond 47 n.
support 218 n.
gait 265 n.
walk 267 vb.
be proud 871 vb.
be vain 873 vb.
be ostentatious 875 vb.
ostentation 875 n.
boast 877 vb.

stub
remainder 41 n.
tobacco 388 n.
label 547 n.

stubble
leavings 41 n.
hair 259 n.
roughness 259 n.
grass 366 n.
rubbish 641 n.

stubborn
strong 162 adj.
rigid 326 adj.
tough 329 adj.
persevering 600 adj.
obstinate 602 adj.
difficult 700 adj.
resisting 715 adj.
impenitent 940 adj.

stubby
short 204 adj.
thick 205 adj.

stub one's toe
collide 279 vb.

stub out
extinguish 382 vb.

stucco
adhesive 47 n.
coat 226 vb.
facing 226 n.

stuck
firm 45 adj.
still 266 adj.
in difficulties 700 adj.
hindered 702 adj.

stuck on
in love 887 adj.

stuck up
affected 850 adj.
be proud 871 vb.
proud 871 adj.

vain 873 adj.

stuck with
hindered 702 adj.

stud
fastening 47 n.
pillar 218 n.
roughen 259 vb.
horse 273 n.
variegate 437 vb.
decorate 844 vb.
jewellery 844 n.
libertine 952 n.

student
enquirer 459 n.
scholar 492 n.
learner 538 n.
student 538 n.

studied
predetermined 608 adj.
affected 850 adj.

studies
study 536 n.

studio
room 194 n.
workshop 687 n.

studious
studious 536 adj.
industrious 678 adj.

study
retreat 192 n.
room 194 n.
musical piece 412 n.
meditate 449 vb.
study 536 n.
study 536 vb.
picture 553 n.
dissertation 591 n.
intend 617 vb.
prepare oneself 669 vb.
workshop 687 n.
seclusion 883 n.

stuff
essential part 5 n.
chief part 52 n.
fill 54 n.
bring together 74 vb.
load 193 vb.
enlarge 197 vb.
textile 222 n.
line 227 n.
cook 301 vb.
matter 319 n.
texture 331 n.
materials 631 n.
be overabundant 637 vb.
preserve 666 vb

satiate 863 vb.
eat to excess 947 vb.

stuff and nonsense
absurdity 497 n.
silly talk 515 n.

stuffed shirt
thing that lacks substance 4 n.
vain person 873 n.

stuffing
increment 36 n.
adjunct 40 n.
contents 193 n.
lining 227 n.
stopper 264 n.
insertion 303 n.
materials 631 n.
satiation 863 n.
gluttonous 947 adj.

stuff oneself
eat 301 vb.

stuffy
warm 379 adj.
fetid 397 adj.
unhealthy 653 adj.
tedious 838 adj.
dull 840 adj.

stuffy (air)
dense 324 adj.

stumble
walk 267 vb.
descent 309 n.
tumble 309 vb.
blunder 495 vb.
be clumsy 695 vb.
be wicked 934 vb.

stumble on or upon
meet with 154 vb.
chance 159 vb.
discover 484 vb.

stumbling block
obstacle 702 n.
restraint 747 n.

stump
remainder 41 n.
piece 53 n.
extremity 69 n.
projection 254 n.
leg 267 n.
walk 267 vb.
puzzle 474 vb.
be difficult 700 vb.

stumped, be
not know 491 vb.
not understand 517 vb.

stumps
leg 267 n.
objective 617 n.
stump up
pay 804 vb.
stumpy
short 204 adj.
stun
strike 279 vb.
make insensitive
375 vb.
be loud 400 vb.
surprise 508 vb.
be wonderful
864 vb.
stung
excited 821 adj.
angry 891 adj.
resentful 891 adj.
stung, be
pay too much
811 vb.
stunned
not expecting
508 adj.
afraid 854 adj.
stunning
super 644 adj.
stunt
make smaller
198 vb.
shorten 204 vb.
fly 271 vb.
contrivance 623 n.
deed 676 n.
pageant 875 n.
stunted
dwarfish 196 adj.
short 204 adj.
deformed 246 adj.
stunt man *or*
woman
athlete 162 n.
doer 676 n.
brave person
855 n.
stupefaction
wonder 864 n.
stupefy
make insensitive
375 vb.
impress 821 vb.
be wonderful
864 vb.
stupendous
prodigious 32 adj.
huge 195 adj.
wonderful 864 adj.
stupid
unintelligent
499 adj.
unskilful 695 adj.

dull 840 adj.
stupidity
unintelligence
499 n.
moral insensibility
820 n.
stupor
insensitivity
375 n.
sluggishness
679 n.
moral insensibility
820 n.
wonder 864 n.
sturdy
stalwart 162 adj.
stutter
speech defect
580 n.
stammer 580 vb.
be clumsy 695 vb.
show feeling
818 vb.
quake 854 vb.
sty
stable 192 n.
enclosure 235 n.
stye
swelling 253 n.
style
mode 7 n.
similarity 18 n.
sort 77 n.
chronology 117 n.
form 243 n.
flower 366 n.
engraving 555 n.
name 561 n.
name 561 n.
style 566 n.
elegance 575 n.
way 624 n.
conduct 688 n.
skill 694 n.
beauty 841 n.
fashion 848 n.
style of address
title 870 n.
styling
hairdressing
843 n.
stylish
elegant 575 adj.
personable
841 adj.
fashionable
848 adj.
stylistic
stylistic 566 adj.
stylus
sharp point 256 n.
music player

414 n.
stymie
be obstructive
702 vb.
obstruct 702 vb.
suave
smooth 258 adj.
courteous 884 adj.
sub
inferior 35 n.
substitute 150 n.
publish 528 vb.
subaltern
inferior 35 adj.
inferior 35 n.
army officer
741 n.
servant 742 n.
subconscious
intuition 476 n.
intuitive 476 adj.
latency 523 n.
latent 523 adj.
subconscious,
the
spirit 447 n.
subcutaneous
interior 224 n.
subdivision
splitting 46 n.
subdivision 53 n.
subdue
moderate 177 vb.
prevail 178 vb.
overcome 727 vb.
subjugate 745 vb.
restrain 747 vb.
subedit
publish 528 vb.
rectify 654 vb.
subgroup
subdivision 53 n.
subhuman
animal 365 adj.
cruel 898 adj.
subject
living model 23 n.
inferior 35 adj.
inferior 35 n.
topic 452 n.
part of speech
564 n.
overcome 727 vb.
subject 742 n.
subject 745 adj.
subject, be
be subject 745 vb.
subjective
special 80 adj.
inward-looking
224 adj.
intuitive 476 adj.

biased 481 adj.
misjudging
481 adj.
subjectivity
introversion 224 n.
subjectivity 320 n.
subject matter
topic 452 n.
meaning 514 n.
subject to
liable 180 adj.
provided 468 adv.
subject 745 adj.
on terms 766 adv.
subject to terms
conditional
766 adj.
subjoin
insert 303 vb.
sub judice
sub judice
480 adv.
subjugate
prevail 178 vb.
subjugate 745 vb.
sublet
lease 784 vb.
lending 784 n.
sub-lieutenant
nautical personnel
270 n.
naval officer
741 n.
sublimate
vaporize 338 vb.
make better
654 vb.
sublime
high 209 adj.
worshipful
866 adj.
proud 871 adj.
divine 965 adj.
subliminal
latent 523 adj.
involuntary
596 adj.
sublimity
height 209 n.
prestige 866 n.
divine attribute
965 n.
submarine
low 210 adj.
deep 211 adj.
depth 211 n.
ship 275 n.
warship 722 n.
submerge
suppress 165 vb.
immerse 303 vb.
descend 309 vb.

plunge 313 vb.
drench 341 vb.
irrigate 341 vb.
be unseen 444 vb.
obliterate 550 vb.
submerse
plunge 313 vb.
submission
argument 475 n.
supposition 512 n.
affirmation 532 n.
submission 721 n.
entreaty 761 n.
submissive
willing 597 adj.
inactive 679 adj.
manageable
701 adj.
peaceful 717 adj.
submitting
721 adj.
obedient 739 adj.
subjected 745 adj.
humble 872 adj.
servile 879 adj.
respectful 920 adj.
submit
propound 512 vb.
affirm 532 vb.
advise 691 vb.
submit 721 vb.
submit a report
communicate
524 vb.
subnormal
inferior 35 adj.
abnormal 84 adj.
unintelligent
499 adj.
having a learning
disability
503 adj.
subordinate
external 6 adj.
inferior 35 adj.
inferior 35 n.
servant 742 n.
subject 745 adj.
subordination
inferiority 35 n.
order 60 n.
arrangement 62 n.
sequence 65 n.
subjection 745 n.
suborn
bribe 612 vb.
subplot
narrative 590 n.
dramatic theory
594 n.
subpoena
command 737 vb.

suet
fat 357 n.
suffer
acquiesce 488 vb.
be ill 651 vb.
permit 756 vb.
be patient 823 vb.
suffer 825 vb.
sufferance
permission 756 n.
suffice
suffice 635 vb.
sufficient
sufficient 635 adj.
suffix
add 38 vb.
adjunct 40 n.
affix 45 vb.
place after 65 vb.
sequel 67 n.
extremity 69 n.
part of speech
  564 n.
suffocate
disable 161 vb.
suppress 165 vb.
kill 362 vb.
murder 362 vb.
be hot 379 vb.
heat 381 vb.
extinguish 382 vb.
be overabundant
  637 vb.
hinder 702 vb.
suffrage
affirmation 532 n.
vote 605 n.
prayers 981 n.
suffragette
female 373 n.
vote 605 n.
suffusion
mixture 43 n.
feeling 818 n.
humiliation 872 n.
Sufism
philosophy 449 n.
religion 973 n.
sugar
food content
  301 n.
sweeten 392 vb.
sweet thing 392 n.
please 826 vb.
darling 890 n.
flatter 925 vb.
sugar cane
grass 366 n.
sugar daddy
patron 707 n.
giver 781 n.
good giver 813 n.

lover 887 n.
libertine 952 n.
sugar the pill
sweeten 392 vb.
deceive 542 vb.
flatter 925 vb.
sugary
sweet 392 adj.
pleasurable
  826 adj.
flattering 925 adj.
suggest
evidence 466 vb.
remind 505 vb.
propound 512 vb.
imply 523 vb.
hint 524 vb.
indicate 547 vb.
represent 551 vb.
advise 691 vb.
offer 759 vb.
suggestion
similarity 18 n.
small quantity
  33 n.
knowledge 490 n.
reminder 505 n.
latency 523 n.
hint 524 n.
plan 623 n.
advice 691 n.
suggestive
influential
  178 adj.
meaningful
  514 adj.
exciting 821 adj.
impure 951 adj.
suicidal
destructive
  165 adj.
murderous
  362 adj.
hopeless 853 adj.
rash 857 adj.
suicide
kill oneself
  362 vb.
suicide 362 n.
suit
uniformity 16 n.
accord 24 vb.
adjust 24 vb.
sort 77 n.
suit 228 n.
following 284 n.
beautify 841 vb.
wooing 889 n.
accusation 928 n.
litigation 959 n.
suit (of cards)
series 71 n.

suitable
circumstantial
  8 adj.
relevant 9 adj.
fit 24 adj.
right 913 adj.
suitcase
box 194 n.
suite
series 71 n.
concomitant 89 n.
flat 192 n.
follower 284 n.
musical piece
  412 n.
suiting
adaptation 24 n.
agreeing 24 adj.
textile 222 n.
suitor
concomitant 89 n.
follower 284 n.
petitioner 763 n.
lover 887 n.
litigant 959 n.
sulk
be discontented
  829 vb.
be dejected
  834 vb.
be rude 885 vb.
sulks
discontent 829 n.
resentment 891 n.
sullenness 893 n.
sulky
carriage 274 n.
discontented
  829 adj.
melancholic
  834 adj.
sullen 893 adj.
sullen
sullen 893 adj.
sully
dim 419 vb.
make unclean
  649 vb.
make ugly 842 vb.
blemish 845 vb.
shame 867 vb.
defame 926 vb.
be impious
  980 vb.
sulphurous
fetid 397 adj.
sultan
sovereign 741 n.
sultana
fruit and vegeta-
  bles 301 n.
sultry
warm 379 adj.

sullen 893 adj.
sum
quantity 26 n.
add 38 vb.
all 52 n.
whole 52 n.
numerical result
  85 n.
numbering 86 n.
funds 797 n.
summarize
shorten 204 vb.
be concise 569 vb.
abstract 592 vb.
summary
brief 114 adj.
shortening 204 n.
concise 569 adj.
description 590 n.
dissertation 591 n.
compendium
  592 n.
lawless 954 adj.
summation
addition 38 n.
whole 52 n.
numbering 86 n.
summer
pass time 108 vb.
period 110 n.
summer 128 n.
be present 189 vb.
beam 218 n.
heyday 730 n.
summerhouse
arbour 194 n.
summery
warm 379 adj.
summing-up
estimate 480 n.
judgment 480 n.
legal trial 959 n.
summit
summit 213 n.
conference 584 n.
council 692 n.
summon
bring together
  74 vb.
command 737 vb.
desire 859 vb.
indict 928 vb.
litigate 959 vb.
summons
call 547 n.
command 737 n.
warrant 737 n.
desire 859 n.
accusation 928 n.
law 953 n.
legal process
  959 n.

summon up
excite 821 vb.
sum of money
funds 797 n.
sump
receptacle 194 n.
base 214 n.
cavity 255 n.
storage 632 n.
sink 649 n.
sumptuous
ostentatious
  875 adj.
sum up
shorten 204 vb.
estimate 480 vb.
judge 480 vb.
abstract 592 vb.
try a case 959 vb.
sun
sun 321 n.
dry 342 vb.
dryness 342 n.
heat 379 n.
light 417 n.
light 420 n.
sunbathe
be hot 379 vb.
sunbeam
light 417 n.
sun bed
beauty treatment
  843 n.
sunburn
burning 381 n.
brown 430 n.
sundae
dessert 301 n.
Sunday
holy day 988 n.
Sunday best
clothing 228 n.
finery 844 n.
sunder
break up 46 vb.
disunite 46 vb.
sundial
timekeeper 117 n.
sundown
evening 129 n.
darkening 418 n.
sundress
beachwear 228 n.
dress 228 n.
sundries
merchandise
  795 n.
sundry
existing in many
  forms 82 adj.
many 104 adj.
sunglasses
shade 226 n.

786 n.
fleece 786 vb.
defraud 788 vb.
swindling 788 vb.
be dishonest
786 vb.
swine
pig 365 n.
cad 938 n.
sensualist 944 n.
swing
periodic recurrence
141 n.
reversion 148 n.
vary 152 vb.
agency 173 n.
range 183 n.
hang 217 vb.
hanging object
217 n.
strike 279 vb.
deviate 282 vb.
deviation 282 n.
fluctuation 317 n.
oscillate 317 vb.
music 412 n.
action 676 n.
scope 744 n.
be punished
963 vb.
swingeing
exorbitant 32 adj.
**swings and
roundabouts**
correlation 12 n.
reversion 148 n.
compromise 770 n.
swing the lead
be false 541 vb.
fail in duty
918 vb.
swipe
knock 279 n.
strike 279 vb.
propulsion 287 n.
strike at 712 vb.
steal 788 vb.
swirl
rotate 315 vb.
whirl 315 n.
eddy 350 n.
swish
faintness 401 n.
sound faint
401 vb.
hiss 406 vb.
hissing 406 n.
fashionable
848 adj.
switch
branch 53 n.
substitute 150 vb.

substitution 150 n.
interchange
151 vb.
hair 259 n.
transpose 272 vb.
deflect 282 vb.
diverge 294 vb.
tool 630 n.
club 723 n.
hairdressing
843 n.
scourge 964 n.
switchback
obliqueness 220 n.
meandering 251 n.
undulatory
251 adj.
vehicle 274 n.
switchboard
focus 76 n.
telecommunication
531 n.
switch off
terminate 69 vb.
cease 145 vb.
switch on
initiate 68 vb.
operate 173 vb.
move 265 vb.
hear 415 vb.
swivel
pivot 218 n.
rotator 315 n.
swiz
trickery 542 n.
fable 543 n.
swollen
great 32 adj.
convex 253 adj.
diseased 651 adj.
proud 871 adj.
swollen head
pride 871 n.
proud person
871 n.
vanity 873 n.
swoon
helplessness
161 n.
insensitivity
375 n.
be fatigued
684 vb.
swoop
move fast 277 vb.
spurt 277 n.
descend 309 vb.
descent 309 n.
plunge 313 n.
swoosh
spurt 277 n.
hiss 406 vb.

hissing 406 n.
sword
destroyer 168 n.
sharp edge 256 n.
side arms 723 n.
badge of rank
743 n.
honours 866 n.
**sword of Damo-
cles**
danger 661 n.
intimidation
854 n.
threat 900 n.
sworn
affirmative
532 adj.
obedient 739 adj.
contractual
765 adj.
obliged 917 adj.
swot
study 536 vb.
learner 538 n.
sycophant
toady 879 n.
flatterer 925 n.
syllabify
spell 558 vb.
syllable
speech sound
398 n.
word 559 n.
phrase 563 vb.
voice 577 n.
syllabus
list 87 n.
compendium
592 n.
sylph
fairy 970 n.
sylph-like
narrow 206 adj.
fairylike 970 adj.
symbiosis
union 45 n.
life 360 n.
subjection 745 n.
symbol
*thing that lacks
substance* 4 n.
number 85 n.
substitute 150 n.
metaphor 519 n.
badge 547 n.
indication 547 n.
image 551 n.
letter 558 n.
symbolic
lacking substance
4 adj.
occult 523 adj.

trivial 639 adj.
ritual 988 adj.
symbolism
metaphor 519 n.
latency 523 n.
indication 547 n.
ritual act 988 n.
symbolize
mean 514 vb.
manifest 522 vb.
indicate 547 vb.
represent 551 vb.
symmetry
equality 28 n.
symmetry 245 n.
sympathetic
agreeing 24 adj.
assenting 488 adj.
feeling 818 adj.
friendly 880 adj.
benevolent
897 adj.
pitying 905 adj.
sympathize
imagine 513 vb.
feel 818 vb.
be friendly 880 vb.
pity 905 vb.
**sympathize
with**
love 887 vb.
pity 905 vb.
sympathy
bond 47 n.
attraction 291 n.
imagination
513 n.
cooperation 706 n.
harmony 710 n.
participation
775 n.
feeling 818 n.
liking 859 n.
friendliness 880 n.
love 887 n.
benevolence 897 n.
condolence 905 n.
pity 905 n.
symphonic
harmonious
410 adj.
musical 412 adj.
symphony
musical piece
412 n.
symposium
accumulation
74 n.
assembly 74 n.
argument 475 n.
conference 584 n.
symptom
concomitant 89 n.

visibility 443 n.
evidence 466 n.
omen 511 n.
manifestation
522 n.
hint 524 n.
indication 547 n.
signal 547 n.
illness 651 n.
diagnosis 658 n.
warning 664 n.
symptomatic
visible 443 adj.
evidential 466 adj.
synagogue
church 990 n.
sync
simultaneousness
123 n.
synchronize
123 vb.
synchronism
simultaneousness
123 n.
synchronize
adjust 24 vb.
combine 50 vb.
synchronize
123 vb.
syncopated
musical 412 adj.
syncopation
tempo 410 n.
music 412 n.
syndicate
publish 528 vb.
association 706 n.
corporation 708 n.
syndrome
concomitant 89 n.
structure 331 n.
evidence 466 n.
omen 511 n.
manifestation
522 n.
indication 547 n.
signal 547 n.
illness 651 n.
diagnosis 658 n.
synergy
concurrence 181 n.
synod
synod 985 n.
synonym
identity 13 n.
equivalence 28 n.
substitute 150 n.
connotation 514 n.
word 559 n.
name 561 n.
synonymous
identical 13 adj.

take by storm
attack 712 vb.
take 786 vb.
take care
be wise 498 vb.
take care of
be mindful
455 vb.
look after 457 vb.
do 676 vb.
take down
lower 311 vb.
record 548 vb.
write 586 vb.
ridicule 851 vb.
**take down a
peg**
abase 311 vb.
depose 752 vb.
shame 867 vb.
humiliate 872 vb.
take effect
operate 173 vb.
be successful
727 vb.
**take exception
to**
deprecate 762 vb.
resent 891 vb.
disapprove 924 vb.
**take for
granted**
assume 471 vb.
certain 473 adj.
postulate 475 vb.
be credulous
487 vb.
suppose 512 vb.
not wonder
865 vb.
be ungrateful
908 vb.
**take French
leave**
be absent 190 vb.
disappear 446 vb.
run away 620 vb.
escape 667 vb.
disobey 738 vb.
be free 744 vb.
take hold
cohere 48 vb.
prevail 178 vb.
take 786 vb.
take ill
be discontented
829 vb.
resent 891 vb.
take in
contain 56 vb.
comprise 78 vb.
load 193 vb.

make smaller
198 vb.
absorb 299 vb.
admit 299 vb.
scan 438 vb.
see 438 vb.
know 490 vb.
understand
516 vb.
fool 542 vb.
store 632 vb.
safeguard 660 vb.
receive 782 vb.
take 786 vb.
**take in one's
stride**
do easily 701 vb.
**take into
account**
meditate 449 vb.
notice 455 vb.
qualify 468 vb.
take into care
look after 457 vb.
**take into con-
sideration**
meditate 449 vb.
notice 455 vb.
take issue with
go to war 718 vb.
take it
*be of the opinion
that* 485 vb.
suppose 512 vb.
knuckle under
721 vb.
take it easy
move slowly
278 vb.
be neglectful
458 vb.
be inactive
679 vb.
rest 683 vb.
**take it on the
chin**
suffer 825 vb.
**take it or leave
it**
have no choice
606 vb.
be indifferent
860 vb.
**take it upon
oneself**
will 595 vb.
taken off guard
unprepared
670 adj.
take note
notice 455 vb.
taken aback, be
not expect 508 vb.

taken short, be
excrete 302 vb.
**taken to the
cleaner's, be**
be defeated
728 vb.
taken with, be
be in love 887 vb.
take off
imitate 20 vb.
grow 36 vb.
subtract 39 vb.
displace 188 vb.
fly 271 vb.
start out 296 vb.
ascend 308 vb.
act 594 vb.
discount 810 vb.
relieve 831 vb.
satirize 851 vb.
takeoff
copy 22 n.
aeronautics 271 n.
air travel 271 n.
departure 296 n.
ascent 308 n.
satire 851 n.
take office
take authority
733 vb.
take on
admit 299 vb.
train 534 vb.
employ 622 vb.
store 632 vb.
attempt 671 vb.
undertake 672 vb.
do 676 vb.
withstand 704 vb.
contend 716 vb.
fight 716 vb.
be discontented
829 vb.
lament 836 vb.
take one back
remind 505 vb.
**take one's
breath away**
surprise 508 vb.
make mute
578 vb.
impress 821 vb.
delight 826 vb.
be beautiful
841 vb.
be wonderful
864 vb.
take one's ease
rest 683 vb.
**take one's hat
off to**
respect 920 vb.

approve 923 vb.
praise 923 vb.
take one's pick
select 605 vb.
take one's time
wait 136 vb.
move slowly
278 vb.
be cautious
858 vb.
take one up on
dissent 489 vb.
defy 711 vb.
take on oneself
be resolute 599 vb.
busy oneself
622 vb.
promise 764 vb.
be insolent
878 vb.
incur a duty
917 vb.
take on trust
believe 485 vb.
be credulous
487 vb.
take orders
take orders
986 vb.
take out
subtract 39 vb.
exclude 57 vb.
extract 304 vb.
court 889 vb.
take over
come after 65 vb.
appropriate
786 vb.
take 786 vb.
takeover
relation 9 n.
transference 272 n.
expropriation
786 n.
purchase 792 n.
takeover bid
offer 759 n.
purchase 792 n.
**take over the
reigns**
take authority
733 vb.
take pains
be attentive
455 vb.
be active 678 vb.
take part
be present 189 vb.
cooperate 706 vb.
take pity on
relieve 831 vb.
pity 905 vb.

take pot luck
be sociable
882 vb.
taker
possessor 776 n.
recipient 782 n.
taker 786 n.
take risks
gamble 618 vb.
take root
stay 144 vb.
prevail 178 vb.
place oneself
187 vb.
be in the habit of
610 vb.
take shape
become 1 vb.
take sides
be biased 481 vb.
choose 605 vb.
**take something
the wrong
way**
be hostile 881 vb.
take steps
prepare 669 vb.
do 676 vb.
take stock of
scan 438 vb.
meditate 449 vb.
take the biscuit
be superior 34 vb.
**take the bit
between one's
teeth**
will 595 vb.
be obstinate
602 vb.
disobey 738 vb.
**take the bull by
the horns**
be resolute 599 vb.
attempt 671 vb.
be active 678 vb.
be courageous
855 vb.
take the chair
direct 689 vb.
**take the floor
or the stand**
orate 579 vb.
take the helm
direct 689 vb.
**take the initia-
tive**
initiate 68 vb.
take the lead
come before 64 vb.
initiate 68 vb.
be in front 237 vb.
precede 283 vb.

amusement 837 n.
telex
communicate
524 vb.
information
524 n.
telecommunication
531 n.
tell
number 86 vb.
inform 524 vb.
divulge 526 vb.
describe 590 vb.
command 737 vb.
accuse 928 vb.
tell against
tell against
467 vb.
teller
informant 524 n.
treasurer 798 n.
**tell its own
story**
evidence 466 vb.
be intelligible
516 vb.
be plain 522 vb.
tell lies
be false 541 vb.
be dishonest
930 vb.
tell off
reprove 924 vb.
punish 963 vb.
tell on
inform 524 vb.
divulge 526 vb.
accuse 928 vb.
telltale
witness 466 n.
informer 524 n.
tell tales
inform 524 vb.
tell-tale sign
disclosure 526 n.
indication 547 n.
tell upon
influence 178 vb.
temerity
rashness 857 n.
temp
deputy 755 n.
temper
temperament 5 n.
state 7 n.
mix 43 vb.
strengthen 162 vb.
moderate 177 vb.
harden 326 vb.
qualify 468 vb.
mature 669 vb.
mental state

817 n.
excitation 821 n.
excitable state
822 n.
relieve 831 vb.
anger 891 n.
be temperate
942 vb.
temperament
temperament 5 n.
moral sensibility
819 n.
irascibility 892 n.
sullenness 893 n.
temperamental
non-uniform
17 adj.
capricious 604 adj.
excitable 822 adj.
irascible 892 adj.
sullen 893 adj.
temperance
virtue 933 n.
virtues 933 n.
temperance 942 n.
temperate
warm 379 n.
temperate 942 adj.
temperature
thermometry
379 n.
illness 651 n.
tempest
storm 176 n.
velocity 277 n.
commotion 318 n.
excitable state
822 n.
tempestuous
disorderly 61 adj.
violent 176 adj.
speedy 277 adj.
windy 352 adj.
excitable 822 adj.
temple
head 213 n.
refuge 662 n.
honours 866 n.
church 990 n.
temple 990 n.
tempo
tendency 179 n.
motion 265 n.
velocity 277 n.
tempo 410 n.
temporal
continuing
108 adj.
transient 114 adj.
temporary
circumstantial
8 adj.

inferior 35 adj.
ephemeral
114 adj.
substituted
150 adj.
**temporary
measure**
substitute 150 n.
temporize
put off 136 vb.
tempt
cause 156 vb.
tempt 612 vb.
temptation
attraction 291 n.
inducement 612 n.
difficulty 700 n.
request 761 n.
desired object
859 n.
liking 859 n.
tempting
tasty 386 adj.
savoury 390 adj.
tempting offer
incentive 612 n.
reward 962 n.
**tempt provi-
dence** *or* **fate**
face danger
661 vb.
be rash 857 vb.
be insolent
878 vb.
ten
over five 99 n.
tenable
rational 475 adj.
credible 485 adj.
invulnerable
660 adj.
tenacious
cohesive 48 adj.
tough 329 adj.
resolute 599 adj.
persevering
600 adj.
obstinate 602 adj.
retentive 778 adj.
tenacity
cohesiveness 48 n.
toughness 329 n.
resolution 599 n.
perseverance
600 n.
obstinacy 602 n.
retention 778 n.
courage 855 n.
tenancy
time 108 n.
possession 773 n.
non-ownership

774 n.
tenant
resident 191 n.
live 192 vb.
possessor 776 n.
tend
tend 179 vb.
look after 457 vb.
practise medicine
658 vb.
serve 742 vb.
tendency
tendency 179 n.
tender
locomotive 274 n.
boat 275 n.
ship 275 n.
follower 284 n.
soft 327 adj.
sentient 374 adj.
painful 377 adj.
soft-hued 425 adj.
lenient 736 adj.
offer 759 n.
offer 759 vb.
sensitive 819 adj.
causing pain
827 adj.
honour 866 vb.
loving 887 adj.
benevolent
897 adj.
pitying 905 adj.
tender age
tender age 130 n.
youth 130 n.
tenderfoot
outsider 59 n.
beginner 538 n.
tender-hearted
feeling 818 adj.
impressible
819 adj.
pitying 905 adj.
tenderize
soften 327 vb.
tender mercies
severity 735 n.
mercy 905 n.
tenderness
weakness 163 n.
softness 327 n.
sensitivity 374 n.
pain 377 n.
leniency 736 n.
moral sensibility
819 n.
painfulness 827 n.
love 887 n.
benevolence 897 n.
tending
possible 469 adj.

tendon
ligature 47 n.
tendril
ligature 47 n.
branch 53 n.
filament 208 n.
coil 251 n.
foliage 366 n.
pincers 778 n.
tenements
flat 192 n.
housing 192 n.
tenet
precept 693 n.
theology 973 n.
tenets
creed 485 n.
tennis
ball game 837 n.
tennis court
arena 724 n.
pleasure ground
837 n.
tennis elbow
rheumatism
651 n.
tenon
joint 45 n.
projection 254 n.
tenor
degree 27 n.
tendency 179 n.
direction 281 n.
stridency 407 n.
vocalist 413 n.
meaning 514 n.
tense
tied 45 adj.
time 108 n.
rigid 326 adj.
grammar 564 n.
feeling 564 n.
fervent 818 adj.
excited 821 adj.
excitable 822 adj.
nervous 854 adj.
tensile
elastic 328 adj.
tension
quantity 26 n.
energy 160 n.
dissension 709 n.
excitation 821 n.
worry 825 n.
enmity 881 n.
tent
live 192 vb.
dwelling 192 n.
pavilion 192 n.
small house
192 n.
canopy 226 n.

be prodigal
815 vb.
throwback
recurrence 106 n.
reversion 148 n.
relapse 657 n.
throw cold
water on
moderate 177 vb.
dissuade 613 vb.
hinder 702 vb.
throw down
demolish 165 vb.
move 265 vb.
let fall 311 vb.
throw down the
gauntlet
be resolute 599 vb.
defy 711 vb.
enrage 891 vb.
throw dust in
one's eye
be unrelated
10 vb.
deflect 282 vb.
blind 439 vb.
deceive 542 vb.
plead 614 vb.
avoid 620 vb.
elude 667 vb.
throw in
introduce 231 vb.
throw in one's
hand
relinquish 621 vb.
resign 753 vb.
throw in one's
lot with
choose 605 vb.
throw in one's
teeth
defy 711 vb.
accuse 928 vb.
throw in the
sponge or the
towel
relinquish 621 vb.
submit 721 vb.
throw into
confusion
throw into confu-
sion 63 vb.
disarrange 63 vb.
throw light on
make bright
417 vb.
interpret 520 vb.
manifest 522 vb.
thrown
formed 243 adj.
thrown, be
tumble 309 vb.

thrown-out
chest
ostentation 875 n.
thrown to the
lions, be
endangered
661 adj.
throw off
disaccustom
611 vb.
throw off the
scent
distract 456 vb.
puzzle 474 vb.
elude 667 vb.
throw one off
the scent
avoid 620 vb.
throw oneself
at
pursue 619 vb.
throw one's hat
in the ring
defy 711 vb.
throw one's
weight about
be vigorous
174 vb.
be proud 871 vb.
be insolent
878 vb.
throw open
open 263 vb.
admit 299 vb.
manifest 522 vb.
throw out
impel 279 vb.
eject 300 vb.
reject 607 vb.
throw out the
baby with the
bath water
overstep 306 vb.
waste 634 vb.
act foolishly
695 vb.
throw over
fool 542 vb.
change one's mind
603 vb.
relinquish 621 vb.
throw the book
at
criticize 924 vb.
indict 928 vb.
punish 963 vb.
throw together
join 45 vb.
throw up
eject 300 vb.
vomit 300 vb.
elevate 310 vb.

resign 753 vb.
thrum
roll 403 vb.
resound 404 vb.
discord 411 vb.
play music
413 vb.
thrush
bird 365 n.
animal disease
651 n.
skin disease
651 n.
thrust
energy 160 n.
vigorousness
174 n.
distortion 246 n.
spurt 277 n.
impel 279 vb.
impulse 279 n.
propellant 287 n.
be active 678 vb.
attack 712 n.
strike at 712 vb.
thrust oneself
forward
be active 678 vb.
thud
impulse 279 n.
faintness 401 n.
sound faint
401 vb.
non-resonance
405 n.
thug
violent creature
176 n.
murderer 362 n.
robber 789 n.
ruffian 904 n.
bad person 938 n.
thumb
joint 45 n.
feeler 378 n.
finger 378 n.
touch 378 vb.
study 536 vb.
signal 547 vb.
thumb a lift
ride 267 vb.
beg 761 vb.
thumb index
indication 547 n.
edition 589 n.
thumbnail
sketch
miniature 196 n.
picture 553 n.
description 590 n.
compendium
592 n.

thumbscrew
pain 377 n.
instrument of pun-
ishment or torture
964 n.
thumbs down
prohibition 757 n.
refusal 760 n.
condemnation
961 n.
thumbs up
assent 488 n.
approbation
923 n.
acquittal 960 n.
thumb-
twiddling
tedium 838 n.
thump
knock 279 n.
strike 279 vb.
faintness 401 n.
sound faint
401 vb.
bang 402 n.
non-resonance
405 n.
thunder
storm 176 n.
be loud 400 vb.
loudness 400 n.
emphasize 532 vb.
be angry 891 vb.
curse 899 vb.
threaten 900 vb.
criticize 924 vb.
thunder and
lightning
storm 176 n.
thunderbolt
lack of expectation
508 n.
thunderclap
loudness 400 n.
bang 402 n.
lack of expectation
508 n.
thunderous
loud 400 adj.
approving 923 adj.
thunderstorm
commotion 318 n.
rain 350 n.
gale 352 n.
thunderstruck
not expecting
508 adj.
thus
thus 8 adv.
hence 158 adv.
thwack
knock 279 n.

strike 279 vb.
thwart
halt 145 vb.
disappoint 509 vb.
negate 533 vb.
be obstructive
702 vb.
oppose 704 vb.
trouble 827 vb.
thyme
herb 301 n.
scent 396 n.
tiara
headgear 228 n.
regalia 743 n.
jewellery 844 n.
vestments 989 n.
tibia
leg 267 n.
tic
spasm 318 n.
vision 438 n.
gesture 547 n.
nervous disorder
651 n.
tick
instant 116 n.
periodic recurrence
141 n.
oscillate 317 vb.
insect 365 n.
faintness 401 n.
sound faint
401 vb.
roll 403 vb.
mark 547 vb.
borrowing 785 n.
purchase 792 vb.
credit 802 n.
approve 923 vb.
ticket
adjunct 40 n.
list 87 n.
credential 466 n.
label 547 n.
mark 547 vb.
electorate 605 n.
policy 623 n.
precept 693 n.
permit 756 n.
tickle
touch 378 vb.
incentive 612 n.
delight 826 vb.
amuse 837 vb.
be ridiculous
849 vb.
endearment 889 n.
tickled pink
pleased 824 adj.
merry 833 adj.
tickled to death
pleased 824 adj.

toot
loudness 400 n.
resound 404 vb.
play music
413 vb.
raise the alarm
665 vb.
tooth
tooth 256 n.
notch 260 vb.
liking 859 n.
toothache
pang 377 n.
tooth and nail
be violent 176 vb.
toothless
ageing 131 adj.
impotent 161 adj.
toothsome
savoury 390 adj.
tootle
resound 404 vb.
play music
413 vb.
too-too
affected 850 adj.
top
superiority 34 n.
fill 54 vb.
put in front 64 vb.
extremity 69 n.
crown 213 vb.
summit 213 n.
topmost 213 adj.
apex 213 n.
covering 226 n.
article of clothing
228 n.
shirt 228 n.
limit 236 vb.
cone 252 n.
stopper 264 n.
climb 308 vb.
rotator 315 n.
completion 725 n.
plaything 837 n.
top brass
bigwig 638 n.
director 690 n.
top drawer
elite 644 n.
fashionable society
848 n.
genteel 868 adj.
upper class 868 n.
top-heavy
unequal 29 adj.
weighty 322 adj.
clumsy 695 adj.
topic
topic 452 n.
topical
present 121 adj.

modern 126 adj.
topical 452 adj.
topless
short 204 adj.
uncovered 229 adj.
top-notch
supreme 34 adj.
best 644 adj.
super 644 adj.
skilful 694 adj.
top out
crown 213 vb.
carry through
725 vb.
topping
covering 226 n.
super 644 adj.
topple
demolish 165 vb.
tumble 309 vb.
tops, the
exceller 644 n.
favourite 890 n.
good person 937 n.
top-secret
occult 523 adj.
concealed 525 adj.
secret 530 n.
topsy-turvy
contrarily 14 adv.
inversely 221 adv.
top to toe
lengthwise
203 adv.
top up
fill 54 vb.
store 632 vb.
replenish 633 vb.
torch
lamp 420 n.
torch 420 n.
toreador
killer 362 n.
combatant 722 n.
torment
give pain 377 vb.
pain 377 n.
bane 659 n.
suffering 825 n.
torment 827 vb.
tornado
turmoil 61 n.
storm 176 n.
whirl 315 n.
gale 352 n.
torpedo
suppress 165 vb.
fire at 712 vb.
bomb 723 n.
torpid
inert 175 adj.
inactive 679 adj.

inexcitable
823 adj.
torpor
inertness 175 n.
inactivity 679 n.
sluggishness
679 n.
torque
quantity 26 n.
loop 250 n.
torrent
great quantity
32 n.
outbreak 176 n.
velocity 277 n.
stream 350 n.
torrential
violent 176 adj.
torrid
hot 379 adj.
warm 379 adj.
torso
remainder 41 n.
chief part 52 n.
piece 53 n.
incompleteness
55 n.
image 551 n.
sculpture 554 n.
tortilla
bread, pastries
and cakes
301 n.
mouthful 301 n.
tortoise
slowcoach 278 n.
animal 365 n.
reptile 365 n.
tortoiseshell
covering 226 n.
variegated
437 adj.
variegation 437 n.
tortuous
convoluted
251 adj.
unclear 568 adj.
dishonest 930 adj.
torture
force 176 vb.
violence 176 n.
pain 377 n.
suffering 825 n.
be malevolent
898 vb.
cruel act 898 n.
corporal punish-
ment 963 n.
torture 963 vb.
to scale
relative 9 adj.
relatively 9 adv.

toss
small quantity
33 n.
disarrange 63 vb.
jumble 63 vb.
voyage 269 n.
propel 287 vb.
propulsion 287 n.
oscillate 317 vb.
agitation 318 n.
be agitated
318 vb.
trifle 639 n.
toss and turn
be excited 821 vb.
toss aside
not respect 921 vb.
toss one's head
be proud 871 vb.
despise 922 vb.
toss up
elevate 310 vb.
gamble 618 vb.
toss-up
equal chance
159 n.
uncertainty 474 n.
tot
child 132 n.
dwarf 196 n.
drink 301 n.
total
quantity 26 n.
consummate
32 adj.
add 38 vb.
addition 38 n.
all 52 n.
whole 52 adj.
complete 54 adj.
inclusive 78 adj.
numerical result
85 n.
number 86 vb.
totalitarianism
uniformity 16 n.
despotism 733 n.
brute force 735 n.
totality
whole 52 n.
completeness 54 n.
totally
completely 54 adv.
tote
counting instru-
ment 86 n.
carry 273 vb.
gambling 618 n.
totem
badge 547 n.
(See also **indica-**
tion.)

deity 966 n.
idol 982 n.
totem pole
idol 982 n.
to the four
winds
widely 183 adv.
to the letter
truly 494 adv.
to the point
relevant 9 adj.
apt 24 adj.
brief 114 adj.
rational 475 adj.
concise 569 adj.
to the purpose
apt 24 adj.
to the utmost
completely 54 adv.
totter
come unstuck
49 vb.
vary 152 vb.
be weak 163 vb.
walk 267 vb.
move slowly
278 vb.
oscillate 317 vb.
be agitated
318 vb.
deteriorate 655 vb.
tot up to
number 86 vb.
touch
be related 9 vb.
small quantity
33 n.
tincture 43 n.
disarrange 63 vb.
be situated
186 vb.
limit 236 n.
have feeling
374 vb.
sense 374 n.
touch 378 n.
touch 378 vb.
gesture 547 n.
objective 617 n.
request 761 n.
excite 821 vb.
children's games
837 n.
touch and go
unreliability
474 n.
unreliable 474 adj.
unsafe 661 adj.
touch down
fly 271 vb.
land 295 vb.
descend 309 vb.

love 887 vb.
darling 890 n.
approve 923 vb.
treasure hunt
search 459 n.
racing 716 n.
treasurer
treasurer 798 n.
treasure trove
discovery 484 n.
benefit 615 n.
acquisition 771 n.
treasury
anthology 592 n.
treasury 799 n.
treat
modify 143 vb.
pleasure 376 n.
dissertate 591 vb.
practise medicine
658 vb.
remedy 658 vb.
behave 688 vb.
contract 765 vb.
give 781 vb.
pay for 804 vb.
enjoyment 824 n.
pleasurableness
826 n.
amusement 837 n.
treat as
substitute 150 vb.
treatise
reading matter
589 n.
dissertation 591 n.
treatment
change 143 n.
painting 553 n.
way 624 n.
use 673 n.
conduct 688 n.
treat with
make terms
766 vb.
treaty
treaty 765 n.
treble
treble 94 adj.
treble 94 vb.
stridency 407 n.
vocalist 413 n.
treble chance
gambling 618 n.
treble figures
hundred 99 n.
trebly
greatly 32 vb.
tree
tree 366 n.
treetop
apex 213 n.

foliage 366 n.
trefoil
three 93 n.
heraldry 547 n.
pattern 844 n.
trek
land travel 267 n.
travel 267 vb.
amuse oneself
837 vb.
trellis
frame 218 n.
network 222 n.
tremble
vary 152 vb.
be weak 163 vb.
be agitated
318 vb.
be cold 380 vb.
sound faint
401 vb.
roll 403 vb.
show feeling
818 vb.
be excited 821 vb.
quake 854 vb.
trembling
agitation 318 n.
(See also **spasm**.)
feeling 818 n.
nervous 854 adj.
nervousness 854 n.
tremendous
prodigious 32 adj.
tremor
outbreak 176 n.
oscillation 317 n.
agitation 318 n.
feeling 818 n.
nervousness 854 n.
tremulousness
agitation 318 n.
trench
gap 201 n.
fence 235 n.
excavation 255 n.
furrow 262 n.
water channel
351 n.
cultivate 370 vb.
refuge 662 n.
defences 713 n.
trenchant
keen 174 adj.
assertive 532 adj.
concise 569 adj.
disapproving
924 adj.
trend
mode 7 n.
similarity 18 n.
continuity 71 n.

tendency 179 n.
form 243 n.
direction 281 n.
fashion 848 n.
liking 859 n.
trend-setter
living model 23 n.
precursor 66 n.
fashionable society
848 n.
trendy
modern 126 adj.
modernist 126 n.
fashionable
848 adj.
trepidation
agitation 318 n.
excitable state
822 n.
fear 854 n.
nervousness 854 n.
trespass
interfere 231 vb.
entering 297 n.
intrude 297 vb.
encroach 306 vb.
disobey 738 vb.
appropriate
786 vb.
do wrong 914 vb.
wrong 914 n.
unjustifed claim
916 n.
be wicked 934 vb.
vice 934 n.
be guilty 936 vb.
guilty act 936 n.
lawbreaking
954 n.
trespasser
outsider 59 n.
offender 904 n.
usurper 916 n.
trestle
frame 218 n.
triad
three 93 n.
musical note
410 n.
triage
choice 605 n.
medical art 658 n.
trial
enquiry 459 n.
empiricism 461 n.
experiment 461 n.
experiment
461 vb.
experimental
461 adj.
bane 659 n.
preparation 669 n.

attempt 671 n.
difficulty 700 n.
contest 716 n.
suffering 825 n.
legal trial 959 n.
punishment 963 n.
trial and error
empiricism 461 n.
trial of strength
hard task 700 n.
contest 716 n.
trial run
enquiry 459 n.
experiment 461 n.
preparation 669 n.
trials
experiment 461 n.
preparation 669 n.
adversity 731 n.
trials and tribu-
lations
painfulness 827 n.
triangle
three 93 n.
angular figure
247 n.
gong 414 n.
triangular
three 93 adj.
tribal
ethnic 11 adj.
national 371 adj.
tribe
family 11 n.
race 11 n.
group 74 n.
breed 77 n.
multitude 104 n.
genealogy 169 n.
native 191 n.
community 708 n.
tribesman
kinsman 11 n.
tribulation
difficulty 700 n.
suffering 825 n.
painfulness 827 n.
tribunal
tribunal 956 n.
tributary
inferior 35 adj.
stream 350 n.
subject 745 adj.
tribute
gift 781 n.
receiving 782 n.
pay 804 n.
payment 804 n.
tax 809 n.
thanks 907 n.
what is due 915 n.
praise 923 n.

reward 962 n.
trice
instant 116 n.
triceps
ligature 47 n.
trick
deceive 542 vb.
fool 542 vb.
trickery 542 n.
habit 610 n.
contrivance 623 n.
skill 694 n.
be cunning
698 vb.
stratagem 698 n.
revel 837 n.
perfidiousness
930 n.
trickery
trickery 542 n.
trickle
small quantity
33 n.
fewness 105 n.
move slowly
278 vb.
be wet 341 vb.
flow 350 vb.
trick out
primp 843 vb.
decorate 844 vb.
tricks of the
trade
trickery 542 n.
stratagem 698 n.
trickster
trickster 545 n.
tricky
deceiving 542 adj.
difficult 700 adj.
tricycle
three 93 n.
bicycle 274 n.
plaything 837 n.
trident
three 93 n.
tried
certain 473 adj.
matured 669 adj.
expert 694 adj.
approved 923 adj.
trustworthy
929 adj.
tried and true
friendly 880 adj.
triennial
seasonal 141 adj.
triennium
three 93 n.
trifle
dessert 301 n.
be inattentive

actor 594 n.
party 708 n.
trousers
trousers 228 n.
trowel
ladle 194 n.
sharp edge 256 n.
conveyor 274 n.
farm and garden
tools 370 n.
truancy
absence 190 n.
relinquishment
621 n.
escape 667 n.
undutifulness
918 n.
truant
absence 190 n.
absent 190 adj.
avoider 620 n.
escaper 667 n.
undutiful 918 adj.
undutifulness
918 n.
truce
lull 145 n.
interval 201 n.
state of rest 266 n.
rescue 668 n.
peace 717 n.
pacification 719 n.
truck
carrier 273 n.
carry 273 vb.
lorry 274 n.
pushcart 274 n.
train 274 n.
trudge
walk 267 vb.
move slowly
278 vb.
true
inimitable 21 adj.
straight 249 adj.
accurate 494 adj.
true 494 adj.
artless 699 adj.
patriotic 901 adj.
true blue
conformable
83 adj.
permanent
144 adj.
political party
708 n.
patriotic 901 adj.
trustworthy
929 adj.
true to life
lifelike 18 adj.
true 494 adj.

descriptive
590 adj.
truffle
fruit and vegeta-
bles 301 n.
truism
truth 494 n.
axiom 496 n.
maxim 496 n.
lack of meaning
515 n.
truly
truly 494 adv.
trump
be superior 34 vb.
masterpiece 694 n.
overcome 727 vb.
success 727 n.
good person 937 n.
trump card
advantage 34 n.
contrivance 623 n.
chief thing 638 n.
success 727 n.
trumped-up
deceiving 542 adj.
spurious 542 adj.
untrue 543 adj.
trumpery
bauble 639 n.
trumpet
resound 404 vb.
shrill 407 vb.
howl 409 vb.
play music
413 vb.
horn 414 n.
proclaim 528 vb.
publicizer 528 n.
call 547 n.
be ostentatious
875 vb.
boast 877 vb.
praise 923 vb.
trump up
fake 541 vb.
truncated
short 204 adj.
concise 569 adj.
truncheon
club 723 n.
badge of office
743 n.
trundle
move 265 vb.
propel 287 vb.
rotate 315 vb.
trunk
remainder 41 n.
chief part 52 n.
piece 53 n.
incompleteness

55 n.
box 194 n.
support 218 n.
cylinder 252 n.
protuberance
254 n.
tree 366 n.
trunks
beachwear 228 n.
legwear 228 n.
truss
tie 45 vb.
bring together
74 vb.
bunch 74 n.
beam 218 n.
support 218 n.
support 218 vb.
trust
transference 272 n.
transport 272 n.
belief 485 n.
believe 485 vb.
expectation 507 n.
association 706 n.
corporation 708 n.
mandate 751 n.
hope 852 n.
hope 852 vb.
trustee
nominee 754 n.
recipient 782 n.
treasurer 798 n.
trustful
credulous 487 adj.
trust in
be certain 473 vb.
trustworthy
credible 485 adj.
trustworthy
929 adj.
trusty
credible 485 adj.
trustworthy
929 adj.
truth
truth 494 n.
maxim 496 n.
truthfulness
540 n.
artlessness 699 n.
divine attribute
965 n.
truthful
true 494 adj.
truthful 540 adj.
trustworthy
929 adj.
try
enquire 459 vb.
judge 480 vb.
be willing 597 vb.

persevere 600 vb.
attempt 671 n.
attempt 671 vb.
avail oneself of
673 vb.
do 676 vb.
exert oneself
682 vb.
torment 827 vb.
be tedious 838 vb.
trying
annoying 827 adj.
try it on
be tentative
461 vb.
deceive 542 vb.
behave 688 vb.
**try one's hand
at**
attempt 671 vb.
try out
experiment
461 vb.
trysting
social round
882 n.
tsarism
despotism 733 n.
tub
vat 194 n.
vessel 194 n.
bulk 195 n.
ship 275 n.
water 339 n.
washing 648 n.
tuba
horn 414 n.
tubby
fat 195 adj.
thick 205 adj.
tube
electronics 160 n.
excavation 255 n.
tube 263 n.
tunnel 263 n.
railway 624 n.
tuber
plant 366 n.
tuberculosis
infection 651 n.
respiratory disease
651 n.
tub-thumping
eloquent 579 adj.
oration 579 n.
oratory 579 n.
tuck
fold 261 n.
food 301 n.
tuck in
place 187 vb.
load 193 vb.

eat 301 vb.
tuck into
insert 303 vb.
tuck up
place 187 vb.
shorten 204 vb.
tuft
bunch 74 n.
fewness 105 n.
hair 259 n.
tug
move 265 vb.
boat 275 n.
ship 275 n.
draw 288 vb.
traction 288 n.
attract 291 vb.
attraction 291 n.
extraction 304 n.
exertion 682 n.
work 682 vb.
tugboat
boat 275 n.
tug of love
opposition 704 n.
contest 716 n.
tug of war
traction 288 n.
opposition 704 n.
contest 716 n.
**tug one's fore-
lock**
greet 884 vb.
tuition
teaching 534 n.
tumble
have sexual inter-
course with
45 vb.
jumble 63 vb.
descent 309 n.
tumble 309 vb.
tumbledown
flimsy 163 adj.
dilapidated
655 adj.
tumbler
athlete 162 n.
cup 194 n.
tumble to
discover 484 vb.
understand
516 vb.
tummy
stomach 194 n.
insides 224 n.
tumour
distension 197 n.
swelling 253 n.
cancer 651 n.
tumult
turmoil 61 n.

be successful
727 vb.
turn over
be inverted
221 vb.
be curved 248 vb.
fold 261 vb.
transfer 272 vb.
search 459 vb.
trade 791 vb.
turnover
*bread, pastries
and cakes*
301 n.
earnings 771 n.
receipt 807 n.
reward 962 n.
**turn over a new
leaf**
change 143 vb.
be turned to
147 vb.
change one's mind
603 vb.
get better 654 vb.
be penitent
939 vb.
turn over to
commission
751 vb.
**turn Queen's
evidence**
inform 524 vb.
confess 526 vb.
accuse 928 vb.
turn round
be inverted
221 vb.
turn round
282 vb.
circle 314 vb.
turnstile
barrier 235 n.
*recording instru-
ment* 549 n.
access 624 n.
obstacle 702 n.
treasury 799 n.
turntable
rotator 315 n.
music player
414 n.
turn tail
regress 286 vb.
run away 620 vb.
be cowardly
856 vb.
**turn the clock
back**
revert 148 vb.
turn the corner
change 143 vb.

get better 654 vb.
be restored 656 vb.
**turn the other
cheek**
be patient 823 vb.
be humble 872 vb.
forgive 909 vb.
turn the scale
predominate
34 vb.
modify 143 vb.
cause 156 vb.
influence 178 vb.
prevail 178 vb.
dominate 733 vb.
**turn the stom-
ach**
be unpalatable
391 vb.
**turn the tables
on**
retaliate 714 vb.
accuse 928 vb.
turn to
be turned to
147 vb.
speak to 583 vb.
avail oneself of
673 vb.
**turn topsy-
turvy**
*throw into confu-
sion* 63 vb.
be inverted
221 vb.
invert 221 vb.
turn up
happen 154 vb.
chance 159 vb.
be present 189 vb.
shorten 204 vb.
fold 261 vb.
arrive 295 vb.
be visible 443 vb.
turn-up
article of clothing
228 n.
fold 261 n.
**turn-up for the
book**
benefit 615 n.
**turn up one's
nose**
be unwilling
598 vb.
reject 607 vb.
be fastidious
862 vb.
despise 922 vb.
**turn up one's
toes**
die 361 vb.

**turn upside
down**
*throw into confu-
sion* 63 vb.
modify 143 vb.
turn up trumps
be successful
727 vb.
get rich 800 vb.
turpitude
disrepute 867 n.
improbity 930 n.
wickedness 934 n.
turquoise
blue 435 adj.
blueness 435 n.
gem 844 n.
turret
high structure
209 n.
fort 713 n.
turtle
reptile 365 n.
tusk
tooth 256 n.
tussle
contend 716 vb.
contention 716 n.
contest 716 n.
fight 716 n.
tussock
bunch 74 n.
tutelage
teaching 534 n.
learning 536 n.
protection 660 n.
subjection 745 n.
tutor
educate 534 vb.
teach 534 vb.
teacher 537 n.
domestic 742 n.
keeper 749 n.
tutorial
educational
534 adj.
teaching 534 n.
tutoring
teaching 534 n.
tut-tut
deprecate 762 vb.
deprecation 762 n.
disapprobation
924 n.
disapprove 924 vb.
tutu
skirt 228 n.
tuxedo
formal dress
228 n.
jacket 228 n.
TV
broadcasting

531 n.
twaddle
absurdity 497 n.
silly talk 515 n.
twain
existence as two
90 n.
twang
sound 398 n.
resound 404 vb.
rasp 407 vb.
stridency 407 n.
play music
413 vb.
pronunciation
577 n.
speech defect
580 n.
tweak
draw 288 vb.
give pain 377 vb.
twee
affected 850 adj.
tweed
textile 222 n.
roughness 259 n.
**Tweedledum
and Tweedle-
dee**
existence as two
90 n.
tweeds
suit 228 n.
**tween, tween-
ager**
young person
132 n.
tweet
howl 409 vb.
tweezers
tool 630 n.
pincers 778 n.
twelfth
*divided into many
parts* 100 adj.
Twelfth Night
holy day 988 n.
twelve
over five 99 n.
twelve o'clock
noon 128 n.
twenty
twenty and over
99 n.
**twenty ques-
tions**
indoor game
837 n.
twerp
fool 501 n.
twice
double 91 adj.

twiddle
rotate 315 vb.
touch 378 vb.
**twiddle one's
thumbs**
not act 677 vb.
be inactive
679 vb.
twig
branch 53 n.
young plant
132 n.
foliage 366 n.
tree 366 n.
know 490 vb.
understand
516 vb.
twilight
evening 129 n.
light 417 n.
darkness 418 n.
dim 419 adj.
half-light 419 n.
deterioration
655 n.
twill
crossed 222 adj.
textile 222 n.
weave 222 vb.
twin
kinsman 11 n.
identity 13 n.
analogue 18 n.
liken 18 vb.
similar 18 adj.
be equal 28 vb.
peer 28 n.
concomitant 89 n.
dual 90 adj.
double 91 adj.
double 91 vb.
contemporary
123 n.
synchronous
123 adj.
child 132 n.
twine
tie 45 n.
cable 47 n.
fibre 208 n.
twine 251 vb.
twine round
cohere 48 vb.
twinge
give pain 377 vb.
pang 377 n.
suffering 825 n.
twinkle
instant 116 n.
vary 152 vb.
agitation 318 n.
be agitated

318 vb.
flash 417 n.
shine 417 vb.
gesticulate 547 vb.
gesture 547 n.
laughter 835 n.
smile 835 vb.
twinkling
instant 116 n.
flash 417 n.
**twinkling of an
eye, the**
instant 116 n.
twins
existence as two
90 n.
twin set
jersey 228 n.
twirl
coil 251 n.
twine 251 vb.
rotate 315 vb.
rotation 315 n.
twist
tie 45 vb.
complexity 61 n.
disarrange 63 vb.
make conform
83 vb.
disable 161 vb.
force 176 vb.
bag 194 n.
fibre 208 n.
obliqueness 220 n.
deform 244 vb.
distort 246 vb.
distortion 246 n.
coil 251 n.
convolution 251 n.
twine 251 vb.
be in motion
265 vb.
deviate 282 vb.
draw 288 vb.
circle 314 vb.
tobacco 388 n.
bias 481 vb.
eccentricity 503 n.
misinterpret
521 vb.
pervert 655 vb.
dance 837 n.
dance 837 vb.
make ugly 842 vb.
twist and turn
meander 251 vb.
twisted
distorted 246 adj.
convoluted
251 adj.
biased 481 adj.
imperfect 647 adj.

unsightly 842 adj.
twister
gale 352 n.
trickster 545 n.
bad person 938 n.
twist one's arm
induce 612 vb.
compel 740 vb.
twit
fool 501 n.
ridicule 851 vb.
not respect 921 vb.
criticize 924 vb.
accusation 928 n.
twitch
draw 288 vb.
agitate 318 vb.
agitation 318 n.
be agitated
318 vb.
spasm 318 n.
feel pain 377 vb.
gesture 547 n.
twitchiness
agitation 318 n.
twitter
agitation 318 n.
be agitated
318 vb.
howl 409 vb.
howling 409 n.
sing 413 vb.
be talkative
581 vb.
twittering
howling 409 n.
two
existence as two
90 n.
two-a-penny
trivial 639 adj.
cheap 812 adj.
two-edged
double 91 adj.
equivocal 518 adj.
**two-edged
weapon**
inexpediency
643 n.
two-faced
dual 90 adj.
double 91 adj.
hypocritical
541 adj.
dishonest 930 adj.
**two-faced per-
son**
recanter 603 n.
twofold
double 91 adj.
two of a kind
analogue 18 n.

twosome
existence as two
90 n.
two-time
deceive 542 vb.
two-way
correlative 12 adj.
double 91 adj.
tycoon
bigwig 638 n.
autocrat 741 n.
rich person 800 n.
type
character 5 n.
uniformity 16 n.
analogue 18 n.
copy 20 vb.
prototype 23 n.
sort 77 n.
example 83 n.
form 243 n.
person 371 n.
indication 547 n.
image 551 n.
letter 558 n.
write 586 vb.
print-type 587 n.
typeface
print-type 587 n.
typescript
script 586 n.
book 589 n.
typewriter
stationery 586 n.
typhoid
digestive disorder
651 n.
infection 651 n.
typhoon
storm 176 n.
gale 352 n.
typical
characteristic
5 adj.
lifelike 18 adj.
general 79 adj.
typical 83 adj.
typify
be uniform 16 vb.
resemble 18 vb.
predict 511 vb.
manifest 522 vb.
indicate 547 vb.
represent 551 vb.
typist
shorthand writer
586 n.
typography
composition 56 n.
printing 555 n.
print 587 n.
tyrannical
violent 176 adj.

authoritative
733 adj.
oppressive 735 adj.
insolent 878 adj.
cruel 898 adj.
lawless 954 adj.
tyrannize
be violent 176 vb.
ill-treat 645 vb.
meddle 678 vb.
rule 733 vb.
oppress 735 vb.
be malevolent
898 vb.
tyranny
influence 178 n.
despotism 733 n.
brute force 735 n.
insolence 878 n.
unjustifed claim
916 n.
tyrant
tyrant 735 n.
autocrat 741 n.
tyre
wheel 250 n.

U

U
well-bred 848 adj.
genteel 868 adj.
über-
supreme 34 adj.
ubiquitous
present everywhere
189 adj.
U-boat
ship 275 n.
warship 722 n.
udder
bosom 253 n.
UFO
spaceship 276 n.
unknown thing
491 n.
ugly
deformed 246 adj.
ugly 842 adj.
sullen 893 adj.
ugly customer
troublemaker
663 n.
low fellow 869 n.
ruffian 904 n.
bad person 938 n.
ugly duckling
eyesore 842 n.
ukulele
stringed instrument
414 n.

ulcer
digestive disorder
651 n.
ulcer 651 n.
painfulness 827 n.
ulterior
extraneous 59 adj.
future 124 adj.
distant 199 adj.
ulterior motive
concealment
525 n.
motive 612
ultimate
supreme 34 adj.
final 69 adj.
fundamental
156 adj.
distant 199 adj.
ultimatum
limit 236 n.
intention 617 n.
requirement 627 n.
warning 664 n.
demand 737 n.
request 761 n.
conditions 766 n.
ultra
extremely 32 vb.
ultra vires
unwarranted
916 adj.
umbelliferous
broad 205 adj.
umbilical
central 225 adj.
umbilical cord
bond 47 n.
obstetrics 167 n.
umbrage
foliage 366 n.
resentment 891 n.
umbrella
shade 226 n.
dome 253 n.
protection 660 n.
shelter 662 n.
umlaut
speech sound
398 n.
punctuation
547 n.
umpire
estimator 480 n.
judge 480 vb.
mediate 720 vb.
mediator 720 n.
judge 957 n.
umpteen
many 104 adj.
unable
powerless 161 adj.

undemanding
easy 701 adj.
lax 734 adj.
lenient 736 adj.
undemocratic
authoritarian
735 adj.
insolent 878 adj.
undemonstra-
tive
impassive 820 adj.
undeniable
undisputed
473 adj.
credal 485 adj.
undependable
unreliable 474 adj.
dishonest 930 adj.
under
low 210 adj.
under 210 adv.
underachieve
fall short 307 vb.
under-age
young 130 adj.
under arrest
imprisoned
747 adj.
captive 750 adj.
underbelly
insides 224 n.
undercapital-
ized
unprovided
636 adj.
undercarriage
frame 218 n.
support 218 n.
carrier 273 n.
aircraft 276 n.
undercharge
cheapen 812 vb.
underclothes
underwear 228 n.
undercoat
layer 207 n.
pigment 425 n.
under control
obedient 739 adj.
restrained 747 adj.
undercover
latent 523 adj.
concealed 525 adj.
undercover
agent
secret service
459 n.
informer 524 n.
undercurrent
current 350 n.
latency 523 n.
undercurrents
cause 156 n.

undercut
sell 793 vb.
cheapen 812 vb.
underdeveloped
incomplete 55 adj.
immature 670 adj.
underdog
inferior 35 n.
loser 728 n.
unlucky person
731 n.
underdone
culinary 301 adj.
unsavoury
391 adj.
uncooked 670 adj.
under duress
by force 740 adv.
underemploy-
ment
inaction 677 n.
underestimate
underestimate
483 vb.
underestimation
483 n.
underexpose
darken 418 vb.
underfed
underfed 636 adj.
underfoot
low 210 adj.
under 210 adv.
underframe
support 218 n.
undergo
meet with 154 vb.
feel 818 vb.
suffer 825 vb.
undergraduate
student 538 n.
underground
low 210 adj.
under 210 adv.
deep 211 adj.
tunnel 263 n.
concealed 525 adj.
hiding-place
527 n.
rebel 738 n.
undergrowth
wood 366 n.
underhand
occult 523 adj.
stealthily 525 adv.
stealthy 525 adj.
dishonest 930 adj.
underinsure
be rash 857 vb.
under investiga-
tion
sub judice

480 adv.
underived
original 21 adj.
underlay
layer 207 n.
underlie
cause 156 vb.
lurk 523 vb.
underline
strengthen 162 vb.
attract notice
455 vb.
emphasize 532 vb.
mark 547 vb.
underling
inferior 35 n.
nonentity 639 n.
servant 742 n.
commoner 869 n.
underlining
vigour 571 n.
underlying
latent 523 adj.
undermanned
deficient 307 adj.
unprovided
636 adj.
undermine
disable 161 vb.
weaken 163 vb.
make concave
255 vb.
descend 309 vb.
tell against
467 vb.
plot 623 vb.
impair 655 vb.
be cunning
698 vb.
hinder 702 vb.
revolt 738 vb.
underneath
under 210 adv.
undernourished
underfed 636 adj.
under one's belt
completed 725 adj.
under one's
nose
near 200 adv.
obvious 443 adj.
visible 443 adj.
under one's
thumb
obedient 739 adj.
subject 745 adj.
underpaid
cheap 812 adj.
unwarranted
916 adj.
underpants
underwear 228 n.

underpass
crossing 222 n.
tunnel 263 n.
passage 305 n.
bridge 624 n.
underpin
support 218 vb.
underprice
underestimate
483 vb.
underprivileged
poor 801 adj.
underprivi-
leged, the
lower classes
869 n.
under protest
by force 740 adv.
underrate
underestimate
483 vb.
not respect 921 vb.
hold cheap
922 vb.
undersea
deep 211 adj.
undershirt
underwear 228 n.
underside
lowness 210 n.
undersign
sign 547 vb.
undersized
small 33 adj.
dwarfish 196 adj.
lean 206 adj.
underskirt
underwear 228 n.
understaffed
unprovided
636 adj.
understand
perceive 447 adj.
understand
516 vb.
imply 523 vb.
understandable
intelligible
516 adj.
understanding
agreement 24 n.
intellect 447 n.
knowledge 490 n.
intelligence 498 n.
imagination
513 n.
harmony 710 n.
pacification 719 n.
pact 765 n.
feeling 818 n.
friendliness 880 n.
friendly 880 adj.

love 887 n.
benevolence 897 n.
pity 905 n.
pitying 905 adj.
understate
moderate 177 adj.
underestimate
483 vb.
understated
soft-hued 425 adj.
understood
tacit 523 adj.
usual 610 adj.
understudy
substitute 150 n.
act 594 vb.
actor 594 n.
deputize 755 vb.
deputy 755 n.
undertake
undertake 672 vb.
undertaker
interment 364 n.
doer 676 n.
undertaking
business 622 n.
undertaking
672 n.
promise 764 n.
under-the-
counter
stealthily 525 adv.
under the sun
existing 1 adj.
widely 183 adv.
undertone
contrariety 14 n.
faintness 401 n.
musical note
410 n.
latency 523 n.
voicelessness
578 n.
undervalue
lessen 37 vb.
misjudge 481 vb.
underestimate
483 vb.
not respect 921 vb.
hold cheap
922 vb.
underwater
deep 211 adj.
under way
moving 265 adj.
in preparation
669 adv.
underwear
underwear 228 n.
underweight
unequal 29 adj.
inferior 35 adj.

weakly 163 adj.
light 323 adj.
underworld
depth 211 n.
lower classes
869 n.
offender 904 n.
wickedness 934 n.
hell 972 n.
underwrite
promise 764 vb.
contract 765 vb.
give security
767 vb.
undeserved
unwarranted
916 adj.
undesirability
inexpediency
643 n.
undesirable
inexpedient
643 adj.
unpleasant
827 adj.
unwanted 860 adj.
bad person 938 n.
undetected
latent 523 adj.
undetermined
irresolute 601 adj.
undeveloped
incomplete 55 adj.
latent 523 adj.
imperfect 647 adj.
immature 670 adj.
unskilled 695 adj.
undeviating
uniform 16 adj.
unchangeable
153 adj.
straight 249 adj.
directed 281 adj.
accurate 494 adj.
orthodox 976 adj.
**undifferenti-
ated**
uniform 16 adj.
indiscriminate
464 adj.
undignified
dishonest 930 adj.
undiluted
unmixed 44 adj.
strong 162 adj.
undiminished
intact 52 adj.
undimmed
undimmed
417 adj.
undiscernible
unintelligible

517 adj.
undiscerning
blind 439 adj.
inattentive
456 adj.
undiscriminating
464 adj.
undisciplined
disorderly 61 adj.
disobedient
738 adj.
intemperate
943 adj.
undisclosed
concealed 525 adj.
undiscovered
unborn 2 adj.
unknown 491 adj.
latent 523 adj.
occult 523 adj.
**undiscriminat-
ing**
approving 923 adj.
undisguised
obvious 443 adj.
genuine 494 adj.
undismayed
unafraid 855 adj.
undisputed
undisputed
473 adj.
undissolved
intact 52 adj.
undistinguished
indiscriminate
464 adj.
middling 732 adj.
undisturbed
tranquil 266 adj.
undivided
intact 52 adj.
complete 54 adj.
orthodox 976 adj.
undivulged
tacit 523 adj.
undo
disunite 46 vb.
destroy 165 vb.
counteract 182 vb.
open 263 vb.
annul 752 vb.
undoing
separation 46 n.
destruction 165 n.
annulment 752 n.
undomesticated
unaccustomed
611 adj.
undone
incomplete 55 adj.
hopeless 853 adj.
undoubted
undisputed

473 adj.
undress
informal dress
228 n.
uniform 228 n.
uncover 229 vb.
uncovering 229 n.
undrinkable
unsavoury
391 adj.
unhealthy 653 adj.
undue
unapt 25 adj.
undulate
crinkle 251 vb.
gait 265 n.
oscillate 317 vb.
undulatory
undulatory
251 adj.
unduly
extremely 32 vb.
undutiful
undutiful 918 adj.
undying
existing 1 adj.
perpetual 115 adj.
unchangeable
153 adj.
remembered
505 adj.
unearned
unwarranted
916 adj.
unearth
eject 300 vb.
extract 304 vb.
exhume 364 vb.
discover 484 vb.
manifest 522 vb.
unearthly
extraneous 59 adj.
non-material
320 adj.
divine 965 adj.
spooky 970 adj.
unearthly hour
earliness 135 n.
unease
evil 616 n.
uneasy
clumsy 695 adj.
nervous 854 adj.
uneatable
unsavoury
391 adj.
uneconomic
wasteful 634 adj.
prodigal 815 adj.
uneconomical
prodigal 815 adj.
unedited
intact 52 adj.

uneducated
uninstructed
491 adj.
unembellished
plain 573 adj.
unembroidered
truthful 540 adj.
unemotional
impassive 820 adj.
unemployable
useless 641 adj.
unemployed
powerless 161 adj.
at rest 266 adj.
non-active
677 adj.
unending
perpetual 115 adj.
unenlightened
ignorant 491 adj.
unwise 499 adj.
unenterprising
cautious 858 adj.
unenthusiastic
unwilling 598 adj.
apathetic 820 adj.
unequal
unequal 29 adj.
unequalled
unequal 29 adj.
supreme 34 adj.
best 644 adj.
unequal to
insufficient
636 adj.
unequipped
unequipped
670 adj.
unequivocal
absolute 32 adj.
certain 473 adj.
positive 473 adj.
intelligible
516 adj.
unerring
certain 473 adj.
accurate 494 adj.
innocent 935 adj.
unescorted
alone 88 adj.
vulnerable
661 adj.
unethical
dishonest 930 adj.
uneven
non-uniform
17 adj.
unequal 29 adj.
discontinuous
72 adj.
fitful 142 adj.
rough 259 adj.

imperfect 647 adj.
unjust 914 adj.
uneventful
tranquil 266 adj.
trivial 639 adj.
**unexception-
able**
guiltless 935 adj.
unexceptional
regular 81 adj.
unexcited
apathetic 820 adj.
unexciting
tedious 838 adj.
unexpected
casual 159 adj.
unexpected
508 adj.
unexplained
uncertain 474 adj.
unknown 491 adj.
puzzling 517 adj.
unexplored
new 126 adj.
neglected 458 adj.
unknown 491 adj.
latent 523 adj.
secluded 883 adj.
unexposed
latent 523 adj.
unexpressed
tacit 523 adj.
unexpurgated
intact 52 adj.
impure 951 adj.
**unfailing regu-
larity**
uniformity 16 n.
frequency 139 n.
unfair
unjust 914 adj.
dishonest 930 adj.
**unfair advan-
tage**
injustice 914 n.
unfaithful
changing 152 adj.
non-observant
769 adj.
hostile 881 adj.
perfidious 930 adj.
unfaithfulness
enmity 881 n.
perfidiousness
930 n.
illicit love 951 n.
unfallen
innocent 935 adj.
pure 950 adj.
unfamiliar
unusual 84 adj.
unknown 491 adj.

84 adj.
rigid 326 adj.
unman
lessen 37 vb.
unman 161 vb.
depress 834 vb.
frighten 854 vb.
unmanageable
wilful 602 adj.
difficult 700 adj.
disobedient
738 adj.
unmanifested
latent 523 adj.
unmanly
female 373 adj.
cowardly 856 adj.
unmanned
impotent 161 adj.
afraid 854 adj.
unmannerly
ill-bred 847 adj.
discourteous
885 adj.
unmarked
neglected 458 adj.
undamaged
646 adj.
unmarried
unsociable
883 adj.
unmask
be plain 522 vb.
disclose 526 vb.
unmatched
best 644 adj.
unmeasured
indiscriminate
464 adj.
unmentionable
prohibited 757 adj.
discreditable
867 adj.
impure 951 adj.
unmentionables
underwear 228 n.
unmercenary
disinterested
931 adj.
unmerciful
pitiless 906 adj.
unmerited
unwarranted
916 adj.
unmethodical
lacking order
61 adj.
unmindful
inattentive
456 adj.
forgetful 506 adj.
unmistakable
visible 443 adj.

certain 473 adj.
intelligible
516 adj.
manifest 522 adj.
unmitigated
consummate
32 adj.
complete 54 adj.
violent 176 adj.
unmixed
unmixed 44 adj.
unmodified
unmixed 44 adj.
unmoor
separate 46 vb.
navigate 269 vb.
start out 296 vb.
unmotivated
spontaneous
609 adj.
unmoved
at rest 266 adj.
apathetic 820 adj.
indifferent
860 adj.
unkind 898 adj.
pitiless 906 adj.
unmoving
still 266 adj.
unmusical
discordant
411 adj.
unnamed
unknown 491 adj.
concealed 525 adj.
anonymous
562 adj.
unnatural
disagreeing 25 adj.
extraneous 59 adj.
abnormal 84 adj.
unusual 84 adj.
affected 850 adj.
cruel 898 adj.
unnavigable
impracticable
470 adj.
difficult 700 adj.
unnecessary
superfluous
637 adj.
unimportant
639 adj.
unneighbourly
unsociable
883 adj.
unnerve
unman 161 vb.
depress 834 vb.
frighten 854 vb.
unnoticed
invisible 444 adj.

neglected 458 adj.
inglorious 867 adj.
unobjectionable
guiltless 935 adj.
unobservant
inattentive
456 adj.
unobstructed
open 263 adj.
unobtainable
absent 190 adj.
impracticable
470 adj.
scarce 636 adj.
unobtrusive
modest 874 adj.
unoccupied
empty 190 adj.
non-active
677 adj.
inactive 679 adj.
leisurely 681 adj.
free 744 adj.
not possessed
774 adj.
unofficial
independent
744 adj.
illegal 954 adj.
lawless 954 adj.
unopened
closed 264 adj.
unorganized
unprepared
670 adj.
unoriginal
usual 610 adj.
dull 840 adj.
unorthodox
unconformable
84 adj.
erroneous 495 adj.
unpack
uncover 229 vb.
open 263 vb.
empty 300 vb.
extract 304 vb.
disclose 526 vb.
unpaid
voluntary 597 adj.
unpalatable
unsavoury
391 adj.
unpleasant
827 adj.
unparalleled
supreme 34 adj.
unusual 84 adj.
best 644 adj.
unpardonable
wrong 914 adj.
heinous 934 adj.

unperceived
unknown 491 adj.
unperceiving
blind 439 adj.
unperfumed
odourless 395 adj.
unperson
outcast 883 n.
unpick
disunite 46 vb.
unpleasant
unpleasant
827 adj.
discourteous
885 adj.
unplug
disunite 46 vb.
open 263 vb.
liberate 746 vb.
unplumbed
deep 211 adj.
unknown 491 adj.
unpolished
rough 259 adj.
dim 419 adj.
inelegant 576 adj.
immature 670 adj.
plebeian 869 adj.
unpolluted
unmixed 44 adj.
unpopular
unpleasant
827 adj.
disreputable
867 adj.
unpossessed
not possessed
774 adj.
unpractical
useless 641 adj.
unskilful 695 adj.
unpraiseworthy
blameworthy
924 adj.
unprecedented
original 21 adj.
first 68 adj.
new 126 adj.
infrequent 140 adj.
unknown 491 adj.
unexpected
508 adj.
not customary
611 adj.
wonderful 864 adj.
unpredictable
non-uniform
17 adj.
changing 152 adj.
uncertain 474 adj.
unreliable 474 adj.
unknown 491 adj.

capricious 604 adj.
unpredicted
unexpected
508 adj.
unprejudiced
just 913 adj.
unpremeditated
involuntary
596 adj.
spontaneous
609 adj.
unintentional
618 adj.
unprepared
670 adj.
unprepared
unprepared
670 adj.
unprepossessing
ugly 842 adj.
unpresentable
ill-bred 847 adj.
unpretentious
truthful 540 adj.
plain 573 adj.
artless 699 adj.
humble 872 adj.
modest 874 adj.
unprincipled
dishonest 930 adj.
wicked 934 adj.
unprintable
prohibited 757 adj.
impure 951 adj.
unprocessed
uncompleted
726 adj.
unproclaimed
tacit 523 adj.
unproductive
unproductive
172 adj.
unprofessed
tacit 523 adj.
unprofitable
unproductive
172 adj.
profitless 641 adj.
inexpedient
643 adj.
unprogressive
non-active
677 adj.
unpromising
unpromising
853 adj.
unprompted
volitional 595 adj.
voluntary 597 adj.
spontaneous
609 adj.
**unpronounce-
able**
inexpressible

517 adj.
unpronounced
tacit 523 adj.
unpropitious
inopportune
138 adj.
opposing 704 adj.
unpromising
853 adj.
unprosperous
not prosperous
731 adj.
unprotected
neglected 458 adj.
vulnerable
661 adj.
unprotesting
humble 872 adj.
unproved
poorly reasoned
477 adj.
unprovided
unprovided
636 adj.
unprovoked
spontaneous
609 adj.
unpublished
tacit 523 adj.
unpunctual
anachronistic
118 adj.
late 136 adj.
ill-timed 138 adj.
unqualified
unmixed 44 adj.
positive 473 adj.
dabbling 491 adj.
unequipped
670 adj.
unskilled 695 adj.
unquestionable
undisputed
473 adj.
true 494 adj.
unquotable
impure 951 adj.
unravel
separate 46 vb.
extract 304 vb.
decipher 520 vb.
unread
neglected 458 adj.
uninstructed
491 adj.
unreal
unreal 2 adj.
imaginary
513 adj.
imaginative
513 adj.
unrealistic
dissimilar 19 adj.

impossible
470 adj.
misjudging
481 adj.
erroneous 495 adj.
unreality
lacking substance
4 n.
non-materiality
320 n.
unreasonable
impossible
470 adj.
illogical 477 adj.
unwise 499 adj.
capricious 604 adj.
wrong 914 adj.
unrecognizable
converted 147 adj.
invisible 444 adj.
unintelligible
517 adj.
disguised 525 adj.
unrecognized
unknown 491 adj.
unreconciled
hostile 881 adj.
impenitent
940 adj.
unredeemed
wicked 934 adj.
unrefined
undiscriminating
464 adj.
inelegant 576 adj.
ill-bred 847 adj.
vulgar 847 adj.
unreformed
impenitent
940 adj.
unrehearsed
spontaneous
609 adj.
unprepared
670 adj.
unrelated
unrelated 10 adj.
unrelenting
obstinate 602 adj.
pitiless 906 adj.
impenitent
940 adj.
unreliable
changing 152 adj.
weak 163 adj.
unreliable 474 adj.
capricious 604 adj.
undutiful 918 adj.
flattering 925 adj.
dishonest 930 adj.
unrelieved
uniform 16 adj.

unremembered
forgotten 506 adj.
unremitting
continuous 71 adj.
persevering
600 adj.
laborious 682 adj.
unrepeated
one 88 adj.
unrepentant
impenitent
940 adj.
**unrepresenta-
tive**
abnormal 84 adj.
unrepresented
absent 190 adj.
unreserved
positive 473 adj.
free 744 adj.
unresisting
inactive 679 adj.
submitting
721 adj.
unresolved
uncertain 474 adj.
irresolute 601 adj.
unresponsive
impassive 820 adj.
indifferent
860 adj.
unrest
motion 265 n.
discontent 829 n.
unrestrained
violent 176 adj.
intemperate
943 adj.
unrestricted
absolute 32 adj.
unrewarding
profitless 641 adj.
unrighteous
wrong 914 adj.
unrightful
unwarranted
916 adj.
unripe
incomplete 55 adj.
young 130 adj.
sour 393 adj.
immature 670 adj.
uncompleted
726 adj.
unrivalled
supreme 34 adj.
unroll
lengthen 203 vb.
straighten 249 vb.
evolve 316 vb.
manifest 522 vb.
disclose 526 vb.

unromantic
true 494 adj.
unruffled
tranquil 266 adj.
impassive 820 adj.
inexcitable
823 adj.
amiable 884 adj.
unruly
disorderly 61 adj.
violent 176 adj.
wilful 602 adj.
disobedient
738 adj.
unsafe
unsafe 661 adj.
unsaid
unknown 491 adj.
tacit 523 adj.
unsaleable
profitless 641 adj.
unsanctified
heathenish
974 adj.
profane 980 adj.
unsanctioned
unwarranted
916 adj.
unsated
unprovided
636 adj.
greedy 859 adj.
unsatisfactory
incomplete 55 adj.
disappointing
509 adj.
inexpedient
643 adj.
bad 645 adj.
unpleasant
827 adj.
unsatisfied
greedy 859 adj.
envious 912 adj.
unsavoury
unsavoury
391 adj.
unsay
recant 603 vb.
unscathed
undamaged
646 adj.
unscented
odourless 395 adj.
unscientific
illogical 477 adj.
erroneous 495 adj.
unscramble
simplify 44 vb.
unscrupulous
dishonest 930 adj.
wicked 934 adj.

unseasonable
ill-timed 138 adj.
inexpedient
643 adj.
unseasoned
unmixed 44 adj.
tasteless 387 adj.
immature 670 adj.
unseat
disunite 46 vb.
disarrange 63 vb.
displace 188 vb.
depose 752 vb.
unseeing
insensitive
375 adj.
blind 439 adj.
inattentive
456 adj.
misjudging
481 adj.
impassive 820 adj.
unseemly
unwise 499 adj.
inexpedient
643 adj.
unsightly 842 adj.
wrong 914 adj.
unseen
invisible 444 adj.
unknown 491 adj.
latent 523 adj.
inglorious 867 adj.
modest 874 adj.
secluded 883 adj.
unselective
undiscriminating
464 adj.
unselfconfident
modest 874 adj.
unselfish
benevolent
897 adj.
disinterested
931 adj.
unsentimental
impassive 820 adj.
unsettle
decompose 51 vb.
disarrange 63 vb.
impress 821 vb.
unsex
unman 161 vb.
unshackle
disencumber
701 vb.
liberate 746 vb.
unshakable
firm 45 adj.
fixed 153 adj.
certain 473 adj.
credal 485 adj.

invert 221 vb.
overturning 221 n.
lowering 311 n.
distract 456 vb.
hinder 702 vb.
impress 821 vb.
trouble 827 vb.
cause discontent
   829 vb.
cause dislike
   861 vb.
enrage 891 vb.
upshot
event 154 n.
effect 157 n.
judgment 480 n.
completion 725 n.
upside down
contrarily 14 adv.
upsides with
equal 28 adj.
upstage
act 594 vb.
stage set 594 n.
proud 871 adj.
insolent 878 adj.
upstairs
up 308 adv.
intelligence 498 n.
upstanding
vertical 215 adj.
upstart
new 126 adj.
commoner 869 n.
insolent person
   878 n.
upsurge
increase 36 n.
ascent 308 n.
upswing
increase 36 n.
elevation 310 n.
improvement
   654 n.
up the creek
in difficulties
   700 adj.
hindered 702 adj.
uptight
excited 821 adj.
nervous 854 adj.
irascible 892 adj.
up to
while 108 adv.
powerful 160 adj.
up-to-date
present 121 adj.
modern 126 adj.
up to one's eyes
busy 678 adj.
up to some-
   thing
dishonest 930 adj.

up to the mark
sufficient 635 adj.
expert 694 adj.
up-to-the-
   minute
present 121 adj.
modern 126 adj.
fashionable
   848 adj.
upturn
increase 36 n.
invert 221 vb.
ascent 308 n.
improvement
   654 n.
upwards
up 308 adv.
upwind
towards 281 adv.
urbane
cunning 698 adj.
well-bred 848 adj.
sociable 882 adj.
courteous 884 adj.
urbanization
housing 192 n.
urchin
young person
   132 n.
urge
impel 279 vb.
affirm 532 vb.
emphasize 532 vb.
be resolute 599 vb.
incite 612 vb.
hasten 680 vb.
advise 691 vb.
compel 740 vb.
animate 821 vb.
desire 859 n.
urgent
strong 162 adj.
resolute 599 adj.
important 638 adj.
hasty 680 adj.
compelling
   740 adj.
urge on
accelerate 277 vb.
urinal
toilet 649 n.
urinate
excrete 302 vb.
urine
excrement 302 n.
urn
vessel 194 n.
inter 364 vb.
interment 364 n.
pottery 381 n.
us
self 80 n.

usable
useful 640 adj.
used 673 adj.
usage
connotation 514 n.
habit 610 n.
use 673 n.
use
habit 610 n.
instrumentality
   628 n.
utility 640 n.
use 673 n.
use 673 vb.
used
used 673 adj.
used to
accustomed to
   610 adj.
useful
useful 640 adj.
useless
useless 641 adj.
user-friendly
computerized
   86 adj.
intelligible
   516 adj.
easy 701 adj.
use up
disable 161 vb.
dispose of 673 vb.
use 673 vb.
expend 806 vb.
usher
accompany 89 vb.
retainer 742 n.
bridal party 894 n.
usher in
come before 64 vb.
initiate 68 vb.
precede 283 vb.
admit 299 vb.
predict 511 vb.
greet 884 vb.
usual
general 79 adj.
usual 610 adj.
usual suspects
practice 610 n.
usurer
lender 784 n.
usurp
encroach 306 vb.
take authority
   733 vb.
appropriate
   786 vb.
deprive 786 vb.
usurper
impostor 545 n.
taker 786 n.

usurper 916 n.
usury
gain 771 n.
lending 784 n.
interest 803 n.
utensil
tool 630 n.
uterus
genitals 167 n.
insides 224 n.
utilitarian
useful 640 adj.
philanthropic
   901 adj.
philanthropist
   901 n.
ethical 917 adj.
utility
utility 640 n.
utilize
find useful
   640 adj.
use 673 vb.
utmost
limit 236 n.
Utopia
fantasy 513 n.
aspiration 852 n.
utter
consummate
   32 adj.
simple 44 adj.
divulge 526 vb.
publish 528 vb.
voice 577 vb.
speak 579 vb.
utterance
voice 577 n.
speech 579 n.
utterly
greatly 32 adv.
completely 54 adv.
uttermost
limit 236 n.
U-turn
change 143 n.
reversion 148 n.
curve 248 n.
return 286 n.
circuitous motion
   314 n.
change of mind
   603 n.

V

vacancy
lacking substance
   4 n.
emptiness 190 n.
job 622 n.

non-ownership
   774 n.
vacant
lacking substance
   4 adj.
empty 190 adj.
unintelligent
   499 adj.
free 744 adj.
not possessed
   774 adj.
vacate
go away 190 vb.
relinquish 621 vb.
vacation
absence 190 n.
leisure 681 n.
rest 683 n.
permit 756 n.
vaccinate
implant 303 vb.
practise medicine
   658 vb.
safeguard 660 vb.
vaccine
preventive 658 n.
vacillate
change 143 vb.
vary 152 vb.
be uncertain
   474 vb.
be irresolute
   601 vb.
be capricious
   604 vb.
vacuous
lacking substance
   4 adj.
empty 190 adj.
mindless 448 adj.
vacuum
non-existence 2 n.
emptiness 190 n.
lack of density
   325 n.
clean 648 vb.
vacuum cleaner
cleaning utensil
   648 n.
vade mecum
guidebook 524 n.
vagabond
wanderer 268 n.
low fellow 869 n.
vagary
foolery 497 n.
conception 513 n.
whim 604 n.
vagina
genitals 167 n.
aperture 263 n.
vagrant
changing 152 adj.

wanderer 268 n.
derelict 779 n.
poor person 801 n.
vague
  lacking substance
    4 adj.
  general 79 adj.
  formless 244 adj.
  shadowy 419 adj.
  indistinct 444 adj.
  uncertain 474 adj.
  reticent 525 adj.
  unclear 568 adj.
vain
  profitless 641 adj.
  useless 641 adj.
  unsuccessful
    728 adj.
  vain 873 adj.
vainglorious
  proud 871 adj.
  vain 873 adj.
valance
  edging 234 n.
  trimming 844 n.
valediction
  farewell 296 n.
valentine
  correspondence
    588 n.
  loved one 887 n.
  love token 889 n.
  darling 890 n.
valet
  clothier 228 n.
  clean 648 vb.
  minister to
    703 vb.
  domestic 742 n.
  serve 742 vb.
valiant
  courageous
    855 adj.
valid
  powerful 160 adj.
  strong 162 adj.
  genuine 494 adj.
  useful 640 adj.
validate
  stabilize 153 vb.
  corroborate
    466 vb.
  testify 466 vb.
  make legal
    953 vb.
validity
  authenticity
    494 n.
  legality 953 n.
valise
  box 194 n.
valley
  valley 255 n.

valour
  courage 855 n.
valuable
  valuable 644 adj.
valuables
  estate 777 n.
valuation
  degree 27 n.
  measurement
    465 n.
  estimate 480 n.
value
  degree 27 n.
  equivalence 28 n.
  appraise 465 vb.
  estimate 480 vb.
  importance 638 n.
  utility 640 n.
  goodness 644 n.
  account 808 vb.
  price 809 n.
  price 809 vb.
  tax 809 vb.
  dearness 811 n.
  have taste 846 vb.
  honour 866 vb.
  love 887 n.
  respect 920 vb.
  approve 923 vb.
valueless
  trivial 639 adj.
  profitless 641 adj.
valuer
  estimator 480 n.
valve
  electronics 160 n.
  stopper 264 n.
  water channel
    351 n.
vampire
  taker 786 n.
  demon 970 n.
van
  beginning 68 n.
  lorry 274 n.
  preceding 283 n.
vandal
  destroyer 168 n.
  violent creature
    176 n.
  troublemaker
    663 n.
vandalism
  destruction 165 n.
  violence 176 n.
  waste 634 n.
  inhumanity 898 n.
vandalize
  waste 634 vb.
  impair 655 vb.
  make ugly 842 vb.
  blemish 845 vb.

vane
  weather 340 n.
  indicator 547 n.
vanguard
  precursor 66 n.
  front 237 n.
  preceding 283 n.
  armed force 722 n.
vanish
  pass away 2 vb.
  be transient
    114 vb.
  go away 190 vb.
  be unseen 444 vb.
  disappear 446 vb.
vanity
  thing that lacks
    substance 4 n.
  overestimation
    482 n.
  vanity 873 n.
vanquish
  overcome 727 vb.
vantage
  advantage 34 n.
vantage point
  view 438 n.
vapid
  tasteless 387 adj.
  feeble 572 adj.
  dull 840 adj.
vaporize
  lighten 323 vb.
  vaporize 338 vb.
vaporizer
  vaporizer 338 n.
  air 340 n.
vaporous
  gaseous 336 adj.
  vaporific 338 adj.
  imaginary
    513 adj.
vapour
  emit 300 vb.
  gas 336 n.
  cloud 355 n.
  fantasy 513 n.
  boast 877 vb.
vapours
  melancholy 834 n.
variable
  circumstantial
    8 adj.
  non-uniform
    17 adj.
  unequal 29 adj.
  number 85 n.
  fitful 142 adj.
  changeable
    143 adj.
  changing 152 adj.
  unreliable 474 adj.

irresolute 601 adj.
capricious 604 adj.
variance
  difference 15 n.
  disagreement 25 n.
  dissension 709 n.
variant
  variant 15 n.
  changing 152 adj.
variation
  contrariety 14 n.
  difference 15 n.
  dissimilarity 19 n.
  change 143 n.
  musical piece
    412 n.
variegated
  variegated
    437 adj.
variety
  difference 15 n.
  variant 15 n.
  non-uniformity
    17 n.
  dissimilarity 19 n.
  disagreement 25 n.
  medley 43 n.
  sort 77 n.
  existence in many
    forms 82 n.
  changeableness
    152 n.
  variegation 437 n.
  stage show 594 n.
variform
  existing in many
    forms 82 adj.
various
  different 15 adj.
  dissimilar 19 adj.
  many 104 adj.
varlet
  low fellow 869 n.
varnish
  coat 226 vb.
  facing 226 n.
  smooth 258 vb.
  smoother 258 n.
  smoothness 258 n.
  resin 357 n.
  use sophistry
    477 vb.
  untruth 543 n.
  exaggerate 546 vb.
  plead 614 vb.
  cleanser 648 n.
  preserve 666 vb.
  decorate 844 vb.
  ostentation 875 n.

extenuate 927 vb.
justify 927 vb.
vary
  differ 15 vb.
  be unequal 29 vb.
  modify 143 vb.
  vary 152 vb.
vase
  bowl 194 n.
  vessel 194 n.
vasectomy
  contraception
    172 n.
  surgery 658 n.
vassal
  dependant 742 n.
  subject 742 n.
  subject 745 adj.
vast
  enormous 32 adj.
  spacious 183 adj.
  huge 195 adj.
  large 195 adj.
vat
  vat 194 n.
Vatican
  church office
    985 n.
  the church 985 n.
  parsonage 986 n.
vaudeville
  stage show 594 n.
vault
  cellar 194 n.
  depth 211 n.
  roof 226 n.
  curve 248 n.
  dome 253 n.
  ascend 308 vb.
  ascent 308 n.
  leap 312 n.
  leap 312 vb.
  tomb 364 n.
  hiding-place
    527 n.
  storage 632 n.
  church interior
    990 n.
vaunt
  boast 877 vb.
veal
  meat 301 n.
vector
  number 85 n.
  infection 651 n.
veer
  change 143 vb.
  vary 152 vb.
  navigate 269 vb.
  deviate 282 vb.
  deviation 282 n.
  blow 352 vb.

veer round
turn back 286 vb.
change one's mind
603 vb.

vegan
eater 301 n.
feeding 301 adj.
abstainer 942 n.
temperate 942 adj.

vegetable
fruit and vegeta-
bles 301 n.
unfeeling person
820 n.

vegetable-like
impassive 820 adj.
inexcitable
823 adj.

vegetarian
eater 301 n.
feeding 301 adj.
abstainer 942 n.
temperate 942 adj.

vegetate
pass time 108 n.
be at rest 266 vb.
vegetate 366 vb.
be inactive
679 vb.
be insensitive
820 vb.

vegetation
inertness 175 n.
plant life 366 n.
inaction 677 n.
moral insensibility
820 n.

vehement
vigorous 174 adj.
violent 176 adj.
assertive 532 adj.
forceful 571 adj.
fervent 818 adj.

vehicle
vehicle 274 n.
instrument 628 n.

veil
cover 226 vb.
shade 226 n.
headgear 228 n.
darken 418 vb.
dim 419 vb.
screen 421 n.
screen 421 vb.
be unseen 444 vb.
invisibility 444 n.
conceal 525 vb.
disguise 527 n.
sham 542 n.
vocation 622 n.

veiled
uncertain 474 adj.

unknown 491 adj.
occult 523 adj.
concealed 525 adj.
secluded 883 adj.
monastic 986 adj.

vein
state 7 n.
small quantity
33 n.
tincture 43 n.
tendency 179 n.
narrowness 206 n.
layer 207 n.
filament 208 n.
tube 263 n.
water channel
351 n.
variegate 437 vb.
style 566 n.
diffuseness 570 n.
store 632 n.
mental state
817 n.

veld
space 183 n.
plain 348 n.

vellum
stationery 586 n.
bookbinding
589 n.

velocity
velocity 277 n.

velour
textile 222 n.
smoothness 258 n.

velvet
textile 222 n.
smoothness 258 n.
softness 327 n.
heyday 730 n.

velvet glove
conduct 688 n.
leniency 736 n.

velvety
smooth 258 adj.
soft 327 adj.

venal
corruptible
930 adj.

vend
trade 791 vb.
sell 793 vb.

vendetta
quarrel 709 n.
enmity 881 n.
revenge 910 n.

vendor
seller 793 n.

veneer
layer 207 n.
shallowness
212 n.

coat 226 vb.
covering 226 n.
facing 226 n.
appearance 445 n.
disguise 527 n.
sham 542 n.
be ostentatious
875 vb.
ostentation 875 n.

venerable
great 32 adj.
olden 127 adj.
ageing 131 adj.

venerate
respect 920 vb.
worship 981 vb.

venereal
connective 45 adj.
diseased 651 adj.
sensual 944 adj.

venereal disease
venereal disease
651 n.

venetian blind
shade 226 n.
curtain 421 n.

vengeance
revenge 910 n.

venial
guiltless 935 adj.

venison
meat 301 n.

venom
poison 659 n.
malevolence
898 n.

venomous
toxic 653 adj.
hostile 881 adj.
malevolent
898 adj.
disapproving
924 adj.

vent
aperture 263 n.
outlet 298 n.
air pipe 353 n.
divulge 526 vb.
means of escape
667 n.

ventilate
aerate 340 vb.
blow 352 vb.
divulge 526 vb.
publish 528 vb.
dissertate 591 vb.
purify 648 vb.
make sanitary
652 vb.
refresh 685 vb.

ventilation
ventilation 352 n.

publicity 528 n.
cleansing 648 n.

ventilator
air 340 n.
ventilation 352 n.

ventricle
compartment
194 n.
insides 224 n.

ventriloquist
imitator 20 n.
entertainer 594 n.

venture
be tentative
461 vb.
gamble 618 vb.
gambling 618 n.
business 622 n.
danger 661 n.
attempt 671 n.
attempt 671 vb.
undertaking
672 n.
speculate 791 vb.
be courageous
855 vb.

venturesome
dangerous 661 adj.
enterprising
672 adj.
courageous
855 adj.
rash 857 adj.

venue
focus 76 n.
locality 187 n.

veracity
truthfulness
540 n.

verandah
lobby 194 n.

verb
part of speech
564 n.

verbal
testimony 466 n.
semantic 514 adj.
informative
524 adj.
verbal 559 adj.
grammatical
564 adj.
speaking 579 adj.

verbalize
form 243 vb.
phrase 563 vb.
voice 577 vb.

verbatim
accurate 494 adj.
true 494 adj.
truly 494 adv.
verbally 559 adv.

verbiage
empty talk 515 n.
word 559 n.
obscurity 568 n.
diffuseness 570 n.

verbose
verbal 559 adj.
diffuse 570 adj.
talkative 581 adj.

verdant
prolific 171 adj.
green 434 adj.

verdict
judgment 480 n.
legal trial 959 n.

verdure
foliage 366 n.
grass 366 n.
greenness 434 n.

verge
extremity 69 n.
tend 179 vb.
nearness 200 n.
edge 234 n.
limit 236 n.
road 624 n.
badge of office
743 n.

verger
officer 741 n.
servant 742 n.
church officer
986 n.

verification
experiment 461 n.
evidence 466 n.
certainty 473 n.
demonstration
478 n.
assent 488 n.
title deed 767 n.

verify
corroborate
466 vb.
make certain
473 vb.
demonstrate
478 vb.
give security
767 vb.

verisimilitude
probability 471 n.
accuracy 494 n.
truth 494 n.
truthfulness
540 n.

verity
truth 494 n.

vermicelli
dish 301 n.

vermin
insect 365 n.

receipt 807 n.
vouch for
promise 764 vb.
give security
767 vb.
vouchsafe
permit 756 vb.
give 781 vb.
vow
affirm 532 vb.
promise 764 n.
promise 764 vb.
offer worship
981 vb.
vowel
speech sound
398 n.
voice 577 n.
vox populi
judgment 480 n.
vote 605 n.
government 733 n.
tribunal 956 n.
voyage
land travel 267 n.
voyage 269 vb.
water travel
269 n.
voyeur
spectator 441 n.
libertine 952 n.
voyeurism
inspection 438 n.
curiosity 453 n.
vroom
move fast 277 vb.
spurt 277 n.
roll 403 vb.
V-sign
gesture 547 n.
sauciness 878 n.
indignity 921 n.
vulcanized
tough 329 adj.
vulgar
general 79 adj.
linguistic 557 adj.
not nice 645 adj.
vulgar 847 adj.
impure 951 adj.
vulgarity
*lack of discrimina-
tion* 464 n.
inelegance 576 n.
wit 839 n.
bad taste 847 n.
ill-breeding 847 n.
scurrility 899 n.
vulnerable
weak 163 adj.
vulnerable
661 adj.

vulture
eater 301 n.
bird 365 n.
taker 786 n.
glutton 947 n.

W

wacky
crazy 503 adj.
wad
piece 53 n.
bunch 74 n.
line 227 vb.
ammunition
723 n.
paper money
797 n.
wadding
contents 193 n.
lining 227 n.
stopper 264 n.
softness 327 n.
waddle
be in motion
265 vb.
gait 265 n.
walk 267 vb.
move slowly
278 n.
oscillate 317 vb.
wade
walk 267 vb.
swim 269 vb.
waders
footwear 228 n.
wadi
stream 350 n.
water channel
351 n.
wads
great quantity
32 n.
funds 797 n.
wealth 800 n.
wafer
adhesive 47 n.
strip 208 n.
*bread, pastries
and cakes*
301 n.
waffle
*bread, pastries
and cakes*
301 n.
mean nothing
515 vb.
be equivocal
518 vb.
be diffuse 570 vb.
diffuseness 570 n.

be talkative
581 vb.
chatter 581 n.
waft
carry 273 vb.
be light 323 vb.
blow 352 vb.
breeze 352 n.
wag
brandish 317 vb.
fluctuation 317 n.
oscillate 317 vb.
agitate 318 vb.
be agitated
318 vb.
humorist 839 n.
wage
do 676 vb.
earnings 771 n.
reward 962 n.
wager
uncertainty 474 n.
gamble 618 vb.
gambling 681 n.
contend 716 vb.
contest 716 n.
wages
pay 804 n.
receipt 807 n.
reward 962 n.
waggle
brandish 317 vb.
oscillate 317 vb.
agitate 318 vb.
be agitated
318 vb.
wagon
cart 274 n.
train 274 n.
waif
wanderer 268 n.
derelict 779 n.
wail
cry 408 n.
cry 408 vb.
howl 409 vb.
be discontented
829 vb.
lament 836 vb.
lamentation
836 n.
weep 836 vb.
wainscotting
lining 227 n.
waistband
belt 228 n.
waistcoat
jacket 228 n.
waistline
centrality 225 n.
article of clothing
228 n.

(See also **belt**.)
wait
continue 108 vb.
wait 136 vb.
go on 146 vb.
wait and see
wait 136 vb.
be tentative
461 vb.
be uncertain
474 vb.
not act 677 vb.
waiter
servant 742 n.
waiting
future 124 adj.
traffic control
305 n.
dubiety 474 n.
expectant 507 adj.
expectation 507 n.
waiting game
caution 858 n.
waiting list
list 87 n.
record 548 n.
waiting room
lobby 194 n.
wait on
result 157 vb.
follow 284 vb.
minister to
703 vb.
court 889 vb.
waitress
servant 742 n.
waive
relinquish 621 vb.
not retain 779 vb.
waiver
resignation 753 n.
loss of right 916 n.
wake
adjunct 40 n.
retinue 67 n.
continuity 71 n.
effect 157 n.
rear 238 n.
water travel
269 n.
follower 284 n.
eddy 350 n.
funeral rites
364 n.
trace 548 n.
excite 821 vb.
lament 836 n.
condolence 905 n.
wakeful
attentive 455 adj.
active 678 adj.
wake up
have feeling

374 vb.
walk
park 192 n.
gait 265 n.
walking 267 n.
walk 267 vb.
path 624 n.
exercise 682 vb.
conduct 688 n.
haunt 970 vb.
walkabout
walking 267 n.
walker
pedestrian 268 n.
traveller 268 n.
walkie-talkie
hearing aid 415 n.
telecommunication
531 n.
walking
motion 265 n.
land travel 267 n.
walking 267 n.
**Walkman
(tdmk)**
music player
414 n.
walk off with
win 727 vb.
steal 788 vb.
walk of life
state 7 n.
vocation 622 n.
conduct 688 n.
duty 917 n.
walk out
cease 145 vb.
walk out 296 vb.
relinquish 621 vb.
resist 715 vb.
deprecate 762 vb.
fail in duty
918 vb.
walkout
stop 145 n.
strike 145 n.
departure 296 n.
going out 298 n.
dissent 489 n.
relinquishment
621 n.
walk out on
change one's mind
603 vb.
walk out with
accompany 89 vb.
court 889 vb.
walkover
easy thing 701 n.
victory 727 n.
wall
exclusion 57 n.

filament 208 n.
network 222 n.
textile 222 n.
weaving 222 n.
texture 331 n.
trap 542 n.
Web, the
Internet 531 n.
webbing
network 222 n.
web-footed
deformed 246 adj.
website
information
524 n.
Internet 531 n.
wed
wed 894 vb.
wedding
wedding 894 n.
**wedding anni-
versary**
anniversary 141 n.
special day 876 n.
wedding 894 n.
wedding march
musical piece
412 n.
wedding 894 n.
wedding ring
jewellery 844 n.
love token 889 n.
wedding 894 n.
ritual object
988 n.
wedge
affix 45 vb.
piece 53 n.
support 218 n.
angular figure
247 n.
sharp edge 256 n.
stopper 264 n.
tool 630 n.
wedlock
union 45 n.
marriage 894 n.
wee
small 33 adj.
little 196 adj.
weed
exclude 57 vb.
cause to be few
105 vb.
weakling 163 n.
plant 366 n.
cultivate 370 vb.
ninny 501 n.
disencumber
701 vb.
weed-killer
poison 659 n.

weed out
lessen 37 vb.
eject 300 vb.
extract 304 vb.
weedy
lean 206 adj.
week
over five 99 n.
period 110 n.
weekday
period 110 n.
weekend
pass time 108 vb.
visit 882 vb.
weekly
periodic 110 adj.
periodically
141 adv.
seasonal 141 adj.
journal 528 n.
weep
emit 300 vb.
excrete 302 vb.
be wet 341 vb.
suffer 825 vb.
be dejected
834 vb.
weep 836 vb.
weep for
be sensitive
819 vb.
pity 905 vb.
weeping
outflow 298 n.
water 339 n.
unhappy 825 adj.
lamentation
836 n.
repentant 939 adj.
weigh
elevate 310 vb.
weigh 322 vb.
meditate 449 vb.
notice 455 vb.
mete out 465 vb.
estimate 480 vb.
motivate 612 vb.
weigh against
tell against
467 vb.
weigh anchor
navigate 269 vb.
start out 296 vb.
weighbridge
scales 322 n.
weigh in
criticize 924 vb.
weigh on
lower 311 vb.
weigh 322 vb.
oppress 735 vb.
weight
having substance
3 n.

quantity 26 n.
power 160 n.
influence 178 n.
bulk 195 n.
size 195 n.
distort 246 vb.
materiality 319 n.
gravity 322 n.
weighing 322 n.
make heavy
322 vb.
scales 322 n.
(See also
**weights and
measures**.)
vigour 571 n.
importance 638 n.
do wrong 914 vb.
weightless
light 323 adj.
weight-lifting
exercise 682 n.
sport 837 n.
**weights and
measures**
weights and meas-
ures 465 n.
weighty
influential
178 adj.
material 319 adj.
weighty 322 adj.
forceful 571 adj.
important 638 adj.
weir
waterfall 350 n.
water channel
351 n.
obstacle 702 n.
weird
unconformable
84 adj.
fate 596 n.
frightening
854 adj.
wonderful 864 adj.
spooky 970 adj.
magical 983 adj.
weirdo
nonconformist
84 n.
welcome
arrival 295 n.
meet 295 vb.
welcome 295 int.
admit 299 vb.
reception 299 n.
pleasant 376 adj.
assent 488 n.
assent 488 vb.
pleasurable
826 adj.

desire 859 vb.
desired 859 adj.
celebrate 876 vb.
celebration 876 n.
be friendly 880 vb.
friendliness 880 n.
be hospitable
882 vb.
sociability 882 n.
courteous act
884 n.
greet 884 vb.
congratulation
886 n.
show respect
920 vb.
applaud 923 vb.
approbation
923 n.
weld
join 45 vb.
joint 45 n.
welder
artisan 686 n.
welfare
good 615 n.
prosperity 730 n.
welfare state
safety 660 n.
shelter 662 n.
political organiza-
tion 733 n.
social care 901 n.
well
greatly 32 vb.
receptacle 194 n.
lowness 210 n.
depth 211 n.
excavation 255 n.
water 339 n.
lake 346 n.
flow 350 vb.
stream 350 n.
well 615 adv.
store 632 n.
healthy 650 adj.
skilfully 694 adv.
well-adjusted
adjusted 24 adj.
accurate 494 adj.
well-advised
wise 498 adj.
well-aimed
apt 24 adj.
accurate 494 adj.
well-appointed
prepared 669 adj.
well-balanced
symmetrical
245 adj.
well-behaved
orderly 60 adj.

obedient 739 adj.
amiable 884 adj.
well-being
euphoria 376 n.
good 615 n.
health 650 n.
healthiness 652 n.
prosperity 730 n.
happiness 824 n.
well-born
worshipful
866 adj.
noble 868 adj.
well-bred
well-bred 848 adj.
well-built
strong 162 adj.
large 195 adj.
beautiful 841 adj.
well-chosen
chosen 605 adj.
**well-connected,
be**
influence 178 vb.
well-considered
wise 498 adj.
well-cut
adjusted 24 adj.
well-deserved
just 913 adj.
due 915 adj.
well-disposed
willing 597 adj.
**well-
documented**
real 1 adj.
evidential 466 adj.
well done
bravo 923 int.
well-done
culinary 301 adj.
well-dressed
personable
841 adj.
fashionable
848 adj.
well-earned
due 915 adj.
well-endowed
gifted 694 adj.
rich 800 adj.
shapely 841 adj.
well-established
permanent
144 adj.
well-fed
fat 195 adj.
well-fitting
adjusted 24 adj.
well-formed
shapely 841 adj.
well-founded
fixed 153 adj.

864 n.
wonderful 864 adj.
sorcery 983 n.
wondrous
wonderful 864 adj.
wonky
flimsy 163 adj.
dilapidated
655 adj.
woo
pursue 619 vb.
request 761 vb.
desire 859 vb.
be in love 887 vb.
court 889 vb.
wood
missile 287 n.
wood 366 n.
wooden 366 adj.
heater 383 n.
fuel 385 n.
wood carving
sculpture 554 n.
wooden
wooden 366 adj.
inelegant 576 adj.
impassive 820 adj.
wooden spoon
rear 238 n.
lack of skill 695 n.
trophy 729 n.
woodwind
blowing 352 n.
orchestra 413 n.
flute 414 n.
musical instrument
414 n.
woodwork
structure 331 n.
ornamental art
844 n.
woodworm
destroyer 168 n.
insect 365 n.
blight 659 n.
woody
tough 329 n.
wooden 366 adj.
woof
weaving 222 n.
howl 409 vb.
wooing
loving 887 adj.
wooing 889 n.
wool
fibre 208 n.
textile 222 n.
hair 259 n.
materials 631 n.
woolgathering
abstracted
456 adj.

abstractedness
456 n.
woolly
jersey 228 n.
smooth 258 adj.
hairy 259 adj.
poorly reasoned
477 adj.
woozy
with one's head
spinning 315 adj.
tipsy 949 adj.
word
component 58 n.
testimony 466 n.
information
524 n.
message 529 n.
news 529 n.
word 559 n.
phrase 563 n.
warning 664 n.
command 737 n.
promise 764 n.
duty 917 n.
word for word
accurate 494 adj.
truly 494 adv.
verbally 559 adv.
word in edge-
ways, a
oration 579 n.
wording
phrase 563 n.
word in the ear
hint 524 n.
address 583 n.
warning 664 n.
word of mouth
tradition 127 n.
testimony 466 n.
information
524 n.
message 529 n.
speech 579 n.
word-perfect
prepared 669 adj.
word-play
equivocalness
518 n.
figure of speech
519 n.
neologism 560 n.
wit 839 n.
word processor
computing 86 n.
words
phrase 563 n.
quarrel 709 n.
contention 716 n.
anger 891 n.
words, the
reading matter

589 n.
words of one
syllable
truthfulness
540 n.
conciseness 569 n.
word to the
wise
hint 524 n.
hush 582 int.
warning 664 n.
advice 691 n.
wordy
long-winded
570 adj.
work
energy 160 n.
product 164 n.
agency 173 n.
operate 173 vb.
influence 178 vb.
form 243 vb.
effervesce 318 vb.
bubble 355 vb.
musical piece
412 n.
variegate 437 vb.
stage play 594 n.
business 622 n.
busy oneself
622 vb.
function 622 vb.
job 622 n.
be instrumental
628 vb.
be expedient
642 vb.
use 673 vb.
action 676 n.
deed 676 n.
labour 682 n.
work 682 vb.
be successful
727 n.
decorate 844 vb.
workable
powerful 160 adj.
possible 469 adj.
workaday
plain 573 adj.
work against
counteract 182 vb.
plot 623 vb.
oppose 704 vb.
workaholic
busy person 678 n.
work at
persevere 600 vb.
busy oneself
622 vb.
deal with 688 vb.
workbox
basket 194 n.

worked up
matured 669 adj.
angry 891 adj.
worker
worker 686 n.
servant 742 n.
workforce
component 58 n.
band 74 n.
means 629 n.
personnel 686 n.
workhouse
retreat 192 n.
poverty 801 n.
work in
introduce 231 vb.
work-in
strike 145 n.
working
instrumental
628 adj.
store 632 n.
action 676 n.
active 678 adj.
labouring 682 adj.
serving 742 adj.
working class
lower classes
869 n.
working day
period 110 n.
job 622 n.
labour 682 n.
working party
enquiry 459 n.
(See also
enquirer.)
nominee 754 n.
workings
structure 331 n.
workmanlike
industrious
678 adj.
work miracles
be successful
727 vb.
be wonderful
864 vb.
work on
influence 178 vb.
work out
happen 154 vb.
result 157 vb.
decipher 520 vb.
mature 669 vb.
exercise 682 vb.
deal with 688 vb.
carry through
725 vb.
amuse oneself
837 vb.
work-out
exercise 682 n.

work party
band 74 n.
workroom
room 194 n.
workshop 687 n.
works
component 58 n.
structure 331 n.
writing 586 n.
machine 630 n.
workshop 687 n.
works, the
all 52 n.
workshop
teaching 534 n.
class 538 n.
workshop 687 n.
work study
management
689 n.
work to rule
strike 145 n.
work up
excite 821 vb.
work wonders
be active 678 vb.
world
great quantity
32 n.
comprehensive
52 adj.
whole 52 n.
affairs 154 n.
space 183 n.
spacious 183 adj.
universe 321 n.
world 321 n.
world, the
fellowship 882 n.
worldly
material 319 adj.
irreligious 974 adj.
worldly goods
property 777 n.
worldly-wise
intelligent 498 adj.
world of
great quantity
32 n.
world of, a
multitude 104 n.
world-shaking
revolutionary
149 adj.
world-view
generality 79 n.
world-weary
bored 838 adj.
worldwide
extensive 32 adj.
comprehensive
52 adj.

The Penguin Concise Thesaurus

Edited by Rosalind Fergusson, Martin Manser and David Pickering

The Penguin Thesaurus offers a vast selection of synonyms and antonyms for
a whole host of words in A–Z order. Each entry is simplicity itself to follow,
and where a particular word has several different senses, these are clearly
indicated and explained. This invaluable and up-to-date Thesaurus is the
ideal first port of call to help you quickly and easily find the best word for
every occasion.

- Contains over 400,000 synonyms and antonyms, listing words
  closest in meaning first
- Arranged in an easy-to-follow A–Z format
- Ranges from standard and formal English to slang and jargon and
  informal and colloquial expressions, as well as the latest buzzwords
- Provides helpful examples to pinpoint the nuances of particular
  words

The Penguin Concise Dictionary

Edited by Robert Allen

This concise edition of the bestselling *Penguin English Dictionary* is the perfect reference book for everyday use, exploring every aspect of the English language as it is used today. Compiled by Britain's foremost lexicographers, meticulously researched, with a wealth of useful additional features, and presented in a clear, easy-to-read format, it is the ideal companion for every home and office.

- Includes over 150,000 words, phrases and clear definitions, with more information than other leading dictionaries
- Covers standard English, as well as scientific and technical vocabulary, slang and jargon
- Provides invaluable guidance on correct usage, commonly confused words, grammar and spelling
- Gives fascinating word histories explaining the origins of words from *hypochondria* to *sideburns*

The Penguin Rhyming Dictionary

Rosalind Fergusson

The Penguin Rhyming Dictionary is an indispensable reference companion for anyone who writes verse – whether lyric poet, songwriter or composer of limericks or jingles. Clearly arranged and easy to use, it offers an astonishingly wide range of suggestions for rhyming words, from the common and everyday to the more difficult and obscure.

- Contains lists of rhymes for well over 40,000 words
- Distinguishes between close rhymes and less exact ones
- Includes separate sections for one-, two- and three-syllable rhymes
- Provides concise explanations of unusual words

'One of the delights of our age – not just a fall-back for poets in a jam, but a treasure-trove for writers of every kind. As it satisfies our search for similar sounds, so it leads us into new thoughts, strange associations, unexpected territories – and always with exuberance, enjoying difference, allowing preference, enriching utterance, extending circumference, reducing ignorance. Everyone who loves words should own a copy'
Andrew Motion

FOURTH EDITION

The Penguin Dictionary of Literary Terms and Literary Theory

J. A. Cuddon

The Penguin Dictionary of Literary Terms and Literary Theory is firmly established as a key work of reference for the terms used today in this complex and varied subject. Now in its fourth edition, it remains the most comprehensive and accessible work of its kind, and is invaluable for students, teachers and general readers alike.

- Gives definitions of technical terms (*hamartia, iamb, zeugma*) and critical jargon (*aporia, binary opposition, intertextuality*)
- Explores literary movements (*neoclassicism, romanticism, vorticism*) and schools of literary theory (*feminist criticism, new historicism, structuralism*)
- Covers genres (*elegy, fabliau, pastoral*) and literary forms (*haiku, ottava rima, sonnet*)
- Provides apt literary quotations to illustrate definitions

The Penguin Guide to Punctuation

R. L. Trask

The Penguin Guide to Punctuation is indispensable for anyone who needs to get to grips with using punctuation in their written work. Whether you are puzzled by colons and semicolons, unsure of where commas should go or baffled by apostrophes, this jargon-free and succinct guide is for you.

- Contains precise definitions of every type of punctuation mark and shows how each should be used
- Provides numerous examples of good and bad usage
- Explains the correct use of capital letters, contractions and abbreviations, italics, boldface and the special characters available on computers
- Covers punctuation in footnotes, references, bibliographies and letters

'Excellent . . . covers almost every point that an editor needs' The Society of Freelance Editors and Proofreaders

'A concise and highly readable reference book . . . tightly-structured, with clear definitions of each type of punctuation' *Sunday Telegraph*